C++ Language Reference

VERSION 5.0

Borland® C++

Borland International, Inc., 100 Borland Way
P.O. Box 660001, Scotts Valley, CA 95067-0001

1E0R0196   WBC1350WW21773
9697989900-9 8 7 6 5 4 3 2 1
D2
ISBN 0-672-30926-2

Contents

v

Chapter 4
Global variables   377

Chapter 5
The preprocessor   391

Part II
Borland C++ DOS programmer's reference   407

Chapter 6
Borland graphics interface   409

Chapter 11
The iostreams classes   607

Chapter 12
The persistent streams classes and macros   637

Chapter 13
The mathematical classes   655

Chapter 14
Class diagnostic macros   665

Chapter 15
Run-time support   671

Part V
Visual Database Tools reference   1007

Chapter 18
Classes, properties, methods, and events   1009

Part VI

Borland Windows Custom Controls reference   1461

Chapter 19
Borland windows custom controls   1463

Part VII
BIVBX library functions reference   1487

Chapter 20
BIVBX library functions   1489

Introduction

This book is a reference manual for the Borland C++ language. Each part in this book has a companion part in the Borland C++ *Programmer's Guide*. This book provides detailed information about specific items such as functions, classes, macros, properties, methods, and events. The Borland C++ *Programmer's Guide* provides the how-to-implement perspective on using Borland C++.

How this book is organized

This book is divided into the following parts:

- **Part I, "Borland C++ programmer's reference,"** is for the advanced programmer. It provides you with detailed information on keywords, runtime functions, global variables, and the preprocessor.

- **Part II, "Borland C++ DOS programmer's reference,"** provides information you might need to develop 16-bit applications that are targeted to run DOS. It provides DOS-only run-time functions, DOS libraries, and DOS global variables.

- **Part III, "Borland C++ class libraries reference,"** provides detailed information about C++ container classes, iostreams classes, persistent streams classes and macros, mathematical classes, class diagnostic macros, and runtime support.

- **Part IV, "Standard C++ class libraries reference,"** documents the Rogue Wave Software, Inc., implementation of the Standard C++ Library.

- **Part V, "Visual Database Tools reference,"** details the Visual Database Tools classes, properties, methods, and events.

- **Part VI, "Borland Windows Custom Controls reference,"** documents the Borland Windows Custom Controls.

- **Part VII, "BIVBX library functions reference,"** provides details about the BIVBX library functions.

Typefaces and icons used in this book

This book uses the following special fonts:

`Monospace`	This type represents text that you type or text as it appears onscreen.
Italics	These are used to emphasize and introduce words, and to indicate variable names (identifiers), function names, class names, and structure names.
Bold	This type indicates reserved keywords words, format specifiers, and command-line options.
Keycap	This type represents a particular key you should press on your keyboard. For example, "Press *Del* to erase the character."
Key1+Key2	This indicates a command that requires you to press *Key1* with *Key2*. For example, *Shift+a* (although not a command) indicates the uppercase letter "A."
ALL CAPS	This type represents disk directories, file names, and application names. (However, header file names are presented in lowercase to be consistent with how these files are usually written in source code.)
Menu | Choice	This represents menu commands. Rather than use the phrase "choose the Save command from the File menu," Borland manuals use the convention "choose File | Save."
Note	This icon indicates material that you should take special notice of.

Borland C++ programmer's reference

Part I contains reference material for the advanced programmer. This part is organized as follows:

- **Chapter 1, "Keywords,"** shows how the lexical tokens for Borland C++ are categorized. It covers the different categories of word-like units, known as *tokens*, recognized by a language.

- **Chapter 2, "Borland C++ library routines,"** contains an overview of the Borland C++ library routines and header files. After describing the static and dynamic-link libraries, the header files are listed; the library routines are grouped according to the tasks they commonly perform.

- **Chapter 3, "Run-time functions,"** is an alphabetical reference of all Borland C++ library functions. Each entry gives syntax, portability information, an operative description, and return values for the function, together with a reference list of related functions.

- **Chapter 4, "Global variables,"** defines and discusses Borland C++'s global variables. You can use these to save yourself a great deal of programming time on commonly needed variables (such as dates, time, error messages, stack size, and so on).

- **Chapter 5, "The preprocessor,"** discusses the CPP and CPP32 preprocessors and the preprocessor functionality built into the Borland C++ compiler.

1

Keywords

Keywords are words reserved for special purposes and must not be used as normal identifier names. You can set options in the IDE or for the command-line compiler to select ANSI keywords only, UNIX keywords only, or to support all keywords—including the Borland C++ extensions.

Keywords (by category)

This section is a categorical listing of the keywords Borland C++ supports.

Borland C++ Extensions	Keywords unique to Borland C++
C++ Specific	Keywords recognized only in C++ programs
Modifiers	Keywords that change one or more attributes of an identifier associated with an object
Operators	Keywords that invoke functions against objects or identifiers
Statements	Keywords that specify program control during execution
Storage Class Specifiers	Keywords that define the location and duration of an identifier
Type Specifiers	Keywords that determine how memory is allocated and bit patterns are interpreted

Borland C++ keyword extensions

Borland C++ provides additional keywords that are not part of the ANSI or UNIX conventions. You cannot use these keywords in your programs if you set the IDE or command-line options to recognize only ANSI or UNIX keywords.

The Borland C++ keyword extensions are:

_asm	_import
__asm	__import
_cdecl	__interrupt
cdecl	_interrupt
_cs	interrupt
__declspec	_loadds
__ds	__loadds
_ds	near
__es	__near
_es	_near
__except	_pascal
__export	__pascal
_export	pascal
far	__rtti
_far	__saveregs
__far	_saveregs
__fastcall	__seg
_fastcall	_seg
__finally	_ss
__huge	__thread
_huge	__try
huge	

C++ specific keywords

There are several keywords specific to C++. They are not available if you are writing a C-only program.

The keywords specific to C++ are:

asm	inline	template	typename
bool	mutable	this	
catch	namespace	throw	
class	new	true	
const_cast	operator	try	
delete	private	typeid	

dynamic_cast	protected	reinterpret_cast
explicit	public	using
false	__rtti	virtual
friend	static_cast	wchar

Modifiers

A declaration uses modifiers to alter aspects of the identifier/object mapping.

The Borland C++ modifiers are:
__cdecl
const
__cs
__declspec
__ds
__es
__export
__far
__fastcall
__huge
__import
__interrupt
__loadds
__near
__pascal
__rtti
__ss
__stdcall
volatile

Operator keywords

Several Borland C++ keywords denote operators that invoke functions against objects and identifiers.

The keyword operators supported by Borland C++ are:

delete	operator	typeid
new	sizeof	

See also Operators

Statement keywords

Statements specify the flow of control in a program. In the absence of specific jumps and selection statements, statements execute sequentially as they appear in the source code.

The statement keywords in Borland C++ are:

break	else	switch
case	__finally	throw
catch	for__try	
continue	goto	try
default	if while	
do	return	
__except		

Storage class specifiers

Storage classes specifiers are also called type specifiers. They dictate the location (data segment, register, heap, or stack) of an object and its duration or lifetime (the entire running time of the program, or during execution of some blocks of code). Storage class can be established by the declaration syntax, by its placement in the source code, or by both of these factors.

The keyword **mutable** does not affect the lifetime of the class member to which it is applied.

The storage class specifiers in Borland C++ are:

auto	mutable	static
__declspec	register	
extern		typedef

Type specifiers

The type determines how much memory is allocated to an object and how the program interprets the bit patterns found in the object's storage allocation. A data type is the set of values (often implementation-dependent) identifiers can assume, together with the set of operations allowed on those values.

The type specifier keywords in Borland C++ are:

char	float	signed	wchar_t
class	int	struct	
double	long	union	
enum	short	unsigned	

Use the *sizeof* operators to find the size in bytes of any predefined or user-defined type.

Register pseudovariables

_AX	_AL	_AH	_SI	_es
_BX	_BL	_BH	_DI	_ss
_CX	_CL	_CH	_BP	_cs
_DX	_DL	_DH	_SP	_ds
_FLAGS				

All but the _FLAGS register pseudovariable are associated with the general purpose, segment, address, and special purpose registers.

Use register pseudovariables anywhere that you can use an integer variable to directly access the corresponding 80x86 register.

The 16-bit flags register contains information about the state of the 80x86 and the results of recent instructions.

Example

```
_AX = 0x4c00;
```

Parameter types and possible registers used

The compiler uses the following rules when deciding which parameters are to be passed in registers.

Parameter type	Registers
char (signed and unsigned)	AL, DL, BL
int (signed and unsigned)	AX, DX, BX
long (signed and unsigned)	DX:AX
near pointer	AX, DX, BX

Only three parameters can be passed in registers to any one function.

Do not assume the assignment of registers will reflect the ordering of the parameters to a function. Far pointer, union, structure, and floating-point (float, double, and long) parameters are pushed on the stack.

Keyword alphabetical reference

asm, _asm, __asm

```
asm <opcode> <operands> <; or newline>
_asm <opcode> <operands> <; or newline>
__asm <opcode> <operands> <; or newline>
```

Use the **asm, _asm,** or **__asm** keyword to place assembly language statements in the middle of your C or C++ source code. Any C++ symbols are replaced by the appropriate assembly language equivalents.

You can group assembly language statements by beginning the block of statements with the **asm** keyword, then surrounding the statements with braces ({ }). The initial brace must be on the same line as the **asm** keyword; placing it on the following line generates a syntax error.

Examples

```
// This example places a single assembler statement in your code:
asm pop dx

// If you want to include several of asm statements,
// surround them with braces:
asm {
  mov ax, 0x0e07
  xor bx, bx
  int 0x10        // makes the system beep
}
```

See also BASM, "Using inline assembly"

auto

[auto] <data-definition> ;
Use the **auto** modifer to define a local variable as having a local lifetime.

This is the default for local variables and is rarely used.

Example

```
int main()
{
  auto int i;
  i = 5;
  return i;
}
```

break

break ;
Use the **break** statement within loops to pass control to the first statement following the innermost enclosing brace.

See also continue, do, for, switch, while

Example

```
/* Illustrates the use of keywords break, case, default, and switch. */
#include <conio.h>
#include <stdio.h>

int main(void) {
    int ch;
```

```
    printf("\tPRESS a, b, OR c. ANY OTHER CHOICE WILL "
        "TERMINATE THIS PROGRAM.");
    for ( /* FOREVER */; ((ch = getch()) != EOF); )
        switch (ch) {
            case 'a' :    /* THE CHOICE OF a HAS ITS OWN ACTION. */
                printf("\nOption a was selected.\n");
                break;
            case 'b' :    /* BOTH b AND c GET THE SAME RESULTS. */
            case 'c' :
                printf("\nOption b or c was selected.\n");
                break;
            default :
                printf("\nNOT A VALID CHOICE!  Bye ...");
                return(-1);
        }
    return(0);
    }
```

bool

bool <identifier>;

Use **bool** and the literals **false** and **true** to make Boolean logic tests.

The **bool** keyword represents a type that can take only the value **false** or **true**. The keywords **false** and **true** are Boolean literals with predefined values. **false** is numericallly zero and **true** is numerically one. These Boolean literals are rvalues; you cannot make an assignment to them.

You can convert an rvalue that is **bool** type to an rvalue that is **int** type. The numerical conversion sets **false** to zero and **true** becomes one.

You can convert arithmetic, enumeration, pointer, or pointer to member rvalue types to an rvalue of type **bool**. A zero value, null pointer value, or null member pointer value is converted to **false**. Any other value is converted to **true**.

See also   if

Example

```
/* How to make Boolean tests with bool, true, and false. */
#include <iostream.h>

bool func() {    // Function returns a bool type
    return NULL;  // NULL is converted to Boolean false
// return false;  // This statement is Boolean equivalent to the one above.
    }

int main() {
    bool val = false;   // Boolean variable
    int i = 1;          // i is neither Boolean-true nor Boolean-false
    int g = 3;
    int *iptr = 0;      // null pointer
    float j = 1.01;     // j is neither Boolean-true nor Boolean-false
```

```
    // Tests on integers
    if (i == true)  cout << "True: value is 1" << endl;
    if (i == false) cout << "False: value is 0" << endl;

    if (g) cout << "g is true.";
    else cout << "g is false.";

    // Test on pointer
    if (iptr == false) cout << "Invalid pointer." << endl;
    if (iptr == true) cout << "Valid pointer." << endl;

    // To test j's truth value, cast it to bool type.
    if (bool(j) == true) cout << "Boolean j is true." << endl;

    // Test Boolean function return value
    val = func();
    if (val == false)
       cout << "func() returned false.";
    if (val == true)
       cout << "func() returned true.";
    return false;  // false is converted to 0
}
```

Output:

```
True: value is 1
Unknown truth value for g.
Invalid pointer.
Boolean j is true.
func() returned false.
```

case

```
switch ( <switch variable> ){
  case <constant expression> : <statement>; [break;]
    ⋮
  default : <statement>;
}
```

Use the **case** statement in conjunction with switches to determine which statements evalute.

The list of possible branch points within *<statement>* is determined by preceding substatements with

```
    case <constant expression> : <statement>;
```

where *<constant expression>* must be an **int** and must be unique.

The *<constant expression>* values are searched for a match for the *<switch variable>*.

If a match is found, execution continues after the matching **case** statement until a **break** statement is encountered or the end of the **switch** statement is reached.

If no match is found, control is passed to the **default** case.

Note   It is illegal to have duplicate **case** constants in the same **switch** statement.

See also   break, default, switch

catch

catch (exception-declaration) compound-statement
The exception handler is indicated by the **catch** keyword. The handler must be used immediately after the statements marked by the try keyword. The keyword **catch** can also occur immediately after another **catch**. Each handler will only evaluate an exception that matches, or can be converted to, the type specified in its argument list.

See also   C++ Exception Handling, throw

cdecl, _cdecl, __cdecl

cdecl <data/function definition> ;
_cdecl <data/function definition> ;
_ _cdecl <data/function definition> ;
Use a **cdecl**, **_cdecl**, or **_ _cdecl** modifier to declare a variable or a function using the C-style naming conventions (case-sensitive, with a leading underscore appended). When you use **cdecl**, **_cdecl**, or **_ _cdecl** in front of a function, it affects how the parameters are passed (last parameter is pushed first, and the caller cleans up the stack). The **_ _cdecl** modifier overrides the compiler directives and IDE options and allows the function to be called as a regular C function.

The **cdecl**, **_cdecl**, and **_ _cdecl** keywords are specific to Borland C++.

Example

```
int cdecl FileCount;
long far cdecl HisFunc(int x);
```

char

[signed|unsigned] char <variable_name>
Use the type specifier **char** to define a character data type. Variables of type **char** are 1 byte in length.

A **char** can be signed, unsigned, or unspecified. By default, **signed char** is assumed.

Objects declared as characters (**char**) are large enough to store any member of the basic ASCII character set.

See also   data types (16-bit), data types (32-bit)

class

<classkey> <classname> [<:baselist>] { <member list> }

- *<classkey>* is either a class, struct, or union.

- *<classname>* can be any name unique within its scope.

- *<baselist>* lists the base class(es) that this class derives from; *<baselist>* is optional.

- *<member list>* declares the class' data members and member functions.

Use the **class** keyword to define a C++ class.

Within a class:

- the data are called data members

- the functions are called member functions

Example

```
class stars {
    int magnitude;        // Data member
    int starfunc(void);   // Member function
};
```

See also   Borland *C++ Programmer's Guide*, Chapter 3, "C++ specifics," private, protected, public, this

const

const <variable name> [= <value>] ;
<function name> (const <type>*<variable name> ;)
<function name> const;
Use the **const** modifier to make a variable value unmodifiable.

Use the **const** modifier to assign an initial value to a variable that cannot be changed by the program. Any future assignments to a **const** result in a compiler error.

A **const** pointer cannot be modified, though the object to which it points can be changed. Consider the following examples.

```
const float pi   = 3.14;
const  maxint  = 12345;    // When used by itself, const is equivalent to int.
char *const str1 = "Hello, world";           // A constant pointer
char const *str2 = "Borland International";  A pointer to a constant character
string.
```

Given these declarations, the following statements are legal.

```
pi   = 3.0;       // Assigns a value to a const.
i    = maxint++;  // Increments a const.
str1 = "Hi, there!" // Points str1 to something else.
```

Using the const keyword in C++ programs

C++ extends **const** to include classes and member functions. In a C++ class definition, use the **const** modifier following a member function declaration. The member function is prevented from modifying any data in the class.

A class object defined with the **const** keyword attempts to use only member functions that are also defined with **const**. If you call a member function that is not defined as **const**, the compiler issues a warning that the a non-**const** function is being called for a **const** object. Using the **const** keyword in this manner is a safety feature of C.

Warning A pointer can indirectly modify a **const** variable, as in the following:

```
*(int *)&my_age = 35;
```

If you use the **const** modifier with a pointer parameter in a function's parameter list, the function cannot modify the variable that the pointer points to. For example,

```
int printf (const char *format, ...);
```

printf is prevented from modifying the format string.

See also const_cast, mutable, volatile

Example 1

```
class X  {
   int j;
public:
   X::X() { j = 0; };
   int lowerBound() const;          // DOES NOT MODIFY ANY DATA MEMBERS
   int dimension(X x1, const X &x2) { // x2 DATA MEMBERS WON'T BE MODIFIED
      x1.j = 3;        // OKAY; x1 OBJECT IS MODIFIABLE
      x2.j = 5;        // ERROR; x2 IS NOT MODIFIABLE
      return x2.j;
      }
};
```

Example 2

```
#include <iostream.h>

class Alpha {
   int num;
public:
   Alpha(int j = 0) { num = j; }
   int func(int i) const {
      cout << "Non-modifying function." << endl;
      return i++;
      }
   int func(int i) {
      cout << "Modify private data" << endl;
      return num = i;
      }
   int f(int i) { cout << "Non-
const function called with i = " << i << endl; return i;}
```

```
    };

    void main() {
        Alpha alpha_mod;          // Calls the non-const functions.
        const Alpha alpha_inst;   // Attempts to call the const functions.

        alpha_mod.func(1);
        alpha_mod.f(1);           // Causes a compiler warning.

        alpha_inst.func(1);
        alpha_inst.f(1);
    }
```

Output

```
    Modify private data
    Non-const function called with i = 1
    Non-modifying function.
    Non-const function called with i = 1
```

continue

continue ;

Use the **continue** statement within loops to pass control to the end of the innermost enclosing brace; at which point the loop continuation condition is re-evaluated.

See also   while, do, for

Example

```
    void main ()
    {
      for (i = 0; i < 20; i++) {
        if (array[i] == 0)
          continue;
        array[i] = 1/array[i];
      }
    }
```

_cs, _ _cs

<type> _cs <pointer definition> ;
<type> _ _cs <pointer definition> ;
Use the _cs and _ _cs keywords to define special versions of near data pointers.

These pointers are 16-bit offsets associated with the specified segment register: CS.

Example

```
char _cs  *s;      /* in cs code segment  */
```

See also   _ds, _ _ds, _es, _ _es, _ss, _ _ss

_ _declspec

_ _declspec(decl-modifier)

Use the _ _**declspec** keyword to indicate the storage class attributes for a DLL.

The _ _**declspec** keyword extends the attribute syntax for storage class modifiers so that their placement in a declarative statement is more flexible. The _ _**declspec** keyword and its argument can appear anywhere in the declarator list, as opposed to the old style modifiers which could only appear immediately preceding the identifier to be modified.

```
_ _export void f(void);                  // illegal
void _ _export f(void)                   // correct
void _ _declspec(dllexport) f(void);     // correct
_ _declspec(dllexport)void f(void);      // correct
class _ _declspec(dllexport) ClassName { }   // correct
```

The *decl-modifier* argument can only be one of *dllexport*, *dllimport*, or *thread*. The meaning of these arguments is equivalent to the following storage class attribute keywords.

Argument	Storage class	Compiler support
dllexport	_ _export	32- and 16-bit
dllimport	_ _import	32- bit (legal, but no effect on 16-bit programs)
thread	_ _thread	32- bit only

See also   _ _export, _ _import, _ _thread

Example

```
/* Examples of  _ _declspec declarations follow. */
_ _declspec(dllimport) void func(void);
_ _declspec(dllimport) int a;
_ _declspec(dllexport) void bar (void);

/** Use thread argument only with static storage data. **/
_ _declspec(thread) int th;
int _ _declspec(thread) th1;
```

default

```
switch ( <switch variable> ){
  case <constant expression> : <statement>; [break;]
     ⋮
  default : <statement>;
}
```

Use the **default** statement in **switch** statement blocks.

- If a **case** match is not found and the **default** statement is found within the **switch** statement, the execution continues at this point.

- If no default is defined in the **switch** statement, control passes to the next statement that follows the **switch** statement block.

See also   break

defined

```
#if defined[(] <identifier> [)]
#elif defined[(] <identifier> [)]
```

Use the **defined** operator to test if an identifier was previously defined using #define. The **defined** operator is only valid in #if and #elif expressions.

Defined evaluates to 1 (true) if a previously defined symbol has not been undefined (using #undef); otherwise, it evaluates to 0 (false).

Defined performs the same function as **#ifdef**.

```
#if defined(mysym)
```

is the same as

```
#ifdef mysym
```

The advantage is that you can use **defined** repeatedly in a complex expression following the **#if** directive; for example,

```
#if defined(mysym) && !defined(yoursym)
```

See also   #ifdef directive, The Preprocessor

delete

```
<::> delete <cast-expression>
<::> delete [ ] <cast-expression>
delete <array-name> [ ];
```

The **delete** operator offers dynamic storage deallocation, deallocating a memory block allocated by a previous call to new. It is similar but superior to the standard library function free.

You should use the **delete** operator to remove arrays that you no longer need. Failure to free memory can result in memory leaks.

See also   "The delete operator with arrays, ""Overloading the operator delete"

The delete operator with arrays

Arrays are deleted by operator **delete[]()**. You must use the syntax **delete []** *expr* when deleting an array. After C++ 2.1, the array dimension should not be specified within the brackets:

```
char * p;

void func()
{
   p = new char[10];     //  allocate 10 chars
   delete[] p;           // delete 10 chars
}
```

C++ 2.0 code required the array size. In order to allow 2.0 code to compile, Borland C++ issues a warning and simply ignores any size that is specified. For example, if the preceding example reads **delete[10] p** and is compiled, the warning is as follows:

```
Warning: Array size for 'delete' ignored in function func()
```

Overloading the operator delete

The global operators, **::operator delete()**, and **::operator delete[]()** cannot be overloaded. However, you can override the default version of each of these operators with your own implementation. Only one instance of the each global **delete** function can exist in the program.

The user-defined operator **delete** must have a **void** return type and **void*** as its first argument; a second argument of type size_t is optional. A class *T* can define at most one version of each of *T*::**operator delete[]()** and *T*::**operator delete()**. To overload the **delete** operators, use the following prototypes:

```
void operator delete(void *Type_ptr, [size_t Type_size]);     // For Non-array

void operator delete[](size_t Type_ptr, [size_t Type_size]); // For arrays
```

do

do <statement> while (<condition>);
The **do** statement executes until the condition becomes **false**.

<statement> is executed repeatedly as long as the value of <condition> remains **true**.

Since the conditon tests after each the loop executes the <statement>, the loop will execute at least once.

Example

```
/* This example prompts users for a password  */
/* and continued to prompt them until they    */
/* enter one that matches the value stored in */
/* checkword.                                  */

#include <stdio.h>
```

```
#include <string.h>

int main ()
{
  char checkword[80] = "password";
  char password[80]   = "";

  do {
    printf ("Enter password: ");
    scanf("%s", password);
  } while (strcmp(password, checkword));

  return 0;
}
```

See also   while, bool

double

[long] double <identifier>

Use the **double** type specifier to define an identifier to be a floating-point data type. The optional modifier **long** extends the accuracy of the floating-point value.

If you use the **double** keyword, the Borland C++ IDE will automatically link the floating-point math package into your program.

See also   data types (16-bit), data types (32-bit), float, long

_ds, _ _ds

<type> _ds <pointer definition> ;
<type> _ _ds <pointer definition> ;

Use the **_ds** and **_ _ds** keywords to define special versions of near data pointers.

These pointers are 16-bit offsets associated with the specified segment register: DS.

Example

```
long _ds  l[4] ;  /* in ds data segment  */
```

See also   _cs, _ _cs, _es, _ _es, _ss, _ _ss

enum

enum [<type_tag>] {<constant_name> [= <value>], ...} [var_list];

- *<type_tag>* is an optional type tag that names the set.

- *<constant_name>* is the name of a constant that can optionally be assigned the value of *<value>*. These are also called enumeration constants.

- *<value>* must be an integer. If <value> is missing, it is assumed to be:

  - *<prev>* + 1

  - where *<prev>* is the value of the previous integer constant in the list. For the first integer constant in the list, the default value is 0.

- *<var_list>* is an optional variable list that assigns variables to the enum type.

Use the **enum** keyword to define a set of constants of type **int**, called an enumeration data type.

An enumeration data type provides mnemonic identifiers for a set of integer values. Borland C++ stores enumerators in a single byte if you uncheck Treat Enums As Ints (O | C | Code Generation) or use the **-b** flag.

Enums are always interpreted as **int**s if the range of values permits, but if they are not **int**s the value gets promoted to an **int** in expressions. Depending on the values of the enumerators, identifiers in an enumerator list are implicitly of type **signed char**, **unsigned char**, or **int**.

In C, an enumerated variable can be assigned any value of type **int**—no type checking beyond that is enforced. In C++, an enumerated variable can be assigned only one of its enumerators.

In C++, lets you omit the **enum** keyword if *<tag_type>* is not the name of anything else in the same scope. You can also omit *<tag_type>* if no further variables of this **enum** type are required.

In the absence of a *<value>* the first enumerator is assigned the value of zero. Any subsequent names without initializers will then increase by one. *<value>* can be any expression yielding a positive or negative integer value (after possible integer promotions). These values are usually unique, but duplicates are legal.

Enumeration tags share the same name space as structure and union tags. Enumerators share the same name space as ordinary variable identifiers.

In C++, enumerators declared within a class are in the scope of that class.

Examples

```
enum days { sun, mon, tues, wed, thur, fri, sat } anyday;
```

Establishes a unique integral type, **enum** *days*, a variable *anyday* of this type, and a set of enumerators (*sun*, *mon*,...) with constant integer values.

```
enum modes { LASTMODE = -1, BW40=0, C40, BW80, C80, MONO = 7 };
/*
    "modes" is the type tag.
```

```
    "LASTMODE", "BW40", "C40", etc. are the constant names.
    The value of C40 is 1 (BW40 + 1); BW80 = 2 (C40 + 1), etc.
*/
```

_es, _ _es

<type> _es <pointer definition> ;
<type> _ _es <pointer definition> ;
Use the **_es** and **_ _es** keywords to define special versions of near data pointers.

These pointers are 16-bit offsets associated with the specified segment register: ES.

Example

```
    char _es  m[8] ;  /* in es segment      */
```

See also   __cs, _ _cs, ds, _ _ds, _ss, _ _ss

__except

_ _except (expression) compound-statement
The **_ _except** keyword specifies the action that should be taken when the exception specified by *expression* has been raised.

explicit

explicit <single-parameter constructor declaration>
Normally, a class with a single-parameter constructor can be assigned a value that matches the constructor type. This value is automatically (implicitly) converted into an object of the class type to which it is being assigned. You can prevent this kind of implicit conversion from occurring by declaring the constructor of the class with the **explicit** keyword. Then all objects of that class must be assigned values that are of the class type; all other assignments result in a compiler error.

Objects of the following class can be assigned values that match the constructor type or the class type:

```
class X {
public:
  X(int);
  X(const char*, int = 0);
};
```

Then, the following assignment statements are legal:

```
void f(X arg) {
  X a = 1;
  X B = "Jessie";
  a = 2;
}
```

However, objects of the following class can be assigned values that match the class type only:

```
class X {
public:
  explicit X(int);
  explicit X(const char*, int = 0);
};
```

The **explicit** constructors then require the values in the following assignment statements to be converted to the class type to which they are being assigned.

```
void f(X arg) {
  X a = X(1);
  X b = X("Jessie",0);
  a = X(2);
}
```

See also   C-Based Structured Exceptions, _ _finally, _ _try, try

_export, __export

Form 1   class _export <class name>

Form 2   return_type _export <function name>

Form 3   data_type _export <data name>
These modifiers are used to export classes, functions, and data.

The linker enters functions flagged with **_export** or **_ _export** into an export table for the module.

Using **_export** or **_ _export** eliminates the need for an EXPORTS section in your module definition file.

Note   Exported functions must be declared as **_ _far**. You can use the FAR type, defined in windows.h.

Functions that are not modified with **_export** or **_ _export** receive abbreviated prolog and epilog code, resulting in a smaller object file and slightly faster execution.

Note   If you use **_export** or **_ _export** to export a function, that function will be exported by name rather than by ordinal (ordinal is usually more efficient).

If you want to change various attributes from the default, you'll need a module definition file.

Prologs, epilogs, and exports: a summary

Prologs and epilogs are required when exporting functions in a 16-bit Windows application. They ensure that the correct data segment is active during callback functions and mark near and far stack frames for Windows stack crawling. Two steps are required to export a function.

1 The compiler must create the correct prolog and epilog for the function.

2 The linker must create an entry for every export function in the header section of the executable.

In 32-bit Windows the binding of data segments does not apply. However, DLLs must have entries in the header so the loader can find the function to link to when an .EXE loads the DLL

If a function is flagged with the _ _**export** keyword and any of the Windows compiler options are used, it will be compiled as exportable and linked as an export.

If a function is *not* flagged with the _ _**export** keyword, then one of the following situations will determine whether the function is exportable:

• If you compile with the -tW/-tWC or -tWD/-tWCD option (or with the All Functions Exportable IDE equivalent), the function will be compiled as exportable.

• If the function is listed in the EXPORTS section of the module definition file, the function will be linked as an export. If it is not listed in the module definition file, or if no module definition file is linked, it won't be linked as an export.

• If you compile with the -tWE or -tWDE/-tWCDE option (or with the Explicit Functions Exported IDE equivalent), the function will *not* be compiled as exportable. Including this function in the EXPORTS section of the module definition will cause it be exported, but, because the prolog is incorrect, the program will run incorrectly. You may get a Windows error message in the 16-bit environment.

See the table, Compiler options and the _export keyword, for a summary of the effect of the combination of the Windows compiler options and the _ _**export** keyword.

See also   _export, _import

Compiler options and the _ _export keyword

This table summarizes the effect of the combination of various Windows options and the _ _**export** keyword:

The compiler option is: *	-tW^2 or -tWD	-tWE^2 or -tWDE	-tW^2 or -tWD	-tWE^2 or -tWDE	-tW^2 or -tWD	-tWE^2 or -tWDE	-tW^2 or -tWD	-tWE^2 or -tWDE
Function flagged with _ _export?	Yes	Yes	Yes	Yes	No	No	No	No
Function^2 listed in EXPORTS?	Yes	Yes	No	No	Yes	Yes	No	No
Is function^2 exportable?	Yes	Yes	Yes	Yes	Yes	No	Yes	No
Will function be exported?	Yes	Yes	Yes	Yes	Yes	Yes **	No ***	No

*Or the 32-bit console-mode application equivalents.

**The function will be exported in some sense, but because the prolog and epilog will not be correct, the function will not work as expected.

***This combination also makes little sense. It is inefficient to compile all functions as exportable if you do not actually export some of them.

See also   _export

Smart callbacks and the _export keyword

If you use the Smart Callbacks IDE option at compile time, callback functions do not need to be listed in the EXPORTS statement or flagged with the **_export** keyword.

Functions compile them so that they are callback functions.

Exportable functions in DLLs

There are two ways to compile a function *f1( )* in a DLL as exportable and then export it.

- Compile the DLL with all functions exportable (with the Windows DLL All Functions Exportable option in the IDE) and list f1( ) in the EXPORTS section of the module definition file, or

- Flag the function f1( ) with the _export keyword.

Using _export with C++ classes

Whenever you declare a class as **_export**, the compiler treats it as huge (with 32-bit pointers), and exports all of its non-inline member functions and static data members.

You cannot declare a class as **_export** and as **_far** or **_huge** (**_export** implies **_huge**, which implies **_far**).

If you declare the class in an include file that is included in both the DLL source files and the source files of the application that use the DLL, declare the class

- as **_export** when compiling the DLL

- as **_huge** when compiling the application

To do this, use the _ _DLL_ _ macro, which the compiler defines when it's building a DLL.

Note   In the mangled name, the compiler encodes the information that a given class member is a member of a huge class. This ensures that the linker will catch any mismatches when a program is using huge and non-huge classes.

extern

extern <data definition> ;
[extern] <function prototype> ;

Use the **extern** modifier to indicate that the actual storage and initial value of a variable, or body of a function, is defined in a separate source code module. Functions declared with **extern** are visible throughout all source files in a program, unless you redefine the function as **static**.

The keyword **extern** is optional for a function prototype.

Use extern "c" to prevent function names from being mangled in C++ programs.

Examples

```
extern int _fmode;
extern void Factorial(int n);
extern "c" void cfunc(int);
```

far, _far, __far

<type> far <pointer definition> ;
<type> far <function definition>
<type> _far <pointer definition> ;
<type> _far <function definition>
<type> __far <pointer definition> ;
<type> __far <function definition>

Use the **far**, **_far** and **__far** modifiers to generate function code for calls and returns using variables that are outside of the data segment.

The first version of **far**, **_far**, or **__far** declares a pointer to be two words with a range of 1 megabyte. Use **__far** when compiling small or compact models to force pointers to be **__far**.

Examples

```
char __far *s;
void * __far * p;
int __far my_func() {}
```

_fastcall, __fastcall

_fastcall function-name
__fastcall function-name

Use the **_fastcall** modifiers to declare functions that expect parameters to be passed in registers.

The compiler treats this calling convention as a new language specifier, along the lines of **_cdecl** and **_pascal**.

Functions declared using **_cdecl** or **_pascal** cannot also have the **_fastcall** modifiers because they use the stack to pass parameters. Likewise, the **_fastcall** modifiers cannot be used together with **_export** or **_loadds**.

The compiler generates a warning if you mix functions of these types or if you use the **_fastcall** modifiers in a dangerous situation. You can, however, use functions that use the **_fastcall** or **__fastcall** conventions in overlaid modules (for example, with modules that will use VROOMM).

The compiler prefixes the **_fastcall** function name with an at-sign ("@"). This prefix applies to both unmangled C function names and to mangled C++ function names.

Note   The **__fastcall** modifier is subject to name mangling. See the description of the **-VC** option.

__finally

__finally {compound-statement}
The **__finally** keyword specifies actions that should be taken regardless of how the flow within the preceding **__try** exits.

The **__finally** keyword is supported only in C programs.

See also   "C-Based Structured Exceptions"

float

float <identifier>
Use the **float** type specifier to define an identifier to be a floating-point data type.

Type	Length	Range
float	32 bits	$3.4 * (10^{**}-38)$ to $3.4 * (10^{**}+38)$

The Borland C++ IDE automatically links the floating-point math package into you program if you use floating-point values or operators.

See also   double

for

for ([<initialization>] ; [<condition>] ; [<increment>]) <statement>
The **for** statement implements an iterative loop.

<statement> is executed repeatedly until the value of *<condition>* is false.

• Before the first iteration of the loop, *<initialization>* initializes variables for the loop.

• After each iteration of the loop, *<increments>* increments a loop counter. Consequently, j++ is functionally the same as ++j.

In C++, *<initialization>* can be an expression or a declaration.

The scope of any identifier declared within the **for** loop extends to the end of the control statement only.

A variable defined in the **for**-*initialization* expression is in scope only within the **for**-block. See the description of the **-Vd** option.

All the expressions are optional. If *<condition>* is left out, it is assumed to be always true.

Examples

```
// An example of the scope of variables in for-expressions.
// The example compiles if you use the -Vd option.
#include <iostream.h>

int main() {
    for (int i = 0; i < 10; i++)
        if (i == 8)
        cout << "\ni = " << i;
    return i;  // Undefined symbol 'i' in function main().
}
```

friend

friend <identifier>;

Use **friend** to declare a function or class with full access rights to the private and protected members of an outside class, without being a member of that class.

In all other respects, the **friend** is a normal function in terms of scope, declarations, and definitions.

Example

```
class stars {
    friend galaxy;
    int magnitude;
    int starfunc(void);
};

class galaxy {
    long int number_of_stars;
    void stars_magnitude(stars&);
    void stars_func(stars*);
}
```

goto

goto <identifier> ;

Use the **goto** statement to transfer control to the location of a local label specified by *<identifier>*.

Labels are always terminated by a colon.

Example

```
Again:          /* this is the label */
;
:
goto Again;
```

huge, _huge, _ _huge

```
<type> huge <pointer-definition> ;
<type> _huge <pointer-definition> ;
<type> _ _huge <pointer-definition> ;
```
The **_huge** modifiers are similar to the **_far** modifier except for two additional features:

- Its segment is normalized during pointer arithmetic so that pointer comparisons are accurate.

- Huge pointers can be incremented without suffering from segment wraparound.

See also   far

if

```
if ( <condition> )  <statement1>;
```

```
if ( <condition> )  <statement1>;
else  <statement2>;
```
Use **if** to implement a conditional statement.

You can declare variables in the *condition* expression. For example,

```
if (int val = func(arg))
```

is valid syntax. The variable *val* is in scope for the **if** statement and extends to an **else** block when it exists.

The condition statement must convert to a **bool** type. Otherwise, the condition is ill-formed.

When *<condition>* evaluates to **true**, *<statement1>* executes.

If *<condition>* is **false**, *<statement2>* executes.

The **else** keyword is optional, but no statements can come between an **if** statement and an **else**.

The #if and #else preprocessor statements (directives) look similar to the **if** and **else** statements, but have very different effects. They control which source file lines are compiled and which are ignored.

See also   bool

Examples

```
if (int val = func(count)) { /* statements */ }
else {
```

```
/* take other action */
cout << "val is false"
}
```

_import, _ _import

Form 1   class _import <class name>

class _ _import <class name>

Form 2   return_type _import <function name> //32-bit only

return_type _ _import <function name> //32-bit only

Form 3   data_type _import <data name> //32-bit only

data_type _ _import <data name> //32-bit only

This keyword can be used as a class modifier for 16-bit programs; and as a class, function, or data modifier in 32-bit programs. If you're importing classes that are declared with the modifier _ _**huge**, you must change the modifier to the keyword _ _**import**. The _ _**huge** modifier merely causes far addressing of the virtual tables (the same effect as the **-Vf** compiler option). The _ _**import** modifier makes all function and static addresses default to _**far**.

inline

inline <datatype> <class>_<function> (<parameters>) { <statements>; }

Use the **inline** keyword to declare or define C++ inline functions.

Inline functions are best reserved for small, frequently used functions.

Example

```
inline char* cat_func(void) { return char*; }
```

int

[signed|unsigned] int <identifier> ;

Use the **int** type specifier to define an integer data type.

Variables of type **int** can be **signed** (default) or **unsigned**.

See also   data types (16-bit), data types (32-bit), double

_ _interrupt functions

interrupt <function-definition> ;

_interrupt <function-definition> ;

_ _interrupt <function-definition> ;

Use the _ _**interrupt** function modifier to define a function as an interrupt handler.

The _ _**interrupt** modifier is specific to Borlalnd C++. _ _**interrupt** functions are designed to be used with interrupt vectors.

Interrupt functions compile with extra function entry and exit code so that all CPU registers are saved. The BP, SP, SS, CS, and IP registers are preserved as part of the C-calling sequence or as part of the interrupt handling itself. The function uses an IRET instruction to return, so that the function can be used as hardware and software interrupts.

Declare interrupt functions to be of type **void** and can be declared in any memory model. For all memory models except **huge**, DS is set to the program data segment. For the huge memory model, DS is set to the module's data segment.

Example

```
void interrupt myhandler()
{
...
}
```

_loadds, __loadds

_loadds <function-name>
_ _loadds <function-name>
Use the _ _**loadds** keyword to indicate that a function should set the DS register, just as a **huge** function does.

These keywords are useful for writing low-level interface routines, such as mouse support routines.

long

long [int] <identifier> ;
[long] double <identifier> ;
When used to modify an **int**, it doubles the number of bytes available to store the integer value.

When used to modify a **double**, it defines a floating-point data type with 80 bits of precision instead of 64.

The Borland C++ IDE links the floating-point math package if you use floating-point values or operators anywhere in your program.

See also   data types (16-bit), data types (32-bit), float

mutable

mutable <variable name>;
Use the **mutable** specifier to make a variable modifiable even though it is in a **const**-qualified expression.

Using the mutable keyword

Only class data members can be declared mutable. The **mutable** keyword cannot be used on **static** or **const** names. The purpose of **mutable** is to specify which data members can be modified by **const** member functions. Normally, a **const** member function cannot modify data members.

See also   const, const_cast, volatile

Example

```
#include <iostream.h>
class Alpha {
    mutable int count;
    mutable const int* iptr;
public:
    int func1(int i = 0) const { // Promises not to change const arguments.
        count = i++;  // But count can be changed.
        iptr = &i;
        cout << *iptr;
        return count;
        }
};

int main(void) {
    Alpha a;

    a.func1(0);
    return 0;
    }
```

near, _near, _ _near

`<type> near <pointer definition> ;`
`<type> near <function definition>`
`<type> _near <pointer definition> ;`
`<type> _near <function definition>`
`<type> _ _near <pointer definition> ;`
`<type> _ _near <function definition>`

Use **near** and **_near** type modifiers to force pointers to be near and to generate function code for a near call and a near return.

The first version of **_near** declares a pointer to be one word with a range of 64K.

Use this type modifier when compiling in the medium, large, or huge memory models to force pointers to be **near**.

When either **near** or **_near** is used with a function declaration, the compiler generates function code for a **near** call and a **near** return.

Example

```
char near *s;
int (near *ip)[10];
int near my_func() {}
```

new

<::> new <placement> type-name <(initializer)>
<::> new <placement> (type-name) <(initializer)>
The **new** operator offers dynamic storage allocation, similar but superior to the standard library function *malloc*. The **new** operator must always be supplied with a data type in place of *type-name*. Items surrounded by angle brackets are optional. The optional arguments can be as follows:

- :: operator, invokes the global version of **new**.

- *placement* can be used to supply additional arguments to **new**. You can use this syntax only if you have have an overloaded version of **new** that matches the optional arguments. See the discussion of the placement syntax.

- *initializer*, if present is used to initialize the allocation. Arrays cannot be initialized by the allocation operator.

A request for non-array allocation uses the appropriate **operator new()** function. Any request for array allocation will call the appropriate **operator new[]()** function. The selection of the allocation operator is done as follows:

Allocation of arrays of *Type*:

- Attempts to use a class-specific array allocator:

  Type::**operator new[]()**

- If the class-specific array allocator is not defined, the global version is used:

  ::**operator new[]()**

Allocation of non-arrays of *Type*:

- Attempts to used the class-specific allocator:

  Type::**operator new()**

- If the class-specific array allocator is not defined, the global version is used:

  ::**operator new()**

Allocation of single objects (that are not class-type) which are not held in arrays:

- Memory allocation for a non-array object is by using the ::**operator new()**. Note that this allocation function is always used for the predefined types. It is possible to overload this global operator function. However, this is generally not advised.

Allocation of arrays:

- Use the global allocation operator:

  ::**operator new[] ()**

Note Arrays of classes require the default constructor.

new tries to create an object of type *Type* by allocating (if possible) sizeof (*Type*) bytes in free store (also called the heap). **new** calculates the size of *Type* without the need for an explicit **sizeof** operator. Further, the pointer returned is of the correct type, "pointer to *Type*," without the need for explicit casting. The storage duration of the **new** object is from the point of creation until the operator **delete** destroys it by deallocating its memory, or until the end of the program.

If successful, **new** returns a pointer to the allocated memory. By default, an allocation failure (such as insufficient or fragmented heap memory) results in the predefined exception *xalloc* being thrown. Your program should always be prepared to catch the *xalloc* exception before trying to access the new object (unless you use a new-handler).

A request for allocation of 0 bytes returns a non-null pointer. Repeated requests for zero-size allocations return distinct, non-null pointers.

Operator new placement syntax

The *placement* syntax for **operator new( )** can be used only if you have overloaded the allocation operator with the appropriate arguments. You can use the *placement* syntax when you want to use and reuse a memory space which you set up once at the beginning of your program.

When you use the overloaded **operator new( )** to specify where you want an allocation to be placed, you are responsible for deleting the allocation. Because you call your version of the allocation operator, you cannot depend on the global **::operator delete( )** to do the cleanup.

To release memory, you make an explicit call on the destructor. This method for cleaning up memory should be used only in special situations and with great care. If you make an explicit call of a destructor before an object that has been constructed on the stack goes out of scope, the destructor will be called again when the stackframe is cleaned up.

Operator new placement syntax example

```
// An example of the placement syntax for operator new()
#include <iostream.h>

class Alpha {
  union {
    char  ch;
    char  buf[10];
    };
public:
    Alpha(char c = '\0') : ch(c) {
       cout << "character constructor" << endl;
       }
    Alpha(char *s) {
       cout << "string constructor" << endl;
       strcpy(buf,s);
       }
```

```
    ~Alpha( ) { cout << "Alpha::~Alpha() " << endl; }

    void * operator new(size_t, void * buf) {
        return buf;
        }
};

void main() {
    char *str = new char[sizeof(Alpha)];

    // Place 'X' at start of str.
    Alpha* ptr = new(str) Alpha('X');
    cout << "str[0] = " << str[0] << endl;

    // Explicit call of the destructor
    ptr -> Alpha::~Alpha();

    // Place a string in str buffer.
    ptr = new(str) Alpha("my string");
    cout << "\n str = " << str << endl;

    // Explicit call of the destructor
    ptr -> Alpha::~Alpha();
    delete[] str;
    }
```

Output

```
character constructor
str[0] = X
Alpha::~Alpha()
string constructor

 str = my string
Alpha::~Alpha()
```

Handling errors for the new operator

You can define a function to be called if the **new** operator fails. To tell the **new** operator about the new-handler function, use *set_new_handler* and supply a pointer to the new-handler. If you want **new** to return null on failure, you must use *set_new_handler(0)* .

The operator new with arrays

If *Type* is an array, the pointer returned by operator **new**[]() points to the first element of the array. When creating multidimensional arrays with **new**, all array sizes must be supplied (although the leftmost dimension doesn't have to be a compile-time constant):

```
mat_ptr = new int[3][10][12];    // OK
mat_ptr = new int[n][10][12];    // OK
mat_ptr = new int[3][][12];      // illegal
mat_ptr = new int[][10][12];     // illegal
```

Although the first array dimension can be a variable, all following dimensions must be constants.

Example of the new and delete operators

```
// ALLOCATE A TWO-DIMENSIONAL SPACE, INITIALIZE, AND DELETE IT.
#include <except.h>
#include <iostream.h>

void display(long double **);
void de_allocate(long double **);

int m = 3;                              // THE NUMBER OF ROWS.
int n = 5;                              // THE NUMBER OF COLUMNS.

int main(void) {
   long double **data;

   try {                                // TEST FOR EXCEPTIONS.
      data = new long double*[m];       // STEP 1: SET UP THE ROWS.
      for (int j = 0; j < m; j++)
         data[j] = new long double[n];  // STEP 2: SET UP THE COLUMNS
      }
   catch (xalloc) {   // ENTER THIS BLOCK ONLY IF xalloc IS THROWN.
      // YOU COULD REQUEST OTHER ACTIONS BEFORE TERMINATING
      cout << "Could not allocate. Bye ...";
      exit(-1);
      }

   for (int i = 0; i < m; i++)
      for (int j = 0; j < n; j++)
         data[i][j] = i + j;            // ARBITRARY INITIALIZATION

   display(data);
   de_allocate(data);
   return 0;
   }

void display(long double **data) {
   for (int i = 0; i < m; i++) {
      for (int j = 0; j < n; j++)
         cout << data[i][j] << " ";
      cout << "\n" << endl;
      }
   }

void de_allocate(long double **data) {
   for (int i = 0; i < m;  i++)
      delete[] data[i];                 // STEP 1: DELETE THE COLUMNS

   delete[] data;                       // STEP 2: DELETE THE ROWS
   }
```

::operator new

By default, if there is no overloaded version of **new**, a request for dynamic memory allocation always uses the global version of **new**, **::operator new()**. A request for array allocation calls **::operator new[]()**. With class objects of type name, a specific operator called *name***::operator new()** or *name***::operator new[]()** can be defined. When **new** is applied to class name objects it invokes the appropriate *name***::operator new** if it is present; otherwise, the global **::operator new** is used.

Only the **operator new()** function will accept an optional initializer. The array allocator version, **operator new[]()**, will not accept initializers. In the absence of explicit initializers, the object created by **new** contains unpredictable data (garbage). The objects allocated by **new**, other than arrays, can be initialized with a suitable expression between parentheses:

```
int_ptr = new int(3);
```

Arrays of classes with constructors are initialized with the default constructor. The user-defined **new** operator with customized initialization plays a key role in C++ constructors for class-type objects.

Overloading the operator new

The global **::operator new()** and **::operator new[]()** can be overloaded. Each overloaded instance must have a unique signature. Therefore, multiple instances of a global allocation operator can coexist in a single program.

Class-specific memory allocation operators can also be overloaded. The operator **new** can be implemented to provide alternative free storage (heap) memory-management routines, or implemented to accept additional arguments. A user-defined operator **new** must return a **void*** and must have a *size_t* as its first argument. To overload the **new** operators, use the following prototypes declared in the new.h header file.

- ```
  void * operator new(size_t Type_size); // For Non-array
  ```
- ```
  void * operator new[](size_t Type_size); // For arrays
  ```

The Borland C++ compiler provides *Type_size* to the **new** operator. Any data type may be substitued for *Type_size* except function names (although a pointer to function is permitted), class declarations, enumeration declarations, **const**, **volatile**.

Example of overloading the new and delete operators

```
#include <stdlib.h>

class X {
    ⋮
public:
    void* operator new(size_t size) { return newalloc(size);}
    void operator delete(void* p) { newfree(p); }
    X() { /* initialize here */ }
    X(char ch) { /* and here */ }
```

```
~X() { /* clean up here */ }
   ⋮
};
```

The *size* argument gives the size of the object being created, and *newalloc* and *newfree* are user-supplied memory allocation and deallocation functions. Constructor and destructor calls for objects of class *X* (or objects of classes derived from *X* that do not have their own overloaded operators **new** and **delete**) will invoke the matching user-defined *X*::**operator new()** and *X*::**operator delete()**, respectively. (Destructors will be called only if you use the **-xd** compiler option and an exception is thrown.)

The *X*::**operator new()**, *X*::**operator new[]()**, *X*::**operator delete()** and *X*::**operator delete[]()** operator functions are static members of *X* whether explicitly declared as static or not, so they cannot be virtual functions.

The standard, predefined (global) **::operator new()**, **::operator new[]()**, **:: operator delete()**, and **::operator delete[]()** operators can still be used within the scope of *X*, either explicitly with the global scope or implicitly when creating and destroying non-*X* or non-*X*-derived class objects. For example, you could use the standard **new** and **delete** when defining the overloaded versions:

```
void* X::operator new(size_t s)
{
   void* ptr = new char[s]; // standard new called
     ⋮
   return ptr;
}

void X::operator delete(void* ptr)
{
     ⋮
   delete (void*) ptr;      // standard delete called
}
```

The reason for the *size* argument is that classes derived from *X* inherit the *X*::**operator new()** and *X*::**operator new[]()**. The size of a derived class object may well differ from that of the base class.

operator

```
operator <operator symbol>( <parameters> )
{
   <statements>;
}
```

Use the **operator** keyword to define a new (overloaded) action of the given operator. When the operator is overloaded as a member function, only one argument is allowed, as *this is implicitly the first argument.

When you overload an operator as a friend, you can specify two arguments.

Example

```
new_complex operator +(complex c1, complex c2)
{
    return complex(c1.real + c2.real, c1.imag + c2.imag);
}
```

See also   class, overloading operators

pascal, _pascal, __pascal

pascal <data-definition/function-definition> ;
_pascal <data-definition/function-definition> ;
_ _pascal <data-definition/function-definition> ;
Use the **pascal**, **_pascal**, and **_ _pascal** keywords to declare a variable or a function using a Pascal-style naming convention (the name is in uppercase).

In addition, **pascal** declares Pascal-style parameter-passing conventions when applied to a function header (first parameter pushed first; the called function cleans up the stack).

In C++ programs, functions declared with the **pascal** modifer will still be mangled.

```
int pascal FileCount;
far pascal long ThisFunc(int x, char *s);
```

private

private: <declarations>
A **private** member can be accessed only by member functions and friends of the class in which it is declared.

Class members are **private** by default.

You can override the default struct access with **private** or **protected** but you cannot override the default **union** access.

Friend declarations are not affected by these access specifiers.

See also   class, friend, protected, public

protected

protected: <declarations>
A **protected** member can be accessed by member functions and friends of the class in which it was declared, and by classes derived from the declared class.

You can override the default struct access with **private** or **protected** but you cannot override the default **union** access.

Friend declarations are not affected by these access specifiers.

See also   class, friend, private, public

public

public: <declarations>
A **public** member can be accessed by any function.

Members of a **struct** or **union** are public by default.

You can override the default **struct** access with **private** or **protected** but you cannot override the default **union** access.

Friend declarations are not affected by these access specifiers.

See also   class, friend, private, protected, struct, union

register

register <data definition> ;
Use the **register** storage class specifier to store the variable being declared in a CPU register (if possible), to optimize access and reduce code.

Items declared with the **register** keyword have a global lifetime.

Note   The Borland C++ compiler can ignore requests for register allocation. Register allocation is based on the compiler's analysis of how a variable is used.

Example

```
register int i;
```

return

return [<expression>] ;
Use the **return** statement to exit from the current function back to the calling routine, optionally returning a value.

Example

```
double sqr(double x)
{
   return (x*x);
}
```

_ _rtti and the -RT option

Run-time type definition (RTTI) is enabled by default in Borland C++. You can use the -**RT** command-line option to disable it (-**RT-**) or to enable it (-**RT**). If RTTI is disabled, or if the argument to **typeid** is a pointer or a reference to a non-polymorphic class, **typeid** returns a reference to a **const** *typeinfo* object that describes the declared type of the pointer or reference, and not the actual object that the pointer or reference is bound to.

In addition, even when RTTI is disabled, you can force all instances of a particular class and all classes derived from that class to provide polymorphic run-time type identification (where appropriate) by using the Borland C++ keyword _ _**rtti** in the class definition.

When you use the **-RT-** compiler option, if any base class is declared _ _**rtti**, then all polymorphic base classes must also be declared _ _**rtti**.

```
struct _ _rtti S1 { virtual s1func(); };   /* Polymorphic */
struct _ _rtti S2 { virtual s2func(); };   /* Polymorphic */
struct X : S1, S2 { };
```

If you turn off the RTTI mechanism (by using the **-RT-** compiler option), RTTI might not be available for derived classes. When a class is derived from multiple classes, the order and type of base classes determines whether or not the class inherits the RTTI capability.

When you have polymorphic and non-polymorphic classes, the order of inheritance is important. If you compile the following declarations with -RT-, you should declare *X* with the _ _**rtti** modifier. Otherwise, switching the order of the base classes for the class *X* results in the compile-time error Can't inherit non-RTTI class from RTTI base '*S1*'.

```
struct _ _rtti S1 { virtual func(); };   /* Polymorphic class */
struct S2 { };                           /*  Non-polymorphic class */
struct _ _rtti X : S1, S2 { };
```

Note   The class X is explicitly declared with _ _**rtti**. This makes it safe to mix the order and type of classes.

In the following example, class X inherits only non-polymorphic classes. Class X does not need to be declared _ _**rtti**.

```
struct _ _rtti S1 { };   // Non-polymorphic class
struct S2 { };
struct X : S2, S1 { };   // The order is not essential
```

Applying either _ _**rtti** or using the **-RT** compiler option will not make a static class into a polymorphic class.

Run-time type identification (RTTI) overview

Run-time type identification (RTTI) lets you write portable code that can determine the actual type of a data object at run time even when the code has access only to a pointer or reference to that object. This makes it possible, for example, to convert a pointer to a virtual base class into a pointer to the derived type of the actual object. Use the dynamic_cast operator to make run-time casts.

The RTTI mechanism also lets you check whether an object is of some particular type and whether two objects are of the same type. You can do this with **typeid** operator, which determines the actual type of its argument and returns a reference to an object of type **const** *typeinfo*, which describes that type.

You can also use a type name as the argument to **typeid**, and **typeid** will return a reference to a **const** *typeinfo* object for that type. The class *typeinfo* provides an **operator==** and an **operator!=** that you can use to determine whether two objects are of the same type. Class *typeinfo* also provides a member function name that returns a pointer to a character string that holds the name of the type.

See also   Bad_typeid class, typeinfo class

_ _rtti Example

```
/* HOW TO GET RUN-TIME TYPE INFORMATION FOR POLYMORPHIC CLASSES.*/
#include <iostream.h>
#include <typeinfo.h>

class _ _rtti Alpha {          /* Provide RTTI for this class and */
                              /* all classes derived from it */

    virtual void func() {};  /* A virtual function makes */
                              /* Alpha a polymorphic class. */
};

class B : public Alpha {};

int main(void) {
    B Binst;              // Instantiate class B
    B *Bptr;              // Declare a B-type pointer
    Bptr = &Binst;        // Initialize the pointer

    // THESE TESTS ARE DONE AT RUN TIME
    try {
       if (typeid( *Bptr ) == typeid( B ) )
           // Ask "WHAT IS THE TYPE FOR *Bptr?"
           cout << "Name is " << typeid( *Bptr ).name();
       if (typeid( *Bptr ) != typeid( Alpha ) )
           cout << "\nPointer is not an Alpha-type.";
       return 0;
       }
    catch (Bad_typeid) {
       cout << "typeid() has failed.";
       return 1;
       }
    }
```

Output

```
Name is B
Pointer is not an Alpha-type.
```

-RT option and destructors

When **-xd** is enabled, a pointer to a class with a virtual destructor can't be deleted if that class is not compiled with **-RT**. The **-RT** and **-xd** options are on by default.

Example

```
class Alpha {
public:
    virtual ~Alpha( ) { }
};
void func( Alpha *Aptr ) {
    delete Aptr;           // Error.  Alpha is not a polymorphic class type
    }
```

_saveregs, _ _saveregs

_saveregs <function-name>;
_ _saveregs <function-name>;

The _ _**saveregs** modifier causes the function to preserve all register values and restore them before returning (except for explicit return values passed in registers such as AX or DX). _ _**saveregs** is not available in flat mode.

Use this keyword with functions; it is useful for writing low-level interface routines, such as mouse support routines.

Note   The _ _**saveregs** modifier is subject to name mangling. See the description of the **-VC** option for more information.

See also   _loadds

_seg, _ _seg

<datatype> _seg *<identifier> ;
<datatype> _ _seg *<identifier> ;

Use _**seg** in 16-bit segment pointer type declarators. _**seg** is not available in flat mode.

Any indirection through *<identifier>* has an assumed offset of 0. In arithmetic involving segment pointers they are treated like pointers except for the following restrictions.

• You cannot use the ++, --, +=, or -= operators with segment pointers.

• You cannot subtract one segment pointer from another.

• If you add a **near** pointer to a segment pointer, the operation creates a **far** pointer result by using the segment from the segment pointer and the offset from the **near** pointer.

  Therefore, the two pointers must point to the same type, or one must be a pointer to **void**.

  There is no multiplication of the offset, regardless of the type pointed to.

• When a segment pointer is used in an indirection expression, it also implicitly converts to a **far** pointer.

• If you add or subtract an integer operand to or from a segment pointer, the result is a **far** pointer. The segment is taken from the segment pointer; the offset is calculated by multiplying the size of the object pointed to by the integer operand.

- Segment pointers can be assigned, initialized, passed into and out of functions, and compared.

Example

```
int _seg *name;
```

short

short int <variable> ;
Use the **short** type modifier when you want a variable smaller than an **int**. This modifier can be applied to the base type **int**.

When the base type is omitted from a declaration, **int** is assumed.

Examples

```
short int i;
short     i;    /* same as "short int i;" */
```

See also   long, signed, unsigned

signed

signed <type> <variable> ;
Use the **signed** type modifier when the variable value can be either positive or negative. The **signed** modifier can be applied to base types **int**, **char**, **long** and **short**.

When the base type is omitted from a declaration, **int** is assumed.

Example

```
signed   int       i;    /* signed is default      */
signed             i;    /* same as "signed int i;" */
unsigned long int  l;    /* int OK, not needed      */
signed   char      ch;   /* unsigned is default     */
```

See also   char, int, long, short, unsigned

sizeof

The **sizeof** operator has two distinct uses:

- **sizeof** *unary-expression*
- **sizeof** (*type-name*)

The result in both cases is an integer constant that gives the size in bytes of how much memory space is used by the operand (determined by its type, with some exceptions). The amount of space that is reserved for each type depends on the machine.

In the first use, the type of the operand expression is determined without evaluating the expression (and therefore without side effects). When the operand is of type **char** (**signed** or **unsigned**), **sizeof** gives the result 1. When the operand is a non-parameter of array type, the result is the total number of bytes in the array (in other words, an array name is not converted to a pointer type). The number of elements in an array equals *sizeof array/ sizeof array[0]* .

If the operand is a parameter declared as array type or function type, **sizeof** gives the size of the pointer. When applied to structures and unions, **sizeof** gives the total number of bytes, including any padding.

You cannot use **sizeof** with expressions of function type, incomplete types, parenthesized names of such types, or with an lvalue that designates a bit field object.

The integer type of the result of **sizeof** is *size_t*, defined in stddef.h.

You can use **sizeof** in preprocessor directives; this is specific to Borland C++.

In C++, *sizeof(classtype)* , where *classtype* is derived from some base class, returns the size of the object (remember, this includes the size of the base class).

Example

```
/*  USE THE sizeof OPERATOR TO GET SIZES OF DIFFERENT DATA TYPES. */
#include <stdio.h>
struct st {
    char *name;     /* 2 BYTES IN SMALL-DATA MODELS; 4 BYTES IN LARGE-DATA MODEL */
    int age;        /* 2 BYTES IN SMALL-DATA MODELS; 4 BYTES IN LARGE-DATA MODEL */
    double height;  /* ALWAYS EIGHT BYTES */
        };

struct st St_Array[]= {  /* AN ARRAY OF structs */
    { "Jr.",     4,  34.20 },  /* ST_Array[0] */
    { "Suzie",  23,  69.75 },  /* ST_Array[1] */
    };
int main() {
    long double LD_Array[] = { 1.3, 501.09, 0.0007, 90.1, 17.08 };

    printf("(\nNumber of elements in LD_Array = %d",
            sizeof(LD_Array) / sizeof(LD_Array[0]));

    /****  THE NUMBER OF ELEMENTS IN THE ST_Array. ****/
    printf("\nSt_Array has %d elements",
            sizeof(St_Array)/sizeof(St_Array[0]));

    /****  THE NUMBER OF BYTES IN EACH ST_Array ELEMENT.  ****/
    printf("\nSt_Array[0] = %d", sizeof(St_Array[0]));

    /****  THE TOTAL NUMBER OF BYTES IN ST_Array.  ****/
        printf("\nSt_Array=%d", sizeof(St_Array));
    return 0;
    }
```

Output

```
Number of elements in LD_Array = 5
St_Array has 2 elements
St_Array[0] = 12
St_Array= 24
```

_ss, _ _ss

<type> _ss <pointer definition> ;
<type> _ _ss <pointer definition> ;
Use the **_ss** and **_ _ss** keywords to define special versions of near data pointers.

These pointers are 16-bit offsets associated with the specified segment register: SS.

Example
```
long _ss  ix ;   /* in ss stack segment  */
```

See also   _cs, _ _cs, _ds, _ _ds, _es, _ _es

static

static <data definition> ;
static <function name> <function definition> ;
Use the **static** storage class specifier with a local variable to preserve the last value between successive calls to that function. A **static** variable acts like a local variable but has the lifetime of an external variable.

In a class, data and member functions can be declared **static**. Only one copy of the **static** data exists for all objects of the class.

A **static** member function of a global class has external linkage. A member of a local class has no linkage. A **static** member function is associated only with the class in which it is declared. Therefore, such member functions cannot be **virtual**.

Static member functions can only call other **static** member functions and only have access to **static** data. Such member functions do not have a **this** pointer.

Example
```
static int i;
static void printnewline(void) {}
```

_stdcall, _ _ stdcall

_ _stdcall <function-name>
_stdcall <function-name>
The **_stdcall** and **_ _stdcall** keywords force the compiler to generate function calls using the Standard calling convention.The resulting function calls are smaller and faster. Functions must pass the correct number and type of arguments; this is unlike normal C use, which permits a variable number of function arguments. Such functions comply with the standard WIN32 argument-passing convention.

Note   The **_ _stdcall** modifier is subject to name mangling. See the description of the -VC option for more information.

struct

```
struct [<struct type name>] {
  [<type> <variable-name[, variable-name, ...]>] ;
  ⋮
} [<structure variables>] ;
```
Use a **struct** to group variables into a single record.

<struct type name>   An optional tag name that refers to the structure type.

<structure variables>   The data definitions, also optional.

Though both *<struct type name>* and *<structure variables>* are optional, one of the two must appear.

You define elements in the record by naming a *<type>*, followed by one or more *<variable-name>* (separated by commas).

Separate different variable types by a semicolon.

To access elements in a structure, use a record selector (.).

To declare additional variables of the same type, use the keyword **struct** followed by the *<struct type name>*, followed by the variable names.

Note   Borland C++ allows the use of anonymous **struct** embedded within another structure.

Example

```
struct my_struct {
  char name[80], phone_number[80];
  int  age, height;
} my_friend;

strcpy(my_friend.name,"Mr. Wizard");   /* accessing an element */

struct my_struct my_friends[100];   /* declaring additional variables */
```
See also   class, public, union, #pragma anon_struct

switch

```
switch ( <switch variable> ) {
  case <constant expression> : <statement>; [break;]
  ⋮
default : <statement>;
}
```
Use the **switch** statement to pass control to a **case** which matches the *<switch variable>*. At which point the statements following the matching **case** are evaluated .

If no **case** satisfies the condition the **default** case evaluates.

To avoid evaluating any other **case**s and reliquish control from the **switch**, terminate each **case** with **break;**.

See also   break, case, default

Example

```
/* Illustrates the use of keywords break, case, default, and switch. */
#include <conio.h>
#include <stdio.h>

int main(void) {
    int ch;

    printf("\tPRESS a, b, OR c. ANY OTHER CHOICE WILL "
           "TERMINATE THIS PROGRAM.");
    for ( /* FOREVER */; ((ch = getch()) != EOF); )
        switch (ch) {
            case 'a' :    /* THE CHOICE OF a HAS ITS OWN ACTION. */
                printf("\nOption a was selected.\n");
                break;
            case 'b' :    /* BOTH b AND c GET THE SAME RESULTS. */
            case 'c' :
                printf("\nOption b or c was selected.\n");
                break;
            default :
                printf("\nNOT A VALID CHOICE!  Bye ...");
                return(-1);
        }
    return(0);
}
```

template

template-declaration:
  template < template-argument-list > declaration

template-argument-list:
  template-argument
  template-argument-list, template argument

template-argument:
  type-argument
  argument-declaration

type-argument:
  class identifier

template-class-name:
  template-name < template-arg-list >

template-arg-list:
  template-arg
  template-arg-list , template-arg

template-arg:
    expression
    type-name

< template-argument-list > declaration

Use templates (also called generics or parameterized types) to construct a family of related functions or classes.

this

class X {
    int a;
public:
    X (int b) {this -> a = b;}

In nonstatic member functions, the keyword **this** is a pointer to the object for which the function is called. All calls to nonstatic member functions pass **this** as a hidden argument.

this is a local variable available in the body of any nonstatic member function. Use it implicitly within the function for member references. It does not need to be declared and it is rarely referred to explicitly in a function definition.

For example, in the call *x.func(y)*, where *y* is a member of *X*, the keyword **this** is set to *&x* and *y* is set to *this->y*, which is equivalent to *x.y*.

Static member functions do not have a **this** pointer because they are called with no particular object in mind. Thus, a static member function cannot access nonstatic members without explicitly specifying an object with . or ->.

See also   ., ->, class, new

throw

throw assignment-expression

When an exception occurs, the **throw** expression initializes a temporary object of the type *T* (to match the type of argument *arg*) used in *throw(T arg)*. Other copies can be generated as required by the compiler. Consequently, it can be useful to define a copy constructor for the exception object.

See also   catch, C++ Exception Handling, try

_ _try

_ _try compound-statement handler-list
_ _try compound-statement termination-statement

The _ _**try** keyword is supported only in C programs. Use try in C++ programs.

A block of code in which an exception can occur must be prefixed by the keyword _ _**try**. Following the **try** keyword is a block of code enclosed by braces. This indicates that the program is prepared to test for the existence of exceptions. If an exception occurs, the normal program flow is interrupted. The program begins a search for a handler that matches the exception. If the exception is generated in a C module, it is possible to handle the structured exception in either a C module or a C++ module.

If a handler can be found for the generated structured exception, the following actions can be taken:

- Execute the actions specified by the handler

- Ignore the generated exception and resume program execution

- Continue the search for some other handler (regenerate the exception)

If no handler is found, the program will call the *terminate* function. If no exceptions are thrown, the program executes in the normal fashion.

See also   C-Based Structured Exceptions, _ _except, catch, _ _finally, throw

Example

```
// In PROG.C
void func(void) {
    // generate an exception
    RaiseException( // specify your arguments );
}

// In CALLER.CPP
// How to test for C++ or C-based exceptions.
#include <excpt.h>
#include <iostream.h>

int main(void) {
    try
    {                // test for C++ exceptions
        try
        {            // test for C-based structured exceptions
            func();
        }
        _ _except( /* filter-expression */ )
        {
        cout << "A structured exception was generated.";
        /* specify actions to take for this structured exception */
        return -1;
        }
        return 0;
    }
    catch ( ... )
    {
    // handler for any C++ exception
    cout << "A C++ exception was thrown.";
    return 1;
    }
}
```

try

try compound-statement handler-list
The **try** keyword is supported only in C++ programs. Use _ _**try** in C programs.

A block of code in which an exception can occur must be prefixed by the keyword **try**. Following the **try** keyword is a block of code enclosed by braces. This indicates that the program is prepared to test for the existence of exceptions. If an exception occurs, the program flow is interrupted. The sequence of steps taken is as follows:

• The program searches for a matching handler

• If a handler is found, the stack is unwound to that point

• Program control is tranferred to the handler

If no handler is found, the program will call the *terminate* function. If no exceptions are thrown, the program executes in the normal fashion.

See also   catch, throw C++ Exception Handling

typedef

typedef <type definition> <identifier> ;
Use the **typedef** keyword to assign the symbol name *<identifier>* to the data type definition *<type definition>*.

typeid

typeid(expression)
typeid(type-name)
You can use **typeid** to get run-time identification of types and expressions. A call to **typeid** returns a reference to an object of type **const** typeinfo. The returned object represents the type of the **typeid** operand.

If the **typeid** operand is a dereferenced pointer or a reference to a polymorphic type, **typeid** returns the dynamic type of the actual object pointed or referred to. If the operand is non-polymorphic, **typeid** returns an object that represents the **static** type.

You can use the **typeid** operator with fundamental data types as well as user-defined types.

If the **typeid** operand is a dereferenced NULL pointer, the *Bad_typeid* exception is thrown.

See also   Bad_typeid class, _ _rtti

Example

```
// HOW TO USE operator typeid, Type_info::before(), AND Type_info::name()
#include <iostream.h>
#include <typeinfo.h>
```

```
class A { };
class B : A { };

void main() {
   char C;
   float X;

   // USE THE typeinfo::operator==()TO MAKE COMPARISON
   if (typeid( C ) == typeid( X ))
      cout << "C and X are the same type." << endl;
   else cout << "C and X are NOT the same type." << endl;

   // USE true AND false LITERALS TO MAKE COMPARISON
   cout << typeid(int).name();
   cout << " before " << typeid(double).name() << ": " <<
        (typeid(int).before(typeid(double)) ? true : false) << endl;
   cout << typeid(double).name();

   cout << " before " << typeid(int).name() << ": " <<
        (typeid(double).before(typeid(int)) ? true : false) << endl;

   cout << typeid(A).name();
   cout << " before " << typeid(B).name() << ": " <<
        (typeid(A).before(typeid(B)) ? true : false) << endl;
}
```

Output

```
C and X are NOT the same type.
int before double: 0
double before int: 1
A before B: 1
```

typename

Form 1   typename <identifier>
Use to reference a type that you have not yet defined. See Example 1.

Form 2   template < typename <identifier> > class <identifier>
Use in place of the **class** keyword in a template declaration. See Example 2.

Example 1

```
/* This example uses the typename keyword to declare variables */
/* as type T::A, which has not yet been defined. */

void f() {
   typedef typename T::A TA;    // declare TA as type T::A
   TA a5;                       // declare a5 as type TA
   typename T::A a6;            // declare a6 as type T::A
   TA * pta6;                   // declare pta6 as pointer to type TA
}
```

Example 2

```
/* This example shows how the typename keyword can be used to replace */
/* the class keyword in a template declaration. */

#include <iostream.h>

template <typename T1, typename T2> T2 convert (T1 t1)
                                // use typename instead of class.
{ return (T2)t1; }

template <typename X, class Y> bool isequal (X x, Y y)
                                // mix typename and class.
{ if (x==y)return 1; return 0; }
```

Example 3

```
typedef unsigned char byte;
typedef char str40[41];
typedef struct {
    double re, im;
    } complex;
```

union

```
union [<union type name>] {
  <type> <variable names> ;
  ...
} [<union variables>] ;
```
Use unions to define variables that share storage space.

Example

```
union int_or_long {
    int     i;
    long    l;
} a_number;
```

The compiler allocates enough storage in *a_number* to accommodate the largest element in the union.

Unlike a **struct**, the variables *a_number.i* and *a_number.l* occupy the same location in memory. Thus, writing into one overwrites the other.

Use the record selector (.) to access elements of a union .

See also   bit fields, class, public, struct

unsigned

unsigned <type> <variable> ;
Use the **unsigned** type modifier when variable values will always be positive. The
unsigned modifer can be applied to base types **int, char, long,** and **short**.

When the base type is omitted from a declaration, **int** is assumed.

Examples

```
unsigned int      i;
unsigned          i;    /* same as "unsigned int i;"   */
unsigned long int l;    /* int OK, not needed          */
unsigned char     ch;   /* unsigned is default for char */
```

See also   char, int, long, short, signed

virtual

virtual class-name
virtual function-name
Use the **virtual** keyword to allow derived classes to provide different versions of a base
class function. Once you declare a function as **virtual**, you can redefine it in any derived
class, even if the number and type of arguments are the same.

The redefined function overrides the base class function.

void

void identifier
void is a special type indicating the absence of any value. Use the **void** keyword as a
function return type if the function does not return a value.

```
void hello(char *name)
{
  printf("Hello, %s.",name);
}
```

Use **void** as a function heading if the function does not take any parameters.

```
int init(void)
{
  return 1;
}
```

Void Pointers

Generic pointers can also be declared as **void**, meaning that they can point to any type.

void pointers cannot be dereferenced without explicit casting because the compiler
cannot determine the size of the pointer object.

Example

```
int x;
float r;
void *p = &x;          /* p points to x */
int main (void)

  *(int *) p = 2;
  p = &r;              /* p points to r */
  *(float *)p = 1.1;
}
```

volatile

volatile <data definition> ;

Use the **volatile** modifier to indicate that a variable can be changed by a background routine, an interrupt routine, or an I/O port. Declaring an object to be **volatile** warns the compiler not to make assumptions concerning the value of the object while evaluating expressions in which it occurs because the value could change at any moment. It also prevents the compiler from making the variable a register variable

The routines in this example (assuming *timer* has been properly associated with a hardware clock interrupt) implement a timed wait of ticks specified by the argument *interval*. A highly optimizing compiler might not load the value of *ticks* inside the test of the **while** loop since the loop doesn't change the value of *ticks*.

Note C++ extends **volatile** to include classes and member functions. If you've declared a **volatile** object, you can use only its **volatile** member functions.

See also const

wchar_t

wchar_t <identifier>;

In C++ programs, **wchar_t** is a fundamental data type that can represent distinct codes for any element of the largest extended character set in any of the supported locales. A **wchar_t** type is the same size, signedness, and alignment requirement as an **int** type.

while

while (<condition>) <statement>

Use the **while** keyword to conditionally iterate a statement.

<statement> executes repeatedly until the value of <condition> is **false**. If no condition is specified, the **while** clause is equivalent to **while(true)**.

The test takes place before <statement> executes. Thus, if <condition> evaluates to **false** on the first pass, the loop does not execute.

Example

```
while (*p == ' ') p++;
```

See also do

Data types

16-bit

Type	Length	Range
unsigned char	8 bits	0 to 255
char	8 bits	-128 to 127
enum	16 bits	-32,768 to 32,767
unsigned int	16 bits	0 to 65,535
short int	16 bits	-32,768 to 32,767
int	16 bits	-32,768 to 32,767
unsigned long	32 bits	0 to 4,294,967,295
long	32 bits	-2,147,483,648 to 2,147,483,647
float	32 bits	3.4 x 10-38 to 3.4 x 10+38
double	64 bits	1.7 x 10-308 to 1.7 x 10+308
long double	80 bits	3.4 x 10-4932 to 1.1 x 10+4932
near (pointer)	16 bits	not applicable
far (pointer)	32 bits	not applicable

32-bit

Type	Length	Range
unsigned char	8 bits	0 to 255
char	8 bits	-128 to 127
short int	16 bits	-32,768 to 32,767
unsigned int	32 bits	0 to 4,294,967,295
int	32 bits	-2,147,483,648 to 2,147,483,647
unsigned long	32 bits	0 to 4,294,967,295
enum	16 bits	-2,147,483,648 to 2,147,483,647
long	32 bits	-2,147,483,648 to 2,147,483,647
float	32 bits	3.4 x 10-38 to 3.4 x 10+38
double	64 bits	1.7 x 10-308 to 1.7 x 10+308
long double	80 bits	3.4 x 10-4932 to 1.1 x 10+4932
near (pointer)	32 bits	not applicable
far (pointer)	32 bits	not applicable

2

Borland C++ library routines

Borland C++ has several hundred classes, functions, and macros that you call from within your C and C++ programs to perform a wide variety of tasks, including low- and high-level I/O, string and file manipulation, memory allocation, process control, data conversion, mathematical calculations, and much more. These classes, functions, and macros are collectively referred to as library routines.

Reasons to access the run-time library source code

The following are some reasons why you might want to obtain the source code for run-time library routines:

- To write a function similar to, but not the same as, a Borland C++ function. With access to the run-time library source code, you can tailor the library function to suit your needs, and avoid having to write a separate function of your own.

- To know more about the internals of a library function when you debug your code.

- To delete the leading underscores on C symbols.

- To learn programming techniques by studying tight, professionally written library source code.

Because Borland believes strongly in the concept of open architecture, the Borland C++ run-time library source code is available for licensing. Just fill out the order form distributed with your Borland C++ package, include your payment, and Borland will ship you the Borland C++ run-time library source code.

Guidelines for selecting run-time libraries

Use the following guidelines when selecting which run-time libraries to us:

- 16-bit DLLs are supported only in the large memory model.

- For 32-bit programs, only the flat memory model is supported.
- 32-bit console and GUI programs require different startup code.
- Multithread applications are supported only in 32-bit programs.

Run-time libraries overview

Borland C++ has several hundred classes, functions, and macros that you call from within your C and C++ programs to perform a wide variety of tasks, including low- and high-level I/O, string and file manipulation, memory allocation, process control, data conversion, mathematical calculations, and much more. These classes, functions, and macros are collectively referred to as library routines.

The Borland C++ run-time libraries are divided into static (OBJ and LIB) and dynamic-link (DLL) versions.

- Static libraries are located in the LIB subdirectory of your installation.
- Dynamic-link libraries are located in the BIN subdirectory of your installation.

Several versions of the run-time libraries are available. For example, there are specific versions for each memory model, debugging, and 16- and 32-bit versions. There are also optional libraries to provide mathematics, containers, ObjectWindows development, and international applications.

Static run-time libraries

Listed below are each of the Borland C++ static library names, the operating environment in which it is available, and its use.

File name	Environment	Use
Directory of BC5\LIB		
BIDSI.LIB	Win 16	16-bit dynamic BIDS import library for BIDS50.DLL
BIDSF.LIB	Win32s, Win32	32-bit BIDS library
BIDSFI.LIB	Win32s, Win32	32-bit dynamic BIDS import library for BIDS50F.DLL
BIDS?.LIB	Win 16	16-bit BIDS library
BWCC.LIB	Win 16	16-bit import library for BWCC.DLL
BWCC32.LIB ·	Win32s, Win32	32-bit import library for BWCC32.DLL
C0D32.OBJ	Win32s, Win32	32-bit DLL startup module
C0D?.OBJ	Win 16	16-bit DLL startup module
C0W32.OBJ	Win32s, Win32	32-bit GUI EXE startup module
C0W?.OBJ	Win 16	16-bit EXE startup module
C0X32.OBJ	Win32	32-bit console-mode EXE startup module
CRTLDLL.LIB	Win 16	16-bit dynamic import library for BC500RTL.DLL
CT.LIB	DOS	tiny library (DOS only)
CW32.LIB	Win32s, Win32	32-bit GUI single-thread library
CW?.LIB	Win 16	16-bit library

File name	Environment	Use
CW32I.LIB	Win32s, Win32	32-bit single-thread, GUI, dynamic RTL import library for CW3220.DLL
CW32MT.LIB	Win32	32-bit GUI multithread library
CW32MTI.LIB	Win32	32-bit multithread, GUI, dynamic RTL import library for CW3220MT.DLL
IMPORT.LIB	Win 16	16-bit import library
IMPORT32.LIB	Win32s, Win32	32-bit import library
MATHW?.LIB	Win 16	16-bit math libraries
NOEH?.LIB	16-bit DOS, DPMI16	Eliminate exception handling code in run-time libraries
NOEHW?.LIB	Win 16, DPMI16	Eliminate exception handling code in run-time libraries
W32SUT16.LIB	Win 16	16-bit universal thunking library
W32SUT32.LIB	Win32s	32-bit universal thunking library
OBSOLETE.LIB	Win 16, Win32, Win32s	Provides obsolete global variables

Directory of BC5\LIB\16-BIT

FILES.C	Win 16	Increases the number of file handles
FILES2.C	Win 16	Increases the number of file handles
MATHERR.C	Win 16	Sample of a user-defined floating-point math exception handler for float and double types
MATHERRL.C	Win 16	Sample of a user-defined floating-point math exception handler for long double type
WILDARG.OBJ	Win 16	Transforms wild-card arguments into an array of arguments to *main()* in console-mode applications

Directory of BC5\LIB\32-BIT

FILES.C	Win32s, Win32	Increases the number of file handles
FILES2.C	Win32s, Win32	Increases the number of file handles
FILEINFO.OBJ	Win32s, Win32	Passes open file-handle information to child processes
GP.OBJ	Win32s, Win32	Prints register-dump information when an exception occurs
MATHERR.C	Win32s, Win32	Sample of a user-defined floating-point math exception handler for float and double types
MATHERRL.C	Win32s, Win32	Sample of a user-defined floating-point math exception handler for long double type
WILDARGS.OBJ	Win32	Transforms wild-card arguments into an array of arguments to *main()* in console-mode applications

Directory of BC5\LIB\STARTUP

BUILD-C0.BAT	Win 16	Batch file to build C0D?.OBJ, C0F?.OBJ, and C0W?.OBJ
C0.ASM	DOS	Source for C0?.OBJ
C0D.ASM	Win 16	Source for C0D?.OBJ
C0W.ASM	Win 16	Source for C0W?.OBJ
RULES.ASI	Win 16	Assembly rules for C0D.ASM and C0W.ASM

Table legend

Each memory model has its own library file and math file that contain versions of the routines written for that particular model.

The **?** placeholder in each of the library file names represents one of the supported memory models (S = small, M = medium, C = compact, and L = large).

For example, the available versions of the 16-bit DLL startup module (C0D?.OBJ) are:

- C0DS.OBJ (small)
- C0DM.OBJ (medium)
- C0DC.OBJ (compact)
- C0DL.OBJ (large)

See also   Default run-time libraries, Dynamic-link libraries, Guidelines for selecting run-time libraries, Obsolete functions, Reasons to access the run-time library source code

Dynamic-link libraries

The dynamic-link library (DLL) version of the run-time library is contained in the BIN subdirectory of your installation. Several versions of the dynamic-link libraries are available. For example, there are 16- and 32-bit–specific versions, and versions that support multithread applications.

In the 16-bit–specific version, only the large-memory model DLL is provided. No other memory model is supported in a 16-bit DLL.

Listed below are each of the Borland C++ DLL names, the operating environment in which it is available, and its use.

Directory: BC5\BIN

File Name	Environment	Use
BC500RTL.DLL	Win 16	16-bit, large memory model
BIDS50.DLL	Win 16	16-bit BIDS
BIDS50F.DLL	Win32s, Win32	32-bit BIDS
CW3220.DLL	Win32s, Win32	32-bit, single thread, GUI mode
CW3220MT.DLL	Win32	32-bit, multithread, GUI mode
LOCALE.BLL	Win 16, Win32s, Win32	Locale library

C++ prototyped routines

Certain routines described in this book have multiple declarations. You must choose the prototype appropriate for your program. In general, the multiple prototypes are required to support the original C implementation and the stricter and sometimes different C++ function declaration syntax. For example, some string-handling routines have multiple prototypes because in addition to the ANSI-C–specified prototype, Borland C++ provides prototypes consistent with the ANSI C++ draft.

Function	Header
getvect	dos.h
max	stdlib.h
memchr	string.h
min	stdlib.h
setvect	dos.h
strchr	string.h
strpbrk	string.h
strrchr	string.h
strstr	string.h

Borland C++ library routines by category

The following sections list the library routines by category.

Classification routines

The following routines classify ASCII characters as letters, control characters, punctuation, uppercase, and so.

These routines are all declared in ctype.h.

isalnum	islower
isalpha	isprint
isascii	ispunct
iscntrl	isspace
isdigit	isupper
isgraph	isxdigit

Console I/O routines

The following routines output text to the screen or read from the keyboard. They cannot be used in a GUI application.

Function	Header	Function	Header
cgets	conio.h	movetext	conio.h
clreol	conio.h	normvideo	conio.h
clrscr	conio.h	putch	conio.h
cprintf	conio.h	puttext	conio.h
cputs	conio.h	_setcursortype	conio.h

Function	Header	Function	Header
delline	conio.h	*textattr*	conio.h
getpass	conio.h	*textbackground*	conio.h
gettext	conio.h	*textcolor*	conio.h
gettextinfo	conio.h	*textmode*	conio.h
gotoxy	conio.h	*ungetc*	stdio.h
highvideo	conio.h	*wherex*	conio.h
insline	conio.h	*wherey*	conio.h
lowvideo	conio.h	*window*	conio.h

Conversion routines

The following routines convert characters and strings from

- Alpha to different numeric representations (floating-point, integers, longs)
- Numeric to alpha representations
- Uppercase to lowercase (and vice versa)

Function	Header	Function	Header
atof	stdlib.h	*strtol*	stdlib.h
atoi	stdlib.h	*_strtold*	stdlib.h
atol	stdlib.h	*strtoul*	stdlib.h
ecvt	stdlib.h	*toascii*	ctype.h
fcvt	stdlib.h	*_tolower*	ctype.h
gcvt	stdlib.h	*tolower*	ctype.h
itoa	stdlib.h	*_toupper*	ctype.h
ltoa	stdlib.h	*toupper*	ctype.h
strtod	stdlib.h	*ultoa*	stdlib.h

Diagnostic routines

The following routines provide built-in troubleshooting capability.

Function	Header
assert	assert.h
_matherr	math.h
_matherrl	math.h
perror	errno.h

Directory control routines

The following routines manipulate directories and path names:

Function	Header	Function	Header
chdir	dir.h	_getdcwd	direct.h
_chdrive	direct.h	getdisk	dir.h
closedir	dirent.h	_makepath	stdlib.h
_dos_findfirst	dos.h	mkdir	dir.h
_dos_findnext	dos.h	mktemp	dir.h
_dos_getdiskfree	dos.h	opendir	direct.h
_dos_getdrive	dos.h	readdir	dirent.h
_dos_setdrive	dos.h	rewinddir	dirent.h
findfirst	dir.h	rmdir	dir.h
findnext	dir.h	_searchenv	stdlib.h
fnmerge	dir.h	searchpath	dir.h
fnsplit	dir.h	_searchstr	stdlib.h
_fullpath	stdlib.h	setdisk	dir.h
getcurdir	dir.h	_splitpath	stdlib.h
getcwd	dir.h		

EasyWin routines

The following routines are portable to EasyWin programs, but are not available in Windows 16-bit programs. They are provided to help you port DOS programs into a Windows 16-bit applications.

Function	Header	Function	Header
clreol	conio.h	printf	stdio.h
clrscr	conio.h	putch	conio.h
fgetchar	stdio.h	putchar	stdio.h
getch	stdio.h	puts	stdio.h
getchar	stdio.h	scanf	stdio.h
getche	stdio.h	vprintf	stdio.h
gets	stdio.h	vscanf	stdio.h
gotoxy	conio.h	wherex	conio.h
kbhit	conio.h	wherey	conio.h
perror	errno.h		

Inline routines

The following routines have inline versions. The compiler will generate code for the inline versions when you use #pragma intrinsic or if you specify program optimization.

Function	Header	Function	Header
abs	math.h	stpcpy	string.h
alloca	malloc.h	strcat	string.h
_crotl	stdlib.h	strchr	string.h
_crotr	stdlib.h	strcmp	string.h
_lrotl	stdlib.h	strcpy	string.h
_lrotr	stdlib.h	strlen	string.h
memchr	mem.h	strncat	string.h
memcmp	mem.h	strncmp	string.h
memcpy	mem.h	strncpy	string.h
memset	mem.h	strnset	string.h
_rotl	stdlib.h	strrchr	string.h
_rotr	stdlib.h	strset	string.h

Input/output routines

The following routines provide stream- and operating-system level I/O capability.

Function	Header	Function	Header
access	io.h	getftime	io.h
chmod	io.h	gets	stdio.h
chsize	io.h	getw	stdio.h
clearerr	stdio.h	ioctl	io.h
close	io.h	isatty	io.h
creat	io.h	kbhit	conio.h
creatnew	io.h	lock	io.h
creattemp	io.h	locking	io.h
cscanf	conio.h	lseek	io.h
_dos_close	dos.h	open	io.h
_pclose	stdio.h	_open_osfhandle	io.h
_dos_creat	dos.h	perror	stdio.h
_dos_creatnew	dos.h	_pipe	io.h
_dos_getfileattr	dos.h	_popen	stdio.h
_dos_getftime	dos.h	printf	stdio.h
_dos_open	dos.h	putc	stdio.h
_dos_read	dos.h	putchar	stdio.h
_dos_setfileattr	dos.h	puts	stdio.h
_dos_setftime	dos.h	putw	stdio.h
_dos_write	dos.h	read	io.h
dup	io.h	remove	stdio.h

Function	Header	Function	Header
dup2	io.h	rename	stdio.h
eof	io.h	rewind	stdio.h
fclose	stdio.h	rmtmp	stdio.h
fcloseall	stdio.h	_rtl_chmod	io.h
fdopen	stdio.h	_rtl_close	io.h
feof	stdio.h	_rtl_creat	io.h
ferror	stdio.h	_rtl_open	io.h
fflush	stdio.h	_rtl_read	io.h
fgetc	stdio.h	_rtl_write	io.h
fgetchar	stdio.h	scanf	stdio.h
fgetpos	stdio.h	setbuf	stdio.h
fgets	stdio.h	setftime	io.h
filelength	io.h	setmode	io.h
fileno	stdio.h	setvbuf	stdio.h
flushall	stdio.h	sopen	io.h
fopen	stdio.h	sprintf	stdio.h
fprintf	stdio.h	sscanf	stdio.h
fputc	stdio.h	strerror	stdio.h
fputchar	stdio.h	_strerror	string.h, stdio.h
fputs	stdio.h	tell	io.h
fread	stdio.h	tempnam	stdio.h
freopen	stdio.h	(class)	file.h
fscanf	stdio.h	tmpfile	stdio.h
fseek	stdio.h	tmpnam	stdio.h
fsetpos	stdio.h	umask	io.h
_fsopen	stdio.h	unlink	dos.h
fstat	sys\stat.h	unlock	io.h
ftell	stdio.h	utime	utime.h
fwrite	stdio.h	vfprintf	stdio.h
get_osfhandle	io.h	vfscanf	stdio.h
getc	stdio.h	vprintf	stdio.h
getch	conio.h	vscanf	stdio.h
getchar	stdio.h	vsprintf	stdio.h
getche	conio.h	vsscanf	io.h

Interface routines (DOS, 8086, BIOS)

The following routines provide operating-system, BIOS, and machine-specific capabilities.

Function	Header	Function	Header
bdos	dos.h	inp	conio.h
bdosptr	dos.h	inpw	conio.h

Function	Header	Function	Header
_bios_equiplist	bios.h	inport	dos.h
biosequip	bios.h	inportb	dos.h
biosmemory	bios.h	int86	dos.h
biostime	bios.h	int86x	dos.h
_chain_intr	dos.h	intdos	dos.h
country	dos.h	intdosx	dos.h
ctrlbrk	dos.h	intr	dos.h
_disable	dos.h	MK_FP	dos.h
disable	dos.h	outp	conio.h
dosexterr	dos.h	outpw	conio.h
_dos_getvect	dos.h	outport	dos.h
_dos_setvect	dos.h	outportb	dos.h
_enable	dos.h	parsfnm	dos.h
enable	dos.h	peek	dos.h
FP_OFF	dos.h	peekb	dos.h
FP_SEG	dos.h	poke	dos.h
geninterrupt	dos.h	pokeb	dos.h
getcbrk	dos.h	segread	dos.h
getdfree	dos.h	setcbrk	dos.h
getdta	dos.h	_setcursortype	conio.h
getfat	dos.h	setdta	dos.h
getfatd	dos.h	setvect	dos.h
getpsp	dos.h	setverify	dos.h
getvect	dos.h	sleep	dos.h
getverify	dos.h		

International API routines

The following routines are affected by the current locale. The current locale is specified by the *setlocale* function and is enabled by defining _ _USELOCALES_ _ with -D command-line option. When you define _ _USELOCALES_ _, only function versions of the following routines are used in the run-time library rather than macros.

Function	Header	Function	Header
cprintf	stdio.h	scanf	stdio.h
cscanf	stdio.h	setlocale	locale.h
fprintf	stdio.h	sprintf	stdio.h
fscanf	stdio.h	sscanf	stdio.h
isalnum	ctype.h	strcoll	string.h
isalpha	ctype.h	strftime	time.h
iscntrl	ctype.h	strlwr	string.h
isdigit	ctype.h	strupr	string.h
isgraph	ctype.h	strxfrm	string.h

Function	Header	Function	Header
islower	ctype.h	*tolower*	ctype.h
isprint	ctype.h	*toupper*	ctype.h
ispunct	ctype.h	*vfprintf*	stdio.h
isspace	ctype.h	*vfscanf*	stdio.h
isupper	ctype.h	*vprintf*	stdio.h
isxdigit	ctype.h	*vscanf*	stdio.h
localeconv	locale.h	*vsprintf*	stdio.h
printf	stdio.h	*vsscanf*	stdio.h

Manipulation routines

The following routines handle strings and blocks of memory: copying, comparing, converting, and searching.

Function	Header	Function	Header
mblen	stdlib.h	*strerror*	string.h
mbstowcs	stdlib.h	*stricmp*	string.h
mbtowc	stdlib.h	*strlen*	string.h
memccpy	mem.h, string.h	*strlwr*	string.h
memchr	mem.h, string.h	*strncat*	string.h
memcmp	mem.h, string.h	*strncmpi*	string.h
memcpy	mem.h, string.h	*strncmp*	string.h
memicmp	mem.h, string.h	*strncpy*	string.h
memmove	mem.h, string.h	*strnicmp*	string.h
memset	mem.h, string.h	*strnset*	string.h
movedata	mem.h, string.h	*strpbrk*	string.h
movmem	mem.h, string.h	*strrchr*	string.h
setmem	mem.h	*strrev*	string.h
stpcpy	string.h	*strset*	string.h
strcat	string.h	*strspn*	string.h
strchr	string.h	*strstr*	string.h
strcmpi	string.h	*strtok*	string.h
strcmp	string.h	*strupr*	string.h
strcoll	string.h	*strxfrm*	string.h
strcpy	string.h	*wcstombs*	stdlib.h
strcspn	string.h	*wctomb*	stdlib.h
strdup	string.h		

Math routines

The following routines perform mathematical calculations and conversions.

Function	Header	Function	Header
abs	complex.h, stdlib.h	*labs*	stdlib.h
acos	complex.h, math.h	*ldexp*	math.h
acosl	math.h	*ldexpl*	math.h
arg	complex.h	*ldiv*	math.h
asin	complex.h, math.h	*log*	complex.h, math.h
asinl	math.h	*logl*	math.h
atan	complex.h, math.h	*log10*	complex.h, math.h
atan2	complex.h, math.h	*log10l*	math.h
atan2l	math.h	*_lrotl*	stdlib.h
atanl	math.h	*_lrotr*	stdlib.h
atof	stdlib.h, math.h	*ltoa*	stdlib.h
atoi	stdlib.h	*_matherr*	math.h
atol	stdlib.h	*_matherrl*	math.h
_atold	math.h	*modf*	math.h
bcd (class)	bcd.h	*modfl*	math.h
cabs	math.h	*norm*	complex.h
cabsl	math.h	*polar*	complex.h
ceil	math.h	*poly*	math.h
ceill	math.h	*polyl*	math.h
_clear87	float.h	*pow*	complex.h, math.h
complex (class)	complex.h	*pow10*	math.h
conj	complex.h	*pow10l*	math.h
_control87	float.h	*powl*	math.h
cos	complex.h, math.h	*rand*	stdlib.h
cosh	complex.h, math.h	*random*	stdlib.h
coshl	math.h	*randomize*	stdlib.h
cosl	math.h	*real*	complex.h
div	math.h	*_rotl*	stdlib.h
ecvt	stdlib.h	*_rotr*	stdlib.h
exp	complex.h, math.h	*sin*	complex.h, math.h
expl	math.h	*sinh*	complex.h, math.h
fabs	math.h	*sinhl*	math.h

Function	Header	Function	Header
fabsl	math.h	*sinl*	complex.h, math.h
fcvt	stdlib.h	*sqrt*	complex.h, math.h
floor	math.h	*sqrtl*	math.h
floorl	math.h	*srand*	stdlib.h
fmod	math.h	*_status87*	float.h
fmodl	math.h	*strtod*	stdlib.h
_fpreset	float.h	*strtol*	stdlib.h
frexp	math.h	*_strtold*	stdlib.h
frexpl	math.h	*strtoul*	stdlib.h
gcvt	stdlib.h	*tan*	complex.h, math.h
hypot	math.h	*tanh*	complex.h, math.h
hypotl	math.h	*tanhl*	complex.h, math.h
imag	complex.h	*tanl*	math.h
itoa	stdlib.h	*ultoa*	stdlib.h

Memory routines

The following routines provide dynamic memory allocation in the small-data and large-data models.

Function	Header	Function	Header
alloca	malloc.h	*heapcheckfree*	alloc.h
_bios_memsize	bios.h	*heapchecknode*	alloc.h
calloc	alloc.h, stdlib.h	*heapwalk*	alloc.h
farcalloc	alloc.h	*malloc*	alloc.h, stdlib.h
farfree	alloc.h	*realloc*	alloc.h, stdlib.h
farmalloc	alloc.h	*set_new_handler*	new.h
free	alloc.h, stdlib.h	*stackavail*	malloc.h
heapcheck	alloc.h		

Miscellaneous routines

The following routines provide non-local goto capabilities and locale.

Function	Header
localeconv	locale.h
longjmp	setjmp.h
setjmp	setjmp.h
setlocale	locale.h

Obsolete functions

The old names of the following functions are available, but the compiler will generate a warning that you are using an obsolete name. Future versions of Borland C++ might not provide support for the old function names.

The following function names have been changed:

Old name	New name	Header file
_chmod	_rtl_chmod	io.h
_close	_rtl_close	io.h
_creat	_rtl_creat	io.h
_heapwalk	_rtl_heapwalk	malloc.h
_open	_rtl_open	io.h
_read	_rtl_read	io.h
_write	_rtl_write	io.h

Process control routines

The following routines invoke and terminate new processes from within another routine.

Function	Header	Function	Header
abort	process.h	exit	process.h
_beginthread	process.h	_expand	process.h
_beginthreadNT	process.h	getpid	process.h
_c_exit	process.h	_pclose	stdio.h
_cexit	process.h	_popen	stdio.h
cwait	process.h	raise	signal.h
_endthread	process.h	signal	signal.h
execle	process.h	spawnle	process.h
execl	process.h	spawnlpe	process.h
execlpe	process.h	spawnlp	process.h
execlp	process.h	spawnl	process.h
execve	process.h	spawnve	process.h
execv	process.h	spawnvpe	process.h
execvpe	process.h	spawnvp	process.h
execvp	process.h	spawnv	process.h
_exit	process.h	wait	process.h

Time and date routines

The following functions are time conversion and time manipulation routines.

Function	Header	Function	Header
asctime	time.h	gmtime	time.h
_bios_timeofday	bios.h	localtime	time.h
ctime	time.h	mktime	time.h
difftime	time.h	stime	time.h
_dos_getdate	dos.h	_strdate	time.h
_dos_gettime	dos.h	strftime	time.h
_dos_setdate	dos.h	_strtime	time.h
_dos_settime	dos.h	TDate (class)	date.h
dostounix	dos.h	time	time.h
ftime	sys\timeb.h	TTime (class)	date.h
getdate	dos.h	tzset	time.h
gettime	dos.h	unixtodos	dos.h

Variable argument list routines

The following routines are for use when accessing variable argument lists (such as with *printf*, *vscanf*, and so on).

Function	Header
va_start	stdarg.h
va_arg	stdarg.h
va_end	stdarg.h

Chapter

3

Run-time functions

This chapter contains a detailed description of each function in the Borland C++ library. The functions are listed in alphabetical order, although a few of the routines are grouped by "family" (the *exec...* and *spawn...* functions, for example) because they perform similar or related tasks.

Note Programming examples for each function are available in the online Help system. You can easily copy them from Help and paste them into your files.

Each function entry provides certain standard information. For instance, the entry for *free*

- Tells you whic header file(s) contains the prototype for *free*

- Summarizes what *free* does

- Gives the syntax for calling *free*

- Gives a detailed description of how *free* is implemented and how it relates to the other memory-allocation routines

- Lists other language compilers that include similar functions

- Refers you to related functions

The following sample library entry lists each entry section and describes the information it contains. The alphabetical listings follow.

Sample function entry   header file name

The *function* is followed by the header file(s) containing the prototype for *function* or definitions of constants, enumerated types, and so on used by *function*.

Syntax
function(modifier *parameter*[,...]);

This gives you the declaration syntax for *function*; parameter names are italicized. The [,...] indicates that other parameters and their modifiers can follow.

Description

Summary of what this *function* does.

This section describes what *function* does, the parameters it takes, and any details you need to use *function* and the related routines listed.

Return value

The value that *function* returns (if any) is given here. If *function* sets any global variables, their values are also listed.

See also

Routines related to *function* that you might want to read about are listed here. If a routine name contains an ellipsis, it indicates that you should refer to a family of functions (for example, *exec...* refers to the entire family of *exec* functions: *excel, execle, execlp, execlpe, execv, execve, execvp,* and *execvpe*).

Portability

Portability is indicated by marks (+) in the columns of the portability table. A sample portability table is shown here:

DOS	UNIX	Win 16	Win 32	ANSI C	ANSI C++	OS/2
+	+	+	+	+	+	+

Each entry in the portability table is described in the following table. Any additional restrictions are discussed in the Description section.

DOS   Available for DOS.

UNIX   Available under UNIX and/or POSIX.

Win 16   Compatible with 16-bit Windows programs running of Microsoft Windows 3.1, Windows for Workgroups 3.1, and Windows for Workgroups 3.11. For information about using certain non-Windows (such as *printf* and *scanf*) in programs that run under Windows.

Win 32   Available to 32-bit Windows programs running on Win32s 1.0 and Windows NT 3.1 applications.

ANSI C   Defined by the ANSI C standard.

ANSI C++   Included in the ANSI C++ proposal.

OS/2   Available for OS/2.

abort

Syntax
void abort(void);

Description
Abnormally terminates a program.

abort causes an abnormal program termination by calling *raise*(SIGABRT). If there is no signal handler for SIGABRT, then *abort* writes a termination message (Abnormal program termination) on stderr, then aborts the program by a call to *_exit* with exit code 3.

Return value
abort returns the exit code 3 to the parent process or to the operating system command processor.

See also
assert, atexit, _c_exit, _cexit, _exit, exit, raise, signal, spawnl

Portability

DOS	UNIX	Win 16	Win 32	ANSI C	ANSI C++	OS/2
+	+	+	+	+	+	+

abs

Syntax
int abs(int x);

Description
Returns the absolute value of an integer.

abs returns the absolute value of the integer argument x. If *abs* is called when stdlib.h has been included, it's treated as a macro that expands to inline code.

If you want to use the *abs* function instead of the macro, include

```
#undef abs
```

in your program, after the #include <stdlib.h>.

This function can be used with *bcd* and *complex* types.

Return value
The *abs* function returns an integer in the range of 0 to INT_MAX, with the exception that an argument with the value INT_MIN is returned as INT_MIN. The values for INT_MAX and INT_MIN are defined in header file limit.h.

See also

bcd, cabs, complex, fabs, labs

Portability

DOS	UNIX	Win 16	Win 32	ANSI C	ANSI C++	OS/2
+	+	+	+	+	+	+

access   io.h

Syntax

int access(const char *filename, int amode);

Description

Determines accessibility of a file.

access checks the file named by *filename* to determine if it exists, and whether it can be read, written to, or executed.

The list of *amode* values is as follows:

06   Check for read and write permission

04   Check for read permission

02   Check for write permission

01   Execute (ignored)

00   Check for existence of file

Under DOS, OS/2, and Windows (16- and 32-bit), all existing files have read access (*amode* equals 04), so 00 and 04 give the same result. Similarly, *amode* values of 06 and 02 are equivalent because under DOS write access implies read access.

If *filename* refers to a directory, *access* simply determines whether the directory exists.

Return value

If the requested access is allowed, *access* returns 0; otherwise, it returns a value of -1, and the global variable *errno* is set to one of the following values:

ENOENT   Path or file name not found

EACCES   Permission denied

See also

chmod, fstat, stat

Portability

DOS	UNIX	Win 16	Win 32	ANSI C	ANSI C++	OS/2
+	+	+	+			

acos, acosl   math.h

Syntax

```
double acos(double x);
long double acosl(long double x);
```

Description

Calculates the arc cosine.

acos returns the arc cosine of the input value.

acosl is the **long double** version; it takes a **long double** argument and returns a **long double** result.

Arguments to *acos* and *acosl* must be in the range -1 to 1, or else *acos* and *acosl* return NAN and set the global variable *errno* to

EDOM   Domain error

This function can be used with *bcd* and *complex* types.

Return value

acos and *acosl* of an argument between -1 and +1 return a value in the range 0 to *pi*. Error handling for these routines can be modified through the functions *_matherr* and *_matherrl*.

See also

asin, atan, atan2, bcd, complex, cos, _matherr, sin, tan

Portability

	DOS	UNIX	Win 16	Win 32	ANSI C	ANSI C++	OS/2
acos	+	+	+	+	+	+	+
acosl	+		+	+			+

alloca   malloc.h

Syntax

```
void *alloca(size_t size);
```

Description

Allocates temporary stack space.

alloca allocates *size* bytes on the stack; the allocated space is automatically freed up when the calling function exits.

Because *alloca* modifies the stack pointer, do not place calls to *alloca* in an expression that is an argument to a function.

The *alloca* function should not be used in the **try**-block of a C++ program. If an exception is thrown, any values placed on the stack by *alloca* will be corrupted.

If the calling function does not contain any references to local variables in the stack, the stack will not be restored correctly when the function exits, resulting in a program crash. To ensure that the stack is restored correctly, use the following code in the calling function:

```
char *p;
char dummy[5];

dummy[0] = 0;
   ⋮
p = alloca(nbytes);
```

Return value

If enough stack space is available, *alloca* returns a pointer to the allocated stack area. Otherwise, it returns NULL.

See also

malloc

Portability

DOS	UNIX	Win 16	Win 32	ANSI C	ANSI C++	OS/2
+	+	+	+			+

asctime   time.h

Syntax

char *asctime(const struct tm *tblock);

Description

Converts date and time to ASCII.

asctime converts a time stored as a structure in **tblock* to a 26-character string of the same form as the *ctime* string:

```
Sun Sep 16 01:03:52 1973\n\0
```

Return value

asctime returns a pointer to the character string containing the date and time. This string is a static variable that is overwritten with each call to *asctime*.

See also

ctime, difftime, ftime, gmtime, localtime, mktime, strftime, stime, time, tzset

Portability

DOS	UNIX	Win 16	Win 32	ANSI C	ANSI C++	OS/2
+	+	+	+	+	+	+

asin, asinl   math.h

Syntax

```
double asin(double x);
long double asinl(long double x);
```

Description

Calculates the arc sine.

asin of a real argument returns the arc sine of the input value.

asinl is the **long double** version; it takes a **long double** argument and returns a **long double** result.

Real arguments to *asin* and *asinl* must be in the range -1 to 1, or else *asin* and *asinl* return NAN and set the global variable *errno* to

EDOM   Domain error

This function can be used with *bcd* and *complex* types.

Return value

asin and *asinl* of a real argument return a value in the range $-pi/2$ to $pi/2$. Error handling for these functions may be modified through the functions *_matherr* and *_matherrl*.

See also

acos, atan, atan2, bcd, complex, cos, _matherr, sin, tan

Portability

	DOS	UNIX	Win 16	Win 32	ANSI C	ANSI C++	OS/2
asin	+	+	+	+	+	+	+
asinl	+		+	+			+

assert

assert.h

Syntax
void assert(int test);

Description
Tests a condition and possibly aborts.

assert is a macro that expands to an **if** statement; if *test* evaluates to zero, *assert* aborts the program (by calling *abort*) and asserts the following a message on stderr:

```
Assertion failed: test, file filename, line linenum
```

The *filename* and *linenum* listed in the message are the source file name and line number where the *assert* macro appears.

If you place the #define NDEBUG directive ("no debugging") in the source code before the #include <assert.h> directive, the effect is to comment out the *assert* statement.

Return value
None.

See also
abort

Portability

DOS	UNIX	Win 16	Win 32	ANSI C	ANSI C++	OS/2
+	+	+	+	+	+	+

atan, atanl

math.h

Syntax
double atan(double x);
long double atanl(long double x);

Description
Calculates the arc tangent.

atan calculates the arc tangent of the input value.

atanl is the **long double** version; it takes a **long double** argument and returns a **long double** result. This function can be used with *bcd* and *complex* types.

Return value
atan and *atanl* of a real argument return a value in the range $-pi/2$ to $pi/2$. Error handling for these functions can be modified through the functions *_matherr* and *_matherrl*.

See also

acos, asin, atan2, bcd, complex, cos, _matherr, sin, tan

Portability

	DOS	UNIX	Win 16	Win 32	ANSI C	ANSI C++	OS/2
atan	+	+	+	+	+	+	+
atanl	+		+	+			+

atan2, atan2l   math.h

Syntax

```
double atan2(double y, double x);
long double atan2l(long double y, long double x);
```

Description

Calculates the arc tangent of y/x.

atan2 returns the arc tangent of y/x; it produces correct results even when the resulting angle is near $pi/2$ or $-pi/2$ (x near 0). If both x and y are set to 0, the function sets the global variable *errno* to EDOM, indicating a domain error.

atan2l is the **long double** version; it takes **long double** arguments and returns a **long double** result.

Return value

atan2 and *atan2l* return a value in the range -*pi* to *pi*. Error handling for these functions can be modified through the functions *_matherr* and *_matherrl*.

See also

acos, asin, atan, cos, _matherr, sin, tan

Portability

	DOS	UNIX	Win 16	Win 32	ANSI C	ANSI C++	OS/2
atan2	+	+	+	+	+	+	+
atan2l	+		+	+			+

atexit   stdlib.h

Syntax

```
int atexit(void (_USERENTRY * func)(void));
```

Description

Registers termination function.

atexit registers the function pointed to by *func* as an exit function. Upon normal termination of the program, *exit* calls *func* just before returning to the operating system. *fcmp* must be used with the _USERENTRY calling convention.

Each call to *atexit* registers another exit function. Up to 32 functions can be registered. They are executed on a last-in, first-out basis (that is, the last function registered is the first to be executed).

Return value

atexit returns 0 on success and nonzero on failure (no space left to register the function).

See also

abort, _c_exit, _cexit, _exit, exit, spawn

Portability

DOS	UNIX	Win 16	Win 32	ANSI C	ANSI C++	OS/2
+		+	+	+	+	+

atof, _atold   math.h

Syntax

```
double atof(const char *s);
long double _atold(const char *s);
```

Description

Converts a string to a floating-point number.

atof converts a string pointed to by *s* to **double**; this function recognizes the character representation of a floating-point number, made up of the following:

- An optional string of tabs and spaces
- An optional sign
- A string of digits and an optional decimal point (the digits can be on both sides of the decimal point)
- An optional *e* or *E* followed by an optional signed integer

The characters must match this generic format:

[whitespace] [sign] [ddd] [.] [ddd] [e | E[sign]ddd]

atof also recognizes +INF and -INF for plus and minus infinity, and +NAN and -NAN for Not-a-Number.

In this function, the first unrecognized character ends the conversion.

_atold is the **long double** version; it converts the string pointed to by *s* to a **long double.** The functions *strtod* and *_strtold* are similar to *atof* and *_atold*; they provide better error detection, and hence are preferred in some applications.

Return value

atof and *_atold* return the converted value of the input string.

If there is an overflow, *atof* (or *_atold*) returns plus or minus HUGE_VAL (or _LHUGE_VAL), *errno* is set to ERANGE (Result out of range), and *_matherr* (or *_matherrl*) is not called.

See also

atoi, atol, ecvt, fcvt, gcvt, scanf, strtod

Portability

	DOS	UNIX	Win 16	Win 32	ANSI C	ANSI C++	OS/2
atof	+	+	+	+	+	+	+
_atold	+		+	+			+

atoi

Syntax

int atoi(const char *s);

Description

Converts a string to an integer.

atoi converts a string pointed to by *s* to **int**; *atoi* recognizes (in the following order)

- An optional string of tabs and spaces
- An optional sign
- A string of digits

The characters must match this generic format:

[ws] [sn] [ddd]

In this function, the first unrecognized character ends the conversion. There are no provisions for overflow in *atoi* (results are undefined).

Return value

atoi returns the converted value of the input string. If the string cannot be converted to a number of the corresponding type (**int**), *atoi* returns 0.

See also

atof, atol, ecvt, fcvt, gcvt, scanf, strtod

Portability

DOS	UNIX	Win 16	Win 32	ANSI C	ANSI C++	OS/2
+	+	+	+	+	+	+

atol   stdlib.h

Syntax

long atol(const char *s);

Description

Converts a string to a long.

atol converts the string pointed to by *s* to **long**. *atol* recognizes (in the following order)

- An optional string of tabs and spaces
- An optional sign
- A string of digits

The characters must match this generic format:

[ws] [sn] [ddd]

In this function, the first unrecognized character ends the conversion. There are no provisions for overflow in *atol* (results are undefined).

Return value

atol returns the converted value of the input string. If the string cannot be converted to a number of the corresponding type (b), *atol* returns 0.

See also

atof, atoi, ecvt, fcvt, gcvt, scanf, strtod, strtol, strtoul

Portability

DOS	UNIX	Win 16	Win 32	ANSI C	ANSI C++	OS/2
+	+	+	+	+	+	+

bdos   dos.h

Syntax

int bdos(int dosfun, unsigned dosdx, unsigned dosal);

Description

Accesses DOS system calls.

bdos provides direct access to many of the DOS system calls. See your DOS reference manuals for details on each system call.

For system calls that require an integer argument, use *bdos*; if they require a pointer argument, use *bdosptr*. In the large data models (compact, large, and huge), it is important to use *bdosptr* instead of *bdos* for system calls that require a pointer as the call argument.

- *dosfun* is defined in your DOS reference manuals.
- *dosdx* is the value of register DX.
- *dosal* is the value of register AL.

Return value
The return value of *bdos* is the value of AX set by the system call.

See also
bdosptr, geninterrupt, int86, int86x, intdos, intdosx

Portability

DOS	UNIX	Win 16	Win 32	ANSI C	ANSI C++	OS/2
+		+				

bdosptr   dos.h

Syntax
int bdosptr(int dosfun, void *argument, unsigned dosal);

Description
Accesses DOS system calls.

bdosptr provides direct access to many of the DOS system calls. See your DOS reference manuals for details of each system call.

For system calls that require an integer argument, use *bdos*; if calls require a pointer argument, use *bdosptr*. In the large data models (compact, large, and huge), it is important to use *bdosptr* for system calls that require a pointer as the call argument. In the small data models, the *argument* parameter to *bdosptr* specifies DX; in the large data models, it gives the DS:DX values to be used by the system call.

dosfun is defined in your DOS reference manuals. *dosal* is the value of register AL.

Return value
The return value of *bdosptr* is the value of AX on success or -1 on failure. On failure, the global variables *errno* and *_doserrno* are set.

See also
bdos, geninterrupt, int86, int86x, intdos, intdosx

Portability

DOS	UNIX	Win 16	Win 32	ANSI C	ANSI C++	OS/2
		+				+

_beginthread   process.h

Syntax
unsigned long _beginthread(_USERENTRY (*start_address)(void *), unsigned stack_size, void *arglist)

Description
Starts execution of a new thread.

Note   The *start_address* must be declared to be _USERENTRY.

The *_beginthread* function creates and starts a new thread. The thread starts execution at *start_address*.

The size of its stack in bytes is *stack_size*; the stack is allocated by the operating system after the stack size is rounded up to the next multiple of 4096. The thread is passed *arglist* as its only parameter; it can be NULL, but must be present. The thread terminates by simply returning, or by calling *_endthread*.

Either this function or *_beginthreadNT* must be used instead of the operating system thread-creation API function because *_beginthread* and *_beginthreadNT* perform initialization required for correct operation of the run-time library functions.

This function is available only in the multithread libraries.

Return value
_beginthread returns the handle of the new thread.

On error, the function returns -1, and the global variable *errno* is set to one of the following values:

EAGAIN   Too many threads

EINVAL   Invalid request

Also see the Win32 description of *GetLastError*.

See also
_beginthreadNT, *_endthread*

Portability

DOS	UNIX	Win 16	Win 32	ANSI C	ANSI C++	OS/2
		+				+

_beginthreadNT

process.h

Syntax

unsigned long _beginthreadNT(void (_USERENTRY *start_address)(void *), unsigned stack_size, void *arglist,
void *security_attrib, unsigned long create_flags, unsigned long *thread_id);

Description

Starts execution of a new thread under Windows NT.

Note   The *start_address* must be declared to be _USERENTRY.

All multithread Windows NT programs must use *_beginthreadNT* or the *_beginthread* function instead of the operating system thread-creation API function because these functions perform initialization required for correct operation of the run-time library functions. The *_beginthreadNT* function provides support for the operating system security. These functions are available only in the multithread libraries.

The *_beginthreadNT* function creates and starts a new thread. The thread starts execution at *start_address*.

The size of its stack in bytes is *stack_size*; the stack is allocated by the operating system after the stack size is rounded up to the next multiple of 4096. The thread *arglist* can be NULL, but must be present. The thread terminates by simply returning, or by calling *_endthread*.

The *_beginthreadNT* function uses the *security_attr* pointer to access the SECURITY_ATTRIBUTES structure. The structure contains the security attributes for the thread. If *security_attr* is NULL, the thread is created with default security attributes. The thread handle is not inherited if *security_attr* is NULL.

_beginthreadNT reads the *create_flags* variable for flags that provide additional information about the thread creation. This variable can be zero, specifying that the thread will run immediately upon creation. The variable can also be CREATE_SUSPENDED; in which case, the thread will not run until the *ResumeThread* function is called. *ResumeThread* is provided by the Win32 API.

_beginthreadNT initializes the *thread_id* variable with the thread identifier.

Return value

On success, *_beginthreadNT* returns the handle of the new thread.

On error, it returns -1, and the global variable *errno* is set to one of the following values:

EAGAIN   Too many threads

EINVAL   Invalid request

See also

_beginthread, _endthread

Portability

DOS	UNIX	Win 16	Win 32	ANSI C	ANSI C++	OS/2
			+			

biosequip   bios.h

Syntax
int biosequip(void);

Description
Checks equipment.

biosequip uses BIOS interrupt 0x11 to return an integer describing the equipment connected to the system.

Return value
The return value is interpreted as a collection of bit-sized fields. The IBM PC values follow:

Bits 14–15	Number of parallel printers installed
	00 = 0 printers
	01 = 1 printer
	10 = 2 printers
	11 = 3 printers
Bit 13	Serial printer attached
Bit 12	Game I/O attached
Bits 9-11	Number of COM ports (DOS only sees two ports but can be pushed to see four; the IBM PS/2 can see up to eight.)
	000 = 0 ports
	001 = 1 port
	010 = 2 ports
	011 = 3 ports
	100 = 4 ports
	101 = 5 ports
	110 = 6 ports
	111 = 7 ports
Bit 8	Direct memory access (DMA)
	0 = Machine has DMA

	1 = Machine does not have DMA; for example, PC Jr.
Bits 6-7	Number of disk drives
	00 = 1 drive
	01 = 2 drives
	10 = 3 drives
	11 = 4 drives, only if bit 0 is 1
Bits 4-5	Initial video mode
	00 = Unused
	01 = 40x25 BW with color card
	10 = 80x25 BW with color card
	11 = 80x25 BW with mono card
Bits 2-3	Motherboard RAM size
	00 = 16K
	01 = 32K
	10 = 48K
	11 = 64K
Bit 1	Floating-point coprocessor
Bit 0	Boot from disk

Portability

DOS	UNIX	Win 16	Win 32	ANSI C	ANSI C++	OS/2
+		+				

_bios_equiplist   bios.h

Syntax
unsigned _bios_equiplist(void);

Description
Checks equipment.

_bios_equiplist uses BIOS interrupt 0x11 to return an integer describing the equipment connected to the system.

Return value

The return value is interpreted as a collection of bit-sized fields. The IBM PC values follow:

Bits 14-15   Number of parallel printers installed

00 = 0 printers

01 = 1 printer

10 = 2 printers

11 = 3 printers

Bit 13   Serial printer attached

Bit 12   Game I/O attached

Bits 9-11   Number of COM ports (DOS only sees two ports but can be pushed to see four; the IBM PS/2 can see up to eight.)

000 = 0 ports

001 = 1 port

010 = 2 ports

011 = 3 ports

100 = 4 ports

101 = 5 ports

110 = 6 ports

111 = 7 ports

Bit 8   Direct memory access (DMA)

0 = Machine has DMA

1 = Machine does not have DMA; for example, PC Jr.

Bits 6-7   Number of disk drives

00 = 1 drive

01 = 2 drives

10 = 3 drives

11 = 4 drives, only if bit 0 is 1

Bits 4-5   Initial video mode

00 = Unused

01 = 40x25 BW with color card

10 = 80x25 BW with color card

11 = 80x25 BW with mono card

Bits 2-3	Motherboard RAM size
	00 = 16K
	01 = 32K
	10 = 48K
	11 = 64K
Bit 1	Floating-point coprocessor
Bit 0	Boot from disk

Portability

DOS	UNIX	Win 16	Win 32	ANSI C	ANSI C++	OS/2
+		+				

biosmemory   bios.h

Syntax
int biosmemory(void);

Description
Returns memory size.

biosmemory returns the size of RAM memory using BIOS interrupt 0x12. This does not include display adapter memory, extended memory, or expanded memory.

Return value
biosmemory returns the size of RAM memory in 1K blocks.

Portability

DOS	UNIX	Win 16	Win 32	ANSI C	ANSI C++	OS/2
	+		+			

_bios_memsize   bios.h

Syntax
unsigned _bios_memsize(void);

Description
Returns memory size.

_bios_memsize returns the size of RAM memory using BIOS interrupt 0x12. This does not include display adapter memory, extended memory, or expanded memory.

Return value

_bios_memsize_ returns the size of RAM memory in 1K blocks.

Portability

DOS	UNIX	Win 16	Win 32	ANSI C	ANSI C++	OS/2
+		+		.		

biostime   bios.h

Syntax

long biostime(int cmd, long newtime);

Description

Reads or sets the BIOS timer.

biostime either reads or sets the BIOS timer. This is a timer counting ticks since midnight at a rate of ticks per second as defined by _BIOS_CLOCKS_PER_SEC. _biostime_ uses BIOS interrupt 0x1A.

If _cmd_ equals 0, _biostime_ returns the current value of the timer. If _cmd_ equals 1, the timer is set to the **long** value in _newtime_. For example:

```
totalsecs = biostime(int cmd, long newtime) / _BIOS_CLK_TCK;
```

The _BIOS_CLOCKS_PER_SEC and _BIOS_CLK_TCK constants are defined in bios.h.

Return value

When _biostime_ reads the BIOS timer (_cmd_ = 0), it returns the timer's current value.

Portability

DOS	UNIX	Win 16	Win 32	ANSI C	ANSI C++	OS/2
+		+				

_bios_timeofday   bios.h

Syntax

unsigned _bios_timeofday(int cmd, long *timep);

Description

Reads or sets the BIOS timer.

_bios_timeofday_ either reads or sets the BIOS timer. This is a timer counting ticks since midnight at a rate of roughly 18.2 ticks per second. _bios_timeofday_ uses BIOS interrupt 0x1A.

The *cmd* parameter can be either of the following values:

_TIME_GETCLOCK   The function stores the current BIOS timer value into the location pointed to by *timep*. If the timer has not been read or written since midnight, the function returns 1. Otherwise, the function returns 0.

_TIME_SETCLOCK   The function sets the BIOS timer to the long value pointed to by *timep*. The function does not return a value.

Return value
The *_bios_timeofday* returns the value in AX that was set by the BIOS timer call.

Portability

DOS	UNIX	Win 16	Win 32	ANSI C	ANSI C++	OS/2
+		+				

bsearch   stdlib.h

Syntax
```
void *bsearch(const void *key, const void *base, size_t nelem, size_t width,
            int (_USERENTRY *fcmp)(const void *, const void *));
```

Description
Binary search of an array.

bsearch searches a table (array) of *nelem* elements in memory, and returns the address of the first entry in the table that matches the search key. The array must be in order. If no match is found, *bsearch* returns 0.

Note   Because this is a binary search, the first matching entry is not necessarily the first entry in the table.

The type *size_t* is defined in stddef.h header file.

- *nelem* gives the number of elements in the table.
- *width* specifies the number of bytes in each table entry.

The comparison routine *fcmp* must be used with the _USERENTRY calling convention.

fcmp is called with two arguments: *elem1* and *elem2*. Each argument points to an item to be compared. The comparison function compares each of the pointed-to items (**elem1* and **elem2*), and returns an integer based on the results of the comparison.

For *bsearch*, the *fcmp* return value is

- < 0 if *elem1 < *elem2
- == 0 if *elem1 == *elem2
- > 0 if *elem1 > *elem2

Return value

bsearch returns the address of the first entry in the table that matches the search key. If no match is found, *bsearch* returns 0.

See also

lfind, lsearch, qsort

Portability

DOS	UNIX	Win 16	Win 32	ANSI C	ANSI C++	OS/2
+	+	+	+	+	+	+

cabs, cabsl   math.h

Syntax

```
double cabs(struct complex z);
long double cabsl(struct _complexl z);
```

Description

cabs calculates the absolute value of a complex number. *cabs* is a macro that calculates the absolute value of *z*, a complex number. *z* is a structure with type *complex*; the structure is defined in math.h as

```
struct complex {
    double x, y;
    };
```

where *x* is the real part, and *y* is the imaginary part.

Calling *cabs* is equivalent to calling *sqrt* with the real and imaginary components of *z*, as shown here:

```
sqrt(z.x * z.x + z.y * z.y)
```

cabsl is the **long double** version; it takes a structure with type *_complexl* as an argument, and returns a **long double** result. The structure is defined in math.h as

```
struct _complexl {
    long double x, y;
};
```

Note   If you are using C++, you may also use the *complex* class defined in complex.h, and use the function *abs* to get the absolute value of a *complex* number.

Return value

cabs (or *cabsl*) returns the absolute value of *z*, a double. On overflow, *cabs* (or *cabsl*) returns HUGE_VAL (or _LHUGE_VAL) and sets the global variable *errno* to

ERANGE   Result out of range

Error handling for these functions can be modified through the functions *_matherr* and *_matherrl*.

See also
abs, *complex*, *errno* (global variable), *fabs*, *labs*, *_matherr*

Portability

	DOS	UNIX	Win 16	Win 32	ANSI C	ANSI C++	OS/2
cabs	+	+	+	+			+
cabsl	+		+	+			+

calloc   stdlib.h

Syntax
void *calloc(size_t nitems, size_t size);

Description
Allocates main memory.

calloc provides access to the C memory heap. The heap is available for dynamic allocation of variable-sized blocks of memory. Many data structures, such as trees and lists, naturally employ heap memory allocation.

All the space between the end of the data segment and the top of the program stack is available for use in the tiny (DOS only), small, and medium data models, except for a small margin immediately before the top of the stack. This margin allows room for the application to grow on the stack, and provides a small amount of room needed by the operating system.

In the large data models (compact, large, and huge), all space beyond the program stack to the end of physical memory is available for the heap.

Note Memory models are available only for 16-bit applications.

calloc allocates a block of size *nitems * size*. The block is cleared to 0. If you want to allocate a block larger than 64K, you must use *farcalloc*.

Return value
calloc returns a pointer to the newly allocated block. If not enough space exists for the new block or if *nitems* or *size* is 0, *calloc* returns NULL.

See also
farcalloc, *free*, *malloc*, *realloc*

Portability

DOS	UNIX	Win 16	Win 32	ANSI C	ANSI C++	OS/2
+	+	+	+	+	+	+

ceil, ceill   math.h

Syntax
double ceil(double x);
long double ceill(long double x);

Description
Rounds up.

ceil finds the smallest integer not less than *x*.

ceill is the **long double** version; it takes a **long double** argument and returns a **long double** result.

Return value
These functions return the integer found as a **double** *(ceil)* or a **long double** *(ceill)*.

See also
floor, fmod

Portability

	DOS	UNIX	Win 16	Win 32	ANSI C	ANSI C++	OS/2
ceil	+	+	+	+	+	+	+
ceill	+		+	+			+

_c_exit   process.h

Syntax
void _c_exit(void);

Description
Performs *_exit* cleanup without terminating the program.

_c_exit performs the same cleanup as *_exit*, except that it does not terminate the calling process.

Return value
None.

See also
abort, atexit, _cexit, exec, _exit, exit, signal, spawn

Portability

DOS	UNIX	Win 16	Win 32	ANSI C	ANSI C++	OS/2
+		+	+			+

_cexit

Syntax

void _cexit(void);

Description

Performs *exit* cleanup without terminating the program.

_cexit performs the same cleanup as *exit*, except that it does not close files or terminate the calling process. Buffered output (waiting to be output) is written, and any registered "exit functions" (posted with *atexit*) are called.

Return value

None.

See also

abort, *atexit*, *_c_exit*, *exec*, *_exit*, *exit*, *signal*, *spawn*

Portability

DOS	UNIX	Win 16	Win 32	ANSI C	ANSI C++	OS/2
+		+	+			+

cgets

Syntax

char *cgets(char *str);

Description

Reads a string from the console.

cgets reads a string of characters from the console, storing the string (and the string length) in the location pointed to by *str*.

cgets reads characters until it encounters a carriage-return/linefeed (CR/LF) combination, or until the maximum allowable number of characters have been read. If *cgets* reads a CR/LF combination, it replaces the combination with a \0 (null terminator) before storing the string.

Before *cgets* is called, set *str*[0] to the maximum length of the string to be read. On return, *str*[1] is set to the number of characters actually read. The characters read start at *str*[2] and end with a null terminator. Thus, *str* must be at least *str*[0] plus 2 bytes long.

Note Do not use this function for Win32s or Win32 GUI applications.

Return value

On success, *cgets* returns a pointer to *str*[2].

See also

cputs, fgets, getch, getche, gets

Portability

DOS	UNIX	Win 16	Win 32	ANSI C	ANSI C++	OS/2
+			+			+

_chain_intr   dos.h

Syntax

void _chain_intr(void (interrupt far *newhandler)());

Description

Chains to another interrupt handler.

_chain_intr passes control from the currently executing interrupt handler to the new interrupt handler whose address is *newhandler*. The current register set is *not* passed to the new handler. Instead, the new handler receives the registers that were stacked (and possibly modified in the stack) by the old handler. The new handler can simply return, as if it were the original handler. The old handler is not entered again.

_chain_intr can be called only by C interrupt functions. It is useful when writing a TSR that needs to insert itself in a chain of interrupt handlers (such as the keyboard interrupt).

Return value

None.

See also

_dos_getvect, _dos_setvect

Portability

DOS	UNIX	Win 16	Win 32	ANSI C	ANSI C++	OS/2
+		+				

chdir   dir.h

Syntax

int chdir(const char *path);

Description

Changes current directory.

chdir causes the directory specified by *path* to become the current working directory; *path* must specify an existing directory.

A drive can also be specified in the path argument, such as

```
chdir("a:\\BC")
```

but this method changes only the current directory on that drive; it does not change the active drive.

- Under Windows, only the current process is affected.
- Under DOS, the function changes the current directory of the parent process.

Return value
Upon successful completion, *chdir* returns a value of 0. Otherwise, it returns a value of -1, and the global variable *errno* is set to

ENOENT   Path or file name not found

See also
getcurdir, getcwd, getdisk, mkdir, rmdir, setdisk, system

Portability

DOS	UNIX	Win 16	Win 32	ANSI C	ANSI C++	OS/2
+	+	+	+			+

_chdrive   direct.h

Syntax
int _chdrive(int drive);

Description
Sets current disk drive.

_chdrive sets the current drive to the one associated with *drive:* 1 for A, 2 for B, 3 for C, and so on.

This function changes the current drive of the parent process.

Return value
_chdrive returns 0 if the current drive was changed successfully; otherwise, it returns -1.

See also
_dos_setdrive

Portability

DOS	UNIX	Win 16	Win 32	ANSI C	ANSI C++	OS/2
+		+	+			+

_chmod

Obsolete function. See _rtl_chmod.

chmod   sys\stat.h

Syntax

int chmod(const char *path, int amode);

Description

Changes file access mode.

chmod sets the file-access permissions of the file given by *path* according to the mask given by *amode*. *path* points to a string.

amode can contain one or both of the symbolic constants S_IWRITE and S_IREAD (defined in sys\stat.h).

Value of *amode*	Access permission
S_IWRITE	Permission to write
S_IREAD	Permission to read
S_IREAD | S_IWRITE	Permission to read and write (write permission implies read permission)

Return value

Upon successfully changing the file access mode, *chmod* returns 0. Otherwise, *chmod* returns a value of -1.

In the event of an error, the global variable *errno* is set to one of the following values:

EACCES   Permission denied

ENOENT   Path or file name not found

See also

access, fstat, open, _rtl_chmod, sopen, stat

Portability

DOS	UNIX	Win 16	Win 32	ANSI C	ANSI C++	OS/2
+	+	+	+			+

chsize   io.h

Syntax

int chsize(int handle, long size);

Description

Changes the file size.

chsize changes the size of the file associated with *handle*. It can truncate or extend the file, depending on the value of *size* compared to the file's original size.

The mode in which you open the file must allow writing.

If *chsize* extends the file, it will append null characters (\0). If it truncates the file, all data beyond the new end-of-file indicator is lost.

Return value

On success, *chsize* returns 0. On failure, it returns -1 and the global variable *errno* is set to one of the following values:

EACCESS   Permission denied

EBADF   Bad file number

ENOSPC   No space left on device

See also

close, creat, open, _rtl_creat

Portability

DOS	UNIX	Win 16	Win 32	ANSI C	ANSI C++	OS/2
+		+	+			+

_clear87   float.h

Syntax

unsigned int _clear87 (void);

Description

Clears floating-point status word.

_clear87 clears the floating-point status word, which is a combination of the 80x87 status word and other conditions detected by the 80x87 exception handler.

Return value

The bits in the value returned indicate the floating-point status before it was cleared. For information on the status word, refer to the constants defined in float.h.

See also

_control87, _fpreset, _status87

Portability

DOS	UNIX	Win 16	Win 32	ANSI C	ANSI C++	OS/2
+		+	+			+

clearerr   stdio.h

Syntax
void clearerr(FILE *stream);

Description
Resets error indication.

clearerr resets the named stream's error and end-of-file indicators to 0. Once the error indicator is set, stream operations continue to return error status until a call is made to *clearerr* or *rewind*. The end-of-file indicator is reset with each input operation.

Return value
None.

See also
eof, feof, ferror, perror, rewind

Portability

DOS	UNIX	Win 16	Win 32	ANSI C	ANSI C++	OS/2
+	+	+	+	+	+	+

clock   time.h

Syntax
clock_t clock(void);

Description
Determines processor time.

clock can be used to determine the time interval between two events. To determine the time in seconds, the value returned by *clock* should be divided by the value of the macro *CLK_TCK*.

Return value
On success, *clock* returns the processor time elapsed since the beginning of the program invocation.

On error (if the processor time is not available or its value cannot be represented), *clock* returns -1.

See also
time

Portability

DOS	UNIX	Win 16	Win 32	ANSI C	ANSI C++	OS/2
+	+	+	+	+	+	+

close   io.h

Syntax
int close(int handle);

Description
Closes a file.

The *close* function closes the file associated with *handle,* a file handle obtained from a call to *creat, creatnew, creattemp, dup, dup2, open, _rtl_creat,* or *_rtl_open.*

It does not write a *Ctrl-Z* character at the end of the file. If you want to terminate the file with a *Ctrl-Z,* you must explicitly output one.

Return value
Upon successful completion, *close* returns 0.

On error (if it fails because *handle* is not the handle of a valid, open file), *close* returns a value of -1 and the global variable *errno* is set to

EBADF   Bad file number

See also
chsize, creat, creatnew, dup, fclose, open, _rtl_close, sopen

Portability

DOS	UNIX	Win 16	Win 32	ANSI C	ANSI C++	OS/2
+	+	+	+			+

closedir   dirent.h

Syntax
void closedir(DIR *dirp);

Description
Closes a directory stream.

On UNIX platforms, *closedir* is available on POSIX-compliant systems.

The *closedir* function closes the directory stream *dirp*, which must have been opened by a previous call to *opendir*. After the stream is closed, *dirp* no longer points to a valid directory stream.

Return value

If *closedir* is successful, it returns 0. Otherwise, *closedir* returns -1 and sets the global variable *errno* to

EBADF   The *dirp* argument does not point to a valid open directory stream

See also

errno (global variable), *opendir, readdir, rewinddir*

Portability

DOS	UNIX	Win 16	Win 32	ANSI C	ANSI C++	OS/2
+	+	+	+			+

clreol   conio.h

Syntax

void clreol(void);

Description

Clears to end of line in text window.

clreol clears all characters from the cursor position to the end of the line within the current text window, without moving the cursor.

Note   This function should not be used in Win32s or Win32 GUI applications.

Return value

None.

See also

clrscr, delline, window

Portability

DOS	UNIX	Win 16	Win 32	ANSI C	ANSI C++	OS/2
+		+	+			+

clrscr

conio.h

Syntax

void clrscr(void);

Description

Clears the text-mode window.

clrscr clears the current text window and places the cursor in the upper left corner (at position 1,1).

Note   Do not use this function for Win32s or Win32 GUI applications.

Return value

None.

See also

clreol, delline, window

Portability

DOS	UNIX	Win 16	Win 32	ANSI C	ANSI C++	OS/2
+		+	+			+

_control87

float.h

Syntax

unsigned int _control87(unsigned int newcw, unsigned int mask);

Description

Manipulates the floating-point control word.

_control87 retrieves or changes the floating-point control word.

The floating-point control word is an **unsigned int** that, bit by bit, specifies certain modes in the floating-point package; namely, the precision, infinity, and rounding modes. Changing these modes lets you mask or unmask floating-point exceptions.

_control87 matches the bits in *mask* to the bits in *newcw*. If a *mask* bit equals 1, the corresponding bit in *newcw* contains the new value for the same bit in the floating-point control word, and *_control87* sets that bit in the control word to the new value.

Here is a simple illustration:

Original control word: 0100	0011	0110	0011
mask:	1000	0001	0100	1111
newcw:	1110	1001	0000	0101
Changing bits:	1*xxx*	*xxx*1	*x*0*xx*	0101

If *mask* equals 0, *_control87* returns the floating-point control word without altering it.

Return value

The bits in the value returned reflect the new floating-point control word. For a complete definition of the bits returned by *_control87*, see the header file float.h.

See also

_clear87, _fpreset, signal, _status87

Portability

DOS	UNIX	Win 16	Win 32	ANSI C	ANSI C++	OS/2
+		+	+			+

cos, cosl   math.h

Syntax

```
double cos(double x);
long double cosl(long double x);
```

Description

Calculates the cosine of a value.

cos computes the cosine of the input value. The angle is specified in radians.

cosl is the **long double** version; it takes a **long double** argument and returns a **long double** result.

This function can be used with *bcd* and *complex* types.

Return value

cos of a real argument returns a value in the range -1 to 1. Error handling for these functions can be modified through *_matherr* (or *_matherrl*).

See also

acos, asin, atan, atan2, bcd, complex, _matherr, sin, tan

Portability

	DOS	UNIX	Win 16	Win 32	ANSI C	ANSI C++	OS/2
cos	+	+	+	+	+	+	+
cosl	+		+	+			+

cosh, coshl   math.h

Syntax

double cosh(double x);
long double coshl(long double x);

Description

Calculates the hyperbolic cosine of a value.

cosh computes the hyperbolic cosine. *coshl* is the **long double** version; it takes a **long double** argument and returns a **long double** result.

This function can be used with *bcd* and *complex* types.

Return value

cosh returns the hyperbolic cosine of the argument.

When the correct value would create an overflow, these functions return the value HUGE_VAL *(cosh)* or _LHUGE_VAL *(coshl)* with the appropriate sign, and the global variable *errno* is set to ERANGE. Error handling for these functions can be modified through the functions *_matherr* and *_matherrl*.

See also

acos, asin, atan, atan2, bcd, complex, cos, _matherr, sin, sinh, tan, tanh

Portability

	DOS	UNIX	Win 16	Win 32	ANSI C	ANSI C++	OS/2
cosh	+	+	+	+	+	+	+
coshl	+		+	+			+

country   dos.h

Syntax

struct COUNTRY *country(int xcode, struct country *cp);

Description

Returns country-dependent information.

country specifies how certain country-dependent data (such as dates, times, and currency) will be formatted. The values set by this function depend on the operating system version being used.

If *cp* has a value of -1, the current country is set to the value of *xcode*, which must be nonzero. The *COUNTRY* structure pointed to by *cp* is filled with the country-dependent information of the current country (if *xcode* is set to zero), or the country given by *xcode*.

The structure *COUNTRY* is defined as follows:

```
struct COUNTRY{
    short co_date;          /* date format */
    char co_curr[5];        /* currency symbol */
    char co_thsep[2];       /* thousands separator */
    char co_desep[2];       /* decimal separator */
    char co_dtsep[2];       /* date separator */
    char co_tmsep[2];       /* time separator */
    char co_currstyle;      /* currency style */
    char co_digits;         /* significant digits in currency */
    char co_time;           /* time format */
    long co_case;           /* case map */
    char co_dasep[2];       /* data separator */
    char co_fill[10];       /* filler */
};
```

The date format in *co_date* is

0   for the U.S. style of month, day, year.

1   for the European style of day, month, year.

2   for the Japanese style of year, month, day.

Currency display style is given by *co_currstyle* as follows:

0   for the currency symbol to precede the value with no spaces between the symbol and the number.

1   for the currency symbol to follow the value with no spaces between the number and the symbol.

2   for the currency symbol to precede the value with a space after the symbol.

3   for the currency symbol to follow the number with a space before the symbol.

Return value

On success, *country* returns the pointer argument *cp*. On error, it returns NULL.

Portability

DOS	UNIX	Win 16	Win 32	ANSI C	ANSI C++	OS/2
+		+				+

cprintf   conio.h

Syntax

int cprintf(const char *format[, argument, ...]);

Description

Writes formatted output to the screen.

cprintf accepts a series of arguments, applies to each a format specifier contained in the format string pointed to by *format*, and outputs the formatted data directly to the current text window on the screen. There must be the same number of format specifiers as arguments.

For details on format specifiers, see "printf Format Specifiers."

The string is written either directly to screen memory or by way of a BIOS call, depending on the value of the global variable *_directvideo*.

Unlike *fprintf* and *printf*, *cprintf* does not translate linefeed characters (\n) into carriage-return/linefeed character pairs (\r\n). Tab characters (specified by \t) are not expanded into spaces.

Note   Do not use this function for Win32s or Win32 GUI applications.

Return value

cprintf returns the number of characters output.

See also

_directvideo (global variable), *fprintf, printf, putch, sprintf, vprintf*

Portability

DOS	UNIX	Win 16	Win 32	ANSI C	ANSI C++	OS/2
+			+			+

cputs   conio.h

Syntax

int cputs(const char *str);

Description

Writes a string to the screen.

cputs writes the null-terminated string *str* to the current text window. It does not append a newline character.

The string is written either directly to screen memory or by way of a BIOS call, depending on the value of the global variable *_directvideo*. Unlike *puts*, *cputs* does not translate linefeed characters (\n) into carriage-return/linefeed character pairs (\r\n).

Note   Do not use this function for Win32s or Win32 GUI applications.

Return value

cputs returns the last character printed.

See also
cgets, fputs, putch, puts

Portability

DOS	UNIX	Win 16	Win 32	ANSI C	ANSI C++	OS/2
+			+			+

_creat

Obsolete function. See *_rtl.creat*.

creat   io.h

Syntax
int creat(const char *path, int amode);

Description
Creates a new file or overwrites an existing one.

Note Remember that a backslash in a path requires '\\'.

creat creates a new file or prepares to rewrite an existing file given by *path*. *amode* applies only to newly created files.

A file created with *creat* is always created in the translation mode specified by the global variable *_fmode* (O_TEXT or O_BINARY).

If the file exists and the write attribute is set, *creat* truncates the file to a length of 0 bytes, leaving the file attributes unchanged. If the existing file has the read-only attribute set, the *creat* call fails and the file remains unchanged.

The *creat* call examines only the S_IWRITE bit of the access-mode word *amode*. If that bit is 1, the file can be written to. If the bit is 0, the file is marked as read-only. All other operating system attributes are set to 0.

amode can be one of the following (defined in sys\stat.h):

Value of *amode*	Access permission
S_IWRITE	Permission to write
S_IREAD	Permission to read
S_IREAD / S_IWRITE	Permission to read and write (write permission implies read permission)

Return value
Upon successful completion, *creat* returns the new file handle, a nonnegative integer; otherwise, it returns -1.

In the event of error, the global variable *errno* is set to one of the following:

EACCES   Permission denied

ENOENT   Path or file name not found

EMFILE   Too many open files

See also
chmod, chsize, close, creatnew, creattemp, dup, dup2, _fmode (global variable), *fopen, open, _rtl_creat, sopen, write*

Portability

DOS	UNIX	Win 16	Win 32	ANSI C	ANSI C++	OS/2
+	+	+	+			+

creatnew   io.h

Syntax
int creatnew(const char *path, int mode);

Description
Creates a new file.

creatnew is identical to *_rtl_creat* with one exception: If the file exists, *creatnew* returns an error and leaves the file untouched.

The *mode* argument to *creatnew* can be zero or an OR-combination of any one of the following constants (defined in dos.h):

FA_HIDDEN   Hidden file

FA_RDONLY   Read-only attribute

FA_SYSTEM   System file

Return value
Upon successful completion, *creat* returns the new file handle, a nonnegative integer; otherwise, it returns -1.

In the event of error, the global variable errno is set to one of the following values:

EACCES   Permission denied

EEXIST   File already exists

EMFILE   Too many open files

ENOENT   Path or file name not found

See also

close, creat, creattemp, _dos_creatnew, dup, _fmode (global variable), *open, _rtl_creat*

Portability

DOS	UNIX	Win 16	Win 32	ANSI C	ANSI C++	OS/2
+		+	+			+

creattemp   io.h

Syntax

int creattemp(char *path, int attrib);

Description

Creates a unique file in the directory associated with the path name.

A file created with *creattemp* is always created in the translation mode specified by the global variable *_fmode* (O_TEXT or O_BINARY).

path is a path name ending with a *backslash* (\). A unique file name is selected in the directory given by *path*. The newly created file name is stored in the *path* string supplied. *path* should be long enough to hold the resulting file name. The file is not automatically deleted when the program terminates.

creattemp accepts *attrib*, a DOS attribute word. Upon successful file creation, the file pointer is set to the beginning of the file. The file is opened for both reading and writing.

The *attrib* argument to *creattemp* can be zero or an OR-combination of any one of the following constants (defined in dos.h):

FA_HIDDEN   Hidden file

FA_RDONLY   Read-only attribute

FA_SYSTEM   System file

Return value

Upon successful completion, the new file handle, a nonnegative integer, is returned; otherwise, -1 is returned.

In the event of error, the global variable *errno* is set to one of the following values:

EACCES   Permission denied

EMFILE   Too many open files

ENOENT   Path or file name not found

See also

close, creat, creatnew, dup, _fmode (global variable), *open, _rtl_creat*

Portability

DOS	UNIX	Win 16	Win 32	ANSI C	ANSI C++	OS/2
+		+	+			+

_crotl, _crotr   stdlib.h

Syntax

unsigned char _crotl(unsigned char val, int count);
unsigned char _crotr(unsigned char val, int count);

Description

Rotates an unsigned char left or right.

_crotl rotates the given *val* to the left *count* bits. _crotr rotates the given *val* to the right *count* bits.

The argument *val* is an **unsigned char**, or its equivalent in decimal or hexadecimal form.

Return value

The functions return the rotated word:

- _crotl returns the value of *val* left-rotated *count* bits.
- _crotr returns the value of *val* right-rotated *count* bits.

See also

_lrotl, _lrotr, _rotl, _rotr

Portability

DOS	UNIX	Win 16	Win 32	ANSI C	ANSI C++	OS/2
+		+	+			+

cscanf   conio.h

Syntax

int cscanf(char *format[, address, ...]);

Description

Scans and formats input from the console.

cscanf scans a series of input fields one character at a time, reading directly from the console. Then each field is formatted according to a format specifier passed to *cscanf* in the format string pointed to by *format*. Finally, *cscanf* stores the formatted input at an address passed to it as an argument following *format*, and echoes the input directly to the screen. There must be the same number of format specifiers and addresses as there are input fields.

Note   For details on format specifiers, see "scanf Format Specifiers."

cscanf might stop scanning a particular field before it reaches the normal end-of-field (whitespace) character, or it might terminate entirely for a number of reasons. See *scanf* for a discussion of possible causes.

Note   Do not use this function for Win32s or Win32 GUI applications.

Return value
cscanf returns the number of input fields successfully scanned, converted, and stored; the return value does not include scanned fields that were not stored. If no fields were stored, the return value is 0.

If *cscanf* attempts to read at end-of-file , the return value is EOF.

See also
fscanf, getche, scanf, sscanf

Portability

DOS	UNIX	Win 16	Win 32	ANSI C	ANSI C++	OS/2
+			+			+

ctime   time.h

Syntax
```
char *ctime(const time_t *time);
```

Description
Converts date and time to a string.

ctime converts a time value pointed to by *time* (the value returned by the function *time*) into a 26-character string in the following form, terminating with a newline character and a null character:

```
Mon Nov 21 11:31:54 1983\n\0
```

All the fields have constant width.

The global long variable *_timezone* contains the difference in seconds between GMT and local standard time (in PST, *_timezone* is 8*60*60). The global variable *_daylight* is nonzero *if and only if* the standard U.S. *_daylight* saving time conversion should be applied. These variables are set by the *tzset* function, not by the user program directly.

Return value

ctime returns a pointer to the character string containing the date and time. The return value points to static data that is overwritten with each call to *ctime*.

See also

asctime, _daylight (global variable), *difftime, ftime, getdate, gmtime, localtime, settime, time, _timezone* (global variable), *tzset*

Portability

DOS	UNIX	Win 16	Win 32	ANSI C	ANSI C++	OS/2
+	+	+	+	+	+	+

ctrlbrk   dos.h

Syntax

void ctrlbrk(int (*handler)(void));

Description

Sets control-break handler.

ctrlbrk sets a new control-break handler function pointed to by *handler*. The interrupt vector 0x23 is modified to call the named function.

ctrlbrk establishes a DOS interrupt handler that calls the named function; the named function is not called directly.

The handler function can perform any number of operations and system calls. The handler does not have to return; it can use *longjmp* to return to an arbitrary point in the program. The handler function returns 0 to abort the current program; any other value causes the program to resume execution.

Return value

ctrlbrk returns nothing.

See also

getcbrk, signal

Portability

DOS	UNIX	Win 16	Win 32	ANSI C	ANSI C++	OS/2
+		+				

cwait   process.h

Syntax

int cwait(int *statloc, int pid, int action);

Description

Waits for child process to terminate.

The *cwait* function waits for a child process to terminate. The process ID of the child to wait for is *pid*. If *statloc* is not NULL, it points to the location where *cwait* will store the termination status. The *action* specifies whether to wait for the process alone, or for the process and all of its children.

If the child process terminated normally (by calling *exit*, or returning from *main*), the termination status word is defined as follows:

Bits 0-7   Zero

Bits 8-15   The least significant byte of the return code from the child process. This is the value that is passed to *exit*, or is returned from *main*. If the child process simply exited from *main* without returning a value, this value will be unpredictable.

If the child process terminated abnormally, the termination status word is defined as follows:

Bits 0-7   **Termination information about the child:**

       1   Critical error abort.

       2   Execution fault, protection exception.

       3   External termination signal.

Bits 8-15   Zero

If *pid* is 0, *cwait* waits for any child process to terminate. Otherwise, *pid* specifies the process ID of the process to wait for; this value must have been obtained by an earlier call to an asynchronous *spawn* function.

The acceptable values for *action* are WAIT_CHILD, which waits for the specified child only, and WAIT_GRANDCHILD, which waits for the specified child *and* all of its children. These two values are defined in process.h.

Return value

When *cwait* returns after a normal child process termination, it returns the process ID of the child.

When *cwait* returns after an abnormal child termination, it returns -1 to the parent and sets *errno* to EINTR (the child process terminated abnormally).

If *cwait* returns without a child process completion, it returns a -1 value and sets *errno* to one of the following values:

ECHILD   No child exists or the pid value is bad

EINVAL   A bad action value was specified

See also
spawnl, wait

Portability

DOS	UNIX	Win 16	Win 32	ANSI C	ANSI C++	OS/2
			+			+

delline

conio.h

Syntax
void delline(void);

Description
Deletes line in text window.

delline deletes the line containing the cursor and moves all lines below it one line up. *delline* operates within the currently active text window.

Note Do not use this function for Win32s or Win32 GUI applications.

Return value
None.

See also
clreol, clrscr, insline, window

Portability

DOS	UNIX	Win 16	Win 32	ANSI C	ANSI C++	OS/2
+		+	+			+

difftime

time.h

Syntax
double difftime(time_t time2, time_t time1);

Description
Computes the difference between two times.

difftime calculates the elapsed time in seconds, from *time1* to *time2*.

Return value
difftime returns the result of its calculation as a **double**.

See also
asctime, ctime, _daylight (global variable), *gmtime, localtime, time, _timezone* (global variable)

Portability

DOS	UNIX	Win 16	Win 32	ANSI C	ANSI C++	OS/2
+	+	+	+	+	+	+

disable, _disable, enable, _enable   dos.h

Syntax
void disable(void);
void _disable(void);
void enable(void);
void _enable(void);

Description
Disables and enables interrupts.

These macros are designed to provide a programmer with flexible hardware interrupt control.

disable and *_disable* macros disable interrupts. Only the NMI (non-maskable interrupt) is allowed from any external device.

enable and *_enable* macros enable interrupts, allowing any device interrupts to occur.

Return value
None.

See also
getvect

Portability

DOS	UNIX	Win 16	Win 32	ANSI C	ANSI C++	OS/2
+	+	+	+			

div   stdlib.h

Syntax
div_t div(int numer, int denom);

Description
Divides two integers, returning quotient and remainder.

div divides two integers and returns both the quotient and the remainder as a *div_t* type. *numer* and *denom* are the numerator and denominator, respectively. The *div_t* type is a structure of integers defined (with **typedef**) in stdlib.h as follows:

```
typedef struct {
    int  quot;      /* quotient */
    int  rem;       /* remainder */
} div_t;
```

Return value
div returns a structure whose elements are *quot* (the quotient) and *rem* (the remainder).

See also
ldiv

Portability

DOS	UNIX	Win 16	Win 32	ANSI C	ANSI C++	OS/2
+		+	+	+	+	+

_dos_close   dos.h

Syntax
unsigned _dos_close(int handle);

Description
Closes a file.

The *_dos_close* function closes the file associated with *handle*; *handle* is a file handle obtained from a *_dos_creat*, *_dos_creatnew*, or *_dos_open* call.

Return value
Upon successful completion, *_dos_close* returns 0. Otherwise, it returns the operating system error code and the global variable *errno* is set to

EBADF   Bad file number

See also
_dos_creat, *_dos_open*, *_dos_read*, *_dos_write*

Portability

DOS	UNIX	Win 16	Win 32	ANSI C	ANSI C++	OS/2
+		+				+

_dos_commit

dos.h

Syntax
unsigned _dos_commit(int handle);

Description
Outputs a file to the disk.

This function makes DOS flush any output that it has buffered for a specific handle to the disk.

Return value
The function returns zero on success. On failure the function returns the DOS error code and sets *errno* to EBADF on failure.

See also
_dos_creat, _dos_write, _rtl_close, _rtl_creat

Portability

DOS	UNIX	Win 16	Win 32	ANSI C	ANSI C++	OS/2
+		+				

_dos_creat

dos.h

Syntax
unsigned _dos_creat(const char *path,int attrib,int *handlep);

Description
Creates a new file or overwrites an existing one.

_dos_creat opens the file specified by *path*. The file is always opened in binary mode. Upon successful file creation, the file pointer is set to the beginning of the file. *_dos_creat* stores the file handle in the location pointed to by *handlep*. The file is opened for both reading and writing.

If the file already exists, its size is reset to 0. (This is essentially the same as deleting the file and creating a new file with the same name.)

The *attrib* argument is an ORed combination of one or more of the following constants (defined in dos.h):

_A_NORMAL	Normal file
_A_RDONLY	Read-only file
_A_HIDDEN	Hidden file
_A_SYSTEM	System file

Return value

On success, _dos_creat returns 0.

On error, it returns the operating system error code and the global variable *errno* is set to one of the following values:

EACCES   Permission denied

ENOENT   Path or file name not found

EMFILE   Too many open files

See also

chsize, close, creat, creatnew, creattemp, _rtl_chmod, _rtl_close

Portability

DOS	UNIX	Win 16	Win 32	ANSI C	ANSI C++	OS/2
+		+				+

_dos_creatnew   dos.h

Syntax

unsigned _dos_creatnew(const char *path, int attrib, int *handlep);

Description

Creates a new file.

_dos_creatnew creates and opens the new file *path*. The file is given the access permission *attrib*, an operating-system attribute word. The file is always opened in binary mode. Upon successful file creation, the file handle is stored in the location pointed to by *handlep,* and the file pointer is set to the beginning of the file. The file is opened for both reading and writing.

If the file already exists, *_dos_creatnew* returns an error and leaves the file untouched.

The *attrib* argument to *_dos_creatnew* is an OR combination of one or more of the following constants (defined in dos.h):

_A_NORMAL   Normal file

_A_RDONLY   Read-only file

_A_HIDDEN   Hidden file

_A_SYSTEM   System file

Return value

Upon successful completion, *_dos_creatnew* returns 0. Otherwise, it returns the operating system error code, and the global variable *errno* is set to one of the following:

EACCES   Permission denied

EEXIST   File already exists

EMFILE   Too many open files

ENOENT   Path or file name not found

See also

creatnew, *_dos_close*, *_dos_creat*, *_dos_getfileattr*, *_dos_setfileattr*

Portability

DOS	UNIX	Win 16	Win 32	ANSI C	ANSI C++	OS/2
+		+				+

dosexterr   dos.h

Syntax

int dosexterr(struct DOSERROR *eblkp);

Description

Gets extended DOS error information.

This function fills in the DOSERROR structure pointed to by *eblkp* with extended error information after a DOS call has failed. The structure is defined as follows:

```
struct  DOSERROR {
    int de_exterror;      /* extended error */
    char de_class;        /* error class */
    char de_action;       /* action */
    char de_locus;        /* error locus */
};
```

The values in this structure are obtained by way of DOS call 0x59. A *de_exterror* value of 0 indicates that the prior DOS call did not result in an error.

Return value

dosexterr returns the value *de_exterror*.

Portability

DOS	UNIX	Win 16	Win 32	ANSI C	ANSI C++	OS/2
+		+				

_dos_findfirst

dos.h

Syntax

unsigned _dos_findfirst(const char *pathname, int attrib, struct find_t *ffblk);

Description

Searches a disk directory.

_dos_findfirst begins a search of a disk directory.

pathname is a string with an optional drive specifier, path, and file name of the file to be found. The file name portion can contain wildcard match characters (such as ? or *). If a matching file is found, the *find_t* structure pointed to by *ffblk* is filled with the file-directory information.

The format of the *find_t* structure is as follows:

```
struct find_t {
    char reserved[21];      /* reserved by the operating system */
    char attrib;            /* attribute found */
    int wr_time;            /* file time */
    int wr_date;            /* file date */
    long size;              /* file size */
    char name[13];          /* found file name */
};
```

attrib is an operating system file-attribute word used in selecting eligible files for the search. *attrib* is an OR combination of one or more of the following constants (defined in dos.h):

_A_NORMAL	Normal file
_A_RDONLY	Read-only attribute
_A_HIDDEN	Hidden file
_A_SYSTEM	System file
_A_VOLID	Volume label
_A_SUBDIR	Directory
_A_ARCH	Archive

For more detailed information about these attributes, refer to your operating system reference manuals.

Note *wr_time* and *wr_date* contain bit fields for referring to the file's date and time. The structure of these fields was established by the operating system.

wr_time:

Bits 0-4	The result of seconds divided by 2 (for example, 10 here means 20 seconds)
Bits 5-10	Minutes

Bits 11-15	Hours
wr_date:	
Bits 0-4	Day
Bits 5-8	Month
Bits 9-15	Years since 1980 (for example, 9 here means 1989)

Return value

_dos_findfirst returns 0 on successfully finding a file matching the search *pathname*. When no more files can be found, or if there is some error in the file name, the operating system error code is returned, and the global variable *errno* is set to

ENOENT   Path or file name not found

See also

_dos_findnext

Portability

DOS	UNIX	Win 16	Win 32	ANSI C	ANSI C++	OS/2
+		+				+

_dos_findnext   dos.h

Syntax

unsigned _dos_findnext(struct find_t *ffblk);

Description

Continues *_dos_findfirst* search.

_dos_findnext is used to fetch subsequent files that match the *pathname* given in *_dos_findfirst*. *ffblk* is the same block filled in by the *_dos_findfirst* call. This block contains necessary information for continuing the search. One file name for each call to *_dos_findnext* is returned until no more files are found in the directory matching the *pathname*.

Return value

_dos_findnext returns 0 on successfully finding a file matching the search *pathname*. When no more files can be found, or if there is some error in the file name, the operating system error code is returned, and the global variable *errno* is set to

ENOENT   Path or file name not found

See also

_dos_findfirst

Portability

DOS	UNIX	Win 16	Win 32	ANSI C	ANSI C++	OS/2
+		+				+

_dos_getdate, _dos_setdate, getdate, setdate   dos.h

Syntax
void _dos_getdate(struct dosdate_t *datep);
unsigned _dos_setdate(struct dosdate_t *datep);
void getdate(struct date *datep);
void setdate(struct date *datep);

Description
Gets and sets system date.

getdate fills in the *date* structure (pointed to by *datep*) with the system's current date.

setdate sets the system date (month, day, and year) to that in the *date* structure pointed to by *datep*. Note that a request to set a date might fail if you do not have the privileges required by the operating system.

The *date* structure is defined as follows:

```
struct date{
    int da_year;      /* current year */
    char da_day;      /* day of the month */
    char da_mon;      /* month (1 = Jan) */
};
```

_dos_getdate fills in the *dosdate_t* structure (pointed to by *datep*) with the system's current date.

The *dosdate_t* structure is defined as follows:

```
struct dosdate_t {
    unsigned char day;        /* 1-31 */
    unsigned char month;      /* 1-12 */
    unsigned int  year;       /* 1980 - 2099 */
    unsigned char dayofweek;  /* 0 - 6 (0=Sunday) */
};
```

Return value
_dos_getdate, *getdate*, and *setdate* do not return a value.

If the date is set successfully, *_dos_setdate* returns 0.

Otherwise, it returns a non-zero value and the global variable *errno* is set to

EINVAL   Invalid date

See also
ctime, gettime, settime

Portability

DOS	UNIX	Win 16	Win 32	ANSI C	ANSI C++	OS/2
+		+				+

_dos_getdiskfree   dos.h

Syntax

unsigned _dos_getdiskfree(unsigned char drive, struct diskfree_t *dtable);

Description

Gets disk free space.

_dos_getdiskfree_ accepts a drive specifier in _drive_ (0 for default, 1 for A, 2 for B, and so on) and fills in the _diskfree_t_ structure pointed to by _dtable_ with disk characteristics.

The _diskfree_t_ structure is defined as follows:

```
struct diskfree_t {
    unsigned avail_clusters;       /* available clusters */
    unsigned total_clusters;       /* total clusters */
    unsigned bytes_per_sector;     /* bytes per sector */
    unsigned sectors_per_cluster;  /* sectors per cluster */
};
```

Return value

_dos_getdiskfree_ returns 0 if successful. Otherwise, it returns a non-zero value and the global variable _errno_ is set to

EINVAL   Invalid drive specified

See also

getfat, getfatd

Portability

DOS	UNIX	Win 16	Win 32	ANSI C	ANSI C++	OS/2
+		+				+

_dos_getdrive, _dos_setdrive   dos.h

Syntax

void _dos_getdrive(unsigned *drivep);
void _dos_setdrive(unsigned drivep, unsigned *ndrives);

Description

Gets and sets the current drive number.

_dos_getdrive gets the current drive number.

_dos_setdrive sets the current drive and stores the total number of drives at the location pointed to by *ndrives*.

The drive numbers at the location pointed to by *drivep* are as follows: 1 for A, 2 for B, 3 for C, and so on.

This function changes the current drive of the parent process.

Return value
None. Use *_dos_getdrive* to verify that the current drive was changed successfully.

See also
getcwd

Portability

DOS	UNIX	Win 16	Win 32	ANSI C	ANSI C++	OS/2
+		+				+

_dos_getfileattr, _dos_setfileattr   dos.h

Syntax
```
int _dos_getfileattr(const char *path, unsigned *attribp);
int _dos_setfileattr(const char *path, unsigned attrib);
```

Description
Changes file access mode.

_dos_getfileattr fetches the file attributes for the file *path*. The attributes are stored at the location pointed to by *attribp*.

_dos_setfileattr sets the file attributes for the file *path* to the value *attrib*. The file attributes can be an OR combination of the following symbolic constants (defined in dos.h):

_A_RDONLY	Read-only attribute
_A_HIDDEN	Hidden file
_A_SYSTEM	System file
_A_VOLID	Volume label
_A_SUBDIR	Directory
_A_ARCH	Archive
_A_NORMAL	Normal file (no attribute bits set)

Return value

Upon successful completion, _dos_getfileattr and _dos_setfileattr return 0. Otherwise, these functions return the operating system error code, and the global variable *errno* is set to

ENOENT   Path or file name not found

See also

chmod, *stat*

Portability

DOS	UNIX	Win 16	Win 32	ANSI C	ANSI C++	OS/2
+		+				+

_dos_getftime, _dos_setftime   dos.h

Syntax

unsigned _dos_getftime(int handle, unsigned *datep, unsigned *timep);
unsigned _dos_setftime(int handle, unsigned date, unsigned time);

Description

Gets and sets file date and time.

_dos_getftime retrieves the file time and date for the disk file associated with the open *handle*. The file must have been previously opened using *_dos_open*, *_dos_creat*, or *_dos_creatnew*. *_dos_getftime* stores the date and time at the locations pointed to by *datep* and *timep*.

-*dos_setftime* sets the file's new date and time values as specified by *date* and *time*.

Note that the date and time values containbit fields for referring to the file's date and timeThe structure of these fields was established by the operating system.

Date:

Bits 0-4   Day

Bits 5-8   Month

Bits 9-15   Years since 1980 (for example, 9 here means 1989)

Time:

Bits 0-4   The result of seconds divided by 2 (for example, 10 here means 20 seconds)

Bits 5-10   Minutes

Bits 11-15   Hours

Return value

_dos_getftime and *_dos_setftime* return 0 on success.

In the event of an error return, the operating system error code is returned and the global variable *errno* is set to one of the following values:

EACCES   Permission denied

EBADF   Bad file number

See also
fstat, stat

Portability

DOS	UNIX	Win 16	Win 32	ANSI C	ANSI C++	OS/2
+		+				+

_dos_gettime, _dos_settime   dos.h

Syntax
```
void _dos_gettime(struct dostime_t *timep);
unsigned _dos_settime(struct dostime_t *timep);
```

Description
Gets and sets system time.

_dos_gettime fills in the *dostime_t* structure pointed to by *timep* with the system's current time.

_dos_settime sets the system time to the values in the *dostime_t* structure pointed to by *timep*.

The *dostime_t* structure is defined as follows:

```
struct dostime_t {
    unsigned char hour;     /* hours 0-23 */
    unsigned char minute;   /* minutes 0-59 */
    unsigned char second;   /* seconds 0-59 */
    unsigned char hsecond;  /* hundredths of seconds 0-99 */
};
```

Return value
_dos_gettime does not return a value.

If *_dos_settime* is successful, it returns 0. Otherwise, it returns the operating system error code, and the global variable *errno* is set to

EINVAL   Invalid time

See also

_dos_getdate, _dos_setdate, _dos_settime, stime, time

Portability

DOS	UNIX	Win 16	Win 32	ANSI C	ANSI C++	OS/2
+		+				+

_dos_getvect   dos.h

Syntax

void interrupt(*_dos_getvect(unsigned interruptno)) ();

Description

Gets interrupt vector.

Every processor of the 8086 family includes a set of interrupt vectors, numbered 0 to 255. The 4-byte value in each vector is actually an address, which is the location of an interrupt function.

_dos_getvect reads the value of the interrupt vector given by *interruptno* and returns that value as a (far) pointer to an interrupt function. The value of *interruptno* can be from 0 to 255.

Return value

_dos_getvect returns the current 4-byte value stored in the interrupt vector named by *interruptno*.

See also

_disable, _enable, _dos_setvect

Portability

DOS	UNIX	Win 16	Win 32	ANSI C	ANSI C++	OS/2
+		+				

_dos_open   fcntl.h, share.h, dos.h

Syntax

unsigned _dos_open(const char *filename, unsigned oflags, int *handlep);

Description

Opens a file for reading or writing.

_dos_open opens the file specified by *filename*, then prepares it for reading or writing, as determined by the value of *oflags*. The file is always opened in binary mode. _dos_open stores the file handle at the location pointed to by *handlep*.

oflags uses the flags from the following two lists. Only one flag from List 1 can be used (and one must be used) and the flags in List 2 can be used in any logical combination.

List 1: read/write flags	Description
O_RDONLY	Open for reading.
O_WRONLY	Open for writing.
O_RDWR	Open for reading and writing.

The following additional values can be included in *oflags* (using an OR operation):

List 2: Other access flags	Description
O_NOINHERIT	The file is not passed to child programs.
SH_COMPAT	Allow other opens with SH_COMPAT. The call will fail if the file has already been opened in any other shared mode.
SH_DENYRW	Only the current handle can have access to the file.
SH_DENWR	Allow only reads from any other open to the file.
SH_DENYRD	Allow only writes from any other open to the file.
SH_DENYNO	Allow other shared opens to the file, but not other SH_COMPAT opens.

Note These symbolic constants are defined in fcntl.h and share.h.

Only one of the SH_DENYxx values can be included in a single _dos_open routine. These file-sharing attributes are in addition to any locking performed on the files.

The maximum number of simultaneously open files is defined by HANDLE_MAX.

Return value

On success, _dos_open returns 0 and stores the file handle at the location pointed to by *handlep*. The file pointer, which marks the current position in the file, is set to the beginning of the file.

On error, it returns the operating system error code and sets the global variable *errno* to one of the following values:

EACCES	Permission denied
EINVACC	Invalid access code
EMFILE	Too many open files
ENOENT	Path or file not found

See also

open, _rtl_read, sopen

Portability

DOS	UNIX	Win 16	Win 32	ANSI C	ANSI C++	OS/2
+		+				+

_dos_read

dos.h

Syntax
unsigned _dos_read(int handle, void *buf, unsigned len, unsigned *nread);

Description
Reads from file.

The _dos_read function reads *len* bytes from the file associated with *handle* into the buffer pointed to by the pointer *buf*. The actual number of bytes read is stored at the location pointed to by *nread*; when an error occurs, or the end-of-file is encountered, this number might be less than *len*.

_dos_read does not remove carriage returns because it treats all files as binary files.

handle is a file handle obtained from a *_dos_creat*, *_dos_creatnew*, or *_dos_open* call.

For *_read*, handle is a file handle obtained from a *creat*, *open*, *dup*, or *dup2* call.

On disk files, _dos_read begins reading at the current file pointer. When the reading is complete, they increment the file pointer by the number of bytes read. On devices, the bytes are read directly from the device.

The maximum number of bytes that _dos_read can read is UINT_MAX -1 (because UINT_MAX is the same as -1, the error return indicator). UINT_MAX is defined in limits.h.

Return value
On success, _dos_read returns 0.

On error, it returns the DOS error code and sets the global variable *errno*.

On success, *_read* returns a positive integer indicating the number of bytes placed in the buffer. On end-of-file, *_read* returns zero. On error, *_read* returns -1, and the global variable *errno* is set to one of the following values:

EACCES   Permission denied

EBADF   Bad file number

See also
_open, *read*, *_rtl_write*

Portability

DOS	UNIX	Win 16	Win 32	ANSI C	ANSI C++	OS/2
+		+				+

_dos_setdate

See *_dos_getdate*.

_dos_setfileattn

See _dos_getfileattr.

_dos_setftime

See _dos_getftime.

_dos_settime

See _dos_gettime.

_dos_setvect   dos.h

Syntax
void _dos_setvect(unsigned interruptno, void interrupt (*isr) ());

Description
Sets interrupt vector entry.

Every processor of the 8086 family includes a set of interrupt vectors, numbered 0 to 255. The 4-byte value in each vector is actually an address, which is the location of an interrupt function.

_dos_setvect sets the value of the interrupt vector named by *interruptno* to a new value, *isr*, which is a far pointer containing the address of a new interrupt function. The address of a C routine can be passed to *isr* only if that routine is declared to be an interrupt routine.

If you use the prototypes declared in dos.h, simply pass the address of an interrupt function to _dos_setvect in any memory model.

Return value
None.

See also
_dos_getvect

Portability

DOS	UNIX	Win 16	Win 32	ANSI C	ANSI C++	OS/2
+		+				

dostounix

dos.h

Syntax

long dostounix(struct date *d, struct time *t);

Description

Converts date and time to UNIX time format.

dostounix converts a date and time as returned from *getdate* and *gettime* into UNIX time format. *d* points to a *date* structure, and *t* points to a *time* structure containing valid date and time information.

The date and time must not be earlier than or equal to Jan 1 1980 00:00:00.

Return value

UNIX version of current date and time parameters: number of seconds since 00:00:00 on January 1, 1970 (GMT).

See also

getdate, gettime, unixtodos

Portability

DOS	UNIX	Win 16	Win 32	ANSI C	ANSI C++	OS/2
+		+				+

_dos_write

dos.h

Syntax

unsigned _dos_write(int handle, const void far *buf, unsigned len, unsigned *nwritten);
unsigned _dos_write(int handle, const void *buf, unsigned len, unsigned *nwritten);

Description

Writes to a file.

_dos_write writes *len* bytes from the buffer pointed to by pointer *buf* to the file associated with *handle*.

_dos_write does not translate a linefeed character (LF) to a CR/LF pair because it treats all files as binary data.

The actual number of bytes written is stored at the location pointed to by *nwritten*. If the number of bytes actually written is less than that requested, the condition should be considered an error and probably indicates a full disk. For disk files, writing always proceeds from the current file pointer. On devices, bytes are directly sent to the device.

Return value

On success, *_dos_write* returns 0.

On error, it returns the operating system error code and sets the global variable errno to one of the following values:

| EACCES | Permission denied |
| EBADF | Bad file number |

See also
_dos_open, _dos_creat, _dos_read

Portability

DOS	UNIX	Win 16	Win 32	ANSI C	ANSI C++	OS/2
+		+				+

dup   io.h

Syntax
int dup(int handle);

Description
Duplicates a file handle.

dup creates a new file handle that has the following in common with the original file handle:

- Same open file or device
- Same file pointer (that is, changing the file pointer of one changes the other)
- Same access mode (read, write, read/write)

handle is a file handle obtained from a call to *creat, open, dup, dup2, _rtl_creat,* or *_rtl_open*.

Return value
Upon successful completion, *dup* returns the new file handle, a nonnegative integer; otherwise, *dup* returns -1.

In the event of error, the global variable *errno* is set to one of the following values:

| EBADF | Bad file number |
| EMFILE | Too many open files |

See also
close, creat, creatnew, creattemp, dup2, fopen, open, _rtl_close, _rtl_creat, _rtl_open

Portability

DOS	UNIX	Win 16	Win 32	ANSI C	ANSI C++	OS/2
+	+	+	+			+

dup2

io.h

Syntax
int dup2(int oldhandle, int newhandle);

Description
Duplicates a file handle (*oldhandle*) onto an existing file handle (*newhandle*).

dup2 creates a new file handle that has the following in common with the original file handle:

- Same open file or device
- Same file pointer (that is, changing the file pointer of one changes the other)
- Same access mode (read, write, read/write)

dup2 creates a new handle with the value of *newhandle*. If the file associated with *newhandle* is open when *dup2* is called, the file is closed.

newhandle and *oldhandle* are file handles obtained from a *creat, open, dup,* or *dup2* call.

Return value
dup2 returns 0 on successful completion, -1 otherwise.

In the event of error, the global variable *errno* is set to one of the following values:

EBADF   Bad file number

EMFILE   Too many open files

See also
close, creat, creatnew, creattemp, dup, fopen, open, _rtl_close, _rtl_creat, _rtl_open

Portability

DOS	UNIX	Win 16	Win 32	ANSI C	ANSI C++	OS/2
+	+	+	+			+

ecvt

stdlib.h

Syntax
char *ecvt(double value, int ndig, int *dec, int *sign);

Description
Converts a floating-point number to a string.

ecvt converts *value* to a null-terminated string of *ndig* digits, starting with the leftmost significant digit, and returns a pointer to the string. The position of the decimal point relative to the beginning of the string is stored indirectly through *dec* (a negative value for *dec* means that the decimal lies to the left of the returned digits). There is no decimal point in the string itself. If the sign of *value* is negative, the word pointed to by *sign* is nonzero; otherwise, it's 0. The low-order digit is rounded.

Return value
The return value of *ecvt* points to static data for the string of digits whose content is overwritten by each call to *ecvt* and *fcvt*.

See also
fcvt, gcvt, sprintf

Portability

DOS	UNIX	Win 16	Win 32	ANSI C	ANSI C++	OS/2
+	+	+	+			+

_ _emit_ _   dos.h

Syntax
void _ _emit_ _(argument, ...);

Description
Inserts literal values directly into code.

_ _emit_ _ is an inline function that lets you insert literal values directly into object code as it is compiling. It is used to generate machine language instructions without using inline assembly language or an assembler.

Generally the arguments of an _ _emit_ _ call are single-byte machine instructions. However, because of the capabilities of this function, more complex instructions, complete with references to C variables, can be constructed.

You should use this function only if you are familiar with the machine language of the 80x86 processor family. You can use this function to place arbitrary bytes in the instruction code of a function; if any of these bytes is incorrect, the program misbehaves and can easily crash your machine. Borland C++ does not attempt to analyze your calls for correctness in any way. If you encode instructions that change machine registers or memory, Borland C++ will not be aware of it and might not properly preserve registers, as it would in many cases with inline assembly language (for example, it recognizes the usage of SI and DI registers in inline instructions). You are completely on your own with this function.

You must pass at least one argument to _ _emit_ _; any number can be given. The arguments to this function are not treated like any other function call arguments in the language. An argument passed to _ _emit_ _ will not be converted in any way.

There are special restrictions on the form of the arguments to _ _emit_ _. Arguments must be in the form of expressions that can be used to initialize a static object. This means that integer and floating-point constants and the addresses of static objects can be used. The values of such expressions are written to the object code at the point of the call, exactly as if they were being used to initialize data. The address of a parameter or auto variable, plus or minus a constant offset, can also be used. For these arguments, the offset of the variable from BP is stored.

The number of bytes placed in the object code is determined from the type of the argument, except in the following cases:

- If a signed integer constant (that is 0x90) appears that fits within the range of 0 to 255, it is treated as if it were a character.

- If the address of an auto or parameter variable is used, a byte is written if the offset of the variable from BP is between -128 and 127; otherwise, a word is written.

Simple bytes are written as follows:

```
_ _emit_ _(0x90);
```

If you want a word written, but the value you are passing is under 255, simply cast it to **unsigned** using one of these methods:

```
_ _emit_ _(0xB8, (unsigned)17);
_ _emit_ _(0xB8, 17u);
```

Two- or four-byte address values can be forced by casting an address to **void near *** or **void far ***, respectively.

Return value
None.

Portability

DOS	UNIX	Win 16	Win 32	ANSI C	ANSI C++	OS/2
+		+	+			+

_endthread   process.h

Syntax
void _endthread(void);

Description
Terminates execution of a thread.

The _endthread function terminates the currently executing thread. The thread must have been started by an earlier call to _beginthread or _beginthreadNT.

This function is available in the multithread libraries; it is not in the single-thread libraries.

Return value
The function does not return a value.

See also

_beginthread, _beginthreadNT

Portability

DOS	UNIX	Win 16	Win 32	ANSI C	ANSI C++	OS/2
			+			+

eof   io.h

Syntax

int eof(int handle);

Description

Checks for end-of-file.

eof determines whether the file associated with *handle* has reached end-of-file.

Return value

If the current position is end-of-file, *eof* returns the value 1; otherwise, it returns 0. A return value of -1 indicates an error; the global variable *errno* is set to

EBADF   Bad file number

See also

clearerr, feof, ferror, perror

Portability

DOS	UNIX	Win 16	Win 32	ANSI C	ANSI C++	OS/2
+		+	+			+

execl, execle, execlp, execlpe, execv, execve, execvp, execvpe   process.h

Syntax

int execl(char *path, char *arg0 *arg1, ..., *argn, NULL);
int execle(char *path, char *arg0, *arg1, ..., *argn, NULL, char **env);

int execlp(char *path, char *arg0,*arg1, ..., *argn, NULL);
int execlpe(char *path, char *arg0, *arg1, ..., *argn, NULL, char **env);

int execv(char *path, char *argv[]);
int execve(char *path, char *argv[], char **env);

```
int execvp(char *path, char *argv[]);
int execvpe(char *path, char *argv[], char **env);
```

Description
Loads and runs other programs.

The functions in the *exec...* family load and run (execute) other programs, known as *child processes*. When an *exec...* call succeeds, the child process overlays the *parent process*. There must be sufficient memory available for loading and executing the child process. *path* is the file name of the called child process. The *exec...* functions search for *path* using the standard search algorithm:

- If no explicit extension is given, the functions search for the file as given. If the file is not found, they add .EXE and search again. If not found, they add .COM and search again. If found, the command processor, COMSPEC (Windows) or COMMAND.COM (DOS), is used to run the batch file.

- If an explicit extension or a period is given, the functions search for the file exactly as given.

The suffixes *l*, *v*, *p*, and *e* added to the *exec...* "family name" specify that the named function operates with certain capabilities.

l   Specifies that the argument pointers (*arg0, arg1, ..., argn*) are passed as separate arguments. Typically, the *l* suffix is used when you know in advance the number of arguments to be passed.

v   Specifies that the argument pointers (*argv[0] ..., arg[n]*) are passed as an array of pointers. Typically, the *v* suffix is used when a variable number of arguments is to be passed.

p   Specifies that the function searches for the file in those directories specified by the PATH environment variable (without the *p* suffix, the function searches only the current working directory). If the *path* parameter does not contain an explicit directory, the function searches first the current directory, then the directories set with the PATH environment variable.

e   Specifies that the argument *env* can be passed to the child process, letting you alter the environment for the child process. Without the *e* suffix, child processes inherit the environment of the parent process.

Each function in the *exec...* family must have one of the two argument-specifying suffixes (either *l* or *v*). The path search and environment inheritance suffixes (*p* and *e*) are optional; for example:

- *execl* is an *exec...* function that takes separate arguments, searches only the root or current directory for the child, and passes on the parent's environment to the child.

- *execvpe* is an *exec...* function that takes an array of argument pointers, incorporates PATH in its search for the child process, and accepts the *env* argument for altering the child's environment.

The *exec...* functions must pass at least one argument to the child process (*arg0 or argv[0]*); this argument is, by convention, a copy of *path*. (Using a different value for this 0th argument won't produce an error.)

path is available for the child process.

When the *l* suffix is used, *arg0* usually points to *path*, and *arg1*, ..., *argn* point to character strings that form the new list of arguments. A mandatory null following *argn* marks the end of the list.

When the *e* suffix is used, you pass a list of new environment settings through the argument *env*. This environment argument is an array of character pointers. Each element points to a null-terminated character string of the form

```
envvar = value
```

where *envvar* is the name of an environment variable, and *value* is the string value to which *envvar* is set. The last element in *env* is null. When *env* is null, the child inherits the parents' environment settings.

The combined length of *arg0* + *arg1* + ... + *argn* (or of *argv[0]* + *argv[1]* + ... + *argn[n]*), including space characters that separate the arguments, must be less than 128 bytes for a 16-bit application, or 260 bytes for a Win32 application. Null terminators are not counted.

When an *exec...* function call is made, any open files remain open in the child process.

Return value
If successful, the *exec...* functions do not return. On error, the *exec...* functions return -1, and the global variable *errno* is set to one of the following values:

EACCES   Permission denied

EMFILE   Too many open files

ENOENT   Path or file name not found

ENOEXEC   Exec format error

ENOMEM   Not enough memory

See also
abort, atexit, _c_exit, _cexit, _exit, exit, _fpreset, searchpath, spawn, system

Portability

DOS	UNIX	Win 16	Win 32	ANSI C	ANSI C++	OS/2
+			+			+

_exit   stdlib.h

Syntax
```
void _exit(int status);Description
```

Terminates program.

_exit terminates execution without closing any files, flushing any output, or calling any exit functions.

The calling process uses *status* as the exit status of the process. Typically a value of 0 is used to indicate a normal exit, and a nonzero value indicates some error.

Return value
None.

See also
abort, atexit, _c_exit, _cexit, exec, exit, spawn

Portability

DOS	UNIX	Win 16	Win 32	ANSI C	ANSI C++	OS/2
+	+	+	+			+

exit   stdlib.h

Syntax
void exit(int status);

Description
Terminates program.

exit terminates the calling process. Before termination, all files are closed, buffered output (waiting to be output) is written, and any registered "exit functions" (posted with *atexit*) are called.

status is provided for the calling process as the exit status of the process. Typically a value of 0 is used to indicate a normal exit, and a nonzero value indicates some error. It can be, but is not required to be, set with one of the following:

EXIT_FAILURE   Abnormal program termination; signal to operating system that program has terminated with an error

EXIT_SUCCESS   Normal program termination

Return value
None.

See also
abort, atexit, _c_exit, _cexit, exec, _exit, signal, spawn

Portability

DOS	UNIX	Win 16	Win 32	ANSI C	ANSI C++	OS/2
+	+	+	+	+	+	+

exp, expl   math.h

Syntax
double exp(double x);
long double expl(long double x);

Description
Calculates the exponential *e* to the *x*.

expl is the **long double** version; it takes a **long double** argument and returns a **long double** result.

This function can be used with bcd and complex types.

Return value
exp returns *e* to the *x*.

Sometimes the arguments passed to these functions produce results that overflow or are incalculable. When the correct value overflows, *exp* returns the value HUGE_VAL and *expl* returns _LHUGE_VAL. Results of excessively large magnitude cause the global variable *errno* to be set to

ERANGE   Result out of range

On underflow, these functions return 0.0, and the global variable errno is not changed. Error handling for these functions can be modified through the functions *_matherr* and *_matherrl*.

See also
frexp, ldexp, log, log10, _matherr, pow, pow10, sqrt

Portability

	DOS	UNIX	Win 16	Win 32	ANSI C	ANSI C++	OS/2
exp	+	+	+	+	+	+	+
expl	+		+	+			+

_expand   malloc.h

Syntax
void *_expand(void *block, size_t size);

Description

Grows or shrinks a heap block in place.

This function attempts to change the size of an allocated memory *block* without moving the block's location in the heap. The data in the *block* are not changed, up to the smaller of the old and new sizes of the block. The block must have been allocated earlier with *malloc*, *calloc*, or *realloc*, and must not have been freed.

Return value

If *_expand* is able to resize the block without moving it, *_expand* returns a pointer to the block, whose address is unchanged. If *_expand* is unsuccessful, it returns a NULL pointer and does not modify or resize the block.

See also

calloc, malloc, realloc

Portability

DOS	UNIX	Win 16	Win 32	ANSI C	ANSI C++	OS/2
			+			+

fabs, fabsl — math.h

Syntax

```
double fabs(double x);
long double fabsl(long double x);
```

Description

Returns the absolute value of a floating-point number.

fabs calculates the absolute value of *x*, a double. *fabsl* is the **long double** version; it takes a **long double** argument and returns a **long double** result.

Return value

fabs and *fabsl* return the absolute value of *x*.

See also

abs, cabs, labs

Portability

	DOS	UNIX	Win 16	Win 32	ANSI C	ANSI C++	OS/2
fabs	+	+	+	+	+	+	+
fabsl	+		+	+			+

farcalloc

alloc.h

Syntax

void far *farcalloc(unsigned long nunits, unsigned long unitsz);

Description

Allocates memory from the far heap.

farcalloc allocates memory from the far heap for an array containing *nunits* elements, each *unitsz* bytes long.

For allocating from the far heap, note that:

* All available RAM can be allocated.

* Blocks larger than 64K can be allocated.

* Far pointers (or huge pointers if blocks are larger than 64K) are used to access the allocated blocks.

In the compact, large, and huge memory models, *farcalloc* is similar, though not identical, to *calloc*. It takes **unsigned long** parameters, while *calloc* takes **unsigned** parameters. For DOS users, a tiny model program cannot use *faralloc*.

Return value

farcalloc returns a pointer to the newly allocated block, or NULL if not enough space exists for the new block.

See also

calloc, farfree, farmalloc, malloc

Portability

DOS	UNIX	Win 16	Win 32	ANSI C	ANSI C++	OS/2
+		+				

farfree

alloc.h

Syntax

void farfree(void far * block);

Description

Frees a block from far heap.

farfree releases a block of memory previously allocated from the far heap.

In the small and medium memory models, blocks allocated by *farmalloc* cannot be freed with normal *free*, and blocks allocated with *malloc* cannot be freed with *farfree*. In these models, the two heaps are completely distinct. For DOS users, a tiny model program cannot use *farfree*.

Return value
None.

See also
farcalloc, farmalloc

Portability

DOS	UNIX	Win 16	Win 32	ANSI C	ANSI C++	OS/2
+		+				

farmalloc   alloc.h

Syntax
void far *farmalloc(unsigned long nbytes);

Description
Allocates from far heap.

farmalloc allocates a block of memory *nbytes* bytes long from the far heap.

For allocating from the far heap, note that:

- All available RAM can be allocated.
- Blocks larger than 64K can be allocated.
- Far pointers are used to access the allocated blocks.

In the compact, large, and huge memory models, *farmalloc* is similar though not identical to *malloc*. It takes **unsigned long** parameters, while *malloc* takes **unsigned** parameters. For DOS users, a tiny model program cannot use *farmalloc*.

Return value
farmalloc returns a pointer to the newly allocated block, or NULL if not enough space exists for the new block.

See also
farcalloc, farfree, farrealloc, malloc

Portability

DOS	UNIX	Win 16	Win 32	ANSI C	ANSI C++	OS/2
+		+				

farrealloc

alloc.h

Syntax

void far *farrealloc(void far *oldblock, unsigned long nbytes);

Description

Adjusts allocated block in far heap.

farrealloc adjusts the size of the allocated block to *nbytes* copying the contents to a new location if necessary.

For allocating from the far heap:

- All available RAM can be allocated.
- Blocks larger than 64K can be allocated.
- Far pointers are used to access the allocated blocks.

For DOS users, a tiny model program cannot use *farrealloc*.

Return value

farrealloc returns the address of the reallocated block which might be different than the address of the original block. If the block cannot be reallocated, *farrealloc* returns NULL.

See also

realloc

Portability

DOS	UNIX	Win 16	Win 32	ANSI C	ANSI C++	OS/2
+		+				

fclose

stdio.h

Syntax

int fclose(FILE *stream);

Description

Closes a stream.

fclose closes the named stream. All buffers associated with the stream are flushed before closing. System-allocated buffers are freed upon closing. Buffers assigned with *setbuf* or *setvbuf* are not automatically freed. (But if *setvbuf* is passed null for the buffer pointer it *will* free it upon close.)

Return value

fclose returns 0 on success. It returns EOF if any errors were detected.

See also

close, fcloseall, fdopen, fflush, flushall, fopen, freopen

Portability

DOS	UNIX	Win 16	Win 32	ANSI C	ANSI C++	OS/2
+	+	+	+	+	+	+

fcloseall

stdio.h

Syntax

int fcloseall(void);

Description

Closes open streams.

fcloseall closes all open streams except:

- stdin
- stdout
- stdprn
- stderr
- stdaux

Note   stdprn and stdaux streams are not available in OS/2 and Win32.

Return value

fcloseall returns the total number of streams it closed. It returns EOF if any errors were detected.

See also

fclose, fdopen, flushall, fopen, freopen

Portability

DOS	UNIX	Win 16	Win 32	ANSI C	ANSI C++	OS/2
+	+	+	+			+

fcvt

stdlib.h

Syntax

char *fcvt(double value, int ndig, int *dec, int *sign);

Description

Converts a floating-point number to a string.

fcvt converts *value* to a null-terminated string digit starting with the leftmost significant digit with *ndig* digits to the right of the decimal point. *fcvt* then returns a pointer to the string. The position of the decimal point relative to the beginning of the string is stored indirectly through *dec* (a negative value for *dec* means to the left of the returned digits). There is no decimal point in the string itself. If the sign of *value* is negative the word pointed to by *sign* is nonzero; otherwise it is 0.

The correct digit has been rounded for the number of digits to the right of the decimal point specified by *ndig*.

Return value

The return value of *fcvt* points to static data whose content is overwritten by each call to *fcvt* and *ecvt*.

See also

ecvt, gcvt, sprintf

Portability

DOS	UNIX	Win 16	Win 32	ANSI C	ANSI C++	OS/2
+	+	+	+			+

fdopen   stdio.h

Syntax

FILE *fdopen(int handle, char *type);

Description

Associates a stream with a file handle.

fdopen associates a stream with a file handle obtained from *creat, dup, dup2,* or *open*.

The type of stream must match the mode of the open *handle*.

The *type* string used in a call to *fdopen* is one of the following values:

Value	Description
r	Open for reading only.
w	Create for writing.
a	Append; open for writing at end-of-file or create for writing if the file does not exist.
r+	Open an existing file for update (reading and writing).
w+	Create a new file for update.
a+	Open for append; open (or create if the file does not exist) for update at the end of the file.

To specify that a given file is being opened or created in text mode, append *t* to the value of the *type* string (for example, *rt* or *w+t*).

Similarly, to specify binary mode, append *b* to the *type* string (for example, *rb* or *w+b*).

If *t* or *b* is not given in the *type* string, the mode is governed by the global variable *_fmode*.

If *_fmode* is set to O_BINARY, files will be opened in binary mode.

If *_fmode* is set to O_TEXT, files will be opened in text mode.

Note The O_... constants are defined in fcntl.h.

When a file is opened for update, both input and output can be done on the resulting stream; however:

- output cannot be directly followed by input without an intervening *fseek* or *rewind*.
- input cannot be directly followed by output without an intervening *fseek*, *rewind*, or an input that encounters end-of-file.

Return value
On successful completion *fdopen* returns a pointer to the newly opened stream. In the event of error it returns NULL.

See also
fclose, fopen, freopen, _get_osfhandle, open

Portability

DOS	UNIX	Win 16	Win 32	ANSI C	ANSI C++	OS/2
+	+	+	+			+

feof   stdio.h

Syntax
int feof(FILE *stream);

Description
Detects end-of-file on a stream.

feof is a macro that tests the given stream for an end-of-file indicator. Once the indicator is set, read operations on the file return the indicator until *rewind* is called or the file is closed. The end-of-file indicator is reset with each input operation.

Return value
feof returns nonzero if an end-of-file indicator was detected on the last input operation on the named stream and 0 if end-of-file has not been reached.

See also
clearerr, eof, ferror, perror

Portability

DOS	UNIX	Win 16	Win 32	ANSI C	ANSI C++	OS/2
+	+	+	+	+	+	+

ferror

stdio.h

Syntax
int ferror(FILE *stream);

Description
Detects errors on stream.

ferror is a macro that tests the given stream for a read or write error. If the stream's error indicator has been set, it remains set until *clearerr* or *rewind* is called or until the stream is closed.

Return value
ferror returns nonzero if an error was detected on the named stream.

See also
clearerr, eof, feof, fopen, gets, perror

Portability

DOS	UNIX	Win 16	Win 32	ANSI C	ANSI C++	OS/2
+	+	+	+	+	+	+

fflush

stdio.h

Syntax
int fflush(FILE *stream);

Description
Flushes a stream.

If the given stream has buffered output *fflush* writes the output for *stream* to the associated file.

The stream remains open after *fflush* has executed. *fflush* has no effect on an unbuffered stream.

Return value
fflush returns 0 on success. It returns EOF if any errors were detected.

See also

fclose, flushall, setbuf, setvbuf

Portability

DOS	UNIX	Win 16	Win 32	ANSI C	ANSI C++	OS/2
+	+	+	+	+	+	+

fgetc

stdio.h

Syntax

int fgetc(FILE *stream);

Description

Gets character from stream.

fgetc returns the next character on the named input stream.

Return value

On success *fgetc* returns the character read after converting it to an **int** without sign extension. On end-of-file or error it returns EOF.

See also

fgetchar, fputc, getc, getch, getchar, getche, ungetc, ungetch

Portability

DOS	UNIX	Win 16	Win 32	ANSI C	ANSI C++	OS/2
+	+	+	+	+	+	+

fgetchar

stdio.h

Syntax

int fgetchar(void);

Description

Gets character from stdin.

fgetchar returns the next character from stdin. It is defined as *fgetc* (stdin).

Note   For Win32s or Win32 GUI applications, stdin must be redirected.

Return value

On success *fgetchar* returns the character read after converting it to an **int** without sign extension. On end-of-file or error it returns EOF.

See also
fgetc, fputchar, freopen, getchar

Portability

DOS	UNIX	Win 16	Win 32	ANSI C	ANSI C++	OS/2
+	+	+	+			+

fgetpos   stdio.h

Syntax
int fgetpos(FILE *stream, fpos_t *pos);

Description
Gets the current file pointer.

fgetpos stores the position of the file pointer associated with the given stream in the location pointed to by *pos*. The exact value is unimportant; its value is opaque except as a parameter to subsequent *fsetpos* calls.

Return value
On success *fgetpos* returns 0. On failure it returns a nonzero value and sets the global variable *errno* to:

EBADF   Bad file number

EINVAL   Invalid number

See also
fseek, fsetpos, ftell, tell

Portability

DOS	UNIX	Win 16	Win 32	ANSI C	ANSI C++	OS/2
+		+	+	+	+	+

fgets   stdio.h

Syntax
char *fgets(char *s, int n, FILE *stream);

Description
Gets a string from a stream.

fgets reads characters from *stream* into the string *s*. The function stops reading when it reads either *n* - 1 characters or a newline character, whichever comes first. *fgets* retains the newline character at the end of *s*. A null byte is appended to *s* to mark the end of the string.

Return value

On success *fgets* returns the string pointed to by *s*; it returns NULL on end-of-file or error.

See also

cgets, fputs, gets

Portability

DOS	UNIX	Win 16	Win 32	ANSI C	ANSI C++	OS/2
+	+	+	+	+	+	+

filelength   io.h

Syntax

long filelength(int handle);

Description

Gets file size in bytes.

filelength returns the length (in bytes) of the file associated with *handle*.

Return value

On success *filelength* returns a **long** value the file length in bytes. On error it returns -1 and the global variable *errno* is set to

EBADF   Bad file number

See also

fopen, lseek, open

Portability

DOS	UNIX	Win 16	Win 32	ANSI C	ANSI C++	OS/2
+		+	+			+

fileno   stdio.h

Syntax

int fileno(FILE *stream);

Description
Gets file handle.

fileno is a macro that returns the file handle for the given stream. If *stream* has more than one handle *fileno* returns the handle assigned to the stream when it was first opened.

Return value
fileno returns the integer file handle associated with *stream*.

See also
fdopen, fopen, freopen, _get_osfhandle

Portability

DOS	UNIX	Win 16	Win 32	ANSI C	ANSI C++	OS/2
+	+	+	+			+

findfirst   dir.h

Syntax
int findfirst(const char *pathname, struct ffblk *ffblk, int attrib);

Description
Searches a disk directory.

findfirst begins a search of a disk directory for files specifed by attributes or wildcards.

pathname is a string with an optional drive specifier path and file name of the file to be found. Only the file name portion can contain wildcard match characters (such as ? or *). If a matching file is found the *ffblk* structure is filled with the file-directory information.

Win16
For Win16, the format of the structure *ffblk* is as follows:

```
struct ffblk {
   char ff_reserved[21];     /* reserved by DOS */
   char ff_attrib;           /* attribute found */
   int ff_ftime;             /* file time */
   int ff_fdate;             /* file date */
   long ff_fsize;            /* file size */
   char ff_name[13];         /* found file name */
   };
```

Win32
For Win32, the format of the structure *ffblk* is as follows:

```
struct ffblk {
   long          ff_reserved;
   long          ff_fsize;       /* file size */
```

```
unsigned long   ff_attrib;      /* attribute found */
unsigned short  ff_ftime;       /* file time */
unsigned short  ff_fdate;       /* file date */
char            ff_name[256];   /* found file name */
};
```

attrib is a file-attribute byte used in selecting eligible files for the search. *attrib* should be selected from the following constants defined in dos.h:

FA_RDONLY	Read-only attribute
FA_HIDDEN	Hidden file
FA_SYSTEM	System file
FA_LABEL	Volume label
FA_DIREC	Directory
FA_ARCH	Archive

A combination of constants can be ORed together.

For more detailed information about these attributes refer to your operating system documentation.

ff_ftime and *ff_fdate* contain bit fields for referring to the current date and time. The structure of these fields was established by the operating system. Both are 16-bit structures divided into three fields.

ff_ftime:

Bits 0 to 4	The result of seconds divided by 2 (for example, 10 here means 20 seconds)
Bits 5 to 10	Minutes
Bits 11 to 15	Hours

ff_fdate:

Bits 0-4	Day
Bits 5-8	Month
Bits 9-15	Years since 1980 (for example, 9 here means 1989)

The structure *ftime* declared in io.h uses time and date bit fields similar in structure to *ff_ftime* and *ff_fdate*.

Return value

findfirst returns 0 on successfully finding a file matching the search *pathname*.

When no more files can be found, or if there is an error in the file name:

- -1 is returned

- *errno* is set to

  ENOENT   Path or file name not found

- _doserrno is set to one of the following values:

  ENMFILE   No more files

  ENOENT   Path or file name not found

See also
findnext, getftime, setftime

Portability

DOS	UNIX	Win 16	Win 32	ANSI C	ANSI C++	OS/2
+		+	+			+

findnext   dir.h

Syntax
int findnext(struct ffblk *ffblk);

Description
Continues *findfirst* search.

findnext is used to fetch subsequent files that match the *pathname* given in *findfirst*. *ffblk* is the same block filled in by the *findfirst* call. This block contains necessary information for continuing the search. One file name for each call to *findnext* will be returned until no more files are found in the directory matching the *pathname*.

Return value
findnext returns 0 on successfully finding a file matching the search *pathname*. When no more files can be found or if there is an error in the file name:

- -1 is returned

- *errno* is set to

  ENOENT   Path or file name not found

- *doserrno* is set to one of the following values:

  ENMFILE   No more files

  ENOENT   Path or file name not found

See Also
findfirst

Portability

DOS	UNIX	Win 16	Win 32	ANSI C	ANSI C++	OS/2
+		+	+			+

floor, floorl   math.h

Syntax
double floor(double x);
long double floorl(long double x);

Description
Rounds down.

floor finds the largest integer not greater than *x*.

floorl is the **long double** version; it takes a **long double** argument and returns a **long double** result.

Return value
floor returns the integer found as a **double**. *floorl* returns the integer found as a **long double**.

See also
ceil, fmod

Portability

	DOS	UNIX	Win 16	Win 32	ANSI C	ANSI C++	OS/2
floor	+	+	+	+	+	+	+
floorl	+		+	+			+

flushall   stdio.h

Syntax
int flushall(void);

Description
Flushes all streams.

flushall clears all buffers associated with open input streams and writes all buffers associated with open output streams to their respective files. Any read operation following *flushall* reads new data into the buffers from the input files. Streams stay open after *flushall* executes.

Return value

flushall returns an integer the number of open input and output streams.

See also

fclose, fcloseall, fflush

Portability

DOS	UNIX	Win 16	Win 32	ANSI C	ANSI C++	OS/2
+	+	+	+			+

_fmemccpy

See *memccpy*.

_fmemchr

See *memchr*.

_fmemcmp

See *memcmp*.

_fmemcpy

See *memcpy*.

_fmemicmp

See *fmemicmp*.

_fmemmove

See *memmove*.

_fmemset

See *memset*.

fmod, fmodl   math.h

Syntax
double fmod(double x, double y);
long double fmodl(long double x, long double y);

Description
Calculates x modulo y, the remainder of x/y.

fmod calculates x modulo y (the remainder f, where $x = ay + f$ for some integer a, and $0 < f < y$).

fmodl is the **long double** version; it takes **long double** arguments and returns a **long double** result.

Return value
fmod and *fmodl* return the remainder f where $x = ay + f$ (as described above). When $y = 0$, *fmod* and *fmodl* return 0.

See also
ceil, floor, modf

Portability

	DOS	UNIX	Win 16	Win 32	ANSI C	ANSI C++	OS/2
fmod	+	+	+	+	+	+	+
fmodl	+		+	+			+

_fmovmem

See *movmem*.

fnmerge   dir.h

Syntax
void fnmerge(char *path, const char *drive, const char *dir, const char *name, const char *ext);

Description
Builds a path from component parts.

fnmerge makes a path name from its components. The new path name is

```
X:\DIR\SUBDIR\NAME.EXT
```

where:

drive = X
dir = \DIR\SUBDIR\
name = NAME
ext = .EXT

If *drive* is empty or NULL, no drive is inserted in the path name. If it is missing a trailing colon (:), a colon is inserted in the path name.

If *dir* is empty or NULL, no directory is inserted in the path name. If it is missing a trailing slash (\ or /), a backslash is inserted in the path name.

If *name* is empty or NULL, no file name is inserted in the path name.

If *ext* is empty or NULL, no extension is inserted in the path name. If it is missing a leading period (.), a period is inserted in the path name.

fnmerge assumes there is enough space in *path* for the constructed path name. The maximum constructed length is MAXPATH. MAXPATH is defined in dir.h.

fnmerge and *fnsplit* are invertible; if you split a given *path* with *fnsplit*, then merge the resultant components with *fnmerge*, you end up with *path*.

Return value
None.

See also
fnsplit

Portability

DOS	UNIX	Win 16	Win 32	ANSI C	ANSI C++	OS/2
+		+	+			+

fnsplit   dir.h

Syntax
int fnsplit(const char *path, char *drive, char *dir, char *name, char *ext);

Description
Splits a full path name into its components.

fnsplit takes a file's full path name *(path)* as a string in the form X:\DIR\SUBDIR\ NAME.EXT and splits *path* into its four components. It then stores those components in the strings pointed to by *drive, dir, name,* and *ext*. All five components must be passed but any of them can be a null, which means the corresponding component will be parsed but not stored. If any path component is null, that component corresponds to a non-NULL, empty string.

The maximum sizes for these strings are given by the constants *MAXDRIVE, MAXDIR, MAXPATH, MAXFILE,* and *MAXEXT* (defined in dir.h) and each size includes space for the null-terminator.

Constant	Max 16-bit	Max 32-bit	String
MAXPATH	80	256	*path*
MAXDRIVE	3	3	*drive*; includes colon (:)
MAXDIR	66	260	*dir*; includes leading and trailing backslashes (\)
MAXFILE	9	256	*name*
MAXEXT	5	256	*ext*; includes leading dot (.)

fnsplit assumes that there is enough space to store each non-null component.

When *fnsplit* splits *path* it treats the punctuation as follows:

- *drive* includes the colon (C:, A:, and so on).

- *dir* includes the leading and trailing backslashes (\BC\include\, \source\, and so on).

- *name* includes the file name.

- *ext* includes the dot preceding the extension (.C, .EXE, and so on).

fnmerge and *fnsplit* are invertible; if you split a given *path* with *fnsplit*, then merge the resultant components with *fnmerge*, you end up with *path*.

Return value

fnsplit returns an integer (composed of five flags defined in dir.h) indicating which of the full path name components were present in *path*. These flags and the components they represent are:

EXTENSION	An extension
FILENAME	A file name
DIRECTORY	A directory (and possibly subdirectories)
DRIVE	A drive specification (see dir.h)
WILDCARDS	Wildcards (* or ?)

See also
fnmerge

Portability

DOS	UNIX	Win 16	Win 32	ANSI C	ANSI C++	OS/2
+	+	+	+			+

fopen

Syntax

FILE *fopen(const char *filename, const char *mode);

Description

Opens a stream.

fopen opens the file named by *filename* and associates a stream with it. *fopen* returns a pointer to be used to identify the stream in subsequent operations.

The *mode* string used in calls to *fopen* is one of the following values:

Value	Description
r	Open for reading only.
w	Create for writing. If a file by that name already exists, it will be overwritten.
a	Append; open for writing at end-of-file or create for writing if the file does not exist.
r+	Open an existing file for update (reading and writing).
w+	Create a new file for update (reading and writing). If a file by that name already exists, it will be overwritten.
a+	Open for append; open (or create if the file does not exist) for update at the end of the file.

To specify that a given file is being opened or created in text mode append a *t* to the *mode* string (*rt w+t* and so on). Similarly to specify binary mode append a *b* to the *mode* string (*wb a+b* and so on). *fopen* also allows the *t* or *b* to be inserted between the letter and the + character in the mode string; for example *rt+* is equivalent to *r+t*.

If a *t* or *b* is not given in the *mode* string the mode is governed by the global variable *_fmode*. If *_fmode* is set to O_BINARY files are opened in binary mode. If *_fmode* is set to O_TEXT they are opened in text mode. These O_... constants are defined in fcntl.h.

When a file is opened for update, both input and output can be done on the resulting stream; however,

- output cannot be directly followed by input without an intervening *fseek* or *rewind*.

- input cannot be directly followed by output without an intervening *fseek*, *rewind*, or an input that encounters end-of-file.

Return value

On successful completion *fopen* returns a pointer to the newly opened stream. In the event of error it returns NULL.

See also

creat, dup, fclose, fdopen, ferror, _fmode (global variable), *fread, freopen, fseek, fwrite, open, rewind, setbuf, setmode*

Portability

DOS	UNIX	Win 16	Win 32	ANSI C	ANSI C++	OS/2
+	+	+	+	+	+	+

FP_OFF, FP_SEG   dos.h

Syntax
unsigned FP_OFF(void far *p);
unsigned FP_SEG(void far *p);

Description
Gets a far address offset or segment.

FP_OFF is a macro that gets or sets the offset of the **far** pointer *p*.

FP_SEG is a macro that gets or sets the segment value of the **far** pointer *p*.

Return value
FP_OFF returns an **unsigned** integer value representing an offset value.

FP_SEG returns an **unsigned** integer representing a segment value.

See also
MK_FP, movedata, segread

Portability

DOS	UNIX	Win 16	Win 32	ANSI C	ANSI C++	OS/2
+	+					

_fpreset   float.h

Syntax
void _fpreset(void);

Description
Reinitializes floating-point math package.

_fpreset reinitializes the floating-point math package. This function is usually used in conjunction with *system* or the *exec...* or *spawn...* functions. It is also used to recover from floating-point errors before calling *longjmp*.

Note   If an 80x87 coprocessor is used in a program a child process (executed by the system, or by an *exec...* or *spawn...* function) might alter the parent process' floating-point state.

If you use an 80x87 take the following precautions:

- Do not call *system* or an *exec...* or *spawn...* function while a floating-point expression is being evaluated.

- Call *_fpreset* to reset the floating-point state after using *system exec...* or *spawn...* if there is *any* chance that the child process performed a floating-point operation with the 80x87.

Return value
None.

See also
_clear87, _control87, _status87

Portability

DOS	UNIX	Win 16	Win 32	ANSI C	ANSI C++	OS/2
+		+	+			+

fprintf stdio.h

Syntax
int fprintf(FILE *stream, const char *format[, argument, ...]);

Description
Writes formatted output to a stream.

fprintf accepts a series of arguments, applies to each a format specifier contained in the format string pointed to by *format,* and outputs the formatted data to a stream. There must be the same number of format specifiers as arguments.

Note For details on format specifiers, see *"printf* Format specifiers".

Return value
fprintf returns the number of bytes output. In the event of error it returns EOF.

See also
cprintf, fscanf, printf, putc, sprintf

Portability

DOS	UNIX	Win 16	Win 32	ANSI C	ANSI C++	OS/2
+	+	+	+	+	+	+

fputc

stdio.h

Syntax
int fputc(int c, FILE *stream);

Description
Puts a character on a stream.

fputc outputs character *c* to the named stream.

Note For Win32s or Win32 GUI applications, stdin must be redirected.

Return value
On success, *fputc* returns the character *c*. On error, it returns EOF.

See also
fgetc, *putc*

Portability

DOS	UNIX	Win 16	Win 32	ANSI C	ANSI C++	OS/2
+	+	+	+			+

fputchar

stdio.h

Syntax
int fputchar(int c);

Description
Outputs a character on stdout.

fputchar outputs character *c* to stdout. *fputchar(c)* is the same as *fputc(cstdout)*.

For Win32s or Win32 GUI applications, stdout must be redirected.

Return value
On success *fputchar* returns the character *c*.

On error it returns EOF.

See also
fgetchar, *freopen*, *putchar*

Portability

DOS	UNIX	Win 16	Win 32	ANSI C	ANSI C++	OS/2
+	+		+	+		+

fputs

Syntax
int fputs(const char *s, FILE *stream);

Description
Outputs a string on a stream.

fputs copies the null-terminated string *s* to the given output stream; it does not append a newline character and the terminating null character is not copied.

Return value
On success *fputs* returns a non-negative value.

On error it returns a value of EOF.

See also
fgets, gets, puts

Portability

DOS	UNIX	Win 16	Win 32	ANSI C	ANSI C++	OS/2
+	+	+	+	+	+	+

fread

Syntax
size_t fread(void *ptr, size_t size, size_t n, FILE *stream);

Description
Reads data from a stream.

fread reads *n* items of data each of length *size* bytes from the given input stream into a block pointed to by *ptr*.

The total number of bytes read is *(n * size)*.

Return value
On success *fread* returns the number of items (not bytes) actually read.

On end-of-file or error it returns a short count (possibly 0).

See also
fopen, fwrite, printf, read

Portability

DOS	UNIX	Win 16	Win 32	ANSI C	ANSI C++	OS/2
+	+	+	+	+	+	+

free

stdlib.h

Syntax
void free(void *block);

Description
Frees allocated block.

free deallocates a memory block allocated by a previous call to *calloc, malloc,* or *realloc.*

Return value
None.

See also
calloc, malloc, realloc, strdup

Portability

DOS	UNIX	Win 16	Win 32	ANSI C	ANSI C++	OS/2
+	+	+	+	+	+	+

freeopen

stdio.h

Syntax
FILE *freopen(const char *filename, const char *mode, FILE *stream);

Description
Associates a new file with an open stream.

freopen substitutes the named file in place of the open stream. It closes *stream* regardless of whether the open succeeds. *freopen* is useful for changing the file attached to stdin, stdout, or stderr.

The *mode* string used in calls to *fopen* is one of the following values:

Value	Description
r	Open for reading only.
w	Create for writing.
a	Append; open for writing at end-of-file or create for writing if the file does not exist.
r+	Open an existing file for update (reading and writing).
w+	Create a new file for update (reading and writing).
a+	Open for append; open (or create if the file does not exist) for update at the end of the file.

To specify that a given file is being opened or created in text mode append a *t* to the *mode* string (*rt w+t* and so on); similarly to specify binary mode append a *b* to the *mode* string (*wb a+b* and so on).

If a *t* or *b* is not given in the *mode* string the mode is governed by the global variable *_fmode*. If *_fmode* is set to O_BINARY files are opened in binary mode. If *_fmode* is set to O_TEXT they are opened in text mode. These O_... constants are defined in fcntl.h.

When a file is opened for update, both input and output can be done on the resulting stream; however:

- output cannot be directly followed by input without an intervening *fseek* or *rewind*.

- input cannot be directly followed by output without an intervening *fseek, rewind,* or an input that encounters end-of-file.

Return value
On successful completion *freopen* returns the argument *stream*.

On error it returns NULL.

See also
fclose, fdopen, fopen, open, setmode

Portability

DOS	UNIX	Win 16	Win 32	ANSI C	ANSI C++	OS/2
+	+	+	+	+	+	+

frexp, frexpl   math.h

Syntax
```
double frexp(double x, int *exponent);
long double frexpl(long double x, int *exponent);
```

Description
Splits a number into mantissa and exponent.

frexp calculates the mantissa *m* (a **double** greater than or equal to 0.5 and less than 1) and the integer value *n* such that *x* (the original **double** value) equals $m * 2n$. *frexp* stores *n* in the integer that *exponent* points to.

frexpl is the **long double** version; it takes a **long double** argument for *x* and returns a **long double** result.

Return value
frexp and *frexpl* return the mantissa *m*. Error handling for these routines can be modified through the functions *_matherr* and *_matherrl*.

See also

exp, ldexp, _matherr

Portability

	DOS	UNIX	Win 16	Win 32	ANSI C	ANSI C++	OS/2
frexp	+	+	+	+	+	+	+
frexpl	+		+	+			+

fscanf   stdio.h

Syntax

int fscanf(FILE *stream, const char *format[, address, ...]);

Description

Scans and formats input from a stream.

fscanf scans a series of input fields one character at a time reading from a stream. Then each field is formatted according to a format specifier passed to *fscanf* in the format string pointed to by *format*. Finally *fscanf* stores the formatted input at an address passed to it as an argument following *format*. The number of format specifiers and addresses must be the same as the number of input fields.

Note For details on format specifiers, see "*scanf* Format specifiers."

fscanf can stop scanning a particular field before it reaches the normal end-of-field character (whitespace) or it can terminate entirely for a number of reasons. See *scanf* for a discussion of possible causes.

Return value

fscanf returns the number of input fields successfully scanned, converted, and stored. The return value does not include scanned fields that were not stored.

If *fscanf* attempts to read at end-of-file, the return value is EOF. If no fields were stored, the return value is 0.

See also

atof, cscanf, fprintf, printf, scanf, sscanf, vfscanf, vscanf, vsscanf

Portability

DOS	UNIX	Win 16	Win 32	ANSI C	ANSI C++	OS/2
+	+	+	+	+	+	+

fseek

stdio.h

Syntax

int fseek(FILE *stream, long offset, int whence);

Description

Repositions a file pointer on a stream.

fseek sets the file pointer associated with *stream* to a new position that is *offset* bytes from the file location given by *whence*. For text mode streams *offset* should be 0 or a value returned by *ftell*.

whence must be one of the values 0, 1, or 2 which represent three symbolic constants (defined in stdio.h) as follows:

Constant	*whence*	File location
SEEK_SET	0	File beginning
SEEK_CUR	1	Current file pointer position
SEEK_END	2	End-of-file

fseek discards any character pushed back using *ungetc*. *fseek* is used with stream I/O; for file handle I/O use *lseek*.

After *fseek* the next operation on an update file can be either input or output.

Return value

fseek returns 0 if the pointer is successfully moved and nonzero on failure.

fseek might return a 0 indicating that the pointer has been moved successfully when in fact it has not been. This is because DOS, which actually resets the pointer, does not verify the setting. *fseek* returns an error code only on an unopened file or device.

In the event of an error return the global variable *errno* is set to one of the following values:

EBADF   Bad file pointer

EINVAL   Invalid argument

ESPIPE   Illegal seek on device

See also

fgetpos, fopen, fsetpos, ftell, lseek, rewind, setbuf, tell

Portability

DOS	UNIX	Win 16	Win 32	ANSI C	ANSI C++	OS/2
+	+	+	+	+	+	+

fsetpos

stdio.h

Syntax

int fsetpos(FILE *stream, const fpos_t *pos);

Description

Positions the file pointer of a stream.

fsetpos sets the file pointer associated with *stream* to a new position. The new position is the value obtained by a previous call to *fgetpos* on that stream. It also clears the end-of-file indicator on the file that *stream* points to and undoes any effects of *ungetc* on that file. After a call to *fsetpos* the next operation on the file can be input or output.

Return value

On success *fsetpos* returns 0.

On failure it returns a nonzero value and also sets the global variable *errno* to a nonzero value.

See also

fgetpos, fseek, ftell

Portability

DOS	UNIX	Win 16	Win 32	ANSI C	ANSI C++	OS/2
+		+	+	+	+	+

_fsopen

stdio.h, share.h

Syntax

FILE *_fsopen(const char *filename, const char *mode, int shflag);

Description

Opens a stream with file sharing.

_fsopen opens the file named by *filename* and associates a stream with it. *_fsopen* returns a pointer that is used to identify the stream in subsequent operations.

The *mode* string used in calls to *_fsopen* is one of the following values:

Mode	Description
r	Open for reading only.
w	Create for writing. If a file by that name already exists, it will be overwritten.
a	Append; open for writing at end-of-file or create for writing if the file does not exist.
r+	Open an existing file for update (reading and writing).
w+	Create a new file for update (reading and writing). If a file by that name already exists, it will be overwritten.
a+	Open for append; open (or create if the file does not exist) for update at the end of the file.

To specify that a given file is being opened or created in text mode append a *t* to the *mode* string (*rt w+t* and so on). Similarly to specify binary mode append a *b* to the *mode* string (*wb a+b* and so on). *_fsopen* also allows the *t* or *b* to be inserted between the letter and the + character in the mode string; for example *rt+* is equivalent to *r+t*. If a *t* or *b* is not given in the *mode* string the mode is governed by the global variable *_fmode*. If *_fmode* is set to O_BINARY files are opened in binary mode. If *_fmode* is set to O_TEXT they are opened in text mode. These O_... constants are defined in fcntl.h.

When a file is opened for update, both input and output can be done on the resulting stream; however:

- output cannot be directly followed by input without an intervening *fseek* or *rewind*.

- input cannot be directly followed by output without an intervening *fseek*, *rewind*, or an input that encounters end-of-file.

shflag specifies the type of file-sharing allowed on the file *filename*. Symbolic constants for *shflag* are defined in share.h.

Note   For DOS users, the file-sharing flags are ignored if SHARE is not loaded.

Value of *shflag*	Description
SH_COMPAT	Sets compatibility mode
SH_DENYRW	Denies read/write access
SH_DENYWR	Denies write access
SH_DENYRD	Denies read access
SH_DENYNONE	Permits read/write access
SH_DENYNO	Permits read/write access

Return value
On successful completion *_fsopen* returns a pointer to the newly opened stream.

On error it returns NULL.

See also
creat, _dos_open, dup, fclose, fdopen, ferror, _fmode (global variable), *fopen, fread, freopen, fseek, fwrite, open, rewind, setbuf, setmode, sopen*

Portability

DOS	UNIX	Win 16	Win 32	ANSI C	ANSI C++	OS/2
+		+	+			+

fstat, stat   sys\stat.h

Syntax
```
int fstat(int handle, struct stat *statbuf);
int stat(const char *path, struct stat *statbuf);
```

Description

Gets open file information.

fstat stores information in the *stat* structure about the file or directory associated with *handle*.

stat stores information about a given file or directory in the *stat* structure. The name of the file is *path*.

statbuf points to the *stat* structure (defined in sys\stat.h). That structure contains the following fields:

st_mode	Bit mask giving information about the file's mode
st_dev	Drive number of disk containing the file or file handle if the file is on a device
st_rdev	Same as *st_dev*
st_nlink	Set to the integer constant 1
st_size	Size of the file in bytes
st_atime	Most recent access (Windows) or last time modified (DOS)
st_mtime	Same as *st_atime*
st_ctime	Same as *st_atime*

The *stat* structure contains three more fields not mentioned here. They contain values that are meaningful only in UNIX.

The *st_mode* bit mask that gives information about the mode of the open file includes the following bits:

One of the following bits will be set:

S_IFCHR	If *handle* refers to a device.
S_IFREG	If an ordinary file is referred to by *handle*.

One or both of the following bits will be set:

S_IWRITE	If user has permission to write to file.
S_IREAD	If user has permission to read to file.

The HPFS and NTFS file-management systems make the following distinctions:

st_atime	Most recent access
st_mtime	Most recent modify
st_ctime	Creation time

Return value

fstat and *stat* return 0 if they successfully retrieved the information about the open file.

On error (failure to get the information) these functions return -1 and set the global variable *errno* to

EBADF   Bad file handle

See also
access, chmod

Portability

DOS	UNIX	Win 16	Win 32	ANSI C	ANSI C++	OS/2
+	+	+	+			+

_fstr*   string.h

Syntax
__far string functions

Description
Provides string operations in a large-code model.

Choose **See also** to see a list of string functions that have a **__far** version. The **__far** version of a string function is prefixed with *_fstr*. The behavior of a **__far** string function is identical to the behavior of the standard function to which it corresponds. The only difference is that arguments and return value (if any) to a **__far** string function are modified by the **__far** keyword. The entry for each of the functions provides a description for the **__far** version.

Return value
The return value for a *_fstr*-type function is a **__far** type.

Note When a far string function returns an **int** or *size_t*, the return value is never modified by the **far** keyword.

See also
strcat, strchr, strcmp, strcpy, strcspn, strdup, stricmp, strlen, strlwr, strncat, strncmp, strncpy, strnicmp, strnset, strpbrk, strrchr, strrev, strset, strspn, strstr, strtok, strupr

Portability

DOS	UNIX	Win 16	Win 32	ANSI C	ANSI C++	OS/2
+		+				

ftell

Syntax

long int ftell(FILE *stream);

Description

Returns the current file pointer.

ftell returns the current file pointer for *stream*. The offset is measured in bytes from the beginning of the file (if the file is binary). The value returned by *ftell* can be used in a subsequent call to *fseek*.

Return value

ftell returns the current file pointer position on success. It returns -1L on error and sets the global variable *errno* to a positive value.

In the event of an error return the global variable *errno* is set to one of the following values:

EBADF   Bad file pointer

ESPIPE   Illegal seek on device

See also

fgetpos, fseek, fsetpos, lseek, rewind, tell

Portability

DOS	UNIX	Win 16	Win 32	ANSI C	ANSI C++	OS/2
+	+	+	+	+	+	+

ftime

Syntax

void ftime(struct timeb *buf)

Description

Stores current time in *timeb* structure.

On UNIX platforms *ftime* is available only on System V systems.

ftime determines the current time and fills in the fields in the *timeb* structure pointed to by *buf*. The *timeb* structure contains four fields: *time, millitm, _timezone,* and *dstflag*:

```
struct timeb {
    long time ;
    short millitm ;
    short _timezone ;
    short dstflag ;
};
```

- *time* provides the time in seconds since 00:00:00 Greenwich mean time (GMT) January 1 1970.

- *millitm* is the fractional part of a second in milliseconds.

- *_timezone* is the difference in minutes between GMT and the local time. This value is computed going west from GMT. *ftime* gets this field from the global variable *_timezone* which is set by *tzset*.

- *dstflag* is set to nonzero if daylight saving time is taken into account during time calculations.

Note   *ftime* calls *tzset*. Therefore it isn't necessary to call *tzset* explicitly when you use *ftime*.

Return value
None.

See also
asctime, ctime, gmtime, localtime, stime, time, tzset

Portability

DOS	UNIX	Win 16	Win 32	ANSI C	ANSI C++	OS/2
+	+	+	+			+

_fullpath   stdlib.h

Syntax
char * _fullpath(char *buffer, const char *path, int buflen);

Description
Converts a path name from relative to absolute.

_fullpath converts the relative path name in *path* to an absolute path name that is stored in the array of characters pointed to by *buffer*. The maximum number of characters that can be stored at *buffer* is *buflen*. The function returns NULL if the buffer isn't big enough to store the absolute path name or if the path contains an invalid drive letter.

If *buffer* is NULL, *_fullpath* allocates a buffer of up to _MAX_PATH characters. This buffer should be freed using *free* when it is no longer needed. _MAX_PATH is defined in stdlib.h.

Return value
If successful the *_fullpath* function returns a pointer to the buffer containing the absolute path name.

On error, this function returns NULL.

See also
_makepath, _splitpath

Portability

DOS	UNIX	Win 16	Win 32	ANSI C	ANSI C++	OS/2
+		+	+			+

fwrite

stdio.h

Syntax

size_t fwrite(const void *ptr, size_t size, size_t n, FILE *stream);

Description

Writes to a stream.

fwrite appends *n* items of data each of length *size* bytes to the given output file. The data written begins at *ptr*. The total number of bytes written is *(n x size)*. *ptr* in the declarations is a pointer to any object.

Return value

On successful completion *fwrite* returns the number of items (not bytes) actually written.

On error it returns a short count.

See also

fopen, fread

Portability

DOS	UNIX	Win 16	Win 32	ANSI C	ANSI C++	OS/2
+	+	+	+	+	+	+

gcvt

stdlib.h

Syntax

char *gcvt(double value, int ndec, char *buf);

Description

Converts a floating-point number to a string.

gcvt converts *value* to a null-terminated ASCII string and stores the string in *buf*. It produces *ndec* significant digits in FORTRAN F format, if possible; otherwise, it returns the value in the *printf* E format (ready for printing). It might suppress trailing zeros.

Return value

gcvt returns the address of the string pointed to by *buf*.

See also
ecvt, fcvt, sprintf

Portability

DOS	UNIX	Win 16	Win 32	ANSI C	ANSI C++	OS/2
+	+	+	+			+

geninterrupt   dos.h

Syntax
void geninterrupt(int intr_num);

Description
Generates a software interrupt.

The *geninterrupt* macro triggers a software trap for the interrupt given by *intr_num*. The state of all registers after the call depends on the interrupt called.

Interrupts can leave registers in unpredictable states.

Return value
None.

See also
bdos, bdosptr, disable, enable, getvect, int86, int86x, intdos, intdosx, intr

Portability

DOS	UNIX	Win 16	Win 32	ANSI C	ANSI C++	OS/2
+		+	+			

getc   stdio.h

Syntax
int getc(FILE *stream);

Description
Gets character from stream.

getc returns the next character on the given input stream and increments the stream's file pointer to point to the next character.

Note   For Win32s or Win32 GUI applications, stdin must be redirected.

Return value

On success, *getc* returns the character read, after converting it to an **int** without sign extension.

On end-of-file or error, it returns EOF.

See also

fgetc, getch, getchar, getche, gets, putc, putchar, ungetc

Portability

DOS	UNIX	Win 16	Win 32	ANSI C	ANSI C++	OS/2
+	+	+	+	+	+	+

getcbrk   dos.h

Syntax
int getcbrk(void);

Description
Gets control-break setting.

getcbrk uses the DOS system call 0x33 to return the current setting of control-break checking.

Return value
getcbrk returns 0 if control-break checking is off, or 1 if checking is on.

See also
ctrlbrk, setcbrk

Portability

DOS	UNIX	Win 16	Win 32	ANSI C	ANSI C++	OS/2
+		+				

getch   conio.h

Syntax
int getch(void);

Description
Gets character from keyboard, does not echo to screen.

getch reads a single character directly from the keyboard, without echoing to the screen.

Note   Do not use this function for Win32s or Win32 GUI applications.

Return value

getch returns the character read from the keyboard.

See also

cgets, cscanf, fgetc, getc, getchar, getche, getpass, kbhit, putch, ungetch

Portability

DOS	UNIX	Win 16	Win 32	ANSI C	ANSI C++	OS/2
+			+			+

getchar   stdio.h

Syntax

int getchar(void);

Description

Gets character from stdin.

getchar is a macro that returns the next character on the named input stream stdin. It is defined to be *getc(stdin)*.

Note   Do not use this function for Win32s or Win32 GUI applications.

Return value

On success, *getchar* returns the character read, after converting it to an **int** without sign extension.

On end-of-file or error, it returns EOF.

See also

fgetc, fgetchar, freopen, getc, getch, getche, gets, putc, putchar, scanf, ungetc

Portability

DOS	UNIX	Win 16	Win 32	ANSI C	ANSI C++	OS/2
+	+		+	+	+	+

getche   conio.h

Syntax

int getche(void);

Description

Gets character from the keyboard, echoes to screen.

getche reads a single character from the keyboard and echoes it to the current text window using direct video or BIOS.

Note Do not use this function for Win32s or Win32 GUI applications.

Return value
getche returns the character read from the keyboard.

See also
cgets, cscanf, fgetc, getc, getch, getchar, kbhit, putch, ungetch

Portability

DOS	UNIX	Win 16	Win 32	ANSI C	ANSI C++	OS/2
+			+			+

getcurdir
dir.h

Syntax
int getcurdir(int drive, char *directory);

Description
Gets current directory for specified drive.

getcurdir gets the name of the current working directory for the drive indicated by *drive*. *drive* specifies a drive number (0 for default, 1 for A, and so on). *directory* points to an area of memory of length MAXDIR where the null-terminated directory name will be placed. The name does not contain the drive specification and does not begin with a backslash.

Return value
getcurdir returns 0 on success or -1 in the event of error.

See also
chdir, getcwd, getdisk, mkdir, rmdir

Portability

DOS	UNIX	Win 16	Win 32	ANSI C	ANSI C++	OS/2
+		+	+			+

getcwd
dir.h

Syntax
char *getcwd(char *buf, int buflen);

Description

Gets current working directory.

getcwd gets the full path name (including the drive) of the current working directory, up to *buflen* bytes long, and stores it in *buf*. If the full path name length (including the null terminator) is longer than *buflen* bytes, an error occurs.

If *buf* is NULL, a buffer *buflen* bytes long is allocated for you with *malloc*. You can later free the allocated buffer by passing the return value of *getcwd* to the function *free*.

Return value

getcwd returns the following values:

- If *buf* is not NULL on input, *getcwd* returns *buf* on success, NULL on error.
- If *buf* is NULL on input, *getcwd* returns a pointer to the allocated buffer.

In the event of an error return, the global variable *errno* is set to one of the following values:

ENODEV	No such device
ENOMEM	Not enough memory to allocate a buffer (*buf* is NULL)
ERANGE	Directory name longer than *buflen* (*buf* is not NULL)

See also

chdir, getcurdir, _getdcwd, getdisk, mkdir, rmdir

Portability

DOS	UNIX	Win 16	Win 32	ANSI C	ANSI C++	OS/2
+		+	+			+

_getdcwd   direct.h

Syntax

```
char * _getdcwd(int drive, char *buffer, int buflen);
```

Description

Gets current directory for specified drive.

_getdcwd gets the full path name of the working directory of the specified drive (including the drive name), up to *buflen* bytes long, and stores it in *buffer*. If the full path name length (including the null-terminator) is longer than *buflen*, an error occurs. The drive is 0 for the default drive, 1=A, 2=B, and so on.

If the working directory is the root directory, the terminating character for the full path is a backslash. If the working directory is a subdirectory, there is no terminating backslash after the subdirectory name.

If *buffer* is NULL, *_getdcwd* allocates a buffer at least *buflen* bytes long. You can later free the allocated buffer by passing the *_getdcwd* return value to the *free* function.

Return value

If successful, *_getdcwd* returns a pointer to the buffer containing the current directory for the specified drive.

Otherwise it returns NULL, and sets the global variable *errno* to one of the following values:

ENOMEM   Not enough memory to allocate a buffer (*buffer* is NULL)

ERANGE   Directory name longer than *buflen* (*buffer* is not NULL)

See also

chdir, getcwd, mkdir, rmdir

Portability

DOS	UNIX	Win 16	Win 32	ANSI C	ANSI C++	OS/2
+		+	+			+

getdfree   dos.h

Syntax

void getdfree(unsigned char drive, struct dfree *dtable);

Description

Gets disk free space.

getdfree accepts a drive specifier in *drive* (0 for default, 1 for A, and so on) and fills the *dfree* structure pointed to by *dtable* with disk attributes.

The *dfree* structure is defined as follows:

```
struct dfree {
    unsigned df_avail;      /* available clusters */
    unsigned df_total;      /* total clusters */
    unsigned df_bsec;       /* bytes per sector */
    unsigned df_sclus;      /* sectors per cluster */
};
```

Return value

getdfree returns no value. In the event of an error, *df_sclus* in the *dfree* structure is set to **(unsigned)** -1.

See also

getfat, getfatd

Portability

DOS	UNIX	Win 16	Win 32	ANSI C	ANSI C++	OS/2
+		+	+			+

getdisk, setdisk   dir.h

Syntax
int getdisk(void);
int setdisk(int drive);

Description
Gets or sets the current drive number.

getdisk gets the current drive number. It returns an integer: 0 for A, 1 for B, 2 for C, and so on.

setdisk sets the current drive to the one associated with *drive*: 0 for A, 1 for B, 2 for C, and so on.

The *setdisk* function changes the current drive of the parent process.

Return value
getdisk returns the current drive number. *setdisk* returns the total number of drives available.

See also
getcurdir, *getcwd*

Portability

DOS	UNIX	Win 16	Win 32	ANSI C	ANSI C++	OS/2
+		+	+			+

getdta   dos.h

Syntax
char far *getdta(void);

Description
Gets disk transfer address.

getdta returns the current setting of the disk transfer address (DTA).

In the small and medium memory models, the current data segment is the assumed segment. If you use C or C++ exclusively, this will be the case, but assembly routines can set the DTA to any hardware address.

In the compact or large models, the address returned by *getdta* is the correct hardware address and can be located outside the program.

Return value
getdta returns a far pointer to the current DTA.

See also
fcb (structure), *setdata*

Portability

DOS	UNIX	Win 16	Win 32	ANSI C	ANSI C++	OS/2
+		+				

getenv   stdlib.h

Syntax
```
char *getenv(const char *name);
```

Description
Gets a string from environment.

getenv returns the value of a specified variable. On DOS and OS/2, *name* must be uppercase. On other systems, *name* can be either uppercase or lowercase. *name* must not include the equal sign (=). If the specified environment variable does not exist, *getenv* returns a NULL pointer.

To delete the variable from the environment, use *getenv("name=")*.

Note   Environment entries must not be changed directly. If you want to change an environment value, you must use *putenv*.

Return value
On success, *getenv* returns the value associated with *name*.

If the specified *name* is not defined in the environment, *getenv* returns a NULL pointer.

See also
_environ (global variable), *getpsp*, *putenv*

Portability

DOS	UNIX	Win 16	Win 32	ANSI C	ANSI C++	OS/2
+	+	+	+	+	+	+

getfat

dos.h

Syntax

void getfat(unsigned char drive, struct fatinfo *dtable);

Description

Gets file allocation table information for given drive.

getfat gets information from the file allocation table (FAT) for the drive specified by *drive* (0 for default, 1 for A, 2 for B, and so on). *dtable* points to the *fatinfo* structure to be filled in. The *fatinfo* structure filled in by *getfat* is defined as follows:

```
struct fatinfo {
    char fi_sclus;          /* sectors per cluster */
    char fi_fatid;          /* the FAT id byte */
    unsigned fi_nclus;      /* number of clusters */
    int fi_bysec;           /* bytes per sector */
};
```

Return value

None.

See also

getdfree, getfatd

Portability

DOS	UNIX	Win 16	Win 32	ANSI C	ANSI C++	OS/2
+		+				

getfatd

dos.h

Syntax

void getfatd(struct fatinfo *dtable);

Description

Gets file allocation table information.

getfatd gets information from the file allocation table (FAT) of the default drive. *dtable* points to the *fatinfo* structure to be filled in.

The *fatinfo* structure filled in by *getfatd* is defined as follows:

```
struct fatinfo {
    char fi_sclus;        /* sectors per cluster */
    char fi_fatid;        /* the FAT id byte */
    int fi_nclus;         /* number of clusters */
    int fi_bysec;         /* bytes per sector */
};
```

Return value

None.

See also

getdfree, getfat

Portability

DOS	UNIX	Win 16	Win 32	ANSI C	ANSI C++	OS/2
+		+				

getftime, setftime   io.h

Syntax

int getftime(int handle, struct ftime *ftimep);
int setftime(int handle, struct ftime *ftimep);

Description

Gets and sets the file date and time.

getftime retrieves the file time and date for the disk file associated with the open *handle*. The *ftime* structure pointed to by *ftimep* is filled in with the file's time and date.

setftime sets the file date and time of the disk file associated with the open *handle* to the date and time in the *ftime* structure pointed to by *ftimep*. The file must not be written to after the *setftime* call or the changed information will be lost. The file must be open for writing; an EACCES error will occur if the file is open for read-only access.

setftime requires the file to be open for writing; an EACCES error will occur if the file is open for read-only access.

The *ftime* structure is defined as follows:

```
struct ftime {
    unsigned ft_tsec: 5;      /* two seconds */
    unsigned ft_min: 6;       /* minutes */
    unsigned ft_hour: 5;      /* hours */
    unsigned ft_day: 5;       /* days */
    unsigned ft_month: 4;     /* months */
    unsigned ft_year: 7;      /* year - 1980*/
    };
```

Return value

getftime and *setftime* return 0 on success.

In the event of an error return -1 is returned and the global variable *errno* is set to one of the following values:

EACCES   Permission denied

EBADF	Bad file number
EINVFNC	Invalid function number

See also
fflush, open, setftime

Portability

DOS	UNIX	Win 16	Win 32	ANSI C	ANSI C++	OS/2
+		+	+			+

_get_osfhandle   io.h

Syntax
long _get_osfhandle(int filehandle);

Description
Associates file handles.

The *_get_osfhandle* function associates an operating system file handle with an existing run-time file handle. The variable *filehandle* is the file handle of your program.

Return value
On success, *_get_osfhandle* returns an operating system file handle corresponding to the variable *filehandle*.

On error, it returns -1 and sets the global variable *errno* to

EBADF	an invalid file handle

See also
fdopen, fileno, _open_osfhandle

Portability

DOS	UNIX	Win 16	Win 32	ANSI C	ANSI C++	OS/2
			+			

getpass   conio.h

Syntax
char *getpass(const char *prompt);

Description
Reads a password.

getpass reads a password from the system console after prompting with the null-terminated string *prompt* and disabling the echo. A pointer is returned to a null-terminated string of up to eight characters (not counting the null-terminator).

Note Do not use this function for Win32s or Win32 GUI applications.

Return value
The return value is a pointer to a static string which is overwritten with each call.

See also
getch

Portability

DOS	UNIX	Win 16	Win 32	ANSI C	ANSI C++	OS/2
+	+		+			+

getpid   process.h

Syntax
unsigned getpid(void)

Description
Gets the process ID of a program.

This function returns the current process ID—an integer that uniquely identifies the process.

Return value
getpid returns the current process' ID.

See also
getpsp

Portability

DOS	UNIX	Win 16	Win 32	ANSI C	ANSI C++	OS/2
+	+	+	+			+

getpsp   dos.h

Syntax
unsigned getpsp(void);

Description
Gets the program segment prefix.

getpsp gets the segment address of the program segment prefix (PSP) using DOS call 0x62.

Return value

getpsp returns the address of the Program Segment Prefix (PSP).

See also

getenv, *_psp* (global variable)

Portability

DOS	UNIX	Win 16	Win 32	ANSI C	ANSI C++	OS/2
+		+				

gets   stdio.h

Syntax

char *gets(char *s);

Description

Gets a string from stdin.

gets collects a string of characters terminated by a new line from the standard input stream stdin and puts it into *s*. The new line is replaced by a null character (\0) in *s*.

gets allows input strings to contain certain whitespace characters (spaces, tabs). *gets* returns when it encounters a new line; everything up to the new line is copied into *s*.

The *gets* function is not length-terminated. If the input string is sufficiently large, data can be overwritten and corrupted. The *fgets* function provides better control of input strings.

Note   For Win32s or Win32 GUI applications, stdin must be redirected.

Return value

On success, *gets* returns the string argument *s*.

On end-of-file or error, it returns NULL.

See also

cgets, ferror, fgets, fopen, fputs, fread, freopen, getc, puts, scanf

Portability

DOS	UNIX	Win 16	Win 32	ANSI C	ANSI C++	OS/2
+	+		+	+	+	+

gettext

conio.h

Syntax

int gettext(int left, int top, int right, int bottom, void *destin);

Description

Copies text from text mode screen to memory.

gettext stores the contents of an onscreen text rectangle defined by *left*, *top*, *right*, and *bottom* into the area of memory pointed to by *destin*.

All coordinates are absolute screen coordinates, not window-relative. The upper left corner is (1,1). *gettext* reads the contents of the rectangle into memory sequentially from left to right and top to bottom.

Each position onscreen takes 2 bytes of memory: The first byte is the character in the cell and the second is the cell's video attribute. The space required for a rectangle w columns wide by h rows high is defined as

bytes = (h rows) x (w columns) x 2

Note Do not use this function for Win32s or Win32 GUI applications.

Return value

gettext returns 1 if the operation succeeds.

On error, it returns 0 (for example, if it fails because you gave coordinates outside the range of the current screen mode).

See also

movetext, puttext

Portability

DOS	UNIX	Win 16	Win 32	ANSI C	ANSI C++	OS/2
+			+			+

gettextinfo

conio.h

Syntax

void gettextinfo(struct text_info *r);

Description

Gets text mode video information.

gettextinfo fills in the *text_info* structure pointed to by *r* with the current text video information.

The *text_info* structure is defined in conio.h as follows:

```
struct text_info {
    unsigned char winleft;          /* left window coordinate */
    unsigned char wintop;           /* top window coordinate */
    unsigned char winright;         /* right window coordinate */
    unsigned char winbottom;        /* bottom window coordinate */
    unsigned char attribute;        /* text attribute */
    unsigned char normattr;         /* normal attribute */
    unsigned char currmode;         /* BW40, BW80, C40, C80, or C4350 */
    unsigned char screenheight;     /* text screen's height */
    unsigned char screenwidth;      /* text screen's width */
    unsigned char curx;             /* x-coordinate in current window */
    unsigned char cury;             /* y-coordinate in current window */
};
```

Note   Do not use this function for Win32s or Win32 GUI applications.

Return value
None. Results are returned in the structure pointed to by *r*.

See also
textattr, textbackground, textcolor, textmode, wherex, wherey, window

Portability

DOS	UNIX	Win 16	Win 32	ANSI C	ANSI C++	OS/2
+			+			+

gettime, settime   dos.h

Syntax
void gettime(struct time *timep);
void settime(struct time *timep);

Description
Gets and sets the system time.

gettime fills in the *time* structure pointed to by *timep* with the system's current time.

settime sets the system time to the values in the *time* structure pointed to by *timep*.

The *time* structure is defined as follows:

```
struct time {
    unsigned char ti_min;       /* minutes */
    unsigned char ti_hour;      /* hours */
    unsigned char ti_hund;      /* hundredths of seconds */
    unsigned char ti_sec;       /* seconds */
};
```

Return value

None.

See also

_dos_gettime, _dos_settime, getdate, setdate, stime, time

Portability

	DOS	UNIX	Win 16	Win 32	ANSI C	ANSI C++	OS/2
gettime	+		+	+			+
settime	+		+				+

getvect, setvect   dos.h

Syntax

```
void interrupt(*getvect(int interruptno)) ();           /* C version */
void interrupt(*getvect(int interruptno)) ( ... );      // C++ version
void setvect(int interruptno, void interrupt (*isr) ());     /* C version */
void setvect(int interruptno, void interrupt (*isr) ( ... )); // C++ version
```

Description

Gets and sets interrupt vector.

Every processor of the 8086 family includes a set of interrupt vectors numbered 0 to 255. The 4-byte value in each vector is actually an address which is the location of an interrupt function.

getvect reads the value of the interrupt vector given by *interruptno* and returns that value as a (far) pointer to an interrupt function. The value of *interruptno* can be from 0 to 255.

setvect sets the value of the interrupt vector named by *interruptno* to a new value, *isr*, which is a far pointer containing the address of a new interrupt function. The address of a C routine can be passed to *isr* only if that routine is declared to be an interrupt routine.

Note In C++, only static member functions or non-member functions can be declared to be an interrupt routine. If you use the prototypes declared in dos.h, simply pass the address of an interrupt function to *setvect* in any memory model.

Return value

getvect returns the current 4-byte value stored in the interrupt vector named by *interruptno*.

setvect does not return a value.

See also

disable, _dos_getvect, _dos_setvect, enable, geninterrupt

Portability

DOS	UNIX	Win 16	Win 32	ANSI C	ANSI C++	OS/2
+		+				

getverify
dos.h

Syntax
int getverify(void);

Description
Returns the state of the operating system verify flag.

getverify gets the current state of the verify flag.

The verify flag controls output to the disk. When verify is off writes are not verified; when verify is on all disk writes are verified to ensure proper writing of the data.

Return value
getverify returns the current state of the verify flag, either 0 (off) or 1 (on).

See also
setverify

Portability

DOS	UNIX	Win 16	Win 32	ANSI C	ANSI C++	OS/2
+		+				+

getw
stdio.h

Syntax
int getw(FILE *stream);

Description
Gets integer from stream.

getw returns the next integer in the named input stream. It assumes no special alignment in the file.

getw should not be used when the stream is opened in text mode.

Return value
getw returns the next integer on the input stream.

On end-of-file or error, *getw* returns EOF.

Note Because EOF is a legitimate value for *getw* to return, *feof* or *ferror* should be used to detect end-of-file or error.

See also
putw

Portability

DOS	UNIX	Win 16	Win 32	ANSI C	ANSI C++	OS/2
+	+	+	+			+

gmtime   time.h

Syntax
struct tm *gmtime(const time_t *timer);

Description
Converts date and time to Greenwich mean time (GMT).

gmtime accepts the address of a value returned by *time* and returns a pointer to the structure of type *tm* containing the time elements. *gmtime* converts directly to GMT.

The global long variable *_timezone* should be set to the difference in seconds between GMT and local standard time (in PST *_timezone* is 8 x 60 x 60). The global variable *_daylight* should be set to nonzero *only* if the standard U.S. daylight saving time conversion should be applied.

This is the *tm* structure declaration from the time.h header file:

```
struct tm {
    int tm_sec;              /* Seconds */
    int tm_min;              /* Minutes */
    int tm_hour;             /* Hour (0 - 23) */
    int tm_mday;             /* Day of month (1 - 31) */
    int tm_mon;              /* Month (0 - 11) */
    int tm_year;             /* Year (calendar year minus 1900) */
    int tm_wday;             /* Weekday (0 - 6; Sunday is 0) */
    int tm_yday;             /* Day of year (0 -365) */
    int tm_isdst;            /* Nonzero if daylight saving time is in effect. */
};
```

These quantities give the time on a 24-hour clock, day of month (1 to 31), month (0 to 11), weekday (Sunday equals 0), year - 1900, day of year (0 to 365), and a flag that is nonzero if daylight saving time is in effect.

Return value
gmtime returns a pointer to the structure containing the time elements. This structure is a static that is overwritten with each call.

See also
asctime, ctime, ftime, localtime, stime, time, tzset

Portability

DOS	UNIX	Win 16	Win 32	ANSI C	ANSI C++	OS/2
+	+	+	+	+	+	+

gotoxy   conio.h

Syntax
```
void gotoxy(int x
int y);
```

Description
Positions cursor in text window.

gotoxy moves the cursor to the given position in the current text window. If the coordinates are in any way invalid the call to *gotoxy* is ignored. An example of this is a call to *gotoxy*(40,30) when (35,25) is the bottom right position in the window. Neither argument to *gotoxy* can be zero.

Note   Do not use this function for Win32s or Win32 GUI applications.

Return value
None.

See also
wherex, wherey, window

Portability

DOS	UNIX	Win 16	Win 32	ANSI C	ANSI C++	OS/2
+		+	+			+

heapcheck   alloc.h

Syntax
```
int heapcheck(void);
```

Description
Checks and verifies the heap.

heapcheck walks through the heap and examines each block, checking its pointers, size, and other critical attributes. For DOS users, *heapcheck* maps to *farheapcheck* in the large and huge memory models.

Return value

The return value is less than 0 for an error and greater than 0 for success. The return values and their meaning are as follows:

_HEAPCORRUPT	Heap has been corrupted
_HEAPEMPTY	No heap
_HEAPOK	Heap is verified

Portability

DOS	UNIX	Win 16	Win 32	ANSI C	ANSI C++	OS/2
+			+			+

heapcheckfree   alloc.h

Syntax

int heapcheckfree(unsigned int fillvalue);

Description

Checks the free blocks on the heap for a constant value.

Return value

The return value is less than 0 for an error and greater than 0 for success. The return values and their meaning are as follows:

_BADVALUE	A value other than the fill value was found
_HEAPCORRUPT	Heap has been corrupted
_HEAPEMPTY	No heap
_HEAPOK	Heap is accurate

Portability

DOS	UNIX	Win 16	Win 32	ANSI C	ANSI C++	OS/2
+			+			+

heapchecknode   alloc.h

Syntax

int heapchecknode(void *node);

Description

Checks and verifies a single node on the heap.

If a node has been freed and *heapchecknode* is called with a pointer to the freed block, *heapchecknode* can return _BADNODE rather than the expected _FREEENTRY. This is because adjacent free blocks on the heap are merged, and the block in question no longer exists.

Return value
One of the following values:

_BADNODE	Node could not be found
_FREEENTRY	Node is a free block
_HEAPCORRUPT	Heap has been corrupted
_HEAPEMPTY	No heap
_USEDENTRY	Node is a used block

Portability

DOS	UNIX	Win 16	Win 32	ANSI C	ANSI C++	OS/2
+			+			+

_heapchk

Syntax
int _heapchk(void);

Description
Checks and verifies the heap.

_heapchk walks through the heap and examines each block, checking its pointers, size, and other critical attributes.

Return value
One of the following values:

_HEAPBADNODE	A corrupted heap block has been found
_HEAPEMPTY	No heap exists
_HEAPOK	The heap appears to be uncorrupted

See also
_heapset, _rtl_heapwalk

Portability

DOS	UNIX	Win 16	Win 32	ANSI C	ANSI C++	OS/2
			+			+

heapfillfree

alloc.h

Syntax

int heapfillfree(unsigned int fillvalue);

Description

Fills the free blocks on the heap with a constant value.

Return value

One of the following values:

_HEAPCORRUPT	Heap has been corrupted
_HEAPEMPTY	No heap
_HEAPOK	Heap is accurate

Portability

DOS	UNIX	Win 16	Win 32	ANSI C	ANSI C++	OS/2
+			+			+

_heapmin

malloc.h

Syntax

int _heapmin(void);

Description

Releases unused heap areas.

The _heapmin function returns unused areas of the heap to the operating system. This allows blocks that have been allocated and then freed to be used by other processes. Due to fragmentation of the heap, _heapmin might not always be able to return unused memory to the operating system; this is not an error.

Return value

_heapmin returns 0 if it is successful, or -1 if an error occurs.

See also

free, malloc

Portability

DOS	UNIX	Win 16	Win 32	ANSI C	ANSI C++	OS/2
+		+	+			+

_heapset

malloc.h

Syntax

int _heapset(unsigned int fillvalue);

Description

Fills the free blocks on the heap with a constant value.

_heapset checks the heap for consistency using the same methods as _heapchk. It then fills each free block in the heap with the value contained in the least significant byte of *fillvalue*. This function can be used to find heap-related problems. It does *not* guarantee that subsequently allocated blocks will be filled with the specified value.

Return value

One of the following values:

_HEAPOK	The heap appears to be uncorrupted
_HEAPEMPTY	No heap exists
_HEAPBADNODE	A corrupted heap block has been found

See also

_heapchk, _rtl_heapwalk

Portability

DOS	UNIX	Win 16	Win 32	ANSI C	ANSI C++	OS/2
			+			+

heapwalk

alloc.h

Syntax

int heapwalk(struct heapinfo *hi);

Description

heapwalk is used to "walk" through the heap, node by node.

heapwalk assumes the heap is correct. Use *heapcheck* to verify the heap before using *heapwalk*. _HEAPOK is returned with the last block on the heap. _HEAPEND will be returned on the next call to *heapwalk*.

heapwalk receives a pointer to a structure of type *heapinfo* (declared in alloc.h). For the first call to *heapwalk*, set the *hi.ptr* field to null. *heapwalk* returns with *hi.ptr* containing the address of the first block. *hi.size* holds the size of the block in bytes. *hi.in_use* is a flag that's set if the block is currently in use.

Return value
One of the following values:

_HEAPEMPTY	No heap exists
_HEAPEND	The end of the heap has been reached
_HEAPOK	The *heapinfo* block contains valid information about the next heap block

Portability

DOS	UNIX	Win 16	Win 32	ANSI C	ANSI C++	OS/2
+			+			+

highvideo   conio.h

Syntax
void highvideo(void);

Description
Selects high-intensity characters.

highvideo selects high-intensity characters by setting the high-intensity bit of the currently selected foreground color.

This function does not affect any characters currently onscreen, but does affect those displayed by functions (such as *cprintf*) that perform direct video, text mode output after *highvideo* is called.

Note   Do not use this function for Win32s or Win32 GUI applications.

Return value
None.

See also
cprintf, cputs, gettextinfo, lowvideo, normvideo, textattr, textcolor

Portability

DOS	UNIX	Win 16	Win 32	ANSI C	ANSI C++	OS/2
+			+			+

hypot, hypotl   math.h

Syntax
double hypot(double x, double y);
long double hypotl(long double x, long double y);

Description

Calculates hypotenuse of a right triangle.

hypot calculates the value z where

$z2 = x2 + y2$ and $z >= 0$

This is equivalent to the length of the hypotenuse of a right triangle, if the lengths of the two sides are x and y.

hypotl is the **long double** version; it takes **long double** arguments and returns a **long double** result.

Return value

On success, these functions return z, a **double** (*hypot*) or a **long double**) (*hypotl*). On error (such as an overflow), they set the global variable errno to

ERANGE   Result out of range

and return the value HUGE_VAL (*hypot*) or _LHUGE_VAL) (*hypotl*). Error handling for these routines can be modified through the functions _matherr and _matherrl.

Portability

	DOS	UNIX	Win 16	Win 32	ANSI C	ANSI C++	OS/2
hypot	+	+	+	+			+
hypotl	+		+	+			+

_InitEasyWin   io.h

Syntax

```
void _InitEasyWin(void);
```

Description

The purpose of EasyWin is to convert DOS applications to Windows programs, quickly and easily. You might, however, occasionally want to use EasyWin from within a true 16-bit Windows program. For example, you might want to add *printf* functions to your program code to help you debug your 16-bit Windows program.

To use EasyWin from within a Windows program, make a call to the *_InitEasyWin* function before doing any standard input or output.

For example:

```
#include <windows.h>
#include <stdio.h>

#pragma argsused
int PASCAL WinMain(HANDLE hInstance, HANDLE hPrevInstance,
                   LPSTR lpszCmdLine, int cmdShow)
{
    _InitEasyWin();
```

```
    /* Normal windows setup */

    printf("Hello, world\n");
    return 0;
}
```

The prototype for _InitEasyWin can be found in stdio.h and iostream.h.

Return value
None.

Portability

DOS	UNIX	Win 16	Win 32	ANSI C	ANSI C++	OS/2
		+				

inp   conio.h

Syntax
int inp(unsigned portid);

Description
Reads a byte from a hardware port.

inp is a macro that reads a byte from the input port specified by *portid*. If *inp* is called when conio.h has been included, it will be treated as a macro that expands to inline code. If you don't include conio.h, or if you do include conio.h and undefine the macro *inp*, you get the *inp* function.

Return value
inp returns the value read.

See also
inpw, outp, outpw

Portability

DOS	UNIX	Win 16	Win 32	ANSI C	ANSI C++	OS/2
+		+				

inport   dos.h

Syntax
int inport(int portid);

Description

Reads a word from a hardware port.

inport works just like the 80x86 instruction *IN*. It reads the low byte of a word from the input port specified by *portid*; it reads the high byte from *portid* + 1.

Return value

inport returns the value read.

See also

inportb, outport, outportb

Portability

DOS	UNIX	Win 16	Win 32	ANSI C	ANSI C++	OS/2
+		+				

inportb   dos.h

Syntax

unsigned char inportb(int portid);

Description

Reads a byte from a hardware port.

inportb is a macro that reads a byte from the input port specified by *portid*.

If *inportb* is called when dos.h has been included, it will be treated as a macro that expands to inline code. If you don't include dos.h, or if you do include dos.h and **#undef** the macro *inportb*, you get the *inportb* function.

Return value

inportb returns the value read.

See also

inport, outport, outportb

Portability

DOS	UNIX	Win 16	Win 32	ANSI C	ANSI C++	OS/2
+		+				

inpw   conio.h

Syntax

unsigned inpw(unsigned portid);

Description

Reads a word from a hardware port.

inpw is a macro that reads a 16-bit word from the inport port specified by *portid*. It reads the low byte of the word from *portid*, and the high byte from *portid* + 1.

If *inpw* is called when conio.h has been included, it will be treated as a macro that expands to inline code. If you don't include conio.h, or if you do include conio.h and **#undef** the macro *inpw*, you get the *inpw* function.

Return value

inpw returns the value read.

See also

inp, outp, outpw

Portability

DOS	UNIX	Win 16	Win 32	ANSI C	ANSI C++	OS/2
+		+				

insline   conio.h

Syntax

void insline(void);

Description

Inserts a blank line in the text window.

insline inserts an empty line in the text window at the cursor position using the current text background color. All lines below the empty one move down one line, and the bottom line scrolls off the bottom of the window.

Note Do not use this function for Win32s or Win32 GUI applications.

Return value

None.

See also

clreol, delline, window

Portability

DOS	UNIX	Win 16	Win 32	ANSI C	ANSI C++	OS/2
+			+			+

int86   dos.h

Syntax
int int86(int intno, union REGS *inregs, union REGS *outregs);

Description
General 8086 software interrupt.

int86 executes an 8086 software interrupt specified by the argument *intno*. Before executing the software interrupt, it copies register values from *inregs* into the registers.

After the software interrupt returns, *int86* copies the current register values to *outregs*, copies the status of the carry flag to the *x.cflag* field in *outregs*, and copies the value of the 8086 flags register to the *x.flags* field in *outregs*. If the carry flag is set, it usually indicates that an error has occurred.

Note   *inregs* can point to the same structure that *outregs* points to.

Return value
int86 returns the value of AX after completion of the software interrupt. If the carry flag is set (*outregs -> x.cflag != 0*), indicating an error, this function sets the global variable *_doserrno* to the error code. Note that when the carry flag is *not* set (*outregs -> x.cflag = 0*), you may or may not have an error. To be certain, always check *_doserrno*.

See also
bdos, bdosptr, geninterrupt, int86x, intdos, intdosx, intr

Portability

DOS	UNIX	Win 16	Win 32	ANSI C	ANSI C++	OS/2
+		+				

int86x   dos.h

Syntax
int int86x(int intno, union REGS *inregs, union REGS *outregs, struct SREGS *segregs);

Description
General 8086 software interrupt interface.

int86x executes an 8086 software interrupt specified by the argument *intno*. Before executing the software interrupt, it copies register values from *inregs* into the registers.

In addition, *int86x* copies the *segregs ->ds* and *segregs ->es* values into the corresponding registers before executing the software interrupt. This feature allows programs that use far pointers or a large data memory model to specify which segment is to be used for the software interrupt.

After the software interrupt returns, *int86x* copies the current register values to *outregs*, the status of the carry flag to the x.cflag field in *outregs*, and the value of the 8086 flags register to the x.flags field in *outregs*. In addition, *int86x* restores DS and sets the *segregs* ->es and *segregs* ->ds fields to the values of the corresponding segment registers. If the carry flag is set, it usually indicates that an error has occurred.

int86x lets you invoke an 8086 software interrupt that takes a value of DS different from the default data segment, and/or takes an argument in ES.

Note   *inregs* can point to the same structure that *outregs* points to.

Return value
int86x returns the value of AX after completion of the software interrupt. If the carry flag is set (*outregs* -> x.cflag != 0), indicating an error, this function sets the global variable _doserrno to the error code. Note that when the carry flag is *not* set (*outregs* -> x.cflag = 0), you may or may not have an error. To be certain, always check _doserrno.

See also
bdos, bdosptr, geninterrupt, intdos, intdosx, int86, intr, segread

Portability

DOS	UNIX	Win 16	Win 32	ANSI C	ANSI C++	OS/2
+		+				

intdos

dos.h

Syntax
int intdos(union REGS *inregs, union REGS *outregs);

Description
General DOS interrupt interface.

intdos executes DOS interrupt 0x21 to invoke a specified DOS function. The value of *inregs* -> h.ah specifies the DOS function to be invoked.

After the interrupt 0x21 returns, *intdos* copies the current register values to *outregs*, copies the status of the carry flag to the x.cflag field in *outregs*, and copies the value of the 8086 flags register to the x.flags field in *outregs*. If the carry flag is set, it indicates that an error has occurred.

Note   *inregs* can point to the same structure that *outregs* points to.

Return value
intdos returns the value of AX after completion of the DOS function call. If the carry flag is set (*outregs* -> x.cflag != 0), indicating an error, it sets the global variable _doserrno to the error code. Note that when the carry flag is *not* set (*outregs* -> x.cflag = 0), you may or may not have an error. To be certain, always check _doserrno.

See also

bdos, bdosptr, geninterrupt, int86, int86x, intdosx, intr

Portability

DOS	UNIX	Win 16	Win 32	ANSI C	ANSI C++	OS/2
+		+				

intdosx   dos.h

Syntax

int intdosx(union REGS *inregs, union REGS *outregs, struct SREGS *segregs);

Description

General DOS interrupt interface.

intdosx executes DOS interrupt 0x21 to invoke a specified DOS function. The value of *inregs -> h.ah* specifies the DOS function to be invoked.

In addition, *intdosx* copies the *segregs ->ds* and *segregs ->es* values into the corresponding registers before invoking the DOS function. This feature allows programs that use far pointers or a large data memory model to specify which segment is to be used for the function execution.

After the interrupt 0x21 returns, *intdosx* copies the current register values to *outregs*, copies the status of the carry flag to the *x.cflag* field in *outregs*, and copies the value of the 8086 flags register to the *x.flags* field in *outregs*. In addition, *intdosx* sets the *segregs ->es* and *segregs ->ds* fields to the values of the corresponding segment registers and then restores DS. If the carry flag is set, it indicates that an error occurred.

intdosx lets you invoke a DOS function that takes a value of DS different from the default data segment and/or takes an argument in ES.

Note *inregs* can point to the same structure that *outregs* points to.

Return value

intdosx returns the value of AX after completion of the DOS function call. If the carry flag is set (*outregs -> x.cflag != 0*), indicating an error, it sets the global variable *_doserrno* to the error code. Note that when the carry flag is *not* set (*outregs -> x.cflag = 0*), you may or may not have an error. To be certain, always check *_doserrno*.

See also

bdos, bdosptr, geninterrupt, int86, int86x, intdos, intr, segread

Portability

DOS	UNIX	Win 16	Win 32	ANSI C	ANSI C++	OS/2
+		+				

intr

dos.h

Syntax

void intr(int intno, struct REGPACK *preg);

Description

Alternate 8086 software interrupt interface.

The *intr* function is an alternate interface for executing software interrupts. It generates an 8086 software interrupt specified by the argument *intno*.

intr copies register values from the REGPACK structure *preg* into the registers before executing the software interrupt. After the software interrupt completes, *intr* copies the current register values into *preg*, including the flags.

The arguments passed to *intr* are as follows:

intno   Interrupt number to be executed

preg   Address of a structure containing

        (a) the input registers before the interrupt call

        (b) the value of the registers after the interrupt call

The REGPACK structure (defined in dos.h) has the following format:

```
struct  REGPACK {
    unsigned  r_ax, r_bx, r_cx, r_dx;
    unsigned  r_bp, r_si, r_di, r_ds, r_es, r_flags;
};
```

Return value

No value is returned. The REGPACK structure *preg* contains the value of the registers after the interrupt call.

See also

geninterrupt, int86, int86x, intdos, intdosx

Portability

DOS	UNIX	Win 16	Win 32	ANSI C	ANSI C++	OS/2
+		+				

ioctl

Syntax

int ioctl(int handle, int func [, void *argdx, int argcx]);

Description

Controls I/0 device.

ioctl is available on UNIX systems, but not with these parameters or functionality. UNIX version 7 and System III differ from each other in their use of *ioctl*. *ioctl* calls are not portable to UNIX and are rarely portable across DOS machines.

DOS 3.0 extends *ioctl* with *func* values of 8 and 11.

This is a direct interface to the DOS call 0x44 (IOCTL).

The exact function depends on the value of *func* as follows:

0	Get device information.
1	Set device information (in *argdx*).
2	Read *argcx* bytes into the address pointed to by *argdx*.
3	Write *argcx* bytes from the address pointed to by *argdx*.
4	Same as 2 except *handle* is treated as a drive number (0 equals default, 1 equals A, and so on).
5	Same as 3 except *handle* is a drive number (0 equals default, 1 equals A, and so on).
6	Get input status.
7	Get output status.
8	Test removability; DOS 3.0 only.
11	Set sharing conflict retry count; DOS 3.0 only.

ioctl can be used to get information about device channels. Regular files can also be used, but only *func* values 0, 6, and 7 are defined for them. All other calls return an EINVAL error for files.

See the documentation for system call 0x44 in your DOS reference manuals for detailed information on argument or return values.

The arguments *argdx* and *argcx* are optional.

ioctl provides a direct interface to DOS device drivers for special functions. As a result, the exact behavior of this function varies across different vendors' hardware and in different devices. Also, several vendors do not follow the interfaces described here. Refer to the vendor BIOS documentation for exact use of *ioctl*.

Return value

For *func* 0 or 1, the return value is the device information (DX of the *ioctl* call). For *func* values of 2 through 5, the return value is the number of bytes actually transferred. For *func* values of 6 or 7, the return value is the device status.

In any event, if an error is detected, a value of -1 is returned, and the global variable *errno* is set to one of the following:

EBADF	Bad file number
EINVAL	Invalid argument
EINVDAT	Invalid data

Portability

DOS	UNIX	Win 16	Win 32	ANSI C	ANSI C++	OS/2
+	+	+				

isalnum ctype.h

Syntax
int isalnum(int c);

Description
Tests for an alphanumeric character.

isalnum is a macro that classifies ASCII-coded integer values by table lookup. The macro is affected by the current locale's LC_CTYPE category. For the default C locale, *c* is a letter (*A* to *Z* or *a* to *z*) or a digit (0 to 9).

You can make this macro available as a function by undefining (**#undef**) it.

Return value
It is a predicate returning nonzero for true and 0 for false. *isalnum* returns nonzero if *c* is a letter or a digit.

Portability

DOS	UNIX	Win 16	Win 32	ANSI C	ANSI C++	OS/2
+	+	+	+	+	+	+

isalpha ctype.h

Syntax
int isalpha(int c);

Description
Classifies an alphabetical character.

isalpha is a macro that classifies ASCII-coded integer values by table lookup. The macro is affected by the current locale's LC_CTYPE category. For the default C locale, *c* is a letter (*A* to *Z* or *a* to *z*).

You can make this macro available as a function by undefining (**#undef**) it.

Return value
isalpha returns nonzero if *c* is a letter.

Portability

DOS	UNIX	Win 16	Win 32	ANSI C	ANSI C++	OS/2
+	+	+	+	+	+	+

isascii   ctype.h

Syntax
int isascii(int c);

Description
Character classification macro.

isascii is a macro that classifies ASCII-coded integer values by table lookup. It is a predicate returning nonzero for true and 0 for false.

isascii is defined on all integer values.

Return value
isascii returns nonzero if *c* is in the range 0 to 127 (0x00-0x7F).

Portability

DOS	UNIX	Win 16	Win 32	ANSI C	ANSI C++	OS/2
+	+	+	+			+

isatty   io.h

Syntax
int isatty(int handle);

Description
Checks for device type.

isatty determines whether *handle* is associated with any one of the following character devices:

- a terminal
- a console
- a printer
- a serial port

Return value
If the device is one of the four character devices listed above, *isatty* returns a nonzero integer. If it is not such a device, *isatty* returns 0.

Portability

DOS	UNIX	Win 16	Win 32	ANSI C	ANSI C++	OS/2
+	+	+	+			+

iscntrl   ctype.h

Syntax
```
int iscntrl(int c);
```

Description
Tests for a control character.

iscntrl is a macro that classifies ASCII-coded integer values by table lookup. The macro is affected by the current locale's LC_CTYPE category. For the default C locale, *c* is a delete character or control character (0x7F or 0x00 to 0x1F).

You can make this macro available as a function by undefining (**#undef**) it.

Return value
iscntrl returns nonzero if *c* is a delete character or ordinary control character.

Portability

DOS	UNIX	Win 16	Win 32	ANSI C	ANSI C++	OS/2
+	+	+	+	+	+	+

isdigit   ctype.h

Syntax
```
int isdigit(int c);
```

Description
Tests for decimal-digit character.

isdigit is a macro that classifies ASCII-coded integer values by table lookup. The macro is affected by the current locale's LC_CTYPE category. For the default C locale, *c* is a digit (0 to 9).

You can make this macro available as a function by undefining (**#undef**) it.

Return value
isdigit returns nonzero if *c* is a digit.

Portability

DOS	UNIX	Win 16	Win 32	ANSI C	ANSI C++	OS/2
+	+	+	+	+	+	+

isgraph   ctype.h

Syntax
int isgraph(int c);

Description
Tests for printing character.

isgraph is a macro that classifies ASCII-coded integer values by table lookup. The macro is affected by the current locale's LC_CTYPE category. For the default C locale, *c* is a printing character except blank space (' ').

You can make this macro available as a function by undefining (**#undef**) it.

Return value
isgraph returns nonzero if *c* is a printing character.

Portability

DOS	UNIX	Win 16	Win 32	ANSI C	ANSI C++	OS/2
+	+	+	+	+	+	+

islower   ctype.h

Syntax
int islower(int c);

Description
Tests for lowercase character.

islower is a macro that classifies ASCII-coded integer values by table lookup. The macro is affected by the current locale's LC_CTYPE category. For the default C locale, *c* is a lowercase letter (*a* to *z*).

You can make this macro available as a function by undefining (**#undef**) it.

Return value

islower returns nonzero if *c* is a lowercase letter.

Portability

DOS	UNIX	Win 16	Win 32	ANSI C	ANSI C++	OS/2
+	+	+	+	+	+	+

isprint   ctype.h

Syntax
int isprint(int c);

Description
Tests for printing character.

isprint is a macro that classifies ASCII-coded integer values by table lookup. The macro is affected by the current locale's LC_CTYPE category. For the default C locale, *c* is a printing character including the blank space (' ').

You can make this macro available as a function by undefining (**#undef**) it.

Return value
isprint returns nonzero if *c* is a printing character.

Portability

DOS	UNIX	Win 16	Win 32	ANSI C	ANSI C++	OS/2
+	+	+	+	+	+	+

ispunct   ctype.h

Syntax
int ispunct(int c);

Description
Tests for punctuation character.

ispunct is a macro that classifies ASCII-coded integer values by table lookup. The macro is affected by the current locale's LC_CTYPE category. For the default C locale, *c* is any printing character that is neither an alphanumeric nor a blank space (' ').

You can make this macro available as a function by undefining (**#undef**) it.

Return value

ispunct returns nonzero if *c* is a punctuation character.

Portability

DOS	UNIX	Win 16	Win 32	ANSI C	ANSI C++	OS/2
+	+	+	+	+	+	+

isspace   ctype.h

Syntax

int isspace(int c);

Description

Tests for space character.

isspace is a macro that classifies ASCII-coded integer values by table lookup. The macro is affected by the current locale's LC_CTYPE category.

You can make this macro available as a function by undefining (**#undef**) it.

Return value

isspace returns nonzero if *c* is a space, tab, carriage return, new line, vertical tab, formfeed (0x09 to 0x0D, 0x20), or any other locale-defined space character.

Portability

DOS	UNIX	Win 16	Win 32	ANSI C	ANSI C++	OS/2
+	+	+	+	+	+	+

isupper   ctype.h

Syntax

int isupper(int c);

Description

Tests for uppercase character.

isupper is a macro that classifies ASCII-coded integer values by table lookup. The macro is affected by the current locale's LC_CTYPE category. For the default C locale, *c* is an uppercase letter (*A* to *Z*).

You can make this macro available as a function by undefining (**#undef**) it.

Return value

isupper returns nonzero if *c* is an uppercase letter.

Portability

DOS	UNIX	Win 16	Win 32	ANSI C	ANSI C++	OS/2
+	+	+	+	+	+	+

isxdigit   ctype.h

Syntax

int isxdigit(int c);

Description

Tests for hexadecimal character.

isxdigit is a macro that classifies ASCII-coded integer values by table lookup. The macro is affected by the current locale's LC_CTYPE category.

You can make this macro available as a function by undefining (**#undef**) it.

Return value

isxdigit returns nonzero if *c* is a hexadecimal digit (0 to 9, *A* to *F*, *a* to *f*) or any other hexadecimal digit defined by the locale.

Portability

DOS	UNIX	Win 16	Win 32	ANSI C	ANSI C++	OS/2
+	+	+	+	+	+	+

itoa   stdlib.h

Syntax

char *itoa(int value, char *string, int radix);

Description

Converts an integer to a string.

itoa converts *value* to a null-terminated string and stores the result in *string*. With *itoa*, *value* is an integer.

radix specifies the base to be used in converting *value*; it must be between 2 and 36, inclusive. If *value* is negative and *radix* is 10, the first character of *string* is the minus sign (-).

Note   The space allocated for *string* must be large enough to hold the returned string, including the terminating null character (\0). *itoa* can return up to 17 bytes.

Return value
itoa returns a pointer to *string*.

See also
ltoa, ultoa

Portability

DOS	UNIX	Win 16	Win 32	ANSI C	ANSI C++	OS/2
+		+	+			+

kbhit   conio.h

Syntax
int kbhit(void);

Description
Checks for currently available keystrokes.

kbhit checks to see if a keystroke is currently available. Any available keystrokes can be retrieved with *getch* or *getche*.

Note Do not use this function for Win32s or Win32 GUI applications.

Return value
If a keystroke is available, *kbhit* returns a nonzero value. Otherwise, it returns 0.

See also
getch, getche

Portability

DOS	UNIX	Win 16	Win 32	ANSI C	ANSI C++	OS/2
+		+	+			+

labs   math.h

Syntax
long labs(long int x);

Description
Gives long absolute value.

labs computes the absolute value of the parameter *x*.

Return value

labs returns the absolute value of *x*.

See also

abs, cabs, fabs

Portability

DOS	UNIX	Win 16	Win 32	ANSI C	ANSI C++	OS/2
+	+	+	+	+	+	+

ldexp, ldexpl   math.h

Syntax

double ldexp(double x, int exp);
long double ldexpl(long double x, int exp);

Description

Calculates $x \times 2^{\text{exp}}$.

lexpl is the **long double** version; it takes a **long double** argument for *x* and returns a **long double** result.

Return value

On success, *ldexp* (or *ldexpl*) returns the value it calculated, $x \times 2^{\text{exp}}$. Error handling for these routines can be modified through the functions *_matherr* and *_matherrl*.

See also

exp, frexp, modf

Portability

	DOS	UNIX	Win 16	Win 32	ANSI C	ANSI C++	OS/2
ldexp	+	+	+	+	+	+	+
ldexpl	+		+	+			+

ldiv   stdlib.h

Syntax

ldiv_t ldiv(long int numer, long int denom);

Description

Divides two **longs**, returning quotient and remainder.

ldiv divides two **longs** and returns both the quotient and the remainder as an *ldiv_t* type. *numer* and *denom* are the numerator and denominator, respectively.

The *ldiv_t* type is a structure of **long**s defined in stdlib.h as follows:

```
typedef struct {
    long int quot;      /* quotient */
    long int rem;       /* remainder */
    } ldiv_t;
```

Return value
ldiv returns a structure whose elements are *quot* (the quotient) and *rem* (the remainder).

See also
div

Portability

DOS	UNIX	Win 16	Win 32	ANSI C	ANSI C++	OS/2
+		+	+	+	+	+

lfind   stdlib.h

Syntax
```
void  *lfind(const void *key, const void *base, size_t *num, size_t width,
int (_USERENTRY *fcmp)(const void *, const void *));
```

Description
Performs a linear search.

lfind makes a linear search for the value of *key* in an array of sequential records. It uses a user-defined comparison routine *fcmp*. The *fcmp* function must be used with the _USERENTRY calling convention.

The array is described as having **num* records that are *width* bytes wide, and begins at the memory location pointed to by *base*.

Return value
lfind returns the address of the first entry in the table that matches the search key. If no match is found, *lfind* returns NULL. The comparison routine must return 0 if **elem1* == **elem2*, and nonzero otherwise (*elem1* and *elem2* are its two parameters).

See also
bsearch, lsearch, qsort

Portability

DOS	UNIX	Win 16	Win 32	ANSI C	ANSI C++	OS/2
+	+	+	+			+

localeconv

locale.h

Syntax

struct lconv *localeconv(void);

Description

Queries the locale for numeric format.

This function provides information about the monetary and other numeric formats for the current locale. The information is stored in a **struct** *lconv* type. The structure can only be modified by the *setlocale*. Subsequent calls to *localeconv* will update the *lconv* structure.

The *lconv* structure is defined in locale.h. It contains the following fields:

Field	Application
char *decimal_point;*	Decimal point used in nonmonetary formats. This can never be an empty string.
char *thousands_sep;*	Separator used to group digits to the left of the decimal point. Not used with monetary quantities.
char *grouping;*	Size of each group of digits. Not used with monetary quantities. See the value listing table below.
char *int_curr_symbol;*	International monetary symbol in the current locale. The symbol format is specified in the ISO 4217 Codes for the Representation of Currency and Funds.
char *currency_symbol;*	Local monetary symbol for the current locale.
char *mon_decimal_point;*	Decimal point used to format monetary quantities.
char *mon_thousands_sep;*	Separator used to group digits to the left of the decimal point for monetary quantities.
char *mon_grouping;*	Size of each group of digits used in monetary quantities. See the value listing table below.
char *positive_sign;*	String indicating nonnegative monetary quantities.
char *negative_sign;*	String indicating negative monetary quantities.
char *int_frac_digits;*	Number of digits after the decimal point that are to be displayed in an internationally formatted monetary quantity.
char *frac_digits;*	Number of digits after the decimal point that are to be displayed in a formatted monetary quantity.
char *p_cs_precedes;*	Set to 1 if *currency_symbol* precedes a nonnegative formatted monetary quantity. If *currency_symbol* is after the quantity, it is set to 0.
char *p_sep_by_space;*	Set to 1 if *currency_symbol* is to be separated from the nonnegative formatted monetary quantity by a space. Set to 0 if there is no space separation.
char *n_cs_precedes;*	Set to 1 if *currency_symbol* precedes a negative formatted monetary quantity. If *currency_symbol* is after the quantity, set to 0.
char *n_sep_by_space;*	Set to 1 if *currency_symbol* is to be separated from the negative formatted monetary quantity by a space. Set to 0 if there is no space separation.
char *p_sign_posn;*	Indicate where to position the positive sign in a nonnegative formatted monetary quantity.
char *n_sign_posn;*	Indicate where to position the positive sign in a negative formatted monetary quantity.

Any of the above strings (except *decimal_point*) that is empty (" ") is not supported in the current locale. The nonstring **char** elements are nonnegative numbers. Any nonstring

char element that is set to CHAR_MAX indicates that the element is not supported in the current locale.

The *grouping* and *mon_grouping* elements are set and interpreted as follows:

Value	Meaning
CHAR_MAX	No further grouping is to be performed.
0	The previous element is to be used repeatedly for the remainder of the digits.
any other integer	Indicates how many digits make up the current group. The next element is read to determine the size of the next group of digits before the current group.

The *p_sign_posn* and *n_sign_posn* elements are set and interpreted as follows:

Value	Meaning
0	Use parantheses to surround the quantity and *currency_symbol*.
1	Sign string precedes the quantity and *currency_symbol*.
2	Sign string succeeds the quatity and *currency_symbol*.
3	Sign string immediately precedes the quantity and *currency_symbol*.
4	Sign string immediately succeeds the quantity and *currency_symbol*.

Return value

Returns a pointer to the filled-in structure of type **struct** *lconv*. The values in the structure will change whenever *setlocale* modifies the LC_MONETARY or LC_NUMERIC categories.

See also

setlocale

Portability

DOS	UNIX	Win 16	Win 32	ANSI C	ANSI C++	OS/2
+		+	+	+	+	+

localtime   time.h

Syntax

struct tm *localtime(const time_t *timer);

Description

Converts date and time to a structure.

localtime accepts the address of a value returned by *time* and returns a pointer to the structure of type *tm* containing the time elements. It corrects for the time zone and possible daylight saving time.

The global long variable *_timezone* contains the difference in seconds between GMT and local standard time (in PST, *_timezone* is 8 x 60 x 60). The global variable *_daylight* contains nonzero *only if* the standard U.S. daylight saving time conversion should be applied. These values are set by *tzset*, not by the user program directly.

This is the **tm** structure declaration from the time.h header file:

```
struct tm {
    int tm_sec;
    int tm_min;
    int tm_hour;
    int tm_mday;
    int tm_mon;
    int tm_year;
    int tm_wday;
    int tm_yday;
    int tm_isdst;
};
```

These quantities give the time on a 24-hour clock, day of month (1 to 31), month (0 to 11), weekday (Sunday equals 0), year - 1900, day of year (0 to 365), and a flag that is nonzero if daylight saving time is in effect.

Return value

localtime returns a pointer to the structure containing the time elements. This structure is a static that is overwritten with each call.

See also

asctime, ctime, ftime, gmtime, stime, time, tzset

Portability

DOS	UNIX	Win 16	Win 32	ANSI C	ANSI C++	OS/2
+	+	+	+	+	+	+

lock
io.h

Syntax

int lock(int handle, long offset, long length);

Description

Sets file-sharing locks. DOS users must be sure to load SHARE.EXE before using *lock*.

lock provides an interface to the operating system file-sharing mechanism.

A lock can be placed on arbitrary, nonoverlapping regions of any file. A program attempting to read or write into a locked region will retry the operation three times. If all three retries fail, the call fails with an error.

Return value

lock returns 0 on success. On error, *lock* returns -1 and sets the global variable *errno* to

EACCES   Locking violation

See also
locking, open, sopen, unlock

Portability

DOS	UNIX	Win 16	Win 32	ANSI C	ANSI C++	OS/2
+		+	+			+

locking

io.h, sys\locking.h

Syntax
int locking(int handle, int cmd, long length);

Description
Sets or resets file-sharing locks. DOS users must be sure to load SHARE.EXE before using *locking*.

locking provides an interface to the operating system file-sharing mechanism. The file to be locked or unlocked is the open file specified by *handle*. The region to be locked or unlocked starts at the current file position, and is *length* bytes long.

Locks can be placed on arbitrary, nonoverlapping regions of any file. A program attempting to read or write into a locked region will retry the operation three times. If all three retries fail, the call fails with an error.

The *cmd* specifies the action to be taken (the values are defined in sys\locking.h):

LK_LOCK	Lock the region. If the lock is unsuccessful, try once a second for 10 seconds before giving up.
LK_RLCK	Same as LK_LOCK.
LK_NBLCK	Lock the region. If the lock if unsuccessful, give up immediately.
LK_NBRLCK	Same as LK_NBLCK.
LK_UNLCK	Unlock the region, which must have been previously locked.

Return value
On successful operations, *locking* returns 0. Otherwise, it returns -1, and the global variable *errno* is set to one of the following values:

EACCES	File already locked or unlocked
EBADF	Bad file number
EDEADLOCK	File cannot be locked after 10 retries (*cmd* is LK_LOCK or LK_RLCK)
EINVAL	Invalid *cmd*, or SHARE.EXE not loaded

See also
_fsopen, lock, open, sopen, unlock

Portability

DOS	UNIX	Win 16	Win 32	ANSI C	ANSI C++	OS/2
+		+	+			+

log, logl

math.h

Syntax

double log(double x);
long double logl(long double x);

Description

Calculates the natural logarithm of *x*.

log calculates the natural logarithm of *x*.

logl is the **long double** version; it takes a **long double** argument and returns a **long double** result.

This function can be used with *bcd* and *complex* types.

Return value

On success, *log* and *logl* return the value calculated, *ln(x)*.

If the argument *x* passed to these functions is real and less than 0, the global variable *errno* is set to

EDOM   Domain error

If *x* is 0, the functions return the value negative HUGE_VAL (*log*) or negative _LHUGE_VAL (*logl*), and set *errno* to ERANGE. Error handling for these routines can be modified through the functions *_matherr* and *_matherrl*.

See also

bcd, complex, exp, log10, sqrt

Portability

	DOS	UNIX	Win 16	Win 32	ANSI C	ANSI C++	OS/2
log	+	+	+	+	+	+	+
logl	+		+	+			+

log10, log10l

math.h

Syntax

double log10(double x);
long double log10l(long double x);

Description
log10 calculates the base 10 logarithm of *x*.

log10l is the **long double** version; it takes a **long double** argument and returns a **long double** result.

This function can be used with *bcd* and *complex* types.

Return value
On success, *log10* (or *log10l*) returns the value calculated, $\log_{10}(x)$.
If the argument *x* passed to these functions is real and less than 0, the global variable *errno* is set to

EDOM   Domain error

If *x* is 0, these functions return the value negative HUGE_VAL (*log10*) or _LHUGE_VAL (*log10l*). Error handling for these routines can be modified through the functions *_matherr* and *_matherrl*.

See also
bcd, complex, exp, log

Portability

	DOS	UNIX	Win 16	Win 32	ANSI C	ANSI C++	OS/2
log10	+	+	+	+	+	+	+
log10l	+		+	+			+

longjmp   setjmp.h

Syntax
void longjmp(jmp_buf jmpb, int retval);

Description
Performs nonlocal goto.

A call to *longjmp* restores the task state captured by the last call to setjmp with the argument *jmpb*. It then returns in such a way that *setjmp* appears to have returned with the value *retval*.

A task state includes the following:

Win 16	Win 32
All segment registers CS, DS, ES, SS	No segment registers are saved
Register variables	Register variables
DI and SI	EBX, EDI, ESI
Stack pointer SP	Stack pointer ESP
Frame pointer BP	Frame pointer EBP
Flags	Flags are not saved

A task state is complete enough that *setjmp* and *longjmp* can be used to implement co-routines.

setjmp must be called before *longjmp*. The routine that called *setjmp* and set up *jmpb* must still be active and cannot have returned before the *longjmp* is called. If this happens, the results are unpredictable.

longjmp cannot pass the value 0; if 0 is passed in *retval*, *longjmp* will substitute 1.

DOS users

You cannot use *setjmp* and *longjmp* for implementing co-routines if your program is overlaid. Normally, *setjmp* and *longjmp* save and restore all the registers needed for co-routines, but the overlay manager needs to keep track of stack contents and assumes there is only one stack. When you implement co-routines, there are usually either two stacks or two partitions of one stack, and the overlay manager will not track them properly.

You can have background tasks that run with their own stacks or sections of stack, but you must ensure that the background tasks do not invoke any overlaid code, and you must not use the overlay versions of *setjmp* or *longjmp* to switch to and from background.

Return value
None.

See also
ctrlbrk, setjmp, signal

Portability

DOS	UNIX	Win 16	Win 32	ANSI C	ANSI C++	OS/2
+	+	+	+	+	+	+

lowvideo   conio.h

Syntax
void lowvideo(void);

Description
Selects low-intensity characters.

lowvideo selects low-intensity characters by clearing the high-intensity bit of the currently selected foreground color.

This function does not affect any characters currently onscreen. It affects only those characters displayed by functions that perform text mode, direct console output *after* this function is called.

Note   Do not use this function for Win32s or Win32 GUI applications.

Return value

None.

See also

highvideo, normvideo, textattr, textcolor

Portability

DOS	UNIX	Win 16	Win 32	ANSI C	ANSI C++	OS/2
+			+			+

_lrotl, _lrotr   stdlib.h

Syntax

unsigned long _lrotl(unsigned long val, int count);
unsigned long _lrotr(unsigned long val, int count);

Description

Rotates an **unsigned long** integer value to the left or right.

lrotl rotates the given *val* to the left *count* bits. *_lrotr* rotates the given *val* to the right *count* bits.

Return value

The functions return the rotated integer:

- *_lrotl* returns the value of *val* left-rotated *count* bits.
- *_lrotr* returns the value of *val* right-rotated *count* bits.

See also

_crotr, _crotl, _rotl, _rotr

Portability

DOS	UNIX	Win 16	Win 32	ANSI C	ANSI C++	OS/2
+		+	+			+

lsearch   stdlib.h

Syntax

void *lsearch(const void *key, void *base, size_t *num, size_t width,
int (_USERENTRY *fcmp)(const void *, const void *));

Description

Performs a linear search.

lsearch searches a table for information. Because this is a linear search, the table entries do not need to be sorted before a call to *lsearch*. If the item that *key* points to is not in the table, *lsearch* appends that item to the table.

- *base* points to the base (0th element) of the search table.
- *num* points to an integer containing the number of entries in the table.
- *width* contains the number of bytes in each entry.
- *key* points to the item to be searched for (the *search key*).

The function *fcmp* must be used with the _USERENTRY calling convention.

The argument *fcmp* points to a user-written comparison routine, that compares two items and returns a value based on the comparison.

To search the table, *lsearch* makes repeated calls to the routine whose address is passed in *fcmp*.

On each call to the comparison routine, *lsearch* passes two arguments:

- *key*—a pointer to the item being searched for
- *elem*—pointer to the element of *base* being compared

fcmp is free to interpret the search key and the table entries in any way.

Return value
lsearch returns the address of the first entry in the table that matches the search key.

If the search key is not identical to **elem*, *fcmp* returns a nonzero integer. If the search key is identical to **elem*, *fcmp* returns 0.

See also
bsearch, lfind, qsort

Portability

DOS	UNIX	Win 16	Win 32	ANSI C	ANSI C++	OS/2
+	+	+	+			+

lseek   io.h

Syntax
long lseek(int handle, long offset, int fromwhere);

Description
Moves file pointer.

lseek sets the file pointer associated with *handle* to a new position *offset* bytes beyond the file location given by *fromwhere*. *fromwhere* must be one of the following symbolic constants (defined in io.h):

fromwhere	File location
SEEK_CUR	Current file pointer position
SEEK_END	End-of-file
SEEK_SET	File beginning

Return value

lseek returns the offset of the pointer's new position measured in bytes from the file beginning. *lseek* returns -1L on error, and the global variable *errno* is set to one of the following values:

EBADF	Bad file handle
EINVAL	Invalid argument
ESPIPE	Illegal seek on device

On devices incapable of seeking (such as terminals and printers), the return value is undefined.

See also

filelength, fseek, ftell, getc, open, sopen, ungetc, _rtl_write, write

Portability

DOS	UNIX	Win 16	Win 32	ANSI C	ANSI C++	OS/2
+	+	+	+			+

ltoa   stdlib.h

Syntax

char *ltoa(long value, char *string, int radix);

Description

Converts a **long** to a string.

ltoa converts *value* to a null-terminated string and stores the result in *string*. *value* is a long integer.

radix specifies the base to be used in converting *value*; it must be between 2 and 36, inclusive. If *value* is negative and *radix* is 10, the first character of *string* is the minus sign (-).

Note   The space allocated for *string* must be large enough to hold the returned string, including the terminating null character (\0). *ltoa* can return up to 33 bytes.

Return value

ltoa returns a pointer to *string*.

See also

itoa, ultoa

Portability

DOS	UNIX	Win 16	Win 32	ANSI C	ANSI C++	OS/2
+		+	+			+

_makepath   stdlib.h

Syntax

void _makepath(char *path, const char *drive, const char *dir, const char *name, const char *ext);

Description

Builds a path from component parts.

_makepath makes a path name from its components. The new path name is

```
X:\DIR\SUBDIR\NAME.EXT
```

where

drive	=	X:
dir	=	\DIR\SUBDIR\
name	=	NAME
ext	=	.EXT

If *drive* is empty or NULL, no drive is inserted in the path name. If it is missing a trailing colon (:), a colon is inserted in the path name.

If *dir* is empty or NULL, no directory is inserted in the path name. If it is missing a trailing slash (\ or /), a backslash is inserted in the path name.

If *name* is empty or NULL, no file name is inserted in the path name.

If *ext* is empty or NULL, no extension is inserted in the path name. If it is missing a leading period (.), a period is inserted in the path name.

_makepath assumes there is enough space in *path* for the constructed path name. The maximum constructed length is _MAX_PATH. _MAX_PATH is defined in stdlib.h.

_makepath and *_splitpath* are invertible; if you split a given *path* with *_splitpath*, then merge the resultant components with *_makepath*, you end up with *path*.

Return value

None.

See also

_fullpath, _splitpath

Portability

DOS	UNIX	Win 16	Win 32	ANSI C	ANSI C++	OS/2
+		+	+			+

malloc

stdlib.h or alloc.h

Syntax
void *malloc(size_t size);

Description
malloc allocates a block of *size* bytes from the memory heap. It allows a program to allocate memory explicitly as it's needed, and in the exact amounts needed.

Allocates main memory. The heap is used for dynamic allocation of variable-sized blocks of memory. Many data structures, for example, trees and lists, naturally employ heap memory allocation.

For 16-bit programs, all the space between the end of the data segment and the top of the program stack is available for use in the small data models, except for a small margin immediately before the top of the stack. This margin is intended to allow the application some room to make the stack larger, in addition to a small amount needed by DOS.

In the large data models, all the space beyond the program stack to the end of available memory is available for the heap.

Return value
On success, *malloc* returns a pointer to the newly allocated block of memory. If not enough space exists for the new block, it returns NULL. The contents of the block are left unchanged. If the argument *size == 0*, *malloc* returns NULL.

See also
calloc, *farcalloc*, *farmalloc*, *free*, *realloc*

Portability

DOS	UNIX	Win 16	Win 32	ANSI C	ANSI C++	OS/2
+	+	+	+	+	+	+

_matherr, _matherrl

math.h

Syntax
int _matherr(struct _exception *e);
int _matherrl(struct _exceptionl *e);

Description

User-modifiable math error handler.

_matherr is called when an error is generated by the math library.

_matherrl is the **long double** version; it is called when an error is generated by the *long double* math functions.

_matherr and *_matherrl* each serve as a user hook (a function that can be customized by the user) that you can replace by writing your own math error-handling routine.

_matherr and *_matherrl* are useful for information on trapping domain and range errors caused by the math functions. They do not trap floating-point exceptions, such as division by zero. See *signal* for information on trapping such errors.

You can define your own *_matherr* or *_matherrl* routine to be a custom error handler (such as one that catches and resolves certain types of errors); this customized function overrides the default version in the C library. The customized *_matherr* or *_matherrl* should return 0 if it fails to resolve the error, or nonzero if the error is resolved. When *_matherr* or *_matherrl* return nonzero, no error message is printed and the global variable *errno* is not changed.

Here are the *_exception* and *_exceptionl* structures (defined in math.h):

```
struct _exception {
    int    type;
    char   *name;
    double arg1, arg2, retval;
};

struct _exceptionl {
    int    type;
    char   *name;
    long double arg1, arg2, retval;
};
```

The members of the *_exception* and *_exceptionl* structures are as follows:

Member	What it is (or represents)
type	The type of mathematical error that occurred; an enum type defined in the typedef *_mexcep* (see definition after this list).
name	A pointer to a null-terminated string holding the name of the math library function that resulted in an error.
arg1, arg2	The arguments (passed to the function that name points to) caused the error; if only one argument was passed to the function, it is stored in *arg1*.
retval	The default return value for *_matherr* (or *_matherrl*); you can modify this value.

The **typedef** *_mexcep*, also defined in math.h, enumerates the following symbolic constants representing possible mathematical errors:

Symbolic constant	Mathematical error
DOMAIN	Argument was not in domain of function, such as *log*(-1).
SING	Argument would result in a singularity, such as *pow*(0, -2).

Symbolic constant	Mathematical error
OVERFLOW	Argument would produce a function result greater than DBL_MAX (or LDBL_MAX), such as *exp*(1000).
UNDERFLOW	Argument would produce a function result less than DBL_MIN (or LDBL_MIN), such as *exp*(-1000).
TLOSS	Argument would produce function result with total loss of significant digits, such as *sin*(10e70).

The macros DBL_MAX, DBL_MIN, LDBL_MAX, and LDBL_MIN are defined in float.h.

The source code to the default *_matherr* and *_matherrl* is on the Borland C++ distribution disks.

The UNIX-style *_matherr* and *_matherrl* default behavior (printing a message and terminating) is not ANSI-compatible. If you want a UNIX-style version of these routines, use MATHERR.C and MATHERRL.C provided on the Borland C++ distribution disks.

Return value

The default return value for *_matherr* and *_matherrl* is 1 if the error is UNDERFLOW or TLOSS, 0 otherwise. *_matherr* and *_matherrl* can also modify *e -> retval*, which propagates back to the original caller.

When *_matherr* and *_matherrl* return 0 (indicating that they were not able to resolve the error), the global variable *errno* is set to 0 and an error message is printed.

When *_matherr* and *_matherrl* return nonzero (indicating that they were able to resolve the error), the global variable *errno* is not set and no messages are printed.

Portability

DOS	UNIX	Win 16	Win 32	ANSI C	ANSI C++	OS/2
+		+	+			+

max

stdlib.h

Syntax
```
(type) max(a, b);
template <class T> T max( T t1, T t2 ); // C++ only
```

Description
Returns the larger of two values.

The C macro and the C++ template function compare two values and return the larger of the two. Both arguments and the routine declaration must be of the same type.

Return value
max returns the larger of two values.

See also
min

Portability

DOS	UNIX	Win 16	Win 32	ANSI C	ANSI C++	OS/2
+		+	+			+

mblen   stdlib.h

Syntax
int mblen(const char *s, size_t n);

Description
Determines the length of a multibyte character.

If *s* is not null, *mblen* determines the number of bytes in the multibyte character pointed to by *s*. The maximum number of bytes examined is specified by *n*.

The behavior of *mblen* is affected by the setting of LC_CTYPE category of the current locale.

Return value
If *s* is null, *mblen* returns a nonzero value if multibyte characters have state-dependent encodings. Otherwise, *mblen* returns 0.

If *s* is not null, *mblen* returns 0 if *s* points to the null character, and -1 if the next *n* bytes do not comprise a valid multibyte character.

See also
mbstowcs, mbtowc, setlocale

Portability

DOS	UNIX	Win 16	Win 32	ANSI C	ANSI C++	OS/2
+		+	+	+	+	+

mbstowcs   stdlib.h

Syntax
size_t mbstowcs(wchar_t *pwcs, const char *s, size_t n);

Description
Converts a multibyte string to a **wchar_t** array.

The function converts the multibyte string *s* into the array pointed to by *pwcs*. No more than *n* values are stored in the array. If an invalid multibyte sequence is encountered, *mbstowcs* returns (*size_t*) -1.

The *pwcs* array will not be terminated with a zero value if *mbstowcs* returns *n*.

Return value

If an invalid multibyte sequence is encountered, *mbstowcs* returns (*size_t*) -1. Otherwise, the function returns the number of array elements modified, not including the terminating code, if any.

See also

mblen, mbtowc, setlocale

Portability

DOS	UNIX	Win 16	Win 32	ANSI C	ANSI C++	OS/2
+		+	+	+	+	+

mbtowc   stdlib.h

Syntax

```
int mbtowc(wchar_t *pwc, const char *s, size_t n);
```

Description

Converts a multibyte character to **wchar_t** code.

If *s* is not null, *mbtowc* determines the number of bytes that comprise the multibyte character pointed to by *s*. Next, *mbtowc* determines the value of the type **wchar_t** that corresponds to that multibyte character. If there is a successful match between **wchar_t** and the multibyte character, and *pwc* is not null, the **wchar_t** value is stored in the array pointed to by *pwc*. At most *n* characters are examined.

Return value

When *s* points to an invalid multibyte character, -1 is returned. When *s* points to the null character, 0 is returned. Otherwise, *mbtowc* returns the number of bytes that comprise the converted multibyte character.

The return value never exceeds MB_CUR_MAX or the value of *n*.

See also

mblen, mbstowcs, setlocale

Portability

DOS	UNIX	Win 16	Win 32	ANSI C	ANSI C++	OS/2
+		+	+	+	+	+

memccpy, _fmemccpy

mem.h

Syntax

```
void *memccpy(void *dest, const void *src, int c, size_t n);
void far * far _fmemccpy(void far *dest, const void far *src, int c, size_t n)
```

Description

Copies a block of *n* bytes.

memccpy is available on UNIX System V systems.

memccpy copies a block of *n* bytes from *src* to *dest*. The copying stops as soon as either of the following occurs:

- The character *c* is first copied into *dest*.
- *n* bytes have been copied into *dest*.

Return value

memccpy returns a pointer to the byte in *dest* immediately following *c*, if *c* was copied; otherwise, *memccpy* returns NULL.

See also

memcpy, memmove, memset

Portability

	DOS	UNIX	Win 16	Win 32	ANSI C	ANSI C++	OS/2
memccpy	+	+	+	+			+
_fmemccpy	+		+				

memchr, _fmemchr

mem.h

Syntax

```
void *memchr(const void *s, int c, size_t n);                        /* C only */
void far * far _fmemchr(const void far *s, int c, size_t n);         /* C only*/

const void *memchr(const void *s, int c, size_t n);                 // C++ only
void *memchr(void *s, int c, size_t n);                             // C++ only
const void far * far _fmemchr(const void far *s, int c, size_t n);  //C++ only
void far * far _fmemchr(void far *s, int c, size_t n);              // C++ only
void *memchr(const void *s, int c, size_t n);
void far * far _fmemchr(const void far *s, int c, size_t n);
```

Description

Searches *n* bytes for character *c*.

memchr is available on UNIX System V systems.

memchr searches the first *n* bytes of the block pointed to by *s* for character *c*.

Return value

On success, *memchr* returns a pointer to the first occurrence of *c* in *s*; otherwise, it returns NULL.

Note   If you are using the intrinsic version of these functions, the case of *n* = 0 will return NULL.

Portability

	DOS	UNIX	Win 16	Win 32	ANSI C	ANSI C++	OS/2
memchr	+	+	+	+	+	+	+
_fmemchr	+		+				

memcmp, _fmemcmp   mem.h

Syntax
```
int memcmp(const void *s1, const void *s2, size_t n);
int far _fmemcmp(const void far *s1, const void far *s2, size_t n)
```

Description
Compares two blocks for a length of exactly *n* bytes.

memcmp is available on UNIX System V systems.

memcmp compares the first *n* bytes of the blocks *s1* and *s2* as **unsigned char**s.

Return value
Because it compares bytes as **unsigned char**s, *memcmp* returns a value that is

- < 0 if *s1* is less than *s2*
- = 0 if *s1* is the same as *s2*
- > 0 if *s1* is greater than *s2*

For example,
```
memcmp("\xFF", "\x7F", 1)
```

returns a value greater than 0.

Note   If you are using the intrinsic version of these functions, the case of *n* = 0 will return NULL.

See also
memicmp

Portability

	DOS	UNIX	Win 16	Win 32	ANSI C	ANSI C++	OS/2
memcmp	+	+	+	+	+	+	+
_fmemcmp	+		+				

memcpy, _fmemcpy

mem.h

Syntax
void *memcpy(void *dest, const void *src, size_t n);
void far *far _fmemcpy(void far *dest, const void far *src, size_t n);

Description
Copies a block of *n* bytes.

memcpy is available on UNIX System V systems.

memcpy copies a block of *n* bytes from *src* to *dest*. If *src* and *dest* overlap, the behavior of *memcpy* is undefined.

Return value
memcpy returns *dest*.

See also
memccpy, memmove, memset, movedata, movmem

Portability

	DOS	UNIX	Win 16	Win 32	ANSI C	ANSI C++	OS/2
memcpy	+	+	+	+	+	+	+
_fmemcpy	+		+				

memicmp, _fmemicmp

mem.h

Syntax
int memicmp(const void *s1, const void *s2, size_t n);
int far _fmemicmp(const void far *s1, const void far *s2, size_t n)

Description
Compares *n* bytes of two character arrays, ignoring case.

memicmp is available on UNIX System V systems.

memicmp compares the first *n* bytes of the blocks *s1* and *s2*, ignoring character case (upper or lower).

Return value

memicmp returns a value that is

- < 0 if *s1* is less than *s2*
- = 0 if *s1* is the same as *s2*
- > 0 if *s1* is greater than *s2*

See also

memcmp

Portability

	DOS	UNIX	Win 16	Win 32	ANSI C	ANSI C++	OS/2
memicmp	+	+	+	+			+
_fmemicmp	+		+				

memmove, _fmemmove   mem.h

Syntax

```
void *memmove(void *dest, const void *src, size_t n);
void far * far _fmemmove (void far *dest, const void far *src, size_t n)
```

Description

Copies a block of *n* bytes.

memmove copies a block of *n* bytes from *src* to *dest*. Even when the source and destination blocks overlap, bytes in the overlapping locations are copied correctly.

_fmemmove is the far version.

Return value

memmove and *_fmemmove* return *dest*.

See also

memccpy, memcpy, movmem

Portability

	DOS	UNIX	Win 16	Win 32	ANSI C	ANSI C++	OS/2
memmove	+	+	+	+	+	+	+
_fmemmove	+		+				

memset, _fmemset   mem.h

Syntax

```
void *memset(void *s, int c, size_t n);
```

void far * far _fmemset (void far *s, int c, size_t n)

Description
Sets *n* bytes of a block of memory to byte *c*.

memset sets the first *n* bytes of the array *s* to the character *c*.

Return value
memset returns *s*.

See also
memccpy, memcpy, setmem

Portability

	DOS	UNIX	Win 16	Win 32	ANSI C	ANSI C++	OS/2
memset	+	+	+	+	+	+	+
_fmemset	+		+				

min   stdlib.h

Syntax
(type) min(a, b);
template <class T> T min(T t1, T t2); // C++ only

Description
Returns the smaller of two values.

The C macro and the C++ template function compare two values and return the smaller of the two. Both arguments and the routine declaration must be of the same type.

Return value
min returns the smaller of two values.

See also
max

Portability

DOS	UNIX	Win 16	Win 32	ANSI C	ANSI C++	OS/2
+	+	+				+

mkdir   dir.h

Syntax
int mkdir(const char *path);

Description

Creates a directory.

mkdir is available on UNIX, though it then takes an additional parameter.

mkdir creates a new directory from the given path name *path*.

Return value

mkdir returns the value 0 if the new directory was created.

A return value of -1 indicates an error, and the global variable *errno* is set to one of the following values:

EACCES   Permission denied

ENOENT   No such file or directory

See also

chdir, getcurdir, getcwd, rmdir

Portability

DOS	UNIX	Win 16	Win 32	ANSI C	ANSI C++	OS/2
+	+	+	+			+

MK_FP   dos.h

Syntax

void far * MK_FP(unsigned seg, unsigned ofs);

Description

Makes a **far** pointer.

MK_FP is a macro that makes a **far** pointer from its component segment (*seg*) and offset (*ofs*) parts.

Return value

MK_FP returns a **far** pointer.

See also

FP_OFF, FP_SEG, movedata, segread

Portability

DOS	UNIX	Win 16	Win 32	ANSI C	ANSI C++	OS/2
+	.	+				

mktemp

dir.h

Syntax

char *mktemp(char *template);

Description

Makes a unique file name.

mktemp replaces the string pointed to by *template* with a unique file name and returns *template*.

template should be a null-terminated string with six trailing Xs. These Xs are replaced with a unique collection of letters plus a period, so that there are two letters, a period, and three suffix letters in the new file name.

Starting with AA.AAA, the new file name is assigned by looking up the name on the disk and avoiding pre-existing names of the same format.

Return value

If *template* is well-formed, *mktemp* returns the address of the *template* string. Otherwise, it returns null.

Portability

DOS	UNIX	Win 16	Win 32	ANSI C	ANSI C++	OS/2
+	+	+	+			+

mktime

time.h

Syntax

time_t mktime(struct tm *t);

Description

Converts time to calendar format.

Converts the time in the structure pointed to by *t* into a calendar time with the same format used by the *time* function. The original values of the fields *tm_sec*, *tm_min*, *tm_hour*, *tm_mday*, and *tm_mon* are not restricted to the ranges described in the *tm* structure. If the fields are not in their proper ranges, they are adjusted. Values for fields *tm_wday* and *tm_yday* are computed after the other fields have been adjusted.

The allowable range of calendar times is Jan 1 1970 00:00:00 to Jan 19 2038 03:14:07.

Return value

On success, *mktime* returns calendar time as described above.

On error (if the calendar time cannot be represented), *mktime* returns -1.

See also
localtime, strftime, time

Portability

DOS	UNIX	Win 16	Win 32	ANSI C	ANSI C++	OS/2
+		+	+	+	+	+

modf, modfl   math.h

Syntax
double modf(double x, double *ipart);
long double modfl(long double x, long double *ipart);

Description
Splits a **double** or **long double** into integer and fractional parts.

modf breaks the **double** x into two parts: the integer and the fraction. *modf* stores the integer in *ipart* and returns the fraction.

modfl is the **long double** version; it takes **long double** arguments and returns a **long double** result.

Return value
modf and *modfl* return the fractional part of x.

See also
fmod, ldexp

Portability

	DOS	UNIX	Win 16	Win 32	ANSI C	ANSI C++	OS/2
modf	+	+	+	+	+	+	+
modfl	+		+	+			+

movedata   mem.h

Syntax
void movedata(unsigned srcseg, unsigned srcoff, unsigned dstseg, unsigned dstoff, size_t n);

Description
Copies n bytes.

movedata copies n bytes from the source address (*srcseg:srcoff*) to the destination address (*dstseg:dstoff*). *movedata* provides a memory-model independent means for moving blocks of data.

Return value

None.

See also

FP_OFF, memcpy, MK_FP, movmem, segread

Portability

DOS	UNIX	Win 16	Win 32	ANSI C	ANSI C++	OS/2
+		+				

movmem, _fmovmem   mem.h

Syntax

```
void movmem(const void *src, void *dest, unsigned length);
void _fmovmem(const void far *src, void far *dest, unsigned length);
```

Description

Moves a block of *length* bytes.

movmem moves a block of *length* bytes from *src* to *dest*. Even if the source and destination blocks overlap, the move direction is chosen so that the data is always moved correctly.

_fmovmem is the far version.

Return value

None.

See also

memcpy, memmove, movedata

Portability

DOS	UNIX	Win 16	Win 32	ANSI C	ANSI C++	OS/2
+		+				

movetext   conio.h

Syntax

```
int movetext(int left, int top, int right, int bottom, int destleft, int desttop);
```

Description

Copies text onscreen from one rectangle to another.

movetext copies the contents of the onscreen rectangle defined by *left, top, right,* and *bottom* to a new rectangle of the same dimensions. The new rectangle's upper left corner is position (*destleft, desttop*).

All coordinates are absolute screen coordinates. Rectangles that overlap are moved correctly.

movetext is a text mode function performing direct video output.

Note   Do not use this function for Win32s or Win32 GUI applications.

Return value
On success, *movetext* returns nonzero.

On error (for example, if it failed because you gave coordinates outside the range of the current screen mode), *movetext* returns 0.

See also
gettext, puttext

Portability

DOS	UNIX	Win 16	Win 32	ANSI C	ANSI C++	OS/2
+			+			+

_msize   malloc.h

Syntax
size_t _msize(void *block);

Description
Returns the size of a heap block.

_msize returns the size of the allocated heap block whose address is *block*. The block must have been allocated with *malloc, calloc,* or *realloc*. The returned size can be larger than the number of bytes originally requested when the block was allocated.

Return value
_msize returns the size of the block in bytes.

See also
malloc, free, realloc

Portability

DOS	UNIX	Win 16	Win 32	ANSI C	ANSI C++	OS/2
			+			+

normvideo

conio.h

Syntax

void normvideo(void);

Description

Selects normal-intensity characters.

normvideo selects normal characters by returning the text attribute (foreground and background) to the value it had when the program started.

This function does not affect any characters currently on the screen, only those displayed by functions (such as *cprintf*) performing direct console output functions after *normvideo* is called.

Note Do not use this function for Win32s or Win32 GUI applications.

Return value

None.

See also

highvideo, lowvideo, textattr, textcolor

Portability

DOS	UNIX	Win 16	Win 32	ANSI C	ANSI C++	OS/2
+			+			+

offsetof

stddef.h

Syntax

size_t offsetof(struct_type, struct_member);

Description

Gets the byte offset to a structure member.

offsetof is available only as a macro. The argument *struct_type* is a **struct** type. *struct_member* is any element of the **struct** that can be accessed through the member selection operators or pointers.

If *struct_member* is a bit field, the result is undefined.

See also Chapter 2 in the *C++ Programmer's Guide* for a discussion of the **sizeof** operator, memory allocation, and alignment of structures.

Return value

offsetof returns the number of bytes from the start of the structure to the start of the named structure member.

Portability

DOS	UNIX	Win 16	Win 32	ANSI C	ANSI C++	OS/2
+	+	+	+	+	+	+

open

fcntl.h, io.h

Syntax

int open(const char *path, int access [, unsigned mode]);

Description

Opens a file for reading or writing.

open opens the file specified by *path*, then prepares it for reading and/or writing as determined by the value of *access*.

To create a file in a particular mode, you can either assign to the global variable *_fmode* or call *open* with the O_CREAT and O_TRUNC options ORed with the translation mode desired.

For example, the call

```
open("XMP",O_CREAT|O_TRUNC|O_BINARY,S_IREAD)
```

creates a binary-mode, read-only file named XMP, truncating its length to 0 bytes if it already existed.

For *open*, *access* is constructed by bitwise ORing flags from the following lists. Only one flag from the first list can be used (and one *must* be used); the remaining flags can be used in any logical combination.

These symbolic constants are defined in fcntl.h.

Read/Write Flags

O_RDONLY	Open for reading only.
O_WRONLY	Open for writing only.
O_RDWR	Open for reading and writing.

Other Access Flags

O_NDELAY	Not used; for UNIX compatibility.
O_APPEND	If set, the file pointer will be set to the end of the file prior to each write.
O_CREAT	If the file exists, this flag has no effect. If the file does not exist, the file is created, and the bits of *mode* are used to set the file attribute bits as in *chmod*.
O_TRUNC	If the file exists, its length is truncated to 0. The file attributes remain unchanged.

O_EXCL	Used only with O_CREAT. If the file already exists, an error is returned.
O_BINARY	Can be given to explicitly open the file in binary mode.
O_TEXT	Can be given to explicitly open the file in text mode.

If neither O_BINARY nor O_TEXT is given, the file is opened in the translation mode set by the global variable _fmode_.

If the O_CREAT flag is used in constructing access, you need to supply the *mode* argument to *open* from the following symbolic constants defined in sys\stat.h:

Value of mode	Access permission
S_IWRITE	Permission to write
S_IREAD	Permission to read
S_IREAD I S_IWRITE	Permission to read and write

Return value
On success, *open* returns a nonnegative integer (the file handle). The file pointer, which marks the current position in the file, is set to the beginning of the file.

On error, *open* returns -1 and the global variable *errno* is set to one of the following values:

EACCES	Permission denied
EINVACC	Invalid access code
EMFILE	Too many open files
ENOENT	No such file or directory

See also
chmod, chsize, close, creat, creatnew, creattemp, dup, dup2, fdopen, filelength, fopen, freopen, getftime, lock, lseek, _open_osfhandle, read, _rtl_creat, _rtl_open, _rtl_write, sopen, write

Portability

DOS	UNIX	Win 16	Win 32	ANSI C	ANSI C++	OS/2
+	+	+	+			+

opendir

dirent.h

Syntax
DIR *opendir(char *dirname);

Description
Opens a directory stream for reading.

opendir is available on POSIX-compliant UNIX systems.

The *opendir* function opens a directory stream for reading. The name of the directory to read is *dirname*. The stream is set to read the first entry in the directory.

A directory stream is represented by the *DIR* structure, defined in dirent.h. This structure contains no user-accessible fields. Multiple directory streams can be opened and read simultaneously. Directory entries can be created or deleted while a directory stream is being read.

Use the *readdir* function to read successive entries from a directory stream. Use the *closedir* function to remove a directory stream when it is no longer needed.

Return value
On success, *opendir* returns a pointer to a directory stream that can be used in calls to *readdir*, *rewinddir*, and *closedir*.

On error (If the directory cannot be opened), it returns NULL and sets the global variable *errno* to

ENOENT   The directory does not exist

ENOMEM   Not enough memory to allocate a DIR object

See also
closedir, readdir, rewinddir

Portability

DOS	UNIX	Win 16	Win 32	ANSI C	ANSI C++	OS/2
+	+	+	+			+

_open_osfhandle   io.h

Syntax
int _open_osfhandle(long osfhandle, int flags);

Description
Associates file handles.

The *_open_osfhandle* function allocates a run-time file handle and sets it to point to the operating system file handle specified by *osfhandle*.

The value *flags* is a bitwise OR combination of one or more of the following manifest constants (defined in fcntl.h):

O_APPEND   Repositions the file pointer to the end of the file before every
              write operation.

O_RDONLY   Opens the file for reading only.

O_TEXT   Opens the file in text (translated) mode.

Return value
On success, _open_osfhandle returns a C run-time file handle. Otherwise, it returns -1.

See also
_get_osfhandle, open

Portability

DOS	UNIX	Win 16	Win 32	ANSI C	ANSI C++	OS/2
			+			

outp
conio.h

Syntax
int outp(unsigned portid, int value);

Description
Outputs a byte to a hardware port.

outp is a macro that writes the low byte of *value* to the output port specified by *portid*.

If *outp* is called when conio.h has been included, it will be treated as a macro that expands to inline code. If you don't include conio.h, or if you do include conio.h and #undef the macro *outp*, you'll get the *outp* function.

Return value
outp returns *value*.

See also
inp, inpw, outpw

Portability

DOS	UNIX	Win 16	Win 32	ANSI C	ANSI C++	OS/2
+		+				

outport, outportb
dos.h

Syntax
void outport(int portid, int value);
void outportb(int portid, unsigned char value);

Description
Outputs a word or byte to a hardware port.

outport works just like the 80x86 instruction OUT. It writes the low byte of the word given by *value* to the output port specified by *portid* and writes the high byte of the word to *portid* +1.

outportb is a macro that writes the byte given by *value* to the output port specified by *portid*.

If you include dos.h, *outportb* will be treated as a macro that expands to inline code. If you do not include dos.h, or if you include dos.h and #undef the macro *outportb*, you will get the *outportb* function.

Return value
None.

See also
inport, inportb

Portability

DOS	UNIX	Win 16	Win 32	ANSI C	ANSI C++	OS/2
+		+				

outpw   conio.h

Syntax
unsigned outpw(unsigned portid, unsigned value);

Description
Outputs a word to a hardware port.

outpw is a macro that writes the 16-bit word given by *value* to the output port specified by *portid*. It writes the low byte of *value* to *portid*, and the high byte of the word to *portid* +1, using a single 16-bit *OUT* instruction.

If *outpw* is called when conio.h has been included, it will be treated as a macro that expands to inline code. If you don't include conio.h, or if you do include conio.h and #undef the macro *outpw*, you'll get the *outpw* function.

Return value
outpw returns *value*.

See also
inp, inpw, outp

Portability

DOS	UNIX	Win 16	Win 32	ANSI C	ANSI C++	OS/2
+		+				

parsfnm

dos.h

Syntax
char *parsfnm(const char *cmdline, struct fcb *fcb, int opt);

Description
Parses the file name.

parsfnm parses a string pointed to by *cmdline* for a file name. The string is normally a command line. The file name is placed in a file control block (FCB) as a drive, file name, and extension. The FCB is pointed to by *fcb*.

The *opt* parameter is the value documented for AL in the DOS parse system call. See your DOS reference manuals under system call 0x29 for a description of the parsing operations performed on the file name.

Return value
On success, *parsfnm* returns a pointer to the next byte after the end of the file name.

On error (in parsing the file name), *parsfnm* returns null.

Portability

DOS	UNIX	Win 16	Win 32	ANSI C	ANSI C++	OS/2
+		+				

_pclose

stdio.h

Syntax
int _pclose(FILE * stream);

Description
Waits for piped command to complete.

_pclose closes a pipe stream created by a previous call to *_popen*, and then waits for the associated child command to complete.

Return value
On success, *_pclose* returns the termination status of the child command. This is the same value as the termination status returned by *cwait*, except that the high and low order bytes of the low word are swapped.

On error, it returns -1.

See also
_pipe, _popen

Portability

DOS	UNIX	Win 16	Win 32	ANSI C	ANSI C++	OS/2
			+			+

peek   dos.h

Syntax
int peek(unsigned segment, unsigned offset);

Description
Returns the word at memory location specified by *segment:offset*.

peek returns the word at the memory location *segment:offset*.

If *peek* is called when dos.h has been included, it is treated as a macro that expands to inline code. If you don't include dos.h, or if you do include it and #undef *peek*, you'll get the function rather than the macro.

Return value
peek returns the word of data stored at the memory location *segment:offset*.

See also
peekb, poke

Portability

DOS	UNIX	Win 16	Win 32	ANSI C	ANSI C++	OS/2
+		+				

peekb   dos.h

Syntax
char peekb(unsigned segment, unsigned offset);

Description
Returns the byte of memory specified by *segment:offset*.

peekb returns the byte at the memory location addressed by *segment:offset*.

If *peekb* is called when dos.h has been included, it is treated as a macro that expands to inline code. If you don't include dos.h, or if you do include it and #undef *peekb*, you'll get the function rather than the macro.

Return value

peekb returns the byte of information stored at the memory location *segment:offset*.

See also

peek, pokeb

Portability

DOS	UNIX	Win 16	Win 32	ANSI C	ANSI C++	OS/2
+		+				

perror

stdio.h

Syntax

```
void perror(const char *s);
```

Description

Prints a system error message.

perror prints to the *stderr* stream (normally the console) the system error message for the last library routine that set the global variable *errno*.

It prints the argument *s* followed by a colon (:) and the message corresponding to the current value of the global variable *errno* and finally a new line. The convention is to pass the file name of the program as the argument string.

The array of error message strings is accessed through the global variable *_sys_errlist*. The global variable *errno* can be used as an index into the array to find the string corresponding to the error number. None of the strings include a newline character.

The global variable *_sys_nerr* contains the number of entries in the array.

The following messages are generated by *perror*:

Table 3.1   Win 16 and Win 32 messages

Arg list too big	Math argument
Attempted to remove current directory	Memory arena trashed
Bad address	Name too long
Bad file number	No child processes
Block device required	No more files
Broken pipe	No space left on device
Cross-device link	No such device
Error 0	No such device or address
Exec format error	No such file or directory
Executable file in use	No such process
File already exists	Not a directory
File too large	Not enough memory
Illegal seek	Not same device
Inappropriate I/O control operation	Operation not permitted
Input/output error	Path not found

Table 3.1   Win 16 and Win 32 messages

Interrupted function call	Permission denied
Invalid access code	Possible deadlock
Invalid argument Resource busy	Read-only file system
Invalid dataResource temporarily unavailable	Resource busy
Invalid environment	Resource temporarily unavailable
Invalid format	Result too large
Invalid function number	Too many links
Invalid memory block address	Too many open files
Is a directory	

Table 3.2   Win 32 only messages

Bad address	No child processes
Block device required	No space left on device
Broken pipe	No such device or address
Executable file in use	No such process
File too large	Not a directory
Illegal seek	Operation not permitted
Inappropriate I/O control	Possible deadlock
Input/output error	Read-only file system
Interrupted function call	Resource busy
Is a directory	Resource temporarily unavailable
Name too long	Too many links

Note   For Win32s or Win32 GUI applications, *stderr* must be redirected.

See also
clearerr, eof, freopen, _strerror, strerror

Portability

DOS	UNIX	Win 16	Win 32	ANSI C	ANSI C++	OS/2
+	+		+	+	+	+

_pipe   fcntl.h, io.h

Syntax
int _pipe(int *handles, unsigned int size, int mode);

Description
Creates a read/write pipe.

The *_pipe* function creates an anonymous pipe that can be used to pass information between processes. The pipe is opened for both reading and writing. Like a disk file, a pipe can be read from and written to, but it does not have a name or permanent storage associated with it; data written to and from the pipe exist only in a memory buffer managed by the operating system.

The read handle is returned to *handles*[0], and the write handle is returned to *handles*[1]. The program can use these handles in subsequent calls to *read*, *write*, *dup*, *dup2*, or *close*. When all pipe handles are closed, the pipe is destroyed.

The size of the internal pipe buffer is *size*. A recommended minimum value is 512 bytes.

The translation mode is specified by *mode*, as follows:

O_BINARY The pipe is opened in binary mode

O_TEXT The pipe is opened in text mode

If *mode* is zero, the translation mode is determined by the external variable *_fmode*.

Return value
On success, *_pipe* returns 0 and returns the pipe handles to *handles*[0] and *handles*[1].

On error, it returns -1 and sets *errno* to one of the following values:

EMFILE Too many open files

ENOMEM Out of memory

See also
_pclose, *_popen*

Portability

DOS	UNIX	Win 16	Win 32	ANSI C	ANSI C++	OS/2
			+			+

poke   dos.h

Syntax
void poke(unsigned segment, unsigned offset, int value);

Description
Stores an integer value at a memory location given by *segment:offset*.

poke stores the integer *value* at the memory location *segment:offset*.

If this routine is called when dos.h has been included, it will be treated as a macro that expands to inline code. If you don't include dos.h, or if you do include it and #undef *poke*, you'll get the function rather than the macro.

Return value
None.

See also

peek, pokeb

Portability

DOS	UNIX	Win 16	Win 32	ANSI C	ANSI C++	OS/2
+		+				

pokeb   dos.h

Syntax

void pokeb(unsigned segment, unsigned offset, char value);

Description

Stores a byte value at memory location *segment:offset*.

pokeb stores the byte *value* at the memory location *segment:offset*.

If this routine is called when dos.h has been included, it will be treated as a macro that expands to inline code. If you don't include dos.h, or if you do include it and #undef *pokeb*, you'll get the function rather than the macro.

Return value

None.

See also

peekb, poke

Portability

DOS	UNIX	Win 16	Win 32	ANSI C	ANSI C++	OS/2
+		+				

poly, polyl   math.h

Syntax

double poly(double x, int degree, double coeffs[]);
long double polyl(long double x, int degree, long double coeffs[]);

Description

Generates a polynomial from arguments.

poly generates a polynomial in *x*, of degree *degree*, with coefficients *coeffs[0]*, *coeffs[1]*, ..., *coeffs[degree]*. For example, if *n* = 4, the generated polynomial is:

$$coeffs[4]\,x^4 + coeffs[3]\,x^3 + coeffs[2]\,x^2 + coeffs[1]\,x + coeffs[0]$$

polyl is the **long double** version; it takes **long double** arguments and returns a **long double** result.

Return value
poly and *polyl* return the value of the polynomial as evaluated for the given *x*.

Portability

	DOS	UNIX	Win 16	Win 32	ANSI C	ANSI C++	OS/2
poly	+	+	+	+			+
polyl	+		+	+			+

_popen   stdio.h

Syntax
FILE *_popen (const char *command, const char *mode);

Description
Creates a command processor pipe.

The *_popen* function creates a pipe to the command processor. The command processor is executed asynchronously, and is passed the command line in *command*. The *mode* string specifies whether the pipe is connected to the command processor's standard input or output, and whether the pipe is to be opened in binary or text mode.

The *mode* string can take one of the following values:

Value	Description
rt	Read child command's standard output (text).
rb	Read child command's standard output (binary).
wt	Write to child command's standard input (text).
wb	Write to child command's standard input (binary).

The terminating *t* or *b* is optional; if missing, the translation mode is determined by the external variable *_fmode*.

Use the *_pclose* function to close the pipe and obtain the return code of the command.

Return value
On success, *_popen* returns a FILE pointer that can be used to read the standard output of the command, or to write to the standard input of the command, depending on the *mode* string.

On error, it returns NULL.

See also
_pclose, _pipe

Portability

	DOS	UNIX	Win 16	Win 32	ANSI C	ANSI C++	OS/2
				+			+

pow, powl
math.h

Syntax

double pow(double x, double y);
long double powl(long double x, long double y);

Description

Calculates *x* to the power of *y*.

powl is the **long double** version; it takes **long double** arguments and returns a **long double** result.

This function can be used with *bcd* and *complex* types.

Return value

On success, *pow* and *powl* return the value calculated of *x* to the power of *y*.

Sometimes the arguments passed to these functions produce results that overflow or are incalculable. When the correct value would overflow, the functions return the value HUGE_VAL (*pow*) or _LHUGE_VAL (*powl*). Results of excessively large magnitude can cause the global variable *errno* to be set to

ERANGE   Result out of range

If the argument *x* passed to *pow* or *powl* is real and less than 0, and *y* is not a whole number, or you call *pow(0,0)*, the global variable *errno* is set to

EDOM   Domain error

Error handling for these functions can be modified through the functions *_matherr* and *_matherrl*.

See also

bcd, *complex*, *exp*, *pow10*, *sqrt*

Portability

	DOS	UNIX	Win 16	Win 32	ANSI C	ANSI C++	OS/2
pow	+	+	+	+	+	+	+
powl	+		+	+			+

pow10, pow10l

math.h

Syntax
double pow10(int p);
long double pow10l(int p);

Description
Calculates 10 to the power of *p*.

pow10l is the **long double** version; it takes **long double** arguments and returns a **long double** result.

Return value
On success, *pow10* returns the value calculated, 10 to the power of *p* and *pow10l* returns a **long double** result.

The result is actually calculated to **long double** accuracy. All arguments are valid, although some can cause an underflow or overflow.

See also
exp, *pow*

Portability

	DOS	UNIX	Win 16	Win 32	ANSI C	ANSI C++	OS/2
pow10	+	+	+	+			+
pow10l	+		+	+			+

printf

stdio.h

Syntax
int printf(const char *format[, argument, ...]);

Description
Writes formatted output to *stdout*.

The *printf* function:

• Accepts a series of arguments
• Applies to each argument a format specifier contained in the format string **format*
• Outputs the formatted data (to the screen, a stream, *stdout*, or a string)

There must be enough arguments for the format. If there are not, the results will be unpredictable and likely disastrous. Excess arguments (more than required by the format) are merely ignored.

Note   For Win32s or Win32 GUI applications, *stdout* must be redirected.

Return value

On success, *printf* returns the number of bytes output.

On error, *printf* returns EOF.

See also

cprintf, ecvt, fprintf, fread, freopen, fscanf, putc, puts, putw, scanf, sprintf, vprintf, vsprintf

Portability

DOS	UNIX	Win 16	Win 32	ANSI C	ANSI C++	OS/2
+	+		+	+	+	+

Format string

The format string, present in each of the *printf* function calls, controls how each function will convert, format, and print its arguments.

Note There must be enough arguments for the format; if not, the results will be unpredictable and possibly disastrous. Excess arguments (more than required by the format) are ignored.

The format string is a character string that contains two types of objects:

- Plain characters are copied verbatim to the output stream.
- Conversion specifications fetch arguments from the argument list and apply formatting to them.

Plain characters are simply copied verbatim to the output stream.

Conversion specifications fetch arguments from the argument list and apply formatting to them.

Printf format specifiers

Print format specifiers have the following form:

```
% [flags] [width] [.prec] [F|N|h|l|L] type_char
```

Each format specifier begins with the percent character (**%**).

After the **%** come the following optional specifiers, in this order:

Optional format string components

These are the general aspects of output formatting controlled by the optional characters, specifiers, and modifiers in the format string:

Component	Optional/required	What it controls or specifies
[flags]	(Optional)	Flag character(s) Output justification, numeric signs, decimal points, trailing zeros, octal and hex prefixes
[width]	(Optional)	Width specifier Minimum number of characters to print, padding with blanks or zeros

Component	Optional/required	What it controls or specifies
[prec]	(Optional)	Precision specifier. Maximum number of characters to print; for integers, minimum number of digits to print.
[flags]	(Optional)	Flag character(s). Output justification, numeric signs, decimal points, trailing zeros, octal and hex prefixes.
[width]	(Optional)	Width specifier. Minimum number of characters to print, padding with blanks or zeros.
[prec]	(Optional)	Precision specifier. Maximum number of characters to print; for integers, minimum number of digits to print.
[F|N|h|1|L]	(Optional)	Input size modifier. Override default size of next input argument: N = **near** pointer F = **far** pointer h = short int l = long L = long double
type_char	(Required)	Conversion-type character.

printf flag characters

They can appear in any order and combination.

Flag	What it means
-	Left-justifies the result, pads on the right with blanks. If not given, it right-justifies the result, pads on the left with zeros or blanks.
+	Signed conversion results always begin with a plus (+) or minus (-) sign.
blank	If value is nonnegative, the output begins with a blank instead of a plus; negative values still begin with a minus.
	Specifies that *arg* is to be converted using an alternate form.

Note Plus (+) takes precedence over blank () if both are given.

Alternate forms for printf conversion

If you use the # flag conversion character, it has the following effect on the argument (*arg*) being converted:

Conversion character	How # affects the argument
c s d iu	No effect.
0	0 is prepended to a nonzero *arg*.
x X	0x (or 0X) is prepended to *arg*.
e E f	The result always contains a decimal point even if no digits follow the point. Normally, a decimal point appears in these results only if a digit follows it.
g G	Same as **e** and **E**, except that trailing zeros are not removed.

Width specifiers

The width specifier sets the minimum field width for an output value.

Width is specified in one of two ways:

- directly, through a decimal digit string
- indirectly, through an asterisk (*)

If you use an asterisk for the width specifier, the next argument in the call (which must be an **int**) specifies the minimum output field width.

Nonexistent or small field widths do *not* cause truncation of a field. If the result of a conversion is wider than the field width, the field is expanded to contain the conversion result.

Width specifier	How output width is affected
n	At least *n* characters are printed. If the output value has less than *n* characters, the output is padded with blanks (right-padded if - flag given, left-padded otherwise).
0*n*	At least *n* characters are printed. If the output value has less than *n* characters, it is filled on the left with zeros.
*	The argument list supplies the width specifier, which must precede the actual argument being formatted.

Precision specifiers

The *printf* precision specifiers set the maximum number of characters (or minimum number of integer digits) to print.

A *printf* precision specification always begins with a period (.) to separate it from any preceding width specifier.

Then, like [width], precision is specified in one of two ways:

- directly, through a decimal digit string
- indirectly, through an asterisk (*)

If you use an * for the precision specifier, the next argument in the call (treated as an **int**) specifies the precision.

If you use asterisks for the width or the precision, or for both, the width argument must immediately follow the specifiers, followed by the precision argument, then the argument for the data to be converted.

[.prec]	How output precision is affected
(none)	Precision set to default: = 1 for d, i, o, u, x, X types = 6 for e, E, f types = All significant digits for g, G types = Print to first null character for s types = No effect on c types
.0	For d, i, o, u, x types, precision set to default; for e, E, f types, no decimal point is printed.

[.prec]	How output precision is affected
.n	n characters or n decimal places are printed.
	If the output value has more than n characters, the output might be truncated or rounded. (Whether this happens depends on the type character.)
.	The argument list supplies the precision specifier, which must precede the actual argument being formatted.

No numeric characters will be output for a field (i.e., the field will be blank) if the following conditions are all met:

- you specify an explicit precision of 0
- the format specifier for the field is one of the integer formats (d, i, o, u, or x)
- the value to be printed is 0

How [.prec] affects conversion

Char Type	Effect of [.prec] (.n) on conversion
d, i, o, u, x, X	Specifies that at least n digits are printed. If input argument has less than n digits, output value is left-padded x with zeros. If input argument has more than n digits, the output value is not truncated.
e, E, f	Specifies that n characters are printed after the decimal point, and the last digit printed is rounded.
g, G	Specifies that at most n significant digits are printed.
c	Has no effect on the output.
s	Specifies that no more than n characters are printed.

Note   Certain conventions accompany some of these format specifiers.

Type char	Expected input	Format of output
Numerics		
d	Integer	Signed decimal integer
i	Integer	Signed decimal integer
o	Integer	Unsigned octal integer
u	Integer	Unsigned decimal integer
x	Integer	Unsigned hexadecimal int (with a, b, c, d, e, f)
X	Integer	Unsigned hexadecimal int (with A, B, C, D, E, F)
f	Floating point	Signed value of the form [-]dddd.dddd.
e	Floating point	Signed value of the form [-]d.dddd or e[+/-]ddd
g	Floating point	Signed value in either e or f form, based on given value and precision. Trailing zeros and the decimal point are printed if necessary.
E	Floating point	Same as e; with E for exponent.
G	Floating point	Same as g; with E for exponent if e format used
Characters		
c	Character	Single character
s	String pointer	Prints characters until a null-terminator is pressed or precision is reached
%	None	Prints the % character

Type char	Expected input	Format of output
Pointers		
n	Pointer to int	Stores (in the location pointed to by the input argument) a count of the chars written so far.
p	Pointer	Prints the input argument as a pointer; format depends on which memory model was used. It will be either XXXX:YYYY or YYYY (offset only).

Infinite floating-point numbers are printed as +INF and -INF.

An IEEE Not-A-Number is printed as +NAN or -NAN.

Input-size modifiers

These modifiers determine how printf functions interpret the next input argument, arg[f].

Modifier	Type of arg	arg is interpreted as ...
F	Pointer (*p, s*,	A **far** pointer
N	and *n*)	A **near** pointer (**Note:** *N* can't be used with any conversion in **huge** model.)
h	*d i o u x X*	A **short int**
l	*d i o u x X*	A **long int**
	e E f g G	A **double**
L	*e E f g G*	A **long double**

These modifiers affect how all the printf functions interpret the data type of the corresponding input argument *arg*.

Both *F* and *N* reinterpret the input variable *arg*. Normally, the *arg* for a %*p*, %*s*, or %*n* conversion is a pointer of the default size for the memory model.

h, *l*, and *L* override the default size of the numeric data input arguments. Neither *h* nor *l* affects character (*c, s*) or pointer (*p, n*) types.

printf format specifier conventions

Certain conventions accompany some of the printf format specifiers for the following conversions:

- %e or %E
- %f
- %g or %G
- %x or %X

Note Infinite floating-point numbers are printed as +INF and -INF. An IEEE Not-a-Number is printed as +NAN or -NAN.

%e or %E conversions
The argument is converted to match the style

```
[-] d.ddd...e[+/-]ddd
```

where:

- One digit precedes the decimal point
- The number of digits after the decimal point is equal to the precision.
- The exponent always contains at least two digits

%f conversions

The argument is converted to decimal notation in the style

```
[-] ddd.ddd...
```

where the number of digits after the decimal point is equal to the precision (if a non-zero precision was given).

%g or %G conversions

The argument is printed in style e, E or f, with the precision specifying the number of significant digits.

Trailing zeros are removed from the result, and a decimal point appears only if necessary.

The argument is printed in style e or f (with some restraints) if g is the conversion character. Style e is used only if the exponent that results from the conversion is either greater than the precision or less than -4.

The argument is printed in style E if G is the conversion character.

%x or %X conversions

For x conversions, the letters **a, b, c, d, e**, and **f** appear in the output.

For **X** conversions, the letters **A, B, C, D, E**, and **F** appear in the output.
The other ...*printf* functions include

fprintf	sends formatted output to a stream
sprintf	sends formatted output to a string
vfprintf	sends formatted output to a stream, using an argument list
vprintf	sends formatted output to *stdout*, using an argument list
vsprintf	sends formatted output to a string, using an argument list

putc

stdio.h

Syntax
int putc(int c, FILE *stream);

Description
Outputs a character to a stream.

putc is a macro that outputs the character *c* to the stream given by *stream*.

Return value

On success, *putc* returns the character printed, *c*.

On error, *putc* returns EOF.

See also

fprintf, fputc, fputchar, fputs, fwrite, getc, getchar, printf, putch, putchar, putw, vprintf

Portability

DOS	UNIX	Win 16	Win 32	ANSI C	ANSI C++	OS/2
+	+	+	+	+	+	+

putch   conio.h

Syntax

int putch(int c);

Description

Outputs character to screen.

putch outputs the character *c* to the current text window. It is a text mode function performing direct video output to the console. *putch* does not translate linefeed characters (\n) into carriage-return/linefeed pairs.

The string is written either directly to screen memory or by way of a BIOS call, depending on the value of the global variable *_directvideo*.

Note   This function should not be used in Win32s or Win32 GUI applications.

Return value

On success, *putch* returns the character printed, *c*. On error, it returns EOF.

See also

cprintf, cputs, getch, getche, putc, putchar

Portability

DOS	UNIX	Win 16	Win 32	ANSI C	ANSI C++	OS/2
+		+	+			+

putchar   stdio.h

Syntax

int putchar(int c);

Description

putchar(c) is a macro defined to be *putc*(c, stdout).

Note For Win32s or Win32 GUI applications, *stdout* must be redirected.

Return value
On success, *putchar* returns the character *c*. On error, *putchar* returns EOF.

See also
fputchar, getc, getchar, printf, putc, putch, puts, putw, freopen, vprintf

Portability

DOS	UNIX	Win 16	Win 32	ANSI C	ANSI C++	OS/2
+	+	+	+	+	+	+

putenv   stdlib.h

Syntax
int putenv(const char *name);

Description
Adds string to current environment.

putenv accepts the string *name* and adds it to the environment of the current process. For example,

```
putenv("PATH=C:\\BC");
```

putenv can also be used to modify an existing *name*. On DOS and OS/2, *name* must be uppercase. On other systems, *name* can be either uppercase or lowercase. *name* must not include the equal sign (=). You can set a variable to an empty value by specifying an empty string on the right side of the '=' sign.

putenv can be used only to modify the current program's environment. Once the program ends, the old environment is restored. The environment of the current process is passed to child processes, including any changes made by *putenv*.

Note that the string given to *putenv* must be static or global. Unpredictable results will occur if a local or dynamic string given to *putenv* is used after the string memory is released.

Return value
On success, *putenv* returns 0; on failure, -1.

See also
getenv

Portability

DOS	UNIX	Win 16	Win 32	ANSI C	ANSI C++	OS/2
+	+	+	+			+

puts

Syntax
int puts(const char *s);

Description
Outputs a string to stdout.

puts copies the null-terminated string *s* to the standard output stream *stdout* and appends a newline character.

Note   For Win32s or Win32 GUI applications, *stdout* must be redirected.

Return value
On successful completion, *puts* returns a nonnegative value. Otherwise, it returns a value of EOF.

See also
cputs, fputs, gets, printf, putchar, freopen

Portability

DOS	UNIX	Win 16	Win 32	ANSI C	ANSI C++	OS/2
+	+	+	+	+		+

puttext

Syntax
int puttext(int left, int top, int right, int bottom, void *source);

Description
Copies text from memory to the text mode screen.

puttext writes the contents of the memory area pointed to by *source* out to the onscreen rectangle defined by *left, top, right,* and *bottom*.

All coordinates are absolute screen coordinates, not window-relative. The upper left corner is (1,1).

puttext places the contents of a memory area into the defined rectangle sequentially from left to right and top to bottom.

Each position onscreen takes 2 bytes of memory: The first byte is the character in the cell, and the second is the cell's video attribute. The space required for a rectangle *w* columns wide by *h* rows high is defined as

$$bytes = (h \text{ rows}) \times (w \text{ columns}) \times 2$$

puttext is a text mode function performing direct video output.

Note This function should not be used in Win32s or Win32 GUI applications.

Return value
puttext returns a nonzero value if the operation succeeds; it returns 0 if it fails (for example, if you gave coordinates outside the range of the current screen mode).

See also
gettext, movetext, window

Portability

DOS	UNIX	Win 16	Win 32	ANSI C	ANSI C++	OS/2
+			+			+

putw   stdio.h

Syntax
int putw(int w, FILE *stream);

Description
Puts an integer on a stream.

putw outputs the integer *w* to the given stream. *putw* neither expects nor causes special alignment in the file.

Return value
On success, *putw* returns the integer *w*. On error, *putw* returns EOF. Because EOF is a legitimate integer, use *ferror* to detect errors with *putw*.

See also
getw, printf

Portability

DOS	UNIX	Win 16	Win 32	ANSI C	ANSI C++	OS/2
+	+	+	+			+

qsort   stdlib.h

Syntax
void qsort(void *base, size_t nelem, size_t width, int (_USERENTRY *fcmp)(const void *, const void *));

Description
Sorts using the quicksort algorithm.

qsort is an implementation of the "median of three" variant of the quicksort algorithm. *qsort* sorts the entries in a table by repeatedly calling the user-defined comparison function pointed to by *fcmp*.

- *base* points to the base (0th element) of the table to be sorted.
- *nelem* is the number of entries in the table.
- *width* is the size of each entry in the table, in bytes.

fcmp, the comparison function, must be used with the _USERENTRY calling convention.

fcmp accepts two arguments, *elem1* and *elem2*, each a pointer to an entry in the table. The comparison function compares each of the pointed-to items (**elem1* and **elem2*), and returns an integer based on the result of the comparison.

- **elem1 < *elem2 fcmp* returns an integer < 0
- **elem1 == *elem2 fcmp* returns 0
- **elem1 > *elem2 fcmp* returns an integer > 0

In the comparison, the less-than symbol (<) means the left element should appear before the right element in the final, sorted sequence. Similarly, the greater-than (>) symbol means the left element should appear after the right element in the final, sorted sequence.

Return value
None.

See also
bsearch, lsearch

Portability

DOS	UNIX	Win 16	Win 32	ANSI C	ANSI C++	OS/2
+	+	+	+	+	+	+

raise   signal.h

Syntax
int raise(int sig);

Description
Sends a software signal to the executing program.

raise sends a signal of type *sig* to the program. If the program has installed a signal handler for the signal type specified by *sig*, that handler will be executed. If no handler has been installed, the default action for that signal type will be taken.

The signal types currently defined in signal.h are noted here:

Signal	Description
SIGABRT	Abnormal termination
SIGFPE	Bad floating-point operation
SIGILL	Illegal instruction
SIGINT	Ctrl-C interrupt
SIGSEGV	Invalid access to storage
SIGTERM	Request for program termination
SIGUSR1	User-defined signal
SIGUSR2	User-defined signal
SIGUSR3	User-defined signal
SIGBREAK	Ctrl-Break interrupt

Note SIGABRT isn't generated by Borland C++ during normal operation. It can, however, be generated by abort, raise, or unhandled exceptions.

Return value
On success, *raise* returns 0.

On error it returns nonzero.

See also
abort, signal

Portability

DOS	UNIX	Win 16	Win 32	ANSI C	ANSI C++	OS/2
+	+	+	+	+	+	+

rand

stdlib.h

Syntax
int rand(void);

Description
Random number generator.

rand uses a multiplicative congruential random number generator with period 2 to the 32nd power to return successive pseudorandom numbers in the range from 0 to RAND_MAX. The symbolic constant RAND_MAX is defined in stdlib.h.

Return value
rand returns the generated pseudorandom number.

See also
random, randomize, srand

Portability

DOS	UNIX	Win 16	Win 32	ANSI C	ANSI C++	OS/2
+	+	+	+	+	+	+

random   stdlib.h

Syntax
int random(int num);

Description
Random number generator.

random returns a random number between 0 and (*num*-1). *random(num)* is a macro defined in stdlib.h. Both *num* and the random number returned are integers.

Return value
random returns a number between 0 and (*num*-1).

See also
rand, randomize, srand

Portability

DOS	UNIX	Win 16	Win 32	ANSI C	ANSI C++	OS/2
+		+	+			+

randomize   stdlib.h, time.h

Syntax
void randomize(void);

Description
Initializes random number generator.

randomize initializes the random number generator with a random value.

Return value
None.

See also
rand, random, srand

Portability

DOS	UNIX	Win 16	Win 32	ANSI C	ANSI C++	OS/2
+		+	+			+

_read

Obsolete function. *See _rtl_read.*

read
io.h

Syntax
int read(int handle, void *buf, unsigned len);

Description
Reads from file.

read attempts to read *len* bytes from the file associated with *handle* into the buffer pointed to by *buf*.

For a file opened in text mode, *read* removes carriage returns and reports end-of-file when it reaches a *Ctrl+Z*.

The file handle *handle* is obtained from a *creat, open, dup,* or *dup2* call.

On disk files, *read* begins reading at the current file pointer. When the reading is complete, it increments the file pointer by the number of bytes read. On devices, the bytes are read directly from the device.

The maximum number of bytes that *read* can read is UINT_MAX -1, because UINT_MAX is the same as -1, the error return indicator. UINT_MAX is defined in limits.h.

Return value
On successful completion, *read* returns an integer indicating the number of bytes placed in the buffer. If the file was opened in text mode, *read* does not count carriage returns or *Ctrl+Z* characters in the number of bytes read.

On end-of-file, *read* returns 0. On error, *read* returns -1 and sets the global variable *errno* to one of the following values:

EACCES   Permission denied

EBADF   Bad file number

See also
open, _rtl_read, write

Portability

DOS	UNIX	Win 16	Win 32	ANSI C	ANSI C++	OS/2
+	+	+	+			+

readdir

dirent.h

Syntax

```
struct dirent *readdir(DIR *dirp);
```

Description

Reads the current entry from a directory stream.

readdir is available on POSIX-compliant UNIX systems.

The *readdir* function reads the current directory entry in the directory stream pointed to by *dirp*. The directory stream is advanced to the next entry.

The *readdir* function returns a pointer to a **dirent** structure that is overwritten by each call to the function on the same directory stream. The structure is not overwritten by a *readdir* call on a different directory stream.

The **dirent** structure corresponds to a single directory entry. It is defined in dirent.h, and contains (in addition to other non-accessible members) the following member:

```
char  d_name[];
```

where *d_name* is an array of characters containing the null-terminated file name for the current directory entry. The size of the array is indeterminate; use *strlen* to determine the length of the file name.

All valid directory entries are returned, including subdirectories, "." and ".." entries, system files, hidden files, and volume labels. Unused or deleted directory entries are skipped.

A directory entry can be created or deleted while a directory stream is being read, but *readdir* might or might not return the affected directory entry. Rewinding the directory with *rewinddir* or reopening it with *opendir* ensures that *readdir* will reflect the current state of the directory.

Return value

On success, *readdir* returns a pointer to the current directory entry for the directory stream.

If the end of the directory has been reached, or *dirp* does not refer to an open directory stream, *readdir* returns NULL.

See also

closedir, opendir, rewinddir

Portability

DOS	UNIX	Win 16	Win 32	ANSI C	ANSI C++	OS/2
+	+	+	+			+

realloc   stdlib.h

Syntax
void *realloc(void *block, size_t size);

Description
Reallocates main memory.

realloc attempts to shrink or expand the previously allocated block to *size* bytes. If *size* is zero, the memory block is freed and NULL is returned. The *block* argument points to a memory block previously obtained by calling *malloc, calloc*, or *realloc*. If *block* is a NULL pointer, *realloc* works just like *malloc*.

realloc adjusts the size of the allocated block to *size*, copying the contents to a new location if necessary.

Return value
realloc returns the address of the reallocated block, which can be different than the address of the original block.

If the block cannot be reallocated, *realloc* returns NULL.

If the value of *size* is 0, the memory block is freed and *realloc* returns NULL.

See also
calloc, farrealloc, free, malloc

Portability

DOS	UNIX	Win 16	Win 32	ANSI C	ANSI C++	OS/2
+	+	+	+	+	+	+

remove   stdio.h

Syntax
int remove(const char *filename);

Description
Removes a file.

remove deletes the file specified by *filename*. It is a macro that simply translates its call to a call to *unlink*. If your file is open, be sure to close it before removing it.

The *filename* string can include a full path.

Return value

On successful completion, *remove* returns 0. On error, it returns -1, and the global variable *errno* is set to one of the following values:

EACCES   Permission denied

ENOENT   No such file or directory

See also
unlink

Portability

DOS	UNIX	Win 16	Win 32	ANSI C	ANSI C++	OS/2
+	+	+	+	+	+	+

rename   stdio.h

Syntax
int rename(const char *oldname, const char *newname);

Description
Renames a file.

rename changes the name of a file from *oldname* to *newname*. If a drive specifier is given in *newname*, the specifier must be the same as that given in *oldname*.

Directories in *oldname* and *newname* need not be the same, so *rename* can be used to move a file from one directory to another. Wildcards are not allowed.

This function will fail (EACCES) if either file is currently open in any process.

Return value
On success, *rename* returns 0.

On error (if the file cannot be renamed), it returns -1 and the global variable *errno* is set to one of the following values:

EACCES   Permission denied: filename already exists or has an invalid path

ENOENT   No such file or directory

ENOTSAM   Not same device

Portability

DOS	UNIX	Win 16	Win 32	ANSI C	ANSI C++	OS/2
+		+	+	+	+	+

rewind

stdio.h

Syntax
void rewind(FILE *stream);

Description
Repositions a file pointer to the beginning of a stream.

rewind(stream) is equivalent to *fseek (stream, 0L, SEEK_SET)*, except that *rewind* clears the end-of-file and error indicators, while *fseek* clears the end-of-file indicator only.

After *rewind*, the next operation on an update file can be either input or output.

Return value
None.

See also
fopen, fseek, ftell

Portability

DOS	UNIX	Win 16	Win 32	ANSI C	ANSI C++	OS/2
+	+	+	+	+	+	+

rewinddir

dirent.h

Syntax
void rewinddir(DIR *dirp);

Description
Resets a directory stream to the first entry.

rewinddir is available on POSIX-compliant UNIX systems.

The *rewinddir* function repositions the directory stream *dirp* at the first entry in the directory. It also ensures that the directory stream accurately reflects any directory entries that might have been created or deleted since the last *opendir* or *rewinddir* on that directory stream.

Return value
None.

See also
closedir, opendir, readdir

Portability

DOS	UNIX	Win 16	Win 32	ANSI C	ANSI C++	OS/2
+	+	+	+			+

rmdir   dir.h

Syntax
int rmdir(const char *path);

Description
Removes a directory.

rmdir deletes the directory whose path is given by *path*. The directory named by *path*

- must be empty
- must not be the current working directory
- must not be the root directory

Return value
rmdir returns 0 if the directory is successfully deleted. A return value of -1 indicates an error, and the global variable *errno* is set to one of the following values:

EACCES   Permission denied

ENOENT   Path or file function not found

See also
chdir, getcurdir, getcwd, mkdir

Portability

DOS	UNIX	Win 16	Win 32	ANSI C	ANSI C++	OS/2
+	+	+	+			+

rmtmp   stdio.h

Syntax
int rmtmp(void);

Description
Removes temporary files.

The *rmtmp* function closes and deletes all open temporary file streams, which were previously created with *tmpfile*. The current directory must the same as when the files were created, or the files will not be deleted.

Return value

rmtmp returns the total number of temporary files it closed and deleted.

See also

tmpfile

Portability

DOS	UNIX	Win 16	Win 32	ANSI C	ANSI C++	OS/2
+		+	+			+

_rotl, _rotr   stdlib.h

Syntax

unsigned short _rotl(unsigned short value, int count);
unsigned short _rotr(unsigned short value, int count);

Description

Bit-rotates an **unsigned** short integer value to the left or right.

_rotl rotates the given *value* to the left *count* bits.

_rotr rotates the given *value* to the right *count* bits.

Return value

_rotl, and *_rotr* return the rotated integer:

_rotl returns the value of *value* left-rotated *count* bits.

_rotr returns the value of *value* right-rotated *count* bits.

See also

_crotl, _crotr, _lrotl, _lrotr

Portability

DOS	UNIX	Win 16	Win 32	ANSI C	ANSI C++	OS/2
+		+	+			+

_rtl_chmod   dos.h, io.h

Syntax

int _rtl_chmod(const char *path, int func [, int attrib]);

Description

Gets or sets file attributes.

Note This function replaces _chmod, which is obsolete

_rtl_chmod can either fetch or set file attributes. If *func* is 0, _rtl_chmod returns the current attributes for the file. If *func* is 1, the attribute is set to *attrib*.

attrib can be one of the following symbolic constants (defined in dos.h):

FA_RDONLY	Read-only attribute
FA_HIDDEN	Hidden file
FA_SYSTEM	System file
FA_LABEL	Volume label
FA_DIREC	Directory
FA_ARCH	Archive

Return value
On success, _rtl_chmod returns the file attribute word.

On error, it returns a value of -1 and sets the global variable *errno* to one of the following values:

ENOENT	Path or filename not found
EACCES	Permission denied

See also
chmod, _rtl_creat

Portability
DOS	UNIX	Win 16	Win 32	ANSI C	ANSI C++	OS/2
+		+	+			

_rtl_close   io.h

Syntax
int _rtl_close(int handle);

Description
Closes a file.

Note This function replaces _close, which is obsolete

The _rtl_close function closes the file associated with *handle*, a file handle obtained from a call to *creat, creatnew, creattemp, dup, dup2, open, _rtl_creat*, or *_rtl_open*.

It does not write a *Ctrl+Z* character at the end of the file. If you want to terminate the file with a *Ctrl+Z*, you must explicitly output one.

Return value

On success, _rtl_close returns 0.

On error (if it fails because *handle* is not the handle of a valid, open file), _rtl_close returns a value of -1 and the global variable *errno* is set to

EBADF   Bad file number

See also

chsize, close, creat, creatnew, dup, fclose, _rtl_creat, _rtl_open, sopen

Portability

DOS	UNIX	Win 16	Win 32	ANSI C	ANSI C++	OS/2
+		+	+			

_rtl_creat   dos.h, io.h

Syntax

int _rtl_creat(const char *pathc, int attrib);

Description

Creates a new file or overwrites an existing one.

Note   This function replaces _creat, which is obsolete

_rtl_creat opens the file specified by *path*. The file is always opened in binary mode. Upon successful file creation, the file pointer is set to the beginning of the file. The file is opened for both reading and writing.

If the file already exists its size is reset to 0. (This is essentially the same as deleting the file and creating a new file with the same name.)

The *attrib* argument is an ORed combination of one or more of the following constants (defined in dos.h):

FA_RDONLY   Read-only attribute

FA_HIDDEN   Hidden file

FA_SYSTEM   System file

Return value

On success, _rtl_creat returns the new file handle (a non-negative integer).

On error, it returns -1 and sets the global variable *errno* to one of the following values:

EACCES   Permission denied

EMFILE   Too many open files

ENOENT   Path or file name not found

See also

chsize, close, creat, creatnew, creattemp, _rtl_chmod, _rtl_close

Portability

DOS	UNIX	Win 16	Win 32	ANSI C	ANSI C++	OS/2
+		+	+			

_rtl_heapwalk   malloc.h

Syntax

int _rtl_heapwalk(_HEAPINFO *hi);

Description

Inspects the heap node by node.

Note   This function replaces *_heapwalk*, which is obsolete.

_rtl_heapwalk assumes the heap is correct. Use _heapchk to verify the heap before using *_rtl_heapwalk*. _HEAPOK is returned with the last block on the heap. _HEAPEND will be returned on the next call to *_rtl_heapwalk*.

_rtl_heapwalk receives a pointer to a structure of type _HEAPINFO (declared in malloc.h).

For the first call to *_rtl_heapwalk*, set the *hi._pentry* field to NULL. *_rtl_heapwalk* returns with *hi._pentry* containing the address of the first block.

hi._size	holds the size of the block in bytes.
hi._useflag	is a flag that is set to _USEDENTRY if the block is currently in use. If the block is free, *hi._useflag* is set to _FREEENTRY.

Return value

This function returns one of the following values:

_HEAPBADNODE	A corrupted heap block has been found
_HEAPBADPTR	The _pentry field does not point to a valid heap block
_HEAPEMPTY	No heap exists
_HEAPEND	The end of the heap has been reached
_HEAPOK	The _heapinfo block contains valid information about the next heap block

See also

_heapchk, _heapset

Portability

DOS	UNIX	Win 16	Win 32	ANSI C	ANSI C++	OS/2
			+			+

_rtl_open   fcntl.h

Syntax
int _rtl_open(const char *filename, int oflags);

Description
Opens a file for reading or writing.

Note This function replaces _open, which is obsolete.

_rtl_open opens the file specified by *filename*, then prepares it for reading or writing, as determined by the value of *oflags*. The file is always opened in binary mode.

oflags uses the flags from the following two lists. Only one flag from List 1 can be used (and one *must* be used) and the flags in List 2 can be used in any logical combination.

List 1: Read/Write

O_RDONLY   Open for reading.

O_WRONLY   Open for writing.

O_RDWR   Open for reading and writing.

The following additional values can be included in *oflags* (using an OR operation):

List 2: Other access flags

O_NOINHERIT The file is not passed to child programs.

SH_COMPAT   Allow other opens with SH_COMPAT. The call will fail if the file has already been opened in any other shared mode.

SH_DENYRW   Only the current handle can have access to the file.

SH_DENWR   Allow only reads from any other open to the file.

SH_DENYRD   Allow only writes from any other open to the file.

SH_DENYNO   Allow other shared opens to the file, but not other SH_COMPAT opens.

Note These symbolic constants are defined in fcntl.h and share.h.

Only one of the SH_DENY*xx* values can be included in a single _rtl_open routine. These file-sharing attributes are in addition to any locking performed on the files.

The maximum number of simultaneously open files is defined by HANDLE_MAX.

Return value

On success: _rtl_open returns a non-negative integer (the file handle). The file pointer, which marks the current position in the file, is set to the beginning of the file.

On error, it returns -1 and sets the global variable *errno* to one of the following values:

EACCES	Permission denied
EINVACC	Invalid access code
EMFILE	Too many open files
ENOENT	Path or file not found

See also

open, _rtl_read, sopen

Portability

DOS	UNIX	Win 16	Win 32	ANSI C	ANSI C++	OS/2
+		+	+			

_rtl_read   dos.h

Syntax

int _rtl_read(int handle, void *buf, unsigned len);

Description

Reads from file.

Note   This function replaces _read, which is obsolete.

This function reads *len* bytes from the file associated with *handle* into the buffer pointed to by *buf*. When a file is opened in text mode, _rtl_read does not remove carriage returns.

The argument *handle* is a file handle obtained from a *creat, open, dup,* or *dup2* call.

On disk files, _rtl_read begins reading at the current file pointer. When the reading is complete, it increments the file pointer by the number of bytes read. On devices, the bytes are read directly from the device.

The maximum number of bytes it can read is UINT_MAX -1 (because UINT_MAX is the same as -1, the error return indicator). UINT_MAX is defined in limits.h.

Return value

On success, _rtl_read returns either

- a positive integer, indicating the number of bytes placed in the buffer
- zero, indicating end-of-file

On error, it returns -1 and sets the global variable *errno* to one of the following values:

EACCES   Permission denied

EBADF   Bad file number

See also
read, _rtl_open, _rtl_write

Portability

DOS	UNIX	Win 16	Win 32	ANSI C	ANSI C++	OS/2
+		+	+			

_rtl_write   io.h

Syntax
int _rtl_write(int handle void *buf unsigned len);

Description
Writes to a file.

Note   This function replaces *_write*, which is obsolete.

_rtl_write attempts to write *len* bytes from the buffer pointed to by *buf* to the file associated with *handle*.

The maximum number of bytes that *_rtl_write* can write is UINT_MAX -1 (because UINT_MAX is the same as -1), which is the error return indicator for *_rtl_write*. UINT_MAX is defined in limits.h. *_rtl_write* does not translate a linefeed character (LF) to a CR/LF pair because all its files are binary files.

If the number of bytes actually written is less than that requested the condition should be considered an error and probably indicates a full disk.

For disk files, writing always proceeds from the current file pointer. On devices, bytes are directly sent to the device.

For files opened with the O_APPEND option, the file pointer is not positioned to EOF before writing the data.

Return value
On success, *_rtl_write* returns number of bytes written.

On error, it returns -1 and sets the global variable *errno* to one of the following values:

EACCES   Permission denied

EBADF   Bad file number

See also
lseek, _rtl_read, write

Portability

DOS	UNIX	Win 16	Win 32	ANSI C	ANSI C++	OS/2
+		+	+			

scanf

Syntax
int scanf(const char *format[, address, ...]);

Description
Scans and formats input from the stdin stream.

To use this I/O function in a Windows application, see EasyWin.

Note   For Win32s or Win32 GUI applications, stdin must be redirected.

The *scanf* function:

- scans a series of input fields one character at a time

- formats each field according to a corresponding format specifier passed in the format string **format*.

- *vsscanf* scans and formats input from a string, using an argument list

There must be one format specifier and address for each input field.

scanf might stop scanning a particular field before it reaches the normal end-of-field (whitespace) character, or it might terminate entirely. For details about why this might happen, see "When ...*scanf* stops scanning".

Warning   *scanf* often leads to unexpected results if you diverge from an expected pattern. You must provide information that tells scanf how to synchronize at the end of a line.

The combination of gets or fgets followed by *sscanf* is safe and easy, and therefore recommended over *scanf*.

Return value
On success, *scanf* returns the number of input fields successfully scanned, converted, and stored. The return value does not include scanned fields that were not stored.

On error:

- if no fields were stored, *scanf* returns 0.
- if *scanf* attempts to read at end-of-file or at end-of-string, it returns EOF.

See also

atof, cscanf, fscanf, freopen, getc, printf, sscanf, vfscanf, vscanf, vsscanf

Portability

DOS	UNIX	Win 16	Win 32	ANSI C	ANSI C++	OS/2
+	+		+	+	+	+

The scanf format string

The format string controls how each *...scanf* function scans, converts, and stores its input fields.

The format string is a character string that contains three types of objects:

- whitespace characters
- non-whitespace characters
- format specifiers

Whitespace characters

The whitespace characters are blank, tab (\t) or newline (\n).

If a *...scanf* function encounters a whitespace character in the format string, it reads, but does not store, all consecutive whitespace characters up to the next non-whitespace character in the input.

Trailing whitespace is left unread (including a newline), unless explicitly matched in the format string.

Non-whitespace characters

The non-whitespace characters are all other ASCII characters except the percent sign (%).

If a *...scanf* function encounters a non-whitespace character in the format string, it will read, but not store, a matching non-whitespace character.

Format specifiers

The format specifiers direct the *...scanf* functions to read and convert characters from the input field into specific types of values, then store them in the locations given by the address arguments.

Warning Each format specifier must have an address argument. If there are more format specs than addresses, the results are unpredictable and likely disastrous.

Excess address arguments (more than required by the format) are ignored.

In *...scanf* format strings, format specifiers have the following form:

```
% [*] [width] [F|N] [h|l|L] type_char
```

Each format specifier begins with the percent character (%).

After the % come the following, in this order:

Component	Optional/required	What it is/does
[*]	(Optional)	*Assignment-suppression character.* Suppresses assignment of the next input field.
[width]	(Optional)	*Width specifier.* Specifies maximum number of characters to read; fewer characters might be read if the *...scanf* function encounters a whitespace or unconvertible character.
[F|N]	(Optional)	*Pointer size modifier.* Overrides default size of address argument: *N* = **near** pointer *F* = **far** pointer
[h|l|L]	(Optional)	*Argument-type modifier.* Overrides default type of address argument: *h* = **short int** *l* = **long int**, if type_char specifies integer conversion *l* = **double**, if type_char specifies floating-point conversion *L* = **long double**, (valid only with floating-point conversion)
type_char	(Required)	Type character

Type characters

The information in this table is based on the assumption that no optional characters, specifiers, or modifiers (*, width, or size) were included in the format specifier.

Note   Certain conventions accompany some of these format specifiers.

Type	Expected input	Type of argument
Numerics		
d	Decimal integer	Pointer to **int** (int *arg)
D	Decimal integer	Pointer to **long** (long *arg)
e,E	Floating point	Pointer to **float** (float *arg)
f	Floating point	Pointer to **float** (float *arg)
g,G	Floating point	Pointer to **float** (float *arg)
o	Octal integer	Pointer to **int** (int *arg)
O	Octal integer	Pointer to **long** (long *arg)
i	Decimal, octal, or hexadecimal integer	Pointer to **int** (int *arg)
I	Decimal, octal, or hexadecimal integer	Pointer to **long** (long *arg)
u	Unsigned decimal integer	Pointer to **unsigned int** (unsigned int *arg)
U	Unsigned decimal integer	Pointer to **unsigned long** (unsigned long *arg)
x	Hexadecimal integer	Pointer to **int** (int *arg)
X	Hexadecimal integer	Pointer to **int** (int *arg)
Characters		
s	Character string	Pointer to array of chars (char arg[])
c	Character	Pointer to **char** (char *arg) if a field width is given along with the c-type character (such as %5c)

Type	Expected input	Type of argument
		Pointer to array of *W* chars (`char arg[W]`)
%	% character	No conversion done; the % is stored
Pointers		
n		Pointer to **int** (`int *arg`). The number of characters read successfully up to %n is stored in this int.
p	Hexadecimal form	Pointer to an object (`far*` or `near*`)
	YYYY:ZZZZ or ZZZZ	%p conversions default to the pointer size native to the memory model

See also

Argument-type Modifiers, Assignment Suppression, Format Specifier Conventions, Format Specifiers, Format String, Input Fields, Pointer-size Modifiers, Width Specifiers, When ...scanf Functions Stop Scanning, ...*scanf* functions

Input fields

In a ...*scanf* function, any one of the following is an input field:

- all characters up to (but not including) the next whitespace character
- all characters up to the first one that can't be converted under the current format specifier (such as an 8 or 9 under octal format)
- up to *n* characters, where *n* is the specified field width

Assignment-suppression character

The assignment-suppression character is an asterisk (`*`), not to be confused with the C indirection (pointer) operator.

If the asterisk follows the percent sign (`%`) in a format specifier, the next input field will be scanned but it won't be assigned to the next address argument.

The suppressed input data is assumed to be of the type specified by the type character that follows the asterisk character.

Width specifiers

The width specifier (*n*), a decimal integer, controls the maximum number of characters to be read from the current input field.

Up to *n* characters are read, converted, and stored in the current address argument.

If the input field contains fewer than *n* characters, the ...*scanf* function reads all the characters in the field, then proceeds with the next field and format specifier.

The success of literal matches and suppressed assignments is not directly determinable.

If the ...*scanf* function encounters a whitespace or non-convertible character before it reads "width" characters, it:

- reads, converts, and stores the characters read so far, then
- attends to the next format specifier.

A non-convertible character is one that can't be converted according to the given format (8 or 9 when the format is octal, *J* or *K* when the format is hexadecimal or decimal, etc.).

Pointer-size and argument-type modifiers

These modifiers affect how *...scanf* functions interpret the corresponding address argument *arg[f]*.

Pointer-size modifiers
Pointer-size modifiers override the default or declared size of *arg*.

Modifier	*arg* Interpreted As...
F	**Far** pointer
N	**Near** pointer (Can't be used with any conversion in huge model)

Argument-type modifiers
Argument-type modifiers indicate which type of the following input data is to be used (h = **short**, l = **long**, L = **long double**).

The input data is converted to the specified version, and the *arg* for that input data should point to an object of corresponding size.

Modifier	For This Type	Convert Input to...
h	d i o u x	**short int**; store in **short** object
	D I O U X	(No effect)
	e f c s n p	(No effect)
l	d i o u x	**long int**; store in **long** object
	e f g	**double**; store in **double** object
	D I O U X	(No effect)
	c s n p	(No effect)
L	e f g	**long double**; store in **long double** object
	(all others)	(No effect)

Format specifier conventions

Certain conventions accompany some of the *...scanf* format specifiers for the following conversions:

- single character (%c)
- character array (%[W]c)
- string (%s)
- floating-point (%e, %E, %f, %g, and %G)
- unsigned (%d, %i, %o, %x, %D, %I, %O, %X, %c, %n)
- search sets (%[...], %[^...])

Single character conversion (%c)

This specification reads the next character, including a whitespace character.

To skip one whitespace character and read the next non-whitespace character, use %1s.

Character array conversion (%[W]c)

[W] = width specification

The address argument is a pointer to an array of characters (char arg[W]).

The array consists of *W* elements.

String conversion (%s)

The address argument is a pointer to an array of characters (char arg[]).

The array size must be *at least* (*n*+1) bytes, where *n* = the length of string *s* (in characters).

A space or newline character terminates the input field.

A null terminator is automatically appended to the string and stored as the last element in the array.

Floating-point conversions (%e, %E, %f, %g, and %G)

Floating-point numbers in the input field must conform to the following generic format:

```
[+/-] dddddddd [.] dddd [E|e] [+/-] ddd
```

where [*item*] indicates that the item is optional, and *ddd* represents digits (decimal, octal, or hexadecimal).

In addition, +INF, -INF, +NAN, and -NAN are recognized as floating-point numbers. The sign (+ or -) and capitalization are required.

Unsigned conversions (%d, %i, %o, %x, %D, %l, %O, %X, %c, and %n)

A pointer to **unsigned** character, **unsigned** integer, or **unsigned long** can be used in any conversion where a pointer to a character, integer, or **long** is allowed.

Search set conversion (%[search_set])

The set of characters surrounded by brackets can be substituted for the *s*-type character.

The address argument is a pointer to an array of characters (char arg[]).

These brackets surround a set of characters that define a *search set* of possible characters making up the string (the input field).

If the first character in the brackets is a caret (^), the search set is inverted to include all ASCII characters except those between the brackets.

(Normally, a caret will be included in the inverted search set unless explicitly listed somewhere after the first caret.)

The input field is a string not delimited by whitespace. *...scanf* reads the corresponding input field up to the first character it reaches that does not appear in the search set (or in the inverted search set).

Rules covering search set ranges

- The character prior to the hyphen (-) must be lexically less than the one after it.

- The hyphen must not be the first or last character in the set (If it is first or last, it is considered to just be the hyphen character, not a range definer.)

- The characters on either side of the hyphen must be the ends of the range and not part of some other range.

Examples

`%[abcd]`   Searches the input field for any of the characters *a, b, c,* and *d*

`%[^abcd]`   Searches the input field for any characters except *a, b, c,* and *d*

You can also use a range facility shortcut `[<first>-<last>]` to define a range of letters or numerals in the search set.

To catch all decimal digits, you could define the search set with the explicit search set: `%[0123456789]` or with the range shortcut: `%[0-9]`

To catch alphanumeric characters, you could use the following shortcuts:

`%[A-Z]`   Catches all uppercase letters

`%[0-9A-Za-z]`   Catches all decimal digits and all letters

`%[A-FT-Z]`   Catches all uppercase letters from *A* through *F* and from *T* through *Z*.

When ...scanf functions stop scanning

A *...scanf* function might stop scanning a particular input field before reaching the normal field-end character (whitespace), or it might terminate entirely.

Stop and skip to next input field

...scanf functions stop scanning and storing the current input field and proceed to the next one if any of the following occurs:

- An assignment-suppression character (*) appears after the % in the format specifier. The current input field is scanned but not stored.

- Width characters have been read.

- The next character read can't be converted under the current format (for example, an *A* when the format is decimal).
- The next character in the input field does not appear in the search set (or does appear in an inverted search set).

When *scanf* stops scanning the current input field for one of these reasons, it assumes that the next character is unread and is either

- the first character of the following input field, or
- the first character in a subsequent read operation on the input.

Terminate

...scanf functions will terminate under the following circumstances:

1 The next character in the input field conflicts with a corresponding non-whitespace character in the format string.

2 The next character in the input field is EOF.

3 The format string has been exhausted.

If a character sequence that is not part of a format specifier occurs in the format string, it must match the current sequence of characters in the input field.

...scanf functions will scan but not store the matched characters.

When a conflicting character occurs, it remains in the input field as if the *...scanf* function never read it.

...scanf functions

The *..scanf* functions include

fscanf	Scans and formats input from a stream
scanf	Scans and formats input from stdin
sscanf	Scans and formats input from a string
vfscanf	Scans and formats input from a stream, using an argument list
vscanf	Scans and formats input from stdin using an argument list
vsscanf	Scans and formats input from a string, using an argument list

_searchenv

stdlib.h

Syntax
char *_searchenv(const char *file, const char *varname, char *buf);

Description
Searches an environment path for a file.

_searchenv attempts to locate *file*, searching along the path specified by the operating system _environment variable *varname*. Typical environment variables that contain paths are PATH, LIB, and INCLUDE.

_searchenv searches for the file in the current directory of the current drive first. If the file is not found there, the environment variable *varname* is fetched, and each directory in the path it specifies is searched in turn until the file is found, or the path is exhausted.

When the file is located, the full path name is stored in the buffer pointed to by *buf*. This string can be used in a call to access the file (for example, with *fopen* or *exec...*). The buffer is assumed to be large enough to store any possible file name. If the file cannot be successfully located, an empty string (consisting of only a null character) will be stored at *buf*.

Return value
None.

See also
_dos_findfirst, *_dos_findnext*, *exec*, *spawn*, *system*

Portability

DOS	UNIX	Win 16	Win 32	ANSI C	ANSI C++	OS/2
+		+	+			+

searchpath

dir.h

Syntax
char *searchpath(const char *file);

Description
Searches the operating system path for a file.

searchpath attempts to locate *file*, searching along the operating system path, which is the PATH=... string in the environment. A pointer to the complete path-name string is returned as the function value.

searchpath searches for the file in the current directory of the current drive first. If the file is not found there, the PATH environment variable is fetched, and each directory in the path is searched in turn until the file is found, or the path is exhausted.

When the file is located, a string is returned containing the full path name. This string can be used in a call to access the file (for example, with *fopen* or *exec...*).

The string returned is located in a static buffer and is overwritten on each subsequent call to *searchpath*.

Return value
searchpath returns a pointer to a file name string if the file is successfully located; otherwise, *searchpath* returns null.

See also
exec, findfirst, findnext, spawn , system

Portability

DOS	UNIX	Win 16	Win 32	ANSI C	ANSI C++	OS/2
+		+	+			+

_searchstr   stdlib.h

Syntax
void _searchstr(const char *file, const char *ipath, char *buf);

Description
Searches a list of directories for a file.

_searchstr attempts to locate *file*, searching along the path specified by the string *ipath*.

_searchstr searches for the file in the current directory of the current drive first. If the file is not found there, each directory in *ipath* is searched in turn until the file is found, or the path is exhausted. The directories in *ipath* must be separated by semicolons.

When the file is located, the full path name is stored in the buffer pointed by by *buf*. This string can be used in a call to access the file (for example, with *fopen* or *exec...*). The buffer is assumed to be large enough to store any possible file name. The constant _MAX_PATH defined in stdlib.h, is the size of the largest file name. If the file cannot be successfully located, an empty string (consisting of only a null character) will be stored at *buf*.

Return value
None.

See also
_searchenv

Portability

DOS	UNIX	Win 16	Win 32	ANSI C	ANSI C++	OS/2
+		+	+			+

segread

dos.h

Syntax
void segread(struct SREGS *segp);

Description
Reads segment registers.

segread places the current values of the segment registers into the structure pointed to by *segp*.

This call is intended for use with *intdosx* and *int86x*.

Return value
None.

See also
FP_OFF, int86, int86x, intdos, intdosx, MK_FP, movedata

Portability

DOS	UNIX	Win 16	Win 32	ANSI C	ANSI C++	OS/2
+		+				

setbuf

stdio.h

Syntax
void setbuf(FILE *stream, char *buf);

Description
Assigns buffering to a stream.

setbuf causes the buffer *buf* to be used for I/O buffering instead of an automatically allocated buffer. It is used after *stream* has been opened.

If *buf* is null, I/O will be unbuffered; otherwise, it will be fully buffered. The buffer must be BUFSIZ bytes long (specified in stdio.h).

stdin and *stdout* are unbuffered if they are not redirected; otherwise, they are fully buffered. *setbuf* can be used to change the buffering style used.

Unbuffered means that characters written to a stream are immediately output to the file or device, while *buffered* means that the characters are accumulated and written as a block.

setbuf produces unpredictable results unless it is called immediately after opening *stream* or after a call to *fseek*. Calling *setbuf* after *stream* has been unbuffered is legal and will not cause problems.

A common cause for error is to allocate the buffer as an automatic (local) variable and then fail to close the file before returning from the function where the buffer was declared.

Return value
None.

See also
fflush, fopen, fseek, setvbuf

Portability

DOS	UNIX	Win 16	Win 32	ANSI C	ANSI C++	OS/2
+	+	+	+	+	+	+

setcbrk   dos.h

Syntax
int setcbrk(int cbrkvalue);

Description
Sets control-break setting.

setcbrk uses the DOS system call 0x33 to turn control-break checking on or off.

| value = 0 | Turns checking off (check only during I/O to console, printer, or communications devices). |
| value = 1 | Turns checking on (check at every system call). |

Return value
setcbrk returns *cbrkvalue*, the value passed.

See also
getcbrk

Portability

DOS	UNIX	Win 16	Win 32	ANSI C	ANSI C++	OS/2
+		+				

_setcursortype   conio.h

Syntax
void _setcursortype(int cur_t);

Description
Selects cursor appearance.
Sets the cursor type to

_NOCURSOR	Turns off the cursor
_NORMALCURSOR	Normal underscore cursor
_SOLIDCURSOR	Solid block cursor

Note Do not use this function for Win32s or Win32 GUI applications.

Return value
None.

Portability

DOS	UNIX	Win 16	Win 32	ANSI C	ANSI C++	OS/2
+			+			+

setdate

See _dos_getdate_.

setdisk

See _getdisk_.

setdta   dos.h

Syntax
void setdta(char far *dta);

Description
Sets disk-transfer address.

setdta changes the current setting of the DOS disk-transfer address (DTA) to the value given by _dta_.

Return value
None.

See also
getdta

Portability

DOS	UNIX	Win 16	Win 32	ANSI C	ANSI C++	OS/2
+		+				

setftime

See *getftime*.

setjmp

Syntax
int setjmp(jmp_buf jmpb);

Description
Sets up for nonlocal goto.

setjmp captures the complete *task state* in *jmpb* and returns 0.

A later call to *longjmp* with *jmpb* restores the captured task state and returns in such a way that *setjmp* appears to have returned with the value *val*.

A task state includes

Win 16	Win 32
All segment registers	No segment registers are saved
CS, DS, ES, SS	
Register variables	Register variables
DI and SI	EBX, EDI, ESI
Stack pointer SP	Stack pointer ESP
Frame pointer BP	Frame pointer EBP
Flags	Flags are not saved

A task state is complete enough that *setjmp* can be used to implement co-routines.

setjmp must be called before *longjmp*. The routine that calls *setjmp* and sets up *jmpb* must still be active and cannot have returned before the *longjmp* is called. If it has returned, the results are unpredictable.

setjmp is useful for dealing with errors and exceptions encountered in a low-level subroutine of a program.

DOS users
You cannot use *setjmp* and *longjmp* for implementing co-routines if your program is overlaid. Normally, *setjmp* and *longjmp* save and restore all the registers needed for co-routines, but the overlay manager needs to keep track of stack contents and assumes there is only one stack. When you implement co-routines there are usually either two

stacks or two partitions of one stack, and the overlay manager will not track them properly.

You can have background tasks that run with their own stacks or sections of stack, but you must ensure that the background tasks do not invoke any overlaid code, and you must not use the overlay versions of *setjmp* or *longjmp* to switch to and from background. When you avoid using overlay code or support routines, the existence of the background stacks does not disturb the overlay manager.

Return value

setjmp returns 0 when it is initially called. If the return is from a call to *longjmp*, *setjmp* returns a nonzero value (as in the example).

See also

longjmp, signal

Portability

DOS	UNIX	Win 16	Win 32	ANSI C	ANSI C++	OS/2
+	+	+	+	+	+	+

setlocale   locale.h

Syntax

char *setlocale(int category, const char *locale);

Description

Selects or queries a locale.

Borland C++ supports the following locales at present:

Module	Locale supported
de_DE	German
fr_FR	French
en_GB	English (Great Britain)
en_US	English (United States)

Note   Future releases of Borland C++ will increase the number of locales supported.

For each locale, the following character sets are supported:

DOS437   English

DOS850   Multilingual (Latin I)

WIN1252   Windows, Multilingual

For a description of DOS character sets, see *MS-DOS User's Guide and Reference*. See also *MS Windows 3.1 Programmer's Reference, Volume 4* for a discussion of the WIN1252 character set.

The possible values for the *category* argument are as follows:

Value	Affect
LC_ALL	Affects all the following categories
LC_COLLATE	Affects *strcoll* and *strxfrm*
LC_CTYPE	Affects single-byte character handling functions. The *mbstowcs* and *mbtowc* functions are not affected.
LC_MONETARY	Affects monetary formatting by the *localeconv* function
LC_NUMERIC	Affects the decimal point of non-monetary data formatting. This includes the *printf* family of functions, and the information returned by *localeconv*.
LC_TIME	Affects *strftime*

The *locale* argument is a pointer to the name of the locale or named locale category. Passing a NULL pointer returns the current locale in effect. Passing a pointer that points to a null string requests *setlocale* to look for environment variables to determine which locale to set. The locale names are case sensitive.

Note The LOCALE.BLL file is installed in BC5\BIN directory.

If you specify a locale other than the default C locale, *setlocale* tries to access the locale library file named LOCALE.BLL to obtain the locale data. This file is located using the following strategies:

1 Searching the directory where the application's executable resides.

2 Searching in the current default directory.

3 Accessing the "PATH" environment variable and searching in each of the specified directories.

If the locale library is not found, *setlocale* terminates.

When *setlocale* is unable to honor a locale request, the preexisting locale in effect is unchanged and a null pointer is returned.

If the *locale* argument is a NULL pointer, the locale string for the category is returned. If *category* is LC_ALL, a complete locale string is returned. The structure of the complete locale string consists of the names of all the categories in the current locale concatenated and separated by semicolons. This string can be used as the locale parameter when calling *setlocale* with LC_ALL. This will reinstate all the locale categories that are named in the complete locale string, and allows saving and restoring of locale states. If the complete locale string is used with a single category, for example, LC_TIME, only that category will be restored from the locale string.

ANSI C states that if an empty string "" is used as the locale parameter an implementation defined locale is used. *setlocale* has been implemented to look for corresponding _environment variables in this instance as POSIX suggests.

If the _environment variable LC_ALL exists, the category will be set according to this variable. If the variable does not exist, the _environment variable that has the same name as the requested category is looked for and the category is set accordingly.

If none of the above are satisfied, the _environment variable named LANG is used. Otherwise, *setlocale* fails and returns a NULL pointer.

To take advantage of dynamically loadable locales in your application, define
_ _USELOCALES_ _ for each module. If _ _USELOCALES_ _ is not defined, all locale-sensitive functions and macros will work only with the default C locale.

If a NULL pointer is used as the argument for the *locale* parameter, *setlocale* returns a
string that specifies the current locale in effect. If the *category* parameter specifies a single
category, such as LC_COLLATE, the string pointed to will be the name of that category.
If LC_ALL is used as the *category* parameter then the string pointed to will be a full
locale string that will indicate the name of each category in effect.

```
     ?
localenameptr = setlocale( LC_COLLATE, NULL );

if (localenameptr)
   printf( "%s\n", localenameptr );
   .
   .
   .
```

The output here will be one of the module names together with the specified code page.
For example, the output could be `fr_FR.DOS850@dbase`.

```
     ?
localenameptr = setlocale( LC_ALL, NULL );

if (localenameptr)
   printf( "%s\n", localenameptr );
   ?
```

An example of the output here could be the following:

```
fr_FR.DOS850@dbase;fr_FR.DOS850;fr_FR.DOS850;fr_FR.DOS850;
fr_FR.DOS850;fr_FR.DOS850;;
```

Each category in this full string is delimited by a semicolon. This string can be copied
and saved by an application and then used again to restore the same locale categories at
another time. Each delimited name corresponds to the locale category constants defined
in locale.h. Therefore, the first name is the name of the LC_COLLATE category, the
second is the LC_CTYPE category, and so on. Any other categories named in the
locale.h header file are reserved for future implementation.

Here are some examples of setting locales by using *setlocale*:

Set all default categories for the specified French locale:

```
setlocale( LC_ALL, "fr_FR.DOS850" );
```

Note   The default collation is named *dbase*. Therefore, whether you specify *dbase* or nothing at
all, you get the same collation. However, *dbase* might not be the default in future
releases.

Set French locale to named collation *dbase*:

```
setlocale( LC_COLLATE, "fr_FR.DOS850@dbase" )
```

When a category is loaded from the locale library, the default category is the one that will be loaded unless a modifier name is used. For example:

```
setlocale( LC_COLLATE, "fr_FR.DOS850" )
```

causes the default LC_COLLATE category to be loaded. It might or might not have a specific name.

```
setlocale( LC_COLLATE, "fr_FR.DOS850@dbase" )
```

specifies that the LC_COLLATE category named dbase to be loaded. This might or might not be the default.

setlocale updates the *lconv* locale structure when a request has been fulfilled.

When an application exits, any allocated memory used for the locale object is deallocated.

Return value
If selection is successful, *setlocale* returns a pointer to a string that is associated with the selected category (or possibly all categories) for the new locale.

On failure, a NULL pointer is returned and the locale is unchanged. All other possible returns are discussed in the Remarks section above.

See also
localeconv

Portability

DOS	UNIX	Win 16	Win 32	ANSI C	ANSI C++	OS/2
+		+	+	+	+	+

setmem   mem.h

Syntax
void setmem(void *dest, unsigned length, char value);

Description
Assigns a value to a range of memory.

setmem sets a block of *length* bytes, pointed to by *dest*, to the byte *value*.

Return value
None.

See also
memset, strset

Portability

DOS	UNIX	Win 16	Win 32	ANSI C	ANSI C++	OS/2
+	+	+	+			+

setmode

io.h

Syntax
int setmode(int handle, int amode);

Description
Sets mode of an open file.

setmode sets the mode of the open file associated with *handle* to either binary or text. The argument *amode* must have a value of either O_BINARY or O_TEXT, never both. (These symbolic constants are defined in fcntl.h.)

Return value
setmode returns the previous translation mode if successful. On error it returns -1 and sets the global variable errno to

EINVAL   Invalid argument

See also
creat, open, _rtl_creat, _rtl_open

Portability

DOS	UNIX	Win 16	Win 32	ANSI C	ANSI C++	OS/2
+		+	+			+

setvbuf

stdio.h

Syntax
int setvbuf(FILE *stream, char *buf, int type, size_t size);

Description
Assigns buffering to a stream.

setvbuf causes the buffer *buf* to be used for I/O buffering instead of an automatically allocated buffer. It is used after the given stream is opened.

If *buf* is null, a buffer will be allocated using *malloc*; the buffer will use *size* as the amount allocated. The buffer will be automatically freed on close. The *size* parameter specifies the buffer size and must be greater than zero.

The parameter size is limited by the constant UINT_MAX as defined in limits.h.

stdin and *stdout* are unbuffered if they are not redirected; otherwise, they are fully buffered. *Unbuffered* means that characters written to a stream are immediately output to the file or device, while *buffered* means that the characters are accumulated and written as a block.

The *type* parameter is one of the following:

_IOFBF
: *fully buffered* file. When a buffer is empty, the next input operation will attempt to fill the entire buffer. On output, the buffer will be completely filled before any data is written to the file.

_IOLBF
: *line buffered* file. When a buffer is empty, the next input operation will still attempt to fill the entire buffer. On output, however, the buffer will be flushed whenever a newline character is written to the file.

_IONBF
: *unbuffered* file. The *buf* and *size* parameters are ignored. Each input operation will read directly from the file, and each output operation will immediately write the data to the file.

A common cause for error is to allocate the buffer as an automatic (local) variable and then fail to close the file before returning from the function where the buffer was declared.

Return value
On success, *setvbuf* returns 0.

On error (if an invalid value is given for *type* or *size*, or if there is not enough space to allocate a buffer), it returns nonzero.

See also
fflush, fopen, setbuf

Portability

DOS	UNIX	Win 16	Win 32	ANSI C	ANSI C++	OS/2
+	+	+	+	+	+	+

setvect

See getvect.

setverify   dos.h

Syntax
void setverify(int value);

Description
Sets the state of the verify flag in the operating system.

setverify sets the current state of the verify flag to *value*, which can be either 0 (off) or 1 (on).

The verify flag controls output to the disk. When verify is off, writes are not verified; when verify is on, all disk writes are verified to ensure proper writing of the data.

Return value
None.

See also
getverify

Portability

DOS	UNIX	Win 16	Win 32	ANSI C	ANSI C++	OS/2
+		+				+

signal   signal.h

Syntax
```
void (_USERENTRY *signal(int sig, void (_USERENTRY *func)
       (int sig[, int subcode])))(int);
```

Description
Specifies signal-handling actions.

signal determines how receipt of signal number *sig* will subsequently be treated. You can install a user-specified handler routine (specified by the argument *func*) or use one of the two predefined handlers, SIG_DFL and SIG_IGN, in signal.h. The function *func* must be used with the _USERENTRY calling convention.

A routine that catches a signal (such as a floating point) also clears the signal. To continue to receive signals, a signal handler must be reinstalled by calling signal again.

Function pointer	Description
SIG_DFL	Terminates the program
SIG_ERR	Indicates an error return from signal
SIG_IGN	Ignore this type signal

The following table shows signal types and their defaults:

Signal type	Description
SIGBREAK	Keyboard must be in raw mode.
SIGABRT	Abnormal termination. Default action is equivalent to calling _exit(3).
SIGFPE	Arithmetic error caused by division by 0, invalid operation, and the like. Default action is equivalent to calling _exit(1).
SIGILL	Illegal operation. Default action is equivalent to calling _exit(1).
SIGINT	Ctrl-C interrupt. Default action is to do an INT 23h.

Signal type	Description
SIGSEGV	Illegal storage access. Default action is equivalent to calling _exit(1).
SIGTERM	Request for program termination. Default action is equivalent to calling _exit(1).
SIGUSR1, SIGUSR2, SIGUSR3	User-defined signals (available only in Win32) can be generated only by calling *raise*. Default action is to ignore the signal.

signal.h defines a type called *sig_atomic_t*, the largest integer type the processor can load or store atomically in the presence of asynchronous interrupts (for the 8086 family, this is a 16-bit word, for 80386 and higher number processors, it is a 32-bit word--a Borland C++ integer).

When a signal is generated by the *raise* function or by an external event, the following two things happen:

- If a user-specified handler has been installed for the signal, the action for that signal type is set to SIG_DFL.

- The user-specified function is called with the signal type as the parameter.

User-specified handler functions can terminate by a return or by a call to *abort*, *_exit*, *exit*, or *longjmp*. If your handler function is expected to continue to receive and handle more signals, you must have the handler function call *signal* again.

Borland C++ implements an extension to ANSI C when the signal type is SIGFPE, SIGSEGV, or SIGILL. The user-specified handler function is called with one or two extra parameters. If SIGFPE, SIGSEGV, or SIGILL has been raised as the result of an explicit call to the *raise* function, the user-specified handler is called with one extra parameter, an integer specifying that the handler is being explicitly invoked. The explicit activation values for SIGFPE, SIGSEGV and SIGILL are as follows

Note   Declarations of these types are defined in float.h.

SIGSEGV signal	Meaning
SIGFPE	FPE_EXPLICITGEN
SIGSEGV	SEGV_EXPLICITGEN
SIGILL	ILL_EXPLICITGEN

If SIGFPE is raised because of a floating-point exception, the user handler is called with one extra parameter that specifies the FPE_xxx type of the signal. If SIGSEGV, SIGILL, or the integer-related variants of SIGFPE signals (FPE_INTOVFLOW or FPE_INTDIV0) are raised as the result of a processor exception, the user handler is called with two extra parameters:

1   The SIGFPE, SIGSEGV, or SIGILL exception type (see float.h for all these types). This first parameter is the usual ANSI signal type.

2   An integer pointer into the stack of the interrupt handler that called the user-specified handler. This pointer points to a list of the processor registers saved when the exception occurred. The registers are in the same order as the parameters to an interrupt function; that is, BP, DI, SI, DS, ES, DX, CX, BX, AX, IP, CS, FLAGS. To have a register value changed when the handler returns, change one of the locations in this list.

For example, to have a new SI value on return, do something like this:

```
*((int*)list_pointer + 2) = new_SI_value;
```

In this way, the handler can examine and make any adjustments to the registers that you want.

The following SIGFPE-type signals can occur (or be generated). They correspond to the exceptions that the 8087 family is capable of detecting, as well as the "INTEGER DIVIDE BY ZERO" and the "INTERRUPT ON OVERFLOW" on the main CPU. (The declarations for these are in float.h.)

SIGFPE signal	Meaning
FPE_INTOVFLOW	INTO executed with OF flag set
FPE_INTDIV0	Integer divide by zero
FPE_INVALID	Invalid operation
FPE_ZERODIVIDE	Division by zero
FPE_OVERFLOW	Numeric overflow
FPE_UNDERFLOW	Numeric underflow
FPE_INEXACT	Precision
FPE_EXPLICITGEN	User program executed *raise*(SIGFPE)
FPE_STACKFAULT	Floating-point stack overflow or underflow
FPE_STACKFAULT	Stack overflow

The FPE_INTOVFLOW and FPE_INTDIV0 signals are generated by integer operations, and the others are generated by floating-point operations. Whether the floating-point exceptions are generated depends on the coprocessor control word, which can be modified with *_control87*. Denormal exceptions are handled by Borland C++ and not passed to a signal handler.

The following SIGSEGV-type signals can occur:

SEGV_BOUND   Bound constraint exception

SEGV_EXPLICITGEN   *raise*(SIGSEGV) was executed

The 8088 and 8086 processors *don't* have a bound instruction. The 186, 286, 386, and NEC V series processors *do* have this instruction. So, on the 8088 and 8086 processors, the SEGV_BOUND type of SIGSEGV signal won't occur. Borland C++ doesn't generate bound instructions, but they can be used in inline code and separately compiled assembler routines that are linked in.

The following SIGILL-type signals can occur:

ILL_EXECUTION   Illegal operation attempted

ILL_EXPLICITGEN   *raise*(SIGILL) was executed

The 8088, 8086, NEC V20, and NEC V30 processors *do not* have an illegal operation exception. The 186, 286, 386, NEC V40, and NEC V50 processors *do* have this exception type. On 8088, 8086, NEC V20, and NEC V30 processors, the ILL_EXECUTION type of SIGILL won't occur.

When the signal type is SIGFPE, SIGSEGV, or SIGILL, a return from a signal handler is generally not advisable if the state of the 8087 is corrupt, the results of an integer division are wrong, an operation that shouldn't have overflowed did, a bound instruction failed, or an illegal operation was attempted. The only time a return is reasonable is when the handler alters the registers so that a reasonable return context exists *or* the signal type indicates that the signal was generated explicitly (for example, FPE_EXPLICITGEN, SEGV_EXPLICITGEN, or ILL_EXPLICITGEN). Generally in this case you would print an error message and terminate the program using _exit, exit, or abort. If a return is executed under any other conditions, the program's action will probably be unpredictable.

Note Take special care when using the *signal* function in a multithread program. The SIGINT, SIGTERM, and SIGBREAK signals can be used only by the main thread (thread one) in a non-Win32 application. When one of these signals occurs, the currently executing thread is suspended, and control transfers to the signal handler (if any) set up by thread one. Other signals can be handled by any thread.

A signal handler should not use C++ run-time library functions, because a semaphore deadlock might occur. Instead, the handler should simply set a flag or post a semaphore, and return immediately.

Return value

On success, *signal* returns a pointer to the previous handler routine for the specified signal type.

On error, *signal* returns SIG_ERR, and the external variable errno is set to EINVAL.

See also

abort, _c_exit, _cexit, _control87, ctrlbrk, *exit, longjmp, raise, setjmp*

Portability

DOS	UNIX	Win 16	Win 32	ANSI C	ANSI C++	OS/2
+	+	+	+	+	+	+

sin, sinl   math.h

Syntax

double sin(double x);
long double sinl(long double x);

Description

Calculates sine.

sin computes the sine of the input value. Angles are specified in radians.

sinl is the **long double** version; it takes a **long double** argument and returns a **long double** result. Error handling for these functions can be modified through the functions *_matherr* and *_matherrl*.

This function can be used with *bcd* and *complex* types.

Return value

sin and *sinl* return the sine of the input value.

See also

acos, asin, atan, atan2, bcd, complex, cos, tan

Portability

	DOS	UNIX	Win 16	Win 32	ANSI C	ANSI C++	OS/2
sin	+	+	+	+	+		+
sinl	+		+	+			+

sinh, sinhl   math.h

Syntax

```
double sinh(double x);
long double sinhl(long double x);
```

Description

Calculates hyperbolic sine.

sinh computes the hyperbolic sine, $(e^x - e^{-x})/2$.

sinl is the **long double** version; it takes a **long double** argument and returns a **long double** result. Error handling for *sinh* and *sinhl* can be modified through the functions *_matherr* and *_matherrl*.

This function can be used with *bcd* and *complex* types.

Return value

sinh and *sinhl* return the hyperbolic sine of *x*.

When the correct value overflows, these functions return the value HUGE_VAL (*sinh*) or _LHUGE_VAL (*sinhl*) of appropriate sign. Also, the global variable *errno* is set to ERANGE.

See also

acos, asin, atan, atan2, bcd, complex, cos, cosh, sin, tan, tanh

Portability

	DOS	UNIX	Win 16	Win 32	ANSI C	ANSI C++	OS/2
sinh	+	+	+	+	+		+
sinhl	+		+	+			+

sleep   dos.h

Syntax
void sleep(unsigned seconds);

Description
Suspends execution for an interval (seconds).

With a call to *sleep*, the current program is suspended from execution for the number of seconds specified by the argument *seconds*. The interval is accurate only to the nearest hundredth of a second or to the accuracy of the operating system clock, whichever is less accurate.

Return value
None.

Portability

DOS	UNIX	Win 16	Win 32	ANSI C	ANSI C++	OS/2
+	+		+			+

sopen   fcntl.h, sys\stat.h, share.h, io.h

Syntax
int sopen(char *path, int access, int shflag[, int mode]);

Description
Opens a shared file.

sopen opens the file given by *path* and prepares it for shared reading or writing, as determined by *access, shflag,* and *mode*.

For *sopen, access* is constructed by ORing flags bitwise from the following lists:

Read/write flags
You can use only one of the following flags:

O_RDONLY   Open for reading only.

O_WRONLY   Open for writing only.

O_RDWR   Open for reading and writing.

Other access flags
You can use any logical combination of the following flags:

O_NDELAY   Not used; for UNIX compatibility.

O_APPEND   If set, the file pointer is set to the end of the file prior to each write.

O_CREA	If the file exists, this flag has no effect. If the file does not exist, the file is created, and the bits of *mode* are used to set the file attribute bits as in *chmod*.
O_TRUNC	If the file exists, its length is truncated to 0. The file attributes remain unchanged.
O_EXCL	Used only with O_CREAT. If the file already exists, an error is returned.
O_BINARY	This flag can be given to explicitly open the file in binary mode.
O_TEXT	This flag can be given to explicitly open the file in text mode.
O_NOINHERIT	The file is not passed to child programs.

Note   These O_... symbolic constants are defined in fcntl.h.

If neither O_BINARY nor O_TEXT is given, the file is opened in the translation mode set by the global variable _fmode.

If the O_CREAT flag is used in constructing *access*, you need to supply the *mode* argument to *sopen* from the following symbolic constants defined in sys\stat.h.

Value of mode	Access permission
S_IWRITE	Permission to write
S_IREAD	Permission to read
S_IREAD|S_IWRITE	Permission to read/write

shflag specifies the type of file-sharing allowed on the file *path*. Symbolic constants for *shflag* are defined in share.h.

Value of *shflag*	What it does
SH_COMPAT	Sets compatibility mode.
SH_DENYRW	Denies read/write access
SH_DENYWR	Denies write access
SH_DENYRD	Denies read access
SH_DENYNONE	Permits read/write access
SH_DENYNO	Permits read/write access

Return value

On success, *sopen* returns a nonnegative integer (the file handle), and the file pointer (that marks the current position in the file) is set to the beginning of the file.

On error, it returns -1, and the global variable errno is set to

EACCES	Permission denied
EINVACC	Invalid access code
EMFILE	Too many open files
ENOENT	Path or file function not found

See also
chmod, close, creat, lock, lseek, open, _rtl_open, unlock, umask

Portability

DOS	UNIX	Win 16	Win 32	ANSI C	ANSI C++	OS/2
+	+	+	+			+

spawnl, spawnle, spawnlp, spawnlpe, spawnv, spawnve, spawnvp, spawnvpe   process.h, stdio.h

Syntax
```
int spawnl(int mode, char *path, char *arg0, arg1, ..., argn, NULL);
int spawnle(int mode, char *path, char *arg0, arg1, ..., argn, NULL, char *envp[]);
int spawnlp(int mode, char *path, char *arg0, arg1, ..., argn, NULL);
int spawnlpe(int mode, char *path, char *arg0, arg1, ..., argn, NULL, char *envp[]);
int spawnv(int mode, char *path, char *argv[]);
int spawnve(int mode, char *path, char *argv[], char *envp[]);
int spawnvp(int mode, char *path, char *argv[]);
int spawnvpe(int mode, char *path, char *argv[], char *envp[]);
```

Note   In *spawnle, spawnlpe, spawnv, spawnve, spawnvp,* and *spawnvpe,* the last string must be NULL.

Description
The functions in the *spawn...* family create and run (execute) other files, known as child processes. There must be sufficient memory available for loading and executing a child process.

The value of *mode* determines what action the calling function (the *parent process*) takes after the *spawn...* call. The possible values of *mode* are

P_WAIT	Puts parent process on hold until child process completes execution.
P_NOWAIT	Continues to run parent process while child process runs. The child process ID is returned, so that the parent can wait for completion using *cwait* or *wait*. This mode is currently not available for 16-bit Windows or 16-bit DOS; using it generates an error value.
P_NOWAITO	Identical to P_NOWAIT except that the child process ID isn't saved by the operating system, so the parent process can't wait for it using *cwait* or *wait*.
P_DETACH	Identical to P_NOWAITO, except that the child process is executed in the background with no access to the keyboard or the display.
P_OVERLAY	Overlays child process in memory location formerly occupied by parent. Same as an *exec...* call.

path is the file name of the called child process. The *spawn...* function calls search for *path* using the standard operating system search algorithm:

- If there is no extension or no period, they search for an exact file name. If the file is not found, they search for files first with the extension EXE, then COM, and finally BAT.

- If an extension is given, they search only for the exact file name.

- If only a period is given, they search only for the file name with no extension.

- If *path* does not contain an explicit directory, *spawn...* functions that have the **p** suffix search the current directory, then the directories set with the operating system PATH environment variable.

The suffixes *p*, *l*, and *v*, and *e* added to the *spawn...* "family name" specify that the named function operates with certain capabilities.

p	The function searches for the file in those directories specified by the PATH environment variable. Without the p suffix, the function searches only the current working directory.
l	The argument pointers *arg0, arg1, ..., argn* are passed as separate arguments. Typically, the *l* suffix is used when you know in advance the number of arguments to be passed.
v	The argument pointers *argv[0], ..., arg[n]* are passed as an array of pointers. Typically, the *v* suffix is used when a variable number of arguments is to be passed.
e	The argument *envp* can be passed to the child process, letting you alter the environment for the child process. Without the *e* suffix, child processes inherit the environment of the parent process.

Each function in the *spawn...* family must have one of the two argument-specifying suffixes (either *l* or *v*). The path search and environment inheritance suffixes (*p* and *e*) are optional.

For example:

- *spawnl* takes separate arguments, searches only the current directory for the child, and passes on the parent's environment to the child.

- *spawnvpe* takes an array of argument pointers, incorporates PATH in its search for the child process, and accepts the *envp* argument for altering the child's environment.

The *spawn...* functions must pass at least one argument to the child process (*arg0 or argv[0]*). This argument is, by convention, a copy of *path*. (Using a different value for this 0 argument won't produce an error.) If you want to pass an empty argument list to the child process, then *arg0* or *argv[0]* must be NULL.

Under DOS 3.x, path is available for the child process; under earlier versions, the child process cannot use the passed value of the 0 argument (*arg0* or *argv[0]*).

When the *l* suffix is used, *arg0* usually points to *path*, and *arg1*, ..., *argn* point to character strings that form the new list of arguments. A mandatory null following *argn* marks the end of the list.

When the *e* suffix is used, you pass a list of new environment settings through the argument *envp*. This environment argument is an array of character pointers. Each element points to a null-terminated character string of the form

```
envvar = value
```

where *envvar* is the name of an environment variable, and *value* is the string value to which *envvar* is set. The last element in *envp[]* is null. When *envp* is null, the child inherits the parents' environment settings.

The combined length of *arg0* + *arg1* + ... + *argn* (or of *argv[0]* + *argv[1]* + ... + *argv[n]*), including space characters that separate the arguments, must be less than 260 bytes for Windows (128 for DOS). Null-terminators are not counted.

When a *spawn...* function call is made, any open files remain open in the child process.

Return value
When successful, the *spawn...* functions, where *mode* is P_WAIT, return the child process' exit status (0 for a normal termination). If the child specifically calls *exit* with a nonzero argument, its exit status can be set to a nonzero value.

If *mode* is P_NOWAIT or P_NOWAITO, the spawn functions return the process ID of the child process. The ID obtained when using P_NOWAIT can be passed to cwait.

On error, the *spawn...* functions return -1, and the global variable errno is set to one of the following values:

E2BIG	Arg list too long
EINVAL	Invalid argument
ENOENT	Path or file name not found
ENOEXEC	Exec format error
ENOMEM	Not enough memory

See also
abort, atexit, _c_exit, _cexit, cwait, _exit, exit, exec, _fpreset, searchpath, system, wait

Portability
DOS	UNIX	Win 16	Win 32	ANSI C	ANSI C++	OS/2
+			+			+

_splitpath   stdlib.h

Syntax
void _splitpath(const char *path, char *drive, char *dir, char *name, char *ext);

Description
Splits a full path name into its components.

splitpath takes a file's full path name (*path*) as a string in the form

```
X:\DIR\SUBDIR\NAME.EXT
```

and splits *path* into its four components. It then stores those components in the strings pointed to by *drive*, *dir*, *name*, and *ext*. (All five components must be passed, but any of them can be a null, which means the corresponding component will be parsed but not stored.) The maximum sizes for these strings are given by the constants _MAX_DRIVE, _MAX_DIR, _MAX_PATH, _MAX_FNAME, and _MAX_EXT (defined in stdlib.h), and each size includes space for the null-terminator. These constants are defined in stdlib.h.

Constant	String
_MAX_PATH	*path*
_MAX_DRIVE	*drive*; includes colon (:)
_MAX_DIR	*dir*; includes leading and trailing backslashes (\)
_MAX_FNAME	name
_MAX_EXT	*ext*; includes leading dot (.)

splitpath assumes that there is enough space to store each non-null component.

When _splitpath_ splits *path*, it treats the punctuation as follows:

• *drive* includes the colon (C:, A:, and so on).

• *dir* includes the leading and trailing backslashes (\BC\include\, \source\, and so on).

• *name* includes the file name.

• *ext* includes the dot preceding the extension (.C, .EXE, and so on).

makepath and _splitpath_ are invertible; if you split a given *path* with _splitpath_, then merge the resultant components with _makepath_, you end up with *path*.

Return value
None.

See also
fullpath, _makepath_

Portability

DOS	UNIX	Win 16	Win 32	ANSI C	ANSI C++	OS/2
+	+	+	+			+

sprintf   stdio.h

Syntax
```
int sprintf(char *buffer, const char *format[, argument, ...]);
```

Description
Writes formatted output to a string.

Note For details on format specifiers, see printf.

sprintf accepts a series of arguments, applies to each a format specifier contained in the format string pointed to by *format*, and outputs the formatted data to a string.

sprintf applies the first format specifier to the first argument, the second to the second, and so on. There must be the same number of format specifiers as arguments.

Return value
On success, *sprintf* returns the number of bytes output. The return value does not include the terminating null byte in the count.

On error, *sprintf* returns EOF.

See also
fprintf, printf

Portability

DOS	UNIX	Win 16	Win 32	ANSI C	ANSI C++	OS/2
+	+	+	+	+	+	+

sqrt, sqrtl   math.h

Syntax
double sqrt(double x);
long double sqrtl(long double x);

Description
Calculates the positive square root.

sqrt calculates the positive square root of the argument *x*.

sqrtl is the **long double** version; it takes a **long double** argument and returns a **long double** result. Error handling for these functions can be modified through the functions _matherr and _matherrl.

This function can be used with *bcd* and *complex* types.

Return value
On success, *sqrt* and *sqrtl* return the value calculated, the square root of *x*. If *x* is real and positive, the result is positive. If *x* is real and negative, the global variable *errno* is set to

EDOM   Domain error

See also
bcd, complex, exp, log, pow

Portability

	DOS	UNIX	Win 16	Win 32	ANSI C	ANSI C++	OS/2
sqrt	+	+	+	+	+		+
sqrtl	+		+	+			+

srand

stdlib.h

Syntax
void srand(unsigned seed);

Description
Initializes random number generator.

The random number generator is reinitialized by calling *srand* with an argument value of 1. It can be set to a new starting point by calling *srand* with a given *seed* number.

Return value
None.

See also
rand, random, randomize

Portability

DOS	UNIX	Win 16	Win 32	ANSI C	ANSI C++	OS/2
+	+	+	+	+	+	+

sscanf

stdio.h

Syntax
int sscanf(const char *buffer, const char *format[, address, ...]);

Description
Scans and formats input from a string.

Note   For details on format specifiers, see *scanf*.

sscanf scans a series of input fields, one character at a time, reading from a string. Then each field is formatted according to a format specifier passed to *sscanf* in the format string pointed to by *format*. Finally, *sscanf* stores the formatted input at an address passed to it as an argument following *format*. There must be the same number of format specifiers and addresses as there are input fields.

sscanf might stop scanning a particular field before it reaches the normal end-of-field (whitespace) character, or it might terminate entirely, for a number of reasons. See *scanf* for a discussion of possible causes.

Return value
On success, *sscanf* returns the number of input fields successfully scanned, converted, and stored; the return value does not include scanned fields that were not stored.

If *sscanf* attempts to read at end-of-string, it returns EOF.

On error (If no fields were stored), it returns 0.

See also
fscanf, scanf

Portability

DOS	UNIX	Win 16	Win 32	ANSI C	ANSI C++	OS/2
+	+	+	+	+	+	+

stackavail   malloc.h

Syntax
size_t stackavail(void);

Description
Gets the amount of available stack memory.

stackavail returns the number of bytes available on the stack. This is the amount of dynamic memory that *alloca* can access.

Return value
stackavail returns a *size_t* value indicating the number of bytes available.

See also
alloca

Portability

DOS	UNIX	Win 16	Win 32	ANSI C	ANSI C++	OS/2
+		+	+			+

_status87   float.h

Syntax
unsigned int _status87(void);

Description

Gets floating-point status.

status87 gets the floating-point status word, which is a combination of the 80 *x*87 status word and other conditions detected by the 80 *x*87 exception handler.

Return value

The bits in the return value give the floating-point status. See float.h for a complete definition of the bits returned by _status87_.

Portability

DOS	UNIX	Win 16	Win 32	ANSI C	ANSI C++	OS/2
+		+	+			+

stime   time.h

Syntax

int stime(time_t *tp);

Description

Sets system date and time.

stime sets the system time and date. *tp* points to the value of the time as measured in seconds from 00:00:00 GMT, January 1, 1970.

Return value

stime returns a value of 0.

See also

asctime, ftime, gettime, gmtime, localtime, time, tzset

Portability

DOS	UNIX	Win 16	Win 32	ANSI C	ANSI C++	OS/2
+	+	+				+

stpcpy   string.h

Syntax

char *stpcpy(char *dest, const char *src);

Description

Copies one string into another.

stpcpy copies the string *src* to *dest*, stopping after the terminating null character of *src* has been reached.

Return value

stpcpy returns *dest* + *strlen(src)*.

See also

strcpy

Portability

DOS	UNIX	Win 16	Win 32	ANSI C	ANSI C++	OS/2
+	+	+	+			+

strcat, _fstrcat

string.h

Syntax

char *strcat(char *dest, const char *src);
char far * far _fstrcat(char far *dest, const char far *src)

Description

Appends one string to another.

strcat appends a copy of *src* to the end of *dest*. The length of the resulting string is *strlen(dest)* + *strlen(src)*.

Return value

strcat returns a pointer to the concatenated strings.

Portability

	DOS	UNIX	Win 16	Win 32	ANSI C	ANSI C++	OS/2
strcat	+	+	+	+	+	+	+
_fstrcat	+		+				

strchr, _fstrchr

string.h

Syntax

char *strchr(const char *s, int c);	/* C only */
char far * far _fstrchr(const char far *s, int c)	/* C only */
const char *strchr(const char *s, int c);	// C++ only
char *strchr(char *s, int c);	// C++ only
const char far * far _fstrchr(const char far *s, int c);	// C++ only
char far * far _fstrchr(char far *s, int c);	// C++ only

Description

Scans a string for the first occurrence of a given character.

strchr scans a string in the forward direction, looking for a specific character. *strchr* finds the *first* occurrence of the character *c* in the string *s*. The null-terminator is considered to be part of the string.

For example:

```
strchr(strs,0)
```

returns a pointer to the terminating null character of the string *strs*.

Return value
strchr returns a pointer to the first occurrence of the character *c* in *s*; if *c* does not occur in *s*, *strchr* returns null.

See also
strcspn, strrchr

Portability

	DOS	UNIX	Win 16	Win 32	ANSI C	ANSI C++	OS/2
strchr	+	+	+	+	+	+	+
_fstrchr	+		+				

strcmp   string.h

Syntax
int strcmp(const char *s1, const char *s2);

Description
Compares one string to another.

strcmp performs an unsigned comparison of *s1* to *s2*, starting with the first character in each string and continuing with subsequent characters until the corresponding characters differ or until the end of the strings is reached.

Return value

If *s1* is...	*strcmp* returns a value that is...
less than *s2*	< 0
the same as *s2*	== 0
greater than *s2*	> 0

See also
strcmpi, strcoll, stricmp, strncmp, strncmpi, strnicmp

Portability

DOS	UNIX	Win 16	Win 32	ANSI C	ANSI C++	OS/2
+	+	+	+	+	+	+

strcmpi   string.h

Syntax
int strcmpi(const char *s1, const char *s2);

Description
Compares one string to another, without case sensitivity.

strcmpi performs an unsigned comparison of *s1* to *s2*, without case sensitivity (same as *stricmp*--implemented as a macro).

It returns a value (< 0, 0, or > 0) based on the result of comparing *s1* (or part of it) to *s2* (or part of it).

The routine *strcmpi* is the same as *stricmp*. *strcmpi* is implemented through a macro in string.h and translates calls from *strcmpi* to *stricmp*. Therefore, in order to use *strcmpi*, you must include the header file string.h for the macro to be available. This macro is provided for compatibility with other C compilers.

Return value

If *s1* is...	*strcmpi* returns a value that is...
less than *s2*	< 0
the same as *s2*	== 0
greater than *s2*	> 0

See also
strcmp, strcoll, stricmp, strncmp, strncmpi, strnicmp

Portability

DOS	UNIX	Win 16	Win 32	ANSI C	ANSI C++	OS/2
+	+		+			+

strcoll   string.h

Syntax
int strcoll(char *s1, char *s2);

Description
Compares two strings.

strcoll compares the string pointed to by *s1* to the string pointed to by *s2*, according to the current locale's LC_COLLATE category.

Return value

If s1 is...	strcoll returns a value that is...
less than *s2*	< 0
the same as *s2*	== 0
greater than *s2*	> 0

See also
strcmp, strcmpi, stricmp, strncmp, strncmpi, strnicmp, strxfrm

Portability

DOS	UNIX	Win 16	Win 32	ANSI C	ANSI C++	OS/2
+	+	+	+	+	+	+

strcpy   string.h

Syntax
char *strcpy(char *dest, const char *src);

Description
Copies one string into another.

Copies string *src* to *dest*, stopping after the terminating null character has been moved.

Return value
strcpy returns *dest*.

See also
stpcpy

Portability

DOS	UNIX	Win 16	Win 32	ANSI C	ANSI C++	OS/2
+	+	+	+	+	+	+

strcspn, _fstrcspn   string.h

Syntax
size_t strcspn(const char *s1, const char *s2);
size_t far *far _fstrcspn(const char far *s1, const char far *s2)

Description

Scans a string for the initial segment not containing any subset of a given set of characters.

The *strcspn* functions search *s1* until any one of the characters contained in *s2* is found. The number of characters which were read in *s1* is the return value. The string termination character is not counted. Neither string is altered during the search.

Return value

strcspn returns the length of the initial segment of string *s1* that consists entirely of characters *not* from string *s2*.

See also

strchr, strrchr

Portability

	DOS	UNIX	Win 16	Win 32	ANSI C	ANSI C++	OS/2
strcspn	+	+	+	+	+	+	+
_fstrcspn	+		+				

_strdate   time.h

Syntax

char * _strdate(char *buf);

Description

Converts current date to string.

_strdate converts the current date to a string, storing the string in the buffer *buf*. The buffer must be at least 9 characters long.

The string has the form MM/DD/YY where MM, DD, and YY are all two-digit numbers representing the month, day, and year. The string is terminated by a null character.

Return value

_strdate returns *buf*, the address of the date string.

See also

asctime, ctime, localtime, strftime, _strtime, time

Portability

DOS	UNIX	Win 16	Win 32	ANSI C	ANSI C++	OS/2
+		+	+			+

strdup, _fstrdup

string.h

Syntax

char *strdup(const char *s);

char far * far _fstrdup(const char far *s)

Description

Copies a string into a newly created location.

strdup makes a duplicate of string *s*, obtaining space with a call to *malloc*. The allocated space is (*strlen(s)* + 1) bytes long. The user is responsible for freeing the space allocated by *strdup* when it is no longer needed.

Return value

strdup returns a pointer to the storage location containing the duplicated string, or returns null if space could not be allocated.

See also

free

Portability

	DOS	UNIX	Win 16	Win 32	ANSI C	ANSI C++	OS/2
strdup	+	+	+	+			+
_fstrdup	+		+				

_strerror

string.h

Syntax

char *_strerror(const char *s);

Description

Builds a customized error message.

_strerror lets you generate customized error messages; it returns a pointer to a null-terminated string containing an error message.

- If *s* is null, the return value points to the most recent error message.

- If *s* is not null, the return value contains *s* (your customized error message), a colon, a space, the most-recently generated system error message, and a new line. *s* should be 94 characters or less.

Return value

_strerror returns a pointer to a constructed error string. The error message string is constructed in a static buffer that is overwritten with each call to *_strerror*.

See also
perror, strerror

Portability

DOS	UNIX	Win 16	Win 32	ANSI C	ANSI C++	OS/2
+		+	+			+

strerror   string.h

Syntax
char *strerror(int errnum);

Description
Returns a pointer to an error message string.

strerror takes an **int** parameter *errnum*, an error number, and returns a pointer to an error message string associated with *errnum*.

Return value
strerror returns a pointer to a constructed error string. The error message string is constructed in a static buffer that is overwritten with each call to *strerror*.

See also
perror, _strerror

Portability

DOS	UNIX	Win 16	Win 32	ANSI C	ANSI C++	OS/2
+		+	+	+	+	+

strftime   time.h

Syntax
size_t strftime(char *s, size_t maxsize, const char *fmt, const struct tm *t);

Description
Formats time for output.

strftime formats the time in the argument *t* into the array pointed to by the argument *s* according to the *fmt* specifications. All ordinary characters are copied unchanged. No more than *maxsize* characters are placed in *s*.

The time is formatted according to the current locale's LC_TIME category.

Return value
On success, *strftime* returns the number of characters placed into *s*.

On error (if the number of characters required is greater than *maxsize*), *strftime* returns 0.

See also
localtime, mktime, time

strftime format string

Consists of zero or more directives and ordinary characters. A directive consists of the % character followed by a character that determines the substitution that is to take place.

ANSI-defined format specifiers for strftime

The following table describes the ANSI-defined specifiers for the format string used with strftime.

Format specifier	Substitutes
%%	Character %
%a	Abbreviated weekday name
%A	Full weekday name
%b	Abbreviated month name
%B	Full month name
%c	Date and time
%d	Two-digit day of month (01 - 31)
%H	Two-digit hour (00 - 23)
%I	Two-digit hour (01 - 12)
%j	Three-digit day of year (001 - 366)
%m	Two-digit month as a decimal number (1 - 12)
%M	2-digit minute (00 - 59)
%p	AM or PM
%S	Two-digit second (00 - 59)
%U	Two-digit week number where Sunday is the first day of the week (00 - 53)
%w	Weekday where 0 is Sunday (0 - 6)
%W	Two-digit week number where Monday is the first day of week the week (00 - 53)
%x	Date
%X	Time
%y	Two-digit year without century (00 to 99)
%Y	Year with century
%Z	Time zone name, or no characters if no time zone

POSIX-defined format specifiers

The following table describes the POSIX-defined specifiers for the format string used with strftime.

Note   You must define __USELOCALES__ in order to use these descriptors.

Format specifier	Substitution
%C	Century as a decimal number (00 - 99). For example, 1992 => 19
%D	Date in the format mm/dd/yy
%e	Day of the month as a decimal number in a two-digit field with leading space (1 -31)
%h	A synonym for %b
%n	Newline character
%r	12-hour time (01 - 12) format with am/pm string i.e. "%I:%M:%S %p"
%t	Tab character
%T	24-hour time (00 - 23) in the format "HH:MM:SS"
%u	Weekday as a decimal number (1 Monday - 7 Sunday)

POSIX-defined format specifier modifiers

The following table describes the POSIX-defined modifiers for the following format string specifiers used with strftime.

Note   You must define __USELOCALES__ in order to use these descriptors.

Descriptor modifier	Substitutes
%Od	Day of the month using alternate numeric symbols
%Oe	Day of the month using alternate numeric symbols
%OH	Hour (24 hour) using alternate numeric symbols
%OI	Hour (12 hour) using alternate numeric symbols
%Om	Month using alternate numeric symbols
%OM	Minutes using alternate numeric symbols
%OS	Seconds using alternate numeric symbols
%Ou	Weekday as a number using alternate numeric symbols
%OU	Week number of the year using alternate numeric symbols
%Ow	Weekday as number using alternate numeric symbols
%OW	Week number of the year using alternate numeric symbols
%Oy	Year (offset from %C) using alternate numeric symbols

%O modifier

When the %O modifier is used before any of the above supported numeric format descriptors (for example, %Od), the numeric value is converted to the corresponding ordinal string, if it exists. If an ordinal string does not exist, the basic format descriptor is used unmodified.

For example, on 4/20/94

- %d produces 20
- %Od produces 20th

Portability

DOS	UNIX	Win 16	Win 32	ANSI C	ANSI C++	OS/2
+		+	+	+	+	+

stricmp, _fstricmp   string.h

Syntax

int stricmp(const char *s1, const char *s2);
int far _fstricmp(const char far *s1, const char far *s2)

Description

Compares one string to another, without case sensitivity.

stricmp performs an unsigned comparison of *s1* to *s2*, starting with the first character in each string and continuing with subsequent characters until the corresponding characters differ or until the end of the strings is reached. The comparison is not case sensitive.

It returns a value (< 0, 0, or > 0) based on the result of comparing *s1* (or part of it) to *s2* (or part of it).

The routines *stricmp* and *strcmpi* are the same; *strcmpi* is implemented through a macro in string.h that translates calls from *strcmpi* to *stricmp*. Therefore, in order to use *stricmp*, you must include the header file string.h for the macro to be available.

Return value

If *s1* is...	*stricmp* returns a value that is...
less than *s2*	< 0
the same as *s2*	== 0
greater than *s2*	> 0

See also

strcmp, strcmpi, strcoll, strncmp, strncmpi, strnicmp

Portability

	DOS	UNIX	Win 16	Win 32	ANSI C	ANSI C++	OS/2
stricmp	+	+	+	+	+	+	+
_fstricmp	+		+				

strlen, _fstrlen
string.h

Syntax
size_t strlen(const char *s);
size_t far _fstrlen(const char far *s)

Description
Calculates the length of a string.

strlen calculates the length of *s*.

Return value
strlen returns the number of characters in *s*, not counting the null-terminating character.

Portability

	DOS	UNIX	Win 16	Win 32	ANSI C	ANSI C++	OS/2
strlen	+	+	+	+	+	+	+
_fstrlen	+		+				

strlwr, _fstrlwr
string.h

Syntax
char *strlwr(char *s);
char far * far _fstrlwr(char char far *s)

Description
Converts uppercase letters in a string to lowercase.

strlwr converts uppercase letters in string *s* to lowercase according to the current locale's LC_CTYPE category. For the C locale, the conversion is from uppercase letters (*A* to *Z*) to lowercase letters (*a* to *z*). No other characters are changed.

Return value
strlwr returns a pointer to the string *s*.

See also
strupr

Portability

	DOS	UNIX	Win 16	Win 32	ANSI C	ANSI C++	OS/2
strlwr	+	+	+	+	+	+	+
_fstrlwr	+		+				

strncat, _fstrncat

Syntax

char *strncat(char *dest, const char *src, size_t maxlen);
char far * far _fstrncat(char far *dest, const char far *src, size_t maxlen)

Description

Appends a portion of one string to another.

strncat copies at most *maxlen* characters of *src* to the end of *dest* and then appends a null character. The maximum length of the resulting string is *strlen(dest) + maxlen*.

Return value

strncat returns *dest*.

Portability

	DOS	UNIX	Win 16	Win 32	ANSI C	ANSI C++	OS/2
strncat	+	+	+	+	+	+	+
_fstrncat	+		+				

strncmp, _fstrncmp

Syntax

int strncmp(const char *s1, const char *s2, size_t maxlen);
int far _fstrncmp(const char far *s1, const char far *s2, size_t maxlen)

Description

Compares a portion of one string to a portion of another.

strncmp makes the same unsigned comparison as *strcmp,* but looks at no more than *maxlen* characters. It starts with the first character in each string and continues with subsequent characters until the corresponding characters differ or until it has examined *maxlen* characters.

Return value

strncmp returns an *int* value based on the result of comparing *s1* (or part of it) to *s2* (or part of it):

- < 0 if *s1* is less than *s2*
- == 0 if *s1* is the same as *s2*
- > 0 if *s1* is greater than *s2*

See also

strcmp, strcoll, stricmp, strncmp, strnicmp

Portability

	DOS	UNIX	Win 16	Win 32	ANSI C	ANSI C++	OS/2
strncmp	+	+	+	+	+	+	+
_fstrncmp	+		+				

strncmpi   string.h

Syntax

int strncmpi(const char *s1, const char *s2, size_t n);

Description

Compares a portion of one string to a portion of another, without case sensitivity.

strncmpi performs a signed comparison of *s1* to *s2*, for a maximum length of *n* bytes, starting with the first character in each string and continuing with subsequent characters until the corresponding characters differ or until *n* characters have been examined. The comparison is not case sensitive. (*strncmpi* is the same as *strnicmp*-- implemented as a macro). It returns a value (< 0, 0, or > 0) based on the result of comparing *s1* (or part of it) to *s2* (or part of it).

The routines *strnicmp* and *strncmpi* are the same; *strncmpi* is implemented through a macro in string.h that translates calls from *strncmpi* to *strnicmp*. Therefore, in order to use *strncmpi*, you must include the header file string.h for the macro to be available. This macro is provided for compatibility with other C compilers.

Return value

If *s1* is...	*strncmpi* returns a value that is...
less than *s2*	< 0
the same as *s2*	== 0
greater than *s2*	> 0

Portability

DOS	UNIX	Win 16	Win 32	ANSI C	ANSI C++	OS/2
+	+	+				

strncpy, _fstrncpy   stdio.h

Syntax

char *strncpy(char *dest, const char *src, size_t maxlen);

char far * far _fstrncpy(char far *dest, const char far *src, size_t maxlen)

Description

Copies a given number of bytes from one string into another, truncating or padding as necessary.

strncpy copies up to *maxlen* characters from *src* into *dest*, truncating or null-padding *dest*. The target string, *dest*, might not be null-terminated if the length of *src* is *maxlen* or more.

Return value
strncpy returns *dest*.

Portability

	DOS	UNIX	Win 16	Win 32	ANSI C	ANSI C++	OS/2
strncpy	+	+	+	+	+	+	+
_fstrncpy	+		+				

strnicmp, _fstrnicmp   string.h

Syntax
```
int strnicmp(const char *s1, const char *s2, size_t maxlen);
int far _fstrnicmp(const char far *s1, const char far *s2, size_t maxlen)
```

Description
Compares a portion of one string to a portion of another, without case sensitivity.

strnicmp performs a signed comparison of *s1* to *s2*, for a maximum length of *maxlen* bytes, starting with the first character in each string and continuing with subsequent characters until the corresponding characters differ or until the end of the strings is reached. The comparison is not case sensitive.

It returns a value (< 0, 0, or > 0) based on the result of comparing *s1* (or part of it) to *s2* (or part of it).

Return value

If s1 is...	strnicmp returns a value that is...
less than *s2*	< 0
the same as *s2*	== 0
greater than *s2*	> 0

Portability

	DOS	UNIX	Win 16	Win 32	ANSI C	ANSI C++	OS/2
strnicmp	+		+	+			+
_fstrnicmp	+		+				

strnset, _fstrnset   string.h

Syntax
```
char *strnset(char *s, int ch, size_t n);
char far * far _fstrnset(char far *s, int ch, size_t n)
```

Description

Sets a specified number of characters in a string to a given character.

strnset copies the character *ch* into the first *n* bytes of the string *s*. If *n* > *strlen(s)*, then *strlen(s)* replaces *n*. It stops when *n* characters have been set, or when a null character is found.

Return value

strnset returns *s*.

Portability

	DOS	UNIX	Win 16	Win 32	ANSI C	ANSI C++	OS/2
strnset	+		+	+			+
_fstrnset	+		+				

strpbrk, _fstrpbrk   string.h

Syntax

```
char *strpbrk(const char *s1, const char *s2);        /* C only */
char far *far _fstrpbrk(const char far *s1,
const char far*s2)                                    /* C only */

const char *strpbrk(const char *s1, const char *s2);  // C++ only
char *strpbrk(char *s1, const char *s2);              // C++ only
const char far *far _fstrpbrk(const char far *s1,
const char far *s2);                                  // C++ only
char far * far _fstrpbrk(char far *s1,
            const char far *s2);                      // C++ only
```

Description

Scans a string for the first occurrence of any character from a given set.

strpbrk scans a string, *s1*, for the first occurrence of any character appearing in *s2*.

Return value

strpbrk returns a pointer to the first occurrence of any of the characters in *s2*. If none of the *s2* characters occur in *s1*, *strpbrk* returns null.

Portability

	DOS	UNIX	Win 16	Win 32	ANSI C	ANSI C++	OS/2
strpbrk	+	+	+	+	+	+	+
_fstpbrk	+		+				

strrchr, _fstrrchr

string.h

Syntax
```
char *strrchr(const char *s, int c);              /* C only */
char far * far _fstrrchr(const char far *s, int c)   /* C only */

const char *strrchr(const char *s, int c);        // C++ only
char *strrchr(char *s, int c);                     // C++ only
const char *_fstrrchr(const char far *s, int c);   // C++ only
char *_fstrrchr(char far *s, int c);               // C++ only
```

Description
Scans a string for the last occurrence of a given character.

strrchr scans a string in the reverse direction, looking for a specific character. *strrchr* finds the *last* occurrence of the character *c* in the string *s*. The null-terminator is considered to be part of the string.

Return value
strrchr returns a pointer to the last occurrence of the character *c*. If *c* does not occur in *s*, *strrchr* returns null.

See also
strcspn, strchr

Portability

	DOS	UNIX	Win 16	Win 32	ANSI C	ANSI C++	OS/2
strrchr	+	+	+	+	+	+	+
_fstrrchr	+		+				

strrev, _fstrrev

string.h

Syntax
```
char *strrev(char *s);
char far * far _fstrrev(char far *s)
```

Description
Reverses a string.

strrev changes all characters in a string to reverse order, except the terminating null character. (For example, it would change *string\0* to *gnirts\0*.)

Return value
strrev returns a pointer to the reversed string.

Portability

	DOS	UNIX	Win 16	Win 32	ANSI C	ANSI C++	OS/2
strrev	+		+	+			+
_fstrrev	+		+				

strset, _fstrset   string.h

Syntax
char *strset(char *s, int ch);
char far * far _fstrset(char far *s, int ch)

Description
Sets all characters in a string to a given character.

strset sets all characters in the string *s* to the character *ch*. It quits when the terminating null character is found.

Return value
strset returns *s*.

See also
setmem

Portability

	DOS	UNIX	Win 16	Win 32	ANSI C	ANSI C++	OS/2
strset	+		+	+			+
_fstrset	+		+				

strspn, _fstrspn   string.h

Syntax
size_t strspn(const char *s1, const char *s2);
size_t far _fstrspn(const char far *s1, const char far *s2)

Description
Scans a string for the first segment that is a subset of a given set of characters.

strspn finds the initial segment of string *s1* that consists entirely of characters from string *s2*.

Return value
strspn returns the length of the initial segment of *s1* that consists entirely of characters from *s2*.

Portability

	DOS	UNIX	Win 16	Win 32	ANSI C	ANSI C++	OS/2
strspn	+	+	+	+	+	+	+
_fstrspn	+		+				

strstr, _fstrstr string.h

Syntax

```
char *strstr(const char *s1, const char *s2);          /* C only */
char far * far _fstrstr(const char far *s1,
const char far*s2);                                     /* C only */

const char *strstr(const char *s1, const char          // C++ only
char *strstr(char *s1, const char *s2);                 // C++ only
const char far *far _fstrstr(const char far *s1, const char far *s2);   // C++ only
char far * far _fstrstr(char far *s1, const char far *s2);              // C++ only
```

Description

Scans a string for the occurrence of a given substring.

strstr scans *s1* for the first occurrence of the substring *s2*.

Return value

strstr returns a pointer to the element in *s1*, where *s2* begins (points to *s2* in *s1*). If *s2* does not occur in *s1*, *strstr* returns null.

Portability

	DOS	UNIX	Win 16	Win 32	ANSI C	ANSI C++	OS/2
strstr	+	+	+	+	+	+	+
_fstrstr	+		+				

_strtime time.h

Syntax

```
char *_strtime(char *buf);
```

Description

Converts current time to string.

_strtime converts the current time to a string, storing the string in the buffer *buf*. The buffer must be at least 9 characters long.

The string has the following form:

```
HH:MM:SS
```

where HH, MM, and SS are all two-digit numbers representing the hour, minute, and second, respectively. The string is terminated by a null character.

Return value
strtime returns *buf*, the address of the time string.

See also
asctime, ctime, localtime, strftime, _strdate, time

Portability

DOS	UNIX	Win 16	Win 32	ANSI C	ANSI C++	OS/2
+		+	+			+

strtod, _strtold   stdlib.h

Syntax
```
double strtod(const char *s, char **endptr);
long double _strtold(const char *s, char **endptr);
```

Description
Convert a string to a **double** or **long double** value.

strtod converts a character string, *s*, to a **double** value. *s* is a sequence of characters that can be interpreted as a **double** value; the characters must match this generic format:

```
[ws] [sn] [ddd] [.] [ddd] [fmt[sn]ddd]
```

where:

[ws]	=	optional whitespace
[sn]	=	optional sign (+ or -)
[ddd]	=	optional digits
[fmt]	=	optional *e* or *E*
[.]	=	optional decimal point

strtod also recognizes +INF and -INF for plus and minus infinity, and +NAN and -NAN for Not-a-Number.

For example, here are some character strings that *strtod* can convert to **double**:

```
+ 1231.1981 e-1
502.85E2
+ 2010.952
```

strtod stops reading the string at the first character that cannot be interpreted as an appropriate part of a **double** value.

If *endptr* is not null, *strtod* sets **endptr* to point to the character that stopped the scan (**endptr = &stopper*). *endptr* is useful for error detection.

strtold is the **long double** version; it converts a string to a **long double** value.

Return value

These functions return the value of _s_ as a **double** (_strtod_) or a **long double** (_strtold_). In case of overflow, they return plus or minus HUGE_VAL (_strtod_) or _LHUGE_VAL (_strtold_).

See also

atof

Portability

	DOS	UNIX	Win 16	Win 32	ANSI C	ANSI C++	OS/2
strtod	+	+	+	+	+	+	+
_strtold	+		+	+			+

strtok, _fstrtok   string.h

Syntax

```
char *strtok(char *s1, const char *s2);
char far * far _fstrtok(char far *s1, const char far *s2)
```

Description

Searches one string for tokens, which are separated by delimiters defined in a second string.

strtok considers the string _s1_ to consist of a sequence of zero or more text tokens, separated by spans of one or more characters from the separator string _s2_.

The first call to _strtok_ returns a pointer to the first character of the first token in _s1_ and writes a null character into _s1_ immediately following the returned token. Subsequent calls with null for the first argument will work through the string _s1_ in this way, until no tokens remain.

The separator string, _s2_, can be different from call to call.

Note Calls to _strtok_ cannot be nested with a function call that also uses _strtok_. Doing so will causes an endless loop.

Return value

strtok returns a pointer to the token found in _s1_. A NULL pointer is returned when there are no more tokens.

Portability

	DOS	UNIX	Win 16	Win 32	ANSI C	ANSI C++	OS/2
strtok	+	+	+	+	+	+	+
_fstrtok	+		+				

strtol

Syntax

long strtol(const char *s, char **endptr, int radix);

Description

Converts a string to a **long** value.

strtol converts a character string, *s*, to a **long** integer value. *s* is a sequence of characters that can be interpreted as a **long** value; the characters must match this generic format:

    [ws] [sn] [0] [x] [ddd]

where:

[ws]	=	optional whitespace
[sn]	=	optional sign (+ or -)
[0]	=	optional zero (0)
[x]	=	optional x or X
[ddd]	=	optional digits

strtol stops reading the string at the first character it doesn't recognize.

If *radix* is between 2 and 36, the long integer is expressed in base *radix*. If *radix* is 0, the first few characters of *s* determine the base of the value being converted.

First character	Second character	String interpreted as...
0	1 - 7	Octal
0	x or X	Hexadecimal
1 - 9		Decimal

If *radix* is 1, it is considered to be an invalid value. If *radix* is less than 0 or greater than 36, it is considered to be an invalid value.

Any invalid value for *radix* causes the result to be 0 and sets the next character pointer **endptr* to the starting string pointer.

If the value in *s* is meant to be interpreted as octal, any character other than 0 to 7 will be unrecognized.

If the value in *s* is meant to be interpreted as decimal, any character other than 0 to 9 will be unrecognized.

If the value in *s* is meant to be interpreted as a number in any other base, then only the numerals and letters used to represent numbers in that base will be recognized. (For example, if *radix* equals 5, only 0 to 4 will be recognized; if *radix* equals 20, only 0 to 9 and *A* to *J* will be recognized.)

If *endptr* is not null, *strtol* sets **endptr* to point to the character that stopped the scan (**endptr* = &*stopper*).

Return value
strtol returns the value of the converted string, or 0 on error.

See also
atoi, atol, strtoul

Portability

DOS	UNIX	Win 16	Win 32	ANSI C	ANSI C++	OS/2
+		+	+	+	+	+

strtoul   stdlib.h

Syntax
unsigned long strtoul(const char *s, char **endptr, int radix);

Description
Converts a string to an **unsigned long** in the given radix.

strtoul operates the same as *strtol*, except that it converts a string *str* to an **unsigned long** value (where *strtol* converts to a **long**). Refer to the entry for *strtol* for more information.

Return value
strtoul returns the converted value, an **unsigned long**, or 0 on error.

See also
atol, strtol

Portability

DOS	UNIX	Win 16	Win 32	ANSI C	ANSI C++	OS/2
+		+	+	+	+	+

strupr, _fstrupr   string.h

Syntax
char *strupr(char *s);
char far * far _fstrupr(char far *s)

Description
Converts lowercase letters in a string to uppercase.

strupr converts lowercase letters in string *s* to uppercase according to the current locale's LC_CTYPE category. For the default C locale, the conversion is from lowercase letters (*a* to *z*) to uppercase letters (*A* to *Z*). No other characters are changed.

Return value
strupr returns *s*.

See also
strlwr

Portability

	DOS	UNIX	Win 16	Win 32	ANSI C	ANSI C++	OS/2
strupr	+		+	+			+
_fstrupr	+		+				

strxfrm   string.h

Syntax
size_t strxfrm(char *target, const char *source, size_t n);

Description
Transforms a portion of a string to a specified collation.

strxfrm transforms the string pointed to by *source* into the string *target* for no more than *n* characters. The transformation is such that if the *strcmp* function is applied to the resulting strings, its return corresponds with the return values of the *strcoll* function.

No more than *n* characters, including the terminating null character, are copied to *target*.

strxfrm transforms a character string into a special string according to the current locale's LC_COLLATE category. The special string that is built can be compared with another of the same type, byte for byte, to achieve a locale-correct collation result. These special strings, which can be thought of as keys or tokenized strings, are not compatible across the different locales.

The tokens in the tokenized strings are built from the collation weights used by *strcoll* from the active locale's collation tables.

Processing stops only after all levels have been processed for the character string or the length of the tokenized string is equal to the *maxlen* parameter.

All redundant tokens are removed from each level's set of tokens.

The tokenized string buffer must be large enough to contain the resulting tokenized string. The length of this buffer depends on the size of the character string, the number of collation levels, the rules for each level and whether there are any special characters in the character string. Certain special characters can cause extra character processing of the string resulting in more space requirements. For example, the French character "oe" will take double the space for itself because in some locales, it expands to collation weights for each level. Substrings that have substitutions will also cause extra space requirements.

There is no safe formula to determine the required string buffer size, but at least (levels * string length) are required.

Return value

Number of characters copied not including the terminating null character. If the value returned is greater than or equal to *n*, the content of *target* is indeterminate.

See also

strcmp, strcoll, strncpy

Portability

DOS	UNIX	Win 16	Win 32	ANSI C	ANSI C++	OS/2
+		+	+	+	+	+

swab   stdlib.h

Syntax

void swab(char *from, char *to, int nbytes);

Description

Swaps bytes.

swab copies *nbytes* bytes from the *from* string to the *to* string. Adjacent even- and odd-byte positions are swapped. This is useful for moving data from one machine to another machine with a different byte order. *nbytes* should be even.

Return value

None.

Portability

DOS	UNIX	Win 16	Win 32	ANSI C	ANSI C++	OS/2
+	+	+	+			+

system   stdlib.h

Syntax

int system(const char *command);

Description

Issues an operating system command.

system invokes the operating system command processor to execute an operating system command, batch file, or other program named by the string *command*, from inside an executing C program.

To be located and executed, the program must be in the current directory or in one of the directories listed in the PATH string in the environment.

The COMSPEC environment variable is used to find the command processor program file, so that file need not be in the current directory.

Return value

If *command* is a NULL pointer, *system* returns nonzero if a command processor is available.

If *command* is not a NULL pointer, *system* returns 0 if the command processor was successfully started.

If an error occurred, a -1 is returned and errno is set to one of the following:

ENOENT   Path or file function not found

ENOEXEC   Exec format error

ENOMEM   Not enough memory

See also

exec..., _fpreset, searchpath, spawn...

Portability

DOS	UNIX	Win 16	Win 32	ANSI C	ANSI C++	OS/2
+	+		+			+

tan, tanl   math.h

Syntax

```
double tan(double x);
long double tanl(long double x);
```

Description

Calculates the tangent.

tan calculates the tangent. Angles are specified in radians.

tanl is the **long double** version; it takes a **long double** argument and returns a **long double** result. Error handling for these routines can be modified through the functions *_matherr* and *_matherrl*.

This function can be used with *bcd* and *complex* types.

Return value

tan and *tanl* return the tangent of *x*, $sin(x)/cos(x)$.

See also

acos, asin, atan, atan2, bcd, complex, cos, sin

Portability

	DOS	UNIX	Win 16	Win 32	ANSI C	ANSI C++	OS/2
tan	+	+	+	+	+	+	+
tanl	+		+	+			+

tanh, tanhl   math.h

Syntax
double tanh(double x);
long double tanhl(long double x);

Description
Calculates the hyperbolic tangent.

tanh computes the hyperbolic tangent, $sinh(x)/cosh(x)$.

tanhl is the **long double** version; it takes a **long double** argument and returns a **long double** result. Error handling for these functions can be modified through the functions *_matherr* and *_matherrl*.

This function can be used with *bcd* and *complex* types.

Return value
tanh and *tanhl* return the hyperbolic tangent of *x*.

See also
bcd, complex, cos, cosh, sin, sinh, tan

Portability;

	DOS	UNIX	Win 16	Win 32	ANSI C	ANSI C++	OS/2
tanh	+	+	+	+	+	+	+
tanhl	+		+	+			+

tell   io.h

Syntax
long tell(int handle);

Description
Gets the current position of a file pointer.

tell gets the current position of the file pointer associated with *handle* and expresses it as the number of bytes from the beginning of the file.

Return value

tell returns the current file pointer position. A return of -1 (**long**) indicates an error, and the global variable errno is set to

EBADF   Bad file number

See also

fgetpos, fseek, ftell, lseek

Portability

DOS	UNIX	Win 16	Win 32	ANSI C	ANSI C++	OS/2
+	+	+	+			+

tempnam

stdio.h

Syntax

char *tempnam(char *dir, char *prefix)

Description

Creates a unique file name in specified directory.

The *tempnam* function creates a unique file name in arbitrary directories. The unique file is not actually created; *tempnam* only verifies that it does not currently exist. It attempts to use the following directories, in the order shown, when creating the file name:

• The directory specified by the TMP environment variable.
• The *dir* argument to *tempnam*.
• The *P_tmpdir* definition in stdio.h. If you edit stdio.h and change this definition, *tempnam* will *not* use the new definition.
• The current working directory.

If any of these directories is NULL, undefined, or does not exist, it is skipped.

The *prefix* argument specifies the first part of the file name; it cannot be longer than 5 characters, and cannot contain a period (.). A unique file name is created by concatenating the directory name, the *prefix*, and 6 unique characters. Space for the resulting file name is allocated with *malloc*; when this file name is no longer needed, the caller should call *free* to free it.

If you do create a temporary file using the name constructed by *tempnam*, it is your responsibility to delete the file name (for example, with a call to *remove*). It is not deleted automatically. (*tmpfile* does delete the file name.)

Return value

If *tempnam* is successful, it returns a pointer to the unique temporary file name, which the caller can pass to *free* when it is no longer needed. Otherwise, if *tempnam* cannot create a unique file name, it returns NULL.

See also
mktemp, tmpfile, tmpnam

Portability

DOS	UNIX	Win 16	Win 32	ANSI C	ANSI C++	OS/2
+	+	+	+			+

textattr

conio.h

Syntax
void textattr(int newattr);

Description
Sets text attributes.

Note Do not use this function for Win32s or Win32 GUI applications.

textattr lets you set both the foreground and background colors in a single call. (Normally, you set the attributes with *textcolor* and *textbackground*.)

This function does not affect any characters currently onscreen; it affects only those characters displayed by functions (such as *cprintf*) performing text mode, direct video output *after* this function is called.

The color information is encoded in the *newattr* parameter as follows:

```
7  6  5  4 │ 3  2  1  0
B  b  b  b │ f  f  f  f
```

In this 8-bit *newattr* parameter:

- *ffff* is the 4-bit foreground color (0 to 15).
- *bbb* is the 3-bit background color (0 to 7).
- *B* is the blink-enable bit.

If the blink-enable bit is on, the character blinks. This can be accomplished by adding the constant BLINK to the attribute.

If you use the symbolic color constants defined in conio.h for creating text attributes with *textattr*, note the following limitations on the color you select for the background:

- You can select only one of the first eight colors for the background.
- You must shift the selected background color left by 4 bits to move it into the correct bit positions.

These symbolic constants are listed in the following table:

Symbolic constant	Numeric value	Foreground or background
BLACK	0	Both
BLUE	1	Both
GREEN	2	Both
CYAN	3	Both
RED	4	Both
MAGENTA	5	Both
BROWN	6	Both
LIGHTGRAY	7	Both
DARKGRAY	8	Foreground only
LIGHTBLUE	9	Foreground only
LIGHTGREEN	10	Foreground only
LIGHTCYAN	11	Foreground only
LIGHTRED	12	Foreground only
LIGHTMAGENTA	13	Foreground only
YELLOW	14	Foreground only
WHITE	15	Foreground only
BLINK	128	Foreground only

Return value

None.

See also

gettextinfo, highvideo, lowvideo, normvideo, textbackground, textcolor

Portability

DOS	UNIX	Win 16	Win 32	ANSI C	ANSI C++	OS/2
+			+			+

textbackground   conio.h

Syntax

void textbackground(int newcolor);

Description

Selects new text background color.

Note   Do not use this function for Win32s or Win32 GUI applications.

textbackground selects the background color. This function works for functions that produce output in text mode directly to the screen. *newcolor* selects the new background color. You can set *newcolor* to an integer from 0 to 7, or to one of the symbolic constants defined in conio.h. If you use symbolic constants, you must include conio.h.

Once you have called *textbackground,* all subsequent functions using direct video output (such as *cprintf*) will use *newcolor. textbackground* does not affect any characters currently onscreen.

The following table lists the symbolic constants and the numeric values of the allowable colors:

Symbolic constant	Numeric value
BLACK	0
BLUE	1
GREEN	2
CYAN	3
RED	4
MAGENTA	5
BROWN	6
LIGHTGRAY	7

Return value
None.

See also
gettextinfo, textattr, textcolor

Portability

DOS	UNIX	Win 16	Win 32	ANSI C	ANSI C++	OS/2
+			+			+

textcolor   conio.h

Syntax
void textcolor(int newcolor);

Description
Selects new character color in text mode.

Note Do not use this function for Win32s or Win32 GUI applications.

textcolor selects the foreground character color. This function works for the console output functions. *newcolor* selects the new foreground color. You can set *newcolor* to an integer as given in the table below, or to one of the symbolic constants defined in conio.h. If you use symbolic constants, you must include conio.h.

Once you have called *textcolor,* all subsequent functions using direct video output (such as *cprintf*) will use *newcolor. textcolor* does not affect any characters currently onscreen.

The following table lists the allowable colors (as symbolic constants) and their numeric values:

Symbolic constant	Numeric value
BLACK	0
BLUE	1
GREEN	2
CYAN	3
RED	4
MAGENTA	5
BROWN	6
LIGHTGRAY	7
DARKGRAY	8
LIGHTBLUE	9
LIGHTGREEN	10
LIGHTCYAN	11
LIGHTRED	12
LIGHTMAGENTA	13
YELLOW	14
WHITE	15
BLINK	128

You can make the characters blink by adding 128 to the foreground color. The predefined constant BLINK exists for this purpose.

For example:

```
textcolor(CYAN + BLINK);
```

Note Some monitors do not recognize the intensity signal used to create the eight "light" colors (8-15). On such monitors, the light colors are displayed as their "dark" equivalents (0-7). Also, systems that do not display in color can treat these numbers as shades of one color, special patterns, or special attributes (such as underlined, bold, italics, and so on). Exactly what you'll see on such systems depends on your hardware.

Return value
None.

See also
gettextinfo, highvideo, lowvideo, normvideo, textattr, textbackground

Portability

DOS	UNIX	Win 16	Win 32	ANSI C	ANSI C++	OS/2
+			+			+

textmode

Syntax

void textmode(int newmode);

Description

Puts screen in text mode.

Note   Do not use this function for Win32s or Win32 GUI applications.

textmode selects a specific text mode.

You can give the text mode (the argument *newmode*) by using a symbolic constant from the enumeration type *text_modes* (defined in conio.h).

The most commonly used *text_modes* type constants and the modes they specify are given in the following table. Some additional values are defined in conio.h.

Symbolic constant	Text mode
LASTMODE	Previous text mode
BW40	Black and white, 40 columns
C40	Color, 40 columns
BW80	Black and white, 80 columns
C80	Color, 80 columns
MONO	Monochrome, 80 columns
C4350	EGA 43-line and VGA 50-line modes

When *textmode* is called, the current window is reset to the entire screen, and the current text attributes are reset to normal, corresponding to a call to *normvideo*.

Specifying LASTMODE to *textmode* causes the most recently selected text mode to be re-selected.

textmode should be used only when the screen or window is in text mode (presumably to change to a different text mode). This is the only context in which *textmode* should be used. When the screen is in graphics mode, use *restorecrtmode* instead to escape temporarily to text mode.

Return value

None.

See also

gettextinfo, window

Portability

DOS	UNIX	Win 16	Win 32	ANSI C	ANSI C++	OS/2
+			+			+

time

Syntax
time_t time(time_t *timer);

Description
Gets time of day.

time gives the current time, in seconds, elapsed since 00:00:00 GMT, January 1, 1970, and stores that value in the location pointed to by *timer*, provided that *timer* is not a NULL pointer.

Return value
time returns the elapsed time in seconds.

See also
asctime, ctime, difftime, ftime, gettime, gmtime, localtime, settime, stime, tzset

Portability

DOS	UNIX	Win 16	Win 32	ANSI C	ANSI C++	OS/2
+	+	+	+	+	+	+

tmpfile

Syntax
FILE *tmpfile(void);

Description
Opens a "scratch" file in binary mode.

tmpfile creates a temporary binary file and opens it for update ($w + b$). If you do not change the directory after creating the temporary file, the file is automatically removed when it's closed or when your program terminates.

Return value
tmpfile returns a pointer to the stream of the temporary file created. If the file can't be created, *tmpfile* returns NULL.

See also
fopen, tmpnam

Portability

DOS	UNIX	Win 16	Win 32	ANSI C	ANSI C++	OS/2
+	+	+	+	+	+	+

tmpnam
stdio.h

Syntax
char *tmpnam(char *s);

Description
Creates a unique file name.

tmpnam creates a unique file name, which can safely be used as the name of a temporary file. *tmpnam* generates a different string each time you call it, up to TMP_MAX times. TMP_MAX is defined in stdio.h as 65,535.

The parameter to *tmpnam*, *s*, is either NULL or a pointer to an array of at least L_*tmpnam* characters. L_*tmpnam* is defined in stdio.h. If *s* is NULL, *tmpnam* leaves the generated temporary file name in an internal static object and returns a pointer to that object. If *s* is not NULL, *tmpnam* overwrites the internal static object and places its result in the pointed-to array, which must be at least L_*tmpnam* characters long, and returns *s*.

If you do create such a temporary file with *tmpnam*, it is your responsibility to delete the file name (for example, with a call to *remove*). It is not deleted automatically. (*tmpfile* does delete the file name.)

Return value
If *s* is NULL, *tmpnam* returns a pointer to an internal static object. Otherwise, *tmpnam* returns *s*.

See also
tmpfile

Portability

DOS	UNIX	Win 16	Win 32	ANSI C	ANSI C++	OS/2
+	+	+	+	+	+	+

toascii
ctype.h

Syntax
int toascii(int c);

Description
Translates characters to ASCII format.

toascii is a macro that converts the integer *c* to ASCII by clearing all but the lower 7 bits; this gives a value in the range 0 to 127.

Return value

toascii returns the converted value of *c*.

Portability

DOS	UNIX	Win 16	Win 32	ANSI C	ANSI C++	OS/2
+	+	+	+			+

_tolower

ctype.h

Syntax

int _tolower(int ch);

Description

_tolower is a macro that does the same conversion as *tolower*, except that it should be used only when *ch* is known to be uppercase (*A to Z*).

To use *_tolower*, you must include ctype.h.

Return value

_tolower returns the converted value of *ch* if it is uppercase; otherwise, the result is undefined.

Portability

DOS	UNIX	Win 16	Win 32	ANSI C	ANSI C++	OS/2
+	+	+	+			+

tolower

ctype.h

Syntax

int tolower(int ch);

Description

Translates characters to lowercase.

tolower is a function that converts an integer *ch* (in the range EOF to 255) to its lowercase value (*a to z*; if it was uppercase, *A to Z*). All others are left unchanged.

Return value

tolower returns the converted value of *ch* if it is uppercase; it returns all others unchanged.

Portability

DOS	UNIX	Win 16	Win 32	ANSI C	ANSI C++	OS/2
+	+	+	+	+	+	+

_toupper
ctype.h

Syntax
int _toupper(int ch);

Description
Translates characters to uppercase.

toupper is a macro that does the same conversion as _toupper_, except that it should be used only when _ch_ is known to be lowercase (_a_ to _z_).

To use _toupper_, you must include ctype.h.

Return value
toupper returns the converted value of _ch_ if it is lowercase; otherwise, the result is undefined.

Portability

DOS	UNIX	Win 16	Win 32	ANSI C	ANSI C++	OS/2
+	+	+	+			+

toupper
ctype.h

Syntax
int toupper(int ch);

Description
Translates characters to uppercase.

toupper is a function that converts an integer _ch_ (in the range EOF to 255) to its uppercase value (_A_ to _Z_; if it was lowercase, _a_ to _z_). All others are left unchanged.

Return value
toupper returns the converted value of _ch_ if it is lowercase; it returns all others unchanged.

Portability

DOS	UNIX	Win 16	Win 32	ANSI C	ANSI C++	OS/2
+	+	+	+	+	+	+

3tzset

Syntax

void tzset(void)

Description

Sets value of global variables _daylight, _timezone, and _tzname.

tzset is available on XENIX systems.

tzset sets the _daylight, _timezone, and _tzname global variables based on the environment variable *TZ*. The library functions *ftime* and *localtime* use these global variables to adjust Greenwich Mean Time (GMT) to the local time zone. The format of the *TZ* environment string is:

```
TZ = zzz[+/-]d[d][lll]
```

where *zzz* is a three-character string representing the name of the current time zone. All three characters are required. For example, the string "PST" could be used to represent Pacific standard time.

[+/-]d[d] is a required field containing an optionally signed number with 1 or more digits. This number is the local time zone's difference from GMT in hours. Positive numbers adjust westward from GMT. Negative numbers adjust eastward from GMT. For example, the number 5 = EST, +8 = PST, and -1 = continental Europe. This number is used in the calculation of the global variable _timezone. _timezone is the difference in seconds between GMT and the local time zone.

lll is an optional three-character field that represents the local time zone, daylight saving time. For example, the string "PDT" could be used to represent pacific daylight saving time. If this field is present, it causes the global variable _daylight to be set nonzero. If this field is absent, _daylight is set to zero.

If the *TZ* environment string isn't present or isn't in the preceding form, a default *TZ* = "EST5EDT" is presumed for the purposes of assigning values to the global variables _daylight, _timezone, and _tzname.

The global variable _tzname[0] points to a three-character string with the value of the time-zone name from the *TZ* environment string. _tzname[1] points to a three-character string with the value of the daylight saving time-zone name from the *TZ* environment string. If no daylight saving name is present, _tzname[1] points to a NULL string.

Return value

None.

See also

asctime, ctime, ftime, gmtime, localtime, stime, time

Portability

DOS	UNIX	Win 16	Win 32	ANSI C	ANSI C++	OS/2
+	+	+	+			+

ultoa

Syntax
char *ultoa(unsigned long value, char *string, int radix);

Description
Converts an **unsigned long** to a string.

ultoa converts *value* to a null-terminated string and stores the result in *string*. *value* is an **unsigned long**.

radix specifies the base to be used in converting *value*; it must be between 2 and 36, inclusive. *ultoa* performs no overflow checking, and if *value* is negative and *radix* equals 10, it does not set the minus sign.

Note The space allocated for *string* must be large enough to hold the returned string, including the terminating null character (\0). *ultoa* can return up to 33 bytes.

Return value
ultoa returns *string*.

See also
itoa, ltoa

Portability

DOS	UNIX	Win 16	Win 32	ANSI C	ANSI C++	OS/2
+		+	+			+

umask

Syntax
unsigned umask(unsigned mode);

Description
Sets file read/write permission mask.

The *umask* function sets the access permission mask used by *open* and *creat*. Bits that are set in *mode* will be cleared in the access permission of files subsequently created by *open* and *creat*.

The *mode* can have one of the following values, defined in sys\stat.h:

Value of mode	Access permission
S_IWRITE	Permission to write
S_IREAD	Permission to read
S_IREAD|S_IWRITE	Permission to read and write

Return value

The previous value of the mask. There is no error return.

See also

creat, *open*

Portability

DOS	UNIX	Win 16	Win 32	ANSI C	ANSI C++	OS/2
+		+	+			+

ungetc

stdio.h

Syntax

int ungetc(int c, FILE *stream);

Description

Pushes a character back into input stream.

Note   Do not use this function for Win32s or Win32 GUI applications.

ungetc pushes the character *c* back onto the named input *stream*, which must be open for reading. This character will be returned on the next call to *getc* or *fread* for that *stream*. One character can be pushed back in all situations. A second call to *ungetc* without a call to *getc* will force the previous character to be forgotten. A call to *fflush, fseek, fsetpos,* or *rewind* erases all memory of any pushed-back characters.

Return value

On success, *ungetc* returns the character pushed back.

On error, it returns EOF.

See also

fgetc, getc, getchar

Portability

DOS	UNIX	Win 16	Win 32	ANSI C	ANSI C++	OS/2
+	+	+	+	+	+	+

ungetch

Syntax

int ungetch(int ch);

Description

Pushes a character back to the keyboard buffer.

Note Do not use this function for Win32s or Win32 GUI applications.

ungetch pushes the character *ch* back to the console, causing *ch* to be the next character read. The *ungetch* function fails if it is called more than once before the next read.

Return value

On success, *ungetch* returns the character *ch*.

On error, it returns EOF.

See also

getch, getche

Portability

DOS	UNIX	Win 16	Win 32	ANSI C	ANSI C++	OS/2
+	+		+			+

unixtodos

Syntax

void unixtodos(long time, struct date *d, struct time *t);

Description

Converts date and time from UNIX to DOS format.

unixtodos converts the UNIX-format time given in *time* to DOS format and fills in the *date* and *time* structures pointed to by *d* and *t*.

time must not represent a calendar time earlier than Jan. 1, 1980 00:00:00.

Return value

None.

See also

dostounix

Portability

DOS	UNIX	Win 16	Win 32	ANSI C	ANSI C++	OS/2
+		+	+			+

unlink   io.h

Syntax
int unlink(const char *filename);

Description
Deletes a file.

unlink deletes a file specified by *filename*. Any drive, path, and file name can be used as a *filename*. Wildcards are not allowed.

Read-only files cannot be deleted by this call. To remove read-only files, first use *chmod* or *_rtl_chmod* to change the read-only attribute.

Note   If your file is open, be sure to close it before unlinking it.

Return value
On success, *unlink* returns 0.

On error, it returns -1 and sets the global variable *errno* to one of the following values:

EACCES   Permission denied

ENOENT   Path or file name not found

See also
chmod, remove

Portability

DOS	UNIX	Win 16	Win 32	ANSI C	ANSI C++	OS/2
+	+	+	+			+

unlock   io.h

Syntax
int unlock(int handle, long offset, long length);

Description
Releases file-sharing locks.

unlock provides an interface to the operating system file-sharing mechanism. *unlock* removes a lock previously placed with a call to *lock*. To avoid error, all locks must be removed before a file is closed. A program must release all locks before completing.

Return value

On success, *unlock* returns 0.

On error, it returns -1.

See also

lock, locking, sopen

Portability

DOS	UNIX	Win 16	Win 32	ANSI C	ANSI C++	OS/2
+		+	+			+

utime

utime.h

Syntax

```
int utime(char *path, struct utimbuf *times);
```

Description

Sets file time and date.

utime sets the modification time for the file *path*. The modification time is contained in the *utimbuf* structure pointed to by *times*. This structure is defined in utime.h, and has the following format:

```
struct utimbuf {
    time_t   actime;    /* access time */
    time_t   modtime;   /* modification time */
    };
```

The FAT (file allocation table) file system supports only a modification time; therefore, on FAT file systems *utime* ignores *actime* and uses only *modtime* to set the file's modification time.

If *times* is NULL, the file's modification time is set to the current time.

Return value

On success, *utime* returns 0.

On error, it returns -1, and sets the global variable *errno* to one of the following values:

EACCES	Permission denied
EMFILE	Too many open files
ENOENT	Path or file name not found

See also

setftime, stat, time

Portability

DOS	UNIX	Win 16	Win 32	ANSI C	ANSI C++	OS/2
+	+	+	+			+

va_arg, va_end, va_start
stdarg.h

Syntax
```
void va_start(va_list ap, lastfix);
type va_arg(va_list ap, type);
void va_end(va_list ap);
```

Description
Implements a variable argument list.

Some C functions, such as *vfprintf* and *vprintf*, take variable argument lists in addition to taking a number of fixed (known) parameters. The *va_arg, va_end*, and *va_start* macros provide a portable way to access these argument lists. They are used for stepping through a list of arguments when the called function does not know the number and types of the arguments being passed.

The header file stdarg.h declares one type (**va_list**) and three macros (*va_start, va_arg,* and *va_end*).

- **va_list**: This array holds information needed by *va_arg* and *va_end*. When a called function takes a variable argument list, it declares a variable *ap* of type **va_list**.

- *va_start*: This routine (implemented as a macro) sets *ap* to point to the first of the variable arguments being passed to the function. *va_start* must be used before the first call to *va_arg* or *va_end*.

- *va_start* takes two parameters: *ap* and *lastfix*. (*ap* is explained under *va_list* in the preceding paragraph; *lastfix* is the name of the last fixed parameter being passed to the called function.)

- *va_arg*: This routine (also implemented as a macro) expands to an expression that has the same type and value as the next argument being passed (one of the variable arguments). The variable *ap* to *va_arg* should be the same *ap* that *va_start* initialized.

Note Because of default promotions, you cannot use **char, unsigned char**, or **float** types with *va_arg*.

The first time *va_arg* is used, it returns the first argument in the list. Each successive time *va_arg* is used, it returns the next argument in the list. It does this by first dereferencing *ap*, and then incrementing *ap* to point to the following item. *va_arg* uses the *type* to both perform the dereference and to locate the following item. Each successive time *va_arg* is invoked, it modifies *ap* to point to the next argument in the list.

- *va_end*: This macro helps the called function perform a normal return. *va_end* might modify *ap* in such a way that it cannot be used unless *va_start* is recalled. *va_end* should be called after *va_arg* has read all the arguments; failure to do so might cause strange, undefined behavior in your program.

Return value

va_start and *va_end* return no values; *va_arg* returns the current argument in the list (the one that *ap* is pointing to).

See also

vprintf, vscanf

Portability

DOS	UNIX	Win 16	Win 32	ANSI C	ANSI C++	OS/2
+	+	+	+	+	+	+

vfprintf   stdio.h

Syntax

int vfprintf(FILE *stream, const char *format, va_list arglist);

Description

Writes formatted output to a stream.

The *v...printf* functions are known as *alternate entry points* for the *...printf* functions. They behave exactly like their *...printf* counterparts, but they accept a pointer to a list of arguments instead of an argument list.

For details on format specifiers, see "printf Format Specifiers."

vfprintf accepts a pointer to a series of arguments, applies to each argument a format specifier contained in the format string pointed to by *format*, and outputs the formatted data to a stream. There must be the same number of format specifiers as arguments.

Return value

On success, *vfprintf* returns the number of bytes output.

On error, it returns EOF.

See also

printf, va_arg, va_end, va_start

Portability

DOS	UNIX	Win 16	Win 32	ANSI C	ANSI C++	OS/2
+	+	+	+	+	+	+

vfscanf   stdio.h

Syntax

int vfscanf(FILE *stream const char *format va_list arglist);

Description
Scans and formats input from a stream.

The *v...scanf* functions are known as *alternate entry points* for the *...scanf* functions. They behave exactly like their *...scanf* counterparts but they accept a pointer to a list of arguments instead of an argument list.

For details on format specifiers, see "scanf Format Specifiers."

vfscanf scans a series of input fields one character at a time reading from a stream. Then each field is formatted according to a format specifier passed to *vfscanf* in the format string pointed to by *format*. Finally *vfscanf* stores the formatted input at an address passed to it as an argument following *format*. There must be the same number of format specifiers and addresses as there are input fields. *vfscanf* might stop scanning a particular field before it reaches the normal end-of-field (whitespace) character or it might terminate entirely for a number of reasons. See *scanf* for a discussion of possible causes.

Return value
vfscanf returns the number of input fields successfully scanned converted and stored; the return value does not include scanned fields that were not stored. If no fields were stored the return value is 0.

If *vfscanf* attempts to read at end-of-file the return value is EOF.

See also
fscanf, scanf, va_arg, va_end, va_start

Portability

DOS	UNIX	Win 16	Win 32	ANSI C	ANSI C++	OS/2
+	+	+	+			+

vprintf

stdarg.h

Syntax
int vprintf(const char *format, va_list arglist);

Description
Writes formatted output to stdout.

Note Do not use this function for Win32s or Win32 GUI applications.

The *v...printf* functions are known as *alternate entry points* for the *...printf* functions. They behave exactly like their *...printf* counterparts, but they accept a pointer to a list of arguments instead of an argument list.

For details on format specifiers, see "printf Format Specifiers."

vprintf accepts a pointer to a series of arguments, applies to each a format specifier contained in the format string pointed to by *format*, and outputs the formatted data to stdout. There must be the same number of format specifiers as arguments.

Note   When you use the SS!=DS flag in 16-bit applications, *vprintf* assumes that the address being passed is in the SS segment.

Return value
vprint returns the number of bytes output. In the event of error, *vprint* returns EOF.

See also
freopen, printf, va_arg, va_end, va_start

Portability

DOS	UNIX	Win 16	Win 32	ANSI C	ANSI C++	OS/2
+	+		+	+		+

vscanf   stdarg.h

Syntax
int vscanf(const char *format, va_list arglist);

Description
Scans and formats input from stdin.

Note   Do not use this function for Win32s or Win32 GUI applications.

The *v...scanf* functions are known as *alternate entry points* for the *...scanf* functions. They behave exactly like their *...scanf* counterparts, but they accept a pointer to a list of arguments instead of an argument list.

For details on format specifiers, see "scanf Format Specifiers."

vscanf scans a series of input fields, one character at a time, reading from stdin. Then each field is formatted according to a format specifier passed to *vscanf* in the format string pointed to by *format*. Finally, *vscanf* stores the formatted input at an address passed to it as an argument following *format*. There must be the same number of format specifiers and addresses as there are input fields.

vscanf might stop scanning a particular field before it reaches the normal end-of-field (whitespace) character, or it might terminate entirely, for a number of reasons. See *scanf* for a discussion of possible causes.

Return value

vscanf returns the number of input fields successfully scanned, converted, and stored; the return value does not include scanned fields that were not stored. If no fields were stored, the return value is 0.

If *vscanf* attempts to read at end-of-file, the return value is EOF.

See also

freopen, fscanf, scanf, va_arg, va_end, va_start

Portability

DOS	UNIX	Win 16	Win 32	ANSI C	ANSI C++	OS/2
+	+	+	+			+

vsprintf   stdarg.h

Syntax
```
int vsprintf(char *buffer, const char *format, va_list arglist);
```

Description
Writes formatted output to a string.

The *v...printf* functions are known as *alternate entry points* for the *...printf* functions. They behave exactly like their *...printf* counterparts, but they accept a pointer to a list of arguments instead of an argument list.

For details on format specifiers, see "pprintf Format Specifiers."

vsprintf accepts a pointer to a series of arguments, applies to each a format specifier contained in the format string pointed to by *format*, and outputs the formatted data to a string. There must be the same number of format specifiers as arguments.

Return value
vsprintf returns the number of bytes output. In the event of error, *vsprintf* returns EOF.

See also
printf, va_arg, va_end, va_start

Portability

DOS	UNIX	Win 16	Win 32	ANSI C	ANSI C++	OS/2
+	+	+	+	+	+	+

vsscanf
stdarg.h

Syntax
int vsscanf(const char *buffer, const char *format, va_list arglist);

Description
Scans and formats input from a stream.

The *v...scanf* functions are known as *alternate entry points* for the *...scanf* functions. They behave exactly like their *...scanf* counterparts, but they accept a pointer to a list of arguments instead of an argument list.

For details on format specifiers, see "Scanf Format Specifiers."

vsscanf scans a series of input fields, one character at a time, reading from a stream. Then each field is formatted according to a format specifier passed to *vsscanf* in the format string pointed to by *format*. Finally, *vsscanf* stores the formatted input at an address passed to it as an argument following *format*. There must be the same number of format specifiers and addresses as there are input fields.

vsscanf might stop scanning a particular field before it reaches the normal end-of-field (whitespace) character, or it might terminate entirely, for a number of reasons. See *scanf* for a discussion of possible causes.

Return value
vsscanf returns the number of input fields successfully scanned, converted, and stored; the return value does not include scanned fields that were not stored. If no fields were stored, the return value is 0.

If *vsscanf* attempts to read at end-of-string, the return value is EOF.

See also
fscanf, scanf, sscanf, va_arg, va_end, va_start, vfscanf

Portability

DOS	UNIX	Win 16	Win 32	ANSI C	ANSI C++	OS/2
+	+	+	+			+

wait
process.h

Syntax
int wait(int *statloc);

Description
Waits for one or more child processes to terminate.

The *wait* function waits for one or more child processes to terminate. The child processes must be those created by the calling program; *wait* cannot wait for grandchildren (processes spawned by child processes). If *statloc* is not NULL, it points to location where *wait* will store the termination status.

If the child process terminated normally (by calling *exit*, or returning from *main*), the termination status word is defined as follows:

Bits 0-7	Zero.
Bits 8-15	The least significant byte of the return code from the child process. This is the value that is passed to *exit*, or is returned from *main*. If the child process simply exited from *main* without returning a value, this value will be unpredictable. If the child process terminated abnormally, the termination status word is defined as follows:
Bits 0-7	Termination information about the child:
	1 Critical error abort.
	2 Execution fault, protection exception.
	3 External termination signal.
Bits 8-15	Zero.

Return value
When *wait* returns after a normal child process termination it returns the process ID of the child.

When *wait* returns after an abnormal child termination it returns -1 to the parent and sets *errno* to EINTR.

If *wait* returns without a child process completion it returns a -1 value and sets errno to

ECHILD	No child process exists

See also
cwait, spawn

Portability

DOS	UNIX	Win 16	Win 32	ANSI C	ANSI C++	OS/2
			+			+

wcstombs

stdlib.h

Syntax
size_t wcstombs(char *s, const wchar_t *pwcs, size_t n);

Description
Converts a **wchar_t** array into a multibyte string.

wcstombs converts the type **wchar_t** elements contained in *pwcs* into a multibyte character string *s*. The process terminates if either a null character or an invalid multibyte character is encountered.

No more than *n* bytes are modified. If *n* number of bytes are processed before a null character is reached, the array *s* is not null terminated.

The behavior of *wcstombs* is affected by the setting of LC_CTYPE category of the current locale.

Return value

If an invalid multibyte character is encountered, *wcstombs* returns (size_t) -1. Otherwise, the function returns the number of bytes modified, not including the terminating code, if any.

Portability

DOS	UNIX	Win 16	Win 32	ANSI C	ANSI C++	OS/2
+	+	+	+	+	+	+

wctomb   stdlib.h

Syntax
int wctomb(char *s, wchar_t wc);

Description
Converts **wchar_t** code to a multibyte character.

If *s* is not null, *wctomb* determines the number of bytes needed to represent the multibyte character corresponding to *wc* (including any change in shift state). The multibyte character is stored in *s*. At most MB_CUR_MAX characters are stored. If the value of *wc* is zero, *wctomb* is left in the initial state.

The behavior of *wctomb* is affected by the setting of LC_CTYPE category of the current locale.

Return value

If *s* is a NULL pointer, *wctomb* returns a nonzero value if multibyte character encodings do have state-dependent encodings, and a zero value if they do not.

If *s* is not a NULL pointer, *wctomb* returns -1 if the *wc* value does not represent a valid multibyte character. Otherwise, *wctomb* returns the number of bytes that are contained in the multibyte character corresponding to *wc*. In no case will the return value be greater than the value of MB_CUR_MAX macro.

Portability

DOS	UNIX	Win 16	Win 32	ANSI C	ANSI C++	OS/2
+	+	+	+	+	+	+

wherex

conio.h

Syntax

int wherex(void);

Description

Gives horizontal cursor position within window.

Note   Do not use this function for Win32s or Win32 GUI applications.

wherex returns the x-coordinate of the current cursor position (within the current text window).

Return value

wherex returns an integer in the range 1 to the number of columns in the current video mode.

See also

gettextinfo, gotoxy, wherey

Portability

DOS	UNIX	Win 16	Win 32	ANSI C	ANSI C++	OS/2
+		+	+			+

wherey

conio.h

Syntax

int wherey(void);

Description

Gives vertical cursor position within window.

Note   Do not use this function for Win32s or Win32 GUI applications.

wherey returns the y-coordinate of the current cursor position (within the current text window).

Return value

wherey returns an integer in the range 1 to the number of rows in the current video mode.

See also

gettextinfo, gotoxy, wherex

Portability

DOS	UNIX	Win 16	Win 32	ANSI C	ANSI C++	OS/2
+		+	+			+

window

Syntax
void window(int left, int top, int right, int bottom);

Description
Defines active text mode window.

Note   Do not use this function for Win32s or Win32 GUI applications.

window defines a text window onscreen. If the coordinates are in any way invalid, the call to *window* is ignored.

left and *top* are the screen coordinates of the upper left corner of the window.

right and *bottom* are the screen coordinates of the lower right corner.

The minimum size of the text window is one column by one line. The default window is full screen, with the coordinates:

```
1,1,C,R
```

where C is the number of columns in the current video mode, and R is the number of rows.

Return value
None.

See also
clreol, clrscr, delline, gettextinfo, gotoxy, insline, lseek, puttext, _rtl_read, textmode, write

Portability

DOS	UNIX	Win 16	Win 32	ANSI C	ANSI C++	OS/2
+			+			+

write

Syntax
int write(int handle, void *buf, unsigned len);

Description
Writes to a file.

write writes a buffer of data to the file or device named by the given *handle*. *handle* is a file handle obtained from a *creat, open, dup,* or *dup2* call.

This function attempts to write *len* bytes from the buffer pointed to by *buf* to the file associated with *handle*. Except when *write* is used to write to a text file, the number of bytes written to the file will be no more than the number requested. The maximum number of bytes that *write* can write is UINT_MAX -1, because UINT_MAX is the same as -1, which is the error return indicator for *write*. On text files, when *write* sees a linefeed (LF) character, it outputs a CR/LF pair. UINT_MAX is defined in limits.h.

If the number of bytes actually written is less than that requested, the condition should be considered an error and probably indicates a full disk. For disks or disk files, writing always proceeds from the current file pointer. For devices, bytes are sent directly to the device. For files opened with the O_APPEND option, the file pointer is positioned to EOF by *write* before writing the data.

Return value

write returns the number of bytes written. A *write* to a text file does not count generated carriage returns. In case of error, *write* returns -1 and sets the global variable *errno* to one of the following values:

EACCES   Permission denied

EBADF   Bad file number

See also

creat, lseek, open, read, _rtl_write

Portability

DOS	UNIX	Win 16	Win 32	ANSI C	ANSI C++	OS/2
+	+	+	+			+

4

Global variables

Borland C++ provides you with predefined global variables for many common needs, such as dates, times, command-line arguments, and so on. These variables are presented in this chapter in alphabetical (ASCII) order.

For a list of obsolete global variables, see the section, "Obsolete global variables," later in this chapter.

_8087   dos.h

extern int _8087;
The _8087 variable is set to a nonzero value if the startup code autodetection logic detects a floating-point coprocessor.

_8087 value	Math coprocessor
1	8087
2	80287
3	80387
0	(none detected)

The autodetection logic can be overridden by setting the 87 environment variable to YES or NO. (The commands are SET 87=YES and SET 87=NO; it is essential that there be no spaces before or after the equal sign.) In this case, the _8087 variable will reflect the override.

Portability

DOS	UNIX	Win 16	Win 32	ANSI C	ANSI C++	OS/2
+		+	+			

_argc

dos.h

```
extern int _argc;
```
_argc has the value of *argc* passed to *main* when the program starts.

Example

```
#include <iostream.h>
#include <dos.h>        // TO GET THE GLOBAL _arg VALUES

void func() {
   cout << "argc= " << _argc << endl;

   for (int i = 0; i < _argc; ++i)
     cout << _argv[i] << endl;
   }

void main(int argc, char ** argv) {
   func(); // THIS FUNCTION KNOWS ALL THE main() ARGUMENTS
   }
```

Portability

DOS	UNIX	Win 16	Win 32	ANSI C	ANSI C++	OS/2
+		+	+			+

_argv

dos.h

```
extern char **_argv;
```
_argv points to an array containing the original command-line arguments (the elements of *argv[]*) passed to *main* when the program starts.

Example

```
#include <iostream.h>
#include <dos.h>        // TO GET THE GLOBAL _arg VALUES

void func() {
   cout << "argc= " << _argc << endl;

   for (int i = 0; i < _argc; ++i)
     cout << _argv[i] << endl;
   }

void main(int argc, char ** argv) {
   func(); // THIS FUNCTION KNOWS ALL THE main() ARGUMENTS
   }
```

Portability

DOS	UNIX	Win 16	Win 32	ANSI C	ANSI C++	OS/2
+		+	+			+

_ctype   ctype.h

extern char _ctype[];

ctype is an array of character attribute information indexed by ASCII value + 1. Each entry is a set of bits describing the character. This array is used by _isdigit_, _isprint_, and so on.

Portability

DOS	UNIX	Win 16	Win 32	ANSI C	ANSI C++	OS/2
+		+	+			+

_daylight   time.h

extern int _daylight;

daylight is used by the time and date functions. It is set by the _tzset_, _ftime_, and _localtime_ functions to 1 for daylight saving time, 0 for standard time.

See also   _timezone, _tzname_

Portability

DOS	UNIX	Win 16	Win 32	ANSI C	ANSI C++	OS/2
+		+	+			+

_directvideo   conio.h

extern int _directvideo;

directvideo controls whether your program's console output goes directly to the video RAM (_directvideo_ = 1) or goes via ROM BIOS calls (_directvideo_ = 0).

The default value is _directvideo_ = 1 (console output goes directly to video RAM). To use _directvideo_ = 1, the video hardware on your system must be identical to IBM display adapters. Setting _directvideo_ = 0 allows your console output to work on any system that is IBM BIOS-compatible.

directvideo should be used only in character-based applications. It is not allowed in 16-bit Windows, Win32s, or Win32 GUI applications.

Portability

DOS	UNIX	Win 16	Win 32	ANSI C	ANSI C++	OS/2
+		+	+			

_environ

dos.h

extern char ** _environ;

_environ is an array of pointers to strings; it is used to access and alter the operating system environment variables. Each string is of the form:

```
envvar = varvalue
```

where *envvar* is the name of an environment variable (such as PATH), and *varvalue* is the string value to which *envvar* is set (such as C:\BIN;C:\DOS). The string *varvalue* can be empty.

When a program begins execution, the operating system environment settings are passed directly to the program. Note that *env*, the third argument to *main*, is equal to the initial setting of *_environ*.

The *_environ* array can be accessed by *getenv*; however, the *putenv* function is the only routine that should be used to add, change, or delete the *_environ* array entries. This is because modification can resize and relocate the process environment array, but *_environ* is automatically adjusted so that it always points to the array.

See also   *getenv, putenv*

Portability

DOS	UNIX	Win 16	Win 32	ANSI C	ANSI C++	OS/2
+		+	+			+

errno

errno.h

extern int errno;

errno is used by *perror* to print error messages when certain library routines fail to accomplish their appointed tasks.

When an error in a math or system call occurs, *errno* is set to indicate the type of error. Sometimes *errno* and *_doserrno* are equivalent. At other times, *errno* does not contain the actual operating system error code, which is contained in *_doserrno*. Still other errors might occur that set only *errno*, not *_doserrno*.

Example

```
/* DISPLAY THE SYSTEM ERRORS. */
#include <errno.h>
#include <stdio.h>

extern char *_sys_errlist[];

main()
{
    int i = 0;

    while(_sys_errlist[i++]) printf("%s\n", _sys_errlist[i]);
```

```
    return 0;
}
```

Portability

DOS	UNIX	Win 16	Win 32	ANSI C	ANSI C++	OS/2
+		+	+			+

_doserrno   errno.h

extern int _doserrno;

doserrno is a variable that maps many operating system error codes to _errno_; however, _perror_ does not use _doserrno_ directly.

When an operating system call results in an error, _doserrno_ is set to the actual operating system error code. _errno_ is a parallel error variable inherited from UNIX.

The following list gives mnemonics for the actual DOS error codes to which _doserrno_ can be set. (This value of _doserrno_ may or may not be mapped (through _errno_) to an equivalent error message string in _sys_errlist_.)

Mnemonic	DOS error code
E2BIG	Bad environ
EACCES	Access denied
EACCES	Bad access
EACCES	Is current dir
EBADF	Bad handle
EFAULT	Reserved
EINVAL	Bad data
EINVAL	Bad function
EMFILE	Too many open
ENOENT	No such file or directory
ENOEXEC	Bad format
ENOMEM	Mcb destroyed
ENOMEM	Out of memory
ENOMEM	Bad block
EXDEV	Bad drive
EXDEV	Not same device

Refer to your DOS reference manual for more information about DOS error return codes.

Example

```
/* DISPLAY THE SYSTEM ERRORS. */
#include <errno.h>
#include <stdio.h>
```

```
extern char *_sys_errlist[];

main()
{
   int i = 0;

   while(_sys_errlist[i++]) printf("%s\n", _sys_errlist[i]);
   return 0;
}
```

Portability

DOS	UNIX	Win 16	Win 32	ANSI C	ANSI C++	OS/2
+		+	+			+

_sys_errlist   errno.h

extern char * _sys_errlist[ ];

_sys_errlist_ is used by perror to print error messages when certain library routines fail to accomplish their appointed tasks.

To provide more control over message formatting, the array of message strings is provided in _sys_errlist_. You can use _errno_ as an index into the array to find the string corresponding to the error number. The string does not include any newline character.

The following table gives mnemonics and their meanings for the values stored in _sys_errlist_. The list is alphabetically ordered for ease your reading convenience. For the numerical ordering, see the header file errno.h.

Mnemonic	16-bit Description	32-bit Description
E2BIG	Arg list too long	Arg list too long
EACCES	Permission denied	Permission denied
EBADF	Bad file number	Bad file number
ECHILD		No child process
ECONTR	Memory blocks destroyed	Memory blocks destroyed
ECURDIR	Attempt to remove CurDir	Attempt to remove CurDir
EDEADLOCK		Locking violation
EDOM	Domain error	Math argument
EEXIST	File already exists	File already exists
EFAULT	Unknown error	Unknown error
EINTR		Interrupted function call
EINVACC	Invalid access code	Invalid access code
EINVAL	Invalid argument	Invalid argument
EINVDAT	Invalid data	Invalid data
EINVDRV	Invalid drive specified	Invalid drive specified
EINVENV	Invalid environment	Invalid environment
EINVFMT	Invalid format	Invalid format
EINVFNC	Invalid function number	Invalid function number

Mnemonic	16-bit Description	32-bit Description
EINVMEM	Invalid memory block address	Invalid memory block address
EIO		input/output error
EMFILE	Too many open files	Too many open files
ENAMETOOLONG		File name too long
ENFILE		Too many open files
ENMFILE	No more files	No more files
ENODEV	No such device	No such device
ENOENT	No such file or directory	No such file or directory
ENOEXEC	Exec format error	Exec format error
ENOFILE	No such file or directory	File not found
ENOMEM	Not enough memory	Not enough core
ENOPATH	Path not found	Path not found
ENOSPC		No space left on device
ENOTSAM	Not same device	Not same device
ENXIO		No such device or address
EPERM		Operation not permitted
EPIPE		Broken pipe
ERANGE	Result out of range	Result too large
EROFS		Read-only file system
ESPIPE		Illegal seek
EXDEV	Cross-device link	Cross-device link
EZERO	Error 0	Error 0

Refer to your DOS reference manual for more information about DOS error return codes.

Example

```
/* DISPLAY THE SYSTEM ERRORS. */
#include <errno.h>
#include <stdio.h>

extern char *_sys_errlist[];

main()
{
   int i = 0;

   while(_sys_errlist[i++]) printf("%s\n", _sys_errlist[i]);
   return 0;
}
```

Portability

DOS	UNIX	Win 16	Win 32	ANSI C	ANSI C++	OS/2
+		+	+			+

_sys_nerr

errno.h

extern int _sys_nerr;

_sys_nerr is used by perror to print error messages when certain library routines fail to accomplish their appointed tasks.

This variable is defined as the number of error message strings in *_sys_errlist*.

Example

```
/* DISPLAY THE SYSTEM ERRORS. */
#include <errno.h>
#include <stdio.h>

extern char *_sys_errlist[];

main()
{
   int i = 0;

   while(_sys_errlist[i++]) printf("%s\n", _sys_errlist[i]);
   return 0;
}
```

Portability

DOS	UNIX	Win 16	Win 32	ANSI C	ANSI C++	OS/2
+		+	+			+

_floatconvert

stdio.h

extern int _floatconvert;

Floating-point output requires linking of conversion routines used by *printf, scanf,* and any variants of these functions. In order to reduce executable size, the floating-point formats are not automatically linked. However, this linkage is done automatically whenever your program uses a mathematical routine or the address is taken of some floating-point number. If neither of these actions occur, the missing floating-point formats can result in a run-time error.

Example

```
/* PREPARE TO OUTPUT FLOATING-POINT NUMBERS. */
#include <stdio.h>
#pragma extref _floatconvert

void main() {
  printf("d = %lf\n", 1);
}
```

Portability

DOS	UNIX	Win 16	Win 32	ANSI C	ANSI C++	OS/2
+		+	+			+

_fmode   fcntl.h

extern int _fmode;

fmode determines in which mode (text or binary) files will be opened and translated. The value of _fmode_ is O_TEXT by default, which specifies that files will be read in text mode. If _fmode_ is set to O_BINARY, the files are opened and read in binary mode. (O_TEXT and O_BINARY are defined in fcntl.h.)

In text mode, carriage-return/linefeed (CR/LF) combinations are translated to a single linefeed character (LF) on input. On output, the reverse is true: LF characters are translated to CR/LF combinations.

In binary mode, no such translation occurs.

You can override the default mode as set by _fmode_ by specifying a _t_ (for text mode) or _b_ (for binary mode) in the argument _type_ in the library functions _fopen, fdopen,_ and _freopen._ Also, in the function _open,_ the argument access can include either O_BINARY or O_TEXT, which will explicitly define the file being opened (given by the _open pathname_ argument) to be in either binary or text mode.

Portability

DOS	UNIX	Win 16	Win 32	ANSI C	ANSI C++	OS/2
+		+	+			+

_new_handler   new.h

typedef void (*pvf)();
pvf _new_handler;

_new_handler_ contains a pointer to a function that takes no arguments and returns **void**. If **operator new()** is unable to allocate the space required, it will call the function pointed to by _new_handler_; if that function returns it will try the allocation again. By default, the function pointed to by _new_handler_ simply terminates the application. The application can replace this handler, however, with a function that can try to free up some space. This is done by assigning directly to _new_handler_ or by calling the function set_new_handler, which returns a pointer to the former handler.

As an alternative, you can set using the function _set_new_handler,_ like this:

```
pvf set_new_handler(pvf p);
```

_new_handler_ is provided primarily for compatibility with C++ version 1.2. In most cases this functionality can be better provided by overloading **operator new()**.

_osmajor   dos.h

extern unsigned char _osmajor;

The major version number of the operating system is available individually through
_osmajor. For example, if you are running DOS version 3.2, _osmajor will be 3.

This variable can be useful when you want to write modules that will run on DOS
versions 2.x and 3.x. Some library routines behave differently depending on the DOS
version number, while others only work under DOS 3.x and higher. For example, refer
to *creatnew*, *ioctl*, and *_rtl_open*.

See also   *_osminor*, *_osversion*, *_version*

_osminor   dos.h

extern unsigned char _osminor;

The minor version number of the operating system is available individually through
_osminor. For example, if you are running DOS version 3.2, _osminor will be 20.

This variables can be useful when you want to write modules that will run on DOS
versions 2.x and 3.x. Some library routines behave differently depending on the DOS
version number, while others only work under DOS 3.x and higher. For example, refer
to *creatnew*, *ioctl*, and *_rtl_open*.

See also   *_osmajor*, *_osversion*, *_version*

_osversion   dos.h

extern unsigned _osversion;

_osversion contains the operating system version number, with the major version
number in the low byte and the minor version number in the high byte. (For DOS
version x.y, the *x* is the major version number, and *y* is the minor version number.)

_osversion is functionally identical to *_version*.

Portability

DOS	UNIX	Win 16	Win 32	ANSI C	ANSI C++	OS/2
+		+	+			+

_psp   dos.h, process.h, stdlib.h

extern unsigned int _psp;

_psp specifies the address of the program segment prefix (PSP) of a program. The PSP is a DOS process descriptor; it contains initial DOS information about the program.

Note   *_psp* cannot be used in DLLs.

Portability

DOS	UNIX	Win 16	Win 32	ANSI C	ANSI C++	OS/2
+		+	+			+

_ _throwExceptionName   except.h

extern char * _ _throwExceptionName;

Use this global variable to get the name of a thrown exception. The output for this variable is a printable character string.

See also   *_ _throwFileName, _ _throwLineNumber*

Portability

DOS	UNIX	Win 16	Win 32	ANSI C	ANSI C++	OS/2
+		+	+			+

_ _throwFileName   except.h

extern char * _ _throwFileName;

Use this global variable to get the name of a thrown exception. The output for this variables is a printable character string.

To get the file name for a thrown exception with *_ _throwFileName*, you must compile the module with the *-xp* compiler option.

See also   *_ _throwExceptionName, _ _throwLineNumber*

Portability

DOS	UNIX	Win 16	Win 32	ANSI C	ANSI C++	OS/2
+		+	+			+

_ _throwLineNumber

except.h

extern char * _ _throwLineNumber;

Use this global variable to get the name of a thrown exception. The output for this variable is a printable character string.

To get the line number for a thrown exception with _throwLineNumber, you must compile the module with the **-xp** compiler option.

See also _ _throwExceptionName, _ _throwFileName

Portability

DOS	UNIX	Win 16	Win 32	ANSI C	ANSI C++	OS/2
+		+	+			+

_threadid

stddef.h

extern long _threadid;

_threadid is a long integer that contains the ID of the currently executing thread. It is implemented as a macro, and should be declared only by including stddef.h.

Portability

DOS	UNIX	Win 16	Win 32	ANSI C	ANSI C++	OS/2
+			+			+

_timezone

time.h

extern long _timezone;

_timezone is used by the time-and-date functions. It is calculated by the tzset function; it is assigned a long value that is the difference, in seconds, between the current local time and Greenwich mean time.

See also _daylight, _tzname

Portability

DOS	UNIX	Win 16	Win 32	ANSI C	ANSI C++	OS/2
+		+	+			+

_tzname

time.h

extern char * _tzname[2]

The global variable _tzname is an array of pointers to strings containing abbreviations for time zone names. _tzname[0] points to a three-character string with the value of the time zone name from the TZ environment string. The global variable _tzname[1] points to a three-character string with the value of the daylight saving time zone name from the

TZ environment string. If no daylight saving name is present, *_tzname*[1] points to a null string.

See also   *_daylight, _timezone*

Portability

DOS	UNIX	Win 16	Win 32	ANSI C	ANSI C++	OS/2
+		+	+			+

_version   dos.h

extern unsigned _version;
_version contains the operating system version number, with the major version number in the low byte and the minor version number in the high byte. (For DOS version *x.y*, the *x* is the major version number, and *y* is the minor.)

See also   *_osmajor, _osminor, _osversion*

Portability

DOS	UNIX	Win 16	Win 32	ANSI C	ANSI C++	OS/2
+		+	+			+

_wscroll   conio.h

extern int _wscroll
_wscroll is a console I/O flag. Its default value is 1. If you set *_wscroll* to 0, scrolling is disabled. This can be useful for drawing along the edges of a window without having your screen scroll.

_wscroll should be used only in character-based applications. It is available for EasyWin but is not allowed in 16-bit Windows, Win32s, or Win32 GUI applications.

Portability

DOS	UNIX	Win 16	Win 32	ANSI C	ANSI C++	OS/2
+		+	+			+

Obsolete global variables

The following global variables have been renamed to comply with ANSI naming requirements. You should always use the new names.

If you link with libraries that were compiled with Borland C++ 3.1 (or earlier) header files, the following message is generated:

```
Error: undefined external <varname> in module <LIBNAME>.LIB
```

You should recompile a library module that results in such an error. If you cannot recompile the code for such libraries, you can link with OBSOLETE.LIB to resolve the external variable names.

The following global variables have been renamed:

Old name	New name	Header file
daylight	_daylight	time.h
directvideo	_directvideo	conio.h
environ	_environ	stdlib.h
sys_errlist	_sys_errlist	errno.h
sys_nerr	_sys_nerr	errno.h
timezone	_timezone	time.h
tzname	_tzname	time.h

5

Preprocessor directives

Preprocessor directives are usually placed at the beginning of your source code, but they can legally appear at any point in a program. The Borland C++ preprocessor detects preprocessor directives (also known as control lines) and parses the tokens embedded in them. Borland C++ supports these preprocessor directives:

(null directive)	ifdef
define	ifndef
elif	include
else	line
endif	pragma
error	undef
if	

Any line with a leading # is taken as a preprocessing directive, unless the # is within a string literal, in a character constant, or embedded in a comment. The initial # can be preceded or followed by whitespace (excluding new lines).

(Null directive)

#

The null directive consists of a line containing the single character #. This line is always ignored.

#define

#define macro_identifier <token_sequence>
The **#define** directive defines a *macro*. Macros provide a mechanism for token replacement with or without a set of formal, function-like parameters.

Each occurrence of *macro_identifier* in your source code following this control line will be replaced in the original position with the possibly empty *token_sequence* (there are some exceptions, which are noted later). Such replacements are known as *macro expansions*. The token sequence is sometimes called the *body* of the macro.

An empty token sequence results in the removal of each affected macro identifier from the source code.

After each individual macro expansion, a further scan is made of the newly expanded text. This allows for the possibility of *nested macros*: The expanded text can contain macro identifiers that are subject to replacement. However, if the macro expands into what looks like a preprocessing directive, such a directive will not be recognized by the preprocessor. There are these restrictions to macro expansion:

- Any occurrences of the macro identifier found within literal strings, character constants, or comments in the source code are not expanded.

- A macro won't be expanded during its own expansion (so #define A A won't expand indefinitely).

Example

```
#define HI "Have a nice day!"
#define empty
#define NIL ""
#define GETSTD #include <stdio.h>
```

See also   "Keywords and protected words as macros," "Macros with parameters," #undef, "Using the -D and -U command-line options"

#undef

#undef macro_identifier
You can undefine a macro using the **#undef** directive. **#undef** detaches any previous token sequence from the macro identifier; the macro definition has been forgotten, and the macro identifier is undefined. No macro expansion occurs within **#undef** lines.

The state of being *defined* or *undefined* turns out to be an important property of an identifier, regardless of the actual definition. The **#ifdef** and **#ifndef** conditional directives, used to test whether any identifier is currently defined or not, offer a flexible mechanism for controlling many aspects of a compilation.

After a macro identifier has been undefined, it can be redefined with **#define**, using the same or a different token sequence.

Attempting to redefine an already defined macro identifier will result in a warning unless the new definition is *exactly* the same token-by-token definition as the existing one. The preferred strategy where definitions might exist in other header files is as follows:

```
#ifndef BLOCK_SIZE
  #define BLOCK_SIZE 512
#endif
```

The middle line is bypassed if BLOCK_SIZE is currently defined; if BLOCK_SIZE is not currently defined, the middle line is invoked to define it.

No semicolon (;) is needed to terminate a preprocessor directive. Any character found in the token sequence, including semicolons, will appear in the macro expansion. The token sequence terminates at the first non-backslashed new line encountered. Any sequence of whitespace, including comments in the token sequence, is replaced with a single-space character.

Example

```
#define BLOCK_SIZE 512
  ⋮
#undef BLOCK_SIZE
/* use of BLOCK_SIZE now would be illegal "unknown" identifier */
  ⋮
#define BLOCK_SIZE 128    /* redefinition */
```

See also   #define, "Using the -D and -U command-line options"

Using the -D and -U command-line options

Identifiers can be defined and undefined using the command-line compiler options -D and -U.

The command line

```
BCC32 -Ddebug=1; paradox=0; X -Umysym myprog.c
```

is equivalent to placing

```
#define debug 1
#define paradox 0
#define X
#undef mysym
```

in the program.

See also   #define, #undef

Keywords and protected words as macros

It is legal but ill-advised to use Borland C++ keywords as macro identifiers:

```
#define int long    /* legal but probably catastrophic */
#define INT long     /* legal and possibly useful */
```

The following predefined global identifiers *cannot* appear immediately following a #define or #undef directive:

_ _DATE_ _	_ _FILE_ _	_ _LINE_ _
_ _STDC_ _	_ _TIME_ _	

Macros with parameters

The following syntax is used to define a macro with parameters:

```
#define macro_identifier(<arg_list>) token_sequence
```

Any comma within parentheses in an argument list is treated as part of the argument, not as an argument delimiter.

Note there can be no whitespace between the macro identifier and the (. The optional *arg_list* is a sequence of identifiers separated by commas, not unlike the argument list of a C function. Each comma-delimited identifier plays the role of a *formal argument* or *placeholder*.

Such macros are called by writing

```
macro_identifier<whitespace>(<actual_arg_list>)
```

in the subsequent source code. The syntax is identical to that of a function call; indeed, many standard library C "functions" are implemented as macros. However, there are some important semantic differences, side effects, and potential pitfalls.

The optional *actual_arg_list* must contain the same number of comma-delimited token sequences, known as actual arguments, as found in the formal *arg_list* of the #define line: There must be an actual argument for each formal argument. An error will be reported if the number of arguments in the two lists is different.

A macro call results in two sets of replacements. First, the macro identifier and the parenthesis-enclosed arguments are replaced by the token sequence. Next, any formal arguments occurring in the token sequence are replaced by the corresponding real arguments appearing in the *actual_arg_list*.

As with simple macro definitions, rescanning occurs to detect any embedded macro identifiers eligible for expansion.

Nesting parentheses and commas

The *actual_arg_list* can contain nested parentheses provided that they are balanced; also, commas appearing within quotes or parentheses are not treated like argument delimiters.

Token pasting with

You can paste (or merge) two tokens together by separating them with ## (plus optional whitespace on either side). The preprocessor removes the whitespace and the ##, combining the separate tokens into one new token. You can use this to construct identifiers.

Converting to strings with

The # symbol can be placed in front of a formal macro argument in order to convert the actual argument to a string after replacement.

Using the backslash (\) for line continuation

A long token sequence can straddle a line by using a backslash (\). The backslash and the following newline are both stripped to provide the actual token sequence used in expansions.

Side effects and other dangers

The similarities between function and macro calls often obscure their differences. A macro call has no built-in type checking, so a mismatch between formal and actual argument data types can produce bizarre, hard-to-debug results with no immediate warning. Macro calls can also give rise to unwanted side effects, especially when an actual argument is evaluated more than once.

#error

#error errmsg

The **#error** directive generates the message:

```
Error: filename line# : Error directive: errmsg
```

This directive is usually embedded in a preprocessor conditional statement that catches some undesired compile-time condition. In the normal case, that condition will be false. If the condition is true, you want the compiler to print an error message and stop the compile. You do this by putting an **#error** directive within a conditional statement that is true for the undesired case.

Example

```
#if (MYVAL != 0 && MYVAL != 1)
#error MYVAL must be defined to either 0 or 1
#endif
```

#if, #elif, #else, and #endif

```
#if constant-expression-1
<section-1>
<#elif constant-expression-2 newline section-2>
⋮
<#elif constant-expression-n newline section-n>
<#else <newline> final-section>
#endif
```

Borland C++ supports conditional compilation by replacing the appropriate source-code lines with a blank line. The lines thus ignored are those lines that are not to be compiled as a result of the directives. All conditional compilation directives must be completed in the source or include file in which they are begun.

The conditional directives **#if**, **#elif**, **#else**, and **#endif** work like the normal C conditional operators. If the *constant-expression-1* (subject to macro expansion) evaluates to nonzero (true), the lines of code (possibly empty) represented by *section-1*, whether preprocessor command lines or normal source lines, are preprocessed and, as appropriate, passed to the Borland C++ compiler. Otherwise, if *constant-expression-1* evaluates to zero (false), *section-1* is ignored (no macro expansion and no compilation).

In the *true* case, after *section-1* has been preprocessed, control passes to the matching **#endif** (which ends this conditional sequence) and continues with *next-section*. In the *false* case, control passes to the next **#elif** line (if any) where constant-expression-2 is evaluated. If true, *section-2* is processed, after which control moves on to the matching **#endif**. Otherwise, if *constant-expression-2* is false, control passes to the next **#elif**, and so on, until either **#else** or **#endif** is reached. The optional **#else** is used as an alternative condition for which all previous tests have proved false. The **#endif** ends the conditional sequence.

The processed section can contain further conditional clauses, nested to any depth; each **#if** must be matched with a closing **#endif**.

The net result of the preceding scenario is that only one section (possibly empty) is passed on for further processing. The bypassed sections are relevant only for keeping track of any nested conditionals, so that each **#if** can be matched with its correct **#endif**.

The constant expressions to be tested must evaluate to a constant integral value.

See also   defined keyword, #ifdef and #ifndef

#ifdef and #ifndef

```
#ifdef identifier
#ifndef identifier
```
The **#ifdef** and **#ifndef** conditional directives let you test whether an identifier is currently defined or not; that is, whether a previous #define command has been processed for that identifier and is still in force. The line

```
#ifdef identifier
```

has exactly the same effect as

```
#if 1
```

if *identifier* is currently defined, and the same effect as

```
#if 0
```

if *identifier* is currently undefined.

#ifndef tests true for the "not-defined" condition, so the line

```
#ifndef identifier
```

has exactly the same effect as

```
#if 0
```

if *identifier* is currently defined, and the same effect as

```
#if 1
```

if *identifier* is currently undefined.

The syntax thereafter follows that of #if, #elif, #else, and #endif.

An identifier defined as NULL is considered to be defined.

See also   defined keyword

#include

```
#include <header_name>
#include "header_name"
#include macro_identifier
```

The **#include** directive pulls in other named files, known as *include files*, *header files*, or *headers*, into the source code. The syntax has three versions:

- The first and second versions imply that no macro expansion will be attempted; in other words, *header_name* is never scanned for macro identifiers. *header_name* must be a valid DOS file name with an extension (traditionally .h for header) and optional path name and path delimiters.

- The third version assumes that neither < nor "appears as the first non-whitespace character following **#include**; further, it assumes a macro definition exists that will expand the macro identifier into a valid delimited header name with either of the *<header_name>* or *"header_name"* formats.

The preprocessor removes the **#include** line and conceptually replaces it with the entire text of the header file at that point in the source code. The source code itself is not changed, but the compiler "sees" the enlarged text. The placement of the **#include** can therefore influence the scope and duration of any identifiers in the included file.

If you place an explicit path in the *header_name*, only that directory will be searched.

The difference between the *<header_name>* and *"header_name"* formats lies in the searching algorithm employed in trying to locate the include file.

Header file search with <header_name>

The *<header_name>* version specifies a standard include file; the search is made successively in each of the include directories in the order they are defined. If the file is not located in any of the default directories, an error message is issued.

Header file search with "header_name"

The *"header_name"* version specifies a user-supplied include file; the file is sought first in the current directory (usually the directory holding the source file being compiled). If the file is not found there, the search continues in the include directories as in the *<header_name>* situation.

Example

This **#include** statement causes it to look for MYINCLUD.H in the standard include directory.

```
#include <stdio.h>
```

This **#include** statement causes it to look for MYINCLUD.H in the current directory, then in the default directories.

```
#include "myinclud.h"
```

After expansion, this **#include** statement causes the preprocessor to look in C:\BC4\ INCLUDE\MYSTUFF.H and nowhere else.

```
#define myinclud "C:\BC4\INCLUDE\MYSTUFF.H"
/* Note: Single backslashes OK here; within a C statement you would
   need "C:\BC4\INCLUDE\\MYSTUFF.H" */
#include  myinclud
/* macro expansion */
```

#line

#line integer_constant <"filename">

You can use the **#line** directive to supply line numbers to a program for cross-reference and error reporting. If your program consists of sections derived from some other program file, it is often useful to mark such sections with the line numbers of the original source rather than the normal sequential line numbers derived from the composite program.

The **#line** directive indicates that the following source line originally came from line number *integer_constant* of *filename*. Once the *filename* has been registered, subsequent **#line** commands relating to that file can omit the explicit *filename* argument.

Macros are expanded in **#line** arguments as they are in the #include directive.

The **#line** directive is primarily used by utilities that produce C code as output, and not in human-written code.

Pragma summary

#pragma directive-name

With **#pragma**, Borland C++ can define the directives it wants without interfering with other compilers that support **#pragma**. If the compiler doesn't recognize *directive-name*, it ignores the **#pragma** directive without any error or warning message.

Borland C++ supports the following **#pragma** directives:

- #pragma argsused
- #pragma anon_struct
- #pragma codeseg
- #pragma comment

- #pragma exit
- #pragma hdrfile
- #pragma hdrstop
- #pragma inline
- #pragma intrinsic
- #pragma message
- #pragma option
- #pragma saveregs
- #pragma startup
- #pragma warn

#pragma argsused

#pragma argused

The **argsused** pragma is allowed only between function definitions, and it affects only the next function. It disables the warning message:

```
"Parameter name is never used in function func-name"
```

#pragma anon_struct

#pragma anon_struct on
#pragma anon_struct off

The **anon_struct** directive allows you to compile anonymous structures embedded in classes.

```
#pragma anon_struct on
struct S {
   int i;
   struct {  // Embedded anonymous struct
      int   j ;
      float x ;
   };
   class {  // Embedded anonymous class
   public:
      long double ld;
   };
S() { i = 1; j = 2; x = 3.3; ld = 12345.5;}
};
#pragma anon_struct off

void main() {
   S mystruct;
   mystruct.x = 1.2;  // Assign to embedded data.
   }
```

#pragma codeseg

#pragma codeseg <seg_name> <"seg_class"> <group>
The **codeseg** directive lets you name the segment, class, or group where functions are allocated. If the pragma is used without any of its options' arguments, the default code segment is used for function allocation.

#pragma comment

#pragma comment (comment type, "string")
The **comment** directive lets you write a comment record into an output file. The *comment type* can be one of the following values:

Value	Explanation
exestr	The linker writes *string* into an .OBJ file. Your specified *string* is placed in the executable file. Such a string is never loaded into memory but can be found in the executable file by use of a suitable file search utility.
lib	Writes a comment record into an .OBJ file. The comment record is used by the linker as a library-search directory. A library module that is not specified in the linker's response-file can be specified by the **comment** LIB directive. The linker includes the library module name specified in *string* as the last library. Multiple modules can be named and linked in the order in which they are named.
user	The compiler writes *string* into the .OBJ file. The specified string is ignored by the linker.

#pragma exit and #pragma startup

#pragma startup function-name <priority>
#pragma exit function-name <priority>
These two pragmas allow the program to specify function(s) that should be called either upon program startup (before the *main* function is called), or program exit (just before the program terminates through **_exit**).

The specified *function-name* must be a previously declared function taking no arguments and returning **void**; in other words, it should be declared as:

```
void func(void);
```

The optional *priority* parameter should be an integer in the range 64 to 255. The highest priority is 0. Functions with higher priorities are called first at startup and last at exit. If you don't specify a priority, it defaults to 100.

Note   Priorities from 0 to 63 are used by the C libraries, and should not be used by the user.

#pragma hdrfile

#pragma hdrfile "filename.CSM"
This directive sets the name of the file in which to store precompiled headers.

If you aren't using precompiled headers, this directive has no effect. You can use the command-line compiler option -H=filename or the Use precompiled headers option to change the name of the file used to store precompiled headers.

#pragma hdrstop

#pragma hdrstop
This directive terminates the list of header files eligible for precompilation. You can use it to reduce the amount of disk space used by precompiled headers.

#pragma inline

#pragma inline
This directive is equivalent to the **-B** command-line compiler option or the IDE inline option.

This is best placed at the top of the file, because the compiler restarts itself with the **-B** option when it encounters #**pragma inline**.

#pragma intrinsic

#pragma intrinsic [-]function-name
Use #**pragma intrinsic** to override command-line switches or IDE options to control the inlining of functions.

When inlining an intrinsic function, always include a prototype for that function before using it.

Example
This example causes the compiler to generate code for *strcpy* in your function:

```
#pragma intrinsic strcpy
```

while this version prevents the compiler from inlining *strcpy*:

```
#pragma intrinsic -strcpy
```

#pragma message

#pragma message ("text" ["text"["text" ...]])
#pragma message text
Use #**pragma message** to specify a user-defined message within your program code.

The first form requires that the text consist of one or more string constants, and the message must be enclosed in parentheses. (This form is compatible with MSC.) The second form uses the text following the #**pragma** for the text of the warning message. With both forms of the #**pragma**, any macro references are expanded before the message is displayed.

Display of user-defined messages is on by default and can be turned on or off with the User-Defined Warnings option in the IDE. This option corresponds to the 16/32 bit compiler's **-wmsg** switch.

See also   #pragma warn

Example
The following example displays either "You are compiling using version xxx of BC++" (where xxx is the version number) or "Sorry, you are not using the Borland C++ compiler".

```
#ifdef __BORLANDC__
#pragma message You are compiling using version __BORLANDC__ of BC++.
#else
#pragma message ("Sorry, you are not using the Borland C++ compiler")
#endif
```

#pragma option

#pragma option [options...]
Use **#pragma option** to include command-line options within your program code.

options can be any command-line option (except those listed in the following paragraph). Any number of options can appear in one directive. Any of the toggle options (such as **-a** or **-K**) can be turned on and off as on the command line. For these toggle options, you can also put a period following the option to return the option to its command-line, configuration file, or option-menu setting. This allows you to temporarily change an option, then return it to its default, without having to remember (or even needing to know) what the exact default setting was.

Options that cannot appear in a **#pragma option** include:

-B	-c	-d*name*
-D*name=string*	-e*filename*	-E
-Fx	-h	-l*filename*
-lexset	-M	-o
-P	-Q	-S
-T	-U*name*	-V
-X	-Y	

You can use **#pragma**s, **#include**s, **#define**, and some **#if**s in the following cases:

- Before the use of any macro name that begins with two underscores (and is therefore a possible built-in macro) in an **#if**, **#ifdef**, **#ifndef**, or **#elif** directive.

- Before the occurrence of the first real token (the first C or C++ declaration).

Certain command-line options can appear only in a **#pragma option** command before these events. These options are:

-E*filename*	-f	-i
-m*	-n*path*	-o*filename*
-u	-W	-z
*		

Other options can be changed anywhere. The following options will only affect the compiler if they get changed between functions or object declarations:

-1	-h	-r
-2	-k	-rd
-a	-N	-v
-ff	-O	-y
-G	-p	-Z

The following options can be changed at any time and take effect immediately:

-A	-g*n*	-zE
-b	-j*n*	-zF
-C	-K	-zH
-d	-w*xxx*	

The options can appear followed by a dot (.) to reset the option to its command-line state.

#pragma saveregs

#pragma saveregs
The **saveregs** pragma guarantees that a **huge** function will not change the value of any of the registers when it is entered. This directive is sometimes needed for interfacing with assembly language code. The directive should be placed immediately before the function definition. It applies to that function alone.

#pragma warn

#pragma warn [+|-|.]www
The **warn** pragma lets you override specific **-w*xxx*** command-line options or check Display Warnings in the Messages options.

Example
If your source code contains the directives:

```
#pragma warn +xxx
#pragma warn -yyy
#pragma warn .zzz
```

the *xxx* warning will be turned on, the *yyy* warning will be turned off, and the *zzz* warning will be restored to the value it had when compilation of the file began. See the command-line options summary for a complete list of the three-letter abbreviations and the warnings to which they apply.

Predefined macros

Borland C++ predefines certain global identifiers known as manifest constants. Most global indentifiers begin and end with two underscores (_).

Note For readability, underscores are often separated by a single blank space. In your source code, you should never insert whitespace between underscores.

See also the description of memory-model macros.

Macro	Value	What macro is/does
_ _BCOPT_ _	1	Defined in any compiler that has an optimizer.
_ _BCPLUSPLUS_ _	0x340	Defined if you've selected C++ compilation; will increase in later releases.
_ _BORLANDC_ _	0x460	Version number.
_ _CDECL_ _	1	Defined if Calling Convention is set to C; otherwise undefined.
_CHAR_UNSIGNED	1	Defined by default indicating that the default **char** is **unsigned char**. Use the **-K** option to undefine this macro.
_ _CONSOLE_ _		Available only for the 32-bit compiler. When defined, the macro indicates that the program is a console application.
_CPPUNWIND	1	Enable stack unwinding.This is true by default; use **-xd-** to disable.
_ _cplusplus	1	Defined if in C++ mode; otherwise, undefined.
_ _DATE_ _	String literal	Date when processing began on the current file.
_ _DLL_ _	1	Defined if Prolog/Epilog Code Generation is set to Windows DLL; otherwise undefined.
_ _FILE_ _	String literal	Name of the current file being processed.
_ _LINE_ _	Decimal constant	Number of the current source file line being processed.
_ _DLL_ _	1	True whenever **-WD** option is used.
_M_IX86	1	Always defined. The default value is 300. You can change the value to 400 or 500 by using the **/4** or **/5** options.
_ _MSDOS_ _	1	Integer constant.
_ _MT_ _	1	Defined only for the 32-bit compiler if the **-WM** option is used. It specifies that the multithread library is to be linked.
_ _OVERLAY_ _	1	Specific to the Borland C and C++ family of compilers. It is predefined as 1 if you compile a module with the **-Y** option (enable overlay support). If you do not enable overlay support, this macro is undefined.
_ _PASCAL_ _	1	Defined if Calling Convention is set to Pascal; otherwise undefined.

Macro	Value	What macro is/does
_ _STDC_ _	1	Defined if you compile with the Keywords option set to ANSI; otherwise, undefined.
_ _TCPLUSPLUS_ _	0x340	Version number.
_ _TEMPLATES_ _	1	Specific to the Borland C++ compilers. It is defined as 1 for C++ files (meaning that Borland C++ supports templates); otherwise, it is undefined.
_ _TIME_ _	String literal	Time when processing began on the current file.
_ _TLS_ _	1	Always true when the 32-bit compiler is used.
_ _TURBOC_ _	0x460	Will increase in later releases.
_WCHAR_T	1	Defined only for C++ programs to indicate that **wchar_t** is an intrinsically defined data type.
_WCHAR_T_DEFINED	1	Defined only for C++ programs to indicate that **wchar_t** is an intrinsically defined data type.
_Windows		Defined for Windows 16- and 32-bit compilations.
_ _WIN32_ _	1	Always defined for the 32-bit compiler. It is defined for console and GUI applications.

Note   _ _DATE_ _, _ _FILE_ _, _ _LINE_ _, _ _STDC_ _, and _ _TIME_ _ **cannot** appear immediately following a #define or #undef directive.

II

Borland C++ DOS programmer's reference

Part II provides information you might need to develop 16-bit applications that are targeted to run under DOS. This part is organized as follows:

- **Chapter 6, "Borland graphics interface,"** is a reference to the functions declared in the graphics.h header file. The functions discussed in this chapter are available only for 16-bit DOS applications. Sample programs for these functions are available in the online Help.

- **Chapter 7, "DOS-only run-time functions,"** is a reference to those functions that are available only in a 16-bit DOS-targeted application. There are many additional functions and C++ classes that can be used in DOS applications (and are also available to other platforms). The online Help provides many sample programs for the functions that are referenced here.

- **Chapter 8, "DOS run-time libraries,"** provides an overview of the libraries and global variables that are available only for 16-bit DOS applications.

- **Chapter 9, "DOS global variables,"** describes the global variables that are available only for 16-bit DOS applications.

C h a p t e r

6

Borland graphics interface

This chapter presents a description, in alphabetical order, of the Borland C++ graphics functions. The graphics functions are available only for 16-bit DOS applications.

arc
graphics.h

Function
Draws an arc.

Syntax
void far arc(int x, int y, int stangle, int endangle, int radius);

Remarks
arc draws a circular arc in the current drawing color centered at (*x*,*y*) with a radius given by *radius*. The *arc* travels from *stangle* to *endangle*. If *stangle* equals 0 and *endangle* equals 360, the call to *arc* draws a complete circle.

The angle for *arc* is reckoned counterclockwise, with 0 degrees at 3 o'clock, 90 degrees at 12 o'clock, and so on.

The *linestyle* parameter does not affect arcs, circles, ellipses, or pie slices. Only the *thickness* parameter is used.

If you're using a CGA in high resolution mode or a monochrome graphics adapter, the examples in online Help that show how to use graphics functions might not produce the expected results. If your system runs on a CGA or monochrome adapter, pass the value 1 to those functions that alter the fill or drawing color (*setcolor*, *setfillstyle*, and *setlinestyle*, for example), instead of a symbolic color constant (defined in graphics.h).

Return value
None.

bar

Function
Draws a two-dimensional bar.

Syntax
void far bar(int left, int top, int right, int bottom);

Remarks
bar draws a filled-in, rectangular, two-dimensional bar. The bar is filled using the current fill pattern and fill color. *bar* does not outline the bar; to draw an outlined two-dimensional bar, use *bar3d* with *depth* equal to 0.

The upper left and lower right corners of the rectangle are given by (*left, top*) and (*right, bottom*), respectively. The coordinates refer to pixels.

Return value
None.

See also
bar3d, rectangle, setcolor, setfillstyle, setlinestyle

bar3d

Function
Draws a three-dimensional bar.

Syntax
void far bar3d(int left, int top, int right, int bottom, int depth, int topflag);

Remarks
bar3d draws a three-dimensional rectangular bar, then fills it using the current fill pattern and fill color. The three-dimensional outline of the bar is drawn in the current line style and color. The bar's depth in pixels is given by *depth*. The *topflag* parameter governs whether a three-dimensional top is put on the bar. If *topflag* is nonzero, a top is put on; otherwise, no top is put on the bar (making it possible to stack several bars on top of one another).

The upper left and lower right corners of the rectangle are given by (*left, top*) and (*right, bottom*), respectively.

To calculate a typical depth for *bar3d*, take 25% of the width of the bar, like this:

```
bar3d(left,top,right,bottom, (right-left)/4,1);
```

Return value
None.

See also
bar, rectangle, setcolor, setfillstyle, setlinestyle

circle   graphics.h

Function
Draws a circle of the given radius with its center at (*x,y*).

Syntax
void far circle(int x, int y, int radius);

Remarks
circle draws a circle in the current drawing color with its center at (*x,y*) and the radius given by *radius*.

Note   The *linestyle* parameter does not affect arcs, circles, ellipses, or pie slices. Only the *thickness* parameter is used.

If your circles are not perfectly round, adjust the aspect ratio.

Return value
None.

See also
arc, ellipse, fillellipse, getaspectratio, sector, setaspectratio

cleardevice   graphics.h

Function
Clears the graphics screen.

Syntax
void far cleardevice(void);

Remarks
cleardevice erases (that is, fills with the current background color) the entire graphics screen and moves the CP (current position) to home (0,0).

Return value
None.

See also
clearviewport

clearviewport   graphics.h

Function
Clears the current viewport.

Syntax
void far clearviewport(void);

Remarks
clearviewport erases the viewport and moves the CP (current position) to home (0,0), relative to the viewport.

Return value
None.

See also
cleardevice, getviewsettings, setviewport

closegraph   graphics.h

Function
Shuts down the graphics system.

Syntax
void far closegraph(void);

Remarks
closegraph deallocates all memory allocated by the graphics system, then restores the screen to the mode it was in before you called *initgraph*. (The graphics system deallocates memory, such as the drivers, fonts, and an internal buffer, through a call to *_graphfreemem*.)

Return value
None.

See also
initgraph, setgraphbufsize

detectgraph

Function
Determines graphics driver and graphics mode to use by checking the hardware.

Syntax
void far detectgraph(int far *graphdriver, int far *graphmode);

Remarks
detectgraph detects your system's graphics adapter and chooses the mode that provides the highest resolution for that adapter. If no graphics hardware is detected, *graphdriver* is set to grNotDetected (–2), and *graphresult* returns grNotDetected (–2).

graphdriver is an integer that specifies the graphics driver to be used. You can give it a value using a constant of the *graphics_drivers* enumeration type, which is defined in graphics.h and listed in the following table.

Table 6.1   detectgraph constants

graphics_drivers constant	Numeric value
CURRENT_DRIVER	–1
DETECT	0 (requests autodetection)
CGA	1
MCGA	2
EGA	3
EGA64	4
EGAMONO	5
IBM8514	6
HERCMONO	7
ATT400	8
VGA	9
PC3270	10

graphmode is an integer that specifies the initial graphics mode (unless *graphdriver* equals DETECT; in which case, *graphmode* is set to the highest resolution available for the detected driver). You can give *graphmode* a value using a constant of the *graphics_modes* enumeration type, which is defined in graphics.h and listed in the following table.

Table 6.2   Graphics drivers information

Graphics driver	*graphics_modes*	Value	Column × row	Palette	Pages
CGA	CGAC0	0	320×200	C0	1
	CGAC1	1	320×200	C1	1
	CGAC2	2	320×200	C2	1
	CGAC3	3	320×200	C3	1
	CGAHI	4	640×200	2 color	1

Table 6.2 Graphics drivers information (continued)

Graphics driver	graphics_modes	Value	Column × row	Palette	Pages
MCGA	MCGAC0	0	320×200	C0	1
	MCGAC1	1	320×200	C1	1
	MCGAC2	2	320×200	C2	1
	MCGAC3	3	320×200	C3	1
	MCGAMED	4	640×200	2 color	1
	MCGAHI	5	640×480	2 color	1
EGA	EGALO	0	640×200	16 color	4
	EGAHI	1	640×350	16 color	2
EGA64	EGA64LO	0	640×200	16 color	1
	EGA64HI	1	640×350	4 color	1
EGA-MONO	EGAMONOHI	3	640×350	2 color	1*
	EGAMONOHI	3	640×350	2 color	2**
HERC	HERCMONOHI	0	720×348	2 color	2
ATT400	ATT400C0	0	320×200	C0	1
	ATT400C1	1	320×200	C1	1
	ATT400C2	2	320×200	C2	1
	ATT400C3	3	320×200	C3	1
	ATT400MED	4	640×200	2 color	1
	ATT400HI	5	640×400	2 color	1
VGA	VGALO	0	640×200	16 color	2
	VGAMED	1	640×350	16 color	2
	VGAHI	2	640×480	16 color	1
PC3270	PC3270HI	0	720×350	2 color	1
IBM8514	IBM8514HI	0	640×480	256 color	
	IBM8514LO	0	1024×768	256 color	

* 64K on EGAMONO card
** 256K on EGAMONO card

Note The main reason to call *detectgraph* directly is to override the graphics mode that *detectgraph* recommends to *initgraph*.

Return value
None.

See also
graphresult, initgraph

drawpoly

graphics.h

Function
Draws the outline of a polygon.

Syntax

void far drawpoly(int numpoints, int far *polypoints);

Remarks

drawpoly draws a polygon with *numpoints* points, using the current line style and color.

*polypoints points to a sequence of (*numpoints* × 2) integers. Each pair of integers gives the *x* and *y* coordinates of a point on the polygon.

To draw a closed figure with *n* vertices, you must pass *n* + 1 coordinates to *drawpoly* where the *n*th coordinate is equal to the 0th.

Return value

None.

See also

fillpoly, floodfill, graphresult, setwritemode

ellipse   graphics.h

Function

Draws an elliptical arc.

Syntax

void far ellipse(int x, int y, int stangle, int endangle, int xradius, int yradius);

Remarks

ellipse draws an elliptical arc in the current drawing color with its center at (*x*,*y*) and the horizontal and vertical axes given by *xradius* and *yradius*, respectively. The ellipse travels from *stangle* to *endangle*. If *stangle* equals 0 and *endangle* equals 360, the call to *ellipse* draws a complete ellipse.

The angle for *ellipse* is reckoned counterclockwise, with 0 degrees at 3 o'clock, 90 degrees at 12 o'clock, and so on.

The *linestyle* parameter does not affect arcs, circles, ellipses, or pie slices. Only the *thickness* parameter is used.

Return value

None.

See also

arc, circle, fillellipse, sector

fillellipse

graphics.h

Function
Draws and fills an ellipse.

Syntax
void far fillellipse(int x, int y, int xradius, int yradius);

Remarks
fillellipse draws an ellipse using (*x,y*) as a center point and *xradius* and *yradius* as the horizontal and vertical axes; fills it with the current fill color and pattern.

Return value
None.

See also
arc, circle, ellipse, pieslice

fillpoly

graphics.h

Function
Draws and fills a polygon.

Syntax
void far fillpoly(int numpoints, int far *polypoints);

Remarks
fillpoly draws the outline of a polygon with *numpoints* points in the current line style and color (just as *drawpoly* does), then fills the polygon using the current fill pattern and fill color.

polypoints points to a sequence of (*numpoints* × 2) integers. Each pair of integers gives the *x* and *y* coordinates of a point on the polygon.

Return value
None.

See also
drawpoly, floodfill, graphresult, setfillstyle

floodfill

graphics.h

Function
Flood-fills a bounded region.

Syntax
void far floodfill(int x, int y, int border);

Remarks
floodfill fills an enclosed area on bitmap devices. (*x,y*) is a "seed point" within the enclosed area to be filled. The area bounded by the color *border* is flooded with the current fill pattern and fill color. If the seed point is within an enclosed area, the inside will be filled. If the seed is outside the enclosed area, the exterior will be filled.

Use *fillpoly* instead of *floodfill* whenever possible so that you can maintain code compatibility with future versions.

Note *floodfill* does not work with the IBM-8514 driver.

Return value
If an error occurs while flooding a region, *graphresult* returns a value of –7.

See also
drawpoly, fillpoly, graphresult, setcolor, setfillstyle

getarccoords

graphics.h

Function
Gets coordinates of the last call to *arc*.

Syntax
void far getarccoords(struct arccoordstype far *arccoords);

Remarks
getarccoords fills in the *arccoordstype* structure pointed to by *arccoords* with information about the last call to *arc*. The *arccoordstype* structure is defined in graphics.h as follows:

```
struct arccoordstype {
    int x, y;
    int xstart, ystart, xend, yend;
};
```

The members of this structure are used to specify the center point (*x,y*), the starting position (*xstart, ystart*), and the ending position (*xend, yend*) of the arc. They are useful if you need to make a line meet at the end of an arc.

Return value
None.

See also
arc, fillellipse, sector

getaspectratio

Function
Retrieves the current graphics mode's aspect ratio.

Syntax
void far getaspectratio(int far *xasp, int far *yasp);

Remarks
The y aspect factor, *$*yasp$*, is normalized to 10,000. On all graphics adapters except the VGA, *$*xasp$* (the x aspect factor) is less than *$*yasp$* because the pixels are taller than they are wide. On the VGA, which has "square" pixels, *$*xasp$* equals *$*yasp$*. In general, the relationship between *$*yasp$* and *$*xasp$* can be stated as

$*yasp$ = 10,000

$*xasp$ <= 10,000

getaspectratio gets the values in *$*xasp$* and *$*yasp$*.

Return value
None.

See also
arc, circle, ellipse, fillellipse, pieslice, sector, setaspectratio

getbkcolor

Function
Returns the current background color.

Syntax
int far getbkcolor(void);

Remarks
getbkcolor returns the current background color. (See the table under *setbkcolor* for details.)

Return value

getbkcolor returns the current background color.

See also

getcolor, getmaxcolor, getpalette, setbkcolor

getcolor   graphics.h

Function

Returns the current drawing color.

Syntax

int far getcolor(void);

Remarks

getcolor returns the current drawing color.

The drawing color is the value to which pixels are set when lines and so on are drawn. For example, in CGAC0 mode, the palette contains four colors: the background color, light green, light red, and yellow. In this mode, if *getcolor* returns 1, the current drawing color is light green.

Return value

getcolor returns the current drawing color.

See also

getbkcolor, getmaxcolor, getpalette, setcolor

getdefaultpalette   graphics.h

Function

Returns the palette definition structure.

Syntax

struct palettetype *far getdefaultpalette(void);

Remarks

getdefaultpalette finds the *palettetype* structure that contains the palette initialized by the driver during *initgraph*.

Return value

getdefaultpalette returns a pointer to the default palette set up by the current driver when that driver was initialized.

See also
getpalette, initgraph

getdrivername

graphics.h

Function
Returns a pointer to a string containing the name of the current graphics driver.

Syntax
char *far getdrivername(void);

Remarks
After a call to *initgraph, getdrivername* returns the name of the driver that is currently loaded.

Return value
getdrivername returns a pointer to a string with the name of the currently loaded graphics driver.

See also
initgraph

getfillpattern

graphics.h

Function
Copies a user-defined fill pattern into memory.

Syntax
void far getfillpattern(char far *pattern);

Remarks
getfillpattern copies the user-defined fill pattern, as set by *setfillpattern*, into the 8-byte area pointed to by *pattern*.

pattern is a pointer to a sequence of 8 bytes, with each byte corresponding to 8 pixels in the pattern. Whenever a bit in a pattern byte is set to 1, the corresponding pixel will be plotted. For example, the following user-defined fill pattern represents a checkerboard:

```
char checkboard[8] = { 0xAA, 0x55, 0xAA, 0x55, 0xAA, 0x55, 0xAA, 0x55 };
```

Return value
None.

See also
getfillsettings, setfillpattern

getfillsettings

graphics.h

Function
Gets information about current fill pattern and color.

Syntax
void far getfillsettings(struct fillsettingstype far *fillinfo);

Remarks
getfillsettings fills in the *fillsettingstype* structure pointed to by *fillinfo* with information about the current fill pattern and fill color. The *fillsettingstype* structure is defined in graphics.h as follows:

```
struct fillsettingstype {
    int pattern;            /* current fill pattern */
    int color;              /* current fill color */
};
```

The functions *bar*, *bar3d*, *fillpoly*, *floodfill*, and *pieslice* all fill an area with the current fill pattern in the current fill color. There are 11 predefined fill pattern styles (such as solid, crosshatch, dotted, and so on). Symbolic names for the predefined patterns are provided by the enumerated type *fill_patterns* in graphics.h (see the following table). In addition, you can define your own fill pattern.

If *pattern* equals 12 (USER_FILL), then a user-defined fill pattern is being used; otherwise, *pattern* gives the number of a predefined pattern.

The enumerated type *fill_patterns*, defined in graphics.h, gives names for the predefined fill patterns, plus an indicator for a user-defined pattern.

Name	Value	Description
EMPTY_FILL	0	Fill with background color
SOLID_FILL	1	Solid fill
LINE_FILL	2	Fill with— —
LTSLASH_FILL	3	Fill with ///
SLASH_FILL	4	Fill with ///, thick lines
BKSLASH_FILL	5	Fill with \\\, thick lines
LTBKSLASH_FILL	6	Fill with \\\
HATCH_FILL	7	Light hatch fill
XHATCH_FILL	8	Heavy crosshatch fill
INTERLEAVE_FILL	9	Interleaving line fill
WIDE_DOT_FILL	10	Widely spaced dot fill
CLOSE_DOT_FILL	11	Closely spaced dot fill
USER_FILL	12	User-defined fill pattern

All but EMPTY_FILL fill with the current fill color; EMPTY_FILL uses the current background color.

Return value

None.

See also

getfillpattern, *setfillpattern*, *setfillstyle*

getgraphmode

graphics.h

Function

Returns the current graphics mode.

Syntax

int far getgraphmode(void);

Remarks

Your program must make a successful call to *initgraph* before calling *getgraphmode*.

The enumeration *graphics_mode*, defined in graphics.h, gives names for the predefined graphics modes. For a table listing these enumeration values, refer to the description for *initgraph*.

Return value

getgraphmode returns the graphics mode set by *initgraph* or *setgraphmode*.

See also

getmoderange, *restorecrtmode*, *setgraphmode*

getimage

graphics.h

Function

Saves a bit image of the specified region into memory.

Syntax

void far getimage(int left, int top, int right, int bottom, void far *bitmap);

Remarks

getimage copies an image from the screen to memory.

left, *top*, *right*, and *bottom* define the screen area to which the rectangle is copied. *bitmap* points to the area in memory where the bit image is stored. The first two words of this area are used for the width and height of the rectangle; the remainder holds the image itself.

Return value
None.

See also
imagesize, putimage, putpixel

getlinesettings

Function
Gets the current line style, pattern, and thickness.

Syntax
void far getlinesettings(struct linesettingstype far *lineinfo);

Remarks
getlinesettings fills a *linesettingstype* structure pointed to by *lineinfo* with information about the current line style, pattern, and thickness.

The *linesettingstype* structure is defined in graphics.h as follows:

```
struct linesettingstype {
    int linestyle;
    unsigned upattern;
    int thickness;
};
```

linestyle specifies in which style subsequent lines will be drawn (such as solid, dotted, centered, dashed). The enumeration *line_styles*, defined in graphics.h, gives names to these operators:

Name	Value	Description
SOLID_LINE	0	Solid line
DOTTED_LINE	1	Dotted line
CENTER_LINE	2	Centered line
DASHED_LINE	3	Dashed line
USERBIT_LINE	4	User-defined line style

thickness specifies whether the width of subsequent lines drawn will be normal or thick.

Name	Value	Description
NORM_WIDTH	1	1 pixel wide
THICK_WIDTH	3	3 pixels wide

upattern is a 16-bit pattern that applies only if *linestyle* is USERBIT_LINE (4). In that case, whenever a bit in the pattern word is 1, the corresponding pixel in the line is drawn in the current drawing color. For example, a solid line corresponds to a *upattern* of 0xFFFF (all pixels drawn), while a dashed line can correspond to a *upattern* of 0x3333 or 0x0F0F. If the *linestyle* parameter to *setlinestyle* is not USERBIT_LINE (!=4), the *upattern* parameter must still be supplied but is ignored.

Return value
None.

See also
setlinestyle

getmaxcolor   **graphics.h**

Function
Returns the maximum color value that can be passed to the *setcolor* function.

Syntax
int far getmaxcolor(void);

Remarks
getmaxcolor returns the highest valid color value for the current graphics driver and mode that can be passed to *setcolor*.

For example, on a 256K EGA, *getmaxcolor* always returns 15, which means that any call to *setcolor* with a value from 0 to 15 is valid. On a CGA in high-resolution mode or on a Hercules monochrome adapter, *getmaxcolor* returns a value of 1.

Return value
getmaxcolor returns the highest available color value.

See also
getbkcolor, getcolor, getpalette, getpalettesize, setcolor

getmaxmode   **graphics.h**

Function
Returns the maximum mode number for the current driver.

Syntax
int far getmaxmode(void);

Remarks

getmaxmode lets you find out the maximum mode number for the currently loaded driver, directly from the driver. This gives it an advantage over *getmoderange*, which works for Borland drivers only. The minimum mode is 0.

Return value

getmaxmode returns the maximum mode number for the current driver.

See also

getmodename, getmoderange

getmaxx   graphics.h

Function

Returns the maximum *x* screen coordinate.

Syntax

int far getmaxx(void);

Remarks

getmaxx returns the maximum (screen-relative) *x* value for the current graphics driver and mode.

For example, on a CGA in 320×200 mode, *getmaxx* returns 319. *getmaxx* is invaluable for centering, determining the boundaries of a region onscreen, and so on.

Return value

getmaxx returns the maximum *x* screen coordinate.

See also

getmaxy, getx

getmaxy   graphics.h

Function

Returns the maximum *y* screen coordinate.

Syntax

int far getmaxy(void);

Remarks

getmaxy returns the maximum (screen-relative) *y* value for the current graphics driver and mode.

For example, on a CGA in 320×200 mode, *getmaxy* returns 199. *getmaxy* is invaluable for centering, determining the boundaries of a region onscreen, and so on.

Return value
getmaxy returns the maximum *y* screen coordinate.

See also
getmaxx, getx, gety

getmodename   graphics.h

Function
Returns a pointer to a string containing the name of a specified graphics mode.

Syntax
```
char *far getmodename(int mode_number);
```

Remarks
getmodename accepts a graphics mode number as input and returns a string containing the name of the corresponding graphics mode. The mode names are embedded in each driver. The return values ("320×200 CGA P1," "640×200 CGA," and so on) are useful for building menus or displaying status.

Return value
getmodename returns a pointer to a string with the name of the graphics mode.

See also
getmaxmode, getmoderange

getmoderange   graphics.h

Function
Gets the range of modes for a given graphics driver.

Syntax
void far getmoderange(int graphdriver, int far *lomode, int far *himode);

Remarks
getmoderange gets the range of valid graphics modes for the given graphics driver, *graphdriver*. The lowest permissible mode value is returned in **lomode*, and the highest permissible value is **himode*. If *graphdriver* specifies an invalid graphics driver, both **lomode* and **himode* are set to –1. If the value of *graphdriver* is –1, the currently loaded driver modes are given.

Return value
None.

See also
getgraphmode, getmaxmode, getmodename, initgraph, setgraphmode

getpalette

Function
Gets information about the current palette.

Syntax
void far getpalette(struct palettetype far *palette);

Remarks
getpalette fills the *palettetype* structure pointed to by *palette* with information about the current palette's size and colors.

The MAXCOLORS constant and the *palettetype* structure used by *getpalette* are defined in graphics.h as follows:

```
#define MAXCOLORS  15

struct palettetype {
   unsigned char size;
   signed char colors[MAXCOLORS + 1];
};
```

size gives the number of colors in the palette for the current graphics driver in the current mode.

colors is an array of *size* bytes containing the actual raw color numbers for each entry in the palette.

Note *getpalette* cannot be used with the IBM-8514 driver.

Return value
None.

See also
getbkcolor, getcolor, getdefaultpalette, getmaxcolor, setallpalette, setpalette

getpalettesize

Function
Returns the size of the palette color lookup table.

Syntax

int far getpalettesize(void);

Remarks

getpalettesize is used to determine how many palette entries can be set for the current graphics mode. For example, the EGA in color mode returns 16.

Return value

getpalettesize returns the number of palette entries in the current palette.

See also

setpalette, setallpalette

getpixel   graphics.h

Function

Gets the color of a specified pixel.

Syntax

unsigned far getpixel(int x, int y);

Remarks

getpixel gets the color of the pixel located at (*x,y*).

Return value

getpixel returns the color of the given pixel.

See also

getimage, putpixel

gettextsettings   graphics.h

Function

Gets information about the current graphics text font.

Syntax

void far gettextsettings(struct textsettingstype far *texttypeinfo);

Remarks

gettextsettings fills the *textsettingstype* structure pointed to by *textinfo* with information about the current text font, direction, size, and justification.

The *textsettingstype* structure used by *gettextsettings* is defined in graphics.h as follows:

```
struct textsettingstype {
    int font;
    int direction;
    int charsize;
    int horiz;
    int vert;
};
```

See *settextstyle* for a description of these fields.

Return value
None.

See also
outtext, outtextxy, registerbgifont, settextjustify, settextstyle, setusercharsize, textheight, textwidth

getviewsettings   graphics.h

Function
Gets information about the current viewport.

Syntax
void far getviewsettings(struct viewporttype far *viewport);

Remarks
getviewsettings fills the *viewporttype* structure pointed to by *viewport* with information about the current viewport.

The *viewporttype* structure used by *getviewport* is defined in graphics.h as follows:

```
struct viewporttype {
    int left, top, right, bottom;
    int clip;
};
```

Return value
None.

See also
clearviewport, getx, gety, setviewport

getx

Function
Returns the current graphics position's x-coordinate.

Syntax
int far getx(void);

Remarks
getx finds the current graphics position's x-coordinate. The value is viewport-relative.

Return value
getx returns the x-coordinate of the current position.

See also
getmaxx, getmaxy, getviewsettings, gety, moveto

gety

Function
Returns the current graphics position's y-coordinate.

Syntax
int far gety(void);

Remarks
gety returns the current graphics position's y-coordinate. The value is viewport-relative.

Return value
gety returns the y-coordinate of the current position.

See also
getmaxx, getmaxy, getviewsettings, getx, moveto

graphdefaults

Function
Resets all graphics settings to their defaults.

Syntax
void far graphdefaults(void);

Remarks

graphdefaults resets all graphics settings to their defaults:

- Sets the viewport to the entire screen.
- Moves the current position to (0,0).
- Sets the default palette colors, background color, and drawing color.
- Sets the default fill style and pattern.
- Sets the default text font and justification.

Return value

None.

See also

initgraph, setgraphmode

grapherrormsg   graphics.h

Function

Returns a pointer to an error message string.

Syntax

char * far grapherrormsg(int errorcode);

Remarks

grapherrormsg returns a pointer to the error message string associated with *errorcode*, the value returned by *graphresult*.

Refer to the entry for *errno* in Chapter 4, "Global variables," for a list of error messages and mnemonics.

Return value

grapherrormsg returns a pointer to an error message string.

See also

graphresult

_graphfreemem   graphics.h

Function

User hook into graphics memory deallocation.

Syntax

void far _graphfreemem(void far *ptr, unsigned size);

Remarks

The graphics library calls _graphfreemem_ to release memory previously allocated through _graphgetmem_. You can choose to control the graphics library memory management by simply defining your own version of _graphfreemem_ (you must declare it exactly as shown in the declaration). The default version of this routine merely calls _free_.

Return value

None.

See also

graphgetmem, _setgraphbufsize_

_graphgetmem   graphics.h

Function

User hook into graphics memory allocation.

Syntax

void far * far _graphgetmem(unsigned size);

Remarks

Routines in the graphics library (not the user program) normally call _graphgetmem_ to allocate memory for internal buffers, graphics drivers, and character sets. You can choose to control the memory management of the graphics library by defining your own version of _graphgetmem_ (you must declare it exactly as shown in the declaration). The default version of this routine merely calls _malloc_.

Return value

None.

See also

graphfreemem, _initgraph_, _setgraphbufsize_

graphresult   graphics.h

Function

Returns an error code for the last unsuccessful graphics operation.

Syntax

int far graphresult(void);

Remarks

graphresult returns the error code for the last graphics operation that reported an error and resets the error level to grOk.

The following table lists the error codes returned by *graphresult*. The enumerated type *graph_errors* defines the errors in this table. *graph_errors* is declared in graphics.h.

Error code	*graph_errors* constant	Corresponding error message string
0	grOk	No error
–1	grNoInitGraph	(BGI) graphics not installed (use *initgraph*)
–2	grNotDetected	Graphics hardware not detected
–3	grFileNotFound	Device driver file not found
–4	grInvalidDriver	Invalid device driver file
–5	grNoLoadMem	Not enough memory to load driver
–6	grNoScanMem	Out of memory in scan fill
–7	grNoFloodMem	Out of memory in flood fill
–8	grFontNotFound	Font file not found
–9	igrNoFontMem	Not enough memory to load font
–10	grInvalidMode	Invalid graphics mode for selected driver
–11	grError	Graphics error
–12	grIOerror	Graphics I/O error
–13	grInvalidFont	Invalid font file
–14	grInvalidFontNum	Invalid font number
–15	grInvalidDeviceNum	Invalid device number
–18	grInvalidVersion	Invalid version number

Note that the variable maintained by *graphresult* is reset to 0 after *graphresult* has been called. Therefore, you should store the value of *graphresult* in a temporary variable and then test it.

Return value

graphresult returns the current graphics error number, an integer in the range –15 to 0; *grapherrormsg* returns a pointer to a string associated with the value returned by *graphresult*.

See also

detectgraph, drawpoly, fillpoly, floodfill, grapherrormsg, initgraph, pieslice, registerbgidriver, registerbgifont, setallpalette, setcolor, setfillstyle, setgraphmode, setlinestyle, setpalette, settextjustify, settextstyle, setusercharsize, setviewport, setvisualpage

imagesize

graphics.h

Function

Returns the number of bytes required to store a bit image.

Syntax

unsigned far imagesize(int left, int top, int right, int bottom);

Remarks

imagesize determines the size of the memory area required to store a bit image. If the size required for the selected image is greater than or equal to 64K – 1 bytes, *imagesize* returns 0xFFFF (–1).

Return value

imagesize returns the size of the required memory area in bytes.

See also

getimage, putimage

initgraph

graphics.h

Function

Initializes the graphics system.

Syntax

void far initgraph(int far *graphdriver, int far *graphmode, char far *pathtodriver);

Remarks

initgraph initializes the graphics system by loading a graphics driver from disk (or validating a registered driver), and putting the system into graphics mode.

To start the graphics system, first call the *initgraph* function. *initgraph* loads the graphics driver and puts the system into graphics mode. You can tell *initgraph* to use a particular graphics driver and mode, or to autodetect the attached video adapter at run time and pick the corresponding driver.

If you tell *initgraph* to autodetect, it calls *detectgraph* to select a graphics driver and mode. *initgraph* also resets all graphics settings to their defaults (current position, palette, color, viewport, and so on) and resets *graphresult* to 0.

Normally, *initgraph* loads a graphics driver by allocating memory for the driver (through _*graphgetmem*), then loading the appropriate .BGI file from disk. As an alternative to this dynamic loading scheme, you can link a graphics driver file (or several of them) directly into your executable program file. See UTILS.TXT (included with your distribution disks) for more information on BGIOBJ.

pathtodriver specifies the directory path where *initgraph* looks for graphics drivers. *initgraph* first looks in the path specified in *pathtodriver*, then (if they're not there) in the current directory. Accordingly, if *pathtodriver* is null, the driver files (*.BGI) must be in the current directory. This is also the path *settextstyle* searches for the stroked character font files (*.CHR).

graphdriver is an integer that specifies the graphics driver to be used. You can give it a value using a constant of the *graphics_drivers* enumeration type, which is defined in graphics.h and listed in Table 6.3.

Table 6.3 Graphics drivers constants

graphics_drivers constant	Numeric value
DETECT	0 (requests autodetection)
CGA	1
MCGA	2
EGA	3
EGA64	4
EGAMONO	5
IBM8514	6
HERCMONO	7
ATT400	8
VGA	9
PC3270	10

graphmode is an integer that specifies the initial graphics mode (unless *graphdriver* equals DETECT, in which case *graphmode* is set by *initgraph* to the highest resolution available for the detected driver). You can give *graphmode* a value using a constant of the *graphics_modes* enumeration type, which is defined in graphics.h and listed in Table 6.5.

Note *graphdriver* and *graphmode* must be set to valid values from Tables 6.3 and 6.5, or you'll get unpredictable results. The exception is *graphdriver* = DETECT.

In Table 6.5, the **Palette** listings C0, C1, C2, and C3 refer to the four predefined four-color palettes available on CGA (and compatible) systems. You can select the background color (entry #0) in each of these palettes, but the other colors are fixed. These palettes are described in greater detail in Chapter 3, and summarized in Table 6.4.

Table 6.4 Color palettes

Palette number	Color assigned to pixel value		
	1	2	3
0	LIGHTGREEN	LIGHTRED	YELLOW
1	LIGHTCYAN	LIGHTMAGENTA	WHITE
2	GREEN	RED	BROWN
3	CYAN	MAGENTA	LIGHTGRAY

After a call to *initgraph*, *graphdriver* is set to the current graphics driver, and *graphmode* is set to the current graphics mode.

Table 6.5 Graphics modes

Graphics driver	graphics_modes	Value	_Column ×row	Palette	Pages
CGA	CGAC0	0	320×200	C0	1
	CGAC1	1	320×200	C1	1
	CGAC2	2	320×200	C2	1
	CGAC3	3	320×200	C3	1
	CGAHI	4	640×200	2 color	1
MCGA	MCGAC0	0	320×200	C0	1
	MCGAC1	1	320×200	C1	1
	MCGAC2	2	320×200	C2	1
	MCGAC3	3	320×200	C3	1
	MCGAMED	4	640×200	2 color	1
	MCGAHI	5	640×480	2 color	1
EGA	EGALO	0	640×200	16 color	4
	EGAHI	1	640×350	16 color	2
EGA64	EGA64LO	0	640×200	16 color	1
	EGA64HI	1	640×350	4 color	1
EGA-MONO	EGAMONOHI	3	640×350	2 color	1*
	EGAMONOHI	3	640×350	2 color	2**
HERC	HERCMONOHI	0	720×348	2 color	2
ATT400	ATT400C0	0	320×200	C0	1
	ATT400C1	1	320×200	C1	1
	ATT400C2	2	320×200	C2	1
	ATT400C3	3	320×200	C3	1
	ATT400MED	4	640×200	2 color	1
	ATT400HI	5	640×400	2 color	1
VGA	VGALO	0	640×200	16 color	2
	VGAMED	1	640×350	16 color	2
	VGAHI	2	640×480	16 color	1
PC3270	PC3270HI	0	720×350	2 color	1
IBM8514	IBM8514HI	1	1024×768	256 color	
	IBM8514LO	0	640×480	256 color	

* 64K on EGAMONO card

** 256K on EGAMONO card

Return value

initgraph always sets the internal error code; on success, it sets the code to 0. If an error occurs, **graphdriver* is set to –2, –3, –4, or –5, and *graphresult* returns the same value as listed here:

grNotDetected	–2	Cannot detect a graphics card
grFileNotFound	–3	Cannot find driver file
grInvalidDriver	–4	Invalid driver
grNoLoadMem	–5	Insufficient memory to load driver

See also

closegraph, detectgraph, getdefaultpalette, getdrivername, getgraphmode, getmoderange, graphdefaults, _graphgetmem, graphresult, installuserdriver, registerbgidriver, registerbgifont, restorecrtmode, setgraphbufsize, setgraphmode

installuserdriver

graphics.h

Function

Installs a vendor-added device driver to the BGI device-driver table.

Syntax

int far installuserdriver(char far *name, int huge (*detect)(void));

Remarks

installuserdriver lets you add a vendor-added device driver to the BGI internal table. The *name* parameter is the name of the new device-driver file (.BGI), and the *detect* parameter is a pointer to an optional autodetect function that can accompany the new driver. This autodetect function takes no parameters and returns an integer value.

There are two ways to use this vendor-supplied driver. Let's assume you have a new video card called the Spiffy Graphics Array (SGA) and that the SGA manufacturer provided you with a BGI device driver (SGA.BGI). The easiest way to use this driver is to install it by calling *installuserdriver* and then passing the return value (the assigned driver number) directly to *initgraph*.

The other, more general way to use this driver is to link in an autodetect function that will be called by *initgraph* as part of its hardware-detection logic (presumably, the manufacturer of the SGA gave you this autodetect function). When you install the driver (by calling *installuserdriver*), you pass the address of this function, along with the device driver's file name.

After you install the device-driver file name and the SGA autodetect function, call *initgraph* and let it go through its normal autodetection process. Before *initgraph* calls its built-in autodetection function (*detectgraph*), it first calls the SGA autodetect function. If the SGA autodetect function doesn't find the SGA hardware, it returns a value of –11 (grError), and *initgraph* proceeds with its normal hardware detection logic (which can include calling any other vendor-supplied autodetection functions in the order in which they were "installed"). If, however, the autodetect function determines that an SGA is present, it returns a nonnegative mode number; then *initgraph* locates and loads SGA.BGI, puts the hardware into the default graphics mode recommended by the autodetect function, and finally returns control to your program.

You can install up to ten drivers at one time.

Return value
The value returned by *installuserdriver* is the driver number parameter you would pass to *initgraph* in order to select the newly installed driver manually.

See also
initgraph, registerbgidriver

installuserfont
graphics.h

Function
Loads a font file (.CHR) that is not built into the BGI system.

Syntax
int far installuserfont(char far *name);

Remarks
name is a file name in the current directory (path name is not supported) of a font file containing a stroked font. Up to twenty fonts can be installed at one time.

Return value
installuserfont returns a font ID number that can then be passed to *settextstyle* to select the corresponding font. If the internal font table is full, a value of –11 (grError) is returned.

See also
settextstyle

line
graphics.h

Function
Draws a line between two specified points.

Syntax
void far line(int x1, int y1, int x2, int y2);

Remarks
line draws a line in the current color, using the current line style and thickness between the two points specified, (*x1,y1*) and (*x2,y2*), without updating the current position (CP).

Return value
None.

See also
getlinesettings, linerel, lineto, setcolor, setlinestyle, setwritemode

linerel

Function
Draws a line a relative distance from the current position (CP).

Syntax
void far linerel(int dx, int dy);

Remarks
linerel draws a line from the CP to a point that is a relative distance (*dx,dy*) from the CP. The CP is advanced by (*dx,dy*).

Return value
None.

See also
getlinesettings, line, lineto, setcolor, setlinestyle, setwritemode

lineto

Function
Draws a line from the current position (CP) to (*x,y*).

Syntax
void far lineto(int x, int y);

Remarks
lineto draws a line from the CP to (*x,y*), then moves the CP to (*x,y*).

Return value
None.

See also
getlinesettings, line, linerel, setcolor, setlinestyle, setvisualpage, setwritemode

moverel

graphics.h

Function
Moves the current position (CP) a relative distance.

Syntax
void far moverel(int dx, int dy);

Remarks
moverel moves the current position (CP) *dx* pixels in the *x* direction and *dy* pixels in the *y* direction.

Return value
None.

See also
moveto

moveto

graphics.h

Function
Moves the current position (CP) to (x,y).

Syntax
void far moveto(int x, int y);

Remarks
moveto moves the current position (CP) to viewport position (x,y).

Return value
None.

See also
moverel

outtext

graphics.h

Function
Displays a string in the viewport.

Syntax
void far outtext(char far *textstring);

Remarks

outtext displays a text string in the viewport, using the current font, direction, and size.

outtext outputs *textstring* at the current position (CP). If the horizontal text justification is LEFT_TEXT and the text direction is HORIZ_DIR, the CP's x-coordinate is advanced by *textwidth(textstring)*. Otherwise, the CP remains unchanged.

To maintain code compatibility when using several fonts, use *textwidth* and *textheight* to determine the dimensions of the string.

Note If a string is printed with the default font using *outtext*, any part of the string that extends outside the current viewport is truncated.

outtext is for use in graphics mode; it will not work in text mode.

Return value

None.

See also

gettextsettings, outtextxy, settextjustify, textheight, textwidth

outtextxy

graphics.h

Function

Displays a string at a specified location.

Syntax

void far outtextxy(int x, int y, char far *textstring);

Remarks

outtextxy displays a text string in the viewport at the given position (x, y), using the current justification settings and the current font, direction, and size.

To maintain code compatibility when using several fonts, use *textwidth* and *textheight* to determine the dimensions of the string.

Note If a string is printed with the default font using *outtext* or *outtextxy*, any part of the string that extends outside the current viewport is truncated.

outtextxy is for use in graphics mode; it will not work in text mode.

Return value

None.

See also

gettextsettings, outtext, textheight, textwidth

pieslice

graphics.h

Function
Draws and fills in a pie slice.

Syntax
void far pieslice(int x, int y, int stangle, int endangle, int radius);

Remarks
pieslice draws and fills a pie slice centered at (*x,y*) with a radius given by *radius*. The slice travels from *stangle* to *endangle*. The slice is outlined in the current drawing color and then filled using the current fill pattern and fill color.

The angles for *pieslice* are given in degrees. They are measured counterclockwise, with 0 degrees at 3 o'clock, 90 degrees at 12 o'clock, and so on.

If you're using a CGA or monochrome adapter, the examples in online Help that show how to use graphics functions might not produce the expected results. If your system runs on a CGA or monochrome adapter, use the value 1 (one) instead of the symbolic color constant, and consult the second online Help example under *arc* on how to use the *pieslice* function.

Return value
None.

See also
fillellipse, fill_patterns (enumerated type), *graphresult, sector, setfillstyle*

putimage

graphics.h

Function
Outputs a bit image to screen.

Syntax
void far putimage(int left, int top, void far *bitmap, int op);

Remarks
putimage puts the bit image previously saved with *getimage* back onto the screen, with the upper left corner of the image placed at (*left,top*). *bitmap* points to the area in memory where the source image is stored.

The *op* parameter to *putimage* specifies a combination operator that controls how the color for each destination pixel onscreen is computed, based on the pixel already onscreen and the corresponding source pixel in memory.

The enumeration *putimage_ops*, as defined in graphics.h, gives names to these operators.

Name	Value	Description
COPY_PUT	0	Copy
XOR_PUT	1	Exclusive or
OR_PUT	2	Inclusive or
AND_PUT	3	And
NOT_PUT	4	Copy the inverse of the source

In other words, COPY_PUT copies the source bitmap image onto the screen, XOR_PUT XORs the source image with the image already onscreen, OR_PUT ORs the source image with that onscreen, and so on.

Return value
None.

See also
getimage, imagesize, putpixel, setvisualpage

putpixel   graphics.h

Function
Plots a pixel at a specified point.

Syntax
void far putpixel(int x, int y, int color);

Remarks
putpixel plots a point in the color defined by *color* at (*x,y*).

Return value
None.

See also
getpixel, putimage

rectangle   graphics.h

Function
Draws a rectangle.

Syntax
void far rectangle(int left, int top, int right, int bottom);

Remarks

rectangle draws a rectangle in the current line style, thickness, and drawing color.

(*left,top*) is the upper left corner of the rectangle, and (*right,bottom*) is its lower right corner.

Return value

None.

See also

bar, bar3d, setcolor, setlinestyle

registerbgifont

graphics.h

Function

Registers linked-in stroked font code.

Syntax

int registerbgifont(void (*font)(void));

Remarks

Calling *registerbgifont* informs the graphics system that the font pointed to by *font* was included at link time. This routine checks the linked-in code for the specified font; if the code is valid, it registers the code in internal tables.

By using the name of a linked-in font in a call to *registerbgifont,* you also tell the compiler (and linker) to link in the object file with that public name.

If you register a user-supplied font, you *must* pass the result of *registerbgifont* to *settextstyle* as the font number to be used.

Return value

registerbgifont returns a negative graphics error code if the specified font is invalid. Otherwise, *registerbgifont* returns the font number of the registered font.

See also

graphresult, initgraph, installuserdriver, registerbgidriver, settextstyle

registerbgidriver

graphics.h

Function

Registers a user-loaded or linked-in graphics driver code with the graphics system.

Syntax

int registerbgidriver(void (*driver)(void));

Remarks

registerbgidriver enables a user to load a driver file and "register" the driver. Once its memory location has been passed to *registerbgidriver*, *initgraph* uses the registered driver. A user-registered driver can be loaded from disk onto the heap, or converted to an .OBJ file (using BGIOBJ.EXE) and linked into the .EXE.

Calling *registerbgidriver* informs the graphics system that the driver pointed to by *driver* was included at link time. This routine checks the linked-in code for the specified driver; if the code is valid, it registers the code in internal tables.

By using the name of a linked-in driver in a call to *registerbgidriver*, you also tell the compiler (and linker) to link in the object file with that public name.

Return value

registerbgidriver returns a negative graphics error code if the specified driver or font is invalid. Otherwise, *registerbgidriver* returns the driver number.

If you register a user-supplied driver, you *must* pass the result of *registerbgidriver* to *initgraph* as the driver number to be used.

See also

graphresult, *initgraph*, *installuserdriver*, *registerbgifont*

restorecrtmode   graphics.h

Function

Restores the screen mode to its pre-*initgraph* setting.

Syntax

void far restorecrtmode(void);

Remarks

restorecrtmode restores the original video mode detected by *initgraph*.

This function can be used in conjunction with *setgraphmode* to switch back and forth between text and graphics modes. *textmode* should not be used for this purpose; use it only when the screen is in text mode, to change to a different text mode.

Return value

None.

See also

getgraphmode, *initgraph*, *setgraphmode*

sector

graphics.h

Function
Draws and fills an elliptical pie slice.

Syntax
void far sector(int x, int y, int stangle, int endangle, int xradius, int yradius);

Remarks
Draws and fills an elliptical pie slice using (x,y) as the center point, *xradius* and *yradius* as the horizontal and vertical radii, respectively, and drawing from *stangle* to *endangle*. The pie slice is outlined using the current color, and filled using the pattern and color defined by *setfillstyle* or *setfillpattern*.

The angles for *sector* are given in degrees. They are measured counterclockwise with 0 degrees at 3 o'clock, 90 degrees at 12 o'clock, and so on.

If an error occurs while the pie slice is filling, *graphresult* returns a value of –6 (grNoScanMem).

Return value
None.

See also
arc, circle, ellipse, getarccoords, getaspectratio, graphresult, pieslice, setfillpattern, setfillstyle, setgraphbufsize

setactivepage

graphics.h

Function
Sets the active page for graphics output.

Syntax
void far setactivepage(int page);

Remarks
setactivepage makes *page* the active graphics page. All subsequent graphics output will be directed to that graphics page.

The active graphics page might not be the one you see onscreen, depending on how many graphics pages are available on your system. Only the EGA, VGA, and Hercules graphics cards support multiple pages.

Return value
None.

See also
setvisualpage

setallpalette   **graphics.h**

Function
Changes all palette colors as specified.

Syntax
void far setallpalette(struct palettetype far *palette);

Remarks
setallpalette sets the current palette to the values given in the *palettetype* structure pointed to by *palette*.

You can partially (or completely) change the colors in the EGA/VGA palette with *setallpalette*.

The MAXCOLORS constant and the *palettetype* structure used by *setallpalette* are defined in graphics.h as follows:

```
#define MAXCOLORS  15

struct palettetype {
   unsigned char size;
   signed char colors[MAXCOLORS + 1];
};
```

size gives the number of colors in the palette for the current graphics driver in the current mode.

colors is an array of *size* bytes containing the actual raw color numbers for each entry in the palette. If an element of *colors* is –1, the palette color for that entry is not changed.

The elements in the *colors* array used by *setallpalette* can be represented by symbolic constants which are defined in graphics.h.

Table 6.6   Actual color table

CGA		EGA/VGA	
Name	Value	Name	Value
BLACK	0	EGA_BLACK	0
BLUE	1	EGA_BLUE	1
GREEN	2	EGA_GREEN	2
CYAN	3	EGA_CYAN	3
RED	4	EGA_RED	4
MAGENTA	5	EGA_MAGENTA	5
BROWN	6	EGA_LIGHTGRAY	7
LIGHTGRAY	7	EGA_BROWN	20

Table 6.6   Actual color table (continued)

CGA		EGA/VGA	
Name	**Value**	**Name**	**Value**
DARKGRAY	8	EGA_DARKGRAY	56
LIGHTBLUE	9	EGA_LIGHTBLUE	57
LIGHTGREEN	10	EGA_LIGHTGREEN	58
LIGHTCYAN	11	EGA_LIGHTCYAN	59
LIGHTRED	12	EGA_LIGHTRED	60
LIGHTMAGENTA	13	EGA_LIGHTMAGENTA	61
YELLOW	14	EGA_YELLOW	62
WHITE	15	EGA_WHITE	63

Note that valid colors depend on the current graphics driver and current graphics mode.

Changes made to the palette are seen immediately onscreen. Each time a palette color is changed, all occurrences of that color onscreen will change to the new color value.

Note   *setallpalette* cannot be used with the IBM-8514 driver.

Return value
If invalid input is passed to *setallpalette*, *graphresult* returns –11 (grError), and the current palette remains unchanged.

See also
getpalette, getpalettesize, graphresult, setbkcolor, setcolor, setpalette

setaspectratio   graphics.h

Function
Changes the default aspect ratio correction factor.

Syntax
void far setaspectratio(int xasp, int yasp);

Remarks
setaspectratio changes the default aspect ratio of the graphics system. The graphics system uses the aspect ratio to make sure that circles are round onscreen. If circles appear elliptical, the monitor is not aligned properly. You could correct this in the hardware by realigning the monitor, but it's easier to change in the software by using *setaspectratio* to set the aspect ratio. To obtain the current aspect ratio from the system, call *getaspectratio*.

Return value
None.

See also
circle, getaspectratio

setbkcolor   **graphics.h**

Function
Sets the current background color using the palette.

Syntax
void far setbkcolor(int color);

Remarks
setbkcolor sets the background to the color specified by *color*. The argument *color* can be a name or a number, as listed in the following table:

Number	Name	Number	Name
0	BLACK	8	DARKGRAY
1	BLUE	9	LIGHTBLUE
2	GREEN	10	LIGHTGREEN
3	CYAN	11	LIGHTCYAN
4	RED	12	LIGHTRED
5	MAGENTA	13	LIGHTMAGENTA
6	BROWN	14	YELLOW
7	LIGHTGRAY	15	WHITE

Note These symbolic names are defined in graphics.h.

For example, if you want to set the background color to blue, you can call

```
ASPROGRAMC setbkcolor(BLUE) /* or */ setbkcolor(1)
```

On CGA and EGA systems, *setbkcolor* changes the background color by changing the first entry in the palette.

Note If you use an EGA or a VGA, and you change the palette colors with *setpalette* or *setallpalette*, the defined symbolic constants might not give you the correct color. This is because the parameter to *setbkcolor* indicates the entry number in the current palette rather than a specific color (unless the parameter passed is 0, which always sets the background color to black).

Return value
None.

See also
getbkcolor, setallpalette, setcolor, setpalette

setcolor

Function
Sets the current drawing color using the palette.

Syntax
void far setcolor(int color);

Remarks
setcolor sets the current drawing color to *color*, which can range from 0 to *getmaxcolor*.

The current drawing color is the value to which pixels are set when lines, and so on are drawn. The following tables show the drawing colors available for the CGA and EGA, respectively.

Table 6.7   Colors available for CGA

Palette number	Constant assigned to color number (pixel value)		
	1	2	3
0	CGA_LIGHTGREEN	CGA_LIGHTRED	CGA_YELLOW
1	CGA_LIGHTCYAN	CGA_LIGHTMAGENTA	CGA_WHITE
2	CGA_GREEN	CGA_RED	CGA_BROWN
3	CGA_CYAN	CGA_MAGENTA	CGA_LIGHTGRAY

Table 6.8   Colors available for EGA

Number	Name	Number	Name
0	BLACK	8	DARKGRAY
1	BLUE	9	LIGHTBLUE
2	GREEN	10	LIGHTGREEN
3	CYAN	11	LIGHTCYAN
4	RED	12	LIGHTRED
5	MAGENTA	13	LIGHTMAGENTA
6	BROWN	14	YELLOW
7	LIGHTGRAY	15	WHITE

You select a drawing color by passing either the color number itself or the equivalent symbolic name to *setcolor*. For example, in CGAC0 mode, the palette contains four colors: the background color, light green, light red, and yellow. In this mode, either *setcolor*(3) or *setcolor*(CGA_YELLOW) selects a drawing color of yellow.

Return value
None.

See also
getcolor, getmaxcolor, graphresult, setallpalette, setbkcolor, setpalette

setfillpattern   graphics.h

Function
Selects a user-defined fill pattern.

Syntax
void far setfillpattern(char far *upattern, int color);

Remarks
setfillpattern is like *setfillstyle*, except that you use it to set a user-defined 8×8 pattern rather than a predefined pattern.

upattern is a pointer to a sequence of 8 bytes, with each byte corresponding to 8 pixels in the pattern. Whenever a bit in a pattern byte is set to 1, the corresponding pixel is plotted.

Return value
None.

See also
getfillpattern, getfillsettings, graphresult, sector, setfillstyle

setfillstyle   graphics.h

Function
Sets the fill pattern and color.

Syntax
void far setfillstyle(int pattern, int color);

Remarks
setfillstyle sets the current fill pattern and fill color. To set a user-defined fill pattern, do *not* give a pattern of 12 (USER_FILL) to *setfillstyle*; instead, call *setfillpattern*.

The enumeration *fill_patterns*, which is defined in graphics.h, gives names for the predefined fill patterns and an indicator for a user-defined pattern.

Name	Value	Description
EMPTY_FILL	0	Fill with background color
SOLID_FILL	1	Solid fill
LINE_FILL	2	Fill with — —
LTSLASH_FILL	3	Fill with / / /
SLASH_FILL	4	Fill with / / /, thick lines
BKSLASH_FILL	5	Fill with \ \ \, thick lines
LTBKSLASH_FILL	6	Fill with \ \ \
HATCH_FILL	7	Light hatch fill

Name	Value	Description
XHATCH_FILL	8	Heavy crosshatch fill
INTERLEAVE_FILL	9	Interleaving line fill
WIDE_DOT_FILL	10	Widely spaced dot fill
CLOSE_DOT_FILL	11	Closely spaced dot fill
USER_FILL	12	User-defined fill pattern

All but EMPTY_FILL fill with the current fill color; EMPTY_FILL use the current background color.

If invalid input is passed to *setfillstyle*, *graphresult* returns –11 (grError), and the current fill pattern and fill color remain unchanged.

Return value
None.

See also
bar, bar3d, fillpoly, floodfill, getfillsettings, graphresult, pieslice, sector, setfillpattern

setgraphmode   graphics.h

Function
Sets the system to graphics mode and clears the screen.

Syntax
void far setgraphmode(int mode);

Remarks
setgraphmode selects a graphics mode different than the default one set by *initgraph*. *mode* must be a valid mode for the current device driver. *setgraphmode* clears the screen and resets all graphics settings to their defaults (current position, palette, color, viewport, and so on).

You can use *setgraphmode* in conjunction with *restorecrtmode* to switch back and forth between text and graphics modes.

Return value
If you give *setgraphmode* an invalid mode for the current device driver, *graphresult* returns a value of –10 (grInvalidMode).

See also
getgraphmode, getmoderange, graphresult, initgraph, restorecrtmode

setgraphbufsize
graphics.h

Function
Changes the size of the internal graphics buffer.

Syntax
unsigned far setgraphbufsize(unsigned bufsize);

Remarks
Some of the graphics routines (such as *floodfill*) use a memory buffer that is allocated when *initgraph* is called and released when *closegraph* is called. The default size of this buffer, allocated by *_graphgetmem*, is 4,096 bytes.

You might want to make this buffer smaller (to save memory space) or bigger (if, for example, a call to *floodfill* produces error –7: Out of flood memory).

setgraphbufsize tells *initgraph* how much memory to allocate for this internal graphics buffer when it calls *_graphgetmem*.

Note You *must* call *setgraphbufsize* before calling *initgraph*. Once *initgraph* has been called, all calls to *setgraphbufsize* are ignored until after the next call to *closegraph*.

Return value
setgraphbufsize returns the previous size of the internal buffer.

See also
closegraph, *_graphfreemem*, *_graphgetmem*, *initgraph*, *sector*

setlinestyle
graphics.h

Function
Sets the current line width and style.

Syntax
void far setlinestyle(int linestyle, unsigned upattern, int thickness);

Remarks
setlinestyle sets the style for all lines drawn by *line, lineto, rectangle, drawpoly*, and so on.

The *linesettingstype* structure is defined in graphics.h as follows:

```
struct linesettingstype {
    int linestyle;
    unsigned upattern;
    int thickness;
};
```

linestyle specifies in which of several styles subsequent lines will be drawn (such as solid, dotted, centered, dashed). The enumeration *line_styles*, which is defined in graphics.h, gives names to these operators:

Name	Value	Description
SOLID_LINE	0	Solid line
DOTTED_LINE	1	Dotted line
CENTER_LINE	2	Centered line
DASHED_LINE	3	Dashed line
USERBIT_LINE	4	User-defined line style

thickness specifies whether the width of subsequent lines drawn will be normal or thick.

Name	Value	Description
NORM_WIDTH	1	1 pixel wide
THICK_WIDTH	3	3 pixels wide

upattern is a 16-bit pattern that applies only if *linestyle* is USERBIT_LINE (4). In that case, whenever a bit in the pattern word is 1, the corresponding pixel in the line is drawn in the current drawing color. For example, a solid line corresponds to a *upattern* of 0xFFFF (all pixels drawn), and a dashed line can correspond to a *upattern* of 0x3333 or 0x0F0F. If the *linestyle* parameter to *setlinestyle* is not USERBIT_LINE (in other words, if it is not equal to 4), you must still provide the *upattern* parameter, but it will be ignored.

Note   The *linestyle* parameter does not affect arcs, circles, ellipses, or pie slices. Only the *thickness* parameter is used.

Return value
If invalid input is passed to *setlinestyle*, *graphresult* returns –11, and the current line style remains unchanged.

See also
arc, bar3d, circle, drawpoly, ellipse, getlinesettings, graphresult, line, linerel, lineto, pieslice, rectangle

setpalette   graphics.h

Function
Changes one palette color.

Syntax
void far setpalette(int colornum, int color);

Remarks

setpalette changes the *colornum* entry in the palette to *color*. For example, *setpalette*(0,5) changes the first color in the current palette (the background color) to actual color number 5. If *size* is the number of entries in the current palette, *colornum* can range between 0 and (*size* –1).

You can partially (or completely) change the colors in the EGA/VGA palette with *setpalette*. On a CGA, you can only change the first entry in the palette (*colornum* equals 0, the background color) with a call to *setpalette*.

The *color* parameter passed to *setpalette* can be represented by symbolic constants which are defined in graphics.h.

CGA		EGA/VGA	
Name	Value	Name	Value
BLACK	0	EGA_BLACK	0
BLUE	1	EGA_BLUE	1
GREEN	2	EGA_GREEN	2
CYAN	3	EGA_CYAN	3
RED	4	EGA_RED	4
MAGENTA	5	EGA_MAGENTA	5
BROWN	6	EGA_LIGHTGRAY	7
LIGHTGRAY	7	EGA_BROWN	20
DARKGRAY	8	EGA_DARKGRAY	56
LIGHTBLUE	9	EGA_LIGHTBLUE	57
LIGHTGREEN	10	EGA_LIGHTGREEN	58
LIGHTCYAN	11	EGA_LIGHTCYAN	59
LIGHTRED	12	EGA_LIGHTRED	60
LIGHTMAGENTA	13	EGA_LIGHTMAGENTA	61
YELLOW	14	EGA_YELLOW	62
WHITE	15	EGA_WHITE	63

Note that valid colors depend on the current graphics driver and current graphics mode.

Changes made to the palette are seen immediately onscreen. Each time a palette color is changed, all occurrences of that color onscreen change to the new color value.

Note *setpalette* cannot be used with the IBM-8514 driver; use *setrgbpalette* instead.

Return value

If invalid input is passed to *setpalette*, *graphresult* returns –11, and the current palette remains unchanged.

See also

getpalette, graphresult, setallpalette, setbkcolor, setcolor, setrgbpalette

setrgbpalette
graphics.h

Function
Lets user define colors for the IBM 8514.

Syntax
void far setrgbpalette(int colornum, int red, int green, int blue);

Remarks
setrgbpalette can be used with the IBM 8514 and VGA drivers.

colornum defines the palette entry to be loaded, while *red*, *green*, and *blue* define the component colors of the palette entry.

For the IBM 8514 display (and the VGA in 256K color mode), *colornum* is in the range 0 to 255. For the remaining modes of the VGA, *colornum* is in the range 0 to 15. Only the lower byte of *red*, *green*, or *blue* is used, and out of each byte, only the 6 most significant bits are loaded in the palette.

Note For compatibility with other IBM graphics adapters, the BGI driver defines the first 16 palette entries of the IBM 8514 to the default colors of the EGA/VGA. These values can be used as is, or they can be changed using *setrgbpalette*.

Return value
None.

See also
setpalette

settextjustify
graphics.h

Function
Sets text justification for graphics functions.

Syntax
void far settextjustify(int horiz, int vert);

Remarks
Text output after a call to *settextjustify* is justified around the current position (CP) horizontally and vertically, as specified. The default justification settings are LEFT_TEXT (for horizontal) and TOP_TEXT (for vertical). The enumeration *text_just* in graphics.h provides names for the *horiz* and *vert* settings passed to *settextjustify*.

Description	Name	Value	Action
horiz	LEFT_TEXT	0	Left-justify text
	CENTER_TEXT	1	Center text
	RIGHT_TEXT	2	Right-justify text

Description	Name	Value	Action
vert	BOTTOM_TEXT	0	Justify from bottom
	CENTER_TEXT	1	Center text
	TOP_TEXT	2	Justify from top

If *horiz* is equal to LEFT_TEXT and *direction* equals HORIZ_DIR, the CP's x component is advanced after a call to *outtext(string)* by *textwidth(string)*.

settextjustify affects text written with *outtext* and cannot be used with text mode and stream functions.

Return value

If invalid input is passed to *settextjustify*, *graphresult* returns –11, and the current text justification remains unchanged.

See also

gettextsettings, graphresult, outtext, settextstyle

settextstyle   graphics.h

Function
Sets the current text characteristics for graphics output.

Syntax
void far settextstyle(int font, int direction, int charsize);

Remarks
settextstyle sets the text font, the direction in which text is displayed, and the size of the characters. A call to *settextstyle* affects all text output by *outtext* and *outtextxy*.

The parameters *font*, *direction*, and *charsize* are described in the following:

font: One 8×8 bit-mapped font and several "stroked" fonts are available. The 8×8 bit-mapped font is the default. The enumeration *font_names*, which is defined in graphics.h, provides names for these different font settings:

Name	Value	Description
DEFAULT_FONT	0	8×8 bit-mapped font
TRIPLEX_FONT	1	Stroked triplex font
SMALL_FONT	2	Stroked small font
SANS_SERIF_FONT	3	Stroked sans-serif font
GOTHIC_FONT	4	Stroked gothic font
SCRIPT_FONT	5	Stroked script font
SIMPLEX_FONT	6	Stroked simplex script font
TRIPLEX_SCR_FONT	7	Stroked triplex script font
COMPLEX_FONT	8	Stroked complex font

Name	Value	Description
EUROPEAN_FONT	9	Stroked European font
BOLD_FONT	10	Stroked bold font

The default bit-mapped font is built into the graphics system. Stroked fonts are stored in *.CHR disk files, and only one at a time is kept in memory. Therefore, when you select a stroked font (different from the last selected stroked font), the corresponding *.CHR file must be loaded from disk.

To avoid this loading when several stroked fonts are used, you can link font files into your program. Do this by converting them into object files with the BGIOBJ utility, then registering them through *registerbgifont*.

direction: Font directions supported are horizontal text (left to right) and vertical text (rotated 90 degrees counterclockwise). The default direction is HORIZ_DIR.

Name	Value	Description
HORIZ_DIR	0	Left to right
VERT_DIR	1	Bottom to top

charsize: The size of each character can be magnified using the *charsize* factor. If *charsize* is nonzero, it can affect bit-mapped or stroked characters. A *charsize* value of 0 can be used only with stroked fonts.

- If *charsize* equals 1, *outtext* and *outtextxy* display characters from the 8×8 bit-mapped font in an 8×8 pixel rectangle onscreen.

- If *charsize* equals 2, these output functions display characters from the 8×8 bit-mapped font in a 16×16 pixel rectangle, and so on (up to a limit of ten times the normal size).

- When *charsize* equals 0, the output functions *outtext* and *outtextxy* magnify the stroked font text using either the default character magnification factor (4) or the user-defined character size given by *setusercharsize*.

Always use *textheight* and *textwidth* to determine the actual dimensions of the text.

Return value
None.

See also
gettextsettings, graphresult, installuserfont, settextjustify, setusercharsize, textheight, textwidth

setusercharsize
graphics.h

Function
Varies character width and height for stroked fonts.

Syntax
void far setusercharsize(int multx, int divx, int multy, int divy);

Remarks
setusercharsize gives you finer control over the size of text from stroked fonts used with graphics functions. The values set by *setusercharsize* are active *only* if *charsize* equals 0, as set by a previous call to *settextstyle*.

With *setusercharsize*, you specify factors by which the width and height are scaled. The default width is scaled by *multx : divx*, and the default height is scaled by *multy : divy*. For example, to make text twice as wide and 50% taller than the default, set

```
multx = 2;  divx = 1;
multy = 3;  divy = 2;
```

Return value
None.

See also
gettextsettings, graphresult, settextstyle

setviewport
graphics.h

Function
Sets the current viewport for graphics output.

Syntax
void far setviewport(int left, int top, int right, int bottom, int clip);

Remarks
setviewport establishes a new viewport for graphics output.

The viewport's corners are given in absolute screen coordinates by (*left,top*) and (*right,bottom*). The current position (CP) is moved to (0,0) in the new window.

The parameter *clip* determines whether drawings are clipped (truncated) at the current viewport boundaries. If *clip* is nonzero, all drawings will be clipped to the current viewport.

Return value

If invalid input is passed to *setviewport*, *graphresult* returns –11, and the current view settings remain unchanged.

See also

clearviewport, getviewsettings, graphresult

setvisualpage   graphics.h

Function

Sets the visual graphics page number.

Syntax

void far setvisualpage(int page);

Remarks

setvisualpage makes *page* the visual graphics page.

Return value

None.

See also

graphresult, setactivepage

setwritemode   graphics.h

Function

Sets the writing mode for line drawing in graphics mode.

Syntax

void far setwritemode(int mode);

Remarks

The following constants are defined:

```
COPY_PUT = 0      /* MOV */
XOR_PUT  = 1      /* XOR */
```

Each constant corresponds to a binary operation between each byte in the line and the corresponding bytes onscreen. COPY_PUT uses the assembly language **MOV** instruction, overwriting with the line whatever is on the screen. XOR_PUT uses the **XOR** command to combine the line with the screen. Two successive **XOR** commands will erase the line and restore the screen to its original appearance.

Note *setwritemode* currently works only with *line, linerel, lineto, rectangle,* and *drawpoly*.

Return value
None.

See also
drawpoly, line, linerel, lineto, putimage

---

textheight   graphics.h

Function
Returns the height of a string in pixels.

Syntax
int far textheight(char far *textstring);

Remarks
The graphics function *textheight* takes the current font size and multiplication factor, and determines the height of *textstring* in pixels. This function is useful for adjusting the spacing between lines, computing viewport heights, sizing a title to make it fit on a graph or in a box, and so on.

For example, with the 8×8 bit-mapped font and a multiplication factor of 1 (set by *settextstyle*), the string *TurboC++* is 8 pixels high.

Note Use *textheight* to compute the height of strings, instead of doing the computations manually. By using this function, no source code modifications have to be made when different fonts are selected.

Return value
textheight returns the text height in pixels.

See also
gettextsettings, outtext, outtextxy, settextstyle, textwidth

textwidth

graphics.h

Function
Returns the width of a string in pixels.

Syntax
int far textwidth(char far *textstring);

Remarks
The graphics function *textwidth* takes the string length, current font size, and multiplication factor, and determines the width of *textstring* in pixels.

This function is useful for computing viewport widths, sizing a title to make it fit on a graph or in a box, and so on.

Note   Use *textwidth* to compute the width of strings, instead of doing the computations manually. When you use this function, no source code modifications have to be made when different fonts are selected.

Return value
textwidth returns the text width in pixels.

See also
gettextsettings, *outtext*, *outtextxy*, *settextstyle*, *textheight*

7

DOS-only run-time functions

Except for the functions *brk* and *sbrk* (which are available on DOS and UNIX), the functions described in this chapter are available only for 16-bit DOS applications. Chapter 2, "Borland C++ library routines," describes additional functions; some of those functions can also be used in 16-bit DOS applications. The descriptions of some of the functions listed in the **See also** entries of this chapter can be found in Chapter 3, "Runtime functions."

absread   dos.h

Function
Reads absolute disk sectors.

Syntax
int absread(int drive, int nsects, long lsect, void *buffer);

Description
absread reads specific disk sectors. It ignores the logical structure of a disk and pays no attention to files, FATs, or directories.

absread uses DOS interrupt 0x25 to read specific disk sectors.

drive	=	drive number to read (0 = A, 1 = B, etc.)
nsects	=	number of sectors to read
lsect	=	beginning logical sector number
buffer	=	memory address where the data is to be read

The number of sectors to read is limited to 64K or the size of the buffer, whichever is smaller.

Return value
If it is successful, *absread* returns 0.

On error, the routine returns –1 and sets the global variable *errno* to the value returned by the system call in the AX register.

See also
abswrite, biosdisk

abswrite

Function
Writes absolute disk sectors.

Syntax
int abswrite(int drive, int nsects, long lsect, void *buffer);

Description
abswrite writes specific disk sectors. It ignores the logical structure of a disk and pays no attention to files, FATs, or directories.

Note If used improperly, *abswrite* can overwrite files, directories, and FATs.

abswrite uses DOS interrupt 0x26 to write specific disk sectors.

drive	=	drive number to write to (0 = A, 1 = B, etc.)
nsects	=	number of sectors to write to
lsect	=	beginning logical sector number
buffer	=	memory address where the data is to be written

The number of sectors to write to is limited to 64K or the size of the buffer, whichever is smaller.

Return value
If it is successful, *abswrite* returns 0.

On error, the routine returns –1 and sets the global variable *errno* to the value of the AX register returned by the system call.

See also
absread, biosdisk

allocmem, _dos_allocmem

Function
Allocates DOS memory segment.

Syntax
int allocmem(unsigned size, unsigned *segp);
unsigned _dos_allocmem(unsigned size, unsigned *segp);

Description

allocmem and *_dos_allocmem* use the DOS system call 0x48 to allocate a block of free memory and return the segment address of the allocated block.

size is the desired size in paragraphs (a paragraph is 16 bytes). *segp* is a pointer to a word that will be assigned the segment address of the newly allocated block.

For *allocmem*, if not enough room is available, no assignment is made to the word pointed to by *segp*.

For *_dos_allocmem*, if not enough room is available, the size of the largest available block will be stored in the word pointed to by *segp*.

All allocated blocks are paragraph-aligned.

Note   *allocmem* and *_dos_allocmem* cannot coexist with *malloc*.

Return value

allocmem returns –1 on success. In the event of error, *allocmem* returns a number indicating the size in paragraphs of the largest available block.

_dos_allocmem returns 0 on success. In the event of error, *_dos_allocmem* returns the DOS error code and sets the word pointed to by *segp* to the size in paragraphs of the largest available block.

An error return from *allocmem* or *_dos_allocmem* sets the global variable *_doserrno* and sets the global variable *errno* to the following:

    ENOMEM   Not enough memory

See also

coreleft, freemem, malloc, setblock

bioscom   bios.h

Function

Performs serial I/O.

Syntax

int bioscom(int cmd, char abyte, int port);

Description

bioscom performs various RS-232 communications over the I/O port given in *port*.

A *port* value of 0 corresponds to COM1, 1 corresponds to COM2, and so forth.

The value of *cmd* can be one of the following:

    0   Sets the communications parameters to the value in *abyte*
    1   Sends the character in *abyte* out over the communications line.

2 Receives a character from the communications line.

3 Returns the current status of the communications port.

abyte is a combination of the following bits (one value is selected from each of the groups):

0x02	7 data bits	0x00	110 baud
0x03	8 data bits	0x20	150 baud
		0x40	300 baud
0x00	1 stop bit	0x60	600 baud
0x04	2 stop bits	0x80	1200 baud
0x00	No parity	0xA0	2400 baud
0x08	Odd parity	0xC0	4800 baud
0x18	Even parity	0xE0	9600 baud

For example, a value of 0xEB (0xE0 | 0x08 | 0x00 | 0x03) for *abyte* sets the communications port to 9600 baud, odd parity, 1 stop bit, and 8 data bits. *bioscom* uses the BIOS 0x14 interrupt.

Return value

For all values of *cmd*, *bioscom* returns a 16-bit integer, of which the upper 8 bits are status bits and the lower 8 bits vary, depending on the value of *cmd*. The upper bits of the return value are defined as follows:

Bit 15 Time out
Bit 14 Transmit shift register empty
Bit 13 Transmit holding register empty
Bit 12 Break detect
Bit 11 Framing error
Bit 10 Parity error
Bit 9 Overrun error
Bit 8 Data ready

If the *abyte* value could not be sent, bit 15 is set to 1. Otherwise, the remaining upper and lower bits are appropriately set. For example, if a framing error has occurred, bit 11 is set to 1.

With a *cmd* value of 2, the byte read is in the lower bits of the return value if there is no error. If an error occurs, at least one of the upper bits is set to 1. If no upper bits are set to 1, the byte was received without error.

With a *cmd* value of 0 or 3, the return value has the upper bits set as defined, and the lower bits are defined as follows:

Bit 7 Received line signal detect
Bit 6 Ring indicator
Bit 5 Data set ready
Bit 4 Clear to send

Bit 3	Change in receive line signal detector
Bit 2	Trailing edge ring detector
Bit 1	Change in data set ready
Bit 0	Change in clear to send

biosdisk

Function
Issues BIOS disk drive services.

Syntax
int biosdisk(int cmd, int drive, int head, int track, int sector, int nsects, void *buffer);

Description
biosdisk uses interrupt 0x13 to issue disk operations directly to the BIOS.

drive is a number that specifies which disk drive is to be used: 0 for the first floppy disk drive, 1 for the second floppy disk drive, 2 for the third, and so on. For hard disk drives, a *drive* value of 0x80 specifies the first drive, 0x81 specifies the second, 0x82 the third, and so forth.

For hard disks, the physical drive is specified, not the disk partition. If necessary, the application program must interpret the partition table information itself.

cmd indicates the operation to perform. Depending on the value of *cmd*, the other parameters might or might not be needed.

Here are the possible values for *cmd* for the IBM PC, XT, AT, or PS/2, or any compatible system:

Value	Description
0	Resets disk system, forcing the drive controller to do a hard reset. All other parameters are ignored.
1	Returns the status of the last disk operation. All other parameters are ignored.
2	Reads one or more disk sectors into memory. The starting sector to read is given by *head*, *track*, and *sector*. The number of sectors is given by *nsects*. The data is read, 512 bytes per sector, into *buffer*.
3	Writes one or more disk sectors from memory. The starting sector to write is given by *head*, *track*, and *sector*. The number of sectors is given by *nsects*. The data is written, 512 bytes per sector, from *buffer*.
4	Verifies one or more sectors. The starting sector is given by *head*, *track*, and *sector*. The number of sectors is given by *nsects*.
5	Formats a track. The track is specified by *head* and *track*. *buffer* points to a table of sector headers to be written on the named *track*. See the *Technical Reference Manual* for the IBM PC for a description of this table and the format operation.

The following cmd values are allowed only for the XT, AT, PS/2, and compatibles:

Value	Description
6	Formats a track and sets bad sector flags.
7	Formats the drive beginning at a specific track.
8	Returns the current drive parameters. The drive information is returned in *buffer* in the first 4 bytes.
9	Initializes drive-pair characteristics.
10	Does a long read, which reads 512 plus 4 extra bytes per sector.
11	Does a long write, which writes 512 plus 4 extra bytes per sector.
12	Does a disk seek.
13	Alternates disk reset.
14	Reads sector buffer.
15	Writes sector buffer.
16	Tests whether the named drive is ready.
17	Recalibrates the drive.
18	Controller RAM diagnostic.
19	Drive diagnostic.
20	Controller internal diagnostic.

Note *biosdisk* operates below the level of files on raw sectors. *It can destroy file contents and directories on a hard disk.*

Return value

biosdisk returns a status byte composed of the following bits:

Bits	Description
0x00	Operation successful.
0x01	Bad command.
0x02	Address mark not found.
0x03	Attempt to write to write-protected disk.
0x04	Sector not found.
0x05	Reset failed (hard disk).
0x06	Disk changed since last operation.
0x07	Drive parameter activity failed.
0x08	Direct memory access (DMA) overrun.
0x09	Attempt to perform DMA across 64K boundary.
0x0A	Bad sector detected.
0x0B	Bad track detected.
0x0C	Unsupported track.
0x10	Bad CRC/ECC on disk read.
0x11	CRC/ECC corrected data error.
0x20	Controller has failed.
0x40	Seek operation failed.
0x80	Attachment failed to respond.

Bits	Description
0xAA	Drive not ready (hard disk only).
0xBB	Undefined error occurred (hard disk only).
0xCC	Write fault occurred.
0xE0	Status error.
0xFF	Sense operation failed.

0x11 is not an error because the data is correct. The value is returned to give the application an opportunity to decide for itself.

See also
absread, abswrite

_bios_disk   bios.h

Function
Issues BIOS disk drive services

Syntax
unsigned _bios_disk(unsigned cmd, struct diskinfo_t *dinfo);

Description
_bios_disk uses interrupt 0x13 to issue disk operations directly to the BIOS. The *cmd* argument specifies the operation to perform, and *dinfo* points to a *diskinfo_t* structure that contains the remaining parameters required by the operation.

The *diskinfo_t* structure (defined in bios.h) has the following format:

```
struct diskinfo_t {
    unsigned drive, head, track, sector, nsectors;
    void far *buffer;
};
```

drive is a number that specifies which disk drive is to be used: 0 for the first floppy disk drive, 1 for the second floppy disk drive, 2 for the third, and so on. For hard disk drives, a *drive* value of 0x80 specifies the first drive, 0x81 specifies the second, 0x82 the third, and so forth.

For hard disks, the physical drive is specified, not the disk partition. If necessary, the application program must interpret the partition table information itself.

Depending on the value of *cmd*, the other parameters in the *diskinfo_t* structure might or might not be needed.

The possible values for *cmd* (defined in bios.h) are the following:

Value	Description
_DISK_RESET	Resets disk system, forcing the drive controller to do a hard reset. All *diskinfo_t* parameters are ignored.
_DISK_STATUS	Returns the status of the last disk operation. All *diskinfo_t* parameters are ignored.

Value	Description
_DISK_READ	Reads one or more disk sectors into memory. The starting sector to read is given by *head*, *track*, and *sector*. The number of sectors is given by *nsectors*. The data is read, 512 bytes per sector, into *buffer*. If the operation is successful, the high byte of the return value will be 0 and the low byte will contain the number of sectors. If an error occurred, the high byte of the return value will have one of the following values:

0x01	Bad command.
0x02	Address mark not found.
0x03	Attempt to write to write-protected disk.
0x04	Sector not found.
0x05	Reset failed (hard disk).
0x06	Disk changed since last operation.
0x07	Drive parameter activity failed.
0x08	Direct memory access (DMA) overrun.
0x09	Attempt to perform DMA across 64K boundary.
0x0A	Bad sector detected.
0x0B	Bad track detected.
0x0C	Unsupported track.
0x10	Bad CRC/ECC on disk read.
0x11	CRC/ECC corrected data error.
0x20	Controller has failed.
0x40	Seek operation failed.
0x80	Attachment failed to respond.
0xAA	Drive not ready (hard disk only).
0xBB	Undefined error occurred (hard disk only).
0xCC	Write fault occurred.
0xE0	Status error.
0xFF	Sense operation failed.

Value	Description
	0x11 is not an error because the data is correct. The value is returned to give the application an opportunity to decide for itself.
_DISK_WRITE	Writes one or more disk sectors from memory. The starting sector to write is given by *head*, *track*, and *sector*. The number of sectors is given by *nsectors*. The data is written, 512 bytes per sector, from *buffer*. See _DISK_READ (above) for a description of the return value.
_DISK_VERIFY	Verifies one or more sectors. The starting sector is given by *head*, *track*, and *sector*. The number of sectors is given by *nsectors*. See _DISK_READ (above) for a description of the return value.
_DISK_FORMAT	Formats a track. The track is specified by *head* and *track*. *buffer* points to a table of sector headers to be written on the named *track*. See the *Technical Reference Manual* for the IBM PC for a description of this table and the format operation.

Return value

_bios_disk returns the value of the AX register set by the INT 0x13 BIOS call.

See also

absread, abswrite, biosdisk

bioskey

bios.h

Function

Keyboard interface, using BIOS services directly.

Syntax

int bioskey(int cmd);

Description

bioskey performs various keyboard operations using BIOS interrupt 0x16. The parameter *cmd* determines the exact operation.

Return value

The value returned by *bioskey* depends on the task it performs, determined by the value of *cmd*:

Value	Description
0	If the lower 8 bits are nonzero, *bioskey* returns the ASCII character for the next keystroke waiting in the queue or the next key pressed at the keyboard. If the lower 8 bits are zero, the upper 8 bits are the extended keyboard codes defined in the IBM PC *Technical Reference Manual*.
1	This tests whether a keystroke is available to be read. A return value of zero means no key is available. The return value is 0xFFFFF (–1) if *Ctrl+Brk* has been pressed. Otherwise, the value of the next keystroke is returned. The keystroke itself is kept to be returned by the next call to *bioskey* that has a *cmd* value of zero.
2	Requests the current shift key status. The value is obtained by ORing the following values together:

Bit 7	0x80	*Insert* on
Bit 6	0x40	*Caps* on
Bit 5	0x20	*Num Lock* on
Bit 4	0x10	*Scroll Lock* on
Bit 3	0x08	*Alt* pressed
Bit 2	0x04	*Ctrl* pressed
Bit 1	0x02	← *Shift* pressed
Bit 0	0x01	→ *Shift* pressed

_bios_keybrd

bios.h

Function

Keyboard interface, using BIOS services directly.

Syntax

unsigned _bios_keybrd(unsigned cmd);

Description

_bios_keybrd performs various keyboard operations using BIOS interrupt 0x16. The parameter *cmd* determines the exact operation.

Return value

The value returned by _bios_keybrd depends on the task it performs, determined by the value of *cmd* (defined in bios.h):

Value	Description
_KEYBRD_READ	If the lower 8 bits are nonzero, _bios_keybrd returns the ASCII character for the next keystroke waiting in the queue or the next key pressed at the keyboard. If the lower 8 bits are zero, the upper 8 bits are the extended keyboard codes defined in the IBM PC *Technical Reference Manual*.
_NKEYBRD_READ	Use this value instead of _KEYBRD_READY to read the keyboard codes for enhanced keyboards, which have additional cursor and function keys.
_KEYBRD_READY	This tests whether a keystroke is available to be read. A return value of zero means no key is available. The return value is 0xFFFF (–1) if *Ctrl+Brk* has been pressed. Otherwise, the value of the next keystroke is returned, as described in _KEYBRD_READ (above). The keystroke itself is kept to be returned by the next call to _bios_keybrd that has a *cmd* value of _KEYBRD_READ or _NKEYBRD_READ.
_NKEYBRD_READY	Use this value to check the status of enhanced keyboards, which have additional cursor and function keys.
_KEYBRD_SHIFTSTATUS	Requests the current shift key status. The value will contain an OR of zero or more of the following values:
	Bit 7 0x80 *Insert* on
	Bit 6 0x40 *Caps* on
	Bit 5 0x20 *Num Lock* on
	Bit 4 0x10 *Scroll Lock* on
	Bit 3 0x08 *Alt* pressed
	Bit 2 0x04 *Ctrl* pressed
	Bit 1 0x02 Left *Shift* pressed
	Bit 0 0x01 Right *Shift* pressed
_NKEYBRD_SHIFTSTATUS	Use this value instead of _KEYBRD_SHIFTSTATUS to request the full 16-bit shift key status for enhanced keyboards. The return value will contain an OR of zero or more of the bits defined above in _KEYBRD_SHIFTSTATUS, and additionally, any of the following bits:
	Bit 15 0x8000 *Sys Req* pressed
	Bit 14 0x4000 *Caps Lock* pressed
	Bit 13 0x2000 *Num Lock* pressed
	Bit 12 0x1000 *Scroll Lock* pressed
	Bit 11 0x0800 Right *Alt* pressed
	Bit 10 0x0400 Right *Ctrl* pressed
	Bit 9 0x0200 Left *Alt* pressed
	Bit 8 0x0100 Left *Ctrl* pressed

biosprint

bios.h

Function
Printer I/O using BIOS services directly.

Syntax
int biosprint(int cmd, int abyte, int port);

Description
biosprint performs various printer functions on the printer identified by the parameter *port* using BIOS interrupt 0x17.

A *port* value of 0 corresponds to LPT1; a *port* value of 1 corresponds to LPT2; and so on.

The value of *cmd* can be one of the following:

0	Prints the character in *abyte*.
1	Initializes the printer port.
2	Reads the printer status.

The value of *abyte* can be 0 to 255.

Return value
The value returned from any of these operations is the current printer status, which is obtained by ORing these bit values together:

Bit 0	0x01	Device time out
Bit 3	0x08	I/O error
Bit 4	0x10	Selected
Bit 5	0x20	Out of paper
Bit 6	0x40	Acknowledge
Bit 7	0x80	Not busy

_bios_printer

bios.h

Function
Printer I/O using BIOS services directly.

Syntax
unsigned _bios_printer(int cmd, int port, int abyte);

Description
_bios_printer performs various printer functions on the printer identified by the parameter *port* using BIOS interrupt 0x17.

A *port* value of 0 corresponds to LPT1; a *port* value of 1 corresponds to LPT2; and so on.

The value of *cmd* can be one of the following values (defined in bios.h):

    _PRINTER_WRITE   Prints the character in *abyte*. The value of *abyte* can be 0 to 255.
    _PRINTER_INIT   Initializes the printer port. The *abyte* argument is ignored.
    _PRINTER_STATUS Reads the printer status. The *abyte* argument is ignored.

Return value

The value returned from any of these operations is the current printer status, which is obtained by ORing these bit values together:

Bit 0	0x01	Device time out
Bit 3	0x08	I/O error
Bit 4	0x10	Selected
Bit 5	0x20	Out of paper
Bit 6	0x40	Acknowledge
Bit 7	0x80	Not busy

_bios_serialcom

bios.h

Function

Performs serial I/O.

Syntax

unsigned _bios_serialcom(int cmd, int port, char abyte);

Description

_bios_serialcom performs various RS-232 communications over the I/O port given in *port*.

A *port* value of 0 corresponds to COM1, 1 corresponds to COM2, and so forth.

The value of *cmd* can be one of the following values (defined in bios.h):

Value	Description
_COM_INIT	Sets the communications parameters to the value in *abyte*.
_COM_SEND	Sends the character in *abyte* out over the communications line.
_COM_RECEIVE	Receives a character from the communications line. The *abyte* argument is ignored.
_COM_STATUS	Returns the current status of the communications port. The *abyte* argument is ignored.

When *cmd* is _COM_INIT, *abyte* is a OR combination of the following bits:

• Select only one of these:

    _COM_CHR7   7 data bits
    _COM_CHR8   8 data bits

- Select only one of these:

  _COM_STOP1   1 stop bit
  _COM_STOP2   2 stop bits

- Select only one of these:

  _COM_NOPARITY   No parity
  _COM_ODDPARITY Odd parity
  _COM_EVENPARITY Even parity

- Select only one of these:

_COM_110	110 baud
_COM_150	150 baud
_COM_300	300 baud
_COM_600	600 baud
_COM_1200	1200 baud
_COM_2400	2400 baud
_COM_4800	4800 baud
_COM_9600	9600 baud

For example, a value of (_COM_9600 | _COM_ODDPARITY | _COM_STOP1 | _COM_CHR8) for *abyte* sets the communications port to 9600 baud, odd parity, 1 stop bit, and 8 data bits. *_bios_serialcom* uses the BIOS 0x14 interrupt.

Return value

For all values of *cmd*, *_bios_serialcom* returns a 16-bit integer of which the upper 8 bits are status bits and the lower 8 bits vary, depending on the value of *cmd*. The upper bits of the return value are defined as follows:

Bit 15	Time out
Bit 14	Transmit shift register empty
Bit 13	Transmit holding register empty
Bit 12	Break detect
Bit 11	Framing error
Bit 10	Parity error
Bit 9	Overrun error
Bit 8	Data ready

If the *abyte* value could not be sent, bit 15 is set to 1. Otherwise, the remaining upper and lower bits are appropriately set. For example, if a framing error has occurred, bit 11 is set to 1.

With a *cmd* value of _COM_RECEIVE, the byte read is in the lower bits of the return value if there is no error. If an error occurs, at least one of the upper bits is set to 1. If no upper bits are set to 1, the byte was received without error.

With a *cmd* value of _COM_INIT or _COM_STATUS, the return value has the upper bits set as defined, and the lower bits are defined as follows:

Bit 7   Received line signal detect
Bit 6   Ring indicator
Bit 5   Data set ready
Bit 4   Clear to send
Bit 3   Change in receive line signal detector
Bit 2   Trailing edge ring detector
Bit 1   Change in data set ready
Bit 0   Change in clear to send

brk   alloc.h

Function
Changes data-segment space allocation.

Syntax
int brk(void *addr);

Description
brk dynamically changes the amount of space allocated to the calling program's heap. The change is made by resetting the program's *break value*, which is the address of the first location beyond the end of the data segment. The amount of allocated space increases as the break value increases.

brk sets the break value to *addr* and changes the allocated space accordingly.

This function will fail without making any change in the allocated space if such a change would allocate more space than is allowable.

Return value
Upon successful completion, *brk* returns a value of 0. On failure, this function returns a value of –1 and the global variable *errno* is set to the following:

ENOMEM   Not enough memory

See also
coreleft, sbrk

coreleft   alloc.h

Function
Returns a measure of unused RAM memory.

Syntax

In the tiny, small, and medium models:
unsigned coreleft(void);

In the compact, large, and huge models:
unsigned long coreleft(void);

Description

coreleft returns a measure of RAM memory not in use. It gives a different measurement value, depending on whether the memory model is of the small data group or the large data group.

Return value

In the small data models, *coreleft* returns the amount of unused memory between the top of the heap and the stack. In the large data models, *coreleft* returns the amount of memory between the highest allocated block and the end of available memory.

See also

allocmem, brk, farcoreleft, malloc

delay   dos.h

Function

Suspends execution for an interval (milliseconds).

Syntax

void delay(unsigned milliseconds);

Description

With a call to *delay*, the current program is suspended from execution for the number of milliseconds specified by the argument *milliseconds*. It is no longer necessary to make a calibration call to delay before using it. *delay* is accurate to a millisecond.

Return value

None.

See also

nosound, sleep, sound

farcoreleft   alloc.h

Function

Returns a measure of unused memory in far heap.

Syntax

unsigned long farcoreleft(void);

Description

farcoreleft returns a measure of the amount of unused memory in the far heap beyond the highest allocated block.

A tiny model program cannot make use of *farcoreleft*.

Return value

farcoreleft returns the total amount of space left in the far heap, between the highest allocated block and the end of available memory.

See also

coreleft, *farcalloc*, *farmalloc*

farheapcheck   alloc.h

Function

Checks and verifies the far heap.

Syntax

int farheapcheck(void);

Description

farheapcheck walks through the far heap and examines each block, checking its pointers, size, and other critical attributes.

Return value

The return value is less than zero for an error and greater than zero for success.

_HEAPEMPTY is returned if there is no heap (value 1).

_HEAPOK is returned if the heap is verified (value 2).

_HEAPCORRUPT is returned if the heap has been corrupted (value –1).

See also

heapcheck

farheapcheckfree   alloc.h

Function

Checks the free blocks on the far heap for a constant value.

Syntax

int farheapcheckfree(unsigned int fillvalue);

Description

farheapcheckfree checks the free blocks on the far heap for a constant value.

Return value

The return value is less than zero for an error and greater than zero for success.

_HEAPEMPTY is returned if there is no heap (value 1).

_HEAPOK is returned if the heap is accurate (value 2).

_HEAPCORRUPT is returned if the heap has been corrupted (value –1).

_BADVALUE is returned if a value other than the fill value was found (value –3).

See also

farheapfillfree, heapcheckfree

farheapchecknode   alloc.h

Function

Checks and verifies a single node on the far heap.

Syntax

int farheapchecknode(void *node);

Description

If a node has been freed and *farheapchecknode* is called with a pointer to the freed block, *farheapchecknode* can return _BADNODE rather than the expected _FREEENTRY. This is because adjacent free blocks on the heap are merged, and the block in question no longer exists.

Return value

The return value is less than zero for an error and greater than zero for success.

_HEAPEMPTY is returned if there is no heap (value 1).

_HEAPCORRUPT is returned if the heap has been corrupted (value –1).

_BADNODE is returned if the node could not be found (value –2).

_FREEENTRY is returned if the node is a free block (value 3).

_USEDENTRY is returned if the node is a used block (value 4).

See also

heapchecknode

farheapfillfree
alloc.h

Function
Fills the free blocks on the far heap with a constant value.

Syntax
int farheapfillfree(unsigned int fillvalue);

Description
farheapfillfree fills the free blocks on the far heap with a constant value.

Return value
The return value is less than zero for an error and greater than zero for success.

_HEAPEMPTY is returned if there is no heap (value 1).

_HEAPOK is returned if the heap is accurate (value 2).

_HEAPCORRUPT is returned if the heap has been corrupted (value –1).

See also
farheapcheckfree, heapfillfree

farheapwalk
alloc.h

Function
farheapwalk is used to "walk" through the far heap node by node.

Syntax
int farheapwalk(struct farheapinfo *hi);

Description
farheapwalk assumes the heap is correct. Use *farheapcheck* to verify the heap before using *farheapwalk*. _HEAPOK is returned with the last block on the heap. _HEAPEND will be returned on the next call to *farheapwalk*.

farheapwalk receives a pointer to a structure of type *heapinfo* (defined in alloc.h). For the first call to *farheapwalk*, set the hi.ptr field to null. *farheapwalk* returns with hi.ptr containing the address of the first block. hi.size holds the size of the block in bytes. hi.in_use is a flag that is set if the block is currently in use.

Return value
_HEAPEMPTY is returned if there is no heap (value 1).

_HEAPOK is returned if the heapinfo block contains valid data (value 2).

_HEAPEND is returned if the end of the heap has been reached (value 5).

See also

heapwalk

freemem, _dos_freemem   dos.h

Function
Frees a previously allocated DOS memory block.

Syntax
int freemem(unsigned segx);
unsigned _dos_freemem(unsigned segx);

Description
freemem frees a memory block allocated by a previous call to *allocmem*.

_dos_freemem frees a memory block allocated by a previous call to *_dos_allocmem*. *segx* is the segment address of that block.

Return value
freemem and *_dos_freemem* return 0 on success.

In the event of error, *freemem* returns –1 and sets *errno*.

In the event of error, *_dos_freemem* returns the DOS error code and sets *errno*.

In the event of error, these functions set global variable *errno* to the following:

    ENOMEM   Insufficient memory

See also
allocmem, _dos_allocmem, free

harderr, hardresume, hardretn   dos.h

Function
Establishes and handles hardware errors.

Syntax
void harderr(int (*handler)());
void hardresume(int axret);
void hardretn(int retn);

Description
The error handler established by *harderr* can call *hardresume* to return to DOS. The return value of the *rescode* (result code) of *hardresume* contains an abort (2), retry (1), or ignore (0) indicator. The abort is accomplished by invoking DOS interrupt 0x23, the control-break interrupt.

The error handler established by *harderr* can return directly to the application program by calling *hardretn*. The returned value is whatever value you passed to *hardretn*.

harderr establishes a hardware error handler for the current program. This error handler is invoked whenever an interrupt 0x24 occurs. (See your DOS reference manuals for a discussion of the interrupt.)

The function pointed to by *handler* is called when such an interrupt occurs. The handler function is called with the following arguments:

```
handler(int errval, int ax, int bp, int si);
```

errval is the error code set in the DI register by DOS. *ax*, *bp*, and *si* are the values DOS sets for the AX, BP, and SI registers, respectively.

- *ax* indicates whether a disk error or other device error was encountered. If *ax* is nonnegative, a disk error was encountered; otherwise, the error was a device error. For a disk error, *ax* ANDed with 0x00FF gives the failing drive number (0 equals A, 1 equals B, and so on).

- *bp* and *si* together point to the device driver header of the failing driver. *bp* contains the segment address, and *si* the offset.

The function pointed to by *handler* is not called directly. *harderr* establishes a DOS interrupt handler that calls the function.

The handler can issue DOS calls 1 through 0xC; any other DOS call corrupts DOS. In particular, any of the C standard I/O or UNIX-emulation I/O calls *cannot* be used.

The handler must return 0 for ignore, 1 for retry, and 2 for abort.

Return value
None.

See also
peek, poke

_harderr   dos.h

Function
Establishes a hardware error handler.

Syntax
void _harderr(int (far *handler)());

Description
_harderr establishes a hardware error handler for the current program. This error handler is invoked whenever an interrupt 0x24 occurs. (See your DOS reference manuals for a discussion of the interrupt.)

The function pointed to by *handler* is called when such an interrupt occurs. The handler function is called with the following arguments:

```
void far handler(unsigned deverr, unsigned errval, unsigned far *devhdr);
```

- *deverr* is the device error code (passed to the handler by DOS in the AX register).

- *errval* is the error code (passed to the handler by DOS in the DI register).

- *devhdr* a far pointer to the driver header of the device that caused the error (passed to the handler by DOS in the BP:SI register pair).

The handler should use these arguments instead of referring directly to the CPU registers.

deverr indicates whether a disk error or other device error was encountered. If bit 15 of *deverr* is 0, a disk error was encountered. Otherwise, the error was a device error. For a disk error, *deverr* ANDed with 0x00FF give the failing drive number (0 equals A, 1 equals B, and so on).

The function pointed to by *handler* is not called directly. *_harderr* establishes a DOS interrupt handler that calls the function.

The handler can issue DOS calls 1 through 0xC; any other DOS call corrupts DOS. In particular, any of the C standard I/O or UNIX-emulation I/O calls *cannot* be used.

The handler does not return a value, and it must exit using *_hardretn* or *_hardresume*.

Return value
None.

See also
_hardresume, *_hardretn*

_hardresume
dos.h

Function
Hardware error handler.

Syntax
void _hardresume(int rescode);

Description
The error handler established by *_harderr* can call *_hardresume* to return to DOS. The return value of the *rescode* (result code) of *_hardresume* contains one of the following values:

_HARDERR_ABORT	Abort the program by invoking DOS interrupt 0x23, the control-break interrupt.
_HARDERR_IGNORE	Ignore the error.

_HARDERR_RETRY	Retry the operation.
_HARDERR_FAIL	Fail the operation.

Return value

The _hardresume_ function does not return a value, and does not return to the caller.

See also

harderr, _hardretn_

_hardretn   dos.h

Function

Hardware error handler.

Syntax

void _hardretn(int retn);

Description

The error handler established by _harderr_ can return directly to the application program by calling _hardretn_.

If the DOS function that caused the error is less than 0x38, and it is a function that can indicate an error condition, then _hardretn_ will return to the application program with the AL register set to 0xFF. The _retn_ argument is ignored for all DOS functions less than 0x38.

If the DOS function is greater than or equal to 0x38, the _retn_ argument should be a DOS error code; it is returned to the application program in the AX register. The carry flag is also set to indicate to the application that the operation resulted in an error.

Return value

The _hardresume_ function does not return a value, and does not return to the caller.

See also

harderr, _hardresume_

keep, _dos_keep   dos.h

Function

Exits and remains resident.

Syntax

void keep(unsigned char status, unsigned size);
void _dos_keep(unsigned char status, unsigned size);

Description

keep and *_dos_keep* return to DOS with the exit status in *status*. The current program remains resident, however. The program is set to *size* paragraphs in length, and the remainder of the memory of the program is freed.

keep and *_dos_keep* can be used when installing TSR programs. *keep* and *_dos_keep* use DOS function 0x31.

Before *_dos_keep* exits, it calls any registered "exit functions" (posted with *atexit*), flushes file buffers, and restores interrupt vectors modified by the startup code.

Return value

None.

See also

abort , *exit*

nosound dos.h

Function

Turns PC speaker off.

Syntax

void nosound(void);

Description

Turns the speaker off after it has been turned on by a call to *sound*.

Return value

None.

See also

delay, *sound*

_OvrInitEms dos.h

Function

Initializes expanded memory swapping for the overlay manager.

Syntax

int _ _cdecl _ _far _OvrInitEms(unsigned emsHandle, unsigned firstPage, unsigned pages);

Description

OvrInitEms checks for the presence of expanded memory by looking for an EMS driver and allocating memory from it. If _emsHandle_ is zero, the overlay manager allocates EMS pages and uses them for swapping. If _emsHandle_ is not zero, then it should be a valid EMS handle; the overlay manager will use it for swapping. In that case, you can specify _firstPage_, where the swapping can start inside that area.

In both cases, a nonzero _pages_ parameter gives the limit of the usable pages by the overlay manager.

Return value

OvrInitEms returns 0 if the overlay manager is able to use expanded memory for swapping.

See also

OvrInitExt, _ovrbuffer_ (global variable)

_OvrInitExt   dos.h

Function

Initializes extended memory swapping for the overlay manager.

Syntax

int _ _cdecl _ _far _OvrInitExt(unsigned long startAddress, unsigned long length);

Description

OvrInitExt checks for the presence of extended memory, using the known methods to detect the presence of other programs using extended memory, and allocates memory from it. If _startAddress_ is zero, the overlay manager determines the start address and uses, at most, the size of the overlays. If _startAddress_ is not zero, then the overlay manager uses the extended memory above that address.

In both cases, a nonzero _length_ parameter gives the limit of the usable extended memory by the overlay manager.

Return value

OvrInitExt returns 0 if the overlay manager is able to use extended memory for swapping.

See also

OvrInitEms, _ovrbuffer_ (global variable)

randbrd   dos.h

Function
Reads random block.

Syntax
int randbrd(struct fcb *fcb, int rcnt);

Description
randbrd reads *rcnt* number of records using the open file control block (FCB) pointed to by *fcb*. The records are read into memory at the current disk transfer address (DTA). They are read from the disk record indicated in the random record field of the FCB. This is accomplished by calling DOS system call 0x27.

The actual number of records read can be determined by examining the random record field of the FCB. The random record field is advanced by the number of records actually read.

Return value
The following values are returned, depending on the result of the *randbrd* operation:

    0   All records are read.

    1   End-of-file is reached and the last record read is complete.

    2   Reading records would have wrapped around address 0xFFFF (as many
         records as possible are read).

    3   End-of-file is reached with the last record incomplete.

See also
getdta, randbwr, setdta

randbwr   dos.h

Function
Writes random block.

Syntax
int randbwr(struct fcb *fcb, int rcnt);

Description
randbwr writes *rcnt* number of records to disk using the open file control block (FCB) pointed to by *fcb*. This is accomplished using DOS system call 0x28. If *rcnt* is 0, the file is truncated to the length indicated by the random record field.

The actual number of records written can be determined by examining the random record field of the FCB. The random record field is advanced by the number of records actually written.

Return value
The following values are returned, depending upon the result of the *randbwr* operation:

0   All records are written.

1   There is not enough disk space to write the records (no records are written).

2   Writing records would have wrapped around address 0xFFFF (as many records as possible are written).

See also
randbrd

sbrk   alloc.h

Function
Changes data segment space allocation.

Syntax
void *sbrk(int incr);

Description
sbrk adds *incr* bytes to the break value and changes the allocated space accordingly. *incr* can be negative, in which case the amount of allocated space is decreased.

sbrk will fail without making any change in the allocated space if such a change would result in more space being allocated than is allowable.

Return value
Upon successful completion, *sbrk* returns the old break value. On failure, *sbrk* returns a value of –1, and the global variable *errno* is set to the following:

ENOMEM   Not enough core

See also
brk

setblock, _dos_setblock   dos.h

Function
Modifies the size of a previously allocated block.

Syntax

int setblock(unsigned segx, unsigned newsize);
unsigned _dos_setblock(unsigned newsize, unsigned segx, unsigned *maxp);

Description

setblock and *_dos_setblock* modify the size of a memory segment. *segx* is the segment address returned by a previous call to *allocmem* or *_dos_allocmem*. *newsize* is the new, requested size in paragraphs. If the segment cannot be changed to the new size, *_dos_setblock* stores the size of the largest possible segment at the location pointed to by *maxp*.

Return value

setblock returns –1 on success. In the event of error, it returns the size of the largest possible block (in paragraphs), and the global variable *_doserrno* is set.

_dos_setblock returns 0 on success. In the event of error, it returns the DOS error code, and the global variable *errno* is set to the following:

ENOMEM   Not enough memory, or bad segment address

See also

allocmem, freemem

sound

dos.h

Function

Turns PC speaker on at specified frequency.

Syntax

void sound(unsigned frequency);

Description

sound turns on the PC speaker at a given frequency. *frequency* specifies the frequency of the sound in hertz (cycles per second). To turn the speaker off after a call to *sound*, call the function *nosound*.

See also

delay, nosound

8

DOS run-time libraries

The static (OBJ and LIB) 16-bit Borland C++ run-time libraries are contained in the LIB subdirectory of your installation. For each of the library file names, the '?' character represents one of the six (tiny, compact, small, medium, large, and huge) distinct memory models supported by Borland. Each model has its own library file and math file containing versions of the routines written for that particular model. See the *C++ Programmer's Guide*, Chapter 13, "DOS memory management," for details on memory models.

Table 8.1 lists the Borland C++ libraries names and uses that are available for 16-bit DOS-only applications. See the *C++ User's Guide* for information on linkers, linker options, requirements, and selection of libraries.

Table 8.1   Run-time libraries

File name	Use
BIDSH.LIB	Huge memory model of Borland classlibs
BIDSDBH.LIB	Diagnostic version of the above library
C?.LIB	DOS-only libraries
C0F?.OBJ	MS compatible startup
C0?.OBJ	BC startup
EMU.LIB	Floating-point emulation
FP87.LIB	For programs that run on machines with 80x87 coprocessor
GRAPHICS.LIB	Borland graphics interface
MATH?.LIB	Math routines
OVERLAY.LIB	Overlay development

DOS run-time libraries overview

The DOS-specific applications use static run-time libraries (OBJ and LIB). These libraries are available only to the 16-bit development tools. Library routines are composed of functions and macros that you can call from within your C and C++ programs to perform a wide variety of tasks. These tasks include low- and high-level I/O, string and file manipulation, memory allocation, process control, data conversion, mathematical calculations, and much more.

Several versions of the run-time library are available. For example, there are memory-model specific versions and diagnostic versions. There are also optional libraries that provide containers, graphics, and mathematics.

DOS interface routines

These routines provide operating-system BIOS and machine-specific capabilities for DOS.

Routine	Header file	Routine	Header file
absread	dos.h	_dos_keep	dos.h
abswrite	dos.h	freemem	dos.h
abswrite	bios.h	_harderr	dos.h
_bios_keybrd	bios.h	harderr	dos.h
_bios_printer	bios.h	hardresume	dos.h
_bios_serialcom	bios.h	_hardresume	dos.h
bioscom	bios.h	hardretn	dos.h
biosdisk	bios.h	_hardretn	dos.h
bioskey	bios.h	keep	dos.h
biosprint	bios.h	randbrd	dos.h
_dos_freemem	dos.h	randbwr	dos.h

DOS memory routines

These routines provide dynamic memory allocation in the small-data and large-data models.

Routine	Header file	Routine	Header file
allocmem	dos.h	farheapcheck	alloc.h
brk	alloc.h	farheapcheckfree	alloc.h
coreleft	alloc.h, stdlib.h	farheapchecknode	dos.h
_dos_allocmem	alloc.h	farheapfillfree	dos.h
_dos_freemem	alloc.h	farheapwalk	alloc.h
_dos_setblock	dos.h	farrealloc	alloc.h
farcoreleft	alloc.h	sbrk	alloc.h

Miscellaneous DOS routines

These routines provide sound effects and time delay.

Routine	Header file
delay	dos.h
nosound	dos.h
sound	dos.h

Chapter

9

DOS global variables

This chapter describes the Borland C++ global variables that are available for 16-bit DOS-only applications.

_heaplen

dos.h

Function
Holds the length of the near heap (available only for 16-bit DOS-only applications).

Syntax
unsigned _heaplen;

Description
heaplen specifies the size (in bytes) of the near heap in the small data models (tiny, small, and medium). _heaplen_ does not exist in the large data models (compact, large, and huge) because they do not have a near heap.

In the small and medium models, the data segment size is computed as follows:

```
data segment [small,medium] = global data + heap + stack
```

where the size of the stack can be adjusted with _stklen_.

If _heaplen_ is set to 0, the program allocates 64K bytes for the data segment, and the effective heap size is

```
64K - (global data + stack) bytes
```

By default, _heaplen_ equals 0, so you'll get a 64K data segment unless you specify a particular _heaplen_ value.

In the tiny model, everything (including code) is in the same segment, so the data segment computations are adjusted to include the code plus 256 bytes for the program segment prefix (PSP).

```
data segment [tiny] = 256 + code + global data + heap + stack
```

If _heaplen_ equals 0 in the tiny model, the effective heap size is obtained by subtracting the PSP, code, global data, and stack from 64K.

In the compact and large models, there is no near heap, and the stack is in its own segment, so the data segment is

```
data segment [compact,large] = global data
```

In the huge model, the stack is a separate segment, and each module has its own data segment.

See also
stklen

_ovrbuffer   dos.h

Function
Changes the size of the overlay buffer (available only for 16-bit DOS applications).

Syntax
unsigned _ovrbuffer = size;

Description
The default overlay buffer size is twice the size of the largest overlay. This is adequate for some applications. Suppose, however, that a particular function of a program is implemented through many modules, each of which is overlaid. If the total size of those modules is larger than the overlay buffer, a substantial amount of swapping will occur if the modules make frequent calls to each other.

The solution is to increase the size of the overlay buffer so that enough memory is available at any given time to contain all overlays that make frequent calls to each other. You can do this by setting the _ovrbuffer_ global variable to the required size in paragraphs. For example, to set the overlay buffer to 128K, include the following statement in your code:

```
unsigned _ovrbuffer = 0x2000;
```

There is no general formula for determining the ideal overlay buffer size.

See also
_OvrInitEms, _OvrInitExt_

_stklen

dos.h

Function
Holds the size of the stack.

Syntax
unsigned _stklen;

Description
_stklen specifies the size of the stack for all six memory models. The minimum stack size allowed is 128 words; if you give a smaller value, *_stklen* is automatically adjusted to the minimum. The default stack size is 4K.

In the small and medium models, the data segment size is computed as follows:

```
data segment [small, medium] = global data + heap + stack
```

The size of the heap can be adjusted with *_heaplen*.

In the tiny model, everything (including code) is in the same segment, so the data segment computations are adjusted to include the code plus 256 bytes for the program segment prefix (PSP).

```
data segment [tiny] = 256 + code + global data + heap + stack
```

In the compact and large models, there is no near heap, and the stack is in its own segment, so the data segment is simply

```
data segment [compact,large] = global data
```

In the huge memory model, the stack is a separate segment, and each module has its own data segment.

See also
_heaplen

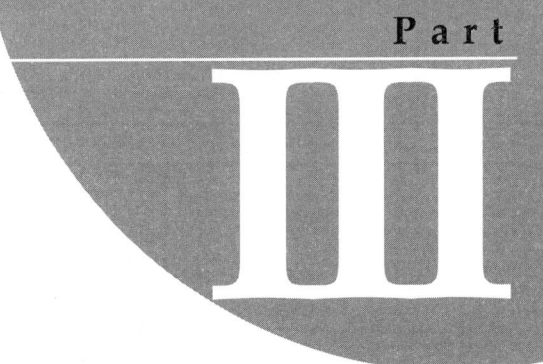

Part

Borland C++ class libraries reference

Part III provides reference material for Borland C++ classes. This part is organized as follows:

- **Chapter 10, "The C++ container classes,"** provides reference material to the Borland C++ container class library.

- **Chapter 11, "The iostreams classes,"** details the iostream classes of the C++ stream class library.

- **Chapter 12, "The persistent streams classes and macros,"** describes the persistent streams and macros supported by Borland to help you develop streamable objects.

- **Chapter 13, "The mathematical classes,"** discusses the C++ mathematical classes.

- **Chapter 14, "Class diagnostic macros,"** details the set of macros for debugging C++ code.

- **Chapter 15, "Run-time support,"** provides a detailed description of the functions and classes that provide runtime support.

- **Chapter 16, "C++ services classes,"** presents the classes you can use for accessing and manipulating time, date, file, and thread classes.

10

The C++ container classes

This chapter is a reference guide to the Borland C++ container class library. This library is organized into thirteen container class families, listed here.

- Array (arrays.h)
- Association (assoc.h)
- Bag (bags.h)
- Binary search tree (binimp.h)
- Dequeue (deques.h)
- Dictionary (dict.h)
- Double list (dlistimp.h)

- Hash table (hashimp.h)
- List (listimp.h)
- Queue (queues.h)
- Set (sets.h)
- Stack (stacks.h)
- Vector (vectimp.h)

Array class template family   arrays.h

An array container manages a group of objects, where objects are placed contiguously within a block of memory and can be accessed with an index operator. This family includes nine container classes, together with their corresponding nine iterator classes.

Introduction

Containers in this family manage objects and pointers to objects, and can sort objects. All arrays can be resized. Some arrays can be sorted. Most classes use the default memory manager *TStandardAllocator*, but you can pass your own memory manager class to managed container class templates.

Class family list
Here is a list of container classes composing this family. See "Template family syntax" for template prototypes for each template. See "Container members" and "Iterator methods" for definitions of members all classes use in common.

Direct templates

- TArrayAsVector
- TMArrayAsVector
- TSArrayAsVector
- TMSArrayAsVector
- TArray

- TArrayAsVectorIterator
- TMArrayAsVectorIterator
- TSASrrayAsVectorIterator
- TMSArrayAsVectorIterator
- TArrayIterator

Indirect templates

- TIArrayAsVector
- TMIArrayAsVector
- TISArrayAsVector
- TMISArrayAsVector

- TIArrayAsVectorIterator
- TMIArrayAsVectorIterator
- TISArrayAsVectorIterator
- TMISArrayAsVectorIterator

Using array classes

Use an array container when you need an automatically resizable container that provides indexed access to its stored elements.

Perform the following steps to use an *Array* class:

1 Set the data type for the element you will store in your array container. Decide whether to store objects themselves in the array, or pointers to those objects. Decide whether to use the default memory manager or to manage memory yourself.

2 Select the array family template that fits your program design. Array classes can store data or pointers to data, can accept either default or user-supplied memory managers, and can automatically sort elements as they are added to the array container.

For example, if you have chosen to store pointers to **long**s and want to build an array that holds your pointers in order sorted by object, instantiate an object *TISArrayAsVector* class.

3 Classes instantiating stored objects of your own user type must provide the functions listed here. Predefined types already provide these functions.

- Default constructor (direct classes)
- Copy constructor (all classes)
- Assignment operator (direct classes)
- Less-than operator (sorted classes)
- Equivalence operator (all classes)

4 If you have decided to use your own memory manager to manage array elements, then you must overload the *new* and *delete* operator member declarations in your memory manager class to support your new user type.

5 If you plan to use *FirstThat*, *LastThat* or *ForEach* member functions to iterate through your array, then you must write implementation functions to act on your stored data.

6 To promote code maintainability, you should **typedef** the container and iterator class templates you have selected to use. This makes it easy to change a class template while minimizing changes you may need to make to your working code.

7 Instantiate an array container class from the class template you have selected to use. Pass the type of the objects you will store in your array container class to the class template upon class instantiation. If you are using a managed class, then you must also pass the type of your memory manager class to the template.

8 Instantiate an array container object. Pass appropriate constructor parameters to your object upon instantiation.

9 Instantiate an array iterator, if you have decided to use an iterator to access elements in your array container. Pass your array container object to your iterator object when you instantiate your iterator object.

Code example

The following example declares an *TArrayAsVector* container named *vect*, that holds ten elements of type **long**. It fills the array, searches the array for the element that holds the value '7', and then deletes that array element. It then calls both *ForEach* and *TArrayAsVectorIterator* to display the contents of the array container. The numbers 1 through 10 display on your screen, minus the number 7.

Note that *ForEach* calls the *iterfunct* function called *Show*, that simply displays the contents of the current array element. *ForEach* then moves to the next element in the array, calls *Show* again, and repeats this process until every element in the array has been displayed.

```
#include<iostream.h>
#include<classlib\arrays.h>
/*  Here is an iterfunct required by the ForEach member function.
  It displays the contents of the current element c.
*/
void Show(long&c, void*){ cout << c << endl; }
/* This wrapper function instantiates an iterator object called
   go, passes the container object called vect into it upon
   instantiation, and shows the contents of each vect array element
   as it is encountered.
*/
void UseIterator(const TArrayAsVector<long> &vect)
   {
   TArrayAsVectorIterator<long>go(vect);
   while(go!=0)
      {
      cout << go.Current() << endl;
      go++;
      }
   }
int main()
{
   /* Instantiate an array container called vect
      that holds 10 longs.
   */
   TArrayAsVector<long>vect(10);
   for(int i=0; i<10; i++)    // Fill the array
      vect.Add(i);
```

```
/* You can now call global or member functions at this point
   to act on data contained in the array. This program detaches
   any object in the array that contains the long value '7'.
*/
vect.Detach(7);
/* Call the vect ForEach member function to iterate through
   the array. Pass an iterfunct called Show to ForEach. This
   function displays the contents of the element it points to
   each time ForEach calls it.
*/
cout << "Using ForEach member function to iterate:\n";
vect.ForEach(Show, 0);
/* Repeat the iteration process using an iterator object.
   The UseIterator function below combines an instantiation
   call with a streams call to display the contents of the
   current element.
*/
cout << "\nUsing an iterator object to iterate:\n";
UseIterator(vect);
return 0;
}
```

Output

```
Using ForEach member function to iterate:
0
1
2
3
4
5
6
8
9
Using an iterator object to iterate:
0
1
2
3
4
5
6
8
9
```

Template family syntax

This section lists template prototypes and definitions for classes in the Array family.

Direct templates

Objects instantiated from classes listed here contain elements of type *T*.

TArrayAsVector

template <class T> class TArrayAsVector

Creates an array container holding elements of type *T*.

TMArrayAsVector

template <class T, class Alloc> class TMArrayAsVector

Creates an array container holding elements of type *T*, managed by a memory manager of type *Alloc*.

TSArrayAsVector

template <class T> class TSArrayAsVector

Creates a sorted array container holding elements of type *T*. Objects passed into this array are automatically placed in sorted order.

TMSArrayAsVector

template <class T, class Alloc> class TMSArrayAsVector

Creates a sorted container array holding elements of type *T*. Objects passed into this array are automatically placed in sorted order. Memory is managed by a user-defined memory manager.

Indirect class templates

Objects instantiated from classes listed here contain pointers to array elements of type *T*.

TIArrayAsVector

template <class T> class TIArrayAsVector

Creates an array container holding pointers to objects of type *T*.

TMIArrayAsVector

template <class T, class Alloc> class TMIArrayAsVector

Creates an array container holding pointers to objects of type *T*. Memory is managed by a user-defined memory manager.

TMISArrayAsVector

template <class T, class Alloc> class TMISArrayAsVector

Creates a sorted array container holding pointers to objects of type *T*. Memory is managed by a user-defined memory manager. Pointers passed into this array are automatically placed in sorted order.

TISArrayAsVector

template <class T, class Alloc> class TISArrayAsVector

Creates a sorted array container holding pointers to objects of type *T*. Pointers passed into this array are automatically placed in sorted order.

Iterator class templates

All iterator classes use their *Current* member to access each object stored in the container they support.

Each iterator class listed here is paired with a container class template that matches its name format. For example, *TIMArrayAsVectorIterator* instantiates an iterator object that takes a *TIMArrayAsVector* container object as its argument. Always use the iterator that matches the container type holding the stored objects you want to access.

Direct templates

TArrayAsVectorIterator
template <class T> class TArrayAsVectorIterator

TMArrayAsVectorIterator
template <class T,class Alloc> class TMArrayAsVectorIterator

TMSArrayAsVectorIterator
template <class T,class Alloc> class TMSArrayAsVectorIterator

TSArrayAsVectorIterator
template <class T> class TSArrayAsVectorIterator

Indirect templates

TIArrayAsVectorIterator
template <class T> TIArrayAsVector

TMIArrayAsVectorIterator
template <class T, class Alloc> TMIArrayAsVectorIterator

TMISArrayAsVectorIterator
template <class T, class Alloc> TMISArrayAsVectorIterator

TISArrayAsVectorIterator
template <class T> class TISArrayAsVectorIterator

Container members

Type definitions

CondFunc
typedef int (*CondFunc) (const T &, void *)

Defines the return type and input parameters for the user-written function used as an input parameter to the *FirstThat* and *LastThat* member functions.

When using *FirstThat* or *LastThat* to iterate through your array, you must write a function taking a const reference to an object of your user type and a **void** pointer. When you call *FirstThat* or *LastThat*, you pass a pointer to this function as an input parameter.

IterFunc
typedef void (*IterFunc) (T &, void *)

Defines the return type and input parameters for the user-written function used as an input parameter to the *ForEach* member function.

When using *ForEach* to iterate through your array, you must write a function taking a reference to an object of your user type and a void pointer. When you call *ForEach*, you pass a pointer to your function as an input parameter.

Public constructors

Constructors

TArrayAsVector (int upper, int lower = 0, int delta = 0)
TMArrayAsVector (int upper, int lower = 0, int delta = 0)
TMSArrayAsVector (int upper, int lower = 0, int delta = 0)
TMCArrayAsVector (int upper, int lower = 0, int delta = 0)
TIArrayAsVector (int upper, int lower = 0, int delta = 0)
TIMArrayAsVector (int upper, int lower = 0, int delta = 0)
TIMSArrayAsVector (int upper, int lower = 0, int delta = 0)
TIMCArrayAsVector (int upper, int lower = 0, int delta = 0)

Creates an array container with an upper bound of *upper*, a lower bound of *lower*, and a growth value of *delta*.

The delta value sets the expansion increment for this array container. Arrays can be expanded to include more objects than they were originally instantiated to hold. When an array container is full and you add one more object, the container automatically resizes itself by the delta value, to store the new object. The expansion increment is measured in terms of the number of objects that the container was instantiated to hold.

Setting *delta* to zero determines that this array container cannot grow to accomodate more objects than its instantiated size, set by *upper*.

Public member functions

Add

Form 1   int Add(const T& t)

Adds the object *t* at the next available index at the end of an array.

Adding an element beyond the upper bound leads to an overflow condition. If an overflow occurs and *delta* is nonzero, the array is expanded (by sufficient multiples of delta bytes) to accommodate the addition. If *delta* is zero; the *add* operation fails. *Add* returns 0 if the object cannot be added to the array. Supports direct array containers.

Form 2   int Add (T *t)

Adds a pointer to the object *t* at the next available index at the end of an array.

Supports indirect array containers.

AddAt

int AddAt (const T& t, int loc)
int AddAt (T *t, int loc)

Adds the object *t* at the specified index. If that index is occupied, it moves objects in the array up to make room for the added object. If *loc* is beyond the upper bound, the array is expanded, provided that this container was instantiated with a nonzero *delta* value. If delta is zero, attempting to *addat* beyond the upper bound throws an exception.

The first prototype supports direct containers. The second prototype adds a pointer to the object *t*. The second prototype supports indirect array containers.

ArraySize

ArraySize unsigned ArraySize() const;

Returns the current number of elements allocated in the container.

Destroy

Form 1
```
int Destroy( const T& t )
int Destroy( int i )
```

Both prototypes support direct containers. The first prototype removes the given object from the array. The second prototype removes the object located at index *i* and deletes it from memory.

Form 2
```
int Destroy( const T *t )
int Destroy( int i )
```

Both prototypes support indirect containers. The first prototype removes the pointer from the array and deletes its object from memory. The second prototype removes the object located at int *i* and deletes it from memory.

Detach

Form 1
```
int Detach( const T& t )
int Detach( int loc )
```

Both prototypes support direct containers.

The first prototype removes the first object that compares equal to the specified object *t*.

The second prototype removes the object stored at index *loc* from the array.

Form 2
```
int Detach( const T *t, DeleteType dt = NoDelete )
int Detach( int loc, DeleteType dt = NoDelete )
```

Both prototypes support indirect containers.

The first prototype removes the specified pointer *t*. The second prototype removes the pointer at the array index specified by *loc*. The value *dt* determines whether the object referenced by the pointer will be deleted from memory.

dt is a function parameter for the *DeleteType* **enum** member. *DeleteType* supports these values:

Value	Description
NoDelete	The object will not be deleted from memory. This is the default value.
DefDelete	The object will be deleted if the container owns its contents, or left in memory if the container does not own its contents.
Delete	The object will be deleted from memory whether or not the container owns its objects.

Find

```
int Find( const T& t ) const
int Find( const T *t ) const
```

Finds the specified object *t* and returns the index of the object, or INT_MAX if the object was not found.

The first prototype supports direct array objects; the second prototype supports indirect array objects.

ForEach

```
void ForEach( IterFunc iter, void *args )
```

ForEach executes the given function *iter* for each element in the array. The *args* argument lets you pass arbitrary data to this function.

IterFunc is a **typedef** that specifies the return type and input parameters for the custom function called by *ForEach* to operate on data stored at the current node.

iter is your function, which operates on data contained in the element that *ForEach* is referencing. You must write *iter* to take a reference to your node data and a **void** type pointer.

When called, *ForEach* positions a pointer at a node and calls your custom function, *iter*. *iter* checks data at that node, and may change that data based on a condition you define. When finished, *iter* returns control to *ForEach*, which moves to the next node in the tree. *ForEach* repeats this process until it has traversed the tree.

FirstThat
T *FirstThat(CondFunc cond, void *args) const

Returns a pointer to the first object in the array that satisfies a given condition, or returns 0 if no object in the array meets the condition. You supply a test-function *cond* that returns **true** for a certain condition. You can pass arbitrary arguments via *args*.

CondFunc is a **typedef** which specifies the type of the function that you pass to *FirstThat*. *cond* is your function, which operates on data contained in the current array element. *cond* returns 0 to *FirstThat* if it determines that iteration should continue, and returns a nonzero value if it determines that the current object is the one being sought.

Flush
void Flush ()
void Flush (DeleteType dt = DefDelete)

Removes all elements from the array without destroying the array.

The first prototype supports direct array containers. The second prototype supports indirect array containers.

For indirect arrays, the value *dt* determines whether the pointers removed from the container should also be deleted from memory. See the *Detach* member function.

GetItemsInContainer
unsigned GetItemsInContainer () const

Returns the number of elements currently stored in the array. Use *ArraySize* to get the size of the array itself.

HasMember
int HasMember(const T& t) const

Returns nonzero if the given object *t* is found in the array.

IsEmpty
int IsEmpty () const

Returns nonzero if the array contains no elements.

IsFull
int IsFull () const

Returns nonzero if the array is full. The array is full if the *delta* input parameter to the template that created this container object is equal to 0, and if the number of items in this container equals the value returned by *ArraySize*.

LastThat
T *LastThat(CondFunc cond, void *args) const

Returns a pointer to the last object in the array that satisfies a given condition. You supply a test function pointer *cond* that returns **true** for a certain condition. You can pass arbitrary arguments to this function via the *args* input parameter. *LastThat* returns 0 if no object in the array meets the condition you specified in your function pointed to by *cond*.

CondFunc is a **typedef** which specifies the type of the function that you pass to *LastThat*. *cond* is your function, which operates on data contained in the current array element. *cond* returns 0 to *LastThat* if it determines that iteration should continue, and returns a nonzero value if it determines that the current object is the one being sought.

LowerBound
int LowerBound() const

Returns the array's lower-bound value.

UpperBound
int UpperBound() const

Returns the array's current upper-bound value.

Operators

operator [ ]
Form 1   T& operator [](int loc)

Returns a reference to the element at the location *loc*. Resizes the array if necessary to make *loc* a valid index.

Form 2   T& operator [](int loc) const

Returns a reference to the element at location *loc*. Throws an exception in the debugging version, if *loc* is an out-of-bounds value.

Protected member functions

ItemAt
const T& ItemAt(int i) const

Returns a copy of the object stored at location *i*.

Iterator methods

Public constructors
Form 1   TArrayAsVectorIterator(const TArrayAsVector<T> & a)
                TIArrayAsVectorIterator(const TIArrayAsVector<T> & a)
                TSArrayAsVectorIterator(const TSArrayAsVector<T> & a)
                TISArrayAsVectorIterator(const TISArrayAsVector<T> & a)

Creates an iterator object to traverse *ArrayAsVector* objects which do not take a memory manager as an input parameter. This is a function template which takes your array element user type as a template parameter.

a is a reference to a *TArrayAsVector* object holding elements of your user type, as an input parameter.

Form 2   TMArrayAsVectorIterator(const TMArrayAsVector<T,Alloc> & a)
           TIMArrayAsVectorIterator(const TIMArrayAsVector<T,Alloc> & a)
           TMSArrayAsVectorIterator(const TMSArrayAsVector<T,Alloc> & a)
           TIMSArrayAsVectorIterator(const TIMSArrayAsVector<T,Alloc> & a)

Creates an iterator object to traverse *ArrayAsVector* objects which take a memory manager as an input parameter.

a is a reference to an *ArrayAsVector* object holding elements of your user type and a memory manager of your user type, as input parameters.

Public member functions

Current
Form 1   const T& Current () const
           For direct containers; returns a reference to the current object.

Form 2   T * Current () const
           For indirect containers; returns a pointer to the current object.

Restart
Form 1   void Restart ()
           Restarts iteration from the beginning of the array.

Form 2   void Restart (unsigned start, unsigned stop)
           Restarts iteration over the specified range.

Operators

operator ++
Form 1   const T& operator ++ (int)
           Moves to the next object and returns the object that was current before the move (postincrement operator).

Form 2   const T& operator ++ ()
           Moves to the next object and returns that object (preincrement operator).

operator int
operator int () const

Converts the iterator to an integer value. This operator is used to test for objects remaining in the iterator. This operator returns a nonzero value if the iterator has not finished operating on the array, or a zero value if it has completed iterating.

Association class template family

assoc.h

Association objects bind a key to a value. When given a specific key-type value, a Dictionary object searches the association objects it stores, and returns the value-type data associated with that key.

Introduction

This class family includes eight classes. Individual classes in this family can contain data, or pointers to data. Most classes use the default memory manager *TStandardAllocator*, but you can pass your own memory manager class to managed association class templates.

Association classes are not containers. They cannot hold an expanding number of elements of your user type. They are designed to hold only one key and one value. Association classes are designed to be contained in a dictionary object.

Class family list

Here is a list of classes composing the association class template family. See "Template family syntax" for individual template prototypes. See "Container members" for definitions of all class members.

Note   There are no iterator classes in this family.

Unmanaged class templates
- TDDAssociation
- TDIAssociation
- TIDAssociation
- TIIAssociation

Managed class templates
- TMDDAssociation
- TMDIAssociation
- TMIDAssociation
- TMIIAssociation

Association class naming convention

The association class family names follow a naming convention that differs slightly from ADT classes. Each association class template carries a key function code and a value function code that indicates whether these members are direct or indirect.

For example,

1   The TIDAssociation class template instantiates an association object that holds a pointer to a key-type value (the letter I) and also holds a value-type value object (the letter D, following the letter I).

2   TMIDAssociation class template is like a TIDAssociation class template, but it also can access a custom memory manager class you pass to it upon instantiation (the letter M).

Using this class family

Use an association template to build a dictionary object. Association objects hold one key and one value data item.

Perform the following steps to use an association class:

1   Select a key type and a value type for your association class. Decide whether to store data directly, or to store pointers to data. For example, to associate a person's name and age, choose a *string* to contain the name, and an *int* to contain that person's age.

2   Select an association family template that supports your program design. Association classes support any combination of direct and indirect keys and values, and can accept either default or user-supplied memory managers.

3   Key and value classes instantiating stored objects of your own user type must provide the functions listed here. Predefined key and value types already provide these functions.

   • Default constructor
   • Assignment operator
   • Less-than operator
   • Equality operator

4   Your association class assumes, either that its key *K* has a *HashValue* member function, or that it can access a global function with one of the following prototypes listed here.

```
unsigned HashValue ( K );
unsigned HashValue ( const K & );
```

5   If you have decided to use your own memory manager to manage association objects, then you must overload the *new* and *delete* operator members in your memory manager class to support your new user type.

6   Instantiate an association class from the association class template you have selected to use. Pass the key and value user types to your class template upon instantiation. Also pass your memory manager user type to your association class, if you have chosen to provide your own memory manager.

7   Instantiate an association object. Pass key and value data as input parameters to your association object upon instantiation. This data is stored in protected *KeyData* and *ValueData* members.

8   Under most conditions, you will also create a dictionary object to hold this association object. The dictionary object also can be direct or indirect, and may or may not support a custom memory manager. See "Dictionary class template family" for details.

Code example

Association objects are designed to work with Dictionary containers. See "Dictionary class template family" for a code example using association objects.

Template family syntax

This section lists template prototypes and definitions for classes in the Association family.

Direct templates

Classes listed here support the default memory manager, which does not need to be explicitly passed to the association object.

TDDAssociation

template <class K class V> class TDDAssociation

Creates an association object which binds a direct key K to a direct value V.

TDIAssociation

template <class K class V> class TDIAssociation

Creates an association object which binds a direct key K with an indirect value V. Class A is the class of your memory manager.

TIDAssociation

template <class K class V> class TIDAssociation

Creates an association object which binds an indirect key K to a direct value V.

TIIAssociation

template <class K class V> class TIIAssociation

Creates an association object which binds an indirect key K with an indirect value V.

Managed association class templates

Classes listed here support a user-written memory manager.

TMIIAssociation

template <class K class V, class A> class TMIIAssociation

Creates a memory-managed association object which binds an indirect key K to an indirect value V. Class A is the class of your memory manager.

TMIDAssociation

template <class K class V, class A> class TMIDAssociation

Creates a memory-managed association object which binds an indirect key K to a direct value V. Class A is the class of your memory manager.

TMDIAssociation

template <class K class V, class A> class TMDIAssociation

Creates a memory-managed association object which binds a direct key K to an indirect value V. Class A is the class of your memory manager.

TMDDAssociation

template <class K class V, class A> class TMDDAssociation

Creates a memory-managed association object which binds a direct key K with a direct value V. Class A is the class of your memory manager.

Association class container members

Protected data members

KeyData
K KeyData

The key data of type K is passed as a parameter into the association class template upon class instantiation. *KeyData* is passed to the association object upon object instantiation.

ValueData
V ValueData

The value data of type V is passed as a parameter into the association class template upon class instantiation. *ValueData* is passed to the association object upon object instantiation.

Public constructors

Default constructors
TDDAssociation ()
TDIAssociation ()
TIDAssociation ()
TIIAssociation ()
TMDDAssociation ()
TMDIAssociation ()
TMIDAssociation ()
TMIIAssociation ()

Form 1   TDDAssociation (const K &k const V &v)
TMDDAssociation (const K &k const V &v)

Constructs an object that associates a key object k with a value object v. The second prototype supports a custom memory manager class.

Form 2   TIDAssociation (K * k, const V &v)
TMIDAssociation (K * k, const V &v)

Constructs an object that associates a pointer to key object k with a value object v. The second prototype supports a custom memory manager class.

Form 3   TDIAssociation (K &k, const V * v)
TMDIAssociation (K &k, const V * v)

Constructs an object that associates a pointer to key object k with a pointer to value object v. The second prototype supports a custom memory manager class.

Form 4   TIIAssociation (K * k, V * v)
TMIIAssociation (K * k, V * v)

Constructs an object that associates a reference to key object k with a pointer to value object v. The second prototype supports a custom memory manager class.

Public member functions

DeleteElements
void DeleteElements ()

Deletes the current association object from a dictionary.

The dictionary object containing the association object calls its *Detach* or *Flush* members to delete association objects. *Detach* or *Flush* determine whether the current association object should be deleted from memory. If so, the current association object calls its *DeleteElements* member to delete its Key and Value data from memory.

HashValue

unsigned HashValue ()

Returns the hash value for the key.

Key

const K& key () const

const K * key () const

Returns *KeyData*, the K parameter passed into the Association class template upon instantiation. The first prototype returns a reference to *KeyData*, and supports association objects storing direct keys. The second prototype returns a pointer to *KeyData*, and supports association classes storing indirect keys.

Value

const V& value () const

const V * value () const

Returns *ValueData*, the V parameter passed into the Association class template upon instantiation. The first prototype returns a reference to *ValueData*, and supports association objects storing direct values. The second prototype returns a pointer to *ValueData*, and supports association classes storing indirect values.

Operator

operator ==

int operator == (const TMDDAssociation<K,V,A> & a) const

Tests for equality between keys.

Bag class template family
bags.h

Bag containers manage bags of objects. A bag is a container that holds any number of objects in any order, and of any value. The bag is the least structured of all the data structures supported by any container in the container class families. The bag family includes four container classes, together with their corresponding four iterator classes.

Introduction

Individual containers in this family manage objects and pointers to objects. Most classes use the default memory manager *TStandardAllocator*, but you can pass your own memory manager class to managed container class templates.

Class family list

Here is a list of container classes composing this family. See "Template family syntax" for template prototypes for each template. See "Container members" and "Iterator methods" for definitions of members all classes use in common.

Direct templates
- TBagAsVector
- TMBagAsVector
- TBagAsVectorIterator
- TMBagAsVectorIterator

Indirect templates
- TIBagAsVector
- TMIBagAsVector
- TIBagAsVectorIterator
- TMIBagAsVectorIterator

Using this class family

Use a bag container to hold objects, when you don't need indexed access to the container, lookup operations are not frequent, and you might need to store duplicate values.

Perform the following steps to use a bag class:

1   Specify the type for the object you will store in your bag container. Decide whether to store objects themselves in the bag, or pointers to those objects. Decide whether to use a default memory manager object, or to manage memory yourself, through your own memory manager object.

2   Select the bag family template that fits your program design. Bag classes can accept objects or pointers to objects, can accept either default or user-supplied memory managers, and can sort elements as they are added to the bag container.

3   The objects that you store in a bag container must provide the following functions:
- Default constructor (direct classes only)
- Copy constructor (all classes)
- Assignment operator (direct classes only)
- Equality operator (all classes)

4   If you have decided to use your own memory manager to manage bag elements, then you must overload the *new* and *delete* operator member declarations in your memory manager class to support your new user type.

In most cases, you can declare these members by copying prototypes declared in class *TStandardAllocator* into your own class prototype, and changing their declared types to your user type. Refer to class *TStandardAllocator* in `allocctr.h`.

5   If you plan to use *FirstThat*, *LastThat* or *ForEach* member functions to iterate through your Bag, then you must write callback functions to act on data stored in your Bag. These functions must conform to a prototype syntax expected by the *FirstThat*, *LastThat* or *ForEach* member function. For coding convenience, these function prototypes are **typedef**ed as listed under "Container members."

6 To promote code maintainability, you should **typedef** the container and iterator class templates you have selected to use. This makes it easy to change a class template while minimizing changes you may need to make to your working code.

7 Instantiate a bag container class from your class template. Pass the type of the object you will store in your bag container to the bag class template upon class instantiation.

8 Instantiate a bag container object.

9 Instantiate a bag iterator, if you have decided to use an iterator to access elements in your bag container. Pass your bag container object to your iterator object when you instantiate your iterator object.

Code example

The following example declares a *TBagAsVector* container named *bag*, that holds ten elements of type *long*. It fills the bag, searches the bag for the element that holds the value 7, and then deletes that bag element. It then calls both *ForEach* and *TBagAsVectorIterator* to display the contents of the bag container. The numbers 1 through 10 display on your screen, minus the number 7.

Note that *ForEach* calls the iteration function called *Show*, that simply displays the contents of the current bag element. *ForEach* then moves to the next element in the bag, calls *Show* again, and repeats this process until every element in the bag has been displayed.

```
#include <iostream.h>
#include <classlib\bags.h>
/* Here is an iteration function required by the ForEach
   member function. It displays the contents of the current element c.
*/
void Show ( long& c, void*)    { cout << c << endl; }
/* This wrapper function instantiates an iterator object called go,
    passes the container object called bag into it upon instantiation,
    and shows the contents of each bag bag element as it is encountered.
*/
void UseIterator ( const TBagAsVector < long > & bag )
{
    TBagAsVectorIterator < long > go (bag);
    while ( go != 0 )
       {
       cout << go.Current( ) << endl;
       go++;
       }
}
int main ( )
{
    /* Instantiate a bag container called bag that holds 10 longs. */
    TBagAsVector < long > bag(10);
    for ( int i = 0; i < 10; i++ ) // fill the Bag
       bag.Add(i);
    /* You can now call global or member functions at this point to
       act on data contained in the Bag. This program detaches any
```

```
         object in the Bag  that contains the long value '7'.
   */
   bag.Detach(7);
   /* Call the bag::ForEach member function to iterate through
      the Bag. Pass an iteration function called Show to ForEach.
      This function displays the contents of the element it points
      to each time ForEach calls it.
   */
   cout << "Using ForEach member function to iterate:\n";
   bag.ForEach ( Show, 0 );
   /* Repeat the iteration process using an iterator object.
      The UseIterator function below combines an instantiation
      call with a streams call, to display the contents of the
      current element.
   */
   cout << "\nUsing an iterator object to iterate:\n";
   UseIterator(bag);
   return 0;
}
```

Output

```
Using ForEach member function to iterate:
0
1
2
3
4
5
6
8
9
Using an iterator object to iterate:
0
1
2
3
4
5
6
8
9
```

Template family syntax

This section lists template prototypes and definitions for classes in the bag family.

Direct templates

Objects instantiated from classes listed here contain literal elements of type *T*.

TBagAsVector

template <class T> TBagAsVector

Creates a bag container storing objects of type *T*.

TMBagAsVector

template <class T, class Alloc> class TMBagAsVector

Creates a bag container storing objects of type *T*, managed by a memory manager of type *Alloc*.

Indirect class templates

Objects instantiated from classes listed here contain pointers to bag elements of type *T*.

TIBagAsVector

template <class T> class TIBagAsVector

Creates a bag container storing pointers to objects of type *T*.

TMIBagAsVector

template <class T, class Alloc> class TMIBagAsVector

Creates a bag container storing pointers to objects of type *T*. Memory is managed by a user-defined memory manager of type *Alloc*. Pass in your memory manager object to the *TMIBagAsVector* object as an input parameter when you instantiate your *TMIBagAsVector* object.

Iterator class templates

All iterator classes use their *Current* member to access each object stored in the container they support.

Each iterator class listed here is paired with a container class template that matches its name format. For example, *TIMBagAsVectorIterator* instantiates an iterator object that takes a *TIMBagAsVector* container object as its argument. Always use the iterator that matches the container type holding the stored objects you want to access.

Direct templates

TBagAsVectorIterator

template <class T> class TBagAsVectorIterator

TMBagAsVectorIterator

template <class T,class Alloc> class TMBagAsVectorIterator

Indirect templates

TIBagAsVectorIterator

template <class T> TIBagAsVector

TMIBagAsVectorIterator

template <class T, class Alloc> TMIBagAsVectorIterator

Container members

Type definitions

CondFunc

typedef int (*CondFunc) (const T &, void *)

Defines the return type and input parameters for the user-written function *cond*. *Condfunc* is used as an input parameter to the *ForEach* member function.

When using *FirstThat* or *LastThat* to iterate through your bag, you must write a function taking a **const** reference to an object of your user type and a **void** pointer. When you call *FirstThat* or *LastThat*, you pass a pointer to your function as an input parameter.

IterFunc

typedef void (*IterFunc) (T &, void *)

Defines the return type and input parameters for the user-written function *iter*. **Iterfunc* is used as an input parameter to the *ForEach* member function.

When using *ForEach* to iterate through your bag, you must write a function taking a reference to an object of your user type and a **void** pointer. When you call *ForEach*, you pass a pointer to your function as an input parameter.

Public constructors

Form 1 TBagAsVector (unsigned sz = DEFAULT_BAG_SIZE)

Creates a bag container holding objects of type *T*. *sz* represents the initial number of slots allocated.

Form 2 TIBagAsVector (unsigned sz = DEFAULT_BAG_SIZE)

Creates an empty bag container holding pointers to objects of type *T*. *sz* represents the initial number of slots allocated.

Form 3 TMBagAsVector (unsigned sz = DEFAULT_BAG_SIZE)

Creates a bag container holding objects of type *T* and using a user-supplied memory manager object of type *Alloc*.

Form 4 TMIBagAsVector (unsigned sz = DEFAULT_BAG_SIZE)

Creates a bag container holding pointers to objects of type *T* and using a user-supplied memory manager object of type *Alloc*.

Public member functions

Add

Form 1 int Add(const T& t)

For direct bag containers. Adds object *t* to the bag container.

Form 2 int Add (T *t)

For indirect bag containers. Adds a pointer to object *t* to the bag container.

Detach

Form 1 int Detach(const T& t)

For direct containers.

Removes the first object that compares equal to the specified object *t*.

Form 2   int Detach(T *t, DeleteType dt = NoDelete)

For indirect containers.

Removes the specified pointer **t*. The value *dt* and the current ownership setting determine whether the object itself will be removed from the bag and also deleted from memory.

dt can be set to one of these three **enum** values:

Value	Description
NoDelete	The object will not be deleted from memory. This is the default value.
DefDelete	The object will be deleted if the container owns its contents, or left in memory if the container does not own its contents.
Delete	The object will be deleted from memory whether or not the container owns its objects.

Find

int Find(const T& t) const

int Find(const T *t) const

Finds the specified object *t* and returns a pointer to that the object, or 0 if the object was not found. The first prototype supports direct bag objects; the second prototype supports indirect bag objects.

ForEach

void ForEach(IterFunc iter, void *args)

ForEach executes the given function *iter* for each object in the bag. The *args* argument lets you pass arbitrary data to this function.

IterFunc is a **typedef** that specifies the return type and input parameters for the function called by *ForEach* to operate on data stored at the current node. This is a predefined **typedef**.

iter is your function, that operates on data contained in the node that *ForEach* references. You must write *iter* to take a reference to your node data and a **void** type pointer.

When called, *ForEach* positions a pointer at an element in the bag, and calls your function, *iter*. *iter* checks data at that element, and may change that data based on a condition you define. When finished, *iter* returns control to *ForEach*, that moves to the next element in the bag. *ForEach* repeats this process until it has visited every object in the bag.

FirstThat

T *FirstThat(CondFunc cond, void *args) const

Returns a pointer to the first object in the bag that satisfies a given condition, or returns zero if no object in the bag meets the condition.

You supply a test-function pointer *cond* that returns **true** for a certain condition. You can pass arbitrary arguments via *args*.

CondFunc is a **typedef** that maps your implementation function to the signature that *FirstThat* recognizes. *cond* is your function, that operates on data contained in the current bag element. Supports indirect bag containers—also *TMBagAsVector*.

Flush

void Flush ()

void Flush (TShouldDelete::DeleteType dt = TShouldDelete::DefDelete)

Removes all elements from the bag without destroying the bag. The first prototype supports direct bag objects; the second prototype supports indirect bag objects.

For indirect bag containers, the value *dt* determines whether elements removed from the container will also be deleted from memory. See *Detach*.

GetItemsInContainer

int GetItemsInContainer() const

Returns the number of items in the bag.

HasMember

int HasMember(const T& t) const

Returns nonzero if the given object *t* is found in the bag.

IsEmpty

int IsEmpty () const

Returns nonzero if the bag contains no elements.

IsFull

int IsFull () const

Always returns zero for a bag container.

LastThat

T *LastThat(CondFunc cond, void *args) const

Returns a pointer to the last object in the bag that satisfies a given condition. You supply a pointer to the test function *cond* that you must write. *cond* takes a pointer to the current object and a **void** pointer. It returns 1 (**true**) for a certain condition, and returns 0 (**false**) if no object in the bag meets the condition you specified. Supports indirect containers.

LastThat is valid only for indirect containers.

Iterator methods

Public constructors

Form 1   TMBagAsVectorIterator
(const TMBagAsVector <class T, class Alloc > & b)

Creates an iterator object to traverse *TMBagAsVector* objects. *Alloc* is the type of your Memory Manager object.

Form 2   TBagAsVectorIterator
(const TBagAsVector < class T > & b)

Creates an iterator object to traverse *TBagAsVector* objects.

Form 3 TMIBagAsVectorIterator(const TMIBagAsVector<T,Alloc> & b)

Creates an iterator object to traverse indirect, memory-managed *BagAsVector* objects as input parameters. This is a function template that takes your user type as a template parameter. *b* is a reference to a *TMIBagAsVector* object holding elements of your user type, as an input parameter.

Form 4 TIBagAsVectorIterator(const TIBagAsVector < T > & b)

Creates an iterator object to traverse a BagAsVector object that takes a pointer to an object of type *T* as an input parameter. *a* is a reference to a *TIBagAsVector* object holding pointers to elements of your user type as an input parameter.

Public member functions

Current

Form 1 const T& Current () const

For direct containers; returns a reference to the current object.

Form 2 T * Current () const

For indirect containers; returns a pointer to the current object.

Restart
void Restart ()

Restarts iteration from the beginning of the bag.

Operators

operator ++
Form 1 const T& operator ++ (int)

Moves to the next object and returns the object that was current before the move (postincrement operator).

Form 2 const T& operator ++ ()

Moves to the next object and returns that object (preincrement operator).

operator int
operator int () const

Converts the iterator to an integer value for testing if objects remain in the iterator. This operator returns a nonzero value if the iterator has not finished opeating on the bag, or a zero value if it has completed.

Binary search tree class template family   binimp.h

Binary tree containers manage data placed into nodes, where each node can connect to one parent and up to two child nodes. This family includes two container classes, together with their corresponding two iterator classes.

Introduction

Individual containers in this family manage objects and pointers to objects. Binary search tree templates use the default memory manager *TStandardAllocator*. You cannot pass your own memory manager to a template in the binary tree family.

By default, binary trees connect nodes in an inorder sequence. This means that binary tree nodes are connected so that the value placed into a parent node is more than the value placed into the left child node and less than the value placed into the right child node. Repeated values are placed into right child nodes on the tree, and the tree is restructured if necessary. This strategy creates an inherently sorted tree that can be searched more quickly than can array, linked list, or hash table containers. You can change default sequencing to preorder or postorder node sequencing from the container constructor, when the container is instantiated.

Binary trees are unbalanced. The order in which you place data into the tree determines the shape of the tree. Binary tree objects do not adjust themselves in order to build more symmetrical shapes.

Binary tree objects adjust themselves automatically when you add or delete data from the tree. If a duplicate value is added or a parent node is deleted, the object promotes the appropriate child node and recursively adjusts the tree without your intervention.

Class family list

Here is a list of container classes composing this family. See "Template family syntax" for template prototypes for each template. See "Container members" and "Iterator methods" for definitions of members all classes use in common.

Direct templates
- TBinarySearchTreeImp
- TBinarySearchTreeIteratorImp

Indirect templates
- TIBinarySearchTreeImp
- TIBinarySearchTreeIteratorImp

Using this class family

Use a binary tree container when lookup speed is important.

Perform the following steps to use a binary search tree class:

1 Determine the type of data you will store in the tree. Decide whether to store objects themselves in the tree, or to store pointers to those objects.

2 Select the tree family template that fits your program design. Binary tree nodes store data or pointers to data.

3 Classes instantiating stored objects of your own user type must provide the functions listed here. Predefined types already provide these functions.

- Copy constructor
- Less-than operator
- Equivalence operator

4 If you plan to use the *ForEach* member function to iterate through your tree, then you must write a function to act on data stored in your tree. This function must support the prototype syntax expected by the *ForEach* member function. For coding convenience, these function prototypes are **typedef**ed as listed under "Container members."

5 To promote code maintainability, you should **typedef** the container and iterator class templates you have selected to use. This makes it easy to change a class template while minimizing the changes you need to make to your working code.

6 Instantiate a binary search tree class from your class template. Pass the user type of the data stored in the binary tree node to the template upon instantiation.

7 Instantiate a binary search tree container object.

8 Instantiate a binary search tree iterator, if you have decided to use an iterator to access elements in your binary search tree container. Pass your binary search tree container object to your iterator object when you instantiate your iterator object.

Code example

This example instantiates a binary tree container to hold **long**s, adds nine random numbers to the tree, and then adds the number 32 to the tree. It uses *ForEach* to display tree contents on your terminal, detaches the number 32, and then uses an iterator object to display the new contents of the tree.

```
#include <iostreams.h>
#include <classlib/binimp.h>
#include <stdlib.h>

typedef TBinarySearchTreeImp < long > tree_type;
typedef TBinarySearchTreeIteratorImp< long > tree_iter;

/* This is the iteration function required by the ForEach member
   function. It displays the contents of the current element c.
*/
void Show ( long& c, void*)  { cout << c << endl; }

void UseIterator(tree_type& tree)
{
   tree_iter go(tree); // instantiate an iterator
   while ( go != 0 )  // current returns a zero when it finishes
      {
      cout << go.Current( ) << endl;
      go++;
      }
}

int main ( )
```

```
{
    randomize();
    tree_type tree;
    tree.Add(32);    // add the number 32 first.

    /* Add nine random numbers between 1 and 64 to the tree. Some
       will be lower and some higher than 32.
    */
    int treesize = 9;
    for ( int i = 0; i < treesize; i++)
        tree.Add( random(63) + 1 );

    cout << "Iterate through the tree using ForEach and "
            "print it out.\nThe number 32 is present." << endl;
    tree.ForEach(Show,0);
    cout << "\n\nDetach the number '32' from the tree. \n\n";

    tree.Detach ( 32 );
    cout << "Use the iterator object to display the\n"
            "contents of all the nodes in the tree.\n"
            "The number 32 is absent." << endl;
    UseIterator ( tree );
    return 0;
}
```

Sample output (output may vary)

```
Iterate through the tree using ForEach and print it out.
The number 32 is present.
2
9
17
25
27
28
32
33
56
58


Detach the number '32' from the tree.

Use the iterator object to display the
contents of all the nodes in the tree.
The number 32 is absent.
2
9
17
25
27
```

```
28
33
56
58
```

Template family syntax

This section lists template prototypes and definitions for classes in the binary tree family.

Direct template

Objects instantiated from class listed here contains data of type *T*.

TBinarySearchTreeImp

template <class T> class TBinarySearchTreeImp

Creates a direct binary tree class storing data of type *T*.

Indirect template

Objects instantiated from class listed here contains pointers to data of type *T*.

TIBinarySearchTreeImp

template <class T> class TIBinarySearchTreeImp

Creates an indirect binary search tree storing pointers to data of type *T*.

Iterator class templates

All iterator classes use their *Current* member to access each object stored in the container they support.

Each iterator class listed here is paired with a container class template which matches its name format. For example, *TIMBinarySearchTreeIteratorImp* instantiates an iterator object which takes a *TIMBinarySearchTree* container object as its argument. Always select to use the iterator which matches the container type holding the stored objects you want to access.

Direct template

TBinarySearchTreeIteratorImp

template <class T> class TBinarySearchTreeIteratorImp

Indirect template

TIBinarySearchTreeIteratorImp

template <class T> class TIBinarySearchTreeIteratorImp

Container members

Type definition

IterFunc

typedef void (*IterFunc) (T &, void *)

Defines the return type and input parameters for the user-written function *iter*. **Iterfunc* is used as an input parameter to the *ForEach* member function.

When using *ForEach* to iterate through your array, you must write a function taking a reference to an object of your user type and a **void** pointer. Your function returns a nonzero value if it has not acted on data, and a zero value if it has acted on data. When you call *ForEach*, you pass a pointer to this function as an input parameter.

Public constructors

All binary search tree class templates build classes which call the default protected constructor in *TBinaryTreeBase*. You do not need to pass parameters to a binary tree object upon instantiation.

Public member functions

Add

int Add(const T& t)

int Add (T * t)

Creates a new binary-tree node and inserts a reference to object *t* into it. The first prototype supports *TBinarySearchTreeImp* objects.

Creates a new binary-tree node on the tree and inserts a pointer to object *t* into that node. The second prototype supports *TIBinarySearchTreeImp* objects.

Detach

int Detach(const T& t)

int Detach(T * t, int del = 0)

Removes the node containing item *t* from the tree. The first prototype supports *TBinarySearchTreeImp* objects.

Removes the node containing a pointer to item *t* from the tree. The item is deleted from memory if *del* equals one. The second prototype supports *TIBinarySearchTreeImp* objects.

Find

Form 1 T * Find(const T& t) const

Returns a pointer to the node containing item *t*. Supports *TBinarySearchTreeImp* objects.

Form 2 T * Find(T * t) const

Returns a pointer to the node containing a pointer to item *t*. Supports *TIBinarySearchTreeImp* objects.

ForEach

void ForEach(IterFunc iter, void *args, IteratorOrder order = InOrder)

ForEach executes the given function *iter* for each node in the tree. The *args* argument lets you pass arbitrary data to this function. *IteratorOrder* sets the searching order for the tree.

IterFunc is a **typedef** which which specifies the return type and input parameters for the function called by *ForEach* to operate on data stored at the current node. This is a predefined **typedef**.

iter is your function, which operates on data contained in the node that *ForEach* is pointing to. You must write *iter* to take a reference to your node data and a **void** type pointer.

When called, *ForEach* positions a pointer at a node and calls your function, *iter*. *iter* checks data at that node, and may change that data based on a condition you define. When finished, *iter* returns control to *ForEach*, which moves to the next node in the tree. *ForEach* repeats this process until it has traversed the tree.

IteratorOrder is an **enum** value that determines the order in which this iterator will traverse the tree. Valid values are *InOrder*, *PreOrder*, and *PostOrder*.

Flush
void Flush ()
void Flush (int del = 0)

Removes all items from the tree without destroying the tree. The first prototype supports *TBinarySearchTreeImp* objects.

For *TIBinarySearchTreeImp* objects, the second prototype removes all items from the tree. They are deleted from memory if *del* equals one. If *del* equals zero, the items are not deleted from memory.

GetItemsInContainer
unsigned GetItemsInContainer()

Returns the number of items currently stored in the tree.

IsEmpty
int IsEmpty ()

Returns a nonzero value if the array contains no elements.

Operators
Binary search tree containers have no operators.

Protected member functions
These protected members implement functions defined in public members. You do not need to call these members directly.

EqualTo
virtual int EqualTo (BinNode * n1, BinNode * n2)

Tests equality between two nodes on the tree. Returns **true** if the values contained at *n1* and *n2* are equal.

LessThan
virtual int LessThan (BinNode * n1, BinNode * n2)

Tests if node n1 is less than node *n2*.

DeleteNode
virtual int DeleteNode (BinNode * node, int del)

Deletes *node*. The second parameter is ignored.

Iterator methods

Public constructors

Form 1   TBinarySearchTreeIteratorImp
    (TBinarySearchTreeImp < T > & tree, .
    TBinarySearchTreeBase::IteratorOrder order
    = TBinarySearchTreeBase::InOrder)

Constructs an iterator object that traverses a *TBinarysearchTreeImp* container handling nodes of type *T*. This object sets its iteration order to equal the *InOrder* setting it finds in the *TBinarySearchTreeBase* class.

Form 2   TIBinarySearchTreeIteratorImp
    (TIBinarySearchTreeImp < T > & tree,
    TBinarySearchTreeBase::IteratorOrder order
    = TBinarySearchTreeBase ::InOrder)

Constructs an iterator object that traverses a *TIBinarysearchTreeImp* container handling pointers to nodes of type *T*. This object sets its iteration order to equal the *InOrder* setting it finds in the *TBinarySearchTreeBase* class.

Form 3   TBinarySearchTreeIteratorImp < TVoidPointer > (tree, order)

Constructs an iterator object that traverses a *TIBinarysearchTreeImp* container handling nodes of type *T*. This object sets its iteration order to equal the *InOrder* setting it finds in the *TBinarySearchTreeBase* class.

Public member functions

Current
Form 1   const T& Current () const

For direct containers; returns a reference to the current object.

Form 2   T * Current () const

For indirect containers; returns a pointer to the current object.

Restart
void Restart ()

Restarts iteration from the root of the tree.

Operators

operator ++
Form 1   const T& operator ++ (int)
    T * operator ++ (int i)

Moves to the next object in the tree and returns the object that was current before the move. The first prototype is the postincrement operator for *TBinarySearchTreeImp*.

Moves to the next object in the tree and returns a pointer to the object that was current before the move. The second prototype is the postincrement operator for *TIBinarySearchTreeImp*.

Form 2   const T& operator ++ ()

T * operator ++ ()

Moves to the next object in the tree and returns that object. The first prototype is the preincrement operator for *TBinarySearchTreeImp*.

Moves to the next object in the tree and returns a pointer to that object. The second prototype is the preincrement operator for *TBinarySearchTreeImp*.

operator int

operator int () const

Converts the iterator to an integer value. This operator is used to test for objects remaining in the iterator. This operator returns a nonzero value if the iterator has not finished operating on the array, or a zero value if it has completed iterating.

Deque class template family   **deques.h**

Deque objects manage a train of objects of type *T*, where objects can be inserted or removed from either the head or the tail of the train. The queue structure stores head and tail objects in the order they were received. A call to the head or the tail surrenders the last object inserted at the head or tail. The queue family includes nine container classes, together with their corresponding nine iterator classes.

Introduction

Individual containers in this family manage objects and pointers to objects. Most classes use the default memory manager *TStandardAllocator*, but you can pass your own memory manager class to managed container class templates.

You can implement deque structures as vectors or as double-linked lists. Both kinds of class templates take the same parameters and present the same list of member functions. For example, if you change your class user type from *TDequeAsVector* to *TDequeAsDoubleList*, you will not need to change calls you made to deque member functions in your source code.

A *DequeAsVector* class cannot be resized; a *DequeAsList* class can be resized.

Class family list

Here is the list of classes composing this family. See "Template family syntax" for template prototypes for each template. See "Container members" and "Iterator methods" for member definitions.

Direct templates

- TDequeAsVector
- TDequeAsDoubleList
- TMDequeAsVector
- TMDequeAsDoubleList
- TDeque

- TDequeAsVectorIterator
- TDequeAsDoubleListIterator
- TMDequeAsVectorIterator
- TMDequeAsDoubleListIterator
- TDequeIterator

Indirect templates

- TIDequeAsVector
- TIDequeAsDoubleList
- TMIDequeAsVector
- TMIDequeAsDoubleList

- TIDequeAsVectorIterator
- TDequeAsDoubleListIterator
- TMIDequeAsVectorIterator
- TMDequeAsDoubleListIterator

Using this class family

Use a deque class when you need access to both ends of a chain of stored objects.

Perform the following steps to use a deque class:

1 Set the data type for the element you will store in your deque container. Decide whether to store objects themselves in the deque, or to store pointers to those objects. Decide whether to use the default memory manager *TStandardAllocator*, or to manage memory yourself.

2 Select the deque family template that fits your program design. Deque classes can store objects or pointers to objects, and can accept either default or user-supplied memory managers. You also may implement your deque as a double-linked list, or as a vector.

For example, if you have chosen to store pointers to **long**s in a deque implemented as a double-linked list, instantiate an object of the *TIDequeAsDoubleList* class.

3 Classes instantiating stored objects of your own user type must provide the functions listed here. Predefined types already provide these functions.

- Default constructor (all classes)
- Copy constructor (all vector classes; indirect double list classes)
- Assignment operator (direct vector classes)
- Equality operator (indirect double list classes)

4 If you have decided to use your own memory manager, then you must overload the *new* and *delete* operator member declarations in your memory manager class to support your new user type.

5 If you plan to use *FirstThat*, *LastThat*, or *ForEach* member functions to iterate through your deque, then you must write functions to act on data stored in your deque. These functions must conform to a prototype syntax expected by the *FirstThat*, *LastThat*, or *ForEach* member function. For coding convenience, these function prototypes are **typedef**ed as listed under "Container members."

6 To promote code maintainability, you should **typedef** the container and iterator class templates you have decided to use. This makes it easy to change a class template without making changes to your working code.

7 Instantiate a deque container class from the class template you have decided to use. Pass the type of the objects you will store in your container class to the class template upon class instantiation. If you are using a managed class, then you must also pass the type of your memory manager class to the template.

8 Instantiate a deque container object.

9 Instantiate a deque iterator, if you have decided to use an iterator to access elements in your deque container. Pass your deque container object to your iterator object when you instantiate your iterator object.

Code example

This example illustrates a deque of strings implemented as a double-linked list.

```
#include <iostream.h>
#include <strstrea.h>
#include <classlib\deques.h>
#include <string.h>

typedef TIDequeAsDoubleList < string > lDeque;

int main ( )
{
    lDeque d;
        for ( int i = 1; i < 5; i++)
            {
            string* s = new string("string ");
            *s += (char)('A' + (i-1));
          // Use alternating left and right insertions
                if ( i & 1 )
                    d.PutLeft ( s );
                else
                    d.PutRight ( s );
            }
        cout << "Deque Contents:" << endl;
        while ( !d.IsEmpty () )
            { // Must dereference when using an indirect container
            string* s = d.GetLeft ( );
            cout << *s << endl;
            delete s;
            }

    return 0;
}
```

```
Deque Contents:
string C
string A
string B
string D
```

Template family syntax

This section lists template prototypes and definitions for classes in the deque family.

Direct templates
Objects instantiated from classes listed here contain data of type *T*.

TDequeAsDoubleList
TDequeAsVector
template <class T> class TDequeAsDoubleList

template <class T> class TDequeAsVector

Creates a deque container holding objects of type *T*. The first prototype implements the deque as a double-linked list. The second prototype implements the deque as a vector.

TMDequeAsDoubleList
TMDequeAsVector
template <class T, class Alloc> class TMDequeAsDoubleList

template <class T, class Alloc> class TMDequeAsVector

Creates a deque container holding objects of type *T*, managed by a memory manager of type *Alloc*. The first prototype implements the deque as a double-linked list. The second prototype implements the deque as a vector.

Indirect class templates
Objects instantiated from classes listed here contain pointers to deque objects of type *T*. The first prototype implements the deque as a double-linked list. The second prototype implements the deque as a vector.

TIDequeAsDoubleList
TIDequeAsVector
template <class T> class TIDequeAsDoubleList

template <class T> class TIDequeAsVector

Creates a deque container holding pointers to objects of type *T*. The first prototype implements the deque as a double-linked list. The second prototype implements the deque as a vector.

TMIDequeAsDoubleList
TMIDequeAsVector
template <class T, class Alloc> class TMIDequeAsDoubleList

template <class T, class Alloc> class TMIDequeAsVector

Creates a deque container holding pointers to objects type *T*. Memory is managed by a user-defined memory manager. The first prototype implements the deque as a double-linked list. The second prototype implements the deque as a vector.

Iterator class templates

All iterator classes use their *Current* member to access each object stored in the container they support.

Each iterator class listed here is paired with a container class template that matches its name format. For example, *TIMDequeAsVectorIterator* instantiates an iterator object that takes a *TIMDequeAsVector* container object as its argument. Always use the iterator that matches the container type holding the stored objects you want to access.

Direct templates

TDequeAsVectorIterator

template <class T> class TDequeAsVectorIterator

TDequeAsDoubleListIterator

template <class T,class Alloc> class TMDequeAsDoubleListIterator

TMDequeAsVectorIterator

template <class T,class Alloc> class TMDequeAsVectorIterator

TMDequeAsDoubleListIterator

template <class T> class TMDequeAsDoubleListIterator

Indirect templates

TIDequeAsVectorIterator

template <class T> class TIDequeAsVectorIterator

TIDequeAsDoubleListIterator

template <class T,class Alloc> class TIDequeAsDoubleListIterator

TIMDequeAsVectorIterator

template <class T,class Alloc> class TIMDequeAsVectorIterator

TIMDequeAsDoubleListIterator

template <class T> class TIMDequeAsDoubleListIterator

Container members

Type definitions

CondFunc

typedef int (*condFunc) (const T &, void *)

Defines the return type and input parameters for the user-written function used as an input parameter to the *FirstThat and LastThat* member functions.

When using *FirstThat* or *LastThat* to iterate through your deque, you must write a function taking a **const** reference to an object of your user type and a **void** pointer. When you call *FirstThat* or *LastThat*, you pass a pointer to this function as as the *cond* input parameter.

IterFunc

typedef void (*IterFunc) (T &, void *)

Defines the return type and input parameters for the user-supplied function used as an input parameter to the *ForEach* member function.

When using *ForEach* to iterate through your deque, you must write a function taking a reference to an object of your user type and a **void** pointer. When you call *ForEach*, you pass a pointer to your function as the *iter* input parameter.

Public constructors

DequeAsList classes call the protected default *TDequeAsDoubleListImp* constructor, which takes no parameters.

Constructors

TDequeAsVector (unsigned max = DEFAULT_DEQUE_SIZE)
TMDequeAsVector (unsigned max = DEFAULT_DEQUE_SIZE)
TIDequeAsVector (unsigned sz = DEFAULT_DEQUE_SIZE)
TMIDequeAsVector (unsigned sz = DEFAULT_DEQUE_SIZE)

Creates a deque container with a default max size of DEFAULT_DEQUE_SIZE.

Public member functions

FirstThat

T *FirstThat(CondFunc cond, void *args) const

Iterates through the deque from head to tail and returns a pointer to the first object in the deque that satisfies a given condition. You supply a pointer to a user-written test-function that returns **true** for a certain condition. You can pass arbitrary arguments via *args*.

CondFunc is a **typedef** that defines parameters for a function passed as an input parameter to *FirstThat*. *cond* is your function, that operates on data contained in the current deque element.

ForEach

void ForEach(IterFunc iter, void *args)

ForEach executes the given function *iter* for each element in the deque. The *args* argument lets you pass arbitrary data to this function. *IteratorOrder* sets the searching order for the deque.

IterFunc is a **typedef** that that specifies the return type and input parameters for the function called by *ForEach* to operate on data stored at the current element.

iter is your function, that operates on data contained in the deque that *ForEach* is pointing to. You must write *iter* to take a reference to your node data and a **void** type pointer.

When called, *ForEach* positions a pointer at a deque and calls your function, *iter*. *iter* checks data at that deque, and may change that data based on a condition you define. When finished, *iter* returns control to *ForEach*, that moves to the element node in the deque. *ForEach* repeats this process until it has iterated through the deque.

Flush

void Flush ()

void Flush (TShouldDelete::DeleteType = TShouldDelete::DefDelete)

Removes all elements from the deque without destroying the deque container. The first prototype supports direct deque objects; the second prototype supports indirect deque objects.

For indirect deques, the ownership status of the deque elements determines whether they will be deleted from memory as well as from the deque container. The value *TShouldDelete::DefDelete* removes items from memory if they are owned by the deque container. *Delete* always removes items, no matter who owns them. *NoDelete* never removes items from memory.

GetItemsInContainer

unsigned GetItemsInContainer() const

Returns the number of items in the deque.

GetLeft

T GetLeft ()

T * GetLeft ()

Returns the object at the left end of the deque and removes it from the deque. The debuggable version throws an exception when the deque is empty.

GetRight

T GetRight ()

T * GetRight ()

Returns the object at the right end of the deque and removes it from the deque. The debuggable version throws an exception when the deque is empty.

IsEmpty

int IsEmpty () const

Returns nonzero if the deque contains no elements.

IsFull

int IsFull () const

Returns nonzero if the deque is full.

LastThat

T *LastThat(CondFunc cond, void *args) const

Iterates through the deque from head to tail and returns a pointer to the last object in the deque that satisfies a given condition.

You must supply a test function pointer *cond* that returns **true** for a condition you define. You can pass arbitrary arguments to this function via the *args* input parameter. *LastThat* returns zero if no object in the deque meets the condition you specified in *cond*.

PeekLeft

const T & PeekLeft () const

T * PeekLeft () const

Returns the object at the left end (head) of the deque. The object stays in the deque.

PeekRight

const T & PeekRight () const

T * PeekRight () const

Returns the object at the right end (tail) of the deque. The object stays in the deque.

PutLeft

void PutLeft (const T &) const

void PutLeft (T * t) const

Adds the object at the left end (head) of the deque.

PutRight

void PutRight (const T &) const

void PutRight (T * t) const

Adds the object at the right end (tail) of the deque.

Protected data members

These are implementation members. You should not need to call them directly.

Data

Vect Data

This data member contains deque data.

Left

unsigned Left

This data member contains the index to the leftmost element of the deque.

Right

unsigned Right

This data member contains the index to the rightmost element of the deque.

Protected member functions

These are implementation members. You do not need to call them directly.

Next

unsigned Next (unsigned index) const

Returns index plus 1. Wraps around to the head of the deque. This is an implementation member. You do not need to call it directly.

Prev

unsigned Prev (unsigned index) const

Returns *index* plus 1. Wraps around to the tail of the deque. This is an implementation member. You do not need to call it directly.

Operators

Deque containers have no operators.

Iterator methods

Public constructors

Form 1   TMDequeAsVectorIterator (const TMDequeAsVector <class T, class Alloc > & d)

Creates an iterator object to traverse *TMDequeAsVector* objects. *Alloc* is the type of your Memory Manager object.

Form 2   TDequeAsVectorIterator (const TDequeAsVector < class T > & d)

             TIDequeAsVectorIterator (const TIDequeAsVector < class T > & d)

Creates an iterator object to traverse objects stored in *TDequeAsVector* and *TIDequeAsVector* containers.

Form 3   TMIDequeAsVectorIterator (const TMIDequeAsVector < T, Alloc > & d)

Creates an iterator object to traverse objects stored in *TMIDequeAsVector* containers.

Public member functions

Current

Form 1   const T& Current () const

For direct containers; returns a reference to the current object.

Form 2   T * Current () const

For indirect containers; returns a pointer to the current object.

Restart

void Restart ()

Restarts iteration from the beginning of the deque.

Operators

operator ++

Form 1   const T& operator ++ (int)

Moves to the next object and returns the object that was current before the move (postincrement operator).

Form 2   const T& operator ++ ()

Moves to the next object and returns that object (preincrement operator).

operator int

operator int ()

Converts the iterator to an integer value. This operator is used to test for objects remaining in the iterator. This operator returns a nonzero value if the iterator has not finished operating on the deque, or a zero value if it has completed iterating.

Dictionary class template family   dict.h

Dictionary containers manage objects holding data. A dictionary object usually stores objects instantiated from an association class, that returns value data given key data.

Introduction

Individual dictionary containers can manage objects or pointers to objects. Two classes use the default memory manager *TStandardAllocator*. Two other classes can accept your own memory manager as an input parameter.

The dictionary class family includes four container classes, together with their corresponding four iterator classes, and two helper classes. Direct classes are base classes. Indirect classes derive from the *TShouldDelete* class.

Class family list

Here is a list of container classes composing this family. See "Template family syntax" for template prototypes for each template. See "Container members" and "Iterator methods" for definitions of members all classes use in common.

Direct templates

- TDictionaryAsHashTable
- TMDictionaryAsHashTable
- TDictionary

- TDictionaryAsHashTableIterator
- TMDictionaryAsHashTableIterator
- TDictionaryIterator

Indirect templates

- TIDictionaryAsHashTable
- TMIDictionaryAsHashTable

- TIDictionaryAsHashTableIterator
- TMIDictionaryAsHashTableIterator

Using this class family

Use a dictionary class when you need to retrieve a stored value based on a key.

Under normal circumstances, you will have selected an association class and determined value and key user types for data stored in objects of that association class. See "Association class template family" for details.

Dictionary objects assume that the association objects they contain include copy constructors, default constructors, and equivalence operators that support their key and value data types.

Perform the following steps to use a *DictionaryAsHashTable* object:

1 Select a dictionary family template that suits your program design. Dictionary classes can hold objects or pointers to objects, and can accept either default or user-supplied memory managers.

2 Classes instantiating stored objects of your own user type must provide the functions listed here. Predefined types already provide these functions.

- Default constructor
- Copy constructor
- Assignment operator
- Less-than operator
- Equality operator

3 If you have decided to use your own memory manager to manage dictionary objects, then you must overload the *new* and *delete* operator members in your memory manager class to support your new user type.

4 If you plan to use the *ForEach* member function in your dictionary object, then you must write a function whose signature conforms to the *IterFunc* **typedef**. *ForEach* iterates through each object stored in your dictionary. Your custom *iter* function operates on each element in turn.

5 To promote code portability, you should **typedef** the dictionary and association container class templates, and the dictionary iterator class template you have decided to use. This makes it easy to change a class template while minimizing changes you may need to make to your working code.

6 Instantiate a dictionary class template with your association class data type.

7 Instantiate an object of your class. Pass appropriate constructor parameters to your object upon instantiation.

8 Instantiate an iterator object, if you have decided to iterate through elements stored in your dictionary object. Pass your dictionary object to the iterator object upon instantiation.

Code example

The following example is a function that places five association objects of type *assoc* into a dictionary object of type *dict*. Each association object stores a name as a key of type *string*, and binds it to an age as value of type **int**. The *assoc* objects are instantiated at the time they are added to the dict object.

The example then calls the dictionary object *find* member function to find the age of a person named "Stevens". It prints out the age corresponding to that name on your terminal screen, and then uses *detach* to remove that association object from the dictionary object. For convenience and readability, association and dictionary class templates are **typedef**ed to *assocType* and *dicType*.

```
#include <string.h>
#include <iostream.h>
#include <classlib\assoc.h>
#include <classlib\dict.h>

typedef TDDAssociation < string, int > assocType;
typedef TDictionaryAsHashTable < assocType > dicType;
typedef TDictionaryAsHashTableIterator < assocType > dicIterType;

unsigned HashValue( const string& t )
{
  return t.hash();
}

// Unrelated program code goes here ...
void main( )
{
    dicType dict;
```

```
    assocType assoc;

    /* Here is one way to add association objects to a dictionary container.*/
    assocType Assoc1("Becker", 14);
    dict.Add(Assoc1);
    assocType Assoc2("Brewster", 9);
    dict.Add(Assoc2);

    /* Here is a second way to add association objects to a dictionary.
       These are unnamed association objects of type assocType.
    */

    dict.Add ( assocType( "Quinn", 21 ) );
    dict.Add ( assocType( "Stevens", 19 ) );
    dict.Add ( assocType( "Torres", 93 ) );

    /* Here is how to find and print out value data in a
       dictionary container.
    */

    assocType* Res = dict.Find(Assoc2);
    if (Res != 0) {
       cout << "Here is Brewster's age:   ";
       cout << Res->Value() << "\n "<< endl;
       }

    /* Here is how to display all dictionary container contents
       on your terminal screen. Note that Current() is an iterator
       function that returns an association object. Key() and
       Value() are association object functions that return key
       and value data respectively.
    */
    dicIterType dicIter (dict);
    cout << "Here are the dictionary contents.\n" << endl;
       while ( dicIter != 0 )
          {
          cout << dicIter.Current().Key() << ":   " ;
          cout << dicIter.Current().Value() << endl;
          dicIter++;
          }
}
```

Output

```
Here is Brewster's age:   9

Here are the dictionary contents.

Quinn:  21
Torres:  93
Stevens:  19
Brewster:  9
Becker:  14
```

Template family syntax

This section lists template prototypes and definitions for classes in the dictionary family.

Direct templates

Objects instantiated from classes listed here contain objects.

TDictionary

template <class T> class TDictionary

Creates a dictionary object containing objects of type *T*, where *T* is the user type of an association class.

This is a convenient synonym for the *TDictionaryAsHashTable* class.

TDictionaryAsHashTable

template <class T> class TDictionaryAsHashTable

Creates a dictionary object containing objects of type *T*, where *T* is the user type of an association class.

TMDictionaryAsHashTable

template <class T, class Alloc> class TMDictionaryAsHashTable

Creates a managed dictionary container, that holds objects of type T. Memory is managed by a user-defined memory manager of type *Alloc*.

Indirect class templates

Classes listed here manage pointers to objects.

TIDictionaryAsHashTable

template <class T> class TIDictionaryAsHashTable

Creates a dictionary object containing pointers to objects of type *T*, where *T* is the user type of an association class.

TMIDictionaryAsHashTable

template <class T, class Alloc> class TMIDictionaryAsHashTable

Creates a dictionary object containing pointers to objects of type *T*, where *T* is the user type of an association class.

Iterator class templates

All iterator classes use their *Current* member to access each object stored in the container they support.

Each iterator class listed here is paired with a container class template that matches its name format. For example, *TIMDictionaryAsHashTableIterator* instantiates an iterator object that takes a *TIMDictionaryAsHashTable* container object as its argument. Always use the iterator that matches the container type holding the stored objects you want to access.

Direct templates

TDictionaryAsHashTableIterator
template <class T> class TDictionaryAsHashTableIterator

TMDictionaryAsHashTableIterator
template <class T,class Alloc> class TMDictionaryAsHashTableIterator

Indirect templates

TIDictionaryAsHashTableIterator
template <class T> TIDictionaryAsHashTable

TMIDictionaryAsHashTableIterator
template <class T, class Alloc> TMIDictionaryAsHashTableIterator

Container members

Protected data members

HashTable
TMHashTableImp < class T,class A > Hashtable;

Implements the underlying hash table. You should not need to call this function directly.

Type definitions

IterFunc
typedef void (*IterFunc) (T &, void *)

Function type used as a parameter to the *ForEach member function.*

When using *ForEach* to iterate through your array, you must write a function taking a reference to an object of your user type and a **void** pointer. When you call *ForEach*, you pass *IterFunc* as an input parameter, that is a pointer to this function.

Public constructors
TDictionaryAsHashTable (unsigned size = DEFAULT_HASH_TABLE_SIZE)
TMDictionaryAsHashTable (unsigned size = DEFAULT_HASH_TABLE_SIZE)
TIDictionaryAsHashTable (unsigned size = DEFAULT_HASH_TABLE_SIZE)
TMIDictionaryAsHashTable (unsigned size = DEFAULT_HASH_TABLE_SIZE)

Creates a dictionary container with the specified size *sz*. This size defaults to DEFAULT_HASH_TABLE_SIZE.

Public member functions

Add
int Add(const T & t)
int Add (T *t)

For direct dictionary objects, the first prototype adds a *T* object to the dictionary.

For indirect dictionary objects, the second prototype adds a pointer to a *T* object to the dictionary.

Detach

int Detach(const T & t, DeleteType dt = DefDelete)
int Detach(T *t, int del = 0)

The first prototype removes the specified object *t* and supports direct dictionaries.

dt is a function parameter for the *DeleteType* **enum** member. *DeleteType* supports these values:

Value	Description
NoDelete	The object will not be deleted from memory. This is the default value.
DefDelete	The object will be deleted if the container owns its contents, or left in memory if the container does not own its contents.
Delete	The object will be deleted from memory whether or not the container owns its objects.

The second prototype removes the specified pointer * *t* and deletes it if *del* = 1. The second prototype supports indirect dictionary containers. The value *del* and the current ownership setting determine whether the object removed from the container will also be deleted from memory.

Find

T * Find(const T& t)
T * Find(T *t)

The first prototype returns a pointer to item *t*. It supports direct containers.

The second prototype supports indirect containers.

ForEach

void ForEach(IterFunc iter, void * args)

Creates an internal iterator that executes the given function *iter* for each item in the container. The *args* argument lets you pass arbitrary data to the *iter* function.

IterFunc is a **typedef** that maps your implementation function to the signature that *ForEach* recognizes.

Flush

void Flush (DeleteType dt = DefDelete)
void Flush (int del = 0)

Removes all elements from the dictionary without destroying the dictionary. Calls *DeleteElements* for each association object in the dictionary.

The second prototype supports indirect dictionary objects. Deletes the item if *del* = 1.

For indirect dictionary objects, the value *del* determines whether the elements themselves are destroyed. By default, the ownership status of the array determines whether they will be deleted from memory as well, as explained in the *Detach* member function.

GetItemsInContainer

inline unsigned GetItemsInContainer()

Returns the number of items contained in the Dictionary object.

IsEmpty
inline int IsEmpty ()

Returns nonzero if this dictionary object contains no elements.

Iterator methods

Public constructors

Form 1 TDictionaryAsHashTableIterator (const TDictionaryAsHashTable <class T > & t)

TIDictionaryAsHashTableIterator (const TIDictionaryAsHashTable <class T > & t)

Creates an iterator object to traverse direct, unmanaged dictionary objects.

Form 2 TMDictionaryAsHashTableIterator (const TMDictionaryAsHashTable <class T, class A > & t)

TMIDictionaryAsHashTableIterator (const TMIDictionaryAsHashTable <class T, class A > & t)

Creates an iterator object to traverse direct or indirect managed dictionary objects. *A* is the type of your Memory Manager object.

Public member functions

Current
Form 1 const T& Current () const

For direct containers; returns a reference to the current object.

Form 2 T * Current () const

For indirect containers; returns a pointer to the current object.

Restart
void Restart ()

Restarts iteration from the beginning of the dictionary.

Operators

operator ++
Form 1 const T& operator ++ (int)

Moves to the next object and returns the object that was current before the move (postincrement operator).

Form 2 const T& operator ++ ()

Moves to the next object and returns that object (preincrement operator).

operator int
operator int ()

Converts the iterator to an integer value. This operator is used to test for objects remaining in the iterator. This operator returns a nonzero value if the iterator has not finished operating on the array, or a zero value if it has completed iterating.

Double list class template family
dlistimp.h

A double list container manages a chain of nodes, where each node supports a pointer to the previous node and a pointer to the next node in the chain. This family includes eight container classes, together with their corresponding eight iterator classes.

Introduction

Individual containers in this family manage node objects and pointers to node objects. Some classes can automatically maintain a sorted double list. Most classes use the default memory manager *TStandardAllocator*, but you can pass your own memory manager class to managed list class templates.

Normally, a list data structure contains a chain of nodes. To build a list, you must define a node. Containers in this family handle this task for you.

All containers in this family use a protected class, *TMDoubleListElement*, to define and instantiate a node object and manage pointers which position it within the list. You never need to instantiate an object of this class directly.

Classes in this family

Here is a list of classes composing this family. See "Template family syntax" for template prototypes for each template. See "Container members" and "Iterator methods" for member definitions.

Direct templates

- TDoubleListImp
- TMDoubleListImp
- TMSDoubleListImp
- TSDoubleListImp

- TDoubleListIteratorImp
- TMDoubleListIteratorImp
- TMSDoubleListIteratorImp
- TSDoubleListIteratorImp

Indirect templates

- TIDoubleListImp
- TMIDoubleListImp
- TMISDoubleListImp
- TISDoubleListImp

- TIDoubleListIteratorImp
- TMIDoubleListIteratorImp
- TMISDoubleListIteratorImp
- TISDoubleListIteratorImp

Using this class family

Use a double list container when you need to access a list of objects from both ends.

Perform the following steps to use a double list class:

1 Determine the user type for the data you will store in your double list container. Decide whether to store objects themselves in the double list, or pointers to those

objects. Decide whether to use the default memory manager *TStandardAllocator*, or to manage memory yourself, through a memory manager object you write.

2 Select the double list family template that fits your program design. Double list classes can store objects or pointers to objects, and can accept either default or user-supplied memory managers.

  For example, if you have chosen to store pointers to **long**s in a list implemented as a double-linked list, instantiate an object of the *TIDoubleListImp* class.

3 Classes instantiating stored objects of your own user type must provide the functions listed here. Predefined types already provide these functions.

  • Default constructor (direct classes only)
  • Copy constructor
  • Assignment operator
  • Less-than operator (sorted classes only)
  • Equality operator

4 If you have decided to use your own memory manager, then you must overload the **new** and **delete** operator member declarations in your memory manager class to support your new user type.

5 If you plan to use *FirstThat, LastThat,* or *ForEach* member functions to iterate through your double list, then you must write functions to act on data stored in your double list. These functions must conform to a prototype syntax expected by the *FirstThat, LastThat* or *ForEach* member function. For coding convenience, these function prototypes are **typedef**ed as listed under "Container members."

6 To promote code maintainability, you should **typedef** the container and iterator class templates you have selected to use. This makes it easy to change a class template without making changes to your working code.

7 Instantiate a double list container class from your class template. Pass the user type of the data you will store in your double list container class to the class template upon class instantiation. If you have decided to use your own memory manager class, then pass the type of your memory manager to your double list template when you instantiate your double list class.

8 Instantiate a double list container.

9 Instantiate a double list iterator object, if you have decided to use an iterator to access elements in your double list container. Pass your double list container object to your iterator object when you instantiate your iterator object.

Code example

The following example declares an *TDoubleListImp* container named *list*, that holds ten elements of type **long**. It writes ten **long**s to the list, searches the list for the element that holds the value '7', and then deletes that list element. It then calls both *ForEach* and *TDoubleListIteratorImp* to display the contents of the list container. The numbers 1 through 10 display on your screen, minus the number 7.

Note that *ForEach* calls the iteration function called *Show*, which simply displays the contents of the current array element. *ForEach* then moves to the next element in the list, calls *Show* again, and repeats this process until every element in the list has been displayed.

```
#include <iostream.h>
#include <classlib\dlistimp.h>

/* This is the iteration function required by the ForEach member
   function. It displays the contents of the current element c.
*/
void Show ( long& c, void*) { cout << c << endl; }

/* This wrapper function instantiates an iterator object
   called go, passes the container object called dlist into
   it upon instantiation, and shows the contents of each
   dlist node as it is encountered.
*/
void UseIterator ( const TDoubleListImp <long> & dlist )
{
     TDoubleListIteratorImp <long> go (dlist ) ;
     while ( go != 0 )
        {
        cout << go.Current ( ) << endl;
        go++;
        }
}

int main ( )
{
   // Instantiate a doublelist container called dlist.
   TDoubleListImp < long > dlist ;

   for ( int i = 0; i < 10; i++ ) // fill the list
      dlist.Add(i);

   /* You can now call global or member functions at this point to
      act on data contained in the list. This program objects
      containing the value '7' from the container.
   */
   dlist.Detach(7);

   /* Call the dlist::ForEach member function to iterate
      through the list of values. Pass an iterfunct called
      Show to ForEach. This function displays the contents
      of the element it points to each time ForEach calls it.
   */
   cout << "Using ForEach member function to iterate:\n";
   dlist.ForEach ( Show, 0 );

   /* Repeat the iteration process using an iterator object.
      The UseIterator function below combines an instantiation
```

```
        call with a streams call, to display the contents of the
        current element.
    */
    cout << "Using an iterator object to iterate:\n";
    UseIterator( dlist );
    return 0;
}
```

Output

```
Using ForEach member function to iterate:
9
8
6
5
4
3
2
1
0
Using an iterator object to iterate:
9
8
6
5
4
3
2
1
0
```

Template family syntax

This section lists template prototypes and definitions for classes in the double list family.

Direct templates

Objects instantiated from classes listed here contain literal elements of type T.

TDoubleListImp

template <class T> class TDoubleListImp

Creates a double list container holding objects of type T.

TMDoubleListImp

template <class T, class Alloc> class TMDoubleListImp

Creates a double list container holding objects of type T, managed by a memory manager of type *Alloc*.

TMSDoubleListImp

template <class T, class Alloc> class TMSDoubleListImp

Creates a double list container holding objects of type *T*, stored in sorted order in the list, and managed by a memory manager of type *Alloc*.

TSDoubleListImp
template <class T, class Alloc> class TSDoubleListImp

Creates a double list container holding objects of type *T*, stored in sorted order in the list.

Indirect class templates

Objects instantiated from classes listed here contain pointers to double list objects of type *T*.

TIDoubleListImp
template <class T> class TIDoubleListImp

Creates a double list container holding pointers to objects of type T.

TMIDoubleListImp
template <class T, class Alloc> class TMIDoubleListImp

Creates a double list container holding pointers to objects of type *T*. Memory is managed by a user-defined memory manager of type *Alloc*.

TMISDoubleListImp
template <class T, class Alloc> class TMISDoubleListImp

Creates a sorted double list container holding pointers to objects of type *T*. Memory is managed by a user-defined memory manager of type *Alloc*.

TISDoubleListImp
template <class T, class Alloc> class TISDoubleListImp

Creates a sorted double list container holding pointers to objects of type *T*.

Iterator class templates

All iterator classes use their *Current* member to access each object stored in the container they support.

Each iterator class listed here is paired with a container class template which matches its name format. For example, *TIMDoubleListIteratorImp* instantiates an iterator object which takes a *TIMDoubleListImp* container object as its argument. Always select to use the iterator which matches the container type holding the stored objects you want to access.

Direct templates

TDoubleListIteratorImp
template <class T> class TDoubleListIteratorImp

TMDoubleListIteratorImp
template <class T,class Alloc> class TMDoubleListIteratorImp

TMSDoubleListIteratorImp
template <class T,class Alloc> class TMSDoubleListIteratorImp

TSDoubleListIteratorImp
template <class T> class TSDoubleListIteratorImp

Indirect templates

TIDoubleListIteratorImp
template <class T> TIDoubleListIteratorImp

TMIDoubleListIteratorImp
template <class T, class Alloc> TMIDoubleListIteratorImp

TMISDoubleListIteratorImp
template <class T, class Alloc> TMISDoubleListIteratorImp

TISDoubleListIteratorImp
template <class T> class TISDoubleListIteratorImp

Container members

Type definitions

CondFunc
typedef int (*CondFunc) (const T &, void *)

Defines the type and input parameters for an implementation function used as a parameter to *FirstThat* and *LastThat* member functions.

When using *FirstThat* or *LastThat* to iterate through your double list, you must write a function taking a **const** reference to an object of your user type and a **void** pointer. When you call *FirstThat* or *LastThat*, you pass a pointer to this function as as the *cond* input parameter.

IterFunc
typedef void (*IterFunc) (T &, void *)

Defines the type and input parameters for an implementation function used as a parameter to the *ForEach* member function.

When using *ForEach* to iterate through your double list, you must write a function taking a reference to an object of your user type and a **void** pointer. When you call *ForEach*, you pass a pointer to your function as athe *iter* input parameter.

Public constructors
All other constructors in this family are private.

TDoubleListImp ()
TMDoubleListImp ()

Creates a managed double list container.

Public member functions

Add

int Add (const T & t);

int Add (const T *t);

Add the given object *t* at the beginning of the double list.

The first prototype supports direct containers. The second prototype supports indirect containers.

AddAtHead

int AddAtHead (const T & t);

int AddAtHead (const T * t);

Add the given object *t* at the beginning of the double list.

The first prototype supports direct containers. The second prototype supports indirect containers.

AddAtTail

int AddAtTail (const T & t);

int AddAtTail (const T * t);

Add the given object *t* at the end of the double list.

The first prototype supports direct containers. The second prototype supports indirect containers.

Detach

int Detach (const T &);

int Detach (T *t, int del = 0);

Removes the first occurrence of the given object *t*, encountered by searching from the beginning of the list. *del* specifies whether the object should be deleted from memory.

The first prototype supports direct containers. The second prototype supports indirect containers.

DetachAtHead

int DetachAtHead ();

int DetachAtHead (int del = 0);

Removes an item from the head of a double list without searching for a match.

The first prototype supports direct containers. The second prototype supports indirect containers.

DetachAtTail

int DetachAtTail ();

int DetachAtTail (int del = 0);

Removes an item from the tail of a double list.

The first prototype supports direct containers. The second prototype supports indirect containers.

FirstThat

T *FirstThat(CondFunc cond, void *args) const

Returns a pointer to the first object in the double list that satisfies a given condition. You supply a test-function pointer *cond* that returns **true** for a certain condition. You can pass arbitrary arguments via *args*.

CondFunc is a **typedef** which maps your implementation function to the signature which *FirstThat* recognizes. *cond* is your function, which operates on data contained in the current double list element.

ForEach
void ForEach(IterFunc iter, void *args)

ForEach executes the given function *iter* for each element in the double list container. The *args* argument lets you pass arbitrary data to this function. *IteratorOrder* sets the searching order for the container.

IterFunc is a **typedef** which which specifies the return type and input parameters for the function called by *ForEach* to operate on data stored at the current element.

iter is your function, which operates on data contained in the deque that *ForEach* is pointing to. You must write *iter* to take a reference to your node data and a **void** type pointer.

When called, *ForEach* positions a pointer at a deque and calls your function, *iter*. *iter* checks data at that deque, and may change that data based on a condition you define. When finished, *iter* returns control to *ForEach*, which moves to the element node in the deque. *ForEach* repeats this process until it has iterated through the deque.

Flush
void Flush ()
void Flush (int = 0)

Removes all nodes from the double list without destroying the container. The first prototype supports direct double list objects; the second prototype supports indirect double list objects.

For indirect double lists, the value *int* determines whether or not the elements themselves are destroyed by default. The ownership status of the double list determines whether its elements should be deleted from memory.

IsEmpty
int IsEmpty () const

Returns nonzero if the double list contains no elements.

LastThat
T *LastThat(CondFunc cond, void *args) const

Returns a pointer to the last object in the double list that satisfies a given condition. You supply a test function pointer *cond* that returns **true** for a certain condition. You can pass arbitrary arguments to this function via the *args* input parameter. *LastThat* returns zero if no object in the double list meets the condition you specified in the *cond* parameter.

PeekHead
Form 1   const T & PeekHead () const

Returns the a reference to the node at the head of the double list. Supports direct containers.

Form 2   T * PeekHead () const

Returns the a pointer to the node at the head of the double list. The object stays in the double list.

PeekTail

Form 1   const T & PeekTail () const

Returns the a reference to the node at the tail of the double list. Supports direct containers.

Form 2   T * PeekTail () const

Returns the a pointer to the node at the tail of the double list. Supports indirect containers. The object stays in the double list.

Iterator methods

Public constructors

Form 1   TMDoubleListIteratorImp (const TMDoubleListImp <T, Alloc > & I)

Creates an iterator object to traverse *TMDoubleListImp* objects. *Alloc* is the type of your Memory Manager class.

Form 2   TDoubleListIteratorImp (const TDoubleListImp < T > & I)
          TIDoubleListIteratorImp (const TIDoubleListImp < T > & I)

Creates an iterator object to traverse *TDoubleListImp* and *TIDoubleListImp* objects.

Form 3   TMIDoubleListIteratorImp (const TMIDoubleListImp < T, Alloc > & I)

Creates an iterator object to traverse *TMIDoubleListImp* objects. This is a function template which takes your user type as a template parameter. *l* is a reference to a *TMIDoubleListImp* object holding elements of your user type, as an input parameter.

Public member functions

Current

Form 1   const T& Current () const

For direct containers; returns a reference to the current object.

Form 2   T * Current () const

For indirect containers; returns a pointer to the current object.

Restart
void Restart ()

Restarts iteration from the beginning of the double list.

Operators

operator ++
Form 1   const T& operator ++ (int)

Moves to the next object and returns the object that was current before the move (postincrement operator).

Form 2   const T& operator ++ ()

Moves to the next object and returns that object (preincrement operator).

operator int

operator int ()

Converts the iterator to an integer value. This operator is used to test for objects remaining in the iterator. This operator returns a nonzero value if the iterator has not finished operating on the array, or a zero value if it has completed iterating.

Hash table class template family   hashimp.h

Hash table containers define a hash table data structure which manages data of type *T*. All container classes in this family use a hash function to assign a unique key to data placed in the table.

Introduction

The hash table class family includes four container classes, together with their corresponding four iterator classes. Two classes use the default memory manager *TStandardAllocator*. Two other classes can accept your own memory manager class as an input parameter.

Hash table classes are used to implement Dictionary classes. Hash table classes can be used independently, provided that your program provides either a global *HashValue* function, or a *HashValue* member within the class providing objects to be stored. The *HashValue* function for built-in types is already provided.

Classes in this family

Here is a list of container classes composing this family. See "Template family syntax" for template prototypes for each template. See "Container members" and "Iterator methods" for definitions of members all classes use in common.

Direct templates
- THashTableImp
- THashTableImpIterator
- TMHashTableImp
- TMHashTableImpIterator

Indirect templates
- TIHashTableImp
- TIHashTableImpIterator
- TMIHashTableImp
- TMIHashTableImpIterator

Using this class family

Use a hash table container when you need to look up values based on keys and your data does not fit into a dictionary class holding association objects.

Perform the following steps to use a hash table object:

1 Select a data type for the data you will store in a hash table. Decide whether you will store the data itself, or pointers to that data.

If you intend to store objects of your own user type, then you must write a function called *HashValue*, which supports your class type.

HashValue functions for built-in data types are already provided.

2 Select a hash table family template that suits your program design. Hash table classes can hold objects or pointers to objects, and can accept either default or user-supplied memory managers.

3 If your hash table container stores objects of your own data-type, those objects must provide the following functions to support that data type:

- Default constructor (*THashTableImp* class only)
- Copy constructor
- Equivalence operator
- *HashValue* function
- Your *HashValue* function takes a reference to an object *t* as the value to be stored, calculates a unique *unsigned int* (a hash value) based on that object, and returns that **unsigned int** as the key (hash) value bound to that object. It must be called *HashValue*.
- You must write this function. You can include *HashValue* as a member of the class that instantiates objects of your user type, or you can make this function a global function.
- A global HashValue function conforms to this prototype:

  ```
  unsigned HashValue ( const T & t );
  ```
- A *HashValue* function included as a member of your class must conform to the following prototype:

  ```
  unsigned HashValue ( ) const
  ```

4 If you have decided to use your own memory manager to manage hash table objects, then you must overload the new and delete operator members in your memory manager class to support your new user type.

Pass in your memory manager user type as the *Alloc* parameter to your class template when you instantiate a hash table class.

5 If you plan to use the *ForEach* member function in your hash table object, then you must write a function whose signature conforms to the *IterFunc* **typedef**. *ForEach* iterates through each object stored in your hash table. Your custom *iter* function operates on each element in turn.

6 To promote code maintainability, you should **typedef** your hash table container and iterator class template you have selected to use. This makes it easy to change a class template while minimizing changes you may need to make to your working code.

7 Instantiate a container class from the class template you have selected to use. Pass the user type of your container class to the class template upon class instantiation. If you are using a managed class, then you must also pass the type of your memory manager class to the template.

8 Instantiate an object of your class.

9 Instantiate an iterator object, if you have decided to iterate through elements stored in your hash table object. Pass your hash table object to the iterator object upon instantiation.

Template family syntax

This section lists template prototypes and definitions for classes in the Hash table family.

Direct templates

Containers instantiated from classes listed here contain objects.

THashTableImp

template <class T> class THashTableImp

Creates a hash table object containing objects of type T.

TMHashTableImp

template <class T, class Alloc> class TMHashTableImp

Creates a managed hash table container, which holds objects of type T. Memory is managed by a user-defined memory manager of type *Alloc*.

Indirect class templates

Classes listed here manage pointers to objects.

TIHashTableImp

template <class T> class TIHashTableImp

Creates a hash table object containing pointers to objects of type T.

TMIHashTableImp

template <class T, class Alloc> class TMIHashTableImp

Creates a hash table object containing pointers to objects of type T.

Iterator class templates

All iterator classes use their *Current* member to access each object stored in the container they support.

Each iterator class listed here is paired with a container class template which matches its name format. For example, *TIMHashTableIteratorImp* instantiates an iterator object which takes a *TIMAsHashTableImp* container object as its argument. Always select to use the iterator which matches the container type holding the stored objects you want to access.

Direct templates

THashTableIteratorImp
template <class T> class THashTableIteratorImp

TMHashTableIteratorImp
template <class T,class Alloc> class TMHashTableIteratorImp

Indirect templates

TIHashTableIteratorImp
template <class T> TIDictionaryAsHashTable

TMIHashTableIteratorImp
template <class T, class Alloc> TMIHashTableIteratorImp

Container members

Type definitions

IterFunc
typedef void (*IterFunc) (T &, void *)
Function type used as a parameter to the *ForEach* member function.

When using *ForEach* to iterate through your hash table, you must write a function taking a reference to an object of your user type and a **void** pointer. When you call *ForEach*, you pass *IterFunc* as an input parameter, which is a pointer to this function.

Public constructors
TMHashTableImp (unsigned aPrime = DEFAULT_HASH_TABLE_SIZE)
THashTableImp (unsigned aPrime = DEFAULT_HASH_TABLE_SIZE)
TMIHashTableImp (unsigned aPrime = DEFAULT_HASH_TABLE_SIZE)
TIHashTableImp (unsigned aPrime = DEFAULT_HASH_TABLE_SIZE)
Constructs a hash table container.

Public member functions

Add
int Add(const T & t)
int Add (T * t)
For direct hash table objects, the first prototype adds object *t* to the hash table.

For indirect hash table objects, the second prototype adds a pointer to object *t* to the hash table.

The first prototype supports direct hash table containers. The second prototype supports indirect hash table containers.

Detach

int Detach(T & t, int del = 0)

int Detach(T * t, int del = 0)

The first prototype removes the specified object *t*. Supports direct containers.

The second prototype removes the specified pointer * *t* and deletes it if *del* = 1. Supports indirect hash table objects. The value *del* and the current ownership setting determine whether the removed object will also be deleted from memory.

Find

T * Find(const T& t) const

T * Find(const T * t) const

For direct containers, the first prototype returns a pointer to item *t*.

For indirect containers, the second prototype returns a pointer to item *t*.

Flush

void Flush ()

void Flush (int del = 0)

For direct containers, the first prototype removes all elements from the hash table without destroying the hash table.

For indirect containers, the value *del* determines whether the elements themselves are destroyed. If *del* =1, the element will be deleted from memory. If *del* = 0; the element will be retained in memory.

ForEach

void ForEach(IterFunc iter, void * args)

ForEach executes the given function *iter* for each element stored in the hash table. The *args* argument lets you pass arbitrary data to this function.

IterFunc is a **typedef** which which specifies the return type and input parameters for the function called by *ForEach* to operate on data stored at the current hash table entry. This is a predefined **typedef**.

iter is your function, which operates on data contained at the table entry that *ForEach* is pointing to. You must write *iter* to take a reference to your node data and a **void** type pointer.

When called, *ForEach* positions a pointer at the first table entry and calls your function, iter. *iter* checks data at that location, and can change that data based on a condition you define. When finished, *iter* returns control to *ForEach*, which moves to the next table entry. *ForEach* repeats this process until it has visited every entry stored on the hash table.

GetItemsInContainer

unsigned GetItemsInContainer() const

Returns the number of items contained in the hash table object.

IsEmpty

int IsEmpty () const

Returns 1 if this hash table object contains no elements.

Container operators

operator delete
operator delete;
Deletes a value from the hash table container.

operator delete [ ]
operator delete [];
Deletes the value stored at the given position in the container.

Iterator methods

Public constructors

Form 1   TMHashTableIteratorImp (const TMHashTableImp < class T, class A > & h)
THashTableIteratorImp (const THashTableImp < class T > & h)
Creates an iterator object to traverse direct hash table objects.

Form 2   TMIHashTableIteratorImp (const TMIHashTableImp < class T, class A > & h)
Creates an iterator object to traverse indirect hash table objects. *A* is the type of your Memory Manager class.

Form 3   THashTableImpIterator (const T_HashTableImp <class T > & t)
Creates an iterator object to traverse direct, unmanaged hash table objects.

Public member functions

Current
Form 1   const T& Current () const
For direct containers; returns a reference to the current object.

Form 2   T * Current () const
For indirect containers; returns a pointer to the current object.

Restart
void Restart ()
Restarts iteration from the beginning of the hash table.

Iterator operators

operator ++
Form 1   const T& operator ++ (int)
const T * operator ++ (int)
Moves to the next object and returns the object that was current before the move (postincrement operator). The second prototype supports indirect containers.

Form 2   const T& operator ++ ()
const T * operator ++ ()
Moves to the next object and returns that object (preincrement operator). The second prototype supports indirect containers.

operator int

operator int ()

Converts the iterator to an integer value. This operator is used to test for objects remaining in the iterator. This operator returns a nonzero value if the iterator has not finished operating on the array, or a zero value if it has completed iterating.

List class template family   listimp.h

List containers manage a chain of nodes containing data of type *T*, where each node supports a pointer to the previous node in the chain. This family includes eight container classes, together with their corresponding eight iterator classes.

Introduction

Individual containers in this family manage node objects and pointers to node objects. Some classes can automatically maintain a sorted list. Most classes use the default memory manager *TStandardAllocator*, but you can pass your own memory manager class to managed container class templates.

Normally, a list data structure contains a chain of nodes. To build a list, you must define a node. Containers in this family handle this task for you.

All containers in this family use a protected class, *TListElement*, to define and instantiate a node object and manage pointers which position it within the list. You never need to instantiate an object of this class directly.

Classes in this family

Here is a list of classes composing this family. See "Template family syntax" for template prototypes for each template. See "Container members" and "Iterator methods" for member definitions.

Direct templates
- TListImp
- TMListImp
- TMSListImp
- TSListImp
- TListIteratorImp
- TMListIteratorImp
- TMSListIteratorImp
- TSListIteratorImp

Indirect templates
- TIListImp
- TMIListImp
- TMISListImp
- TISListImp
- TIListIteratorImp
- TMIListIteratorImp
- TMISListIteratorImp
- TISListIteratorImp

Using this class family

Use a list container when you need to insert and remove stored objects from only one end of the list.

Perform the following steps to use a list class:

1 Determine the type for the data you will store in your list container. Decide whether to store objects themselves in the list, or pointers to those objects. Decide whether to use the default memory manager *TStandardAllocator*, or to manage memory yourself.

2 Select the list family template that fits your program design. List classes can store objects or pointers to objects, and can accept either default or user-supplied memory managers.

   For example, if you have chosen to store pointers to longs in a list implemented as a double-linked list, instantiate an object of the *TIListImp* class.

3 Classes instantiating stored objects of your own user type must provide the functions listed here. Predefined types already provide these functions.
   - Default constructor (direct classes only)
   - Copy constructor
   - Assignment operator
   - Less-than operator (sorted classes only)
   - Equality operator

4 If you have decided to use your own memory manager, then you must overload the *new* and *delete* operator member declarations in your memory manager class to support your new user type.

5 If you plan to use *FirstThat*, *LastThat* or *ForEach* member functions to iterate through your list, then you must write functions to act on data stored in your list. These functions must conform to a prototype syntax expected by the *FirstThat*, *LastThat* or *ForEach* member function. For coding convenience, these function prototypes are **typedef**ed as listed under "Container members."

6 To promote code maintainability, you should **typedef** the container and iterator class templates you have selected to use. This makes it easy to change a class template without making changes to your working code.

7 Instantiate a list container class from the class template you have selected to use. Pass the data type of the objects you will store in your list container class to the class template upon class instantiation. If you are using a managed class, then you must also pass the type of your memory manager class to the template.

8 Instantiate a list container object.

9 Instantiate a list iterator object, if you have decided to use an iterator to access elements in your list container. Pass your list container object to your iterator object when you instantiate your iterator object.

Code example

The following example declares an *TListImp* container named *list*, that holds ten elements of type *long*. It writes ten **long**s to the list, searches the list for the element that holds the value '7', and then deletes that list element. It then calls both *ForEach* and

TListIteratorImp to display the contents of the list container. The numbers 1 through 10 display on your screen, minus the number 7.

Note that *ForEach* calls the iteration function called *Show*, which simply displays the contents of the current array element. *ForEach* then moves to the next element in the list, calls *Show* again, and repeats this process until every element in the list has been displayed.

```
#include <iostream.h>
#include <classlib\listimp.h>

/* This is the iteration function required by the ForEach member
   function. It displays the contents of the current element c.
*/
void Show ( long& c, void*) { cout << c << endl; }

/* This wrapper function instantiates an iterator object called go,
   passes the container object called list into it upon instantiation,
   and shows the contents of each list node as it is encountered.
*/
void UseIterator ( const TListImp <long> & list )
{
    TListIteratorImp <long> go(list);
        while ( go != 0 )
            {
            cout << go.Current( ) << endl;
            go++;
            }
}

int main ( )
{
    /* Instantiate a List container called list. */
    TListImp < long > list;

    for (int i = 0; i < 10; i++ ) // fill the array
        list.Add ( i );

    /* You may now call global or member functions at this point to
       act on data contained in the list. This program detaches any
       object in the list which contains the long value '7'.
    */
    list.Detach(7);

    /* Call the list ForEach member function to iterate through the
       list of values. Pass an iteration function called Show to
       ForEach. This function displays the contents of the element
       it points to each time ForEach calls it.
    */
    cout << "Using ForEach member function to iterate:\n";
    list.ForEach ( Show, 0 );

    /* Repeat the iteration process using an iterator object.
```

```
              The UseIterator function below combines an instantiation
              call with a streams call, to display the contents of the
              current element.
        */
        cout << "\nUsing an iterator object to iterate:\n";
        UseIterator(list);
        return 0;
}
```

Output

```
Using ForEach member function to iterate:
9
8
6
5
4
3
2
1
0

Using an iterator object to iterate:
9
8
6
5
4
3
2
1
0
```

Template family syntax

Direct templates
Objects instantiated from classes listed here contain data of type *T*.

TListImp
template <class T> class TListImp
Creates a list container holding objects of type *T*.

TMListImp
template <class T, class Alloc> class TMListImp
Creates a list container holding objects of type *T*, managed by a memory manager of type *Alloc*.

TMSListImp
template <class T, class Alloc> class TMSListImp

Creates a list container holding objects of type *T*, stored in sorted order in the list, and managed by a memory manager of type *Alloc*.

TSListImp

template <class T, class Alloc> class TSListImp

Creates a list container holding objects of type *T*, stored in sorted order in the list.

Indirect class templates

Objects instantiated from classes listed here contain pointers to list objects of type *T*.

TIListImp

template <class T> class TIListImp

Creates a list container holding pointers to objects of type *T*.

TMIListImp

template <class T, class Alloc> class TMIListImp

Creates a list container holding pointers to objects of type *T*. Memory is managed by a user-defined memory manager.

TMISListImp

template <class T, class Alloc> class TMISListImp

Creates a sorted list container holding pointers to objects of type *T*. Memory is managed by a user-defined memory manager.

TISListImp

template <class T, class Alloc> class TISListImp

Creates a sorted list container holding pointers to objects of type *T*.

Iterator class templates

All iterator classes use their *Current* member to access each object stored in the container they support.

Each iterator class listed here is paired with a container class template which matches its name format. For example, *TIMListIteratorImp* instantiates an iterator object which takes a *TIMListImp* container object as its argument. Always use the iterator which matches the container type holding the stored objects you want to access.

Direct templates

TListIteratorImp

template <class T> class TListIteratorImp

TMListIteratorImp

template <class T,class Alloc> class TMListIteratorImp

TMSListIteratorImp

template <class T,class Alloc> class TMSListIteratorImp

TSListIteratorImp

template <class T> class TSListIteratorImp

Indirect templates

TIListIteratorImp
template <class T> TIListIteratorImp

TMIListIteratorImp
template <class T, class Alloc> TMIListIteratorImp

TMISListIteratorImp
template <class T, class Alloc> TMISListIteratorImp

TISListIteratorImp
template <class T> class TISListIteratorImp

Container members

Type definitions

CondFunc
typedef int (*CondFunc) (const T &, void *)

Defines the type and input parameters for an implementation function used as a parameter to *FirstThat* and *LastThat* member functions.

When using *FirstThat* or *LastThat* to iterate through your list, you must write a function taking a **const** reference to an object of your user type and a **void** pointer. When you call *FirstThat* or *LastThat*, you pass a pointer to this function as as the *cond* input parameter.

IterFunc
typedef void (*IterFunc) (T &, void *)

Defines the type and input parameters for an implementation function used as a parameter to the *ForEach* member function.

When using *ForEach* to iterate through your list, you must write a function taking a reference to an object of your user type and a **void** pointer. When you call *ForEach*, you pass a pointer to your function as the *iter* input parameter.

Public constructors

Constructors for indirect list classes are private.
TListImp ()
TMListImp ()
Creates an empty list container.

Public member functions

Add
int Add (const T & t);
int Add (const T *t);
Add the given object *t* at the beginning of the list.

The first prototype supports direct containers. The second prototype supports indirect containers.

Detach

int Detach (const T &);

int Detach (T *t, int del = 0);

Removes the first occurence of the given object *t*, encountered by searching from the beginning of the list. *del* = 0 specifies that the object will be removed from the container but kept in memory. *del* = 1 specifies that the object will be removed from the container but kept in memory.

The first prototype supports direct containers. The second prototype supports indirect containers.

DetachAtHead

int DetachAtHead ();

int DetachAtHead (int del = 0);

Removes an item from the head of a list without searching for a match.

The first prototype supports direct containers. The second prototype supports indirect containers.

FirstThat

T *FirstThat(CondFunc cond, void *args) const

Returns a pointer to the first object in the list that satisfies a given condition. You supply a test-function pointer *cond* that returns **true** for a certain condition. You can pass arbitrary arguments via *args*.

CondFunc is a **typedef** which maps your implementation function to the signature which *FirstThat* recognizes. *cond* is your callback function, which operates on data contained in the current list node.

ForEach

void ForEach(IterFunc iter, void *args)

ForEach executes the given function *iter* for each element in the list container. The *args* argument lets you pass arbitrary data to this function. *IteratorOrder* sets the searching order for the container.

IterFunc is a **typedef** which which specifies the return type and input parameters for the function called by *ForEach* to operate on data stored at the current element.

iter is your function, which operates on data contained in the deque that *ForEach* is pointing to. You must write *iter* to take a pointer to your node data and a **void** type pointer.

When called, *ForEach* positions a pointer at a list node and calls your function, *iter*. *iter* checks data at that node, and may change that data based on a condition you define. When finished, *iter* returns control to *ForEach*, which moves to the node in the list. *ForEach* repeats this process until it has iterated through the list.

Flush

void Flush ()

void Flush (int del = 0)

Removes all nodes from the list without destroying the container.

The first prototype supports direct list objects; the second prototype supports indirect list objects.

For indirect lists, *del* determines whether or objects referenced by their pointers will be deleted from memory. Set *del* to a nonzero value to delete objects from memory. Set *del* to zero to keep objects in memory.

IsEmpty

int IsEmpty () const

Returns nonzero if the list contains no elements.

LastThat

T *LastThat(CondFunc cond, void *args) const

Returns a pointer to the last object in the list that satisfies a given condition. You supply a test function pointer *cond* that returns **true** for a certain condition. You can pass arbitrary arguments to this function via the *args* input parameter. *LastThat* returns zero if no object in the list meets the condition you specified in your function pointed to by *cond*.

PeekHead

const T & PeekHead () const

T * PeekHead () const

Returns the a reference to the node at the head of the list. The object stays in the list.

Iterator methods

Public constructors

Form 1   TMListIteratorImp (const TMListImp <T, Alloc > & I)

Creates an iterator object to traverse *TMListImp* objects. *Alloc* is the type of your Memory Manager.

Form 2   TListIteratorImp (const TListImp < T > & I)

TIListIteratorImp (const TIListImp < T > & I)

Creates an iterator object to traverse *TListImp* and *TIListImp* objects.

Form 3   TMIListIteratorImp (const TMIListImp < T, Alloc > & I)

Creates an iterator object to traverse *TMIListImp* objects. This is a function template which takes your user type as a template parameter. *I* is a reference to a *TMIListImp* object holding elements of your user type, as input parameters.

Public member functions

Current

Form 1   const T& Current () const

For direct containers; returns a reference to the current object.

Form 2   T * Current () const

For indirect containers; returns a pointer to the current object.

Restart

void Restart ()

Restarts iteration from the beginning of the list.

Operators

operator ++

Form 1   const T& operator ++ (int)

Moves to the next object and returns the object that was current before the move (postincrement operator).

Form 2   const T& operator ++ ()

Moves to the next object and returns that object (preincrement operator).

operator int

operator int ()

Converts the iterator to an integer value. This operator is used to test for objects remaining in the iterator. This operator returns a nonzero value if the iterator has not finished operating on the array, or a zero value if it has completed iterating.

Queue class template family   queues.h

A queue container manages a train of objects, where objects are added to the train from the tail position, and removed from the train from the head position. This family includes nine container classes, together with their corresponding nine iterator classes.

Introduction

Individual containers in this family manage objects and pointers to objects. Most classes use the default memory manager *TStandardAllocator*, but you can pass your own memory manager class to managed container class templates.

You can implement queue structures as vectors or as double-linked lists. Both kinds of class templates take the same parameters and present the same list of member functions. For example, if you change your class user type from *TQueueAsVector* to *TQueueAsDoubleList, you* will not need to change calls you made to queue member functions in your source code.

A *QueueAsVector* class can not be resized; a *QueueAsList* class can be resized.

Class family list

Here is a list of classes composing this family. See "Template family syntax" for template prototypes for each template. See "Container members" and "Iterator methods" for member definitions.

Direct templates

- TQueueAsVector
- TQueueAsDoubleList
- TMQueueAsVector
- TMQueueAsDoubleList
- TQueue

- TQueueAsVectorIterator
- TQueueAsDoubleListIterator
- TMQueueAsVectorIterator
- TMQueueAsDoubleListIterator
- TQueueIterator

Indirect templates

- TIQueueAsVector
- TIQueueAsDoubleList
- TMIQueueAsVector
- TMIQueueAsDoubleList

- TIQueueAsVectorIterator
- TIQueueAsDoubleListIterator
- TMIQueueAsVectorIterator
- TMIQueueAsDoubleListIterator

Using this class family

Use a queue container when you need to store data in a FIFO structure.

Perform the following steps to use a queue class:

1   Determine the data type for the element you will store in your queue container. Decide whether to store objects themselves in the queue, or to store pointers to those objects. Decide whether to use the default memory manager *TStandardAllocator*, or to manage memory yourself.

2   Select the queue family template that fits your program design. Queue classes can store objects or pointers to objects, and can accept either default or user-supplied memory managers. You also may select to implement your queue as a double-linked list, or as a vector.

3   For example, if you have chosen to store pointers to longs in a queue implemented as a double-linked list, instantiate an object of the *TIQueueAsDoubleList* class.

4   Classes instantiating stored objects of your own user type must provide the functions listed here. Predefined types already provide these functions.
    - Default constructor (all classes)
    - Copy constructor (all vector classes; indirect double list classes)
    - Assignment operator (direct vector classes)
    - Equality operator (indirect double list classes)

5   If you have decided to use your own memory manager, then you must overload the **new** and **delete** operator member declarations in your memory manager class to support your new user type.

    If you plan to use *FirstThat, LastThat,* or *ForEach* member functions to iterate through your queue, then you must write functions to act on data stored in your queue. These functions must conform to a prototype syntax expected by the *FirstThat, LastThat,* or *ForEach* member function. For coding convenience, these function prototypes are **typedef**ed as listed under "Container members."

6   To promote code maintainability, you should **typedef** the container and iterator class templates you have selected to use. This makes it easy to change a class template without making changes to your working code.

7 Instantiate a queue container class from the class template you have selected to use. Pass the data type of the objects you will store in your queue container class to the class template upon class instantiation. If you are using a managed class, then you must also pass the type of your memory manager class to the template.

8 Instantiate a queue container object. Pass the default queue size to this object upon instantiation.

9 Instantiate a queue iterator object, if you have decided to use an iterator to access elements in your queue container. Pass your queue container object to your iterator object when you instantiate your iterator object.

Code example

This example illustrates a queue storing pointers to strings implemented as a double-linked list.

```
#include <iostream.h>
#include <strstrea.h>
#include <classlib\queues.h>
#include <string.h>

typedef TIQueueAsDoubleList < string > lQueue;

int main ( )
{
    lQueue d;

    for ( int i = 1; i < 5; i++)
        {
        string* s = new string("string ");
        *s += (char)('0' + i);
        d.Put ( s );
        }
    cout << "Queue Contents:" << endl;

    while ( !d.IsEmpty () )
        {
        // Must dereference when using an indirect container
        string* s = d.Get ( );
        cout << *s << endl;
        delete s;
        }
    return 0;
}
```

Output

```
Queue Contents:
string 1
string 2
string 3
string 4
```

Template family syntax

This section lists template prototypes and definitions for classes in the queue family.

Direct templates

Objects instantiated from classes listed here contain elements of type T.

TQueueAsDoubleList
TQueueAsVector

template <class T> class TQueueAsDoubleList

template <class T> class TQueueAsVector

Creates a queue container holding objects of type T. The first prototype implements the queue as a double-linked list. The second prototype implements the queue as a vector.

TMQueueAsDoubleList
TMQueueAsVector

template <class T, class Alloc> class TMQueueAsDoubleList

template <class T, class Alloc> class TMQueueAsVector

Creates a queue container holding objects of type T, managed by a memory manager of type *Alloc*. The first prototype implements the queue as a double-linked list. The second prototype implements the queue as a vector.

Indirect class templates

Objects instantiated from classes listed here contain pointers to queue objects of type T.

TIQueueAsDoubleList
TIQueueAsVector

template <class T> class TIQueueAsDoubleList

template <class T> class TIQueueAsVector

Creates a queue container holding pointers to objects of type T. The first prototype implements the queue as a double-linked list. The second prototype implements the queue as a vector.

TMIQueueAsDoubleList
TMIQueueAsVector

template <class T, class Alloc> class TMIQueueAsDoubleList

template <class T, class Alloc> class TMIQueueAsVector

Creates a queue container holding pointers to objects of type T. Memory is managed by a user-defined memory manager. The first prototype implements the queue as a double-linked list. The second prototype implements the queue as a vector.

Iterator class templates

All iterator classes use their *Current* member to access each object stored in the container they support.

Each iterator class listed here is paired with a container class template that matches its name format. For example, *TIMQueueAsVectorIterator* instantiates an iterator object that takes a *TIMQueueAsVector* container object as its argument. Always select to use the iterator that matches the container type holding the stored objects you want to access.

Direct templates

TQueueAsVectorIterator
template <class T> class TQueueAsVectorIterator

TQueueAsListIterator
template <class T,class Alloc> class TMQueueAsListIterator

TMQueueAsVectorIterator
template <class T,class Alloc> class TMQueueAsVectorIterator

TMQueueAsListIterator
template <class T> class TMQueueAsListIterator

Indirect templates

TIQueueAsVectorIterator
template <class T> class TIQueueAsVectorIterator

TIQueueAsListIterator
template <class T,class Alloc> class TIQueueAsListIterator

TIMQueueAsVectorIterator
template <class T,class Alloc> class TIMQueueAsVectorIterator

TIMQueueAsListIterator
template <class T> class TIMQueueAsListIterator

Container members

Type definitions

CondFunc
typedef int (*CondFunc) (const T &, void *)

Defines the return type and input parameters for the user-written function used as an input parameter to the *FirstThat* and *LastThat* member functions.

When using *FirstThat* or *LastThat* to iterate through your queue, you must write a function taking a **const** reference to an object of your user type and a **void** pointer. When you call *FirstThat* or *LastThat*, you pass a pointer to this function as as the *cond* input parameter.

IterFunc
typedef void (*IterFunc) (T &, void *)

Defines the return type and input parameters for the user-written function used as an input parameter to the *ForEach* member function.

When using *ForEach* to iterate through your queue, you must write a function taking a reference to an object of your user type and a **void** pointer. When you call *ForEach*, you pass a pointer to your function as the *iter* input parameter.

Public constructors

QueueAsList classes call the protected default *TQueueAsDoubleListImp* constructor, which takes no parameters.

TQueueAsVector (unsigned max = DEFAULT_QUEUE_SIZE)
TMQueueAsVector (unsigned max = DEFAULT_QUEUE_SIZE)
TIQueueAsVector (unsigned sz = DEFAULT_QUEUE_SIZE)
TMIQueueAsVector (unsigned sz = DEFAULT_QUEUE_SIZE)

Creates a queue container with a default maximum size of DEFAULT_QUEUE_SIZE.

Public member functions

FirstThat

T *FirstThat(CondFunc cond, void *args) const

Iterates through the queue from head to tail and returns a pointer to the first object in the queue that satisfies a given condition. You supply a pointer *cond* to a user-written test-function that returns **true** for a certain condition. You can pass arbitrary arguments via *args*.

CondFunc is a **typedef** that defines parameters for a function passed as an input parameter to *FirstThat*. *cond* is your function, that operates on data contained in the current queue element.

ForEach

void ForEach(IterFunc iter, void *args)

ForEach executes the given function *iter* for each element in the queue. The args argument lets you pass arbitrary data to this function. *IteratorOrder* sets the searching order for the queue.

IterFunc is a **typedef** that specifies the return type and input parameters for the function called by *ForEach* to operate on data stored at the current element.

iter is your function, that operates on data contained in the queue that *ForEach* is pointing to. You must write *iter* to take a reference to an element and a **void** type pointer.

When called, *ForEach* positions a pointer at a queue and calls your function, *iter*. *iter* checks data at that queue, and may change that data based on a condition you define. When finished, *iter* returns control to *ForEach*, that moves to the element in the queue. *ForEach* repeats this process until it has iterated through the queue.

Flush

void Flush ()

void Flush (TShouldDelete::DeleteType dt = TShouldDelete::DefDelete)

Removes all elements from the queue without destroying it.

The first prototype supports direct queue objects; the second prototype supports indirect queue objects.

For indirect queues, *Flush* removes pointers to data. The ownership status of the queue determines whether objects referenced by those pointers will be deleted from memory. The value *TShouldDelete::DefDelete* sets items to be removed from memory if they are owned by the queue container. *Delete* always removes items, no matter who owns them. *NoDelete* never removes items from memory.

Get
T Get ()

T * Get ()

Removes and returns the object pointer from the queue. If the queue is empty, it returns 0. If the queue is empty, it throws the *PRECONDITION* exception in the debug version. In the non-debug version, *Get* returns a meaningless object if the queue is empty.

The first prototype supports direct templates. The second prototype supports indirect templates.

GetItemsInContainer
unsigned GetItemsInContainer() const

Returns the number of items in the queue.

IsEmpty
int IsEmpty () const

Returns nonzero if the queue contains no elements.

IsFull
int IsFull () const

Returns nonzero if the queue is full.

LastThat
T *LastThat(CondFunc cond, void *args) const

Iterates through the queue from head to tail and returns a pointer to the last object in the queue that satisfies a given condition.

You must supply a test function pointer *cond* that returns **true** for a condition you define. You can pass arbitrary arguments to this function via the *args* input parameter. *LastThat* returns zero if no object in the queue meets the condition you specified in *cond*.

Put
void Put (const T &) const

void Put (T * t) const

Adds the object to the tail of the queue.

The first prototype supports direct templates. The second prototype supports indirect templates.

Operators
Queue containers have no operators.

Iterator methods

Iterator constructors
Form 1   TMQueueAsVectorIterator (const TMQueueAsVector <class T, class Alloc > & d)

Creates an iterator object to traverse objects stored in *TMQueueAsVector* containers. *Alloc* is the type of your Memory Manager object.

Form 2   TQueueAsVectorIterator (const TQueueAsVector < class T > & d)

TIQueueAsVectorIterator (const TIQueueAsVector < class T > & d)

Creates an iterator object to traverse objects stored in *TQueueAsVector* and *TIQueueAsVector* containers.

Form 3   TMIQueueAsVectorIterator (const TMIQueueAsVector < T, Alloc > & d)

TMIQueueAsVectorIterator (const TMIQueueAsVector<T,Alloc>&);

Creates an iterator object to traverse objects stored in *TMIQueueAsVector* containers.

Public member functions

Current
Form 1   const T& Current () const

For direct containers; returns a reference to the current object.

Form 2   T * Current () const

For indirect containers; returns a pointer to the current object.

Restart
void Restart ()

Restarts iteration from the beginning of the queue.

Operators

operator ++
Form 1   const T& operator ++ (int)

Moves to the next object and returns the object that was current before the move (postincrement operator).

Form 2   const T& operator ++ ()

Moves to the next object and returns that object (preincrement operator).

operator int
operator int ()

Converts the iterator to an integer value. This operator is used to test for objects remaining in the iterator. This operator returns a nonzero value if the iterator has not finished operating on the array, or a zero value if it has completed iterating.

Set class template family   sets.h

Set containers manage data items as an unordered group of non-repeating objects. The set family includes four container classes, together with their corresponding four iterator classes.

Introduction

Individual containers in this family manage objects and pointers to objects. Most classes use the default memory manager *TStandardAllocator*, but you can pass your own memory manager object to managed container classes upon instantiation.

Class family list

Here is a list of container classes composing this family. See "Template family syntax" for template prototypes for each template. See "Container members" and "Iterator methods" for definitions of members all classes use in common.

Direct templates
- TSetAsVector
- TMSetAsVector

- TSetAsVectorIterator
- TMSetAsVectorIterator

Indirect templates
- TISetAsVector
- TMISetAsVector

- TISetAsVectorIterator
- TMISetAsVectorIterator

Using this class family

Use a set container when you need to store data in an unstructured container, and do not want to retain duplicated data.

Perform the following steps to use a set class:

1 Determine the data type for the element you will store in your set container. Decide whether to store objects themselves in the set, or pointers to those objects. Decide whether to use a default memory manager.

2 Select the set family template that fits your program design. Set classes can accept objects or pointers to objects, can accept either default or user-supplied memory managers, and can sort elements as they are added to the set container.

3 Classes instantiating stored objects of your own user type must provide the functions listed here. Predefined types already provide these functions.
- Default constructor (direct classes only)
- Copy constructor (all classes)
- Assignment operator (direct classes only)
- Equivalence operator (all classes)

4 If you have decided to use your own memory manager to manage set elements, then you must overload the *new* and *delete* operator member declarations in your memory manager class to support your new user type.

5 If you plan to use *FirstThat*, *LastThat*, or *ForEach* member functions to iterate through your Set, then you must write functions to act on data stored in your Set. These functions must conform to a prototype syntax expected by the *FirstThat*, *LastThat*, or *ForEach* member function. For coding convenience, these function prototypes are **typedef**ed as listed under "Container members."

6 To promote code maintainability, you should **typedef** the container and iterator class templates you have selected to use. This makes it easy to change a class template while minimizing changes you may need to make to your working code.

7 Instantiate a set container class from the class template you have selected to use. Pass the data type of the objects you will store in your set container, to the class template upon class instantiation. If you are using a managed class, then you must also pass the type of your memory manager class to the template.

8 Instantiate a set container object.

9 Instantiate a set iterator, if you have decided to use an iterator to access elements in your set container. Pass your set container object to your iterator object when you instantiate your iterator object.

Code example

The following example below declares a *TSetAsVector* container named *set*, that holds ten elements of type **long**. It fills the set, searches the set for the element that holds the value '7', and then deletes that set element. It then calls both *ForEach* and *TSetAsVectorIterator* to display the contents of the set container. The numbers 1 through 10 display on your screen, minus the number 7.

Note that *ForEach* calls the iteration function called *Show*, which simply displays the contents of the current set element. *ForEach* then moves to the next element in the set, calls *Show* again, and repeats this process until every element in the set has been displayed.

```
#include <iostream.h>
#include<classlib\sets.h>

/* Here is an iteration function required by the ForEach member function.
   It displays the contents of the current element c.
*/
void Show ( long& c, void*)  { cout << c << endl; }

/* This wrapper function instantiates an iterator object called go,
   passes the container object called set into it upon instantiation,
   and shows the contents of each set set element as it is encountered.
*/
void UseIterator ( const TSetAsVector < long > & set )
   {
   TSetAsVectorIterator < long > go (set);
   while ( go != 0 )
      {
      cout << go.Current( ) << endl;
      go++;
      }
   }

int main ( )
   {
```

```
        // Instantiate a set container called set that holds 10 longs.
        TSetAsVector < long > set( 10 );

        for ( int i = 0; i < 10; i++ ) // fill set
            set.Add( i );

        /* You can now call global or member functions at this point to
           act on data contained in the Set. This program detaches any
           object in the Set which contains the long value '7'.
        */
        set.Detach ( 7 );

        /* Call the set ForEach member function to iterate through the Set.
           Pass an iteration function called Show to ForEach. This function
           displays the contents of the element it points to each time
           ForEach calls it.
        */
        cout << "Using ForEach member function to iterate:\n";
        set.ForEach( Show, 0 );

        /* Repeat the iteration process using an iterator object.
           The UseIterator function below combines an instantiation
           call with a streams call, to display the contents of the
           current element.
        */
        cout << "\nUsing an iterator object to iterate:\n";
        UseIterator ( set );
        return 0;
}
```

Output

```
Using ForEach member function to iterate:
0
1
2
3
4
5
6
8
9

Using an iterator object to iterate:
0
1
2
3
4
5
6
8
9
```

Template family syntax

This section lists template prototypes and definitions for classes in the set family.

Direct templates

Objects instantiated from classes listed here contain elements of type T.

TSetAsVector

template <class T> class TSetAsVector

Creates a set container storing objects of type T.

TMSetAsVector

template <class T, class Alloc> class TMSetAsVector

Creates a set container storing objects of type T, managed by a memory manager of type *Alloc*.

Indirect class templates

Objects instantiated from classes listed here contain pointers to set elements of type T.

TISetAsVector

template <class T> class TISetAsVector

Creates a set container storing pointers to objects of type T.

TMISetAsVector

template <class T, class Alloc> class TMISetAsVector

Creates a set container storing pointers to objects of type T. Memory is managed by a user-defined memory manager of type *Alloc*.

Iterator class templates

All iterator classes use their *Current* member to access each object stored in the container they support.

Each iterator class listed here is paired with a container class template which matches its name format. For example, *TIMSetAsVectorIterator* instantiates an iterator object which takes a *TIMSetAsVector* container object as its argument. Always use the iterator which matches the container type holding the stored objects you want to access.

Direct templates

TSetAsVectorIterator

template <class T> class TSetAsVectorIterator

TMSetAsVectorIterator

template <class T,class Alloc> class TMSetAsVectorIterator

Indirect templates

TISetAsVectorIterator

template <class T> class TISetAsVectorIterator

TIMSetAsVectorIterator

template <class T,class Alloc> class TIMSetAsVectorIterator

Container members

Type definitions

CondFunc

typedef int (*condFunc) (const T &, void *)

Defines input parameters for a function which is used as a parameter to *FirstThat* and *LastThat* member functions.

When using *FirstThat* or *LastThat* to iterate through your set, you must write a function taking a **const** reference to an object of your user type and a **void** pointer. When you call *FirstThat* or *LastThat*, you pass a pointer to your function as an input parameter.

IterFunc

typedef void (*IterFunc) (T &, void *)

Defines input parameters for a function, which is used as a parameter to *ForEach* member function.

When using *ForEach* to iterate through your set, you must write a function taking a reference to an object of your user type and a **void** pointer. When you call *ForEach*, you pass a pointer to your function as an input parameter.

Public constructors

Form 1   TSetAsVector (unsigned sz = DEFAULT_SET_SIZE)

Creates a set container holding objects of type *T*. *sz* represents the initial number of slots allocated.

Form 2   TISetAsVector (unsigned sz = DEFAULT_SET_SIZE)

Creates an empty set container holding pointers to objects of type *T*. *sz* represents the initial number of slots allocated.

Form 3   TMSetAsVector (unsigned sz = DEFAULT_SET_SIZE)

Creates a set container holding objects of type *T* and using a user-supplied memory manager object of type *Alloc*.

Form 4   TMISetAsVector (unsigned sz = DEFAULT_SET_SIZE)

Creates a set container holding pointers to objects of type *T* and using a user-supplied memory manager object of type *Alloc*.

Public member functions

Add

Form 1   int Add(const T& t)

Supports direct set objects. Adds object *t* to the container.

Form 2   int Add (T *t)

For indirect set objects. Adds a pointer to object *t* to the container.

Detach

Form 1   int Detach(const T& t)

Supports direct containers. Removes the first object that compares equal to the specified object *t*.

Form 2   int Detach(T *t, DeleteType dt = NoDelete)

Supports indirect containers. Removes the specified object pointer *t. *dt* determines whether the object referenced by the pointer will be deleted from memory. *dt* can be set equal to one of three *DeleteType* **enum** values:

Value	Description
NoDelete	The object will not be deleted from memory. This is the default value.
DefDelete	The object will be deleted if the container owns its contents, or left in memory if the container does not own its contents.
Delete	The object will be deleted from memory whether or not the container owns its objects.

Find

int Find(const T& t) const

int Find(const T *t) const

Finds the specified object *t* and returns a pointer to that the object, or zero, if the object was not found. The first prototype supports direct set containers; the second prototype supports indirect set containers.

ForEach

void ForEach(IterFunc iter, void *args)

ForEach executes the given function *iter* for each object in the set. The *args* argument lets you pass arbitrary data to this function.

IterFunc is a **typedef** which which specifies the return type and input parameters for the function called by *ForEach* to operate on data stored at the current node. This is a predefined **typedef**.

iter is your function, which operates on data contained in the node that *ForEach* is pointing to. You must write *iter* to take a reference to your node data and a **void** type pointer.

When called, *ForEach* positions a pointer at an element in the set, and calls your function, *iter*. *iter* checks data at that element, and may change that data based on a condition you define. When finished, *iter* returns control to *ForEach*, which moves to the next element in the set. *ForEach* repeats this process until it has traversed the tree.

FirstThat

T *FirstThat(CondFunc cond, void *args) const

Returns a pointer to the first object in the set that satisfies a given condition, or zero, if no object in the set meets the condition.

You supply a test-function pointer *cond* that returns **true** for a certain condition. You can pass arbitrary arguments via *args*.

CondFunc is a **typedef** which maps your implementation function to the signature which *FirstThat* recognizes. *cond* is your function, which operates on data contained in the current set element. Supports indirect set containers—also *TMSetAsVector*.

FirstThat is valid only for direct containers.

Flush

```
void Flush ()
void Flush ( TShouldDelete::DeleteType dt = TShouldDelete::DefDelete )
```

Removes all elements from the set without destroying the set. The first prototype supports direct set objects; the second prototype supports indirect set objects.

For indirect set containers, *dt* determines whether elements removed from the container will also be deleted from memory. See *Detach*.

GetItemsInContainer

```
int GetItemsInContainer() const
```

Returns the number of items in the set.

HasMember

```
int HasMember( const T& t ) const
```

Returns nonzero if the given object *t* is found in the set.

IsEmpty

```
int IsEmpty () const
```

Returns one if the set contains no elements.

IsFull

```
int IsFull () const
```

Always returns zero for a set container.

LastThat

```
T *LastThat( CondFunc cond, void *args ) const
```

Returns a pointer to the last object in the set that satisfies a given condition. You supply a reference to the test function *cond* that you must write. *cond* takes a pointer to the current object and a **void** pointer. It returns **true** for a certain condition, and returns zero if no object in the set meets the condition you specified.

LastThat is valid only for indirect containers.

Iterator methods

Public constructors

Form 1
```
TMSetAsVectorIterator
( const TMSetAsVector <class T, class Alloc > & b )
```
Creates an iterator object to traverse *TMSetAsVector* objects. *Alloc* is the type of your Memory Manager.

Form 2
```
TSetAsVectorIterator
( const TSetAsVector < class T > & b )
```
Creates an iterator object to traverse *TSetAsVector* objects.

Form 3
```
TMISetAsVectorIterator( const TMISetAsVector<T,Alloc> & s )
```

Creates an iterator object to traverse indirect, memory-managed *SetAsVector* objects as input parameters. This is a function template which takes your user type as a template parameter. *s* is a reference to a *TMISetAsVector* object holding elements of your user type as an input parameter.

Form 4   TISetAsVectorIterator(const TISetAsVector < T > & s)

Creates an iterator object to traverse a *SetAsVector* object which takes a pointer to an object of type *T* as an input parameter. *s* is a reference to a *TISetAsVector* object holding pointers to elements of your user type as an input parameter.

Public member functions

Current

Form 1   const T& Current () const

For direct containers; returns a reference to the current object.

Form 2   T * Current () const

For indirect containers; returns a pointer to the current object.

Restart

void Restart ()

Restarts iteration from the beginning of the set.

Iterator operators

operator ++

Form 1   const T& operator ++ (int)

Moves to the next object and returns the object that was current before the move (postincrement operator).

Form 2   const T& operator ++ ()

Moves to the next object and returns that object (preincrement operator).

operator int

operator int () const

Converts the iterator to an integer value. This operator is used to test for objects remaining in the iterator. This operator returns a nonzero value if the iterator has not finished operating on the array, or a zero value if it has completed iterating.

Stack class template family   stacks.h

Stack containers manage an ordered chain of objects of type *T*, where objects are sequenced in the order they were placed onto the chain, and objects can be added or deleted only from the first (top) position in the chain. This is commonly called "last-in, first-out" order. This family includes eight container classes, together with their corresponding eight iterator classes.

Introduction

Individual containers in this family manage objects and pointers to objects. Most classes use the default memory manager *TStandardAllocator*, but you can pass your own memory manager object to managed container classes upon instantiation.

You can implement stack structures as vectors or as linked lists. Both kinds of class templates take the same parameters and present the same list of member functions. For example, if you change your class user type from *TStackAsVector* to *TStackAsList*, *you* will not need to change calls you made to stack member functions in your source code.

A *StackAsVector* class can not be resized; a *StackAsList* class can be resized.

Class family list

Here is a list of classes composing this family. See "Template family syntax" for template prototypes for each template. See "Container members" and "Iterator methods" for member definitions.

Direct templates
- TStackAsVector
- TStackAsList
- TMStackAsVector
- TMStackAsList
- TStack

- TStackAsVectorIterator
- TStackAsListIterator
- TMStackAsVectorIterator
- TMStackAsListIterator
- TStackIterator

Indirect templates
- TIStackAsVector
- TIStackAsList
- TMIStackAsVector
- TMIStackAsList

- TIStackAsVectorIterator
- TStackAsListIterator
- TMIStackAsVectorIterator
- TMStackAsListIterator

Using this class family

Perform the following steps to use a stack class:

1 Select the user type for the element you will store in your stack container. Decide whether to store objects themselves in the stack, or to store pointers to those objects. Decide whether to use the default memory manager *TStandardAllocator*, or to manage memory yourself, through your own memory manager.

2 Select the stack family template that fits your program design. Stack classes can store objects or pointers to objects, and can accept either default or user-supplied memory managers. You also may select to implement your stack as a linked list, or as a vector.

For example, if you have chosen to store pointers to **long**s in a deque implemented as a linked list, instantiate an object of the *TIStackAsList* class.

3 Classes instantiating stored objects of your own user type must provide the functions listed here. Predefined types already provide these functions.
- Default constructor (all classes)

- Copy constructor (all vector classes; indirect list classes)
- Assignment operator (direct vector classes)
- Equality operator (indirect list classes)

4 If you have decided to use your own memory manager, then you must overload the **new** and **delete** operator member declarations in your memory manager class to support your new user type.

5 If you plan to use *FirstThat*, *LastThat*, or *ForEach* member functions to iterate through your stack, then you must write functions to act on data stored in your stack. These functions must conform to a prototype syntax expected by the *FirstThat*, *LastThat*, or *ForEach* member function. For coding convenience, these function prototypes are **typedef**ed as listed under "Container members."

6 To promote code maintainability, you should **typedef** the container and iterator class templates you have selected to use. This makes it easy to change a class template without making changes to your working code.

7 Instantiate a stack container class from the class template you have selected to use. Pass the user type of your stack container class to the class template upon class instantiation. If you are using a managed class, then you must also pass the type of your memory manager class to the template.

8 Instantiate a stack container object.

9 Instantiate a stack iterator object, if you have decided to use an iterator to access elements in your stack container. Pass your stack container object to your iterator object when you instantiate your iterator object.

Code example

This code example implements a stack of *ints* using a vector as the underlying FDS. It places ten **int**s onto the stack in ascending order. It then pops those **int**s and displays them on your terminal.

Note that for an indirect stack object, you must change the **typedef** and change The code here includes three alternate lines needed to change from a direct stack managing **int**s, to an indirect stack managing pointers to **int**s.

```
#include <classlib\stacks.h>
#include <iostream.h>

    typedef TStackAsVector < int > IntStack; // direct
// typedef TIStackAsVector <int > IntStack; ...indirect

int main ()
{
    IntStack intStack;
    for ( int i = 0; i < 10; i++ )
        intStack.Push ( i );     // direct push code
//      intStack.Push ( new int(i)); ....... indirect push code

    for ( i = 0; i < 10; i++ )
```

```
        cout <<  intStack.Pop ( ) << "  ";  // direct
// this line is for indirect templates
//      cout << *intStack.Top ( ) << "intStack.Pop();

    cout << endl;
    return ( 0 );
}
```

Output

```
9  8  7  6  5  4  3  2  1  0
```

Template family syntax

Direct templates
Objects instantiated from classes listed here contain data of type *T*.

TStackAsList
TStackAsVector
template <class T> class TStackAsList

template <class T> class TStackAsVector

Creates a stack container holding objects of type *T*. The first prototype implements the stack as a linked list. The second prototype implements the stack as a vector.

TMStackAsList
TMStackAsVector
template <class T, class Alloc> class TMStackAsList

template <class T, class Alloc> class TMStackAsVector

Creates a stack container holding objects of type *T*, managed by a memory manager of type *Alloc*. The first prototype implements the stack as a linked list. The second prototype implements the stack as a vector.

Indirect class templates
Objects instantiated from classes listed here contain pointers to stack objects of type *T*. The first prototype implements the stack as a double-linked list. The second prototype implements the stack as a vector.

TIStackAsList
TIStackAsVector
template <class T> class TIStackAsList

template <class T> class TIStackAsVector

Creates a stack container holding pointers to objects of type *T*. The first prototype implements the stack as a double-linked list. The second prototype implements the stack as a vector.

TMIStackAsList
TMIStackAsVector

template <class T, class Alloc> class TMIStackAsList

template <class T, class Alloc> class TMIStackAsVector

Creates a stack container holding pointers to objects of type *T*. Memory is managed by a user-defined memory manager. The first prototype implements the stack as a double-linked list. The second prototype implements the stack as a vector.

Iterator class templates

All iterator classes use their *Current* member to access each object stored in the container they support.

Each iterator class listed here is paired with a container class template which matches its name format. For example, *TIMStackAsVectorIterator* instantiates an iterator object which takes a *TIMStackAsVector* container object as its argument. Always use the iterator which matches the container type holding the stored objects you want to access.

Direct templates

TStackAsVectorIterator

template <class T> class TStackAsVectorIterator

TStackAsListIterator

template <class T,class Alloc> class TMStackAsListIterator

TMStackAsVectorIterator

template <class T,class Alloc> class TMStackAsVectorIterator

TMStackAsListIterator

template <class T> class TMStackAsListIterator

Indirect templates

TIStackAsVectorIterator

template <class T> class TIStackAsVectorIterator

TIStackAsListIterator

template <class T,class Alloc> class TIStackAsListIterator

TIMStackAsVectorIterator

template <class T,class Alloc> class TIMStackAsVectorIterator

TIMStackAsListIterator

template <class T> class TIMStackAsListIterator

Container members

Type definitions

CondFunc

typedef int (*CondFunc) (const T &, void *)

Defines the return type and input parameters for the user-written function used as an input parameter to the *FirstThat* and *LastThat* member functions.

When using *FirstThat* or *LastThat* to iterate through your stack, you must write a function taking a **const** reference to an object of your user type and a **void** pointer. When you call *FirstThat* or *LastThat*, you pass a pointer to this function as as the *cond* input parameter.

IterFunc

typedef void (*IterFunc) (T &, void *)

Defines the return type and input parameters for the user-written function used as an input parameter to the *ForEach* member function.

When using *ForEach* to iterate through your stack, you must write a function taking a reference to an object of your user type and a **void** pointer. When you call *ForEach*, you pass a pointer to your function as the *iter* input parameter.

Public constructors

StackAsList classes call the protected default *TStackAsListImp* constructor, which takes no parameters.

TStackAsVector (unsigned max = DEFAULT_STACK_SIZE)
TMStackAsVector (unsigned max = DEFAULT_STACK_SIZE)
TIStackAsVector (unsigned sz = DEFAULT_STACK_SIZE)
TMIStackAsVector (unsigned sz = DEFAULT_STACK_SIZE)

Creates a stack container with a default max size of DEFAULT_STACK_SIZE.

Public member functions

FirstThat

T *FirstThat(CondFunc cond, void *args) const

Iterates through the stack from head to tail and returns a pointer to the first object in the stack that satisfies a given condition. You supply a pointer *cond* to a user-written test-function that returns **true** for a certain condition. You can pass arbitrary arguments via *args*.

CondFunc is a **typedef** which defines parameters for a function passed as an input parameter to *FirstThat*. *cond* is your function, which operates on data contained in the current stack element.

ForEach

void ForEach(IterFunc iter, void *args)

ForEach executes the given function *iter* for each element in the stack. The *args* argument lets you pass arbitrary data to this function. *IteratorOrder* sets the searching order for the stack.

IterFunc is a **typedef** which which specifies the return type and input parameters for the function called by *ForEach* to operate on data stored at the current element.

iter is your function, which operates on data contained in the stack that *ForEach* is pointing to. You must write *iter* to take a pointer to your node data and a **void** type pointer.

When called, *ForEach* positions a pointer at a stack and calls your function, *iter. iter* checks data at that stack, and may change that data based on a condition you define. When finished, *iter* returns control to *ForEach*, which moves to the element node in the stack. *ForEach* repeats this process until it has iterated through the stack.

Flush
void Flush ()

void Flush (TShouldDelete::DeleteType dt = TShouldDelete::DefDelete)

Removes all elements from the stack without destroying it.

The first prototype supports direct stack objects; the second prototype supports indirect stack objects.

For indirect stacks, *Flush* removes pointers to data. The ownership status of the stack determines whether objects referenced by those pointers will be deleted from memory.

dt is a DeleteType variable that sets whether objects will be deleted from memory. It supports these values:

Value	Description
NoDelete	The object will not be deleted from memory.
DefDelete	The object will be deleted if the container owns its contents, or left in memory if the container does not own its contents. This is the default value.
Delete	The object will be deleted from memory whether or not the container owns its objects.

GetItemsInContainer
unsigned GetItemsInContainer() const

Returns the number of items in the stack.

IsEmpty
int IsEmpty () const

Returns nonzero if the stack contains no elements.

IsFull
int IsFull () const

Returns nonzero if the stack is full.

LastThat
T *LastThat(CondFunc cond, void *args) const

Iterates through the stack from head to tail and returns a pointer to the last object in the stack that satisfies a given condition.

You must supply a test function pointer *cond* that returns **true** for a condition you define. You can pass arbitrary arguments to this function via the *args* input parameter. *LastThat* returns zero if no object in the stack meets the condition you specified in *cond*.

Pop
T Pop ()

T * Pop ()

Returns the object at the left end of the stack and removes it from the stack. The debuggable version throws an exception when the stack is empty.

Push

void Push (const T &) const

void Push (T * t) const

Adds object *t* to the top of the stack.

Top

const T & Top () const

T * Top () const

Returns the object at the top of the stack. The object stays in the stack.

Iterator methods

Public constructors

Form 1   TMStackAsVectorIterator (const TMStackAsVector <class T, class Alloc > & d)

Creates an iterator object to traverse *TMStackAsVector* objects. *Alloc* is the type of your memory manager object.

Form 2   TStackAsVectorIterator (const TStackAsVector < class T > & d)

TIStackAsVectorIterator (const TIStackAsVector < class T > & d)

Creates an iterator object to traverse objects stored in *TStackAsVector* and *TIStackAsVector* containers.

Form 3   TMIStackAsVectorIterator (const TMIStackAsVector < T, Alloc > & d)

TMIStackAsVectorIterator (const TMIStackAsVector<T,Alloc>&);

Creates an iterator object to traverse objects stored in *TMIStackAsVector* containers. This is a function template which takes your user type as a template parameter. *d* is a reference to a *TMIStackAsVector* container holding elements of your data type, as an input parameter.

Public member functions

Current

Form 1   const T& Current () const

For direct containers; returns a reference to the current object.

Form 2   T * Current () const

For indirect containers; returns a pointer to the current object.

Restart

void Restart ()

Restarts iteration from the beginning of the stack.

Operators

operator ++

Form 1   const T& operator ++ (int)

Moves to the next object and returns the object that was current before the move (postincrement operator).

Form 2   const T& operator ++ ()

Moves to the next object and returns that object (preincrement operator).

operator int

operator int ()

Converts the iterator to an integer value. This operator is used to test for objects remaining in the iterator. This operator returns a nonzero value if the iterator has not finished operating on the array, or a zero value if it has completed iterating.

TShouldDelete class   shddel.h

TShouldDelete maintains the ownership state for an indirect container. If a container owns the objects it contains, it may remove those objects and also delete those objects from memory. If a container does not own the objects it contains, then it may remove those objects, but the objects remain in memory. When a container is destroyed, this class also determines the fate of the objects it held.

As a virtual base class, *TShouldDelete* provides ownership control for all containers classes. The member function *OwnsElements* can either report or change the ownership status of a container. The member *DelObj* determines whether objects in containers should be deleted.

Using this class family

Refer to Chapter 15, "Using Borland container classes" of the C++ *Programmer's Guide* for a procedure using members contained in this class.

Template syntax

class TShouldDelete

Container members

Public data members

DeleteType

enum DeleteType { NoDelete, DefDelete, Delete }

Enumerates values to determine whether or not an object should be deleted upon removal from a container.

Public constructor

TShouldDelete (DeleteType dt = Delete)

Creates a *TShouldDelete* object.

Public member functions

OwnsElements

Form 1   int OwnsElements ()

Returns nonzero if the container owns its elements, or zero if it does not.

Form 2   void OwnsElements (int del)

Changes the ownership status as follows: If *del* equals zero, ownership is turned off and the stored object can be removed from the container but can not be deleted from memory. Otherwise ownership is turned on and the stored object will be deleted from memory.

Protected member functions

DelObj

int DelObj (DeleteType dt)

Tests the state of ownership and returns one if the contained objects should be deleted or zero if the contained elements should not be deleted. The factors determining this are the current ownership state, and the value of *dt*, as shown in the following table:

	DelObj	
ownsElements	No	Yes
NoDelete	No	No
DefDelete	No	Yes
Delete	Yes	Yes

delObj returns 1 if (*dt* is *Delete*) or (*dt* is *DefDelete* and the container currently owns its elements). Thus a *dt* of *NoDelete* returns 0 (don't delete) regardless of ownership; a *dt* of *Delete* returns 1 (do delete) regardless of ownership; and a *dt* of *DefDelete* returns 1 (do delete) if the elements are owned, but a zero (don't delete) if the objects are not owned.

Vector class template family   vectimp.h

Vector containers manage contiguous blocks of memory, where each block contains an object of type *T*. This family includes thirteen container classes, together with their corresponding thirteen iterator classes.

Introduction

Individual containers in this family manage objects and pointers to objects, and can sort and count objects. Most classes use the default memory manager *TStandardAllocator*, but you can pass your own memory manager object to managed container object upon instantiation.

Classes in this family

Here is a list of container classes composing this family. See "Template family syntax" for template prototypes for each template. See "Container members" and "Iterator methods" for definitions of members all classes use in common.

Direct templates
- TVectorImp
- TMVectorImp
- TMCVectorImp
- TMSVectorImp
- TCVectorImp
- TSVectorImp
- TVector

- TVectorIteratorImp
- TMVectorIteratorImp
- TSVectorIteratorImp
- TMSVectorIteratorImp
- TCVectorIteratorImp
- TSVectorIteratorImp
- TVectorIteratorImp

Indirect templates
- TIVectorImp
- TMIVectorImp
- TMICVectorImp
- TMISVectorImp
- TICVectorImp
- TISVectorImp

- TIVectorIteratorImp
- TMIVectorIteratorImp
- TMICVectorIteratorImp
- TMISVectorIteratorImp
- TICVectorIteratorImp
- TISVectorIteratorImp

Using this class family

Use a vector class when you must guarantee which data will be stored in order in contiguous memory and need to use an index operator to access which data.

Perform the following steps to use a vector class:

1 Determine the data type for the element you will store in your vector container. Decide whether to store objects themselves in the vector, or pointers to those objects. Decide whether to use the default memory manager or to manage memory yourself.

2 Select the vector family template which fits your program design. Some vector classes can store data or pointers to data, can accept either default or user-supplied memory managers, and can automatically sort elements as they are added to the vector container.

   For example, if you have chosen to store pointers to **long**s and want to build a vector which holds your pointers in sorted order, instantiate an object of the *TISVectorImp* class.

3 Classes instantiating stored objects of your own user type must provide the functions listed here. Predefined types already provide these functions.
   - Default constructor (direct classes only)
   - Copy constructor direct classes only)
   - Assignment operator (direct classes only)

- Less-than operator (required for sorted vector classes)
- Equality operator (all classes)

4 If you have decided to use your own memory manager to manage vector elements, then you must overload the *new* and *delete* operator member declarations in your memory manager class to support your new user type.

5 If you plan to use *FirstWhich, LastWhich,* or *ForEach* member functions to iterate through your vector, then you must write implementation functions to act on your stored data. These functions must conform to prototype syntaxes expected by the *FirstWhich, LastWhich,* or *ForEach* member functions. For coding convenience, these function signatures are **typedef**ed as listed under "Container members."

6 To promote code maintainability, you should **typedef** the container and iterator class templates you have selected to use. This makes it easy to change a class template while minimizing changes you may need to make to your working code.

7 Instantiate a vector container class from the class template you have selected to use. Pass the user type of the data you will store in your vector container class to the class template upon class instantiation. If you are using a managed class, then you must also pass the type of your memory manager class to the template.

8 Instantiate a vector container object. Pass appropriate constructor parameters to your object upon instantiation.

9 Instantiate a vector iterator, if you have decided to use an iterator to access elements in your vector container. Pass your vector container object to your iterator object when you instantiate your iterator object.

Code example

The following example declares a *TVectorImp* container named *vect*, which holds ten elements of type **long**. It fills the vector, searches the vector for the element which holds the value '7', and then deletes the vector element. It then calls both *ForEach* and *TVectorIteratorImp* to display the contents of the vector container. The numbers 1 through 10 display on your screen, minus the number 7.

Note which *ForEach* calls the iteration function called *Show*, which simply displays the contents of the current vector element. *ForEach* then moves to the next element in the vector, calls *Show* again, and repeats this process until every element in the vector has been displayed.

```
#include <iostream.h>
#include <classlib\vectimp.h>

/* This is the iteration function required by the ForEach member
   function. It displays the contents of the current element c.
*/
void Show ( long& c, void*)  { cout << c << endl; }

/* This function instantiates an iterator object called go, passes
   the container object called vect into it upon instantiation,
   and shows the contents of each vect element as it is encountered.
*/
void UseIterator ( const TCVectorImp<long> & vect )
```

```
        {
        TCVectorIteratorImp<long> go (vect );
            while ( go != 0 )
                {
                cout << go.Current( ) << endl;
                go++;
                }
        }


    int main ( )
    {
        /* Instantiate a vector container called vect that holds 10 longs. */
        TCVectorImp < long > vect (10);

        for ( int i = 0; i < 10; i++ ) // fill the vector
            vect.Add (i);

        /* You can now call global or member functions at this point to act
           on data contained in the vector. This program detaches any object
           in the vector that contains the long value '7'.
        */
        vect.Detach((long)7);   // The cast removes ambiguity.

        /* Call the vect::ForEach member function to iterate through the
           vector. Pass an iteration function called Show to ForEach. This
           function displays the contents of the element it points to
           each time ForEach calls it.
        */
        cout << "Using ForEach member function to iterate:\n";
        vect.ForEach ( Show, 0 );

        /* Repeat the iteration process using an iterator object.
           The UseIterator function below combines an instantiation
           call with a streams call, to display the contents of the
           current element.
        */
        cout << "\nUsing an iterator object to iterate:\n";
        UseIterator ( vect ) ;
        return 0;
    }
```

Output

```
Using ForEach member function to iterate:
0
1
2
3
4
5
6
```

```
8
9

Using an iterator object to iterate:
0
1
2
3
4
5
6
8
9
```

Template family syntax

This section lists template prototypes and definitions for classes in the vector family.

Direct templates

Objects instantiated from classes listed here contain elements of type *T*.

TVectorImp

template <class T> class TVectorImp

Creates a vector container holding elements of type *T*.

TMVectorImp

template <class T, class Alloc> class TMVectorImp

Creates a managed vector container holding elements of type *T*, managed by a memory manager of type *Alloc*.

TMCVectorImp

template <class T, class Alloc> class TMCVectorImp

Creates a managed, counted vector container holding elements of type *T*, managed by a memory manager of type *Alloc*.

TMSVectorImp

template <class T, class Alloc> class TMSVectorImp

Creates a managed, sorted vector container holding elements of type *T*, managed by a memory manager of type *Alloc*.

TCVectorImp

template <class T > class TCVectorImp

Creates a counted vector container holding elements of type *T*.

TSVectorImp

template <class T > class TSVectorImp

Creates a sorted vector container holding elements of type *T*.

Indirect class templates

Objects instantiated from classes listed here contain pointers to vector elements of type *T*.

TIVectorImp

template <class T> class TIVectorImp

Creates a vector container holding pointers to elements of type T.

TMIVectorImp

template <class T, class Alloc> class TMIVectorImp

Creates a managed vector container holding pointers to elements of type T, managed by a memory manager of type *Alloc*.

TMICVectorImp

template <class T, class Alloc> class TMICVectorImp

Creates a managed, counted vector container holding pointers to elements of type T, managed by a memory manager of type *Alloc*.

TMISVectorImp

template <class T, class Alloc> class TMISVectorImp

Creates a managed, sorted vector container holding pointers to elements of type T, managed by a memory manager of type *Alloc*.

TICVectorImp

template <class T > class TICVectorImp

Creates a counted vector container holding pointers to elements of type T.

TISVectorImp

template <class T > class TISVectorImp

Creates a sorted vector container holding pointers to elements of type T.

Iterator class templates

All iterator classes use their *Current* member to access each object stored in the container they support.

Each iterator class listed here is paired with a container class template which matches its name format. For example, *TIMVectorIteratorImp* instantiates an iterator object which takes a *TIMVectorImp* container object as its argument. Always use the iterator which matches the container type holding the stored objects you want to access.

Direct templates

TVectorIteratorImp

template <class T> class TVectorIteratorImp

TMVectorIteratorImp

template <class T,class Alloc> class TMVectorIteratorImp

TMSVectorIteratorImp

template <class T,class Alloc> class TMSVectorIteratorImp

TMCVectorIteratorImp

template <class T,class Alloc> class TMCVectorIteratorImp

TCVectorIteratorImp

template <class T> class TCVectorIteratorImp

TSVectorIteratorImp

template <class T> class TSVectorIteratorImp

Indirect templates

TIVectorIteratorImp

template <class T> TIVectorImp

TMIVectorIteratorImp

template <class T, class Alloc> TMIVectorIteratorImp

TMISVectorIteratorImp

template <class T, class Alloc> TMISVectorIteratorImp

TMICVectorIteratorImp

template <class T, class Alloc> TMICVectorIteratorImp

TICVectorIteratorImp

template <class T> class TICVectorIteratorImp

TISVectorIteratorImp

template <class T> class TISVectorIteratorImp

Container members

Type definitions

CondFunc

typedef int (*CondFunc) (const T &, void *)

Defines input parameters for a function, which is used as a parameter to *FirstWhich* and *LastWhich* member functions.

When using *FirstWhich* or *LastWhich* to iterate through your vector, you must write a function taking a **const** reference to an object of your user type and a **void** pointer. When you call *FirstWhich* or *LastWhich*, you pass a pointer to this function as an input parameter.

IterFunc

typedef void (*IterFunc) (T &, void *)

Defines input parameters for a function, which is used as a parameter to the *ForEach* member function.

When using *ForEach* to iterate through your vector, you must write a function taking a reference to an object of your user type and a **void** pointer. When you call *ForEach*, you pass a pointer to your function as an input parameter.

Public constructors

Form 1   TVectorImp ()

TMVectorImp ()
TCVectorImp ()
TMCVectorImp ()
TMSVectorImp ()
TSVectorImp ()
Constructs an empty vector container.

Form 2   TVectorImp (unsigned sz, unsigned d = 0)
TMVectorImp (unsigned sz, unsigned d = 0)
TMCVectorImp (unsigned sz, unsigned d = 0)
TCVectorImp (unsigned sz, unsigned d = 0)
TMCVectorImp (unsigned sz, unsigned d = 0)
TMSVectorImp (unsigned sz, unsigned d = 0)
TSVectorImp (unsigned sz, unsigned d = 0)
Constructs a vector of *sz* objects. *d* is the delta value for this container. Each object is initialized by default to zero.

The delta value *d* sets how many objects of type *T* can be added past the end of this vector at once. Setting *d* to zero determines which this vector container cannot grow to accommodate more objects than its instantiated size, which was set by *upper*.

Form 3   TMVectorImp (const TMVectorImp < T, Alloc) &
Copy constructor.

Form 4   TMIVectorImp (unsigned sz)
Constructs a managed vector of pointers to objects. *sz* is the size of the vector.

Form 5   TIVectorImp (unsigned sz, unsigned d = 0)
TICVectorImp (unsigned sz, unsigned d = 0)
TISVectorImp (unsigned sz, unsigned d = 0)
TMICVectorImp (unsigned sz, unsigned d = 0)
TMISVectorImp (unsigned sz, unsigned d = 0)
Constructs a vector of pointers to objects. *sz* represents the vector size. *d* represents the initialization value.

Public member functions

Add
Form 1   int Add(const T& t)
Adds object *t* to the vector. Also increments the *Count_* value for direct counted containers.

Form 2   int Add (T *t)
For indirect vector objects. Adds a pointer to the object *t*.

AddAt
int AddAt (const T& t, unsigned)
Adds an object to the container at the specified location and increments *Count_* for counted vector containers.

Count

unsigned Count () const

Returns *Count_*, which is the current number of objects stored in the vector. Supports *TMCVectorImp* objects.

Detach

int Detach(const T& loc)

int Detach(unsigned loc)

Supports direct containers.

Removes the object by specifying its vector index.

Find

Form 1 virtual unsigned Find(const T&) const

Finds the specified object and returns the object's index; otherwise returns INT_MAX.

Form 2 int Find(const T *t) const

Finds the specified object *t* and returns the index of the object, or INT_MAX if the object was not found.

FirstWhich

T *FirstWhich(CondFunc cond, void *args, unsigned start, unsigned stop) const

T *FirstWhich(CondFunc cond, void *args) const

Returns a pointer to the first object in the vector that satisfies a given condition, or returns zero if no object in the vector meets this condition. You supply a test-function pointer *cond* which returns **true** for a certain condition. You can pass arbitrary arguments via *args*.

CondFunc is a **typedef** which specifies the type of the function which you pass to *FirstWhich*. *cond* is your function, which operates on data contained in the current vector element. *cond* returns zero to *FirstWhich* if it determines which iteration should continue, and returns a nonzero value if it determines which the current object is the one being sought.

The first prototype specifies a range to be searched.

The second prototype searches the entire vector and returns zero if no item was found. This prototype supports *TMIVectorImp* objects.

Flush

void Flush (unsigned stop = UINT_MAX, unsigned start = 0)

void Flush(unsigned del = 0,unsigned stop = UINT_MAX,unsigned start = 0)

The first prototype removes all elements from the container without destroying the container. It supports direct containers.

The second prototype provides start and stop values for a specified range to be flushed. The first parameter sets whether or not objects removed from the container will also be deleted from memory. Default values define this member to remove all stored objects but keep them in memory. This prototype supports indirect objects.

Objects removed from the vector are also removed from memory if the vector owns those objects. The *del* parameter specifies ownership in the second prototype. A value of zero keeps objects in memory. A nonzero value deletes objects from memory.

ForEach

void ForEach(IterFunc iter, void *args)

void ForEach(IterFunc iter, void *, unsigned start, unsigned stop)

ForEach executes the given function *iter* for each element in the vector. The *args* argument lets you pass arbitrary data to this function.

IterFunc is a **typedef** which which specifies the return type and input parameters for the function called by *ForEach* to operate on data stored at the current node. This is a predefined **typedef**.

iter is your function, which operates on data contained in the node which *ForEach* is pointing to. You must write *iter* to take a reference to your node data and a **void** type pointer.

When called, *ForEach* positions a pointer at a node and calls your function, *iter*. *iter* checks data stored in which element, and may change which data based on a condition you define. When finished, *iter* returns control to *ForEach*, which moves to the next element in the vector. *ForEach* repeats this process until it has visited every element in the vector.

The second prototype allows you to specify an iteration range. It supports managed indirect vector containers.

GetDelta

virtual unsigned GetDelta () const

Returns the growth delta for the vector. Delta is set by the *d* parameter in the container constructor upon instantiation.

LastWhich

T *LastWhich(CondFunc cond, void *args, unsigned start, unsigned stop) const

T *LastWhich(CondFunc cond, void *args) const

Returns a pointer to the last object in the vector that satisfies a given condition, or returns zero if no object in the vector meets this condition. You supply a test-function pointer *cond* which returns **true** for a certain condition. You can pass arbitrary arguments via *args*. The first prototype allows you to specify a range.

CondFunc is a **typedef** which specifies the type of the function which you pass to *FirstWhich*. *cond* is your function, which operates on data contained in the current vector element. *cond* returns zero to *LastWhich* if it determines which iteration should continue, and returns a nonzero value if it determines which the current object is the one being sought.

The first prototype specifies a range to be searched.

The second prototype searches the entire vector and returns zero if no item was found. This prototype supports *TMIVectorImp* objects.

Limit

unsigned Limit () const

Returns the maximum number of objects this container can hold without being resized. This value is initialized to the *upper* parameter passed in to the constructor upon instantiation.

Resize

void Resize (unsigned sz, unsigned offset = 0)

Creates a new vector of size *sz*. The existing vector is copied to the expanded vector, then deleted. In a vector of pointers, the entries are zeroed. In a vector of objects, the default constructor is invoked for each unused element. *offset* is the location in the new vector where the first element of the old vector should be copied. This is needed when the vector has to be extended downward.

Top

virtual unsigned Top () const

Returns the index of the next location which will be filled in the vector. This function is used by counted vectors. For direct vectors, *top* returns *lim*; for counted and sorted vectors, *top* returns the current insertion point.

Zero

virtual void Zero (unsigned, unsigned)

Sets contents for this container to zero begining at the index passed as the first parameter, and ending at the index which is one less than the second parameter.

Zero is valid for direct vector containers, but does nothing. For indirect containers, it zeroes stored pointers.

Operators

operator [ ]

Form 1   T & operator [](unsigned index) const

Returns a reference to an object of type *T*, stored at the location *index*. You can assign a different pointer value to this reference, and it will modify the underlying pointer.

Form 2   T * & operator [] (unsigned index) const

Returns a reference to a pointer to an object of type *T*, where the pointer is stored at the location *index*.

operator =

const TMVectorImp<T, Alloc> & operator = (const TMVectorImp<T, Alloc> &)

Vector assignment operator.

Protected data members

Count_

unsigned Count_

Maintains the number of objects in the vector for counted containers.

Delta

unsigned Delta

Specifies the size increment to be used when the vector grows. This value is set by the *d* input parameter in the constructor.

Lim
unsigned Lim

Lim stores the maximum number of objects of type *T* which this vector can contain without being resized. It is initialized to the *upper* input parameter for the constructor which initialized this object.

Protected member functions

Find
virtual unsigned Find (void *) const

Finds the specified pointer and returns its index for indirect counted containers.

Zero
virtual void Zero (unsigned, unsigned)

Sets contents for this container to zero begining at the index passed as the first parameter, and ending at the index which is one less than the second parameter.

Zero is valid for direct vector containers, but does nothing. For indirect containers, it zeroes stored pointers.

Iterator methods

Public constructors

Form 1 TVectorIteratorImp (const TVectorImp < T > & v)
TCVectorIteratorImp (const TCVectorImp < T > & v)
TSVectorIteratorImp (const TSVectorImp < T > & v)
TIVectorIteratorImp (const TIVectorImp < T > & v)
TICVectorIteratorImp (const TICVectorImp < T > & v)
TISVectorIteratorImp (const TISVectorImp < T > & v)

Creates an iterator object to traverse vectors holding objects of type *T*.

v is a reference to an iterator object which takes a vector container holding elements of your type, as an input parameter.

Form 2 TMVectorIteratorImp (const TMCVectorImp < T, Alloc > & v)
TMIVectorIteratorImp (const TMCVectorImp < T, Alloc > & v)
TMCVectorIteratorImp (const TMCVectorImp < T, Alloc > & v)
TMSVectorIteratorImp (const TMVectorImp < T, Alloc > & v)
TMICVectorIteratorImp (const TMICVectorImp < T, Alloc > & v)
TMISVectorIteratorImp (const TMISVectorImp < T, Alloc > & v)

Creates an iterator object to traverse a vector holding objects of type *T*, and which also takes the type of your memory manager as an input parameter.

v is a reference to an iterator object which takes a vector container holding elements of your user type, as an input parameter.

Form 3   TCVectorIteratorImp (const TCVectorIteratorImp<T,Alloc> & v, unsigned start, unsigned stop)
           TMVectorIteratorImp (const TMVectorIteratorImp<T,Alloc> & v, unsigned start, unsigned stop)
           TMSVectorIteratorImp (const TMSVectorIteratorImp<T,Alloc> & v, unsigned start, unsigned stop)
           TMIVectorIteratorImp (const TMIVectorIteratorImp<T,Alloc> & v, unsigned l, unsigned u)
           TMICVectorIteratorImp (const TMICVectorIteratorImp<T,Alloc> & v, unsigned l, unsigned u)
           TICVectorIteratorImp (const TICVectorIteratorImp<T,Alloc> & v, unsigned l, unsigned u)
           TMISVectorIteratorImp (const TMISVectorImp<T,Alloc> & v, unsigned l, unsigned u)
           TISVectorIteratorImp (const TISVectorIteratorImp<T,Alloc> & v, unsigned l, unsigned u)

Creates an iterator object to traverse vector objects which take a memory manager as an input parameter. *start* and *stop* allow you to specify a range over which this object will iterate.

v is a reference to a container object holding elements of your data type, as an input parameter.

l and *u* are stand for *lower* and *upper*. You do not need to pass these values into this constructor. These parameters are used internally.

Public member functions

Current

Form 1   const T & Current ()
           const T & Current () const

For direct containers; returns a reference to the current object.

Form 2   T * Current () const

For indirect containers; returns a pointer to the current object.

Restart

Form 1   void Restart ()

Restarts iteration from the beginning of the vector.

Form 2   void Restart (unsigned start, unsigned stop)

Restarts iteration over the specified range.

Operators

operator ++

Form 1   const T& operator ++ (int)

Moves to the next object and returns the object which was current before the move (postincrement operator).

Form 2   const T& operator ++ ()

Moves to the next object and returns which object (preincrement operator).

operator int

operator int () const

Converts the iterator to an integer value. This operator is used to test for objects remaining in the iterator. This operator returns a nonzero value if the iterator has not finished operating on the array, or a zero value if it has completed iterating.

11

The iostreams classes

The stream class library in C++ consists of several classes distributed in two separate hierarchical trees. See the C++ *Programmer's Guide*, Chapter 18, "Using the iostreams classes," for an illustration of the class hierarchies. This reference presents some of the most useful details of these classes, in alphabetical order. The following cross-reference table tells which classes belong to which header files.

Header file	Includes	Classes
constrea.h	CONIO.H, IOMANIP.H, IOSTREAM.H	conbuf, constream
fstream.h	IOSTREAM.H	filebuf, fstream, fstreambase, ifstream, ofstream
iostream.h	MEM.H	ios, iostream, iostream_withassign, istream, istream_withassign, ostream, ostream_withassign, streambuf
strstrea.h	IOSTREAM.H	istrstream, ostrstream, strstreambase, strstreambuf

conbuf class   constrea.h

Specializes *streambuf* to handle console output.

Note   *conbuf* is available only for console-mode applications.

Public constructor

conbuf()
Makes an unattached *conbuf*.

Public member functions

clreol
void clreol( )
Clears to end of line in text window.

clrscr
void clrscr( )
Clears the defined screen.

delline
void delline( )
Deletes a line in the window.

gotoxy
void gotoxy(int x, int y)
Positions the cursor in the window at the specified location.

highvideo
void highvideo( )
Selects high-intensity characters.

insline
void insline( )
Inserts a blank line.

lowvideo
void lowvideo( )
Selects low-intensity characters.

normvideo
void normvideo( )
Selects normal-intensity characters.

overflow
virtual int overflow(int = EOF)
Flushes the *conbuf* to its destination.

setcursortype
void setcursortype(int cur_type)
Selects the cursor appearance.

textattr
void textattr(int newattribute)
Selects the cursor appearance.

textbackground
void textbackground(int newcolor)
Selects the text background color.

textcolor
void textcolor(int newcolor)
Selects character color in text mode.

textmode
static void textmode(int newmode)
Puts the screen in text mode.

wherex
int wherex( )
Gets the horizontal cursor position.

wherey
int wherey( )
Gets the vertical cursor position.

window
void window(int left, int top, int right, int bottom)
Defines the active window.

constream class   constrea.h

Provides console output streams. This class is derived from *ostream*.

Note   *constream* is available only for console-mode applications.

Public constructor

constream( )
Provides an unattached output stream to the console.

Public member functions

clrscr
void clrscr( )
Clears the screen.

rdbuf
conbuf *rdbuf( )
Returns a pointer to this *constream*'s assigned *conbuf*.

textmode
void textmode(int newmode)
Puts the screen in text mode.

window
void window(int left, int top, int right, int bottom)
Defines the active window.

filebuf class

fstream.h

Specializes *streambuf* to handle files for input and output of characters. (Since *streambuf* does not provide streams for input or output, the derived classes of *streambuf* must do so.)

The I/O functions of classes *istream* and *ostream* make calls to the functions of *filebuf* to do the actual insertion or extraction on the streams. This occurs if the 'bp' (pointer to *streambuf*) *fdata* member of class *ios* has been assigned a pointer to class *filebuf*.

Example

```
// OPERATIONS WITH filebuf

#include <fstream.h>
const char *OUTF = "_junk_.$$$";

int main(void) {
    filebuf fbuf;  // Unattached file buffer.

    fbuf.open(OUTF, ios::out);
    if (!fbuf.is_open() ) {
        cerr << "Error opening input file " << OUTF;
        return(-1);
        }
  return(0);
    }

//***********************************************************
// OPERATIONS WITH filebuf(fd)
#include <fstream.h>
#include <io.h>
#include <fcntl.h>

int main(void) {
    const char *filename = "_junk_.$$$";
    int fd;  // The file descriptor.

    fd = open(filename, O_RDWR | O_CREAT); // Open file; get descriptor

    // Make a filebuf; use file descriptor.
    filebuf iofile(fd);

    if (!iofile.is_open()) {
        cerr << "The filebuf is not open.";
      return(1);
        }

    // Do things with filebuf.
    iofile.sputn("Borland International", 21);

    return(0);
    }
```

Public constructors

Form 1   filebuf::filebuf();
Makes a *filebuf* that isn't attached to a file.

Form 2   filebuf::filebuf(int fd);
Makes a *filebuf* attached to a file by file descriptor *fd*.

Form 3   filebuf::filebuf(int fd, char *, int n);
Makes a *filebuf* attached to a file specified by the file descriptor *fd*, and uses *buf* as the storage area. The size of *buf* is sufficient to store *n* bytes. If *buf* is NULL or *n* is non-positive, the *filebuf* is unbuffered.

Public data member

openprot
static const int openprot;
The *openprot* data member is the default file protection. It sets the permissions to read and write. File sharing is not allowed.

Public member functions

attach
filebuf* attach(int);
Attaches this closed *filebuf* to opened file descriptor.

close
filebuf* close();
Flushes and closes the file. Returns 0 on error.

fd
int fd();
The *fd* member function returns the file descriptor or EOF.

is_open
int is_open();
The *is_open* member function returns nonzero if the file is open.

open
filebuf* open(const char *name, int mode, int prot = filebuf::openprot);
Opens a file for the specific class object. The *mode* parameter can be set using the *open_mode* enumeration defined in class *ios*.

Class	*mode* parameter
fstream	ios::in
ofstream	ios::out

prot corresponds to the DOS access permission, and it is used unless *ios::nocreate* is specified in *mode*. The default parameter is set to read and write permission.

overflow
virtual int overflow(int = EOF);
Flushes a buffer to its destination. Every derived class should define the actions to be taken.

seekoff
virtual streampos seekoff(streamoff offset, ios::seek_dir, int mode);
Moves the file pointer relative to the current position in the direction of *seek_dir*.

seek_dir is set using the *seek_dir* enumeration definition in class *ios*.

ios::beg	Seek from beginning of file.
ios::cur	Seek from current location.
ios::end	Seek from end of file.

Since the long can be a negative value, seeking can occur "backward" in the file from the end or current location.

mode specifies the move to be in get or put area of the internal buffer by using *ios::in*, *ios::out*, or both.

When this virtual member function is redefined in a derived class, it could be seeking into the stream and not *streambuf*'s internal buffer.

setbuf
virtual streambuf* setbuf(char*, int);
Specifies a buffer of a specified size for the class object. When used as a *strstreambuf* and the function is overloaded, the first argument is not meaningful and should be set to zero.

sync
virtual int sync();
Synchronizes the internal data structures and the external stream representation.

underflow
Form 1　virtual int underflow();
Makes input available. This is called when no more data exists in the input buffer. Every derived class should define the actions to be taken.

fstream class　　　　　　　　　　　　　　　fstream.h

Provides for simultaneous input and output on a *filebuf*.

Input and output are initiated using the functions of the base classes *istream* and *ostream*. For example, *fstream* can use the function *istream::getline()* to extract characters from the file.

Example

```
// Create a file stream.
#include <fstream.h>

void main(void) {
    char ch;
    const char *name = "_junk_.$$$";
    int mode = ios::in | ios::app;

    fstream outf( name, mode );   // Output file stream.
    cout << "Ready for input: Use Control-Z to end.";
    while ( cin.get(ch) )
        outf.put( ch );
}
```

Public constructors

Form 1   fstream();
Makes an *fstream* that is not attached to a file.

Form 2   fstream(const char *name, int mode = ios::in, int prot = filebuf::openprot);
Makes an *fstream*, opens a file with access specified by *mode*, and connects to it.

Form 3   fstream(int fd);
Makes an *fstream*, and connects to an open file descriptor specified by *fd*.

Form 4   fstream(int fd, char *buf, int n);
Makes an *fstream* specified by the file descriptor *fd*, and uses *buf* as the storage area. The size of *buf* is sufficient to store *n* bytes. If *buf* is NULL or *n* is non-positive, the *fstream* is unbuffered.

Public member functions

open
void open(const char *name, int mode, int prot=filebuf::openprot);
Opens a file for the specific class object.

The *mode* parameter can be set using the *open_mode* enumeration defined in class *ios*.

Class	*mode* parameter
fstream	ios::in
ofstream	ios::out

prot corresponds to the DOS access permission, and it is used unless *ios::nocreate* is specified in *mode*. The default parameter is set to read and write permission.

rdbuf
filebuf* rdbuf();
Returns the buffer used.

fstreambase class

fstream.h

fstreambase provides access to *filebuf* functions not accessible through *ios::bp* to *fstreambase* and its derived classes.

If a member function of *filebuf* is not a **virtual** member of *filebuf*'s base class (*streambuf*), it is not accessible. For example: *attach*, *open*, and *close* are not accessible.

The constructors of *fstreambase* initialize the *ios::bp* data member to point to the *filebuf*.

Public constructors

Form 1   fstreambase();
Makes an *fstreambase* that is not attached to a file.

Form 2   fstreambase(const char *name, int mode, int = filebuf::openprot);
Makes an *fstreambase*, opens a file specified by *name* in the mode specified by *mode*, and connects to it.

Form 3   fstreambase(int fd);
Makes an *fstreambase* and connects to an open file descriptor specified by *fd*.

Form 4   fstreambase(int fd, char *buf, int len);
Makes an *fstreambase* connected to an open file descriptor specified by *fd* and uses a buffer specified by *buf* with a size specified by *len*.

Public member functions

attach
void attach(int);
Connects to an open file descriptor.

close
void close();
Closes the associated *filebuf* and file.

open
void open(const char *name, int mode,int prot=filebuf::openprot);
Opens a file for the specific class object.

The *mode* parameter can be set using the *open_mode* enumeration defined in class *ios*.

Class	*mode* parameter
fstream	ios::in
ofstream	ios::out

prot corresponds to the DOS access permission, and it is used unless *ios::nocreate* is specified in *mode*. The default parameter is set to read and write permission.

rdbuf

filebuf* rdbuf();

Returns the buffer used.

setbuf

void setbuf(char*, int);

Assigns a user-specified buffer to the *filebuf*.

ifstream class

Provides an input stream to input from a file using a *filebuf*.

Public constructors

Form 1   ifstream();

Makes an *ifstream* that is not attached to a file.

Form 2   ifstream(const char *name, int mode = ios::in, int = filebuf::openprot);

Makes an *ifstream*, opens an input file in protected mode, and connects to it. The existing file contents are preserved; new writes are appended. By default, a file is not created if it does not already exist.

Form 3   ifstream(int fd);

Makes an *ifstream* and connects to an open-file descriptor *fd*.

Form 4   ifstream(int fd, char *buf, int buf_len);

Makes an *ifstream* connected to an open file specified by its descriptor, *fd*. The *ifstream* uses the buffer specified by *buf* of length *buf_len*.

Public member functions

open

void open(const char *name, int mode, int prot=filebuf::openprot);

Opens a file for the specific class object.

The *mode* parameter can be set using the *open_mode* enumeration defined in class *ios*.

Class	*mode* parameter
fstream	ios::in
ofstream	ios::out

prot corresponds to the DOS access permission, and it is used unless *ios::nocreate* is specified in *mode*. The default parameter is set to read and write permission.

rdbuf

filebuf* rdbuf();

Returns the buffer used.

ios class

iostream.h

Provides operations common to both input and output. Its derived classes (*istream*, *ostream*, and *iostream*) specialize I/O with high-level formatting operations. The *ios* base class is a base for *istream*, *ostream*, *fstreambas*e, and *strstreambase*.

Protected constructor

ios(); // PROTECTED
Constructs an *ios* object that has no corresponding *streambuf*. A derived class should call *ios::init(streambuf *)* to provide a *streambuf*.

Public constructor

ios(streambuf *);
Associates a given *streambuf* with the stream by assigning the pointer *ios::bp* to point to the *streambuf* passed in as a parameter.

Protected data members

bp
streambuf *bp(); // PROTECTED
The *bp* data member points to the associated *streambuf*.

state
int state; // PROTECTED
The *state* data member is the current state of the *streambuf*.

x_fill
int x_fill; // PROTECTED
Use the *x_fill* data member for padding characters on output.

x_flags
long x_flags; // PROTECTED
Use the *x_flags* data member for formatting flag bits.

x_precision
int x_precision; // PROTECTED
Use the *x_precision* data member for floating-point precision on output.

*x_tie
ostream *x_tie
Use the **x_tie data* member to specify the tied *ostream*, if any.

x_width
int x_width; // PROTECTED
Use the *x_width* data member to specify the field width on output.

Public data members

seek_dir
enum seek_dir { beg=0, cur=1, end=2 };
Stream seek direction.

open_mode
enum open_mode {

app,	// Append data—always write at end of file.
ate,	// Seek to end of file upon original open.
in,	// Open for input (default for ifstreams).
out,	// Open for output (default for ofstreams).
binary,	// Open file in binary mode.
trunc,	// Discard contents if file exists (default if out is specified and neither ate nor app is specified).
nocreate,	// If file does not exist, open fails.
noreplace,	// If file exists, open for output fails unless ate or app is set.

};
Stream operation mode. These parameters can be logically ORed.

adjustfield
static const long adjustfield;
Use the *adjustfield* data member with *setf* to control padding to the left, right, or for internal fill.

Examples

```
cout<<setf(ios::left, ios::adjustfield)<<hex<<0xFE;
```
Result: 000xFE   left filled

```
cout<<setf(ios::internal, ios::adjustfield)<<hex<<0xFE;
```
Result: 0x00FE   internal filled

basefield
static const long basefield;
Use the *basefield* data member with *setf* to set the notation to a decimal, octal, or hexidecimal base.

Example
The following example sets a decimal base.

```
cout<<setf(ios::dec, ios::basefield)<<i;
```

floatfield
static const long floatfield;
Use the *floatfield* data member with *setf* to set the floating-point notation to scientific or fixed.

Example
The following example sets scientific notation.

```
cout<<setf(ios::scientific, ios::floatfield)<<f;
```

Protected member functions

init
void init(streambuf *); // PROTECTED
The *init* member function associates the *ios* with the specified *streambuf*.

setstate
void setstate(int); // PROTECTED
Sets specified status bits.

Public member functions

bad
int bad();
The *bad* member function returns nonzero if error occured by checking *ios::badbit* and *ios::hardfail* in *ios::state*.

bitalloc
static long bitalloc();
The *bitalloc* member function acquires a new flag bit set.

The return value may be used to set, clear, and test the flag. This is for user-defined formatting flags.

clear
void clear(int = 0);
The *clear* member function sets the stream state to the given value by setting *ios::state* to the given value.

The constants of the *io_state* enumeration in class *ios* are normally used as the parameter.

The values of *io_state* can be ORed together to set more than one bit in *state*.

eof
int eof();
The *eof* member function returns nonzero on end of file by checking the *ios::eofbit* in *ios::state*.

fail
int fail();
The *fail* member function returns nonzero if an operation failed by checking the *ios::failbit, ios::badbit,* or *ios::hardfail* bits in *ios::state*.

fill
Form 1 char fill();
Returns the current fill character.

Form 2 char fill(char);
Resets the fill character; returns the previous one.

flags

Form 1   long flags();

Returns the current format flags, which can be compared to the values in the formatting flags enumeration of class *ios*. *flags(0)* resets the formatting flags as the default value.

Form 2   long flags(long);

Sets the format flags to be identical to the given **long**. The flags of the **long** are set using the values in the formatting flags enumeration in class *ios*. It returns the previous flags. *flags(0)* resets the default format.

good

int good();

The *good* member function returns nonzero if no state bits were set (no errors occurred) in *ios::state*.

precision

Form 1   int precision(int);

Sets the floating-point precision, and returns the previous setting. This must be reset for each data item being output if a precision other than the default is desired.

Form 2   int precision();

Returns the current floating-point precision.

rdbuf

streambuf* rdbuf();

Returns a pointer to this stream's assigned *streambuf*.

rdstate

int rdstate();

Returns the stream state by returning the value of the data member state of class *ios*.

setf

Form 1   long setf(long setbits, long field);

Clears the bits corresponding to those marked in *field* in the data member *x_flags*, and then resets those marked in *setbits*. *setbits* can be specifed by using the constants in the format flags enumeration of class *ios*.

Form 2   long setf(long);

Sets the flags corresponding to those marked in the given **long**. The flags are set in *ios::x_flags*. The **long** can be specified by using the constants in the formatting flags enumeration of class *ios*. It returns the previous settings.

sync_with_stdio

static void sync_with_stdio();

The *sync_with_stdio* member function synchronizes *stdio* files and *iostreams*.

Note   Do not use in new code. It will slow performance.

tie

Form 1   ostream* tie();

Returns the tied stream, or 0 if none. Tied streams are streams that are connected so that when one is used, the other is affected in some way. For example, *cin* and *cout* are tied; when *cin* is used, it flushes *cout* first.

Form 2   ostream* tie(ostream*);

Ties another stream to this one and returns the previously tied stream, if any. When an input stream has characters to be consumed, or if an output stream needs more characters, the tied stream is first flushed automatically. By default, *cin, cerr,* and *clog* are tied to *cout*.

unsetf

long unsetf(long);

The *unsetf* member function clears the bits corresponding to those marked in the given **long**.

The bits are cleared in *ios::x_flags*.

The flags of the **long** can be set using the constants in the format flags enumeration of class *ios*.

unsetf returns the previous settings.

width

Form 1   int width();

Returns the current width setting.

Form 2   int width(int);

Sets the width, and returns the previous width. This must be reset for each data item input or output if a width other than the default is desired.

xalloc

static int xalloc();

The *xalloc* member function returns an array index of previously unused words that can be used as user-defined formatting flags.

Format flag	Description
enum {	
skipws,	Skip whitespace on input.
left,	Left-adjust output.
right,	Right-adjust output.
internal,	Pad after sign or base indicator.
dec,	Decimal conversion.
oct,	Octal conversion.
hex,	Hexadecimal conversion.
showbase,	Show base indicator on output.
showpoint,	Show decimal point for floating-point output.
uppercase,	Uppercase hex output.
showpos,	Show '+' with positive integers.
scientific,	Suffix floating-point numbers with exponential (E) notation on output.
fixed,	Use fixed decimal point for floating-point numbers.
unitbuf,	Flush all streams after insertion.
stdio,	Flush *stdout, stderr* after insertion.
};	

iostream class   iostream.h

This class, derived from *istream* and *ostream*, is a mixture of its base classes, allowing both input and output on a stream. It is a base for *fstream* and *strstream*.

The stream is implemented by the class *ios::bp* is pointing to. Depending on which derived class of *streambuf bp* is pointing to, determines if the input stream and output stream will be the same.

For example, *iostream* using a *filebuf* will input and output to the same file. Yet *iostream* using a *strstreambuf* can have the input and output stream go to the same or different memory locations.

Public constructor

iostream(streambuf *);
Associates a given *streambuf* with the class.

Public member functions

None.

iostream_withassign class   iostream.h

This class is an *iostream* that overloads the = operator, which allows you to reassign *ios::bp* to a different derived class of *streambuf*.

Public constructor

iostream_withassign();
Null constructor (calls the default constructor for *iostream*).

Public member functions

None (although the = operator is overloaded).

istream class   iostream.h

Provides formatted and unformatted input from a derived class of class *streambuf* via *ios::bp*.

An instance of class *istream* does not perform the actual input, but the member functions of class *istream* call the member functions of the class *bp* is pointing to extract the characters from the input stream.

The >> operator, which is overloaded for all fundamental types, can then format the data.

istream provides the generic code for formatting the data after it is extracted from the input stream.

Example

```
// Illustrates positioning within an input stream.
#include <iostream.h>
#include <fstream.h>
void main(void) {
   const char *filename = "_junk_.$$$";
   int size = 0;
   ifstream inf( filename, ios::in | ios::nocreate );
   inf.seekg(0L, ios::end );
   if ( (size = inf.tellg()) < 0) {
      cerr << filename << " not found";
      return;
      }
   cout << filename << " size = " << size;
   }
```

Public constructor

istream(streambuf *);
Associates a given derived class of *streambuf* to the class, thus providing an input stream. This is done by assigning *ios::bp* to the parameter of the constructor.

Protected member function

eatwhite
void eatwhite(); // PROTECTED
Extracts consecutive whitespace.

Public member functions

gcount
int gcount();
The *gcount* member function returns the number of unformatted characters last extracted. Unformatted extraction occurs within the member functions *get*, *getline*, and *read*.

Example

```
#include <iostream.h>

void main(void) {
  char *name;
```

```
      int buf_size = 100;
      int count = 0;           // Character counter.

      name = new char[buf_size];

      // Notice that the output buffer is flushed.
      cout << "\n Enter your name:" << endl;
      cin.getline(name, buf_size);

      count = cin.gcount();
      // Since getline() retains the linefeed, gcount()
      // will count it as input.
      cout << "\nName character count: " << count - 1;
   }
```

get
Form 1   int get();
Extracts the next character or EOF.

Form 2   istream& get(char*, int len, char = '\n');
istream& get(signed char*, int len, char = '\n');
istream& get(unsigned char*, int len, char = '\n')
Extracts characters into the given **char*** until the delimiter (third parameter) or end-of-file is encountered, or until (*len* - 1) bytes have been read. A terminating null is always placed in the output string. The delimiter is not extracted from the input stream. Fails only if no characters were extracted.

Form 3   istream& get(char&);
istream& get(signed char&);
istream& get(unsigned char&);
Extracts a single character into the given character reference.

Form 4   istream& get(streambuf&, char = '\n');
Extracts characters into the given *streambuf* until the delimiter is encountered.

getline
istream& getline(char*, int, char = '\n');
istream& getline(signed char*, int, char = '\n');
istream& getline(unsigned char*, int, char = '\n');
The *getline* member function extracts up to the delimiter, puts the characters in the buffer, removes the delimiter from the input stream and does not put the delimiter into the buffer.

Example
```
#include <iostream.h>

void main(void) {
  char *name;
  int buf_size = 100;
  int count = 0;           // Character counter.

  name = new char[buf_size];
```

```
                // Notice that the output buffer is flushed.
                cout << "\n Enter your name:" << endl;
                cin.getline(name, buf_size);

                count = cin.gcount();
                // Since getline() retains the linefeed, gcount()
                // will count it as input.
                cout << "\nName character count: " << count - 1;
            }
```

ignore

istream& ignore(int n = 1, int delim = EOF);

The *ignore* member function causes up to *n* characters in the input stream to be skipped; stops if *delim* is encountered.

The deliminator is extracted from the stream.

ipfx

istream& ipfx(int n = 0);

The *ipfx* function is called by input functions prior to fetching from an input stream. Functions which perform formatted input call *ipfx(0)*; unformatted input functions call *ipfx(1)*.

peek

int peek();

The *peek* member function returns the next character without extraction.

putback

istream& putback(char);

The *putback* member function pushes back a character into the stream.

read

istream& read(char*, int);
istream& read(signed char*, int);
istream& read(unsigned char*, int);

The *read* member function extracts a given number of characters into an array. Use *gcount( )* for the number of characters actually extracted if an error occurred.

seekg

Form 1   istream& seekg(streampos pos);

Moves to an absolute position (as returned from *tellg*).

Form 2   istream& seekg(streamoff offset, seek_dir dir);

Moves *offset* number of bytes relative to the current position for the input stream. The offset is in the direction specified by *dir* following the definition: *enum seek_dir {beg, cur, end};*.

Use *ostream::seekp* for positioning in an output stream.

Use *seekpos* or *seekoff* for positioning in a stream buffer.

tellg

long tellg();

The *tellg* member function returns the current stream position.

istream_withassign class

iostream.h

This class is an *istream* that overloads the = operator and lets you reassign the pointer *ios::bp* to a different derived class of *streambuf*.

Public constructor

istream_withassign()
Default constructor (calls the default constructor for *istream*).

Public member functions

None (although the = operator is overloaded).

ofstream class

fstream.h

Provides an output stream to extract from a file using a *filebuf*.

Public constructors

Form 1 ofstream();
Makes an *ofstream* that is not attached to a file.

Form 2 ofstream(const char *name, int mode = ios::out, int prot = filebuf::openprot);
Makes an *ofstream*, opens a file for writing, and connects to it.

Form 3 ofstream(int fd);
Makes an *ofstream* and connects to an open file descriptor specified by *fd*.

Form 4 ofstream(int fd, char *buf, int len);
Makes an *ofstream* connected to an open file descriptor specified by *fd*. The buffer specified by *buf* of *len* is used by the *ofstream*.

Public member functions

open
void open(const char *name, int mode, int prot=filebuf::openprot);
Opens a file for the specific class object.

The *mode* parameter can be set using the *open_mode* enumeration defined in class *ios*.

Class	*mode* parameter
fstream	ios::in
ofstream	ios::out

prot corresponds to the DOS access permission, and it is used unless *ios::nocreate* is specified in *mode*. The default parameter is set to read and write permission.

rdbuf
filebuf* rdbuf();
Returns the buffer used.

ostream class

ostream provides formatted and unformatted output to a *streambuf*.

An instance of class *ostream* will not perform the actual output, but the member functions of *ostream* will call the member functions of the class *bp* is pointing to and insert the characters to the output stream.

The overloaded operator << formats the data before it is sent to *bp*.

ostream provides the generic code for formatting the data before it is inserted to the output stream.

Public constructors

ostream(streambuf *buf);
Associates a given *streambuf* to the class, providing an output stream. This is done by assigning the pointer *ios::bp* to *buf*.

Public member functions

flush
ostream& flush();
This member function flushes the stream.

opfx
int opfx();
The *opfx* function is called by output functions prior to inserting to an output stream. *opfx* returns 0 if the *ostream* has a nonzero error state. Otherwise, *opfx* returns a nonzero value.

osfx
void osfx();
The *osfx* function performs post output operations. If *ios::unitbuf* is on, *osfx* flushes the ostream. On failure, *osfx* sets *ios::failbit*.

put
ostream& put(char ch);
ostream& put(signed char ch);
ostream& put(unsigned char ch);
The *put* member function inserts the character.

seekp

Form 1   ostream& seekp(streampos);
Moves to an absolute position (as returned from *tellp*).

Form 2   ostream& seekp(streamoff, seek_dir);
Moves to a position relative to the current position, following the definition: **enum** *seek_dir beg, cur, end*.

tellp

streampos tellp( );
The *tellp* member function returns the current stream position.

write

ostream& write(const char*, int n);
ostream& write(const signed char*, int n);
ostream& write(const unsigned char*, int n);
The *write* member function inserts *n* characters (nulls included).

ostream_withassign class   iostream.h

This class is an *ostream* that overloads the = operator and allows you to reassign the pointer *ios::bp* to a different derived class of *streambuf*.

Public constructor

ostream_withassign( );
Null constructor (calls the default constructor for *ostream*).

Public member functions

None (although the = operator is overloaded).

streambuf class   iostream.h

This is a base class for all other buffering classes. It provides a buffer interface between your data and storage areas such as memory or physical devices. The buffers created by *streambuf* are referred to as get, put, and reserve areas. The contents are accessed and manipulated by pointers that point between characters.

Buffering actions performed by *streambuf* are rather primitive. Normally, applications gain access to buffers and buffering functions through a pointer to *streambuf* that is set by *ios*. Class *ios* provides a pointer to *streambuf* that provides a transparent access to buffer services for high-level classes. The high-level classes provide I/O formatting.

Example

```
// Operations with streambufs.
#include <iostream.h>
#include <fstream.h>

int main(void) {
   int c;
   const char *filename = "_junk_.$$$";
   ofstream outfile;
   streambuf *out, *input = cin.rdbuf();

   // Position at the end of file. Append all text.
   outfile.open( filename, ios::ate | ios::app);
   if (!outfile) {
      cerr << "Could not open " << filename;
      return(-1);
      }

   out = outfile.rdbuf();  // Connect ofstream and streambuf.

   clog << "Input some text. Use Control-Z to end." << endl;
   while ( (c = input -> sbumpc() ) != EOF) {
      cout << char(c);                         // Echo to screen.
      if (out -> sputc(c) == EOF)
         cerr << "Output error";
      }
   return(0);
   }
```

Public constructors

Form 1   streambuf();
Creates an empty buffer object.

Form 2   streambuf(char *buf, int size);
Constructs an empty buffer *buf* and sets up a reserve area for *size* number of bytes.

Protected member functions

allocate
int allocate(); // PROTECTED
The *allocate* member function sets up a buffer area.

base
char *base(); // PROTECTED
The *base* member function returns the start of the buffer area.

blen
int blen(); // PROTECTED
The *blen* member function returns the length of the buffer area.

eback
char *eback(); // PROTECTED
The *eback* member function returns the base of putback section of get area.

ebuf
char *ebuf(); // PROTECTED
The *ebuf* member function returns the end+1 of the buffer area.

egptr
char *egptr(); // PROTECTED
The *egptr* member function returns the end+1 of the get area.

epptr
char *epptr(); // PROTECTED
The *epptr* member function returns the end+1 of the put area.

gbump
void gbump(int n); // PROTECTED
The *gbump* member function advances the get pointer by *n* which may be positive or negative.

No checks are performed on the new value.

gptr
char *gptr(); // PROTECTED
The *gptr* member function returns the next location in get area.

pbase
char *pbase(); // PROTECTED
The *pbase* member function returns the start of put area.

pptr
char *pptr(); // PROTECTED
The *pptr* member function returns a pointer to the next location in the put area.

setb
void setb(char *, char *, int = 0); // PROTECTED
The *setb* member function sets the buffer area.

setg
void setg(char *, char *, char *); // PROTECTED
The *setg* member function initializes the get pointers.

setp
void setp(char *, char *); // PROTECTED
The *setp* member function initializes the put pointers.

unbuffered
Form 1 void unbuffered(int);
Sets the buffering state.

Form 2 int unbuffered(); // PROTECTED
Returns nonzero if not buffered.

Public member functions

in_avail
int in_avail();
The *in_avail* member function returns the number of characters remaining in the internal input buffer.

This may be the input stream, depending on which derived class of *streambuf* the function call originated from.

out_waiting
int out_waiting();
The *out_waiting* member function returns the number of characters remaining in the internal output buffer.

This may be the output stream, depending on which derived class of *streambuf* the function call originated from.

pbump
void pbump(int); // PROTECTED
The *pbump* member function increments the put pointer *pptr()* by *n* which may be positive or negative.

No checks are performed on the new value of *pptr()*.

sbumpc
int sbumpc();
The *sbumpc* member function returns the current character from the internal input buffer, then advances.

This may be the input stream depending on which derived class of *streambuf* the function call originated from.

seekoff
virtual streampos seekoff(streamoff offset, ios::seek_dir, int mode);
Moves the file pointer relative to the current position in the direction of *seek_dir*.

seek_dir is set using the *seek_dir* enumeration definition in class *ios*.

ios::beg	Seek from beginning of file.
ios::cur	Seek from current location.
ios::end	Seek from end of file.

Since the long can be a negative value, seeking can occur "backward" in the file from the end or current location.

mode specifies the move to be in get or put area of the internal buffer by using *ios::in*, *ios::out*, or both.

When this virtual member function is redefined in a derived class, it could be seeking into the stream and not *streambuf*'s internal buffer.

seekpos

virtual streampos seekpos(streampos, int = (ios::in | ios::out));
The *seekpos* member function moves the get and/or put pointer to an absolute position in the internal buffer of the *streambuf*.

Because *seekpos* is **virtual**, it may be redefined in a derived class to reposition in the input and/or ouput stream.

setbuf

streambuf* setbuf(unsigned char*, int);
Uses the specified array for the internal buffer.

sgetc

int sgetc();
The *setc* member function peeks at the next character in the internal input buffer.

sgetn

int sgetn(char*, int n);
The *sgetn* member function gets the next *n* characters from the internal input buffer.

snextc

int snextc();
The *snextc* member function advances to and returns the next character from the internal input buffer.

sputbackc

int sputbackc(char);
The *sputbackc* member function returns a character to the internal input buffer.

sputc

int sputc(int);
The *sputc* member function puts one character into the internal output buffer.

sputn

int sputn(const char*, int n);
The *sputn* member function puts *n* characters into the internal output buffer.

stossc

void stossc();
The *stossc* member function advances to the next character in the internal input buffer.
The *setb* member function sets the buffer area.

istrstream class

strstrea.h

Provides input operations on a *strstreambuf*.

The cluster (*ios, istream, ostream, iostream,* and *streambuf*) provides a base for specialized clusters that deal with memory.

Public constructors

Form 1   istrstream(unsigned char *);
          istrstream(char *);
          istrstream(signed char *);
          Makes an *istrstream* with a specified string (a null character is never extracted).

Form 2   istrsteam(signed char *str, int);
          istrstream(char *str, int n);
          istrstream(unsigned char *str, int);
          Makes an *istrstream* using up to *n* bytes of *str*.

Member functions

None.

ostrstream class   strstrea.h

Provides an output stream to insert from an array using a *strstreambuf*.

Public constructors

Form 1   ostrstream();
          Makes an *ostrstream* with a dynamic array for the input stream.

Form 2   ostrstream(char *buf, int len, int mode = ios::out);
          ostrstream(signed char *buf, int len, int mode = ios::out);
          ostrstream(unsigned char *buf, int len, int mode = ios::out);
          Makes an *ostrstream* with a buffer specified by *buf* and size specified by *len*. If *mode* is
          ios::app or *ios::ate,* the get/put pointer is positioned at the null character of the string.

Public member functions

pcount
int *pcount();
The *pcount* member function returns the number of bytes currently stored in the buffer.

str
char *str();
Returns and freezes the buffer. The user must deallocate it if the buffer was dynamic.

strstream class   strstrea.h

Provides simultaneous input and output to and from an array using a *strstreambuf*.
Input and output is initiated using the functions of the base classes *istream* and *ostream*.

For example, *strstream* can use the function *istream::getline( )* to extract characters from the buffer.

Public constructors

Form 1   strstream( );
Makes a *strstream* with the base class *strstreambase's streambuf* data member's buffer dynamically allocated the first time it is used. The put area and get areas are the same.

Form 2   strstream(char*, int sz, int mode);
Makes a *strstream* with a specified *n*-byte buffer. If *mode* is *ios::app* or *ios::ate,* the get/put pointer is positioned at the null character of the string.

Form 3   strstream(signed char*, int sz, int mode);
Makes a *strstream* with a specified *n*-byte buffer. If *mode* is *ios::app* or *ios::ate,* the get/put pointer is positioned at the null character of the string.

Form 4   strstream(unsigned char*, int sz, int mode);
Makes a *strstream* with a specified *n*-byte buffer. If *mode* is *ios::app* or *ios::ate,* the get/put pointer is positioned at the null character of the string.

Public member function

str
char *str( );
Returns and freezes the buffer. The user must deallocate it if the buffer was dynamic.

strstreambase class   strstrea.h

Specializes *ios* to string streams by initializing *ios::bp* to point to a *strstreambuf.* This provides the condition checks necessary for any string I/O in memory. For this reason, *strstreambase* is almost entirely protected and accessible only to derived classes which perform I/O. It makes virtual use of *ios.*

Public constructors

Form 1   strstreambase( );
Makes a *strstreambase* with its *streambuf* data member's buffer dynamically allocated the first time it is used. The put area and get areas are the same.

Form 2   strstreambase(const char*, int, char *start);
Makes a *strstreambase* with a specified buffer and starting position.

Public member function

rdbuf
strstreambuf * rdbuf( );
Returns a pointer to the *strstreambuf* associated with this object.

strstreambuf class

strstreambuf specializes *streambuf* to create a buffer for in-memory string formatting.

strstreambuf is one of the two classes defined in the C++ stream library which provide a place for input to be gathered from and a place for output to go. The other class is *filebuf*.

The I/O functions of *istream* and *ostream* make calls to the functions of *strstreambuf* to do the actual insertion or extraction on the streams.

Public constructors

Form 1   strstreambuf();
Makes a dynamic *strstreambuf*. Memory will be dynamically allocated as needed. The put area and get areas are the same.

Form 2   strstreambuf(void * (*alloc)(long n), void (*release)(void *buffer));
Makes a dynamic buffer with specified allocation and free functions.

Form 3   strstreambuf(int n);
Makes a dynamic *strstreambuf*, initially allocating a buffer of at least *n* bytes.

Form 4   strstreambuf(char *buf, int n, char *strt = 0);
           strstreambuf(signed char *buf, int n, signed char *strt = 0);
           strstreambuf(unsigned char *buf, int n, unsigned char *strt = 0);
This *strstreambuf* constructor creates a static *strstreambuf*. The *streambuf* uses *n* bytes starting at the position pointed to by *buf*. The *buf* pointer indicates the get area.

N = 0   *buf* points to a null-terminated string which constitutes the *strstreambuf*.

N < 0   *strstreambuf* is not terminated and continues indefinitely.

N > 0   Indicates the number of bytes used by *strstreambuf* beginning at the position pointed to by *buf*.

Public member functions

doallocate
virtual int doallocate ();
Performs low-level buffer allocation.

freeze
void freeze(int = 1);
The *freeze* member function disallows storing any characters in the buffer, if the input parameter is nonzero.

Unfreeze the buffer by passing a zero.

overflow
virtual int overflow(int = EOF);
Flushes a buffer to its destination. Every derived class should define the actions to be taken.

seekoff
virtual streampos seekoff(streamoff offset, ios::seek_dir, int mode);
Moves the file pointer relative to the current position in the direction of *seek_dir*.

seek_dir is set using the *seek_dir* enumeration definition in class *ios*.

ios::beg	Seek from beginning of file.
ios::cur	Seek from current location.
ios::end	Seek from end of file.

Since the long can be a negative value, seeking can occur "backward" in the file from the end or current location.

mode specifies the move to be in get or put area of the internal buffer by using *ios::in, ios::out* or both.

When this virtual member function is redefined in a derived class, it could be seeking into the stream and not *streambuf*'s internal buffer.

setbuf
virtual streambuf* setbuf(char*, int);
Specifies a buffer of a specified size for the class object. When used as a *strstreambuf* and the function is overloaded, the first argument is not meaningful and should be set to zero.

str
char *str();
Returns and freezes the buffer. The user must deallocate it if the buffer was dynamic.

sync
virtual int sync();
Establishes consistency between internal data structures and the external stream representation.

underflow
virtual int underflow();
Makes input available. This is called when no more data exists in the input buffer. Every derived class should define the actions to be taken.

12

The persistent streams classes and macros

Borland support for persistent streams consists of a class hierarchy and macros to help you develop streamable objects. These topics are a reference for these classes and macros.

Streamable classes

They alphabetically list and describe all the public classes that support persistent objects.

fpbase class   objstrm.h

class fpbase : virtual public pstream

Provides the basic operations common to all object file stream I/O. It is a base class for handling streamable objects on file streams.

Public constructors

Form 1   fpbase();
          Creates a buffered *fpbase* object.

Form 2   fpbase(const char *name, int omode, int prot = filebuf::openprot);
          Creates a buffered *fpbase* object. It opens the file specified by *name*, using the mode *omode* and protection *prot*; and attaches this file to the stream.

Form 3   fpbase(int f);
          Creates a buffered *fpbase* object, and attaches the file specified by the file descriptor *f* to the stream.

Form 4   fpbase(int f, char *b, int len);

Creates a buffered *fpbase* object. It initializes the file buffer to be associated with the file descriptor *f*, and to use the buffer specified by *b* with a length of *len*.

Public member functions

attach
void attach(int f);

Attaches the file with descriptor *f* to this stream if possible and sets *ios::state* accordingly.

close
void close( );

Closes the stream and associated file.

open
void open(const char *name, int mode, int prot = filebuf::openprot);

Opens the named file in the given *mode* (*app*, *ate*, *in*, *out*, *binary*, *trunc*, *nocreate*, or *noreplace*) and protection. The opened file is attached to this stream.

rdbuf
filebuf * rdbuf( );

Returns a pointer to the current file buffer.

setbuf
void setbuf(char *buf, int len);

Sets the location of the buffer to *buf* and the buffer size to *len*.

ifpstream class   objstrzm.h

class ifpstream : public fpbase, public ipstream

ifpstream is a simple "mix" of its bases, *fpbase* and *ipstream*. It provides the base class reading (extracting) streamable objects from file streams.

Public constructors

Form 1   ifpstream( );

Creates a buffered *ifpstream* object using a default buffer.

Form 2   ifpstream(const char *name, int mode=ios::in, int prot = filebuf::openprot);

Creates a buffered *ifpstream* object. It opens the file specified by *name* using the mode *mode* and protection *prot*; and attaches this file to the stream.

Form 3   ifpstream(int f);

Creates a buffered *ifpstream* object and attaches the file specified by the file descriptor *f* to the stream.

Form 4   ifpstream(int f, char *b, int len);

Creates a buffered *ifpstream* object. It initializes the file buffer to be associated with the file descriptor *f* and to use the buffer specified by *b* with a length of *len*.

Public member functions

open
void open(const char *name, int mode, int prot = filebuf::openprot);

It opens the named file in the given *mode* (*app*, *ate*, *in*, *out*, *binary*, *trunc*, *nocreate*, or *noreplace*) and protection. The default *mode* for *ifpstream* is *ios::in* (input) with *openprot* protection. The opened file is attached to this stream.

rdbuf
filebuf * rdbuf();

Returns a pointer to the current file buffer.

ipstream class   objstrm.h

class ipstream : virtual public pstream

ipstream, a specialized input stream derivative of *pstream*, is the base class for reading (extracting) streamable objects.

Public and protected constructors

Form 1   ipstream(streambuf *buf);

Creates a buffered *ipstream* with the given buffer. The state is set to 0.

Form 2   ipstream();   // PROTECTED

Creates a buffered *ipstream* without initializing the buffer pointer, *bp*. Use *psteam::init* to set the buffer and state.

Public member functions

find
TStreamableBase * Find(P_id_type Id);

Returns a pointer to the object corresponding to *Id*.

freadBytes
void freadBytes(void *data, size_t sz);

Reads the number of bytes specified by *sz* into the supplied buffer (*data*).

freadString
Form 1   char *freadString();

Reads a string from the stream. It determines the length of the string and allocates a far character array of the appropriate length. It reads the string into this array and returns a pointer to the string. The caller is expected to free the allocated memory block.

Form 2   char *freadString(char *buf, unsigned maxLen);

Reads a string from the stream into the supplied far buffer (*buf*). If the length of the string is greater than *maxLen*–1, it reads nothing. Otherwise, it reads the string into the buffer and appends a null-terminating byte.

getVersion

getVersion() const;

Returns the object version number.

readByte

uint8 readByte();

Returns the byte at the current stream position.

readBytes

void readBytes(void data, size_t sz);

Reads *sz* bytes from current stream position, and writes them to *data*.

readString

Form 1   char * readString();

Allocates a buffer large enough to contain the string at the current stream position and reads the string into the buffer. The caller must free the buffer.

Form 2   char * readString(char *buf, unsigned maxLen);

Reads the string at the current stream position into the buffer specified by *buf*. If the length of the string is greater than *maxLen*–1, it reads nothing. Otherwise, it reads the string into the buffer and appends a null-terminating byte.

readWord

uint32 readWord();

Returns the word at the current stream position.

readWord16

uint16 readWord16();

Returns the 16-bit word at the current stream position.

readWord32

uint32 readWord32();

Returns the 32-bit word at the current stream position.

registerObject

void registerObject(TStreamableBase * adr);

Registers the object pointed to by *adr*.

seekg

Form 1   ipstream& seekg(streampos pos);

Moves the stream position to the absolute position given by *pos*.

Form 2   ipstream& seekg(streamoff off, ios::seek_dir);

Moves to a position relative to the current position by an offset *off* (+ or –) starting at *ios::seek_dir*. You can set *ios::seek_dir* to one of the following:

- *beg* (start of stream)
- *cur* (current stream position)
- *end* (end of stream)

tellg

streampos tellg();

Returns the (absolute) current stream position.

Protected member functions

readData
void * readData(const ObjectBuilder * ,TStreamableBase *& mem);

If *mem* is 0, it calls the appropriate *build* function to allocate memory and initialize the virtual table pointer for the object.

Finally, it invokes the appropriate read function to read the object from the stream into the memory pointed to by *mem*.

readPrefix
const ObjectBuilder * readPrefix( );

Returns the *TStreamableClass* object corresponding to the class *name* stored at the current position in the stream.

readSuffix
void readSuffix( );

Reads and checks the suffix of the object.

readVersion
void readVersion( );

Reads the version number of the input stream.

Friend operator

operator >>
friend ipstream& operator >> (ipstream& ps, signed char & ch);
friend ipstream& operator >> (ipstream& ps, unsigned char & ch);
friend ipstream& operator >> (ipstream& ps, signed short & sh);
friend ipstream& operator >> (ipstream& ps, unsigned short & sh);
friend ipstream& operator >> (ipstream& ps, signed int & i);
friend ipstream& operator >> (ipstream& ps, unsigned int & i);
friend ipstream& operator >> (ipstream& ps, signed long & l);
friend ipstream& operator >> (ipstream& ps, unsigned long & l);
friend ipstream& operator >> (ipstream& ps, float & f);
friend ipstream& operator >> (ipstream& ps, double & d);
friend ipstream& operator >> (ipstream& ps, long double & d);
friend ipstream& operator >> (ipstream& ps, TStreamableBase t);
friend ipstream& operator >> (ipstream& ps, void *t);

This friend operator of *ipstream* extracts (reads) from the *ipstream ps*, to the given argument. It returns a reference to the stream that lets you chain **>>** operations in the usual way.

The data type of the argument determines how the read is performed. For example, reading a **signed** *char* is implemented using *readByte*.

ofpstream class   objstrm.h

class ofpstream : public fpbase, public opstream

Provides the base class for writing (inserting) streamable objects to file streams.

Public constructors

Form 1   ofpstream();
Creates a buffered *ofpstream* object using a default buffer.

Form 2   ofpstream(const char *name, int mode = ios::out, int prot = filebuf::openprot);
Creates a buffered *ofpstream* object. It opens the file specified by *name*, using the mode *mode*, and protection *prot*, and attaches this file to the stream

Form 3   ofpstream(int f);
Creates a buffered *ofpstream* object and attaches the file specified by the file descriptor, *f* to the stream.

Form 4   ofpstream(int f, char *b, int len);
Creates a buffered *ofpstream* object. It initializes the file buffer to be associated with the file descriptor *f* and to use the buffer specified by *b* with a length of *len*.

Public member functions

open
void open(char *name, int mode = ios::out, int prot = filebuf::openprot);
Opens the named file in the given *mode* (*app, ate, in, out, binary, trunc, nocreate,* or *noreplace*) and protection. The default mode for ofpstream is *ios::out* (output) with *openprot* protection. The opened file is attached to this stream.

rdbuf
filebuf * rdbuf();
Returns a pointer to the current file buffer.

opstream class   objstrm.h

class opstream : virtual public pstream

opstream, a specialized derivative of *pstream*, is the base class for writing (inserting) streamable objects.

Public and protected constructors

Form 1   opstream(streambuf *buf);
Creates a buffered *opstream* with the given buffer and sets the *bp* data member to *buf*. The state is set to 0.

Form 2   opstream(); // PROTECTED

Creates an *opstream* object without initializing the buffer pointer, *bp*. Use *pstream::init* to set the buffer and state.

Public member functions

findObject
P_id_type findObject(TStreamableBase *adr);
Returns the type ID for the object pointed to by *adr*.

findVB
P_id_type findVB(TStreamableBase *adr);
Returns a pointer to the **virtual** base.

flush
opstream& flush();
Flushes the stream.

fwriteBytes
void fwriteBytes(const void *data, size_t sz);
Writes the specified number of bytes (*sz*) from the supplied buffer (*data*) to the stream.

fwriteString
void fwriteString(const char *str);
Writes the specified far character string (*str*) to the stream.

registerObject
void registerObject(TStreamableBase *adr);
Registers the class of the object pointed to by *adr*.

registerVB
void registerVB(TStreamableBase *adr);
Registers a **virtual** base class.

seekp
Form1   opstream& seekp(streampos pos);
Moves the current position of the stream to the absolute position given by *pos*.

Form2   opstream& seekp(streamoff off,ios::seek_dir);
Moves to a position relative to the current position by an offset *off* (+ or −) starting at *ios::seek_dir*. You can set *ios::seek_dir* to one if the following:

- *beg* (start of stream)
- *cur* (current stream position)
- *end* (end of stream)

tellp
streampos tellp();
Returns the (absolute) current stream position.

writeByte
void writeByte(uint8 ch);
Writes the byte *ch* to the stream.

writeBytes

Form 1   void writeBytes(const void *data, size_t sz);

Writes *sz* bytes from the *data* buffer to the stream.

Form 2   void writeBytes(const void far *data, size_t sz);

Writes *sz* bytes from the *data* buffer to the stream.

writeObject

void writeObject(const TStreamableBase *t, int isPtr = 0, ModuleId mid = GetModuleId( ));

Writes the object, pointed to by *t*, to the output stream. The *isPtr* argument indicates whether the object was allocated from the heap.

writeObjectPointer

void writeObjectPointer(const TStreamableBase *t, ModuleId mid = GetModuleId( ));

Writes the object pointer *t* to the output stream.

writeString

void writeString(const char *str);

Writes *str* to the stream.

writeWord

void writeWord(uint32 us);

Writes the 32-bit word *us* to the stream.

writeWord16

void writeWord16(uint16 us);

Writes the 16-bit word *us* to the stream.

writeWord32

void writeWord32(uint32 us);

Writes the 32-bit word *us* to the stream.

Protected member functions

writeData

void writeData(TStreamableBase *t);

Writes data to the stream by calling the *write* member function of the appropriate class for the object being written.

writePrefix

void writePrefix(const TStreamableBase *t);

Writes the class name prefix to the stream. The << operator uses this function to write a prefix and suffix around the data written with *writeData*. The prefix/suffix is used to ensure typesafe stream I/O.

writeSuffix

void writeSuffix(const TStreamableBase *t);

Writes the class name suffix to the stream. The << operator uses this function to write a prefix and suffix around the data written with *writeData*. The prefix/suffix is used to ensure typesafe stream I/O.

Friend operator

opstream::<<

friend opstream& operator << (opstream& ps, signed char ch);
friend opstream& operator << (opstream& ps, unsigned char ch);
friend opstream& operator << (opstream& ps, signed short sh);
friend opstream& operator << (opstream& ps, unsigned short sh);
friend opstream& operator << (opstream& ps, signed int i);
friend opstream& operator << (opstream& ps, unsigned int i);
friend opstream& operator << (opstream& ps, signed long l);
friend opstream& operator << (opstream& ps, unsigned long l);
friend opstream& operator << (opstream& ps, float f);
friend opstream& operator << (opstream& ps, double d);
friend opstream& operator << (opstream& ps, long double d);
friend opstream& operator << (opstream& ps, TStreamableBase& t);

This **friend** operator of *opstream* inserts (writes) the given argument to the given *ipstream* object.

The data type of the argument determines the form of write operation employed.

pstream class   objstrm.h

class pstream
Provides the base class for handling streamable objects.

Public and protected constructor

Form 1   pstream(streambuf *buf);
Creates a buffered *pstream* with the given buffer. The state is set to 0.

Form 2   pstream(); // PROTECTED
Creates a *pstream* without initializing the buffer pointer *bp* or state. Use *init* to set the buffer and *setstate* to set the state.

Public data member

PointerTypes
enum PointerTypes (ptNull, ptIndexed, ptObject);
Enumerates object pointer types.

Protected data members

bp
streambuf *bp;
The *bp* data member is a pointer to the stream buffer.

state
int state;
Formats state flags. Use *rdstate* to access the current state.

Public member functions

bad
int bad() const;
Returns nonzero if an error occurs.

clear
void clear(int aState = 0);
Sets the stream state to the given value (defaults to 0).

eof
int eof() const;
Returns nonzero on end of stream.

fail
int fail() const;
Returns nonzero if a previous stream operation failed.

good
int good() const;
Returns nonzero if no error states have been recorded for the stream (that is, no errors have occurred).

rdbuf
streambuf * rdbuf() const;
Returns the *pb* pointer to the buffer assigned to the stream.

rdstate
int rdstate() const;
Returns the current state value.

Protected member functions

init
void init(streambuf *sbp);
The *init* member function initializes the stream and sets state to 0 and bp to *sbp*.

setstate
void setstate(int b);
Updates the *state* data member with *state* |= (*b* & *0xFF*).

Operators

operator void *()
operator void * () const;
Converts to a **void** pointer.

operator ! ()

int operator ! () const;

Overloads the NOT operator. Returns 0 if the operation has failed (that is, if *pstream::fail* returned nonzero); otherwise, returns nonzero.

TStreamableBase class   objstrm.h

class TStreamableBase

Classes that inherit from *TStreamableBase* are known as streamable classes (their objects can be written to and read from streams). If you develop your own streamable classes, make sure that *TStreamableBase* is somewhere in their ancestry.

Using an existing streamable class as a base is the easiest way to create a streamable class. If your class must also fit into an existing class hierarchy, you can use multiple inheritance to derive a class from *TStreamableBase*.

Type definition

Type_id

typedef const char *Type_id;

Describes type identifiers.

Public member functions

CastableID

virtual Type_id CastableID() const = 0;

Provides support for typesafe downcasting. Returns string containing the type name.

Note   This function is available only when the library is built without run-time type identification (RTTI).

FindBase

virtual void *FindBase(Type_id id) const;

Returns a pointer to the base class.

Note   This function is available only when the library is built without run-time type identification (RTTI).

MostDerived

virtual void *MostDerived() const = 0;

Returns a **void** pointer to the actual streamed object.

Note   This function is available only when the library is built without run-time type identification (RTTI).

TStreamableClass class   streambl.h

class TStreamableClass : public ObjectBuilder

TStreamableClass is used by the private database class and *pstream* in the registration of streamable classes.

Public constructor

TStreamableClass(const char *n, BUILDER b, int d=NoDelta, ModuleId mid=GetModuleId());

Creates a *TStreamableClass* object with the given name (*n*) and the given builder function (*b*), then registers the type.

For example, each streamable has a *Build* member function of type BUILDER. For typesafe object-stream I/O, the stream manager needs to access the names and the type information for each class. To ensure that the appropriate functions are linked into any application using the stream manager, you must provide a reference such as

```
TStreamableClass RegClassName;
```

where *TClassName* is the name of the class for which objects need to be streamed. (Note that *RegClassName* is a single identifier.) This not only registers *TClassName* (telling the stream manager which *Build* function to use), it also automatically registers any dependent classes. You can register a class more than once without any harm or overhead.

Invoke this function to provide raw memory of the correct size into which an object of the specified class can be read. Because the *Build* procedure invokes a special constructor for the class, all virtual table pointers are initialized correctly.

The distance, in bytes, between the base of the streamable object and the beginning of the *TStreamableBase* component of the object is *d*. Calculate *d* by using the _ _DELTA macro.

Example

```
TStreamableClass RegTClassName = TStreamableClass("TClassName", TClassName::build,
                    _ _DELTA(TClassName));
```

Friend classes

ipstream, opstream

TStreamer class   objstrm.h

class TStreamer

Provides a base class for all streamable objects.

Protected constructor

TStreamer(TStreamableBase *obj)

Constructs the *TStreamer* object, and initializes the streamable object pointer.

Public and protected member functions

GetObject

TStreamableBase *GetObject( ) const

Returns the address of the *TStreamableBase* component of the streamable object.

Read

virtual void *Read(ipstream&, uint32) const = 0;

This pure virtual member function must be redefined for every streamable class. It must read the necessary data members for the streamable class from the supplied *ipstream*.

StreamableName

virtual const char *StreamableName( ) const = 0;

This pure **virtual** member function must be redefined for every streamable class. It returns the name of the streamable class, which is used by the stream manager to register the streamable class. The name returned must be a zero-terminated string.

Write

virtual void Write(opstream&) const = 0;

This pure **virtual** function must be redefined for every streamable class. It must write the necessary streamable class data members to the supplied *opstream* object. *Write* is usually implemented by calling the *Write* member function (if available) of a base class, and then inserting any additional data members for the derived class.

Streaming macros

These macros are provided to simplify the declaration and definition of streamable classes.

DECLARE_STREAMABLE macro   objstrm.h

DECLARE_STREAMABLE(exp, cls, ver)

The DECLARE_STREAMABLE macro is used within a class definition to add the members that are needed for streaming. Since it contains access specifiers, it should be followed by an access specifier or be used at the end of the class definition.

- The first parameter should be a macro, which in turn should conditionally expand to either _ _**import** and _ _**export**, depending on whether the class is to be imported or exported from a DLL.

- The second parameter is the streamable class name.

- The third parameter is the object version number.

DECLARE_STREAMABLE_FROM_BASE macro objstrm.h

DECLARE_STREAMABLE_FROM_BASE(exp, cls, ver)

This macro is used in the same way as DECLARE_STREAMABLE, but in the case where the class being defined can be written and read using *Read* and *Write* functions defined in its base class without change. This usually occurs when a derived class overrides **virtual** functions in its base or provides different constructors, but does not add any data members.

If you used DECLARE_STREAMABLE in this case, you would have to write *Read* and *Write* functions that merely called the base's *Read* and *Write* functions. Using DECLARE_STREAMABLE_FROM_BASE prevents this.

DECLARE_ABSTRACT_STREAMABLE macro objstrm.h

DECLARE_ABSTRACT_STREAMABLE(exp, cls, ver)

This macro is used in an abstract class. DECLARE_STREAMABLE doesn't work with an abstract class because an asbtract class can never be instantiated, and the code that attempts to instantiate the object (*Build*) causes compiler errors.

DECLARE_STREAMER macro objstrm.h

DECLARE_STREAMER(exp, cls, ver)

This macro defines a nested class within your streamable class, and contains the core of the streaming code. DECLARE_STREAMER declares the *Read* and *Write* function declarations, whose definitions you must provide, and the *Build* function that calls the *TStreamableClass* constructor.

- The first parameter should be a macro, which in turn should conditionally expand to either _ _import or _ _export, depending on whether or not the class is to be imported or exported from a DLL.

- The second parameter is the streamable class name.

- The third parameter is the object version number.

DECLARE_STREAMER_FROM_BASE macro objstrm.h

DECLARE_STREAMER_FROM_BASE(exp, cls, ver)

This macro is used by DECLARE_STREAMABLE_FROM_BASE. It declares a nested *Streamer* class without the *Read* and *Write* functions.

- The first parameter should be a macro, which in turn should conditionally expand to either _ _import or _ _export, depending on whether or not the class is to be imported or exported from a DLL.

- The second parameter is the streamable class name.

- The third parameter is the object version number.

DECLARE_ABSTRACT_STREAMER macro   objstrm.h

DECLARE_ABSTRACT_STREAMER (exp, cls, ver)

This macro is used by DECLARE_ABSTRACT_STREAMABLE. It declares a nested *Streamer* class without the *Build* function.

- The first parameter should be a macro, which in turn should conditionally expand to either **__import** or **__export**, depending on whether or not the class is to be imported or exported from a DLL.

- The second parameter is the streamable class name.

- The third parameter is the object version number.

DECLARE_CASTABLE macro   objstrm.h

DECLARE_CASTABLE

This macro provides declarations that provide a rudimentary typesafe downcast mechanism. This is useful for compilers that don't support run-time type information.

DECLARE_STREAMABLE_OPS macro   objstrm.h

DECLARE_STREAMABLE_OPS(cls)

Declares the inserters and extractors. For template classes, DECLARE_STREAMABLE_OPS must use *class<...>* as the macro argument; other DECLAREs take only the class name.

DECLARE_STREAMABLE_CTOR macro   objstrm.h

DECLARE_STREAMABLE_CTOR(cls)

Declares the constructor called by the *Streamer::Build* function.

IMPLEMENT_STREAMABLE macros   objstrm.h

IMPLEMENT_STREAMABLE(cls)
IMPLEMENT_STREAMABLE1(cls, base1)
IMPLEMENT_STREAMABLE2(cls, base1, base2)
IMPLEMENT_STREAMABLE3(cls, base1, base2, base3)
IMPLEMENT_STREAMABLE4(cls, base1, base2, base3, base4)
IMPLEMENT_STREAMABLE5(cls, base1, base2, base3, base4, base5)

These macros generate the registration object for the class via IMPLEMENT_STREAMABLE_CLASS, and generate the various member functions that are needed for a streamable class via IMPLEMENT_ABSTRACT_STREAMABLE.

IMPLEMENT_STREAMABLE is used when the class has no base classes other than *TStreamableBase*. Its only parameter is the name of the class. The numbered versions (IMPLEMENT_STREAMABLE1, IMPLEMENT_STREAMABLE2, and so on) are for classes that have bases. Each base class, including all **virtual** bases, must be listed in the IMPLEMENT_STREAMABLE macro invocation.

The individual components comprising the above macros can be used separately for special situations, such as custom constructors.

IMPLEMENT_STREAMABLE_CLASS macro objstrm.h

IMPLEMENT_STREAMABLE_CLASS(cls)
Constructs a *TStreamableClass* class instance.

IMPLEMENT_STREAMABLE_CTOR macros objstrm.h

IMPLEMENT_STREAMABLE_CTOR(cls)
IMPLEMENT_STREAMABLE_CTOR1(cls, base1)
IMPLEMENT_STREAMABLE_CTOR2(cls, base1, base2)
IMPLEMENT_STREAMABLE_CTOR3(cls, base1, base2, base3)
IMPLEMENT_STREAMABLE_CTOR4(cls, base1, base2, base3, base4)
IMPLEMENT_STREAMABLE_CTOR5(cls, base1, base2, base3, base4, base5)
Defines the constructor called by the *Build* function. All base classes must be listed in the appropriate macro.

IMPLEMENT_STREAMABLE_POINTER macro objstrm.h

IMPLEMENT_STREAMABLE_POINTER(cls)
Creates the instance pointer extraction operator (>>).

IMPLEMENT_CASTABLE_ID macro objstrm.h

IMPLEMENT_CASTABLE_ID(cls)
Sets the typesafe downcast identifier.

IMPLEMENT_CASTABLE macros objstrm.h

IMPLEMENT_CASTABLE(cls)
IMPLEMENT_CASTABLE1(cls)

IMPLEMENT_CASTABLE2(cls)
IMPLEMENT_CASTABLE3(cls)
IMPLEMENT_CASTABLE4(cls)
IMPLEMENT_CASTABLE5(cls)

These macros implement code that supports the typesafe downcast mechanism.

IMPLEMENT_STREAMER macro   objstrm.h

IMPLEMENT_STREAMER(cls)
Defines the *Streamer* constructor.

IMPLEMENT_ABSTRACT_STREAMABLE macros   objstrm.h

IMPLEMENT_ABSTRACT_STREAMABLE(cls)
IMPLEMENT_ABSTRACT_STREAMABLE1(cls)
IMPLEMENT_ABSTRACT_STREAMABLE2(cls)
IMPLEMENT_ABSTRACT_STREAMABLE3(cls)
IMPLEMENT_ABSTRACT_STREAMABLE4(cls)
IMPLEMENT_ABSTRACT_STREAMABLE5(cls)

This macro expands to

- IMPLEMENT_STREAMER (defines the *Streamer* constructor)

- IMPLEMENT_STREAMABLE_CTOR (defines the *TStreamableClass* constructor)

- IMPLEMENT_STREAMABLE_POINTER (defines the instance pointer extraction operator)

IMPLEMENT_STREAMABLE_FROM_BASE macro   objstrm.h

IMPLEMENT_STREAMABLE_FROM_BASE(cls, base1)
This macro expands to

- IMPLEMENT_STREAMABLE_CLASS (constructs a *TStreamableClass* instance)

- IMPLEMENT_STREAMABLE_CTOR1 (defines a one base class constructor that is called by *Build*)

- IMPLEMENT_STREAMABLE_POINTER (defines the instance pointer extraction operator)

13

The mathematical classes

The C++ mathematical classes provide mathematical operations that are available only in C++ programs. C++ programs, however, that use these classes, the numerical types that they define, or any of their **friend** and member functions can use any of the ANSI C standard mathematical routines.

These classes construct numerical types, define the functions used to carry out operations with their respective types (for example, converting to and from the *bcd* and *complex* type), and overload all necessary operators. These classes are independent of any hierarchy, but each class includes the iostream.h header file.

The C++ mathematical classes are

- *bcd*
- *complex*

bcd class   bcd.h

Creates binary-coded decimals (BCD) from integers or floating-point numerical types. The **friend** function *real* converts *bcd* numbers back to **long double**.

Example

```
/* Show thction can handle the bcd, */
/*   complex, and double types. Use the tan() function. */
#include <bcd.h>
#include <complex.h>

void main(void) {
    double PI = 3.1416;         /* Use to define radian angles. */

    double  x = (PI * 0.250);   /* 45 degree angle approximation. */
    bcd     y = bcd(x);
    complex z = complex(x);
```

```
cout   <<  " double x = "   << x << "\t\t tan(x) = " << tan(x)
       <<  "\n bcd y = "       << y << "\t\t\t tan(y) = " << tan(y)
       <<  "\n complex z = " << z << "\t tan(z) = " << tan(z);
}
```

Program output

```
double x = 0.7854        tan(x) = 1.000004
bcd y = 0.7854           tan(y) = 1.000004
complex z = (0.7854, 0)  tan(z) = (1.000004, 0)
```

Portability

DOS	UNIX	Win16	Win 32	ANSI C	ANSI C++	OS/2
+		+	+			+

Public constructors

Once you construct BCD numbers, you can freely mix them in expressions with **int**s, **double**s, and other numeric types.

Form 1   bcd();

Default used to declare a variable of type BCD.

```
bcd i;        // Construct a bcd-type number.
bcd j = 37;   // Construct and initialize a bcd-type number.
```

Form 2   bcd(int x);

Defines a BCD variable from an **int** variable or directly from an integer. For example,

```
int i = 15;
bcd j = bcd(i);   // Initialize j with a previously declared type.
bcd k = bcd(12);  // Construct k from the integer provided.
```

The previous example produces

```
i=15,j=15,k=12.
```

Form 3   bcd(unsigned int x);

Defines a BCD variable from one that was previously declared to be an **unsigned int** type. An unsigned integer can be provided directly to the constructor.

Form 4   bcd(long x);

Defines a BCD variable from a **long** variable or directly from a **long** value.

Form 5   bcd(unsigned long x);

Defines a BCD variable from one that was previously declared to be an **unsigned long** type.

Form 6   bcd(double x, int decimals = Max);

Defines a BCD variable from one that was previously declared to be a floating point **double** type. The constructor also creates a variable directly from a **double** value.

To specify a precision level (that is, the number of digits after the decimal point) that is different from the default, use the variable *decimals*. Here is an example:

```
double x = 1.2345;   // Declare and initialize in the usual manner.
bcd y = bcd(x, 2);   // Create a bcd numerical type from x.
```

The precision level for *y* is set to 2. Therefore, *y* is initialized with 1.23.

Form 7   bcd(long double x, int decimals = Max);

Defines a BCD variable from one that was previously declared to be a floating point **long double** type. Alternately, you can supply a **long double** value directly in the place of *x*.

To specify a precision level (that is, the number of digits after the decimal point) that is different from the default, use the variable *decimals*.

Friend functions

real

long double real (bcd number)

You can use the *real* function to convert a binary coded decimal number back to a **long double**. See the *C++ Programmer's Guide*, Chapter 2, for a discussion about arithmetic conversions.

You can use BCD numbers in any of the ANSI C standard math functions. The following ANSI C math functions are overloaded to operate with BCD types:

```
friendbcdabs(bcd&);
friendbcdacos(bcd&);
friendbcdasin(bcd&);
friendbcdatan(bcd&);
friendbcdcos(bcd&);
friendbcdcosh(bcd&);
friendbcdexp(bcd&);
friendbcdlog(bcd&);
friendbcdlog10(bcd&);
friendbcdpow(bcd&base,bcd&expon);
friendbcdsin(bcd&);
friendbcdsinh(bcd&);
friendbcdsqrt(bcd&);
friendbcdtan(bcd&);
friendbcdtanh(bcd&);
```

Operators

The *bcd* class overloads the operators +, –, *, /, +=, –=, *=, /=, =, ==, and !=. These operators provide BCD arithmetic manipulation as when used with the standard mathematical functions.

The operators << and >> are overloaded for stream input and output of BCD numbers, as they are for other data types in iostream.h.

Range

The BCD numbers have about 17 decimal digits precision, and a range of 1×10^{-125} to 1×10^{125} (approximately).

Note The number is rounded according to the rules of banker's rounding, which means round to nearest whole number, with ties being rounded to an even digit.

complex class   complex.h

Creates *complex* numbers. The *real* function converts *complex* numbers back to **long double**. The **friend** function returns the real part of a *complex* number or converts a *complex* number back to **double**. The data associated to a *complex* number consists of two floating-point numbers. *real* returns the one considered to be the real part.

Example

```
/* Show that an ANSI math function can handle the bcd, */
/*  complex, and double types. Use the tan() function. */
#include <bcd.h>
#include <complex.h>

void main(void) {
    double PI = 3.1416;         /* Use to define radian angles. */

    double  x = (PI * 0.250);  /* 45 degree angle approximation. */
    bcd     y = bcd(x);
    complex z = complex(x);

    cout  << " double x = "  << x << "\t\t tan(x) = " << tan(x)
          << "\n bcd y = "    << y << "\t\t\t tan(y) = " << tan(y)
          << "\n complex z = " << z << "\t tan(z) = " << tan(z);
}
```

Program output

```
double x = 0.7854       tan(x) = 1.000004
bcd y = 0.7854          tan(y) = 1.000004
complex z = (0.7854, 0)  tan(z) = (1.000004, 0)
```

Public constructors

Once you construct complex numbers, you can freely mix them in expressions with **ints**, **doubles**, and other numeric types.

Note If you do not want to program in C++, but instead want to program in C, the only constructs available to you are **struct** *complex* and *cabs*, which give the absolute value of a complex number. Both of these alternates are defined in math.h.

```
complex();
```

The default typically used to declare a variable of type *complex*. Here is an example:

```
complex i;      /* Construct a complex-type number. */
complex j = 37;  /* Construct and initialize a complex-type number. */
complex(double real, double imag = 0);
```

Creates a *complex* numerical type out of a **double**. Upon construction, a real and an imaginary part are provided. The imaginary part is taken to be zero if *imag* is omitted.

Friend functions

You can also use complex numbers in any of the ANSI C standard mathematical functions.

abs
friend double abs(complex& val);
Returns the absolute value of a complex number.

The complex version of *abs* returns a **double**. All other math functions return a *complex* type when *val* is *complex* type.

acos
friend complex acos(complex& z);
Calculates the arc cosine.

The complex inverse cosine is defined by

```
acos(z) = -i * log(z + i sqrt(1 - z))
arg
```

arg
double arg(complex x);
arg gives the angle, in radians, of the number in the complex plane.

The positive real axis has angle 0, and the positive imaginary axis has angle pi/2. If the argument passed to *arg* is *complex 0* (zero), *arg* returns zero.

$arg(x)$ returns $atan2(imag(x), real(x))$.

Example
```
// Illustrate the use of each of the complex friend functions.
#include <complex.h>  // This also includes iostream.h.

int main(void)
{
   complex z(3.1, 4.2);
   cout << "z = " << z << "\n";
   cout << "  has real part = " << real(z) << "\n";
   cout << "  and imaginary part = " << imag(z) << "\n";
   cout << "z has complex conjugate = " << conj(z) << "\n";

   double mag = sqrt(norm(z));
   double ang = arg(z);
```

```
        cout << "The polar form of z is:\n";
        cout << "    magnitude = " << mag << "\n";
        cout << "    angle (in radians) = " << ang << "\n";
        cout << "Reconstructing z from its polar form gives:\n";
        cout << "    z = " << polar(mag,ang) << "\n";
        return 0;
    }
```

Program output

```
z = (3.1, 4.2)
    has real part = 3.1
    and imaginary part = 4.2
z has complex conjugate = (3.1, -4.2)
The polar form of z is:
    magnitude = 5.220153
    angle (in radians) = 0.934958
Reconstructing z from its polar form gives:
    z = (3.1, 4.2)
```

asin

friend complex asin(complex& z);

Calculates the arc sine.

The complex inverse sine is defined by

```
asin(z) = -i * log(i * z + sqrt(1 - z ))
atan
```

atan

friend complex atan(complex& z);

Calculates the arc tangent.

The complex inverse tangent is defined by

```
atan(z) = -0.5 i log((1 + i z)/(1 - i z))
```

conj

complex conj(complex z);

Returns the complex conjugate of a complex number.

conj(z) is the same as *complex(real(z), –imag(z))*.

cos

friend complex cos(complex& z);

Calculates the cosine of a value.

The complex cosine is defined by

```
cos(z) = ( exp(i * z) + exp(-i * z) ) / 2
```

cosh

friend complex cosh(complex& z);

Calculates the hyperbolic cosine of a value.

The complex hyperbolic cosine is defined by

```
cosh(z) = ( exp(z) + exp(-z) ) / 2
exp
```

exp

friend complex exp(complex& y);

Calculates the exponential *e* to the *y*.

The complex exponential function is defined by

```
exp(x + y * i) = exp(x) (cos(y) + i * sin(y) )
```

imag

double imag(complex x);

Returns the imaginary part of a complex number.

The data associated to a complex number consists of two floating-point (**double**) numbers. *imag* returns the one considered to be the imaginary part.

log

friend complex log(complex& z);

Calculates the natural logarithm of *z*.

The complex natural logarithm is defined by

```
log(z) = log( abs(z) ) + i * arg(z)
```

log10

friend complex log10(complex& z);

Calculates $\log_{10}(z)$.

The complex common logarithm is defined by

```
log10(z) = log(z) / log(10)
```

norm

double norm(complex x);

Returns the square of the absolute value. *norm(x)* returns the magnitude *real(x) * real(x) + imag(x) * imag(x)*.

norm can overflow if either the real or imaginary part is sufficiently large.

polar

complex polar(double mag, double angle = 0);

Returns a complex number with a given magnitude (absolute value) and angle.

polar(mag, angle) is the same as *complex(mag * cos(angle), mag * sin(angle))*.

pow

friend complex pow(complex& base, double expon);
friend complex pow(double base, complex& expon);
friend complex pow(complex& base, complex& expon);

Calculates *base* to the power of *expon*.

The complex *pow* is defined by

```
pow(base, expon) = exp(expon * log(base))
```

real

long double real(bcd number);

double real(complex x);

Converts a BCD or complex number back to a **long double** or returns the real part of complex number. The data associated to a complex number consists of two floating-point numbers; *real* returns the one considered to be the real part.

Example

```
/* Show that an ANSI math function can handle the bcd, */
/*  complex, and double types. Use the tan() function. */
#include <bcd.h>
#include <complex.h>

void main(void) {
    double PI = 3.1416;        /* Use to define radian angles. */

    double  x = (PI * 0.250);  /* 45 degree angle approximation. */
    bcd     y = bcd(x);
    complex z = complex(x);

    cout  << " double x = "  << x << "\t\t tan(x) = " << tan(x)
          << "\n bcd y = "    << y << "\t\t\t tan(y) = " << tan(y)
          << "\n complex z = " << z << "\t tan(z) = " << tan(z);
    }
```

Program output

```
double x = 0.7854        tan(x) = 1.000004
bcd y = 0.7854           tan(y) = 1.000004
complex z = (0.7854, 0)  tan(z) = (1.000004, 0)
```

sin

friend complex sin(complex& z);

Calculates the trigonometric sine.

The complex sine is defined by

```
sin(z) = ( exp(i * z) - exp(-i * z) ) / (2 * i)
```

sinh

friend complex sinh(complex& z);

Calculates the hyperbolic sine.

The complex hyperbolic sine is defined by

```
sinh(z) = ( exp(z) - exp(-z) ) / 2
```

sqrt

friend complex sqrt(complex& x);

Calculates the positive square root.

For any complex number *x*, *sqrt(x)* gives the complex root whose *arg* is *arg(x)*/2.

The complex square root is defined by

```
sqrt(x) = sqrt(abs(x)) (cos( arg(x) / 2) + i * sin(arg(x)/2))
```

tan

friend complex tan(complex& z);
Calculates the trigonometric tangent.

The complex tangent is defined by

```
tan(z) = sin(z) / cos(z)
```

tanh

friend complex tanh(complex& z);
Calculates the hyperbolic tangent.

The complex hyperbolic tangent is defined by

```
tanh(z) = sinh(z) / cosh(z)
```

Operators

The *complex* class overloads the operators +, –, *, /, +=, –=, *=, /=, =, ==, and !=. These operators provide complex arithmetic manipulation in the usual sense.

The operators << and >> are overloaded for stream input and output of complex numbers, as they are for other data types in iostream.h.

14

Class diagnostic macros

Borland provides a set of macros for debugging C++ code. They are located in checks.h. There are two types of macros, *default* and *extended*. The default macros are

- CHECK
- PRECONDITION
- TRACE
- WARN

The extended macros are

- CHECKX
- PRECONDITIONX
- TRACEX
- WARNX

Default macros provide straightforward value checking and message output. The extended macros let you create macro groups that you can selectively enable or disable. Extended macros also let you selectively enable or disable within a group based on a numeric threshold level.

Three preprocessor symbols control diagnostic macro expansion: _ _DEBUG, _ _TRACE, and _ _WARN. If one of these symbols is defined when compiling, then the corresponding macros expand and diagnostic code is generated. If none of these symbols is defined, then the macros do not expand and no diagnostic code is generated. These symbols can be defined on the command line using the **-D** switch, or by using #define statements within your code.

	_ _DEBUG=1	_ _DEBUG=2	_ _TRACE	_ _WARN
PRECONDITION	X	X		
PRECONDITIONX	X	X		
CHECK		X		
CHECKX		X		

	_ _DEBUG=1	_ _DEBUG=2	_ _TRACE	_ _WARN
TRACE			X	
TRACEX			X	
WARN				X
WARNX				X

To create a diagnostic version of an executable, place the diagnostic macros at strategic points within the program code and compile with the appropriate preprocessor symbols defined. Diagnostic versions of the Borland class libraries are built in a similar manner.

The following sections describe the default and extended diagnostic macros, give examples of their use, and explain message output and run-time control.

Default diagnostic macros   checks.h

CHECK
CHECK(<cond>)
Throws an exception if *<cond>* equals 0. Use CHECK to perform value checking within a function.

PRECONDITION
PRECONDITION(<cond>)
Throws an exception if *<cond>* equals 0. Use PRECONDITION on entry to a function to check the validity of the arguments and to do any other checking to determine if the function has been invoked correctly.

TRACE
TRACE(<msg>)
Outputs *<msg>*. TRACE is used to output general messages that are not dependent upon a particular condition.

WARN
WARN(<cond>,<msg>)
Outputs *<msg>* if *<cond>* is nonzero. It is used to output conditional messages.

Example of TRACE and WARN macros

The following program illustrates the use of the default TRACE and WARN macros:

```
#include <checks.h>

int main()
{
   TRACE( "Hello World" );
   WARN( 5 != 5, "Math is broken!" );
   WARN( 5 != 7, "Math still works!" );

   return 0;
}
```

When the previous code is compiled with _ _TRACE and _ _WARN defined, it produces the following output when run:

```
Trace PROG.C 5: [Def] Hello World
Warning PROG.C 7: [Def] Math still works!
```

This output indicates that the message "Hello World" was output by the default TRACE macro on line 5 of PROG.C, and the message "Math still works!" was output by the default WARN macro on line 7 of PROG.C.

Default diagnostic macros expand to extended diagnostic macros with the group set to "Def" and the level set to 0. This "Def" group controls the behavior of the default macros and is initially enabled with a threshold level of 0.

Extended diagnostic macros   checks.h

The extended macros CHECKX and PRECONDITIONX augment CHECK and PRECONDITION by letting you provide a message to be output when the condition fails.

The extended macros TRACEX and WARNX augment TRACE and WARN by providing a way to specify macro groups that can be independently enabled or disabled. TRACEX and WARNX require additional arguments that specify the group to which the macro belong, and the threshold level at which the macro should be executed. The macro is excuted only if the specified group is enabled and has a threshold level that is greater than or equal to the threshhold level argument used in the macro.

CHECKX
CHECKX(<cond>,<msg>)
Outputs <*msg*> and throws an exception if <*cond*> equals 0. Use CHECKX to perform value checking within a function.

PRECONDITIONX
PRECONDITIONX(<cond>,<msg>)
Outputs <*msg*> and throws an exception if <*cond*> equals 0. Use PRECONDITIONX on entry to a function to check the validity of the arguments and to do any other checking to determine if the function has been invoked correctly.

TRACEX
TRACEX(<group>,<level>,<msg>)
Trace only if <*group*> and <*level*> are enabled.

WARNX
WARNX(<group>,<cond>,<level>,<msg>)
Warn only if <*group*> and <*level*> are enabled.

DIAG_DECLARE_GROUP
DIAG_DECLARE_GROUP(<name>)
Declare a group named <*name*>. You cannot use DIAG_DECLARE_GROUP and DIAG_DEFINE_GROUP in the same compilation unit.

DIAG_DEFINE_GROUP
DIAG_DEFINE_GROUP(<name>,<enabled>,<level>)

Define a group named *<name>*. You cannot use DIAG_DECLARE_GROUP and DIAG_DEFINE_GROUP in the same compilation unit.

DIAG_ENABLE
DIAG_ENABLE(<group>,<state>)

Sets *<group>*'s enable flag to *<state>*.

DIAG_ISENABLED
DIAG_ISENABLED(<group>)

Returns nonzero if *<group>* is enabled.

DIAG_SETLEVEL
DIAG_SETLEVEL(<group>,<level>)

Sets *<group>*'s threshold level to *<level>*.

DIAG_GETLEVEL
DIAG_GETLEVEL(<group>)

Gets *<group>*'s threshold level.

Threshold levels are arbitrary numeric values that establish a threshold for enabling macros. A macro with a level greater than the group threshold level will not be executed. For example, if a group has a threshold level of 0 (the default value), all macros that belong to that group and have levels of 1 or greater are ignored.

Example of extended diagnostics macros

The following PROG.C example defines two diagnostic groups, *Group1* and *Group2*, which are used as arguments to extended diagnostic macros:

```
#include <checks.h>

DIAG_DEFINE_GROUP(Group1,1,0);
DIAG_DEFINE_GROUP(Group2,1,0);

void    main( int argc, char **argv )
{
   TRACE( "Always works, argc=" << argc );

   TRACEX( Group1, 0, "Hello" );
   TRACEX( Group2, 0, "Hello" );

   DIAG_DISABLE(Group1);

   TRACEX( Group1, 0, "Won't execute - group is disabled!" );
   TRACEX( Group2, 3, "Won't execute - level is too high!" );
}
```

When the above code is compiled with _ _TRACE defined and run, it produces the following output:

```
Trace PROG.C 8: [Def] Always works, argc=1
Trace PROG.C 10: [Group1] Hello
Trace PROG.C 11: [Group2] Hello
```

Note that the last two macros are not executed. In the first case, the group *Group1* is disabled. In the second case, the macro level exceeds *Group2*'s threshold level (set by default to 0).

Macro message output

The TRACE, TRACEX, WARN, and WARNX macros take a *<msg>* argument that is conditionally inserted into an output stream. This means that a sequence of objects can be inserted into the output stream as in this example

```
TRACE( "Mouse @ " << x << "," << y ); )
```

The use of streams is extensible to different object types and allows for parameters within trace messages.

Diagnostic macro message output can be viewed while the program is running. If the target environment is Windows, the output is sent to the *OutputDebugString* function, and can be viewed with the DBWIN.EXE or OX.SYS utilities. If Turbo Debugger is running, the output will be sent to its log window. If the target environment is DOS, the output is sent to the standard output stream and can be easily redirected at the command line.

Run-time macro control

Diagnostic groups can be controlled at runtime by using the control macros within your program or by directly modifying the group information within the debugger.

This group information is contained in a template class named *TDiagGroup<TDiagGroupClass##Group>*, where *##Group* is the name of the group. This class contains a static structure *Flags*, which in turn contains the enabled flag and the threshold level. For example, to enable the group *Group1*, you would set the variable *TDiagGroup<TDiagGroupClassGroup1>::Flags.Enabled* to 1.

15

Run-time support

These topics provide a detailed description of the functions and classes that provide run-time support. Any class operators or member functions are listed immediately after the class constructor.

See Chapter 1, "Keywords," for a discussion of how to use exception-handling keywords.

The following portability table applies to all classes and functions in this chapter except *set_new_handler*.

Portability

DOS	UNIX	Win 16	Win 32	ANSI C	ANSI C++	OS/2
+		+	+		+	

Bad_cast class   typeinfo.h

When **dynamic_cast** fails to make a cast to reference, the expression can throw *Bad_cast*. Note that when **dynamic_cast** fails to make a cast to pointer type, the result is the null pointer.

Bad_typeid class   typeinfo.h

When the operand of **typeid** is a dereferenced null pointer, the **typeid** operator can throw *Bad_typeid*.

set_new_handler
new.h

```
typedef void (new * new_handler)() throw(xalloc);
new_handler set_new_handler(new_handler my_handler);
```

set_new_handler installs the function to be called when the global **operator new()** or **operator new[]()** cannot allocate the requested memory. By default the **new** operators throw an *xalloc* exception if memory cannot be allocated. You can change this default behavior by calling *set_new_handler* to set a new handler. To retain the traditional version of **new**, which does not throw exceptions, you can use *set_new_handler(0)*.

If **new** cannot allocate the requested memory, it calls the handler that was set by a previous call to *set_new_handler*. If there is no handler installed by *set_new_handler*, **new** returns 0. *my_handler* should specify the actions to be taken when **new** cannot satisfy a request for memory allocation. The *new_handler* type, defined in new.h, is a function that takes no arguments and returns **void**. A *new_handler* can throw an *xalloc* exception.

The user-defined *my_handler* should do one of the following:

- Return after freeing memory
- Throw an *xalloc* exception or an exception derived from *xalloc*
- Call *abort* or *exit* functions

If *my_handler* returns, then **new** will again attempt to satisfy the request.

Ideally, *my_handler* would free up memory and return. **new** would then be able to satisfy the request and the program would continue. However, if *my_handler* cannot provide memory for **new**, *my_handler* must throw an exception or terminate the program. Otherwise, an infinite loop will be created.

Preferably, you should overload **operator new()** and **operator new[]()** to take appropriate actions for your applications.

Return value
set_new_handler returns the old handler, if one has been registered.

The user-defined argument function, *my_handler*, should not return a value.

Portability

DOS	UNIX	Win 16	Win 32	ANSI C	ANSI C++	OS/2
+			+	+		+	+

set_terminate
except.h

```
typedef void (*terminate_function)();
terminate_function set_terminate(terminate_function t_func);
```

set_terminate lets you install a function that defines the program's termination behavior when a handler for the exception cannot be found. The actions are defined in *t_func*, which is declared to be a function of type *terminate_function*. A *terminate_function* type, defined in except.h, is a function that takes no arguments, and returns **void**.

By default, an exception for which no handler can be found results in the program calling the *terminate* function. This will normally result in a call to *abort*. The program then ends with the message Abnormal program termination. If you want some function other than *abort* to be called by the *terminate* function, you should define your own *t_func* function. Your *t_func* function is installed by *set_terminate* as the termination function. The installation of *t_func* lets you implement any actions that are not taken by *abort*.

Return value

The previous function given to *set_terminate* will be the return value.

The definition of *t_func* must terminate the program. Such a user-defined function must not return to its caller, the *terminate* function. An attempt to return to the caller results in undefined program behavior. It is also an error for *t_func* to throw an exception.

set_unexpected   except.h

```
typedef void ( * unexpected_function )();
unexpected_function set_unexpected(unexpected_function unexpected_func);
```

set_unexpected lets you install a function that defines the program's behavior when a function throws an exception not listed in its exception specification. The actions are defined in *unexpected_func*, which is declared to be a function of type *unexpected_function*. An *unexpected_function* type, defined in except.h, is a function that takes no arguments, and returns **void**.

By default, an unexpected exception causes *unexpected* to be called. If *unexpected_func* is defined, it is subsequently called by *unexpected*. Program control is then turned over to the user-defined *unexpected_func*. Otherwise, *terminate* is called.

Return value

The previous function given to *set_unexpected* will be the return value.

The definition of *unexpected_func* must not return to its caller, the *unexpected* function. An attempt to return to the caller results in undefined program behavior.

unexpected_func can also call *abort*, *exit*, or *terminate*.

terminate   except.h

```
void terminate();
```

The function *terminate* can be called by *unexpected* or by the program when a handler for an exception cannot be found. The default action by *terminate* is to call *abort*. Such a default action causes immediate program termination.

You can modify the way that your program will terminate when an exception is generated that is not listed in the exception specification. If you do not want the program to terminate with a call to *abort*, you can instead define a function to be called. Such a function (called a *terminate_function*) will be called by *terminate* if it is registered with *set_terminate*.

Return value

None.

typeinfo class   typeinfo.h

Provides information about a type.

Example

```
TYPE INFORMATION.
#include <iostream.h>
#include <typeinfo.h>

class __rtti Alpha {
   virtual void func() {};  // This makes Alpha a polymorphic class type.
};

class B : public Alpha {};

int main(void) {
   B Binst;            // Instantiate class B
   B *Bptr;            // Declare a B-type pointer
   Bptr = &Binst;      // Initialize the pointer

   // THESE TESTS ARE DONE AT RUNTIME

   if (typeid( *Bptr ) == typeid( B ) )
       // Ask "WHAT IS THE TYPE FOR *Bptr?"
       cout << "Name is " << typeid( *Bptr).name();

   if (typeid( *Bptr ) != typeid( Alpha ) )
       cout << "\nPointer is not an Alpha-type.";

   return 0;
   }

// Program Output
// Name is B
// Pointer is not an Alpha-type.
```

Public constructor

Only a private constructor is provided. You cannot create *typeinfo* objects. By declaring your objects to be **_ _rtti** types, or by using the **–RT** compiler switch, the compiler provides your objects with the elements of *typeinfo*. *typeinfo* references are generated by the **typeid** operator.

See Chapter 3 in the *C++ Programmer's Guide* for a discussion of the **typeid** operator.

Public member functions

The functions, *fname* and *name*, perform identically. Use *fname* in large memory-model programs.

name
const char* name( ) const;
const char*__for fname( ) const;
This function returns a printable string that identifies the type *name* of the operand to **typeid**. The space for the character string is overwritten on each call.

before
int before(const typeinfo&);
Use this function to compare the lexical order of types. For example, to compare two types, *T1* and *T2*, use the following syntax:

```
typeid ( T1 ).before(typeid( T2 ));
```

The *before* function returns 0 or 1.

Operators

operator ==
int operator==(const typeinfo &) const;
Provides comparison of *typeinfos*.

operator !=
int operator!=(const typeinfo &) const;
Provides comparison of *typeinfos*.

unexpected   except.h

void unexpected( );
The *unexpected* function is called when a function throws an exception not listed in its exception specification. The program calls *unexpected*, which by default calls any user-defined function registered by *set_unexpected*. If no function is registered with *set_unexpected*, the *unexpected* function then calls *terminate*.

Return value
None, although *unexpected* may throw an exception.

xalloc class

Reports an error on allocation request.

Public constructor

xalloc(const string &msg, size_t size);

The *xalloc* class has no default constructor. Every use of *xalloc* must define the message to be reported when a *size* allocation cannot be fulfilled. The *string* type is defined in cstring.h header file.

Public member functions

raise
void raise() throw(xalloc);

Calling *raise* causes an *xalloc* to be thrown. In particular, it throws ***this**.

requested
size_t requested() const;

Returns the number of bytes that were requested for allocation.

xmsg class

Reports a message related to an exception.

Public constructor

xmsg(string msg);

There is no default constructor for *xmsg*. Every *xmsg* object must have a *string* message explicitly defined. The *string* type is defined in cstring.h header file.

Public member functions

raise
void raise() throw(xmsg);

Calling *raise* causes an *xmsg* to be thrown. In particular, it throws ***this**.

why
const string _FAR & why() const;

Reports the string used to construct an *xmsg*. Because every *xmsg* must have its message explicitly defined, every instance should have a unique message.

Chapter

16

C++ services classes

These are the C++ service classes you can use for accessing and manipulating time, date, file, and thread classes.

Class type	Header file
Date class	date.h
File class	file.h
String classes	cstring.h, regexp.h
Thread classes	thread.h
Time class	time.h

The header files for these classes are found in either \BC5\INCLUDE or \BC5\ INCLUDE\CLASSLIB.

Header file	Includes	Classes
classlib\date.h	_DEFS.H	*TDate*
file.h	DATE.H, _DEFS.H, FCNTL.H, STDLIB.H, STDIO.H, SHARE.H, SYS\STAT.H, SYS\TYPES.H, THREAD.H, TIME.H	*TFile*
cstring.h	CTYPE.H, EXCEPT.H, REF.H, STDDEF.H, STRING.H, WINDOWS.H	*string, TSubstring*
thread.h	CSTRING. H, CHECKS.H, _DEFS.H	*TCriticalSection, TSync, TThread*

string class   cstring.h

class string;

This class uses a technique called "copy-on-write." Multiple instances of a string can refer to the same piece of data so long as it is in a "read only" situation. If a string writes to the data, then a copy is automatically made if more than one string is referring to it.

8Chapter 16, C++ services classes   677

Public constructors

Form 1   string();
             The default constructor. Creates a string of length zero.

Form 2   string(const string _FAR &s);
             Copy constructor. Creates a string that contains a copy of the contents of string *s*.

Form 3   string(const string _FAR &s, size_t start, size_t n = NPOS);
             A string containing a copy of the *n* bytes beginning at position start of string *s* is created.

Form 4   string(const char _FAR *cp);
             A string containing a copy of the bytes from the location pointed to by *cp* through the first 0 byte is created (conversion from **char***).

Form 5   string(const char _FAR *cp, size_t start, size_t n = NPOS);
             A string containing a copy of the *n* bytes beginning at the location pointed to by *cp* is created.

Form 6   string(char c);
             Constructs a string containing the character *c*.

Form 7   string(char c, size_t n = NPOS);
             Constructs a string containing the character *c* repeated *n* times.

Form 8   string(signed char c);
             Constructs a string containing the character *c*.

Form 9   string(signed char c, size_t n = NPOS);
             Constructs a string containing the character *c* repeated *n* times.

Form 10   string(unsigned char c);
             Constructs a string containing the character *c*.

Form 11   string(unsigned char c, size_t n = NPOS);
             Constructs a string containing the character c repeated *n* times.

Form 12   string(const TSubString _FAR &ss);
             Constructs a string from the substring *ss*.

Form 13   string(const char __far *cp);
             Constructs strings for Windows small and medium memory model.

Form 14   string(const char __far *cp, size_t start, size_t n = NPOS);
             Constructs strings for Windows small and medium memory model.

Form 15   string(HINSTANCE instance, UINT id, int len = 255);
             Windows version for constructing a string from a resource.

Public data member

StripType
enum StripType { Leading, Trailing, Both };
Enumerates type of stripping.

Public member functions

ansi_to_oem
void ansi_to_oem();
Converts the target string from the ANSI character set into the OEM-defined character set.

append
Form 1   string _FAR & append(const string _FAR &s);
Appends string *s* to the target string.

Form 2   string _FAR & append(const string _FAR &s, size_t start, size_t n = NPOS);
Beginning from the start position in *s*, appends the next *n* characters of string *s* to the target string.

Form 3   string _FAR & append(const char _FAR *cp, size_t start, size_t n = NPOS);
Beginning from the start position of the character array *cp*, appends the next *n* characters to the target string.

assign
Form 1   string _FAR & assign(const string _FAR &s);
Assigns string *s* to target string.

Form 2   string _FAR & assign(const string _FAR &s, size_t start, size_t n = NPOS);
Beginning from the start position in *s*, copies *n* characters to target string.

compare
Form 1   int compare(const string _FAR &s) const throw();
Compares the target string to the string *s*. *compare* returns an integer less than, equal to, or greater than 0, depending on whether the target string is less than, equal to, or greater than *s*.

Form 2   int compare(const string _FAR &s, size_t orig, size_t n = NPOS) const throw();
Compares not more than *n* characters of string *s*, beginning at character position *orig*, with this string.

contains
Form 1   int contains(const char _FAR * pat) const;
Returns 1 if *pat* is found in the target string, 0 otherwise.

Form 2   int contains(const string _FAR & s) const;
Returns 1 if string *s* is found in the target string, 0 otherwise.

copy
Form 1   size_t copy(char _FAR *cb, size_t n = NPOS);
Copies at most *n* characters from the target string into the **char** array pointed to by *cb*. *copy* returns the number of characters copied.

Form 2   size_t copy(char _FAR *cb, size_t n, size_t pos);
Copies at most *n* characters beginning at position *pos* from the target string into the **char** array pointed to by *cb*. *copy* returns the number of characters copied.

Form 3   string copy() const throw(xalloc).;

Returns a distinct copy of the string.

c_str

const char _FAR *c_str() const;

Returns a pointer to a zero-terminated character array, that holds the same characters contained in the string. The returned pointer may point to the actual contents of the string, or it may point to an array that the string allocates for this function call. The effects of any direct modification to the contents of this array are undefined, and the results of accessing this array after the execution of any non-**const** member function on the target string are undefined.

Conversions from a string object to a **char*** are inherently dangerous, because they violate the class boundary and can lead to dangling pointers. For this reason class *string* does not have an implicit conversion to *char**, but provides *c_str* for use when this conversion is needed.

find

Form 1   size_t find(const string _FAR &s);

Locates the first occurrence of the string *s* in the target string. If the string is found, it returns the position of the beginning of *s* within the target string. If the string *s* is not found, it returns *NPOS*.

Form 2   size_t find(const string _FAR &s, size_t pos);

Locates the first occurrence of the string *s* in the target string, beginning at the position *pos*. If the string is found, it returns the position of the beginning of *s* within the target string. If *s* is not found, it returns *NPOS*, and does not change *pos*.

Form 3   size_t find(const TRegexp _FAR &pat, size_t i = 0);

Searches the string for patterns matching regular expression *pat* beginning at location *i*. It returns the position of the beginning of *pat* within the target string. If the *pat* is not found, it returns *NPOS*, and does not change *pos*.

Form 4   size_t find(const TRegexp _FAR &pat, size_t _FAR *ext, size_t i = 0) const;

Searches the string for patterns matching regular expression *pat* beginning at location *i*. Parameter *ext* returns the length of the matching string if found. It returns the position of the beginning of *pat* within the target string. If the *pat* is not found, it returns *NPOS*, and does not change *pos*.

find_first_of

Form 1   size_t find_first_of(const string _FAR &s) const;

Locates the first occurrence in the target string of any character contained in string *s*. If the search is successful *find_first_of* returns the character location. If the search fails, *find_first_of* returns *NPOS*.

Form 2   size_t find_first_of(const string _FAR &s, size_t pos) const;

Locates the first occurrence in the target string of any character contained in string *s*. If the search is successful, the function returns the character position within the target string, and *find_first_of* returns 1. If the search fails or if pos > length(), *find_first_of* returns *NPOS*.

find_first_not_of

Form 1   size_t find_first_not_of(const string _FAR &s) const;

Locates the first occurrence in the target string of any character not contained in string *s*. If the search is successful, *find_first_not_of* returns the character position within the target string. If the search fails it returns *NPOS*.

Form 2   size_t find_first_not_of(const string _FAR &s, size_t pos) const;

Locates the first occurrence in the target string of any character not contained in string *s*. If the search is successful, *find_first_not_of* returns the character position within the target string. If the search fails or if `pos > length()`, *find_first_not_of* returns *NPOS*.

find_last_of
Form 1   size_t find_last_of(const string _FAR &s) const;

Locates the last occurrence in the target string of any character contained in string *s*. If the search is successful *find_last_of* returns the character position within the target string. If the search fails it returns *NPOS*.

Form 2   size_t find_last_of(const string _FAR &s, size_t pos) const;

Locates the last occurrence in the target string of any character contained in string *s* after position *pos*. If the search is successful, *find_last_of* returns the character position within the target string. If the search fails or if `pos > length()`, *find_last_of* returns *NPOS*.

find_last_not_of
Form 1   size_t find_last_not_of(const string _FAR &s) const;

Locates the last occurrence in the target string of any character not contained in string *s*. If the search is successful *find_last_not_of* returns the character position within the target string. If the search fails it returns *NPOS*.

Form 2   size_t find_last_not_of(const string _FAR &s, size_t pos) const;

Locates the last occurrence in the target string of any character not contained in string *s* after position *pos*. If the search is successful, *find_last_not_of* returns the character position within the target string. If the search fails or if `pos > length()`, *find_last_not_of* returns *NPOS*.

get_at
char get_at(size_t pos) const throw(outofrange);

Returns the character at the specified position. If `pos > length()-1`, an *outofrange* exception is thrown.

get_case_sensitive_flag
static int get_case_sensitive_flag();

Returns 0 if the string comparisons are case sensitive, 1 if not.

get_initial_capacity
static unsigned get_initial_capacity();

Returns the number of characters that will fit in the string without resizing.

get_max_waste
static unsigned get_max_waste();

After a string is resized, returns the amount of free space available.

get_paranoid_check
static int get_paranoid_check();

Returns 1 if paranoid checking is enabled, 0 if not.

get_resize_increment
static unsigned get_resize_increment();
Returns the string resizing increment.

get_skipwhitespace_flag
static int get_skipwhitespace_flag();
Returns 1 if whitespace is skipped, 0 if not.

hash
unsigned hash() const;
Returns hash value.

initial_capacity
static size_t initial_capacity(size_t ic = 63);
Sets initial string allocation capacity.

insert
Form 1   string _FAR &insert(size_t pos, const string _FAR &s);

Inserts string *s* at position *pos* in the target string. *insert* returns a reference to the resulting string.

Form 2   string _FAR &insert(size_t pos, const string _FAR &s, size_t start, size_t n = NPOS);

Beginning at position *start* in *s*, the insert function inserts not more than *n* characters from the target string to the string *s* at position *pos* in the target string. *insert* returns a reference to the resulting string. If *pos* is invalid, insert throws the *outofrange* exception.

is_null
int is_null() const;
Returns 1 if the string is empty, 0 otherwise.

length
unsigned length() const;
Returns the number of characters in the target string. Since null characters can be stored in a string, *length()* might be greater than *strlen(c_str())*.

MaxWaste
static size_t MaxWaste(size_t mw = 63);
Sets the maximum empty space size and resizes the string.

oem_to_ansi
void oem_to_ansi();
Windows function for converting the target string from the ANSI character set to the OEM-defined character set.

prepend
Form 1   string _FAR &prepend(const string _FAR &s);

Prepends string *s* to the target string.

Form 2   string _FAR &prepend(const string _FAR &s, size_t start, size_t n = NPOS);

Beginning from start position in *s*, the prepend function prefixes the target string with *n* characters taken from string *s*.

Form 3	string _FAR &prepend(const char _FAR *cp);

Prepends the character array *cp* to the target string.

Form 4	string _FAR &prepend(const char _FAR *cp, size_t start, size_t n = NPOS);

Beginning from start position in *cp*, the *prepend* function prefixes the target string with *n* characters taken from character array *cp*.

put_at
void put_at(size_t pos, char c) throw(outofrange);

Replaces the character at *pos* with *c*. If *pos* is greater than or equal to *length( )* an *outofrange* exception is thrown.

read_file
istream _FAR &read_file(istream _FAR &is);

Reads from input stream *is* until an EOF or a null terminator is reached.

read_line
istream _FAR &read_line(istream _FAR &is);

Reads from input stream *is* until an EOF or a newline is reached.

read_string
istream _FAR &read_string(istream _FAR &is);

Reads from input stream *is* until an EOF or a null terminator is reached.

read_to_delim
istream _FAR &read_to_delim(istream _FAR &is, char delim = '\n');

Reads from input stream *is* until an EOF or a *delim* is reached.

read_token
istream _FAR &read_token(istream _FAR &is);

Reads from input stream *is* until whitespace is reached. Note that this function skips any initial whitespace.

rfind
Form 1	size_t rfind(const string _FAR &s);

Locates the last occurrence of the string *s* in the target string. If the string is found, it returns the position of the beginning of the string *s* within the target string. If *s* is not found, it returns *NPOS*.

Form 2	size_t rfind(const string _FAR &s, size_t pos);

Locates the last occurrence of the string *s*, that is not beyond the position *pos* in the target string. If the string is found, it returns the position of the beginning of *s* within the target string. If *s* is not found it returns *NPOS*, and does not change *pos*.

remove
Form 1	string _FAR &remove(size_t pos);

Removes the characters from *pos* to the end of the target string and returns a reference to the resulting string.

Form 2	string _FAR &remove(size_t pos, size_t n = NPOS);

Removes at most *n* characters from the target string beginning at *pos* and returns a reference to the resulting string.

replace

Form 1   string _FAR &replace(size_t pos, size_t n = NPOS, const string _FAR &s);

Removes at most *n* characters from the target string beginning at *pos*, and replaces them with a copy of the string *s*. *replace* returns a reference to the resulting string.

Form 2   string _FAR &replace(size_t pos, size_t n1, const string _FAR &s, size_t start, size_t n2);

Removes at most *n1* characters from the target string beginning at *pos*, and replaces them with *n2* characters of string *s* beginning at *start*. *replace* returns a reference to the resulting string.

reserve

Form 1   size_t reserve() const;

Returns an implementation-dependent value that indicates the current internal storage size. The returned value is always greater than or equal to *length( )*.

Form 2   void reserve(size_t ic);

Suggests to the implementation that the target string may eventually require *ic* bytes of storage.

resize

void resize(size_t m);

Resizes the string to *m* characters, truncating or adding blanks as necessary.

resize_increment

static size_t resize_increment (size_t ri = 64);

Sets the resize increment for automatic resizing.

set_case_sensitive

static int set_case_sensitive(int tf = 1);

Sets case sensitivity. 1 is case sensitive; 0 is not case sensitive.

set_paranoid_check

static int set_paranoid_check(int ck = 1);

String searches use a hash value scheme to find the strings. There is a possibility that more than one string could hash to the same value. Calling *set_paranoid_check* with *ck* set to 1 forces checking the string found against the desired string with the C library function *strcmp*. When *set_paranoid_check* is called with *ck* set to 0, this final check is not made.

skip_whitespace

static int skip_whitespace(int sk = 1);

Set to 1 to skip whitespace after a token read, 0 otherwise.

strip

TSubString strip(StripType s = Trailing, char c=' ');

Strips away *c* characters from the beginning, end, or both (beginning and end) of string *s*, depending on *StripType*.

substr

Form 1   string substr(size_t pos) const;

Creates a string containing a copy of the characters from *pos* to the end of the target string.

Form 2   string substr(size_t pos, size_t n = NPOS) const;

Creates a string containing a copy of not more than *n* characters from *pos* to the end of the target string.

substring

Form 1   TSubString substring(const char _FAR *cp);

Creates a *TSubString* object containing a copy of the characters pointed to by **cp*.

Form 2   const TSubString substring(const char _FAR *cp) const;

Creates a *TSubString* object containing a copy of the characters pointed to by **cp*.

Form 3   TSubString substring(const char _FAR *cp, size_t start);

Creates a *TSubString* object containing a copy of the characters pointed to by **cp*, starting at character start.

Form 4   const TSubString substring(const char _FAR *cp, size_t start) const;

Creates a *TSubString* object containing a copy of the characters pointed to by **cp*, starting at character start.

to_lower
void to_lower();
Changes the string to lowercase.

to_upper
void to_upper();
Changes target string to uppercase.

Protected member functions

assert_element
void assert_element(size_t pos) const;
Throws an *outofrange* exception if an invalid element is given.

assert_index
void assert_index(size_t pos) const;
Throws an *outofrange* exception if an invalid index is given.

cow
void cow();
Copy-on-write. Multiple instances of a string can refer to the same piece of data as long as it is in a read-only situation. If a string writes to the data, then *cow* (copy-on-write) is called to make a copy if more than one string is referring to it.

valid_element
int valid_element(size_t pos) const;
Returns 1 if *pos* is an element of the string, 0 otherwise.

valid_index

int valid_index(size_t pos) const;

Returns 1 if *pos* is a valid index of the string, 0 otherwise.

Operators

operator =

string _FAR & operator=(const string _FAR &s);

If the target string is the same object as the parameter passed to the assignment, the assignment operator does nothing. Otherwise it performs any actions necessary to free up resources allocated to the target string, then copies *s* into the target string.

operator +=

Form 1   string _FAR & operator += (const string _FAR &s);

Appends the contents of the string *s* to the target string.

Form 2   string _FAR & operator+=(const char _FAR *cp);

Appends the contents of *cp* to the target string.

operator +

friend string _Cdecl _FARFUNC operator+(const string _FAR &s, const char _FAR *cp);

Concatenates string *s* and *cp*.

operator []

Form 1   char _FAR & operator[](size_t pos);

Returns a reference to the character at position *pos*.

Form 2   char operator[](size_t pos) const;

Returns the character at position *pos*.

operator ()

Form 1   char _FAR & operator()(size_t pos);

Returns a reference to the character at position *pos*.

Form 2   TSubString operator()(size_t start, size_t len);

Returns the substring beginning at location *start* and spanning *len* bytes.

Form 3   TSubString operator()(const TRegexp _FAR & re);

Returns the first occurrence of a substring matching regular expression *re*.

Form 4   TSubString operator()(const TRegexp _FAR & re, size_t start);

Returns the first occurrence of a substring matching regular expression *re*, beginning at location *start*.

Form 5   char operator()(size_t pos) const;

Returns the character at position *pos*.

Form 6   const TSubString operator()(size_t start, size_t len) const;

Returns the substring beginning at location *start* and spanning *len* bytes.

Form 7   const TSubString operator()(const TRegexp _FAR & pat) const;

Returns the first occurrence of a substring matching regular expression *re*.

Form 8   const TSubString operator()(const TRegexp _FAR & pat, size_t start) const;
Returns the first occurrence of a substring matching regular expression *re*, beginning at location *start*.

operator ==
Form 1   friend int operator == (const string _FAR &s1, const string _FAR &s2);
Tests for equality of string *s1* and string *s2*. Two strings are equal if they have the same length, and if the same location in each string contains characters that compare equally. operator == returns a 1 to indicate that the strings are equal, and a 0 to indicate that they are not equal.

Form 2   friend int operator == (const string _FAR &s, const char _FAR *cp);
Tests for equality of string *s1* and **char** **cp*. The two are equal if they have the same length, and if the same location in each string contains characters that compare equally. operator == returns a 1 to indicate that the strings are equal, and a 0 to indicate that they are not equal.

Form 3   friend int operator == (const char _FAR *cp, const string _FAR &s);
Tests for equality of string *s1* and **char** **cp*. The two are equal if they have the same length, and if the same location in each string contains characters that compare equally. operator == returns a 1 to indicate that the strings are equal, and a 0 to indicate that they are not equal.

operator !=
Form 1   friend int operator != (const string _FAR &s1, const string _FAR &s2);
Tests for inequality of strings *s1* and *s2*. Two strings are equal if they have the same length, and if the same location in each string contains characters that compare equally. operator != returns a 1 to indicate that the strings are not equal, and a 0 to indicate that they are equal.

Form 2   friend int operator != (const string _FAR &s, const char _FAR *cp);
Tests for inequality between string *s* and **char** **cp*. The two are equal if they have the same length, and if the same location in each string contains characters that compare equally. operator != returns a 1 to indicate that the strings are not equal, and a 0 to indicate that they are equal.

Form 3   friend int operator != (const char _FAR *cp, const string _FAR &s);
Tests for inequality between string *s* and **char** **cp*. The two are equal if they have the same length, and if the same location in each string contains characters that compare equally. operator != returns a 1 to indicate that the strings are not equal, and a 0 to indicate that they are equal.

operator <
Form 1   friend int operator < (const string _FAR &s1, const string _FAR &s2);
Compares the string *s1* to string *s2*. Returns 1 if string s1 is less than *s2*, 0 otherwise.

Form 2   friend int operator < (const string _FAR &s, const char _FAR *cp);
Compares the string *s1* to **cp2*. Returns 1 if the left side of the expression is less than the right side, 0 otherwise.

Form 3   friend int operator < (const char _FAR *cp, const string _FAR &s);

Compares the string *s1* to **cp2*. Returns 1 if the left side of the expression is less than the right side, 0 otherwise.

operator <=

Form 1   friend int operator <= (const string _FAR &s1, const string _FAR &s2);

Compares string *s1* to **cp*. Returns 1 if the left side of the expression is less than or equal to the right side, 0 otherwise.

Form 2   friend int operator <= (const string _FAR &s, const char _FAR *cp);

Compares the string *s1* to string *s2*. Returns 1 if string *s1* is less than or equal to *s2*, 0 otherwise.

Form 3   friend int operator <= (const char _FAR *cp, const string _FAR &s);

Compares string *s1* to **cp*. Returns 1 if the left side of the expression is less than or equal to the right side, 0 otherwise.

operator >

Form 1   friend int operator > (const string _FAR &s1, const string _FAR &s2);

Compares the string *s1* to string *s2*. Returns 1 if string *s1* is greater than *s2*, 0 otherwise.

Form 2   friend int operator > (const string _FAR &s, const char _FAR *cp);

Compares string *s1* to **cp2*. Returns 1 if the left side of the expression is greater than the right side, 0 otherwise.

Form 3   friend int operator > (const char _FAR *cp, const string _FAR &s);

Compares string *s1* to **cp2*. Returns 1 if the left side of the expression is greater than the right side, 0 otherwise.

operator >=

Form 1   friend int operator >= (const string _FAR &s1, const string _FR &s2);

Compares string *s1* to string *s2*. Returns 1 if string *s1* is greater than or equal to *s2*, 0 otherwise.

Form 2   friend int operator >= (const string _FAR &s, const char _FAR *cp);

Compares string *s1* to **cp*. Returns 1 if the left side of the expression is greater than or equal to the right side, 0 otherwise.

Form 3   friend int operator >= (const char _FAR *cp, const string _FAR &s);

Compares string *s1* to **cp*. Returns 1 if the left side of the expression is greater than or equal to the right side, 0 otherwise.

Related global operators and functions

operator >>

Form 1   friend ipstream _FAR & operator >> (ipstream _FAR & is, string _FAR & str);

Extracts string *str* from input stream *is*.

Form 2   istream _FAR & _Cdecl _FARFUNC operator>>(istream _FAR &is, string _FAR &s);

Behaves the same as **operator >>** (*istream&*, **char** ***), and returns a reference to *is*.

operator <<

Form 1   ostream _FAR & _Cdecl _FARFUNC operator<<(ostream _FAR &os, const string _FAR & s);

Behaves the same as **operator << (***ostream&,* **const char** *)* except that it does not terminate when it encounters a null character in the string. Returns a reference to *os*.

Form 2   opstream _FAR& _Cdecl operator << (opstream _FAR & os, const string _FAR & str);

Inserts string *str* into persistent output stream *os*.

operator +

Form 1   string _Cdecl _FARFUNC operator + (const char _FAR *cp, const string _FAR &s);

Concatenates **cp* and string *s*.

Form 2   string _Cdecl _FARFUNC operator + (const string _FAR &s1, const string _FAR &s2);

Concatenates string *s1* and *s2*.

getline

Form 1   istream _FAR & _Cdecl getline(istream _FAR &is, string _FAR &s);

Behaves the same as *istream::getline(chptr, NPOS)*, except that instead of storing into a **char** array, it stores into a *string. getline* returns a reference to *is*.

Form 2   istream _FAR & _Cdecl getline(istream _FAR &is, string _FAR &s, char c);

Behaves the same as *istream::getline(cb, NPOS, c)*, except that instead of storing into a **char** array, it stores into a *string. getline* returns a reference to *is*.

to_lower

string _Cdecl _FARFUNC to_lower(const string _FAR &s);

Changes string *s* to lowercase.

to_upper

string _Cdecl _FARFUNC to_upper(const string _FAR &s);

Changes string *s* to uppercase.

TDate class   date.h

class TDate

The *TDate* class represents a date. It has members that read, write, and store dates, and that convert dates to Gregorian calendar dates.

Type definitions

DayTy

typedef unsigned DayTy;

Day type.

HowToPrint

enum HowToPrint{ Normal, Terse, Numbers, EuropeanNumbers, European };

Lists different print formats.

JulTy
typedef unsigned long JulTy;
Julian calendar type.

MonthTy
typedef unsigned MonthTy;
Month type.

YearTy
typedef unsigned YearTy;
Year type.

Public constructors

Form 1   TDate();
Constructs a *TDate* object with the current date.

Form 2   TDate(DayTy day, YearTy year);
Constructs a *TDate* object with the given day and year. The base date for this computation is December 31 of the previous year. If year == 0, it constructs a *TDate* with January 1, 1901, as the "day zero." For example, *TDate*(–1,0) = December 31, 1900, and *TDate*(1,0) = January 2, 1901.

Form 3   TDate(DayTy day, const char* month, YearTy year);
Constructs a *TDate* object for the given day, month, and year.

Form 4   TDate(DayTy day, MonthTy month, YearTy year);
Constructs a *TDate* object for the given day, month, and year.

Form 5   TDate(istream& is);
Constructs a *TDate* object, reading the date from input stream *is*.

Form 6   TDate(const TTime& time);
Constructs a *TDate* object from *TTime* object time.

Public member functions

AsString
string AsString() const;
Converts the *TDate* object to a string object.

Between
int Between(const TDate& d1, const TDate& d2) const;
Returns 1 if this *TDate* object is between *d1* and *d2*, inclusive.

CompareTo
int CompareTo(const TDate &) const;
Returns 1 if the target *TDate* is greater than parameter *TDate*, –1 if the target is less than the parameter, and 0 if the dates are equal.

Day
DayTy Day() const;
Returns the day of the year (1–365).

DayName
const char *DayName(DayTy weekDayNumber);
Returns a string name for the day of the week, where Monday is 1 and Sunday is 7.

DayOfMonth
DayTy DayOfMonth() const;
Returns the day of the month (1–31).

DayOfWeek
DayTy DayOfWeek(const char* dayName);
Returns the number associated with a string naming the day of the week, where Monday is 1 and Sunday is 7.

DaysInYear
DayTy DaysInYear(YearTy);
Returns the number of days in the year specified (365 or 366).

DayWithinMonth
int DayWithinMonth(MonthTy, DayTy, YearTy);
Returns 1 if the given day is within the given month for the given year.

FirstDayOfMonth
Form 1   DayTy FirstDayOfMonth() const;
Returns the number of the first day of the month for this *TDate*.

Form 2   DayTy FirstDayOfMonth(MonthTy month) const;
Returns the number of the first day of a given month. Returns 0 if *month* is outside the range 1 through 12.

Hash
unsigned Hash() const;
Returns a hash value for the date.

IndexOfMonth
MonthTy IndexOfMonth(const char *monthName);
Returns the number (1–12) of the month *monthName*.

IsValid
int IsValid() const;
Returns 1 if this *TDate* is valid, 0 otherwise.

Jday
JulTy Jday(MonthTy, DayTy, YearTy);
Converts the given Gregorian calendar date to the corresponding Julian day number. Gregorian calendar started on Sep. 14, 1752. This function is not valid before that date. Returns 0 if the date is invalid.

Leap

int Leap() const;

Returns 1 if this *TDate's* year is a leap year, 0 otherwise.

Max

TDate Max(const TDate& dt) const;

Compares this *TDate* with *dt* and returns the date with the greater Julian number.

Min

TDate Min(const TDate& dt) const;

Compares this *TDate* with *dt* and returns the date with the lesser Julian number.

Month

MonthTy Month() const;

Returns the month number for this *TDate*.

MonthName

const char *MonthName(MonthTy monthNumber);

Returns the string name for the given *monthNumber* (1–12). Returns 0 for an invalid *monthNumber*.

NameOfDay

const char *NameOfDay() const;

Returns this *TDate's* day string name.

NameOfMonth

const char *NameOfMonth() const;

Returns this *TDate's* month string name.

Previous

Form 1   TDate Previous(const char *dayName) const;

Returns the *TDate* of the previous *dayName*.

Form 2   TDate Previous(DayTy day) const;

Returns the *TDate* of the previous day.

SetPrintOption

HowToPrint SetPrintOption(HowToPrint h);

Sets the print option for all *TDate* objects and returns the old setting.

WeekDay

DayTy WeekDay() const;

Returns 1 (Monday) through 7 (Sunday).

Year

YearTy Year() const;

Returns the year of this *TDate*.

Protected member functions

AssertIndexOfMonth
static int AssertIndexOfMonth(MonthTy m);
Returns 1 if *m* is between 1 and 12 inclusive, otherwise returns 0.

AssertWeekDayNumber
static int AssertWeekDayNumber(DayTy d);
Returns 1 if *d* is between 1 and 7 inclusive, otherwise returns 0.

Operators

operator <
int operator < (const TDate& date) const;
Returns 1 if this *TDate* precedes *date*, otherwise returns 0.

operator <=
int operator <= (const TDate& date) const;
Returns 1 if this *TDate* is less than or equal to *date*, otherwise returns 0.

operator >
int operator > (const TDate& date) const;
Returns 1 if this *TDate* is greater than *date*, otherwise returns 0.

operator >=
int operator >= (const TDate& date) const;
Returns 1 if this *TDate* is greater than or equal to *date*, otherwise returns 0.

operator ==
int operator == (const TDate& date) const;
Returns 1 if this *TDate* is equal to *date*, otherwise returns 0.

operator !=
int operator != (const TDate& date) const;
Returns 1 if this *TDate* is not equal to *date*, otherwise returns 0.

operator -
JulTy operator - (const TDate& dt) const;
Subtracts *dt* from this *TDate* and returns the difference.

operator +
Form 1 friend TDate operator + (const TDate& dt, int dd);

Form 2 friend TDate operator + (int dd, const TDate& dt);
Returns a new *TDate* containing the sum of this *TDate* and *dd*.

operator ++
void operator ++ ();
Increments this *TDate* by 1.

operator --
void operator -- ();
Decrements this *TDate* by 1.

operator +=
void operator += (int dd);
Adds *dd* to this *TDate*.

operator -=
void operator -= (int dd);
Subtracts *dd* from this *TDate*.

operator <<
friend ostream& operator << (ostream& os, const TDate& date);
Inserts *date* into output stream *os*.

operator >>
friend istream& operator >> (istream& is, TDate& date);
Extracts *date* from input stream *is*.

Friend operator

operator -
friend TDate operator - (const TDate& dt, int dd);
Subtracts *dd* from this *TDate* and returns the difference.

TFile class   file.h

class TFile
The *TFile* class encapsulates standard file characteristics and operations.

Public constructors

Form 1   TFile();
Creates a *TFile* object with a file handle of *FileNull*.

Form 2   TFile(int handle);
Creates a *TFile* object with a file handle of *handle*.

Form 3   TFile(const TFile& file);
Creates a *TFile* object with the same file handle file.

Form 4   TFile(const char* name, uint16 access=ReadOnly, uint16 permission=PermRdWr);
Creates a *TFile* object and opens file name with the given attributes. The file is created if it does not exist.

Public data members

FileNull
enum { FileNull };

Represents a null file handle.

File flags
File translation modes and sharing capabilities:

```
enum{
    ReadOnly    = O_RDONLY,
    ReadWrite   = O_RDWR,
    WriteOnly   = O_WRONLY,
    Create      = O_CREAT | O_TRUNC,
    CreateExcl  = O_CREAT | O_EXCL,
    Append      = O_APPEND,
#if defined( _ _FLAT_ _ )
    Compat      = SH_COMPAT,
    DenyNone    = SH_DENYNONE,
#else
    DenyRead    = SH_DENYRD,
    DenyWrite   = SH_DENYWR,
#endif
    DenyRdWr    = SH_DENYRW,
    NoInherit   = O_NOINHERIT
    };
```

File read and write permissions:

```
enum{
    PermRead    = S_IREAD,
    PermWrite   = S_IWRITE,
    PermRdWr    = S_IREAD | S_IWRITE
    };
```

File types:

```
enum{
    Normal      = 0x00,
    RdOnly      = 0x01,
    Hidden      = 0x02,
    System      = 0x04,
    Volume      = 0x08,
    Directory   = 0x10,
    Archive     = 0x20
    };
```

File pointer seek direction:

```
enum seek_dir
    {
    beg = 0,
    cur = 1,
    end = 2
    };
```

TFileStatus structure:

```
struct TFileStatus
{
    TTime createTime;
    TTime modifyTime;
    TTime accessTime;
    long size;
    uint8 attribute;
    char fullName[_MAX_PATH];
};
```

Public member functions

Close
int Close();
Closes the file. Returns nonzero if successful, 0 otherwise.

Flush
void Flush();
Performs any pending I/O functions.

GetHandle
int GetHandle() const;
Returns the file handle.

GetStatus
Form 1   int GetStatus(TFileStatus& status) const;
Fills *status* with the current file status. Returns nonzero if successful, 0 otherwise.

Form 2   int GetStatus(const char *name, TFileStatus& status);
Fills *status* with the status for *name*. Returns nonzero if successful, 0 otherwise.

IsOpen
int IsOpen() const;
Returns 1 if the file is open, 0 otherwise.

Length
Form 1   long Length() const;
Returns the file length.

Form 2   void Length(long newLen);
Resizes file to *newLen*.

LockRange
void LockRange(long position, uint32 count);
Locks *count* bytes, beginning at *position* of the associated file.

Open
int Open(const char* name, uint16 access, uint16 permission);
Opens file *name* with the given attributes. The file will be created if it does not exist. Returns 1 if successful, 0 otherwise.

Position
long Position() const;

Returns the current position of the file pointer. Returns –1 to indicate an error.

Read
Form 1   int Read(void *buffer, int numBytes);

Reads *numBytes* from the file into *buffer*.

Form 2   long Read(void huge *buffer, long numBytes);

Reads *numBytes* from the file into *buffer*. (32-bit Windows version)

Remove
static void Remove(const char *name);

Removes file *name*. Returns 0 if successful, –1 if unsuccessful.

Rename
static void Rename(const char *oldName, const char *newName);

Renames file *oldName* to *newName*.

Seek
long Seek(long offset, int origin = beg);

Repositions the file pointer to *offset* bytes from the specified *origin*.

SeekToBegin
long SeekToBegin();

Repositions the file pointer to the beginning of the file.

SeekToEnd
long SeekToEnd();

Repositions the file pointer to the end of the file.

SetStatus
static int SetStatus(const char *name, const TFileStatus& status);

Sets file name's status to *status*.

UnlockRange
void UnlockRange(long Position, uint32 count);

Unlocks the range at the given *Position*.

Write
Form 1   int Write(const void *buffer, int numBytes);

Writes *numbytes* of *buffer* to the file.

Form 2   long Write(const void huge *buffer, long numBytes);

Writes *numbytes* of *buffer* to the file. (32-bit Windows version).

TSubString class   cstring.h

class TSubString;

This class allows selected elements to be addressed.

Public member functions

get_at
char get_at(size_t pos) const;
Returns the character at the specified position. If *pos* > *length*() – 1, an exception is thrown.

is_null
int is_null() const;
Returns 1 if the string is empty, 0 otherwise.

length
size_t length() const;
Returns the substring length.

put_at
void put_at(size_t pos, char c);
Replaces the character at pos with c. If pos == length(), *put_at* appends c to the target string. If pos > length() an exception is thrown.

start
int start() const;
Returns the index of the starting character.

to_lower
void to_lower();
Changes the substring to lowercase.

to_upper
void to_upper();
Changes the substring to uppercase.

Protected member function

assert_element
int assert_element(size_t pos) const;
Returns 1 if *pos* represents a valid index into the substring, 0 otherwise.

Operators

operator =
TSubString _FAR & operator=(const string _FAR &s);
Copies *s* into the target substring.

operator ==
Form 1   int operator ==(const char _FAR * cp) const;
Tests for equality between the target substring and *cp. The two are equal if they have the same length, and if the same location in each string contains the same character. operator == returns a 1 to indicate that the strings are equal, and a 0 to indicate that they are not equal.

Form 2   int operator ==(const string _FAR & s) const;

Tests for equality between the target substring and string *s*. Two are equal if they have the same length, and if the same location in each string contains the same character. operator == returns a 1 to indicate that the strings are equal, and a 0 to indicate that they are not equal.

operator !=

Form 1   int operator !=(const char _FAR * cp) const;

Tests for inequality between the target string and **cp*. Two strings are equal if they have the same length, and if the same location in each string contains the same character. operator != returns a 1 to indicate that the strings are not equal, and a 0 to indicate that they are equal.

Form 2   int operator !=(const string _FAR & s) const;

Tests for inequality between the target string and string *s*. Two strings are equal if they have the same length, and if the same location in each string contains the same character. operator != returns a 1 to indicate that the strings are not equal, and a 0 to indicate that they are equal.

operator ()

Form 1   char _FAR & operator ()(size_t pos);

Returns a reference to the character at position *pos*.

Form 2   char operator ()(size_t pos) const;

Returns the character at position *pos*.

operator []

Form 1   char _FAR & operator [](size_t pos);

Returns a reference to the character at position *pos*.

Form 2   char operator [](size_t pos) const;

Returns the character at position *pos*.

operator !

int operator !() const;

Detects null substrings. Returns 1 if the substring is not null.

TRegexp class   regexp.h

This class represents regular expressions. *TRegexp* is a support class used by the *string* class for string searches.

Regular expressions use these special characters:

. [ ] - ^ * ? + $

General rules

Characters other than the special characters match themselves. For example "yardbird" matches "yardbird."

A backslash (\) followed by a special character matches the special character itself. For example, "Pardon\?" matches "Pardon?".

The following escape codes can be used to match control characters:

Code	Explanation
\b	*Backspace*
\e	*Esc*
\f	Formfeed
\n	Newline
\r	Carriage return
\t	*Tab*
\x*ddd*	The literal hex number 0xddd
\^*x*	Where *x* matches some control code (for example \^c, \^c)

One-character regular expressions

The . special character matches any single character except a newline character. For example ".ive" would match "jive" or "five."

The [and] special characters are used to denote one-character regular expressions that will match any of the characters within the brackets. For example, "[aeiou]" would match either "a," "e," "i," "o," or "u."

The - special character is used within the [ ] special characters to denote a range of characters to match. For example, "[a–z]" would match any lowercase alphabetic character between a and z.

The ^ special character is used to specify search for any character but those specified. For example, "[^g–v]" would match on any lowercase alphabetic character NOT between g and v.

Multiple-character regular expressions

The * special character following a one-character regular expression matches zero or more occurrences of that regular expression. For example, "[a–z]*" matches zero or more occurrences of lowercase alphabetic characters.

The + special character following a one-character regular expression matches one or more occurrences of that regular expression. For example, "[0-9]+" matches one or more occurrences of lowercase alphabetic characters.

The ? special character specifies that the following character is optional. For example, "xy?z" matches "xy" or "xyz."

Regular expressions can be concatentated. For example, "[A-Z][a-z]*" matches capitalized words.

Matching at the beginning and end of a line

If the ^ special character is at the beginning of a regular expression, then a match occurs only if the string is at the beginning of a line. For example, "^[A-Z][a-z]*" matches capitalized words at the beginning of a line.

If the $ special character is at the end of a regular expression, then a match occurs only if the string is at the end of a line. For example, "[A-Z][a-z]*$" matches capitalized words at the end of a line.

Type definitions

StatVal

enum StatVal{OK=0, ILLEGAL, TOOLONG};

StatVal enumerates the status conditions returned by *TRegexp::status*, where

Status	Description
OK	Means the given regular expression is legal
ILLEGAL	Means the pattern was illegal
TOOLONG	Means the pattern exceeded maximum length (128)

Public constructors

Form1:   TRegexp(const char far* cp);
Constructs a regular expression object using the pattern given pointed to by *cp*.

Form2:   TRegexp(const TRegexp far& r);
Constructs a copy of regular expression object *r*.

Public member functions

find

size_t find(const string& s, size_t* len, size_t start=0)

Finds the first instance in string *s* that matches this regular expression. The search begins at index *start*, and *len* returns the length of the matching string if found. The return value contains the index of the the beginning of the matching string. If no match is found, *len* is 0, and –1 is returned.

status

StatVal status()

Returns the status of this regular expression. Status values are

Status	Description
OK	means the given regular expression is legal
ILLEGAL	means the pattern was illegal
TOOLONG	means the pattern exceeded maximum length (128)

Operators

operator =

Form 1   TRegexp& operator=(const TRegexp& r)

Sets this regular expression to a copy of *r*, using value semantics.

Form 2   TRegexp& operator=(const char* cp)

Sets this regular expression to the pattern given by *cp*.

TCriticalSection class   thread.h

class TCriticalSection

TCriticalSection provides a system-independent interface to critical sections in threads. *TCriticalSection* objects can be used in conjunction with *TCriticalSection::Lock* objects to guarantee that only one thread can be executing any of the code sections protected by the lock at any given time.

Public constructor and destructor

Constructor

TCriticalSection();

Constructs a *TCriticalSection* object.

Destructor

~TCriticalSection();

Destroys a *TCriticalSection* object.

TCriticalSection::Lock class   thread.h

class Lock

This nested class handles locking and unlocking critical sections.

Example

Only one thread of execution will be allowed to execute the critical code inside function *f* at any one time.

```
TCriticalSection LockF;
void f()
{
    TCriticalSection::Lock(LockF);

    // critical processing here
}
```

Public constructor and destructor

Constructor
Lock(const TCriticalSection&);
Requests a lock on the *TCriticalSection* object. If no other *Lock* object holds a lock on that *TCriticalSection* object, the lock is allowed and execution continues. If another *Lock* object holds a lock on that object, the requesting thread is blocked until the lock is released.

Destructor
~Lock();
Releases the lock.

TMutex class   thread.h

TT*Mutex* provides a system-independent interface to critical sections in threads. *TMutex* objects can be used in conjunction with *TMutex::Lock* class objects to guarantee that only one thread can be executing any of the code sections protected by the lock at any given time.

The differences between the classes *TCriticalSection* and *TMutex* are that a timeout can be specified when creating a *Lock* on a *TMutex* object, and that a *TMutex* object has an *HMTX* that can be used outside the class. This mirrors the distinction made in Windows NT between a CRITICALSECTION and a *Mutex*. Under NT a *TCriticalSection* object is much faster than a *TMutex* object. Under operating systems that do not make this distinction a *TCriticalSection* object can use the same underlying implementation as a *TMutex*, losing the speed advantage that it has under NT.

Public constructor and destructor

Constructor
TMutex();
Constructs a *TMutex* object.

Destructor
~TMutex();
Destroys a *TMutex* object.

Operator

operator HMTX
operator HMTX() const;
Returns a handle to the underlying *TMutex* object, for use in operating system calls that require it.

TMutex::Lock class   thread.h

This nested class handles locking and unlocking *TMutex* objects.

Public constructor

Lock(const TMutex&, unsigned long timeOut = NoLimit);
Requests a lock on the *TMutex* object. If no *Lock* object in another thread holds a lock on that *TMutex* object, the lock is allowed and execution continues. If a *Lock* object in another thread holds a lock on that object, the requesting thread is blocked until the lock is released.

Public member function

Release
void Release();
Releases the lock on the *TMutex* object.

TSync class   thread.h

TSync provides a system-independent interface for building classes that act like monitors—classes in which only one member can execute on a particular instance at any one time. *TSync* uses *TCriticalSection*, has no public members, and can only be used as a base class.

Example

```
class ThreadSafe : private TSync
{
public:
    void f();
    void g();
private:
    int i;
};

void ThreadSafe::f()
{
    Lock(this);
```

```
        if( i == 2 )
            i = 3;
    }

    void ThreadSafe::g()
    {
        Lock(this);
        if( i == 3 )
            i = 2;
    }
```

Protected constructors

Form 1   TSync();
Default constructor.

Form 2   TSync(const TSync&);
Copy constructor. Does not copy the *TCriticalSection* object.

Protected operator

operator =
const TSync& operator = (const TSync& s)
Assigns *s* to the target, and does not copy the *TCriticalSection* object.

TSync::Lock class   thread.h

class Lock : private TCriticalSection::Lock
This nested class handles locking and unlocking critical sections.

Public constructor and destructor

Constructor
Lock(const TSync *s);
Requests a lock on the critical section of the *TSync* object pointed to by *s*. If no other *Lock* object holds a lock on that *TCriticalSection* object, the lock is allowed and execution continues. If another *Lock* object holds a lock on that object, the requesting thread is blocked until the lock is released.

Destructor
~Lock();
Releases the lock.

TThread class

class TThread

The *TThread* class provides a system-independent interface to threads.

Example

```
class TimerThread : private TThread
{
public:
    TimerThread() : Count(0) {}
private:
    unsigned long Run();
    int Count;
};

unsigned long TimerThread::Run()
{
    // loop 10 times
    while( Count++ < 10 )
    {
        sleep(1000);     // delay 1 second
        cout << "Iteration " << Count << endl;
    }
    return 0L;
}

int main()
{
    TimerThread timer;
    timer.Start();
    Sleep( 20000 );      // delay 20 seconds
    return 0;
}
```

Protected constructors and destructor

Constructor
Form 1   TThread();
Constructs an object of type *TThread*.

Form 2   TThread(const TThread&);
Copy constructor. Puts the target object into the *Created* state.

Destructor
virtual ~TThread();
Destroys the *TThread* object.

Type definition

Status

enum Status { Created, Running, Suspended, Finished, Invalid };

Describes the state of the thread, as follows:

Thread state	Description
Created	The object has been created but its thread has not been started. The only valid transition from this state is to *Running*, which happens on a call to *Start*. In particular, a call to *Suspend* or *Resume* when the object is in this state is an error and will throw an exception.
Running	The thread has been started successfully. There are two transitions from this state: •When the user calls *Suspend*, the object moves into the *Suspended* state. •When the thread exits the object moves into the *Finished* state. Calling *Resume* on an object that is in the *Running* state is an error and will throw an exception.
Suspended	The thread has been suspended by the user. Subsequent calls to *Suspend* nest, so there must be as many calls to *Resume* as there were to *Suspend* before the thread resumes execution.
Finished	The thread has finished executing. There are no valid transitions out of this state. This is the only state from which it is legal to invoke the destructor for the object. Invoking the destructor when the object is in any other state is an error and will throw an exception.

Public member functions

GetPriority

int GetPriority( ) const;

Gets the thread priority.

GetStatus

Status GetStatus( ) const;

Returns the current status of the thread. See the previous table under "Type Definition".

Resume

unsigned long Resume( );

Resumes execution of a suspended thread.

SetPriority

int SetPriority(int);

Sets the thread priority.

Start

HANDLE Start( );

Begins execution of the thread, and returns the thread handle.

Suspend

unsigned long Suspend( );

Suspends execution of the thread.

Terminate

void Terminate( );

Sets an internal flag that indicates that the thread should exit. The derived class can check the state of this flag by calling *ShouldTerminate*.

TerminateAndWait

void TerminateAndWait(unsigned long timeout = NoLimit);

Combines the behavior of *Terminate* and *WaitForExit*. Sets an internal flag that indicates that the thread should exit and blocks the calling thread until the internal thread exits or until the time specified by timeout, in milliseconds, expires. A timeout of –1 says to wait indefinitely.

WaitForExit

void WaitForExit(unsigned long timeout = NoLimit);

Blocks the calling thread until the internal thread exits or until the time specified by timeout, in milliseconds, expires. A timeout of –1 says wait indefinitely.

Protected member function

ShouldTerminate

int ShouldTerminate( ) const;

Returns a nonzero value to indicate that *Terminate* or *TerminateAndWait* has been called and that the thread will finish its processing and exit.

Protected operator

operator =

const TThread& operator = (const TThread&);

The *TThread* assignment operator. The target object must be in either the *Created* or *Finished* state. If so, assignment puts the target object into the *Created* state. If the object is not in either state, an exception will be thrown.

TThread::TThreadError class   thread.h

class TThreadError

TThreadError defines the exceptions that are thrown when a threading error occurs.

Type definitions

ErrorType

enum ErrorType
   {
   SuspendBeforeRun,
   ResumeBeforeRun,
   ResumeDuringRun,
   SuspendAfterExit,
   ResumeAfterExit,

CreationFailure,
DestroyBeforeExit,
AssignError
};

Identifies the type of error that occurred. The following list explains each error type:

Error type	Description
SuspendBeforeRun	The user called *Suspend* on an object before calling *Start*.
ResumeBeforeRun	The user called *Resume* on an object before calling *Start*.
ResumeDuringRun	The user called *Resume* on a thread that was not suspended.
SuspendAfterExit	The user called *Suspend* on an object whose thread had already exited.
ResumeAfterExit	The user called *Resume* on an object whose thread had already exited.
CreationFailure	The operating system was unable to create the thread.
DestroyBeforeExit	The destructor of the object was invoked before its thread had exited.
AssignError	An attempt was made to assign to an object that was not in either the *Created* or *Finished* state.

Public member function

GetErrorType
ErrorType GetErrorType( ) const;
Returns the *ErrorType* for the error that occurred.

TTime class

class TTime
The *TTime* class encapsulates time functions and characteristics.

Type definitions

typedef unsigned HourTy;
typedef unsigned MinuteTy;
typedef unsigned SecondTy;
typedef unsigned long ClockTy;
Type definitions for hours, minutes, and seconds since January 1, 1901.

Public constructors

Form 1   TTime();
Constructs a *TTime* object with the current time.

Form 2   TTime(ClockTy s);
Constructs a *TTime* object with the given *s* (seconds since January 1, 1901).

Form 3   TTime(HourTy h, MinuteTy m, SecondTy s = 0);
Constructs a *TTime* object with the given time and today's date.

Form 4   TTime(const TDate&, HourTy h=0, MinuteTy m=0, SecondTy s=0);
Constructs a *TTime* object with the given time and date.

Protected data members

MaxDate
static const TDate MaxDate;
The maximum valid date for *TTime* objects.

RefDate
static const TDate RefDate;
The minimum valid date for *TTime* objects: January 1, 1901.

Public member functions

AsString
string AsString( ) const;
Returns a string object containing the time.

BeginDST
static TTime BeginDST(unsigned year);
Returns the start of daylight saving time for the given *year*.

Between
int Between(const TTime& a, const TTime& b) const;
Returns 1 if the target date is between *TTime a* and *TTime b*, 0 otherwise.

CompareTo
int CompareTo(const TTime &) const;
Compares *t* to this *TTime* object and returns 0 if the times are equal, 1 if *t* is earlier, and −1 if *t* is later.

EndDST
static TTime EndDST(unsigned year);
Returns the time when daylight saving time ends for the given *year*.

Hash
unsigned Hash( ) const;
Returns seconds since January 1, 1901.

Hour
HourTy Hour( ) const;
Returns the hour in local time.

HourGMT
HourTy HourGMT( ) const;
Returns the hour in Greenwich mean time.

IsDST
int IsDST() const;
Returns 1 if the time is in daylight saving time, 0 otherwise.

IsValid
int IsValid() const;
Returns 1 if this *TTime* object contains a valid time, 0 otherwise.

Max
TTime Max(const TTime& t) const;
Returns either this *TTime* object or *t*, whichever is greater.

Min
TTime Min(const TTime& t) const;
Returns either this *TTime* object or *t*, whichever is less.

Minute
MinuteTy Minute() const;
Returns the minute in local time.

MinuteGMT
MinuteTy MinuteGMT() const;
Returns the minute in Greenwich Mean Time.

PrintDate
static int PrintDate(int flag);
Set *flag* to 1 to print the date along with the time; set to 0 to not print the date. Returns the old setting.

Second
SecondTy Second() const;
Returns seconds.

Seconds
ClockTy Seconds() const;
Returns seconds since January 1, 1901.

Protected member functions

AssertDate
static int AssertDate(const TDate& d);
Returns 1 if *d* is between the earliest valid date (*RefDate*) and the latest valid date (*MaxDate*).

Operators

operator <
int operator < (const TTime& t) const;
Returns 1 if the target time is less than time *t*, 0 otherwise.

operator <=

int operator <= (const TTime& t) const;

Returns 1 if the target time is less than or equal to time *t*, 0 otherwise.

operator >

int operator > (const TTime& t) const;

Returns 1 if the target time is greater than time *t*, 0 otherwise.

operator >=

int operator >= (const TTime& t) const;

Returns 1 if the target time is greater than or equal to time *t*, 0 otherwise.

operator ==

int operator == (const TTime& t) const;

Returns 1 if the target time is equal to time *t*, 0 otherwise.

operator !=

int operator != (const TTime& t) const;

Returns 1 if the target time is not equal to time *t*, 0 otherwise.

operator ++

void operator++();

Increments the time by 1 second.

operator --

void operator--();

Decrements the time by 1 second.

operator +=

void operator+=(long s);

Adds *s* seconds to the time.

operator -=

void operator-=(long s);

Subtracts *s* seconds from the time.

operator +

friend TTime operator + (const TTime& t, long s);

friend TTime operator + (long s, const TTime& t);

Adds *s* seconds to time *t*.

operator -

friend TTime operator - (const TTime& t, long s);

friend TTime operator - (long s, const TTime& t);

Performs subtraction, in seconds, between *s* and *t*.

operator <<

Form 1   friend ostream& operator << (ostream& os, const TTime& t);

Inserts time *t* into output stream *os*.

Form 2   friend opstream& operator << (opstream& s, const TTime& d);

Inserts time *t* into persistent stream *s*.

operator >>

friend ipstream& operator >> (ipstream& s, TTime& d);

Extracts time *t* from persistent stream *s*.

Standard C++ class libraries reference

Part IV documents the Rogue Wave Software, Inc., implementation of the ANSI/ISO Standard C++ Library. This reference is a companion to Part IV, Standard class libraries guide, of the C++ *Programmer's Guide*. The Programmer's Guide introduces you to the standard class libraries and presents material from the how-to-implement perspective.

This part provides the details about Rogue Wave's implementation of the ANSI/ISO Standard Library.

Part IV, "Standard Class Libraries Guide" documents Rogue Wave's implementation of the Standard C++ Library.

Based on ANSI's Working Paper for Draft Proposed International Standard for Information Systems—Programming Language C++. April 28, 1995.

Typeface conventions used in this part

We have presented both *class_names* and *function_names()* in a distinctive font the first time they are introduced. In addition, when we wish to refer to a function name or algorithm name but not draw attention to the arguments, we will follow the function name with an empty pair of parenthesis. We do this even when the actual function invocation requires additional arguments. We have used the term *algorithm* to refer to the functions in the generic algorithms portion of the standard library, so as to avoid confusion with member functions, argument functions, and functions defined by the programmer. Note that both class names and function names in the standard library follow the convention of using an underline character as a separator. Throughout the text, examples and file names are printed in the same *italics* font used for function names.

In the text, it is common to omit printing the class name in the distinctive font after it has been introduced. This is intended to make the appearance of the text less visually disruptive. However, we return to the distinctive font to make a distinction between several different possibilities, as for example between the classes ***vector*** and ***list*** used as containers in constructing a ***stack***.

Standard class libraries reference

This chapter presents an alphabetical listing of all the classes, algorithms, and function objects provided by this release of Rogue Wave's Standard C++ Library. The heading of each entry indicates the category (that is, algorithms, containers, and so on) that the class belongs to. Table 17.1 provides a list of the classes organized by category.

For each class, the reference begins with a brief summary of the class, and a synopsis that indicates the header file(s), a declaration and definition of a class object, and any type definitions for the class. The reference continues with a description and, in most cases, an example. All methods associated with a class, including constructors, operators, member functions, and so on, are grouped in categories according to their general use and described. The categories, although not a part of the C++ language, provide a way of organizing the methods.

Throughout the documentation, there are frequent references to "self," which should be understood to mean "*this*".

Standards conformance

The information presented in this reference conforms with the requirements of the ANSI X3J16/ISO WG21 Joint C++ Committee.

Table 17.1 Categories of classes

Category	#include Syntax	Class
Algorithms	#include <algorithm>	adjacent_find
		binary_search
		copy
		copy_backward
		count
		count_if

Table 17.1   Categories of classes (continued)

Category	#include Syntax	Class
		equal
		equal_range
		fill
		fill_n
		find
		find_first_of
		find_if
		for_each
		generate
		generate_n
		includes
		inplace_merge
		iter_swap
		lexicographical_compare
		lower_bound
		make_heap
		max
		max_element
		merge
		min
		min_element
		mismatch
		next_permutation
		nth_element
		partial_sort
		partial_sort_copy
		partition
		pop_heap
		prev_permutation
		push_heap
		random_shuffle
		remove
		remove_copy
		remove_copy_if
		remove_if
		replace
		replace_copy
		replace_copy_if
		replace_if
		reverse
		reverse_copy
		rotate

Table 17.1 Categories of classes (continued)

Category	#include Syntax	Class
		rotate_copy
		search
		set_difference
		set_intersection
		set_symmetric_difference
		set_union
		sort
		sort_heap
		stable_partition
		stable_sort
		swap
		swap_ranges
		transform
		unique
		unique_copy
		upper_bound
Complex number library	#include <complex>	complex
Containers	#include <deque>	deque
	#include <list>	list
	#include <map>	map
	#include <map>	multimap
	#include <set>	multiset
	#include <queue>	priority_queue
	#include <queue>	queue
	#include <set>	set
	#include <stack>	stack
	#include <vector>	vector
Function adaptors	#include <functional>	bind1st
		bind2nd
		not1
		not2
		ptr_fun
Function objects	#include <functional>	binary_function
		binary_negate
		binder1st
		binder2nd
		divides
		equal_to
		greater
		greater_equal
		less

Table 17.1 Categories of classes (continued)

Category	#include Syntax	Class
		less_equal
		logical_and
		logical_not
		logical_or
		minus
		modulus
		negate
		not_equal_to
		plus
		pointer_to_binary_function
		pointer_to_unary_function
		times
		unary_function
Generalized numeric operations	#include <numeric>	accumulate
		adjacent_difference
		inner_product
		partial_sum
Insert iterators	#include <iterator>	back_insert_iterator
		back_inserter
		front_insert_iterator
		front_inserter
		insert_iterator
		inserter
Iterators	#include <iterator>	bidirectional iterator
		forward iterator
		input iterator
		output iterator
		random access iterator
		reverse_bidirectional_iterator
		reverse_iterator
Iterator operations	#include<iterator>	advance
		distance
Memory-handling primitives	#include <memory>	allocate
		construct
		deallocate
		destroy
		get_temporary_buffer
		return_temporary_buffer
Memory management	#include <memory>	raw_storage_iterator
		uninitialized_copy
		uninitialized_fill
		uninitialized_fill_n

Table 17.1 Categories of classes (continued)

Category	#include Syntax	Class
Numeric limits library	#include <limits>	numeric limits
String library	#include <string>	basic_string
		string
		wstring
Utility classes	#include <utility>	pair
Utility operators	#include <utility>	operator!=
		operator>
		operator<=
		operator>=

accumulate   Generalized numeric operation

Summary
Accumulate all elements within a range into a single value.

Synopsis
```
#include <numeric>
template <class InputIterator, class T>
T accumulate (InputIterator first,
        InputIterator last,
        T init);

template <class InputIterator,
        class T,
        class BinaryOperation>
T accumulate (InputIterator first,
        InputIterator last,
        T init,
        BinaryOperation binary_op);
```

Description
This algorithm accumulates, or "sums" all elements in range *[first, last)* into a single value. For instance, applying *accumulate* to the sequence {1,2,3} will produce {6}.

The first version of the algorithm uses plus (+) as the default operator. The second version lets you specify any binary operation.

To avoid the problem of accumulating an empty range, *accumulate* requires an initial value, *init*, that is used as the de facto first element of the accumulation. Usually *init* is the identity value for the binary operation of *accumulate*. (For example, in the default version of the algorithm, *init* is normally equal to 0. If you specify that *binary_op* is multiplication, then *init* would normally be equal to 1.)

Accumulation is done by initializing the accumulator *acc* with the initial value *init* and then modifying it with *acc = acc + *i* or *acc = binary_op(acc, *i)* for every iterator *i* in the range *[first, last)* in order. If the sequence is empty, *accumulate* returns *init*.

Complexity

accumulate performs exactly *last-first* applications of the binary operation.

Example

```
#include <numeric>    //for accumulate
#include <vector>     //for vector
#include <functional> //for times
using namespace std;

int main()
{
  //Typedef for vector iterators
  typedef vector<int>::iterator iterator;

  //Initialize a vector using an array of ints
  int d1[10] = {1,2,3,4,5,6,7,8,9,10};
  vector<int> v1(d1, d1+10);

  //Accumulate sums and products
  int sum = accumulate(v1.begin(), v1.end(), 0);
  int prod = accumulate(v1.begin(), v1.end(),
            1, times<int>());

  //Output the results
  cout << "For the series: ";
  for(iterator i = v1.begin(); i != v1.end(); i++)
  cout << *i << " ";

  cout << " where N = 10." << endl;
  cout << "The sum = (N*N + N)/2 = " << sum << endl;
  cout << "The product = N! = " << prod << endl;
  return 0;
}
```

adjacent_difference

Generalized numeric operation

Summary

Outputs a sequence of the differences between each adjacent pair of elements in a range.

Synopsis

#include <numeric>

```
template <class InputIterator, class OutputIterator>
OutputIterator adjacent_difference (InputIterator first,
                    InputIterator last,
                    OutputIterator result);


template <class InputIterator,
        class OutputIterator,
        class BinaryOperation>
OutputIterator adjacent_difference (InputIterator first,
                    InputIterator last,
                    OutputIterator result,
                    BinaryOperation bin_op);
```

Description

Informally, *adjacent_difference* fills a sequence with the differences between successive elements in a container. The result is a sequence in which the first element is equal to the first element of the sequence being processed, and the remaining elements are equal to the the calculated differences between adjacent elements. For instance, applying *adjacent_difference* to {1,2,3,5} will produce a result of {1,1,1,2}.

By default, subtraction is used to compute the difference, but you can supply any binary operator. The binary operator is then applied to adjacent elements. For example, by supplying the plus (+) operator, the result of applying *adjacent_difference* to {1,2,3,5} is the sequence {1,3,5,8}.

Formally, *adjacent_difference* assigns to every element referred to by iterator *i* in the range *[result + 1, result + (last - first))* a value equal to the appropriate one of the following lines of code:

```
*(first  + (i - result)) - *(first + (i - result) - 1)
```

or

```
binary_op (*(first + (i - result)), *(first + (i - result) - 1))
```

result is assigned the value of **first*.

The iterator that *adjacent_difference* returns is equal to *result + (last - first)*.

result can be equal to *first*. This allows you to place the results of applying *adjacent_difference* into the original sequence.

Complexity

This algorithm performs exactly *(last-first) - 1* applications of the default operation (-) or *binary_op*.

Example

```
#include<numeric>        //For adjacent_difference
#include<vector>         //For vector
#include<functional>     //For times
using namespace std;
```

```
int main()
{
  //Initialize a vector of ints from an array
  int arr[10] = {1,1,2,3,5,8,13,21,34,55};
  vector<int> v(arr,arr+10);

  //Two uninitialized vectors for storing results
  vector<int> diffs(10), prods(10);

  //Calculate difference(s) using default operator (minus)
  adjacent_difference(v.begin(),v.end(),diffs.begin());

  //Calculate difference(s) using the times operator
  adjacent_difference(v.begin(), v.end(), prods.begin(),
        times<int>());

  //Output the results
  cout << "For the vector: " << endl << "      ";
  copy(v.begin(),v.end(),ostream_iterator<int>(cout," "));
  cout << endl << endl;

  cout << "The differences between adjacent elements are: "
        << endl << "      ";
  copy(diffs.begin(),diffs.end(),
        ostream_iterator<int>(cout," "));
  cout << endl << endl;

  cout << "The products of adjacent elements are: "
        << endl << "      ";
  copy(prods.begin(),prods.end(),
        ostream_iterator<int>(cout," "));

  cout << endl;

  return 0;
}
```

adjacent_find   **Algorithm**

Summary
Find the first adjacent pair of elements in a sequence that are equivalent.

Synopsis
#include <algorithm>

template <class ForwardIterator>
 ForwardIterator
 adjacent_find(ForwardIterator first, ForwardIterator last);

```
template <class ForwardIterator, class Predicate>
 ForwardIterator
 adjacent_find(ForwardIterator first, ForwardIterator last,
         Predicate pred);
```

Description

There are two versions of the *adjacent_find* algorithm. The first finds equal adjacent
elements in the sequence defined by iterators *first* and *last* and returns an iterator *i*
pointing to the first of the equal elements. The second version lets you specify your own
binary function to test for a condition. It returns an iterator *i* pointing to the first of the
pair of elements that meet the conditions of the binary function. In other words,
adjacent_find returns the first iterator *i* such that both *i* and *i + 1* are in the range
[first, last) for which one of the following conditions holds:

```
   *i  ==  *(i  +  1)
```

or

```
   pred(*i,*(i  +  1))  ==  true
```

If *adjacent_find* does not find a match, it returns *last*.

Complexity

adjacent_find performs exactly *find(first,last,value) - first* applications of the corresponding
predicate.

Example

```
#include <vector>
#include <algorithm>
using namespace std;

int main()
{
  typedef vector<int>::iterator iterator;
  int d1[10] = {0,1,2,2,3,4,2,2,6,7};

  // Set up a vector
  vector<int> v1(d1,d1 + 10);

  // Try find
  iterator it1 = find(v1.begin(),v1.end(),3);
  // it1 = v1.begin() + 4;

  // Try find_if
  iterator it2 =
      find_if(v1.begin(),v1.end(),bind1st(equal_to<int>(),3));
  // it2 = v1.begin() + 4

  // Try both adjacent_find variants
  iterator it3 = adjacent_find(v1.begin(),v1.end());
```

```
    // it3 = v1.begin() +2

    iterator it4 =
        adjacent_find(v1.begin(),v1.end(),equal_to<int>());
    // v4 = v1.begin() + 2

    // Output results
    cout << *it1 << " " << *it2 << " " << *it3 << " "
        << *it4 << endl;

    return 0;
}
```

advance Iterator operation

Summary
Move an iterator forward or backward (if available) by a certain distance.

Synopsis
#include <iterator>

template <class InputIterator, class Distance>
void advance (InputIterator& i, Distance n);

Description
The *advance* template function allows an iterator to be advanced through a container by some arbitrary distance. For bidirectional and random access iterators, this distance may be negative. This function uses operator + and operator - for random access iterators, which provides a constant time implementation. For input, forward, and bidirectional iterators, *advance* uses operator ++ to provide linear time implementations. *advance* also uses operator -- with bidirectional iterators operator to provide linear time implementations of negative distances.

If n is positive, *advance* increments iterator reference i by n. For negative n, *advance* decrements reference i. Remember that *advance* accepts a negative argument n for random access and bidirectional iterators only.

Example
```
#include<iterator>
#include<list>
using namespace std;

int main()
{
  //Initialize a list using an array
  int arr[6] = {3,4,5,6,7,8};
  list<int> l(arr,arr+6);
```

```
//Declare a list iterator, s.b. a ForwardIterator
list<int>::iterator itr = l.begin();

//Output the original list
cout << "For the list: ";
copy(l.begin(),l.end(),ostream_iterator<int>(cout," "));
cout << endl << endl;
cout << "When the iterator is initialized to l.begin(),"
     << endl << "it points to " << *itr << endl << endl;

// operator+ is not available for a ForwardIterator,
// so use advance.

advance(itr, 4);
cout << "After advance(itr,4), the iterator points to "
     << *itr << endl;
return 0;
}
```

Algorithms

Summary
Generic algorithms for performing various operations on containers and sequences.

Synopsis
The synopsis of each algorithm appears in its entry in the reference guide.

Description
The Standard C++ Library provides a very flexible framework for applying generic algorithms to containers. The library also provides a rich set of these algorithms for searching, sorting, merging, transforming, scanning, and much more.

Each algorithm can be applied to a variety of containers, including those defined by a user of the library. The following design features make algorithms generic:

- Generic algorithms access the collection through iterators.

- Algorithms are templated on iterator types.

- Each algorithm is designed to require the least number of services from the iterators it uses.

In addition to requiring certain iterator capabilities, algorithms may require a container to be in a specific state. For example, some algorithms can only work on previously sorted containers.

There are several ways to group algorithms. The broadest categorization groups the algorithms based on whether or not they change the elements in the sequence. Those algorithms that alter (or mutate) the contents of a container fall into the mutating group. All others are considered non-mutating. Algorithms can also be grouped according to the type of operations they perform. Finally, because most algorithms rely on iterators to gain access to data, they can be grouped according to the type of iterator they require. The following three sections provide lists of algorithms grouped according to these criteria.

Algorithms by mutating/non-mutating function

The broadest categorization groups algorithms into two main types: mutating and non-mutating. Those algorithms that alter (or mutate) the contents of a container fall into the mutating group. All others are considered non-mutating.For example, both *fill* and *sort* are mutating algorithms, while *find* and *for_each* are non-mutating.

Non-mutating operations		
accumulate	find	max
adjacent_find	find_if	max_element
binary_search	find_first_of	min
count	for_each	min_element
count_if	includes	mismatch
equal	lexicographical_compare	nth_element
equal_range	lower_bound mismatch search	
Mutating operations		
copy	merge	reverse
copy_backward	nth_element	reverse_copy
fill	next_permutation	rotate swap
fill_n	partial_sort	rotate_copy
generate	partial_sort_copy	set_difference
generate_n	replace	set_symmetric_difference
inplace_merge	replace_copy	set_intersection
iter_swap	replace_copy_if	set_union
make_heap	replace_if	sort

Note that the library provides both in place and copy versions of many algorithms, such as *replace* and *replace_copy*. The library also provides versions of algorithms that allow the use of default comparators and comparators supplied by the user. Often these functions are overloaded, but in some cases (where overloading proved impractical or impossible) the names differ (e.g., *replace*, which will use equality to determine replacement, and *replace_if*, which accesses a user provided compare function).

Algorithms by operation

We can further distinguish algorithms by the kind of operations they perform. The following lists all algorithms by loosely grouping them into similar operations.

Binary search operations (elements must be sorted)	
binary_search	lower_bound
equal_range	upper_bound

Compare operations	
equal	mismatch
lexicographical_compare	

Copy operations	
copy	copy_backward

Heap operations	
make_heap	push_heap
pop_heap	sort_heap

Initializing operations	
fill	generate
fill_n	generate_n

Merge operations (elements must be sorted)	
inplace_merge	merge

Minimum and maximum	
max	min
max_element	min_element

Permutaton generators	
next_permutation	prev_permutation

Remove operations	
remove	remove_if
remove_copy	unique
remove_copy_if	unique_copy

Scanning operations	
accumulate	for_each

Search operations	
adjacent_find	find_if
count	find_first_of
count_if	search
find	

Set operations	
includes	set_symmetric_difference
set_difference	set_union
set_intersection	

Sorting operations	
nth_element	sort
partial_sort	stable_sort
partial_sort_copy	

Swap operations	
swap	swap_ranges

Transforming operations	
partition	reverse
random_shuffle	reverse_copy
replace	rotate
replace_copy	rotate_copy
replace_copy_if	stable_partition
replace_if	transform

Algorithms by iterator category

Each algorithm requires certain kinds of iterators (for a description of the iterators and their capabilities see the *iterator* entry in this manual). The following set of lists groups the algorithms according to the types of iterators they require.

Algorithms that use no iterators		
max	min	swap

Algorithms that require only input iterators		
accumulate	for_each	inner_product
count	find	lexicographical_compare
count_if	find_if	mismatch
equal	includes	

Algorithms that require only output iterators		
fill_n	generate_n	

Algorithms that read from input iterators and write to output iterators		
adjacent_difference	remove_copy_if	set_symmetric_difference
copy	replace_copy	set_union
merge	replace_copy_if	transform
partial_sum	set_difference	unique_copy
remove_copy	set_intersedtion	

Algorithms that require forward iterators		
adjacent_find	lower_bound	rotate

binary_search	max_element	search
equal_range	min_element	swap_ranges
fill	remove	unique
find_first_of	remove_if	upper_bound
generate	replace	
iter_swap	replace_if	

Algorithm that reads from forward iterators and writes to output iterators

rotate_copy

Algorithms that require bidirectional iterators

copy_backward	partition	stable_permutation
inplace_merge	prev_permutation	
next_permutation	reverse	

Algorithm that reads from bidirectional iterators and writes to output iterators

reverse_copy

Algorithms that require random access iterators

make_heap	pop_heap	sort
nth_element	push_heap	sort_heap
partial_sort	random_shuffle	stable_sort

Algorithm that reads from input iterators and write to random access iterators

partial_sort_copy

Complexity
The complexity for each of these algorithms is given in the manual page for that algorithm.

See also
Manual pages for each of the algorithms named in the lists above.

allocate   Memory handling primitive

Summary
Pointer based primitive for handling memory

Synopsis
```
#include <memory>

template <class T>
 T* allocate (ptrdiff_t n, T*);
```

Description

allocate reserves an unitialized memory buffer of size *n* sizeof(T)*, in system memory and returns a typed pointer to that buffer.

See also

Other memory handling primitives: *deallocate, construct, get_temporary_buffer, return_temporary_buffer*

associative containers

Summary

Associative containers are ordered containers. These containers provide member functions that allow the efficient insertion, retrieval and manipulation of keys. The standard library provides the *map, multimap, set* and *multiset* associative containers. *map* and *multimap* associate values with the keys and allow for fast retrieval of the value, based upon fast retrieval of the key. *set* and *multiset* store only keys, allowing fast retrieval of the key itself.

See also

For more information about associative containers, see the *C++ Programmer's Guide*, Chapter 21, "Container classes," or see the section on the specific container.

auto_ptr   Memory management

Summary
A simple, smart pointer class.

Synopsis
```
#include <memory>

template <class X> class auto_ptr {

public:

// constructor/copy/destroy

explicit auto_ptr (X* p = 0);
auto_ptr (auto_ptr<X>&);
void operator= (auto_ptr<X>&);
~auto_ptr ();

// members

X& operator* () const;
```

```
    X* operator-> () const;
    X* get () const;
    X* release ();
    void reset (X* p = 0);
};
```

Description

The template class *auto_ptr* holds onto a pointer obtained via *new* and deletes that object when the *auto_ptr* object itself is destroyed (such as when leaving block scope). *auto_ptr* can be used to make calls to operator *new* exception-safe. The *auto_ptr* class provides semantics of strict ownership: an object may be safely pointed to by only one *auto_ptr*, so copying an *auto_ptr* copies the pointer *and* transfers ownership to the destination.

Constructor

```
explicit
auto_ptr (X* p = 0);
```
Constructs an object of class *auto_ptr<X>*, initializing the held pointer to *p*. Requires that *p* points to an object of class *X* or a class derived from *X* for which *delete p* is defined and accessible, or that *p* is a null pointer.

```
auto_ptr (auto_ptr<X>& a);
```
Constructs an object of class *auto_ptr<X>*, and copies the argument *a* to *this. *this becomes the new owner of the underlying pointer.

Destructor

```
~auto_ptr ();
```
Deletes the underlying pointer.

Operators

```
void
operator= (auto_ptr<X>& a);
```
Assignment operator. Copies the argument *a* to *this. *this becomes the new owner of the underlying pointer. If *this already owned a pointer, then that pointer is deleted first.

```
X&
operator* () const;
```
Returns a reference to the object to which the underlying pointer points.

```
X*
operator-> () const;
```
Returns the underlying pointer.

Member functions

```
X*
get () const;
```
Returns the underlying pointer.

X*

release();

Releases ownership of the underlying pointer. Returns that pointer.

void

reset (X* p = 0);

Requires that *p* points to an object of class *X* or a class derived from *X* for which *delete p* is defined and accessible, or *p* is a null pointer. Deletes the current underlying pointer, then resets it to *p*.

Example

```
//
// stdlib/examples/manual/auto_ptr.cpp
//
#include <iostream.h>
#include <memory>
using namespace std;

//
// A simple structure.
//
struct X
{
    X (int i = 0) : m_i(i) { }
    int get() const { return m_i; }
    int m_i;
};

int main ()
{
    //
    // b will hold a pointer to an X.
    //
    auto_ptr<X> b(new X(12345));
    //
    // a will now be the owner of the underlying pointer.
    //
    auto_ptr<X> a = b;
    //
    // Output the value contained by the underlying pointer.
    //
    cout << a->get() << endl;
    //
    // The pointer will be deleted when a is destroyed on leaving scope.
    //
    return 0;
}
```

back_insert_iterator, back_inserter
Insert iterator

Summary
An insert iterator used to insert items at the end of a collection.

Synopsis
#include <iterator>

template <class Container>
 class back_insert_iterator : public output_iterator {

protected:
   Container& container;
public:
   back_insert_iterator (Container& x);
   back_insert_iterator<Container>&
   operator= (const Container::value_type& value);
   back_insert_iterator<Container>& operator* ();
   back_insert_iterator<Container>& operator++ ();
   back_insert_iterator<Container> operator++ (int);
};

template <class Container>
 back_insert_iterator<Container> back_inserter (Container& x)

Description
Insert iterators let you *insert* new elements into a collection rather than copy a new element's value over the value of an existing element. The class *back_insert_iterator* is used to insert items at the end of a collection. The function *back_inserter* creates an instance of a *back_insert_iterator* for a particular collection type. A *back_insert_iterator* can be used with *vectors*, *deques*, and *lists*, but not with *maps* or *sets*.

Example
```
/***************************************************************
 *
 * ins_itr.cpp - Example program of insert iterator.
 *
 * $Id: ins_itr.cpp,v 1.7 1995/10/06 18:18:03 hart Exp $
 *
 * $$RW_INSERT_HEADER "slyrs.str"
 *
 ***************************************************************/

#include <iterator>
#include <deque>
using namespace std;

int main ()
{
   //
   // Initialize a deque using an array.
```

```
        //
        int arr[4] = { 3,4,7,8 };
        deque<int> d(arr+0, arr+4);
        //
        // Output the original deque.
        //
        cout << "Start with a deque: " << endl << "     ";
        copy(d.begin(), d.end(), ostream_iterator<int>(cout," "));
        //
        // Insert into the middle.
        //
        insert_iterator<deque<int> > ins(d, d.begin()+2);
        *ins = 5; *ins = 6;
        //
        // Output the new deque.
        //
        cout << endl << endl;
        cout << "Use an insert_iterator: " << endl << "     ";
        copy(d.begin(), d.end(), ostream_iterator<int>(cout," "));
        //
        // A deque of four 1s.
        //
        deque<int> d2(4, 1);
        //
        // Insert d2 at front of d.
        //
        copy(d2.begin(), d2.end(), front_inserter(d));
        //
        // Output the new deque.
        //
        cout << endl << endl;
        cout << "Use a front_inserter: " << endl << "     ";
        copy(d.begin(), d.end(), ostream_iterator<int>(cout," "));
        //
        // Insert d2 at back of d.
        //
        copy(d2.begin(), d2.end(), back_inserter(d));
        //
        // Output the new deque.
        //
        cout << endl << endl;
        cout << "Use a back_inserter: " << endl << "     ";
        copy(d.begin(), d.end(), ostream_iterator<int>(cout," "));
        cout << endl;

        return 0;
    }
```

Constructor

back_insert_iterator (Container& x);
Constructor. Creates an instance of a *back_insert_iterator* associated with container *x*.

Operators

back_insert_iterator<Container>&
operator = (const Container::value_type& value);
Inserts a copy of *value* on the end of the container, and returns **this*.

back_insert_iterator<Container>&
operator* ();
Returns **this*.

back_insert_iterator<Container>&
operator++ ();

back_insert_iterator<Container>
operator++ (int);
Increments the input iterator and returns **this*.

Helper function

template <class Container>
back_insert_iterator<Container>
back_inserter (Container& x)
Returns a *back_insert_iterator* that will insert elements at the end of container *x*. This function allows you to create insert iterators inline.

See also
insert iterators

basic_string   Strings Library

Summary
A templated class for handling sequences of character-like entities. *string* and *wstring* are specialized versions of *basic_string* for *char*s and *wchar_t*s respectively.

```
typedef basic_string <char> string;
typedef basic_string <wchar_t> wstring;
```

Synopsis
#include <string>

template <class charT,
    class traits = string_char_traits<charT>,
    class Allocator = allocator>

class basic_string {

public:

```
// Types

typedef traits                    traits_type;
typedef typename traits::char_type      value_type;

typedef typename Allocator::size_type       size_type;
typedef typename Allocator::difference_type  difference_type;

typedef typename Allocator::reference       reference;
typedef typename Allocator::const_reference  const_reference;
typedef typename Allocator::pointer          pointer;
typedef typename Allocator::const_pointer    const_pointer;

typedef typename Allocator::pointer          iterator;
typedef typename Allocator::const_pointer    const_iterator;

typedef reverse_iterator<const iterator,
           value_type,
           const reference,
           difference_type>
const_reverse_iterator;

typedef reverse_iterator<iterator,
           value_type,
           reference,
           difference_type>   reverse_iterator;

static const size_type npos = -1;

// Constructors/Destructors

explicit basic_string(Allocator& = Allocator());
basic_string(const basic_string& str, size_type pos = 0,
        size_type n = npos, Allocator& = Allocator());
basic_string(const charT* s, size_type n,
        Allocator& = Allocator());
basic_string(const charT* s, Allocator& = Allocator());
basic_string(size_type n, charT c,
        Allocator& = Allocator());
template <class InputIterator>
basic_string(InputIterator begin, InputIterator end,
        Allocator& = Allocator());
~basic_string();

// Assignment operators
```

```
basic_string& operator=(const basic_string& str);
basic_string& operator=(const charT* s);
basic_string& operator=(charT c);

// Iterators
iterator      begin();
const_iterator begin() const;
iterator      end();
const_iterator end() const;

reverse_iterator      rbegin();
const_reverse_iterator rbegin() const;
reverse_iterator      rend();
const_reverse_iterator rend() const;

// Capacity
size_type     size() const;
size_type     length() const;
size_type     max_size() const;
void          resize(size_type n, charT c);
void          resize(size_type n);
size_type     capacity() const;
void          reserve(size_type res_arg);
bool          empty() const;

// Element access
charT         operator[](size_type pos) const;
reference     operator[](size_type pos);
const_reference at(size_type n) const;
reference      at(size_type n);

// Modifiers
basic_string& operator+=(const basic_string& rhs);
basic_string& operator+=(const charT* s);
basic_string& operator+=(charT c);
basic_string& append(const basic_string&,
              size_type pos = 0,
              size_type = npos);
basic_string& append(const charT* s, size_type n);
basic_string& append(const charT* s);
basic_string& append(size_type n, charT c = charT());
template<class InputIterator>
basic_string& append(InputIterator, InputIterator);

basic_string& assign(const basic_string& str,
```

```
                        size_type pos = 0,
                        size_type n = npos);
        basic_string& assign(const charT* s, size_type n);
        basic_string& assign(const charT* s);
        basic_string& assign(size_type n, charT c );
        template<class InputIterator>
        basic_string& assign(InputIterator, InputIterator);

        basic_string& insert(size_type pos1,
                        const basic_string& str,
                        size_type pos = 0,
                        size_type n = npos);
        basic_string& insert(size_type pos, const charT* s,
                        size_type n);
        basic_string& insert(size_type pos, const charT* s);
        basic_string& insert(size_type pos, size_type n,
                        charT c );
        iterator insert(iterator p, charT c = charT());
        iterator insert(iterator p, size_type n,
                        charT c );
        template<class InputIterator>
        void insert(iterator p, InputIterator first,
                        InputIterator last);

        basic_string& remove(size_type pos = 0,
                        size_type n = npos);
        basic_string& remove(iterator position);
        basic_string& remove(iterator first, iterator last);

        basic_string& replace(size_type pos, size_type n1,
                        const charT* s, size_type n2);
        basic_string& replace(size_type pos1, size_type n1,
                        const basic_string& str,
                        size_type pos2 = 0,
                        size_type n2 = npos);
        basic_string& replace(size_type pos, size_type n,
                        const charT* s);
        basic_string& replace(size_type pos, size_type n,
                        size_type n2, charT c);
        basic_string& replace(iterator i1, iterator i2,
                        const basic_string& str);
        basic_string& replace(iterator i1, iterator i2,
                        const charT* s, size_type n);
        basic_string& replace(iterator i1, iterator i2,
                        const charT* s);
```

```
basic_string& replace(iterator i1, iterator i2,
            size_type n, charT c );
template<class InputIterator>
basic_string& replace(iterator i1, iterator i2,
            InputIterator j1,
            InputIterator j2);

size_type copy(charT* s, size_type n, size_type pos = 0);
void swap(basic_string<charT, traits, Allocator>&);

// String operations
const charT* c_str() const;
const charT* data() const;

size_type find(const basic_string& str,
        size_type pos = 0) const;
size_type find(const charT* s,
        size_type pos, size_type n) const;
size_type find(const charT* s, size_type pos = 0) const;
size_type find(charT c, size_type pos = 0) const;

size_type rfind(const basic_string& str,
        size_type pos = npos) const;
size_type rfind(const charT* s,
        size_type pos, size_type n) const;
size_type rfind(const charT* s,
        size_type pos = npos) const;
size_type rfind(charT c, size_type pos = npos) const;

size_type find_first_of(const basic_string& str,
            size_type pos = 0) const;
size_type find_first_of(const charT* s,
            size_type pos,
            size_type n) const;
size_type find_first_of(const charT* s,
            size_type pos = 0) const;
size_type find_first_of(charT c,
            size_type pos = 0) const;

size_type find_last_of(const basic_string& str,
            size_type pos = npos) const;
size_type find_last_of(const charT* s,
            size_type pos, size_type n) const;
size_type find_last_of(const charT* s,
            size_type pos = npos) const;
```

```
        size_type find_last_of(charT c,
                  size_type pos = npos) const;

        size_type find_first_not_of(const basic_string& str,
                      size_type pos = 0) const;
        size_type find_first_not_of(const charT* s,
                      size_type pos,
                      size_type n) const;
        size_type find_first_not_of(const charT* s,
                      size_type pos = 0) const;
        size_type find_first_not_of(charT c,
                  size_type pos = 0) const;

        size_type find_last_not_of(const basic_string& str,
                      size_type pos = npos) const;
        size_type find_last_not_of(const charT* s,
                      size_type pos,
                      size_type n) const;
        size_type find_last_not_of(const charT* s,
                      size_type pos = npos) const;
        size_type find_last_not_of(charT c,
                  size_type pos = npos) const;

        basic_string substr(size_type pos = 0,
                  size_type n = npos) const;
        int compare(const basic_string& str, size_type pos = 0,
              size_type n = npos) const;
        int compare(charT* s, size_type pos, size_type n) const;
        int compare(charT* s, size_type pos = 0) const;

    };
```

Description

basic_string<charT, traits, allocator> is a homogeneous collection of character-like entities. It provides general string functionality such as compare, append, assign, insert, remove, replace and various searches. *basic_string* also functions as an STL sequence container, providing random access iterators. This allows some of the generic algorithms to apply to strings.

Any underlying character-like type may be used as long as an appropriate *string_char_traits* class is provided or the default traits class is applicable.

Examples

```
#include<string>
using namespace std;
```

```
int main()
{
  string test, result;

  //Type in a string over five characters long
  while(test.empty() || test.size() <= 5)
  {
    cout << "Type a string between 5 and 100 characters long. "
            << endl;
    cin >> test;
  }

  //Test operator[] access
  cout << endl << "You typed in: " << test << endl << endl;
  cout << "Changing the third character from " << test[2] <<
          " to * " << endl;
  test[3] = '*';
  cout << "now its: " << test << endl << endl;

  //Try the insertion member function
  cout << "Identifying the middle: ";
  test.insert(test.size() / 2, "(the middle is here!)");
  cout << test << endl << endl;

  //Try replacement
  cout << "I didn't like the word 'middle',so instead,I'll say:"
          << endl;
  test.replace(test.find("middle",0), 6, "center");
  cout << test << endl;

  return 0;
}
```

Constructors and destructors

In all cases, the *Allocator* parameter specifies the storage for the constructed string.

explicit
basic_string (const Allocator& a = Allocator());
The default constructor. Creates a *basic_string* of length zero.

explicit
basic_string (size_type size, const Allocator& a = Allocator());
Creates a string of *size* entities.

basic_string (const basic_string<T, traits, Allocator>& s);
Creates a string that is a copy of *s*.

basic_string (const basic_string<T, traits, Allocator>&s,
        size_type pos,
        const Allocator& a = Allocator());
Creates a string that is a copy of *s* starting at character *pos*.

```
basic_string (const charT * s, size_type n,
        const Allocator& a = Allocator());
```
Creates a string that contains the first *n* characters of *s*.

```
basic_string (const charT * s,
        const Allocator& a = Allocator());
```
Creates a string containing all characters in *s* up to, but not including, a *traits::eos()* character. *s* cannot be a null pointer.

```
basic_string (size_type n, charT c,
        const Allocator& a  = Allocator());
```
Creates a string containing *n* repetitions of *c*.

```
template <class InputIterator>
basic_string  (InputIterator first, InputIterator last,
        const Allocator& a = Allocator());
```
Creates a *basic_string* of length *last - first*, filled with all values obtained by dereferencing the *InputIterators* on the range *[first, last)*.

```
~basic_string ();
```
Releases any allocated memory for this *basic_string*.

Operators

```
basic_string
operator = (const basic_string& str);
```
Sets the contents of this string to be the same as str.

```
basic_string
operator = (const charT * s);
```
Sets the contents of this string to be the same as *s* up to, but not including, the *traits::eos()* character.

```
basic_string
operator = (charT c);
```
Sets the contents of this string to be equal to the single *charT c*.

```
charT
operator [ ] (size_type pos) const;
```

```
reference
operator [ ] (size_type pos);
```
If *pos < size()*, returns the element at position *pos* in this string. If *pos == size()*, the *const* version returns *traits::eos()*, the behavior of the non-*const* version is undefined. The reference returned is invalidated by any call to *c_str()*, *data()*, or any non-*const* member function.

```
basic_string&
operator  += (const basic_string& s);
```

```
basic_string&
operator += (const charT* s);
```

```
basic_string&
operator += (charT c);
```

Concatenates a string onto the current contents of this string. The second member operator uses *traits::length()* to determine the number of elements from *s* to add. The third member operator adds the single character *c*. All return a reference to this string after completion.

Iterators

```
iterator begin ();
iterator begin () const;
```

Return an iterator initialized to the first element of the string.

```
iterator end ();
iterator end () const;
```

Return an iterator initialized to the position after the last element of the string.

```
iterator rbegin ();
iterator rbegin () const;
```

Returns an iterator equivalent to *reverse_iterator(end())*.

```
iterator rend ();
iterator rend () const;
```

Returns an iterator equivalent to *reverse_iterator(begin())*.

Member functions

```
basic_string&
append (const basic_string& s, size_type
    pos = 0, size_type n = npos);

basic_string&
append (const charT* s, size_type n);

basic_string&
append (const charT* s);

basic_string&
append (charT c);

basic_string&
append (size_type n, charT c );

template<class InputIterator>
basic_string&
append (InputIterator first, InputIterator last);
```

Append another string to the end of this string. The first function appends the lesser of *n* and *s.size() - pos* characters of *s*, beginning at position *pos* to this string. This member will throw an *out_of_range* exception if *pos > str.size()*. The second member appends *n* characters of the array pointed to by *s*. The third variation appends elements from the array pointed to by *s* up to, but not including, a *traits::eos()* character. The fourth and fifth variations append one or *n* repetitions of *c*, respectively. The final *append* function appends the elements specified in the range *[first, last)*.

All functions will throw a *length_error* exception if the resulting length will exceed *max_size()*. All return a reference to this string after completion.

```
basic_string&
assign (const basic_string& s,
    size_type pos = 0, size_type n = npos);

basic_string&
assign (const charT* s, size_type n);

basic_string&
assign (const charT* s);

basic_string&
assign (charT c);

basic_string&
assign (size_type n, charT c );

template<class InputIterator>
basic_string&
assign (InputIterator first, InputIterator last);
```

Replace the value of this string with the value of another.

All versions of the function assign values to this string. The first variation assigns the lesser of *n* and *s.size() - pos* characters of *s*, beginning at position *pos*. It throws an *out_of_range* exception if *pos > str.size()*. The second version of the function assigns *n* characters of the array pointed to by *s*. The third version assigns elements from the array pointed to by *s* up to, but not including, a *traits::eos()* character. The fourth and fifth assign one or *n* repetitions of *c*, respectively. The last variation assigns the members specified by the range *[first, last)*.

All functions will throw a *length_error* exception if the resulting length will exceed *max_size()*. All return a reference to this string after completion.

```
const_reference
at (size_type n) const;

reference
at (size_type n);
```

If *n < size()*, returns the element at position *n* in this string. Otherwise, an *out_of_range* exception is thrown.

```
size_type
capacity () const;
```

Returns the current storage capacity of the string. This is guaranteed to be at least as large as *size()*.

```
int
compare (const basic_string& str,
    size_type pos = 0, size_type n = npos);
```

Returns the result of a lexographical comparison between elements of this string and elements of *str*. Throws an *out_of_range* exception if *pos* > *size()*. The return value is:

```
traits::compare (data()+pos, str.data(),
                    min{n, size()-pos, str.size()}).
```

int
compare (const charT* s, size_type pos,
    size_type n) const;

int
compare (const charT* s, size_type pos = 0) const;

Return the result of a lexographical comparison between elements of this string and a given comparison string. The members return, respectively:

```
compare(basic_string(s, n), pos)
compare(basic_string(s), pos)
```

size_type
compare (charT* s, size_type n, size_type pos = 0);

Replaces elements in memory with copies of elements from this string. An *out_of_range* exception will be thrown if *pos* > *size()*. The lesser of *n* and *size()* - *pos* elements of this string, starting at position *pos* are copied into the array pointed to by *s*. No terminating null is appended to *s*.

const charT*
c_str () const;

Return a pointer to the initial element of an array whose first *size()* elements are copies of the elements in this string. A *traits::eos()* element is appended to the end. The elements of the array may not be altered, and the returned pointer is only valid until a non-*const* member function of this string is called. If *size()* is zero, the *c_str()* returns a pointer to a *traits::eos()* character. See also the *data()* function.

const charT*
data () const;

Return a pointer to the initial element of an array whose first *size()* elements are copies of the elements in this string. A *traits::eos()* element is appended to the end. The elements of the array may not be altered, and the returned pointer is only valid until a non-*const* member function of this string is called. If *size()* is zero, the *data()* function returns a *NULL* pointer. See also the *c_str()* function.

bool **empty** () const;
Returns *size() == 0*.

size_type
find (const basic_string& str, size_type pos = 0) const;

Searches for the first occurance of the substring specified by *str* in this string, starting at position *pos*. If found, it returns the index of the first character of the matching substring. If not found, returns *npos*. Equality is defined by *traits::eq()*.

size_type
find (const charT* s, size_type pos, size_type n) const;

size_type

find (const charT* s, size_type pos = 0) const;

size_type
find (charT c, size_type pos = 0) const;

Search for the first sequence of characters in this string that match a specified string. The variations of this function return, respectively:

```
find(basic_string(s,n), pos)
find(basic_string(s), pos)
find(basic_string(1, c), pos)
```

size_type
find_first_not_of (const basic_string& str,
                size_type pos = 0) const;

Searches for the first element of this string at or after position *pos* that is not equal to any element of *str*. If found, *find_first_not_of* returns the index of the non-matching character. If all of the characters match, the function returns *npos*. Equality is defined by *traits::eq()*.

size_type
find_first_not_of (const charT* s,
                size_type pos, size_type n) const;

size_type
find_first_not_of (const charT* s,
                size_type pos = 0) const;

size_type
find_first_not_of (charT c, size_type pos = 0) const;

Search for the first element in this string at or after position *pos* that is not equal to any element of a given set of characters. The members return, respectively:

```
find_first_not_of(basic_string(s,n), pos)
find_first_not_of(basic_string(s), pos)
find_first_not_of(basic_string(1, c), pos)
```

size_type
find_first_of (const basic_string& str,
          size_type pos = 0) const;

Searches for the first occurence at or after position *pos* of any element of *str* in this string. If found, the index of this matching character is returned. If not found, *npos* is returned. Equality is defined by *traits::eq()*.

size_type
find_first_of (const charT* s, size_type pos,
          size_type n) const;

size_type
find_first_of (const charT* s, size_type pos = 0) const;

size_type
find_first_of (charT c, size_type pos = 0) const;

Search for the first occurence in this string of any element in a specified string. The *find_first_of* variations return, respectively:

```
find_first_of(basic_string(s,n), pos)
find_first_of(basic_string(s), pos)
find_first_of(basic_string(1, c), pos)
```

size_type
find_last_not_of (const basic_string& str,
   size_type pos = npos) const;

Searches for the last element of this string at or before position *pos* that is not equal to any element of *str*. If *find_last_not_of* finds a non-matching element, it returns the index of the character. If all the elements match, the function returns *npos*. Equality is defined by *traits::eq()*.

size_type
find_last_not_of (const charT* s,
   size_type pos, size_type n) const;

size_type
find_last_not_of (const charT* s, size_type pos = 0) const;

size_type
find_last_not_of (charT c, size_type pos = 0) const;

Search for the last element in this string at or before position *pos* that is not equal to any element of a given set of characters. The members return, respectively:

```
find_last_not_of(basic_string(s,n), pos)
find_last_not_of(basic_string(s), pos)
find_last_not_of(basic_string(1, c), pos)
```

size_type
find_last_of (const basic_string& str,
   size_type pos = npos) const;

Searches for the last occurence of any element of *str* at or before position *pos* in this string. If found, *find_last_of* returns the index of the matching character. If not found *find_last_of* returns *npos*. Equality is defined by *traits::eq()*.

size_type
find_last_of (const charT* s, size_type pos,
   size_type n) const;

size_type
find_last_of (const charT* s, size_type pos = 0) const;

size_type
find_last_of (charT c, size_type pos = 0) const;

Search for the last occurence in this string of any element in a specified string. The members return, respectively:

```
find_last_of(basic_string(s,n), pos)
find_last_of(basic_string(s), pos)
find_last_of(basic_string(1, c), pos)
```

basic_string&
insert (size_type pos, const basic_string& s,
  size_type pos2 = 0, size_type n = npos);

basic_string&
insert (size_type pos, const charT* s, size_type n);

basic_string&
insert (size_type pos, const charT* s);

basic_strint&
insert (size_type pos, charT c);

basic_string&
insert (size_type pos, size_type n, charT c);

Insert additional elements at position *pos* in this string. All of the variants of this function will throw an *out_of_range* exception if *pos > size()*. All variants will also throw a *length_error* if the resulting string will exceed *max_size()*. Elements of this string will be moved apart as necessary to accommodate the inserted elements. All return a reference to this string after completion.

The first variation of this function inserts the lesser of *n* and *s.size() - pos2* characters of *s*, beginning at position *pos2* in this string. This version will throw an *out_of_range* exception if *pos2 > s.size()*. The second version inserts *n* characters of the array pointed to by *s*. The third inserts elements from the array pointed to by *s* up to, but not including, a *traits::eos()* character. Finally, the fourth and fifth variations insert one or *n* repetitions of *c*.

iterator
insert (iterator p, charT c = charT());

iterator
insert (iterator p, size_type n, charT c);

template<class InputIterator>
void
insert (iterator p, InputIterator first, InputIterator last);

Insert additional elements in this string immediately before the character referred to by *p*. All of these versions of *insert* require that *p* is a valid iterator on this string. The first version inserts a copy of *c*. The second version inserts *n* repetitions of *c*. The third version inserts characters in the range *[first, last)*. The first two versions return *p*.

size_type
length () const;

Return the number of elements contained in this string.

size_type
max_size () const

Returns the maximum possible size of the string.

size_type
rfind (const basic_string& str, size_type pos = npos) const;

Searches for the last occurrence of the substring specified by *str* in this string, starting at position *pos*. Note that only the first character of the substring must be <= *pos*; the remaining characters may extend beyond *pos*. If found, the index of the first character of that matches substring is returned. If not found, *npos* is returned. Equality is defined by *traits::eq()*.

```
size_type
```
rfind (const charT* s, size_type pos, size_type n) const;

```
size_type
```
rfind (const charT* s, size_type pos = 0) const;

```
size_type
```
rfind (charT c, size_type pos = 0) const;

Searches for the last sequence of characters in this string matching a specified string. The *rfind* variations return, respectively:

```
rfind(basic_string(s,n), pos)
rfind(basic_string(s), pos)
rfind(basic_string(1, c), pos)
```

```
basic_string&
```
remove (size_type pos = 0, size_type n = npos);

```
basic_string&
```
remove (iterator p);

```
basic_string&
```
remove (iterator first, iterator last);

This function removes elements from the string, collapsing the remaining elements, as necessary, to remove any space left empty. The first version of the function removes the smaller of *n* and *size() - pos* starting at position *pos*. An *out_of_range* exception will be thrown if *pos > size()*. The second version requires that *p* is a valid iterator on this string, and removes the character referred to by *p*. The last version of *remove* requires that both *first* and *last* are valid iterators on this string, and removes the characters defined by the range *[first, last)*. The destructors for all removed characters are called. All versions of *remove* return a reference to this string after completion.

```
basic_string&
```
replace (size_type pos, size_type n1, const basic_string& s,
    size_type pos2 = 0, size_type n2 = npos);

```
basic_string&
```
replace (size_type pos, size_type n1, const charT* s, size_type n2);

```
basic_string&
```
replace (size_type pos, size_type n1, const charT* s);

```
basic_string&
```
replace (size_type pos, size_type n1, size_type n2, charT c);

The *replace* function replaces selected elements of this string with an alternate set of elements. All of these versions insert the new elements in place of *n1* elements in this string, starting at position *pos*. They each throw an *out_of_range* exception if *pos1 > size()* and a *length_error* exception if the resulting string size exceeds *max_size()*.

The first version replaces elements of the original string with *n2* characters from string *s* starting at position *pos2*. It will throw the *out_of_range* exception if *pos2 > s.size()*. The second variation of the function replaces elements in the original string with *n2* elements from the array pointed to by *s*. The third version replaces elements in the string with elements from the array pointed to by *s*, up to, but not including, a *traits::eos()* character. The fourth replaces *n* elements with *n2* repetitions of character *c*.

basic_string&
replace (iterator i1, iterator i2,
    const basic_string& str);

basic_string&
replace (iterator i1, iterator i2, const charT* s,
    size_type n);

basic_string&
replace (iterator i1, iterator i2, const charT* s);

basic_string&
replace (iterator i1, iterator i2, size_type n,
    charT c);

template<class InputIterator>
basic_string&

replace (iterator i1, iterator i2,
    InputIterator j1, InputIterator j2);

Replace selected elements of this string with an alternative set of elements. All of these versions of *replace* require iterators *i1* and *i2* to be valid iterators on this string. The elements specified by the range *[i1, i2)* are replaced by the new elements.

The first version shown here replaces with all members in *str*. The second version starts at position *i1*, and replaces the next *n* characters with *n* characters of the array pointed to by *s*. The third variation replaces string elements with elements from the array pointed to by *s* up to, but not including, a *traits::eos()* character. The fourth version replaces string elements with *n* repetitions of *c*. The last variation shown here replaces string elements with the members specified in the range *[j1, j2)*.

void **reserve** (size_type res_arg);
Assures that the storage capacity is at least *res_arg*.

void
resize (size_type n, charT c)

void
resize (size_type n)

Changes the capacity of this string to *n*. If the new capacity is smaller than the current size of the string, then it is truncated. If the capacity is larger, then the string is padded with *c* characters. The latter *resize* member pads the string with default characters specified by *traits::eos()*.

size_type
size () const;
Return the number of elements contained in this string.

basic_string
substr (size_type pos = 0, size_type n = npos) const;

Returns a string composed of copies of the lesser of *n* and *size()* characters in this string starting at index *pos*. Throws an out_of_range exception if *pos* <= *size()*.

void
swap (basic_string& s);
Swaps the contents of this string with the contents of *s*.

Non-member operators

template<class charT, class traits, class Allocator>
basic_string
operator + (const basic_string& lhs, const basic_string& rhs)

Returns a string of length *lhs.size()* + *rhs.size()*, where the first *lhs.size()* elements are copies of the elements of *lhs*, and the next *rhs.size()* elements are copies of the elements of *rhs*.

template<class charT, class traits, class Allocator>
basic_string
operator + (const charT* lhs, const basic_string& rhs)

template<class charT, class traits, class Allocator>
basic_string
operator + (charT lhs, const basic_string& rhs)

template<class charT, class traits, class Allocator>
basic_string
operator + (const basic_string& lhs, const charT* rhs)

template<class charT, class traits, class Allocator>
basic_string
operator + (const basic_string& lhs, charT rhs)

Returns a string that represents the concatenation of two string-like entities. These functions return, respectively:

```
basic_string(lhs) + rhs
basic_string(1, lhs) + rhs
lhs + basic_string(rhs)
lhs + basic_string(1, rhs)
```

template<class charT, class traits, class Allocator>
bool
operator == (const basic_string& lhs, const
basic_string& rhs)

Returns a Boolean value of *true* if *lhs* and *rhs* are equal, and *false* if they are not. Equality is defined by the *compare()* member function.

template<class charT, class traits, class Allocator>
bool
operator == (const charT* lhs, const basic_string& rhs)

template<class charT, class traits, class Allocator>
bool

operator == (const basic_string& lhs, const charT* rhs)

Returns a Boolean value indicating whether *lhs* and *rhs* are equal. Equality is defined by the *compare()* member function. These functions return, respectively:

```
basic_string(lhs) == rhs
lhs == basic_string(rhs)
```

template<class charT, class traits, class Allocator>
bool
operator != (const basic_string& lhs,
        const basic_string& rhs)

Returns a Boolean value representing the inequality of *lhs* and *rhs*. Inequality is defined by the *compare()* member function.

template<class charT, class traits, class Allocator>
bool
operator != (const charT* lhs, const basic_string& rhs)

template<class charT, class traits, class Allocator>
bool
operator != (const basic_string& lhs, const charT* rhs)

Returns a Boolean value representing the inequality of *lhs* and *rhs*. Inequality is defined by the *compare()* member function. The members return, respectively:

```
basic_string(lhs) != rhs
lhs != basic_string(rhs)
```

template<class charT, class traits, class Allocator>
bool
operator < (const basic_string& lhs, const basic_string& rhs)

Returns a Boolean value representing the lexigraphical less-than relationship of *lhs* and *rhs*. Less-than is defined by the *compare()* member.

template<class charT, class traits, class Allocator>
bool
operator < (const charT* lhs, const basic_string& rhs)

template<class charT, class traits, class Allocator>
bool
operator < (const basic_string& lhs, const charT* rhs)

Returns a Boolean value representing the lexigraphical less-than relationship of *lhs* and *rhs*. Less-than is defined by the *compare()* member function. These functions return, respectively:

```
basic_string(lhs) < rhs
lhs < basic_string(rhs)
```

template<class charT, class traits, class Allocator>
bool
operator > (const basic_string& lhs, const basic_string& rhs)

Returns a Boolean value representing the lexigraphical greater-than relationship of *lhs* and *rhs*. Greater-than is defined by the *compare()* member function.

```
template<class charT, class traits, class Allocator>
bool
operator > (const charT* lhs, const basic_string& rhs)
```

```
template<class charT, class traits, class Allocator>
bool operator > (const basic_string& lhs, const charT* rhs)
```

Returns a Boolean value representing the lexigraphical greater-than relationship of *lhs* and *rhs*. Greater-than is defined by the *compare()* member. The members return, respectively:

```
basic_string(lhs) > rhs
lhs > basic_string(rhs)
```

```
template<class charT, class traits, class Allocator>
bool
operator <= (const basic_string& lhs,
        const basic_string& rhs)
```

Returns a Boolean value representing the lexigraphical less-than-or-equal relationship of *lhs* and *rhs*. Less-than-or-equal is defined by the *compare()* member function.

```
template<class charT, class traits, class Allocator>
bool
operator <= (const charT* lhs, const
basic_string& rhs)
```

```
template<class charT, class traits, class Allocator>
bool
operator <= (const basic_string& lhs, const
charT* rhs)
```

Returns a Boolean value representing the lexigraphical less-than-or-equal relationship of *lhs* and *rhs*. Less-than-or-equal is defined by the *compare()* member function. These functions return, respectively:

```
basic_string(lhs) <= rhs
lhs <= basic_string(rhs)
```

```
template<class charT, class traits, class Allocator>
bool
operator >= (const basic_string& lhs,
        const basic_string& rhs)
```

Returns a Boolean value representing the lexigraphical greater-than-or-equal relationship of *lhs* and *rhs*. Greater-than-or-equal is defined by the *compare()* member function.

```
template<class charT, class traits, class Allocator>
bool
operator >= (const charT* lhs, const basic_string& rhs)
```

```
template<class charT, class traits, class Allocator>
bool
operator >= (const basic_string& lhs, const charT* rhs)
```

Returns a Boolean value representing the lexigraphical greater-than-or-equal relationship of *lhs* and *rhs*. Greater-than-or-equal is defined by the *compare()* member. The members return, respectively:

```
basic_string(lhs) >= rhs
lhs >= basic_string(rhs)
```

```
template<class charT, class traits, class Allocator>
basic_istream<charT>&
operator >> (basic_istream<charT>& is,
        basic_string<charT,
        traits, Allocator>& str);
```

Reads *basic_string<charT, traits, Allocator>* from *is* using *traits::char_in* until a *traits::is_del()* element is read. All elements read, except the delimiter, are placed in *str*. After the read, the function returns *is*.

```
template<class charT, class traits, class Allocator>
basic_ostream<charT>&
operator << (basic_ostream<charT>& os,
        const basic_string<charT,
        traits, Allocator>& str);
```

Writes all elements of *str* to *os* in order from first to last, using *traits::char_out()*. After the write, the function returns *os*.

Non-member function

```
template <class charT, class IS_traits, class STR_traits,
        class STR_Alloc>
basic_istream<charT, IS_traits>&
getline (basic_istream<charT, IS_traits>& is,
        basic_string<charT, STR_traits, STR_Alloc>& str,
        charT delim = IS_traits::newline() );
```

An unformatted input function that extracts characters from *is* into *str* until *npos - 1* characters are read, the end of the input sequence is reached, or the character read is *delim*. The characters are read using *STR_traits::char_in()*.

If the new *iostreams* is not available on your system, we provide the equivalent *operator >>*, *operator <<*, and *getline* functions that work with the old *iostreams*.

bidirectional iterator   Iterator

Summary
An iterator that can both read and write and can traverse a container in both directions

Description
Note For a complete discussion of iterators, see the C++ *Programmer's Guide*, Chapter 19, "Iterators."

Iterators are a generalization of pointers that allow a C++ program to uniformly interact with different data structures. Bidirectional iterators can move both forwards and backwards through a container, and have the ability to both read and write data. These iterators satisfy the requirements shown in Table 17.2.

Note that most of these requirements are also the requirements for forward iterators. The following key pertains to the iterator descriptions listed:

a and b	values of type X
n	value of *distance* type
u, *Distance*, *tmp*, and m	identifiers
r	value of type $X\&$
t	value of type T

Table 17.2   Requirements for bidirectional iterators

Expression	Requirement
$X\ u$	u might have a singular value
$X()$	$X()$ might be singular
$X(a)$	copy constructor, $a == X(a)$
$X\ u(a)$	copy constructor, $u == a$
$X\ u = a$	assignment, $u == a$
$a == b, a\ != b$	return value convertable to *bool*
$*a$	return value convertable to $T\&$
$++r$	returns $X\&$
$r++$	return value convertable to const $X\&\&$
$*r++$	returns $T\&$
$--r$	returns $X\&$
$r--$	return *value* convertable to *const* $X\&$
$*r--$	returns $T\&$

Like forward iterators, bidirectional iterators have the condition that $a == b$ implies $*a== *b$.

There are no restrictions on the number of passes an algorithm may make through the structure.

See also
Chapter 19, "Iterators," and Chapter 21, "Container classes," in the C++ *Programmer's Guide*.

binary_function   Function object

Summary
Base class for creating binary function objects.

Synopsis
#include <functional>

```
template <class Arg1, class Arg2, class Result>
    struct binary_function{
        typedef Arg1 first_argument_type;
        typedef Arg2 second_argument_type;
        typedef Result result_type;
    };
```

Description
Function objects are objects with an *operator()* defined. They are important for the
effective use of the standard library's generic algorithms, because the interface for each
algorithmic template can accept either an object with an *operator()* defined or a pointer to
a function. The Standard C++ Library provides both a standard set of function objects,
and a pair of classes that you can use as the base for creating your own function objects.

Function objects that take two arguments are called *binary function objects*. Binary function objects are required to provide the typedefs *first_argument_type*,
second_argument_type, and *result_type*. The *binary_function* class makes the task of creating
templated binary function objects easier by providing the necessary typedefs for a binary
function object. You can create your own binary function objects by inheriting from
binary_function.

See also
function objects, unary_function, the "Function objects" section of Chapter 20 in the *C++
Programmer's Guide*.

binary_negate   Function object

Summary
Function object that returns the complement of the result of its binary predicate

Synopsis
#include <functional>

```
template<class Predicate>
class binary_negate
  : public binary_function<Predicate::first_argument_type,
                Predicate::second_argument_type,
```

```
            bool                 >
{

public:
    explicit binary_negate (const Predicate& pred);
    bool operator() (const first_argument_type& x,
              const second_argument_type& y) const;
};

template <class Predicate>
binary_negate<Predicate> not2 (const Predicate& pred);
```

Description

binary_negate is a function object class that provides a return type for the function adaptor *not2*. *not2* is a function adaptor, known as a negator, that takes a binary predicate function object as its argument and returns a binary predicate function object that is the complement of the original.

Note that *not2* works only with function objects that are defined as subclasses of the class *binary_function*.

Constructor

explicit binary_negate (const Predicate& pred);
Construct a `binary_negate` object from predicate *pred*.

Operator

bool operator ( ) (const first_argument_type& x,
          const second_argument_type& y) const;
Return the result of *pred(x,y)*.

See also

binary_function, *unary_negate*

binary_search   Algorithm

Summary

Performs a binary search for a value on a container.

Synopsis

```
#include <algorithm>
template <class ForwardIterator, class T>
    bool
    binary_search(ForwardIterator first, ForwardIterator last,
            const T& value);
```

```
template <class ForwardIterator, class T, class Compare>
bool
binary_search(ForwardIterator first, ForwardIterator last,
              const T& value, Compare comp);
```

Description

The *binary_search* algorithm, like other related algorithms (*equal_range, lower_bound* and *upper_bound*) performs a binary search on ordered containers. All binary search algorithms have two versions. The first version uses the less than operator (*operator <*) to perform the comparison, and assumes that the sequence has been sorted using that operator. The second version allows you to include a function object of type *Compare*, which it assumes was the function used to sort the sequence. The function object must be a binary predicate.

The *binary_search* algorithm returns *true* if a sequence contains an element equivalent to the argument *value*. The first version of *binary_search* returns *true* if the sequence contains at least one element that is equal to the search value. The second version of the *binary_search* algorithm returns *true* if the sequence contains at least one element that satisfies the conditions of the comparison function. Formally, *binary_search* returns *true* if there is an iterator *i* in the range *[first, last)* that satisfies the corresponding conditions:

```
!(*i < value) && !(value < *i)
```

or

```
comp(*i, value)  == false && comp(value, *i) == false
```

Complexity

binary_search performs at most *log(last - first)* + 2 comparisons.

Examples

```
#include <vector>
#include <algorithm>
using namespace std;

int main()
{
  typedef vector<int>::iterator iterator;
  int d1[10] = {0,1,2,2,3,4,2,2,6,7};

  // Set up a vector
  vector<int> v1(d1,d1 + 10);
  sort(v1.begin(),v1.end());

  // Try binary_search variants
  bool b1 = binary_search(v1.begin(),v1.end(),3);
  // b1 = true

  bool b2 =
      binary_search(v1.begin(),v1.end(),11,less<int>());
```

```
    // b = false

    // Output results
    cout << "In the vector: ";
    copy(v1.begin(),v1.end(),
            ostream_iterator<int>(cout," "));

    cout << endl << "The number 3 was "
         << (b1 ? "FOUND" : "NOT FOUND");
    cout << endl << "The number 11 was "
         << (b2 ? "FOUND" : "NOT FOUND") << endl;
    return 0;
  }
```

See also
equal_range, lower_bound, upper_bound

bind1st, bind2nd, binder1st, binder2nd   **Function object**

Summary
Templatized utilities to bind values to function objects

Synopsis
#include <functional>

```
// Class binder1st
template <class Operation>
class binder1st
  : public unary_function<Operation::second_argument_type,
                Operation::result_type> {

protected:
  Operation op; argument_type value;
public:
  binder1st(const Operation& x, const
        Operation::first_argument_type& y) : op(x). value(y) {}
  result_type operator() (const argument_type& x) const
};

// Creator bind1st
template<class Operation, class T>
binder1st <Operation> bind1st(const Operation& op, const T& x)

// Class binder2nd
template <class Operation>
class binder2nd
```

```
              : public unary_function<Operation::first_argument_type,
                          Operation::result_type> {

      protected:
        Operation op; argument_type value;
      public:
        binder2nd(const Operation& x, const
              Operation::second_argument_type& y) : op(x). value(y) {}
        result_type operator() (const argument_type& x) const
      };

      // Creator bind2nd
      template<class Operation, class T>
      binder2nd <Operation> bind2nd(const Operation& op, const T& x)
```

Description

Because so many functions provided by the standard library take other functions as arguments, the library includes classes that let you build new function objects out of old ones. Both *bind1st()* and *bind2nd()* are functions that take as arguments a binary function object *f* and a value *x*, and return, respectively, classes *binder1st* and *binder2nd*. The underlying function object must be a subclass of *binary_function*.

Class *binder1st* binds the value to the first argument of the binary function, and *binder2nd* does the same thing for the second argument of the function. The resulting classes can be used in place of a unary predicate in other function calls.

The *bind1st()* and *bind2nd()* member functions are used inline to create the unary predicates. For example, you could use the *count_if* algorithm to count all elements in a vector that are less than or equal to 7, using the following:

```
    count_if (v.begin, v.end, bind1st(greater <int> (),7), littleNums)
```

This function adds one to *littleNums* each time the predicate is *true*, i.e., each time 7 is greater than the element.

Examples

```
      #include <functional>
      #include <algorithm>
      #include <vector>
      using namespace std;

      int main()
      {
        typedef vector<int>::iterator iterator;
        int d1[4] = {1,2,3,4};

        // Set up a vector
        vector<int> v1(d1,d1 + 4);

        // Create an 'equal to 3' unary predicate by binding 3 to
```

```
    // the equal_to binary predicate.
    binder1st<equal_to<int> > equal_to_3 =
        bind1st(equal_to<int>(),3);

    // Now use this new predicate in a call to find_if
    iterator it1 = find_if(v1.begin(),v1.end(),equal_to_3);
    // it1 = v1.begin() + 2

    // Even better, construct the new predicate on the fly
    iterator it2 =
        find_if(v1.begin(),v1.end(),bind1st(equal_to<int>(),3));
    // it2 = v1.begin() + 2

    // And now the same thing using bind2nd
    // Same result since == is commutative
    iterator it3 =
        find_if(v1.begin(),v1.end(),bind2nd(equal_to<int>(),3));
    // it3 = v1.begin() + 2

    // Output results
    cout << *it1 << " " << *it2 << " " << *it3 << endl;
    return 0;
}
```

bitset

Container

Summary
A template class and related functions for storing and manipulating fixed-size sequences of bits.

Synopsis
#include <bitset>

template <size_t N>
 class bitset {

public:

// bit reference:

 class reference {
 public:

  ~reference()
  reference& operator=(bool x);
  reference& operator=(const reference&);
  bool operator~() const;

```
    operator bool() const;
   reference& flip();
  };
```

// Constructors

```
  bitset ();
  bitset (unsigned long val);
  explicit bitset (const string& str,
           size_t pos = 0,
           size_t n = size_t(-1));
```

// Bitwise Operators and Bitwise Operator Assignment

```
  bitset<N>& operator&= (const bitset<N>& rhs);
  bitset<N>& operator|= (const bitset<N>& rhs);
  bitset<N>& operator^= (const bitset<N>& rhs);
  bitset<N>& operator<<= (size_t pos);
  bitset<N>& operator>>= (size_t pos);
```

// Set, Reset, Flip

```
  bitset<N>& set ();
  bitset<N>& set (size_t pos, int val = 1);
  bitset<N>& reset ();
  bitset<N>& reset (size_t pos);
  bitset<N> operator~() const;
  bitset<N>& flip ();

  bitset<N>& flip (size_t pos);
```

// element access
```
  reference operator[] (size_t pos);
  unsigned long to_ulong() const;
  string to_string() const;
  size_t count() const;
  size_t size() const;
  bool operator== (const bitset<N>& rhs) const;
  bool operator!= (const bitset<N>& rhs) const;
  bool test (size_t pos) const;
  bool any() const;
  bool none() const;
  bitset<N> operator<< (size_t pos) const;
  bitset<N> operator>> (size_t pos) const;
```

```
private:
//implementation


};


// bitset operators


template <size_t N>
bitset<N> operator& (const bitset<N>&, const bitset<N>&);


template <size_t N>
bitset<N> operator| (const bitset<N>&, const bitset<N>&);


template <size_t N>
bitset<N> operator^ (const bitset<N>&, const bitset<N>&);


template <size_t N>
istream& operator>> (istream& is, bitset<N>& x);


template <size_t N>
ostream& operator<< (ostream& os, const bitset<N>& x);
```

Description

bitset<N> is a class that describes objects that can store a sequence consisting of a fixed number of bits, *N*. Each bit represents either the value zero (*reset*) or one (*set*) and has a non-negative position pos.

Errors and exceptions

Bitset constructors and member functions may report the following three types of errors — each associated with a distinct exception:

- Invalid-argument error or *invalid_argument()* exception;
- Out-of-range error or *out_of_range()* exception;
- Overflow error or *over-flow_error()* exception;

If exceptions are not supported on your compiler, then you will get an assertion failure instead of an exception.

Constructors

bitset();

Constructs an object of class *bitset<N>*, initializing all bit values to zero.

bitset(unsigned long val);

Constructs an object of class *bitset<N>*, initializing the first *M* bit values to the corresponding bits in *val*. *M* is the smaller of *N* and the value *CHAR_BIT* * *sizeof(unsigned long)*. If *M* < *N*, remaining bit positions are initialized to zero. Note: *CHAR_BIT* is defined in *<climits>*.

explicit
bitset (const string& str, size_t pos = 0,
    size_t n = size_t(-1));

Determines the effective length *rlen* of the initializing string as the smaller of *n* and *str.size() - pos*. The function throws an *invalid_argument* exception if any of the *rlen* characters in *str*, beginning at position *pos*,is other than 0 or 1. Otherwise, the function constructs an object of class *bitset<N>*, initializing the first *M* bit positions to values determined from the corresponding characters in the string *str*. *M* is the smaller of *N* and *rlen*. This constructor requires that *pos <= str.length()*, otherwise it throws an *out_of_range* exception.

Operators

bool
operator == (const bitset<N>& rhs) const;

Returns *true* if the value of each bit in * *this* equals the value of each corresponding bit in *rhs*. Otherwise returns *false*.

bool
operator != (const bitset<N>& rhs) const;

Returns *true* if the value of any bit in **this* is not equal to the value of the corresponding bit in *rhs*. Otherwise returns *false*.

bitset<N>&
operator &= (const bitset<N>& rhs);

Clears each bit in **this* for which the corresponding bit in *rhs* is clear and leaves all other bits unchanged.

bitset<N>&
operator |= (const bitset<N>& rhs);

Sets each bit in **this* for which the corresponding bit in *rhs* is set, and leaves all other bits unchanged.

bitset<N>&
operator ^= (const bitset<N>& rhs);

Toggles each bit in **this* for which the corresponding bit in *rhs* is set, and leaves all other bits unchanged.

bitset<N>&
operator <<= (size_t pos);

Replaces each bit at position *I* with 0 if *I < pos* or with the value of the bit at *I - pos* if *I >= pos*.

bitset<N>&
operator >>= (size_t pos);

Replaces each bit at position *I* with 0 if *pos >= N-I* or with the value of the bit at position *I + pos* if *pos < N-I*.

bitset<N>&
operator >> (size_t pos) const;

Returns *bitset<N>(*this) >>= pos*.

bitset<N>&
operator << (size_t pos) const;
Returns *bitset<N>(*this) <<= pos*.

bitset<N>
operator ~ ();
Returns the bitset that is the logical complement of each bit in **this*.

bitset<N>
operator & (const bitset<N>& lhs,
  const bitset<N>& rhs);
lhs gets logical *AND* of *lhs* with *rhs*.

bitset<N>
operator | (const bitset<N>& lhs,
  const bitset<N>& rhs);
lhs gets logical *OR* of *lhs* with *rhs*.

bitset<N>
operator ^ (const bitset<N>& lhs,
  const bitset<N>& rhs);
lhs gets logical *XOR* of *lhs* with *rhs*.

template <size_t N>
istream&
operator >> (istream& is, bitset<N>& x);
Extracts up to *N* characters (single-byte) from *is*. Stores these characters in a temporary object *str* of type *string*, then evaluates the expression *x = bitset<N>(str)*. Characters are extracted and stored until any of the following occurs:

- *N* characters have been extracted and stored
- An end-of-file occurs on the input sequence
- The next character is neither '0' nor '1'. In this case, the character is not extracted.

template <size_t N>
ostream&
operator << (ostream& os, const bitset<N>& x);
Returns *os << x.to_string()*

Member functions

bool
any () const;
Returns *true* is any bit in **this* is set. Otherwise returns *false*.

size_t
count () const;
Returns a count of the number of bits set in **this*.

bitset<N>&
flip();

Flips all bits in **this*, and returns **this*.

bitset<N>&
flip (size_t pos) const;

Flips the bit at position *pos* in **this*. Throws an *out_of_range* exception if *pos* does not correspond to a valid bit position.

bool
none () const;

Returns *true* is no bit in **this* is set. Otherwise returns *false*.

bitset<N>&
reset();

Resets all bits in **this*, and returns **this*.

bitset<N>&
reset (size_t pos);

Resets the bit at position *pos* in **this*. Throws an *out_of_range* exception if *pos* does not correspond to a valid bit position.

bitset<N>&
set();

Sets all bits in **this*, and returns **this*.

bitset<N>&
set (size_t pos, int val = 1);

Stores a new value in the bits at position *pos* in **this*. If *val* is nonzero, the stored value is one, otherwise it is zero. Throws an *out_of_range* exception if *pos* does not correspond to a valid bit position.

size_t
size () const;

Returns the template parameter *N*.

bool
test (size_t pos) const;

Returns *true* is the bit at position *pos* is set. Throws an *out_of_range* exception if *pos* does not correspond to a valid bit position.

string
to_string() const;

Returns an object of type *string*, *N* characters long.
Each position in the new string is initialized with a character ('0' for zero and '1' for one) representing the value stored in the corresponding bit position of **this*. Character position *N - 1* corresponds to bit position 0. Subsequent decreasing character positions correspond to increasing bit positions.

unsigned long
to_ulong() const;

Returns the integral value corresponding to the bits in **this*. Throws an *overflow_error* if these bits cannot be represented as type *unsigned long*.

compare

Summary
A binary function or a function object that returns true or false. *compare* is used for ordering elements.

complex   Complex number library

Summary
C++ complex number library

Specializations
complex <float>
complex <double>
complex <long double>

Synopsis
#include <complex>

template <class T>
class complex {

public:

  complex ();
  complex (T re);
  complex (T re , T im);
  template <class X> complex
   (const complex<X>&);

  T real () const;
  T imag () const;

  template <class X>
   complex<T> operator= (const complex<X>&);
  template <class X>
   complex<T> operator+= (const complex<X>&);
  template <class X>
   complex<T> operator-= (const complex<X>&);
  template <class X>
   complex<T> operator*= (const complex<X>&);
  template <class X>
   complex<T> operator/= (const complex<X>&);
};

```
// Operators

template<class T>
 complex<T> operator+
  (const complex<T>&, const complex<T>&);
template<class T>
 complex<T> operator+
  (const complex<T>&, T);
template<class T>
 complex<T> operator+
  (T, const complex<T>&);

template<class T>
 complex<T> operator-

  (const complex<T>&, const complex<T>&);
template<class T>
 complex<T> operator-
  (const complex<T>&, T);
template<classT>
 complex<T> operator-
  (T, const complex<T>&);

template<class T>
 complex<T> operator*
  (const complex<T>&, const complex<T>&);
template<class T>
 complex<T> operator*
  (const complex<T>&, T);
template<class T>
 complex<T> operator*
  (T, const complex<T>&);

template<class T>
 complex<T> operator/
  (const complex<T>&, const complex<T>&);
template<class T>
 complex<T> operator/
  (const complex<T>&, T);
template<class T>
 complex<T> operator/
  (T, const complex<T>&);

template<class T>
```

```
 complex<T> operator+
 (const complex<T>&);
template<class T>
 complex<T> operator-
 (const complex<T>&);

template<class T>
 bool operator==
 (const complex<T>&, const complex<T>&);
template<class T>
 bool operator==
 (const complex<T>&, T);
template<class T>
 bool operator==
 (T, const complex<T>&);

template<class T>
 bool operator!=
 (const complex<T>&, const complex<T>&);
template<class T>
 bool operator!=
 (const complex<T>&, T);

template<class T>
 bool operator!=
 (T, const complex<T>&);

template <class X>
 istream& operator>>
 (istream&, complex<X>&);
template <class X>
 ostream& operator<<
 (ostream&, const complex<X>&);

// Values

template<class T> T real
 (const complex<T>&);
template<class T> T imag
 (const complex<T>&);

template<class T> T abs
 (const complex<T>&);
template<class T> T arg
 (const complex<T>&);
```

```
template<class T> T norm
 (const complex<T>&);

template<class T> complex<T> conj
 (const complex<T>&);
template<class T> complex<T> polar
 (T, T);

// Transcendentals

template<class T> complex<T> acos
 (const complex<T>&);
template<class T> complex<T> asin
 (const complex<T>&);
template<class T> complex<T> atan
 (const complex<T>&);
template<class T> complex<T> atan2
 (const complex<T>&, const complex<T>&);
template<class T> complex<T> atan2
 (const complex<T>&, T);
template<class T> complex<T> atan2
 (T, const complex<T>&);
template<class T> complex<T> cos
 (const complex<T>&);
template<class T> complex<T> cosh
 (const complex<T>&);
template<class T> complex<T> exp
 (const complex<T>&);
template<class T> complex<T> log
 (const complex<T>&);

template<class T> complex<T> log10
 (const complex<T>&);

template<class T> complex<T> pow
 (const complex<T>&, int);
template<class T> complex<T> pow
 (const complex<T>&, T);
template<class T> complex<T> pow
 (const complex<T>&, const complex<T>&);
template<class T> complex<T> pow
 (T, const complex<T>&);

template<class T> complex<T> sin
 (const complex<T>&);
```

```
template<class T> complex<T> sinh
 (const complex<T>&);
template<class T> complex<T> sqrt
 (const complex<T>&);
template<class T> complex<T> tan
 (const complex<T>&);
template<class T> complex<T> tanh
 (const complex<T>&);
```

Description

complex<T> is a class that supports complex numbers. A complex number has a real part and an imaginary part. The *complex* class supports equality, comparison and basic arithmetic operations. In addition, mathematical functions such as exponentiation, logarithmic, power, and square root are also available.

Warnings

On compilers that don't support member function templates, the arithmetic operators will not work on any arbitrary type. (They will work only on float, double and long doubles.) You also will only be able to perform binary arithmetic on types that are the same.

Compilers that don't support non-converting constructors will permit unsafe downcasts (i.e., long double to double, double to float, long double to float).

Examples

```
#include <complex>
using namespace std;

int main()
{
  complex<double> a(1.2, 3.4);
  complex<double> b(-9.8, -7.6);

  a += b;
  a /= sin(b) * cos(a);
  b *= log(a) + pow(b, a);

  cout << "a = " << a << ", b = " << b << endl;

  return 0;
}
```

Constructors

complex
(const T& re_arg = 0, const T& im_arg = 0);

Constructs an object of class *complex*, initializing *re_arg* to the real part and *im_arg* to the imaginary part.

template <class X> complex
(const complex<X>&);

Copy constructor. Constructs a complex number from another complex number.

Assignment operators

template <class X>
complex<T>
operator = (const complex<X>& c);

Assignment operator. Assigns c to itself.

template <class X>
complex<T>
operator += (const complex<X>& c);

Adds c to itself, then returns the result.

template <class X>
complex<T>
operator-= (const complex<X>& c);

Subtracts c from itself, then returns the result.

template <class X>
complex<T>
operator *= (const complex<X>& c);

Multiplies itelf by c then returns the result.

template <class X>
complex<T>
operator /= (const complex<X>& c);

Divides itself by c, then returns the result.

Operators

template<class T> complex<T>
operator + (const complex<T>& lhs,const complex<T>& rhs);

template<class T> complex<T>
operator + (const complex<T>& lhs, T rhs);

template<class T> complex<T>
operator + (T lhs, const complex<T>& rhs);

Returns the sum of *lhs* and *rhs*.

template<class T> complex<T>
operator – (const complex<T>& lhs,const complex<T>& rhs);

template<class T> complex<T>
operator – (const complex<T>& lhs, T rhs);

template<class T> complex<T>
operator – (T lhs, const complex<T>& rhs);

Returns the difference of *lhs* and *rhs*.

template<class T> complex<T>
operator * (const complex<T>& lhs,const complex<T>& rhs);
template<class T> complex<T>
operator * (const complex<T>& lhs, T rhs);
template<class T> complex<T>
operator * (T lhs, const complex<T>& rhs);
Returns the product of *lhs* and *rhs*.

template<class T> complex<T>
operator / (const complex<T>& lhs,const complex<T>& rhs);

template<class T> complex<T>
operator / (const complex<T>& lhs, T rhs);

template<class T> complex<T>
operator / (T lhs, const complex<T>& rhs);
Returns the quotient of *lhs* divided by *rhs*.

template<class T> complex<T>
operator + (const complex<T>& rhs);
Returns *rhs*.

template<class T> complex<T>
operator – (const complex<T>& lhs);
Returns *complex<T>(- lhs.real,() - lhs.imag())*.

template<class T> bool
operator == (const complex<T>& x, const complex<T>& y);
Returns *true* if the real and imaginary parts of x and y are equal.

template<class T> bool
operator == (const complex<T>& x, T y);
Returns *true* if y is equal to the real part of x and the imaginary part of x is equal to 0.

template<class T> bool
operator == (T x, const complex<T>& y);
Returns *true* if x is equal to the real part of y and the imaginary part of y is equal to 0.

template<class T> bool
operator != (const complex<T>& x, const complex<T>& y);
Returns *true* if either the real or the imaginary part of x and y are not equal.

template<class T> bool
operator != (const complex<T>& x, T y);
Returns *true* if y is not equal to the real part of x or the imaginary part of x is not equal to 0.

template<class T> bool
operator != (T x, const complex<T>& y);
Returns *true* if x is not equal to the real part of y or the imaginary part of y is not equal to 0.

template <class X> istream&

operator >> (istream& is, complex<X>& x);

Reads a complex number x into the input stream *is*. x may be of the form u, (u), or (u,v) where u is the real part and v is the imaginary part. If bad input is encountered, the *ios::badbit flag* is set.

template <class X> ostream&
operator << (ostream& os, const complex<X>& x);

Returns $os << "(" << x.real() << "," << x.imag() << ")"$.

Member functions

template<class T> T
abs (const complex<T>& c);

Returns the absolute value or magnitude of c (the square root of the norm).

template<class T> complex<T>
acos (const complex<T>& c);

Returns the arccosine of c.

template<class T> T
arg (const complex<T>& c);

Returns the phase angle of c.

template<class T> complex<T>
asin (const complex<T>& c);

Returns the arcsine of c.

template<class T> complex<T>
atan (const complex<T>& c);

Returns the arctangent of c.

template<class T> complex<T>
atan2 (T a, const complex<T>& b);

Returns the arctangent of a/b.

template<class T> complex<T>
atan2 (const complex<T>& a, T b);

Returns the arctangent of a/b.

template<class T> complex<T>
atan2 (const complex<T>& a, const complex<T>& b);

Returns the arctangent of a/b.

template<class T> complex<T>
conj (const complex<T>& c);

Returns the conjugate of c.

template<class T> complex<T>
cos (const complex<T>& c);

Returns the cosine of c.

template<class T> complex<T>

cosh (const complex<T>& c);
Returns the hyperbolic cosine of c.

template<class T> complex<T>
exp (const complex<T>& x);
Returns e raised to the x power.

T
imag() const;
Returns the imaginary part of the complex number.

template<class T> T
imag (const complex<T>& c) const;
Returns the imaginary part of c.

template<class T> complex<T>
log (const complex<T>& x);
Returns the natural logarithm of x.

template<class T> complex<T>
log10 (const complex<T>& x);
Returns the logarithm base 10 of x.

template<class T> T
norm (const complex<T>& c);
Returns the squared magnitude of c. (The sum of the squares of the real and imaginary parts.)

template<class T> complex<T>
polar (const T& m, const T& a);
Returns the complex value of a complex number whose magnitude is m and phase angle is a, measured in radians.

template<class T> complex<T>
pow (const complex<T>& x, int y);

template<class T> complex<T>
pow (const complex<T>& x, T y);

template<class T> complex<T>
pow (const complex<T>& x, const complex<T>& y);

template<class T> complex<T>
pow (T x, const complex<T>& y);
Returns x raised to the y power.

T
real() const;
Returns the real part of the complex number.

template<class T> T
real (const complex<T>& c);
Returns the real part of c.

template<class T> complex<T>
sin (const complex<T>& c);
Returns the sine of *c*.

template<class T> complex<T>
sinh (const complex<T>& c);
Returns the hyperbolic sine of *c*.

template<class T> complex<T>
sqrt (const complex<T>& x);
Returns the square root of *x*.

template<class T> complex<T>
tan (const complex<T>& x);
Returns the tangent of *x*.

template<class T> complex<T>
tanh (const complex<T>& x);
Returns the hyperbolic tangent of *x*.

construct Memory handling primitive

Summary
Pointer based primitive for initializing memory

Synopsis
#include <memory>

template <class T1, class T2>
 void construct (T1 *p, const T2& value)

Description
The *construct* templated function initializes memory location *p* to *value*.

See also
Other memory handling primitives: *allocate, deallocate, get_temporary_buffer, return_temporary_buffer*

Containers

Summary
A standard template library (STL) collection.

Description

Within the standard template library, collection classes are often described as containers. A container stores a collection of other objects and provides certain basic functionality that supports the use of generic algorithms. Containers come in two basic flavors: sequences, and associative containers. They are further distinguished by the type of iterator they support.

A *sequence* supports a linear arrangement of single elements. *vector*, *list*, *deque*, and *string* fall into this category. *Associative containers* map values onto keys, which provides efficient retrieval of the values based on the keys. The STL provides the *map*, *multimap*, *set* and *multiset* associative containers. *map* and *multimap* store the value and the key separately and allow for fast retrieval of the a value, base upon fast retrieval of the key. *set* and *multiset* store only keys allowing fast retrieval of the key itself.

Container Requirements

Containers within the STL must meet the following requirements:

- A container allocates all storage for the objects it holds.

- A container *X* of objects of type *T* provides the following types:

X::*value_type*	a *T*
X::*reference*	*lvalue* of *T*
X::*const_reference*	*const lvalue* of *T*
X::*iterator*	An iterator type pointing to *T*. X::*iterator* cannot be an output iterator.
X::*const_iterator*	An iterator type pointing to *const T*. May be of any iterator type except output.
X::*difference_type*	A signed integral type (must be the same as the distance type for X::*iterator* and X::*const_iterator*
X::*size_type*	An unsigned integral type representing any non-negative value of *difference_type*

- A container provides a default constructor, a copy constructor, an assignment operator, and a full complement of comparison operators.

- A container provides the following member functions:

begin()	Returns an iterator pointing to the first element in the collection
end()	Returns an iterator pointing just beyond the last element in the collection
swap(container)	Swaps elements between this container and the swap's argument.
size()	Returns the number of elements in the collection as a *size_type*.

max_size()	Returns the largest possible number of elements for this type of container as a *size_type*.
empty()	Returns *true* if the container is empty, *false* otherwise.

Reversible Containers

A container may be reversible. Essentially, a reversible container provides a reverse iterator that allows traversel of the collection in a direction opposite that of the default iterator. A reversible container must meet the following requirements in addition to those listed above:

- A reversible container provides the following types:

X::*reverse_iterator*	An iterator type pointing to *T*.
X::*const_reverse_iterator*	An iterator type pointing to *T*

- A reversible container provides the following member functions:

rbegin()	Returns a *reverse_iterator* pointing past the end of the collection
rend()	Returns a *reverse_iterator* pointing to the first element in the collection.

Sequences

In addition to the requirements for containers, the following requirements hold for sequences:

- *iterator* and *const_iterator* must be forward iterators, bidirectional iterators or random access iterators.

- A sequence provides the following constructors:

X(n, t)	Constructs a container with *n* elements *t*.
X(i, j)	Constructs a container with elements from the range [*i,j*).

- A sequence must provides the following member functions:

insert(p,t)	Inserts the element *t* in front of the position identified by the iterator *p*.
insert(p,n,t)	Inserts *n* elements *t* in front of the position identified by the iterator *p*.
insert(p,i,j)	Inserts elements from the range [*i,j*) in front of the position identified by the the iterator *p*.
erase(q)	Erases the element pointed to by the iterator *q*.
erase(q1,q2)	Erases the elements in the range [*q1,q2*).

- A sequence may also provide the following member functions if they can be implemented with constant time complexity.

front()	Returns the element pointed to by *begin()*
back()	Returns the element pointed to by *end()*
push_front(x)	Inserts the element *x* at *begin()*
push_back(x)	Inserts the element *x* at *end()*
pop_front()	Erases the element at *begin()*
pop_back()	Erases the element at *end() -1*
operator[](n)	Returns the element at *a.begin() + n*

Associative Containers

In addition to the requirements for a container, the following requirements hold for associative containers:

- For an associative container *iterator* and *const_iterator* must be *bidirectional_iterators*. Associative containers are inherently sorted. Their iterators proceed through the container in the non-descending order of keys (where non-descending order is defined by the comparison object that was used to construct the container).

- An associative container provides the following types:

X::key_type	the type of the *Key*
X::key_compare	the type of the comparison to use to put the keys in order
X::value_compare	the type of the comparison used on values

- The default constructor and copy constructor for associative containers use the template parameter comparison class.

- An associative container provides the following additional constructors:

X(c)	Construct an empty container using *c* as the comparision object
X(i,j,c)	Constructs a container with elements from the range *[i,j)* and the comparison object *c*.
X(i, j)	Constructs a container with elements from the range *[i,j)* using the template parameter comparison object.

- An associative container provides the following member functions:

key_comp()	Returns the comparison object used in constructing the associative container.
value_comp()	Returns the value comparison object used in constructing the associative container.

a_uniq.insert(t)	Inserts *t* if and only if there is no element in the container with key equal to the key of *t*. Returns a *pair<iterator,bool>*. The *bool* component of the returned pair indicates the success or failure of the operation and the *iterator* component points to the element with key equal to key of *t*.
insert(t)	Insert the element *t* and returns an iterator pointing to the newly inserted element.
insert(p,t)	If the container does *not* support redundant key values then this function only inserts *t* if there is no key present that is equal to the key of *t*. If the container *does* support redundant keys then this function always inserts the element *t*. The iterator *p* serves as a hint of where to start searching, allowing for some optimization of the insertion. It does not restrict the algorithm from inserting ahead of that location if necessary.
insert(i,j)	Inserts elements from the range *[i,j)*.
erase(k)	Erases all elements with key equal to *k*.
erase(q1,q2)	Erases the elements in the range *[q1,q2)*.
find(k)	Returns an iterator pointing to an element with key equal to *k* or *end()* if such and element is not found.
count(k)	Returns the number of elements with key equal to *k*.
lower_bound(k)	Returns an iterator pointing to the first element with a key not less than *k*.
upper_bound(k)	Returns an iterator pointing to the first element with a key greater than *k*.
equal_range(k)	Returns a pair of iterators such that the first element of the pair is equivelent to *lower_bound(k)* and the second element equivelent to *upper_bound(k)*.

copy, copy_backward   **Algorithm**

Summary
Copies a range of elements

Synopsis
#include <algorithm>

```
template <class InputIterator, class OutputIterator>
  OutputIterator
  copy(InputIterator first, InputIterator last,
      OutputIterator result);

template <class InputIterator, class OutputIterator>
```

```
OutputIterator
copy_backward(InputIterator first, InputIterator last,
        OutputIterator result);
```

Description

The *copy* algorithm copies values from the range specified by *[first ,last)* to the range that specified by *[result,result + (last - first))*. *copy* can be used to copy values from one container to another, or to copy values from one location in a container to another location in the *same* container, as long as *result* is not within the range *[first-last)*. *copy* returns *result + (last - first)*. For each non-negative integer *n < (last - first)*, *copy* assigns **(first + n)* to **(result + n)*. The result of *copy* is undefined if *result* is in the range *[first, last)*.

Unless *result* is an insert iterator, *copy* assumes that at least as many elements follow *result* as are in the range *[first, last)*.

The *copy_backward* algorithm copies elements in the range specified by *[first, last)* into the range specified by [*result - (last - first), result)*, starting from the end of the sequence (*last-1*) and progressing to the front (*first*). Note that *copy_backward* does *not* reverse the order of the elements, it simply reverses the order of transfer. *copy_backward* returns *result - (last - first)*. You should use *copy_backward* instead of *copy* when *last* is in the range *[result - (last - first), result)*. For each positive integer *n <= (last - first)*, *copy_backward* assigns **(last - n)* to **(result - n)*. The result of *copy_backward* is undefined if *result* is in the range *[first, last)*.

Unless *result* is an insert iterator, *copy_backward* assumes that there are at least as many elements ahead of *result* as are in the range *[first, last)*.

Complexity

Both *copy* and *copy_backward* perform exactly *last - first* assignments.

Examples

```cpp
#include <algorithm>
#include <vector>
using namespace std;

int main()
{
  int d1[4] = {1,2,3,4};
  int d2[4] = {5,6,7,8};

  // Set up three vectors
  vector<int> v1(d1,d1 + 4), v2(d2,d2 + 4), v3(d2,d2 + 4);
  // Set up one empty vector
  vector<int> v4;

  // Copy v1 to v2
  copy(v1.begin(),v1.end(),v2.begin());
```

```
                // Copy backwards v1 to v3
                copy_backward(v1.begin(),v1.end(),v3.end());

                // Use insert iterator to copy into empty vector
                copy(v1.begin(),v1.end(),back_inserter(v4));

                // Copy all four to cout
                ostream_iterator<int> out(cout," ");
                copy(v1.begin(),v1.end(),out);
                cout << endl;
                copy(v2.begin(),v2.end(),out);
                cout << endl;
                copy(v3.begin(),v3.end(),out);
                cout << endl;
                copy(v4.begin(),v4.end(),out);
                cout << endl;

                return 0;
            }
```

count, count_if   **Algorithm**

Summary
Count the number of elements in a container that satisfy a given condition.

Synopsis
#include <algorithm>

template <class InputIterator, class T, class Size>
 void
 count(InputIterator first, InputIterator last,
     const T& value, Size& n);

template <class InputIterator, class Predicate, class Size>
 void
 count_if(InputIterator first, InputIterator last,
     Predicate pred, Size& n);

Description
The *count* algorithm compares *value* to elements in the sequence defined by iterators *first* and *last*, and increments a counting value *n* each time it finds a match. i.e., *count* adds to *n* the number of iterators *i* in the range *[first, last)* for which the following condition holds:

```
    *i == value
```

The *count_if* algorithm lets you specify a predicate, and increments *n* each time an element in the sequence satisfies the predicate. That is, *count_if* adds to *n* the number of iterators *i* in the range *[first, last)* for which the following condition holds:

```
pred(*i) == true.
```

Complexity

Both *count* and *count_if* perform exactly *last-first* applications of the corresponding predicate.

Examples

```cpp
#include <vector>
#include <algorithm>
using namespace std;

int main()
{
  int sequence[10] = {1,2,3,4,5,5,7,8,9,10};
  int i=0,j=0,k=0;

  // Set up a vector
  vector<int> v(sequence,sequence + 10);

  count(v.begin(),v.end(),5,i);   // Count fives
  count(v.begin(),v.end(),6,j);   // Count sixes
  // i = 2, j = 0

  // Count all less than 8
  count_if(v.begin(),v.end(),bind2nd(less<int>(),8),k);
  // k = 7

  cout << i << " " << j << " " << k << endl;
  return 0;
}
```

deallocate   Memory handling primitive

Summary

A pointer based primitive for handling memory.

Synopsis

#include <memory>

template <class T>
 void deallocate (T* buffer);

Description

The *deallocate* templated function frees the memory used by *buffer* for system-wide use.

See also
Other memory handling primitives: *allocate, construct, get_temporary_buffer, return_temporary_buffer*

deque

Summary
A sequence that supports random access iterators and efficient insertion/deletion at both beginning and end.

Synopsis

```
#include <deque>

template <class T>
 class deque {

public:

// Types

    typedef typename reference;
    typedef typename const_reference;
    typedef typename iterator;
    typedef typename const_iterator;
    typedef typename size_type;
    typedef typename difference_type;
    typedef T value_type;
    typedef reverse_iterator<iterator,
        value_type, reference,
        difference_type> reverse_iterator;
    typedef reverse_iterator<const_iterator,
        value_type, const_reference,
        difference_type> const_reverse_iterator;

// Construct/Copy/Destroy

    explicit deque ();
    explicit deque (size_type, const T& = T());
    deque (const deque<T>&);
    template <class InputIterator>
     deque (InputIterator, InputIterator);
    ~deque ();
    deque<T> operator= (const deque<T>);
    template <class InputIterator>
```

```
  assign (InputIterator, InputIterator);
  template <class Size, class T>
   void assign (Size n, const T& t = T());
```

// Iterators

```
  iterator begin ();
  const_iterator begin () const;
  iterator end ();
  const_iterator end () const;
  reverse_iterator rbegin ();

  const_reverse_iterator rbegin () const;
  reverse_iterator rend ();
  const_reverse_iterator rend () const;
```

// Capacity

```
  size_type size () const;
  size_type max_size () const;
  void resize (size_type,T c = T());
  bool empty () const;
```

// Element access

```
  reference operator[] (size_type);
  const_reference operator[] (size_type) const;
  reference at (size_type n);
  const_reference at (size_type n) const;
  reference front ();
  const_reference front () const;
  reference back ();
  const_reference back () const;
```

// Modifiers

```
  void push_front (const T&);
  void push_back (const T&);
  iterator insert (iterator, const T& = T());
  void insert (iterator, size_type, const T& = T());
  template <class InputIterator>
   void insert (iterator, InputIterator, InputIterator);

  void pop_front ();
  void pop_back ();
```

```
    void erase (iterator);
    void erase (iterator, iterator);
    void swap (deque<T>&);


};


// Comparison


template <class T>
 bool operator== (const deque<T>&, const deque <T>&);


template <class T>
 bool operator< (const deque<T>, const deque <T>&);
```

Description

deque<T> is a type of sequence that supports random access iterators. It supports constant time insert and erase operations at the beginning or the end of the container; insertion and erase in the middle take linear time. Storage management is handled automatically.

Any type used for the template parameter *T* must provide the following (where *T* is the *type, t* is a *value* of *T,* and *u* is a *const value* of *T*):

Default constructor	`T()`
Copy constructors	`T(t)` and `T(u)`
Destructor	`t.~T()`

Caveats

Member function templates are used in all containers provided by the Standard Template Library. An example of this is the constructor for *deque<T>* that takes two templated iterators:

```
template <class InputIterator>
 deque (InputIterator, InputIterator);
```

deque also has an insert function of this type. These functions, when not restricted by compiler limitations, allow you to use any type of input iterator as arguments. For compilers that do not support this feature we provide substitute functions that allow you to use an iterator obtained from the same type of container as the one you are constructing (or calling a member function on), or you can use a pointer to the type of element you have in the container.

For example, if your compiler does not support member function templates you can construct a *deque* in the following two ways:

```
int intarray[10];
deque<int> first_deque(intarray,intarray + 10);
```

```
                  deque<int>
                  second_deque(first_deque.begin(),first_deque.end());
```

But not this way:

```
                  deque<long>
                  long_deque(first_deque.begin(),first_deque.end());
```

since the *long_deque* and *first_deque* are not the same type.

Examples

```
                  #include <deque>
                  #include <string>
                  using namespace std;

                  deque<string> deck_of_cards;
                  deque<string> current_hand;

                  void initialize_cards(deque<string>& cards) {
                    cards.push_front("aceofspades");
                    cards.push_front("kingofspades");
                    cards.push_front("queenofspades");
                    cards.push_front("jackofspades");
                    cards.push_front("tenofspades");
                    // etc.
                  }

                  template <class It, class It2>
                  void print_current_hand(It start, It2 end)
                  {
                    while (start < end)
                    cout << *start++ << endl;
                  }

                  template <class It, class It2>
                  void deal_cards(It, It2 end) {
                    for (int i=0;i<5;i++) {
                      current_hand.insert(current_hand.begin(),*end);
                      deck_of_cards.erase(end++);
                    }
                  }

                  void play_poker() {
                    initialize_cards(deck_of_cards);
                    deal_cards(current_hand.begin(),deck_of_cards.begin());
                  }

                  int main()
                  {
                    play_poker();
                    print_current_hand(current_hand.begin(),current_hand.end());
                    return 0;
                  }
```

Constructors and destructor

explicit
deque ();
The default constructor. Creates a deque of zero elements.

explicit
deque (size_type n, const T& value = T());
Creates a deque of length *n*, containing *n* copies of *value*.

deque (const deque<T>& x);
Copy constructor. Creates a copy of *x*.

template <class InputIterator>
deque (InputIterator first, InputIterator last);
Creates a deque of length *last - first*, filled with all values obtained by dereferencing the *InputIterators* on the range *[first, last)*.

~deque ();
The destructor. Releases any allocated memory for self.

Iterators

iterator **begin** ();
Returns a random access iterator that points to the first element.

const_iterator **begin** () const;
Returns a constant random access iterator that points to the first element.

iterator **end** ();
Returns a random access iterator that points to the past-the-end value.

const_iterator **end** () const;
Returns a constant random access iterator that points to the past-the-end value.

reverse_iterator **rbegin** ();
Returns a random access iterator that points to the past-the-end value.

const_reverse_iterator **rbegin** () const;
Returns a constant random access iterator that points to the past-the-end value.

reverse_iterator **rend** ();
Returns a random access iterator that points to the first element.

const_reverse_iterator **rend** () const;
Returns a constant random access iterator that points to the first element.

Assignment operator

deque<T>&
operator= (const deque<T>& x);
Assignment operator. Erases all elements in self then inserts nto self a copy of each element in *x*. Returns a reference to self.

Reference operators

reference operator[] (size_type n);

Returns a reference to element *n* of self. The result can be used as an lvalue. The index *n* must be between 0 and the size less one.

const_reference operator[] (size_type) const;

Returns a constant reference to element *n* of self. The index *n* must be between 0 and the size less one.

Comparison operators

template <class T>
bool
operator== (const deque<T>& x, const deque T>& y);

Equality operator. Returns *true* if *x* is the same as *y*.

template <class T>
bool
operator< (const deque<T>& x, const deque T>& y);

Returns *true* if the elements contained in *x* are lexicographically less than the elements contained in *y*.

Member functions

template <class InputIterator>
void
assign (InputIterator first, InputIterator last);

Erases all elements contained in self, then inserts new elements from the range *[first, last)*.

template <class Size, class T>
void
assign (Size n, const T& t = T());

Erases all elements contained in self, then inserts *n* instances of the value of *t*.

reference
at (size_type n);

Returns a reference to element *n* of self. The result can be used as an *lvalue*. The index *n* must be between 0 and the size less one.

const_reference
at (size_type) const;

Returns a constant reference to element *n* of self. The index *n* must be between 0 and the size less one.

reference
back ();

Returns a reference to the last element.

const_reference

back () const;
Returns a constant reference to the last element.

bool
empty () const;
Returns true if the size of self is zero.

void
erase (iterator position);
Removes the element pointed to by *position*.

void
erase (iterator first, iterator last);
Removes the elements in the range *[first, last)*.

reference
front ();
Returns a reference to the first element.

const_reference
front () const;
Returns a constant reference to the first element.

iterator
insert (iterator position, const T& x = T());
Inserts *x* before *position*. The return value points to the inserted *x*.

void
insert (iterator position, size_type n, const T& x =T());
Inserts *n* copies of *x* before *position*.

template <class InputIterator>
void
insert (iterator position, InputIterator first,
         InputIterator last);
Inserts copies of the elements in the range *(first, last]* before *position*.

size_type
max_size () const;
Returns *size ()* of the largest possible deque.

void
pop_back ();
Removes the last element. Note that this function does not return the element.

void
pop_front ();
Removes the first element. Note that this function does not return the element

push_back (const T& x);

Appends a copy of x to the end.

void
push_front (const T& x);

Inserts a copy of x at the front.

void
resize (size_type sz, T c = T());

Alters the size of self. If the new size (sz) is greater than the current size then sz-$size()$ c's are inserted at the end of the deque. If the new size is smaller than the current capacity, then the deque is truncated by erasing $size()$-sz elements off the end. If sz is equal to *capacity*, no action is taken.

size_type
size () const;

Returns the number of elements.

void
swap (deque<T>& x);

Exchanges self with x.

destroy   Memory handling primitive

Summary
Invoke the destructor for values pointed to by iterators or pointers.

Synopsis
#include <memory>

template <class ForwardIterator>
void destroy (ForwardIterator first, ForwardIterator last)

template <class T>
void destroy (T* pointer)

Description
template <class T>
void
destroy (T* pointer)

Invokes the destructor for the value pointed to by the argument pointer.

template <class ForwardIterator>
void
destroy (ForwardIterator first, ForwardIterator last)

Destroys all of the values in the range *[first, last)*.

See also
algorithms, stl_iter_memory, stl_ptr_memory

distance

Summary

Computes the distance between two iterators

Synopsis

#include <iterator>

```
template <class InputIterator, class Distance>
void distance (InputIterator first,
          InputIterator last,
          Distance& n);
```

Description

The *distance* template function computes the distance between two iterators and stores that value in *n*. The last iterator must be reachable from the first iterator.

distance increments *n* by the number of times it takes to get from *first* to *last*. *distance* must be a three argument function that stores the result into a reference instead of returning the result, because the distance type cannot be deduced from built-in iterator types such as *int**.

Examples

```
#include<iterator>
#include<vector>
using namespace std;

int main()
{
  //Initialize a vector using an array
  int arr[6] = {3,4,5,6,7,8};
  vector<int> v(arr,arr+6);
  //Declare a list iterator, s.b. a ForwardIterator
  vector<int>::iterator itr = v.begin()+3;
  //Output the original vector
  cout << "For the vector: ";
  copy(v.begin(),v.end(),ostream_iterator<int>(cout," "));
  cout << endl << endl;

  cout << "When the iterator is initialized to point to "
       << *itr << endl << endl;
  // Use of distance
  vector<int>::difference_type dist = 0;
  distance(v.begin(), itr, dist);
```

```
        cout << "The distance between the beginning and itr is "
            << dist << endl;
        return 0;
    }
```

See also
sequence, random_iterator

divides

Summary
Returns the result of dividing its first argument by its second.

Synopsis
#include <functional>

```
template <class T>
  struct divides : binary_function<T, T, T> {
    T operator() (const T& x, const T& y) const
        { return x / y; }
  };
```

Description
divides is a binary function object. Its *operator()* returns the result of dividing *x* by *y*. You can pass a *divides* object to any algorithm that requires a binary function. For example, the *transform* algorithm applies a binary operation to corresponding values in two collections and stores the result. *divides* would be used in that algorithm in the following manner:

```
vector<int> vec1;
vector<int> vec2;
vector<int> vecResult;
?
transform(vec1.begin(), vec1.end(),
          vec2.begin(), vec2.end(),
          vecResult.begin(), divides<int>());
```

After this call to *transform, vecResult[n]* will contain *vec1[n]* divided by *vec2[n]*.

See also
function objects

equal

Summary
Compares two ranges for equivalence.

Synopsis

```
#include <algorithm>

template <class InputIterator1, class InputIterator2>
  bool
  equal(InputIterator1 first1, InputIterator1 last1,
      InputIterator2 first2);

template <class InputIterator1, class InputIterator2,
      class BinaryPredicate>
  bool
  equal(InputIterator1 first1, InputIterator1 last1,
      InputIterator2 first2, BinaryPredicate binary_pred);
```

Description

The *equal* algorithm does a pairwise comparison of all of the elements in one range with all of the elements in another range to see if they match. The first version of *equal* uses the equal operator (==) as the comparison function, and the second version allows you to specify a binary predicate as the comparison function. The first version returns *true* if all of the corresponding elements are equal to each other. The second version of *equal* returns *true* if for each pair of elements in the two ranges, the result of applying the binary predicate is *true*. In other words, *equal* returns *true* if both of the following are true:

- There are at least as many elements in the second range as in the first;

- For every iterator *i* in the range *[first1, last1)* the following corresponding conditions hold:

```
    *i == *(first2 + (i - first1))
```

  or

```
    binary_pred(*i, *(first2 + (i - first1))) == true
```

Otherwise, *equal* returns *false*.

This algorithm assumes that there are at least as many elements available after *first2* as there are in the range *[first1, last1)*.

Complexity

equal performs at most *last1-first1* comparisons or applications of the predicate.

Examples

```
#include <algorithm>
#include <vector>
using namespace std;

int main()
{
    int d1[4] = {1,2,3,4};
    int d2[4] = {1,2,4,3};
```

```
// Set up two vectors
vector<int> v1(d1,d1 + 4), v2(d2,d2 + 4);

// Check for equality
bool b1 = equal(v1.begin(),v1.end(),v2.begin());
bool b2 = equal(v1.begin(),v1.end(),
                v2.begin(),equal_to<int>());

// Both b1 and b2 are false
cout << (b1 ? "TRUE" : "FALSE")  << " "
     << (b2 ? "TRUE" : "FALSE") << endl;
return 0;
}
```

equal_range   Algorithm

Summary
Determines the valid range for insertion of a value in a container.

Synopsis
#include <algorithm>
template <class ForwardIterator, class T>
  pair<ForwardIterator, ForwardIterator>
  equal_range(ForwardIterator first, ForwardIterator last,
        const T& value);

template <class ForwardIterator, class T, class Compare>
  pair<ForwardIterator, ForwardIterator>
  equal_range(ForwardIterator first, ForwardIterator last,
        const T& value, Compare comp);

Description
The *equal_range* algorithm performs a binary search on an ordered container to determine where the element *value* can be inserted without violating the container's ordering. The library provides two versions of the algorithm. The first version uses the less than operator (*operator <*) to search for the valid insertion range, and assumes that the sequence was sorted using the less than operator. The second version allows you to specify a function object of type *compare*, and assumes that *compare* was the function used to sort the sequence. The function object must be a binary predicate.

equal_range returns a pair of iterators, *i* and *j* that define a range containing elements equivalent to *value*, i.e., the first and last valid insertion points for *value*. If *value* is not an element in the container, *i* and *j* are equal. Otherwise, *i* will point to the first element not "less" than value, and *j* will point to the first element greater than value. In the second version, "less" is defined by the comparison object. Formally, *equal_range* returns a sub-range [*i*, *j*) such that *value* can be inserted at any iterator *k* within the range. Depending upon the version of the algorithm used, *k* must satisfy one of the following conditions:

```
!(*k <  value)  &&  !(value  <  *k)
```

or

```
comp(*k,value) == false && comp(value, *k) == false
```

Complexity

equal_range performs at most *2 * log(last - first) + 1* comparisons.

Examples

```
#include <vector>
#include <algorithm>
using namespace std;

int main()
{
  typedef vector<int>::iterator iterator;
  int d1[11] = {0,1,2,2,3,4,2,2,2,6,7};

  // Set up a vector
  vector<int> v1(d1,d1 + 11);

  // Try equal_range variants
  pair<iterator,iterator> p1 =
      equal_range(v1.begin(),v1.end(),3);
  // p1 = (v1.begin() + 4,v1.begin() + 5)

  pair<iterator,iterator> p2 =
      equal_range(v1.begin(),v1.end(),2,less<int>());
  // p2 = (v1.begin() + 4,v1.begin() + 5)

  // Output results
  cout << endl  << "The equal range for 3 is: "
      << "( " << *p1.first << " , "
      << *p1.second << " ) " << endl << endl;

  cout << endl << "The equal range for 2 is: "
      << "( " << *p2.first << " , "
      << *p2.second << " ) " << endl;
  return 0;
}
```

equal_to   Function object

Summary

Binary function object that returns *true* if its first argument equals its second

Synopsis

#include <functional>

```
template <class T>
struct equal_to : binary_function<T, T, bool> {
    bool operator() (const T& x, const T& y) const
        { return x == y; }
};
```

Description

equal_to is a binary function object. Its *operator()* returns *true* if x is equal to y. You can pass an *equal_to* object to any algorithm that requires a binary function. For example, the *transform* algorithm applies a binary operation to corresponding values in two collections and stores the result. *equal_to* would be used in that algorithm in the following manner:

```
vector<int> vec1;
vector<int> vec2;
vector<int> vecResult;
?
transform(vec1.begin(), vec1.end(),
          vec2.begin(), vec2.end(),
          vecResult.begin(), equal_to<int>());
```

After this call to *transform*, *vecResult(n)* will contain a "1" if *vec1(n)* was equal to *vec2(n)* or a "0" if *vec1(n)* was not equal to *vec2(n)*.

See also

function objects

exception   standard exception

Summary
Classes supporting logic and runtime errors.

Synopsis
#include <stdexcept>

```
class exception {
  public:

    exception () throw();
    exception (const exception&) throw();
    exception& operator= (const exception&) throw();
    virtual ~exception () throw();
    virtual const char* what () const throw();
};
class logic_error : public exception {
  public:
```

```
          logic_error (const string& what_arg);
        };
        class domain_error : public logic_error {
          public:
            domain_error (const string& what_arg);
        };
        class invalid_argument : public logic_error {
          public:
            invalid_argument (const string& what_arg);
        };
        class length_error : public logic_error {
          public:
            length_error (const string& what_arg);
        };
        class out_of_range : public logic_error {
          public:
            out_of_range (const string& what_arg);
        };
        class runtime_error : public exception {
          public:
            runtime_error (const string& what_arg);
        };
        class range_error : public runtime_error {
          public:
            range_error (const string& what_arg);
        };
        class overflow_error : public runtime_error {
          public:
            overflow_error (const string& what_arg);
        };
```

Description

The class exception defines the base class for the types of objects thrown as exceptions by Standard C++ Library components, and certain expressions, to report errors detected during program execution. User's can also use these exceptions to report errors in their own programs.

Constructors

exception () throw();
Constructs an object of class exception.

exception (const exception&) throw();
The copy constructor. Copies an exception object.

Destructor

virtual
~exception() throw();
Destroys an object of class exception.

Operators

exception&
operator= (const exception&) throw();
The assignment operator. Copies an exception object.

Member function

virtual const char*
what()const throw();
Returns an implementation-defined, null-terminated byte string representing a human-readable message describing the exception. The message may be a null-terminated multibyte string, suitable for conversion and display as a *wstring*.

Constructors for derived classes

logic_error::logic_error (const string& what_arg);
Constructs an object of class *logic_error*.

domain_error::domain_error (const string& what_arg);
Constructs an object of class *domain_error*.

invalid_argument::invalid_argument (const string& what_arg);
Constructs an object of class *invalid_argument*.

length_error::length_error (const string& what_arg);
Constructs an object of class *length_error*.

out_of_range::out_of_range (const string& what_arg);
Constructs an object of class *out_of_range*.

runtime_error::runtime_error (const string& what_arg);
Constructs an object of class *runtime_error*.

range_error::range_error (const string& what_arg);
Constructs an object of class *range_error*.

overflow_error::overflow_error (const string& what_arg);
Constructs an object of class *overflow_error*.

Examples

```
//
// stdlib/examples/manual/exception.cpp
//
#include <iostream.h>
#include <stdexcept>
```

```
using namespace std;

static void f() { throw runtime_error("a runtime error"); }

int main ()
{
    //
    // By wrapping the body of main in a try-catch block we can
    // be assured that we'll catch all exceptions in the
    // exception hierarchy.  You can simply catch exception as is
    // done below, or you can catch each of the exceptions in
       // which you have an interest.
    //
    try
    {
        f();
    }
    catch (const exception& e)
    {
        cout << "Got an exception: " << e.what() << endl;
    }
    return 0;
}
```

fill, fill_n   Algorithm

Summary
Initializes a range with a given value.

Synopsis
#include <algorithm>

template <class ForwardIterator, class T>
 void
 fill(ForwardIterator first, ForwardIterator last,
     const T& value);

template <class OutputIterator, class Size, class T>
 void fill_n(OutputIterator first, Size n, const T& value);

Description
The *fill* and *fill_n* algorithms are used to assign a value to the elements in a sequence. *fill* assigns the value to all the elements designated by iterators in the range *[first, last)*.

The *fill_n* algorithm assigns the value to all the elements designated by iterators in the range *[first, first + n)*. *fill_n* assumes that there are at least *n* elements following *first*, unless *first* is an insert iterator.

Complexity

fill makes exactly *last - first* assignments, and *fill_n* makes exactly *n* assignments.

Examples

```
#include <algorithm>
#include <vector>
using namespace std;

int main()
{
  int d1[4] = {1,2,3,4};

  // Set up two vectors
  vector<int> v1(d1,d1 + 4), v2(d1,d1 + 4);
  // Set up one empty vector
  vector<int> v3;

  // Fill all of v1 with 9
  fill(v1.begin(),v1.end(),9);

  // Fill first 3 of v2 with 7
  fill_n(v2.begin(),3,7);

  // Use insert iterator to fill v3 with 5 11's
  fill_n(back_inserter(v3),5,11);

  // Copy all three to cout
  ostream_iterator<int> out(cout," ");
  copy(v1.begin(),v1.end(),out);
  cout << endl;
  copy(v2.begin(),v2.end(),out);
  cout << endl;
  copy(v3.begin(),v3.end(),out);
  cout << endl;

  // Fill cout with 3 5's
  fill_n(ostream_iterator<int>(cout," "),3,5);
  cout << endl;

  return 0;
}
```

find

Algorithm

Summary

Find an occurence of value in a sequence

Synopsis

#include <algorithm>

```
template <class InputIterator, class T>
  InputIterator
  find(InputIterator first, InputIterator last,
      const T& value);
```

Description

The *find* algorithm lets you search for the first occurence of a particular value in a sequence. *find* returns the first iterator *i* in the range *[first, last)* for which the following condition holds:

```
*i == value.
```

If *find* does not find a match for *value*, it returns the iterator *last*.

Complexity

find peforms at most *last-first* comparisons.

Examples

```
#include <vector>
#include <algorithm>
using namespace std;

int main()
{
  typedef vector<int>::iterator iterator;
  int d1[10] = {0,1,2,2,3,4,2,2,6,7};

  // Set up a vector
  vector<int> v1(d1,d1 + 10);

  // Try find
  iterator it1 = find(v1.begin(),v1.end(),3);
  // it1 = v1.begin() + 4;

  // Try find_if
  iterator it2 =
      find_if(v1.begin(),v1.end(),bind1st(equal_to<int>(),3));
  // it2 = v1.begin() + 4

  // Try both adjacent_find variants
  iterator it3 = adjacent_find(v1.begin(),v1.end());
  // it3 = v1.begin() +2

  iterator it4 =
      adjacent_find(v1.begin(),v1.end(),equal_to<int>());
  // v4 = v1.begin() + 2

  // Output results
  cout << *it1 << " " << *it2 << " " << *it3 << " " << *it4 << endl;

  return 0;
}
```

See also
adjacent_find, find_first_of, find_if

find_first_of   **Algorithm**

Summary
Finds a match for a given subsequence within a sequence.

Synopsis
```
#include <algorithm>

template <class ForwardIterator1, class ForwardIterator2>
ForwardIterator1 find_first_of (ForwardIterator1 first1,
          ForwardIterator1 last1,
          ForwardIterator2 first2,
          ForwardIterator2 last2);

template <class ForwardIterator1, class ForwardIterator2,
     class BinaryPredicate>
ForwardIterator1 find_first_of (ForwardIterator1 first1,
          ForwardIterator1 last1,
          ForwardIterator2 first2,
          ForwardIterator2 last2,
          BinaryPredicate pred);
```

Description
The *find_first_of* algorithm finds a subsequence, specified by *first2,last2*, in a sequence specified by *first1, last1*. Two versions of the algorithm exist. The first uses the equality operator as the default binary predicate, and the second allows you to specify a binary predicate. The algorithm returns an iterator in the range *[first1,last1)* that points to the first element of the matching subsequence. If the subsequence is not located in the sequence, *find_first_of* returnes *last1*.

In other words, *find_first_of* returns an iterator *i* in the range *[first1,last1)* such that for some *j* in the range *[first2,last2)*:

```
*i ==*(first2 + n)
```

or

```
pred(i, first2+n)==true
```

Complexity
find_first_of performs at most *(last1 - first1)* applications of the corresponding predicate.

Examples
```
#include <vector>
```

```
#include <iterator>
#include <algorithm>
using namespace std;

int main()
{
  typedef vector<int>::iterator iterator;
  int d1[10] = {0,1,2,2,3,4,2,2,6,7};
  int d2[2] = {6,4};

  // Set up two vectors
  vector<int> v1(d1,d1 + 10), v2(d2,d2 + 2);

  // Try both find_first_of variants
  iterator it1 =
    find_first_of(v1.begin(),v1.end(),v2.begin(),v2.end());
  find_first_of(v1.begin(),v1.end(),v2.begin(),v2.end(),
                equal_to<int>());

  // Output results
  cout << "For the vectors: ";
  copy(v1.begin(),v1.end(),
      ostream_iterator<int>(cout," " ));
  cout << " and ";
  copy(v2.begin(),v2.end(),
      ostream_iterator<int>(cout," " ));
  cout << endl << endl
      << "both versions of find_first_of point to: "
      << *it1;

  return 0;
}
```

See also

adjacent_find, find, find_if

find_if   Algorithm

Summary
Find an occurence of value in a sequence

Synopsis
#include <algorithm>

template <class InputIterator, class Predicate>
  InputIterator
  find_if(InputIterator first, InputIterator last,
      Predicate pred);

Description

The *find_if* algorithm allows you to search for the first element in a sequence that satisfies a particular condition. The sequence is defined by iterators *first* and *last*, while the condition is defined by *find_if*'s third argument: a predicate function that returns a Boolean value. *find_if* returns the first iterator *i* in the range *[first, last)* for which the following condition holds:

```
pred(*i) == true.
```

If no such iterator is found, *find_if* returns *last*.

Complexity

find_if performs at most *last-first* applications of the corresponding predicate.

Example

```cpp
#include <vector>
#include <algorithm>
using namespace std;

int main()
{
  typedef vector<int>::iterator iterator;
  int d1[10] = {0,1,2,2,3,4,2,2,6,7};

  // Set up a vector
  vector<int> v1(d1,d1 + 10);

  // Try find
  iterator it1 = find(v1.begin(),v1.end(),3);
  // it1 = v1.begin() + 4;

  // Try find_if
  iterator it2 =
      find_if(v1.begin(),v1.end(),bind1st(equal_to<int>(),3));
  // it2 = v1.begin() + 4

  // Try both adjacent_find variants
  iterator it3 = adjacent_find(v1.begin(),v1.end());
  // it3 = v1.begin() +2

  iterator it4 =
      adjacent_find(v1.begin(),v1.end(),equal_to<int>());
  // v4 = v1.begin() + 2

  // Output results
  cout << *it1 << " " << *it2 << " " << *it3 << " "
      << *it4 << endl;

  return 0;
}
```

See also
adjacent_find, find, find_first_of

for_each

Summary
Applies a function to each element in a range.

Synopsis
#include <algorithm>

template <class InputIterator, class Function>
 void for_each(InputIterator first, InputIterator last,
        Function f);

Description
The *for_each* algorithm applies function *f* to all members of the sequence in the range *[first, last)*, where *first* and *last* are iterators that define the sequence. Since this a non-mutating algorithm, the function *f* cannot make any modifications to the sequence, but it can achieve results through side effects (such as copying or printing). If *f* returns a result, the result is ignored.

Complexity
The function *f* is applied exactly *last - first* times.

Example

```
#include <vector>
#include <algorithm>
using namespace std;

// Function class that outputs its argument times x
template <class Arg>
class out_times_x :  private unary_function<Arg,void>
{
  private:
    Arg multiplier;

  public:
    out_times_x(const Arg& x) : multiplier(x) { }
    void operator()(const Arg& x)
      { cout << x * multiplier << " " << endl; }
};

int main()
{
  int sequence[5] = {1,2,3,4,5};
```

```
    // Set up a vector
    vector<int> v(sequence,sequence + 5);


    // Setup a function object
    out_times_x<int> f2(2);

    for_each(v.begin(),v.end(),f2);    // Apply function

    return 0;
}
```

forward iterator

Summary
A forward-moving iterator that can both read and write.

Description

Note For a complete discussion of iterators, see the C++ *Programmer's Guide*, Chapter 19, "Iterators,"

Iterators are a generalization of pointers that allow a C++ program to uniformly interact with different data structures. Forward iterators are forward moving, and have the ability to both read and write data. These iterators satisfy the requirements listed in Table 17.3. The following key pertains to the iterator descriptions listed:

a and *b*	values of type X
n	value of *distance* type
u, Distance, tmp, and *m*	identifiers
r	value of type $X\&$
t	value of type T

Requirements for forward iterators
The expressions presented in Table 17.3 must be valid for forward iterators:

Table 17.3 Requirements for bidirectional iterators

Expression	Requirement
X u	*u might have a singular value*
X()	*X() might be singular*
X(a)	*copy constructor, a == X(a).*
X u(a)	*copy constructor, u == a*
X u = a	*assignment, u == a*
a == b, a != b	*return value convertible to bool*
*a	*return value convertible to T&*

Expression	Requirement
++r	returns X&
r++	return value convertable to const X&
*r++	returns T&

Forward iterators have the condition that $a == b$ implies $*a == *b$.

There are no restrictions on the number of passes an algorithm may make through the structure.

See also
Iterators, Bidirectional Iterators

See Chapter 19 of the C++ *Programmer's Guide*

front_insert_iterator, front_inserter   Insert iterator

Summary
An insert iterator used to insert items at the beginning of a collection.

Synopsis
```
#include <iterator>

template <class Container>
 class front_insert_iterator : public output_iterator {

protected:
  Container& container;
public:
  front_insert_iterator (Container& x);
  front_insert_iterator<Container>&
  operator= (const Container::value_type& value);
  front_insert_iterator<Container>& operator* ();
  front_insert_iterator<Container>& operator++ ();
  front_insert_iterator<Container> operator++ (int);
};

  template <class Container>
  front_insert_iterator<Container> front_inserter (Container& x)
```

Description
Insert iterators let you *insert* new elements into a collection rather than copy a new element's value over the value of an existing element. The class *front_insert_iterator* is used to insert items at the beginning of a collection. The function *front_inserter* creates

an instance of a *front_insert_iterator* for a particular collection type. A *front_insert_iterator* can be used with *deque*s and *list*s, but not with *map*s or *set*s.

Note that a *front_insert_iterator* makes each element that it inserts the new front of the container. This has the effect of reversing the order of the inserted elements. For example, if you use a *front_insert_iterator* to insert "1" then "2" then "3" onto the front of container *exmpl*, you will find, after the three insertions, that the first three elements of *exmpl* are "3 2 1".

Example

```
/****************************************************************
 *
 * ins_itr.cpp - Example program of insert iterator.
 *
 * $Id: ins_itr.cpp,v 1.7 1995/10/06 18:18:03 hart Exp $
 *
 * $$RW_INSERT_HEADER "slyrs.str"
 *
 ****************************************************************/

#include <iterator>
#include <deque>
using namespace std;

int main ()
{
  //
  // Initialize a deque using an array.
  //
  int arr[4] = { 3,4,7,8 };
  deque<int> d(arr+0, arr+4);
  //
  // Output the original deque.
  //
  cout << "Start with a deque: " << endl << "     ";
  copy(d.begin(), d.end(), ostream_iterator<int>(cout," "));
  //
  // Insert into the middle.
  //
  insert_iterator<deque<int> > ins(d, d.begin()+2);
  *ins = 5; *ins = 6;
  //
  // Output the new deque.
  //
  cout << endl << endl;
  cout << "Use an insert_iterator: " << endl << "     ";
  copy(d.begin(), d.end(), ostream_iterator<int>(cout," "));
  //
  // A deque of four 1s.
  //
  deque<int> d2(4, 1);
  //
```

```
    // Insert d2 at front of d.
    //
    copy(d2.begin(), d2.end(), front_inserter(d));
    //
    // Output the new deque.
    //
    cout << endl << endl;
    cout << "Use a front_inserter: " << endl << "      ";
    copy(d.begin(), d.end(), ostream_iterator<int>(cout," "));
    //
    // Insert d2 at back of d.
    //
    copy(d2.begin(), d2.end(), back_inserter(d));
    //
    // Output the new deque.
    //
    cout << endl << endl;
    cout << "Use a back_inserter: " << endl << "      ";
    copy(d.begin(), d.end(), ostream_iterator<int>(cout," "));
    cout << endl;

    return 0;
}
```

Constructor

front_insert_iterator (Container& x);
Constructor. Creates an instance of a *front_insert_iterator* associated with container *x*.

Operators

front_insert_iterator<Container>&
operator = (const Container::value_type& value);
Inserts a copy of *value* on the front of the container, and returns **this*.

front_insert_iterator<Container>&
operator* ();
Returns **this* (the input iterator itself).

front_insert_iterator<Container>&
operator++ ();

front_insert_iterator<Container>
operator++ (int);
Increments the insert iterator and returns **this*.

Helper function

template <class Container>
back_insert_iterator<Container>
front_inserter (Container& x)

Returns a *front_insert_iterator* that will insert elements at the beginning of container *x*. This function allows you to create front insert iterators inline.

See also
insert iterators

function object

Summary
Objects with an *operator()* defined. Function objects are used in place of pointers to functions as arguments to templated algorithms.

Synopsis
#include<functional>

// typedefs

```
template <class Arg, class Result>
struct unary_function{
    typedef Arg argument_type;
    typedef Result result_type;
};


template <class Arg1, class Arg2, class Result>
struct binary_function{
    typedef Arg1 first_argument_type;
    typedef Arg2 second_argument_type;
    typedef Result result_type;
};
```

// Arithmetic Operations

```
template<class T>
struct plus : binary_function<T, T, T> {
    T operator() (const T& x, const T& y) const
        { return x + y; }
};

template <class T>
struct minus : binary_function<T, T, T> {
    T operator() (const T& x, const T& y) const
        { return x - y; }
};
```

```
template <class T>
struct times : binary_function<T, T, T> {
    T operator() (const T& x, const T& y) const
        { return x * y; }
};

template <class T>
struct divides : binary_function<T, T, T> {
    T operator() (const T& x, const T& y) const
        { return x / y; }
};

template <class T>
struct modulus : binary_function<T, T, T> {
    T operator() (const T& x, const T& y) const
        { return x % y; }
};

template <class T>
struct negate : unary_function<T, T, T> {
    T operator() (const T& x) const
        { return -x; }
};

// Comparisons

template <class T>
struct equal_to : binary_function<T, T, bool> {
    bool operator() (const T& x, const T& y) const
        { return x == y; }
};

template <class T>
struct not_equal_to : binary_function<T, T, bool> {
    bool operator() (const T& x, const T& y) const
        { return x != y; }
};

template <class T>
PD 0 struct greater : binary_function<T, T, bool> {
    bool operator() (const T& x, const T& y) const
        { return x > y; }
};

template <class T>
```

```
    struct less : binary_function<T, T, bool> {
        bool operator() (const T& x, const T& y) const
            { return x < y; }
    };

    template <class T>
    struct greater_equal : binary_function<T, T, bool> {
        bool operator() (const T& x, const T& y) const
            { return x >= y; }
    };

    template <class T>
    struct less_equal : binary_function<T, T, bool> {
        bool operator() (const T& x, const T& y) const
            { return x <= y; }
    };

// Logical Comparisons

    template <class T>
    struct logical_and : binary_function<T, T, bool> {
        bool operator() (const T& x, const T& y) const
            { return x && y; }
    };

    template <class T>
    struct logical_or : binary_function<T, T, bool> {
        bool operator() (const T& x, const T& y) const
            { return x || y; }
    };

    template <class T>
    struct logical_not : unary_function<T, T, bool> {
        bool operator() (const T& x, const T& y) const
            { return !x; }
    };
```

Description

Function objects are objects with an *operator()* defined. They are important for the effective use of the standard library's generic algorithms, because the interface for each algorithmic template can accept either an object with an *operator()* defined, or a pointer to a function. The standard library provides both a standard set of function objects, and a pair of classes that you can use as the base for creating your own function objects.

Function objects that take one argument are called *unary function objects*. Unary function objects are required to provide the typedefs *argument_type* and *result_type*. Similarly, function objects that take two arguments are called *binary function objects* and, as such, are required to provide the typedefs *first_argument_type*, *second_argument_type*, and *result_type*.

The classes *unary_function* and *binary_function* make the task of creating templated function objects easier. The necessary typedefs for a unary or binary function object are provided by inheriting from the appropriate function object class.

The function objects provided by the standard library are listed in Table 17.4, together with a brief description of their operation. This class reference also includes an alphabetic entry for each function.

Table 17.4   Function objects in the standard class library

Function category	Function name	Operation
arithmetic functions	*plus*	addition $x + y$
	minus	subtraction $x - y$
	times	multiplication $x * y$
	divides	division x / y
	modulus	remainder $x \% y$
	negate	negation $- x$
comparison functions	*equal_to*	equality test $x == y$
	not_equal_to	inequality test $x != y$
	greater	greater comparison $x > y$
	less	less-than compari
	greater_equal	greater than or equal comparison $x >= y$
	less_equal	less than or equal comparison $x <= y$
logical functions	*logical_and*	logical conjunction $x \&\& y$
	logical_or	logical disjunction $x \mid\mid y$
	logical_not	logical negation $! x$

Examples

```
#include<functional>
#include<deque>
#include<vector>
#include<algorithm>
using namespace std;

//Create a new function object from unary_function
template<class Arg>
class factorial : public unary_function<Arg, Arg>
{
  public:

  Arg operator()(const Arg& arg)
  {
    Arg a = 1;
    for(Arg i = 2; i <= arg; i++)
      a *= i;
    return a;
```

```
    }
};

int main()
{
  //Initialize a deque with an array of ints
  int init[7] = {1,2,3,4,5,6,7};
  deque<int> d(init, init+7);

  //Create an empty vector to store the factorials
  vector<int> v((size_t)7);

  //Transform the numbers in the deque to their factorials and
  // store in the vector
  transform(d.begin(), d.end(), v.begin(), factorial<int>());

  //Print the results
  cout << "The following numbers: " << endl << "     ";
  copy(d.begin(),d.end(),ostream_iterator<int>(cout," "));

  cout << endl << endl;
  cout << "Have the factorials: " << endl << "     ";
  copy(v.begin(),v.end(),ostream_iterator<int>(cout," "));

  return 0;
}
```

generate, generate_n   Algorithm

Summary
Initialize a container with values produced by a value-generator class.

Synopsis
#include <algorithm>

template <class ForwardIterator, class Generator>
 void
 generate(ForwardIterator first, ForwardIterator last,
     Generator gen);

template <class OutputIterator, class Size, class Generator>
 void
 generate_n(OutputIterator first, Size n, Generator gen);

Description
A value-generator function returns a value each time it is invoked. The algorithms
generate and *generate_n* initialize (or reinitialize) a sequence by assigning the return value

of the generator function *gen* to all the elements designated by iterators in the range *[first, last)* or *[first, first + n)*. The function *gen* takes no arguments. (*gen* can be a function or a class with an *operator ()* defined that takes no arguments.)

generate_n assumes that there are at least *n* elements following *first*, unless *first* is an insert iterator.

Complexity
The *generate* and *generate_n* algorithms invoke *gen* and assign its return value exactly *last - first* (or *n*) times.

Example

```cpp
#include <algorithm>
#include <vector>
using namespace std;

// Value generator simply doubles the current value
// and returns it
template <class T>
class generate_val
{
  private:
    T val_;
  public:
    generate_val(const T& val) : val_(val) {}
    T& operator()() { val_ += val_; return val_; }
};

int main()
{
  int d1[4] = {1,2,3,4};
  generate_val<int> gen(1);

  // Set up two vectors
  vector<int> v1(d1,d1 + 4), v2(d1,d1 + 4);
  // Set up one empty vector
  vector<int> v3;

  // Generate values for all of v1
  generate(v1.begin(),v1.end(),gen);

  // Generate values for first 3 of v2
  generate_n(v2.begin(),3,gen);

  // Use insert iterator to generate 5 values for v3
  generate_n(back_inserter(v3),5,gen);

  // Copy all three to cout
  ostream_iterator<int> out(cout," ");
  copy(v1.begin(),v1.end(),out);
  cout << endl;
```

```
copy(v2.begin(),v2.end(),out);
cout << endl;
copy(v3.begin(),v3.end(),out);
cout << endl;

// Generate 3 values for cout
generate_n(ostream_iterator<int>(cout," "),3,gen);
cout << endl;

return 0;
}
```

get_temporary_buffer   Memory handling primitive

Summary
Pointer based primitive for handling memory

Synopsis
#include <memory>

template <class T>
 pair<T*, ptrdiff_t> get_temporary_buffer (ptrdiff_t n, T*);

Description
The *get_temporary_buffer* templated function reserves from system memory the largest possible buffer that is less than or equal to the size requested (*n*sizeof(T)*), and returns a *pair<T* ptrdiff_t>* containing the address and size of that buffer. The units used to describe the capacity are in *sizeof(T)*.

See also
Other memory handling primitives: *allocate, construct, deallocate, return_temporary_buffer.*

greater   Function object

Summary
Binary function object that returns *true* if its first argument is greater than its second

Synopsis
#include <functional>

```
template <class T>
    struct greater : binary_function<T, T, bool> {
    bool operator() (const T& x, const T& y) const
        { return x > y; }
```

```
};
```

Description

greater is a binary function object. Its *operator()* returns *true* if *x* is greater than *y*. You can pass a *greater* object to any algorithm that requires a binary function. For example, the *transform* algorithm applies a binary operation to corresponding values in two collections and stores the result of the function. *greater* would be used in that algorithm in the following manner:

```
vector<int> vec1;
vector<int> vec2;
vector<int> vecResult;
?
transform(vec1.begin(), vec1.end(),
          vec2.begin(), vec2.end(),
          vecResult.begin(), greater<int>());
```

After this call to *transform*, *vecResult(n)* will contain a "1" if *vec1(n)* was greater than *vec2(n)* or a "0" if *vec1(n)* was less than or equal to *vec2(n)*.

See also

function objects

greater_equal   Function object

Summary

Binary function object that returns *true* if its first argument is greater than or equal to its second

Synopsis

#include <functional>

```
template <class T>
struct greater_equal : binary_function<T, T, bool> {
    bool operator() (const T& x, const T& y) const
        { return x >= y; }
};
```

Description

greater_equal is a binary function object. Its *operator()* returns *true* if *x* is greater than or equal to *y*. You can pass a *greater_equal* object to any algorithm that requires a binary function. For example, the *sort* algorithm can acceept a binary function as an alternate comparison object to sort a sequence. *greater_equal* would be used in that algorithm in the following manner:

```
vector<int> vec1;
?
sort(vec1.begin(), vec1.end(),greater_equal<int>());
```

After this call to *sort*, *vec1* will be sorted in descending order.

See also
function objects

Heap operations   Algorithm

See the entries for *make_heap*, *pop_heap*, *push_heap* and *sort_heap*

includes   Algorithm

Summary
Basic set operation for sorted sequences.

Synopsis
#include <algorithm>

```
template <class InputIterator1, class InputIterator2>
 bool
includes (InputIterator1 first1, InputIterator1 last1,
      InputIterator2 first2, InputIterator2 last2);
```

```
template <class InputIterator1, class InputIterator2, class Compare>
 bool
includes (InputIterator1 first1, InputIterator1 last1,
      InputIterator2 first2, InputIterator2 last2, Compare comp);
```

Description
The *includes* algorithm compares two sorted sequences and returns *true* if every element in the range [*first2, last2*) is contained in the range [*first1, last1*). It returns *false* otherwise. *include* assumes that the sequences are sorted using the default comparison operator less than (<), unless an alternative comparison operator (*comp*) is provided.

Complexity
At most *((last1 - first1) + (last2 - first2)) * 2 -1* comparisons are performed.

Examples
```
#include<algorithm>
#include<set>
using namespace std;

int main()
{
```

```
//Initialize some sets
int a1[10] = {1,2,3,4,5,6,7,8,9,10};
int a2[6]  = {2,4,6,8,10,12};
int a3[4]  = {3,5,7,8};
set<int, less<int> > all(a1, a1+10), even(a2, a2+6),
                         small(a3,a3+4);

//Demonstrate includes
cout << "The set: ";
copy(all.begin(),all.end(),
      ostream_iterator<int>(cout," "));
bool answer = includes(all.begin(), all.end(),
                 small.begin(), small.end());
cout << endl
      << (answer ? "INCLUDES " : "DOES NOT INCLUDE ");
copy(small.begin(),small.end(),
      ostream_iterator<int>(cout," "));
answer = includes(all.begin(), all.end(),
                    even.begin(), even.end());
cout << ", and" << endl
      << (answer ? "INCLUDES" : "DOES NOT INCLUDE ");
copy(even.begin(),even.end(),
      ostream_iterator<int>(cout," "));
cout << endl << endl;

return 0;
}
```

See also
The other set operations:

set_union, set_intersection, set_difference, set_symmetric_difference

inner_product   Generalized numeric operation

Summary
Computes the inner product *A X B* of two ranges *A* and *B*.

Synopsis
#include <numeric>

```
template <class InputIterator1,
       class InputIterator2,
       class T        >
T inner_product (InputIterator1 first1,
       InputIterator1 last1,
       InputIterator2 first2, T init);
```

```
template <class InputIterator1,
        class InputIterator2,
        class T,
        class BinaryOperation1,
        class BinaryOperation last1>
T inner_product (InputIterator1 first1,
        InputIterator1 last1,
        InputIterator2 first2,
        T init,
        BinaryOperation1 binary_op1,
        BinaryOperation binary_op2);
```

Description

There are two versions of *inner_product*. The first computes an inner product using the default multiplication and addition operators, while the second allows you to specify binary operations to use in place of the default operations.

The first version of the function computes its result by initializing the accumulator *acc* with the initial value *init* and then modifying it with:

```
acc = acc + (*i1) * (*i2)
```

for every iterator *i1* in the range *[first1, last1).* and iterator *i2* in the range *[first2, first2 + (last1 - first1))* in order. The algorithm returns *acc*.

The second version of the function initializes *acc* with *init*, then computes the result:

```
acc  = binary_op1(acc, binary_op2(*i1,  *i2))
```

for every iterator *i1* in the range *[first1, last1)* and iterator *i2* in the range *[first2, first2 + (last1 - first1))* in order.

Complexity

The *inner_product* algorithm computes exactly *(last1 - first1)* applications of either

```
acc + (*i1) * (*i2)
```

or

```
binary_op1(acc, binary_op2(*i1, *i2)).
```

Examples

```
#include <numeric>       //For inner_product
#include <list>          //For list
#include <vector>        //For vectors
#include <functional>    //For plus and minus
using namespace std;

int main()
{
  //Initialize a list and an int using arrays of ints
  int a1[3] = {6, -3, -2};
```

```
            int a2[3] = {-2, -3, -2};

            list<int>   l(a1, a1+3);
            vector<int> v(a2, a2+3);

            //Calculate the inner product of the two sets of values
            int inner_prod =
                inner_product(l.begin(), l.end(), v.begin(), 0);

            //Calculate a wacky inner product using the same values
            int wacky =
                inner_product(l.begin(), l.end(), v.begin(), 0,
                              plus<int>(), minus<int>());

            //Print the output
            cout << "For the two sets of numbers: " << endl
                 << "       ";
            copy(v.begin(),v.end(),ostream_iterator<int>(cout," "));
            cout << endl << " and   ";
            copy(l.begin(),l.end(),ostream_iterator<int>(cout," "));

            cout << "," << endl << endl;
            cout << "The inner product is: " << inner_prod << endl;
            cout << "The wacky result is: " << wacky << endl;

            return 0;
        }
```

inplace_merge   Algorithm

Summary
Merge two sorted sequences into one.

Synopsis
```
#include <algorithm>
template <class BidirectionalIterator>
 void
 inplace_merge(BidirectionalIterator first,
         BidirectionalIterator middle,
         BidirectionalIterator last);


template <class BidirectionalIterator, class Compare>
 void
 inplace_merge(BidirectionalIterator first,
         BidirectionalIterator middle,
         BidirectionalIterator last, Compare comp);
```

Description

The *inplace_merge* algorithm merges two sorted consecutive ranges *[first, middle)* and *[middle, last)*,and puts the result of the merge into the range *[first, last)*. The merge is stable, that is, if the two ranges contain equivalent elements, the elements from the first range always precede the elements from the second.

There are two versions of the *inplace_merge* algorithm. The first version uses the less than (<) operator as the default for comparison, and the second version accepts a third argument that specifies a comparison operator.

Complexity

When enough additional memory is available, *inplace_merge* does at most *(last - first) -1* comparisons. If no additional memory is available, an algorithm with *O(NlogN)* complexity may be used.

Examples

```
#include <algorithm>
#include <vector>
using namespace std;

int main()
{
  int d1[4] = {1,2,3,4};
  int d2[8] = {11,13,15,17,12,14,16,18};

  // Set up two vectors
  vector<int> v1(d1,d1 + 4), v2(d1,d1 + 4);

  // Set up four destination vectors
  vector<int> v3(d2,d2 + 8),v4(d2,d2 + 8),
              v5(d2,d2 + 8),v6(d2,d2 + 8);
  // Set up one empty vector
  vector<int> v7;

  // Merge v1 with v2
  merge(v1.begin(),v1.end(),v2.begin(),v2.end(),v3.begin());
  // Now use comparator
  merge(v1.begin(),v1.end(),v2.begin(),v2.end(),v4.begin(),
        less<int>());

  // In place merge v5
  vector<int>::iterator mid = v5.begin();
  advance(mid,4);
  inplace_merge(v5.begin(),mid,v5.end());
  // Now use a comparator on v6
  mid = v6.begin();
  advance(mid,4);
  inplace_merge(v6.begin(),mid,v6.end(),less<int>());

  // Merge v1 and v2 to empty vector using insert iterator
```

```
merge(v1.begin(),v1.end(),v2.begin(),v2.end(),
    back_inserter(v7));

// Copy all cout
ostream_iterator<int> out(cout," ");
copy(v1.begin(),v1.end(),out);
cout << endl;
copy(v2.begin(),v2.end(),out);
cout << endl;
copy(v3.begin(),v3.end(),out);
cout << endl;
copy(v4.begin(),v4.end(),out);
cout << endl;

copy(v5.begin(),v5.end(),out);
cout << endl;
copy(v6.begin(),v6.end(),out);
cout << endl;
copy(v7.begin(),v7.end(),out);
cout << endl;

// Merge v1 and v2 to cout
merge(v1.begin(),v1.end(),v2.begin(),v2.end(),
    ostream_iterator<int>(cout," "));
cout << endl;

return 0;
}
```

See also
merge

input iterator

Iterator

Summary
A read-only, forward moving iterator.

Description

Note   For a complete discussion of iterators, see the *Borland C++ Programmer's Guide*, Chapter 19, "Iterators,"

Iterators are a generalization of pointers that allow a C++ program to uniformly interact with different data structures. Input iterators are read-only, forward-moving iterators that satisfy the requirements listed in Table 17.5.

Requirements for Input Iterators

The following key pertains to the iterator descriptions listed :

a and *b*	values of type *X*
n	value of *distance* type
u, *Distance*, *tmp*, and *m*	identifiers
r	value of type *X&*
t	value of type *T*

The expressions presented in Table 17.5 must be valid for input iterators:

Table 17.5   Requirements for bidirectional iterators

Expression	Requirement
X(a)	*copy constructor, a == X(a)*
X u(a)	*copy constructor, u == a*
X u = a	*assignment, u == a*
a == b, a != b	*return value convertable to bool*
*a	*a == b implies *a == *b*
++r	*returns X&*
r++	*return value convertable to const X&*
*r++	*returns type T*

For input iterators, $a == b$ does not imply that $++a == ++b$.

Algorithms using input iterators should be single pass algorithms. That is they should not pass through the same iterator twice.

The value of type *T* does not have to be an *lvalue*.

See also

iterators, output iterators

insert_iterator, inserter   Insert iterator

Summary

An insert iterator used to insert items into a collection rather than overwrite the collection.

Synopsis

```
#include <iterator>

template <class Container>
 class insert_iterator : public output_iterator {

protected:
    Container& container;
```

```
      Container::iterator iter;
public:
   insert_iterator (Container& x, Container::iterator i);
   insert_iterator<Container>&
   operator= (const Container::value_type& value);
   insert_iterator<Container>& operator* ();
   insert_iterator<Container>& operator++ ();
   insert_iterator<Container> operator++ (int);
};


template <class Container>
insert_iterator<Container> inserter (Container& x, Iterator i)
```

Description

Insert iterators let you *insert* new elements into a collection rather than copy a new element's value over the value of an existing element. The class *insert_iterator* is used to insert items into a specified location of a collection. The function *inserter* creates an instance of an *insert_iterator* given a particular collection type and iterator. An *insert_iterator* can be used with *vector*s, *deque*s, *list*s, *map*s and *set*s.

Example

```cpp
#include<iterator>
#include<vector>
using namespace std;

int main()
{
   //Initialize a vector using an array
   int arr[4] = {3,4,7,8};
   vector<int> v(arr,arr+4);

   //Output the original vector
   cout << "Start with a vector: " << endl << "     ";
   copy(v.begin(),v.end(),ostream_iterator<int>(cout," "));

   //Insert into the middle
   insert_iterator<vector<int> >  ins(v, v.begin()+2);
   *ins = 5;
   *ins = 6;

   //Output the new vector
   cout << endl << endl;
   cout << "Use an insert_iterator: " << endl << "     ";
   copy(v.begin(),v.end(),ostream_iterator<int>(cout," "));

   return 0;
}
```

Constructor

insert_iterator (Container& x, Container::iterator i);

Constructor. Creates an instance of an *insert_iterator* associated with container *x* and iterator *i*.

Operators

insert_iterator<Container>&
operator= (const Container::value_type& value);

Inserts a copy of *value* into the container at the location specified by the *insert_iterator*, increments the iterator, and returns *this*.

insert_iterator<Container>&
operator* ();

Returns *this* (the input iterator itself).

insert_iterator<Container>&
operator++ ();

insert_iterator<Container>
operator++ (int);

Increments the insert iterator and returns *this*.

Helper function

template <class Container, class Iterator>
insert_iterator<Container>
inserter (Container& x, Iterator i)

Returns an *insert_iterator* that will insert elements into container *x* at location *i*. This function allows you to create insert iterators inline.

See also

Insert Iterators

Insert Iterator

Insert iterator

Summary

Iterator adaptor that allows an iterator to insert into a container rather than overwrite elements in the container.

Synopsis

#include <iterator>

template <class Container>
 class back_insert_iterator : public output_iterator {

protected:

```
      Container& container;
   public:
     back_insert_iterator (Container& x);
     back_insert_iterator<Container>&
     operator= (const Container::value_type& value);
     back_insert_iterator<Container>& operator* ();
     back_insert_iterator<Container>& operator++ ();
     back_insert_iterator<Container> operator++ (int);
   };

   template <class Container>
    class front_insert_iterator : public output_iterator {

   protected:
     Container& container;
   public:
     front_insert_iterator (Container& x);
     front_insert_iterator<Container>&
     operator= (const Container::value_type& value);
     front_insert_iterator<Container>& operator* ();
     front_insert_iterator<Container>& operator++ ();
     front_insert_iterator<Container> operator++ (int);
   };

   template <class Container>
    class insert_iterator : public output_iterator {

   protected:
      Container& container;
      Container::iterator iter;
   public:
     insert_iterator (Container& x, Container::iterator i);
     insert_iterator<Container>&
     operator= (const Container::value_type& value);
     insert_iterator<Container>& operator* ();

   insert_iterator<Container>& operator++ ();
     insert_iterator<Container> operator++ (int);
   };

   template <class Container>
   back_insert_iterator<Container> back_inserter (Container& x)

   template <class Container>
   front_insert_iterator<Container> front_inserter (Container& x)
```

```
template <class Container>
insert_iterator<Container> inserter (Container& x, Iterator i)
```

Description

Insert iterators are iterator adaptors that let an iterator *insert* new elements into a collection rather than overwrite existing elements when copying to a container. There are several types of insert iterator classes.

- The class *back_insert_iterator* is used to insert items at the end of a collection. The function *back_inserter* can be used with an iterator inline, to create an instance of a *back_insert_iterator* for a particular collection type.

- The class *front_insert_iterator* is used to insert items at the start of a collection. The function *front_inserter* creates an instance of a *front_insert_iterator* for a particular collection type.

- An *insert_iterator* inserts new items into a collection at a location defined by an iterator supplied to the constructor. Like the other insert iterators, *insert_iterator* has a helper function called *inserter*, which takes a collection and an iterator into that collection, and creates an instance of the *insert_iterator*.

See also

back_insert_iterator, front_insert_iterator, insert_iterator

istream_iterator   Iterators

Summary

Stream iterator that provides iterator capabilities for istreams. This iterator allows generic algorithms to be used directly on streams.

Synopsis

```
#include <iterator>

Istream iterator

template <class T, class Distance = ptrdiff_t>
 class istream_iterator : public input_iterator<T, Distance>
 {

 public:
   istream_iterator();
   istream_iterator (istream& s);
   istream_iterator (const istream_iterator <T, Distance>& x);
   ~istream_itertor ();

   const T& operator*() const;
```

```
    istream_iterator <T, Distance>& operator++();
    istream_iterator <T, Distance>  operator++ (int)
};
```

Description

Stream iterators provide the standard iterator interface for input and output streams.

The class *istream_iterator* reads elements from an input stream. A value of *T* is retrieved and stored when the iterator is constructed and each time *operator++* is called. The iterator will be equal to the end-of-stream iterator value if the end-of-file is reached. Use the constructor with no arguments to create an end-of-stream iterator. The only valid use of this iterator is to compare to other iterators when checking for end of file. Do not attempt to dereference the end-of-stream iterator; it plays the same role as the past-the-end iterator provided by the *end()* function of containers. Since an *istream_iterator* is an input iterator, you cannot assign to the value returned by dereferencing the iterator. This also means that *istream_iterators* can only be used for single pass algorithms.

Since a new value is read every time the *operator++* is used on an *istream_iterator*, that operation is not equality-preserving. This means that *i* == *j* does *not* mean that ++*i* == ++*j* (although two end-of-stream iterators are always equal).

Constructors

istream_iterator ();
Construct an end-of-stream iterator. This iterator can be used to compare against and end-of-file condition. Use it to provide end iterators to algorithms

istream_iterator (istream& s);
Construct an *istream_iterator* on the given stream.

istream_iterator (const istream_iterator<T, Distance>& x);
Copy constructor.

Destructors

~istream_iterator ();
Destructor.

Operators

const T& operator* () const;
Return the current value stored by the iterator.

istream_iterator<T, Distance>&
operator++ ()

istream_iterator<T, Distance>
operator++ (int)

Retrieve the next element from the input stream.

Examples

```cpp
#include <iterator>
#include <vector>
#include <numeric>
using namespace std;

int main ()
{
  vector<int> d;
  int total = 0;
  //
  // Collect values from cin until end of file
  // Note use of default constructor to get ending iterator
  //
  cout << "Enter a sequence of integers (eof to quit): " ;
  copy(istream_iterator<int,vector<int>::difference_type>(cin),
       istream_iterator<int,vector<int>::difference_type>(),
       inserter(d,d.begin()));
  //
  // stream the whole vector and the sum to cout
  //
  copy(d.begin(),d.end()-1,ostream_iterator<int>(cout," + "));
  if (d.size())
    cout << *(d.end()-1) << " = " <<
         accumulate(d.begin(),d.end(),total) << endl;
  return 0;
}
```

See also
iterators, ostream_iterators

Iterators

Summary
Pointer generalizations for traversal and modification of collections.

Description
Iterators are a generalization of pointers that allow a C++ program to uniformly interact with different data structures. The illustration below displays the five iterator categories defined by the standard library, and shows their heirarchical relationship. Because standard library iterator categories are hierarchical, each category includes all the requirements of the categories above it.

Because iterators are used to traverse and access containers, the nature of the container determines what type of iterator it generates. And, because algorithms require specific iterator types as arguments, it is iterators that, for the most part, determine which standard library algorithms can be used with which standard library containers.

To conform to the C++ standard, all container and sequence classes must provide their own iterators. An instance of a container or sequence's iterator may be declared using either of the following:

```
class name ::iterator
class name ::const_iterator
```

Containers and sequences must also provide *const* iterators to the beginning and end of their collections. These may be accessed using the class members, *begin()* and *end()*.

The semantics of iterators are a generalization of the semantics of C++ pointers. Every template function that takes iterators will work using C++ pointers for processing typed contiguous memory sequences.

Iterators may be constant or mutable depending upon whether the result of the *operator* * behaves as a reference or as a reference to a constant. Constant iterators cannot satisfy the requirements of an *output_iterator*.

Every iterator type guarantees that there is an iterator value that points past the last element of a corresponding container. This value is called the *past-the-end value*. No guarantee is made that this value is dereferencable.

Every function provided by an iterator is required to be realized in amortized constant time.

Requirements for Input Iterators

The following key pertains to all the iterator requirements descriptions in Table 17.6:

a and *b*	values of type *X*
n	value of *distance* type
u, Distance, tmp, and *m*	identifiers
r	value of type *X&*
t	value of type *T*

The expressions listed in Table 17.6 must be valid for input iterators:

Table 17.6   Requirements for inputiterators

Expression	Requirement
X(a)	*copy constructor, a == X(a)*
X u(a)	*copy constructor, u == a*
X u = a	*assignment, u == a*
a == b, a != b	
	return value convertible to bool
*a	*a == b implies *a == *b*
++r	*returns X&*
r++	*return value convertible to const X&*
*r++	*returns type T*

For input iterators, *a == b* does not imply that *++a == ++b*.

Algorithms using input iterators should be single pass algorithms. That is they should not pass through the same iterator twice.

The value of type T does not have to be an *lvalue*.

Requirements for output iterators
The expressions listed in Table 17.7 must be valid for output iterators:

Table 17.7   Requirements for output iterators

Expression	Requirement
X(a)	*copy constructor, a == X(a).*
X u(a)	*copy constructor, u == a*
X u = a	*assignment, u == a*
*a = t	*result is not used*
++r	*returns X&*
r++	*return value convertable to const X&*
*r++ = t	*result is not used*

The only valid use for the *operator* * is on the left hand side of the assignment statement.

Algorithms using output iterators should be single pass algorithms. That is they should not pass through the same iterator twice.

Requirements for forward Iterators
The expressions listed in Table 17.8 must be valid for forward iterators:

Table 17.8   Requirements for forward iterators

Expression	Requirement
X u	*u might have a singular value*
X()	*X() might be singular*
X(a)	*copy constructor, a == X(a).*
X u(a)	*copy constructor, u == a*
X u = a	*assignment, u == a*
a == b, a != b	*return value convertable to bool*
*a	*return value convertable to T&*
++r	*returns X&*
r++	*return value convertable to const X&*
*r++	*returns T&*

Forward iterators have the condition that $a == b$ implies $*a == *b$.

There are no restrictions on the number of passes an algorithm may make through the structure.

Requirements for bidirectional iterators

A bidirectional iterator must meet all the requirements for forward iterators. In addition, the expressions listed in Table 17.9 must be valid:

Table 17.9 Requirements for bidrectional iterators

Expression	Requirement
--r	returns X&
r--	return value convertable to const X&
*r--	returns T&

Requirements for random-access iterators

A random access iterator must meet all the requirements for bidirectional iterators. In addition, the expressions in Table 17.10 must be valid:

Table 17.10 Requirementrs for fandom-access iterators

Expression	Requirement
r += n	Semantics of --r or ++r n times depending on the sign of n
a + n, n + a	returns type X
r -= n	returns X&, behaves as r += -n
a - n	returns type X
b - a	returns Distance
a[n]	*(a+n), return value convertable to T
a < b	total ordering relation
a > b	total ordering relation opposite to <
a <= b	!(a < b)
a >= b	!(a > b)

All relational operators return a value convertable to *bool*.

iter_swap   **Algorithm**

Summary

Exchange values pointed at in two locations

Synopsis

```
#include <algorithm>

template <class ForwardIterator1, class ForwardIterator2>
 void iter_swap (ForwardIterator1 a, ForwardIterator2 b);
```

Description
The *iter_swap* algorithm exchanges the values pointed at by the two iterators *a* and *b*.

Example
```
/******************************************************************
 *
 * swap.cpp - Example program of swap algorithm.
 *
 * $Id: swap.cpp,v 1.7 1995/10/06 20:05:43 hart Exp $
 *
 * $$RW_INSERT_HEADER "slyrs.str"
 *
 ******************************************************************/
#include <vector>
#include <algorithm>
using namespace std;

int main ()
{
   int d1[] = {6, 7, 8, 9, 10, 1, 2, 3, 4, 5};
   //
   // Set up a vector.
   //
   vector<int> v(d1+0, d1+10);
   //
   // Output original vector.
   //
   cout << "For the vector: ";
   copy(v.begin(), v.end(), ostream_iterator<int>(cout," "));
   //
   // Swap the first five elements with the last five elements.
   //
   swap_ranges(v.begin(), v.begin()+5, v.begin()+5);
   //
   // Output result.
   //
   cout << endl << endl
        << "Swaping the first 5 elements with the last 5 gives: "
        << endl << "      ";
   copy(v.begin(), v.end(), ostream_iterator<int>(cout," "));
   //
   // Now an example of iter_swap -- swap first and last elements.
   //
   iter_swap(v.begin(), v.end()-1);
```

```
    //
    // Output result.
    //
    cout << endl << endl
         << "Swaping the first and last elements gives: "
         << endl << "        ";
    copy(v.begin(), v.end(), ostream_iterator<int>(cout," "));
    cout << endl;

    return 0;
}
```

See also
swap, swap_ranges

less   Function object

Summary
Binary function object that returns *true* if its first argument is less than its second

Synopsis
#include<functional>

```
template <class T>
    struct less : binary_function<T, T, bool> {
    bool operator() (const T& x, const T& y) const
        { return x < y; }
};
```

Description
less is a binary function object. Its *operator()* returns *true* if *x* is less than *y*. You can pass a *less* object to any algorithm that requires a binary function. For example, the *transform* algorithm applies a binary operation to corresponding values in two collections and stores the result of the function. *less* would be used in that algorithm in the following manner:

```
vector<int> vec1;
vector<int> vec2;
vector<int> vecResult;
    .
    .
    .
transform(vec1.begin(), vec1.end(),
          vec2.begin(), vec2.end(),
          vecResult.begin(), less<int>());
```

After this call to *transform*, *vecResult(n)* will contain a "1" if *vec1(n)* was less than *vec2(n)* or a "0" if *vec1(n)* was greater than or equal to *vec2(n)*.

less_equal — Function object

Summary
Binary function object that returns *true* if its first argument is less than or equal to its second

Synopsis
```
#include<functional>

template <class T>
struct less_equal : binary_function<T, T, bool> {
    bool operator() (const T& x, const T& y) const
        { return x <= y; }
};
```

Description
less_equal is a binary function object. Its *operator()* returns *true* if *x* is less than or equal to *y*. You can pass a *less_equal* object to any algorithm that requires a binary function. For example, the *sort* algorithm can accept a binary function as an alternate comparison object to sort a sequence. *less_equal* would be used in that algorithm in the following manner:
```
vector<int> vec1;
?
sort(vec1.begin(), vec1.end(),greater_equal<int>());
```
After this call to *sort*, *vec1* will be sorted in ascending order.

See also
function objects

lexicographical_compare — Algorithm

Summary
Compares two ranges lexicographically.

Synopsis
```
#include <algorithm>

template <class InputIterator1, class InputIterator2>
 bool
 lexicographical_compare(InputIterator1 first,
```

```
                    InputIterator2 last1,
                    InputIterator2 first2,
                    InputIterator last2);

template <class InputIterator1, class InputIterator2,
        class Compare>
bool
lexicographical_compare(InputIterator1 first,
                    InputIterator2 last1,
                    InputIterator2 first2,
                    InputIterator last2, Compare comp);
```

Description

The *lexicographical_compare* functions compare each element in the range *[first1, last1)* to the corresponding element in the range *[first2, last2)* using iterators *i* and *j*.

The first version of the algorithm uses "<" as the default comparison operator. It immediately returns *true* if it encounters any pair in which **i* is less than **j*, and immediately returns *false* if **j* is less than **i*. If the algorithm reaches the end of the first sequence before reaching the end of the second sequence, it also returns *true*.

The second version of the function takes an argument *comp* that defines a comparison function that used in place of the default "<" operator.

The *lexicographic_compare* functions can be used with all the datatypes provided by the standard library.

Complexity

lexicographical_compare performs at most *min((last1 - first1), (last2 - first2))* applications of the comparison function.

Examples

```cpp
#include <algorithm>
#include <vector>
using namespace std;

int main(void)
{
  int d1[5] = {1,3,5,32,64};
  int d2[5] = {1,3,2,43,56};

  // set up vector
  vector<int> v1(d1,d1 + 5), v2(d2,d2 + 5);

  // Is v1 less than v2 (I think not)
  bool b1 = lexicographical_compare(v1.begin(),
          v1.end(), v2.begin(), v2.end());

  // Is v2 less than v1 (yup, sure is)
```

```
    bool b2 =  lexicographical_compare(v2.begin(),
            v2.end(), v1.begin(), v1.end(), less<int>()));
  cout << (b1 ? "TRUE" : "FALSE") << " "
        << (b2 ? "TRUE" : "FALSE") << endl;

  return 0;
}
```

limits   Numeric Limits library

Refer to the C++ *Programmer's Guide*, Chapter 35, "Numeric limits,"

list   Container

Summary
A sequence that supports bidirectional iterators

Synopsis
#include <list>

template <class T>
 class list {

public:

// typedefs

```
  typedef typename iterator;
  typedef typename const_iterator;
  typedef typename reference;
  typedef typename const_reference;
  typedef typename size_type;
  typedef typename difference_type;
  typedef T value_type;
  typedef  reverse_iterator<iterator, value_type,
        reference, difference_type> reverse_iterator;
  typedef const_reverse_iterator<const_iterator,
        value_type, reference,
        difference_type> const_reverse_iterator;
```

// Construct/Copy/Destroy

```
  explicit list ();
  explicit list (size_type n, const T& value = T());
```

```
template <class InputIterator>
 list (InputIterator first, InputIterator last);
list(const list<T>& x);
~list();
list<T>& operator= (const list<T>&);
template <class InputIterator>
 void assign (InputIterator first, InputIterator last);
template <class Size, class T>
 void assign (Size n, const T& t = T());
```

// Iterators

```
iterator begin ();
const_iterator begin () const;
iterator end ();
const_iterator end () const;
reverse_iterator rbegin ();
const_reverse_iterator rbegin () const;
reverse_iterator rend ();

const_reverse_iterator rend () const;
```

// Capacity

```
bool empty () const;

size_type size () const;
size_type max_size () const;
void resize (size_type sz, T c = T());
```

// Element Access

```
reference front ();
const_reference front () const;
reference back ();
const_reference back () const;
```

// Modifiers

```
void push_front (const T& x);
void pop_front ();
void push_back (const T& x);
void pop_back ();
```

iterator insert (iterator position, const T& x = T());
void insert (iterator position, size_type n, const T& x =
T());
template <class InputIterator>
 void insert (iterator position, InputIterator first,
InputIterator last);

 void erase (iterator position);
 void erase (iterator position, iterator last);

 void swap (list<T>& x);

// Special mutative operations on list

 void splice (iterator position, list<T>& x);
 void splice (iterator position, list<T>& x, iterator i);
 void splice (iterator position, list<T>& x,
        iterator first,iterator last);

 void remove (const T& value);
 template <class Predicate>
 void remove_if (Predicate pred);

 void unique ();

 template <class BinaryPredicate>
 void unique (BinaryPredicate binary_pred);

 void merge (list<T>& x);
 template <class Compare>
 void merge (list<T>& x, Compare comp);

 void sort ();
 template <class Compare>
 void sort (Compare comp);

 void reverse();

};

// Non-member List Operators

template <class T>
 bool operator== (const list<T>&, const list<T>&);

template <class T>

```
bool operator< (const list<T>&, const list<T>&);
```

Description

list<T> is a type of sequence that supports bidirectional iterators. A *list<T>* allows constant time insert and erase operations anywhere within the sequence, with storage management handled automatically. Constant time random access is not supported.

Any type used for the template parameter *T* must provide the following (where *T* is the type, *t* is a *value* of *T*, and *u* is a *const value* of *T*):

```
Default constructor   T()
Copy constructors     T(t) and T(u)
Destructor            t.~T()
Address of            &t and &u yeilding T* and
                        const T* respectively
Assignment            t = a where a is a
                        (possibly const) value of T
```

Caveats

Member function templates are used in all containers provided by the Standard Template Library. An example of this feature is the constructor for *list<T>* that takes two templated iterators:

```
template <class InputIterator>
  list (InputIterator, InputIterator);
```

list also has an *insert* function of this type. These functions, when not restricted by compiler limitations, allow you to use any type of input iterator as arguments. For compilers that do not support this feature, we provide substitute functions that allow you to use an iterator obtained from the same type of container as the one you are constructing (or calling a member function on), or you can use a pointer to the type of element you have in the container.

For example, if your compiler does not support member function templates you can construct a list in the following two ways:

```
int intarray[10];
list<int> first_list(intarray,intarray + 10);
list<int> second_list(first_list.begin(),first_list.end());
```

But not this way:

```
list<long> long_list(first_list.begin(),first_list.end());
```

since the *long_list* and *first_list* are not the same type.

Examples

```
#include <list>
#include <string>
using namespace std;

// Print out a list of strings
ostream& operator<<(ostream& out, const list<string>& l)
```

```
  {
    copy(l.begin(), l.end(), ostream_iterator<string>(cout," "));
    return out;
  }

  int main(void)
  {
    // create a list of critters
    list<string> critters;
    int i;

    // insert several critters
    critters.insert(critters.begin(),"antelope");
    critters.insert(critters.begin(),"bear");
    critters.insert(critters.begin(),"cat");

    // print out the list
    cout << critters << endl;

    // Change cat to cougar
    *find(critters.begin(),critters.end(),"cat") = "cougar";
    cout << critters << endl;

    // put a zebra at the beginning
    // an ocelot ahead of antelope
    // and a rat at the end
    critters.push_front("zebra");
    critters.insert(find(critters.begin(),critters.end(),
                  "antelope"),"ocelot");
    critters.push_back("rat");
    cout << critters << endl;

    // sort the list (Use list's sort function since the
    // generic algorithm requires a random access iterator
    // and list only provides bidirectional)
    critters.sort();
    cout << critters << endl;

    // now let's erase half of the critters
    int     half = critters.size() >> 1;
    for(i = 0; i < half; ++i) {
      critters.erase(critters.begin());
    }
    cout << critters << endl;

    return 0;
  }
```

Constructors and destructors

explicit list();
Creates a list of zero elements.

explicit list (size_type n, const T& value = T());
Creates a list of length *n*, containing *n* copies of *value*.

template <class InputIterator>
list (InputIterator first, InputIterator last);
Creates a list of length *last - first*, filled with all values obtained by dereferencing the *InputIterator s* on the range *[first, last)*.

list (const list<T>& x);
Copy constructor. Creates a copy of *x*.

~list ();
The destructor. Releases any allocated memory for this list.

Assignment operator

list<T>& operator= (const list<T>& x)
Assignment operator. Erases all elements in self then inserts into self a copy of each element in *x*. Returns a reference to **this*.

Iterators

iterator **begin** ();
Returns a bidirectional iterator that points to the first element.

const_iterator **begin** () const;
Returns a constant bidirectional iterator that points to the first element.

iterator **end** ();
Returns a bidirectional iterator that points to the past-the-end value.

const_iterator **end** () const;
Returns a constant bidirectional iterator that points to the past-the-end value.

reverse_iterator **rbegin** ();
Returns a bidirectional iterator that points to the past-the-end value.

const_reverse_iterator **rbegin** () const;
Returns a constant bidirectional iterator that points to the past-the-end value.

reverse_iterator **rend** ();
Returns a bidirectional iterator that points to the first element.

const_reverse_iterator **rend** () const;
Returns a constant bidirectional iterator that points to the first element.

Member functions

template <class InputIterator>
void
assign (InputIterator first, InputIterator last);
Erases all elements contained in self, then inserts new elements from the range *[first, last)*.

```
template <class Size, class T>
void
```
assign (Size n, const T& t = T());
Erases all elements contained in self, then inserts *n* instances of the *value* of *t*.

reference
back ();
Returns a reference to the last element.

const_reference
back () const;

Returns a constant reference to the last element.

bool
empty () const;
Returns *true* if the *size* is zero.

void
erase (iterator position);
Removes the element pointed to by *position*.

void
erase (iterator first, iterator last);
Removes the elements in the range *[first, last)*.

reference
front ();
Returns a reference to the first element.

const_reference
front () const;
Returns a constant reference to the first element.

iterator
insert (iterator position, const T& x = T());
Inserts *x* before *position*. Returns an iterator that points to the inserted *x*.

void
insert (iterator position, size_type n, const T& x = T());
Inserts *n* copies of *x* before *position*.

```
template <class InputIterator>
void
```
insert (iterator position, InputIterator first,InputIterator last);
Inserts copies of the elements in the range *[first, last)* before *position*.

max_size () const;
Returns *size()* of the largest possible list.

void **merge** (list<T>& x);

Merges a sorted x with a sorted self using operator<. For equal elements in the two lists, elements from self will always precede the elements from x. The *merge* function leaves x empty.

```
template <class Compare>
void
merge (list<T>& x, Compare comp);
```

Merges a sorted x with sorted self using a compare function object, *comp*. For same elements in the two lists, elements from self will always precede the elements from x. The *merge* function leaves x empty.

```
void
pop_back ();
```

Removes the last element.

```
void
pop_front ();
```

Removes the first element.

```
void
void push_back (const T& x);
```

Appends a copy of x to the end.

```
push_front (const T& x);
```

Appends a copy of x to the front of the list.

```
void
remove (const T& value);
```

```
template <class Predicate>
void
remove_if (Predicate pred);
```

Removes all elements in the list referred by the list iterator i for which
$*i == value$ or $pred(*i) == true$, whichever is applicable. This is a stable operation, the relative order of list items that are not removed is preserved.

```
void
resize (size_type sz, T c = T());
```

Alters the size of self. If the new size (sz) is greater than the current size, $sz-size()$ c's are inserted at the end of the list. If the new size is smaller than the current capacity, then the list is truncated by erasing $size()-sz$ elements off the end. If sz is equal to capacity no action is taken.

```
void
reverse ();
```

Reverses the order of the elements.

```
size_type
size () const;
```

Returns the number of elements.

void
sort ();
Sorts self according to the *operator<*. *sort* maintains the relative order of equal elements.

template <class Compare>
void
sort (Compare comp);

Sorts self according to a comparison function object, *comp*. This is also a stable sort.

void
splice (iterator position, list<T>& x);
Inserts *x* before position leaving *x* empty.

void
splice (iterator position, list<T>& x, iterator i);
Moves the elements pointed to by iterator *i* in *x* to self, inserting it before *position*. The element is removed from *x*.

void
splice (iterator position, list<T>& x, iterator first, iterator last);
Moves the elements in the range *[first, last)* in *x* to self, inserting before *position*. The elements in the range *[first, last)* are removed from *x*.

void
swap (list<T>& x);
Exchanges self with *x*.

void
unique ();
Erases copies of consecutive repeated elements leaving the first occurrrence.

template <class BinaryPredicate>
void
unique (BinaryPredicate binary_pred);
Erases consecutive elements matching a true condition of the *binary_pred*. The first occurrence is not removed.

Non-member operators

template <class T, class Allocator>
bool
operator== (const list<T>& x, const list <T>& y);
Equality operator. Returns *true* if *x* is the same as *y*.

template <class T, class Allocator>
bool
operator< (const list<T>& x, const list <T>& y);
Returns *true* if the sequence defined by the elements contaned in *x* is lexicographically less than the sequence defined by the elements contained in *y*.

See also
Containers

logical_and   Function object

Summary
Binary function object that returns *true* if both of its arguments are *true*.

Synopsis
#include <functional>

```
template <class T>
struct logical_and : binary_function<T, T, bool> {
    bool operator() (const T& x, const T& y) const
        { return x && y; }
};
```

Description
logical_and is a binary function object. Its *operator()* returns *true* if both *x* and *y* are *true*.
You can pass a *logical_and* object to any algorithm that requires a binary function. For
example, the *transform* algorithm applies a binary operation to corresponding values in
two collections and stores the result of the function. *logical_and* is used in that algorithm
in the following manner:

```
vector<bool> vec1;
vector<bool> vec2;
vector<bool> vecResult;
    .
    .
    .
transform(vec1.begin(), vec1.end(),
          vec2.begin(), vec2.end(),
          vecResult.begin(), logical_and<bool>());
```

After this call to *transform*, *vecResult(n)* will contain a "1" (*true*) if both *vec1(n)* and *vec2(n)*
are *true* or a "0" (*false*) if either *vec1(n)* or *vec2(n)* is *false*.

See also
function objects

logical_not   Function object

Summary
Unary function object that returns *true* if its argument is *false*.

Synopsis
#include<functional>

```
template <class T>
struct logical_not : unary_function<T, T, bool> {
    bool operator() (const T& x, const T& y) const
        { return !x; }
};
```

Description
logical_not is a unary function object. Its *operator()* returns *true* if its argument is *false*. You can pass a *logical_not* object to any algorithm that requires a unary function. For example, the *replace_if* algorithm replaces an element with another value if the result of a unary operation is true. *logical_not* is used in that algorithm in the following manner:

```
vector<int> vec1;
?
void replace_if(vec1.begin(), vec1.end(),
                logical_not<int>(),1);
```

This call to *replace_if* replaces all zeros in the *vec1* with "1".

See also
function objects

logical_or   Function object

Summary
Binary function object that returns *true* if either of its arguments are *true*.

Synopsis
#include<functional>

```
template <class T>
struct logical_or : binary_function<T, T, bool> {
    bool operator() (const T& x, const T& y) const
        { return x || y; }
};
```

Description
logical_or is a binary function object. Its *operator()* returns *true* if either *x* or *y* are *true*. You can pass a *logical_or* object to any algorithm that requires a binary function. For example, the *transform* algorithm applies a binary operation to corresponding values in two collections and stores the result of the function. *logical_or* is used in that algorithm in the following manner:

```
vector<bool> vec1;
```

```
vector<bool> vec2;
vector<bool> vecResult;
?
transform(vec1.begin(), vec1.end(),
          vec2.begin(), vec2.end(),
          vecResult.begin(), logical_or<bool>());
```

After this call to *transform*, *vecResult(n)* will contain a "1" (*true*) if either *vec1(n)* or *vec2(n)* is *true* or a "0" (*false*) if both *vec1(n)* and *vec2(n)* are *false*.

See also

function objects

lower_bound   **Algorithm**

Summary
Determine the first valid position for an element in a sorted container.

Synopsis
template <class ForwardIterator, class T>
  ForwardIterator
  lower_bound(ForwardIterator first, ForwardIterator last,
      const T& value);

template <class ForwardIterator, class T, class Compare>
  ForwardIterator
  lower_bound(ForwardIterator first, ForwardIterator last,
      const T& value, Compare comp);

Description
The *lower_bound* algorithm compares a supplied *value* to elements in a sorted container and returns the first postition in the container that *value* can occupy without violating the container's ordering. There are two versions of the algorithm. The first uses the less than operator (*operator <*) to perform the comparison, and assumes that the sequence has been sorted using that operator. The second version lets you include a function object of type *compare*, and assumes that *compare* is the function used to sort the sequence. The function object must be a binary predicate.

lower_bound's return value is the iterator for the first element in the container that is *greater than or equal to value*, or, when the comparison operator is used, the first element that does not satisfy the comparison function. Formally, the algorithm returns an iterator *i* in the range *[first, last)* such that for any iterator *j* in the range *[first, i)* the following corresponding conditions hold:

```
*j < value
```

or

```
comp(*j, value) == true
```

Complexity

lower_bound performs at most *log(last - first) + 1* comparisons.

Examples

```cpp
#include <vector>
#include <algorithm>
using namespace std;

int main()
{
  typedef vector<int>::iterator iterator;
  int d1[11] = {0,1,2,2,3,4,2,2,2,6,7};

  // Set up a vector
  vector<int> v1(d1,d1 + 11);

  // Try lower_bound variants
  iterator it1 = lower_bound(v1.begin(),v1.end(),3);
  // it1 = v1.begin() + 4

  iterator it2 =
      lower_bound(v1.begin(),v1.end(),2,less<int>());
  // it2 = v1.begin() + 4

  // Try upper_bound variants
  iterator it3 = upper_bound(v1.begin(),v1.end(),3);
  // it3 = vector + 5

  iterator it4 =
     upper_bound(v1.begin(),v1.end(),2,less<int>());
  // it4 = v1.begin() + 5

  cout << endl << endl
      << "The upper and lower bounds of 3: ( "
      << *it1 << " , " << *it3 << " ]" << endl;

  cout << endl << endl
      << "The upper and lower bounds of 2: ( "
      << *it2 << " , " << *it4 << " ]" << endl;

  return 0;
}
```

See also

upper_bound

make_heap

Algorithm

Summary
Creates a heap.

Synopsis
```
#include <algorithm>

template <class RandomAccessIterator>
 void
 make_heap(RandomAccessIterator first,
       RandomAccessIterator last);
template <class RandomAccessIterator, class Compare>
 void
 make_heap(RandomAccessIterator first,
       RandomAccessIterator last, Compare comp);
```

Description
A heap is a particular organization of elements in a range between two random access iterators *[a, b)*. Its two key properties are:

- **a* is the largest element in the range.

- **a* may be removed by the *pop_heap* algorithm, or a new element can be added by the *push_heap* algorithm, in *O(logN)* time.

These properties make heaps useful as priority queues.

The heap algorithms use the less than (<) operator as the default comparison. In all of the algorithms, an alternate comparison operator can be specified.

The first version of the *make_heap* algorithm arranges the elements in the range *[first, last)* into a heap using the less than (<) operator to perform comparisons. The second version uses the comparison operator *comp* to perform the comparisons. Since the only requirements for a heap are the two listed above, *make_heap* is not required to do anything within the range *(first, last-1)*.

Complexity
This algorithm makes at most *3 * (last - first)* comparisons.

Examples
```
#include <algorithm>
#include <vector>
using namespace std;

int main(void)
{
  int d1[4] = {1,2,3,4};
  int d2[4] = {1,3,2,4};

  // Set up two vectors
```

```
vector<int> v1(d1,d1 + 4), v2(d2,d2 + 4);

// Make heaps
make_heap(v1.begin(),v1.end());
make_heap(v2.begin(),v2.end(),less<int>());
// v1 = (4,x,y,z)   and   v2 = (4,x,y,z)
// Note that x, y and z represent the remaining
// values in the container (other than 4).
// The definition of the heap and heap operations
// does not require any particular ordering
// of these values.

// Copy both vectors to cout
ostream_iterator<int> out(cout," ");
copy(v1.begin(),v1.end(),out);
cout << endl;
copy(v2.begin(),v2.end(),out);
cout << endl;

// Now let's pop
pop_heap(v1.begin(),v1.end());
pop_heap(v2.begin(),v2.end(),less<int>());
// v1 = (3,x,y,4) and v2 = (3,x,y,4)

// Copy both vectors to cout
copy(v1.begin(),v1.end(),out);
cout << endl;
copy(v2.begin(),v2.end(),out);
cout << endl;

// And push
push_heap(v1.begin(),v1.end());
push_heap(v2.begin(),v2.end(),less<int>());
// v1 = (4,x,y,z) and v2 = (4,x,y,z)

// Copy both vectors to cout
copy(v1.begin(),v1.end(),out);
cout << endl;
copy(v2.begin(),v2.end(),out);
cout << endl;

// Now sort those heaps
sort_heap(v1.begin(),v1.end());
sort_heap(v2.begin(),v2.end(),less<int>());
// v1 = v2 = (1,2,3,4)

// Copy both vectors to cout
copy(v1.begin(),v1.end(),out);
cout << endl;
copy(v2.begin(),v2.end(),out);
cout << endl;
```

```
        return 0;
    }
```

See also
pop_heap, *push_heap* and *sort_heap*

map

Container

Summary
An associative container providing access to non-key values using unique keys. A *map* supports bidirectional iterators.

Synopsis
#include <map>

template <class Key, class T, class Compare = less<Key> >
 class map {

public:

// types

    typedef Key key_type;
    typedef pair<const Key, T> value_type;
    typedef Compare key_compare;
    typedef typename reference;
    typedef typename const_reference;
    typedef typename iterator;
    typedef typename const_iterator;
    typedef typename size_type;
    typedef typename difference_type;
    typedef reverse_iterator<iterator,
            value_type,
            reference,
            difference_type> reverse_iterator;
    typedef reverse_iterator<const_iterator,
            value_type,
            const_reference,
            difference_type> const_reverse_iterator;

    class value_compare
      : public binary_function<value_type, value_type, bool>
    {
      friend class map;
```
```

```
    protected :
      Compare comp;
      value_compare(Compare c) : comp(c) {}
    public :
      bool operator() (const value_type& x,
                const value_type& y) const
        { return comp(x.first, y.first); }
  };

// Construct/Copy/Destroy

  explicit map (const Compare& comp = Compare());
  template <class InputIterator>
   map (InputIterator first,

      InputIterator last,
      const Compare& comp = Compare());
  map (const map<Key, T, Compare>& x);
  ~map();
  map<Key, Compare>& operator= (const map<Key, T, Compare>&
  x);

// Iterators

  iterator begin();
  const_iterator begin() const;
  iterator end();
  const_iterator end() const;
  reverse_iterator rbegin();
  const_reverse_iterator rbegin() const;
  reverse_iterator rend();
  const_reverse_iterator rend() const;

// Capacity

  bool empty() const;
  size_type size() const;
  size_type max_size() const;

// Element Access

  T& operator[] (const key_type& x);
  const T& operator[] (const key_type& x) const;

// Modifiers
```

```
  pair<iterator, bool> insert (const value_type& x);
  iterator insert (iterator position, const value_type& x);
  template <class InputIterator>
   void insert (InputIterator first, InputIterator last);

  void erase (iterator position);
  size_type erase (const key_type& x);
  void erase (iterator first, iterator last);
  void swap (map<Key, Compare>& x);

// Observers

  key_compare key_comp() const;
  value_compare value_comp() const;

// Map operations

  iterator find (const key_value& x);
  const_iterator find (const key_value& x) const;
  size_type count (const key_type& x) const;
  iterator lower_bound (const key_type& x);
  const_iterator lower_bound (const key_type& x) const;
  iterator upper_bound (const key_type& x);
  const_iterator upper_bound (const key_type& x) const;
  pair<iterator, iterator> equal_range (const key_type& x);
  pair<const_iterator, const_iterator>
    equal_range (const key_type& x) const;
};

template <class Key,
      class T,
      class Compare>
bool operator== (const map<Key, T, Compare>& x,
        const map<Key, T, Compare>& y);

template <class Key,
      class T,
      class Compare>
bool operator< (const map<Key, T, Compare>& x,
        const map<Key, T, Compare>& y);
```

Description

map provides fast access to stored values of type *T* which are indexed by unique keys of a separate type. The default operation for key comparison is the < operator.

map provides bidirectional iterators that point to an instance of *pair<const Key x, T y>* where *x* is the key and *y* is the stored value associated with that key. The definition of *map* provides a *typedef* to this pair called *value_type*.

The types used for both the template parameters *Key* and *T* must provide the following (where *T* is the *type*, *t* is a *value* of *T* and *u* is a *const value* of *T*):

```
Copy constructors -  T(t) and T(u)
Destructor        -  t.~T()
Address of        -  &t and &u yeilding T* and
                     const T* respectively
Assignment        -  t = a where a is a
                     (possibley const) value of T
```

The type used for the *Compare* template parameter must satisfy the requirements for binary functions.

Caveats

Member function templates are used in all containers provided by the Standard Template Library. An example of this feature is the constructor for *map<Key,Compare>* that takes two templated iterators:

```
template <class InputIterator>
  map (InputIterator, InputIterator, Compare);
```

map also has an insert function of this type. These functions, when not restricted by compiler limitations, allow you to use any type of input iterator as arguments. For compilers that do not support this feature we provide substitute functions that allow you to use an iterator obtained from the same type of container as the one you are constructing (or calling a member function on), or you can use a pointer to the type of element you have in the container.

For example, if your compiler does not support member function templates, you can construct a *map* in the following two ways:

```
map<int,int,less<int> >::value_type intarray[10];
map<int,int,less<int> > first_map(intarray,intarray + 10);
map<int, less<int> >
second_map(first_map.begin(),first_map.end());
```

But not this way:

```
map<long, long,less<long> >
long_map(first_map.begin(),first_map.end());
```

Since the *long_map* and *first_map* are not the same type.

Also, many compilers do not support default template arguments. If your compiler is one of these, you need to always supply the *Compare* template argument.

Examples

```
#include <string>
#include <map>
```

```
using namespace std;

typedef map<string, int, less<string> > months_type;

// Print out a pair
template <class First, class Second>
ostream& operator<<(ostream& out,
                    const pair<First,Second> & p)
{
  cout << p.first << " has " << p.second << " days";
  return out;
}

// Print out a map
ostream& operator<<(ostream& out, const months_type & l)
{
  copy(l.begin(),l.end(), ostream_iterator
              <months_type::value_type>(cout,"\n"));
  return out;
}

int main(void)
{
  // create a map of months and the number of days
  // in the month
  months_type months;

  typedef months_type::value_type value_type;

  // Put the months in the multimap
  months.insert(value_type(string("January"),   31));
  months.insert(value_type(string("Febuary"),    28));
  months.insert(value_type(string("Febuary"),    29));
  months.insert(value_type(string("March"),      31));
  months.insert(value_type(string("April"),      30));
  months.insert(value_type(string("May"),        31));
  months.insert(value_type(string("June"),       30));
  months.insert(value_type(string("July"),       31));
  months.insert(value_type(string("August"),     31));
  months.insert(value_type(string("September"),  30));
  months.insert(value_type(string("October"),    31));
  months.insert(value_type(string("November"),   30));
  months.insert(value_type(string("December"),   31));

  // print out the months
  // Second Febuary is not present
  cout << months << endl;

  // Find the Number of days in June
  months_type::iterator p = months.find(string("June"));

  // print out the number of days in June
```

```
if (p != months.end())
    cout << endl << *p << endl;

return 0;
}
```

Constructors and destructors

explicit map (const Compare& comp = Compare());

Default constructor. Constructs an empty map that will use the relation *Compare* to order keys, if it is supplied.

template <class InputIterator>
map (InputIterator first, InputIterator last,
    const Compare& comp = Compare());

Constructs a map containing values in the range *[first, last)*. Creation of the new map is only guaranteed to succeed if the iterators *first* and *last* return values of type *pair<class Key, class Value>* and all values of *Key* in the *range[first, last)* are unique.

map (const map<Key, T, Compare>& x);

Copy constructor. Creates a new map by copying all pairs of *key* and *value* from *x*.

~map ();

The destructor. Releases any allocated memory for this map.

Iterators

iterator **begin**() ;

Returns a iterator pointing to the first element stored in the map. "First" is defined by the map's comparison operator, *Compare*.

const_iterator **begin**() const;

Returns a *const_iterator* pointing to the first element stored in the map.

iterator **end**() ;

Returns a iterator pointing to the last element stored in the map, i.e., the off-the-end value.

const_iterator **end**() const;

Returns a *const_iterator* pointing to the last element stored in the map.

reverse_iterator **rbegin**() ;

Returns a *reverse_iterator* pointing to the first element stored in the map. "First" is defined by the map's comparison operator, *Compare*.

const_reverse_iterator **rbegin**() const;

Returns a *const_reverse_iterator* pointing to the first element stored in the map.

reverse_iterator rend() ;

Returns a *reverse_iterator* pointing to the last element stored in the map, i.e., the off-the-end value.

const_reverse_iterator rend() const;

Returns a *const_reverse_iterator* pointing to the last element stored in the map

Member operators

map<Key, T, Compare>&
operator= (const map<Key, T, Compare>& x);
Assignment. Replaces the contents of **this* with a copy of the map *x*.

T& operator [ ] (const key_type& x);
If an element with the key *x* exists in the map, then a reference to its associated value will be returned. Otherwise the pair *x,T()* will be inserted into the map and a reference to the default object *T()* will be returned.

Member functions

size_type
count (const key_type& x) const;
Returns a 1 if a value with the key *x* exists in the map, otherwise returns a 0.

bool
empty() const;
Returns *true* is the map is empty, *false* otherwise.

pair<iterator,iterator>
equal_range (const key_type& x)
Returns the pair, *(lower_bound(x), upper_bound(x))*.

pair<const_iterator,const_iterator>
equal_range (const key_type& x) const;
Returns the pair, *(lower_bound(x), upper_bound(x))*.

void
erase (iterator position);
Erases the map element pointed to by the iterator *position*.

size_type
erase (const key_type& x);
Erases the element with the key value *x* from the map, if one exists.

void
erase (iterator first, iterator last);
Providing the iterators *first* and *last* point to the same map and *last* is reachable from *first*, all elements in the range *[first, last)* will be erased from the map.

iterator
find (const key_type& x);
Searches the map for a pair with the key value *x* and returns an iterator to that pair if it is found. If such a pair is not found the value *end()* is returned.

const_iterator **find** (const key_type& x) const;
Same as *find* above but returns a *const_iterator*.

pair<iterator, bool>
insert (const value_type& x);

iterator
insert (iterator position, const value_type& x);

If a *value_type* with the same key as *x* is not present in the map, then *x* is inserted into the map. A position may be supplied as a hint regarding where to do the insertion. If the insertion may be done right after *position* then it takes amortized constant time. Otherwise it will take *O(log N)* time.

template <class InputIterator>
void
insert (InputIterator first, InputIterator last);

Copies of each element in the range *[first, last)* which posess a unique key, one not already in the map, will be inserted into the map. The iterators *first* and *last* must return values of *type pair<T1,T2>*. This operation takes approximately *O(N*log(size()+N))* time.

key_compare
key_comp () const;

Returns a function object capable of comparing key values using the comparison operation, *Compare*, of the current map.

iterator
lower_bound (const key_type& x)

Returns an iterator to the smallest map element whose key is greater or equal to *x*. If no such element exists then *end()* is returned.

const_iterator
lower_bound (const key_type& x) const;

Same as *lower_bound* above but returns a *const_iterator*.

size_type
max_size() const;

Returns the maximum possible size of the map. This size is only constrained by the number of unique keys which can be represented by the type *Key*.

size_type
size() const;

Returns the number of elements in the map.

void **swap** (map<Key, T, Compare>& x);

Swaps the contents of the map *x* with the current map, **this*.

iterator
upper_bound (const key_type& x)

Returns an iterator to the largest map element whose key is smaller or equal to *x*. If no such element exists then *end()* is returned.

const_iterator
upper_bound (const key_type& x) const;

Same as *upper_bound* above but returns a *const_iterator*.

value_compare
value_comp () const;

Returns a function object capable of comparing key values using the comparison operation, *Compare*, of the current map. This function is identical to *key_comp* for sets.

Non-member operators

bool operator== (const map<Key, T, Compare>& x,
const map<Key, T, Compare>& y);

Returns *true* if all elements in x are element-wise equal to all elements in y, using *(T::operator==)*. Otherwise it returns *false*.

bool operator< (const map<Key, T, Compare>& x,
const map<Key, T, Compare>& y);

Returns *true* if x is lexicographically less than y. Otherwise, it returns *false*.

max
Algorithm

Summary
Find and return the maximum of a pair of values

Synopsis
#include <algorithm>

template <class T>
 const T& max(const T& a, const T& b);

template <class T, class Compare>
 const T& max(const T& a, const T& b, Compare comp);

Description
The *max* algorithm determines and returns the maximum of a pair of values. The optional argument *comp* defines a comparison function that can be used in place of the default "<" operator. This function can be used with all the datatypes provided by the standard library.

max returns the first argument when the arguments are equal.

Examples
```
#include <algorithm>
using namespace std;

int main(void)
{
   double  d1 = 10.0, d2 = 20.0;

   // Find minimum
```

```
double val1 = min(d1, d2);
// val1 = 10.0

// the greater comparator returns the greater of the
// two values.
double val2 = min(d1, d2, greater<double>());
// val2 = 20.0;

// Find maximum
double val3 = max(d1, d2);
// val3 = 20.0;

// the less comparator returns the smaller of the two values.
// Note that, like every comparison in the STL, max is
// defined in terms of the < operator, so using less here
// is the same as using the max algorithm with a default
// comparator.
double val4 = max(d1, d2, less<double>());
// val4 = 20

cout << val1 << " " << val2 << " "
     << val3 << " " << val4 << endl;

return 0;
}
```

See also
max_element, min, min_element

max_element   Algorithm

Summary
Finds maximum value in a range.

Synopsis
#include <algorithm>

template <class ForwardIterator>
 InputIterator
 max_element(ForwardIterator first, ForwardIterator last);

template <class ForwardIterator, class Compare>
 InputIterator
 max_element(ForwardIterator first, ForwardIterator last,
        Compare comp);

Description

The *max_element* algorithm returns an iterator that denotes the maximum element in a sequence. If the sequence contains more than one copy of the element, the iterator points to its first occurrence. The optional argument *comp* defines a comparison function that can be used in place of the default less than (<) operator. This function can be used with all the datatypes provided by the standard library.

Algorithm *max_element* returns the first iterator *i* in the range *[first, last)* such that for any iterator *j* in the same range the following corresponding conditions hold:

```
!(*i < *j)
```

or

```
comp(*i, *j) == false.
```

Complexity

Exactly *max((last - first) - 1, 0)* applications of the corresponding comparisons are done for *max_element*.

Examples

```
#include <algorithm>
#include <vector>
using namespace std;

int main(void)
{
  typedef vector<int>::iterator iterator;
  int d1[5] = {1,3,5,32,64};

  // set up vector
  vector<int>      v1(d1,d1 + 5);

  // find the largest element in the vector
  iterator it1 = max_element(v1.begin(), v1.end());
  // it1 = v1.begin() + 4

  // find the largest element in the range from
  // the beginning of the vector to the 2nd to last
  iterator it2 = max_element(v1.begin(), v1.end()-1,
                  less<int>());
  // it2 = v1.begin() + 3

  // find the smallest element
  iterator it3 = min_element(v1.begin(), v1.end());
  // it3 = v1.begin()

  // find the smallest value in the range from
  // the beginning of the vector plus 1 to the end
  iterator it4 = min_element(v1.begin()+1, v1.end(),
                  less<int>());
  // it4 = v1.begin() + 1
```

```
    cout << *it1 << " " << *it2 << " "
        << *it3 << " " << *it4 << endl;

    return 0;
}
```

See also
max, min, min_element

merge   Algorithm

Summary
Merge two sorted sequences into a third sequence.

Synopsis
#include <algorithm>

```
template <class InputIterator1, class InputIterator2,
      class OutputIterator>
OutputIterator
merge(InputIterator first1, InputIterator1 last1,
      InputIterator2 first2, InputIterator last2,
      OutputIterator result);

template <class InputIterator1, class InputIterator2,
      class OutputIterator, class Compare>
OutputIterator
merge(InputIterator1 first1, InputIterator1 last1,
      InputIterator2 first2, InputIterator last2,
      OutputIterator result, Compare comp);
```

Description
The *merge* algorithm merges two sorted seqeunces, specified by *[first1, last1)* and
[first2, last2), into the sequence specified by *[result, result + (last1 - first1) + (last2 - first2))*.
The first version of the *merge* algorithm uses the less than operator (<) to compare
elements in the two sequences. The second version uses the comparision function
provided by the function call. If a comparison function is provided, *merge* assumes that
both sequences were sorted using that comparison function.

The merge is stable. This means that if the two original sequences contain equivalent elements, the elements from the first sequence will always precede the matching elements
from the second in the resulting sequence. The size of the result of a *merge* is equal to the
sum of the sizes of the two argument sequences. *merge* returns an iterator that points to
the end of the resulting sequence, i.e., *result + (last1 - first1) + (last2 -first2)*. The result of
merge is undefined if the resulting range overlaps with either of the original ranges.

merge assumes that there are at least *(last1 - first1) + (last2 - first2)* elements following *result*, unless *result* has been adapted by an insert iterator.

Complexity
For *merge* at most *(last - first1) + (last2 - first2) - 1* comparisons are performed.

Examples

```cpp
#include <algorithm>
#include <vector>
using namespace std;

int main()
{
  int d1[4] = {1,2,3,4};
  int d2[8] = {11,13,15,17,12,14,16,18};

  // Set up two vectors
  vector<int> v1(d1,d1 + 4), v2(d1,d1 + 4);
  // Set up four destination vectors
  vector<int> v3(d2,d2 + 8),v4(d2,d2 + 8),
              v5(d2,d2 + 8),v6(d2,d2 + 8);
  // Set up one empty vector
  vector<int> v7;

  // Merge v1 with v2
  merge(v1.begin(),v1.end(),v2.begin(),v2.end(),v3.begin());
  // Now use comparator
  merge(v1.begin(),v1.end(),v2.begin(),v2.end(),v4.begin(),
        less<int>());

  // In place merge v5
  vector<int>::iterator mid = v5.begin();
  advance(mid,4);
  inplace_merge(v5.begin(),mid,v5.end());
  // Now use a comparator on v6
  mid = v6.begin();
  advance(mid,4);
  inplace_merge(v6.begin(),mid,v6.end(),less<int>());

  // Merge v1 and v2 to empty vector using insert iterator
  merge(v1.begin(),v1.end(),v2.begin(),v2.end(),
        back_inserter(v7));

  // Copy all cout
  ostream_iterator<int> out(cout," ");
  copy(v1.begin(),v1.end(),out);
  cout << endl;
  copy(v2.begin(),v2.end(),out);
  cout << endl;
  copy(v3.begin(),v3.end(),out);
```

```
        cout << endl;
        copy(v4.begin(),v4.end(),out);
        cout << endl;
        copy(v5.begin(),v5.end(),out);
        cout << endl;
        copy(v6.begin(),v6.end(),out);
        cout << endl;
        copy(v7.begin(),v7.end(),out);
        cout << endl;

        // Merge v1 and v2 to cout
        merge(v1.begin(),v1.end(),v2.begin(),v2.end(),
            ostream_iterator<int>(cout," "));
        cout << endl;

        return 0;
    }
```

min   Algorithm

Summary
Find and return the minimum of a pair of values

Synopsis
#include <algorithm>

template <class T>
 const T& min(const T& a, const T& b);

template <class T, class Compare>
 const T& min(const T& a, const T& b, Compare comp);

Description
The *min* algorithm determines and returns the minimum of a pair of values. In the second version of the algorithm, the optional argument *comp* defines a comparison function that can be used in place of the default "<" operator. This function can be used with all the datatypes provided by the standard library.

min returns the first argument when the two arguments are equal.

Examples
```
    #include <algorithm>
    using namespace std;

    int main(void)
    {
        double  d1 = 10.0, d2 = 20.0;
```

```
        // Find minimum
        double val1 = min(d1, d2);
        // val1 = 10.0

        // the greater comparator returns the greater of the
        // two values.
        double val2 = min(d1, d2, greater<double>());
        // val2 = 20.0;

        // Find maximum
        double val3 = max(d1, d2);
        // val3 = 20.0;

        // the less comparator returns the smaller of the
        // two values.
        // Note that, like every comparison in the STL, max is
        // defined in terms of the < operator, so using less here
        // is the same as using the max algorithm with a default
        // comparator.
        double val4 = max(d1, d2, less<double>());
        // val4 = 20

        cout << val1 << " " << val2 << " "
            << val3 << " " << val4 << endl;

        return 0;
    }
```

See also
max, max_element, min_element

min_element   **Algorithm**

Summary
Finds the minimum value in a range.

Synopsis
#include <algorithm>

template <class ForwardIterator>
ForwardIterator
min_element(ForwardIterator first, ForwardIterator last);

template <class ForwardIterator, class Compare>
InputIterator
min_element(ForwardIterator first, ForwardIterator last,
        Compare comp);

Description

The *min_element* algorithm returns an iterator that denotes the minimum element in a sequence. If the sequence contains more than one copy of the minimum element, the iterator points to the first occurrence of the element. In the second version of the function, the optional argument *comp* defines a comparison function that can be used in place of the default less than (<) operator. This function can be used with all the datatypes provided by the standard library.

Algorithm *min_element* returns the first iterator *i* in the range *[first, last)* such that for any iterator *j* in the range same range, the following corresponding conditions hold:

```
!(*j < *i)
```

or

```
comp(*j, *i) == false.
```

Complexity

min_element performs exactly *max((last - first) - 1, 0)* applications of the corresponding comparisons.

Examples

```
#include <algorithm>
#include <vector>
using namespace std;

int main(void)
{
  typedef vector<int>::iterator iterator;
  int d1[5] = {1,3,5,32,64};
  // set up vector
  vector<int>     v1(d1,d1 + 5);

  // find the largest element in the vector
  iterator it1 = max_element(v1.begin(), v1.end());
  // it1 = v1.begin() + 4

  // find the largest element in the range from
  // the beginning of the vector to the 2nd to last
  iterator it2 = max_element(v1.begin(), v1.end()-1,
                  less<int>());
  // it2 = v1.begin() + 3

  // find the smallest element
  iterator it3 = min_element(v1.begin(), v1.end());
  // it3 = v1.begin()

  // find the smallest value in the range from
  // the beginning of the vector plus 1 to the end
  iterator it4 = min_element(v1.begin()+1, v1.end(),
                  less<int>());
  // it4 = v1.begin() + 1
```

```
   cout << *it1 << " " << *it2 << " "
        << *it3 << " " << *it4 << endl;

   return 0;
 }
```

See also

max, max_element, min

minus

Summary

Returns the result of subtracting its second argument from its first.

Synopsis

#include<functional>

```
template <class T>
struct minus : binary_function<T, T, T> {
    T operator() (const T& x, const T& y) const
        { return x - y; }
};
```

Description

minus is a binary function object. Its *operator()* returns the result of *x* minus *y*. You can pass a *minus* object to any algorithm that requires a binary function. For example, the *transform* algorithm applies a binary operation to corresponding values in two collections and stores the result. *minus* would be used in that algorithm in the following manner:

```
vector<int> vec1;
vector<int> vec2;
vector<int> vecResult;
   .
   .
   .
transform(vec1.begin(), vec1.end(),
          vec2.begin(), vec2.end(),
          vecResult.begin(), minus<int>());
```

After this call to *transform, vecResult(n)* will contain *vec1(n)* minus *vec2(n)*.

See also

function objects

mismatch

Summary

Compares elements from two sequences and returns the first two elements that don't match each other.

Synopsis

#include <algorithm>

```
template <class InputIterator1, class InputIterator2>
  pair<InputIterator1,InputIterator2>
  mismatch(InputIterator1 first1, InputIterator1 last1,
        InputIterator2 first2);

template <class InputIterator1, class InputIterator2,
        class BinaryPredicate>
  pair<InputIterator1, Inputiterator2>
  mismatch(InputIterator first1, InputIterator1 last1,
        InputIterator2 first2,
        BinaryPredicate binary_pred);
```

Description

The *mismatch* algorithm compares members of two sequences and returns two iterators (*i* and *j*) that point to the first location in each sequence where the sequences differ from each other. Notice that the algorithm denotes both a starting position and an ending position for the first sequence, but denotes only a starting position for the second sequence. *mismatch* assumes that the second sequence has at least as many members as the first sequence. If the two sequences are identical, *mismatch* returns a pair of iterators that point to the end of the first sequence and the corresponding location at which the comparison stopped in the second sequence.

The first version of *mismatch* checks members of a sequence for equality, while the second version lets you specify a comparison function. The comparison function must be a binary predicate.

The iterators *i* and *j* returned by *mismatch* are defined as follows:

```
j  == first2  +  (i  -  first1)
```

and *i* is the first iterator in the range *[first1, last1)* for which the appropriate one of the following conditions hold:

```
!(*i  ==  *(first2  +  (i  -  first1)))
```

or

```
binary_pred(*i, *(first2 + (i - first1))) == false
```

If all of the members in the two sequences match, *mismatch* returns a pair of *last1* and *first2 + (last1 - first1)*.

Complexity

At most *last1 - first1* applications of the corresponding predicate are done.

Examples

```
#include <algorithm>
#include <vector>
using namespace std;

int main(void)
{
  typedef vector<int>::iterator  iterator;
  int d1[4] = {1,2,3,4};
  int d2[4] = {1,3,2,4};

  // Set up two vectors
  vector<int> vi1(d1,d1 + 4), vi2(d2,d2 + 4);

  // p1 will contain two iterators that point to the
  // first pair of elements that are different between
  // the two vectors
  pair<iterator, iterator> p1 = mismatch(vi1.begin(), vi1.end(),
                                         vi2.begin());

  // find the first two elements such that an element in the
  // first vector is greater than the element in the second
  // vector.
  pair<iterator, iterator> p2 = mismatch(vi1.begin(), vi1.end(),
                                         vi2.begin(),
                                         less_equal<int>());

  // Output results
  cout << *p1.first << ", " << *p1.second << endl;
  cout << *p2.first << ", " << *p2.second << endl;

  return 0;
}
```

modulus   Function object

Summary

Returns the remainder obtained by dividing the first argument by the second argument.

Synopsis

```
#include<functional>

template <class T>
struct modulus : binary_function<T, T, T> {
    T operator() (const T& x, const T& y) const
```

```
    { return x % y; }
};
```

Description

modulus is a binary function object. Its *operator()* returns the remainder resulting from of *x* divided by *y*. You can pass a *modulus* object to any algorithm that requires a binary function. For example, the *transform* algorithm applies a binary operation to corresponding values in two collections and stores the result. *modulus* would be used in that algorithm in the following manner:

```
vector<int> vec1;
vector<int> vec2;
vector<int> vecResult;
    .
    .
    .
transform(vec1.begin(), vec1.end(),
          vec2.begin(), vec2.end(),
          vecResult.begin(), modulus<int>());
```

After this call to *transform*, *vecResult(n)* will contain the remainder of *vec1(n)* divided by *vec2(n)*.

See also

function object

multimap   Container

Summary

An associative container providing access to non-key values using keys. *multimap* keys are not required to be unique. A *multimap* supports bidirectional iterators.

Synopsis

```
#include <map>

template <class Key, class T, class Compare = less<Key> >
 class multimap {

public:

// types

  typedef Key key_type;
  typedef pair<const Key, T> value_type;
  typedef Compare key_compare;
  typedef typename reference;
  typedef typename const_reference;
```

```
        typedef typename iterator;
        typedef typename const_iterator;
        typedef typename size_type;
        typedef typename difference_type;
        typedef reverse_iterator<iterator,
                value_type,
                reference,
                difference_type> reverse_iterator;
        typedef reverse_iterator<const_iterator,
                value_type,
                const_reference,
                difference_type> const_reverse_iterator;

        class value_compare
          : public binary_function<value_type, value_type, bool>

// Construct/Copy/Destroy

        explicit multimap (const Compare& comp = Compare());

        template <class InputIterator>
         multimap (InputIterator first,
            InputIterator last,
            const Compare& comp = Compare());
        multimap (const multimap<Key, T, Compare>& x);
         ~multimap ();
     multimap<Key, T, Compare>& operator=
            const multimap<Key, T, Compare>& x);

// Iterators

        iterator begin ();
        const_iterator begin () const;
        iterator end ();
        const_iterator end () const;
        reverse_iterator rbegin ();
        const_reverse_iterator rbegin () const;
        reverse_iterator rend ();
        const_reverse_iterator rend () const;

// Capacity

        bool empty () const;
        size_type size () const;
        size_type max_size () const;
```

// Modifiers

```
  iterator insert (const value_type& x);
  iterator insert (iterator position, const value_type& x);
  template <class InputIterator>
   void insert (InputIterator first, InputIterator last);

  void erase (iterator position);
  size_type erase (const key_type& x);
  void erase (iterator first, iterator last);
  void swap (multimap<Key, T, Compare>& x);
```

// Observers

```
  key_compare key_comp () const;
  value_compare value_comp () const;
```

// Multimap operations

```
  iterator find (const key_value& x);
  const_iterator find (const key_value& x) const;
  size_type count (const key_type& x) const;

  iterator lower_bound (const key_type& x);
  const_iterator lower_bound (const key_type& x) const;
  iterator upper_bound (const key_type& x);
  const_iterator upper_bound (const key_type& x) const;
  pair<iterator, iterator> equal_range (const key_type& x);
  pair<const_iterator, const_iterator>
    equal_range (const key_type& x) const;
};

template <class Key,class T,class Compare>
 bool operator==
   (const multimap<Key, T, Compare>& x,
    const multimap<Key, T, Compare>& y);

template <class Key,
      class T,
      class Compare>
 bool operator<
   (const multimap<Key, T, Compare>& x,
    const multimap<Key, T, Compare>& y);
```

Description

multimap provides fast access to stored values of type *T* which are indexed by keys of a separate type. The default operation for key comparison is the < operator. Unlike *map*, *multimap* allows insertion of duplicate keys.

multimap provides bidirectional iterators which point to an instance of *pair<const Key x, T y>* where *x* is the key and *y* is the stored value associated with that key. The definition of *multimap* provides a *typedef* to this pair called *value_type*.

The types used for both the template parameters *Key* and *T* must provide the following (where *T* is the *type*, *t* is a value of *T* and *u* is a *const value* of *T*):

```
Copy constructors -  T(t) and T(u)
Destructor        -  t.~T()
Address of        -  &t and &u yeilding T* and
                     const T* respectively
Assignment        -  t = a where a is a
                     (possibley const) value of T
```

The type used for the *Compare* template parameter must satisfy the requirements for binary functions.

Caveats

Member function templates are used in all containers provided by the Standard Template Library. An example of this feature is the constructor for *multimap<Key,Compare>* that takes two templated iterators:

```
template <class InputIterator>
 multimap (InputIterator, InputIterator, Compare);
```

multimap also has an *insert* function of this type. These functions, when not restricted by compiler limitations, allow you to use any type of input iterator as arguments. For compilers that do not support this feature we provide substitute functions that allow you to use an iterator obtained from the same type of container as the one you are constructing (or calling a member function on), or you can use a pointer to the type of element you have in the container.

For example, if your compiler does not support member function templates you can construct a multimap in the following two ways:

```
multimap<int,int,less<int> > ::value_type intarray[10];
multimap<int,int,less<int> >
    first_multimap(intarray,intarray + 10);
multimap<int, less<int> >
    second_multimap(first_multimap.begin(),first_multimap.end());
```

but not this way:

```
multimap<long, long, less<long> >
long_multimap(first_multimap.begin(),first_multimap.end());
```

since the *long_multimap* and *first_multimap* are not the same type.

Also, many compilers do not support default template arguments. If your compiler is one of these you need to always supply the *Compare* template argument.

Examples

```cpp
#include <string>
#include <map>
using namespace std;

typedef multimap<int, string, less<int> > months_type;

// Print out a pair
template <class First, class Second>
ostream& operator<<(ostream& out,
                    const pair<First,Second>& p)
{
  cout << p.second << " has " << p.first << " days";
  return out;
}

// Print out a multimap
ostream& operator<<(ostream& out, months_type l)
{
  copy(l.begin(),l.end(), ostream_iterator
              <months_type::value_type>(cout,"\n"));
  return out;
}

int main(void)
{
  // create a multimap of months and the number of
  // days in the month
  months_type months;

  typedef months_type::value_type value_type;

  // Put the months in the multimap
  months.insert(value_type(31, string("January")));
  months.insert(value_type(28, string("Febuary")));
  months.insert(value_type(31, string("March")));
  months.insert(value_type(30, string("April")));
  months.insert(value_type(31, string("May")));
  months.insert(value_type(30, string("June")));
  months.insert(value_type(31, string("July")));
  months.insert(value_type(31, string("August")));
  months.insert(value_type(30, string("September")));
  months.insert(value_type(31, string("October")));
  months.insert(value_type(30, string("November")));
  months.insert(value_type(31, string("December")));

  // print out the months
  cout << "All months of the year" << endl << months << endl;
```

```
            // Find the Months with 30 days
            pair<months_type::iterator,months_type::iterator> p =
                    months.equal_range(30);

            // print out the 30 day months
            cout << endl << "Months with 30 days" << endl;
            copy(p.first,p.second,
                    ostream_iterator<months_type::value_type>(cout,"\n"));

            return 0;
        }
```

Constructors and destructors

explicit multimap (const Compare& comp = Compare());

Default constructor. Constructs an empty multimap that will use the optional relation *comp* to order keys, if it is supplied.

template <class InputIterator>
multimap (InputIterator first,
    InputIterator last,
    const Compare& comp = Compare());

Constructs a multimap containing values in the range *[first, last)*. Creation of the new multimap is only guaranteed to succeed if the iterators *first* and *last* return values of type *pair<class Key, class Value>*.

multimap (const multimap<Key, T, Compare>& x);

Copy constructor. Creates a new multimap by copying all pairs of *key* and *value* from *x*.

~multimap ();

The destructor. Releases any allocated memory for this multimap.

Assignment operator

multimap<Key, T, Compare>&
operator= (const multimap<Key, T, Compare>& x);

Assignment operator. Replaces the contents of **this* with a copy of the multimap *x*.

Iterators

iterator **begin**() ;

Returns a bidirectional iterator pointing to the first element stored in the multimap. "First" is defined by the multimap's comparison operator, *Compare*.

const_iterator **begin**() const;

Returns a *const_iterator* pointing to the first element stored in the multimap. "First" is defined by the multimap's comparison operator, *Compare*.

iterator **end**() ;

Returns a *iterator* pointing to the last element stored in the multimap, i.e. the off-the-end value.

const_iterator **end**() const;

Returns a *const_iterator* pointing to the last element stored in the multimap.

reverse_iterator **rbegin**() ;

Returns a *reverse_iterator* pointing to the first element stored in the multimap. "First" is defined by the multimap's comparison operator, *Compare*.

const_reverse_iterator **rbegin**() const;

Returns a *const_reverse_iterator* pointing to the first element stored in the multimap.

reverse_iterator **rend**() ;

Returns a *reverse_iterator* pointing to the last element stored in the multimap, i.e., the off-the-end value.

const_reverse_iterator **rend**() const;

Returns a *const_reverse_iterator* pointing to the last element stored in the multimap.

Member functions

size_type
count (const key_type& x) const;

Returns the number of elements in the multimap with the key value *x*.

bool
empty() const;

Returns *true* if the multimap is empty, *false* otherwise.

pair<iterator,iterator>
equal_range (const key_type& x)

Returns the pair *(lower_bound(x), upper_bound(x))*.

pair<const_iterator,const_iterator>
equal_range (const key_type& x) const;

Returns the pair *(lower_bound(x), upper_bound(x))*.

void
erase (iterator position);

Erases the multimap element pointed to by the iterator *position*.

size_type
erase (const key_type& x);

Erases all elements with the key value *x* from the multimap, if any exist. Returns the number of erased elements.

void
erase (iterator first, iterator last);

Providing the iterators *first* and *last* point to the same multimap and *last* is reachable from *first*, all elements in the range *[first, last)* will be erased from the multimap.

iterator
find (const key_type& x);

Searches the multimap for a pair with the key value *x* and returns an iterator to that pair if it is found. If such a pair is not found the value *end()* is returned.

const_iterator
find (const key_type& x) const;

Same as find above but returns a *const_iterator*.

iterator
insert (const value_type& x);

iterator
insert (iterator position, const value_type& x);

x is inserted into the multimap. A position may be supplied as a hint regarding where to do the insertion. If the insertion may be done right after *position* then it takes amortized constant time. Otherwise it will take *O(log N)* time.

template <class InputIterator>
void
insert (InputIterator first, InputIterator last);

Copies of each element in the range *[first, last)* will be inserted into the multimap. The iterators *first* and *last* must return values of type *pair<T1,T2>*. This operation takes approximately *O(N*log(size()+N))* time.

key_compare
key_comp() const;

Returns a function object capable of comparing key values using the comparison operation, *Compare*, of the current multimap.

iterator
lower_bound (const key_type& x)

Returns an iterator to the smallest multimap element whose *key* is greater or equal to *x*. If no such element exists then *end()* is returned.

const_iterator
lower_bound (const key_type& x)

Same as *lower_bound* above but returns a *const_iterator*.

size_type
max_size() const;

Returns the maximum possible size of the multimap.

size_type
size() const;

Returns the number of elements in the multimap.

void
swap (multimap<Key, T, Compare>& x);

Swaps the contents of the multimap *x* with the current multimap, **this*.

upper_bound (const key_type& x)

Returns an iterator to the largest multimap element whose key is smaller or equal to *x*. If no such element exists then *end()* is returned.

const_iterator
upper_bound (const key_type& x)

Same as *upper_bound* above but returns a *const_iterator*.

value_compare
value_comp() const;

Returns a function object capable of comparing *value_types* (*key,value* pairs) using the comparison operation, *Compare*, of the current multimap.

Non-member operators

bool operator==(const multimap<Key, T, Compare>& x,
        const multimap<Key, T, Compare>& y);

Returns *true* if all elements in *x* are element-wise equal to all elements in *y*, using *(T::operator==)*. Otherwise it returns *false*.

bool operator< (const multimap<Key, T, Compare>& x,
        const multimap<Key, T, Compare>& y);

Returns *true* if *x* is lexicographically less than *y*. Otherwise, it returns *false*.

See also

containers

multiset

Container Class

Summary

An associative container providing fast access to stored key values. Storage of duplicate keys is allowed. A *multiset* supports bidirectional iterators.

Synopsis
#include <set>

template <class Key, class Compare = less<Key> >
 class multiset {

public:

// typedefs

    typedef Key key_type;
    typedef Key value_type;
    typedef Compare key_compare;
    typedef Compare value_compare;
    typedef typename reference;
    typedef typename const_reference;
    typedef typename iterator;

```
        typedef typename const_iterator;
        typedef typename size_type;
        typedef difference_type;
        typedef reverse_iterator<iterator,
                    value_type,
                    reference,
                    difference_type> reverse_iterator;

        typedef reverse_iterator<const_iterator,
                    value_type,
                    const_reference,
                    difference_type>
    const_reverse_iterator;

    // Construct/Copy/Destroy

        explicit multiset (const Compare& comp = Compare());
        template <class InputIterator>
        multiset (InputIterator first, InputIterator last,
            const Compare& comp = Compare());
        multiset (const multiset<Key, Compare>& x);
        ~multiset ();
        multiset<Key, Compare>& operator= (const multiset<Key,
        Compare>& x);

    // Iterators

        iterator begin ();
        const_iterator begin () const;
        iterator end ();
        const_iterator end () const;
        reverse_iterator rbegin ();
        const_reverse_iterator rbegin () const;
        reverse_iterator rend ();
        const_reverse_iterator rend () const;

    // Capacity

        bool empty () const;
        size_type size () const;
        size_type max_size () const;

    // Modifiers

        iterator insert (const value_type& x);
```

```
   iterator insert (iterator position, const value_type& x);
   template <class InputIterator>
    void insert (InputIterator first, InputIterator last);

   void erase (iterator position);
   size_type erase (const key_type& x);
   void erase (iterator first, iterator last);
   void swap (multiset<Key, Compare>& x);

// Observers

   key_compare key_comp () const;
   value_compare value_comp () const;

// Multiset operations

   iterator find (const key_value& x) const;
   size_type count (const key_type& x) const;
   iterator lower_bound (const key_type& x) const;
   iterator upper_bound (const key_type& x) const;
   pair<iterator, iterator> equal_range (const key_type& x) const;
   };

template <class Key,
      class Compare>
 bool operator==
   (const multiset<Key, Compare>& x,
    const multiset<Key, Compare>& y);

template <class Key,
      class Compare>
 bool operator<
   (const multiset<Key, Compare>& x,

    const multiset<Key, Compare>& y);
```

Description

multiset provides fast access to stored key values. The default operation for key comparison is the < operator. Insertion of duplicate keys is allowed with a multiset.

multiset provides bidirectional iterators which point to a stored key.

Any type used for the template parameter *Key* must provide the following (where *T* is the type, *t* is a value of *T*, and *u* is a *const value* of *T*):

```
   Copy constructors     T(t) and T(u)
   Destructor            t.~T()
```

```
        Address of            &t and &u yeilding T* and
                              const T* respectively
        Assignment            t = a where a is a
                              (possibley const) value of T
```

The *type* used for the *Compare* template parameter must satisfy the requirements for binary functions.

Caveats

Member function templates are used in all containers provided by the Standard Template Library. An example of this feature is the constructor for *multiset<Key,Compare>*, which takes two templated iterators:

```
template <class InputIterator>
multiset (InputIterator, InputIterator);
```

multiset also has an *insert* function of this type. These functions, when not restricted by compiler limitations, allow you to use any type of input iterator as arguments. For compilers that do not support this feature we provide substitute functions that allow you to use an iterator obtained from the same type of container as the one you are constructing (or calling a member function on). You can also use a pointer to the type of element you have in the container.

For example, if your compiler does not support member function templates, you can construct a *multiset* in the following two ways:

```
int intarray[10];
multiset<int,less<int> > first_multiset(intarray,intarray +10);
multiset<int,              less<int>               >
second_multiset(first_multiset.begin(),first_multiset.end());
```

but not this way:

```
multiset<long,            less<long>              >
long_multiset(first_multiset.begin(),first_multiset.end());
```

since the *long_multiset* and *first_multiset* are not the same type.

Also, many compilers do not support default template arguments. If your compiler is one of these you need to always supply the *Compare* template argument.

Examples

```
#include <set>

typedef multiset<int,less<int> > set_type;

ostream& operator<<(ostream& out, const set_type& s)
{
  copy(s.begin(),s.end(),
        ostream_iterator<set_type::value_type>(cout," "));
  return out;
}
```

```
int main(void)
{
  // create a multiset  of int's
  set_type  si;
  int  i;

  for (int j = 0; j < 2; j++)
  {
    for(i = 0; i < 10; ++i) {
      // insert values with a hint
      si.insert(si.begin(), i);
    }
  }

  // print out the multiset
  cout << si << endl;

  // Make another int multiset and an empty multiset
  set_type si2, siResult;
  for (i = 0; i < 10; i++)
      si2.insert(i+5);
  cout << si2 << endl;

  // Try a couple of set algorithms
  set_union(si.begin(),si.end(),si2.begin(),si2.end(),
         inserter(siResult,siResult.begin()));
  cout << "Union:" << endl << siResult << endl;

  siResult.erase(siResult.begin(),siResult.end());
  set_intersection(si.begin(),si.end(),
         si2.begin(),si2.end(),
         inserter(siResult,siResult.begin()));
  cout << "Intersection:" << endl << siResult << endl;

  return 0;
}
```

Constructor and destructor

explicit multiset (const Compare& comp = Compare());
Default constructor. Constructs an empty multiset which will use the optional relation *Compare* to order keys, if it is supplied.

template <class InputIterator>
multiset (InputIterator first,
         InputIterator last,
         const Compare& comp = Compare());
Constructs a multiset containing values in the range *[first, last)*.

multiset (const multiset<Key, Compare>& x);
Copy constructor. Creates a new multiset by copying all key values from *x*.

~multiset ();

The destructor. Releases any allocated memory for this multiset.

Assignment operator

multiset<Key, Compare>&
operator= (const multiset<Key, Compare>& x);

Assignment operator. Replaces the contents of *this* with a copy of the contents of *x*.

Iterators

iterator **begin**()

Returns an iterator pointing to the first element stored in the multiset. "First" is defined by the multiset's comparison operator, *Compare*.

const_iterator **begin**()

Returns a *const_iterator* pointing to the first element stored in the multiset.

iterator **end**()

Returns an iterator pointing to the last element stored in the multiset, i.e., the off-the-end value.

const_iterator **end**()

Returns a *const_iterator* pointing to the last element stored in the multiset, i.e., the off-the-end value.

reverse_iterator **rbegin**()

Returns a *reverse_iterator* pointing to the first element stored in the multiset. "First" is defined by the multiset's comparison operator, *Compare*.

const_reverse_iterator **rbegin**()

Returns a *const_reverse_iterator* pointing to the first element stored in the multiset.

reverse_iterator **rend**()

Returns a *reverse_iterator* pointing to the last element stored in the multiset, i.e., the off-the-end value.

const_reverse_iterator **rend**()

Returns a *const_reverse_iterator* pointing to the last element stored in the multiset, i.e., the off-the-end value.

Member functions

size_type
count (const key_type& x) const;

Returns the number of elements in the multiset with the key value *x*.

bool
empty () const;

Returns *true* if the multiset is empty, *false* otherwise.

pair<iterator,iterator>
equal_range (const key_type& x)const;

Returns the pair *(lower_bound(x), upper_bound(x))*.

void
erase (iterator position);

Erases the multiset element pointed to by the iterator *position*.

size_type
erase (const key_type& x);

Erases all elements with the key value *x* from the multiset, if any exist. Returns the number of erased elements.

void
erase (iterator first, iterator last);

Providing the iterators *first* and *last* point to the same multiset and *last* is reachable from *first*, all elements in the range *[first, last)* will be erased from the multiset.

iterator
find (const key_type& x) const;

Searches the multiset for a key value *x* and returns an iterator to that key if it is found. If such a value is not found the iterator *end()* is returned.

iterator
insert (const value_type& x);

iterator
insert (iterator position, const value_type& x);

x is inserted into the multiset. A position may be supplied as a hint regarding where to do the insertion. If the insertion may be done right after position then it takes amortized constant time. Otherwise it will take *O(log N)* time.

template <class InputIterator>
void
insert (InputIterator first, InputIterator last);

Copies of each element in the range *[first, last)* will be inserted into the multiset. This *insert* takes approximately *O(N*log(size()+N))* time.

key_compare
key_comp () const;

Returns a function object capable of comparing key values using the comparison operation, *Compare*, of the current multiset.

iterator
lower_bound (const key_type& x) const;

Returns an iterator to the smallest multiset element whose key is greater or equal to *x*. If no such element exists, *end()* is returned.

size_type
max_size () const;

Returns the maximum possible size of the multiset *size_type*.

size () const;

Returns the number of elements in the multiset.

void

swap (multiset<Key, Compare >& x);

Swaps the contents of the multiset *x* with the current multiset, **this*.

iterator

upper_bound (const key_type& x) const;

Returns an iterator to the largest multiset element whose key is smaller or equal to *x*. If no such element exists then *end()* is returned.

value_compare

value_comp () const;

Returns a function object capable of comparing key values using the comparison operation, *Compare*, of the current multiset. This function is identical to *key_comp* for sets.

Non-member operators

operator==(const multiset<Key, Compare>& x,
const multiset<Key, Compare>& y);

Returns *true* if all elements in *x* are element-wise equal to all elements in *y*, using *(T::operator==)*. Otherwise it returns *false*.

operator< (const multiset<Key, Compare>& x,
const multiset<Key, Compare>& y);

Returns *true* if *x* is lexicographically less than *y*. Otherwise, it returns *false*.

negate   Function object

Summary

Unary function object that returns the negation of its argument.

Synopsis

#include <functional>

```
template <class T>
struct negate : unary_function<T, T, T> {
    T operator() (const T& x) const
        { return -x; }
};
```

Description

negate is a unary function object. Its *operator()* returns the negation of its argument, i.e., *true* if its argument is *false*, or *false* if its arguement is *true*. You can pass a *negate* object to any algorithm that requires a unary function. For example, the *transform* algorithm applies a unary operation to the values in a collection and stores the result. *negate* could be used in that algorithm in the following manner:

```
vector<int> vec1;
vector<int> vecResult;
```

```
           ⋮
transform(vec1.begin(), vec1.end(),
          vecResult.begin(), negate<int>());
```

After this call to *transform, vecResult(n)* will contain the negation of the element in *vec1(n)*.

See also

function objects

negators   Function object

Summary
Function adaptors and function objects used to reverse the sense of predicate function objects.

Synopsis
#include <functional>

template <class Predicate>
class unary_negate
  : public unary_function<Predicate::argument_type, bool> {

public:
   explicit unary_negate (const Predicate& pred);
   bool operator() (const argument_type& x) const;
};

template<class Predicate>
unary_negate <Predicate> not1 (const Predicate& pred);

template<class Predicate>
class binary_negate
  : public binary_function<Predicate::first_argument_type,
                 Predicate::second_argument_type,
                 bool   >
{
public:
   explicit binary_negate (const Predicate& pred);
   bool operator() (const first_argument_type& x,
            const second_argument_type& y) const;
};

template <class Predicate>
binary_negate<Predicate> not2 (const Predicate& pred);

Description

Negators *not1* and *not2* are functions that take predicate function objects as arguments and return predicate function objects with the opposite sense. Negators work only with function objects defined as subclasses of the classes *unary_function* and *binary_function*. *not1* accepts and returns unary predicate function objects. *not2* accepts and returns binary predicate function objects.

unary_negate and *binary_negate* are function object classes that provide return types for the negators, *not1* and *not2*.

Example

```
#include<functional>
#include<algorithm>
using namespace std;

//Create a new predicate from unary_function
template<class Arg>
class is_odd : public unary_function<Arg, bool>
{
  public:
  bool operator()(const Arg& arg1) const
  {
    return (arg1 % 2 ? true : false);
  }
};

int main()
{
  less<int> less_func;

  // Use not2 on less
  cout << (less_func(1,4) ? "TRUE" : "FALSE") << endl;
  cout << (less_func(4,1) ? "TRUE" : "FALSE") << endl;
  cout << (not2(less<int>())(1,4) ? "TRUE" : "FALSE")
       << endl;
  cout << (not2(less<int>())(4,1) ? "TRUE" : "FALSE")
       << endl;

  //Create an instance of our predicate
  is_odd<int> odd;

  // Use not1 on our user defined predicate
  cout << (odd(1) ? "TRUE" : "FALSE") << endl;
  cout << (odd(4) ? "TRUE" : "FALSE") << endl;
  cout << (not1(odd)(1) ? "TRUE" : "FALSE") << endl;
  cout << (not1(odd)(4) ? "TRUE" : "FALSE") << endl;

  return 0;
}
```

See also
function_object, algorithm

next_permutation

Algorithm

Summary
Generate successive permutations of a sequence based on an ordering function.

Synopsis
#include <algorithm>

template <class BidirectionalIterator>
bool next_permutation (BidirectionalIterator first,
            BidirectionalIterator last);

template <class BidirectionalIterator, class Compare>
bool next_permutation (BidirectionalIterator first,
            BidirectionalIterator last, Compare comp);

Description
The permutation-generating algorithms (*next_permutation* and *prev_permutation*) assume that the set of all permutions of the elements in a sequence is lexicographically sorted with respect to *operator <* or *comp*. So, for example, if a sequence includes the integers 1 2 3, that sequence has six permutations, which, in order from first to last are: 1 2 3, 1 3 2, 2 1 3, 2 3 1, 3 1 2, and 3 2 1.

The *next_permutation* algorithm takes a sequence defined by the range *[first, last)* and transforms it into its next permutation, if possible. If such a permutation does exist, the algorithm completes the transformation and returns *true*. If the permutation does not exist, *next_permutation* returns *false*, and transforms the permutation into its "first" permutation (according to the lexicographical ordering defined by either *operator <*, the default used in the first version of the algorithm, or *comp*, which is user-supplied in the second version of the algorithm.)

For example, if the sequence defined by *[first, last)* contains the integers 3 2 1 (in that order), there is *not* a "next permutation." Therefore, the algorithm transforms the sequence into its first permutation (1 2 3) and returns *false*.

Complexity
At most *(last - first)/2* swaps are performed.

Examples
```
#include <numeric>     //for accumulate
#include <vector>      //for vector
#include <functional>  //for less
using namespace std;
```

```cpp
int main()
{
 //Initialize a vector using an array of ints
 int  a1[] = {0,0,0,0,1,0,0,0,0,0};
 char a2[] = "abcdefghji";
 //Create the initial set and copies for permuting
 vector<int>  m1(a1, a1+10);
 vector<int>  prev_m1((size_t)10), next_m1((size_t)10);
 vector<char> m2(a2, a2+10);
 vector<char> prev_m2((size_t)10), next_m2((size_t)10);
 copy(m1.begin(), m1.end(), prev_m1.begin());
 copy(m1.begin(), m1.end(), next_m1.begin());
 copy(m2.begin(), m2.end(), prev_m2.begin());
 copy(m2.begin(), m2.end(), next_m2.begin());
 //Create permutations
 prev_permutation(prev_m1.begin(),
                   prev_m1.end(),less<int>());
 next_permutation(next_m1.begin(),
                   next_m1.end(),less<int>());
 prev_permutation(prev_m2.begin(),
                   prev_m2.end(),less<int>());
 next_permutation(next_m2.begin(),
                   next_m2.end(),less<int>());
 //Output results
 cout << "Example 1: " << endl << "     ";
 cout << "Original values:     ";
 copy(m1.begin(),m1.end(),
     ostream_iterator<int>(cout," "));
 cout << endl << "     ";
 cout << "Previous permutation: ";
 copy(prev_m1.begin(),prev_m1.end(),
     ostream_iterator<int>(cout," "));
 cout << endl<< "     ";
 cout << "Next Permutation:     ";
 copy(next_m1.begin(),next_m1.end(),
     ostream_iterator<int>(cout," "));
 cout << endl << endl;
 cout << "Example 2: " << endl << "     ";
 cout << "Original values: ";
 copy(m2.begin(),m2.end(),
     ostream_iterator<char>(cout," "));
 cout << endl << "     ";
 cout << "Previous Permutation: ";
 copy(prev_m2.begin(),prev_m2.end(),
     ostream_iterator<char>(cout," "));
 cout << endl << "     ";
 cout << "Next Permutation:     ";
 copy(next_m2.begin(),next_m2.end(),
     ostream_iterator<char>(cout," "));
 cout << endl << endl;
```

```
        return 0;
    }
```

See also
prev_permutation

not1   Function adaptor

Summary
Function adaptor used to reverse the sense of a unary predicate function object.

Synopsis
#include <functional>

template<class Predicate>
unary_negate <Predicate> not1 (const Predicate& pred);

Description
not1 is a function adaptor, known as a negator, that takes a unary predicate function object as its argument and returns a unary predicate function object that is the complement of the original. *unary_negate* is a function object class that provides a return type for the *not1* negator.

Note that *not1* works only with function objects that are defined as subclasses of the class *unary_function*.

See also
negators, not2, unary_function, unary_negate, pointer_to_unary_function

not2   Function adaptor

Summary
Function adaptor used to reverse the sense of a binary predicate function object.

Synopsis
#include <functional>

template <class Predicate>
binary_negate<Predicate> not2 (const Predicate& pred);

Description
not2 is a function adaptor, known as a negator, that takes a binary predicate function object as its argument and returns a binary predicate function object that is the

complement of the original. *binary_negate* is a function object class that provides a return type for the *not2* negator.

Note that *not2* works only with function objects that are defined as subclasses of the class *binary_function*.

See also

binary_function, binary_negate, negators, not1, pointer_to_binary_function

not_equal_to   Function object

Summary
Binary function object that returns *true* if its first argument is not equal to its second.

Synopsis
#include <functional>

```
template <class T>
struct not_equal_to : binary_function<T, T, bool> {
    bool operator() (const T& x, const T& y) const
        { return x != y; }
};
```

Description
not_equal_to is a binary function object. Its *operator()* returns *true* if *x* is not equal to *y*. You can pass a *not_equal_to* object to any algorithm that requires a binary function. For example, the *transform* algorithm applies a binary operation to corresponding values in two collections and stores the result. *not_equal_to* would be used in that algorithm in the following manner:

```
vector<int> vec1;
vector<int> vec2;
vector<int> vecResult;
   .
   .
   .
transform(vec1.begin(), vec1.end(),
          vec2.begin(), vec2.end(),
          vecResult.begin(), not_equal_to<int>());
```

After this call to *transform, vecResult(n)* will contain a "1" if *vec1(n)* was not equal to *vec2(n)* or a "1" if *vec1(n)* was equal to *vec2(n)*.

See also
function object

nth_element
Algorithm

Summary

Rearranges a collection so that all elements lower in sorted order than the nth element come before it and all elements higher in sorter order than the nth element come after it.

Synopsis

```
#include <algorithm>

template <class RandomAccessIterator>
 void nth_element (RandomAccessIterator first,
          RandomAccessIterator nth,
          RandomAccessIterator last);

template <class RandomAccessIterator, class Compare>
 void nth_element (RandomAccessIterator first,
          RandomAccessIterator nth,
          RandomAccessIterator last,
          Compare comp);
```

Description

The *nth_element* algorithm rearranges a collection according to either the default comparison operator (>) or the provided comparison operator. After the algorithm applies, three things are true:

- The element that would be in the nth position if the collection were completely sorted is in the nth position

- All elements prior to the nth position would precede that position in an ordered collection

- All elements following the nth position would follow that position in an ordered collection

That is, for any iterator i in the range *[first, nth)* and any iterator j in the range *[nth, last)* it holds that *!(*i > *j)* or *comp(*i, *j) == false*.

Note that the elements that precede or follow the nth postion are not necessarily sorted relative to each other. The *nth_element* algorithm does *not* sort the entire collection.

Complexity

The algorithm is linear, on average, where N is the size of the range *[first,last)*.

Examples

```
#include<algorithm>
#include<vector>
using namespace std;
```

```
template<class RandomAccessIterator>
void quik_sort(RandomAccessIterator start,
               RandomAccessIterator end)
{
  size_t dist = 0;
  distance(start, end, dist);

  //Stop condition for recursion
  if(dist > 2)
  {
    //Use nth_element to do all the work for quik_sort
    nth_element(start, start+(dist/2), end);

    //Recursive calls to each remaining unsorted portion
    quik_sort(start, start+(dist/2-1));
    quik_sort(start+(dist/2+1), end);
  }

  if(dist == 2 && *end < *start)
    swap(start, end);
}

int main()
{
  //Initialize a vector using an array of ints
  int arr[10] = {37, 12, 2, -5, 14, 1, 0, -1, 14, 32};
  vector<int> v(arr, arr+10);

  //Print the initial vector
  cout << "The unsorted values are: " << endl << "     ";
  vector<int>::iterator i;
  for(i = v.begin(); i != v.end(); i++)
    cout << *i << ", ";
  cout << endl << endl;

  //Use the new sort algorithm
  quik_sort(v.begin(), v.end());

  //Output the sorted vector
  cout << "The sorted values are: " << endl << "     ";
  for(i = v.begin(); i != v.end(); i++)
    cout << *i << ", ";
  cout << endl << endl;

  return 0;
}
```

numeric_limits

Summary

A class for representing information about scalar types.

Specializations

numeric_limits<float>
numeric_limits<double>
numeric_limits<long double>
numeric_limits<short>
numeric_limits<unsigned short>
numeric_limits<int>
numeric_limits<unsigned int>
numeric_limits<long>
numeric_limits<unsigned long>
numeric_limits<char>
numeric_limits<wchar_t>
numeric_limits<unsigned char>
numeric_limits<signed char>
numeric_limits<bool>

Synopsis

```
#include <limits>

template <class T>
 class numeric_limits {

public:

// General -- meaningful for all specializations.

    static const bool is_specialized ;
    static T min ();
    static T max ();
    static const int radix ;
    static const int digits ;
    static const int digits10 ;
    static const bool is_signed ;
    static const bool is_integer ;
    static const bool is_exact ;
    static const bool traps ;
    static const bool is_modulo ;
    static const bool is_bounded ;

 // Floating point specific.

    static T epsilon ();
```

```
        static T round_error ();
        static const int min_exponent10 ;
        static const int max_exponent10 ;
        static const int min_exponent ;

        static const int max_exponent ;
        static const bool has_infinity ;
        static const bool has_quiet_NaN ;
        static const bool has_signaling_NaN ;
        static const bool is_iec559 ;
        static const bool has_denorm ;
        static const bool tinyness_before ;
        static const float_round_style round_style ;
        static T denorm_min ();
        static T infinity ();
        static T quiet_NaN ();
        static T signaling_NaN ();
    };

    enum float_round_style {
      round_indeterminate     = -1,
      round_toward_zero       = 0,
      round_to_nearest        = 1,
      round_toward_infinity   = 2,
      round_toward_neg_infinity = 3
    };
```

Description

numeric_limits is a class for representing information about scalar types. Specializations are provided for each fundamental type, both floating point and integer, including *bool*.

This class encapsulates information that is contained in the *<climits>* and *<cfloat>* headers, as well as providing additional information that is not contained in any existing C or C++ header.

Not all of the information provided by members is meaningful for all specializations of *numeric_limits*. Any value which is not meaningful for a particular type is set to *0* or *false*.

Warning

The specializations for *wide chars* and *bool* will only be available if your compiler has implemented them as real types and not simulated them with typedefs.

Example

```
    #include <limits>
    using namespace std;

    int main()
```

```
{
    numeric_limits<float> float_info;
    if (float_info.is_specialized && float_info.has_infinity)
    {
        // get value of infinity
        float finfinity=float_info.infinity();
    }
    return 0;
}
```

Member fields and functions

static T
denorm_min ();

Returns the minimum denormalized value. Meaningful for all floating point types. For types that do not allow denormalized values, this method must return the minimum normalized value.

static const int
digits ;

Number of radix digits which can be represented without change. For built-in integer types, *digits* will usually be the number of non-sign bits in the representation. For floating point types, *digits* is the number of radix digits in the mantissa. This member is meaningful for all specializations that declare *is_bounded* to be *true*.

static const int
digits10 ;

Number of base 10 digits that can be represented without change. Meaningful for all specializations that declare *is_bounded* to be *true*.

static T
epsilon ();

Returns the machine epsilon (the difference between 1 and the least value greater than 1 that is representable). This function is meaningful for floating point types only.

static const bool
has_denorm ;

This field is *true* if the type allows denormalized values (variable number of exponent bits). It is meaningful for floating point types only.

static const bool
has_infinity ;

This field is *true* if the type has a representation for positive infinity. It is meaningful for floating point types only. This field must be *true* for any type claiming conformance to IEC 559.

static const bool
has_quiet_NaN ;

This field is *true* is the type has a representation for a quiet (non-signaling) "Not a Number". It is meaningful for floating point types only and must be *true* for any type claiming conformance to IEC 559.

static const bool

has_signaling_NaN ;

This field is *true* if the type has a representation for a signaling "Not a Number". It is meaningful for floating point types only, and must be *true* for any type claiming conformance to IEC 559.

static T

infinity ();

Returns the representation of positive infinity, if available. This member function is meaningful for only those specializations that declare *has_infinity* to be *true*. Required for any type claiming conformance to IEC 559.

static const bool

is_bounded ;

This field is *true* if the set of values representable by the type is finite. All built-in C types are bounded; this member would be *false* for arbitrary precision types.

static const bool

is_exact ;

This static member field is *true* if the type uses an exact representation. All integer types are exact, but not vice versa. For example, rational and fixed-exponent representations are exact but not integer. This member is meaningful for all specializations.

static const bool

is_iec559 ;

This member is *true* if and only if the type adheres to the IEC 559 standard. It is meaningful for floating point types only. Must be *true* for any type claiming conformance to IEC 559.

static const bool

is_integer ;

This member is *true* if the type is integer. This member is meaningful for all specializations.

static const bool

is_modulo ;

This field is *true* if the type is modulo. Generally, this is *false* for floating types, *true* for unsigned integers, and *true* for signed integers on most machines. A type is modulo if it is possible to add two positive numbers, and have a result that wraps around to a third number, which is less.

static const bool

is_signed ;

This member is *true* if the type is signed. This member is meaningful for all specializations.

static const bool

is_specialized ;

Indicates whether *numeric_limits* has been specialized for type *T*. This flag must be *true* for all specializations of *numeric_limits*. In the default *numeric_limits<T>* template, this flag must be *false*.

```
static T
max ();
```

Returns the maximum finite value. This function is meaningful for all specializations that declare *is_bounded* to be *true*.

```
static const int
max_exponent ;
```

Maximum positive integer such that the radix raised to that power is in range. This field is meaningful for floating point types only.

```
static const int
max_exponent10 ;
```

Maximum positive integer such that 10 raised to that power is in range. This field is meaningful for floating point types only.

```
static T
min ();
```

Returns the minimum finite value. For floating point types with denormalization, *min()*must return the minimum normalized value. The minimum denormalized value is provided by *denorm_min()*. This function is meaningful for all specializations that declare *is_bounded* to be *true*.

```
static const int
min_exponent ;
```

Minimum negative integer such that the radix raised to that power is in range. This field is meaningful for floating point types only.

```
static const int
min_exponent10 ;
```

Minimum negative integer such that 10 raised to that power is in range. This field is meaningful for floating point types only.

```
static T
quiet_NaN ();
```

Returns the representation of a quiet "Not a Number", if available. This function is meaningful only for those specializations that declare *has_quiet_NaN* to be true. This field is required for any type claiming conformance to IEC 559.

```
static const int
radix ;
```

For floating types, specifies the base or radix of the exponent representation (often 2). For integer types, this member must specify the base of the representation. This field is meaningful for all specializations.

```
static T
round_error ();
```

Returns the measure of the maximum rounding error. This function is meaningful for floating point types only.

```
static const float_round_style
round_style ;
```

The rounding style for the type. Specializations for integer types must return *round_toward_zero*. This is meaningful for all floating point types.

static T

signaling_NaN();

Returns the representation of a signaling "Not a Number", if available. This function is meaningful for only those specializations that declare *has_signaling_NaN* to be *true*. This function must be meaningful for any type claiming conformance to IEC 559.

static const bool

tinyness_before ;

This member is *true* if tinyness is detected before rounding. It is meaningful for floating point types only.

static const bool

traps ;

This field is *true* if trapping is implemented for this type. The *traps* field is meaningful for all specializations.

See also

IEEE Standard for Binary Floating-Point Arithmetic, 345 East 47th Street, New York, NY 10017

Language Independent Arithmetic (LIA-1)

operator!=, operator>, operator<=, operator>=   Utility operators

Summary
Operators for the C++ Standard Template Library

Synopsis
#include <utility>

template <class T>
 bool operator!= (const T& x, const T& y)

template <class T>
 bool operator> (const T& x, const T& y)

template <class T>
 bool operator<= (const T& x, const T& y)

template <class T>
 bool operator>= (const T& x, const T& y)

Description

To avoid redundant definitions of *operator !=* out of *operator ==* and of *operators* >, <=, and >= out of *operator<*, the library provides these definitions:

```
operator != returns !(x==y),
operator >  returns y<x,
operator <= returns !(y<x), and
operator >= returns !(x<y).
```

ostream_iterator   Iterator

Summary

Stream iterators provide iterator capabilities for ostreams and istreams. They allow generic algorithms to be used directly on streams.

Synopsis

```
#include <iterator>

template <class T>
 class ostream_iterator : public output_iterator<T, Distance>
{
public:
   ostream_iterator(ostream& s);
   ostream_iterator (ostream& s, const char* delimiter);
   ostream_iterator (const ostream_iterator<T>& x);
   ~ostream_itertor ();

   ostream_iterator<T>& operator=(const  T&  value);
   ostream_iterator<T>& operator* () const;
   ostream_iterator<T>& operator++ ();
   ostream_iterator<T>  operator++ (int);
};

template <class T, class Distance> inline  bool
operator== (const istream_iterator<T, Distance>& x,
       const istream_iterator<T, Distance>& y);
```

Description

Stream iterators provide the standard iterator interface for input and output streams.

The class *ostream_iterator* writes elements to an output stream. If you use the constructor that has a second, *char ** argument, then that string will be written after every element . (The string must be null-terminated.) Since an ostream iterator is an output iterator, it is not possible to get an element out of the iterator. You can only assign to it.

Constructors

ostream_iterator (ostream& s);
Construct an *ostream_iterator* on the given stream.

ostream_iterator (ostream& s, const char* delimiter);
Construct an *ostream_iterator* on the given stream. The null terminated string delimitor is written to the stream after every element.

ostream_iterator (const ostream_iterator<T>& x);
Copy constructor.

Destructor

~ostream_iterator ();
 Destructor

Operators

const T& operator= (const T& value);
Shift the value *T* onto the output stream.

const T& ostream_iterator<T>&
operator* ();

ostream_iterator<T>&
operator++();

ostream_iterator<T>
operator++ (int);
These operators all do nothing. They simply allow the iterator to be used in common constructs.

Examples

```
#include <iterator>
#include <numeric>
#include <deque>
using namespace std;

int main ()
{
  //
  // Initialize a vector using an array.
  //
  int arr[4] = { 3,4,7,8 };
  int total=0;
  deque<int> d(arr+0, arr+4);
  //
  // stream the whole vector and a sum to cout
  //
  copy(d.begin(),d.end()-1,ostream_iterator<int>(cout," + "));
  cout << *(d.end()-1) << " = " <<
```

```
        accumulate(d.begin(),d.end(),total) << endl;
    return 0;
}
```

See also
istream_iterator, iterators

output iterator   Iterator

Summary
A write-only, forward moving iterator.

Description

Note   For a complete discussion of iterators, see the C++ *Programmer's Guide*, Chapter 19, "Iterators,"

Iterators are a generalization of pointers that allow a C++ program to uniformly interact with different data structures. Output iterators are read-only, forward moving iterators that satisfy the requirements listed below. Note that unlike other iterators used with the standard library, output iterators cannot be constant.

Requirements for Output Iterators
The following key pertains to the iterator descriptions listed:

a and *b*	values of type *X*
n	value of *distance* type
u, *Distance*, *tmp*, and *m*	identifiers
r	value of type *X&*
t	value of type *T*

The following expressions must be valid for output iterators:

Table 17.11 Requirements for output iterators

Expression	Requirement
X(a)	copy constructor, *a* == X(*a*).
X u(a)	copy constructor, *u* == *a*
X u = a	assignment, *u* == *a*
*a = t	result is not used
++r	returns *X&*
r++	return value convertable to *const X&*
*r++ = t	result is not used

The only valid use for the *operator* * is on the left hand side of the assignment statement.

Algorithms using output iterators should be single pass algorithms. That is, they should not pass through the same iterator twice.

See also
Iterators, Input iterators

pair Utility class

Summary
A template for heterogenous pairs of values.

Synopsis
```
#include <utility>

template <class T1, class T2>
 struct pair {
     T1 first;
     T2 second;
     pair (const T1& x, const T2& y);
};

template <class T1, class T2>
 bool operator== (const pair<T1, T2>& x,
         const pair T1, T2>& y);

template <class T1, class T2>
 bool operator< (const pair<T1, T2>& x,
         const pair T1, T2>& y);

template <class T1, class T2>
 pair<T1,T2> make_pair (const T1&, const T2&);
```

Description
The *pair* class provides a template for encapsulating pairs of values that may be of different types.

Constructor

```
pair (const T1& x, const T2& y);
```
The constructor creates a pair of types *T1* and *T2*, making the necessary conversions in *x* and *y*.

Operators

```
template <class T1, class T2>
```

```
bool operator== (const pair<T1, T2>& x,
          const pair T1, T2>& y);
```
Returns *true* if *(x.first == y.first && x.second == y.second)* is *true*. Otherwise it returns *false*.

```
template <class T1, class T2>
 bool operator< (const pair<T1, T2>& x,
          const pair T1, T2>& y);
```
Returns *true* if *(x.first < y.first || (!(y.first < x.first) && x.second < y.second))* is *true*. Otherwise it returns *false*.

Member functions

```
template <class T1, class T2>
pair<T1,T2>
make_pair(x,y)
```
make_pair(x,y) creates a pair by deducing and returning the types of *x* and *y*.

partial_sort   Algorithm

Summary
Templated algorithm for sorting collections of entities.

Synopsis
```
#include <algorithm>

template <class RandomAccessIterator>
 void partial_sort (RandomAccessIterator first,
          RandomAccessIterator middle,
          RandomAccessIterator last);

template <class RandomAccessIterator, class Compare>
 void partial_sort (RandomAccessIterator first,
          RandomAccessIterator middle,
          RandomAccessIterator last, Compare comp);
```

Description
The *partial_sort* algorithm takes the range *[first,last)* and places the first *middle-first* values into sorted order. The result is that the range *[first,middle)*is sorted like it would be if the entire range (*[first,last)*) were sorted. The remaining elements in the range (those in *[middle, last)*) are not in any defined order. The first version of the algorithm uses less than (<) as the comparison operator for the sort. The second version uses the comparision function *comp*.

Complexity
partial_sort does approximately *(last - first) * log(middle-first)* comparisons.

See also

sort, *stable_sort*, *partial_sort_copy*

partial_sort_copy   **Algorithm**

Summary
Templated algorithm for sorting collections of entities.

Synopsis
#include <algorithm>

```
template <class InputIterator,
        class RandomAccessIterator>
void partial_sort_copy (InputIterator first,
                InputIterator last,
                RandomAccessIterator result_first,
                RandomAccessIterator result_last);


template <class InputIterator,
        class RandomAccessIterator,
        class Compare>
void partial_sort_copy (InputIterator first,
                InputIterator last,
                RandomAccessIterator result_first,
                RandomAccessIterator result_last,
                Compare comp);
```

Description
The *partial_sort_copy* algorithm places the smaller of *last-first* and *result_last - result_first* sorted elements from the range *[first,last)* into the range beginning at *result_first*. (i.e., the range: *[result_first, result_first+min(last-first, result_last- result_first))*. Basically, the effect is as if the range *[first,last)* were placed in a temporary buffer, sorted and then as many elements as possible were coppied into the range *[result_first,result_last)*.

The first version of the algorithm uses less than (<) as the comparison operator for the sort. The second version uses the comparision function *comp*.

Complexity
partial_sort_copy does approximately *(last-first) * log(min(last-first, result_last-result_first))* comparisons.

Example
```
/****************************************************************
 *
 * partsort.cpp - Example program of partial sort.
```

```
 *
 * $Id: partsort.cpp,v 1.6 1995/10/06 19:03:56 hart Exp $
 *
 * $$RW_INSERT_HEADER "slyrs.str"
 *
 ****************************************************************/
#include <vector>
#include <algorithm>

int main()
{
  int d1[20] = {17, 3,   5,   -4, 1, 12, -10, -1, 14, 7,
                -6, 8, 15, -11, 2, -2,  18,   4, -3, 0};
  //
  // Set up a vector.
  //
  vector<int> v1(d1+0, d1+20);
  //
  // Output original vector.
  //
  cout << "For the vector: ";
  copy(v1.begin(), v1.end(), ostream_iterator<int>(cout," "));
  //
  // Partial sort the first seven elements.
  //
  partial_sort(v1.begin(), v1.begin()+7, v1.end());
  //
  // Output result.
  //
  cout << endl << endl << "A partial_sort of 7 elements gives: "
       << endl << "      ";
  copy(v1.begin(), v1.end(), ostream_iterator<int>(cout," "));
  cout << endl;
  //
  // A vector of ten elements.
  //
  vector<int> v2(10, 0);
  //
  // Sort the last ten elements in v1 into v2.
  //
  partial_sort_copy(v1.begin()+10, v1.end(), v2.begin(),
                    v2.end());
  //
  // Output result.
  //
  cout << endl << "A partial_sort_copy of the last ten elements
                   gives: " << endl << "      ";
  copy(v2.begin(), v2.end(), ostream_iterator<int>(cout," "));
  cout << endl;

  return 0;
}
```

See also
sort, stable_sort, partial_sort

partial_sum **Generalized numeric operation**

Summary

Calculates successive partial sums of a range of values.

Synopsis

```
#include <numeric>

template <class InputIterator, class OutputIterator>
OutputIterator partial_sum (InputIterator first,
                 InputIterator last,
                 OutputIterator result);

template <class InputIterator,
          class OutputIterator,
          class BinaryOperation>
OutputIterator partial_sum (InputIterator first,
                 InputIterator last,
                 OutputIterator result,
                 BinaryOperation binary_op);
```

Description

The *partial_sum* algorithm creates a new sequence in which every element is formed by adding all the values of the previous elements, or, in the second form of the algorithm, applying the operation *binary_op* successively on every previous element. That is, *partial_sum* assigns to every iterator *i* in the range *[result, result + (last - first))* a value equal to:

```
((...(*first + *(first + 1)) + ... ) + *(first + (i - result)))
```

or, in the second version of the algorithm:

```
binary_op(binary_op(..., binary_op (*first, *(first + 1)),...),*(first + (i -
result)))
```

For instance, applying *partial_sum* to (1,2,3,4,) will yield (1,3,6,10).

The *partial_sum* algorithm returns *result + (last - first)*.

If *result* is equal to *first*, the elements of the new sequence successively replace the elements in the original sequence, effectively turning *partial_sum* into an inplace transformation.

Complexity

Exactly *(last - first) - 1* applications of the default + operator or *binary_op* are performed.

Examples

```cpp
#include <numeric>    //for accumulate
#include <vector>     //for vector
#include <functional> //for times
using namespace std;

int main()
{
  //Initialize a vector using an array of ints
  int d1[10] = {1,2,3,4,5,6,7,8,9,10};
  vector<int> v(d1, d1+10);

  //Create an empty vectors to store results
  vector<int> sums((size_t)10), prods((size_t)10);

  //Compute partial_sums and partial_products
  partial_sum(v.begin(), v.end(), sums.begin());
  partial_sum(v.begin(), v.end(), prods.begin(), times<int>());

  //Output the results
  cout << "For the series: " << endl << "      ";
  copy(v.begin(),v.end(),ostream_iterator<int>(cout," "));
  cout << endl << endl;

  cout << "The partial sums: " << endl << "      " ;
  copy(sums.begin(),sums.end(),
      ostream_iterator<int>(cout," "));
  cout <<" should each equal (N*N + N)/2" << endl << endl;

  cout << "The partial products: " << endl << "      ";
  copy(prods.begin(),prods.end(),
      ostream_iterator<int>(cout," "));
  cout << " should each equal N!" << endl;

  return 0;
}
```

permutation   Algorithm

Summary

Generate successive permutations of a sequence based on an ordering function.

See the entries for *next_permutation* and *prev_permutation*.

partition

Algorithm

Summary

Places all of the entities that satisfy the given predicate before all of the entities that do not.

Synopsis

```
#include <algorithm>

template <class BidirectionalIterator, class Predicate>
BidirectionalIterator
partition (BidirectionalIterator first,
        BidirectionalIterator last,
        Predicate pred);
```

Description

The *partition* algorithm places all the elements in the range *[first, last)* that satisfy *pred* before all the elements that do not satisfy *pred*. It returns an iterator that is one past the end of the group of elements that satisfy *pred*. In other words, *partition* returns *i* such that for any iterator *j* in the range*[first, i), pred(*j) == true*, and, for any iterator *k* in the range *[i, last), pred(*j) == false*.

Note that *partition* does not necessarily maintain the relative order of the elements that match and elements that do not match the predicate. Use the algorithm *stable_partition* if relative order is important.

Complexity

The *partition* algorithm does at most *(last - first)/2* swaps, and applies the predicate exactly *last - first* times.

Example

```
/*************************************************************
 *
 * prtition.cpp - Example program for partition.
 *
 * $Id: prtition.cpp,v 1.7 1995/10/06 19:18:57 hart Exp $
 *
 * $$RW_INSERT_HEADER "slyrs.str"
 *
 *************************************************************/
#include<functional>
#include<deque>
#include<algorithm>

//
// Create a new predicate from unary_function.
//
template<class Arg>
class is_even : public unary_function<Arg, bool>
{
  public:
```

```
    bool operator()(const Arg& arg1) { return (arg1 % 2) == 0; }
  };

  int main ()
  {
    //
    // Initialize a deque with an array of integers.
    //
    int init[10] = { 1,2,3,4,5,6,7,8,9,10 };
    deque<int> d1(init+0, init+10);
    deque<int> d2(init+0, init+10);
    //
    // Print out the original values.
    //
    cout << "Unpartitioned values: " << "\t\t";
    copy(d1.begin(), d1.end(), ostream_iterator<int>(cout," "));
    cout << endl;
    //
    // A partition of the deque according to even/oddness.
    //
    partition(d2.begin(), d2.end(), is_even<int>());
    //
    // Output result of partition.
    //
    cout << "Partitioned values: " << "\t\t";
    copy(d2.begin(), d2.end(), ostream_iterator<int>(cout," "));
    cout << endl;
    //
    // A stable partition of the deque according to even/oddness.
    //
    stable_partition(d1.begin(), d1.end(), is_even<int>());
    //
    // Output result of partition.
    //
    cout << "Stable partitioned values: " << "\t";
    copy(d1.begin(), d1.end(), ostream_iterator<int>(cout," "));
    cout << endl;

    return 0;
  }
```

See also

stable_partition

plus   Function object

Summary

A binary function object that returns the result of adding its first and second arguments.

Synopsis

#include <functional>

```
template<class T>
struct plus : binary_function<T, T, T> {
    T operator() (const T& x, const T& y) const
        { return x + y; }
};
```

Description

plus is a binary function object. Its *operator()* returns the result of adding *x* and *y*. You can pass a *plus* object to any algorithm that uses a binary function. For example, the *transform* algorithm applies a binary operation to corresponding values in two collections and stores the result. *plus* would be used in that algorithm in the following manner:

```
vector<int> vec1;
vector<int> vec2;
vector<int> vecResult;
?
transform(vec1.begin(), vec1.end(),
          vec2.begin(), vec2.end(),
          vecResult.begin(), plus<int>());
```

After this call to *transform, vecResult(n)* will contain *vec1(n)* plus *vec2(n)*.

See also

Function objects

pointer_to_binary-function   Function object

Summary

A function object which adapts a pointer to a binary function to work where a *binary_function* is called for.

Synopsis

#include <functional>

```
template <class Arg1, class Arg2, class Result>
 class pointer_to_binary_function : public binary_function<Arg1, Arg2, Result> {

 public:
    explicit pointer_to_binary_function (Result (*f)(Arg1, Arg2));
    Result operator() (const Arg1& x, const Arg2& y) const;
};

template<class Arg1, class Arg2, class Result>
```

```
pointer_to_binary_function<Arg1, Arg2, Result>
 ptr_fun (Result (*x)(Arg1, Arg2));
```

Description

The *pointer_to_binary_function* class encapsulates a pointer to a two-argument function. The class provides an *operator()* so that the resulting object serves as a binary function object for that function.

The *ptr_fun* function is overloaded to create instances of a *pointer_to_binary_function* when provided with the appropriate pointer to a function.

See also

function_objects, pointer_to_unary_function, ptr_fun

pointer_to_unary_function   Function object

Summary

A function object class that adapts a *pointer to a function* to work where a *unary_function* is called for.

Synopsis
```
#include <functional>

template <class Arg, class Result>
 class pointer_to_unary_function : public unary_function<Arg, Result> {

 public:
    explicit pointer_to_unary_function (Result (*f)(Arg));
    Result operator() (const Arg& x) const;
};

template<class Arg, class Result>
pointer_to_unary_function<Arg, Result>
 ptr_fun (Result (*f)(Arg));
```

Description

The *pointer_to_unary_function* class encapsulates a pointer to a single-argument function. The class provides an *operator()* so that the resulting object serves as a function object for that function.

The *ptr_fun* function is overloaded to create instances of *pointer_to_unary_function* when provided with the appropriate pointer to a function.

See also

function_objects, pointer_to_binary_function, ptr_fun

pop_heap

Algorithms

Summary
Moves the largest element off the heap.

Synopsis
```
template <class RandomAccessIterator>
 void
 pop_heap(RandomAccessIterator first,
        RandomAccessIterator last);

template <class RandomAccessIterator, class Compare>
 void
 pop_heap(RandomAccessIterator first,
        RandomAccessIterator last, Compare comp);
```

Description
A heap is a particular organization of elements in a range between two random access iterators *[a, b)*. Its two key properties are:

- **a* is the largest element in the range.

- **a* may be removed by the *pop_heap* algorithm or a new element added by the *push_heap* algorithm, in *O(logN)* time.

These properties make heaps useful as priority queues.

The *pop_heap* algorithm uses the less than (<) operator as the default comparison. An alternate comparison operator can be specified.

The *pop_heap* algorithm can be used as part of an operation to remove the largest element from a heap. It assumes that the range *[first, last)* is a valid heap (i.e., that *first* is the largest element in the heap or the first element based on the alternate comparison operator). It then swaps the value in the location *first* with the value in the location *last - 1* and makes *[first, last -1)*back into a heap. You can then access the element in *last* using the vector or deque *back()* member function, or remove the element using the *pop_back* member function. Note that *pop_heap* does not actually remove the element from the data structure, you must use another function to do that.

Complexity
pop_heap performs at most *2 * log(last - first)* comparisons.

Example
```
#include <algorithm>
#include <vector>
using namespace std;

int main(void)
```

```
{
  int d1[4] = {1,2,3,4};
  int d2[4] = {1,3,2,4};

  // Set up two vectors
  vector<int> v1(d1,d1 + 4), v2(d2,d2 + 4);

  // Make heaps
  make_heap(v1.begin(),v1.end());
  make_heap(v2.begin(),v2.end(),less<int>());
  // v1 = (4,x,y,z)   and   v2 = (4,x,y,z)
  // Note that x, y and z represent the remaining
  // values in the container (other than 4).
  // The definition of the heap and heap operations
  // does not require any particular ordering
  // of these values.

  // Copy both vectors to cout
  ostream_iterator<int> out(cout," ");
  copy(v1.begin(),v1.end(),out);
  cout << endl;
  copy(v2.begin(),v2.end(),out);
  cout << endl;

  // Now let's pop
  pop_heap(v1.begin(),v1.end());
  pop_heap(v2.begin(),v2.end(),less<int>());
  // v1 = (3,x,y,4) and v2 = (3,x,y,4)

  // Copy both vectors to cout
  copy(v1.begin(),v1.end(),out);
  cout << endl;
  copy(v2.begin(),v2.end(),out);
  cout << endl;

  // And push
  push_heap(v1.begin(),v1.end());
  push_heap(v2.begin(),v2.end(),less<int>());
  // v1 = (4,x,y,z) and v2 = (4,x,y,z)

  // Copy both vectors to cout
  copy(v1.begin(),v1.end(),out);
  cout << endl;
  copy(v2.begin(),v2.end(),out);
  cout << endl;

  // Now sort those heaps
  sort_heap(v1.begin(),v1.end());
  sort_heap(v2.begin(),v2.end(),less<int>());
  // v1 = v2 = (1,2,3,4)

  // Copy both vectors to cout
```

```
    copy(v1.begin(),v1.end(),out);
    cout << endl;
    copy(v2.begin(),v2.end(),out);
    cout << endl;

    return 0;
}
```

See also
make_heap, push_heap, sort_heap

predicate

Summary
A function or a function object that returns a Boolean (true/false) value or an integer value.

prev_permutation   Algorithm

Summary
Generate successive permutations of a sequence based on an ordering function.

Synopsis
#include <algorithm>

template <class BidirectionalIterator>
 bool prev_permutation (BidirectionalIterator first,
            BidirectionalIterator last);

template <class BidirectionalIterator, class Compare>
 bool prev_permutation (BidirectionalIterator first,
            BidirectionalIterator last, Compare comp);

Description
The permutation-generating algorithms (*next_permutation* and *prev_permutation*) assume that the set of all permutions of the elements in a sequence is lexicographically sorted with respect to *operator* < or *comp*. So, for example, if a sequence includes the integers 1 2 3, that sequence has six permutations, which, in order from first to last, are: 1 2 3 , 1 3 2, 2 1 3, 2 3 1, 3 1 2, and 3 2 1.

The *prev_permutation* algorithm takes a sequence defined by the range *[first, last)* and transforms it into its previous permutation, if possible. If such a permutation does exist, the algorithm completes the transformation and returns *true*. If the permutation does not exist, *prev_permutation* returns *false*, and transforms the permutation into its "last" permutation (according to the lexicographical ordering defined by either *operator <*, the default used in the first version of the algorithm, or *comp*, which is user-supplied in the second version of the algorithm.)

For example, if the sequence defined by *[first, last)* contains the integers 1 2 3 (in that order), there is *not* a "previous permutation." Therefore, the algorithm transforms the sequence into its last permutation (3 2 1) and returns *false*.

Complexity
At most *(last - first)/2* swaps are performed.

Examples
```
#include <numeric>    //for accumulate
#include <vector>         //for vector
#include <functional> //for less
using namespace std;

int main()
{
  //Initialize a vector using an array of ints
  int  a1[] = {0,0,0,0,1,0,0,0,0,0};
  char a2[] = "abcdefghji";

  //Create the initial set and copies for permuting
  vector<int>  m1(a1, a1+10);
  vector<int>  prev_m1((size_t)10), next_m1((size_t)10);
  vector<char> m2(a2, a2+10);
  vector<char> prev_m2((size_t)10), next_m2((size_t)10);

  copy(m1.begin(), m1.end(), prev_m1.begin());
  copy(m1.begin(), m1.end(), next_m1.begin());
  copy(m2.begin(), m2.end(), prev_m2.begin());
  copy(m2.begin(), m2.end(), next_m2.begin());

  //Create permutations
  prev_permutation(prev_m1.begin(),
                   prev_m1.end(),less<int>());
  next_permutation(next_m1.begin(),
                   next_m1.end(),less<int>());
  prev_permutation(prev_m2.begin(),
                   prev_m2.end(),less<int>());
  next_permutation(next_m2.begin(),
                   next_m2.end(),less<int>());
  //Output results
  cout << "Example 1: " << endl << "      ";
  cout << "Original values:      ";
  copy(m1.begin(),m1.end(),
       ostream_iterator<int>(cout," "));
  cout << endl << "      ";
  cout << "Previous permutation: ";
```

```
        copy(prev_m1.begin(),prev_m1.end(),
            ostream_iterator<int>(cout," "));

        cout << endl<< "      ";
        cout << "Next Permutation:      ";
        copy(next_m1.begin(),next_m1.end(),
            ostream_iterator<int>(cout," "));
        cout << endl << endl;

        cout << "Example 2: " << endl << "      ";
        cout << "Original values: ";
        copy(m2.begin(),m2.end(),
            ostream_iterator<char>(cout," "));
        cout << endl << "      ";
        cout << "Previous Permutation: ";
        copy(prev_m2.begin(),prev_m2.end(),
            ostream_iterator<char>(cout," "));
        cout << endl << "      ";

        cout << "Next Permutation:      ";
        copy(next_m2.begin(),next_m2.end(),
            ostream_iterator<char>(cout," "));
        cout << endl << endl;

        return 0;
    }
```

See also
next_permutation

priority_queue   **Container**

Summary
A container adapter which behaves like a priority queue. Items popped from the queue
are in order with respect to a "priority."

Synopsis
#include <queue>

```
template <class T,
    class Container = vector<T>,
    class Compare = less<Container::value_type>>
 class priority_queue {

public:

// typedefs
```

```
   typedef typename Container::value_type value_type;
   typedef typename Container::size_type size_type;

protected:

   Container c;
   Compare comp;

public:

   explicit priority_queue (const Compare& x = Compare());
   template <class InputIterator>
    priority_queue (InputIterator first,
              InputIterator last,
              const Compare& x = Compare());
   bool empty () const;
   size_type size () const;
   const value_type& top () const;
   void push (const value_type& x)
   void pop()
};
```

Description

priority_queue is a container adaptor which allows a container to act as a priority queue. This means that the item with the highest priority, as determined by either the default comparison operator (*operator <*) or the comparison *comp*, is brought to the front of the queue whenever anything is pushed onto or popped off the queue.

priority_queue adapts any container that provides *front()*, *push_back()* and *pop_back()*.

Caveats

If your compiler does not support default template parameters, you must always provide a container template parameter when declaring an instance of *priority_queue*. For example, you would not be able to write,

```
priority_queue<int> var;
```

Instead, you would have to write,

```
priority_queue<int, vector<int>> var;
```

Examples

```
#include <queue>
#include <deque>
#include <vector>
#include <string>
using namespace std;
```

```cpp
int main(void)
{
  // Make a priority queue of int  using a deque container
  priority_queue<int, vector<int>, less<int> > pq;

  // Push a couple of values
  pq.push(1);
  pq.push(2);

  // Pop a couple of values and examine the ends
  cout << pq.top() << endl;
  pq.pop();
  cout << pq.top() << endl;
  pq.pop();

  // Make a priority queue of strings
  priority_queue<string,deque<string>, less<string> > pqs;

  // Push on a few strings then pop them back off
  int i;
  for (i = 0; i < 10; i++)
  {
    pqs.push(string(i+1,'a'));
    cout << pqs.top() << endl;
  }
  for (i = 0; i < 10; i++)
  {
    cout << pqs.top() << endl;
    pqs.pop();
  }

  // Make a priority queue of strings using greater
  priority_queue<string,deque<string>, greater<string> > pgqs;

  // Push on a few strings then pop them back off
  for (i = 0; i < 10; i++)
  {
    pgqs.push(string(i+1,'a'));
    cout << pgqs.top() << endl;
  }

  for (i = 0; i < 10; i++)
  {
    cout << pgqs.top() << endl;
    pgqs.pop();
  }

  return 0;
}
```

Constructor

explicit priority_queue (const Compare& x = Compare());

Default constructor. Constructs a priority queue that uses *Container* for its underlying implementation and *Compare* as its standard for determining priority.

template <class InputIterator>
   priority_queue (InputIterator first, InputIterator last,
        const Compare& x = Compare());

Constructs a new priority queue and places into it every entity in the range *[first, last)*.

Member functions

bool
empty () const;
Returns *true* if the priority_queue is empty, *false* otherwise.

void
pop();
Removes the item with the highest priority from the queue.

void
push (const value_type& x);
Adds *x* to the queue.

size_type
size () const;
Returns the number of elements in the priority_queue.

const value_type&
top () const;
Returns a reference to the element in the queue with the highest priority.

ptr_fun Function adaptor

Summary

A function that is overloaded to adapt a *pointer to a function* to work where a function is called for.

Synopsis

#include <functional>

template<class Arg, class Result>
pointer_to_unary_function<Arg, Result>
  ptr_fun (Result (*f)(Arg));

template<class Arg1, class Arg2, class Result>
pointer_to_binary_function<Arg1, Arg2, Result>

```
ptr_fun (Result (*x)(Arg1, Arg2));
```

Description

The *pointer_to_unary_function* and *pointer_to_binary_function* classes encapsulate a pointers to functions. and provide an *operator()* so that the resulting object serves as a function object for the function.

The *ptr_fun* function is overloaded to create instances of *pointer_to_unary_function* or *pointer_to_binary_function* when provided with the appropriate pointer to a function.

Example

```cpp
#include<functional>
#include<deque>
#include<vector>
#include<algorithm>
using namespace std;

//Create a function
int factorial(int x)
{
  int result = 1;
  for(int i = 2; i <= x; i++)
  result *= i;
  return result;
}

int main()
{
  //Initialize a deque with an array of ints
  int init[7] = {1,2,3,4,5,6,7};
  deque<int> d(init, init+7);

  //Create an empty vector to store the factorials
  vector<int> v((size_t)7);

  //Transform the numbers in the deque to their factorials and
  //store in the vector
  transform(d.begin(), d.end(), v.begin(), ptr_fun(factorial));

  //Print the results
  cout << "The following numbers: " << endl << "     ";
  copy(d.begin(),d.end(),ostream_iterator<int>(cout," "));

  cout << endl << endl;
  cout << "Have the factorials: " << endl << "     ";
  copy(v.begin(),v.end(),ostream_iterator<int>(cout," "));

  return 0;
}
```

See also
function_objects, pointer_to_binary_function, pointer_to_unary_function

push_heap ·   Algorithms

Summary
Places a new element into a heap.

Synopsis
```
#include <algorithm>

template <class RandomAccessIterator>
  void
  push_heap(RandomAccessIterator first,
        RandomAccessIterator last);

template <class RandomAccessIterator, class Compare>
  void
  push_heap(RandomAccessIterator first,
        RandomAccessIterator last, Compare comp);
```

Description
A heap is a particular organization of elements in a range between two random access iterators *[a, b)*. Its two key properties are:

- **a* is the largest element in the range.

- **a* may be removed by the *pop_heap* algorithm, or a new element added by the *push_heap* algorithm, in *O(logN)* time.

These properties make heaps useful as priority queues.

The *push_heap* algorithms uses the less than (<) operator as the default comparison. As with all of the heap manipulation algorithms, an alternate comparison function can be specified.

The *push_heap* algorithm is used to add a new element to the heap. First, a new element for the heap is added to the end of a range. (For example, you can use the vector or deque member function *push_back()*to add the element to the end of either of those containers.) The *push_heap* algorithm assumes that the range *[first, last - 1)* is a valid heap. It then properly positions the element in the location *last - 1* into its proper position in the heap, resulting in a heap over the range *[first, last)*.

Note that the *push_heap* algorithm does not place an element into the heap's underlying container. You must user another function to add the element to the end of the container before applying *push_heap*.

Complexity

For *push_heap* at most *log(last - first)* comparisons are performed.

Examples

```
#include <algorithm>
#include <vector>
using namespace std;

int main(void)
{
  int d1[4] = {1,2,3,4};
  int d2[4] = {1,3,2,4};

  // Set up two vectors
  vector<int> v1(d1,d1 + 4), v2(d2,d2 + 4);

  // Make heaps
  make_heap(v1.begin(),v1.end());
  make_heap(v2.begin(),v2.end(),less<int>());
  // v1 = (4,x,y,z)  and  v2 = (4,x,y,z)
  // Note that x, y and z represent the remaining
  // values in the container (other than 4).
  // The definition of the heap and heap operations
  // does not require any particular ordering
  // of these values.

  // Copy both vectors to cout
  ostream_iterator<int> out(cout," ");
  copy(v1.begin(),v1.end(),out);
  cout << endl;
  copy(v2.begin(),v2.end(),out);
  cout << endl;

  // Now let's pop
  pop_heap(v1.begin(),v1.end());
  pop_heap(v2.begin(),v2.end(),less<int>());
  // v1 = (3,x,y,4) and v2 = (3,x,y,4)

  // Copy both vectors to cout
  copy(v1.begin(),v1.end(),out);
  cout << endl;
  copy(v2.begin(),v2.end(),out);
  cout << endl;

  // And push
  push_heap(v1.begin(),v1.end());
  push_heap(v2.begin(),v2.end(),less<int>());
  // v1 = (4,x,y,z) and v2 = (4,x,y,z)

  // Copy both vectors to cout
  copy(v1.begin(),v1.end(),out);
```

```
    cout << endl;
    copy(v2.begin(),v2.end(),out);
    cout << endl;

    // Now sort those heaps
    sort_heap(v1.begin(),v1.end());
    sort_heap(v2.begin(),v2.end(),less<int>());
    // v1 = v2 = (1,2,3,4)


  / Copy both vectors to cout
    copy(v1.begin(),v1.end(),out);
    cout << endl;
    copy(v2.begin(),v2.end(),out);
    cout << endl;

    return 0;
  }
```

See also
make_heap, pop_heap, sort_heap

queue   Container

Summary
A container adaptor that behaves like a queue (first in, first out).

Synopsis
#include <queue>

template <class T, class Container = deque<T>>
 class queue {

public:

// typedefs

  typedef typename Container::value_type value_type;
  typedef typename Container::size_type size_type;

protected:

  Container c;

public:

```
// Accessors

    bool empty () const { return c.empty; }
    size_type size () const { return c.size; }
    value_type& front () { return c.front; }
    const value_type& front () const { return c.front(); }
    value_type& back () { return c.back; }
    const value_type& back () const { return c.back(); }
    void push (const value_type& x) { c.push_back(x); }
    void pop () { c.pop_back(); }
};

template <class T, class Container>
 bool operator== (const queue<T, Container>& x,
            const queue<T Container>& y)
   { return x.c == y.c; }


template <class T, class Container>
 bool operator< (const queue<T, Container>& x,
            const queue<T, Container>& y)
   { return x.c < y.c; }
```

Description

The *queue* container adaptor lets a container function as a queue. In a queue, items are pushed onto the back of the container and removed from the front. The first items pushed onto the queue are the first items to be popped off of the queue (first in, first out, or "FIFO").

queue can adapt any container that supports the *front()*, *back()*, *push_back()* and *pop_front()* operations. In particular *list* and *deque* can be used.

Caveats

If your compiler does not support default template parameters, you must always provide a container template parameter. For example you would not be able to write:

```
queue<int> var;
```

rather, you would have to write,

```
queue<int, deque<int>> var;
```

Examples

```
#include <queue>
#include <string>
#include <deque>
#include <list>
using namespace std;

int main(void)
```

```
{
    // Make a queue using a deque container
    queue<int, list<int> > q;

    // Push a couple of values on then pop them off
    q.push(1);
    q.push(2);
    cout << q.front() << endl;
    q.pop();
    cout << q.front() << endl;
    q.pop();

    // Make a queue of strings using a deque container
    queue<string,deque<string> > qs;

    // Push on a few strings then pop them back off
    int i;
    for (i = 0; i < 10; i++)
    {
        qs.push(string(i+1,'a'));
        cout << qs.front() << endl;
    }
    for (i = 0; i < 10; i++)
    {
        cout << qs.front() << endl;
        qs.pop();
    }

    return 0;
}
```

Member functions

value_type&
back ();
Returns the item at the back of the queue (the last item pushed into the queue).

const value_type&
back() const;
Returns the item at the back of the queue as a *const value_type*.

bool
empty () const;
Returns *true* if the queue is empty, otherwise *false*.

value_type&
front ();
Returns the item at the front of the queue. This will be the first item pushed onto the queue unless *pop()* has been called since then.

const value_type&
front () const;

Returns the item at the front of the queue as a *const value_type*.

void
pop ();
Removes the item at the front of the queue.

void
push (const value_type& x);
Pushes *x* onto the back of the queue.

size_type
size () const;
Returns the number of elements on the queue.

See also
Containers

random access iterator   Iterator

Summary
An iterator that reads and writes, and provides random access to a container.

Description

Note   For a complete discussion of iterators, see the *Borland C++ Programmer's Guide*, Chapter 19, "Iterators."

Iterators are a generalization of pointers that allow a C++ program to uniformly interact with different data structures. Random access iterators can read and write, and provide random access to the containers they serve. These iterators satisfy the requirements listed in Table 17.12.

Requirements for random-access iterators
The following key pertains to the iterator descriptions listed:

a and *b*	values of type *X*
n	value of *distance* type
u, Distance, tmp, and *m*	identifiers
r	value of type *X&*
t	value of type *T*

The expressions in Table 17.12 must be valid for random access iterators:

Table 17.12 Requirements for random-access iterators

Expression	Requirement
$X\ u$	u might have a singular value
$X()$	$X()$ might be singular
$X(a)$	copy constructor, $a == X(a)$.
$X\ u(a)$	copy constructor, $u == a$
$X\ u = a$	assignment, $u == a$
$a == b, a\ != b$	return value convertible to $bool$
$*a$	return value convertible to $T\&$
$++r$	returns $X\&$
$r++$	return value convertible to const $X\&$
$*r++$	returns $T\&$
$--r$	returns $X\&$
$r--$	return $value$ convertible to $const\ X\&$
$*r--$	returns $T\&$
$r += n$	Semantics of $--r$ or $++r$ n times depending on the sign of n
$a + n, n + a$	returns type X
$r -= n$	returns $X\&$, behaves as $r += -n$
$a - n$	returns type X
$b - a$	returns $Distance$
$a[n]$	$*(a+n)$, return value convertible to T
$a < b$	total ordering relation
$a > b$	total ordering relation opposite to $<$
$a <= b$	$!(a < b)$
$a >= b$	$!(a > b)$

Like forward iterators, random access iterators have the condition that $a == b$ implies $*a== *b$.

There are no restrictions on the number of passes an algorithm may make through the structure.

All relational operators return a value convertible to $bool$.

See also
Iterators, Forward Iterators, Bidirectional Iterators

random_shuffle   **Algorithm**

Summary
Randomly shuffles elements of a collection.

Synopsis

#include <algorithm>

```
template <class RandomAccessIterator>
void random_shuffle (RandomAccessIterator first,
            RandomAccessIterator last);

template <class RandomAccessIterator,
        class RandomNumberGenerator>
void random_shuffle (RandomAccessIterator first,
            RandomAccessIterator last,
            RandomNumberGenerator& rand);
```

Description

The *random_shuffle* algorithm shuffles the elements in the range *[first, last)* with uniform distribution. *random_shuffle* can take a particular random number generating function object *rand* , where *rand* takes a positive argument *n* of distance *type* of the *RandomAccessIterator* and returns a randomly chosen value between *0* and *n - 1*.

Complexity

The *random_shuffle* algorithm *(last - first) -1* swaps are done.

Example

```
#include<algorithm>
#include<vector>
using namespace std;
int main()
{
  //Initialize a vector with an array of ints
  int arr[10] = {1,2,3,4,5,6,7,8,9,10};
  vector<int> v(arr, arr+10);
  //Print out elements in original (sorted) order
  cout << "Elements before random_shuffle: " << endl << "     ";
  copy(v.begin(),v.end(),ostream_iterator<int>(cout," "));
  cout << endl << endl;
  //Mix them up with random_shuffle
  random_shuffle(v.begin(), v.end());
  //Print out the mixed up elements
  cout << "Elements after random_shuffle: " << endl << "     ";
  copy(v.begin(),v.end(),ostream_iterator<int>(cout," "));
  cout << endl;

  return 0;
}
```

raw_storage_iterator

Summary
Enables iterator-based algorithms to store results into uninitialized memory.

Synopsis
#include <memory>

```
template <class OutputIterator, class T>
 class raw_storage_iterator : public output_iterator {

public:
  explicit raw_storage_iterator (OutputIterator x);
  raw_storage_iterator<OutputIterator, t>& operator*();
  raw_storage_iterator<OutputIterator, T>&
    operator= (const T& element);
  raw_storage_iterator<OutputIterator>& operator++();
  raw_storage_iterator<OutputIterator> operator++ (int);
};
```

Description
Class *raw_storage_iterator* enables iterator-based algorithms to store their results in uninitialized memory. The template parameter, *OutputIterator* is required to have its *operator* * return an object for which *operator* & is both defined and returns a pointer to *T*.

Constructor
raw_storage_iterator (OutputIterator x);
Initializes the iterator to point to the same value that x points to.

Member operators
raw_storage_iterator <OutputIterator, T> &
operator =(const T& element);
Constructs an instance of *T*, initialized to the value *element*, at the location pointed to by the iterator.

raw_storage_iterator <OutputIterator, T>&
operator++()
Pre-increment: advances the iterator and returns a reference to the updated iterator.

raw_storage_iterator<OutputIterator>
operator++ (int);
Post-increment: advances the iterator and returns the old value of the iterator.

remove

Algorithm

Summary

Move desired elements to the front of a container, and return an iterator that describes where the sequence of desired elements ends.

Synopsis

```
#include <algorithm>

template <class ForwardIterator, class T>
ForwardIterator
remove (ForwardIterator first,
            ForwardIterator last,
            const T& value);
```

Description

The *remove* algorithm eliminates all the elements referred to by iterator *i* in the range *[first, last)* for which the following condition holds: **i == value*. *remove* returns an iterator that designates the end of the resulting range. *remove* is stable, that is, the relative order of the elements that are not removed is the same as their relative order in the original range.

remove does not actually reduce the size of the sequence. It actually operates by: 1) copying the values that are to be *retained* to the front of the sequence, and 2) returning an iterator that describes where the sequence of retained values ends. Elements that are after this iterator are simply the original sequence values, left unchanged. Here's a simple example:

Say we want to remove all values of "2" from the following sequence:

```
354621271
```

Applying the *remove* algorithm results in the following sequence:

```
3546171|XX
```

The vertical bar represents the position of the iterator returned by *remove*. Note that the elements to the left of the vertical bar are the original sequence with the "2's" removed.

Complexity

Exactly *last1 - first1* applications of the corresponding predicate are done.

Examples

```
#include<algorithm>
#include<vector>
#include<iterator>
using namespace std;

template<class Arg>
struct all_true : public unary_function<Arg, bool>
{
```

```
   bool operator()(const Arg& x){ return 1; }
};

int main ()
{
   int arr[10] = {1,2,3,4,5,6,7,8,9,10};
   vector<int> v(arr, arr+10);

   copy(v.begin(),v.end(),ostream_iterator<int>(cout," "));
   cout << endl << endl;

   // remove the 7
   vector<int>::iterator result =
            remove(v.begin(), v.end(), 7);
   // delete dangling elements from the vector
   v.erase(result, v.end());

   copy(v.begin(),v.end(),ostream_iterator<int>(cout," "));
   cout << endl << endl;

   // remove everything beyond the fourth element
   result = remove_if(v.begin()+4,
                      v.begin()+8, all_true<int>());
   // delete dangling elements
   v.erase(result, v.end());

   copy(v.begin(),v.end(),ostream_iterator<int>(cout," "));
   cout << endl << endl;

   return 0;
}
```

See also
remove_if, remove_copy, remove_copy_if

remove_copy   Algorithm

Summary
Move desired elements to the front of a container, and return an iterator that describes where the sequence of desired elements ends.

Synopsis
#include <algorithm>

template <class InputIterator,
        class OutputIterator,
        class T>
 OutputIterator remove_copy (InputIterator first,

```
                    InputIterator last,
                    OutputIterator result,
                    const T& value);
```

Description

The *remove_copy* algorithm copies all the elements referred to by the iterator *i* in the range *[first, last)* for which the following corresponding condition does *not* hold: **i == value*. *remove_copy* returns the end of the resulting range. *remove_copy* is stable, that is, the relative order of the elements in the resulting range is the same as their relative order in the original range. The elements in the original sequence are not altered by *remove_copy*.

Complexity

Exactly *last1 - first1* applications of the corresponding predicate are done.

Example

```cpp
/***************************************************************
 *
 * remove.cpp - Example program of remove algorithm.
 *
 * $Id: remove.cpp,v 1.9 1995/10/06 20:59:40 hart Exp $
 *
 * $$RW_INSERT_HEADER "slyrs.str"
 *
 ***************************************************************/
#include <algorithm>
#include <vector>
#include <iterator>
using namespace std;

template<class Arg>
struct all_true : public unary_function<Arg, bool>
{
  bool operator() (const Arg&) { return 1; }
};

int main ()
{
  int arr[10] = {1,2,3,4,5,6,7,8,9,10};
  vector<int> v(arr+0, arr+10);

  copy(v.begin(),v.end(),ostream_iterator<int>(cout," "));
  cout << endl << endl;
  //
  // Remove the 7.
  //
  vector<int>::iterator result = remove(v.begin(), v.end(), 7);
  //
  // Delete dangling elements from the vector.
  //
```

```
        v.erase(result, v.end());

        copy(v.begin(),v.end(),ostream_iterator<int>(cout," "));
        cout << endl << endl;
        //
        // Remove everything beyond the fourth element.
        //
        result = remove_if(v.begin()+4, v.begin()+8, all_true<int>());
        //
        // Delete dangling elements.
        //
        v.erase(result, v.end());

        copy(v.begin(),v.end(),ostream_iterator<int>(cout," "));
        cout << endl << endl;
        //
        // Now remove all 3s on output.
        //
        remove_copy(v.begin(), v.end(),
                    ostream_iterator<int>(cout," "), 3);
        cout << endl << endl;
        //
        // Now remove everything satisfying predicate on output.
        // Should yield a NULL vector.
        //
        remove_copy_if(v.begin(), v.end(),
                       ostream_iterator<int>(cout," "),
                     all_true<int>());

    return 0;
}
```

See also
remove, remove_if, remove_copy_if

remove_copy_if   Algorithm

Summary
Move desired elements to the front of a container, and return an iterator that describes where the sequence of desired elements ends.

Synopsis
```
#include <algorithm>

template <class InputIterator,
          class OutputIterator,
          class Predicate>
OutputIterator remove_copy_if (InputIterator first,
```

```
            InputIterator last,
            OutputIterator result,
            Predicate pred);
```

Description

The *remove_copy_if* algorithm copies all the elements referred to by the iterator *i* in the range *[first, last)* for which the following condition does *not* hold: *pred(*i) == true*. *remove_copy_if* returns the end of the resulting range. *remove_copy_if* is stable, that is, the relative order of the elements in the resulting range is the same as their relative order in the original range.

Example

```cpp
/***************************************************************
 *
 * remove.cpp - Example program of remove algorithm.
 *
 * $Id: remove.cpp,v 1.9 1995/10/06 20:59:40 hart Exp $
 *
 * $$RW_INSERT_HEADER "slyrs.str"
 *
 ***************************************************************/
#include <algorithm>
#include <vector>
#include <iterator>
using namespace std;

template<class Arg>
struct all_true : public unary_function<Arg, bool>
{
  bool operator() (const Arg&) { return 1; }
};

int main ()
{
  int arr[10] = {1,2,3,4,5,6,7,8,9,10};
  vector<int> v(arr+0, arr+10);

  copy(v.begin(),v.end(),ostream_iterator<int>(cout," "));
  cout << endl << endl;
  //
  // Remove the 7.
  //
  vector<int>::iterator result = remove(v.begin(), v.end(), 7);
  //
  // Delete dangling elements from the vector.
  //
  v.erase(result, v.end());

  copy(v.begin(),v.end(),ostream_iterator<int>(cout," "));
  cout << endl << endl;
```

```
    //
    // Remove everything beyond the fourth element.
    //
    result = remove_if(v.begin()+4, v.begin()+8, all_true<int>());
    //
    // Delete dangling elements.
    //
    v.erase(result, v.end());

    copy(v.begin(),v.end(),ostream_iterator<int>(cout," "));
    cout << endl << endl;
    //
    // Now remove all 3s on output.
    //
    remove_copy(v.begin(), v.end(),
                ostream_iterator<int>(cout," "), 3);
    cout << endl << endl;
    //
    // Now remove everything satisfying predicate on output.
    // Should yield a NULL vector.
    //
    remove_copy_if(v.begin(), v.end(),
                   ostream_iterator<int>(cout," "),
                   all_true<int>());

    return 0;
}
```

Complexity

Exactly *last1 - first1* applications of the corresponding predicate are done.

See also

remove, remove_if, remove_copy

remove_if   Algorithm

Summary

Move desired elements to the front of a container, and return an iterator that describes where the sequence of desired elements ends.

Synopsis

```
#include <algorithm>

template <class ForwardIterator, class Predicate>
 ForwardIterator remove_if (ForwardIterator first,
                ForwardIterator last,
                Predicate pred);
```

Description

The *remove_if* algorithm eliminates all the elements referred to by iterator *i* in the range *[first, last)* for which the following corresponding condition holds: *pred(*i) == true*. *remove_if* returns the end of the resulting range. *remove_if* is stable, that is, the relative order of the elements that are not removed is the same as their relative order in the original range.

remove_if does not actually reduce the size of the sequence. It actually operates by: 1) copying the values that are to be *retained* to the front of the sequence, and 2) returning an iterator that describes where the sequence of retained values ends. Elements that are after this iterator are simply the original sequence values, left unchanged. Here's a simple example:

Say we want to remove all even numbers from the following sequence:

```
123456789
```

Applying the *remove_if* algorithm results in the following sequence:

```
13579 | XXXX
```

The vertical bar represents the position of the iterator returned by *remove_if*. Note that the elements to the left of the vertical bar are the original sequence with the even numbers removed. The elements to the right of the bar are simply the untouched original members of the original sequence.

Complexity

Exactly *last1 - first1* applications of the corresponding predicate are done.

Examples

```cpp
#include<algorithm>
#include<vector>
#include<iterator>
using namespace std;

template<class Arg>
struct all_true : public unary_function<Arg, bool>
{
  bool operator()(const Arg& x){ return 1; }
};

int main ()
{
  int arr[10] = {1,2,3,4,5,6,7,8,9,10};
  vector<int> v(arr, arr+10);

  copy(v.begin(),v.end(),ostream_iterator<int>(cout," "));
  cout << endl << endl;

  // remove the 7
  vector<int>::iterator result =
          remove(v.begin(), v.end(), 7);
```

```
    // delete dangling elements from the vector
    v.erase(result, v.end());

    copy(v.begin(),v.end(),ostream_iterator<int>(cout," "));
    cout << endl << endl;

    // remove everything beyond the fourth element
    result = remove_if(v.begin()+4,
                       v.begin()+8, all_true<int>());
    // delete dangling elements
    v.erase(result, v.end());

    copy(v.begin(),v.end(),ostream_iterator<int>(cout," "));
    cout << endl << endl;

    return 0;
}
```

See also
remove, remove_copy, remove_copy_if

replace   Algorithm

Summary
Substitutes elements stored in a collection with new values.

Synopsis
#include <algorithm>

template <class ForwardIterator, class T>
void replace (ForwardIterator first,
        ForwardIterator last,
        const T& old_value,
        const T& new_value);

Description
The *replace* algorithm replaces elements referred to by iterator *i* in the range *[first, last)* with *new_value* when the following condition holds: **i == old_value*

Complexity
Exactly *last - first* comparisons or applications of the corresponding predicate are done.

Examples
```
    #include<algorithm>
    #include<vector>
    #include<iterator>
    using namespace std;
```

```
template<class Arg>
struct all_true : public unary_function<Arg, bool>
{
  bool operator()(const Arg&){ return 1; }
};

int main()
{

  //Initialize a vector with an array of integers
  int arr[10] = {1,2,3,4,5,6,7,8,9,10};
  vector<int> v(arr, arr+10);

  //Print out original vector
  cout << "The original list: " << endl << "       ";
  copy(v.begin(),v.end(),ostream_iterator<int>(cout," "));
  cout << endl << endl;

  //Replace the number 7 with 11
  replace(v.begin(), v.end(), 7, 11);

  // Print out vector with 7 replaced,
  // s.b.  1 2 3 4 5 6 11 8 9 10
  cout << "List after replace " << endl << "       ";
  copy(v.begin(),v.end(),ostream_iterator<int>(cout," "));
  cout << endl << endl;

  //Replace 1 2 3 with 13 13 13
  replace_if(v.begin(), v.begin()+3, all_true<int>(), 13);

  // Print out the remaining vector,
  // s.b. 13 13 13 4 5 6 11 8 9 10
  cout << "List after replace_if " << endl << "       ";
  copy(v.begin(),v.end(),ostream_iterator<int>(cout," "));
  cout << endl << endl;

  return 0;
}
```

See also

replace_if, replace_copy, replace_copy_if

replace_copy   Algorithm

Summary

Substitutes elements stored in a collection with new values.

Synopsis

#include <algorithm>

```
template <class InputIterator,
        class OutputIterator,
        class T>
OutputIterator replace_copy (InputIterator first,
                    InputIterator last,
                    OutputIterator result,
                    const T& old_value,
                    const T& new_value);
```

Description

The *replace_copy* algorithm leaves the original sequence intact and places the revised sequence into *result*. The algorithm compares elements referred to by interator *i* in the range *[first, last)* with *old_value*. If **i* does not equal *old_value*, then the *replace_copy* copies **i* to *result+(first-i)*. If **i==old_value*, then *replace_copy* copies *new_value* to *result+(first-i)*. *replace_copy* returns *result+(last-first)*.

Complexity

Exactly *last - first* comparisons between values are done.

Example

```
/*******************************************************
 *
 * replace.cpp - Example program of replace algorithm
 *
 * $Id: replace.cpp,v 1.9 1995/10/06 21:01:02 hart Exp $
 *
 * $$RW_INSERT_HEADER "slyrs.str"
 *
 *******************************************************/
#include <algorithm>
#include <vector>
#include <iterator>
using namespace std;

template<class Arg>
struct all_true : public unary_function<Arg, bool>
{
  bool operator() (const Arg&) { return 1; }
};

int main ()
{
  //
  // Initialize a vector with an array of integers.
  //
  int arr[10] = { 1,2,3,4,5,6,7,8,9,10 };
  vector<int> v(arr+0, arr+10);
  //
```

```
                // Print out original vector.
                //
                cout << "The original list: " << endl << "      ";
                copy(v.begin(), v.end(), ostream_iterator<int>(cout," "));
                cout << endl << endl;
                //
                // Replace the number 7 with 11.
                //
                replace(v.begin(), v.end(), 7, 11);
                //
                // Print out vector with 7 replaced.
                //
                cout << "List after replace:" << endl << "      ";
                copy(v.begin(), v.end(), ostream_iterator<int>(cout," "));
                cout << endl << endl;
                //
                // Replace 1 2 3 with 13 13 13.
                //
                replace_if(v.begin(), v.begin()+3, all_true<int>(), 13);
                //
                // Print out the remaining vector.
                //
                cout << "List after replace_if:" << endl << "      ";
                copy(v.begin(), v.end(), ostream_iterator<int>(cout," "));
                cout << endl << endl;
                //
                // Replace those 13s with 17s on output.
                //
                cout << "List using replace_copy to cout:" << endl << "      ";
                replace_copy(v.begin(), v.end(),
                            ostream_iterator<int>(cout, " "), 13, 17);
                cout << endl << endl;
                //
                // A simple example of replace_copy_if.
                //
                cout << "List w/ all elements output as 19s:" << endl << "      ";
                replace_copy_if(v.begin(), v.end(),
                            ostream_iterator<int>(cout, " "),
                            all_true<int>(), 19);
                cout << endl;

                return 0;
        }
```

See also

replace, replace_if, replace_copy_if

replace_copy_if   **Algorithm**

Summary
Substitutes elements stored in a collection with new values.

Synopsis
```
#include <algorithm>
template <class InputIterator,
        class OutputIterator,
        class Predicate,
        class T>
OutputIterator replace_copy_if (InputIterator first,
                InputIterator last,
                OutputIterator result,
                Predicate pred,
                const T& new_value);
```

Description
The *replace_copy_if* algorithm leaves the original sequence intact and places a revised sequence into *result*. The algorithm compares each element **i* in the range *[first,last)* with the conditions specified by *pred*. If *pred(*i)==false*, *replace_copy_if* copies **i* to *result+(first-i)*. If *pred(*i)==true*, then *replace_copy* copies *new_value* to *result+(first-i)*. *replace_copy_if* returns *result+(last-first)*.

Complexity
Exactly *last - first* applications of the predicate are performed.

Example
```
/*************************************************************
 *
 * replace.cpp - Example program of replace algorithm
 *
 * $Id: replace.cpp,v 1.9 1995/10/06 21:01:02 hart Exp $
 *
 * $$RW_INSERT_HEADER "slyrs.str"
 *
 *************************************************************/
#include <algorithm>
#include <vector>
#include <iterator>
using namespace std;

template<class Arg>
struct all_true : public unary_function<Arg, bool>
{
  bool operator() (const Arg&) { return 1; }
};

int main ()
{
```

```
//
// Initialize a vector with an array of integers.
//
int arr[10] = { 1,2,3,4,5,6,7,8,9,10 };
vector<int> v(arr+0, arr+10);
//
// Print out original vector.
//
cout << "The original list: " << endl << "     ";
copy(v.begin(), v.end(), ostream_iterator<int>(cout," "));
cout << endl << endl;
//
// Replace the number 7 with 11.
//
replace(v.begin(), v.end(), 7, 11);
//
// Print out vector with 7 replaced.
//
cout << "List after replace:" << endl << "     ";
copy(v.begin(), v.end(), ostream_iterator<int>(cout," "));
cout << endl << endl;
//
// Replace 1 2 3 with 13 13 13.
//
replace_if(v.begin(), v.begin()+3, all_true<int>(), 13);
//
// Print out the remaining vector.
//
cout << "List after replace_if:" << endl << "     ";
copy(v.begin(), v.end(), ostream_iterator<int>(cout," "));
cout << endl << endl;
//
// Replace those 13s with 17s on output.
//
cout << "List using replace_copy to cout:" << endl << "     ";
replace_copy(v.begin(), v.end(),
             ostream_iterator<int>(cout, " "), 13, 17);
cout << endl << endl;
//
// A simple example of replace_copy_if.
//
cout << "List w/ all elements output as 19s:" << endl << "   ";
replace_copy_if(v.begin(), v.end(),
                ostream_iterator<int>(cout, " "),
                all_true<int>(), 19);
cout << endl;

return 0;
}
```

See also
replace, replace_if, replace_copy

replace_if   **Algorithm**

Summary
Substitutes elements stored in a collection with new values.

Synopsis
#include <algorithm>

```
template <class ForwardIterator,
        class Predicate,
        class T>
void replace_if (ForwardIterator first,
            ForwardIterator last,
            Predicate pred
            const T& new_value);
```

Description
The *replace_if* algorithm replaces element referred to by iterator *i* in the range *[first, last)* with *new_value* when the following condition holds: *pred(*i) == true*.

Complexity
Exactly *last - first* applications of the predicate are done.

Examples
```
#include<algorithm>
#include<vector>
#include<iterator>
using namespace std;

template<class Arg>
struct all_true : public unary_function<Arg, bool>
{
  bool operator()(const Arg&){ return 1; }
};

int main()
{

  //Initialize a vector with an array of integers
  int arr[10] = {1,2,3,4,5,6,7,8,9,10};
  vector<int> v(arr, arr+10);

  //Print out original vector
  cout << "The original list: " << endl << "     ";
```

```
        copy(v.begin(),v.end(),ostream_iterator<int>(cout," "));
        cout << endl << endl;

        //Replace the number 7 with 11
        replace(v.begin(), v.end(), 7, 11);

        // Print out vector with 7 replaced,
        // s.b. 1 2 3 4 5 6 11 8 9 10
        cout << "List after replace " << endl << "      ";
        copy(v.begin(),v.end(),ostream_iterator<int>(cout," "));
        cout << endl << endl;

        //Replace 1 2 3 with 13 13 13
        replace_if(v.begin(), v.begin()+3, all_true<int>(), 13);

        // Print out the remaining vector,
        // s.b. 13 13 13 4 5 6 11 8 9 10
        cout << "List after replace_if " << endl << "      ";
        copy(v.begin(),v.end(),ostream_iterator<int>(cout," "));
        cout << endl << endl;

        return 0;
    }
```

See also
replace, replace_copy, replace_copy_if

return_temporary_buffer   Memory handling primitive

Summary
Pointer based primitive for handling memory

Synopsis
#include <memory>

template <class T>
  void return_temporary_buffer (T* p, T*);

Description
The *return_temporary_buffer* templated function returns a buffer, previously allocated through *get_temporary_buffer*, to available memory. Parameter *p* points to the buffer.

See also
Other memory handling primitives: *allocate, deallocate, construct, get_temporary_buffer*

reverse

Algorithm

Summary
Reverse the order of elements in a collection.

Synopsis
#include <algorithm>

template <class BidirectionalIterator>
 void reverse (BidirectionalIterator first,
         BidirectionalIterator last);

Description
The algorithm *reverse* reverses the elements in a sequence so that the last element becomes the new first element, and the first element becomes the new last. For each non-negative integer $i <= (last - first)/2$, *reverse* applies *swap* to all pairs of iterators *first + i,(last - i)-1*.

Because the iterators are assumed to be bidirectional, *reverse* does not return anything.

Complexity
reverse performs exactly *(last - first)/2* swaps.

Examples
```
#include<algorithm>
#include<vector>
using namespace std;

int main()
{
  //Initialize a vector with an array of ints
  int arr[10] = {1,2,3,4,5,6,7,8,9,10};
  vector<int> v(arr, arr+10);

  //Print out elements in original (sorted) order
  cout << "Elements before reverse: " << endl << "     ";
  copy(v.begin(),v.end(),ostream_iterator<int>(cout," "));
  cout << endl << endl;

  //Reverse the ordering
  reverse(v.begin(), v.end());

  //Print out the reversed elements
  cout << "Elements after reverse: " << endl << "     ";
  copy(v.begin(),v.end(),ostream_iterator<int>(cout," "));
  cout << endl;

  return 0;
}
```

See also

reverse_copy, swap

reverse_bidirectional_iterator, reverse_iterator   Iterator

An iterator that traverses a collection backwards.

Synopsis

```
#include <iterator>

template <class BidirectionalIterator,
        class T,
        class Reference = T&,
        class Distance = ptrdiff_t>
class reverse_bidirectional_iterator
  : public bidirectional_iterator<T, Distance>  {
 protected:
  BidirectionalIterator current;
 public:
  reverse_bidirectional_iterator ();
  explicit reverse_bidirectional_iterator
    (BidirectionalIterator x);
  BidirectionalIterator base ();
  Reference operator* ();
  reverse_bidirectional_iterator <BidirectionalIterator,
                T,
                Reference,
                Distance> &
   operator++ ();
  reverse_bidirectional_iterator <BidirectionalIterator,
                T,
                Reference,
                Distance>
   operator++ (int);
  reverse_bidirectional_iterator <BidirectionalIterator,
                T,
                Reference,
                Distance> &
   operator-- ();
  reverse_bidirectional_iterator <BidirectionalIterator,
                T,
                Reference,
                Distance>
   operator-- (int);
 };
```

```
template <class BidirectionalIterator,
        class T,
        class Reference,
        class Distance>
bool operator== (
  const reverse_bidirectional_iterator
    <BidirectionalIterator,
    T,
    Reference,
    Distance>& x,
    const reverse_bidirectional_iterator
    <BidirectionalIterator,
    T,
    Reference,
    Distance>& y);


template <class RandomAccessIterator,
        class T,
        class Reference = T&,
        class Distance = ptrdiff_t>
class reverse_iterator
  : public random_access_iterator<T, Distance> {

  protected:
    RandomAccessIterator current;

  public:
    reverse_iterator ();
    explicit reverse_iterator (RandomAccessIterator x);
    RandomAccessIterator base ();
    Reference operator* ();
    reverse_iterator <RandomAccessIterator,
            T,
            Reference,
            Distance> &
      operator++ ();
    reverse_iterator <RandomAccessIterator,
            T,
            Reference,
            Distance>
      operator++ (int);
    reverse_iterator <RandomAccessIterator,
            T,
            Reference,
```

```
                    Distance> &
        operator-- ();
    reverse_iterator <RandomAccessIterator,
                    T,
                    Reference,
                    Distance>
        operator-- (int);

    reverse_iterator <RandomAccessIterator,
                    T,
                    Reference,
                    Distance>
        operator+ (Distance n) const;
    reverse_iterator <RandomAccessIterator,
                    T,
                    Reference,
                    Distance> &
        operator+= (Distance n);
    reverse_iterator <RandomAccessIterator,
                    T,
                    Reference,
                    Distance>
        operator- (Distance n) const;
    reverse_iterator <RandomAccessIterator,
                    T,
                    Reference,
                    Distance> &
        operator-= (Distance n);
    Reference operator[] (Distance n);

    template <class RandomAccessIterator,
            class T,
            class Reference,
            class Distance> bool operator== (
        const reverse_iterator
          <RandomAccessIterator,
           T,
           Reference,
           Distance>& x,
        const reverse_iterator
          <RandomAccessIterator,
           T,
           Reference,
           Distance>& y);
```

```
template <class RandomAccessIterator,
        class T,
        class Reference,
        class Distance> bool operator< (
    const reverse_iterator
      <RandomAccessIterator,
      T,
      Reference,
      Distance>& x,
    const reverse_iterator
      <RandomAccessIterator,
      T,
      Reference,
      Distance>& y);

template <class RandomAccessIterator,
        class T,
        class Reference,
        class Distance> Distance operator- (
    const reverse_iterator
      <RandomAccessIterator,
      T,
      Reference,
      Distance>& x,
    const reverse_iterator
      <RandomAccessIterator,
      T,
      Reference,
      Distance>& y);

template <class RandomAccessIterator,
        class T,
        class Reference,
        class Distance>
reverse_iterator<RandomAccessIterator,
          T,
          Reference,
          Distance> operator+ (
    Distance n,
    const reverse_iterator
      <RandomAccessIterator,
      T,
      Reference,
      Distance>& x);
};
```

Description

The iterators *reverse_iterator* and *reverse_bidirectional_iterator* correspond to *random_access_iterator* and *bidirectional_iterator*, except they traverse the collection they point to in the opposite direction. The fundamental relation between a reverse iterator and its corresponding iterator *i* is established by the identity:

```
&*(reverse_iterator(i)) == &*(i-1);
```

This mapping is dictated by the fact that, while there is always a pointer past the end of a container, there might not be a valid pointer before its beginning.

The following are true for *reverse_bidirectional_iterators* :

- These iterators may be instantiated with the default constructor or by a single argument constructor that initializes the new *reverse_bidirectional_iterator* with a *bidirectional_iterator*.

- *operator** returns a reference to the current value pointed to.

- *operator++* advances the iterator to the previous item (*--current*) and returns a reference to **this*.

- *operator++(int)* advances the iterator to the previous item (*--current*) and returns the old value of **this*.

- *operator--* advances the iterator to the following item (*++current*) and returns a reference to **this*.

- *operator--(int)* Advances the iterator to the following item (*++current*) and returns the old value of **this*.

- *operator==* This non-member operator returns *true* if theiterators *x* and *y* point to the same item.

The following are true for *reverse__iterators* :

- These iterators may be instantiated with the default constructor or by a single argument constructor which initializes the new *reverse_iterator* with a *random_access_iterator*.

- *operator** returns a reference to the current value pointed to.

- *operator++* advances the iterator to the previous item (*--current*) and returns a reference to **this*.

- *operator++(int)* advances the iterator to the previous item (*--current*) and returns the old value of **this*.

- *operator--* advances the iterator to the following item (*++current*) and returns a reference to **this*.

- *operator--(int)* advances the iterator to the following item (*++current*) and returns the old value of **this*.

- *operator==* is a non-member operator returns *true* if the iterators *x* and *y* point to the same item.

- The remaining operators (<, +, - , +=, -=) are redefined to behave exactly as they would in a *random_access_iterator*, except with the sense of direction reversed.

Complexity
All iterator operations are required to take at most amortized constant time.

Example
```
#include<iterator>
#include<vector>
using namespace std;

int main()
{
  //Initialize a vector using an array
  int arr[4] = {3,4,7,8};
  vector<int> v(arr,arr+4);

  //Output the original vector
  cout << "Traversing vector with iterator: " << endl << "      ";
  for(vector<int>::iterator i = v.begin(); i != v.end(); i++)
    cout << *i << " ";

  //Declare the reverse_iterator
  vector<int>::reverse_iterator rev(v.end());
  vector<int>::reverse_iterator rev_end(v.begin());

  //Output the vector backwards
  cout << endl << endl;
  cout << "Same vector, same loop, reverse_itertor: " << endl
       << "      ";
  for(; rev != rev_end; rev++)
    cout << *rev << " ";

  return 0;
}
```

See also
iterators

reverse_copy   Algorithm

Summary
Reverse the order of elements in a collection while copying them to a new collecton.

Synopsis
#include <algorithm>

template <class BidirectionalIterator, class OutputIterator>

```
OutputIterator reverse_copy (BidirectionalIterator first,
                             BidirectionalIterator last,
                             OutputIterator result);
```

Description

The *reverse_copy* algorithm copies the range *[first, last)* to the range *[result, result + (last - first))* such that for any non- negative integer *i < (last - first)*, the following assignment takes place:

```
*(result + (last - first) -i) = *(first + i)
```

reverse_copy returns *result + (last - first)*. The ranges *[first, last)* and *[result, result + (last - first))* must not overlap.

Complexity

reverse_copy performs exactly *(last - first)* assignments.

Example

```cpp
/****************************************************************
 *
 * reverse.cpp - Example program reverse algorithm.
 *               See Class Reference Section
 *
 * $Id: reverse.cpp,v 1.7 1995/10/06 19:35:37 hart Exp $
 *
 * $$RW_INSERT_HEADER "slyrs.str"
 *
 ****************************************************************/
#include <algorithm>
#include <vector>
using namespace std;

int main ()
{
  //
  // Initialize a vector with an array of integers.
  //
  int arr[10] = { 1,2,3,4,5,6,7,8,9,10 };
  vector<int> v(arr+0, arr+10);
  //
  // Print out elements in original (sorted) order.
  //
  cout << "Elements before reverse: " << endl << "    ";
  copy(v.begin(), v.end(), ostream_iterator<int>(cout," "));
  cout << endl << endl;
  //
  // Reverse the ordering.
  //
  reverse(v.begin(), v.end());
  //
```

```
// Print out the reversed elements.
//
cout << "Elements after reverse: " << endl << "      ";
copy(v.begin(), v.end(), ostream_iterator<int>(cout," "));
cout << endl << endl;

cout << "A reverse_copy to cout: " << endl << "      ";
reverse_copy(v.begin(), v.end(),
              ostream_iterator<int>(cout, " "));
cout << endl;

return 0;
}
```

See also
reverse

reverse_iterator

See the *reverse_bidirectional_iterator* section of this chapter.

rotate, rotate_copy   **Algorithm**

Summary
Left rotates the order of items in a collection, placing the first item at the end, second item first, etc., until the item pointed to by a specified iterator is the first item in the collection.

Synopsis
#include <algorithm>

template <class ForwardIterator>
void rotate (ForwardIterator first,
        ForwardIterator middle,
        ForwardIterator last);

template <class ForwardIterator, class OutputIterator>
OutputIterator rotate_copy (ForwardIterator first,
                ForwardIterator middle,
                ForwardIterator last,
                OutputIterator result);

Description
The *rotate* algorithm takes three iterator arguments, *first*, which defines the start of a sequence, *last*, which defines the end of the sequence, and *middle* which defines a point

within the sequence. *rotate* "swaps" the segment that contains elements from *first* through *middle-1* with the segment that contains the elements from *middle* through *last*. After *rotate* has applied, the element that was in position *middle*, is in position *first*, and the other elements in that segment are in the same order relative to each other. Similarly, the element that was in position *first* is now in position *last-middle +1*. An example will illustrate how *rotate* works:

Say that we have the sequence:

   2 4 6 8 1 3 5

If we call *rotate* with *middle=5*, the two segments are

   2 4 6 8 and 1 3 5

After we apply rotate, the new sequence will be:

   1 3 5 2 4 6 8

Note that the element that was in the fifth position is now in the first position, and the element that was in the first position is in position 4 (*last - first +1*, or 8 - 5 +1 =4).

The formal description of this algorithms is: for each non-negative integer *i < (last - first)*, *rotate* places the element from the position *first + i* into position *first + (i + (last - middle)) % (last - first)*. *[first, middle)* and *[middle, last)* are valid ranges.

rotate_copy rotates the elements as described above, but instead of swapping elements within the same sequence, it copies the result of the rotation to a container specified by *result*. *rotate_copy* copies the range *[first, last)* to the range *[result, result + (last - first))* such that for each non- negative integer *i < (last - first)* the following assignment takes place:

```
*(result + (i + (last - middle)) % (last -first)) = *(first + i).
```

The ranges *[first, last)* and *[result, result, + (last - first))* may not overlap.

Complexity

For *rotate* at most *last - first* swaps are performed.

For *rotate_copy* *last - first* assignments are performed.

Examples

```
#include<algorithm>
#include<vector>
using namespace std;

int main()
{
  //Initialize a vector with an array of ints
  int arr[10] = {1,2,3,4,5,6,7,8,9,10};
  vector<int> v(arr, arr+10);

  //Print out elements in original (sorted) order
  cout << "Elements before rotate: " << endl << "     ";
```

```
    copy(v.begin(),v.end(),ostream_iterator<int>(cout," "));
    cout << endl << endl;

    //Rotate the elements
    rotate(v.begin(), v.begin()+4, v.end());

    //Print out the rotated elements
    cout << "Elements after rotate: " << endl << "      ";
    copy(v.begin(),v.end(),ostream_iterator<int>(cout," "));
    cout << endl;

    return 0;
}
```

search Algorithm

Summary
Finds a subsequence within a sequence of values that is element-wise equal to the values in an indicated range.

Synopsis
#include <algorithm>

template <class ForwardIterator1, class ForwardIterator2>
ForwardIterator1 search (ForwardIterator1 first1,
            ForwardIterator1 last1,
            ForwardIterator2 first2,
            ForwardIterator2 last2);

template <class ForwardIterator1,
      class ForwardIterator2,
      class BinaryPredicate>
ForwardIterator1 search (ForwardIterator1 first1,
            ForwardIterator1 last1,
            ForwardIterator2 first2,
            ForwardIterator2 last2,
            BinaryPredicate binary_pred);

Description
The *search* algorithm searches for a subsequence (*first2, last2*) within a sequence (*first1, last1*), and returns the beginning location of the subsequence. If it does not find the subsequence, *search* returns *last1*. The first version of *search* uses the equality (==) operator as a default, and the second version allows you to specify a binary predicate to perform the comparison.

Complexity

search performs at most *(last1 - first1)**(last2-first2) applications of the corresponding predicate.

Examples

```
#include<algorithm>
#include<list>
using namespace std;

int main()
{
  // Initialize a list sequence and
  // subsequence with characters
  char seq[40] = "Here's a string with a substring in it";
  char subseq[10] = "substring";
  list<char> sequence(seq, seq+39);
  list<char> subseqnc(subseq, subseq+9);

  //Print out the original sequence
  cout << endl << "The subsequence, " << subseq
       << ", was found at the ";
  cout << endl << "location identified by a '*'"
       << endl << "      ";

  // Create an iterator to identify the location of
  // subsequence within sequence
  list<char>::iterator place;

  //Do search
  place = search(sequence.begin(), sequence.end(),
                 subseqnc.begin(), subseqnc.end());

  //Identify result by marking first character with a '*'
  *place = '*';

  //Output sequence to display result
  for(list<char>::iterator i = sequence.begin();
          i != sequence.end(); i++)
    cout << *i;
  cout << endl;

  return 0;
}
```

Sequence

Summary

A *sequence* is a container that organizes a set of objects, all the same type, into a linear arrangement. . *vector*, *list*, *deque*, and *string* fall into this category.

Sequences offer different complexity trade-offs. *vector* offers fast inserts and deletes from the end of the container. *deque* is useful when insertions and deletions will take place at the beginning or end of the sequence. Use *list* when there are frequent insertions and deletions from the middle of the sequence.

See also

For more information about sequences and their requirements, see C++ *Programmer's Guide*, Chapter 21, "Container classes," or see the section on the specific container.

set   Container

Summary

An associative container that supports unique keys. A *set* supports bidirectional iterators.

Synopsis
```
#include <set>

template <class Key, class Compare = less<Key>>
 class set {

public:

// types

  typedef Key key_type;
  typedef Key value_type;
  typedef typename reference;
  typedef typename const_reference;
  typedef Compare key_compare;
  typedef Compare value_compare;
  typedef typename iterator;
  typedef typename const_iterator;
  typedef typename size_type;
  typedef difference_type;
  typedef reverse_iterator<iterator, value_type,
      reference, difference_type> reverse_iterator;
  typedef const_reverse_iterator<const_iterator,
      value_type, reference  difference_type>
      const_reverse_iterator;

// Construct/Copy/Destroy

  explicit set (const Compare& = Compare());
```

```
        template <class InputIterator>
         set (InputIterator, InputIterator, const Compare& = Compare());
        set (const set<Key, Compare>&);
        ~set ();
        set<Key, Compare>& operator= (const set Key, Compare>&);

    // Iterators

        iterator begin () const;
        iterator end () const;
        reverse_iterator rbegin ();
        reverse_iterator rend ();

    // Capacity

        bool empty () const;

        size_type size () const;
        size_type max_size () const;

    // Modifiers

        pair<iterator, bool> insert (const value_type&);
        iterator insert (iterator, const value_type&);
        template <class InputIterator>
         void insert (iterator, InputIterator, InputIterator);
        void erase (iterator);
        size_type erase (const key_type&);
        void erase (iterator, iterator);
        void swap (set<Key, Compare>&);

    // Observers

        key_compare key_comp () const;
        value_compare value_comp () const;

    // Set operations

        size_type count (const key_type&) const;
        pair<iterator, iterator> equal_range (const  key_type&) const;
        iterator find (const key_value&) const;
        iterator lower_bound (const key_type&) const;
        iterator upper_bound (const key_type&) const

    };
```

// Comparison

```
template <class Key, class Compare>
 bool operator== (const set<Key, Compare>& x,
          const set <Key,Compare>& y);


template <class Key, class Compare>
 bool operator< (const set <Key, Compare>& x,
          const set <Key, Compare>& y);
```

Description

set<T,Compare> is a kind of associative container that supports unique keys and provides for fast retrieval of the keys. A set contains at most one of any key value. The keys are sorted using *Compare*.

Since a set maintains a total order on its elements, you cannot alter the key values directly. Instead, you must insert new elements with an *insert_iterator*.

Any type used for the template parameter *Key* must provide the following (where *T* is the *type*, *t* is a *value* of *T* and *u* is a *const value* of *T*):

```
Copy constructors    T(t) and T(u)
Destructor           t.~T()
Address of           &t and &u yeilding T* and
                     const T* respectively
Assignment           t = a where a is a
                     (possibly const) value of T
```

The *type* used for the *Compare* template parameter must satisfy the requirements for binary functions.

Caveats

Member function templates are used in all containers provided by the Standard Template Library. An example of this feature is the constructor for set *<Key,Compare>* that takestwo templated iterators:

```
template <class InputIterator>
 set (InputIterator, InputIterator);
```

set also has an insert function of this type. These functions, when not restricted by compiler limitations, allow you to use any type of input iterator as arguments. For compilers that do not support this feature we provide substitute functions that allow you to use an iterator obtained from the same type of container as the one you are constructing (or calling a member function on), or you can use a pointer to the type of element you have in the container.

For example, if your compiler does not support member function templates you can construct a set in the following two ways:

```
int intarray[10];
set<int,less<int> > first_set(intarray,intarray + 10);
set<int, less<int> >
second_set(first_set.begin(),first_set.end());
```

but not this way:

```
set<long, less<long> >
long_set(first_set.begin(),first_set.end());
```

since the *long_se*t and *first_set* are not the same type.

Also, many compilers do not support default template arguments. If your compiler is one of these you need to always supply the *Compare* template argument.

Examples

```
#include <set>

typedef set<double,less<double> > set_type;

ostream& operator<<(ostream& out, const set_type& s)
{
  copy(s.begin(), s.end(),
       ostream_iterator<set_type::value_type>(cout," "));
  return out;
}

int main(void)
{
  // create a set of double's, and one of int's
  set_type    sd;
  int         i;

  for(i = 0; i < 10; ++i) {
    // insert values
    sd.insert(i);
  }

  // print out the set
  cout << sd << endl << endl;

  // now let's erase half of the elements in the set
  int      half = sd.size() >> 1;
  set_type::iterator sdi = sd.begin();
  advance(sdi,half);

  sd.erase(sd.begin(),sdi);

  // print it out again
  cout << sd << endl << endl;

  // Make another set and an empty result set
  set_type sd2, sdResult;
```

```
    for (i = 1; i < 9; i++)
        sd2.insert(i+5);
    cout << sd2 << endl;

    // Try a couple of set algorithms
    set_union(sd.begin(),sd.end(),sd2.begin(),sd2.end(),
            inserter(sdResult,sdResult.begin()));
    cout << "Union:" << endl << sdResult << endl;

    sdResult.erase(sdResult.begin(),sdResult.end());
    set_intersection(sd.begin(),sd.end(),
            sd2.begin(),sd2.end(),
            inserter(sdResult,sdResult.begin()));
    cout << "Intersection:" << endl << sdResult << endl;

    return 0;
}
```

Constructors and destructors

explicit
set (const Compare& comp = Compare());

The default constructor. Creates a set of zero elements. If the function object *comp* is supplied, it is used to compare elements of the set. Otherwise, the default function object in the template argument is used. The template argument defaults to *less (<)*.

template <class InputIterator>
set (InputIterator first, InputIterator last, const Compare& comp = Compare ());

Creates a set of length *last - first*, filled with all values obtained by dereferencing the *InputIterators* on the range *[first, last)*. If the function object *comp* is supplied, it is used to compare elements of the set. Otherwise, the default function object in the template argument is used. The template argument defaults to *less (<)*.

set (const set<Key, Compare>& x);

Copy constructor. Creates a copy of *x*.

~set ();

The destructor. Releases any allocated memory for self.

Assignment operator

set<Key, Compare>&
operator= (const set Key, Compare>& x);

Assignment operator. Self will share an implementation with *x*. Returns a reference to self.

Iterators

iterator **begin** ();

Returns an iterator that points to the first element in self.

const_iterator **begin** () const;

Returns a *const_iterator* that points to the first element in self.

iterator **end** ();

Returns an iterator that points to the past-the-end value.

const_iterator **end** () const;

Returns a *const_iterator* that points to the past-the-end value.

reverse_iterator **rbegin** ();

Returns a *reverse_iterator* that points to the past-the-end value.

const_reverse_iterator **rbegin** () const;

Returns a *const_reverse_iterator* that points to the past-the-end value.

reverse_iterator **rend** ();

Returns a *reverse_iterator* that points to the first element.

const_reverse_iterator **rend** () const;

Returns a *const_reverse_iterator* that points to the first element.

Public Member functions

size_type
count (const key_type& x) const;

Returns the number of elements equal to x. Since a set supports unique keys, *count* will always return 1 or 0.

bool
empty () const;

Returns *true* if the size is zero.

pair<iterator, iterator>
equal_range (const key_type& x) const;

Returns *pair<lower_bound(),upper_bound()>*. The *equal_range* function indicates the valid range for insertion of x into the set.

void
erase (iterator position);

Removes the element pointed to by *position*.

size_type
erase (const key_type& x);

Removes all the elements matching x. Returns the number of elements erased. Since a set supports unique keys, *erase* will always return 1.

void
erase (iterator first, iterator last);

Removes the elements in the range *[first, last)*.

iterator
find (const key_value& x) const;

Returns an iterator that points to the element equal to x. If there is no such element, the iterator points to the past-the-end value.

pair<iterator, bool>
insert (const value_type& x);

Inserts *x* in self according to the comparison function object. The template's default comparison function object is *less (<)*.

iterator
insert (iterator position, const value_type& x);

The return value points to the inserted *x*.

template <class InputIterator>
void
insert(InputIterator first, InputIterator last);

Inserts copies of the elements in the range *[first, last]*.

key_compare
key_comp () const;

Returns the comparison function object for the set.

iterator
lower_bound (const key_type& x) const;

Returns an iterator that points to the first element that is greater than or equal to *x*. If there is no such element, the iterator points to the past-the-end value.

size_type
max_size () const;

Returns *size ()* of the largest possible set.

size_type
size () const;

Returns the number of elements.

void
swap (set<Key, Compare>& x);

Exchanges self with *x*.

iterator
upper_bound (const key_type& x) const

Returns an iterator that points to the first element that is greater than *x*. If there is no such element, the iterator points to the past-the-end value.

value_compare
value_comp () const;

Returns the set's comparison object.

Global operators

template <class Key, class Compare>
 bool operator== (const set<Key, Compare>& x,
        const set<Key, Compare>& y);

Equality operator. Returns *true* if *x* is the same as *y*.

template <class Key, class Compare>

```
bool operator< (const set <Key, Compare>& x,
        const set <Key, Compare>& y);
```

Returns true if the elements contained in *x* are lexicographically less than the elements contained in *y*.

See also

container, lexicographical_compare, allocator, bidirectional_iterator

set_difference   Algorithm

Summary

Basic set operation for sorted sequences.

Synopsis

```
#include <algorithm>

template <class InputIterator1, class InputIterator2,
        class OutputIterator>
OutputIterator
set_difference (InputIterator1 first1, InputIterator1 last1,
        InputIterator2 first2, InputIterator2 last2,
        OutputIterator result);

template <class InputIterator1, class InputIterator2,
        class OutputIterator, class Compare>
OutputIterator
set_difference (InputIterator1 first1, InputIterator1 last1,
        InputIterator2 first2, InputIterator2 last2,
        OutputIterator result, Compare comp);
```

Description

The *set_difference* algorithm constructs a sorted difference that includes copies of the elements that are present in the range *[first1, last1)* but are not present in the range *[first2, last2)*. It returns the end of the constructed range.

As an example, assume we have the following two sets:

    1 2 3 4 5

and

    3 4 5 6 7

The result of applying *set_difference* is the set:

    1 2

The result of *set_difference* is undefined if the result range overlaps with either of the original ranges.

set_difference assumes that the ranges are sorted using the default comparision operator less than (<), unless an alternative comparison operator (*comp*) is provided.

Use the *set_symetric_difference* algorithm to return a result that contains all elements that are not in common between the two sets.

Complexity
At most *((last1 - first1) + (last2 - first2)) * 2 -1* comparisons are performed.

Examples
```
#include<algorithm>
#include<set>
using namespace std;

int main()
{

  //Initialize some sets
  int a1[10] = {1,2,3,4,5,6,7,8,9,10};
  int a2[6]  = {2,4,6,8,10,12};

  set<int, less<int> > all(a1, a1+10), even(a2, a2+6),
                       odd;

  //Create an insert_iterator for odd
  insert_iterator<set<int, less<int> > >
                  odd_ins(odd, odd.begin());

  //Demonstrate set_difference
  cout << "The result of:" << endl << "{";
  copy(all.begin(),all.end(),
      ostream_iterator<int>(cout," "));
  cout << "} - {";
  copy(even.begin(),even.end(),
      ostream_iterator<int>(cout," "));
  cout << "} =" << endl << "{";
  set_difference(all.begin(), all.end(),
                 even.begin(), even.end(), odd_ins);
  copy(odd.begin(),odd.end(),
      ostream_iterator<int>(cout," "));
  cout << "}" << endl << endl;

  return 0;
}
```

See also
The other set operations:

includes, set_union, set_intersection, set_symmetric_difference

set_intersection   Algorithm

Summary
Basic set operation for sorted sequences.

Synopsis
```
#include <algorithm>

template <class InputIterator1, class InputIterator2,
        class OutputIterator>
OutputIterator
set_intersection (InputIterator1 first1, InputIterator1 last1,
            InputIterator2 first2, InputIterator last2,
            OutputIterator result);


template <class InputIterator1, class InputIterator2,
        class OutputIterator, class Compare>
 OutputIterator
set_intersection (InputIterator1 first1, InputIterator1 last1,
            InputIterator2 first2, InputIterator2 last2,
            OutputIterator result, Compare comp);
```

Description
The *set_intersection* algorithm constructs a sorted intersection of elements from the two ranges. It returns the end of the constructed range. When it finds an element present in both ranges, *set_intersection* always copies the element from the first range into *result*. This means that the result of *set_intersection* is guaranteed to be stable. The result of *set_intersection* is undefined if the result range overlaps with either of the original ranges.

set_intersection assumes that the ranges are sorted using the default comparision operator less than (<), unless an alternative comparison operator (*comp*) is provided.

Complexity
At most *((last1 - first1) + (last2 - first2)) * 2 -1* comparisons are performed.

Examples
```
#include<algorithm>
#include<set>
using namespace std;

int main()
{

    //Initialize some sets
    int a1[10] = {1,3,5,7,9,11};
    int a3[4]  = {3,5,7,8};
    set<int, less<int> > odd(a1, a1+6),
```

```
                        result, small(a3,a3+4);

        //Create an insert_iterator for result
        insert_iterator<set<int, less<int> > >
                    res_ins(result, result.begin());

        //Demonstrate set_intersection
        cout << "The result of:" << endl << "{";
        copy(small.begin(),small.end(),
            ostream_iterator<int>(cout," "));
        cout << "} intersection {";
        copy(odd.begin(),odd.end(),
            ostream_iterator<int>(cout," "));
        cout << "} =" << endl << "{";
        set_intersection(small.begin(), small.end(),
                    odd.begin(), odd.end(), res_ins);
        copy(result.begin(),result.end(),
        .    ostream_iterator<int>(cout," "));
        cout << "}" << endl << endl;

        return 0;
    }
```

See also
The other set operations: *includes, set_union, set_difference, set_symmetric_difference*

set_symmetric_difference   Algorithm

Summary
Basic set operation for sorted sequences.

Synopsis
#include <algorithm>

template <class InputIterator1, class InputIterator2,
      class OutputIterator>
OutputIterator
set_symmetric_difference (InputIterator1 first1,
                InputIterator1 last1,
                InputIterator2 first2,
                InputIterator2 last2,
                OutputIterator result);

template <class InputIterator1, class InputIterator2,
      class OutputIterator, class Compare>
OutputIterator
set_symmetric_difference (InputIterator1 first1,

```
            InputIterator1 last1,
            InputIterator2 first2,
            InputIterator2 last2,
            OutputIterator result, Compare comp);
```

Description

set_symmetric_difference constructs a sorted symmetric difference of the elements from the two ranges. This means that the constructed range includes copies of the elements that are present in the range *[first1, last1)* but not present in the range *[first2, last2)and* copies of the elements that are present in the range *[first2, last2)* but not in the range *[first1, last1)*. It returns the end of the constructed range.

For example, suppose we have two sets:

1 2 3 4 5

and

3 4 5 6 7

The *set_symmetric_difference* of these two sets is:

1 2 6 7

The result of *set_symmetric_difference* is undefined if the result range overlaps with either of the original ranges.

set_symmetric_difference assumes that the ranges are sorted using the default comparision operator less than (<), unless an alternative comparison operator (*comp*) is provided.

Use the *set_symmetric_difference* algorithm to return a result that includes elements that are present in the first set and not in the second.

Complexity

At most ((*last1* - *first1*) + (*last2* - *first2*)) * 2 -1 comparisons are performed.

Examples

```
#include<algorithm>
#include<set>

int main()
{

  //Initialize some sets
  int a1[] = {1,3,5,7,9,11};
  int a3[] = {3,5,7,8};
  set<int, less<int> > odd(a1,a1+6), result,
                       small(a3,a3+4);

  //Create an insert_iterator for result
  insert_iterator<set<int, less<int> > >
            res_ins(result, result.begin());
```

```
//Demonstrate set_symmetric_difference
cout << "The symmetric difference of:" << endl << "{";
copy(small.begin(),small.end(),
    ostream_iterator<int>(cout," "));
cout << "} with {";
copy(odd.begin(),odd.end(),
    ostream_iterator<int>(cout," "));
cout << "} =" << endl << "{";
set_symmetric_difference(small.begin(), small.end(),
                    odd.begin(), odd.end(), res_ins);
copy(result.begin(),result.end(),
    ostream_iterator<int>(cout," "));
cout << "}" << endl << endl;

    return 0;
}
```

See also
The other set operations: *includes*, *set_union*, *set_intersection*, *set_difference*

set_union
Algorithm

Summary
Basic set operation for sorted sequences.

Synopsis
#include <algorithm>

template <class InputIterator1, class InputIterator2, class OutputIterator>
OutputIterator
set_union (InputIterator1 first1, InputIterator1 last1,
        InputIterator2 first2, InputIterator2 last2,
        OutputIterator result);

template <class InputIterator1, class InputIterator2,
        class OutputIterator, class Compare>
OutputIterator
set_union (InputIterator1 first1, InputIterator1 last1,
        InputIterator2 first2, InputIterator2 last2,
        OutputIterator result, Compare comp);

Description
The *set_union* algorithm constructs a sorted union of the elements from the two ranges. It returns the end of the constructed range. *set_union* is stable, that is, if an element is present in both ranges, the one from the first range is copied. The result of of *set_union* is

undefined if the result range overlaps with either of the original ranges. Note that *set_union* does not merge the two sorted sequences. If an element is present in both sequences, only the element from the first sequence is copied to *result*. (Use the *merge* algorithm to create an ordered merge of two sorted sequences that contains all the elements from both sequences.)

set_union assumes that the sequences are sorted using the default comparision operator less than (<), unless an alternative comparison operator (*comp*) is provided.

Complexity
At most *((last1 - first1) + (last2 - first2)) * 2 -1* comparisons are performed.

Examples

```
#include<algorithm>
#include<set>
using namespace std;

int main()
{

  //Initialize some sets
  int a2[6]  = {2,4,6,8,10,12};
  int a3[4]  = {3,5,7,8};
  set<int, less<int> > even(a2, a2+6),
                       result, small(a3,a3+4);

  //Create an insert_iterator for result
  insert_iterator<set<int, less<int> > >
               res_ins(result, result.begin());

  //Demonstrate set_union
  cout << "The result of:" << endl << "{";
  copy(small.begin(),small.end(),
       ostream_iterator<int>(cout," "));
  cout << "} union {";
  copy(even.begin(),even.end(),
       ostream_iterator<int>(cout," "));
  cout << "} =" << endl << "{";
  set_union(small.begin(), small.end(),
            even.begin(), even.end(), res_ins);
  copy(result.begin(),result.end(),
       ostream_iterator<int>(cout," "));
  cout << "}" << endl << endl;

  return 0;
}
```

See also
merge, and the other set operations: *includes, set_intersection, set_difference, set_symmetric_difference*

sort

Summary
Templated algorithm for sorting collections of entities.

Synopsis
#include <algorithm>

```
template <class RandomAccessIterator>
 void sort (RandomAccessIterator first,
       RandomAccessIterator last);

template <class RandomAccessIterator, class Compare>
 void sort (RandomAccessIterator first,
       RandomAccessIterator last, Compare comp);
```

Description
The *sort* algorithm sorts the elements in the range *[first, last)* using either the less than (<) operator or the comparison operator *comp*. If the worst case behavior is important *stable_sort* or *partial_sort* should be used.

Complexity
sort performs approximately *NlogN*, where *N* equals *last - first*, comparisons on the average.

Examples
```
#include <vector>
#include <algorithm>
#include <functional>
using namespace std;

struct associate
{
  int num;
  char chr;

  associate(int n, char c) : num(n), chr(c){};
  associate() : num(0), chr('\0'){};
};

bool operator<(const associate &x, const associate &y)
{
  return x.num < y.num;
}

ostream& operator<<(ostream &s, const associate &x)
{
  return s << "<" << x.num << ";" << x.chr << ">";
}
```

```
int main ()
{
  vector<associate>::iterator i, j, k;

  associate arr[20] =
        {associate(-4, ' '), associate(16, ' '),
         associate(17, ' '), associate(-3, 's'),
         associate(14, ' '), associate(-6, ' '),
         associate(-1, ' '), associate(-3, 't'),
         associate(23, ' '), associate(-3, 'a'),
         associate(-2, ' '), associate(-7, ' '),
         associate(-3, 'b'), associate(-8, ' '),
         associate(11, ' '), associate(-3, 'l'),
         associate(15, ' '), associate(-5, ' '),
         associate(-3, 'e'), associate(15, ' ')};

  // Set up vectors
  vector<associate> v(arr, arr+20), v1((size_t)20),
             v2((size_t)20);

  // Copy original vector to vectors #1 and #2
  copy(v.begin(), v.end(), v1.begin());
  copy(v.begin(), v.end(), v2.begin());

  // Sort vector #1
  sort(v1.begin(), v1.end());

  // Stable sort vector #2
  stable_sort(v2.begin(), v2.end());

  // Display the results
  cout << "Original    sort      stable_sort" << endl;
  for(i = v.begin(), j = v1.begin(), k = v2.begin();
    i != v.end(); i++, j++, k++)
  cout << *i << "      " << *j << "      " << *k << endl;

  return 0;
}
```

See also
stable_sort, partial_sort, partial_sort_copy

sort_heap   Algorithm

Summary
Converts a heap into a sorted collection.

Synopsis

```
#include <algorithm>
template <class RandomAccessIterator>
  void
  sort_heap(RandomAccessIterator first,
        RandomAccessIterator last);

template <class RandomAccessIterator, class Compare>
  void
  sort_heap(RandomAccessIterator first,
        RandomAccessIterator last, Compare comp);
```

Description

A heap is a particular organization of elements in a range between two random access iterators *[a, b)*. Its two key properties are:

- **a* is the largest element in the range.

- **a* may be removed by *pop_heap()*, or a new element added by *push_heap()*, in *O(logN)* time.

These properties make heaps useful as priority queues.

The *sort_heap* algorithm converts a heap into a sorted collection over the range *[first, last)*using either the default operator (<) or the comparison function supplied with the algorithm. Note that *sort_heap* is not stable, i.e., the elements may not be in the same relative order after *sort_heap* is applied.

Complexity

sort_heap performs at most *NlogN* comparisons where *N* is equal to *last - first*.

Examples

```
#include <algorithm>
#include <vector>
using namespace std;

int main(void)
{
  int d1[4] = {1,2,3,4};
  int d2[4] = {1,3,2,4};

  // Set up two vectors
  vector<int> v1(d1,d1 + 4), v2(d2,d2 + 4);

  // Make heaps
  make_heap(v1.begin(),v1.end());
  make_heap(v2.begin(),v2.end(),less<int>());
  // v1 = (4,x,y,z)   and   v2 = (4,x,y,z)
  // Note that x, y and z represent the remaining
  // values in the container (other than 4).
```

```
                    // The definition of the heap and heap operations
                    // does not require any particular ordering
                    // of these values.

                    // Copy both vectors to cout
                    ostream_iterator<int> out(cout," ");
                    copy(v1.begin(),v1.end(),out);
                    cout << endl;
                    copy(v2.begin(),v2.end(),out);
                    cout << endl;

                    // Now let's pop
                    pop_heap(v1.begin(),v1.end());
                    pop_heap(v2.begin(),v2.end(),less<int>());
                    // v1 = (3,x,y,4) and v2 = (3,x,y,4)

                    // Copy both vectors to cout
                    copy(v1.begin(),v1.end(),out);
                    cout << endl;
                    copy(v2.begin(),v2.end(),out);
                    cout << endl;

                    // And push
                    push_heap(v1.begin(),v1.end());
                    push_heap(v2.begin(),v2.end(),less<int>());
                    // v1 = (4,x,y,z) and v2 = (4,x,y,z)

                    // Copy both vectors to cout
                    copy(v1.begin(),v1.end(),out);
                    cout << endl;
                    copy(v2.begin(),v2.end(),out);
                    cout << endl;

                    // Now sort those heaps
                    sort_heap(v1.begin(),v1.end());
                    sort_heap(v2.begin(),v2.end(),less<int>());
                    // v1 = v2 = (1,2,3,4)

                    // Copy both vectors to cout
                    copy(v1.begin(),v1.end(),out);
                    cout << endl;
                    copy(v2.begin(),v2.end(),out);
                    cout << endl;

                    return 0;
                }
```

stable_partition   **Algorithm**

Summary
Places all of the entities that satisfy the given predicate before all of the entities that do not, while maintaining the relative order of elements in each group.

Synopsis
```
#include <algorithm>

template <class BidirectionalIterator, class Predicate>
BidirectionalIterator
stable_partition (BidirectionalIterator first,
            BidirectionalIterator last,
            Predicate pred);
```

Description
The *stable_partition* algorithm places all the elements in the range *[first, last)* that satisfy *pred* before all the elements that do not satisfy it. It returns an iterator *i* that is one past the end of the group of elements that satisfy *pred*. In other words *stable_partition* returns *i* such that for any iterator *j* in the range *[first, i)*, *pred(*j) == true*, and for any iterator *k* in the range *[i, last)*, *pred(*j) == false*. The relative order of the elements in both groups is preserved.

The *partition* algorithm can be used when it is not necessary to maintain the relative order of elements within the groups that do and do not match the predicate.

Complexity
The *stable_partition* algorithm does at most *(last - first) * log(last - first)* swaps. and applies the predicate exactly *last - first* times.

Examples
```
#include<functional>
 #include<deque>
 #include<algorithm>
using namespace std;

//Create a new predicate from unary_function
template<class Arg>
class is_even : public unary_function<Arg, bool>
{
  public:
  bool operator()(const Arg& arg1)
  {
     return (arg1 % 2) == 0;
  }
};

int main()
```

```
    {
        //Initialize a deque with an array of ints
        int init[10] = {1,2,3,4,5,6,7,8,9,10};
        deque<int> d(init, init+10);

        //Print out the original values
        cout << "Unpartitioned values: " << endl << "     ";
        copy(d.begin(),d.end(),ostream_iterator<int>(cout," "));
        cout << endl << endl;

        //Partition the deque according to even/oddness
        stable_partition(d.begin(), d.end(), is_even<int>());

        //Output result of partition
        cout << "Partitioned values: " << endl << "     ";
        copy(d.begin(),d.end(),ostream_iterator<int>(cout," "));

        return 0;

    }
```

See also
partition

stable_sort   **Algorithm**

Summary
Templated algorithm for sorting collections of entities.

Synopsis
#include <algorithm>

template <class RandomAccessIterator>
 void stable_sort (RandomAccessIterator first,
          RandomAccessIterator last);

template <class RandomAccessIterator, class Compare>
 void stable_sort (RandomAccessIterator first,
          RandomAccessIterator last,
          Compare comp);

Description
The *stable_sort* algorithm sorts the elements in the range *[first, last)*. The first version of the algorithm uses less than (<) as the comparison operator for the sort. The second version uses the comparision function *comp*.

The *stable_sort* algorithm is considered stable because the relative order of the equal elements is preserved.

Complexity

stable_sort does at most *N(logN)* **2, where *N* equals *last -first*, comparisons; if enough extra memory is available, it is *NlogN*.

Examples

```
#include <vector>
#include <algorithm>
#include <functional>
using namespace std;

struct associate
{
  int num;
  char chr;

  associate(int n, char c) : num(n), chr(c){};
  associate() : num(0), chr('\0'){};
};

bool operator<(const associate &x, const associate &y)
{
  return x.num < y.num;
}

ostream& operator<<(ostream &s, const associate &x)
{
  return s << "<" << x.num << ";" << x.chr << ">";
}

int main ()
{
  vector<associate>::iterator i, j, k;

  associate arr[20] =
      {associate(-4, ' '), associate(16, ' '),
       associate(17, ' '), associate(-3, 's'),
       associate(14, ' '), associate(-6, ' '),
       associate(-1, ' '), associate(-3, 't'),
       associate(23, ' '), associate(-3, 'a'),
       associate(-2, ' '), associate(-7, ' '),
       associate(-3, 'b'), associate(-8, ' '),
       associate(11, ' '), associate(-3, 'l'),
       associate(15, ' '), associate(-5, ' '),
       associate(-3, 'e'), associate(15, ' ')};

  // Set up vectors
  vector<associate> v(arr, arr+20), v1((size_t)20),
              v2((size_t)20);

  // Copy original vector to vectors #1 and #2
  copy(v.begin(), v.end(), v1.begin());
```

```
        copy(v.begin(), v.end(), v2.begin());

        // Sort vector #1
        sort(v1.begin(), v1.end());

        // Stable sort vector #2
        stable_sort(v2.begin(), v2.end());

        // Display the results
        cout << "Original    sort      stable_sort" << endl;
        for(i = v.begin(), j = v1.begin(), k = v2.begin();
        i != v.end(); i++, j++, k++)
        cout << *i << "      " << *j << "      " << *k << endl;

        return 0;
    }
```

See also
sort, partial_sort, partial_sort_copy

stack   Container

Summary
A container adaptor which behaves like a stack (last in, first out).

Synopsis
#include <stack>

template <class T, class Container = deque<T>>
 class stack {

public:

// typedefs

  typedef Container::value_type value_type;
  typedef Container::size_type size_type;

protected:
  Container c;

public:

// Accessors

  bool empty () const;

```
  size_type size () const;
  value_type& top ();
  const value_type& top () const;
  void push (const value_type& x);
  void pop ();
};

template <class T, class Container = deque<T>>
 bool operator== (const stack<Container>& x, const
stack<Container>& y);

template <class T, class Container = deque<T>>
 bool operator< (const stack<Container>& x, const
stack<Container>& y);
```

Description

The *stack* container adaptor causes a container to behave like a "last in, first out" (LIFO) stack. The last item that was put ("pushed") onto the stack is the first item removed ("popped" off). The stack can adapt to any container that provides the operations, *back()*, *push_back()*, and *pop_back()*. In particular, *vector*, *list*, and *deque* can be used.

Caveats

If your compiler does not support template parameter defaults, you are required to supply a template parameter for *Container*. For example:

You would not be able to write,

```
stack<int> var;
```

Instead, you would have to write,

```
stack<int, deque<int>> var;
```

Examples

```
#include <stack>
#include <vector>
#include <deque>
#include <string>
using namespace std;

int main(void)
{
  // Make a stack using a vector container
  stack<int,vector<int> > s;

  // Push a couple of values on the stack
  s.push(1);
  s.push(2);
  cout << s.top() << endl;
```

```
                    // Now pop them off
                    s.pop();
                    cout << s.top() << endl;
                    s.pop();

                    // Make a stack of strings using a deque
                    stack<string,deque<string> > ss;

                    // Push a bunch of strings on then pop them off
                    int i;
                    for (i = 0; i < 10; i++)
                    {
                        ss.push(string(i+1,'a'));
                        cout << ss.top() << endl;
                    }
                    for (i = 0; i < 10; i++)
                    {
                        cout << ss.top() << endl;
                        ss.pop();
                    }

                    return 0;
                }
```

Member functions

bool
empty () const;
Returns *true* if the stack is empty, otherwise *false*.

void
pop ();
Removes the item at the top of the stack.

void
push (const value_type& x);
Pushes *x* onto the stack.

size_type
size () const;
Returns the number of elements on the stack.

value_type&
top ();
Returns the item at the top of the stack. This will be the last item pushed onto the stack unless *pop()* has been called since then.

const value_type&
top () const;
Returns the item at the top of the stack as a *const value_type*.

See also
Containers

Stream iterators

Iterators

Summary
Stream iterators provide iterator capabilities for ostreams and istreams. They allow generic algorithms to be used directly on streams.

See the sections *istream_iterator* and *ostream_iterator* for a description of these iterators.

string

String library

Summary
A specialization of the *basic_string* class. For more information about strings, see the entry *basic_string*.

swap

Algorithm

Summary
Exchange values stored in two locations

Synopsis
#include <algorithm>

template <class T>
 void **swap** (T& a, T& b);

Description
The *swap* algorithm exchanges the values in *a* and *b*.

Examples
```
/**********************************************************
 *
 * swap.cpp - Example program of swap algorithm.
 *
 * $Id: swap.cpp,v 1.7 1995/10/06 20:05:43 hart Exp $
 *
 * $$RW_INSERT_HEADER "slyrs.str"
 *
 **********************************************************/
#include <vector>
#include <algorithm>
using namespace std;
```

```
int main ()
{
  int d1[] = {6, 7, 8, 9, 10, 1, 2, 3, 4, 5};
  //
  // Set up a vector.
  //
  vector<int> v(d1+0, d1+10);
  //
  // Output original vector.
  //
  cout << "For the vector: ";
  copy(v.begin(), v.end(), ostream_iterator<int>(cout," "));
  //
  // Swap the first five elements with the last five elements.
  //
  swap_ranges(v.begin(), v.begin()+5, v.begin()+5);
  //
  // Output result.
  //
  cout << endl << endl
       << "Swaping the first 5 elements with the last 5 gives: "
       << endl << "       ";
  copy(v.begin(), v.end(), ostream_iterator<int>(cout," "));
  //
  // Now an example of iter_swap -- swap first and last elements.
  //
  iter_swap(v.begin(), v.end()-1);
  //
  // Output result.
  //
  cout << endl << endl
       << "Swapping the first and last elements gives: "
       << endl << "       ";
  copy(v.begin(), v.end(), ostream_iterator<int>(cout," "));
  cout << endl;

  return 0;
}
```

See also
iter_swap, swap_ranges

swap_ranges   **Algorithm**

Summary
Exchange a range of values in one location with those in another

Synopsis
#include <algorithm>

```
template <class ForwardIterator1, class ForwardIterator2>
 ForwardIterator2 swap_ranges (ForwardIterator1 first1,
                    ForwardIterator last1,
                    ForwardIterator2 first2);
```

Description
The *swap_ranges* algorithm exchanges corresponding values in two ranges, in the following manner:

For each non-negative integer *n < (last - first)* the function exchanges **(first1 + n)* with **(first2 + n))*. After completing all exchanges, *swap_ranges* returns an iterator that points to the end of the second container, i.e., *first2 + (last1 -first1)*. The result of *swap_ranges* is undefined if the two ranges *[first, last)* and *[first2, first2 + (last1 - first1))* overlap.

Examples
```
  #include <vector>
   #include <algorithm>
  using namespace std;

  int main()
  {
    int d1[] = {6, 7, 8, 9, 10, 1, 2, 3, 4, 5};

    // Set up a vector
    vector<int> v(d1,d1 + 10);

    // Output original vector
    cout << "For the vector: ";
    copy(v.begin(),v.end(),ostream_iterator<int>(cout," "));

    // Swap the first five elements with the last five elements
    swap_ranges(v.begin(),v.begin()+5, v.begin()+5);

    // Output result
    cout << endl << endl
        << "Swapping the first five elements "
        << "with the last five gives: "
        << endl << "      ";
    copy(v.begin(),v.end(),ostream_iterator<int>(cout," "));

    return 0;
  }
```

See also
iter_swap, swap

times
Function object

Summary
A binary function object that returns the result of multiplying its first and second arguments.

Synopsis
#include<functional>

```
template <class T>
struct times : binary_function<T, T, T> {
    T operator() (const T& x, const T& y) const
        { return x * y; }
};
```

Description
times is a binary function object. Its *operator()* returns the result of multiplying x and y. You can pass a *times* object to any algorithm that uses a binary function. For example, the *transform* algorithm applies a binary operation to corresponding values in two collections and stores the result. *times* would be used in that algorithm in the following manner:

```
vector<int> vec1;
vector<int> vec2;
vector<int> vecResult;
?
transform(vec1.begin(), vec1.end(),
          vec2.begin(), vec2.end(),
          vecResult.begin(), times<int>());
```

After this call to *transform*, *vecResult(n)* will contain *vec1(n)* times *vec2(n)*.

See also
Function objects

transform
Algorithm

Summary
Applies an operation to a range of values in a collection and stores the result.

Synopsis
#include <algorithm>

```
template <class InputIterator,
          class OutputIterator,
          class UnaryOperation>
```

```
OutputIterator transform (InputIterator first,
                InputIterator last,
                OutputIterator result,
                UnaryOperation op);


template <class InputIterator1,
        class InputIterator2,
        class OutputIterator,
        class BinaryOperation>
OutputIterator transform (InputIterator1 first1,
                InputIterator1 last1,
                InputIterator2 first2,
                OutputIterator result,
                BinaryOperation binary_op);
```

Description

The *transform* algorithm has two forms. The first form applies unary operation *op* to each element of the range *[first,last)*, and sends the result to the output iterator *result*. For example, this version of *transform*, could be used to square each element in a vector. If the output iterator (*result*) is the same as the input iterator used to traverse the range, *transform*, performs its transformation inplace.

The second form of *transform* applies a binary operation, *binary_op*, to corresponding elements in the range *[first1, last1)* and the range that begins at *first2*, and sends the result to *result*. For example, *transform* can be used to add corresponding elements in two sequences, and store the set of sums in a third. The algorithm assumes, but does not check, that the second sequence has at least as many elements as the first sequence. Note that the output iterator *result* can be a third sequence, or either of the two input sequences.

Formally, *transform* assigns through every iterator *i* in the range *[result, result + (last1 - first1))* a new corresponding value equal to:

```
op(*(first1 + (i - result))
```

or

```
binary_op(*(first1 + (i - result), *(first2 + (i - result)))
```

transform returns *result + (last1 - first1)*. *op* and *binary_op* must not have any side effects. *result* may be equal to *first* in case of unary transform, or to *first1* or *first2* in case of binary transform.

Complexity

Exactly *last1 - first1* applications of *op* or *binary_op* are performed.

Examples

```
#include<functional>
#include<deque>
#include<algorithm>
#include<iomanip.h>
```

```
using namespace std;

int main()
{
  //Initialize a deque with an array of ints
  int arr1[5] = {99, 264, 126, 330, 132};
  int arr2[5] = {280, 105, 220, 84, 210};
  deque<int> d1(arr1, arr1+5), d2(arr2, arr2+5);

  //Print the original values
  cout << "The following pairs of numbers: "
       << endl << "      ";
  deque<int>::iterator i1;
  for(i1 = d1.begin(); i1 != d1.end(); i1++)
    cout << setw(6) << *i1 << " ";
  cout << endl << "      ";
  for(i1 = d2.begin(); i1 != d2.end(); i1++)
    cout << setw(6) << *i1 << " ";

  // Transform the numbers in the deque to their
  // factorials and store in the vector
  transform(d1.begin(), d1.end(), d2.begin(),
            d1.begin(), times<int>());

  //Display the results
  cout << endl << endl;
  cout << "Have the products: " << endl << "      ";
  for(i1 = d1.begin(); i1 != d1.end(); i1++)
    cout << setw(6) << *i1 << " ";

  return 0;
}
```

unary_function   Function object

Summary
Base class for creating unary function objects.

Synopsis
#include <functional>

```
template <class Arg, class Result>
struct unary_function{
    typedef Arg argument_type;
    typedef Result result_type;
};
```

Description

Function objects are objects with an *operator()* defined. They are important for the effective use of the standard library's generic algorithms, because the interface for each algorithmic template can accept either an object with an *operator()* defined or a pointer to a function. The standard library provides both a standard set of function objects, and a pair of classes that you can use as the base for creating your own function objects.

Function objects that take one argument are called *unary function objects.* Unary function objects are required to provide the typedefs *argument_type* and *result_type.* The *unary_function* class makes the task of creating templated unary function objects easier by providing the necessary typedefs for a unary function object. You can create your own unary function objects by inheriting from *unary_function.*

See also

function objects, and Chapter 20, "Functions and predicates," in the C++ *Programmer's Guide.*

unary_negate   Function adaptor (negator)

Summary

Function object that returns the complement of the result of its unary predicate

Synopsis

```
#include<functional>

template <class Predicate>
class unary_negate
  : public unary_function<Predicate::argument_type, bool> {

public:
    explicit unary_negate (const Predicate& pred);
    bool operator() (const argument_type& x) const;
};

template<class Predicate>
unary_negate <Predicate> not1 (const Predicate& pred);
```

Description

unary_negate is a function object class that provides a return type for the function adaptor *not1.* *not1* is a function adaptor, known as a negator, that takes a unary predicate function object as its argument and returns a unary predicate function object that is the complement of the original.

Note that *not1* works only with function objects that are defined as subclasses of the class *unary_function.*

Constructor
explicit unary_negate (const Predicate& pred);
Construct a *unary_negate* object from predicate *pred*.

Operator
bool operator ( ) (const argument_type& x) const;
Return the result of *pred(x)*

See also
unary_function, binary_negate

uninitialized_copy   Memory management

Summary
An algorithms that uses *construct* to copy values from one range to another location.

Synopsis
#include <memory>

template <class InputIterator, class ForwardIterator>
ForwardIterator uninitialized_copy (InputIterator first,
                InputIterator last,
                ForwardIterator result);

Description
uninitialized_copy copies all items in the range *[first, last)* into the location beginning at *result* using the *construct* algorithm.

See also
construct

uninitialized_fill   Memory management

Summary
Algorithm that uses the *construct* algorithm for setting values in a collection.

Synopsis
#include <memory>

template <class ForwardIterator, class T>
void uninitialized_fill(ForwardIterator first,
                ForwardIterator last,
                const T& x);

Description

uninitialized_fill initializes all of the items in the range *[first,last)* to the value *x*, using the *construct* algorithm.

See also

construct

uninitialized_fill_n   Memory management

Summary

Algorithm that uses the *construct* algorithm for setting values in a collection.

Synopsis

```
#include <memory>

template <class ForwardIterator,
        class Size, class T>
void uninitialized_fill_n (ForwardIterator first,
                Size n, const T& x);
```

Description

unitialized_fill_n starts at the iterator *first* and initializes the first *n* items to the value *x*, using the *construct* algorithm.

See also

construct

unique, unique_copy   Algorithm

Summary

Removes consecutive duplicates from a range of values and places the resulting unique values into the result.

Synopsis

```
#include <algorithm>

template <class ForwardIterator>
ForwardIterator unique (ForwardIterator first,
                ForwardIterator last);

template <class ForwardIterator, class BinaryPredicate>
ForwardIterator unique (ForwardIterator first,
                ForwardIterator last,
```

```
                        BinaryPredicate binary_pred);

    template <class InputIterator, class OutputIterator>
    OutputIterator unique_copy (InputIterator first,
                    InputIterator last,
                    OutputIterator result);

    template <class InputIterator,
          class OutputIterator,
          class BinaryPredicate>
    OutputIterator unique_copy (InputIterator first,
                    InputIterator last,
                    OutputIterator result,
                    BinaryPredicate binary_pred);
```

Description

The *unique* algorithm moves through a sequence and eliminates all but the first element from every consecutive group of equal elements. There are two versions of the algorithm, one tests for equality, and the other tests whether a binary predicate applied to adjacent elements is true. An element is unique if it does not meet the corresponding condition listed here:

```
    *i  ==  *(i  -  1)
```

or

```
    binary_pred(*i, *(i - 1)) == true.
```

If an element is unique, it is copied to the front of the sequence, overwriting the existing elements. Once all unique elements have been identified. The remainder of the sequence is left unchanged, and *unique* returns the end of the resulting range.

The *unique_copy* algorithm copies the first element from every consecutive group of equal elements, to an OutputIterator. The *unique_copy* algorithm, also has two versions--one that tests for equality and a second that tests adjacent elements against a binary predicate.

unique_copy returns the end of the resulting range.

Complexity

Exactly *(last - first) - 1* applications of the corresponding predicate are performed.

Examples

```
    #include<algorithm>
    #include<vector>
    using namespace std;

    int main()
    {
      //Initialize two vectors
      int a1[20] = {4, 5, 5, 9, -1, -1, -1, 3, 7, 5,
```

```
                    5, 5, 6, 7, 7, 7, 4, 2, 1, 1};
    vector<int> v(a1, a1+20), result;

    //Create an insert_iterator for results
    insert_iterator<vector<int> > ins(result,
                             result.begin());

    //Demonstrate includes
    cout << "The vector: " << endl << "    ";
    copy(v.begin(),v.end(),ostream_iterator<int>(cout," "));

    //Find the unique elements
    unique_copy(v.begin(), v.end(), ins);

    //Display the results
    cout << endl << endl
        << "Has the following unique elements:"
        << endl << "    ";
    copy(result.begin(),result.end(),
        ostream_iterator<int>(cout," "));

    return 0;
}
```

upper_bound   **Algorithm**

Summary
Determines the last valid position for a value in a sorted container.

Synopsis
#include <algorithm>
template <class ForwardIterator, class T>
  ForwardIterator
  upper_bound(ForwardIterator first, ForwardIterator last,
        const T& value);
template <class ForwardIterator, class T, class Compare>
  ForwardIterator
  upper_bound(ForwardIterator first, ForwardIterator last,
        const T& value, Compare comp);

Description
The *upper_bound* algorithm is part of a set of binary search algorithms. All of these
algorithms perform binary searches on ordered containers. Each algorithm has two
versions. The first version uses the less than operator (*operator <*) to perform the
comparison, and assumes that the sequence has been sorted using that operator. The
second version allows you to include a function object of type *compare*, and assumes that

compare is the function used to sort the sequence. The function object must be a binary predicate.

The *upper_bound* algorithm finds the *last* position in a container that *value* can occupy without violating the container's ordering. *upper_bound's* return value is the iterator for the first element in the container that is *greater than value*, or, when the comparison operator is used, the first element that does *not* satisfy the comparison function. Because the algorithm is restricted to using the less than operator or the user-defined function to perform the search, *upper_bound* returns an iterator *i* in the range *[first, last)* such that for any iterator *j* in the range *[first, i)* the appropriate version of the following conditions holds:

```
!(value < *j)
```

or

```
comp(value, *j) == false
```

Complexity
upper_bound performs at most *log(last - first) + 1* comparisons.

Examples
```cpp
#include <vector>
#include <algorithm>
using namespace std;

int main()
{
  typedef vector<int>::iterator iterator;
  int d1[11] = {0,1,2,2,3,4,2,2,2,6,7};

  // Set up a vector
  vector<int> v1(d1,d1 + 11);

  // Try lower_bound variants
  iterator it1 = lower_bound(v1.begin(),v1.end(),3);
  // it1 = v1.begin() + 4

  iterator it2 =
      lower_bound(v1.begin(),v1.end(),2,less<int>());
  // it2 = v1.begin() + 4

  // Try upper_bound variants
  iterator it3 = upper_bound(v1.begin(),v1.end(),3);
  // it3 = vector + 5

  iterator it4 =
     upper_bound(v1.begin(),v1.end(),2,less<int>());
  // it4 = v1.begin() + 5

  cout << endl << endl
       << "The upper and lower bounds of 3: ( "
       << *it1 << " , " << *it3 << " ]" << endl;
```

```
        cout << endl << endl
            << "The upper and lower bounds of 2: ( "
            << *it2 << " , " << *it4 << " ]" << endl;

        return 0;
    }
```

See also
lower_bound

vector

Summary
Sequence that supports random access iterators.

Synopsis
#include <vector>

template <class T>
 class vector {

public:

// Types

  typedef typename reference;
  typedef typename const_reference;
  typedef typename iterator;
  typedef typename const_iterator;
  typedef typename size_type;
  typedef typename difference_type;
  typedef T value_type;
  typedef reverse_iterator<iterator, value_type,
      reference, difference_type> reverse_iterator;
  typedef const_reverse_iterator<const_iterator,
      value_type,   reference,   difference_type>
const_reverse_iterator;

// Construct/Copy/Destroy

  explicit vector ();
  explicit vector (size_type, const T& = T());
  vector (const vector<T>&);
  template <class InputIterator>

```
 vector (InputIterator, InputIterator);
 ~vector ();
 vector<T>& operator= (const vector<T>&);
 template <class InputIterator>
 void assign (InputIterator first, InputIterator last);
 template <class Size, class T>
 void assign (Size n, const T& t = T());

// Iterators

 iterator begin ();
 const_iterator begin () const;
 iterator end ();
 const_iterator end () const;
 reverse_iterator rbegin ();
 const_reverse_iterator rbegin () const;
 reverse_iterator rend ();
 const_reverse_iterator rend () const;

// Capacity

 size_type size () const;
 size_type max_size () const;
 void resize (size_type,T c = T());
 size_type capacity () const;
 bool empty () const;
 void reserve (size_type);

// Element Access

 reference operator[] (size_type);
 const_reference operator[] (size_type) const;
 reference at (size_type n);
 const_reference at (size_type n) const;
 reference front ();
 const_reference front () const;
 reference back ();
 const_reference back () const;

// Modifiers

 void push_back (const T&);
 void pop_back ();
 iterator insert (iterator, const T& = T());
 void insert (iterator, size_type, const T& = T());
```

```
template <class InputIterator>
 void insert (iterator, InputIterator, InputIterator);
 void erase (iterator);
 void erase (iterator, iterator);
 void swap (vector<T>&);


};


// Comparison


template <class T>
 bool operator== (const vector<T>&, const vector <T>&);


template <class T>
 bool operator< (const vector<T>&, const vector<T>&);
```

Description

vector<T> is a type of sequence that supports random access iterators. In addition, it supports amortized constant time insert and erase operations at the end. Insert and erase in the middle take linear time. Storage management is handled automatically. In *vector, iterator* is a random access iterator referring to *T. const_iterator* is a constant random access iterator referring to *const T*. A constructor for *iterator* and *const_iterator* is guaranteed. *size_type* is an unsigned integral type. *difference_type* is a signed integral type.

Any type used for the template parameter *T* must provide the following (where *T* is the *type, t* is a *value* of *T* and *u* is a *const value* of *T*):

```
Default constructor    T()
Copy constructors      T(t) and T(u)
Destructor             t.~T()
Address of             &t and &u yeilding T* and
                        const T* respectively
Assignment             t = a where a is a
                        (possibly const) value of T
```

Special Case

Vectors of bit values (Boolean 1/0 values) are handled as a special case by the standard library, so that they can be efficiently packed several elements to a word. The operations for a boolean vector, *vector<bool>*, are a superset of those for an ordinary vector, only the implementation is more efficient.

Two member functions are available to the the boolean vector data type. One is *flip()*, which inverts all the bits of the vector. Boolean vectors also return as reference an internal value that also supports the *flip()* member function. The other *vector<bool>*-specific member function is a second form of the *swap()* function.

Caveats

Member function templates are used in all containers provided by the Standard Template Library. An example of this feature is the constructor for *vector<T>* that takes two templated iterators:

```
template <class InputIterator>
  vector (InputIterator, InputIterator);
```

vector also has an insert function of this type. These functions, when not restricted by compiler limitations, allow you to use any type of input iterator as arguments. For compilers that do not support this feature we provide substitute functions that allow you to use an iterator obtained from the same type of container as the one you are constructing (or calling a member function on), or you can use a pointer to the type of element you have in the container.

For example, if your compiler does not support member function templates you can construct a vector in the following two ways:

```
int intarray[10];
vector<int> first_vector(intarray,intarray + 10);
vector<int>
second_vector(first_vector.begin(),first_vector.end());
```

but not this way:

```
vector<long>
long_vector(first_vector.begin(),first_vector.end());
```

since the *long_vector* and *first_vector* are not the same type.

Examples

```
#include <vector>
using namespace std;

ostream& operator<<(ostream& out, const vector<int>& v)
{
  copy(v.begin(), v.end(), ostream_iterator<int>(out," "));
  return out;
}

int main(void)
{
  // create a vector of double's, and one of int's
  vector<int>        vi;
  int                i;

  for(i = 0; i < 10; ++i) {
    // insert values before the beginning
    vi.insert(vi.begin(), i);
  }

  // print out the vector
  cout << vi << endl;
```

```
    // now let's erase half of the elements
    int      half = vi.size() >> 1;

    for(i = 0; i < half; ++i) {
      vi.erase(vi.begin());
    }

    // print ir out again
    cout << vi << endl;

    return 0;
  }
```

Constructors and destructors

explicit vector ();

The default constructor. Creates a vector of length zero.

explicit vector (size_type n, const T& value = T());

Creates a vector of length *n*, containing *n* copies of value.

vector (const vector<T>& x);

Creates a copy of *x*.

template <class InputIterator>
vector (InputIterator first, InputIterator last);

Creates a vector of length *last - first*, filled with all values obtained by dereferencing the *InputIterators* on the range *[first, last)*;

~vector ();

The destructor. Releases any allocated memory for this vector.

Iterators

iterator **begin** ();

Returns a random access iterator that points to the first element.

const_iterator **begin** () const;

Returns a constant random access iterator that points to the first element.

iterator **end** ();

Returns a random access iterator that points to the past-the-end value.

const_iterator **end** () const;

Returns a constant random access iterator that points to the past-the-end value.

reverse_iterator **rbegin** ();

Returns a random access iterator that points to the past-the-end value.

const_reverse_iterator **rbegin** () const;

Returns a constant random access iterator that points to the past-the-end value.

reverse_iterator **rend** ();

Returns a random access iterator that points to the first element.

const_reverse_iterator **rend** () const;

Returns a constant random access iterator that points to the first element.

Assignment operator

vector<T>& operator= (const vector<T>& x);

Assignment operator. Erases all elements in self then inserts into self a copy of each element in *x*. Returns a reference to self.

Reference operators

reference operator[] (size_type n);

Returns a reference to element *n* of self. The result can be used as an lvalue. The index *n* must be between 0 and the *size* less one.

const_reference operator[] (size_type n) const;

Returns a constant reference to element *n* of self. The index *n* must be between 0 and the *size* less one.

Member functions

template <class InputIterator>
void
assign (InputIterator first, InputIterator last);

Erases all elements contained in self, then inserts new elements from the range *[first, last)*.

template <class Size, class T>
void
assign (Size n, const T& t = T());

Erases all elements contained in self, then inserts *n* instances of the value of *t*.

reference
at(size_type n);

Returns a reference to element *n* of self. The result can be used as an lvalue. The index *n* must be between 0 and the *size* less one.

const_reference
at (size_type) const;

Returns a constant reference to element *n* of self. The index *n* must be between 0 and the *size* less one.

reference
back ();

Returns a reference to the last element.

const_reference
back () const;

Returns a constant reference to the last element.

size_type
capacity () const;
Returns the size of the allocated storage.

bool
empty () const;
Returns *true* if the *size* is zero.

void
erase (iterator position);
Removes the element pointed to by *position*.

void
erase (iterator first, iterator last);
Removes the elements in the range *[first, last)*.

void
flip();
Flips all the bits in the vector. *This member function is only defined for vector<bool>.*

reference
front ();
Returns a reference to the first element.

const_reference
front () const;
Returns a constant reference to the first element.

iterator
insert (iterator position, const T& x = T());
Inserts *x* before *position*. The return value points to the inserted *x*.

void
insert (iterator position, size_type n, const T& x = T());
Inserts *n* copies of *x* before *position*.

template <class InputIterator>
void
insert (iterator position, InputIterator first, InputIterator last);
Inserts copies of the elements in the range *[first, last]* before *position*.

size_type
max_size () const;
Returns *size()* of the largest possible vector.

void
pop_back ();
Removes the last element of self.

void
push_back (const T& x);
Inserts a copy of *x* to the end of self.

void
reserve (size_type n);

Increases the capacity of self in anticipation of adding new elements. *reserve* itself does not add any new elements. After a call to *reserve, capacity()* is greater than or equal to *n* and subsequent insertions will not cause a reallocation until the size of the vector exceeds *n*. Reallocation does not occur if *n* is less than *capacity()*. If reallocation does occur, then all iterators and references pointing to elements in the vector are invalidated. *reserve* takes at most linear time in the size of self.

void
resize (size_type sz, T c = T());

Alters the size of self. If the new size (*sz*) is greater than the current size, then *sz-size()* *c*'s are inserted at the end of the vector. If the new size is smaller than the current *capacity*, then the vector is truncated by erasing *size()-sz* elements off the end. If *sz* is equal to *capacity* then no action is taken.

size_type
size () const;

Returns the number of elements.

void
swap (vector<T>& x);

Exchanges self with *x*.

void
swap(reference x, reference y);

Swaps the values of *x* and *y*. This is a member function of *vector<bool>* only.

Non-member operators

template <class T>
bool operator== (const vector<T>& x, const vector <T>& y);

Returns *true* if *x* is the same as *y*.

template <class T>
bool operator< (const vector<T>& x, const vector <T>& y);

Returns *true* if the elements contained in *x* are lexicographically less than the elements contained in *y*.

See also

containers, lexicographical_compare

wstring   String library

Summary

A specialization of the *basic_string* class. For more information about strings, see the entry *basic_string*.

V

Visual Database Tools reference

Part V is a reference for Visual Database Tools. Classes, properties, methods, and events are described in detail and are presented in alphabetical (ASCII) order for easy reference. Information provided includes syntax, descriptions, and examples.

18

Classes, properties, methods, and events

Visual Database Tools provide the C++ programmer with database components that simplify the development of Windows database applications.

There are two types of database components: data-access components and data-aware components. Your database applications require both types.

Data-access components provide the means to access the data in your database, whether it exists in a local, desktop database, or on a remote SQL server. Examples of data-access components are TTable, TQuery, and TDataSource. Data-access components have a visual representation while you are building your form in Resource Workshop. You can set their property values at this time. When you run your application, however, these components do not appear, but you can access their properties, methods, and events by the code you write.

Most of the data-access components provided by Visual Database Tools are descendants of TPersistent. Any of these components are legitimate values when a property or method requires a parameter of type TPersistent.

The components descended from TPersistent are:

- TBatchMove
- TDataBase
- TDataSet and its descendants TDBDataSet, TQuery, TStoredProc, and TTable
- TDataSource
- All TField components
- TParams
- TStrings

Many of TPersistent's descendants also inherit from its direct descendant TBCDComponent. The only TPersistent data-access components that do not descend from TBCDComponent are TParams and TStrings components.

Data-aware components are used to build a user interface for your database applications. These components resemble the familiar Windows controls such as edit boxes, list boxes, and so on, but they are connected to fields in a dataset. Users use them to view the data in a dataset and to modify the data. Data-aware components are visible at both design time and run time. You can set their property values in the IDE, and you change these values, call methods of these components, and respond to the events of these components through the code you write.

For both data-access and data-aware components, this is the model you will use most frequently to program with Visual Database Tools:

- In the Dialog editor of Resource Workshop, select a Visual Database Tools component from the Tools palette and add it to the form (a dialog box or window).

- Set property values for the component using the Property Inspector.

- At run time, respond to events that might occur to the component. To respond, you write an event handler that contains the code that executes when the event occurs.

For detailed information on how to perform these steps, see the Part VI, "Visual Database Tools Developer's Guide," in the C++ *Programmer's Guide*.

How to use this chapter

The rest of this chapter is an alphabetical listing of the classes, properties, methods, and events associated with the data-access and data-aware components of Borland C++. The classes are listed under T (TBatchMove, TQuery).

Methods, properties, and events have their own entry outside the class or classes they belong to. For example, the About property is common to all data-aware controls. Instead of several redundant entries in each data-aware class, there is only one entry under the term "About property."

AbortOnKeyViol property

Applies to   TBatchMove component

bool AbortOnKeyViol;

The value of the AbortOnKeyViol property determines whether a batch move operation terminates when an integrity key violation occurs. If AbortOnKeyViol is true (the default), the Execute method terminates when an integrity key violation occurs. If AbortOnKeyViol is false, the batch operation continues.

Note   If you set AbortOnKeyViol to false, you should provide a KeyViolTableName so that all records with key violations can be posted to that table.

Example

```
BatchMove1.AbortOnKeyViol = false;
```

AbortOnProblem property

Applies to   TBatchMove component

bool AbortOnProblem;

The value of the AbortOnProblem property determines whether a batch move operation terminates when a problem occurs because of data type conversion errors. If AbortOnProblem is true (the default), the Execute method terminates when a record cannot be moved successfully to the destination table. If AbortOnProblem is false, the batch operation continues.

Note   If you set AbortOnProblem to false, you should provide a ProblemTableName so that all records with data type conversion errors can be posted to that table.

Example

```
BatchMove1.AbortOnProblem = false;
```

About property

Applies to   All components you can see at design time.

Description   Use the About property to display information about components at design time. Click the About property in the Property Inspector. The About box displays information on the source of the control, whether Borland or third party.

Example

```
TDBEdit.About ( );
```

Action property

Applies to   TDBComboBox, TDBListBox components

TOwnerDrawAction Action;

Run-time and read only. Use the Action property to determine the drawing action required of the OnDrawItem event.

The possible values are as follows:

Value	Meaning
oaDrawEntire	Draw the entire control.
oaFocus	The control has lost or gained focus. Check the State parameter of the OnDrawItem event to determine which.
oaSelect	The selection state of the control has changed. Check the State parameter of the OnDrawItem event to determine how.

Example

```
void List1::OnDraw( short sIndex, TRect rc, TOwnerDrawState odState )
{
  TOwnerDrawAction odAction = Action;
  //Show that the control has focus
  if( odAction.odFocus )
      Canvas->DrawFocusRect( rc.left, rc.top, rc.right, rc.bottom );
  // . . .
}
```

Active property

Applies to   TDataSet, TDBDataSet, TQuery, TStoredProc, TTable components

bool Active;

The value of the Active property determines whether a dataset is open. When Active is set to true, the dataset opens in Browse state (the State property is dsBrowse). This is equivalent to calling the Open method of a dataset. Setting Active to false closes the dataset and is equivalent to calling the Close method.

For TQuery and TStoredProc, if the SQL statement or stored procedure does not return a result set, then setting Active to true raises an EDatabaseError.exception.

Note   Post is not called implicitly by setting Active to false. Use the BeforeClose event to post any pending edits explicitly.

Example

```
// Close the dataset
Table1.Active = false;
// Open the dataset
Table1.Active = true;
```

Add method

Applies to   TFieldDefs, TIndexDefs, TStrings, TVarRecs components

Add method for TFieldDefs components

Applies to   TFieldDefs component

void Add(const string& Name, TFieldType Type, uint16 Size, bool Required);

The Add method creates a new TFieldDefs component using the Name, Type, and Size parameters, and adds it to the Items property. Except for special purposes, you do not need to use this method because the Items property array is filled for you when you open the dataset, or because Update fills Items without opening the dataset.

The value of the Required parameter determines whether the newly added field definition is a required field. If the Required parameter is true, the value of the Required property of the TFieldDefs component is also true. If the Required parameter is false, the value of the Required property is also false.

Add method for TIndexDefs components

Applies to   TIndexDefs component

void Add(const string& name, const string& fields, TIndexOptions options);
The Add method creates a new TIndexDefs component using the name, fields, and options parameters, and adds it to the Items property of the TIndexDefs component. Generally, you won't need to use this method because the dataset has already filled Items for you when it opens, or the Update method fills Items without opening the dataset.

Add method for TStrings components

Applies to   TStrings component

int Add(const string& s);
The Add method adds a new string to a string component. The s parameter is the new string. Add returns the position of the item in the list; the first item in the list has a value of 0.

For TStrings components, the new string is appended to the end of the list unless the Sorted property is true. In such a case the string is inserted into the list of strings to maintain the sort order.

Example   This code adds a new string to a list box:

```
DBListBox1.Items->Add( "New string" );
```

Add method for TVarRecs components

Applies to   TVarRecs component

void Add(TVarRec& var);
The Add method adds a data item to a TVarRecs component. The var parameter is the new data item.

AddFieldDesc method

Applies to   TFieldDefs component

void AddFieldDesc(pFLDDesc FieldDesc, bool Required, uint16 FieldNo);
AddFieldDesc creates a new TFieldDefs component using the information provided by the Borland Database Engine in the FieldDesc parameter, and adds it to the Items property of the TFieldDefs component. Except for special purposes, you do not need to use this method because the Items property is filled for you when you open the dataset, or because Update fills Items without opening the dataset.

AddIndex method

Applies to   TTable component

void AddIndex(const string& name, const string& fields, TIndexOptions options);

The AddIndex method creates a new index for the TTable component. The name parameter contains the name of the new index. The fields parameter holds the list of the fields to include in the index. Separate field names with a semicolon. The options parameter holds one or more of the TIndexOptions values listed below. You can combine options using the bitwise "or" operator (|).

Value	Meaning
ixPrimary	The new index is the table's primary index.
ixUnique	The new index is unique.
ixDescending	The new index sorts in descending order.
ixCaseInsensitive	The new index is case insensitive.
ixExpression	The new index is made up of an expression, such as one that concatenates two fields.

Note   You can't add an index to a dBASE table with the index option ixCaseInsensitive. For example, the following code returns an error if Table1 is a dBASE table:

```
Table1.AddIndex( Name, Fields, ixCaseInsensitive );
Table1.AddIndex( "byLastName", "LastName", ixCaseInsensitive );
```

Example

```
Table1.AddIndex( "NewIndex", "CustNo;CustName", ixUnique| ixCaseInsensitive );
```

AddObject method

Applies to   TStrings component

int AddObject(const string& s, LPVOID object);

The AddObject method adds both a string and an object to a string component. The string and the object are appended to the list of strings. Specify the string to be added as the value of the s parameter, and specify the object to be added as the value of the object parameter. The string and object will always be paired and handled as a single object. There is no restriction as to the kind of object.

Example   This code adds the string "Orange" and a bitmap of an orange to an owner-draw list box:

```
MyFormClass::EvButtonClick( )
{
  TIcon Icon( GetApplication( )->GetInstance( ), "ORANGE.ICO", 1 );
  ListBox1.Items->AddObject( "Orange", ( LPVOID )Icon);
}
```

AddParam method

Applies to   TParams component

void AddParam(TParam& p);

The AddParam method adds the parameter specified with p to the Items property of the parameters component. Use AddParam to build the TParams for a SQL query or a stored procedure.

Example

```
//  Move all parameter info from Params2 to Params1
while( Params2.Count != 0 )
{
  // Grab the first parameter from Params2
  TParam TempParam = Params2[0];
  // Remove it from Params2
  Params2.RemoveParam( TempParam );
  // And add it to Params1
  Params1.AddParam( TempParam );
}
```

AddPassword method

Applies to   TSession component

void AddPassword(const string& p);

The AddPassword method is used to add a new password to the current TSession component for use with Paradox tables. When an application opens a Paradox table that requires a password, the user is prompted to enter a password unless the session has a valid password for the table. If you want to avoid prompting the user, call the AddPassword method before you open the table.

Example

```
Session.AddPassword( "Asecret" );
```

AddStrings method

Applies to   TStrings component

void AddStrings(TStrings& s);

The AddStrings method adds a group of strings to the list of strings in a string component. The new strings are appended to the existing strings. Specify a string component containing the list of strings you want added as the value of the s parameter.

Example   This code appends the contents of a file to the end of a memo control:

```
MyFormClass::EvButton1Click( )
{
```

```
    TStrings Contents;
    Contents.LoadFromFile( "NEWSTUFF.TXT" );
    DBMemo1.Lines->AddStrings( Contents );
}
```

This code adds the list of strings contained in ListBox1.Items to the end of the ListBox2.Items list of strings:

```
MyFormClass::EvButton1Click( )
{
    ListBox2.Items->AddStrings( ListBox1.Items );
}
```

AfterCancel event

Applies to   TDataSet, TDBDataSet, TQuery, TStoredProc, TTable components

Description   The AfterCancel event is activated when the dataset finishes a call to the Cancel method. This event is the last action before Cancel returns to the caller. The Cancel method only activates an AfterCancel event if the dataset is in the Edit state or when changes to the dataset are pending.

By assigning a method to this property, you can take any special actions required by the event.

Source declaration   This declaration of the event source is in the header file:

```
TDatasetNotifySource AfterCancelSource;
```

Sink declaration   Include this declaration of the event sink in the class definition for your sink object:

```
TDatasetNotifySink AfterCancelSink;
```

Handler   Put a prototype for the handler method in the class definition for your sink object:

```
void AfterCancel( TDatasetNotifySink& sink, TDataset& sender );
```

And connect the handler method, which you have implemented, to the event sink by including the following in the class constructor:

```
AfterCancelSink( TDatasetNotify_MFUNCTOR( *this, &TForm::AfterCancel ))
```

Attachment   Attach the event source to the event sink by including the following in your program:

```
TDataset dataset;    //Instantiate the source component
TForm form;          //Instantiate the sink component
dataset.AfterCancelSource += form.AfterCancelSink;
```

AfterClose event

Applies to   TDataSet, TDBDataSet, TQuery, TStoredProc, TTable components

Description   The AfterClose event is activated after a dataset is closed, either by calling the Close method or by setting the Active property to false. This event is the last action before Close returns to the caller. Typically, the AfterClose event handler closes any private lookup tables opened by the BeforeOpen event.

By assigning a method to this property, you can take any special actions required by the event.

Source declaration   This declaration of the event source is in the header file:

```
TDatasetNotifySource AfterCloseSource;
```

Sink declaration   Include this declaration of the event sink in the class definition for your sink object:

```
TDatasetNotifySink AfterCloseSink;
```

Handler   Put a prototype for the handler method in the class definition for your sink object:

```
void AfterClose( TDatasetNotifySink& sink, TDataset& sender );
```

And connect the handler method, which you have implemented, to the event sink by including the following in the class constructor:

```
AfterCloseSink( TDatasetNotify_MFUNCTOR( *this, &TForm::AfterClose ))
```

Attachment   Attach the event source to the event sink by including the following in your program:

```
TDataset dataset;      //Instantiate the source component
TForm form;          //Instantiate the sink component
dataset.AfterCloseSource += form.AfterCloseSink;
```

AfterDelete event

Applies to   TDataSet, TDBDataSet, TQuery, TStoredProc, TTable components

Description   The AfterDelete event is activated when the dataset finishes a call to the Delete method. This event is the last action before Delete returns to the caller. When AfterDelete is called, the deleted record has already been removed from the dataset, and the dataset cursor is on the following record.

By assigning a method to this property, you can take any special actions required by the event.

Source declaration   This declaration of the event source is in the header file:

```
TDatasetNotifySource AfterDeleteSource;
```

Sink declaration   Include this declaration of the event sink in the class definition for your sink object:

```
TDatasetNotifySink AfterDeleteSink;
```

Handler   Put a prototype for the handler method in the class definition for your sink object:

```
void AfterDelete( TDatasetNotifySink& sink, TDataset& sender );
```

And connect the handler method, which you have implemented, to the event sink by including the following in the class constructor:

```
AfterDeleteSink( TDatasetNotify_MFUNCTOR( *this, &TForm::AfterDelete ))
```

Attachment   Attach the event source to the event sink by including the following in your program:

```
TDataset dataset;      //Instantiate the source component
TForm form;            //Instantiate the sink component
dataset.AfterDeleteSource += form.AfterDeleteSink;
```

AfterEdit event

Applies to   TDataSet, TDBDataSet, TQuery, TStoredProc, TTable components

Description   The AfterEdit event is activated when a dataset finishes a call to the Edit method. This event is the last action before Edit returns to the caller.

Note   The event occurs before any changes are made to the current record.

By assigning a method to this property, you can take any special actions required by the event.

Source declaration   This declaration of the event source is in the header file:

```
TDatasetNotifySource AfterEditSource;
```

Sink declaration   Include this declaration of the event sink in the class definition for your sink object:

```
TDatasetNotifySink AfterEditSink;
```

Handler   Put a prototype for the handler method in the class definition for your sink object:

```
void AfterEdit( TDatasetNotifySink& sink, TDataset& sender );
```

And connect the handler method, which you have implemented, to the event sink by including the following in the class constructor:

```
AfterEditSink( TDatasetNotify_MFUNCTOR( *this, &TForm::AfterEdit ))
```

Attachment   Attach the event source to the event sink by including the following in your program:

```
TDataset dataset;      //Instantiate the source component
TForm form;            //Instantiate the sink component
dataset.AfterEditSource += form.AfterEditSink;
```

AfterInsert event

Applies to   TDataSet, TDBDataSet, TQuery, TStoredProc, TTable components

Description   The AfterInsert event is activated when a dataset finishes a call to the Insert or Append methods. This event is the last action before Insert or Append returns to the caller.

Note   This event occurs before a new record has been added to the component.

By assigning a method to this property, you can take any special actions required by the event.

Source declaration   This declaration of the event source is in the header file:

```
TDatasetNotifySource AfterInsertSource;
```

Sink declaration   Include this declaration of the event sink in the class definition for your sink object:

```
TDatasetNotifySink AfterInsertSink;
```

Handler   Put a prototype for the handler method in the class definition for your sink object:

```
void AfterInsert( TDatasetNotifySink& sink, TDataset& sender );
```

And connect the handler method, which you have implemented, to the event sink by including the following in the class constructor:

```
AfterInsertSink( TDatasetNotify_MFUNCTOR( *this, &TForm::AfterInsert ))
```

Attachment   Attach the event source to the event sink by including the following in your program:

```
TDataset dataset;      //Instantiate the source component
TForm form;         //Instantiate the sink component
dataset.AfterInsertSource += form.AfterInsertSink;
```

AfterOpen event

Applies to   TDataSet, TDBDataSet, TQuery, TStoredProc, TTable components

Description   The AfterOpen event is activated after a dataset is opened, either by calling the Open method or by setting the Active property to true. This event is the last action before Open returns to the caller.

By assigning a method to this property, you can take any special actions required by the event.

Source declaration   This declaration of the event source is in the header file:

```
TDatasetNotifySource AfterOpenSource;
```

Sink declaration   Include this declaration of the event sink in the class definition for your sink object:

```
TDatasetNotifySink AfterOpenSink;
```

Handler   Put a prototype for the handler method in the class definition for your sink object:

```
void AfterOpen( TDatasetNotifySink& sink, TDataset& sender );
```

And connect the handler method, which you have implemented, to the event sink by including the following in the class constructor:

```
AfterOpenSink( TDatasetNotify_MFUNCTOR( *this, &TForm::AfterOpen ))
```

Attachment   Attach the event source to the event sink by including the following in your program:

```
TDataset dataset;      //Instantiate the source component
TForm form;         //Instantiate the sink component
dataset.AfterOpenSource += form.AfterOpenSink;
```

AfterPost event

Applies to   TDataSet, TDBDataSet, TQuery, TStoredProc, TTable components

Description   The AfterPost event is activated after a call to the Post method. This event is the last action before Post returns to the caller.

If a TTable component has a range filter in effect (a range filter is set with the ApplyRange method), and if the key value of the newly posted record falls outside the range, the cursor is not positioned on the newly posted record when AfterPost occurs.

By assigning a method to this property, you can take any special actions required by the event.

Source declaration   This declaration of the event source is in the header file:

```
TDatasetNotifySource AfterPostSource;
```

Sink declaration   Include this declaration of the event sink in the class definition for your sink object:

```
TDatasetNotifySink AfterPostSink;
```

Handler   Put a prototype for the handler method in the class definition for your sink object:

```
void AfterPost( TDatasetNotifySink& sink, TDataset& sender );
```

And connect the handler method, which you have implemented, to the event sink by including the following in the class constructor:

```
AfterPostSink( TDatasetNotify_MFUNCTOR( *this, &TForm::AfterPost ));
```

Attachment   Attach the event source to the event sink by including the following in your program:

```
TDataset dataset;      //Instantiate the source component
TForm form;         //Instantiate the sink component
dataset.AfterPostSource += form.AfterPostSink;
```

AliasName property

Applies to   TDataBase component

```
string AliasName;
```
AliasName is the name of an existing BDE alias defined with the BDE Configuration Utility. TDatabase obtains its default parameter settings from the alias. If you specify a

value for the DriverName property, AliasName clears. If you try to change the AliasName value of a TDatabase component when its Connected property value is true, an EDatabaseError exception is raised.

Example
```
Database1.AliasName = "DBDEMOS";
```

Align property

Applies to   All data-aware controls

TAlign Align;
The Align property determines how the controls align within their container (or parent control). These are the possible values:

Value	Meaning
alnNone	The component remains where you place it in the form. This is the default value.
alnTop	The component moves to the top of the form and resizes to fill the width of the form. The height of the component is not affected.
alnBottom	The component moves to the bottom of the form and resizes to fill the width of the form. The height of the component is not affected.
alnLeft	The component moves to the left side of the form and resizes to fill the height of the form. The width of the component is not affected.
alnRight	The component moves to the right side of the form and resizes to fill the height of the form. The width of the component is not affected.
alnClient	The component resizes to fill the client area of a form. If a component already occupies part of the client area, the component resizes to fit within the remaining client area.

If the form or a component containing other components is resized, the components realign within the form or control.

Using the Align property is useful when you want a control to stay in one position on the form, even if the size of the form changes. For example, you could use a panel component with a various controls on it as a tool palette. By changing Align to alLeft, you guarantee that the tool palette always remains on the left side of the form and always equals the client height of the form.

Example
```
DBEdit1.Align = alnRight;
```

Alignment property

Applies to   TDBCheckBox, TDBMemo, TDBText components

Description   The Alignment property aligns text or captions in components.

Alignment property for TDBMemo components

Applies to   TDBMemo component

TAlignment Alignment;
The Alignment property specifies how text is aligned within the component.

These are the possible values:

Value	Meaning
taLeftJustify	Align text to the left side of the control
taCenter	Center text horizontally in the control
taRightJustify	Align text to the right side of the control

Example   This code aligns text to the right side of a label named Label1 in response to a click on a button named RightAlign:

```
MyFormClass::EvRightAlignClick( )
{
   Label1.Alignment = taRightJustify;
}
```

Alignment property for text components

Applies to   TDBText component

TAlignment Alignment;
The Alignment property specifies how text is aligned within the component.

These are the possible values:

Value	Meaning
taLeftJustify	Align text to the left side of the control
taCenter	Center text horizontally in the control
taRightJustify	Align text to the right side of the control

Example   This code aligns text to the right side of a label named Label1 in response to a click on a button named RightAlign:

```
MyFormClass::EvRightAlignClick( )
{
Label1.Alignment = taRightJustify;
}
```

Alignment property for check boxes

Applies to   TDBCheckBox component

TLeftRight Alignment;
For check boxes, the control's caption is always left-aligned within the text area. If the check box is two-dimensional, Alignment determines the placement of that caption area

relative to the control's check box. If the check box is three dimensional, the value of the Alignment property has no effect on the check box.

These are the possible values:

Value	Meaning
lrLeftJustify	Place the caption to the left of the check box.
lrRightJustify	Place the caption to the right of the check box.

Example   This code puts the check box on the left side of the text:

```
MyFormClass::EvButton1Click( )
{
  CheckBox1.Alignment = taLeftJustify;
}
```

AllowGrayed property

Applies to   TDBCheckBox components

bool AllowGrayed;

The value of the AllowGrayed property determines if a check box can have two or three possible states. If AllowGrayed is false, the default value, clicking a check box alternately checks and unchecks it. If AllowGrayed is true, clicking a check box either checks, grays, or unchecks it.

Example   This example uses a check box on a form. When the application runs, the check box is initially checked. When the user clicks it, the check box is unchecked. Clicking it again grays the check box.

```
MyFormClass::FormCreate( )
{
  CheckBox1.AllowGrayed = true;
  CheckBox1.State = cbChecked;
}
```

AllowResize property

Applies to   TBDGrid component

bool AllowResize;

Set the AllowResize property to true to allow users to resize the columns in the data grid. A column can't be resized, however, until its field has been added to the grid. To add a field to the grid, choose Add from the Fields editor.

Example

```
DBGrid1.AllowResize = true;
```

AllowTabs property

Applies to   TBDGrid component

bool AllowTabs;
Set the AllowTabs property to true to allow users to move among the columns of the
data grid by pressing the *Tab* or *Shift+Tab* keys.

Example
```
DBGrid1.AllowTabs = true;
```

Append method

Applies to   TDataSet, TDBDataSet, TQuery, TStoredProc, TTable components

void Append(void);
The Append method moves the cursor to the end of the dataset, puts the dataset into
Insert state, and opens a new, empty record. When an application calls Post, the new
record is inserted in the dataset in a position based on its index, if defined. To discard
the new record, use Cancel.

This method is valid only for datasets that return a live result set.

Note   For indexed tables, both the Append and Insert methods put the new record in the
correct location in the table, based on the table's index. If no index is defined on the
underlying table, then the record maintains its position. Append adds the record to the
end of the table, and Insert inserts it at the current cursor position.

Example   The following code adds a new record when the user clicks a button called
AddRecord:
```
MyFormClass::EvAddRecordClick( )
{
  Table1.Append( );
  Table1.FieldByName( "CustNo" )->AsString = "9999";
  // Fill in other fields here
  if ( you are sure you want to do this )
  {
      Table1.Post( );
  }
  else if ( you changed your mind )
  {
      Table1.Cancel( );
  }
}
```

AppendRecord method

Applies to TDataSet, TDBDataSet, TQuery, TStoredProc, TTable components

void AppendRecord(TVarRecs& values);

The AppendRecord method appends a new record to the dataset using the field values passed in the values parameter. The values are assigned to fields in the record sequentially. For example, the first element is assigned to the first field, the second to the second, and so on. The number of field values passed in values can be fewer than the number of actual fields in the record; any remaining fields are left unassigned and are NULL. The type of each values element must be compatible with the data type of the field.

This method is valid only for datasets that return a live result set.

Note For indexed tables, the AppendRecord and InsertRecord methods both put the new record in the correct location in the table, based on the table's index. If no index is defined on the underlying table, the record maintains its position—AppendRecord adds the record to the end of the table, and InsertRecord inserts it at the current cursor position. In either case, posting a new record in a data grid may cause all the rows before and after the new record to change as the dataset follows the new row to its indexed position and then fetches data to fill the grid around it.

Example The following code appends a record to a table, assigning values to the first five fields of the new record. Notice that the fourth field has a blank value. If you don't want to assign a value to a field, but do want to assign a value to a field that is next in sequential order in the table, you must assign a blank value to the field you want to skip. If the record contains more than five fields, all the remaining fields receive a blank value.

```
TVarRecs values;
values.Add( 999 )
values.Add( "Doe" );
values.Add( "John" );
values.Add( " " );
values.Add( 2045 );
Table1.AppendRecord( &values );
```

ApplyRange method

Applies to TTable component

void ApplyRange(void);

The ApplyRange method applies the range established with the SetRangeStart and SetRangeEnd methods or the EditRangeStart and EditRangeEnd methods to the table. Setting a range reduces the number of records accessible to the application. This is most useful when searching a large table. By narrowing the scope of the search, the search executes more quickly.

Note When comparing fields for range purposes, a NULL field is always less than any other possible value.

Example   This code limits the range from "Goleta" to "Santa Barbara":

```
MyTable.EditRangeStart;      \\ Set the beginning key
MyTable.FieldByName( "City" )->AsString = "Goleta";
MyTable.EditRangeEnd;        \\ Set the ending key
MyTable.FieldByName( "City" )->AsString = "Santa Barbara";
MyTable.ApplyRange;          \\ Tell the dataset to establish the range
```

AsBCD property

Applies to   TParam component

double AsBCD;

Assigning a value to the AsBCD property sets the DataType property value of the TParam component to ftBCD and saves the value as the current data for the parameter. Use the TParam component to set parameters for a SQL query or for a stored procedure.

AsBoolean property

Applies to   TParam, TField components

AsBoolean property for TParam components

Applies to   TParam component

bool AsBoolean;

Assigning a value to the AsBoolean property sets the DataType property value to ftBoolean and saves the value as the current data for the parameter. Accessing the AsBoolean property attempts to convert the current data to a Boolean value and returns that value.

AsBoolean property for fields

Applies to   all TField components

bool AsBoolean;

Run-time only. This is a conversion property that sets or reads a field value as Boolean. For a TBooleanField, AsBoolean can be used to read or set the value of the field, but the Value property should be used for this purpose instead.

For a TStringField, AsBoolean returns true on reading the value of the field if its text begins with the letters Y, y, T or t (for Yes or true), and false otherwise. Using AsBoolean to write a TStringField's value sets the string to T or F.

Example
```
if ( Table1.FieldByName( "BackOrdered" )->AsBoolean )
{
  . . .
}
```

AsCurrency property

Applies to TParam component

double AsCurrency;
Assigning a value to the AsCurrency property sets the DataType property value to ftCurrency and saves the value as the current data for the parameter. Accessing the AsCurrency property attempts to convert the current data to a Double value and returns that value.

AsDate property

Applies to TParam component

DATE AsDate;
Assigning a value to the AsDate property sets the DataType property to ftDate and saves the value as the current data for the parameter. Accessing the AsDate property attempts to convert the current data to a TDateTime value and returns that value.

AsDateTime property

Applies to TParam; all TField components

AsDateTime property for TParam components

Applies to TParam component

DATE AsDateTime;
Assigning a value to the AsDateTime property sets the DataType property to ftDateTime and saves the value as the current data for the parameter. Accessing the AsDateTime property attempts to convert the current data to a TDateTime value and returns that value.

AsDateTime property for fields

Applies to All TField components

DATE AsDateTime;
Run-time only. This is a conversion property. For TDateField, TDateTimeField, or TTimeField, the Value property, not AsDateTime, should be used to read or set the value of the field.

For a TStringField, AsDateTime converts a date to a string on assigning a value to the string field, and converts a string to a date when reading from the field.

Example   The following statement converts a string to a date for insertion into a date field:

```
Table1.FieldByName( "TimeStamp" )->AsDateTime = time( 0 );
```

AsFloat property

Applies to   All TField, TParam components

AsFloat property for TParam components

Applies to   TParam component

double AsFloat;
Assigning a value to the AsFloat property sets the DataType property value to ftFloat and saves the value as the current data for the parameter. Accessing the AsFloat property attempts to convert the current data to a Double value and returns that value.

AsFloat property for fields

Applies to   All TField components

double AsFloat;
Run-time only. This is a conversion property. For a TFloatField, TBCDField, or TCurrencyField, Value should be used (not AsFloat) to read or set the value of the field as a Double.

For a TStringField, AsFloat converts a float to a string on assigning a value to the field, and converts a string to a float when reading from the field.

AsInteger property

Applies to   TParam, all TField components

AsInteger property for TParam components

Applies to   TParam component

int32 AsInteger;
Assigning a value to the AsInteger property sets the DataType property to ftInteger and saves the value as the current data for the parameter. Accessing the AsInteger property attempts to convert the current data to an int32 value and returns that value.

AsInteger property for fields

Applies to   All TField components

int32 AsInteger;
Run-time only. This is a conversion property. For a TIntegerField, TSmallintField, or TWordField, the Value property, not AsInteger, should be used to read or set the value of the field as an int32.

For a TStringField, AsInteger converts an integer to a string on assigning a value to the field, and converts a string to an integer when reading from the field.

Assign method

Applies to   TBatchMove, TDatabase, TDataSet, TDataSource, TDBDataSet, all TField, TFieldDefs, TIndexDefs, TQuery, TParam, TParams, TSession, TStoredProc, TStrings components

Assign method for TFieldDefs components

Applies to   TFieldDefs component

void Assign(TFieldDefs& f);
The Assign method creates a new set of TFieldDefs components in the Items property from the f parameter, clearing any previous field definitions in Items.

Assign method for TIndexDefs components

Applies to   TIndexDefs component

void Assign(TIndexDefs& i);
The Assign method creates a new set of TIndexDefs components in the Items property from the i parameter, clearing any previous index definitions in Items.

Assign method for fields

Applies to   all TField components

void Assign(TPersistent& f);
Assign copies data from one field to another. Both fields must be valid and have the same DataType and Size, and the DataSize of the f parameter must be 255 bytes or less.

The restrictions on type compatibility and size do not apply to TBlobField, TBytesField, TGraphicField, TMemoField, or TVarBytesField. For these components the source (f parameter) can be TBlobField, TBytesField, TGraphicField, TMemoField, TVarBytesField, or TStrings.

Example
```
// Copy one date-time field to another
DateTimeField1.Assign( DateTimeField2 );
// Copy a graphic field to a blob field
BlobField1.Assign( GraphicField1 );
// Copy strings in a TMemo to a TMemoField
MemoField1.Assign( Memo1.Lines );
```

Assign method for TParam components

Applies to   TParam component

void Assign(TParam& p);

The Assign method transfers all the data from the p parameter to the TParam component that calls it. If, however, you specified a value for the ParamType property of the TParam component that calls Assign, the data in the p parameter is not assigned to the TParam component.

Example

```
// Copy the CustNo parameter from Query1 to Query2
Query2.ParamByName( "CustNo" ).Assign(Query1.ParamByName( "CustNo" ) );
```

Assign method for TParams components

Applies to   TParams component

void Assign(TParams& p);

If the p parameter is another TParams component, the Assign method discards any current parameter information in a TParams component and replaces it with the information from p. If the parameter is any other type of object, the Assign method calls its inherited method. Use this method to save and restore a set of parameter information or copy another component's parameter information to the calling TParams component.

Example

```
TParams params1;
TParams params2;
...
// Get the parameters for Query1
params1 = Query1.Params;
// Get the params for Query2
params2 = Query2.Params;
// Assign Query1 params to Query2
params2.Assign( params1 );
// Set new Query2 params
Query2.Params = params;
```

Assign method for other components

Applies to   TBatchMove, TDatabase, TDataSet, TDataSource, TDBDataSet, TQuery, TSession, TStoredProc, TStrings components

void Assign(TPersistent& s);

The Assign method discards the current strings in the list and replaces them with the strings in the s parameter. The general form of a call to Assign is

```
Destination.Assign(Source);
```

which tells the Destination object to assign the contents of the Source object to itself.

In general, the statement "Destination = Source" is not the same as the statement "Destination.Assign(Source)". The statement "Destination = Source" makes Destination reference the same object as Source, whereas "Destination.Assign(Source)" copies the contents of the object referenced by Source into the object referenced by Destination.

The actions performed by Assign depend on the actual types of Destination and Source. For example, if Destination and Source are string objects (TStrings), the strings contained in Source are copied into Destination.

Although the compiler allows any two TPersistent objects to be used in a call to Assign, the call succeeds at run time only if the objects involved "know" how to perform an assignment.

Example   The following code changes the font family of a label so that it matches the font of the button when the user clicks the button:

```
MyFormClass::EvButton1Click( )
{
    Label1.FontName.Assign( Button1.FontName );
}
```

AssignField method

Applies to   TParam component

void AssignField(TField& f);

The AssignField method transfers the DataType and Name values from the TField component specified with the f parameter. Use AssignField to set a parameter from a TField component.

Example

```
// Copy the CustNo field value from Query1 to the CustNo parameter of Query2
Query2.ParamByName( "CustNo" ).AssignField( Query1.FieldByName( "CustNo" ) );
```

AssignValue method

Applies to   All TField components

void AssignValue(TVarRec& v);

The AssignValue method sets the field to v using one of the AsInteger, AsBoolean, AsString, or AsFloat properties, depending on the type of v.

Example

```
Field1.AssignValue( "new string" );
```

AssignValues method

Applies to   TParams component

void AssignValues(TParams& p);

For each entry in Items, the AssignValues method attempts to find a parameter with the same Name property value in p. If successful, the parameter information (type and current data) from the p parameter is assigned to the Items entry. If no match is found, nothing happens.

Example

```
TParams SavedParams;
TParams params;
...
// Save the parameters for Query1
SavedParams = Query1.Params;
// Get params from Query2
params = Query2.Params;
// transfer values from Query1 to Query2
params.AssignValues( SaveParams );
// Restore the parameters to Query2
Query2.Params = params;
```

AsSmallInt property

Applies to   TParam component

int32 AsSmallInt;

Assigning a value to the AsSmallInt property sets the DataType property to fsSmallInt and saves the value as the current data for the parameter. Accessing the AsSmallInt property attempts to convert the current data to an int32 value and returns that value.

AsString property

Applies to   TParam and all TField components

AsString property for TParam components

Applies to   TParam component

string AsString;

Assigning a value to the AsString property sets the DataType property to ftString and saves the value as the current data for the parameter. Accessing the AsString property attempts to convert the current data to a string value and returns that value.

AsString property for fields

Applies to   All TField components

string AsString;
Run-time only. This a conversion property. For a TStringField, the Value property, not AsString, should be used to read or set the value of the field as a string.

For TBCDField, TCurrencyField, TDateField, TDateTimeField, TFloatField, TIntegerField, TSmallintField, TTimeField, and TWordField, AsString converts a string to the appropriate type on inserting or updating the field, and converts the type to a string when reading from the field.

For TBooleanField, on insert or update AsString sets the value to true if the text begins with the letter Y, y, T or t and to false otherwise. When reading from a Boolean field, AsString returns T or F.

For a TMemoField, AsString should only be used to read from the field. It sets the string value to "(Memo)". An exception is raised if AsString is used to write to a TMemoField.

For a TGraphicField, AsString should only be used to read from the field. It sets the string value to "(Graphic)". An exception is raised if AsString is used to write to a TGraphicField.

For a TBlobField, AsString should only be used to read from the field. It sets the string value to "(Blob)". An exception is raised if AsString is used to write to a TBlobField.

For a TBytesField, AsString should only be used to read from the field. It sets the string value to "(Bytes)". An exception is raised if AsString is used to write to a TBytesField.

For a TVarBytesField, AsString should only be used to read from the field. It sets the string value to "(Var Bytes)". An exception is raised if AsString is used to write to a TVarBytesField.

AsTime property

Applies to   TParam component

DATE AsTime;
Assigning a value to the AsTime property sets the DataType property to ftTime and saves the value as the current data for the parameter. Accessing the AsTime property attempts to convert the current data to a TDateTime value and returns that value.

AsWord property

Applies to   TParam component

int32 AsWord;
Assigning a value to the AsWord property sets the DataType property to ftWord and saves the value as the current data for the parameter. Accessing the AsWord property attempts to convert the current data to an int32 value and returns that value.

AtBOF property

Applies to   TDataSet, TDBDataSet, TQuery, TStoredProc, TTable components

bool AtBOF;

Run-time and read only. AtBOF is a Boolean property that indicates whether a dataset is known to be at its first row. The AtBOF property returns a value of true only after:

- An application first opens a table
- A call to a table's First method
- A call to a table's Prior method fails

Example
```
Table1.Last( );
while( ! Table1.AtBOF( ) )
{
  // DoSomething
  Table1.Prior( );
}
```

AtEOF property

Applies to   TDataSet, TDBDataSet, TQuery, TStoredProc, TTable components

bool AtEOF;

Run-time and read only. AtEOF is a Boolean property that indicates whether a dataset is known to be at its last row. The AtEOF property returns a value of true after:

- An application opens an empty dataset
- A call to a table's Last method
- A call to a table's Next fails because the cursor is on the last row

Example
```
Table1.First;
while( !Table1.AtEOF )
{
  // Do Something
  Table1.Next( );
}
```

AutoCalcFields property

Applies to   TDataSet, TDBDataSet, TQuery, TStoredProc, TTable components

bool AutoCalcFields;

The AutoCalcFields property determines when the OnCalcFields event is called. OnCalcFields is always called whenever an application retrieves a record from the database. If AutoCalcFields is true, OnCalcFields is called also whenever a field in a dataset is edited.

If AutoCalcFields is true, OnCalcFields should not perform any actions that modify the dataset (or the linked dataset if it is part of a master-detail relationship), because this can lead to recursion. For example, if OnCalcFields performs a Post, and AutoCalcFields is true, OnCalcFields is called again, leading to another Post, and so on.

AutoDisplay property

Applies to TDBImage, TDBMemo components

bool AutoDisplay;

The value of the AutoDisplay property determines whether to automatically display the contents of a memo or graphic BLOB in a database memo or database image control.

If AutoDisplay is true (the default value), the control automatically displays new data when the underlying BLOB field changes (such as when moving to a new record).

If AutoDisplay is false, the control clears whenever the underlying BLOB field changes. To display the data, the user can double-click on the control or select it and press Enter. In addition, by calling the LoadMemo method of a database memo or the LoadPicture method of a database image you can ensure that the control is showing data.

You might want to change the value of AutoDisplay to false if the automatic loading of BLOB fields seems to take too long.

Example The following code displays the text BLOB in DBMemo1:

```
DBMemo1.AutoDisplay = true;
```

AutoEdit property

Applies to TDataSource component

bool AutoEdit;

Note This was deleted from the print documentation. Verify that it has been implemented before delivering the help file.

AutoEdit determines if data-aware controls connected to a TDataSource component automatically place the current record into edit mode by calling the table's Edit method when the user begins typing within one of them. AutoEdit is true by default; To prevent the data from being unintentionally modified, set AutoEdit to false. When AutoEdit is false, you can still call the Edit method to modify a field.

AutoSelect property

Applies to TDBEdit, TDBLookupCombo components

bool AutoSelect;

The value of the AutoSelect property determines if the text in the edit box or combo box is automatically selected when the user tabs to the control. If AutoSelect is true, the text is selected. If AutoSelect is false, the text is not selected.

The default value is true.

AutoSize property

Applies to   TDBEdit, TDBImage, TDBText components

AutoSize property for database image components

Applies to   TDBImage component

bool AutoSize;

When the AutoSize property is true, the database image control resizes to accommodate the image it contains (specified by the Picture property). When AutoSize is false, the image control remains the same size, regardless of the size of the image. If the image control is smaller than the image, only the portion of the picture that fits inside the image component is visible.

The default value is false.

Note   You must remember to set the AutoSize property to true before loading the picture, or AutoSize has no effect.

To resize the image to fill an image control completely when the control is larger than the native size of the image, use the Stretch property.

Example   This example uses an image control and a button. Resize the image control so that it is too small to display the entire bitmap. When the user clicks the button, the bitmap is loaded into the image control, and the image control resizes to display the bitmap in its entirety.

```
MyFormClass::EvButton1Click( )
{
  Image1.AutoSize = true;
  Image1.Picture = TheHpic;
}
```

AutoSize property for database edit box components

Applies to   TDBEdit component

bool AutoSize;

When the AutoSize property is true, the height of the edit box changes to accommodate font size changes to the text. When AutoSize is false, the edit box remains the same size, regardless of any font changes. The default value is true.

If an edit box has no border, changing the value of AutoSize has no effect. In other words, the BorderStyle property must have a value of bsSingle.

AutoSize property for database text components

Applies to TDBText component

bool AutoSize;

When the AutoSize property is true, the label component resizes to the width and length of the current string in the database text control's Caption property. If you type text for a database text control while AutoSize is true, it grows for each character you type. If you change the font size of the text, the database text control resizes to the new font size. When AutoSize is false, the size of the database text control is not affected by the length of the string in its Caption property.

The default value of AutoSize is true.

Example The following code keeps the size of the label control constant, even though the length of the label's caption changes. As a result, the caption of the label is probably too long to display in the label when the user clicks the button:

```
MyFormClass::EvButton1Click( )
{
  Label1.AutoSize = false;
  Label1.Caption = "This string is too long as the caption of this label";
}
```

BackColor property

Applies to TDBCheckBox, TDBComboBox, TDBEdit, TDBImage, TDBListBox, TDBLookupCombo, TDBLookupList, TDBMemo, TDBRadioGroup, TDBText components

COLORREF BackColor;

For all components, the BackColor property determines the background color of a control.

At design time, set the BackColor property by choosing it in the Property Inspector and clicking on the ellipsis button. This brings up the Windows Color Dialog and you choose a color in the usual way.

At run time, set the BackColor property by using the hexadecimal value for the desired color, or you can use the Windows RGB macro.

Example
```
DBEdit1.BackColor = 0xff00ff;
```

BatchMove method

Applies to   TTable component

int32 BatchMove(TDataSet& t, TBatchMode m);

The BatchMove method copies, appends, updates, or deletes records in a table. The t parameter specifies a dataset component linked to a database table containing the source records. Specify the copy mode as the m parameter; it can be any of the elements of TBatchMode as listed below.

Value	Meaning
batAppend	Append records to the destination table. The destination table must already exist. (The destination must not have any records with the key of the any of the records in the source.)
batUpdate	Update records in the destination table with matching records from the source table. The destination table must exist and must have an index defined to match records.
batAppendUpdate	If a matching record exists in the destination table, update it. Otherwise, append records to the destination table. The destination table must exist and must have an index defined to match records.
batCopy	Create the destination table based on the structure of the source table. The destination table must not already exist—if it does, the operation will delete it.
batDelete	Delete records in the destination table that match records in the source table. The destination table must already exist and must have an index defined.

BatchMove returns the number of records operated on.

Example

```
Table1.BatchMove( Table2, batAppend );
```

BDTException object   bdtc.h

The BDTException object is the base class for all exceptions in Visual Database Tools. All exceptions inherit its methods and properties. The Message data member is a string that describes the exception. The Whow member function displays the message in a Windows MessageBox.

BDTException has two descendant objects. For errors thrown by database components, or by the Borland Database Engine, use the EDatabaseError exception. For errors thrown by TStrings components, use the EListError exception.

EDatabaseError object   bdtc.h

The EDatabaseError is an exception thrown when an error is made in a database component. For example, if you try to open a table that doesn't exist, an EDatabaseError exception is thrown.

```
void TestEDatabaseError( void )
{
   // Try to open a table that doesn't exist
   // and catch the EDatabaseError exception.
TTable table1;
   table1.DatabaseName = "DivePlan";
   table1.TableName = "noexist.db";
   try
   {
       table1.Open( );
   }
   catch( EDatabaseError e )
   {
       e.Show( "EDatabaseError" );
   }
}
```

BeforeCancel event

Applies to   TDataSet, TDBDataSet, TQuery, TStoredProc, TTable components

Description   The BeforeCancel event is activated at the beginning of a call to the Cancel method. This event is the first action taken by Cancel if the dataset is in the Edit State or if changes are pending. Otherwise, the Cancel method does not call BeforeCancel.

By assigning a method to this property, you can take any special actions required by the event. By raising an exception in this event handler, you can prevent the Cancel operation from occurring.

Source declaration   This declaration of the event source is in the header file:

```
TDatasetNotifySource BeforeCancelSource;
```

Sink declaration   Include this declaration of the event sink in the class definition for your sink object:

```
TDatasetNotifySink BeforeCancelSink;
```

Handler   Put a prototype for the handler method in the class definition for your sink object:

```
void BeforeCancel( TDatasetNotifySink& sink, TDataset& sender );
```

And connect the handler method, which you have implemented, to the event sink by including the following in the class constructor:

```
BeforeCancelSink( TDatasetNotify_MFUNCTOR( *this, &TForm::BeforeCancel ))
```

Attachment   Attach the event source to the event sink by including the following in your program:

```
TDataset dataset;      //Instantiate the source component
TForm form;        //Instantiate the sink component
dataset.BeforeCancelSource += form.BeforeCancelSink;
```

BeforeClose event

Applies to   TDataSet, TDBDataSet, TQuery, TStoredProc, TTable components

Description   The BeforeClose event is activated before the dataset is closed, either by calling the Close method or by setting the Active property to false.

By assigning a method to this property, you can take any special actions required by the event. By raising an exception in this event handler, you can prevent the Close operation from occurring.

Source declaration   This declaration of the event source is in the header file:

```
TDatasetNotifySource BeforeCloseSource;
```

Sink declaration   Include this declaration of the event sink in the class definition for your sink object:

```
TDatasetNotifySink BeforeCloseSink;
```

Handler   Put a prototype for the handler method in the class definition for your sink object:

```
void BeforeClose( TDatasetNotifySink& sink, TDataset& sender );
```

And connect the handler method, which you have implemented, to the event sink by including the following in the class constructor:

```
BeforeCloseSink( TDatasetNotify_MFUNCTOR( *this, &TForm::BeforeClose ))
```

Attachment   Attach the event source to the event sink by including the following in your program:

```
TDataset dataset;//Instantiate the event source component
TForm form;//Instantiate the event sink component
dataset.BeforeCloseSource += form.BeforeCloseSink;
```

BeforeDelete event

Applies to   TDataSet, TDBDataSet, TQuery, TStoredProc, TTable components

Description   The BeforeDelete event is activated when the dataset begins a call to the Delete method.

By assigning a method to this property, you can take any special actions required by the event. By raising an exception in this event handler, you can prevent the Delete operation from occurring.

Source declaration   This declaration of the event source is in the header file:

```
TDatasetNotifySource BeforeDeleteSource;
```

Sink declaration   Include this declaration of the event sink in the class definition for your sink object:

```
TDatasetNotifySink BeforeDeleteSink;
```

Handler   Put a prototype for the handler method in the class definition for your sink object:

```
void BeforeDelete( TDatasetNotifySink& sink, TDataset& sender );
```

And connect the handler method, which you have implemented, to the event sink by including the following in the class constructor:

```
BeforeDeleteSink( TDatasetNotify_MFUNCTOR( *this, &TForm::BeforeDelete ))
```

Attachment   Attach the event source to the event sink by including the following in your program:

```
TDataset dataset;//Instantiate the event source component
TForm form;//Instantiate the event sink component
dataset.BeforeDeleteSource += form.BeforeDeleteSink;
```

BeforeEdit event

Applies to   TDataSet, TDBDataSet, TQuery, TStoredProc, TTable components

Description   The BeforeEdit event is activated when the dataset begins a call to the Edit method.

By assigning a method to this property, you can take any special actions required by the event. By raising an exception in this event handler, you can prevent the Edit operation from occurring.

Source declaration   This declaration of the event source is in the header file:

```
TDatasetNotifySource BeforeEditSource;
```

Sink declaration   Include this declaration of the event sink in the class definition for your sink object:

```
TDatasetNotifySink BeforeEditSink;
```

Handler   Put a prototype for the handler method in the class definition for your sink object:

```
void BeforeEdit( TDatasetNotifySink& sink, TDataset& sender );
```

And connect the handler method, which you have implemented, to the event sink by including the following in the class constructor:

```
BeforeEditSink( TDatasetNotify_MFUNCTOR( *this, &TForm::BeforeEdit ))
```

Attachment   Attach the event source to the event sink by including the following in your program:

```
TDataset dataset;//Instantiate the event source component
TForm form;//Instantiate the event sink component
dataset.BeforeEditSource += form.BeforeEditSink;
```

BeforeInsert event

Applies to   TDataSet, TDBDataSet, TQuery, TStoredProc, TTable components

Description   The BeforeInsert event is activated when the dataset begins a call to the Insert or Append methods.

By assigning a method to this property, you can take any special actions required by the event. By raising an exception in this event handler, you can prevent the Insert or Append operation from occurring.

Source declaration   This declaration of the event source is in the header file:

```
TDatasetNotifySource BeforeInsertSource;
```

Sink declaration   Include this declaration of the event sink in the class definition for your sink object:

```
TDatasetNotifySink BeforeInsertSink;
```

Handler   Put a prototype for the handler method in the class definition for your sink object:

```
void BeforeInsert( TDatasetNotifySink& sink, TDataset& sender );
```

And connect the handler method, which you have implemented, to the event sink by including the following in the class constructor:

```
BeforeInsertSink( TDatasetNotify_MFUNCTOR( *this, &TForm::BeforeInsert ))
```

Attachment   Attach the event source to the event sink by including the following in your program:

```
TDataset dataset;//Instantiate the event source component
TForm form;//Instantiate the event sink component
dataset.BeforeInsertSource += form.BeforeInsertSink;
```

BeforeOpen event

Applies to   TDataSet, TDBDataSet, TQuery, TStoredProc, TTable components

Description   The BeforeOpen event is activated before the dataset is opened, either by calling the Open method or by setting the Active property to true. Typically, the BeforeOpen event handler opens any private lookup tables used by other event handlers in the dataset.

By assigning a method to this property, you can take any special actions required by the event. By raising an exception in this event handler, you can prevent the Open operation from occurring.

Source declaration   This declaration of the event source is in the header file:

```
TDatasetNotifySource BeforeOpenSource;
```

Sink declaration   Include this declaration of the event sink in the class definition for your sink object:

```
TDatasetNotifySink BeforeOpenSink;
```

Handler   Put a prototype for the handler method in the class definition for your sink object:

```
void BeforeOpen( TDatasetNotifySink& sink, TDataset& sender );
```

And connect the handler method, which you have implemented, to the event sink by including the following in the class constructor:

```
BeforeOpenSink( TDatasetNotify_MFUNCTOR( *this, &TForm::BeforeOpen ))
```

Attachment   Attach the event source to the event sink by including the following in your program:

```
TDataset dataset;//Instantiate the event source component
TForm form;//Instantiate the event sink component
dataset.BeforeOpenSource += form.BeforeOpenSink;
```

BeforePost event

Applies to   TDataSet, TDBDataSet, TQuery, TStoredProc, TTable components

The BeforePost event is activated at the beginning of a call to the Post method. This event is the first action taken by the Post method, after it calls the UpdateRecord method to reflect any changes made to the record by data controls. The BeforePost event can be used to validate a record before it is posted. By raising an exception, a BeforePost event handler can prevent the posting of an invalid record.

By assigning a method to this property, you can take any special actions required by the event. By raising an exception in this event handler, you can prevent the Post operation from occurring.

Source declaration   This declaration of the event source is in the header file:

```
TDatasetNotifySource BeforePostSource;
```

Sink declaration   Include this declaration of the event sink in the class definition for your sink object:

```
TDatasetNotifySink BeforePostSink;
```

Handler   Put a prototype for the handler method in the class definition for your sink object:

```
void BeforePost( TDatasetNotifySink& sink, TDataset& sender );
```

And connect the handler method, which you have implemented, to the event sink by including the following in the class constructor:

```
BeforePostSink( TDatasetNotify_MFUNCTOR( *this, &TForm::BeforePost ))
```

Attachment   Attach the event source to the event sink by including the following in your program:

```
TDataset dataset;//Instantiate the event source component
TForm form;//Instantiate the event sink component
dataset.BeforePostSource += form.BeforePostSink;
```

BeginDrag method

Applies to   All data-aware controls

void BeginDrag(bool Immediate);
The BeginDrag method starts the dragging of a control. Immediate is a reserved parameter that is always true.

Your application needs to call the BeginDrag method to begin dragging only when the DragMode property value for the control is dmManual.

BorderStyle property

Applies to   TDBEdit, TDBImage, TDBListBox, TDBLookupList, TDBMemo, TDBText components

TBorderStyle BorderStyle;
The BorderStyle property of database edit boxes, images, list boxes, and memo controls determines whether these components have a border. These are the possible values:

Value	Meaning
bsNone	Do not draw a visible border.
bsSingle	Draw a single-line border.

Example   The following example puts a single-line border around the edit box, Edit1:

```
DBEdit1.BorderStyle = bsSingle;
```

Bound property

Applies to   TParam component

bool Bound;
The Bound property determines whether a value has been assigned to the parameter. If Bound is true, a value has been assigned. If Bound is false, the parameter has no value assigned to it. If you attempt to open a parameterized query before all the parameters of the query have values assigned to them, an exception occurs. Therefore, you can use the Bound property to be sure all parameters have values assigned before running the query.

BoundsRect property

Applies to   All data-aware controls

TRect BoundsRect;

The BoundsRect property returns the bounding rectangle of the control, expressed in the coordinate system of the parent control. The statement

```
TRect R = Control.BoundsRect;
```

corresponds to

```
TRect R =
{
  Control.Left,
  Control.Top,
  Control.Left + Control.Width,
  Control.Top + Control.Height
};
```

Example   This code resizes a button control to twice as wide and half as high:

```
void TForm1::Button1Click()
{
  TRect Rect = Button2.BoundsRect;
  Rect.Right = Rect.Left + 2 * (Rect.Right - Rect.Left);
  Rect.Bottom = Rect.Top + (Rect.Bottom - Rect.Top)/2;
  Button2.BoundsRect = Rect;
}
```

BringToFront method

Applies to   All data-aware controls

void BringToFront( );
The BringToFront method puts the component in front of all other components within its parent component or form. You can use it to reorder overlapping components within a form.

The order in which controls stack on top of each order (also called the Z order) depends on the order in which you create them. If you put a database navigator on a form, then create a database check box, the database check box is on top. If you call BringToFront for the database navigator, the navigator moves to the top.

BtnCancel property

Applies to   TDBNavigator component

TBtnState BtnCancel;
The BtnCancel property determines the state of the button on the database navigator that cancels the current edit when the user clicks it. These are the possible values:

Value	Meaning
btnOff	Do not display the Cancel button on the navigator.

Value	Meaning
btnOn	Display the Cancel button on the navigator and enable it.
btnDisabled	Display the Cancel button on the navigator, but disable and dim it.

BtnDelete property

Applies to   TDBNavigator component

TBtnState BtnDelete;

The BtnDelete property determines the state of the button on the database navigator that deletes the current record when the user clicks it. These are the possible values:

Value	Meaning
btnOff	Do not display the Delete button on the navigator.
btnOn	Display the Delete button on the navigator and enable it.
btnDisabled	Display the Delete button on the navigator, but disable and dim it.

BtnEdit property

Applies to   TDBNavigator component

TBtnState BtnEdit;

The BtnEdit property determines the state of the button on the database navigator that puts the current record into Edit mode when the user clicks it. These are the possible values:

Value	Meaning
btnOff	Do not display the Edit button on the navigator.
btnOn	Display the Edit button on the navigator and enable it.
btnDisabled	Display the Edit button on the navigator, but disable and dim it.

BtnFirst property

Applies to   TDBNavigator component

TBtnState BtnFirst;

The BtnFirst property determines the state of the button on the database navigator that takes the user to the first record when the user clicks it. These are the possible values:

Value	Meaning
btnOff	Do not display the First button on the navigator.
btnOn	Display the First button on the navigator and enable it.
btnDisabled	Display the First button on the navigator, but disable and dim it.

BtnInsert property

Applies to   TDBNavigator component

TBtnState BtnInsert;
The BtnInsert property determines the state of the button on the database navigator that inserts a blank record when the user clicks it. These are the possible values:

Value	Meaning
btnOff	Do not display the Insert button on the navigator.
btnOn	Display the Insert button on the navigator and enable it.
btnDisabled	Display the Insert button on the navigator, but disable and dim it

BtnLast property

Applies to   TDBNavigator component

TBtnState BtnLast;
The BtnLast property determines the state of the button on the database navigator that takes the user to the last record when the user clicks it. These are the possible values:

Value	Meaning
btnOff	Do not display the Last button on the navigator.
btnOn	Display the Last button on the navigator and enable it.
btnDisabled	Display the Last button on the navigator, but disable and dim it.

BtnNext property

Applies to   TDBNavigator component

TBtnState BtnNext;
The BtnNext property determines the state of the button on the database navigator that takes the user to the next record when the user clicks it. These are the possible values:

Value	Meaning
btnOff	Do not display the Next button on the navigator.
btnOn	Display the Next button on the navigator and enable it.
btnDisabled	Display the Next button on the navigator, but disable and dim it.

BtnPost property

Applies to   TDBNavigator component

TBtnState BtnPost;

The BtnPost property determines the state of the button on the database navigator that posts the current record when the user clicks it. These are the possible values:

Value	Meaning
btnOff	Do not display the Post button on the navigator.
btnOn	Display the Post button on the navigator and enable it.
btnDisabled	Display the Post button on the navigator, but disable and dim it.

BtnPrevious property

Applies to   TDBNavigator component

TBtnState BtnPrevious;

The BtnPrevious property determines the state of the button on the database navigator that takes the user to the previous record when the user clicks it. These are the possible values:

Value	Meaning
btnOff	Do not display the Previous button on the navigator.
btnOn	Display the Previous button on the navigator and enable it.
btnDisabled	Display the Previous button on the navigator, but disable and dim it.

BtnRefresh property

Applies to   TDBNavigator component

TBtnState BtnRefresh;

The BtnRefresh property determines the state of the button on the database navigator that refreshes the data in the dataset when the user clicks it. These are the possible values:

Value	Meaning
btnOff	Do not display the Refresh button on the navigator.
btnOn	Display the Refresh button on the navigator and enable it.
btnDisabled	Display the Refresh button on the navigator, but disable and dim it.

Calculated property

Applies to   All TField components

bool Calculated;

The Calculated property determines if the value in the field is the result of a calculation. Calculated is true if the value of the field is calculated by the OnCalcFields event handler.

Calculated fields can be created with the Fields editor, but are not stored in or retrieved from the physical tables underlying a dataset. Instead they are calculated for each record in the table by the dataset's OnCalcFields event handler, which typically uses expressions involving values from other fields in the record to generate a value for each calculated field.

For example, a table might have non-calculated fields for Quantity and UnitPrice, and a calculated field for ExtendedPrice, which would be calculated by multiplying the values of the Quantity and UnitPrice fields. Calculated fields are also useful for performing lookups in other tables. For example, a part number can be used to retrieve a part description for display in an invoice line item.

Cancel method

Applies to   TDataSet, TDBDataSet, TQuery, TStoredProc, TTable components

void Cancel(void);
The Cancel method returns the dataset to Browse state and discards any changes to the current record.

CancelRange method

Applies to   TTable component

void CancelRange(void);
The CancelRange method removes any range on a table set with either the ApplyRange or SetRange methods.

Example
```
Table1.CancelRange( );
```

CanFocus method

Applies to   All data-aware controls

bool CanFocus( );
The CanFocus method determines whether a control can receive focus. CanFocus returns true if both the control and its parent(s) have their Visible and Enabled properties set to true. If all the Visible and Enabled properties of the control and the components from which the control descends are **not** true, then CanFocus returns false.

Example   This example uses a group box, a label, and a button on a form. The group box contains a check box. When the application runs, the group box is disabled (Enabled is set to false). Because the group box is the parent of the check box, the user can never tab to the check box. When the user clicks the button, the caption of the label reports that the check box cannot receive the input focus:

```
MyFormClass::SetupWindow( )
{
  ...
  GroupBox1.Enabled = true;
  ...
}
MyFormClass::EvButton1Click( )
{
  if( CheckBox1.CanFocus( ) )
  {
      Label1.SetText( "The check box can focus" );
  }
  else
  {
      Label1.SetText( "The check box cannot focus" );
  }
}
```

CanModify property

Applies to   TDataSet, TDBDataSet, all TField, TQuery, TStoredProc, TTable
components

CanModify property for dataset components

Applies to   TDataSet, TDBDataSet, TQuery, TStoredProc, TTable components

bool CanModify;

Run-time and read only. CanModify specifies whether an application can modify the
data in a dataset. When CanModify is false, then the dataset is read-only, and cannot be
put into Edit or Insert state. When CanModify is true, the dataset can enter Edit or Insert
state.

Even if CanModify is true, it is not a guarantee that a user can to insert or update records
in a table. Other factors may come in to play, such as SQL access privileges, for example.

A TTable component has a ReadOnly property that requests write privileges when set
to false. When ReadOnly is true, CanModify is automatically set to false. When
ReadOnly is false, CanModify is true if the database allows read and write privileges for
the dataset and the underlying table.

Example

```
if( Table1.CanModify( )
{
// Do this only if the dataset can be modified
  Table1.GetFieldByName( "CustNo" )->AsInteger = 1234;
}
```

CanModify property for fields

Applies to   All TField components

bool CanModify;
Run-time and read only. Specifies if a field can be modified for any reason, such as during a SetKey operation. CanModify is true if the value of the field can be modified. If the ReadOnly property of the field is true, or the ReadOnly property of the dataset is true, then CanModify is false.

Canvas property

Applies to   TDBComboBox, TDBListBox components

TDC* Canvas;
Run-time and read only. The Canvas property gives you access to a drawing surface that you can use when implementing a handler for the OnDrawItem event of an owner-drawn list box or combo box control.

Example

```
void MyCombo::OnMyDrawItem( short, TRect& rc, TOwnerDrawState )
{
  // Create blue background
  Canvas->FillRect( rc.left, rc.top, rc.right, rc.bottom, TBrush(0, 0, 255) );
  int iOldMode = Canvas->SetBkMode( TRANSPARENT );
  // Write the selected value
  string Val = Value;
  Canvas->TextOut(0, 0, Val.c_str() );
  // Restore previous BkMode
  Canvas->SetBkMode( iOldMode );
}
```

See also   Action property, ItemHeight property, OnDrawItem event, Style property

Caption property

Applies to   All data-aware controls

string Caption;
The Caption property specifies text that appears in a control. To underline a character in a string, include an ampersand (&) before the character. This type of character is called an accelerator character. The user can then select the control or menu item by pressing *Alt* while typing the underlined character. The default value is the name of the component.

The Caption property of a data grid is available at run time only.

Example   This code changes the caption of a group box:

```
MyFormClass::EvButton1Click( )
```

```
{
    GroupBox1.Caption = "Fancy options";
}
```

Center property

Applies to   TDBImage component

bool Center;

The Center property determines whether a database image is centered in the image control. If Center is true, the image is centered. If Center is false, the image aligns with the top left corner of the control. The default value is true.

ChangedCount property

Applies to   TBatchMove component

int32 ChangedCount;

Run-time and read only. The value of the ChangedCount property is the number of records that were deleted or replaced in the Destination table as the result of a batch move operation. If you specified a table to be the ChangedTableName property value, the number of records in this table will equal the value of ChangedCount after the batch move.

ChangedCount is the number of records added to the table specified by ChangedTableName. If ChangedTableName is not specified, the count is still valid.

Example

```
BatchMove1.Execute();
    if( BatchMove1.ChangedCount != Source.RecordCount )
    {
    // something went wrong
    }
```

ChangedTableName property

Applies to   TBatchMove component

string ChangedTableName;

If you specify the name of a table for the ChangedTableName property, the batch move operation creates a local Paradox table containing all records in the destination table that changed as a result of the batch operation. The number of records placed in the new table is reported in the ChangedCount property.

Example

```
BatchMove1.ChangedTableName = "oldrecs.db";
```

CharCase property

Applies to   TDBEdit component

TEditCharCase CharCase;
The CharCase property determines the case of the Caption property of the database edit box. These are the possible values:

Value	Meaning
ccLower	Display the text of the edit box in lowercase.
ccNormal	Display the text of the edit box in mixed case.
ccUpper	Display the text of the edit box in uppercase.

If the user tries to enter a different case than the current value of CharCase, the characters the user enters appear in the case specified by CharCase. For example, if the value of CharCase is ccLower, only lowercase characters appear in the edit box, even if the user tries to enter uppercase characters.

Example   This example uses an edit box and group box containing three radio buttons. When the user selects the first radio button, the text in the edit box becomes lowercase, and any text the user types in the edit box also appears in lowercase. When the user selects the second radio button, the text in the edit box becomes uppercase, and any text the user types in the edit box also appears in uppercase. When the user selects the third radio button, the text in the edit box remains unchanged, but the user can type using either upper- or lowercase characters:

```
void MyFormClass::EvRadioButton1Click( )
{
  Edit1.CharCase = ecLowerCase;
}
void MyFormClass::EvRadioButton2Click( )
{
  Edit1.CharCase = ecUpperCase;
}
void MyFormClass::EvRadioButton3Click( )
{
  Edit1.CharCase = ecNormal;
}
```

CheckBrowseMode method

Applies to   TDataSet, TDBDataSet, TQuery, TStoredProc, TTable components

void CheckBrowseMode(void);
The CheckBrowseMode method verifies that the dataset is open and has no pending changes. If the dataset's State property is dsEdit, dsInsert, or dsSetKey, the Post method is called to post any pending changes. If the dataset is closed, an EDatabaseError exception is raised.

Checked property

Applies to   TDBCheckBox component

bool Checked;
Run-time only. The Checked property determines whether the database check box is checked, and therefore, selected. If Checked is true, the check box is checked. If Checked is false, the check box is not checked. The value of the Checked property is false if the State of the check box is cbGrayed (the check box is grayed) or cbUnChecked (the check box is unchecked).

Clear method

Applies to   all TField, TDBComboBox, TDBEdit, TDBListBox, TDBMemo, TDBText, TFieldDefs, TIndexDefs, TParam, TParams, TStrings, TVarRecs components

Clear method for fields

Applies to   All TField components

void Clear(void);
Clear sets the value of the field to NULL.

Clear method for other data-aware controls

Applies to   TDBComboBox, TDBEdit, TDBListBox, TDBMemo components

void Clear (void);
The Clear method deletes all text from the control.

Example
```
Edit1.Clear( );
```

Clear method for string lists

Applies to   TStrings, TDBText components

void Clear (void);
The Clear method deletes all items from the component.

Example
```
DBText1.Clear( );
```

Clear method for TFieldDefs components

Applies to   TFieldDefs component

void Clear(void);
The Clear method frees all of the entries in the Items property, effectively removing all TFieldDefs components from a TFieldDefs component.

Clear method for TIndexDefs components

Applies to   TIndexDefs component

void Clear(void);
The Clear method removes all of the entries in the Items property.

Clear method for TParam components

Applies to   TParam component

void Clear(void);
The Clear method sets the parameter to NULL, erasing all previously assigned data. The Name, DataType, and ParamType property values are not altered.

Example

```
// Clear the CustNo parameter for Query1
Query1.ParamByName( "CustNo" )->Clear( );
```

Clear method for TParams components

Applies to   TParams component

void Clear(void);
The Clear method removes all parameter information from the Items property of a TParams component.

Example

```
Params1.Clear( );
```

Clear method for TVarRecs components

Applies to   TVarRecs component

void Clear (void);
The Clear method deletes all data items from the TVarRecs component.

ClearFields method

Applies to   TDataSet, TDBDataSet, TQuery, TStoredProc, TTable components

void ClearFields(void);

The ClearFields method clears all fields of the current record to their default values (normally NULL). The dataset must be in Edit state or an EDatabaseError exception is raised.

ClearSelection method

Applies to   TDBEdit, TDBMemo components

void ClearSelection( );
The ClearSelection method deletes text selected in a database edit box or memo control. If no text is selected in the control when ClearSelection is called, nothing happens.

Example   This code uses a memo control named MyMemo and a button on a form. When the user clicks the button, the text the user selected in the memo control is deleted.

```
MyFormClass::EvButton1Click( )
{
   MyMemo.ClearSelection( );
}
```

ClickButton method

Applies to   TDBNavigator component

void ClickButton(TNavigateBtn);
The ClickButton method simulates a button click on the database navigator, invoking the action of the button. Specify which button ClickButton should operate on as the value of the Index parameter.

Example   This line of code simulates the clicking of the Next button on a database navigator control, which makes the next record in the dataset the current record:

```
DBNavigator1.ClickButton( nbNext );
```

ClientToScreen method

Applies to   All data-aware controls

TPoint ClientToScreen(TPoint pt);
The ClientToScreen method translates the given point from client area coordinates to global screen coordinates. In client area coordinates, 0, 0 corresponds to the upper left corner of the control's client area. In screen coordinates, 0, 0 corresponds to the upper left corner of the screen.

Using the ClientToScreen and ScreenToClient methods you can convert from one control's coordinate system to another control's coordinate system. For instance, the following example converts P from the coordinates in SourceControl to the coordinates in TargetControl:

```
TPoint P = { 0, 0 };
// Translate from SourceControl to Screen
P = SourceControl.ClientToScreen( P );
// Translate from Screen to TargetControl
P = TargetControl.ScreenToClient( P );
// P now holds the position of the upper left corner of
// SourceControl relative to the client area of TargetControl
```

Example   This example uses two edit boxes on a form. When the user clicks a point on the form, the X screen coordinate appears in Edit1, and the Y screen coordinate appears in Edit2.

```
MyFormClass::EvFormLMouseDown( uint modKeys , TPoint P )
{
  TPoint Q;
  char buf[5];
  Q = ClientToScreen(P);              // Q is the TPoint for the screen
  wsprintf( buf, "%d", Q.x );
  Edit1.SetText( buf );
  wsprintf( buf, "%d", Q.y );
  Edit2.SetText( buf );
}
```

Close method

Applies to   TDataBase, TDataSet, TDBDataSet, TQuery, TStoredProc, TTable components

Close method for datasets

Applies to   TDataSet, TDBDataSet, TQuery, TStoredProc, TTable components

void Close(void);
The Close method closes the dataset, returning it to Inactive state. Calling Close is equivalent to setting the Active property to false.

Note   Post is not called implicitly by the Close method. Use the BeforeClose event to post any pending edits explicitly.

Close method for TDatabase components

Applies to   TDatabase component

void Close(void);
The Close method closes the database specified with a TDatabase component and all the dataset components linked to it. This is the same as setting the Connected property to false.

Example
```
Database1.Close( );
```

CloseDatabase method

Applies to TSession component

void CloseDatabase(TDatabase& d);

The CloseDatabase method closes a TDatabase component. The d parameter specifies the TDatabase component to close. Normally, this is handled automatically when an application closes the last table in the database associated with a TDatabase component. CloseDatabase decrements the Session's reference count of the number of open database connections.

Whenever you call OpenDatabase, you should remember to call the CloseDatabase method later in your code to ensure the database connections are handled properly.

Example

```
Database = Session.OpenDatabase( "DBDEMOS" );
//Do Something
// handle exception and close the database
Session.CloseDatabase( "DBDEMOS" );
```

CloseDatasets method

Applies to TDataBase component

void CloseDatasets(void);

The CloseDatasets method closes all of the datasets linked to the TDatabase component, but does not close the database connection itself.

Example

```
Database1.CloseDatasets( );
```

CloseUp method

Applies to TDBLookupCombo component

void CloseUp( );

The CloseUp method closes an opened or "dropped-down" database lookup combo box.

Columns property

Applies to TDBRadioGroup component

int Columns;

The Columns property denotes the number of columns in a database radio group box. Specify the number of columns you want for the radio group box as the value of Columns.

Example

```
RadioGroup1.Columns = 3;
```

Commit method

Applies to   TDataBase component

void Commit(void);

The Commit method commits or finalizes the current transactions and therefore all modifications made to the database since the last call to StartTransaction. If no transaction is active, an EDatabaseError exception is raised. Use this method only when connected to a server database.

Example

```
Database1.StartTransaction( );
// Update one or more records in tables linked to Database1
...
Database1.Commit( );
```

ComponentIndex property (Index at design time)

Applies to   All components

int ComponentIndex;

Read only at run time. The ComponentIndex property indicates the position of the component in its owner's components property list. The first component in the list has a ComponentIndex value of 0, the second has a value of 1, and so on.

When you access the ComponentIndex property at design time, use the VBX standard property name Index.

ConfirmDelete property

Applies to   TDBNavigator component

bool ConfirmDelete;

The ConfirmDelete property determines whether a message box appears, asking you to confirm the deletion when the user uses the database navigator to delete the current record in the dataset. If ConfirmDelete is true, a prompting message box appears and the record isn't deleted unless the user chooses the OK button. If ConfirmDelete is false, no message box appears and the record is deleted.

The default value is true.

Connected property

Applies to TDataBase component

bool Connected;

The Connected property indicates whether the TDatabase component has established a connection to a database. Connected is set to true when an application opens a table in a database (logging in to a server, if required). It is set back to false when the table is closed (unless KeepConnection is true). Set Connected to true to establish a connection to a database without opening a table. Set Connected to false to close a database connection.

The KeepConnection property of TDatabase specifies whether to maintain database connections when no tables in the database are open. The KeepConnections property of TSession specifies whether to maintain database connections when there is no explicit TDatabase component for the database.

Example

```
Database1.Connected = true;
```

CopyFrom method

Applies to TMemoryStream component

int32 CopyFrom(TMemoryStream& Source, int32 Count);

The CopyFrom method copies the number of bytes specified with Count from the stream component specified as Source to the calling stream component. It returns the number of bytes copied.

CopyParams method

Applies to TStoredProc component

void CopyParams(TParams& value);

The CopyParams method copies all of the parameter information from the stored procedure component to value. Use this method to copy parameters from one stored procedure component to another.

Example

```
// Copy all parameters from StoredProc1 to StoredProc2
StoredProc1.CopyParams( StoredProc2.Params );
```

CopyToClipboard method

Applies to   TDBEdit, TDBImage, TDBMemo components

CopyToClipboard method for TDBEdit and TDBMemo

Applies to   TDBEdit, TDBMemo components

void CopyToClipboard( );
The CopyToClipboard method copies the text selected in the control to the Clipboard, replacing any text that exists there. If no text is selected, nothing is copied.

Example   This line of code copies text selected in the database memo control to the Clipboard:

```
DBMemo1.CopyToClipboard( );
```

CopyToClipboard method for TDBImage components

Applies to   TDBImage component

void CopyToClipboard( );
The CopyToClipboard method copies the image of the database image component to the Clipboard.

Example   The following code copies the contents of DBImage1 to the Clipboard:

```
DBImage1.CopyToClipboard( );
```

Count method

Applies to   TParams component

int Count(void);
The Count method returns the number of entries in the Items property of the TParams component.

Example

```
// Assign 999 to any integer parameter which does not have a value
for( i = 0; i < Params.Count ; ++i )
{
  if ( ( Params.Items[i].IsNull ) && (Params.Items[i]->DataType == ftInteger) )
  {
      Params.Items[i]->AsInteger = 999;
  }
}
```

Count property

Applies to   TIndexDefs, TFieldDefs, TParams, TStrings ,TVarRecs components

Count property for TStrings components

Applies to   *T*Strings component

int Count;
Run-time and read only. The *Count* property contains the number of strings in a TStrings component.

Example   The following code snippet retrieves the number of indexes for a table by getting the IndexNames property and counting the number of names returned

```
TStrings strings;
int indexCount;
Table1.GetIndexNames( strings );
indexCount = strings.Count( );
```

Count property for field definitions

Applies to   TFieldDefs component

int Count;
The Count property specifies the total number of TFieldDef components in the TFieldDefs component.

Count property for index definitions

Applies to   TIndexDefs component

int Count;
Run-time and read only. The Count property holds the number of entries in the Items property of the TIndexDefs component.

Count property for TParams components

Applies to   TParams component

int Count;
The Count property specifies the total number of TParam components in the TParams component.

Count property for TVarRecs components

Applies to   *T*VarRecs component

int Count;

Run-time and read only. The Count property contains the number of data items (TVarRec) in a TVarRecs component.

Example   The following code snippet retrieves the number of indexes for a table by getting the IndexNames property and counting the number of names returned

```
TStrings strings;
int indexCount;
Table1.GetIndexNames( strings );
indexCount = strings.Count( );
```

CreateField method

Applies to   *TFieldDef* component

TField CreateField(TBDTComponent& owner);
CreateField creates a TField component of the appropriate type that corresponds to the TFieldDef component itself. The owner parameter is the dataset component containing the field.

CreateParam method

Applies to   *TParams* component

PTParam CreateParam(TFieldType fldType, const string& name, TParamType paramType);
The CreateParam method attempts to add a new entry in Items property of the TParams component. Specify the name of the parameter as name, the field type as fldType, and the parameter type as paramType.

Example
```
TParam param;
// Create a new parameter for CustNo and assign a value of 999 to it
Params.CreateParam( ftInteger, "CustNo", ptInput );
param = Params.ParamByName( "CustNo" );
param.AsInteger = 999;
```

CreateTable method

Applies to   *TTable* component

void CreateTable(void);
The CreateTable method creates a new empty database table. Before calling this method, the DatabaseName, TableName, TableType, FieldDefs, and IndexDefs properties must be assigned values.

Example
```
Table1.Active = false;
  Table1.DatabaseName = "VDT_Demos";
  Table1.TableName = "CustInfo";
```

```
Table1.TableType = ttParadox;
Table1.FieldDefs->Clear( );
Table1.FieldDefs->Add( "Field1", ftInteger, 0, false );
Table1.FieldDefs->Add( "Field2", ftInteger, 0, false );
Table1.IndexDefs->Clear( );
Table1.IndexDefs->Add( "Field1Index", "Field1", ixPrimary|ixUnique );
CreateTable( );
```

Currency property

Applies to   TBCDField, TCurrencyField, TFloatField components

bool Currency;

Run-time only. The Currency property is used to control the format of the value of a TBCDField, TCurrencyField, and TFloatField when both DisplayFormat and EditFormat properties are not assigned.

Currency is true by default for TCurrencyField and false for TFloatField and TBCDField.

Cursor property (MousePointer at design time)

Applies to   All data-aware controls

TCursor Cursor;

The Cursor property is the image used when the mouse passes into the region covered by the control. These are the possible images:

Value	Image	Value	Image	Value	Image
crDefault		crSize		crSizeWE	
crArrow		crSizeNESW		crUpArrow	
crCross		crSizeNS		crHourglass	
crIBeam		crSizeNWSE		crNoDrop	
crIcon					

When you access the Cursor property at design time, use the VBX standard property name MousePointer.

Example   This line of code changes the display of the image to the cross cursor when the user moves the mouse pointer over DBEdit1:

```
DBEdit1.Cursor = crCross;
```

CursorPosChanged method

Applies to   TDataSet, TDBDataSet, TTable, TQuery, TStoredProc components

void CursorPosChanged(void);
The CursorPosChanged method is needed only if you use the Handle property to make direct calls to the Borland Database Engine API which cause the cursor position to change. To notify the dataset that the underlying BDE cursor's position has changed, call CursorPosChanged after the direct calls to the BDE.

CutToClipboard method

Applies to   TDBEdit, TDBImage, TDBMemo components

void CutToClipboard( );
The CutToClipboard method deletes the text selected in the control and copies it to the Clipboard, replacing any text that exists there. If no text is selected, nothing is copied.

For database images, CutToClipboard deletes the image in the control and copies it to the Clipboard, replacing the contents of the Clipboard.

Example
```
DBMemo1.CutToClipboard( );
```

Database property

Applies to   TDBDataSet, TQuery, TStoredProc, TTable components

TDatabase Database;
Run-time and read only. Database specifies the database (TDatabase) component associated with the dataset component. If you did not create a TDatabase at design time, one is created automatically at run time. Use the Database property to refer to the properties and methods of the database.

Example
```
// Do a transaction
Table1.Database->StartTransaction( );
// Post some records with Table1
Table1.Database->Commit( );
```

DatabaseCount property

Applies to   TSession component

int DatabaseCount;

Run-time and read only. DatabaseCount is the number of TDataBase components currently attached to the Session.

Example

```
// Close all databases
while( Session.DatabaseCount != 0 )
{
  Session.Databases[0]->Close( );
}
```

DatabaseName property

Applies to   TDataBase, TDBDataSet, TQuery, TStoredProc, TTable components

Description   DatabaseName for databases and datasets

DatabaseName property for databases

Applies to   TDataBase component

string DatabaseName;

The DatabaseName property is used to define an application-specific alias. Dataset components can reference this name instead of a BDE alias, directory path, or database name. In other words, this is the name of an application-specific alias defined by the dataset component that will show up in the DatabaseName drop-down list of TTable, TQuery, and TStoredProc components.

If you try to change the value of the DatabaseName property when the value of Connected is true, an EDatabaseError exception is raised.

Example

```
Database1.DatabaseName = "VDT_Demos";
```

DatabaseName property for datasets

Applies to   TDBDataSet, TQuery, TStoredProc, TTable components

string DatabaseName;

Set the DatabaseName property to specify the database to access. This property can specify:

- A defined BDE alias,
- A directory path for desktop database files,
- A directory path and file name for a Local InterBase Server database,
- An application-specific alias defined by a TDatabase component

Note   Use the Close method to put a dataset in Inactive state before changing DatabaseName.

Example The following example attempts to open the database, first by using a defined BDE alias, and then by specifying the directory path.

```
// First close the DBDataSet
Table1.Active = false;
try
{
  // First try to use an alias
  Table1.DatabaseName = "VDT_Demos";
  Table1.Active = true;
}
catch (EDatabaseError)
{
  // If that fails, try to use the drive and directory
  Table1.DatabaseName = "c:\\demos\\database";
  Table1.Active = true;
}
```

Databases property

Applies to *T*Session component

TDatabase Databases[int i];
Run-time and read only. The Databases property returns a specified database from the list of all of the currently active TDatabase components within the session. The database returned is the database whose index position in the list of databases is specified with the i parameter.

Example
```
// Close all databases
while( Session.DatabaseCount != 0 )
{
   Session.Databases[0]->Close( );
}
```

DataChanged property

Applies to TDBCheckBox, TDBComboBox, TDBEdit, TDBImage, TDBListBox, TDBLookupCombo, TDBLookupList, TDBMemo, TDBRadioGroup, TDBText components

bool DataChanged;
Run-time only. If DataChanged is true, the data in the control has been changed from that actually in the current record.

When the control moves to another record, an OnValidate event occurs. If DataChanged is true at that time, the control calles the Edit and UpdateRecord methods to write the changes in the control back to the record in the database. To prevent an update, set DataChanged to false.

Example

```
int TMyFormClass::CanClose( )
{
  if( DBMemo1.DataChanged == true )
  {
    MessageBox( "Changed records will be posted", "Information" , MB_OK );
  }
  return true;
}
```

DataField property

Applies to   All data-aware controls except TDBNavigator

PTField DataField;

The DataField property identifies the field the data-aware control displays. The dataset the field is located in is specified in a data source component (TDataSource). The DataSource property of the data-aware control specifies which data source component.

If the DataField value of a database edit box (TDBEdit) is an integer or floating-point value, only characters that are valid in such a field can be entered in the edit box. Characters that are not legal are not accepted.

Example   The following code specifies that the DataField of DBEdit1 is "FNAME."

```
// Change the DataField to the "FNAME" field
DBEdit1.DataField = DBEdit1.DataSource->DataSet->FieldByName( "FNAME" );
```

DataSet property

Applies to   TDataSource, all TField components

DataSet property for data sources

Applies to   TDataSource component

TDataSet DataSet;

DataSet specifies the dataset component (TTable, TQuery, and TStoredProc) that is providing data to the data source. The advantage of this interface approach to connecting data components is that the dataset, data source, and data-aware controls can be connected and disconnected from each other through the TDataSource component.

Example

```
DataSource1.DataSet = Table1; //get data from this form's Table1
DataSource1.DataSet = Form2->Table1; //get data from Form2's Table1
```

DataSet property for fields

Applies to   All TField components

TDataSet DataSet;
Run-time only. The DataSet property identifies the dataset to which a TField component belongs. Assign a value to this property only if you are programmatically creating a TField component.

DataSetColumnName property

Applies to   TDBGrid component

bool DataSetColumnName;
Set the DataSetColumnName property to true to display the field names as column headings on a data grid.

DatasetCount property

Applies to   TDataBase component

int DatasetCount;
Read-only and run time only. The DatasetCount property specifies the number of dataset components that are currently using the TDatabase component.

Example
```
// Check to see if any record associated with this database has pending updates
bool Changed = false;
for( int i = 0; i < Database1.DatasetCount ; i++ )
{
  Changed |= Database1.DataSets[i]->Modified;
}
```

Datasets property

Applies to   TDataBase component

TDBDataSet Datasets[int i];
Run-time and read only. The value of the Datasets property is the dataset indicated by its index position in the list of datasets. Specify its index as the value of the i parameter.

Example
```
//Check to see if any record associated with this database has pending updates
bool Changed = false;
for( int i = 0; i < Database1.DatasetCount; i++ )
{
    Changed |= Database1.DataSets[i]->Modified;
}
```

DataSize property

Applies to   All TField components

int DataSize;
Run-time and read only. The value of DataSize is the number of bytes required to store the field in memory.

DataSource property

Applies to   All data-aware controls; TDataSet, TDBDataSet, TQuery, TStoredProc, TTable components

DataSource property for data-aware controls

Applies to   All data-aware controls

PTDataSource DataSource;
The DataSource property determines where the the data-aware control obtains the data to display. Specify the data source component that identifies the dataset the data is found in.

Example   The following code specifies DataSource1 to be the DataSource of DBGrid1.

```
DBGrid1.DataSource = DataSource1;
```

DataSource property for datasets

Applies to   TDataSet, TDBDataSet, TQuery, TStoredProc, TTable components

TDataSource DataSource;
Set the DataSource property to a TDataSource component in the application to assign values to parameters not bound to values programmatically with Params or ParamByName. If the unbound parameter names match any column names in the specified data source, the current values of those fields are bound to the corresponding parameters. This capability enables applications to have linked queries.

Example   The LINKQRY sample application illustrates the use of the DataSource property to link a query in a master-detail form. The form contains a TQuery component (named Orders) with the following in its SQL property:

```
SELECT Orders.CustNo, Orders.OrderNo, Orders.SaleDate
   FROM Orders
   WHERE Orders.CustNo = :CustNo
```

The form also contains:

- A TDataSource named OrdersSource, linked to Orders by its DataSet property.

- A TTable component (named Cust).

- A TDataSource named CustSource linked to Cust.
- Two data grids; one linked to CustSource and the other to OrdersSource.

Orders' DataSource property is set to CustSource. Because the parameter :CustNo does not have any value assigned to it, at run time an attempt is made to match it with a column name in CustSource, which gets its data from the Customer table through Cust. Because there is a CustNo column in Cust, the current value of CustNo in the Cust table is assigned to the parameter, and the two data grids are linked in a master-detail relationship. Each time the Cust table moves to a different row, the Orders query automatically re-executes to retrieve all the orders for the current customer.

DataType property

Applies to   TField, TFieldDef, TParam components

DataType property for field definitions

Applies to   TFieldDef component

TFieldType DataType;
Run-time and read only. The DataType property contains the type of a physical field. Possible values are those of the TFieldType type: ftUnknown, ftString, ftSmallint, ftInteger, ftWord, ftBoolean, ftFloat, ftCurrency, ftBCD, ftDate, ftTime, ftDateTime, ftBytes, ftVarBytes, ftBlob, ftMemo, or ftGraphic.

DataType property for fields

Applies to   All TField components

TFieldType DataType;
Run-time and read only. DataType identifies the data type of the TField component. Possible values are those of the TFieldType type: ftBoolean, ftBCD, ftBlob, ftBytes, ftCurrency, ftDate, ftDateTime, ftFloat, ftGraphic, ftInteger, ftMemo, ftSmallint, ftString, ftTime, ftUnknown, ftVarBytes, and ftWord.

DataType property for TParam components

Applies to   TParam component

TFieldType DataType;
The DataType property is the type of the parameter. Possible values are those of the TFieldType type: ftUnknown, ftString, ftSmallint, ftInteger, ftWord, ftBoolean, ftFloat, ftCurrency, ftBCD, ftDate, ftTime, ftDateTime, ftBytes, ftVarBytes, ftBlob, ftMemo, or ftGraphic.

Example

```
for( int i = 0; i < Query1.Params->Count ; i++ )
{
  if( Query1.Params->Items[i]->DataType == ftUnknown )
  {
    char message[100];
    wsprintf( message , "Parameter %d is undefined" , i );
    MessageBox( message , "Warning" , MB_OK , 0 );
  }
}
```

DBHandle property

Applies to   TDBDataSet, TQuery, TStoredProc, TTable components

hDBIDb DBHandle;

Run-time and read only. The DBHandle property enables an application to make direct calls to the Borland Database Engine (BDE) API. Many BDE function calls require a database handle. This property provides the requisite database handle.

You should not need to use this property unless your application requires some functionality not encapsulated in the Visual Database Tools.

DBLocale property

Applies to   TDBDataSet, TQuery, TStoredProc, TTable components

TLocale DBLocale;

Run-time and read only. The DBLocale property allows you to make direct calls to the Borland Database Engine using this specification of the language driver. You should not need to use this property unless your application requires some functionality not encapsulated in Visual Database Tools.

DefaultFields property

Applies to   TDataSet, TDBDataSet, TQuery, TStoredProc, TTable components

bool DefaultFields;

The DefaultFields property determines whether TField components for the dataset were created at design time using the Fields Editor. If DefaultFields is true, fields were created at design time. If DefaultFields is false, TField components are created automatically for each of the fields in the dataset using the default field descriptions and layout of the dataset.

Delete method

Applies to   TDataSet, TDBDataSet, TQuery, TStoredProc, TStrings, TTable components

Delete method for TStrings components

Applies to   TStrings component

void Delete(int index);
The Delete method removes the item specified with the index parameter from a string component.

The index is zero-based, so the first item has an index value of 0, the second item has an index value of 1, and so on.

If a string is deleted from a string component, the reference to its associated component is also deleted.

Example

```
// Create a TStrings object with three strings and delete the second one
TStrings tempStrings;
tempStrings.Add( "first string" );
tempStrings.Add( "old second string" );
tempString.Add( "new second string" );
// delete the second string leaving: "first string" and "new second string"
tempString.Delete( 1 );  // deleting second string in zero based TStrings object
```

Delete method for datasets

Applies to   TDataSet, TDBDataSet, TQuery, TStoredProc, TTable components

void Delete(void);
The Delete method deletes the current record from the dataset. The next record then becomes the new current record. If the record deleted was the last record in the dataset, then the previous record becomes the current record.

This method is valid only for datasets that return a live result set.

DeleteIndex method

Applies to   TTable component

void DeleteIndex(const string& n);
The DeleteIndex method deletes a secondary index for a TTable component. The n parameter specifies the name of the index. You must have opened the table with exclusive access (the value of the Exclusive property is true) before you can call DeleteIndex.

Example   This code deletes the NewIndex index for Table1:

```
Table1.DeleteIndex( "NewIndex" );
```

DeleteTable method

Applies to   TTable component

void DeleteTable(void);

The DeleteTable method deletes an existing database table. Before calling this method, the DatabaseName, TableName,and TableType properties must be assigned values. The table must be closed.

Example

```
Table1.Active = false;
Table1.DatabaseName = "DBDEMOS";
Table1.TableName = "Customer";
Table1.TableType = ttParadox;
Table1.DeleteTable( );
```

DescriptionsAvailable property

Applies to   TStoredProc component

bool DescriptionsAvailable(void);

The DescriptionsAvailable property indicates whether stored procedure parameter information is available from the server. If the information is available, it returns true. Otherwise, it returns false. Different servers might require additional information to obtain the parameter information. If DescriptionsAvailable returns false, you must build a TParams component in your code explicity to be used as the value of the Params property for the stored procedure.

Example

```
if( !StoredProc1.DescriptionsAvailable )
{
  // Build the Parameters property explicitly
}
```

Destination property

Applies to   TBatchMove component

TTable Destination;

Destination specifies a TTable component corresponding to the database table that will be the destination of the batch move operation. The destination table might or might not already exist. If it doesn't exist, the table is created during the batch move operation.

Example   This code makes DestTable the destination table for the batch move operation:

```
BatchMove1.Destination = DestTable;
```

DisableControls method

Applies to   TDataSet, TDBDataSet, TQuery, TStoredProc, TTable components

void DisableControls(void);

The DisableControls method temporarily disconnects the dataset from all TDataSource components. While the data sources are disconnected, associated data-aware controls do not reflect changes to datasets. When iterating over a dataset with Next or Prior methods, calling DisableControls first speeds the process, eliminating the need to update the screen each time.

Use EnableControls to restore the connection. The dataset maintains a count of the number of calls to DisableControls and EnableControls, so only the last call to EnableControls will actually update the data sources.

Example

```
Table1.DisableControls( );
// Move forward five records
  for( int i = 1; i <= 5; i++ )
  {
    Table1.Next( );
  }
  // Update the controls to the current record
  Table1.EnableControls( );
```

DisableControls method

Applies to   TDataSet, TDBDataSet, TQuery, TStoredProc, TTable components

void DisableControls(void);

The DisableControls method temporarily disconnects the dataset from all TDataSource components. While the data sources are disconnected, associated data-aware controls do not reflect changes to datasets. When iterating over a dataset with Next or Prior methods, calling DisableControls first speeds the process, eliminating the need to update the screen each time.

Use EnableControls to restore the connection. The dataset maintains a count of the number of calls to DisableControls and EnableControls, so only the last call to EnableControls will actually update the data sources.

Example

```
Table1.DisableControls( );
// Move forward five records
  for( int i = 1; i <= 5; i++ )
  {
    Table1.Next( );
  }
  // Update the controls to the current record
  Table1.EnableControls( );
```

DisableControls method

Applies to   TDataSet, TDBDataSet, TQuery, TStoredProc, TTable components

void DisableControls(void);

The DisableControls method temporarily disconnects the dataset from all TDataSource components. While the data sources are disconnected, associated data-aware controls do not reflect changes to datasets. When iterating over a dataset with Next or Prior methods, calling DisableControls first speeds the process, eliminating the need to update the screen each time.

Use EnableControls to restore the connection. The dataset maintains a count of the number of calls to DisableControls and EnableControls, so only the last call to EnableControls will actually update the data sources.

Example

```
Table1.DisableControls( );
// Move forward five records
  for( int i = 1; i <= 5; i++ )
  {
    Table1.Next( );
  }
  // Update the controls to the current record
  Table1.EnableControls( );
```

DisplayFormat property

Applies to   TBCDField, TCurrencyField, TDateField, TDateTimeField, TFloatField, TIntegerField, TSmallintField, TTimeField, TWordField components

string DisplayFormat;

The DisplayFormat property is used to override the automatic formatting of a field for display purposes.

DisplayFormat property for numeric fields

Applies to   TBCDField, TCurrencyField, TFloatField, TIntegerField, TSmallintField, TWordField components

string DisplayFormat;

Use the DisplayFormat property to override automatic formatting of a field for display purposes. For TFloat, TBCDField, and TCurrencyField components, the Currency property must be set to false for DisplayFormat to take effect.

The following format specifiers are supported in the format string:

Specifier	Represents
0	Digit placeholder. If the value being formatted has a digit in the position where the "0" appears in the format string, then that digit is copied to the output string. Otherwise, a "0" is stored in that position in the output string.
#	Digit placeholder. If the value being formatted has a digit in the position where the "#" appears in the format string, then that digit is copied to the output string. Otherwise, nothing is stored in that position in the output string.
.	Decimal point. The first "." character in the format string determines the location of the decimal separator in the formatted value; any additional "." characters are ignored. The actual character used as a the decimal separator in the output string is determined by the DecimalSeparator global variable. The default value of DecimalSeparator is specified in the Number Format of the International section in the Windows Control Panel.
,	Thousand separator. If the format string contains one or more "," characters, the output will have thousand separators inserted between each group of three digits to the left of the decimal point. The placement and number of "," characters in the format string does not affect the output, except to indicate that thousand separators are wanted. The actual character used as a the thousand separator in the output is determined by the ThousandSeparator global variable. The default value of ThousandSeparator is specified in the Number Format of the International section in the Windows Control Panel.
E+	Scientific notation. If any of the strings "E+," "E-," "e+," or "e-" are contained in the format string, the number is formatted using scientific notation. A group of up to four "0" characters can immediately follow the "E+," "E-," "e+," or "e-" to determine the minimum number of digits in the exponent. The "E+" and "e+" formats cause a plus sign to be output for positive exponents and a minus sign to be output for negative exponents. The "E-" and "e-" formats output a sign character only for negative exponents.
'xx'/"xx"	Characters enclosed in single or double quotes are output as-is, and do not affect formatting.
;	Separates sections for positive, negative, and zero numbers in the format string.

The locations of the leftmost "0" before the decimal point in the format string and the rightmost "0" after the decimal point in the format string determine the range of digits that are always present in the output string.

The number being formatted is always rounded to as many decimal places as there are digit placeholders ("0" or "#") to the right of the decimal point. If the format string contains no decimal point, the value being formatted is rounded to the nearest whole number.

If the number being formatted has more digits to the left of the decimal separator than there are digit placeholders to the left of the "." character in the format string, the extra digits are output before the first digit placeholder.

To allow different formats for positive, negative, and zero values, the format string can contain between one and three sections separated by semicolons.

- One section: The format string applies to all values.

- Two sections: The first section applies to positive values and zeros, and the second section applies to negative values.

- Three sections: The first section applies to positive values, the second applies to negative values, and the third applies to zeros.

If the section for negative values or the section for zero values is empty, that is if there is nothing between the semicolons that delimit the section, the section for positive values is used instead.

If the section for positive values is empty, or if the entire format string is empty, the value is formatted using general floating-point formatting with 15 significant digits. General floating-point formatting is also used if the value has more than 18 digits to the left of the decimal point and the format string does not specify scientific notation.

Example   The following table shows some sample formats and the results produced when the formats are applied to different values:

Format string	Results			
	1234	-1234	0.5	0
	1234	-1234	0.5	0
0	1234	-1234	1	0
0.00	1234.00	-1234.00	0.50	0.00
#.##	1234	-1234	.5	
#,##0.00	1,234.00	-1,234.00	0.50	0.00
#,##0.00;(#,##0.00)	1,234.00	(1,234.00)	0.50	0.00
#,##0.00;;Zero	1,234.00	-1,234.00	0.50	Zero
0.000E+00	1.234E+03	-1.234E+03	5.000E-01	0.000E+00
#.###E-0	1.234E3	-1.234E3	5E-1	0E0

DisplayFormat property for date and time fields

Applies to   TDateField, TDateTimeField, TTimeField components

string DisplayFormat;

Use the DisplayFormat property to override automatic formatting of a field for display purposes. If you do not override, the value is formatted according to the default Windows specifications in the [International] section of the WIN.INI file.

The following format specifiers are supported:

Specifier	Displays
c	Displays the date using the format given by the ShortDateFormat global variable, followed by the time using the format given by the LongTimeFormat global variable. The time is not displayed if the fractional part of the DateTime value is zero.
d	Displays the day as a number without a leading zero (1-31).
dd	Displays the day as a number with a leading zero (01-31).
ddd	Displays the day as an abbreviation (Sun-Sat) using the strings given by the ShortDayNames global variable.
dddd	Displays the day as a full name (Sunday-Saturday) using the strings given by the LongDayNames global variable.
ddddd	Displays the date using the format given by the ShortDateFormat global variable.

Specifier	Displays
dddddd	Displays the date using the format given by the LongDateFormat global variable.
m	Displays the month as a number without a leading zero (1-12). If the m specifier immediately follows an h or hh specifier, the minute rather than the month is displayed.
mm	Displays the month as a number with a leading zero (01-12). If the mm specifier immediately follows an h or hh specifier, the minute rather than the month is displayed.
mmm	Displays the month as an abbreviation (Jan-Dec) using the strings given by the ShortMonthNames global variable.
mmmm	Displays the month as a full name (January-December) using the strings given by the LongMonthNames global variable.
yy	Displays the year as a two-digit number (00-99).
yyyy	Displays the year as a four-digit number (0000-9999).
h	Displays the hour without a leading zero (0-23).
hh	Displays the hour with a leading zero (00-23).
n	Displays the minute without a leading zero (0-59).
nn	Displays the minute with a leading zero (00-59).
s	Displays the second without a leading zero (0-59).
ss	Displays the second with a leading zero (00-59).
t	Displays the time using the format given by the ShortTimeFormat global variable.
tt	Displays the time using the format given by the LongTimeFormat global variable.
am/pm	Uses the 12-hour clock for the preceding h or hh specifier, and displays "am" for any hour before noon, and "pm" for any hour after noon. The am/pm specifier can use lower, upper, or mixed case, and the result is displayed accordingly.
a/p	Uses the 12-hour clock for the preceding h or hh specifier, and displays "a" for any hour before noon, and "p" for any hour after noon. The a/p specifier can use lower, upper, or mixed case, and the result is displayed accordingly.
ampm	Uses the 12-hour clock for the preceding h or hh specifier, and displays the contents of the TimeAMString global variable for any hour before noon, and the contents of the TimePMString global variable for any hour after noon.
/	Displays the date separator character given by the DateSeparator global variable.
:	Displays the time separator character given by the TimeSeparator global variable.
'xx'/"xx"	Characters enclosed in single or double quotes are displayed as-is, and do not affect formatting.

Format specifiers may be written in upper case as well as in lower case letters; both produce the same result.

If the string given by the Format parameter is empty, the date and time value is formatted as if a "c" format specifier had been given.

DisplayText property

Applies to   All TField components

string DisplayText;

Run-time and read only. The string value for the field when it is displayed in a data-aware control that is not in Edit mode. Data-aware controls such as TDBEdit rely on DisplayText to provide the formatting for each field.

The default string depends on a field's data type. You can control the strings returned by DisplayText by specifying a DisplayFormat string or by providing an OnGetText event handler.

For a TStringField, the contents of the field is formatted using the EditMask property.

For a TCurrencyField, if DisplayFormat has been assigned a value it overrides the formatting provided by the Currency property.

Example

```
// Display a message that the current value is invalid
char message[100];
wsprintf( message , "%s is invalid" , Field1.DisplayText->c_str() );
MessageBox( message , "Warning", MB_OK );
```

DisplayValue property

Applies to   TDBLookupCombo, TDBLookupList components

string DisplayValue;
Run-time only. The DisplayValue is the string that appears in the database lookup combo box or database lookup list box. Its value is the string contained in the current record's field specified as the LookupDisplay field. The current value of the Value property, which determines the current record in the lookup table, also determines which string is the DisplayValue string.

DisplayValues property

Applies to   TBooleanField component

string DisplayValues;
DisplayValues controls the manner in which the TBooleanField is translated to and from display format. Set DisplayValues to "T;F" to use "T" and "F" for values of true and false. You can use any pair of phrases you want, separated by a semicolon. If one phrase is omitted, no text is displayed and a data-aware control with no text assigns the corresponding value to the field. The default value is "True;False."

Example

```
Field1.DisplayValues = "Yes;No";
Field2.DisplayValues = "Oui;Non";
```

DragCursor property (DragIcon at design time)

Applies to   All data-aware controls

HPIC DragCursor;
The DragCursor property determines the shape of the mouse pointer when the pointer is over a component that will accept an component being dragged.

When you access the DragCursor property at design time, use the VBX standard property name DragIcon.

DragIcon property (DragCursor at run time)

Applies to   All data-aware controls

HPIC DragIcon;
The DragIcon property determines the shape of the mouse pointer when the pointer is over a component that will accept a component being dragged.

When accessing the DragIcon property at run time, use the name DragCursor.

DragMode property

Applies to   All data-aware controls

TDragMode DragMode;
The DragMode property determines the drag and drop behavior of a control. These are the possible values:

Value	Meaning
dmAutomatic	If dmAutomatic is selected, the control is ready to be dragged; the user just clicks and drags it.
dmManual	If dmManual is selected, the control can't be dragged until the application calls the BeginDrag method.

If a control's DragMode property value is dmAutomatic, the application can disable the drag and drop capability at run time by changing the DragMode property value to dmManual.

Example   This code determines whether the drag mode of the database check box on the form is manual. If it is, then dragging the check box becomes possible.

```
if( DBCheckBox1.DragMode == dmManual )
  {
    DBCheckBox1.BeginDrag( true );
  }
```

DriverName property

Applies to   TDataBase component

string DriverName;
DriverName is the name of a BDE driver, such as STANDARD (for dBASE and Paradox), ORACLE, SYBASE, INFORMIX or INTERBASE. This property clears if the value of AliasName changes, because an AliasName specifies a driver type. Conversely, setting this DriverName clears AliasName.

If you try to set DriverName of a TDatabase for which Connected is true, an EDatabaseError exception is raised.

DropConnections method

Applies to   TSession component

void DropConnections(void);
The DropConnections method drops all inactive database connections. By default, temporary database components keep their connections to the server open even when not in use so that they do not have to log in to the server each time a dataset component is opened.

DropDown method

Applies to   TDBLookupCombo component

void DropDown( );
The DropDown method opens or "drops down" the database lookup combo box so the user has a list of values to choose from.

DropDownCount property

Applies to   TDBComboBox, TDBLookupCombo components

int DropDownCount;
The DropDownCount property determines how long the drop-down list of a combo box is. By default, the drop-down list is long enough to contain eight items without requiring the user to scroll to see them all. If you would like the drop-down list to be smaller or larger, specify a number larger or smaller than eight as the DropDownCount value.

If the DropDownCount value is larger than the number of items in the drop-down list, the drop-down list is just large enough to hold all the items and no larger. For example, if the list contains three items, the drop-down list is only long enough to display the three items, even if the DropDownCount is eight.

Example   The following code assigns three to the DropDownCount property of DBComboBox1. To see more than three items in the drop-down list, the user must scroll.

```
DBComboBox1.DropDownCount = 3;
```

DropDownWidth property

Applies to   TDBComboBox, TDBLookupCombo components

int DropDownWidth;

The DropDownWidth property determines how wide the drop-down list of the combo box is in pixels. The default value is 0, which means the drop-down list is the same width as the combo box.

The DropDownWidth property is useful when you are displaying multiple fields, and therefore, multiple columns in the database lookup combo box.

Example   This code displays three fields in the drop-down list of the database lookup combo box. Each column has a title and is separated from the other columns by a line. The combo box displays ten items at a time; therefore, the user must scroll to view the rest of the items. The drop-down list is 600 pixels wide so all the fields fit in the drop-down list.

```
MyFormClass::SetupWindow( )
{
  DBLookupCombo1.LookupDisplay = "Company;City;Country";
  DBLookupCombo1.DropDownCount = 10;
  DBLookupCombo1.DropDownWidth = 600;
}
```

Duplicates property

Applies to   TStrings component

TDuplicates Duplicates;

The Duplicates property determines whether duplicate strings are allowed in the sorted list of strings of a string list component. If the list is not sorted, the value of Duplicates has no effect. These are the possible values:

Value	Meaning
dupIgnore	Any attempt to add a duplicate string to a sorted string is ignored..
dupAccept	Add duplicate strings to a sorted string list.
dupError	Throw an EListError exception upon an attempt to add a duplicate string.

Example   The following code makes Strings1 ignore duplicate entries.

```
Strings1.Duplicates = dupIgnore;
```

Edit method

Applies to   TDataSet, TDBDataSet, TDataSource, TQuery, TStoredProc, TTable components

Edit method for datasets

Applies to   TDataSet, TDBDataSet, TQuery, TStoredProc, TTable components

void Edit(void);

The Edit method prepares the current record of the dataset for changes and puts the dataset in Edit state, setting the State property to dsEdit. Data-aware controls cannot modify existing records unless the dataset is in Edit state.

Calling this method for a dataset that cannot be modified raises an EDatabaseError exception. The CanModify property will be true for datasets that can be modified.

This method is valid for datasets that return a live result set only.

Edit method for data sources

Applies to   TDataSource component

void Edit(void);

The Edit method of a data source calls the Edit method of the table specified as the value of the DataSet property if the table's AutoEdit property value is true and its State property value is dsBrowse.

EditFormat property

Applies to   TBCDField, TCurrencyField, TFloatField, TIntegerField, TSmallintField, TWordField components

string EditFormat;

Run-time only. Use the EditFormat property to override formatting of a field for editing purposes. If you do not assign a string to EditFormat but the DisplayFormat property does have a value, the DisplayFormat string is used. For TBCDField, TCurrencyField, and TFloatField components, if neither property has a string the Currency property is used to format the field.

The following format specifiers are supported in the format string:

Specifier	Represents
0	Digit placeholder. If the value being formatted has a digit in the position where the "0" appears in the format string, then that digit is copied to the output string. Otherwise, a "0" is stored in that position in the output string.
#	Digit placeholder. If the value being formatted has a digit in the position where the "#" appears in the format string, then that digit is copied to the output string. Otherwise, nothing is stored in that position in the output string.

Specifier	Represents
.	Decimal point. The first "." character in the format string determines the location of the decimal separator in the formatted value; any additional "." characters are ignored. The actual character used as a the decimal separator in the output string is determined by the DecimalSeparator global variable. The default value of DecimalSeparator is specified in the Number Format of the International section in the Windows Control Panel.
,	Thousand separator. If the format string contains one or more "," characters, the output will have thousand separators inserted between each group of three digits to the left of the decimal point. The placement and number of "," characters in the format string does not affect the output, except to indicate that thousand separators are wanted. The actual character used as a the thousand separator in the output is determined by the ThousandSeparator global variable. The default value of ThousandSeparator is specified in the Number Format of the International section in the Windows Control Panel.
E+	Scientific notation. If any of the strings "E+," "E-," "e+," or "e-" are contained in the format string, the number is formatted using scientific notation. A group of up to four "0" characters can immediately follow the "E+," "E-," "e+," or "e-" to determine the minimum number of digits in the exponent. The "E+" and "e+" formats cause a plus sign to be output for positive exponents and a minus sign to be output for negative exponents. The "E-" and "e-" formats output a sign character only for negative exponents.
'xx'/"xx"	Characters enclosed in single or double quotes are output as-is, and do not affect formatting.
;	Separates sections for positive, negative, and zero numbers in the format string.

The locations of the leftmost "0" before the decimal point in the format string and the rightmost "0" after the decimal point in the format string determine the range of digits that are always present in the output string.

The number being formatted is always rounded to as many decimal places as there are digit placeholders ("0" or "#") to the right of the decimal point. If the format string contains no decimal point, the value being formatted is rounded to the nearest whole number.

If the number being formatted has more digits to the left of the decimal separator than there are digit placeholders to the left of the "." character in the format string, the extra digits are output before the first digit placeholder.

To allow different formats for positive, negative, and zero values, the format string can contain between one and three sections separated by semicolons.

- One section: The format string applies to all values.

- Two sections: The first section applies to positive values and zeros, and the second section applies to negative values.

- Three sections: The first section applies to positive values, the second applies to negative values, and the third applies to zeros.

If the section for negative values or the section for zero values is empty, that is if there is nothing between the semicolons that delimit the section, the section for positive values is used instead.

If the section for positive values is empty, or if the entire format string is empty, the value is formatted using general floating-point formatting with 15 significant digits.

General floating-point formatting is also used if the value has more than 18 digits to the left of the decimal point and the format string does not specify scientific notation.

EditKey method

Applies to TTable component

void EditKey(void);

The EditKey method is used to modify the contents of a search key buffer.

The SetKey method prepares the dataset for a search using the contents of one or more indexed fields as the search criterion. First call the SetKey method, which puts the dataset in SetKey mode (the State property is dsSetKey), then specify the values that make up the search key. For example,

```
MyTable.SetKey( );
MyTable.FieldByName( "State" )->AsString = "CA";
MyTable.FieldByName( "City" )->AsString = "Scotts Valley";
```

Call the GotoKey method to start the search. Once a key has been created, you can edit the search key by calling EditKey, then specify the new field values. Finally call GotoKey to search once again. For example,

```
MyTable.EditKey( );
MyTable.FieldByName( "City" )->AsString = "Ben Lomond";
MyTable.GotoKey( );
```

EditKey differs from SetKey in that the latter clears all the elements of the search key buffer to the default values (or blank). EditKey leaves the elements of the search key buffer with their current values.

Example

```
Table1.EditKey( );
Table1.FieldByName( "State" )->AsString = "CA";
Table1.FieldByName( "City" )->AsString = "Santa Barbara";
Table1.GotoKey( );
```

EditMask property

Applies to All TField components

string EditMask;

Run-time only. The EditMask property is the mask that is used to limit the data that can be put into a data field. A mask restricts the characters the user can enter to valid characters and formats. If the user attempts to enter a character that is not valid in the field, the character is not accepted. Validation is performed on a character-by-character basis. Use an OnValidate event to validate the entire input.

A mask consists of three fields with semicolons separating the fields. The first part of the mask is the mask itself. The second part is the character that determines whether the literal characters of a mask are saved as part of the data. The third part of the mask is the character used to represent a blank in the mask.

These are the special characters used to create masks:

Character	Meaning in mask
!	Leading blanks don't appear in the data. If a ! character is not present, trailing blanks don't appear in the data.
>	All characters that follow are in uppercase until the end of the mask or until a < character is encountered.
<	All characters that follow are in lowercase until the end of the mask or until a > character is encountered.
<>	No case checking is done and the data is formatted with the case the user uses to enter the data.
\	The character that follows is a literal character. Use this the backslash character to allow any of the mask special characters as a literal in the data.
L	Requires an alphabetic character only in this position. For the US, this is A-Z, a-z.
l	Permits only an alphabetic character in this position, but doesn't require it.
A	Requires an alphanumeric character only in this position. For the US, this is A-Z, a-z, 0-9.
a	Permits an alphanumeric character in this position, but doesn't require it.
C	Requires a character in this position.
c	Rermits a character in this position, but doesn't require it.
0	Requires a numeric character only in this position.
9	Permits a numeric character in this position, but doesn't require it.
#	Permits a numeric character or a plus or minus sign in this position, but doesn't require it.
:	Separates hours, minutes, and seconds in times. If the character that separates hours, minutes, and seconds is different in the International settings of the Control Panel utility on your computer system, that character is used instead of :.
/	Separates months, days, and years in dates. If the character that separates months, days, and years is different in the International settings of the Control Panel utility on your computer system, that character is used instead of /.
;	Separates masks.
_	Inserts a blank the edit box. When the user enters characters in the field, the cursor skips the blank character.

Example   The following is an example of a mask for an American telephone number.

```
MyField.EditMask = "!\(999\)000-000;1";
```

EditRangeEnd method

Applies to   TTable component

void EditRangeEnd(void);

The EditRangeEnd method is used to modify the end of a previously specified range applied to the table.

Before using EditRangeEnd, you must establish a range on the table. To specify a range, you call the SetRangeStart method and assign values to one or more fields that establish the beginning of the range. Then you call the SetRangeEnd method and assign values to the same fields that establish the end of the range. Finally, you call ApplyRange to apply the range to the table.

Once you have a range established, you can change it. To change the end of the range, you call EditRangeEnd. Then assign new values to the fields used to establish the range end. These new values become the new end of the range as soon as you call the ApplyRange method again.

EditRangeEnd differs from SetRangeEnd in that the latter clears all the elements of the search key buffer to the default values (NULL). EditRangeEnd leaves the elements of search key buffer with their current values.

Note   For Paradox or dBASE tables, these methods work only with indexed fields. For SQL databases, they can work with any columns specified in the IndexFieldNames property.

Example

```
// Limit the range from "Goleta" to "Santa Barbara"
Table1.EditRangeStart( ); // Set the beginning key
Table1.FieldByName( "City" )->AsString = "Goleta";
Table1.EditRangeEnd( ); // Set the ending key
Table1.FieldByName( "City" )->AsString = "Santa Barbara";
Table1.ApplyRange; // Tell the dataset to establish the range
```

EditRangeStart method

Applies to   TTable component

void EditRangeStart(void);

The EditRangeStart method is used to modify the beginning of a previously specified range applied to the table.

Before you can use EditRangeStart, you must establish a range on the table. To specify a range, you call the SetRangeStart method and assign values to one or more fields that establish the beginning of the range. You can then call the SetRangeEnd method and assign values to the same fields that establish the end of the range. Finally, you call ApplyRange to apply the range to the table.

Once you have established a range, you can change it. To change the beginning of the range, call EditRangeStart. Then assign new values to the fields used to establish the range start. These new values become the new beginning of the range as soon as you call the ApplyRange method again.

EditRangeStart differs from SetRangeStart in that the latter clears all the elements of the search key buffer to the default values (NULL). EditRangeStart leaves the elements of the search key buffer with their current values.

Note   For Paradox or dBASE tables, these methods work only with indexed fields. For SQL databases, they can work with any columns specified in the IndexFieldNames property.

Example

```
// Limit the range from "Goleta" to "Santa Barbara"
Table1.EditRangeStart( ); // Set the beginning key
Table1.FieldByName( "City" )->AsString = "Goleta";
Table1.EditRangeEnd; // Set the ending key
Table1.FieldByName( "City" )->AsString = "Santa Barbara";
Table1.ApplyRange( ); // Tell the dataset to establish the range
```

EListError object   bdtc.h

The EListError is an exception that is thrown when an error is made in a list, string, or
string list object. List error exceptions commonly occur when your application refers to
an item in a list that is out of the list's range. For example, the following code is an event
handler that attempts to access an item in a list box that does not exist. The EListError is
thrown and caught:

```
void TestEListErrorRange( void )
{
  TStrings strings;
  // Add values for the first six items
  strings.Add( "zero" );
  strings.Add( "one" );
  strings.Add( "two" );
  strings.Add( "three" );
  strings.Add( "four" );
  strings.Add( "five" );
// Try to read the value of the ninth (nonexistant) item
  try
  {
      strings.Strings[8] = string( "eight" );
  }
// Catch the exception
  catch(EListError e )
  {
      e.Show( "EListError" );
  }
}
```

Also, a list error occurs when your application tries to add a duplicate string to a string
list object when the value of the Duplicates property is dupError.

A list error exception is thrown when you insert a string into a sorted string list, as the
string you insert at the specified position may put the string list out of sorted order. For
example, this code throws the list error exception:

```
void TestEListErrorSorted( void )
{
  TStrings sortedStrings;
sortedStrings.Sorted = true;
  // Add values for the first five items
  strings.Add( "A" );
  strings.Add( "B" );
```

```
        strings.Add( "C" );
        strings.Add( "D" );
        strings.Add( "E" );
    // Try to insert a string out of sort order
        try
        {
            sortedStrings.Insert( 0, "Try to insert here" );
        }
    // Catch the exception
        catch(EListError e )
        {
            e.Show( "EListError" );
        }
    }
```

See also   BDTException object, EDatabaseError object

EmptyTable method

Applies to   TTable component

void EmptyTable(void);

The EmptyTable method deletes all records from the database table specified by TableName. Before calling this method, the DatabaseName, TableName and TableType properties must be assigned values.

Note   If the table is open, it must have been opened with the Exclusive property set to true before your application can call EmptyTable.

Example

```
    Table1.Active = false;
    Table1.DatabaseName = "VDT_Demos";
    Table1.TableName = "CustInfo";
    Table1.TableType = ttParadox;
    Table1.EmptyTable( );
```

EnableControls method

Applies to   TDataSet, TDBDataSet, TQuery, TStoredProc, TTable components

void EnableControls(void);

The EnableControls method restores the connections from the dataset to all TDataSource components that were disconnected by a call to the DisableControls method. While the data sources are disconnected, changes in the active record are reflected in them. The dataset maintains a count of the number of calls to DisableControls and EnableControls, so only the last call to EnableControls actually updates the data sources.

Example

```
Table1.DisableControls( );
// Move forward five records
for( int i = 1; i < 6 ; i++ )
  {
      Table1.Next( );
  }
// Update the controls to the current record
Table1.EnableControls( );
```

Enabled property

Applies to   All data-aware controls; TDataSource component

Description   The Enabled property determines if the control responds to mouse, keyboard, or timer events, or if the data-aware controls update each time the dataset they are connected to changes.

Enabled property for data-aware controls

Applies to   All data-aware controls

bool Enabled;

The Enabled property controls whether the control responds to mouse, keyboard, and timer events. If Enabled is true, the control responds normally. If Enabled is false, the control ignores mouse and keyboard events. Disabled controls appear dimmed.

This code alternately dims or enables a menu command when a user clicks the button:

```
TMyFormClass::Button1Click( )
{
  if( OpenCommand.Enabled )
      OpenCommand.Enabled = false;
  else
      OpenCommand.Enabled = true;
}
```

Enabled property for TDataSource

Applies to   TDataSource component

bool Enabled;

Enabled specifies if the display in data-aware controls connected to TDataSource is updated when the current record in the dataset changes. For example, when Enabled is true and the Next method of a dataset component is called many times, each call updates all controls. Setting Enabled to false allows the Next calls to be made without performing updates to the controls. Once you reach the desired record, set Enabled to true to update the controls to that record.

Note   Setting Enabled to false clears the display in data-aware controls until you set it to true again. If you want to leave the controls with their current contents while moving through the table or query, call the DisableControls and EnableControls methods.

EndDrag method

Applies to   All data-aware controls

void EndDrag(bool Drop);

The EndDrag method stops a component from being dragged any further. If the Drop parameter is true, the component being dragged is dropped. If the Drop parameter is false, the component is not dropped and dragging is canceled.

Example   The following code cancels the dragging of a database edit control without dropping the component.

```
DBEdit1.EndDrag( false );
```

Equals method

Applies to   TStrings component

bool Equals(TStrings& s);

The Equals method compares two strings. Pass a second TStrings component as the s parameter. If the two strings components contain the same number of strings, and the objects in each list are identical, Equals returns true.

Exchange method

Applies to   TStrings component

void Exchange(int index1, int index2);

The Exchange method exchanges the position of two items in the list of strings of a string component. The items are specified with their index values in the index1 and index2 parameters. Because the indexes are zero-based, the first item in the list has an index value of 0, the second item has an index value of 1, and so on.

If a string in a string component has an associated object, Exchange changes the position of both the string and the object.

Example   When this code runs, items 2 and 3 in the database list box switch places:

```
DBListBox1.Items->Exchange( 1, 2 );
```

Exclusive property

Applies to   TTable component

bool Exclusive;

The Exclusive property determines whether other users can access a table while your application has access. To prevent another user from accessing the table, set Exclusive to true. If it doesn't matter if other users have access, you can set Exclusive to false, the default value.

If other users are accessing the table when you try to open it, your exception handler will have to wait for those users to release it. If you do not provide an exception handler and another user already has the table open, your application is terminated.

Note Set the Active property to false before changing Exclusive to prevent an EDatabaseError exception.

Do not set both Active and Exclusive to true in the Property Inspector. Because the Property Inspector will have the table open, your application won't be able to open it.

Set Exclusive to true only when you must have complete control over the table.

Example

```
// Try to open Table1 with Exclusive true
// First, close Table1
Table1.Active = false;
while( true ) // until successful or Cancel button is pressed
{
  try
  {
      Table1.Exclusive = true; // See if it will open
      Table1.Active = true;
      break; // If no error, exit the loop
  }
  catch( EDatabaseError x )
  {
      // Ask if it is OK to retry
      if( MessageBox( "Could not open Table1 exclusively -
OK to retry?", "Error" , MB_OKCANCEL ) != IDOK )
      {
      throw x; // If not, reraise to abort
      }
  // Otherwise resume the repeat loop
  }
}
```

ExecProc method

Applies to TStoredProc component

void ExecProc(void);
The ExecProc method executes the stored procedure on the server.

Example

```
// Execute the stored procedure
StoredProc1.ExecProc( );
```

ExecSQL method

Applies to   TQuery component

void ExecSQL(void);

The ExecSQL method executes an SQL statement assigned to the SQL property of a TQuery if the statement does not return a result set.

Use ExecSQL if the SQL statement is an INSERT, UPDATE, DELETE, or any DDL statement. If the SQL statement is a SELECT statement, call the Open instead to execute the query.

Example

```
Query1.Close( );
Query1.SQL->Clear( );
Query1.SQL->Add( "Delete from Country where Name = \"Argentina\"" );
Query1.ExecSQL( );
```

Execute method

Applies to   TBatchMove component

void Execute(void);

The Execute method performs the batch move operation specified by Mode from the Source table to the Destination table.

Expression property

Applies to   TIndexDef component

string Expression;

Run-time and read only. The Expression property contains an expression in a dBASE index.

FieldByName method

Applies to   TDataSet, TDBDataSet, TQuery, TStoredProc, TTable components

void FieldByName(const string& n, TField* f);

The FieldByName method returns the TField with the name passed as the argument in n. Using FieldByName protects your application from a change in the order of the fields in the dataset. If the field cannot be found, FieldByName raises an exception. If you are not certain whether a field with the requested name exists, use the FindField method.

Example

```
// This is the safe way to change "CustNo" field
Table1.FieldByName( "CustNo" )->AsString = "1234";
// This is *not* the safe way to change "CustNo" field
Table1.Fields[0]->AsString = "1234";
```

FieldCount property

Applies to   TDataSet, TDBDataSet, TQuery, TStoredProc, TTable components

int FieldCount;

Run-time and read only. The FieldCount property specifies the number of fields (columns) in a dataset. It may not be the same as the number of fields in the underlying database table, because you can add calculated fields and remove fields with the Fields Editor.

Example   The following code displays the number of fields in Table1 in a message box:

```
char message[10];
wsprintf( message, "%d fields", Table1.Fieldcount );
MessageBox( message , "Information" , MB_OK );
```

FieldDefs property

Applies to   TDataSet, TDBDataSet, TQuery, TStoredProc, TTable components

TFieldDefs FieldDefs;

Run-time only. The FieldDefs property holds information about each TFieldDef in the dataset. You can use this property to determine which fields are in the dataset, their name, type, and size.

FieldName property

Applies to   All TField components

string FieldName;
FieldName is the name of the physical column in the underlying dataset to which a TField component is bound. For calculated fields, supply a FieldName when you define the field. For non-calculated fields, an exception occurs if a FieldName is not a column name in the physical table.

FieldNo property

Applies to   All TField, TFieldDef components

Description   FieldNo property for field definitions and fields

FieldNo property for field definitions

Applies to   TFieldDef component

int FieldNo;
Run-time and read only. FieldNo is the physical field number used by the Borland Database Engine to refer to the field.

Example

```
// Display the field name and number
char message[50];
wsprintf( message, "%s is field %d", FieldDef1.Name->c_str(), FieldDef1.FieldNo );
MessageBox( message , "Information" , MB_OK );
```

FieldNo property for fields

Applies to   All TField components

int FieldNo;
Run-time and read only. FieldNo is the ordinal of the TField component in its dataset. This property is available for programs that make direct calls to the Borland Database Engine.

Fields property

Applies to   TDataSet, TDBDataSet, TIndexDef, TQuery, TStoredProc, TTable components

Fields property for datasets

Applies to   TDataSet, TDBDataSet, TQuery, TStoredProc, TTable components

TField Fields[int index];
Run-time and read only. The Fields property returns a specific field in the dataset. Specify the field using the index parameter, with the first field in the dataset having an index value of 0.

Example

The following code displays a field's name.

```
char message[1--];
wsprintf( message, "FieldName is %s", table.Fields[0]->FieldName->c_str() );
MessageBox( message, "Information", MB_OK );
```

Fields property for index definitions

Applies to   TIndexDef component

string Fields;
Run-time and read only. Fields is a string consisting of the names or numbers of the fields comprising the index, separated by semicolons (";"). When numbers are used, they are the physical field numbers in the table; for example, 1..N.

Find method

Applies to   TFieldDefs, TStrings components

Find method for TStrings components

Applies to   TStrings component

bool Find(const string& s, int& lpindex);
The Find method searches for a specified string in the list of strings kept in a string component. If the string specified as the value of the s parameter is found, Find returns true and the position of the string in the string component is stored as the value of the lpindex parameter. Because the index is zero-based, the first string in the list of strings has an index value of 0, the second string has an index value of 1, and so on.

Find returns false if the specified string is not found.

Example

```
// Display the field name and number
char message[50];
wsprintf( message , "CustNo is field %d" , FieldDefs.Find( "CustNo" ),FieldNo );
MessageBox( message , "Information" , MB_OK );
```

Find method for field definitions

Applies to   TFieldDefs component

TFieldDef Find(const string& n);
The Find method returns a pointer to an entry in the Items property whose Name
property matches the n parameter. Use this method to obtain information about a
particular TFieldDef component.

Example

```
// Display the field name and number
char message[50];
wsprintf( message , "CustNo is field %d" , FieldDefs.Find( "CustNo" )->FieldNo );
MessageBox( message , "Information" , MB_OK );
```

FindDatabase method

Applies to   TSession component

PTDatabase FindDatabase(const string& n);
The FindDatabase method attempts to find a TDatabase component in the Databases
collection with a DatabaseName property value that matches the n parameter. If there is
no such database, FindDatabase returns a NULL pointer.

Example

```
MyDatabase = Session.FindDatabase( "MYDB" );
```

FindField method

Applies to   TDataSet, TDBDataSet, TQuery, TStoredProc, TTable components

PTField FindField(const string& n);
The FindField method returns the field with the name passed in n. While calling
FindField is slightly slower than a direct reference to the Fields property, using
FindField protects your application from a change in the order of the fields in the
component. If the field cannot be found, FindField returns a NULL pointer.

Example

```
// This is the safe way to change "CustNo" field
Table1.FindField( "CustNo" )->AsString = "1234";
// This is *not* the safe way to change "CustNo" field
Table1.Fields[0]->AsString = "1234";
```

FindIndexForFields method

Applies to   TIndexDefs component

TIndexDef FindIndexForFields(const string& fields);
Run-time and read only. The FindIndexForFields method returns the TIndexDef
component that is present in Items corresponding to a semicolon-separated list of fields.

FindKey method

Applies to   TTable component

bool FindKey(TVarRecs& values);
The FindKey method searches the database table to find a record whose index fields
match those passed in values. FindKey takes an array of values as its argument, where
each value corresponds to a index column in the underlying table. If the number of
values supplied is less than the number of columns in the database table, then the
remaining values are assumed to be blank. FindKey will search for values specified in
the array in the current index.

FindKey does the following:

- Puts the Table in SetKey state.

- Finds the record in the table that matches the specified values. If a matching record is
  found, it moves the cursor there, and returns true.

- If a matching record is not found, it does not move the cursor, and returns false.

Example   This code searches for the record with the customer number of 1234:

```
TVarRecs values;
values.Add(1234);
CustTable.FindKey(values);
```

FindNearest method

Applies to   TTable component

void FindNearest(TVarRecs& values);

The FindNearest method moves the cursor to the first record whose index fields' values are greater than or equal to those passed in values. The search begins at the first record, not at the current cursor position. This method can be used to match columns of string data type only. If you do not supply values for each field in the index key, any unassigned fields will use a NULL value.

FindNearest works by default on the primary index column. To search the table for values in other indexes, you must specify the field name in the table's IndexFieldNames property or the name of the index in the IndexName property.

The KeyExclusive property indicates whether a search will position the cursor on or after the specified record being searched for.

Note   With Paradox or dBASE tables, FindNearest works only with indexed fields. With SQL databases, it can work with any columns specified in the IndexFieldNames property.

Example   This code searches for the first customer number in a CustTable table that is equal to or greater than 1234:

```
TVarRecs values;
values.Add(1234);
CustTable.FindNearest(values);
```

First method

Applies to   TDataSet, TDBDataSet, TQuery, TStoredProc, TTable components

void First(void);

The First method moves the cursor to the first record in the active range of records of the dataset. The active range of records is affected by the filter established with ApplyRange.

If the dataset is in Edit or Insert state, First will perform an implicit Post of any pending data.

Focused method

Applies to   All data-aware controls

bool Focused( );

The Focused method is used to determine whether a control has the focus. If Focused returns true, the control currently is the focused control.

FontBold property

Applies to TDBCheckBox, TDBComboBox, TDBEdit, TDBListBox, TDBLookupCombo, TDBLookupList, TDBMemo, TDBRadioGroup, TDBText components

bool FontBold;
The FontBold property specifies whether the text in a component is boldfaced. If the property is true, the text is boldfaced. If it is false, the text in the component is not boldfaced.

FontItalic property

Applies to TDBCheckBox, TDBComboBox, TDBEdit, TDBListBox, TDBLookupCombo, TDBLookupList, TDBMemo, TDBRadioGroup, TDBText components

bool FontItalic;
The FontItalic property specifies whether the text in a control is italicized. If the property is true, the text is Italic. If it is false, the text in the control is not italicized.

FontName property

Applies to TDBCheckBox, TDBComboBox, TDBEdit, TDBListBox, TDBLookupCombo, TDBLookupList, TDBMemo, TDBRadioGroup, TDBText components

string FontName;
The FontName property specifies the font name (family) for the text in a component.

FontSize property

Applies to TDBCheckBox, TDBComboBox, TDBEdit, TDBListBox, TDBLookupCombo, TDBLookupList, TDBMemo, TDBRadioGroup, TDBText components

int FontSize;
The FontSize property specifies the size in points of the text in a component. If you need to work with the size in pixels, use the Height property.

FontStrikethru property

Applies to TDBCheckBox, TDBComboBox, TDBEdit, TDBListBox, TDBLookupCombo, TDBLookupList, TDBMemo, TDBRadioGroup, TDBText components bool FontStrikethru;

The FontStrikethru property specifies whether the text in a control is displayed with a line struck through it. If the property is true, the text is displayed in strikeout (this is ~~strikeout~~). If it is false, the text in the control is normal.

FontUnderline property

Applies to   TDBCheckBox, TDBComboBox, TDBEdit, TDBListBox, TDBLookupCombo, TDBLookupList, TDBMemo, TDBRadioGroup, TDBText components

bool FontUnderline;

The FontUnderline property specifies whether the text in a control is underlined. If the property is true, the text is underlined. If it is false, the text in the control is not underlined.

ForeColor property

Applies to   TDBCheckBox, TDBComboBox, TDBEdit, TDBImage, TDBListBox, TDBLookupCombo, TDBLookupList, TDBMemo, TDBRadioGroup, TDBText components

COLORREF ForeColor;

For all components, the ForeColor property determines the color of text in a control.

At design time, you set the ForeColor property by choosing it in the Property Inspector and clicking on the ellipsis button. This brings up the Windows Color Dialog, and you choose a color in the usual way.

At run time, set the ForeColor property by using the hexadecimal value for the desired color, or you can use the Windows RGB macro.

Example
```
DBEdit1.ForeColor = RGB( 255,127,255 );
DBEdit2.ForeColor = 0xff00ff;
```

FreeBookmark method

Applies to   TDataSet, TDBDataSet, TQuery, TStoredProc, TTable components

void FreeBookmark(TBookmark bm);

Use the FreeBookmark method in combination with the GetBookmark and GotoBookmark methods. FreeBookmark releases the system resources reserved during a call to GetBookmark. Specify the bookmark to be released as the value of the bm parameter.

Example

```
TBookmark MyBookmark;
// Save the current record position in MyBookmark
MyBookmark = Table1.GetBookmark( );
... // Other code here
// Return to the record associated with MyBookmark
Table1.GotoBookmark( MyBookmark );
// Release the resources for MyBookmark
Table1.FreeBookmark( MyBookmark );
```

GetAliasNames method

Applies to   TSession component

void GetAliasNames(TStrings& list)
The GetAliasNames method clears the strings of the list parameter and adds to it the
names of all defined BDE aliases. Application-specific aliases are not included.

Example

```
Session.GetAliasNames( MyStringList );
```

GetAliasParams method

Applies to   TSession component

void GetAliasParams(const string& n, TStrings& list);
The GetAliasParams method clears the strings of the list parameter and adds to it the
parameters associated with the BDE alias passed in the n parameter.

Example

```
string sDatabaseAlias;
Session.GetAliasParams( sDatabaseAlias , MyStringList );
```

GetBookmark method

Applies to   TDataSet, TDBDataSet, TQuery, TStoredProc, TTable components

TBookmark GetBookmark(void);
The GetBookmark method saves the current record information of the dataset to allow
you to return to that record with a later call to the GotoBookmark method. The
bookmark should be eventually be passed to the FreeBookmark method to release the
resources reserved during the call to GetBookmark. If the dataset is empty or not in
Browse state, GetBookmark returns a NULL pointer.

Note   All bookmarks are invalidated when a dataset is closed and when a table's index is
changed.

Example

```
TBookmark MyBookmark;
// Save the current record position in MyBookmark
MyBookmark = Table1.GetBookmark( );
... // Other code here
// Return to the record associated with MyBookmark
Table1.GotoBookmark( MyBookmark );
// Release the resources for MyBookmark
Table1.FreeBookmark( MyBookmark );
```

GetCurrentRecord method

Applies to   TDataSet, TDBDataSet, TQuery, TStoredProc, TTable components

bool GetCurrentRecord(LPSTR buffer);

The GetCurrentRecord fetches the current record within the dataset and stores it in the buffer specified with the buffer parameter. Before getting the current record, you should allocate sufficient memory for the buffer by using the RecordSize property of the dataset, which returns the size of one record in the dataset.

If the GetCurrentRecord was able to fetch the current record and place it in buffer, it returns true. If the record could not be placed into buffer, it returns false.

Example

```
LPSTR  recBuf = new char[ Table1.RecordSize + 1 ];
Table1.GetCurrentRecord( recBuf );
// do something with the data
// free the buffer
delete[] recBuf;
```

GetData method

Applies to   TField, TParam components

GetData method for TField components

Applies to   All TField components

bool GetData(LPVOID buffer);

The GetData method is used to obtain data from the field in its raw form. Unlike the AsString, and Text properties, GetData performs no translation or interpretation of the data. The buffer must have sufficient space allocated for the data. Use the DataSize property to determine the space required. If the data is NULL, GetData returns false and no data is transferred to Buffer. Otherwise, it returns true.

Example

```
// Retrieve the "raw" data from Field1
// Allocate space
LPVOID Buffer = new BYTE[ field1.DataSize ];
```

```
if( !Field1.GetData( Buffer ) )
{
  char message[50];
  wsprintf( message , "%s is NULL" , Field1.FieldName );
  MessageBox( message , "Information" , MB_OK );
}
else
{
    // Do something with the data
}
// Free the space
delete[] Buffer;
```

GetData method for TParam components

Applies to   TParam component

void GetData(LPVOID buffer);
The GetData method copies the current value of the parameter in native format to
buffer. The buffer must have enough space to hold the information; use the GetDataSize
method to determine the requirement.

Example

```
LPVOID Buffer;
// Allocate enough space to hold the CustNo data
Buffer = new BYTE[ Query1.ParamByName( "CustNo" ).GetDataSize( ) ];
// Retrieve the data
Query1.ParamByName( "CustNo" )->GetData( Buffer );
delete[] Buffer;
```

GetDatabaseNames method

Applies to   TSession component

void GetDatabaseNames(TStrings& list);
The GetDatabaseNames method clears the strings of the list parameter and adds to it the
names of all BDE and application-specific aliases.

Example

```
Session.GetDatabaseNames( MyStringList );
```

GetDataSize method

Applies to   TParam component

uint16 GetDataSize(void);
The GetDataSize method returns the number of bytes required to hold the parameter's
value. Use GetDataSize in conjunction with the GetData method to allocate memory for
the parameter's data.

Example

```
LPVOID Buffer;
// Allocate enough space to hold the CustNo data
Buffer = new BYTE[ Query1.ParamByName( "CustNo" ).GetDataSize( ) ];
// Retrieve the data
Query1.ParamByName( "CustNo" )->GetData( Buffer );
delete[] Buffer;
```

GetDriverNames method

Applies to   TSession component

void GetDriverNames(TStrings& list);
The GetDriverNames method clears the strings of the list parameter and adds to it the
names of all BDE drivers currently installed. This will not include "PARADOX" or
"DBASE," because these databases are handled by the driver named "STANDARD."

Example

```
Session.GetDriverNames( MyStringList );
```

GetDriverParams method

Applies to   TSession component

void GetDriverParams(const string& n, TStrings& list);
The GetDriverParams method clears the strings of the list parameter and adds to it the
default parameters for the driver named in the n parameter. The driver named
"STANDARD" (used for Paradox and dBASE tables) has only one parameter,
"PATH=." SQL drivers have varying numbers of parameters.

Example

```
Session.GetDriverParams( "STANDARD", MyStringList );
```

GetFieldNames method

Applies to   TDataSet, TDBDataSet, TQuery, TStoredProc, TTable components

void GetFieldNames(TStrings& list);
The GetFieldNames method obtains a list of the field names for the dataset and places it
in the list parameter.

Example

```
TStrings myList;
Table1.GetFieldNames( &myList );
```

GetIndexNames method

Applies to   TTable component

void GetIndexNames(TStrings& list);
The GetIndexNames method adds the names of all available indexes for the table to the strings component specified by the list parameter.

Example

```
TStrings  MyList;
Table1.GetIndexNames( &MyList );
// Do something with the names
```

GetPassword method

Applies to   TSession component

bool GetPassword(void);
The GetPassword method invokes the OnPassword event (if any) or displays the default password dialog box. It then returns true if the user chose the OK button and false if the user chose the Cancel button.

GetResults method

Applies to   TStoredProc component

void GetResults(void);
You only need to call this method with a Sybase stored procedure that returns a result set. GetResults returns the output parameter values from the stored procedure. Usually, TStoredProc does this automatically, but Sybase stored procedures do not return the values until the cursor reaches the end of the result set, so you must call GetResults explicitly.

Example

```
StoredProc1.Open( )
while( ! StoredProc.AtEOF )
{
  StoredProc1.Next( );
  // Do Something
}
StoredProc1.GetResults( );
DBEdit1.Text = StoredProc1.ParamByName( "Output" );
```

GetSelTextBuf method

Applies to   TDBEdit, TDBMemo components

int GetSelTextBuf (Buffer LPSTR, BufSize int);

The GetSelTextBuf method copies the selected text from the database edit box or memo control into the buffer pointed to by Buffer, up to a maximum of BufSize characters, and returns the number of characters copied.

Example

```
LPSTR Buffer;
UINT  Size;
// Get length of selected text in DBEdit1
Size = DBEdit1.SelLength;
// Creates Buffer dynamic variable
Buffer = new BYTE[ Size + 1 ];
// Puts DBEdit1.Text into Buffer
DBEdit1.GetSelTextBuf( Buffer,Size );
// do something with the text string
delete Buffer;    // Frees memory allocated to Buffer
```

GetStoredProcNames method

Applies to   TSession component

void GetStoredProcNames(const string& DatabaseName, TStrings& list);

GetStoredProcNames returns a list of all stored procedures defined for the specified SQL database in the list parameter. This method is not valid for Paradox or dBASE databases.

Example

```
Session.GetStoredProcNames( "IB_EMPLOYEE", MyStringList );
```

GetTableNames method

Applies to   TSession component

void GetTableNames(const string& DatabaseName, const string& Pattern, bool Extensions,
        bool SystemTables, TStrings& list);

The GetTableNames method clears the strings of the list parameter and then adds to the string component the names of all the tables in the database referenced by DatabaseName. The Pattern parameter limits the table names to those matching the Pattern string.

For SQL servers, set SystemTables to true to obtain system tables in addition to user tables. For desktop (non-SQL) databases, set Extensions to true to include file-name extensions in the table names.

Example
```
Session.GetTableNames( "DBDEMOS", "*.db", false, false, MyStringList );
```

GetText method

Applies to   TStrings component

void GetText(string& s);
The GetText method returns the text in the TStrings object with <carriage return><line feed> characters between the string items. GetText is useful when working with components that contain blocks of text made up of more than one string. For example, there can be many strings in the SQL property of a TQuery component. When you want to return the entire list of strings in that property all at once, use the GetText method.

GetTextBuf method

Applies to   All data-aware controls

SHORT GetTextBuf(LPSTR Buff, SHORT Len);
The GetTextBuf method retrieves the control's text and copies it into the buffer pointed to by Buff, up to the number of characters given by Len, and returns the number of characters copied.

To find out how many characters the buffer needs to hold the entire text, you can call the GetTextLen method before calling GetTextBuf.

Example   This example copies the text in a database edit box into a dynamic variable:
```
//Get length of string in DBEdit1
UINT  Size = DBEdit1.GetTextLen( );
//Creates Buffer dynamic variable
LPSTR Buffer = new  char[ Size + 1];
//Puts DBEdit1.Text into Buffer
DBEdit1.GetTextBuf( Buffer,Size );
//Frees memory allocated to Buffer
delete[] Buffer;
```

GetTextLen method

Applies to   All data-aware controls

SHORT GetTextLen( );
The GetTextLen method returns the length of the control's text. The most common use of GetTextLen is to find the size needed for a text buffer in the GetTextBuf method.

GotoBookmark method

Applies to   TDataSet, TDBDataSet, TQuery, TStoredProc, TTable components

void GotoBookmark(TBookmark bm);

The GotoBookmark method moves the cursor to the record corresponding to the bookmark specified with the bm parameter obtained through a call to GetBookmark. While you must eventually call the FreeBookmark method to release the resources reserved during the call to GetBookmark, you are free to make as many calls to GotoBookmark as you wish before calling FreeBookmark. If the bm parameter is NULL, GotoBookmark does nothing.

Example

```
TBookmark MyBookmark;
// Save the current record position in MyBookmark
  MyBookmark = Table1.GetBookMark( );
  ... // Other code here
// Return to the record associated with MyBookmark
  Table1.GotoBookMark( MyBookMark );
// Release the resources for MyBookmark
  Table1.FreeBookmark( MyBookmark );
```

GotoCurrent method

Applies to   TTable component

void GotoCurrent(TTable& t);

The GotoCurrent method synchronizes the positions of two TTable components that use the same database table. GotoCurrent changes the position of the table to match that of the t parameter.

Note   Both tables must have the same DatabaseName and TableName or a "table mismatch" exception is raised.

Example

```
Table1.GotoCurrent( Table2 );
```

GotoKey method

Applies to   TTable component

void GotoKey(void);

The GotoKey method is used with the SetKey or EditKey method to move to a specific record in a TTable.

To establish a search key call SetKey to put the table in SetKey state. The next field assignments you make indicate the values to search for in the indexed fields. GotoKey then moves the cursor to the first row in the table within the active range that matches those field values.

To edit a search key, call EditKey. The next field assignments you make indicate the values to search for in the indexed fields. GotoKey then moves the cursor to the first row in the table within the active range that matches those field values.

If the search is unsuccessful, the position of the cursor doesn't change.

Note   If you want to search on a subset of fields in a multiple-field key, you must set the KeyFieldCount property to the number of fields on which you want to search.

Example

```
Table1.EditKey( );
Table1.FieldByName( "CustNo" )->AsFloat = 610;
Table1.GotoKey( );
```

GotoNearest method

Applies to   TTable component

void GotoNearest(void);

The GotoNearest method moves the cursor to the record whose indexed fields are greater than or equal to those in the IndexFields property.

Call EditKey or SetKey to prepare the dataset for a search, then assign new values to the indexed fields, and finally call GotoNearest to start the search.

The KeyExclusive property indicates whether a search positions the cursor on or after the specified record being searched for.

Note   You do not have to assign a value for each field in the index key. Any unassigned field uses a NULL value.

The search begins at the first record in the table, not at the current cursor position.

Example

```
Table1.SetKey( );
Table1.FieldByName( "State" )->AsString = "CA";
Table1.FieldByName( "City" )->AsString = "Santa";
Table1.GotoNearest( );
```

Handle property

Applies to   TDatabase, TDataSet, TDBDataSet, TQuery, TSession, TStoredProc, TTable components

Handle property for sessions

Applies to   TSession component

hDBISes Handle;
Run-time and read only. The Handle property allows you to make direct calls to the Borland Database Engine using this handle to the session (TSession). Under most circumstances you should not need to use this property, unless your application requires some functionality not encapsulated in Visual Database Tools.

Handle property for datasets

Applies to   TDataSet, TDBDataSet, TQuery, TStoredProc, TTable components

hDBICur Handle;
Run-time and read only. The Handle property enables an application to make direct calls to the Borland Database Engine API using this handle of a dataset component.

Under most circumstances you should not need to use this property, unless your application requires some functionality not encapsulated in Visual Database Tools.

Handle property for databases

Applies to   TDataBase component

hDBIDb Handle;
Run-time and read only. Use the Handle property to make direct calls to the Borland Database Engine API that require a database handle. Under most circumstances you should not need to use this property, unless your application requires some functionality not encapsulated in Visual Database Tools.

Height property

Applies to   All data-aware controls

int Height;
The Height property of a control is the vertical size of a database list box control:

Example   The following code doubles the height of a list box control:

```
DBListBox1.Height = DBListBox1.Height * 2;
```

HelpContext property (HelpContextID at design time)

Applies to   All data-aware controls

long HelpContext;
The HelpContext property provides a context number for use in calling context-sensitive online Help. Each screen in the Help system should have a unique context

number. When a component is selected in the application, pressing F1 displays a Help screen. Which Help screen appears depends on the value of the HelpContext property.

When you access the HelpContext property at design time, Resource Workshop uses the VBX standard property name HelpContextID.

HelpContextID property (HelpContext at run time)

Applies to   All data-aware controls

long HelpContextID;
The HelpContextID property provides a context number for use in calling context-sensitive online Help. Each screen in the Help system should have a unique context number. When a component is selected in the application, pressing F1 displays a Help screen. Which Help screen appears depends on the value of the HelpContextID property.

When you access the HelpContextID property programmatically, refer to it as HelpContext.

Hide method

Applies to   All data-aware controls

void Hide( );
The Hide method makes a control invisible by setting the Visible property of the form or control to false. Although a form or control that is hidden is not visible, you can still set the properties of the form or control, or call its methods.

Index property (ComponentIndex at run time)

Applies to   All data-aware controls

int Index;
Read only at run-time. The Index property indicates the position of the component in its owner's components property list. The first component in the list has a Index value of 0, the second has a value of 1, and so on.

When you access the Index property programmatically, refer to it as ComponentIndex.

Index property (TField components)

Applies to   All TField components

int Index;
Index is a field's index number into the Fields property of the dataset. It corresponds to the order of the field in the dataset. You can change the order of a field's position in the

dataset by changing its Index property. A better way to change field order, however, is by dragging and dropping fields in the Fields Editor at design time.

IndexDefs property

Applies to   TTable component

TIndexDefs IndexDefs;
Run-time and read only. The IndexDefs property holds information about all the indexes for a TTable component.

Note   The IndexDefs property may not always reflect the current set of indexes. Before examining any property of IndexDefs, call its Update method to ensure that it has the most recent set of information.

Example

```
// Get the current available indices
Table1.IndexDefs->Update( );
//
 Find one which combines Customer Number ( "CustNo" ) and Order Number ( "OrderNo" )
for( int I = 0; I < Table1.IndexDefs->Count; I++ )
{
  if( Table1.IndexDefs->Items[I]->Fields == "CustNo;OrderNo" )
  {
      break;
  }
}
```

IndexFieldCount property

Applies to   TTable component

int IndexFieldCount;
Run-time only. The IndexFieldCount property is the number of actual fields for the current index. If the table is not Active, the value of IndexFieldCount is zero.

Example

```
int TotalLen = 0;
// Calculate the total length of the index
  for( int i = 0; i < Table1.IndexFieldCount; i++ )
  {
      TotalLen += Table1.IndexFields[i]->DataSize;
  }
```

IndexFieldNames property

Applies to   TTable component

string IndexFieldNames;
The IndexFieldNames property is used with an SQL server to identify the columns to be used as an index for the TTable component. Separate the column names with semicolon characters (";"). If you have too many column names or the names are too long to fit within the 255 character limit, use column numbers instead of names.

Note   IndexFieldNames and IndexName are mutually exclusive. Setting one will clear the other.

Example
```
Query1.IndexFieldNames = "CustNo;OrderNo";
```

IndexFields property

Applies to   TTable component

TField IndexFields[int i];
Run-time only. The IndexFields property gives you access to information about each field of the current index for the dataset. The Active property must be true or the information will not be valid.

Example
```
string S;
// Create a composite string with the index's names separated by "@"
for( i = 0; i < Table1.IndexFieldCount; i++ )
{
  S = S + "@" + Table1.IndexFields[i]->FieldName;
}
```

IndexName property

Applies to   TTable component

string IndexName;
The IndexName property identifies a secondary index for the TTable component. If no value is assigned to IndexName, the table's primary index is used to order the records.

For dBASE tables, the index must reside in the table's master index file. The master index file is determined by taking the TableName property and replacing any file extension with "MDX". Non-maintained indexes are not supported.

Note   IndexFieldNames and IndexName are mutually exclusive. Setting one will clear the other.

Example
```
Table1.IndexName = "CustNoIndex";
```

IndexOf method

Applies to   TFieldDefs, TIndexDefs, TStrings components

Description   The IndexOf method returns the position of an item in a component.

IndexOf method for TStrings components

Applies to   TStrings components

int IndexOf(const string& s);
The IndexOf method returns the position of a string in a list of strings in a component. Specify the string you want to locate as the value of the s parameter. The first position in the list of strings is 0. If the string is not in the string list, IndexOf returns -1.

IndexOf method for index definitions

Applies to   TIndexDefs object

int IndexOf(const string& n);
The IndexOf method returns the index of the entry in the Items parameter whose Name property matches the n parameter.

IndexOf method for field definitions

Applies to   TFieldDefs component

int IndexOf(const string& n);
The IndexOf method returns the index number of the entry in the Items property whose Name property matches the n parameter.

IndexOfObject method

Applies to   TStrings component

int IndexOfObject(LPVOID object);
The IndexOfObject method returns the position of an object stored in the Objects property of a string component. Specify the object you want to locate as the value of the object parameter. The first position in the list of objects is 0. If the object is not in the list of objects, IndexOfObject returns -1.

Insert method

Applies to   TDataSet, TDBDataSet, TQuery, TStoredProc, TStrings, TTable components

Description   The Insert method inserts an item into a component.

Insert method for TStrings components

Applies to   TStrings component

```
void Insert( int index, const string& s );
```
The Insert method inserts a string into the list of strings in a string component. The string s is inserted into the position in the list indicated by the value of index. The index is zero-based, so the first position in the list has an index value of 0.

Example   This code adds five strings to a database list box and then inserts one more at the top of the list box:

```
int i;
for( i = 0; i < 6; i++ )
{
    char buf[15];
    wsprintf( buf , "Item %d" , i );
    DBListBox1.Items->Add( buf );
}
DBListBox1.Items->Insert( 0, "Inserted here" );
```

Insert method for datasets

Applies to   TDataSet, TDBDataSet, TQuery, TStoredProc, TTable components

```
void Insert( void );
```
The Insert method puts the dataset into Insert state and opens a new, empty record at the current cursor location. When an application calls the Post method, the new record is inserted in the dataset in a position based on its index, if defined. To discard the new record, call the Cancel method.

This method is valid only for datasets that return a live result set.

Note   For indexed tables, both the Append and Insert methods put the new record in the correct location in the table, based on the table's index. If no index is defined on the underlying table, then the record maintains its position and Append adds the record to the end of the table, while Insert inserts it at the current cursor position.

Example
```
// Move to the end of the component
Table1.Last( );
Table1.Insert( );
Table1.FieldByName( "CustNo" ).AsString = "9999";
// Fill in other fields here
```

```
    if // you are sure you want to do this
        Table1.Post( );
    else // if you changed your mind
        Table1.Cancel( );
```

InsertObject method

Applies to TStrings component

void InsertObject(int index, const string& s, LPVOID object);

The InsertObject method inserts a string into the list of strings and an component into the list of components in a string or string list component. Specify the string you want to insert as the value of the s parameter, and the component you want to insert as the value of the object parameter. The index parameter identifies the position of the string and component in their respective string and object lists. Because the index is zero-based, the first position in each list has an index value of 0.

If your application calls InsertObject when the list of items is sorted, an EListError exception is raised.

InsertRecord method

Applies to TDataSet, TDBDataSet, TQuery, TStoredProc, TTable components

void InsertRecord(TVarRecs& values);

The InsertRecord method inserts a new record into the dataset using the field values passed in the values parameter. The assignment of the elements of values to fields in the record is sequential; the first element is assigned to the first field, the second to the second, etc.

The number of field values passed in values may be fewer than the number of actual fields in the record; any remaining fields are left unassigned and are NULL. The type of each element of values must be compatible with the type of the field in that the field must be able to perform the assignment using AsString, AsInteger, etc., according the type of the Values element.

This method is valid only for datasets that return a live result set.

Note For indexed tables, the AppendRecord and InsertRecord methods both put the new record in the correct location in the table, based on the table's index. If no index is defined in the underlying table, then the record maintains its position. AppendRecord adds the record to the end of the table, and InsertRecord inserts it at the current cursor position. In either case, posting a new record in a data grid may cause all the rows before and after the new record to change as the dataset follows the new row to its indexed position and then fetches data to fill the grid around it.

Example This example inserts a record into a table with field values assigned for the first five fields. Note that the code assigns a blank value to the fourth field. If you want to skip a field and not assign it a value, but you do want to assign a value to the next sequential field, you must assign a blank value to the field you want to skip. If the record contains more than five fields, all the remaining fields are assigned a blank value.

```
TVarRecs values;
values.Add( 9998 );
values.Add( "Camgros" );
values.Add( "Vickie" );
values.Add( " " );
values.Add( 78000 );
MyTable.InsertRecord( values );
```

IntegralHeight property

Applies to   TDBListBox, TDBLookupList components

bool IntegralHeight;
The IntegralHeight property controls the way the database list box represents itself on the form. If IntegralHeight is true, the list box shows only entries that fit completely in the vertical space, and the bottom of the list box moves up to the bottom of the last completely drawn item in the list. If IntegralHeight is false, the bottom of the list box is at the location determined by its ItemHeight property, and the bottom item visible in the list might not be complete.

If the list box has a Style property value of lbOwerDrawVariable, setting the IntegralHeight property to true has no effect.

If the Style property value of the list box is lsOwnerDrawFixed, the height of the list box at design time is always an increment of the ItemHeight value.

Invalidate method

Applies to   All data-aware controls

void Invalidate( );
The Invalidate method forces a control to repaint as soon as possible.

IsIndexField property

Applies to   All TField components

bool IsIndexField;
Run-time and read only. The IsIndexField property specifies whether or not a field is indexed. If true, the field is an index field.

IsLinkedTo method

Applies to   TDataSet, TDBDataSet, TDataSource, TQuery, TStoredProc, TTable components

IsLinkedTo method for datasets

Applies to   TDataSet, TDBDataSet, TQuery, TStoredProc, TTable components

bool IsLinkedTo(TDataSource& source);

The IsLinkedTo method determines whether the dataset is linked to the TDataSource component specified as the value of the source parameter. If it is linked to the named data source, IsLinkedTo returns true. If IsLinkedTo is false, the dataset is not linked to the named data source.

Example   This example links the TQuery component Query1 to the TDataSource component dataSource1 if they are not already linked.

```
if( !Query1.IsLinkedTo( dataSource1 ) )
{
  Query1.DataSource = dataSource1;
}
```

IsLinkedTo method for data sources

Applies to   TDataSource component

bool IsLinkedTo(TDataSet& DataSet);

The IsLinkedTo method determines whether the datasource is linked to the TDataSet component specified as the value of the DataSet parameter. If it is linked to the named data set, IsLinkedTo returns true. If IsLinkedTo is false, the datasource is not linked to the named data set.

IsNull property

Applies to   All TField, TParam components

IsNull property for TParam components

Applies to   TParam component

bool IsNull;

Run-time and read only. IsNull returns true if the parameter has no data assigned to it. This should only occur if an application has called:

- Assign with another parameter that has no data assigned.
- AssignField with a TField whose data is NULL.
- The Clear method.

Example

```
// Set the CustNo parameter to 999 if it is null
if( Params.ParamByName( "CustNo" )->IsNull )
{
  Params.ParamByName( "CustNo" )->AsInteger = 999;
}
```

IsNull property for fields

Applies to   All TField components

bool IsNull;
Run-time and read only. IsNull returns true if the value of the field is NULL. If the field contains data, IsNull is false.

IsSQLBased property

Applies to   TDataBase component

bool IsSQLBased;
Run-time and read only. IsSQLBased is true if the TDatabase component uses any driver other than "STANDARD". If you are accessing a dBASE or Paradox database or an ASCII file, IsSQLBased will be false.

IsValidChar method

Applies to   All TField components

bool IsValidChar(char c);
Use IsValidChar to determine if a particular character entered in the field is valid for the field. TIntegerField, TSmallintField and TWordField allow "+", "-" and "0" to "9". TBCDField and TFloatField also allow "E", "e", and the DecimalSeparator character. All other fields accept all characters.

ItemAtPos method

Applies to   TDBListBox component

SHORT ItemAtPos(TPoint Pos, bool Existing);
The ItemAtPos method returns the index of the list box indicated by the coordinates of a point on the control. The Pos parameter is the point in the control in window coordinates.

If Pos is beyond the last item in the list box, the value of the Existing variable determines the returned value. If you set Existing to true, ItemAtPos returns -1, indicating that no item exists at that point. If you set Existing to false, ItemAtPos returns the position of the last item in the list box.

ItemAtPos is useful for detecting if an item exists at a particular point in the control.

Example   When this code runs, the index value of the item in the database list box that contains the point specified in the code appears in the database edit box:

```
int Value;
TPoint APoint;
char sIndex[5];
```

```
APoint.X = 30;
APoint.Y = 50;
Value = DBListBox1.ItemAtPos( APoint, false );
wsprintf( sIndex, "%d", Value );
DBEdit1.Text = sIndex;
```

ItemHeight property

Applies to   TDBComboBox, TDBListBox,TDBLookupCombo, TDBLookupList
components

int ItemHeight;

For database list boxes, the ItemHeight property is the height of an item in the list box in pixels when the list box's Style property is lsOwnerDrawFixed. If the Style property is lsStandard or lsOwnerDrawVariable, the value of ItemHeight is ignored. You can control the height of an item in a fixed owner-draw list box by changing the height of ItemHeight.

For database combo boxes, the ItemHeight property is the height of an item in the combo box list in pixels when the combo box's Style property is csOwnerDrawFixed. If the Style property is any other setting, the value of ItemHeight is ignored. You can control the height of an item in a fixed owner-draw combo box by changing the height of ItemHeight.

ItemIndex property

Applies to   TDBComboBox, TDBListBox,TDBLookupCombo,
TDBLookupList,TDBRadioGroup components

int ItemIndex;

Run-time only. The value of the ItemIndex property is the ordinal number of the selected item in the control's item list. If no item is selected, the value is -1 (the default). To select an item at run time, set the value of ItemIndex to the index of the item in the list you want selected, with 0 being the first item in the list.

ItemRect method

Applies to   TDBListBox component

TRect ItemRect (SHORT Item);

The ItemRect method returns the rectangle that surrounds the item specified in the Item parameter.

Items property

Applies to   TDBComboBox, TDBListBox,TDBRadioGroup, TFieldDefs, TIndexDefs, TParams, TVarRecs components

Description   The Items property specifies the items of a component. It behaves differently depending on which component you are using.

Items property for data-aware controls

Applies to   TDBComboBox, TDBListBox, TDBRadioGroup components

PTStrings Items;
The Items property contains the strings that appear in the database list box or combo box, or as radio buttons in a database radio group box. Because Items is an component of type TStrings, you can add, delete, insert, and move items using the Add, Delete, Insert, Exchange, and Move methods of the TStrings component.

The ItemIndex property determines which item is selected, if any.

To determine if a particular item in the list of strings that makes up the Items property for a database list box or combo box is selected, use the Selected property.

Example   When this code runs, the text in the database edit box is added as a string in the database list box:

```
DBListBox1.Items->Add( DBEdit1.Text );
```

Items property for index definitions

Applies to   TIndexDefs component

TIndexDef Items[int i];
Run-time and read only. Items holds the TIndexDef components that describe each index of the dataset. The number of entries is given by the Count property; there will be one entry for each index of the dataset.

Items property for TParams components

Applies to   TParams component

TParam Items[uint16 i];
Run-time and read only. The Items property holds the parameters (TParam components). While you can use Items to reference a particular parameter by its index, the ParamByName method is recommended to avoid depending on the order of the parameters.

Example

```
// Assign 99999 to any integer parameter which does not have a value
for( int i = 0; i < Params.Count; Ii++ )
{
  if( ( Params.Items[i]->IsNull ) && ( Params.Items[i]->DataType == ftInteger ) )
  {
      Params.Items[i]->AsInteger = 99999;
  }
}
```

Items property for field definitions

Applies to   TFieldDefs component

TFieldDef Items[int i];
Items is an array of pointers to the TFieldDef components that describe each field in the dataset. There is one pointer for each component in the dataset.

Items property for TVarRecs components

Applies to   TVarRecs component

TVarRec Items(int i);
Run-time and read only. The Items property contains all the data items in a TVarRecs component. By specifying an index as the value of the i parameter, Items returns the data item at that position in the TVarRecs component.

KeepConnection property

Applies to   TDataBase component

bool KeepConnection;
The KeepConnection property specifies whether an application remains connected to a database server even when no tables are open. If an application needs to open and close several tables in a single database, it is more efficient to set KeepConnection to true. That way, the application remains connected to the database even when it does not have any tables open. It can then open and close tables repeatedly without incurring the overhead of connecting to the database each time. If KeepConnection is false, the database must log in to the server each time the Connected property is set to true.

The TSession component has an application-wide KeepConnections property that determines the initial state of the KeepConnection property for temporary (those created automatically) TDatabase components.

KeepConnections property

Applies to   TSession component

bool KeepConnections;
Run-time only. KeepConnections specifies whether a virtual TDatabase component maintains database connections even if no tables in the database are open. Databases that have an explicit TDatabase component use TDatabase's KeepConnection property instead to determine if connections are persistent.

If KeepConnections is true (the default), the application maintains database connections until the application exits or calls the DropConnections method. If KeepConnections is false, the application disconnects from the database when all datasets connected to tables in the database are closed.

Note   KeepConnections has no effect on connections to databases for which an application has an explicit TDatabase component.

KeyExclusive property

Applies to   TTable component

bool KeyExclusive;
The KeyExclusive property indicates whether range and search functions will exclude the matching records specified by the functions. KeyExclusive is false by default.

For the SetRangeStart and SetRangeEnd methods, KeyExclusive determines whether the filtered range excludes the range boundaries. The default is false, which means rows are in the filtered range if they are greater than or equal to the start range specified and less than or equal to the end range specified. If KeyExclusive is true, only records greater than the start range value and less than the end range value are included in the search results.

For the GotoNearest and FindNearest methods, KeyExclusive indicates whether a search will position the cursor on or after the record being searched for. If KeyExclusive is false, GoToNearest and FindNearest will move the cursor to the record that matches the specified values, if found. If true, then the methods go to the record immediately following the matching record, if found.

Example
```
// Limit the range from 1351 to 1356, excluding both 1351 and 1356
// Set the beginning key
Table1.EditRangeStart( );
Table1.IndexFields[0]->AsString = "1351";
// Exclude 1351 itself
Table1.KeyExclusive = true;
// Set the ending key
Table1.EditRangeEnd( );
Table1.IndexFields[0]->AsString = "1356";
```

```
// Exclude 1356 itself
Table1.KeyExclusive = true;
// Tell the dataset to establish the range
Table1.ApplyRange( );
```

KeyFieldCount property

Applies to   TTable component

int KeyFieldCount;

KeyFieldCount specifies the number of key fields to use with search functions (GotoKey, FindKey, EditKey, and so on) if you don't want to search on all the fields in the key.

For example, if the search key is made up of four fields, you can limit the search key to three by changing the KeyFieldCount property to three before calling GotoKey.

KeyViolCount property

Applies to   TBatchMove component

int32 KeyViolCount;

Run-time and read only. KeyViolCount reports the number of records which could not be replaced, added, or deleted from the Destination property because of integrity key violations. If the AbortOnKeyViol property is true, KeyViolCount is never greater than one, as the first violation termates the batch move operation.

Example

```
BatchMove1.Execute( );
    if( BatchMove1.KeyViolCount != 0 )
    {
        // something went wrong
    }
```

KeyViolTableName property

Applies to   TBatchMove component

string KeyViolTableName;

The value of the KeyViolTableName property determines if all records found to have key violations during the batch move operation are placed in a table with the name entered as the KeyViolTableName property value. If you specify a name for KeyViolTableName, a local Paradox table is created. If no table is specified, no table is created.

If the AbortOnKeyViol property value is true, then there is at most one record in this table as the operation aborts with that first record. The number of records placed in the new table is reported in the KeyViolCount property.

Example
```
BatchMove1.KeyViolTableName = "KeyViol";
```

Last method

Applies to   TDataSet, TDBDataSet, TQuery, TStoredProc, TTable components

void Last(void);
The Last method moves the cursor to the last record in the active range of records of the dataset. The active range of records is affected by the filter established with SetRangeEnd.

If the dataset is in Insert or Edit state, Last performs an implicit Post of any pending data.

Left property

Applies to   All data-aware controls

int Left;
The Left property determines the horizontal coordinate of the left edge of a component relative to the container in pixels. The default value is -1.

Lines property

Applies to   TDBMemo component

PTStrings Lines;
Run-time only. The Lines property contains the text lines in a database memo component.

Example   This code loads the contents of the system's AUTOEXEC.BAT file in to the database memo, and the sixth line of the file is printed:
```
DBMemo1.Lines.LoadFromFile("C:\\AUTOEXEC.BAT");
printf("The 6th line of AUTOEXEC.BAT is: %s", DBMemo1.Lines[5]->c_str() );
```

LoadFromBitmap method

Applies to   TGraphicField component

void LoadFromBitmap(HBITMAP hbitmap, HPALETTE hpalette);
The LoadFromBitmap method loads a bitmap and palette into the TGraphicField component. Use this method when writing to a graphic field.

LoadFromFile method

Applies to   TBlobField, TGraphicField, TMemoField, TStrings components

LoadFromFile method for fields

Applies to   TBlobField, TGraphicField, TMemoField components

void LoadFromFile(const string& filename);
The LoadFromFile method reads a file with the name passed in filename and loads the contents in TBlobField, TMemoField, or TGraphicField.

Note   For TMemoField and TGraphicField, the file should have been created by the SaveToFile or SaveToStream method.

Example

```
// Load a blob field with the contents of autoexec.bat
BlobField1.LoadFromFile( "C:\\autoexec.bat" );
```

LoadFromFile method for TStrings components

Applies to   TStrings component

void LoadFromFile(const string& filename);
The LoadFromFile method reads the file specified in filename and loads the text into the string component.

Example   This example loads a stored SQL statement from the file test.sql into the SQL property of Query1.

```
Query1.SQL->LoadFromFile( "test.SQL" );
```

LoadFromStream method

Applies to   TBlobField, TGraphicField, TMemoField, TStrings components

void LoadFromStream(TMemoryStream& stream);
The LoadFromStream method reads Stream and stores the contents in TBlobField, TMemoField, or TGraphicField.

Note   For a TMemoField or TGraphicField, the file should have been created by the SaveToFile or SaveToStream method.

Example

```
// Load a blob field from an existing stream1
BlobField1.LoadFromStream( Stream1 );
```

LoadMemo method

Applies to   TDBMemo component

void LoadMemo( );
The LoadMemo method loads a text BLOB into the database memo control.

If the value of the AutoDisplay property is true, the text of a memo is automatically loaded and there is no need to call LoadMemo. If AutoDisplay is false, you can control when the text is loaded at run time by calling LoadMemo when you want the text to appear in the control.

LoadPicture method

Applies to   TDBImage component

void LoadPicture( );
The LoadPicture method loads the image specified as the value of the Picture property into the database image control.

If the value of the AutoDisplay property is true, the image of a database image control is automatically loaded, so there is no need to call LoadPicture. If AutoDisplay is false, you can control when the image is loaded at run time by calling LoadPicture when you want the image to appear in the control.

Local property

Applies to   TQuery component

bool Local;
Run-time and read only. The Local property specifies if the table referred to by the TQuery is a local dBASE or Paradox table or an SQL server table. If Local is true, then the table is a dBASE or Paradox table. If Local is false, the table is an SQL table.

For remote SQL tables, some operations (such as record counts) may take longer than for local tables, owing to network constraints.

Example
```
// If the table is local, allow the data-aware controls
// to display the changes
DataSource1.Enabled = Query1.Local;
```

Locale property

Applies to TDataBase, TDataSet, TDBDataSet, TQuery, TSession, TStoredProc, TTable components

Locale property for datasets

Applies to TDataSet, TDBDataSet, TQuery, TStoredProc, TTable components

TLocale Locale;

Run-time and read only. The Locale property identifies the language driver used with the dataset for use with direct calls to the Borland Database Engine API.

You should not need to use this property unless your application requires some functionality not encapsulated in Visual Database Tools.

Locale property for sessions

Applies to TSession component

TLocale Locale;

Run-time and read only. The Locale property identifies the language driver used with the TSession component. It enables you to reference the language driver when making direct calls to the Borland Database Engine API. You should not need to use this property unless your application requires some functionality not encapsulated in Visual Database Tools.

Locale property for databases

Applies to TDataBase component

TLocale Locale;

Run-time and read only. The Locale property identifies the language driver used with the TDatabase component. It allows you to make direct calls to the Borland Database Engine API. You should not need to use this property unless your application requires some functionality not encapsulated in Visual Database Tools.

LockTable method

Applies to TTable component

void LockTable(TLockType t);

The LockTable method locks the table. The type of lock is specified with the t parameter; these are the possible values:

Value	Meaning
ltReadLock	The session placing a read lock prevents other sessions from writing to the physical table underlying a TTable component. Other sessions will still be able to read the table, but they won't be able to write to it, nor will they be able to place a write lock on it. Other TTable components in the same session will still be able to read and write to the physical .table.
ltWriteLock	The session placing a write lock on the table prevents all other sessions from placing any locks on the physical table underlying a TTable component. Other sessions will be able to read the table, but they won't be able to write to it, nor will they be able to place any type of lock on it. Other TTable components in the same session will still be able to read and write to the physical table.

You can place multiple locks of different types on a physical table. For each lock placed, you must make a corresponding call to the UnlockTable method using the same lock type, or the table remains locked.

An exception is raised if the table is closed or the requested lock can't be obtained.

These methods are primarily intended for use with Paradox and dBASE tables. For dBASE tables, read locks are automatically promoted to write locks. For SQL tables, read and write are the same, and the behavior varies according to the server.

LoginPrompt property

Applies to   TDataBase component

bool LoginPrompt;

The LoginPrompt property is used to control how security is handled for SQL databases.

If true, (the default), the standard Login dialog box opens when the application attempts to establish a database connection. The user must then enter a proper user name and password to connect to a database on the server.

If false, then an application looks for login parameters in the Params property of the TDatabase component. These are the USERNAME and PASSWORD parameters. For example,

```
database1.Params->Add( "USERNAME=SYSDBA" );
database1.Params->Add( "PASSWORD=MASTERKEY" );
```

This is not recommended because it compromises server security.

LookupDisplay property

Applies to   TDBLookupCombo, TDBLookupList components

string LookupDisplay;

The LookupDisplay property determines which field in the lookup table displays in the database lookup combo box or database lookup list box. Before you specify a LookupDisplay field, link the two datasets using the LookupField property.

You can choose to display multiple fields from the lookup dataset. Each field appears in a separate column. To specify more than one field to display, separate each field name with a semicolon. For example, this line of code displays three columns in the drop-down list of a database lookup combo box. Column 1 is the name of the company, column 2 is the city where the company is located, and column 3 is the country.

```
DBLookupCombo1.LookupDisplay = "Company;City;Country";
```

You can include titles for the field columns and you can draw lines between rows and columns using the Options property.

Example   The following code specifies that the "Company" field is displayed in DBLookupCombo1.

```
DBLookupCombo1.LookupDisplay = "Company";
```

LookupField property

Applies to   TDBLookupCombo, TDBLookupList components

PTField LookupField;

The LookupField property links the dataset the database lookup combo box or database lookup list box uses to "look up" data to the primary dataset you are working with.

Although the name of the field specified as the LookupField does not have to be the same as the name of the field specified as the DataField, the two fields must contain the same values. For example, the LookupField value can be CustomerNumber and the DataField value can be CustNo as along as both fields use the same number to identify a particular customer. When you specify a LookupField, the current value of that field appears in the control, if the Active property of both datasets is true.

After you specify a LookupField field, you can choose which field to display in the control with the LookupDisplay property.

Example   This code displays the name of the lookup field in a message box:

```
char buf[ 64 ];
wsprintf( buf, "LookupField Name is %\n", DBLookupList1.LookupField->FieldName );
MessageBox( NULL, buf, NULL, MB_OK );
```

LookupSource property

Applies to   TDBLookupCombo, TDBLookupList components

PTDataSource LookupSource;

The LookupSource of a database lookup combo box or lookup list box is the data source component (TDataSource) that identifies the dataset you want the control to use to "look up" the information you want displayed in the control.

Example   The following code specifies that DataSource1 is the lookup source for DBLookupCombo1.

```
DBLookupCombo1.LookupSource = &DataSource1;
```

Mappings property

Applies to   TBatchMove component

TStrings Mappings;

By default TBatchMove matches columns based on their position in the source and destination tables. That is, the first column in the source is matched with the first column in the destination, and so on.

To override the default column mappings, use the Mappings property. This is a list of column mappings (one per line) in one of two forms. To map the column ColName in the source table to the column of the same name in the destination table use:

```
ColName
```

Or, to map the column named SourceColName in the source table to the column named DestColName in the destination table:

```
BatchMove1.Mappings->Add( "CustNo = CustomerID" );
```

If source and destination column data types are not the same, the batch move operation performs a "best fit". It trims character data types, if necessary, and attempts to perform a limited amount of conversion, if possible. For example, mapping a CHAR(10) column to a CHAR(5) column trims the last five characters from the source column.

As an example of conversion, if a source column of character data type is mapped to a destination of type int, the batch move operation converts a character value of "5" to the corresponding int value. Values that cannot be converted generate errors.

Fields in Destination that have no entry in Mappings are set to NULL.

Example

```
TStrings maps;
...
maps.Clear( );
// Map the CustomerNum field to CustNo
maps.Add( "CustNo=CustomerNum" );
MatchMove1.Mappings = maps;
```

MasterFields property

Applies to   TTable component

string MasterFields;

Use the MasterFields property to specify the column(s) to link a detail table with a master table that is specified by the MasterSource property. MasterFields is a string consisting of one or more column names that join the two tables. Separate multiple column names with semicolons. Each time the current record in the master table changes, the new values in those fields are used to select corresponding records from the detail table for display.

Example   Suppose you have a master table named Customer that contains a CustNo field, and you also have a detail table named Orders that also has a CustNo field. To display only those records in Orders that have the same CustNo value as the current record in Customer, write this code:

```
Customer.MasterFields = "CustNo";
```

If you want to display only the records in the detail table that match more than one field value in the master table, specify each field and separate them with a semicolon.

```
Customer.MasterFields = "CustNo;SaleDate";
```

MasterSource property

Applies to   TTable component

TDataSource MasterSource;
The value of the MasterSource property identifies the TDataSource component that specifies the dataset the detail TTable component gets its data from for the master table.

Example

```
Table2.MasterSource = DataSource1;
```

MaxLength property

Applies to   TDBEdit, TDBLookupCombo, TDBComboBox, TDBMemo components

int MaxLength;
The MaxLength property specifies the maximum number of characters the user can enter in a database edit box, database memo, or database combo box. The default setting for MaxLength is 0, which means that there is no limit on the number of characters the control can contain. Any other number limits the number of characters the control can accept.

Example   The following example sets the maximum number of characters for an edit box to 80:

```
DBEdit1.MaxLength = 80;
```

MaxValue property

Applies to   TCurrencyField, TFloatField, TIntegerField, TSmallintField, TWordField components

double MaxValue; // TFloatField, TBCDField, and TCurrencyField
int32 MaxValue; // TIntegerField, TSmallIntField, and TWordField

The MaxValue property limits the maximum value in the field. Assigning a value greater than MaxValue raises an exception.

Example

```
// Limit a field to 1 to 10
Field1.MaxValue = 10;
Field1.MinValue = 1;
```

See also   MinValue property

MinValue property

Applies to   TCurrencyField, TFloatField, TIntegerField, TSmallintField, TWordField component

double MinValue; // TFloatField, TBCDField, and TCurrencyField
int32 MinValue; // TIntegerField, TSmallIntField, and TWordField

The MinValue property limits the minimum value in the field. Assigning a value less than MinValue raises an exception.

Example

```
// Limit the field to 1 to 10
Field1.MaxValue = 10;
Field1.MinValue = 1;
```

Mode property

Applies to   TBatchMove component

TBatchModevclTBatchModeType Mode;

The Mode property specifies what happens during the batch move operation. These are the possible values:

Value	Meaning
batAppend	Append records to the destination table. The destination table must already exist. This is the default mode.
batUpdate	Update records in the destination table with matching records from the source table. The destination table must exist and must have an index defined to match records.
batAppendUpdate	Update any matching record in the destination table. Otherwise, append records to the destination table. The destination table must exist and must have an index defined to match records.
batCopy	Create the destination table based on the structure of the source table. The destination table must not already exist—if it does, the operation will delete it.
batDelete	Delete records in the destination table that match records in the source table. The destination table must already exist and must have an index defined.

Example

This line of code specifies that the batch move operation will update any matching record in the destination table; if no match exists, the records are appended to the destination table:

```
BatchMove1.Mode = batAppendUpdate;
```

Modified property

Applies to   TDataSet, TDBDataSet, TDBEdit, TDBMemo, TQuery, TStoredProc, TTable components

Description   The Modified property specifies if a component's contents have been modified.

Modified property for TDBEdit and TDBMemo components

Applies to   TDBEdit, TDBMemo components

bool Modified;

Run-time only. The Modified property determines whether the text of an database edit box or memo control was changed since it was created or since the last time the Modified property was set to false. If Modified is true, the text was changed. If Modified is false, the text was not changed.

Modified property for datasets

Applies to   TDataSet, TDBDataSet, TQuery, TStoredProc, TTable components

bool Modified;

Run-time and read only. The Modified property is true if a field in the current record has been changed. It is reset to false when the record is updated through a call to the Cancel or Post methods.

MousePointer property (Cursor at run time)

Applies to   All data-aware controls

TCursor MousePointer;

The MousePointer property is the image used when the mouse passes into the region covered by the control. These are the possible images:

Value	Image	Value	Image	Value	Image
crDefault		crSize		crSizeWE	
crArrow		crSizeNESW		crUpArrow	
crCross		crSizeNS		crHourglass	
crIBeam		crSizeNWSE		crNoDrop	
crIcon					

When you access the MousePointer property programmatically, refer to it as Cursor.

Move method

Applies to   TStrings component

void Move(int curIndex, int newIndex);

The Move method changes the position of an item in the list of a list component or in a list of strings in a string component by giving the item a new index value. The curIndex parameter is the item's current index, and the newIndex parameter is the item's new index value.

If a string in a string component has an associated object in the Objects property, Move moves both the string and the object.

Example   This example uses a list box and a button on a form. Five items are added to the database list box, and then the fifth item is moved to the top of the list box:

```
int i;
for( i = 0; i < 5; i++ )
{
    char index[10];
    sprintf( index , "Item %d" , i );
    DBListBox1.Items->Add( index );
}
DBListBox1.Items->Move( 4, 0 );
```

See also   Add method, Delete method, Exchange method, Objects property, Strings property

MoveBy method

Applies to   TDataSet, TDBDataSet, TQuery, TStoredProc, TTable components

void MoveBy(int distance);

The MoveBy method moves the dataset cursor by the number of records specified with the distance parameter. If distance is negative, the move is backward. If distance is positive, the movement is forward. If distance is zero, no move occurs.

If the dataset is in Insert or Edit state, MoveBy performs an implicit Post of any pending data.

Example

```
// Skip three records forward
Table1.MoveBy( 3 );
```

MovedCount property

Applies to   TBatchMove component

int32 MovedCount;

Run-time and read only. MovedCount is the number of records which were actually processed by the Execute method. This includes any records which had integrity or data size problems.

Example   This code executes a batch move operation and reports the number of records moved in a message box:

```
char message[ 25 ];
BatchMove1.Execute( );
sprint( message, "%ld records were moved", BatchMove1.MovedCount );
MessageBox( message , "Information", MB_OK );
```

Name property

Applies to   All data-aware controls; all TField, TDatabase, TFieldDef, TIndexDef, TParam, TSession components

Description   The Name property uniquely identifies a component.

Name property for other components (CtlName at design time)

Applies to   All components visible at design time; all TFieldvclTFieldComponent, , TSessionvclTSessionComponent components

string Name;

The Name property contains the name of the control as referenced by other components. The default names are made up of the type of component combined with the order the control was placed on a dialog box or form at design time, such as "TDBComboBox101", "TDBListBox102", and so on. You may change these to suit your needs.

Note Change component names only at design time.

Name property for index definitions

Applies to TIndexDef component

string Name;
Run-time and read only. Name is the name of the index.

Name property for TParam components

Applies to TParam component

string Name;
The Name property is the name of the parameter.

Example

```
// Change the name of the first parameter column to "CustNo"
Params[0].Name = "CustNo";
```

Name property for field definitions

Applies to TFieldDef component

string Name;
Run-time and read only. Name is the name of the physical field within the table.

Example

```
// Display the field name and number
char message[ 25 ];
sprintf( message, "%s is field number %d", FieldDef1.Name-
>c_str(), FieldDef1.FieldNo );
MessageBox( message , "Information" , MB_OK );
```

NetFileDir property

Applies to TSession component

string NetFileDir;
Run-time only. For Paradox databases only. The NetFileDir property specifies the directory that contains the BDE network control file, PDOXUSRS.NET. This property enables multiple users to share Paradox tables on network drives. NetFileDir overrides the specification defined for the Paradox driver in the BDE Configuration Utility.

All applications that need to share the same Paradox database must specify the same directory, and all must have read/write/create rights for the directory.

Next method

Applies to   TDataSet, TDBDataSet, TQuery, TStoredProc, TTable components

void Next(void);

The Next method moves the cursor forward by one record. If the cursor is already on the last record in the active range, it does not move. If the dataset is in Insert or Edit state, Next performs an implicit Post of any pending data.

Example

```
// Move to the next record
Table1.Next( );
if( Table1.AtEOF )
// No more records
```

Objects property

Applies to   TStrings components

LPVOID Objects[int index];

Run-time only. The Objects property gives you access to an object in the list of objects associated with the list of strings. Each string in the list of strings can have an associated object.

The most common use of objects in a string and string list objects is to associate bitmaps with strings so that you can use the bitmaps in owner-draw controls. For example, if you have an owner-draw list box, you can add a string "Banana" and a bitmap of a banana to the Items property of the list box using the AddObject method. You can then access the "Banana" string using the Strings property or the bitmap using the Objects property.

Specify the object you want to access with its position in the list as the value of the index parameter. The index is zero-based, so the first object in the list of objects has a value of 0, the second object has a value of 1, and so on.

To associate an object with an existing string, assign the object to the Objects property using the same index as that of the existing string in the Strings property. For example, if a string object named Fruits contains the string "Banana" and an existing bitmap of a banana called BananaBitmap, you could make the following assignment:

```
Fruits->Objects[ Fruits.IndexOf( "Banana" ) ] = BananaBitmap;
```

Example   The following code allows the user to specify a bitmap file with the OpenDialog1 open dialog box component when Form1 is created. Then, the bitmap file specified is added to the Items list of ListBox1.

If ListBox1 is an owner-draw control (specified by a Style property of lbOwnerDrawFixed or lbOwnerDrawVariable), the second procedure is the OnDrawItem event handler for ListBox1. The bitmap in the Object property and the text of an item are retrieved and displayed in Listbox1.

```
TMyFormClass::SetupWindow( )
{
  TBitmap TheBitmap;
// ... additional SetupWindow() code
  if( OpenDialog1.Execute( ) )
  {
      TheBitmap.LoadFromFile( OpenDialog1.Data.FileName );
      ListBox1.Items->AddObject( OpenDialog1.Data.FileName, TheBitmap );
  }
}
TMyFormClass::ListBox1DrawItem(SHORT Index, TRect Rect, TOwnerDrawState State )
{
  TIcon picture( _hInstance , ListBox1.Items->Objects[Index] );
ListBox1.Canvas->DrawIcon( Rect.Left, Rect.Top + 4, picture );
  ListBox1.Canvas->TextOut( Rect.Left + 2, Rect.Top + 2, ListBox1.Items-
>Strings[Index] );
}
```

OnCalcFields event

Applies to   TDataSet, TDBDataSet, TQuery, TStoredProc, TTable components

The OnCalcFields event is used to set the values of calculated fields. OnCalcFields is called when a dataset reads a record from the database. In addition, if the dataset's AutoCalcFields property is true, OnCalcFields is called when a non-calculated field is modified while the dataset is in Edit or Insert state.

Typically, the OnCalcFields event is called often, so it should be kept short. OnCalcFields should not perform any actions that modify the dataset (or the linked dataset if it is part of a master-detail relationship), because this can lead to recursion.

While the OnCalcFields event executes, a dataset is put in CalcFields state. When a dataset is in CalcFields state, you cannot set the values of any fields other than calculated fields. After OnCalcFields is completed, the dataset returns to its previous state.

The first call to the OnCalcFields event handler may occur before all components in your application have been initialized. If your handler requires access to another component, make sure the component is created before the first OnCalcFields event occurs.

Source declaration   This declaration of the event source is in the header file:

```
TDatasetNotifySource OnCalcFieldsSource;
```

Sink declaration   Include this declaration of the event sink in the class definition for your sink object:

```
TDatasetNotifySink OnCalcFieldsSink;
```

Handler   Put a prototype for the handler method in the class definition for your sink object:

```
void OnCalcFields( TDatasetNotifySink& sink, TDataset& sender );
```

And connect the handler method, which you have implemented, to the event sink by including the following in the class constructor:

```
OnCalcFieldsSink( TDatasetNotify_MFUNCTOR( *this, &TForm::OnCalcFields ))
```

Attachment   Attach the event source to the event sink by including the following in your program:

```
TDataset strings;      //Instantiate the source component
TForm form;            //Instantiate the sink component
strings.OnCalcFieldsSource += form.OnCalcFieldsSink;
```

OnChange event

Applies to   All TField, TDBComboBox, TDBEdit, TDBImage, TDBLookupCombo, TDBMemo, TDBRadioGroup, TStrings components

Description   An OnChange event occurs when a component changes.

OnChange event for data-aware controls

Applies to   TDBComboBox, TDBNavigator, TDBImage, TDBListBox, TDBMemo, TDBRadioGroup, TDBText components

Header file   dbcombo.h, dbimage.h, dblist.h, dbmemo.h, dbradio.h, dbtext.h

Description   The OnChange event for data-aware controls occurs when the contents of the field the control is accessing changes. Specify any special processing you want to occur at that time in the OnChange event handler.

OnChange event for the TDBComboBox component
This declaration of the event source is in the dbcombo.h header file:

```
TDBComboBoxNotifySource OnChangeSource;
```

Include this declaration of the event sink in the class definition of your sink object:

```
TDBComboBoxNotifySink OnChangeSink;
```

Put a prototype for the handler method in the class definition for your sink object:

```
void OnChange( TDBComboBoxNotifySink& sink, TDBComboBox& sender );
```

Connect the handler method to the event sink by including the following in the class constructor:

```
OnChangeSink( TDBComboBoxNotify_MFUNCTOR( *this, &TForm::OnChange));
```

Attach the event source to the event sink by including the following code in your program:

```
TDBComboBox DBComboBox;        //Instantiate the source component
TForm form                     //Instantiate the sink component
DBComboBox.OnChangeSource += form.OnChangeSink;
```

OnChange event for the TDBEdit component

This declaration of the event source is in the dbedit.h header file:

```
TDBEditNotifySource OnChangeSource;
```

Include this declaration of the event sink in the class declaration of your sink object:

```
TDBEditNotifySink OnChangeSink;
```

Put a prototype for the handler method in the class declaration for your sink object:

```
void OnChange( TDBEditNotifySink& sink, TDBEdit& sender );
```

Connect the handler method to the event sink by including the following in the class constructor:

```
OnChangeSink( TDBEditNotify_MFUNCTOR( *this, &TForm::OnChange ));
```

Attach the event source to the event sink by including the following code in your program:

```
TDBEdit DBEdit;              //Instantiate the source component
TForm form                   //Instantiate the sink component
DBEdit.OnChangeSource += form.OnChangeSink;
```

OnChange event for the TDBLookupCombo component

This declaration of the event source is in the dblkupcb.h header file:

```
TDBLookupComboNotifySource OnChangeSource;
```

Include this declaration of the event sink in the class declaration of your sink object:

```
TDBLookupComboNotifySink OnChangeSink;
```

Put a prototype for the handler method in the class declaration for your sink object:

```
void OnChange( TDBLookupComboNotifySink& sink, TDBLookupCombo& sender );
```

Connect the handler method to the event sink by including the following in the class constructor:

```
OnChangeSink( TDBLookupComboNotify_MFUNCTOR( *this, &TForm::OnChange ));
```

Attach the event source to the event sink by including the following code in your program:

```
TDBLookupCombo DBLookupCombo;     //Instantiate the source component
TForm form                        //Instantiate the sink component
DBLookupCombo.OnChangeSource += form.OnChangeSink;
```

OnChange event for the TDBMemo component

This declaration of the event source is in the dbmemo.h header file:

```
TDBMemoNotifySource OnChangeSource;
```

Include this declaration of the event sink in the class declaration of your sink object:

```
TDBMemoNotifySink OnChangeSink;
```

Put a prototype for the handler method in the class declaration for your sink object:

```
void OnChange( TDBMemoNotifySink& sink, TDBMemo& sender );
```

Connect the handler method to the event sink by including the following in the class constructor:

```
OnChangeSink( TDBMemoNotify_MFUNCTOR( *this, &TForm::OnChange ));
```

Attach the event source to the event sink by including the following code in your program:

```
TDBMemo DBMemo;          //Instantiate the source component
TForm form               //Instantiate the sink component
DBMemo.OnChangeSource += form.OnChangeSink;
```

OnChange event for the TDBRadioGroup component

This declaration of the event source is in the dbradio.h header file:

```
TDBRadioGroupNotifySourcTDBRadioGroupNotifySource OnChangeSource;
```

Include this declaration of the event sink in the class declaration of your sink object:

```
TDBRadioGroupNotifySink OnChangeSink;
```

Put a prototype for the handler method in the class declaration for your sink object:

```
void OnChange( TDBRadioGroupNotifySink& sink,TDBRadioGroup& sender );
```

Connect the handler method to the event sink by including the following in the class constructor:

```
OnChangeSink(TDBRadioGroupNotify_MFUNCTOR( *this,&TForm::OnChange ));
```

Attach the event source to the event sink by including the following code in your program:

```
TDBRadioGroup DBRadioGroup;    //Instantiate the source component
TForm form                     //Instantiate the sink component
DBRadioGroup.OnChangeSource += form.OnChangeSink;
```

OnChange event for fields

Applies to   All TField components

OnChange is activated when the contents of the field are modified. If a data-aware control is linked to the field, OnChange is not activated until the control attempts to store the changes into the current record.

You can take any special actions required by the event by assigning a method to this event.

Source declaration   This declaration of the event source is in the header file:

```
TFieldNotifySource OnChangeSource;
```

Sink declaration   Include this declaration of the event sink in the class declaration for your sink object:

```
TFieldNotifySink OnChangeSink;
```

Handler   Put a prototype for the handler method in the class declaration for your sink object:

```
void OnChange( TFieldNotifySink& sink, TField& sender );
```

And connect the handler method, which you have implemented, to the event sink by including the following in the class constructor:

```
OnChangeSink( TFieldNotify_MFUNCTOR( *this, &TForm::OnChange ))
```

Attachment   Attach the event source to the event sink by including the following in your program:

```
TField field;      //Instantiate the source component
TForm form;        //Instantiate the sink component
field.OnChangeSource += form.OnChangeSink;
```

OnChange event for strings

Applies to   TStrings components

The OnChange event occurs when the contents of a TStrings component changes. You can take any special actions required by the event by assigning a method to this event.

Source declaration   This declaration of the event source is in the header file:

```
TStringsNotifySource OnChangeSource;
```

Sink declaration   Include this declaration of the event sink in the class declaration for your sink object:

```
TStringsNotifySink OnChangeSink;
```

Handler   Put a prototype for the handler method in the class declaration for your sink object:

```
void OnChange( TStringsNotifySink& sink, TStrings& sender );
```

And connect the handler method, which you have implemented, to the event sink by including the following in the class constructor:

```
OnChangeSink( TStringsNotify_MFUNCTOR( *this, &TForm::OnChange ))
```

Attachment   Attach the event source to the event sink by including the following in your program:

```
TStrings strings;     //Instantiate the source component
TForm form;           //Instantiate the sink component
strings.OnChangeSource += form.OnChangeSink;
```

OnClick event

Applies to TDBCheckBox, TDBComboBox, TDBListBox, TDBMemo, TDBRadioGroup, TDBText components

Header files dbchkbx.h, dbcombo.h, dbedit.h, dbgrid.h, dbimage,h, dblist.h, dblkupcb.h, dblkuplb.h dbmemo.h, dbradio.h, dbtext.h

Description The OnClick event occurs when the user clicks the component. Typically, this is when the user presses and releases the primary mouse button with the mouse pointer over the component. This event can also occur when

- The user selects an item in a data grid, list box, or combo box by pressing an arrow key.
- The user presses Spacebar while a button or check box has focus.
- The user presses the accelerator key for a button or check box. For example, if the value of the Caption property of a database check box is "&Bold", the B is underlined at run time and the OnClick event of the check box is triggered when the user presses Alt+B.
- The Checked property of a radio button is set to true.
- The value of the Checked property of a check box is changed.

OnClick event for the TDBCheckBox component

This declaration of the event source is in the dbchkbx.h header file:

```
TDBCheckBoxNotifySource OnClickSource;
```

Include this declaration of the event sink in the class declaration of your sink object:

```
TDBCheckBoxNotifySink OnClickSink;
```

Put a prototype for the handler method in the class declaration for your sink object:

```
void OnClick( TDBCheckBoxNotifySink& sink, TDBCheckBox& sender );
```

Connect the handler method to the event sink by including the following in the class constructor:

```
OnClickSink( TDBCheckBoxNotify_MFUNCTOR( *this, &TForm::OnClick ));
```

Attach the event source to the event sink by including the following code in your program:

```
TDBCheckBox DBCheckBox;          //Instantiate the source component
TForm form                       //Instantiate the sink component
DBCheckBox.OnClickSource += form.OnClickSink;
```

OnClick event for the TDBComboBox component

This declaration of the event source is in the dbcombo.h header file:

```
TDBComboBoxNotifySource OnClickSource;
```

Include this declaration of the event sink in the class declaration of your sink object:

```
TDBComboBoxNotifySink OnClickSink;
```

Put a prototype for the handler method in the class declaration for your sink object:

```
void OnClick( TDBComboBoxNotifySink& sink, TDBComboBox& sender );
```

Connect the handler method to the event sink by including the following in the class constructor:

```
OnClickSink( TDBComboBoxNotify_MFUNCTOR( *this, &TForm::OnClick ));
```

Attach the event source to the event sink by including the following code in your program:

```
TDBComboBox DBComboBox;        //Instantiate the source component
TForm form                     //Instantiate the sink component
DBComboBox.OnClickSource += form.OnClickSink;
```

OnClick event for the TDBEdit component

This declaration of the event source is in the dbedit.h header file:

```
TDBEditNotifySource OnClickSource;
```

Include this declaration of the event sink in the class declaration of your sink object:

```
TDBEditNotifySink OnClickSink;
```

Put a prototype for the handler method in the class declaration for your sink object:

```
void OnClick( TDBEditNotifySink& sink, TDBEdit& sender );
```

Connect the handler method to the event sink by including the following in the class constructor:

```
OnClickSink( TDBEditNotify_MFUNCTOR( *this, &TForm::OnClick ));
```

Attach the event source to the event sink by including the following code in your program:

```
TDBEdit DBEdit;               //Instantiate the source component
TForm form                    //Instantiate the sink component
DBEdit.OnClickSource += form.OnClickSink;
```

OnClick event for the TDBGrid component

This declaration of the event source is in the dbgrid.h header file:

```
TDBGridNotifySource OnClickSource;
```

Include this declaration of the event sink in the class declaration of your sink object:

```
TDBGridNotifySink OnClickSink;
```

Put a prototype for the handler method in the class declaration for your sink object:

```
void OnClick( TDBGridNotifySink& sink, TDBGrid& sender );
```

Connect the handler method to the event sink by including the following in the class constructor:

```
OnClickSink( TDBGridNotify_MFUNCTOR( *this, &TForm::OnClick ));
```

Attach the event source to the event sink by including the following code in your program:

```
TDBGrid DBGrid;           //Instantiate the source component
  TForm form              //Instantiate the sink component
  DBGrid.OnClickSource += form.OnClickSink;
```

OnClick event for the TDBImage component

This declaration of the event source is in the dbimage.h header file:

```
TDBImageNotifySource OnClickSource;
```

Include this declaration of the event sink in the class declaration of your sink object:

```
TDBImageNotifySink OnClickSink;
```

Put a prototype for the handler method in the class declaration for your sink object:

```
void OnClick( TDBImageNotifySink& sink, TDBImage& sender );
```

Connect the handler method to the event sink by including the following in the class constructor:

```
OnClickSink( TDBImageNotify_MFUNCTOR( *this, &TForm::OnClick ));
```

Attach the event source to the event sink by including the following code in your program:

```
TDBImage DBImage;         //Instantiate the source component
 TForm form               //Instantiate the sink component
 DBImage.OnClickSource += form.OnClickSink;
```

OnClick event for the TDBListBox component

This declaration of the event source is in the dblist.h header file:

```
TDBListBoxNotifySource OnClickSource;
```

Include this declaration of the event sink in the class declaration of your sink object:

```
TDBListBoxNotifySink OnClickSink;
```

Put a prototype for the handler method in the class declaration for your sink object:

```
void OnClick( TDBListBoxNotifySink& sink, TDBListBox& sender );
```

Connect the handler method to the event sink by including the following in the class constructor:

```
OnClickSink( TDBListBoxNotify_MFUNCTOR( *this, &TForm::OnClick ));
```

Attach the event source to the event sink by including the following code in your program:

```
TDBListBox DBListBox;     //Instantiate the source component
 TForm form               //Instantiate the sink component
 DBListBox.OnClickSource += form.OnClickSink;
```

OnClick event for the TDBLookupCombo component

This declaration of the event source is in the dblkupcb.h header file:

```
TDBLookupComboNotifySource TDBLookupComboNotifySourceOnClickSource;
```

Include this declaration of the event sink in the class declaration of your sink object:

```
TDBLookupComboNotifySink OnClickSink;
```

Put a prototype for the handler method in the class declaration for your sink object:

```
void OnClick( TDBLookupComboNotifySink& sink, TDBLookupCombo& sender );
```

Connect the handler method to the event sink by including the following in the class constructor:

```
OnClickSink( TDBLookupComboNotify_MFUNCTOR( *this, &TForm::OnClick ));
```

Attach the event source to the event sink by including the following code in your program:

```
TDBLookupCombo DBLookupCombo;        //Instantiate the source component
TForm form                           //Instantiate the sink component
DBLookupCombo.OnClickSource += form.OnClickSink;
```

OnClick event for the TDBLookupList component

This declaration of the event source is in the dblkuplb.h header file:

```
TDBLookupListNotifySource OnClickSource;
```

Include this declaration of the event sink in the class declaration of your sink object:

```
TDBLookupListNotifySink OnClickSink;
```

Put a prototype for the handler method in the class declaration for your sink object:

```
void OnClick( TDBLookupListNotifySink& sink, TDBLookupList& sender );
```

Connect the handler method to the event sink by including the following in the class constructor:

```
OnClickSink( TDBLookupListNotify_MFUNCTOR( *this, &TForm::OnClick ));
```

Attach the event source to the event sink by including the following code in your program:

```
TDBLookupList DBLookupList;        //Instantiate the source component
TForm form                         //Instantiate the sink component
DBLookupList.OnClickSource += form.OnClickSink;
```

OnClick event for the TDBMemo component

This declaration of the event source is in the dbmemo.h header file:

```
TDBMemoNotifySource OnClickSource;
```

Include this declaration of the event sink in the class declaration of your sink object:

```
TDBMemoNotifySink OnClickSink;
```

Put a prototype for the handler method in the class declaration for your sink object:

```
void OnClick( TDBMemoNotifySink& sink, TDBMemo& sender );
```

Connect the handler method to the event sink by including the following in the class constructor:

```
OnClickSink( TDBMemoNotify_MFUNCTOR( *this, &TForm::OnClick ));
```

Attach the event source to the event sink by including the following code in your program:

```
TDBMemo DBMemo;          //Instantiate the source component
TForm form               //Instantiate the sink component
DBMemo.OnClickSource += form.OnClickSink;
```

OnClick event for the TDBRadioGroup component

This declaration of the event source is in the dbradio.h header file:

```
TDBRadioGroupNotifySource OnClickSource;
```

Include this declaration of the event sink in the class declaration of your sink object:

```
TDBRadioGroupNotifySink OnClickSink;
```

Put a prototype for the handler method in the class declaration for your sink object:

```
void OnClick( TDBRadioGroupNotifySink& sink, TDBRadioGroup& sender );
```

Connect the handler method to the event sink by including the following in the class constructor:

```
OnClickSink( TDBRadioGroupNotify_MFUNCTOR( *this, &TForm::OnClick ));
```

Attach the event source to the event sink by including the following code in your program:

```
TDBRadioGroup DBRadioGroup;     //Instantiate the source component
TForm form                      //Instantiate the sink component
DBRadioGroup.OnClickSource += form.OnClickSink;
```

OnClick event for the DBText component

This declaration of the event source is in the dbtext.h header file:

```
TDBTextNotifySource OnClickSource;
```

Include this declaration of the event sink in the class declaration of your sink object:

```
TDBTextNotifySink OnClickSink;
```

Put a prototype for the handler method in the class declaration for your sink object:

```
void OnClick( TDBTextNotifySink& sink, TDBText& sender );
```

Connect the handler method to the event sink by including the following in the class constructor:

```
OnClickSink( TDBTextNotify_MFUNCTOR( *this, &TForm::OnClick ));
```

Attach the event source to the event sink by including the following code in your program:

```
TDBText DBText;              //Instantiate the source component
TForm form                  //Instantiate the sink component
DBText.OnClickSource += form.OnClickSink;
```

OnClick event for the TDBNavigator component

Applies to   TDBNavigator

The OnClick event occurs when the user clicks one of the buttons on the database navigator, or when the user presses the Spacebar while the navigator has focus. Calling the BtnClick method also triggers the OnClick event.

This is the prototype of the OnClick event handler in your code:

```
void OnClick( TDBNavigatorClickSink& sink, TDBNavigator& sender,
          TNavigatorBtn button);
```

The button parameter can be any of these values:

BtnFirst	The button that moves to the first record in the dataset
BtnPrevious	The button that moves to the previous record in the dataset
BtnNext	The button that moves to the next record in the dataset
BtnLast	The button that moves to the last record in the dataset
BtnInsert	The button that puts the dataset in Insert state
BtnDelete	The button that deletes the current record from the dataset
BtnEdit	The button that puts the dataset in Edit state
BtnPost	The button that posts the current record to the dataset
BtnCancel	The button that cancels changes made to the current record
BtnRefresh	The button that refreshes the display of the dataset

Source declaration   This declaration of the event source is in the header file:

```
TDBNavigatorClickSource OnClickSource;
```

Sink declaration   Include this declaration of the event sink in the class declaration for your sink object:

```
TDBNavigatorClickSink OnClickSink;
```

Handler   Put a prototype for the handler method in the class declaration for your sink object:

```
void OnClick( TDBNavigatorClickSink& sink, TDBNavigator& sender,
          TNavigatorBtn button);
```

And connect the handler method, which you have implemented, to the event sink by including the following in the class constructor:

```
OnClickSink( TDBNavigatorClick_MFUNCTOR( *this, &TForm::OnClick ))
```

Attachment   Attach the event source to the event sink by including the following in your program:

```
TDataSource datasource;//Instantiate the source component
TForm form;        //Instantiate the sink component
datasource.OnClickSource += form.OnClickSink;
```

OnDataChange event

Applies to   TDataSource component

The OnDataChange occurs when the State property changes from dsInactive, or when a data-aware control notifies the TDataSource that something has changed.

Notification occurs when the following items change because of field modification or scrolling to a new record: field component, record, dataset component, content, and layout.

This will be the declaration for the OnDataChange event handler in your code:

```
void OnDataChange( TDataChangeSink& sink, TDataSource& sender, TField* field );
```

The field parameter to the method may be NULL if more than one of the fields changed simultaneously (as in a move to a different record). Otherwise, field is the field that changed.

Source declaration   This declaration of the event source is in the header file:

```
TDataChangeSource OnDataChangeSource;
```

Sink declaration   Include this declaration of the event sink in the class declaration for your sink object:

```
TDataChangeSink OnDataChangeSink;
```

Handler   Put a prototype for the handler method in the class declaration for your sink object:

```
void OnDataChange( TDataChangeSink& sink, TDataSource& sender, TField* field );
```

And connect the handler method, which you have implemented, to the event sink by including the following in the class constructor:

```
OnDataChangeSink( TDataChange_MFUNCTOR( *this, &TForm::OnDataChange ))
```

Attachment   Attach the event source to the event sink by including the following in your program:

```
TDataSource datasource;    //Instantiate the source component
TForm form;                //Instantiate the sink component
datasource.OnDataChangeSource += form.OnDataChangeSink;
```

OnDblClick event

Applies to   TDBEdit, TDBGrid, TDBImage, TDBListBox, TDBLookupCombo, TDBLookupList, TDBMemo, TDBNavigator, TDBText components

Header file   dbedit.h, dbgrid.h, dbimage.h, dblist.h, dblkupcb.h, dblkuplb.h, dbmemo, dbnvgtr.h, dbtext.h

Description   The OnDblClick event occurs when the user double-clicks the mouse button while the mouse pointer is over the control.

OnDblClick event for the TDBComboBox component

This declaration of the event source is in the dbcombo.h header file:

```
TDBComboBoxNotifySource OnDblClickSource;
```

Include this declaration of the event sink in the class declaration of your sink object:

```
TDBComboBoxNotifySink OnDblClickSink;
```

Put a prototype for the handler method in the class declaration for your sink object:

```
void OnDblClick( TDBComboBoxNotifySink& sink, TDBComboBox& sender );
```

Connect the handler method to the event sink by including the following in the class constructor:

```
OnDblClickSink( TDBComboBoxNotify_MFUNCTOR( *this, &TForm::OnDblClick ));
```

Attach the event source to the event sink by including the following code in your program:

```
TDBComboBox DBComboBox;      //Instantiate the source component
TForm form                   //Instantiate the sink component
DBComboBox.OnDblClickSource += form.OnDblClickSink;
```

OnDblClick event for the TDBEdit component

This declaration of the event source is in the dbedit.h header file:

```
TDBEditNotifySource OnDblClickSource;
```

Include this declaration of the event sink in the class declaration of your sink object:

```
TDBEditNotifySink OnDblClickSink;
```

Put a prototype for the handler method in the class declaration for your sink object:

```
void OnDblClick( TDBEditNotifySink& sink, TDBEdit& sender );
```

Connect the handler method to the event sink by including the following in the class constructor:

```
OnDblClickSink( TDBEditNotify_MFUNCTOR( *this, &TForm::OnDblClick ));
```

Attach the event source to the event sink by including the following code in your program:

```
TDBEdit DBEdit;                 //Instantiate the source component
TForm form                      //Instantiate the sink component
DBEdit.OnDblClickSource += form.OnDblClickSink;
```

OnDblClick event for the TDBGrid component

This declaration of the event source is in the dbgrid.h header file:

```
TDBGridNotifySource OnDblClickSource;
```

Include this declaration of the event sink in the class declaration of your sink object:

```
TDBGridNotifySink OnDblClickSink;
```

Put a prototype for the handler method in the class declaration for your sink object:

```
void OnDblClick( TDBGridNotifySink& sink, TDBGrid& sender );
```

Connect the handler method to the event sink by including the following in the class constructor:

```
OnDblClickSink( TDBGridNotify_MFUNCTOR( *this, &TForm::OnDblClick ));
```

Attach the event source to the event sink by including the following code in your program:

```
TDBGrid DBGrid;         //Instantiate the source component
TForm form              //Instantiate the sink component
DBGrid.OnDblClickSource += form.OnDblClickSink;
```

OnDblClick event for the TDBImage component

This declaration of the event source is in the dbimage.h header file:

```
TDBImageNotifySource OnDblClickSource;
```

Include this declaration of the event sink in the class declaration of your sink object:

```
TDBImageNotifySink OnDblClickSink;
```

Put a prototype for the handler method in the class declaration for your sink object:

```
void OnDblClick( TDBImageNotifySink& sink, TDBImage& sender );
```

Connect the handler method to the event sink by including the following in the class constructor:

```
OnDblClickSink( TDBImageNotify_MFUNCTOR( *this, &TForm::OnDblClick ));
```

Attach the event source to the event sink by including the following code in your program:

```
TDBImage DBImage;        //Instantiate the source component
TForm form               //Instantiate the sink component
DBImage.OnDblClickSource += form.OnDblClickSink;
```

OnDblClick event for the TDBListBox component

This declaration of the event source is in the dblist.h header file:

```
TDBListBoxNotifySource OnDblClickSource;
```

Include this declaration of the event sink in the class declaration of your sink object:

```
TDBListBoxNotifySink OnDblClickSink;
```

Put a prototype for the handler method in the class declaration for your sink object:

```
void OnDblClick( TDBListBoxNotifySink& sink, TDBListBox& sender );
```

Connect the handler method to the event sink by including the following in the class constructor:

```
OnDblClickSink( TDBListBoxNotify_MFUNCTOR( *this, &TForm::OnDblClick ));
```

Attach the event source to the event sink by including the following code in your program:

```
TDBListBox DBListBox;     //Instantiate the source component
TForm form                //Instantiate the sink component
DBListBox.OnDblClickSource += form.OnDblClickSink;
```

OnDblClick event for the TDBLookupCombo component

This declaration of the event source is in the dblkupcb.h header file:

```
TDBLookupComboNotifySource OnDblClickSource;
```

Include this declaration of the event sink in the class declaration of your sink object:

```
TDBLookupComboNotifySink OnDblClickSink;
```

Put a prototype for the handler method in the class declaration for your sink object:

```
void OnDblClick( TDBLookupComboNotifySink& sink, TDBLookupCombo& sender );
```

Connect the handler method to the event sink by including the following in the class constructor:

```
OnDblClickSink( TDBLookupComboNotify_MFUNCTOR( *this, &TForm::OnDblClick ));
```

Attach the event source to the event sink by including the following code in your program:

```
TDBLookupCombo DBLookupCombo;     //Instantiate the source component
TForm form                        //Instantiate the sink component
DBLookupCombo.OnDblClickSource += form.OnDblClickSink;
```

OnDblClick event for the TDBLookupList component

This declaration of the event source is in the dblkuplb.h header file:

```
TDBLookupListNotifySource OnDblClickSource;
```

Include this declaration of the event sink in the class declaration of your sink object:

```
TDBLookupListNotifySink OnDblClickSink;
```

Put a prototype for the handler method in the class declaration for your sink object:

```
void OnDblClick( TDBLookupListNotifySink& sink, TDBLookupList& sender );
```

Connect the handler method to the event sink by including the following in the class constructor:

```
OnDblClickSink( TDBLookupListNotify_MFUNCTOR( *this, &TForm::OnDblClick ));
```

Attach the event source to the event sink by including the following code in your program:

```
TDBLookupList DBLookupList;     //Instantiate the source component
TForm form                      //Instantiate the sink component
DBLookupList.OnDblClickSource += form.OnDblClickSink;
```

OnDblClick event for the TDBMemo component

This declaration of the event source is in the dbmemo.h header file:

```
TDBMemoNotifySource OnDblClickSource;
```

Include this declaration of the event sink in the class declaration of your sink object:

```
TDBMemoNotifySink OnDblClickSink;
```

Put a prototype for the handler method in the class declaration for your sink object:

```
void OnDblClick( TDBMemoNotifySink& sink, TDBMemo& sender );
```

Connect the handler method to the event sink by including the following in the class constructor:

```
OnDblClickSink( TDBMemoNotify_MFUNCTOR( *this, &TForm::OnDblClick ));
```

Attach the event source to the event sink by including the following code in your program:

```
TDBMemo DBMemo;        //Instantiate the source component
TForm form             //Instantiate the sink component
DBMemo.OnDblClickSource += form.OnDblClickSink;
```

OnDblClick event for the TDBRadioGroup component

This declaration of the event source is in the dbradio.h header file:

```
TDBRadioGroupNotifySource OnDblClickSource;
```

Include this declaration of the event sink in the class declaration of your sink object:

```
TDBRadioGroupNotifySink OnDblClickSink;
```

Put a prototype for the handler method in the class declaration for your sink object:

```
void OnDblClick( TDBRadioGroupNotifySink& sink, TDBRadioGroup& sender );
```

Connect the handler method to the event sink by including the following in the class constructor:

```
OnDblClickSink( TDBRadioGroupNotify_MFUNCTOR( *this, &TForm::OnDblClick ));
```

Attach the event source to the event sink by including the following code in your program:

```
TDBRadioGroup DBRadioGroup;     //Instantiate the source component
TForm form                      //Instantiate the sink component
DBRadioGroup.OnDblClickSource += form.OnDblClickSink;
```

OnDblClick event for the DBText component

This declaration of the event source is in the dbtext.h header file:

```
TDBTextNotifySource OnDblClickSource;
```

Include this declaration of the event sink in the class declaration of your sink object:

```
TDBTextNotifySink OnDblClickSink;
```

Put a prototype for the handler method in the class declaration for your sink object:

```
void OnDblClick( TDBTextNotifySink& sink, TDBText& sender );
```

Connect the handler method to the event sink by including the following in the class constructor:

```
OnDblClickSink( TDBTextNotify_MFUNCTOR( *this, &TForm::OnDblClick ));
```

Attach the event source to the event sink by including the following code in your program:

```
TDBText DBText;                 //Instantiate the source component
TForm form                      //Instantiate the sink component
DBText.OnDblClickSource += form.OnDblClickSink;
```

OnDragDrop event

Applies to TDBCheckBox, TDBComboBox, TDBEdit, TDBGrid, TDBImage, TDBListBox, TDBLookupCombo, TDBLookupList, TDBMemo, TDBNavigator, TDBRadioGroup, TDBText components

Header file dbchkbx.h, dbcombo.h, dbedit.h, dbgrid.h, dbimage.h, dblist.h, dblkupcb.h, dblkuplb.h, dbmemo.h, dbnvgtr.h, dbradio.h, dbtext.h

Description The OnDragDrop event occurs when the user drops an object being dragged. Use the OnDragDrop event handler to specify what you want to happen when the user drops an object.

This will be the declaration for the OnDragDrop event handler for a database check box; if your handler is for another Visual Database Tools control, substitute the name of that control for TDBCheckBox:

```
void OnDragDrop( TDBCheckBoxDragSink& sink, TDBCheckBox& sender,
              TVbxControl& source, SHORT x, SHORT y );
```

The source parameter of the OnDragDrop event is the object being dropped, and the sender is the control the object is being dropped on. The x and y parameters are the coordinates of the mouse positioned over the control in pixels.

OnDragDrop event for the TDBCheckBox component

This declaration of the event source is in the dbchkbx.h header file:

```
TDBCheckBoxDragSource OnDragDropSource;
```

Include this declaration of the event sink in the class declaration of your sink object:

```
TDBCheckBoxDragSink OnDragDropSink;
```

Put a prototype for the handler method in the class declaration for your sink object:

```
void OnDragDrop( TDBCheckBoxDragSink& sink, TDBCheckBox& sender,
              TVbxControl& source, SHORT x, SHORT y );
```

Connect the handler method to the event sink by including the following in the class constructor:

```
OnDragDropSink( TDBCheckBoxDrag_MFUNCTOR( *this, &TForm::OnDragDrop ));
```

Attach the event source to the event sink by including the following code in your program:

```
TDBCheckBox DBCheckBox;        //Instantiate the source component
TForm form                     //Instantiate the sink component
DBCheckBox.OnDragDropSource += form.OnDragDropSink;
```

OnDragDrop event for the TDBComboBox component

This declaration of the event source is in the dbcombo.h header file:

```
TDBComboBoxDragSource OnDragDropSource;
```

Include this declaration of the event sink in the class declaration of your sink object:

```
TDBComboBoxDragSink OnDragDropSink;
```

Put a prototype for the handler method in the class declaration for your sink object:

```
void OnDragDrop( TDBComboBoxDragSink& sink, TDBComboBox& sender,
                TVbxControl& source, SHORT x, SHORT y );
```

Connect the handler method to the event sink by including the following in the class constructor:

```
OnDragDropSink( TDBComboBoxDrag_MFUNCTOR( *this, &TForm::OnDragDrop ));
```

Attach the event source to the event sink by including the following code in your program:

```
TDBComboBox DBComboBox;        //Instantiate the source component
TForm form                     //Instantiate the sink component
DBComboBox.OnDragDropSource += form.OnDragDropSink;
```

OnDragDrop event for the TDBEdit component

This declaration of the event source is in the dbedit.h header file:

```
TDBEditDragSource OnDragDropSource;
```

Include this declaration of the event sink in the class declaration of your sink object:

```
TDBEditDragSink OnDragDropSink;
```

Put a prototype for the handler method in the class declaration for your sink object:

```
void OnDragDrop( TDBEditDragSink& sink, TDBEdit& sender,
                TVbxControl& source, SHORT x, SHORT y );
```

Connect the handler method to the event sink by including the following in the class constructor:

```
OnDragDropSink( TDBEditDrag_MFUNCTOR( *this, &TForm::OnDragDrop ));
```

Attach the event source to the event sink by including the following code in your program:

```
TDBEdit DBEdit;                //Instantiate the source component
TForm form                     //Instantiate the sink component
DBEdit.OnDragDropSource += form.OnDragDropSink;
```

OnDragDrop event for the TDBGrid component

This declaration of the event source is in the dbgrid.h header file:

```
TDBGridDragSource OnDragDropSource;
```

Include this declaration of the event sink in the class declaration of your sink object:
```
TDBGridDragSink OnDragDropSink;
```

Put a prototype for the handler method in the class declaration for your sink object:

```
void OnDragDrop( TDBGridDragSink& sink, TDBGrid& sender,
                TVbxControl& source, SHORT x, SHORT y );
```

Connect the handler method to the event sink by including the following in the class constructor:

```
OnDragDropSink( TDBGridDrag_MFUNCTOR( *this, &TForm::OnDragDrop ));
```

Attach the event source to the event sink by including the following code in your program:

```
TDBGrid DBGrid;          //Instantiate the source component
TForm form               //Instantiate the sink component
DBGrid.OnDragDropSource += form.OnDragDropSink;
```

OnDragDrop event for the TDBImage component

This declaration of the event source is in the dbimage.h header file:

```
TDBImageDragSource OnDragDropSource;
```

Include this declaration of the event sink in the class declaration of your sink object:

```
TDBImageDragSink OnDragDropSink;
```

Put a prototype for the handler method in the class declaration for your sink object:

```
void OnDragDrop( TDBImageDragSink& sink, TDBImage& sender,
                 TVbxControl& source, SHORT x, SHORT y );
```

Connect the handler method to the event sink by including the following in the class constructor:

```
OnDragDropSink( TDBImageDrag_MFUNCTOR( *this, &TForm::OnDragDrop ));
```

Attach the event source to the event sink by including the following code in your program:

```
TDBImage DBImage;         //Instantiate the source component
TForm form                //Instantiate the sink component
DBImage.OnDragDropSource += form.OnDragDropSink;
```

OnDragDrop event for the TDBListBox component

This declaration of the event source is in the dblist.h header file:

```
TDBListBoxDragSource OnDragDropSource;
```

Include this declaration of the event sink in the class declaration of your sink object:

```
TDBListBoxDragSink OnDragDropSink;
```

Put a prototype for the handler method in the class declaration for your sink object:

```
void OnDragDrop( TDBListBoxDragSink& sink, TDBListBox& sender,
                 TVbxControl& source, SHORT x, SHORT y );
```

Connect the handler method to the event sink by including the following in the class constructor:

```
OnDragDropSink( TDBListBoxDrag_MFUNCTOR( *this, &TForm::OnDragDrop ));
```

Attach the event source to the event sink by including the following code in your program:

```
TDBListBox DBListBox;        //Instantiate the source component
TForm form                   //Instantiate the sink component
DBListBox.OnDragDropSource += form.OnDragDropSink;
```

OnDragDrop event for the TDBLookupCombo component
This declaration of the event source is in the dblkupcb.h header file:

```
TDBLookupComboDragSource OnDragDropSource;
```

Include this declaration of the event sink in the class declaration of your sink object:

```
TDBLookupComboDragSink OnDragDropSink;
```

Put a prototype for the handler method in the class declaration for your sink object:

```
void OnDragDrop( TDBLookupComboDragSink& sink, TDBLookupCombo& sender,
            TVbxControl& source, SHORT x, SHORT y );
```

Connect the handler method to the event sink by including the following in the class constructor:

```
OnDragDropSink( TDBLookupComboDrag_MFUNCTOR( *this, &TForm::OnDragDrop ));
```

Attach the event source to the event sink by including the following code in your program:

```
TDBLookupCombo DBLookupCombo;      //Instantiate the source component
TForm form                         //Instantiate the sink component
DBLookupCombo.OnDragDropSource += form.OnDragDropSink;
```

OnDragDrop event for the TDBLookupList component
This declaration of the event source is in the dblkuplb.h header file:

```
TDBLookupListDragSource OnDragDropSource;
```

Include this declaration of the event sink in the class declaration of your sink object:

```
TDBLookupListDragSink OnDragDropSink;
```

Put a prototype for the handler method in the class declaration for your sink object:

```
void OnDragDrop( TDBLookupListDragSink& sink, TDBLookupList& sender,
            TVbxControl& source, SHORT x, SHORT y );
```

Connect the handler method to the event sink by including the following in the class constructor:

```
OnDragDropSink( TDBLookupListDrag_MFUNCTOR( *this, &TForm::OnDragDrop ));
```

Attach the event source to the event sink by including the following code in your program:

```
TDBLookupList DBLookupList;        //Instantiate the source component
TForm form                         //Instantiate the sink component
DBLookupList.OnDragDropSource += form.OnDragDropSink;
```

OnDragDrop event for the TDBMemo component

This declaration of the event source is in the dbmemo.h header file:

```
TDBMemoDragSource OnDragDropSource;
```

Include this declaration of the event sink in the class declaration of your sink object:

```
TDBMemoDragSink OnDragDropSink;
```

Put a prototype for the handler method in the class declaration for your sink object:

```
void OnDragDrop( TDBMemoDragSink& sink, TDBMemo& sender,
                 TVbxControl& source, SHORT x, SHORT y );
```

Connect the handler method to the event sink by including the following in the class constructor:

```
OnDragDropSink( TDBMemoDrag_MFUNCTOR( *this, &TForm::OnDragDrop ));
```

Attach the event source to the event sink by including the following code in your program:

```
TDBMemo DBMemo;          //Instantiate the source component
TForm form               //Instantiate the sink component
DBMemo.OnDragDropSource += form.OnDragDropSink;
```

OnDragDrop event for the TDBNavigator component

This declaration of the event source is in the dbNavigator.h header file:

```
TDBNavigatorDragSource OnDragDropSource;
```

Include this declaration of the event sink in the class declaration of your sink object:

```
TDBNavigatorDragSink OnDragDropSink;
```

Put a prototype for the handler method in the class declaration for your sink object:

```
void OnDragDrop( TDBNavigatorDragSink& sink, TDBNavigator& sender,
                 TVbxControl& source, SHORT x, SHORT y );
```

Connect the handler method to the event sink by including the following in the class constructor:

```
OnDragDropSink( TDBNavigatorDrag_MFUNCTOR( *this, &TForm::OnDragDrop ));
```

Attach the event source to the event sink by including the following code in your program:

```
TDBNavigator DBNavigator;        //Instantiate the source component
TForm form               //Instantiate the sink component
DBNavigator.OnDragDropSource += form.OnDragDropSink;
```

OnDragDrop event for the TDBRadioGroup component

This declaration of the event source is in the dbradio.h header file:

```
TDBRadioGroupDragSource OnDragDropSource;
```

Include this declaration of the event sink in the class declaration of your sink object:

```
TDBRadioGroupDragSink OnDragDropSink;
```

Put a prototype for the handler method in the class declaration for your sink object:

```
void OnDragDrop( TDBRadioGroupDragSink& sink, TDBRadioGroup& sender,
                 TVbxControl& source, SHORT x, SHORT y );
```

Connect the handler method to the event sink by including the following in the class constructor:

```
OnDragDropSink( TDBRadioGroupDrag_MFUNCTOR( *this, &TForm::OnDragDrop ));
```

Attach the event source to the event sink by including the following code in your program:

```
TDBRadioGroup DBRadioGroup;     //Instantiate the source component
TForm form                      //Instantiate the sink component
DBRadioGroup.OnDragDropSource += form.OnDragDropSink;
```

OnDragDrop event for the DBText component

This declaration of the event source is in the dbtext.h header file:

```
TDBTextDragSource OnDragDropSource;
```

Include this declaration of the event sink in the class declaration of your sink object:

```
TDBTextDragSink OnDragDropSink;
```

Put a prototype for the handler method in the class declaration for your sink object:

```
void OnDragDrop( TDBTextDragSink& sink, TDBText& sender,
                 TVbxControl& source, SHORT x, SHORT y );
```

Connect the handler method to the event sink by including the following in the class constructor:

```
OnDragDropSink( TDBTextDrag_MFUNCTOR( *this, &TForm::OnDragDrop ));
```

Attach the event source to the event sink by including the following code in your program:

```
TDBText DBText;                 //Instantiate the source component
TForm form                      //Instantiate the sink component
DBText.OnDragDropSource += form.OnDragDropSink;
```

OnDragOver event

Applies to   TDBCheckBox, TDBComboBox, TDBEdit, TDBGrid, TDBImage, TDBListBox, TDBLookupCombo, TDBLookupList, TDBNavigator, TDBNavigator, TDBRadioGroup, TDBText components

Header file   dbchkbx.h, dbcombo.h, dbedit.h, dbgrid.h, dbimage.h, dblist.h, dblkupcb.h, dblkuplb.h, dbNavigator.h, dbnvgtr.h, dbradio.h, dbtext.h

Description   The OnDragOver event occurs when the user drags an object over a component.

This will be the declaration for the OnDragOver event handler for a database check box; if your handler is for another Visual Database Tools control, substitute the name of that control for TDBCheckBox:

```
void OnDragOver( TDBCheckBoxDragOverSink& sink, TDBCheckBox& sender,
                 TVBxControl& source, SHORT x, SHORT y, TDragState state );
```

The source parameter can be any data-aware control. The x and y parameters are the horizontal and vertical positions, respectively, of the mouse pointer within the target control.

The State parameter specifies the drag state of a dragged control in relationship to another control. These are the possible values:

Value	Meaning
0	The dragged object enters a control in which it can be dropped.
1	The dragged object is moved within a control in which it can be dropped.
2	The dragged object leaves a control in which it can be dropped.

Usually, you will want the cursor to change shape, indicating that the control can accept the dragged object if the user drops it. You can change the shape of the cursor by changing the value of the DragCursor property for the control at run time before an OnDragOver event occurs.

OnDragOver event for the TDBCheckBox component

This declaration of the event source is in the dbchkbx.h header file:

```
TDBCheckBoxDragOverSource OnDragOverSource;
```

Include this declaration of the event sink in the class declaration of your sink object:

```
TDBCheckBoxDragOverSink OnDragOverSink;
```

Put a prototype for the handler method in the class declaration for your sink object:

```
void OnDragOver( TDBCheckBoxDragOverSink& sink, TDBCheckBox& sender,
                 TVBxControl& source, SHORT x, SHORT y, TDragState state );
```

Connect the handler method to the event sink by including the following in the class constructor:

```
OnDragOverSink( TDBCheckBoxDragOver_MFUNCTOR( *this, &TForm::OnDragOver ));
```

Attach the event source to the event sink by including the following code in your program:

```
TDBCheckBox DBCheckBox;          //Instantiate the source component
TForm form                       //Instantiate the sink component
DBCheckBox.OnDragOverSource += form.OnDragOverSink;
```

OnDragOver event for the TDBComboBox component

This declaration of the event source is in the dbcombo.h header file:

```
TDBComboBoxDragOverSource OnDragOverSource;
```

Include this declaration of the event sink in the class declaration of your sink object:

```
TDBComboBoxDragOverSink OnDragOverSink;
```

Put a prototype for the handler method in the class declaration for your sink object:

```
void OnDragOver( TDBComboBoxDragOverSink& sink, TDBComboBox& sender,
                 TVBxControl& source, SHORT x, SHORT y, TDragState state );
```

Connect the handler method to the event sink by including the following in the class constructor:

```
OnDragOverSink( TDBComboBoxDragOver_MFUNCTOR( *this, &TForm::OnDragOver ));
```

Attach the event source to the event sink by including the following code in your program:

```
TDBComboBox DBComboBox;      //Instantiate the source component
TForm form                   //Instantiate the sink component
DBComboBox.OnDragOverSource += form.OnDragOverSink;
```

OnDragOver event for the TDBEdit component

This declaration of the event source is in the dbedit.h header file:

```
TDBEditDragOverSource OnDragOverSource;
```

Include this declaration of the event sink in the class declaration of your sink object:

```
TDBEditDragOverSink OnDragOverSink;
```

Put a prototype for the handler method in the class declaration for your sink object:

```
void OnDragOver( TDBEditDragOverSink& sink, TDBEdit& sender,
                 TVBxControl& source, SHORT x, SHORT y, TDragState state );
```

Connect the handler method to the event sink by including the following in the class constructor:

```
OnDragOverSink( TDBEditDragOver_MFUNCTOR( *this, &TForm::OnDragOver ));
```

Attach the event source to the event sink by including the following code in your program:

```
TDBEdit DBEdit;              //Instantiate the source component
TForm form                   //Instantiate the sink component
DBEdit.OnDragOverSource += form.OnDragOverSink;
```

OnDragOver event for the TDBGrid component

This declaration of the event source is in the dbgrid.h header file:

```
TDBGridDragOverSource OnDragOverSource;
```

Include this declaration of the event sink in the class declaration of your sink object:

```
TDBGridDragOverSink OnDragOverSink;
```

Put a prototype for the handler method in the class declaration for your sink object:

```
void OnDragOver( TDBGridDragOverSink& sink, TDBGrid& sender,
                 TVBxControl& source, SHORT x, SHORT y, TDragState state );
```

Connect the handler method to the event sink by including the following in the class constructor:

```
OnDragOverSink( TDBGridDragOver_MFUNCTOR( *this, &TForm::OnDragOver ));
```

Attach the event source to the event sink by including the following code in your program:

```
TDBGrid DBGrid;          //Instantiate the source component
TForm form               //Instantiate the sink component
DBGrid.OnDragOverSource += form.OnDragOverSink;
```

OnDragOver event for the TDBImage component

This declaration of the event source is in the dbimage.h header file:

```
TDBImageDragOverSource OnDragOverSource;
```

Include this declaration of the event sink in the class declaration of your sink object:

```
TDBImageDragOverSink OnDragOverSink;
```

Put a prototype for the handler method in the class declaration for your sink object:

```
void OnDragOver( TDBImageDragOverSink& sink, TDBImage& sender,
                 TVBxControl& source, SHORT x, SHORT y, TDragState state );
```

Connect the handler method to the event sink by including the following in the class constructor:

```
OnDragOverSink( TDBImageDragOver_MFUNCTOR( *this, &TForm::OnDragOver ));
```

Attach the event source to the event sink by including the following code in your program:

```
TDBImage DBImage;        //Instantiate the source component
TForm form               //Instantiate the sink component
DBImage.OnDragOverSource += form.OnDragOverSink;
```

OnDragOver event for the TDBListBox component

This declaration of the event source is in the dblist.h header file:

```
TDBListBoxDragOverSource OnDragOverSource;
```

Include this declaration of the event sink in the class declaration of your sink object:

```
TDBListBoxDragOverSink OnDragOverSink;
```

Put a prototype for the handler method in the class declaration for your sink object:

```
void OnDragOver( TDBListBoxDragOverSink& sink, TDBListBox& sender,
                 TVBxControl& source, SHORT x, SHORT y, TDragState state );
```

Connect the handler method to the event sink by including the following in the class constructor:

```
OnDragOverSink( TDBListBoxDragOver_MFUNCTOR( *this, &TForm::OnDragOver ));
```

Attach the event source to the event sink by including the following code in your program:

```
TDBListBox DBListBox;      //Instantiate the source component
TForm form                //Instantiate the sink component
DBListBox.OnDragOverSource += form.OnDragOverSink;
```

OnDragOver event for the TDBLookupCombo component

This declaration of the event source is in the dblkupcb.h header file:

```
TDBLookupComboDragOverSource OnDragOverSource;
```

Include this declaration of the event sink in the class declaration of your sink object:

```
TDBLookupComboDragOverSink OnDragOverSink;
```

Put a prototype for the handler method in the class declaration for your sink object:

```
void OnDragOver( TDBLookupComboDragOverSink& sink, TDBLookupCombo& sender,
               TVBxControl& source, SHORT x, SHORT y, TDragState state );
```

Connect the handler method to the event sink by including the following in the class constructor:

```
OnDragOverSink( TDBLookupComboDragOver_MFUNCTOR( *this, &TForm::OnDragOver ));
```

Attach the event source to the event sink by including the following code in your program:

```
TDBLookupCombo DBLookupCombo;      //Instantiate the source component
TForm form                        //Instantiate the sink component
DBLookupCombo.OnDragOverSource += form.OnDragOverSink;
```

OnDragOver event for the TDBLookupList component

This declaration of the event source is in the dblkuplb.h header file:

```
TDBLookupListDragOverSource OnDragOverSource;
```

Include this declaration of the event sink in the class declaration of your sink object:

```
TDBLookupListDragOverSink OnDragOverSink;
```

Put a prototype for the handler method in the class declaration for your sink object:

```
void OnDragOver( TDBLookupListDragOverSink& sink, TDBLookupList& sender,
               TVBxControl& source, SHORT x, SHORT y, TDragState state );
```

Connect the handler method to the event sink by including the following in the class constructor:

```
OnDragOverSink( TDBLookupListDragOver_MFUNCTOR( *this, &TForm::OnDragOver ));
```

Attach the event source to the event sink by including the following code in your program:

```
TDBLookupList DBLookupList;      //Instantiate the source component
TForm form                      //Instantiate the sink component
DBLookupList.OnDragOverSource += form.OnDragOverSink;
```

OnDragOver event for the TDBMemo component

This declaration of the event source is in the dbMemo.h header file:

```
TDBMemoDragOverSource OnDragOverSource;
```

Include this declaration of the event sink in the class declaration of your sink object:

```
TDBMemoDragOverSink OnDragOverSink;
```

Put a prototype for the handler method in the class declaration for your sink object:

```
void OnDragOver( TDBMemoDragOverSink& sink, TDBMemo& sender,
            TVBxControl& source, SHORT x, SHORT y, TDragState state );
```

Connect the handler method to the event sink by including the following in the class constructor:

```
OnDragOverSink( TDBMemoDragOver_MFUNCTOR( *this, &TForm::OnDragOver ));
```

Attach the event source to the event sink by including the following code in your program:

```
TDBMemo DBMemo;          //Instantiate the source component
TForm form              //Instantiate the sink component
DBMemo.OnDragOverSource += form.OnDragOverSink;
```

OnDragOver event for the TDBNavigator component

This declaration of the event source is in the dbNavigator.h header file:

```
TDBNavigatorDragOverSource OnDragOverSource;
```

Include this declaration of the event sink in the class declaration of your sink object:

```
TDBNavigatorDragOverSink OnDragOverSink;
```

Put a prototype for the handler method in the class declaration for your sink object:

```
void OnDragOver( TDBNavigatorDragOverSink& sink, TDBNavigator& sender,
            TVBxControl& source, SHORT x, SHORT y, TDragState state );
```

Connect the handler method to the event sink by including the following in the class constructor:

```
OnDragOverSink( TDBNavigatorDragOver_MFUNCTOR( *this, &TForm::OnDragOver ));
```

Attach the event source to the event sink by including the following code in your program:

```
TDBNavigator DBNavigator;         //Instantiate the source component
TForm form             //Instantiate the sink component
DBNavigator.OnDragOverSource += form.OnDragOverSink;
```

OnDragOver event for the TDBRadioGroup component

This declaration of the event source is in the dbradio.h header file:

```
TDBRadioGroupDragOverSource OnDragOverSource;
```

Include this declaration of the event sink in the class declaration of your sink object:

```
TDBRadioGroupDragOverSink OnDragOverSink;
```

Put a prototype for the handler method in the class declaration for your sink object:

```
void OnDragOver( TDBRadioGroupDragOverSink& sink, TDBRadioGroup& sender,
            TVBxControl& source, SHORT x, SHORT y, TDragState state );
```

Connect the handler method to the event sink by including the following in the class constructor:

```
OnDragOverSink( TDBRadioGroupDragOver_MFUNCTOR( *this, &TForm::OnDragOver ));
```

Attach the event source to the event sink by including the following code in your program:

```
TDBRadioGroup DBRadioGroup;     //Instantiate the source component
TForm form                      //Instantiate the sink component
DBRadioGroup.OnDragOverSource += form.OnDragOverSink;
```

OnDragOver event for the DBText component

This declaration of the event source is in the dbtext.h header file:

```
TDBTextDragOverSource OnDragOverSource;
```

Include this declaration of the event sink in the class declaration of your sink object:

```
TDBTextDragOverSink OnDragOverSink;
```

Put a prototype for the handler method in the class declaration for your sink object:

```
void OnDragOver( TDBTextDragOverSink& sink, TDBText& sender,
            TVBxControl& source, SHORT x, SHORT y, TDragState state );
```

Connect the handler method to the event sink by including the following in the class constructor:

```
OnDragOverSink( TDBTextDragOver_MFUNCTOR( *this, &TForm::OnDragOver ));
```

Attach the event source to the event sink by including the following code in your program:

```
TDBText DBText;                 //Instantiate the source component
TForm form                      //Instantiate the sink component
DBText.OnDragOverSource += form.OnDragOverSink;
```

OnDrawItem event

Applies to   TDBComboBox, TDBListBox components

Header file   dbcombo.h, dblist.h

Description   The OnDrawItem event occurs whenever an item in an owner-draw database list box or combo box needs to be redisplayed. For example, it occurs when the user selects an item or scrolls the database list box or combo box. OnDrawItem events occur only for database list boxes with the Style values lbOwnerDrawFixed or lbOwnerDrawVariable, and for combo boxes with the Style values csOwnerDrawFixed or csOwnerDrawVariable.

This will be the declaration of the OnDrawItem event handler for a database combo box; if your event handler is for a database list box, substitute TDBListBox for TDBComboBox:

```
void OnDrawItem( TDBComboBoxDrawItemSink& sink, TDBComboBox& sender,
                 SHORT index, TRect rc, TOwnerDrawState state );
```

OnDrawItem passes these to its handler describing the item to be drawn:

Value	Meaning
index	The index of the item in that control that identifies the position of the item in the list box
rc	A rectangle in which to draw
state	The state of the item (selected, disabled, grayed, or checked)

These are the possible values of the state parameter:

Value	Meaning
odChecked	The menu item is to be checked. This is used only in a menu.
odGrayed	The item is to be grayed. This is used only in a menu.
odDisabled	The item is disabled.
odSelected	The item is selected.

The size of the rectangle that contains the item is determined either by the ItemHeight property for fixed owner-draw controls or by the response to the OnMeasureItem event for variable owner-draw controls.

OnDrawItem event for the TDBComboBox component

This declaration of the event source is in the dbcombo.h header file:

```
TDBComboBoxDrawItemSource OnDrawItemSource;
```

Include this declaration of the event sink in the class declaration of your sink object:

```
TDBComboBoxDrawItemSink OnDrawItemSink;
```

Put a prototype for the handler method in the class declaration for your sink object:

```
void OnDrawItem( TDBComboBoxDrawItemSink& sink, TDBComboBox& sender,
                 SHORT index, TRect rc, TOwnerDrawState state );
```

Connect the handler method to the event sink by including the following in the class constructor:

```
OnDrawItemSink( TDBComboBoxDrawItem_MFUNCTOR( *this, &TForm::OnDrawItem ));
```

Attach the event source to the event sink by including the following code in your program:

```
TDBComboBox DBComboBox;      //Instantiate the source component
TForm form                   //Instantiate the sink component
DBComboBox.OnDrawItemSource += form.OnDrawItemSink;
```

OnDrawItem event for the TDBListBox component

This declaration of the event source is in the dblist.h header file:

```
TDBListBoxDrawItemSource OnDrawItemSource;
```

Include this declaration of the event sink in the class declaration of your sink object:

```
TDBListBoxDrawItemSink OnDrawItemSink;
```

Put a prototype for the handler method in the class declaration for your sink object:

```
void OnDrawItem( TDBListBoxDrawItemSink& sink, TDBListBox& sender,
                SHORT index, TRect rc, TOwnerDrawState state );
```

Connect the handler method to the event sink by including the following in the class constructor:

```
OnDrawItemSink( TDBListBoxDrawItem_MFUNCTOR( *this, &TForm::OnDrawItem ));
```

Attach the event source to the event sink by including the following code in your program:

```
TDBListBox DBListBox;       //Instantiate the source component
TForm form                  //Instantiate the sink component
DBListBox.OnDrawItemSource += form.OnDrawItemSink;
```

OnDropDown event

Applies to   TDBComboBox, TDBLookupCombo components

Header file   dbcombo.h, dblkupcb.h

Description   The OnDropDown event occurs when the user opens (drops down) a database combo box or lookup combo box.

OnDropDown event for the TDBCombBox component

This declaration of the event source is in the dblist.h header file:

```
TDBComboBoxNotifySource OnDropDownSource;
```

Include this declaration of the event sink in the class declaration for your sink object:

```
TDBComboBoxNotifySink OnDropDownSink;
```

Put a prototype for the handler method in the class declaration for your sink object:

```
void OnDrop ( TDBComboBoxNotifySink& sink, TDBComboBox& sender )
```

Connect the handler method to the event sink by including the following in the class constructor:

```
OnDropDownSink( TDBComboBoxNotify_MFUNCTOR( *this, &TForm::OnDropDown ));
```

Attach the event source to the event sink by including the following code in your program:

```
TDBComboBox DBComboBox;          //Instantiate the source component
TForm form                       //Instantiate the sink component
DBComboBox.OnDropDownSource += form.OnDropDownSink;
```

OnDropDown event for the TDBLookupCombo component

This declaration of the event source is in the dblist.h header file:

```
TDBLookupComboNotifySource OnDropDownSource;
```

Include this declaration of the event sink in the class declaration for your sink object:

```
TDBLookupComboNotifySink OnDropDownSink;
```

Put a prototype for the handler method in the class declaration for your sink object:

```
void OnDrop ( TDBLookupComboNotifySink& sink, TDBLookupCombo& sender )
```

Connect the handler method to the event sink by including the following in the class constructor:

```
OnDropDownSink( TDBLookupComboNotify_MFUNCTOR( *this, &TForm::OnDropDown ));
```

Attach the event source to the event sink by including the following code in your program:

```
TDBLookupCombo DBLookupCombo;        //Instantiate the source component
TForm form                           //Instantiate the sink component
DBLookupCombo.OnDropDownSource += form.OnDropDownSink;
```

OnEndDrag event

Applies to   TDBCheckBox, TDBComboBox, TDBEdit, TDBGrid, TDBImage, TDBListBox, TDBLookupCombo, TDBNavigator, TDBNavigator, TDBRadioGroup, TDBText components

Header file   dbchkbx.h, dbcombo.h, dbedit.h, dbgrid.h, dbimage.h, dblist.h, dblkupcb.h, dbNavigator.h, dbnvgtr.h, dbradio.h, dbtext.h

Description   The OnEndDrag event occurs whenever the dragging of an object ends, either by dropping the object or by canceling the dragging. Use the OnEndDrag event handler to specify any special processing you want to occur when dragging stops.

This will be the declaration for the OnEnd event handler for a database check box; if your handler is for another Visual Database Tools control, substitute the name of that control for TDBCheckBox:

```
void OnEndDrag( TDBCheckBoxDragSink& sink, TDBCheckBox& sender,
         TVbxControl& source, SHORT x, SHORT y );
```

The source parameter of the OnDragDrop event is the object being dropped, and the sender is the control the object is being dropped on. The x and y parameters are the coordinates of the mouse positioned over the control in pixels.

OnEndDrag event for the TDBCheckBox component

This declaration of the event source is in the dbchkbx.h header file:

```
TDBCheckBoxDragSource OnEndDragSource;
```

Include this declaration of the event sink in the class declaration of your sink object:

```
TDBCheckBoxDragSink OnEndDragSink;
```

Put a prototype for the handler method in the class declaration for your sink object:

```
void OnEndDrag( TDBCheckBoxDragSink& sink, TDBCheckBox& sender,
                TVbxControl& source, SHORT x, SHORT y );
```

Connect the handler method to the event sink by including the following in the class constructor:

```
OnEndDragSink( TDBCheckBoxDrag_MFUNCTOR( *this, &TForm::OnEndDrag ));
```

Attach the event source to the event sink by including the following code in your program:

```
TDBCheckBox DBCheckBox;        //Instantiate the source component
TForm form                     //Instantiate the sink component
DBCheckBox.OnEndDragSource += form.OnEndDragSink;
```

OnEndDrag event for the TDBComboBox component

This declaration of the event source is in the dbcombo.h header file:

```
TDBComboBoxDragSource OnEndDragSource;
```

Include this declaration of the event sink in the class declaration of your sink object:

```
TDBComboBoxDragSink OnEndDragSink;
```

Put a prototype for the handler method in the class declaration for your sink object:

```
void OnEndDrag( TDBComboBoxDragSink& sink, TDBComboBox& sender,
                TVbxControl& source, SHORT x, SHORT y );
```

Connect the handler method to the event sink by including the following in the class constructor:

```
OnEndDragSink( TDBComboBoxDrag_MFUNCTOR( *this, &TForm::OnEndDrag ));
```

Attach the event source to the event sink by including the following code in your program:

```
TDBComboBox DBComboBox;        //Instantiate the source component
TForm form                     //Instantiate the sink component
DBComboBox.OnEndDragSource += form.OnEndDragSink;
```

OnEndDrag event for the TDBEdit component

This decaration of the event source is in the dbedit.h header file:

```
TDBEditDragSource OnEndDragSource;
```

Include this declaration of the event sink in the class declaration of your sink object:

```
TDBEditDragSink OnEndDragSink;
```

Put a prototype for the handler method in the class declaration for your sink object:

```
void OnEndDrag( TDBEditSink& sink, TDBEdit& sender, TVbxControl& source,
                SHORT x, SHORT y );
```

Connect the handler method to the event sink by including the following in the class constructor:

```
OnEndDragSink( TDBEditDrag_MFUNCTOR( *this, &TForm::OnEndDrag ));
```

Attach the event source to the event sink by including the following code in your program:

```
TDBEdit DBEdit;            //Instantiate the source component
TForm form                 //Instantiate the sink component
DBEdit.OnEndDragSource += form.OnEndDragSink;
```

OnEndDrag event for the TDBGrid component

This declaration of the event source is in the dbgrid.h header file:

```
TDBGridDragSource OnEndDragSource;
```

Include this declaration of the event sink in the class declaration of your sink object:

```
TDBGridDragSink OnEndDragSink;
```

Put a prototype for the handler method in the class declaration for your sink object:

```
void OnEndDrag( TDBGridDragSink& sink, TDBGrid& sender, TVbxControl& source,
            SHORT x, SHORT y );
```

Connect the handler method to the event sink by including the following in the class constructor:

```
OnEndDragSink( TDBGridDrag_MFUNCTOR( *this, &TForm::OnEndDrag ));
```

Attach the event source to the event sink by including the following code in your program:

```
TDBGrid DBGrid;           //Instantiate the source component
TForm form                //Instantiate the sink component
DBGrid.OnEndDragSource += form.OnEndDragSink;
```

OnEndDrag event for the TDBImage component

This declaration of the event source is in the dbimage.h header file:

```
TDBImageDragSource OnEndDragSource;
```

Include this declaration of the event sink in the class declaration of your sink object:

```
TDBImageDragSink OnEndDragSink;
```

Put a prototype for the handler method in the class declaration for your sink object:

```
void OnEndDrag( TDBImageDragSink& sink, TDBImage& sender, TVbxControl& source,
            SHORT x, SHORT y );
```

Connect the handler method to the event sink by including the following in the class constructor:

```
OnEndDragSink( TDBImageDrag_MFUNCTOR( *this, &TForm::OnEndDrag ));
```

Attach the event source to the event sink by including the following code in your program:

```
TDBImage DBImage;          //Instantiate the source component
TForm form                 //Instantiate the sink component
DBImage.OnEndDragSource += form.OnEndDragSink;
```

OnEndDrag event for the TDBListBox component

This declaration of the event source is in the dblist.h header file:

```
TDBListBoxDragSource OnEndDragSource;
```

Include this declaration of the event sink in the class declaration of your sink object:

```
TDBListBoxDragSink OnEndDragSink;
```

Put a prototype for the handler method in the class declaration for your sink object:

```
void OnEndDrag( TDBListBoxDragSink& sink, TDBListBox& sender,
           TVbxControl& source, SHORT x, SHORT y );
```

Connect the handler method to the event sink by including the following in the class constructor:

```
OnEndDragSink( TDBListBoxDrag_MFUNCTOR( *this, &TForm::OnEndDrag ));
```

Attach the event source to the event sink by including the following code in your program:

```
TDBListBox DBListBox;      //Instantiate the source component
TForm form                 //Instantiate the sink component
DBListBox.OnEndDragSource += form.OnEndDragSink;
```

OnEndDrag event for the TDBLookupCombo component

This declaration of the event source is in the dblkupcb.h header file:

```
TDBLookupComboDragSource OnEndDragSource;
```

Include this declaration of the event sink in the class declaration of your sink object:

```
TDBLookupComboDragSink OnEndDragSink;
```

Put a prototype for the handler method in the class declaration for your sink object:

```
void OnEndDrag( TDBLookupComboDragSink& sink, TDBLookupCombo& sender,
           TVbxControl& source, SHORT x, SHORT y );
```

Connect the handler method to the event sink by including the following in the class constructor:

```
OnEndDragSink( TDBLookupComboDrag_MFUNCTOR( *this, &TForm::OnEndDrag ));
```

Attach the event source to the event sink by including the following code in your program:

```
TDBLookupCombo DBLookupCombo;      //Instantiate the source component
TForm form                         //Instantiate the sink component
DBLookupCombo.OnEndDragSource += form.OnEndDragSink;
```

OnEndDrag event for the TDBLookupList component

This declaration of the event source is in the dblkuplb.h header file:

```
TDBLookupListDragSource OnEndDragSource;
```

Include this declaration of the event sink in the class declaration of your sink object:

```
TDBLookupListDragSink TDBLookupListDragSinkOnEndDragSink;
```

Put a prototype for the handler method in the class declaration for your sink object:

```
void OnEndDrag( TDBLookupListDragSink& sink, TDBLookupList& sender,
                TVbxControl& source, SHORT x, SHORT y );
```

Connect the handler method to the event sink by including the following in the class constructor:

```
OnEndDragSink( TDBLookupListDrag_MFUNCTOR( *this, &TForm::OnEndDrag ));
```

Attach the event source to the event sink by including the following code in your program:

```
TDBLookupList DBLookupList;    //Instantiate the source component
TForm form                     //Instantiate the sink component
DBLookupList.OnEndDragSource += form.OnEndDragSink;
```

OnEndDrag event for the TDBMemo component

This declaration of the event source is in the dbmemo.h header file:

```
TDBMemoDragSource OnEndDragSource;
```

Include this declaration of the event sink in the class declaration of your sink object:

```
TDBMemoDragSink OnEndDragSink;
```

Put a prototype for the handler method in the class declaration for your sink object:

```
void OnEndDrag( TDBMemoDragSink& sink, TDBMemo& sender, TVbxControl& source,
                SHORT x, SHORT y );
```

Connect the handler method to the event sink by including the following in the class constructor:

```
OnEndDragSink( TDBMemoDrag_MFUNCTOR( *this, &TForm::OnEndDrag ));
```

Attach the event source to the event sink by including the following code in your program:

```
TDBMemo DBMemo;       //Instantiate the source component
TForm form            //Instantiate the sink component
DBMemo.OnEndDragSource += form.OnEndDragSink;
```

OnEndDrag event for the TDBNavigator component

This declaration of the event source is in the dbNavigator.h header file:

```
TDBNavigatorDragSource OnEndDragSource;
```

Include this declaration of the event sink in the class declaration of your sink object:

```
TDBNavigatorDragSink OnEndDragSink;
```

Put a prototype for the handler method in the class declaration for your sink object:

```
void OnEndDrag( TDBNavigatorDragSink& sink, TDBNavigator& sender,
                TVbxControl& source, SHORT x, SHORT y );
```

Connect the handler method to the event sink by including the following in the class constructor:

```
OnEndDragSink( TDBNavigatorDrag_MFUNCTOR( *this, &TForm::OnEndDrag ));
```

Attach the event source to the event sink by including the following code in your program:

```
TDBNavigator DBNavigator;            //Instantiate the source component
TForm form               //Instantiate the sink component
DBNavigator.OnEndDragSource += form.OnEndDragSink;
```

OnEndDrag event for the TDBRadioGroup component

This declaration of the event source is in the dbradio.h header file:

```
TDBRadioGroupDragSource OnEndDragSource;
```

Include this declaration of the event sink in the class declaration of your sink object:

```
TDBRadioGroupDragSink OnEndDragSink;
```

Put a prototype for the handler method in the class declaration for your sink object:

```
void OnEndDrag( TDBRadioGroupDragSink& sink, TDBRadioGroup& sender,
                TVbxControl& source, SHORT x, SHORT y );
```

Connect the handler method to the event sink by including the following in the class constructor:

```
OnEndDragSink( TDBRadioGroupDrag_MFUNCTOR( *this, &TForm::OnEndDrag ));
```

Attach the event source to the event sink by including the following code in your program:

```
TDBRadioGroup DBRadioGroup;      //Instantiate the source component
TForm form                       //Instantiate the sink component
DBRadioGroup.OnEndDragSource += form.OnEndDragSink;
```

OnEndDrag event for the DBText component

This declaration of the event source is in the dbtext.h header file:

```
TDBTextDragSource OnEndDragSource;
```

Include this declaration of the event sink in the class declaration of your sink object:

```
TDBTextDragSink OnEndDragSink;
```

Put a prototype for the handler method in the class declaration for your sink object:

```
void OnEndDrag( TDBTextDragSink& sink, TDBText& sender,
                TVbxControl& source, SHORT x, SHORT y );
```

Connect the handler method to the event sink by including the following in the class constructor:

```
OnEndDragSink( TDBTextDrag_MFUNCTOR( *this, &TForm::OnEndDrag ));
```

Attach the event source to the event sink by including the following code in your program:

```
TDBText DBText;              //Instantiate the source component
TForm form                  //Instantiate the sink component
DBText.OnEndDragSource += form.OnEndDragSink;
```

OnEnter event

Applies to   All data-aware controls

Header file   dbchkbx.h, dbcombo.h, dbedit.h, dbgrid.h, dbimage.h, dblist.h, dblkupcb.h, dblkuplb.h, dbNavigator.h, dbnvgtr.h, dbradio.h, dbtext.h

Description   The OnEnter event occurs when a control becomes active or receives the input focus. Use the OnEnter event handler to specify any special processing you want to occur when the control becomes active.

OnEnter event for the TDBCheckBox component

This declaration of the event source is in the dbchkbx.h header file:

```
TDBCheckBoxNotifySource OnEnterSource;
```

Include this declaration of the event sink in the class declaration of your sink object:

```
TDBCheckBoxNotifySink OnEnterSink;
```

Put a prototype for the handler method in the class declaration for your sink object:

```
void OnEnter( TDBCheckBoxNotifySink& sink, TDBCheckBox& sender );
```

Connect the handler method to the event sink by including the following in the class constructor:

```
OnEnterSink( TDBCheckBoxNotify_MFUNCTOR( *this, &TForm::OnEnter ));
```

Attach the event source to the event sink by including the following code in your program:

```
TDBCheckBox DBCheckBox;       //Instantiate the source component
TForm form                    //Instantiate the sink component
DBCheckBox.OnEnterSource += form.OnEnterSink;
```

OnEnter event for the TDBComboBox component

This declaration of the event source is in the dbcombo.h header file:

```
TDBComboBoxNotifySource OnEnterSource;
```

Include this declaration of the event sink in the class declaration of your sink object:

```
TDBComboBoxNotifySink OnEnterSink;
```

Put a prototype for the handler method in the class declaration for your sink object:

```
void OnEnter( TDBComboBoxNotifySink& sink, TDBComboBox& sender );
```

Connect the handler method to the event sink by including the following in the class constructor:

```
OnEnterSink( TDBComboBoxNotify_MFUNCTOR( *this, &TForm::OnEnter ));
```

Attach the event source to the event sink by including the following code in your program:

```
TDBComboBox DBComboBox;     //Instantiate the source component
TForm form                  //Instantiate the sink component
DBComboBox.OnEnterSource += form.OnEnterSink;
```

OnEnter event for the TDBEdit component

This declaration of the event source is in the dbedit.h header file:

```
TDBEditNotifySource OnEnterSource;
```

Include this declaration of the event sink in the class declaration of your sink object:

```
TDBEditNotifySink OnEnterSink;
```

Put a prototype for the handler method in the class declaration for your sink object:

```
void OnEnter( TDBEditNotifySink& sink, TDBEdit& sender );
```

Connect the handler method to the event sink by including the following in the class constructor:

```
OnEnterSink( TDBEditNotify_MFUNCTOR( *this, &TForm::OnEnter ));
```

Attach the event source to the event sink by including the following code in your program:

```
TDBEdit DBEdit;             //Instantiate the source component
TForm form                  //Instantiate the sink component
DBEdit.OnEnterSource += form.OnEnterSink;
```

OnEnter event for the TDBGrid component

This declaration of the event source is in the dbgrid.h header file:

```
TDBGridNotifySource OnEnterSource;
```

Include this declaration of the event sink in the class declaration of your sink object:

```
TDBGridNotifySink OnEnterSink;
```

Put a prototype for the handler method in the class declaration for your sink object:

```
void OnEnter( TDBGridNotifySink& sink, TDBGrid& sender );
```

Connect the handler method to the event sink by including the following in the class constructor:

```
OnEnterSink( TDBGridNotify_MFUNCTOR( *this, &TForm::OnEnter ));
```

Attach the event source to the event sink by including the following code in your program:

```
TDBGrid DBGrid;           //Instantiate the source component
TForm form                //Instantiate the sink component
DBGrid.OnEnterSource += form.OnEnterSink;
```

OnEnter event for the TDBImage component

This declaration of the event source is in the dbimage.h header file:

```
TDBImageNotifySource OnEnterSource;
```

Include this declaration of the event sink in the class declaration of your sink object:

```
TDBImageNotifySink OnEnterSink;
```

Put a prototype for the handler method in the class declaration for your sink object:

```
void OnEnter( TDBImageNotifySink& sink, TDBImage& sender );
```

Connect the handler method to the event sink by including the following in the class constructor:

```
OnEnterSink( TDBImageNotify_MFUNCTOR( *this, &TForm::OnEnter ));
```

Attach the event source to the event sink by including the following code in your program:

```
TDBImage DBImage;         //Instantiate the source component
TForm form                //Instantiate the sink component
DBImage.OnEnterSource += form.OnEnterSink;
```

OnEnter event for the TDBListBox component

This declaration of the event source is in the dblist.h header file:

```
TDBListBoxNotifySource OnEnterSource;
```

Include this declaration of the event sink in the class declaration of your sink object:

```
TDBListBoxNotifySink OnEnterSink;
```

Put a prototype for the handler method in the class declaration for your sink object:

```
void OnEnter( TDBListBoxNotifySink& sink, TDBListBox& sender );
```

Connect the handler method to the event sink by including the following in the class constructor:

```
OnEnterSink( TDBListBoxNotify_MFUNCTOR( *this, &TForm::OnEnter ));
```

Attach the event source to the event sink by including the following code in your program:

```
TDBListBox DBListBox;     //Instantiate the source component
TForm form                //Instantiate the sink component
DBListBox.OnEnterSource += form.OnEnterSink;
```

OnEnter event for the TDBLookupCombo component

This declaration of the event source is in the dblkupcb.h header file:

```
TDBLookupComboNotifySource OnEnterSource;
```

Include this declaration of the event sink in the class declaration of your sink object:

```
TDBLookupComboNotifySink OnEnterSink;
```

Put a prototype for the handler method in the class declaration for your sink object:

```
void OnEnter( TDBLookupComboNotifySink& sink, TDBLookupCombo& sender );
```

Connect the handler method to the event sink by including the following in the class constructor:

```
OnEnterSink( TDBLookupComboNotify_MFUNCTOR( *this, &TForm::OnEnter ));
```

Attach the event source to the event sink by including the following code in your program:

```
TDBLookupCombo DBLookupCombo;       //Instantiate the source component
TForm form                          //Instantiate the sink component
DBLookupCombo.OnEnterSource += form.OnEnterSink;
```

OnEnter event for the TDBLookupList component

This declaration of the event source is in the dblkuplb.h header file:

```
TDBLookupListNotifySource OnEnterSource;
```

Include this declaration of the event sink in the class declaration of your sink object:

```
TDBLookupListNotifySink OnEnterSink;
```

Put a prototype for the handler method in the class declaration for your sink object:

```
void OnEnter( TDBLookupListNotifySink& sink, TDBLookupList& sender );
```

Connect the handler method to the event sink by including the following in the class constructor:

```
OnEnterSink( TDBLookupListNotify_MFUNCTOR( *this, &TForm::OnEnter ));
```

Attach the event source to the event sink by including the following code in your program:

```
TDBLookupList DBLookupList;       //Instantiate the source component
TForm form                        //Instantiate the sink component
DBLookupList.OnEnterSource += form.OnEnterSink;
```

OnEnter event for the TDBMemo component

This declaration of the event source is in the dbmemo.h header file:

```
TDBMemoNotifySource OnEnterSource;
```

Include this declaration of the event sink in the class declaration of your sink object:

```
TDBMemoNotifySink OnEnterSink;
```

Put a prototype for the handler method in the class declaration for your sink object:

```
void OnEnter( TDBMemoNotifySink& sink, TDBMemo& sender );
```

Connect the handler method to the event sink by including the following in the class constructor:

```
OnEnterSink( TDBMemoNotify_MFUNCTOR( *this, &TForm::OnEnter ));
```

Attach the event source to the event sink by including the following code in your program:

```
TDBMemo DBMemo;           //Instantiate the source component
TForm form                //Instantiate the sink component
DBMemo.OnEnterSource += form.OnEnterSink;
```

OnEnter event for the DBText component

This declaration of the event source is in the dbtext.h header file:

```
TDBTextNotifySource OnEnterSource;
```

Include this declaration of the event sink in the class declaration of your sink object:

```
TDBTextNotifySink OnEnterSink;
```

Put a prototype for the handler method in the class declaration for your sink object:

```
void OnEnter( TDBTextNotifySink& sink, TDBText& sender );
```

Connect the handler method to the event sink by including the following in the class constructor:

```
OnEnterSink( TDBTextNotify_MFUNCTOR( *this, &TForm::OnEnter ));
```

Attach the event source to the event sink by including the following code in your program:

```
TDBText DBText;           //Instantiate the source component
TForm form                //Instantiate the sink component
DBText.OnEnterSource += form.OnEnterSink;
```

OnExit event

Applies to   All data-aware controls

Header file   dbchkbx.h, dbcombo.h, dbedit.h, dbgrid.h, dbimage.h, dblist.h, dblkupcb.h, dblkuplb.h, dbNavigator.h, dbnvgtr.h, dbradio.h, dbtext.h

Description   The OnExit event occurs when the input focus shifts away from one control to another. Use the OnExit event handler when you want special processing to occur when this control ceases to be active.

OnExit event for the TDBCheckBox component

This declaration of the event source is in the dbchkbx.h header file:

```
TDBCheckBoxNotifySource OnExitSource;
```

Include this declaration of the event sink in the class declaration of your sink object:

```
TDBCheckBoxNotifySink OnExitSink;
```

Put a prototype for the handler method in the class declaration for your sink object:

```
void OnExit( TDBCheckBoxNotifySink& sink, TDBCheckBox& sender );
```

Connect the handler method to the event sink by including the following in the class constructor:

```
OnExitSink( TDBCheckBoxNotify_MFUNCTOR( *this, &TForm::OnExit ));
```

Attach the event source to the event sink by including the following code in your program:

```
TDBCheckBox DBCheckBox;         //Instantiate the source component
TForm form                      //Instantiate the sink component
DBCheckBox.OnExitSource += form.OnExitSink;
```

OnExit event for the TDBComboBox component

This declaration of the event source is in the dbcombo.h header file:

```
TDBComboBoxNotifySource OnExitSource;
```

Include this declaration of the event sink in the class declaration of your sink object:

```
TDBComboBoxNotifySink OnExitSink;
```

Put a prototype for the handler method in the class declaration for your sink object:

```
void OnExit( TDBComboBoxNotifySink& sink, TDBComboBox& sender );
```

Connect the handler method to the event sink by including the following in the class constructor:

```
OnExitSink( TDBComboBoxNotify_MFUNCTOR( *this, &TForm::OnExit ));
```

Attach the event source to the event sink by including the following code in your program:

```
TDBComboBox DBComboBox;        //Instantiate the source component
TForm form                     //Instantiate the sink component
DBComboBox.OnExitSource += form.OnExitSink;
```

OnExit event for the TDBEdit component

This declaration of the event source is in the dbedit.h header file:

```
TDBEditNotifySource OnExitSource;
```

Include this declaration of the event sink in the class declaration of your sink object:

```
TDBEditNotifySink OnExitSink;
```

Put a prototype for the handler method in the class declaration for your sink object:

```
void OnExit( TDBEditNotifySink& sink, TDBEdit& sender );
```

Connect the handler method to the event sink by including the following in the class constructor:

```
OnExitSink( TDBEditNotify_MFUNCTOR( *this, &TForm::OnExit ));
```

Attach the event source to the event sink by including the following code in your program:

```
TDBEdit DBEdit;              //Instantiate the source component
TForm form                   //Instantiate the sink component
DBEdit.OnExitSource += form.OnExitSink;
```

OnExit event for the TDBGrid component

This declaration of the event source is in the dbgrid.h header file:

```
TDBGridNotifySource OnExitSource;
```

Include this declaration of the event sink in the class declaration of your sink object:

```
TDBGridNotifySink OnExitSink;
```

Put a prototype for the handler method in the class declaration for your sink object:

```
void OnExit( TDBGridNotifySink& sink, TDBGrid& sender );
```

Connect the handler method to the event sink by including the following in the class constructor:

```
OnExitSink( TDBGridNotify_MFUNCTOR( *this, &TForm::OnExit ));
```

Attach the event source to the event sink by including the following code in your program:

```
TDBGrid DBGrid;              //Instantiate the source component
TForm form                   //Instantiate the sink component
DBGrid.OnExitSource += form.OnExitSink;
```

OnExit event for the TDBImage component

This declaration of the event source is in the dbimage.h header file:

```
TDBImageNotifySource OnExitSource;
```

Include this declaration of the event sink in the class declaration of your sink object:

```
TDBImageNotifySink OnExitSink;
```

Put a prototype for the handler method in the class declaration for your sink object:

```
void OnExit( TDBImageNotifySink& sink, TDBImage& sender );
```

Connect the handler method to the event sink by including the following in the class constructor:

```
OnExitSink( TDBImageNotify_MFUNCTOR( *this, &TForm::OnExit ));
```

Attach the event source to the event sink by including the following code in your program:

```
TDBImage DBImage;        //Instantiate the source component
TForm form              //Instantiate the sink component
DBImage.OnExitSource += form.OnExitSink;
```

OnExit event for the TDBListBox component

This declaration of the event source is in the dblist.h header file:

```
TDBListBoxNotifySource OnExitSource;
```

Include this declaration of the event sink in the class declaration of your sink object:

```
TDBListBoxNotifySink OnExitSink;
```

Put a prototype for the handler method in the class declaration for your sink object:

```
void OnExit( TDBListBoxNotifySink& sink, TDBListBox& sender );
```

Connect the handler method to the event sink by including the following in the class constructor:

```
OnExitSink( TDBListBoxNotify_MFUNCTOR( *this, &TForm::OnExit ));
```

Attach the event source to the event sink by including the following code in your program:

```
TDBListBox DBListBox;     //Instantiate the source component
TForm form               //Instantiate the sink component
DBListBox.OnExitSource += form.OnExitSink;
```

OnExit event for the TDBLookupCombo component

This declaration of the event source is in the dblkupcb.h header file:

```
TDBLookupComboNotifySource OnExitSource;
```

Include this declaration of the event sink in the class declaration of your sink object:

```
TDBLookupComboNotifySink OnExitSink;
```

Put a prototype for the handler method in the class declaration for your sink object:

```
void OnExit( TDBLookupComboNotifySink& sink, TDBLookupCombo& sender );
```

Connect the handler method to the event sink by including the following in the class constructor:

```
OnExitSink( TDBLookupComboNotify_MFUNCTOR( *this, &TForm::OnExit ));
```

Attach the event source to the event sink by including the following code in your program:

```
TDBLookupCombo DBLookupCombo;        //Instantiate the source component
TForm form                           //Instantiate the sink component
DBLookupCombo.OnExitSource += form.OnExitSink;
```

OnExit event for the TDBLookupList component

This declaration of the event source is in the dblkuplb.h header file:

```
TDBLookupListNotifySource OnExitSource;
```

Include this declaration of the event sink in the class declaration of your sink object:

```
TDBLookupListNotifySink OnExitSink;
```

Put a prototype for the handler method in the class declaration for your sink object:

```
void OnExit( TDBLookupListNotifySink& sink, TDBLookupList& sender );
```

Connect the handler method to the event sink by including the following in the class constructor:

```
OnExitSink( TDBLookupListNotify_MFUNCTOR( *this, &TForm::OnExit ));
```

Attach the event source to the event sink by including the following code in your program:

```
TDBLookupList DBLookupList;       //Instantiate the source component
TForm form                        //Instantiate the sink component
DBLookupList.OnExitSource += form.OnExitSink;
```

OnExit event for the TDBMemo component

This declaration of the event source is in the dbmemo.h header file:

```
TDBMemoNotifySource OnExitSource;
```

Include this declaration of the event sink in the class declaration of your sink object:

```
TDBMemoNotifySink OnExitSink;
```

Put a prototype for the handler method in the class declaration for your sink object:

```
void OnExit( TDBMemoNotifySink& sink, TDBMemo& sender );
```

Connect the handler method to the event sink by including the following in the class constructor:

```
OnExitSink( TDBMemoNotify_MFUNCTOR( *this, &TForm::OnExit ));
```

Attach the event source to the event sink by including the following code in your program:

```
TDBMemo DBMemo;        //Instantiate the source component
TForm form             //Instantiate the sink component
DBMemo.OnExitSource += form.OnExitSink;
```

OnExit event for the DBText component

This declaration of the event source is in the dbtext.h header file:

```
TDBTextNotifySource OnExitSource;
```

Include this declaration of the event sink in the class declaration of your sink object:

```
TDBTextNotifySink OnExitSink;
```

Put a prototype for the handler method in the class declaration for your sink object:

```
void OnExit( TDBTextNotifySink& sink, TDBText& sender );
```

Connect the handler method to the event sink by including the following in the class constructor:

```
OnExitSink( TDBTextNotify_MFUNCTOR( *this, &TForm::OnExit ));
```

Attach the event source to the event sink by including the following code in your program:

```
TDBText DBText;          //Instantiate the source component
TForm form               //Instantiate the sink component
DBText.OnExitSource += form.OnExitSink;
```

OnGetText event

Applies to   all TField components

Description   The OnGetText event is activated when the DisplayText or Text properties are accessed.

This will be the declaration of the OnGetText event handler in your code:

```
void OnGetText( TFieldGetTextSink& sink, TField& sender, string& text,
              bool displaytext );
```

The text parameter refers to the text contained in the field.

The displaytext parameter indicates if the event should supply the text in display format or in edit format for the Text property. If OnGetText has been assigned a method, the default processing for DisplayText or Text does not occur; the event handler is expected to perform any conversion required to display the value.

By assigning a method to this property, you can take any special actions required by the event.

Source declaration   This declaration of the event source is in the header file:

```
TFieldGetTextSource OnGetTextSource;
```

Sink declaration   Include this declaration of the event sink in the class declaration for your sink object:

```
TFieldGetTextSink OnGetTextSink;
```

Handler   Put a prototype for the handler method in the class declaration for your sink object:

```
void OnGetText( TFieldGetTextSink& sink, TField& sender, string& text,
            bool displaytext );
```

And connect the handler method, which you have implemented, to the event sink by including the following in the class constructor:

```
OnGetTextSink( TFieldGetText_MFUNCTOR( *this, &TForm::OnGetText ))
```

Attachment   Attach the event source to the event sink by including the following in your program:

```
TField field;      //Instantiate the source component
TForm form;        //Instantiate the sink component
field.OnGetTextSource += form.OnGetTextSink;
```

OnKeyDown event

Applies to   TDBCheckBox, TDBComboBox, TDBEdit, TDBGrid, TDBImage, TDBListBox, TDBLookupCombo, TDBNavigator components

Header file   dbchkbx.h, dbcombo.h, dbedit.h, dbgrid.h, dbimage.h, dblist.h, dblkupcb.h, dbnavigator.h

Description   The OnKeyDown event occurs when a user presses any key while the control has focus. Use the OnKeyDown event handler to specify special processing to occur when a key is pressed. The OnKeyDown handler can respond to all keyboard keys including function keys and keys combined with the *Shift*, *Ctrl*, and *Alt* keys.

This will be the declaration for the OnKeyDown event handler for a database check box; if your event handler is for another control, substitute the name of that control for TDBCheckBox:

```
void OnKeyDown( TDBCheckBoxKeySink& sink, TDBCheckBox& sender, SHORT* scancode,
            TShiftState shift );
```

The scancode parameter of the OnKeyDown event is a virtual key code. You can find a list of virtual key codes in the Windows API Help.

The shift parameter may be one or a combination of these possible states:

Value	Meaning
0	No special keys are held down when the key is pressed.
1	The Shift key is held down.
2	The Ctrl key is held down.
4	The Alt key is held down.

OnKeyDown event for the TDBCheckBox component

This declaration of the event source is in the dbchkbx.h header file:

```
TDBCheckBoxKeySource OnKeyDownSource;
```

Include this declaration of the event sink in the class declaration of your sink object:

```
TDBCheckBoxKeySink OnKeyDownSink;
```

Put a prototype for the handler method in the class declaration for your sink object:

```
void OnKeyDown( TDBCheckBoxKeySink& sink, TDBCheckBox& sender, SHORT* scancode,
         TShiftState shift );
```

Connect the handler method to the event sink by including the following in the class constructor:

```
OnKeyDownSink( TDBCheckBoxKey_MFUNCTOR( *this, &TForm::OnKeyDown ));
```

Attach the event source to the event sink by including the following code in your program:

```
TDBCheckBox DBCheckBox;        //Instantiate the source component
TForm form                     //Instantiate the sink component
DBCheckBox.OnKeyDownSource += form.OnKeyDownSink;
```

OnKeyDown event for the TDBComboBox component

This declaration of the event source is in the dbcombo.h header file:

```
TDBComboBoxKeySource OnKeyDownSource;
```

Include this declaration of the event sink in the class declaration of your sink object:

```
TDBComboBoxKeySink OnKeyDownSink;
```

Put a prototype for the handler method in the class declaration for your sink object:

```
void OnKeyDown( TDBComboBoxKeySink& sink, TDBComboBox& sender, SHORT* scancode,
         TShiftState shift );
```

Connect the handler method to the event sink by including the following in the class constructor:

```
OnKeyDownSink( TDBComboBoxKey_MFUNCTOR( *this, &TForm::OnKeyDown ));
```

Attach the event source to the event sink by including the following code in your program:

```
TDBComboBox DBComboBox;        //Instantiate the source component
TForm form                     //Instantiate the sink component
DBComboBox.OnKeyDownSource += form.OnKeyDownSink;
```

OnKeyDown event for the TDBEdit component

This declaration of the event source is in the dbedit.h header file:

```
TDBEditKeySource OnKeyDownSource;
```

Include this declaration of the event sink in the class declaration of your sink object:

```
TDBEditKeySink OnKeyDownSink;
```

Put a prototype for the handler method in the class declaration for your sink object:

```
void OnKeyDown( TDBEditKeySink& sink, TDBEdit& sender, SHORT* scancode,
          TShiftState shift );
```

Connect the handler method to the event sink by including the following in the class constructor:

```
OnKeyDownSink( TDBEditKey_MFUNCTOR( *this, &TForm::OnKeyDown ));
```

Attach the event source to the event sink by including the following code in your program:

```
TDBEdit DBEdit;              //Instantiate the source component
TForm form                   //Instantiate the sink component
DBEdit.OnKeyDownSource += form.OnKeyDownSink;
```

OnKeyDown event for the TDBGrid component

This declaration of the event source is in the dbgrid.h header file:

```
TDBGridKeySource OnKeyDownSource;
```

Include this declaration of the event sink in the class declaration of your sink object:

```
TDBGridKeySink OnKeyDownSink;
```

Put a prototype for the handler method in the class declaration for your sink object:

```
void OnKeyDown( TDBGridKeySink& sink, TDBGrid& sender, SHORT* scancode,
          TShiftState shift );
```

Connect the handler method to the event sink by including the following in the class constructor:

```
OnKeyDownSink( TDBGridKey_MFUNCTOR( *this, &TForm::OnKeyDown ));
```

Attach the event source to the event sink by including the following code in your program:

```
TDBGrid DBGrid;           //Instantiate the source component
TForm form                //Instantiate the sink component
DBGrid.On\KeyDownSource += form.OnKeyDownSink;
```

OnKeyDown event for the TDBImage component

This declaration of the event source is in the dbimage.h header file:

```
TDBImageKeySource OnKeyDownSource;
```

Include this declaration of the event sink in the class declaration of your sink object:

```
TDBImageKeySink OnKeyDownSink;
```

Put a prototype for the handler method in the class declaration for your sink object:

```
void OnKeyDown( TDBImageKeySink& sink, TDBImage& sender, SHORT* scancode,
          TShiftState shift );
```

Connect the handler method to the event sink by including the following in the class constructor:

```
OnKeyDownSink( TDBImageKey_MFUNCTOR( *this, &TForm::OnKeyDown ));
```

Attach the event source to the event sink by including the following code in your program:

```
TDBImage DBImage;          //Instantiate the source component
TForm form                 //Instantiate the sink component
DBImage.OnKeyDownSource += form.OnKeyDownSink;
```

OnKeyDown event for the TDBListBox component

This declaration of the event source is in the dblist.h header file:

```
TDBListBoxKeySource OnKeyDownSource;
```

Include this declaration of the event sink in the class declaration of your sink object:

```
TDBListBoxKeySink OnKeyDownSink;
```

Put a prototype for the handler method in the class declaration for your sink object:

```
void OnKeyDown( TDBListBoxKeySink& sink, TDBListBox& sender, SHORT* scancode,
          TShiftState shift );
```

Connect the handler method to the event sink by including the following in the class constructor:

```
OnKeyDownSink( TDBListBoxKey_MFUNCTOR( *this, &TForm::OnKeyDown ));
```

Attach the event source to the event sink by including the following code in your program:

```
TDBListBox DBListBox;      //Instantiate the source component
TForm form                 //Instantiate the sink component
DBListBox.OnKeyDownSource += form.OnKeyDownSink;
```

OnKeyDown event for the TDBLookupCombo component

This declaration of the event source is in the dblkupcb.h header file:

```
TDBLookupComboKeySource OnKeyDownSource;
```

Include this declaration of the event sink in the class declaration of your sink object:

```
TDBLookupComboKeySink OnKeyDownSink;
```

Put a prototype for the handler method in the class declaration for your sink object:

```
void OnKeyDown( TDBLookupComboKeySink& sink, TDBLookupCombo& sender,
          SHORT* scancode, TShiftState shift );
```

Connect the handler method to the event sink by including the following in the class constructor:

```
OnKeyDownSink( TDBLookupComboKey_MFUNCTOR( *this, &TForm::OnKeyDown ));
```

Attach the event source to the event sink by including the following code in your program:

```
TDBLookupCombo DBLookupCombo;      //Instantiate the source component
TForm form                        //Instantiate the sink component
DBLookupCombo.OnKeyDownSource += form.OnKeyDownSink;
```

OnKeyDown event for the TDBLookupList component

This declaration of the event source is in the dblkuplb.h header file:

```
TDBLookupListKeySource OnKeyDownSource;
```

Include this declaration of the event sink in the class declaration of your sink object:

```
TDBLookupListKeySink OnKeyDownSink;
```

Put a prototype for the handler method in the class declaration for your sink object:

```
void OnKeyDown( TDBLookupListKeySink& sink, TDBLookupList& sender,
             SHORT* scancode, TShiftState shift );
```

Connect the handler method to the event sink by including the following in the class constructor:

```
OnKeyDownSink( TDBLookupListKey_MFUNCTOR( *this, &TForm::OnKeyDown ));
```

Attach the event source to the event sink by including the following code in your program:

```
TDBLookupList DBLookupList;      //Instantiate the source component
TForm form                       //Instantiate the sink component
DBLookupList.OnKeyDownSource += form.OnKeyDownSink;
```

OnKeyDown event for the TDBMemo component

This declaration of the event source is in the dbmemo.h header file:

```
TDBMemoKeySource OnKeyDownSource;
```

Include this declaration of the event sink in the class declaration of your sink object:

```
TDBMemoKeySink OnKeyDownSink;
```

Put a prototype for the handler method in the class declaration for your sink object:

```
void OnKeyDown( TDBMemoKeySink& sink, TDBMemo& sender, SHORT* scancode,
             TShiftState shift );
```

Connect the handler method to the event sink by including the following in the class constructor:

```
OnKeyDownSink( TDBMemoKey_MFUNCTOR( *this, &TForm::OnKeyDown ));
```

Attach the event source to the event sink by including the following code in your program:

```
TDBMemo DBMemo;          //Instantiate the source component
TForm form               //Instantiate the sink component
DBMemo.OnKeyDownSource += form.OnKeyDownSink;
```

OnKeyPress event

Applies to   TDBCheckBox, TDBComboBox, TDBEdit, TDBGrid, TDBImage, TDBListBox, TDBLookupCombo, TDBNavigator components

Header file   dbchkbx.h, dbcombo.h, dbedit.h, dbgrid.h, dbimage.h, dblist.h, dblkupcb.h, dbNavigator.h

Description   The OnKeyPress event occurs when a user presses a single character key. Use the OnKeyPress event handler when you want something to happen as a result of pressing a single key.

This will be the declaration for the OnKeyPress event handler for a database checkbox; if your event handler is for another component, substitute the name of that component for TDBCheckBox:

```
void OnKeyPress( TDBCheckBoxKeyPressSink& sink, TDBCheckBox& sender,
                SHORT keycode );
```

The keycode parameter in the OnKeyPress event handler returns a standard numeric ANSI key code. keycode can be any printable keyboard character, the Ctrl key combined with an alphabetic character, or the Enter or Backspace key.

You can use the OnKeyPress event to intercept keystrokes and test them to see if they are valid or to format the typed characters.

If you want your application to respond to key events that are not ANSI key codes, such as function keys, cursor keys, and any Ctrl, Alt, or Shift key combinations, use the use the OnKeyUp or OnKeyDown events.

OnKeyPress event for the TDBCheckBox component

This declaration of the event source is in the dbchkbx.h header file:

```
TDBCheckBoxKeyPressSource OnKeyPressSource;
```

Include this declaration of the event sink in the class declaration of your sink object:

```
TDBCheckBoxKeyPressSink OnKeyPressSink;
```

Put a prototype for the handler method in the class declaration for your sink object:

```
void OnKeyPress( TDBCheckBoxKeyPressSink& sink, TDBCheckBox& sender,
                SHORT keycode );
```

Connect the handler method to the event sink by including the following in the class constructor:

```
OnKeyPressSink( TDBCheckBoxKey_MFUNCTOR( *this, &TForm::OnKeyPress ));
```

Attach the event source to the event sink by including the following code in your program:

```
TDBCheckBox DBCheckBox;          //Instantiate the source component
TForm form                       //Instantiate the sink component
DBCheckBox.OnKeyPressSource += form.OnKeyPressSink;
```

OnKeyPress event for the TDBComboBox component

This declaration of the event source is in the dbcombo.h header file:

```
TDBComboBoxKeyPressSource OnKeyPressSource;
```

Include this declaration of the event sink in the class declaration of your sink object:

```
TDBComboBoxKeyPressSink OnKeyPressSink;
```

Put a prototype for the handler method in the class declaration for your sink object:

```
void OnKeyPress( TDBComboBoxKeyPressSink& sink, TDBComboBox& sender,
                 SHORT keycode );
```

Connect the handler method to the event sink by including the following in the class constructor:

```
OnKeyPressSink( TDBComboBoxKey_MFUNCTOR( *this, &TForm::OnKeyPress ));
```

Attach the event source to the event sink by including the following code in your program:

```
TDBComboBox DBComboBox;          //Instantiate the source component
TForm form                       //Instantiate the sink component
DBComboBox.OnKeyPressSource += form.OnKeyPressSink;
```

OnKeyPress event for the TDBEdit component

This declaration of the event source is in the dbedit.h header file:

```
TDBEditKeyPressSource OnKeyPressSource;
```

Include this declaration of the event sink in the class declaration of your sink object:

```
TDBEditKeyPressSink OnKeyPressSink;
```

Put a prototype for the handler method in the class declaration for your sink object:

```
void OnKeyPress( TDBEditKeyPressSink& sink, TDBEdit& sender, SHORT keycode );
```

Connect the handler method to the event sink by including the following in the class constructor:

```
OnKeyPressSink( TDBEditKey_MFUNCTOR( *this, &TForm::OnKeyPress ));
```

Attach the event source to the event sink by including the following code in your program:

```
TDBEdit DBEdit;                  //Instantiate the source component
TForm form                       //Instantiate the sink component
DBEdit.OnKeyPressSource += form.OnKeyPressSink;
```

OnKeyPress event for the TDBGrid component

This declaration of the event source is in the dbgrid.h header file:

```
TDBGridKeyPressSource OnKeyPressSource;
```

Include this declaration of the event sink in the class declaration of your sink object:

```
TDBGridKeyPressSink OnKeyPressSink;
```

Put a prototype for the handler method in the class declaration for your sink object:

```
void OnKeyPress( TDBGridKeyPressSink& sink, TDBGrid& sender, SHORT keycode );
```

Connect the handler method to the event sink by including the following in the class constructor:

```
OnKeyPressSink( TDBGridKey_MFUNCTOR( *this, &TForm::OnKeyPress ));
```

Attach the event source to the event sink by including the following code in your program:

```
TDBGrid DBGrid;          //Instantiate the source component
TForm form               //Instantiate the sink component
DBGrid.OnKeyPressSource += form.OnKeyPressSink;
```

OnKeyPress event for the TDBImage component

This declaration of the event source is in the dbimage.h header file:

```
TDBImageKeyPressSource OnKeyPressSource;
```

Include this declaration of the event sink in the class declaration of your sink object:

```
TDBImageKeyPressSink OnKeyPressSink;
```

Put a prototype for the handler method in the class declaration for your sink object:

```
void OnKeyPress( TDBImageKeyPressSink& sink, TDBImage& sender, SHORT keycode );
```

Connect the handler method to the event sink by including the following in the class constructor:

```
OnKeyPressSink( TDBImageKey_MFUNCTOR( *this, &TForm::OnKeyPress ));
```

Attach the event source to the event sink by including the following code in your program:

```
TDBImage DBImage;        //Instantiate the source component
TForm form               //Instantiate the sink component
DBImage.OnKeyPressSource += form.OnKeyPressSink;
```

OnKeyPress event for the TDBListBox component

This declaration of the event source is in the dblist.h header file:

```
TDBListBoxKeyPressSource OnKeyPressSource;
```

Include this declaration of the event sink in the class declaration of your sink object:

```
TDBListBoxKeyPressSink OnKeyPressSink;
```

Put a prototype for the handler method in the class declaration for your sink object:

```
void OnKeyPress( TDBListBoxKeyPressSink& sink, TDBListBox& sender,
                 SHORT keycode );
```

Connect the handler method to the event sink by including the following in the class constructor:

```
OnKeyPressSink( TDBListBoxKey_MFUNCTOR( *this, &TForm::OnKeyPress ));
```

Attach the event source to the event sink by including the following code in your program:

```
TDBListBox DBListBox;      //Instantiate the source component
TForm form                 //Instantiate the sink component
DBListBox.OnKeyPressSource += form.OnKeyPressSink;
```

OnKeyPress event for the TDBLookupCombo component

This declaration of the event source is in the dblkupcb.h header file:

```
TDBLookupComboKeyPressSource OnKeyPressSource;
```

Include this declaration of the event sink in the class declaration of your sink object:

```
TDBLookupComboKeyPressSink OnKeyPressSink;
```

Put a prototype for the handler method in the class declaration for your sink object:

```
void OnKeyPress( TDBLookupComboKeyPressSink& sink, TDBLookupCombo& sender,
                 SHORT keycode );
```

Connect the handler method to the event sink by including the following in the class constructor:

```
OnKeyPressSink( TDBLookupComboKey_MFUNCTOR( *this, &TForm::OnKeyPress ));
```

Attach the event source to the event sink by including the following code in your program:

```
TDBLookupCombo DBLookupCombo;     //Instantiate the source component
TForm form                        //Instantiate the sink component
DBLookupCombo.OnKeyPressSource += form.OnKeyPressSink;
```

OnKeyPress event for the TDBLookupList component

This declaration of the event source is in the dblkuplb.h header file:

```
TDBLookupListKeyPressSource OnKeyPressSource;
```

Include this declaration of the event sink in the class declaration of your sink object:

```
TDBLookupListKeyPressSink OnKeyPressSink;
```

Put a prototype for the handler method in the class declaration for your sink object:

```
void OnKeyPress( TDBLookupListKeyPressSink& sink, TDBLookupList& sender,
                 SHORT keycode );
```

Connect the handler method to the event sink by including the following in the class constructor:

```
OnKeyPressSink( TDBLookupListKey_MFUNCTOR( *this, &TForm::OnKeyPress ));
```

Attach the event source to the event sink by including the following code in your program:

```
TDBLookupList DBLookupList;    //Instantiate the source component
TForm form                     //Instantiate the sink component
DBLookupList.OnKeyPressSource += form.OnKeyPressSink;
```

OnKeyPress event for the TDBMemo component

This declaration of the event source is in the dbmemo.h header file:

```
TDBMemoKeyPressSource OnKeyPressSource;
```

Include this declaration of the event sink in the class declaration of your sink object:

```
TDBMemoKeyPressSink OnKeyPressSink;
```

Put a prototype for the handler method in the class declaration for your sink object:

```
void OnKeyPress( TDBMemoKeyPressSink& sink, TDBMemo& sender, SHORT keycode );
```

Connect the handler method to the event sink by including the following in the class constructor:

```
OnKeyPressSink( TDBMemoKey_MFUNCTOR( *this, &TForm::OnKeyPress ));
```

Attach the event source to the event sink by including the following code in your program:

```
TDBMemo DBMemo;            //Instantiate the source component
TForm form                 //Instantiate the sink component
DBMemo.OnKeyPressSource += form.OnKeyPressSink;
```

OnKeyUp event

Applies to   TDBCheckBox, TDBComboBox, TDBEdit, TDBGrid, TDBImage, TDBListBox, TDBLookupCombo, TDBNavigator components

Header file   dbchkbx.h, dbcombo.h, dbedit.h, dbgrid.h, dbimage.h, dblist.h, dblkupcb.h, dbNavigator.h

Description   The OnKeyUp event occurs when the user releases a key that has been pressed. Use the OnKeyUp event handler when you want special processing to occur when a key is released. The OnKeyUp handler can respond to all keyboard keys including function keys and Shift, Ctrl, and Alt key combinations.

This will be the declaration for the OnKeyDown event handler for a database check box; if your event handler is for another control, substitute the name of that control for TDBCheckBox:

```
void OnKeyUp( TDBCheckBoxKeySink& sink, TDBCheckBox& sender, SHORT* scancode,
             TShiftState shift );
```

The scancode parameter of the OnKeyDown event is a virtual key code. You can find a list of virtual key codes in the Windows API Help.

The shift parameter may be one or a combination of these possible states:

Value	Meaning
0	No special keys are held down when the key is pressed.
1	The Shift key is held down.
2	The Ctrl key is held down.
4	The Alt key is held down.

OnKeyUp event for the TDBCheckBox component

This declaration of the event source is in the dbchkbx.h header file:

```
TDBCheckBoxKeySource OnKeyUpSource;
```

Include this declaration of the event sink in the class declaration of your sink object:

```
TDBCheckBoxKeySink OnKeyUpSink;
```

Put a prototype for the handler method in the class declaration for your sink object:

```
void OnKeyUp( TDBCheckBoxKeySink& sink, TDBCheckBox& sender, SHORT* scancode,
        TShiftState shift );
```

Connect the handler method to the event sink by including the following in the class constructor:

```
OnKeyUpSink( TDBCheckBoxKey_MFUNCTOR( *this, &TForm::OnKeyUp ));
```

Attach the event source to the event sink by including the following code in your program:

```
TDBCheckBox DBCheckBox;         //Instantiate the source component
TForm form                      //Instantiate the sink component
DBCheckBox.OnKeyUpSource += form.OnKeyUpSink;
```

OnKeyUp event for the TDBComboBox component

This declaration of the event source is in the dbcombo.h header file:

```
TDBComboBoxKeySource OnKeyUpSource;
```

Include this declaration of the event sink in the class declaration of your sink object:

```
TDBComboBoxKeySink OnKeyUpSink;
```

Put a prototype for the handler method in the class declaration for your sink object:

```
void OnKeyUp( TDBComboBoxKeySink& sink, TDBComboBox& sender, SHORT* scancode,
        TShiftState shift );
```

Connect the handler method to the event sink by including the following in the class constructor:

```
OnKeyUpSink( TDBComboBoxKey_MFUNCTOR( *this, &TForm::OnKeyUp ));
```

Attach the event source to the event sink by including the following code in your program:

```
TDBComboBox DBComboBox;      //Instantiate the source component
TForm form                  //Instantiate the sink component
DBComboBox.OnKeyUpSource += form.OnKeyUpSink;
```

OnKeyUp event for the TDBEdit component

This declaration of the event source is in the dbedit.h header file:

```
TDBEditKeySource OnKeyUpSource;
```

Include this declaration of the event sink in the class declaration of your sink object:

```
TDBEditKeySink OnKeyUpSink;
```

Put a prototype for the handler method in the class declaration for your sink object:

```
void OnKeyUp( TDBEditKeySink& sink, TDBEdit& sender, SHORT* scancode,
              TShiftState shift );
```

Connect the handler method to the event sink by including the following in the class constructor:

```
OnKeyUpSink( TDBEditKey_MFUNCTOR( *this, &TForm::OnKeyUp ));
```

Attach the event source to the event sink by including the following code in your program:

```
TDBEdit DBEdit;             //Instantiate the source component
TForm form                  //Instantiate the sink component
DBEdit.OnKeyUpSource += form.OnKeyUpSink;
```

OnKeyUp event for the TDBGrid component

This declaration of the event source is in the dbgrid.h header file:

```
TDBGridKeySource OnKeyUpSource;
```

Include this declaration of the event sink in the class declaration of your sink object:

```
TDBGridKeySink OnKeyUpSink;
```

Put a prototype for the handler method in the class declaration for your sink object:

```
void OnKeyUp( TDBGridKeySink& sink, TDBGrid& sender, SHORT* scancode,
              TShiftState shift );
```

Connect the handler method to the event sink by including the following in the class constructor:

```
OnKeyUpSink( TDBGridKey_MFUNCTOR( *this, &TForm::OnKeyUp ));
```

Attach the event source to the event sink by including the following code in your program:

```
TDBGrid DBGrid;            //Instantiate the source component
TForm form                 //Instantiate the sink component
DBGrid.OnKeyUpSource += form.OnKeyUpSink;
```

OnKeyUp event for the TDBImage component

This declaration of the event source is in the dbimage.h header file:

```
TDBImageKeySource OnKeyUpSource;
```

Include this declaration of the event sink in the class declaration of your sink object:

```
TDBImageKeySink OnKeyUpSink;
```

Put a prototype for the handler method in the class declaration for your sink object:

```
void OnKeyUp( TDBImageKeySink& sink, TDBImage& sender, SHORT* scancode,
           TShiftState shift );
```

Connect the handler method to the event sink by including the following in the class constructor:

```
OnKeyUpSink( TDBImageKey_MFUNCTOR( *this, &TForm::OnKeyUp ) );
```

Attach the event source to the event sink by including the following code in your program:

```
TDBImage DBImage;          //Instantiate the source component
TForm form                 //Instantiate the sink component
DBImage.OnKeyUpSource += form.OnKeyUpSink;
```

OnKeyUp event for the TDBListBox component

This declaration of the event source is in the dblist.h header file:

```
TDBListBoxKeySource OnKeyUpSource;
```

Include this declaration of the event sink in the class declaration of your sink object:

```
TDBListBoxKeySink OnKeyUpSink;
```

Put a prototype for the handler method in the class declaration for your sink object:

```
void OnKeyUp( TDBListBoxKeySink& sink, TDBListBox& sender, SHORT* scancode,
           TShiftState shift );
```

Connect the handler method to the event sink by including the following in the class constructor:

```
OnKeyUpSink( TDBListBoxKey_MFUNCTOR( *this, &TForm::OnKeyUp ) );
```

Attach the event source to the event sink by including the following code in your program:

```
TDBListBox DBListBox;      //Instantiate the source component
TForm form                 //Instantiate the sink component
DBListBox.OnKeyUpSource += form.OnKeyUpSink;
```

OnKeyUp event for the TDBLookupCombo component

This declaration of the event source is in the dblkupcb.h header file:

```
TDBLookupComboKeySource OnKeyUpSource;
```

Include this declaration of the event sink in the class declaration of your sink object:

```
TDBLookupComboKeySink OnKeyUpSink;
```

Put a prototype for the handler method in the class declaration for your sink object:

```
void OnKeyUp( TDBLookupComboKeySink& sink, TDBLookupCombo& sender,
              SHORT* scancode, TShiftState shift );
```

Connect the handler method to the event sink by including the following in the class constructor:

```
OnKeyUpSink( TDBLookupComboKey_MFUNCTOR( *this, &TForm::OnKeyUp ));
```

Attach the event source to the event sink by including the following code in your program:

```
TDBLookupCombo DBLookupCombo;      //Instantiate the source component
TForm form                        //Instantiate the sink component
DBLookupCombo.OnKeyUpSource += form.OnKeyUpSink;
```

OnKeyUp event for the TDBLookupList component

This declaration of the event source is in the dblkuplb.h header file:

```
TDBLookupListKeySource OnKeyUpSource;
```

Include this declaration of the event sink in the class declaration of your sink object:

```
TDBLookupListKeySink OnKeyUpSink;
```

Put a prototype for the handler method in the class declaration for your sink object:

```
void OnKeyUp( TDBLookupListKeySink& sink, TDBLookupList& sender,
              SHORT* scancode, TShiftState shift );
```

Connect the handler method to the event sink by including the following in the class constructor:

```
OnKeyUpSink( TDBLookupListKey_MFUNCTOR( *this, &TForm::OnKeyUp ));
```

Attach the event source to the event sink by including the following code in your program:

```
TDBLookupList DBLookupList;      //Instantiate the source component
TForm form                      //Instantiate the sink component
DBLookupList.OnKeyUpSource += form.OnKeyUpSink;
```

OnKeyUp event for the TDBMemo component

This declaration of the event source is in the dbmemo.h header file:

```
TDBMemoKeySource OnKeyUpSource;
```

Include this declaration of the event sink in the class declaration of your sink object:

```
TDBMemoKeySink OnKeyUpSink;
```

Put a prototype for the handler method in the class declaration for your sink object:

```
void OnKeyUp( TDBMemoKeySink& sink, TDBMemo& sender, SHORT* scancode,
              TShiftState shift );
```

Connect the handler method to the event sink by including the following in the class constructor:

```
OnKeyUpSink( TDBMemoKey_MFUNCTOR( *this, &TForm::OnKeyUp ));
```

Attach the event source to the event sink by including the following code in your program:

```
TDBMemo DBMemo;          //Instantiate the source component
TForm form               //Instantiate the sink component
DBMemo.OnKeyUpSource += form.OnKeyUpSink;
```

OnLogin Event

Applies to   TDataBase component

Description   The OnLogin event is activated whenever a TDatabase component assigned to an SQL database is opened and the LoginPrompt property is true. Use the OnLogin event to set login parameters.

This is the declaration of the OnLogin event handler in your code:

```
void OnLogin( TLoginSink& sink, TDatabase& sender, TStrings& loginparams );
```

The OnLogin event obtains a copy of the TDatabase component's login parameters array, Params. Use the Values property to change these parameters:

```
LoginParams.Values["SERVER NAME"] = "MYSERVERNAME";
LoginParams.Values["USER NAME"] = "MYUSERNAME";
LoginParams.Values["PASSWORD"] = "MYPASSWORD";
```

When control returns from your OnLogin event handler, these parameters will be used to establish a connection.

Note   For Paradox, dBASE, and ASCII databases, the only possible parameter is PATH, so the OnLogin event is not activated.

Source declaration   This declaration of the event source is in the header file:

```
TLoginSource OnLoginSource;
```

Sink declaration   Include this declaration of the event sink in the class declaration for your sink object:

```
TLoginSink OnLoginSink;
```

Handler   Put a prototype for the handler method in the class declaration for your sink object:

```
void OnLogin( TLoginSink& sink, TDatabase& sender, TStrings& loginparams );
```

And connect the handler method, which you have implemented, to the event sink by including the following in the class constructor:

```
OnLoginSink( TLogin_MFUNCTOR( *this, &TForm::OnLogin ))
```

Attachment   Attach the event source to the event sink by including the following in your program:

```
TDatabase database;      //Instantiate the source component
TForm form;        //Instantiate the sink component
database.OnLoginSource += form.OnLoginSink;
```

OnMeasureItem event

Applies to   TDBComboBox, TDBListBox components

Header file   dbcombo.h, dblist.h

Description   The OnMeasureItem event occurs whenever an application needs to redisplay an item in an owner-draw list box or combo box with a variable style. That is, for a list box, the Style property is lbOwnerDrawVariable, or for a combo box, the Style property is csOwnerDrawVariable.

This is the declaration of the OnMeasureItem event handler for a database combo box; if your event handler is for a database list box, substitute the name of TDBListBox for TDBComboBox:

```
void OnMeasureItem( TDBComboBoxMeasureItemSink& sink, TDBComboBox& sender,
               SHORT index, SHORT* height );
```

The OnMeasureItem event passes these parameters to its handler describing the item to measure:

Value	Meaning
index	The index of the item in the control
height	The height of the item

The OnMeasureItem event handler should specify the height in pixels that the given item will occupy in the control. Initially the height parameter contains the default height of the item or the height of the item text in the control's font. The handler can set height to a value appropriate to the contents of the item, such as the height of a graphical image to be displayed within the item.

After the OnMeasureItem event occurs, the OnDrawItem event occurs, rendering the item with the measured size.

OnMeasureItem event for the TDBComboBox component

This declaration of the event source is in the dbcombo.h header file:

```
TDBComboBoxMeasureItemSource OnMeasureItemSource;
```

Include this declaration of the event sink in the class declaration of your sink object:

```
TDBComboBoxMeasureItemSink OnMeasureItemSink;
```

Put a prototype for the handler method in the class declaration for your sink object:

```
void OnMeasureItem( TDBComboBoxMeasureItemSink& sink, TDBComboBox& sender,
               SHORT index, SHORT* height );
```

Connect the handler method to the event sink by including the following in the class constructor:

```
OnMeasureItemSink( TDBComboBoxMeasureItem_MFUNCTOR( *this,
            &TForm::OnMeasureItem ));
```

Attach the event source to the event sink by including the following code in your program:

```
TDBComboBox DBComboBox;        //Instantiate the source component
TForm form                     //Instantiate the sink component
DBComboBox.OnMeasureItemSource += form.OnMeasureItemSink;
```

OnMeasureItem event for the TDBListBox component

This declaration of the event source is in the dblist.h header file:

```
TDBListBoxMeasureItemSource OnMeasureItemSource;
```

Include this declaration of the event sink in the class declaration of your sink object:

```
TDBListBoxMeasureItemSink OnMeasureItemSink;
```

Put a prototype for the handler method in the class declaration for your sink object:

```
void OnMeasureItem( TDBListBoxMeasureItemSink& sink, TDBListBox& sender,
            SHORT index, SHORT* height );
```

Connect the handler method to the event sink by including the following in the class constructor:

```
OnMeasureItemSink( TDBListBoxMeasureItem_MFUNCTOR( *this,
            &TForm::OnMeasureItem ));
```

Attach the event source to the event sink by including the following code in your program:

```
TDBListBox DBListBox;        //Instantiate the source component
TForm form                   //Instantiate the sink component
DBListBox.OnMeasureItemSource += form.OnMeasureItemSink;
```

OnMouseDown event

Applies to TDBCheckBox, TDBEdit, TDBImage, TDBListBox, TDBLookupCombo, TDBNavigator, TDBNavigator, TDBText components

Header file dbchkbx.h, dbedit.h, dbimage.h, dblist.h, dblkupcb.h, dbNavigator.h, dbnvgtr.h, dbtext.h

Description The OnMouseDown event occurs when the user presses a mouse button with the mouse pointer over a control. Use the OnMouseDown event handler when you want some processing to occur as a result of pressing a mouse button.

This is the declaration for an OnMouseDown event handler for a database check box control; if your event handler is for another control, substitute the name of that control for TDBCheckBox:

```
void OnMouseDown( TDBCheckBoxMouseSink& sink, TDBCheckBox& sender,
                  TMouseButton button, TShiftState state, SHORT x, SHORT y );
```

The button parameter of the OnMouseDown event identifies which mouse button was pressed. These are the possble values:

Value	Meaning
1	Left mouse button
2	Right mouse button
4	Middle mouse button

By using the shift parameter of the OnMouseDown event handler, you can respond to the state of the mouse buttons and shift keys. *Shift* keys are the *Shift*, *Ctrl*, and *Alt* keys. These are the possible values for the shift parameter:

Value	Meaning
1	*Shift* key
2	*Ctrl* key
4	*Alt* key

x and y are the screen pixel coordinates of the mouse pointer.

OnMouseDown event for the TDBCheckBox component

This declaration of the event source is in the dbchkbx.h header file:

```
TDBCheckBoxMouseSource OnMouseDownSource;
```

Include this declaration of the event sink in the class declaration of your sink object:

```
TDBCheckBoxMouseSink OnMouseDownSink;
```

Put a prototype for the handler method in the class declaration for your sink object:

```
void OnMouseDown( TDBCheckBoxMouseSink& sink, TDBCheckBox& sender,
                  TMouseButton button, TShiftState state, SHORT x, SHORT y );
```

Connect the handler method to the event sink by including the following in the class constructor:

```
OnMouseDownSink( TDBCheckBoxMouse_MFUNCTOR( *this, &TForm::OnMouseDown ));
```

Attach the event source to the event sink by including the following code in your program:

```
TDBCheckBox DBCheckBox;        //Instantiate the source component
TForm form                     //Instantiate the sink component
DBCheckBox.OnMouseDownSource += form.OnMouseDownSink;
```

OnMouseDown event for the TDBEdit component

This declaration of the event source is in the dbedit.h header file:

```
TDBEditMouseSource OnMouseDownSource;
```

Include this declaration of the event sink in the class declaration of your sink object:

```
TDBEditMouseSink OnMouseDownSink;
```

Put a prototype for the handler method in the class declaration for your sink object:

```
void OnMouseDown( TDBEditMouseSink& sink, TDBEdit& sender, TMouseButton button,
                TShiftState state, SHORT x, SHORT y );
```

Connect the handler method to the event sink by including the following in the class constructor:

```
OnMouseDownSink( TDBEditMouse_MFUNCTOR( *this, &TForm::OnMouseDown ));
```

Attach the event source to the event sink by including the following code in your program:

```
TDBEdit DBEdit;              //Instantiate the source component
TForm form                   //Instantiate the sink component
DBEdit.OnMouseDownSource += form.OnMouseDownSink;
```

OnMouseDown event for the TDBImage component

This declaration of the event source is in the dbimage.h header file:

```
TDBImageMouseSource OnMouseDownSource;
```

Include this declaration of the event sink in the class declaration of your sink object:

```
TDBImageMouseSink OnMouseDownSink;
```

Put a prototype for the handler method in the class declaration for your sink object:

```
void OnMouseDown( TDBImageMouseSink& sink, TDBImage& sender,
                TMouseButton button, TShiftState state, SHORT x, SHORT y );
```

Connect the handler method to the event sink by including the following in the class constructor:

```
OnMouseDownSink( TDBImageMouse_MFUNCTOR( *this, &TForm::OnMouseDown ));
```

Attach the event source to the event sink by including the following code in your program:

```
TDBImage DBImage;         //Instantiate the source component
TForm form                //Instantiate the sink component
DBImage.OnMouseDownSource += form.OnMouseDownSink;
```

OnMouseDown event for the TDBListBox component

This declaration of the event source is in the dblist.h header file:

```
TDBListBoxMouseSource OnMouseDownSource;
```

Include this declaration of the event sink in the class declaration of your sink object:

```
TDBListBoxMouseSink OnMouseDownSink;
```

Put a prototype for the handler method in the class declaration for your sink object:

```
void OnMouseDown( TDBListBoxMouseSink& sink, TDBListBox& sender,
                TMouseButton button, TShiftState state, SHORT x, SHORT y );
```

Connect the handler method to the event sink by including the following in the class constructor:

```
OnMouseDownSink( TDBListBoxMouse_MFUNCTOR( *this, &TForm::OnMouseDown ));
```

Attach the event source to the event sink by including the following code in your program:

```
TDBListBox DBListBox;       //Instantiate the source component
TForm form                  //Instantiate the sink component
DBListBox.OnMouseDownSource += form.OnMouseDownSink;
```

OnMouseDown event for the TDBLookupCombo component

This declaration of the event source is in the dblkupcb.h header file:

```
TDBLookupComboMouseSource OnMouseDownSource;
```

Include this declaration of the event sink in the class declaration of your sink object:

```
TDBLookupComboMouseSink OnMouseDownSink;
```

Put a prototype for the handler method in the class declaration for your sink object:

```
void OnMouseDown( TDBLookupComboMouseSink& sink, TDBLookupCombo& sender,
                  TMouseButton button, TShiftState state, SHORT x, SHORT y );
```

Connect the handler method to the event sink by including the following in the class constructor:

```
OnMouseDownSink( TDBLookupComboMouse_MFUNCTOR( *this, &TForm::OnMouseDown ));
```

Attach the event source to the event sink by including the following code in your program:

```
TDBLookupCombo DBLookupCombo;     //Instantiate the source component
TForm form                        //Instantiate the sink component
DBLookupCombo.OnMouseDownSource += form.OnMouseDownSink;
```

OnMouseDown event for the TDBMemo component

This declaration of the event source is in the dbmemo.h header file:

```
TDBMemoMouseSource OnMouseDownSource;
```

Include this declaration of the event sink in the class declaration of your sink object:

```
TDBMemoMouseSink OnMouseDownSink;
```

Put a prototype for the handler method in the class declaration for your sink object:

```
void OnMouseDown( TDBMemoMouseSink& sink, TDBMemo& sender, TMouseButton button,
                  TShiftState state, SHORT x, SHORT y );
```

Connect the handler method to the event sink by including the following in the class constructor:

```
OnMouseDownSink( TDBMemoMouse_MFUNCTOR( *this, &TForm::OnMouseDown ));
```

Attach the event source to the event sink by including the following code in your program:

```
TDBMemo DBMemo;          //Instantiate the source component
TForm form               //Instantiate the sink component
DBMemo.OnMouseDownSource += form.OnMouseDownSink;
```

OnMouseDown event for the TDBText component

This declaration of the event source is in the dbText.h header file:

```
TDBTextMouseSource OnMouseDownSource;
```

Include this declaration of the event sink in the class declaration of your sink object:

```
TDBTextMouseSink OnMouseDownSink;
```

Put a prototype for the handler method in the class declaration for your sink object:

```
void OnMouseDown( TDBTextMouseSink& sink, TDBText& sender, TMouseButton button,
                  TShiftState state, SHORT x, SHORT y );
```

Connect the handler method to the event sink by including the following in the class constructor:

```
OnMouseDownSink( TDBTextMouse_MFUNCTOR( *this, &TForm::OnMouseDown ));
```

Attach the event source to the event sink by including the following code in your program:

```
TDBText DBText;          //Instantiate the source component
TForm form               //Instantiate the sink component
DBText.OnMouseDownSource += form.OnMouseDownSink;
```

OnMouseMove event

Applies to   TDBCheckBox, TDBEdit, TDBImage, TDBListBox, TDBLookupCombo, TDBNavigator, TDBNavigator components

Header file   dbchkbx.h, dbedit.h, dbimage.h, dblist.h, dblkupcb.h, dbnvgtr.h

Description   The OnMouseMove occurs when the user moves the mouse pointer when the mouse pointer is over a control. Use the OnMouseMove event handler when you want something to happen when the mouse pointer moves within the control.

This is the declaration for an OnMouseMove event handler for a database check box control; if your event handler is for another control, substitute the name of that control for TDBCheckBox:

```
void OnMouseMove( TDBCheckBoxMouseSink& sink, TDBCheckBox& sender,
                  TMouseButton button, TShiftState state, SHORT x, SHORT y );
```

The button parameter of the OnMouseMove event identifies which mouse button was pressed. These are the possible values:

Value	Meaning
1	Left mouse button
2	Right mouse button
4	Middle mouse button

By using the shift parameter of the OnMouseMove event handler, you can respond to the state of the mouse buttons and shift keys. Shift keys are the *Shift*, *Ctrl*, and *Alt* keys. These are the possible values for the shift parameter:

Value	Meaning
1	*Shift* key
2	*Ctrl* key
4	*Alt* key

x and y are the screen pixel coordinates of the mouse pointer.

OnMouseMove event for the TDBCheckBox component

This declaration of the event source is in the dbchkbx.h header file:

```
TDBCheckBoxMouseSource OnMouseMoveSource;
```

Include this declaration of the event sink in the class declaration of your sink object:

```
TDBCheckBoxMouseSink OnMouseMoveSink;
```

Put a prototype for the handler method in the class declaration for your sink object:

```
void OnMouseMove( TDBCheckBoxMouseSink& sink, TDBCheckBox& sender,
            TMouseButton button, TShiftState state, SHORT x, SHORT y );
```

Connect the handler method to the event sink by including the following in the class constructor:

```
OnMouseMoveSink( TDBCheckBoxMouse_MFUNCTOR( *this, &TForm::OnMouseMove ));
```

Attach the event source to the event sink by including the following code in your program:

```
TDBCheckBox DBCheckBox;      //Instantiate the source component
TForm form                   //Instantiate the sink component
DBCheckBox.OnMouseMoveSource += form.OnMouseMoveSink;
```

OnMouseMove event for the TDBEdit component

This declaration of the event source is in the dbedit.h header file:

```
TDBEditMouseSource OnMouseMoveSource;
```

Include this declaration of the event sink in the class declaration of your sink object:

```
TDBEditMouseSink OnMouseMoveSink;
```

Put a prototype for the handler method in the class declaration for your sink object:

```
void OnMouseMove( TDBEditMouseSink& sink, TDBEdit& sender, TMouseButton button,
                  TShiftState state, SHORT x, SHORT y );
```

Connect the handler method to the event sink by including the following in the class constructor:

```
OnMouseMoveSink( TDBEditMouse_MFUNCTOR( *this, &TForm::OnMouseMove ));
```

Attach the event source to the event sink by including the following code in your program:

```
TDBEdit DBEdit;            //Instantiate the source component
TForm form                 //Instantiate the sink component
DBEdit.OnMouseMoveSource += form.OnMouseMoveSink;
```

OnMouseMove event for the TDBImage component

This declaration of the event source is in the dbimage.h header file:

```
TDBImageMouseSource OnMouseMoveSource;
```

Include this declaration of the event sink in the class declaration of your sink object:

```
TDBImageMouseSink OnMouseMoveSink;
```

Put a prototype for the handler method in the class declaration for your sink object:

```
void OnMouseMove( TDBImageMouseSink& sink, TDBImage& sender, TMouseButton button,
                  TShiftState state, SHORT x, SHORT y );
```

Connect the handler method to the event sink by including the following in the class constructor:

```
OnMouseMoveSink( TDBImageMouse_MFUNCTOR( *this, &TForm::OnMouseMove ));
```

Attach the event source to the event sink by including the following code in your program:

```
TDBImage DBImage;      //Instantiate the source component
TForm form             //Instantiate the sink component
DBImage.OnMouseMoveSource += form.OnMouseMoveSink;
```

OnMouseMove event for the TDBListBox component

This declaration of the event source is in the dblist.h header file:

```
TDBListBoxMouseSource OnMouseMoveSource;
```

Include this declaration of the event sink in the class declaration of your sink object:

```
TDBListBoxMouseSink OnMouseMoveSink;
```

Put a prototype for the handler method in the class declaration for your sink object:

```
void OnMouseMove( TDBListBoxMouseSink& sink, TDBListBox& sender,
                  TMouseButton button, TShiftState state, SHORT x, SHORT y );
```

Connect the handler method to the event sink by including the following in the class constructor:

```
OnMouseMoveSink( TDBListBoxMouse_MFUNCTOR( *this, &TForm::OnMouseMove ));
```

Attach the event source to the event sink by including the following code in your program:

```
TDBListBox DBListBox;        //Instantiate the source component
TForm form                   //Instantiate the sink component
DBListBox.OnMouseMoveSource += form.OnMouseMoveSink;
```

OnMouseMove event for the TDBLookupCombo component

This declaration of the event source is in the dblkupcb.h header file:

```
TDBLookupComboMouseSource OnMouseMoveSource;
```

Include this declaration of the event sink in the class declaration of your sink object:

```
TDBLookupComboMouseSink OnMouseMoveSink;
```

Put a prototype for the handler method in the class declaration for your sink object:

```
void OnMouseMove( TDBLookupComboMouseSink& sink, TDBLookupCombo& sender,
                  TMouseButton button, TShiftState state, SHORT x, SHORT y );
```

Connect the handler method to the event sink by including the following in the class constructor:

```
OnMouseMoveSink( TDBLookupComboMouse_MFUNCTOR( *this, &TForm::OnMouseMove ));
```

Attach the event source to the event sink by including the following code in your program:

```
TDBLookupCombo DBLookupCombo;       //Instantiate the source component
TForm form                          //Instantiate the sink component
DBLookupCombo.OnMouseMoveSource += form.OnMouseMoveSink;
```

OnMouseMove event for the TDBMemo component

This declaration of the event source is in the dbmemo.h header file:

```
TDBMemoMouseSource OnMouseMoveSource;
```

Include this declaration of the event sink in the class declaration of your sink object:

```
TDBMemoMouseSink OnMouseMoveSink;
```

Put a prototype for the handler method in the class declaration for your sink object:

```
void OnMouseMove( TDBMemoMouseSink& sink, TDBMemo& sender, TMouseButton button,
                  TShiftState state, SHORT x, SHORT y );
```

Connect the handler method to the event sink by including the following in the class constructor:

```
OnMouseMoveSink( TDBMemoMouse_MFUNCTOR( *this, &TForm::OnMouseMove ));
```

Attach the event source to the event sink by including the following code in your program:

```
TDBMemo DBMemo;          //Instantiate the source component
TForm form               //Instantiate the sink component
DBMemo.OnMouseMoveSource += form.OnMouseMoveSink;
```

OnMouseMove event for the TDBText component

This declaration of the event source is in the dbtext.h header file:

```
TDBTextMouseSource OnMouseMoveSource;
```

Include this declaration of the event sink in the class declaration of your sink object:

```
TDBTextMouseSink OnMouseMoveSink;
```

Put a prototype for the handler method in the class declaration for your sink object:

```
void OnMouseMove( TDBTextMouseSink& sink, TDBText& sender, TMouseButton button,
                  TShiftState state, SHORT x, SHORT y );
```

Connect the handler method to the event sink by including the following in the class constructor:

```
OnMouseMoveSink( TDBTextMouse_MFUNCTOR( *this, &TForm::OnMouseMove ));
```

Attach the event source to the event sink by including the following code in your program:

```
TDBText DBText;          //Instantiate the source component
TForm form               //Instantiate the sink component
DBText.OnMouseMoveSource += form.OnMouseMoveSink;
```

OnMouseUp event

Applies to   TDBCheckBox, TDBEdit, TDBImage, TDBListBox, TDBLookupCombo, TDBNavigator, TDBNavigator, TDBText components

Header file   dbchkbx.h, dbedit.h, dbimage.h, dblist.h, dblkupcb.h, dbnvgtr.h, dbtext.h

Description   The OnMouseUp event occurs when the user releases a mouse button that was pressed with the mouse pointer over a component. Use the OnMouseUp event handler to start processing when the user releases a mouse button.

This is the declaration for an OnMouseUp event handler for a database check box control; if your event handler is for another control, substitute the name of that control for TDBCheckBox:

```
void OnMouseUp( TDBCheckBoxMouseSink& sink, TDBCheckBox& sender,
                TMouseButton button, TShiftState state, SHORT x, SHORT y );
```

The button parameter of the OnMouseUp event identifies which mouse button was pressed. These are the possible values:

Value	Meaning
1	Left mouse button
2	Right mouse button
4	Middle mouse button

By using the shift parameter of the OnMouseUp event handler, you can respond to the state of the mouse buttons and shift keys. Shift keys are the *Shift, Ctrl,* and *Alt* keys. These are the possible values for the shift parameter:

Value	Meaning
1	*Shift* key
2	*Ctrl* key
4	*Alt* key

X and Y are the screen pixel coordinates of the mouse pointer.

OnMouseUp event for the TDBCheckBox component

This declaration of the event source is in the dbchkbx.h header file:

```
TDBCheckBoxMouseSource OnMouseUpSource;
```

Include this declaration of the event sink in the class declaration of your sink object:

```
TDBCheckBoxMouseSink OnMouseUpSink;
```

Put a prototype for the handler method in the class declaration for your sink object:

```
void OnMouseUp( TDBCheckBoxMouseSink& sink, TDBCheckBox& sender,
                TMouseButton button, TShiftState state, SHORT x, SHORT y );
```

Connect the handler method to the event sink by including the following in the class constructor:

```
OnMouseUpSink( TDBCheckBoxMouse_MFUNCTOR( *this, &TForm::OnMouseUp ));
```

Attach the event source to the event sink by including the following code in your program:

```
TDBCheckBox DBCheckBox;              //Instantiate the source component
TForm form                           //Instantiate the sink component
DBCheckBox.OnMouseUpSource += form.OnMouseUpSink;
```

OnMouseUp event for the TDBEdit component

This declaration of the event source is in the dbedit.h header file:

```
TDBEditMouseSource OnMouseUpSource;
```

Include this declaration of the event sink in the class declaration of your sink object:

```
TDBEditMouseSink OnMouseUpSink;
```

Put a prototype for the handler method in the class declaration for your sink object:

```
void OnMouseUp( TDBEditMouseSink& sink, TDBEdit& sender, TMouseButton button,
                TShiftState state, SHORT x, SHORT y );
```

Connect the handler method to the event sink by including the following in the class constructor:

```
OnMouseUpSink( TDBEditMouse_MFUNCTOR( *this, &TForm::OnMouseUp ));
```

Attach the event source to the event sink by including the following code in your program:

```
TDBEdit DBEdit;              //Instantiate the source component
TForm form                   //Instantiate the sink component
DBEdit.OnMouseUpSource += form.OnMouseUpSink;
```

OnMouseUp event for the TDBImage component

This declaration of the event source is in the dbimage.h header file:

```
TDBImageMouseSource OnMouseUpSource;
```

Include this declaration of the event sink in the class declaration of your sink object:

```
TDBImageMouseSink OnMouseUpSink;
```

Put a prototype for the handler method in the class declaration for your sink object:

```
void OnMouseUp( TDBImageMouseSink& sink, TDBImage& sender, TMouseButton button,
                TShiftState state, SHORT x, SHORT y );
```

Connect the handler method to the event sink by including the following in the class constructor:

```
OnMouseUpSink( TDBImageMouse_MFUNCTOR( *this, &TForm::OnMouseUp ));
```

Attach the event source to the event sink by including the following code in your program:

```
TDBImage DBImage;            //Instantiate the source component
TForm form                   //Instantiate the sink component
DBImage.OnMouseUpSource += form.OnMouseUpSink;
```

OnMouseUp event for the TDBListBox component

This declaration of the event source is in the dblist.h header file:

```
TDBListBoxMouseSource OnMouseUpSource;
```

Include this declaration of the event sink in the class declaration of your sink object:

```
TDBListBoxMouseSink OnMouseUpSink;
```

Put a prototype for the handler method in the class declaration for your sink object:

```
void OnMouseUp( TDBListBoxMouseSink& sink, TDBListBox& sender,
            TMouseButton button, TShiftState state, SHORT x, SHORT y );
```

Connect the handler method to the event sink by including the following in the class constructor:

```
OnMouseUpSink( TDBListBoxMouse_MFUNCTOR( *this, &TForm::OnMouseUp ));
```

Attach the event source to the event sink by including the following code in your program:

```
TDBListBox DBListBox;       //Instantiate the source component
TForm form                  //Instantiate the sink component
DBListBox.OnMouseUpSource += form.OnMouseUpSink;
```

OnMouseUp event for the TDBLookupCombo component

This declaration of the event source is in the dblkupcb.h header file:

```
TDBLookupComboMouseSource OnMouseUpSource;
```

Include this declaration of the event sink in the class declaration of your sink object:

```
TDBLookupComboMouseSink OnMouseUpSink;
```

Put a prototype for the handler method in the class declaration for your sink object:

```
void OnMouseUp( TDBLookupComboMouseSink& sink, TDBLookupCombo& sender,
            TMouseButton button, TShiftState state, SHORT x, SHORT y );
```

Connect the handler method to the event sink by including the following in the class constructor:

```
OnMouseUpSink( TDBLookupComboMouse_MFUNCTOR( *this, &TForm::OnMouseUp ));
```

Attach the event source to the event sink by including the following code in your program:

```
TDBLookupCombo DBLookupCombo;        //Instantiate the source component
TForm form                           //Instantiate the sink component
DBLookupCombo.OnMouseUpSource += form.OnMouseUpSink;
```

OnMouseUp event for the TDBMemo component

This declaration of the event source is in the dbmemo.h header file:

```
TDBMemoMouseSource OnMouseUpSource;
```

Include this declaration of the event sink in the class declaration of your sink object:

```
TDBMemoMouseSink OnMouseUpSink;
```

Put a prototype for the handler method in the class declaration for your sink object:

```
void OnMouseUp( TDBMemoMouseSink& sink, TDBMemo& sender, TMouseButton button,
            TShiftState state, SHORT x, SHORT y );
```

Connect the handler method to the event sink by including the following in the class constructor:

```
OnMouseUpSink( TDBMemoMouse_MFUNCTOR( *this, &TForm::OnMouseUp ) );
```

Attach the event source to the event sink by including the following code in your program:

```
TDBMemo DBMemo;          //Instantiate the source component
TForm form               //Instantiate the sink component
DBMemo.OnMouseUpSource += form.OnMouseUpSink;
```

OnMouseUp event for the TDBText component

This declaration of the event source is in the dbtext.h header file:

```
TDBTextMouseSource OnMouseUpSource;
```

Include this declaration of the event sink in the class declaration of your sink object:

```
TDBTextMouseSink OnMouseUpSink;
```

Put a prototype for the handler method in the class declaration for your sink object:

```
void OnMouseUp( TDBTextMouseSink& sink, TDBText& sender, TMouseButton button,
                TShiftState state, SHORT x, SHORT y );
```

Connect the handler method to the event sink by including the following in the class constructor:

```
OnMouseUpSink( TDBTextMouse_MFUNCTOR( *this, &TForm::OnMouseUp ) );
```

Attach the event source to the event sink by including the following code in your program:

```
TDBText DBText;          //Instantiate the source component
TForm form               //Instantiate the sink component
DBText.OnMouseUpSource += form.OnMouseUpSink;
```

OnNewRecord event

Applies to   TDataSet, TDBDataSet, TQuery, TStoredProc, TTable components

Header file   bdto.h

Description   The OnNewRecord event is activated whenever a new record is added to the dataset. The event occurs after the BeforeInsert event and before the AfterInsert event. OnNewRecord enables you to initialize any fields of the record without marking the record as Modified. Any changes to the record after this event changes the value of the Modified property.

Source declaration   This declaration of the event source is in the header file:

```
TDatasetDragSource OnNewRecordSource;
```

Sink declaration   Include this declaration of the event sink in the class declaration for your sink object:

```
TDatasetDragSink OnNewRecordSink;
```

Handler Put a prototype for the handler method in the class declaration for your sink object:

```
void OnNewRecord( TDatasetDragSink& sink, TDataSet& sender );
```

And connect the handler method, which you have implemented, to the event sink by including the following in the class constructor:

```
OnNewRecordSink( TDatasetDrag_MFUNCTOR( *this, &TForm::OnNewRecord ))
```

Attachment Attach the event source to the event sink by including the following in your program:

```
TDataSet dataset;      //Instantiate the source component
TForm form;            //Instantiate the sink component
dataset.OnNewRecordSource += form.OnNewRecordSink;
```

OnPassword event

Applies to TSession component

Run-time only. The OnPassword event is activated whenever a Paradox table is opened and the Borland Database Engine reports that the application does not have sufficient access rights.

This is the declaration for the OnPassword event handler in your code:

```
void OnPassword( TPasswordSink& sink, TSession& sender, bool& continue );
```

The value of sender is the Session component. The value of the continue parameter determines whether the caller will make another attempt to access the database. The procedure should add any available additional passwords and set continue to true. If there are no additional passwords available, set continue to false.

If no OnPassword event is defined, Session will create a default dialog box for the user to enter a new password.

Source declaration This declaration of the event source is in the header file:

```
TPasswordSource OnPasswordSource;
```

Sink declaration Include this declaration of the event sink in the class declaration for your sink object:

```
TPasswordSink OnPasswordSink;
```

Handler Put a prototype for the handler method in the class declaration for your sink object:

```
void OnPassword( TPasswordSink& sink, TSession& sender, bool& continue );
```

And connect the handler method, which you have implemented, to the event sink by including the following in the class constructor:

```
OnPasswordSink( TPassword_MFUNCTOR( *this, &TForm::OnPassword ))
```

Attachment   Attach the event source to the event sink by including the following in your program:

```
TSession session;      //Instantiate the source component
TForm form;            //Instantiate the sink component
session.OnPasswordSource += form.OnPasswordSink;
```

OnResize event

Applies to   TDBNavigator component

The OnResize event occurs whenever the database Navigator is resized while an application is running. Use the OnResize event handler when you want something to happen in your application when the database Navigator is resized.

Source declaration   This declaration of the event source is in the dbnvgtr.h header file:

```
TDBNavigatorNotifySource OnResizeSource;
```

Sink declaration   Include this declaration of the event sink in the class declaration for your sink object:

```
TDBNavigatorNotifySink OnResizeSink;
```

Handler   Put a prototype for the handler method in the class declaration for your sink object:

```
void OnResize( TDBNavigatorNotifySink& sink, TDBNavigator& sender );
```

And connect the handler method, which you have implemented, to the event sink by including the following in the class constructor:

```
OnResizeSink( TDBNavigatorNotify_MFUNCTOR( *this, &TForm::OnResize ));
```

Attachment   Attach the event source to the event sink by including the following in your program:

```
TDBNavigator DBNavigator;         //Instantiate the source component
TForm form                        //Instantiate the sink component
DBNavigator.OnReSizeSource += form.OnReSizeSink;
```

OnSetText event

Applies to   TField component

The OnSetText event is activated when the Text property is assigned a value. If OnSetText has been assigned a method, the default processing for Text does not occur. The event handler must store the text provided by Text. By assigning a method to this property, you can take any special actions required by the event.

This is the declaration for the OnSetText event handler in your code:

```
void OnSetText( TFieldSetTextSink& sink, TField& sender, const string& text );
```

The text parameter is the text contained within the field.

Source declaration   This declaration of the event source is in the header file:

```
TFieldSetTextSource OnSetTextSource;
```

Sink declaration   Include this declaration of the event sink in the class declaration for your sink object:

```
TFieldSetTextSink OnSetTextSink;
```

Handler   Put a prototype for the handler method in the class declaration for your sink object:

```
void OnSetText( TFieldSetTextSink& sink, TField& sender, const string& text );
```

And connect the handler method, which you have implemented, to the event sink by including the following in the class constructor:

```
OnSetTextSink( TFieldSetText_MFUNCTOR( *this, &TForm::OnSetText ))
```

Attachment   Attach the event source to the event sink by including the following in your program:

```
TField Field;        //Instantiate the source component
TForm form;          //Instantiate the sink component
Field.OnSetTextSource += form.OnSetTextSink;
```

OnStateChange event

Applies to   TDataSource component

The OnStateChange event occurs when the State property changes.

By assigning a method to this property, you can react programmatically to state changes. For example, this event is useful for enabling or disabling buttons (for example, enabling an edit button only when a table is in edit mode), or displaying processing messages.

Note   OnStateChange can occur even for NULL datasets, so it is important to protect any reference to the DataSet property with a test for a NULL dataset.

Source declaration   This declaration of the event source is in the header file:

```
TDataSourceNotifySource OnStateChangeSource;
```

Sink declaration   Include this declaration of the event sink in the class declaration for your sink object:

```
TDataSourceNotifySink OnStateChangeSink;
```

Handler   Put a prototype for the handler method in the class declaration for your sink object:

```
void OnStateChange( TDataSourceNotifySink& sink, TDataSource& sender, );
```

And connect the handler method, which you have implemented, to the event sink by including the following in the class constructor:

```
OnStateChangeSink( TDataSourceNotify_MFUNCTOR( *this, &TForm::OnStateChange ))
```

Attachment Attach the event source to the event sink by including the following in your program:

```
TDataSource DataSource;  //Instantiate the source component
TForm form;         //Instantiate the sink component
DataSource.OnStateChangeSource += form.OnStateChangeSink;
```

OnUpdateData event

Applies to TDataSource component

OnUpdateData is activated by the Post or UpdateRecord method of a dataset component when the current record is about to be updated in the database. It causes all data-aware controls connected to the data source to be notified of the pending update, allowing them to change their associated fields to the current values in the controls. writing on OnUpdateData event handler, you can react programmatically to updates.

Source declaration This declaration of the event source is in the header file:

```
TDataSourceNotifySource OnUpdateDataSource;
```

Sink declaration Include this declaration of the event sink in the class declaration for your sink object:

```
TDataSourceNotifySink OnUpdateDataSink;
```

Handler Put a prototype for the handler method in the class declaration for your sink object:

```
void OnUpdateData( TDataSourceNotifySink& sink, TDataSource& sender );
```

And connect the handler method, which you have implemented, to the event sink by including the following in the class constructor:

```
OnUpdateDataSink( TDataSourceNotify_MFUNCTOR( *this, &TForm::OnUpdateData ))
```

Attachment Attach the event source to the event sink by including the following in your program:

```
TDataSource DataSource;  //Instantiate the source component
TForm form;         //Instantiate the sink component
DataSource.OnUpdateDataSource += form.OnUpdateDataSink;
```

OnValidate event

Applies to TField components

The OnValidate event is activated when a field is modified. If a data-aware control is linked to the field, changes in the control do not activate OnValidate until the control attempts to store the results of those changes into the current record.

By assigning a method to this property, you can perform any special validation required for the field.

Source declaration   This declaration of the event source is in the header file:

```
TFieldNotifySource OnValidateSource;
```

Sink declaration   Include this declaration of the event sink in the class declaration for your sink object:

```
TFieldNotifySink OnValidateSink;
```

Handler   Put a prototype for the handler method in the class declaration for your sink object:

```
void OnValidate( TFieldNotifySink& sink, TField& sender );
```

And connect the handler method, which you have implemented, to the event sink by including the following in the class constructor:

```
OnValidateSink( TFieldNotify_MFUNCTOR( *this, &TForm::OnValidate ))
```

Attachment   Attach the event source to the event sink by including the following in your program:

```
TField field;      //Instantiate the source component
TForm form;        //Instantiate the sink component
field.OnValidateSource += form.OnValidateSink;
```

Open method

Applies to   TDatabase, TDataSet, TDBDataSet, TQuery, TStoredProc, TTable components

Open method for databases

Applies to   TDataBase component

void Open(void);
The Open method connects the TDatabase component to the server (or the Borland Database Engine for Paradox and dBASE databases). This is the same as setting Connected to true.

Example
```
Database1.Open();
```

Open method for datasets

Applies to   TDataSet, TDBDataSet, TQuery, TStoredProc, TTable components

void Open(void);
The Open method opens the dataset, putting it in Browse state. It is equivalent to setting the Active property to true.

For TQuery, Open executes the SELECT statement in the SQL property. If the statement does not return a result set (for example, an INSERT or UPDATE statement), use ExecSQL instead of Open.

For TStoredProc, use Open to execute the stored procedure if the procedure returns a result set. If the stored procedure returns a single row, use ExecProc instead.

Example
```
try {
  Table1.Open( );
}
catch( EDatabaseError x ) {
  // The dataset could not be opened
  x.Show( );
}
```

OpenDatabase method

Applies to   TSession component

TDatabase OpenDatabase(const string& n);
The OpenDatabase method attempts to find a TDatabase component with a DatabaseName property matching the DatabaseName parameter by calling the FindDatabase method. If no such database can be found, it creates a new database component. OpenDatabase returns either the found database component or the one created. The database returned will be opened during this process. OpenDatabase increments the Session's reference count of the number of open database connections.

Example
```
Database = Session.OpenDatabase( "DBDEMOS" );
//Do Something
Session.CloseDatabase( "DBDEMOS" );
```

Options property

Applies to   TDBLookupCombo, TDBLookupList, TIndexDef components

Options property for lookup boxes

Applies to   TDBLookupCombo, TDBLookupList components

TDBLookupListOptions Options;
The Options property determines how multiple columns in database lookup combo boxes and database lookup list boxes appear. You specify the options you want by choosing one or more of these flags:

Value	Meaning
loColLines	Lines appear between the columns.
loRowLines	Lines appear between the rows.
loOptTitles	The field names appear as titles above the columns in the control.

For example, if you want a database lookup list box to have lines between the columns and you want the field names of the dataset to appear as titles above the columns, you would write this code:

```
MyDBLookupList.Options = loColLines | loOptTitles;
```

To display multiple columns, use the LookupDisplay property.

Example   This code displays three fields in a database lookup list box, displays the field names as titles for the columns, and separates the columns with lines:

```
TMyFormClass.SetupWindow( )
{
  DBLookupList1.LookupDisplay = "Company;City;Country";
  DBLookupList1.Options = loColLines|loTitles;
}
```

Options property for index definitions

Applies to   TIndexDef component

TIndexOptions Options;
Run-time and read only. Options is the set of characteristics of the index. These are the possible values:

Value	Meaning
ixPrimary	The index is a primary index.
ixUnique	Each indexed value must be different from all other indexed values.
ixDescending	The index is in descending order.
ixNonMaintained	The index is not maintained.
ixCaseInsensitive	The index is not sensitive to case.

Overload property

Applies to   TStoredProc component

uint16 Overload;
Oracle servers allow overloading of stored procedures in an Oracle pacge; that is, different procedures with the same name.

Set the Overload property to specify the procedure to execute on an Oracle server. If Overload is zero (the default), there is assumed to be no overloading. If Overload is one (1), the first stored procedure with the overloaded name executes; if it is two (2), the second executes, and so on.

Owner property

Applies to   All data-aware controls

TWindow* Owner;
Run-time and read only. The Owner property indicates which component owns the component.

The form owns all components that are on it. In turn, the form is owned by the application.

When one component is owned by another, the memory for the owned component is freed when its owner's memory is freed. This means that when a form is destroyed, all the components on the form are destroyed also. Finally, when the memory for the application itself is freed, the memory for the form (and all its owned components) is also freed.

Don't confuse ownership of a component with being the parent of a component. A parent is a windowed control that contains a child window. The parent and the owner of a component can be different components.

ParamBindMode property

Applies to   TStoredProc component

TParamBindMode ParamBindMode;
ParamBindMode determines how the elements of the Params array are matched with stored procedure parameters. These are the possible values:

Value	Meaning
pbByName	If ParamBindMode is set to pbByName (the default), parameters are bound based on their names in the stored procedure.
pbByNumber	If ParamBindMode is set to pbByNumber, parameters are bound based on the order in which they are defined in the stored procedure. Use this setting if you are building your parameters list and you don't want to use the parameter names defined in the stored procedure.

ParamByName method

Applies to   TParams; TQuery, TStoredProc components

ParamByName method for TParams components

Applies to   TParams component

TParam* ParamByName(const string& name);
The ParamByName method finds a parameter with the name passed in value. If a match is found, ParamByName returns the parameter. Otherwise, a BDTException exception is raised. Use this method rather than a direct reference to the Items property to keep a specific parameter from depending on the order of the entries.

Example

```
try
{   // Assign a value of 999 to the CustNo parameter
  Params.ParamByName("CustNo")->AsInteger = 999;
}
catch( EDatabaseError x )
{
// If it doesn't exist, then
// Ceate a new parameter for
// CustNo and assign a value of 999 to it
  Params.CreateParam(ftInteger, "CustNo", ptInput).AsInteger = 999;
}
```

ParamByName method for queries and stored procedures

Applies to   TQuery, TStoredProc components

TParam* ParamByName(string& value);
The ParamByName method returns the element of the Params property whose Name property matches the value parameter. Use it to assign values to parameters in a dynamic query by name.

Example   This code assigns the string "1231" to the CustNo parameter:

```
Query1.ParamByName("CustNo")->AsString = "1231";
```

ParamCount property

Applies to   TQuery, TStoredProc component

ParamCount property for queries

Applies to   TQuery component

uint16 ParamCount;
Run-time and read only. The ParamCount property specifies how many entries a TQuery component has in its Params property, that is, how many parameters the query has. Adding a new item to Params automaticallys increase the value; removing an item automatically decreases the value.

Example   This code assigns an integer to each parameter of the query:

```
for( i = 0; i< Query1.ParamCount; i++ )
  Query1.Params->Items[i]->AsInteger = i;
```

ParamCount property for stored procedures

Applies to   TStoredProc component

uint16 ParamCount;
Run-time and read only. ParamCount specifies the total number of input and output parameters to the stored procedure, and is automatically maintained by changes to the Params property. Use ParamCount to iterate over the parameters

Example

```
// Set all parameters to an empty string
  for( i = 0; i < StoredProc1.ParamCount; i++ )
      StoredProc1.Params->Items[i]->AsString = " ";
```

Params property

Applies to   TDatabase, TQuery, TStoredProc component

Params property for stored procedures

Applies to   TStoredProc component

TParams Params;
The Params property holds the parameters to be passed to the stored procedure.

Example

```
// Copy all parameters from StoredProc1 to StoredProc2
StoredProc1.CopyParams(StoredProc2.Params);
```

Params property for queries

Applies to   TQuery component

TParams Params;
Run-time only. The Params property contains the values that are supplied to a dynamic SQL statement.

Example   For example, suppose a TQuery component named Query2 has the following statement for its SQL property:

```
INSERT
  INTO COUNTRY (NAME, CAPITAL, POPULATION)
  VALUES (:Name, :Capital, :Population)
```

An application could use Params to specify the values of the parameters as follows:

```
Query2.Params->Items[0]->AsString = "Lichtenstein";
Query2.Params->Items [1]->AsString = "Vaduz";
Query2.Params->Items [2]->AsInteger = 420000;
```

These statements would bind the value "Lichtenstein" to the :Name parameter, "Vaduz" to the :Capital parameter, and 420000 to the :Population parameter.

Params property for databases

Applies to   TDataBase component

TStrings Params;
The Params property holds the parameters required to open a database on an SQL server. By default, these parameters are specified in the BDE Configuration Utility. You

can customize these parameters for an application-specific alias with the Database Parameters Editor.

For desktop databases, Params specifies only the directory path for the database. For server databases, Params specifies a variety of parameters, including the server name, database name, user name, and password.

Example

```
database1.Params->Values[ "USERNAME"] = "LIZZIEVINSEL";
```

ParamType property

Applies to   TParam component

TParamType ParamType;

ParamType is used to identify the type of the parameter for a stored procedure. Possible values are those of the TParamType type as listed below. Normally this property is set automatically, but if the server does not provide the necessary information, you may have to set it yourself.

These are the possible values:

Value	Meaning
ptUnknown	The parameter type is unknown.
ptInput	This is an input parameter.
ptOutput	This is an output parameter.
ptInputOutput	This is an input/output parameter

Example   This code specifies that the CustNo parameter is an input parameter:

```
StoredProc1. ParamByName("CustNo")->ParamType = ptInput;
```

Parent property

Applies to   All data-aware controls

TWindow* Parent;

The Parent property contains a pointer to the parent of the control. The parent of a control is the control that contains the control. If one control (parent) contains others, the contained controls are child controls of the parent. For example, if your application includes three radio buttons in a group box, the group box is the parent of the three radio buttons, and the radio buttons are the child controls of the group box.

Don't confuse the Parent property with the Owner property. A form is the owner of all the components on it. A child control is always a windowed control contained within another windowed control (its parent). If you put three radio buttons in a group box on a form, the owner of the radio buttons is still the form, while the parent is the group box.

If you are creating a new control, you must assign a Parent property value for the new control. Usually, this is a form, panel, group box, or some control that is designed to contain another. It is possible to assign any control as the parent, but the contained control is likely to be painted over.

When the parent of a control is destroyed, all controls that are its children are also destroyed.

PasswordChar property

Applies to   TDBEdit component

char PasswordChar;

The PasswordChar property lets you create a database edit box that displays special characters in place of the entered text. By default, PasswordChar is the NULL character (ANSI character zero), meaning that the control displays its text normally. If you set PasswordChar to any other character, the control displays that character in place of each character in the control's text.

Example   The following code displays asterisks for each character in an edit box called PasswordField:

```
PasswordField.PasswordChar = "*";
```

PasteFromClipboard method

Applies to   TDBEdit, TDBImage, TDBMemo components

void PasteFromClipboard( );

The PasteFromClipboard method copies the contents of the Clipboard to the control, inserting the contents where the cursor is positioned.

Example   This example uses two edit boxes and a button on a form. When the user clicks the button, text is cut from the Edit1 edit box and pasted into the Edit2 edit box:

```
TMyFormClass::Button1Click()
{
  DBEdit1.SelectAll( );
  DBEdit1.CutToClipboard( );
  DBEdit2.Clear( );
  DBEdit2.PasteFromClipboard( );
  DBEdit1.SetFocus( );
}
```

Picture property

Applies to   TDBImage component

HPIC Picture;

The Picture property determines the image that appears on the image control. The property value is a TPicture object which can contain an icon, metafile, or bitmap graphic.

Example This example uses two picture components. When the dialog first appears, two bitmaps are loaded into the image components and stretched to fit the size of the components. To try this code, substitute names of bitmaps you have available.

```
void AboutDlg::EvLButtonDown (uint modKeys, TPoint& point)
{
  // call the base class for default handling
  TDialog::EvLButtonDown(modKeys, point);
  // load a bitmap from disk and show the image in the image control
  // Note: the following properties are defined in the class:
  // TDib* TheDib; TPalette* ThePalette; TBitmap* TheBitMap;
  // First load the resource from the file. It's in device
  // independent bitmap on disk so we need to use a TDib class
  TheDib = new TDib("c:\\windows\\media\\bitmaps\\arches.bmp");
  // now we want to convert the dib into a device dependent bitmap
  // first thing is to get the palette information from the TDib
  ThePalette = new TPalette(*TheDib);
  // now we can create the device dependent bitmap using
  //  the OWL class. it gets passed the dib and palette
  TheBitMap = new TBitmap(*TheDib, ThePalette);
  // next step is to create a VB PICTURE for the VBX control.
  PICTURE ThePicture;
  // set the type of the PICTURE to a bitmap
  ThePicture.Type = PICTURE_BMP;
  // set the Bitmap and Palette fields in the
  // PICTURE struct's  bitmap union
  ThePicture.Data.Bitmap.Bitmap  = *TheBitMap;
  ThePicture.Data.Bitmap.Palette  = *ThePalette;
  // create the PICTURE getting back the handle
  // needed for theimage control.
  HPIC TheHpic = VBXCreatePicture(&ThePicture);
  // tell the image control to automatically size itself to the image
  Image1.AutoSize = true;
  // and load the image into the image control.
  Image1.Picture = TheHpic;
}
```

Position property

Applies to TMemoryStream component

int32 Position;
The Position property returns the current position within the stream. To change the current position, give Position a new value.

Position is used to implement the Seek method.

Post method

Applies to TDataSet, TDBDataSet, TQuery, TStoredProc, TTable components

void Post(void);

The Post method writes the current record to the database. Post should be called after calling Append or Insert and making any desired changes to the fields of the current record.

Post behaves differently depending on a dataset's state.

- In Edit state, Post modifies the current record.

- In Insert state, Post inserts or appends a new record.

- In SetKey state, Post commits the changes to the search key buffer, and returns the dataset to Browse state.

Posting can be done explicitly, or implicitly as part of another procedure. When an application moves off the current record it calls Post implicitly. Calls to the Next, MoveBy, Prior, First, and Last methods perform a Post if the table is in Edit or Insert state. The Append and Insert methods also implicitly perform a Post of any pending data.

Note   If the record cannot be written to the database for some reason, the dataset will remain in Edit state.

Example

```
Table1.Append();
Table1.FieldByName("CustNo").AsString = "9999";
// Fill in other fields here
if // you are sure you want to do this
  Table1.Post();
else // if you changed your mind
  Table1.Cancel();
```

Precision property

Applies to   TBCDField, TCurrencyField, TFloatField components

int Precision;

The Precision property is used in formatting numeric fields. The value of Precision is the number of decimal places to the right of the decimal point the numeric value should be formatted to before rounding begins. The default value is 15 decimal places.

Prepare method

Applies to   TQuery, TStoredProc components

Description   Prepare method for queries and stored procedures

Prepare method for stored procedures

Applies to   TStoredProc component

void Prepare(void);
The Prepare method prepares the stored procedure to be executed. This allows the server to load the procedure and otherwise prepare for execution.

Prepare method for queries

Applies to TQuery component (dynamic queries only)

void Prepare(void);
The Prepare method sends a parameterized query to the database engine for parsing and optimization. A call to Prepare is not required to use a parameterized query. It is strongly recommended, however, because it improves performance for dynamic queries that are executed more than once. If a query is not explicitly prepared, each time the query runs, it is automatically prepared.

If a query has been executed, an application must call Close before calling Prepare again. Generally, an application should call Prepare once, and set parameters using the Params property, and finally call Open or ExecSQL to execute the query. Each time the query runs with different parameter values, your application must call Close, set the parameter values, and then execute the query with Open or ExecSQL.

Prepared property

Applies to TQuery, TStoredProc components

Description Prepared property for queries and stored procedures

Prepared is a Boolean property of a TQuery component that indicates if a query has been prepared.

Prepared property for stored procedures

Applies to TStoredProc component

bool Prepared;
Run-time only. The Prepared property is true if the stored procedure has been submitted to the server for optimization purposes. Setting Prepared to true does not execute the procedure; it simply advises the server that the procedure needs to be executed at some future time. Setting Prepared to true is equivalent to calling the Prepare method; setting it to false is equivalent to calling the UnPrepare method.

Example

```
// Make sure that the server is aware that we will be executing the procedure
if( ! StoredProc1.Prepared )
  StoredProc1.Prepared = true;
```

Prepared property for queries

Applies to TQuery component

bool Prepared;
Run-time only. The Prepared property specifies if the Prepare method has been called to prepare the TQuery. While preparing a query is not required, it is highly recommended in most cases.

Note Close the TQuery component by setting the Active property to false before changing the value of Prepared.

Prior method

Applies to TDataSet, TDBDataSet, TQuery, TStoredProc, TTable components

void Prior(void);
The Prior method moves the current record position of the dataset backward by one record. If the dataset is in Insert or Edit state, Prior performs an implicit Post of any pending data.

Example
```
// Move to the previous record
Table1.Prior();
if( Table1.AtBOF )
// No more records
```

PrivateDir property

Applies to TSession component

string PrivateDir;
Run-time only. The PrivateDir property specifies the path of the directory in which to store temporary files (for example, files used to process local SQL statements). You should set this property if there will be more than one instance of the application running at a time. Otherwise, the temporary files from multiple application instances will interfere with each other.

ProblemCount property

Applies to TBatchMove component

int32 ProblemCount;
Run-time and read-only. The ProblemCount property reports the number of records that could not be added to the table specified as the value of the Destination property without loss of data due to field width constraints. If the value of the AbortOnProblem property is true, this number is 1 and the operation aborts when the problem occurs.

Example   This code displays the number of problem records in a message box:

```
char message[50];
sprintf( message , "l%d records had problems", BatchMove1.ProblemCount );
MessageBox( message , "Information" , MB_OK );
```

ProblemTableName property

Applies to   TBatchMove component

string ProblemTableName;
If the Execute method is unable to move a record to the table specified as the value of the
Destination property without data loss (caused by a field-width conflict), the record is
placed in a new table with the name supplied as the value of ProblemTableName. If the
value of the AbortOnProblem property is true, there can be at most one record in this
table and the operation aborts with that first problem record. The ProblemCount
property contains the number of records placed in the new table. If ProblemTableName
is not specified, the data in the record is trimmed and placed in the destination table.

Example   This line of code specifies the name of the table holding the problem records:

```
BatchMove1.ProblemTableName = "PROB.DB";
```

Read method

Applies to   TMemoryStream component

int32 Read(LPVOID Buffer, int32 Count);
The Read method reads the number of bytes indicated by the Count parameter from the
stream into the buffer. It returns the number of bytes read.

Example   This line of code reads 4096 bytes into the MyBuf buffer:

```
BlobStream1.Read(MyBuf, 4096);
```

ReadBuffer method

Applies to   TMemoryStream component

void ReadBuffer(LPVOID Buffer, int32 Count);
The ReadBuffer method copies up to Count bytes from the current position in the
stream to Buffer. Buffer must have at least Count bytes allocated for it. Transfers which
require crossing a selector boundary in the destination will be handled correctly.

ReadOnly property

Applies to   All TField, TDBCheckBox, TDBComboBox, TDBEdit, TDBGrid, TDBImage,
TDBListBox, TDBLookupCombo, TDBLookupList, TDBMemo, TDBRadioGroup,
TTable components

ReadOnly property for data-aware controls

Applies to TDBCheckBox, TDBComboBox, TDBEdit, TDBImage, TDBGrid, TDBListBox, TDBLookupCombo, TDBLookupList, TDBMemo, TDBRadioGroup components

bool ReadOnly;

The ReadOnly property determines if the user can change the contents of the control. If ReadOnly is true, the user can't change the contents. If ReadOnly is false, the user can modify the contents. The default value is false.

For data-aware controls, the ReadOnly property determines whether the user can use the data-aware control to change the value of the field of the current record, or if the user can use the control only to display data. If ReadOnly is false, the user can change the field's value as long as the dataset is in edit mode.

When the ReadOnly property of a data grid is true, the user can no longer use the Insert key to insert a new row in the grid, nor can the user append a new row at the end of the data grid with the *Down Arrow* key.

ReadOnly property for tables

Applies to TTable component

bool ReadOnly;

The ReadOnly property determines whether users are able to change data in a table. If ReadOnly is true, users can edit the data; if ReadOnly is false, users cannot edit the data.

Note Before changing the value of ReadOnly, set the Active property of the table to false.

Example This code prevents the users from being able to change values in Table1:

```
Table1.Active = false;
Table1.ReadOnly = true;
Table1.Active = true;
```

ReadOnly property for fields

Applies to All TField components

bool ReadOnly;

The ReadOnly property determines whether the value of a field can be modified. If ReadOnly is false, the default value, a field can be modified. To prevent a field from being modified, set ReadOnly to true.

RecordCount property

Applies to   TBatchMove, TDataSet, TDBDataSet, TQuery, TStoredProc, TTable components

int32 RecordCount;

For a batch move component, the RecordCount property is used to control the maximum number of records that are moved. If zero, all records are moved, beginning with the first record in dataset specified as the value of the Source property. If RecordCount is not zero, a maximum of RecordCount records are moved, beginning with the current record. If RecordCount exceeds the number of records remaining in Source, no wraparound occurs and the operation terminates.

For a query, table, or stored procedure, RecordCount contains the number of records in the dataset.

Example

```
// Limit the move to the first 1000 records
BatchMove1.RecordCount = 1000;
```

RecordSize property

Applies to   TDataSet, TDBDataSet, TQuery, TStoredProc, TTable components

unit16 RecordSize;

Run-time and read-only.The RecordSize property reports the size of a record in the dataset. You can use RecordSize to allocate sufficient memory for a record, then call the GetCurrentRecord to fetch the current record.

Example

```
// allocate a buffer to hold the current record information
LPSTR curRec = new char[Table1.RecordSize];
// get the current record
Table1.GetCurrentRecord( curRec );
// do something with the record
// free the allocated memory
delete[ ] curRec;
```

Refresh method

Applies to   All data-aware controls; TDataSet, TDBDataSet, TQuery, TStoredProc, TTable components

Refresh method for data-aware controls

Applies to   All data-aware controls

void Refresh( );

The Refresh method erases whatever image is on the screen and then repaints the entire control. Within the implementation of Refresh, the Invalidate and then the Update methods are called.

Refresh method for datasets

Applies to   TDataSet, TDBDataSet, TQuery, TStoredProc, TTable components

void Refresh(void);

The Refresh method rereads all records from the dataset. Use Refresh to be certain that data controls display the latest information from the dataset. Calling Refresh may unexpectedly change the displayed data, potentially confusing the user.

RemoveAllPasswords method

Applies to   TSession component

void RemoveAllPasswords(void);

Paradox databases only. The RemoveAllPasswords method causes all previously entered password information to be discarded. Any future access requires that new password information be supplied before the table can be opened.

RemoveParam method

Applies to   TParams component

void RemoveParam(TParam& p);

The RemoveParam method removes the parameter specified as p from the Items property.

Example

```
// Move all parameter info from Params2 to Params1
while( Params2.Count != 0 )
{
  // Grab the first parameter from Params2
  TParam TempParam = Params2[0];
  // Remove it from Params2
  Params2.RemoveParam(TempParam);
  // And add it to Params1
  Params1.AddParam(TempParam);
}
```

RemovePassword method

Applies to   TSession component

void RemovePassword(const string& p);
Paradox databases only. The RemovePassword method removes the password specified by the p parameter from the known set of authorizations. Any future access requires that new password information be supplied before the table can be opened.

Example   This line of code removes the MySecret password:

```
Session.RemovePassword("MySecret");
```

RenameTable method

Applies to   TTable component

void RenameTable(const string& newname);
The RenameTable method renames a table to the name specified in the newname parameter.

Repaint method

Applies to   All data-aware controls

void Repaint( );
The Repaint method forces the control to repaint its image on the screen, but without erasing what already appears there. To erase before repainting, call the Refresh method instead of Repaint.

Example   The following code repaints the database image:

```
DBImage1.Repaint();
```

RequestLive property

Applies to   TQuery component

bool RequestLive;
The RequestLive property determines whether a query returns a live result set that users can then modify, or a read-only result set. To allow users to modify the results of a query, set RequestLive to true. The Borland Database Engine then returns a live result set if the SELECT syntax of the query conforms to the syntax requirements for a live result set. If RequestLive is true, but the syntax does not conform to the requirements, the Borland Database Engine returns a read-only result set (for local SQL) or an error return code (for passthrough SQL). If a query returns a live result set, the CanModify property is set to true.

To prevent the results of query from being modified, set RequestLive to false, the default value.

RequestLive	CanModify	Type of result set
False	False	Read-only result set
True—SELECT syntax meets requirements	True	Live result set
True—SELECT syntax does not meet requirements	False	Read-only result set

Required property

Applies to   All TField, TFieldDef components

Required property for fields

Applies to   All TField components

bool Required;

The Required property determines whether a field must contain a non-NULL value. The default value is false, meaning a field does not require a value. Set Required to true for fields that must get values (for example, a password or part number), and write an OnValidate event handler for the field. Before a record is posted, exceptions are raised for any required fields that have NULL values.

Required property for field definitions

Applies to   TFieldDef component

bool Required;

Run-time and read-only. The Required property determines whether a value for a physical field in an underlying value is required. If Required is true, a value is required; if Required is false, a value is not required.

Example

```
// Is field required?
if( FieldDef1.Required )
  MessageBox( "This is a required field" , "Information" , MB_OK );
```

Rollback method

Applies to   TDatabase component

void Rollback(void);

The Rollback method rolls back the current transaction and thus cancels all modifications made to the database since the last call to StartTransaction. Use this method only when connected to a server database.

Example   This code rolls back the database to the condition before the transaction began:

```
Database1.StartTransaction();
// Update one or more records in tables linked to Database1
...
Database1.Rollback();
```

SaveToBitmap method

Applies to   TGraphicField component

void SaveToBitmap(HBITMAP& hbitmap, HPALETTE& hpalette);
The SaveToBitmap method creates an hbitmap and hpalette from the graphic field. Use this method to save the bitmap from the graphic field to those graphic handles. Free the new hbitmap and hpalette by calling the Windows API function DeleteObject().

SaveToFile method

Applies to   TBlobField, TGraphicField, TMemoField, TStrings components

void SaveToFile(const string& filename);
For a BLOB, memo, or graphic field component, the SaveToFile method saves the contents of the field to the file specified as the value of the filename parameter. For a string component, this method saves the text of the string component to the named file.

Example   This example stores a BLOB field into a file:

```
// Store a blob field into a temporary file
BlobField1.SaveToFile( "c:\\windows\\temp\\myblob.blb" );
```

SaveToStream method

Applies to   TBlobField, TGraphicField, TMemoField, TStrings components

void SaveToStream(TMemoryStream& Stream);
The SaveToStream method writes a stream with the name passed in Stream with the contents of TBlobField, TMemoField, or TGraphicField.

Example

```
// Store a blob field into a stream
BlobField1.SaveToStream(Stream1);
```

ScaleBy method

Applies to   All data-aware controls

void ScaleBy (int M, int D);

The ScaleBy method scales a control to a percentage of its former size. The M parameter is the multiplier and the D parameter is the divisor. For example, if you want a control to be 75% of its original size, specify the value of M as 75, and the value of D as 100 (75/100). You could also obtain the same results by specifying the value of M as 3, and the value of D as 4 (3/4). Both fractions are equal and result in the control being scaled by the same amount, 75%.

If you want the control to be 33% larger than its previous size, specify the value of M as 133, and the value of D as 100 (133/100). You can also obtain the same results by specifying the value of M as 4, and the value of D as 3 (4/3), as the fraction 133/100 is approximately equal to 4/3.

Example The following code scales DBListBox1 to half its original size:

```
DBListBox1.ScaleBy( 50, 50 );
```

ScreenToClient method

Applies to All data-aware controls

Tpoint ScreenToClient(Tpoint pt);

The ScreenToClient method is used to determine the control coordinates in pixels of a point on the screen. ScreenToClient returns X and Y coordinates in a record of type TPoint.

Example The following code converts the origin of the screen (0, 0) to the client coordinates of DBEdit2:

```
TPoint ScreenOrgin, ClientPoint;
ScreenOrgin.X = 0;
ScreenOrgin.Y = 0;
ClientPoint = DBEdit2.ScreenToClient(ScreenOrgin);
```

ScrollBars property

Applies to TDBMemo component

TScrollStyle ScrollBars;

The ScrollBars property controls whether data grid of database memo control has any scroll bars. You can set ScrollBars to any of the following values:

Value	Meaning
ssNone	No scroll bar.
ssHorizontal	Put a scroll bar on the right edge.
ssVertical	Put a scroll bar on the bottom edge.
ssBoth	Put a scroll bar on both the right and bottom edges.

By default, data grids have both vertical and horizontal scroll bars, while database memo controls have none.

Example The following example adds a scroll bar to the bottom of database memo control DBMemo1:

```
DBMemo1.ScrollBars = sbHorizontal;
```

ScrollBy method

Applies to All data-aware controls

void ScrollBy(int DeltaX, int DeltaY);
The ScrollBy method scrolls the contents of a control.

The DeltaX parameter is the change in pixels along the X axis. A positive DeltaX value scrolls the contents to the right; a negative value scrolls the contents to the left. The DeltaY parameter is the change in pixels along the Y axis. A positive DeltaY value scrolls the contents down; a negative value scrolls the contents up.

Seek method

Applies to TMemoryStream component

int32 Seek(int32 Offset, uint16 Origin);
The Seek method resets the current position within the TMemoryStream.

If Origin is 0, the new position is Offset (seek absolute). If Origin is 1, the new position is Position + Offset (seek relative). If Origin is 2, the new position is Size + Offset (seek absolute from end of data). Seek returns the new position, relative to the beginning of the stream.

Use these values (of the TSeekOrigin type) when specifying the seek origin:

Value	Meaning
0	soFromBeginning
1	soFromCurrent
2	soFromEnd

Note When Origin is 0, Offset must be >= 0. When Origin is 2, Offset must be <= 0.

Example

```
// Move to the end of the data so we can add more to it
BlobStream1.Seek(0, soFromEnd);
```

SelectAll method

Applies to   TDBComboBox, TDBEdit, TDBMemo components

void SelectAll( );
The SelectAll method selects the entire block of text in the control. If you want to select only part of the text, use the SelStart and SelLength properties.

Example   The following code selects all the text in DBMemo1:

```
DBMemo1.SelectAll();
```

SelectedField property

Applies to   TDBLookupList component

TField SelectedField;
Run-time and read-only. The value of the SelectedField property indicates which field is selected in the data grid or database lookup list box.

Example   The following code colors the database lookup list box a light aqua if the selected field is "CustNo":

```
if( DBLookupList1.SelectedField.FieldName == "CustNo" )
    DBLookupList1.BackColor == 0x00ffff80;
```

SelLength property

Applies to   TDBComboBox, TDBLookupCombo, TDBEdit, TDBMemo components

int SelLength;
The SelLength property returns the length (in characters) of the control's selected text. By using SelLength along with the SelStart property, you specify which part of the text in the control is selected. You can change the number of selected characters by changing the value of SelLength. When the SelStart value changes, the SelLength value changes accordingly.

The database edit box or memo must be the active control when you change the value of SelLength, or nothing appears to happen.

SelStart property

Applies to   TDBComboBox, TDBLookupCombo, TDBEdit, TDBMemo components

int SelStart;
The SelStart property returns the starting position of the selected part of the control's text, with the first character in the text having a value of 0. You can use SelStart with the SelLength property to select a portion of the text. Specify the character you want the selected text to start with by its position in the text as the value of SelStart.

When the SelStart value changes, the SelLength value changes accordingly.

The edit box or memo must be the active control when you change the value of SelStart, or nothing appears to happen.

SelText property

Applies to   TDBComboBox, TDBLookupCombo, TDBEdit, TDBMemo components

string SelText;

The SelText property contains the selected part of the control's text. You can use it to determine what the selected text is, or you can change the contents of the selected text by specifying a new string. If no text is currently selected, the SelText string is inserted in the text at the cursor.

SendToBack method

Applies to   All data-aware controls

void SendToBack( );

The SendToBack method puts the component behind all other components within its parent component or form. You can use it to reorder overlapping components within a form.

The order in which controls stack on top of each order (also called the Z order) depends on the order in which you create them. If you put a database navigator on a form, then create a database check box, the database check box is on top. If you call SendToBack for the database check box, the check box moves to the bottom.

Session variable   bdto.h

TSession Session;

The Session variable is responsible for maintaining all of the database components used by your application. It is created automatically as part of your application's initialization and destroyed as part of your application's termination. The Session variable must remain active at all times; it can not be destroyed and recreated.

SetBounds method

Applies to   All data-aware controls

virtual void SetBounds(int l, int t, int w, int h);

The SetBounds method sets the component's boundary properties, Left, Top, Width, and Height, to the values passed in l, t, w, and h, respectively.

SetBounds enables you to set more than one of the component's boundary properties at a time. Although you can always set the individual boundaries, using SetBounds enables you to make several changes at once without repainting the control for each change.

Example The following code doubles the size of a database edit box:

```
DBEdit1.SetBounds(DBEdit1.Left, DBEdit1.Top, DBEdit1.Height * 2, DBEdit1.Width * 2;
```

Note that you could use the following code instead, but each click would result in the database edit box being redrawn twice: once to change the height and once to change the width:

```
DBEdit1.Height = DBEdit1.Height * 2;
DBEdit1.Width = DBEdit1.Width * 2;
```

SetData method

Applies to   All TField, TParam components

SetData method for TParam components

Applies to   TParam component

void SetData(LPVOID buffer);
The SetData method copies a new value for the parameter in native format from the value specified in the buffer parameter.

Example
```
long i;
i = 1221;
// Set the data
Query1.ParamByName("CustNo")->SetData(&i);
```

SetData method for fields

Applies to   all TField components

void SetData(LPVOID Buffer);
The SetData method assigns "raw" data to the field. Unlike the AsString or Text properties, SetData performs no translation or interpretation of the data. Buffer must have sufficient space allocated to hold the data. Use the DataSize property to determine the space required. To set the data to a blank value, pass NULL for the Buffer parameter.

Example
```
// Assign "raw" data to Field1
//  Allocate space
Buffer = new BYTE[ Field1.DataSize ];
// Fill Buffer with the desired data
...
// Do the assignment
Field1.SetData(Buffer)
// Free the space
delete Buffer;
```

SetFields method

Applies to   TDataSet, TDBDataSet, TQuery, TStoredProc, TTable components

void SetFields(TVarRecs& values);
The SetFields method assigns the values specified in the Values parameter to the fields in the dataset. If Values has fewer elements than there are fields, the remaining elements are unchanged.

Before calling this method, an application must first call Edit to put the dataset in Edit state. To then modify the current record in the database, it must then call Post.

Because this method depends explicitly on the structure of the underlying table, an application should use it only if the table structure will not change.

Example   This example assigns new values to the first two fields of the current record:
```
TVarRecs values;
values.Add(208);
values.Add(23.1);
MyTable.SetFields(values);
```

SetKey method

Applies to   TTable component

void SetKey(void);
The SetKey method puts a table in SetKey state (the State property is set to dsSetKey). This enables an application to search for values in database tables. In SetKey state, you can set the values of the search key buffer. The search key buffer is a set of fields corresponding to the table's key fields. Assign values you want to search for to these key fields. After setting the values of the search key buffer fields, call GotoKey, GotoNearest, FindKey, or FindNearest to move the cursor to the matching record.

SetKey differs from EditKey in that the former clears all the elements of the search key buffer. EditKey leaves the elements of the search key buffer with their current values, but enables you to edit them.

Example

```
{
    Table1.SetKey();
    Table1.FieldByName("State")->AsString = "CA";
    Table1.FieldByName("City")->AsString = "Scotts Valley";
    Table1.GotoKey();
}
```

SetRange method

Applies to   TTable component

void SetRange(TVarRecs& startValues, TVarRecs& endValues);

The SetRange method combines the functionality of the SetRangeStart, SetRangeEnd, and ApplyRange methods. SetRange assigns the elements you specify as the value of the startValues parameter to the beginning index key, the elements you specify as the value of the endValues parameter to the ending index key, and then calls ApplyRange, which applies the range. This enables an application to filter the data visible to the dataset. Any subsequent search occurs only with this range.

If either startValues or endValues has fewer elements than the number of fields in the current index, then the remaining entries are set to NULL.

Note   With Paradox or dBASE tables, these methods work only with indexed fields. With SQL databases, they can work with any columns specified in the IndexFieldNames property.

Example   This code establishes a new range on a table:

```
TVarRecs startValues;
TVarRecs endValues;
startValues.Add(1000);
endValues.Add(2000);
MyTable.SetRange(&startValues, &endValues);
```

SetRangeEnd method

Applies to   TTable component

void SetRangeEnd(void);

The SetRangeEnd method prepares the table to have the next assignments to key fields become the end values of a range.

To establish a range on a table, call the SetRangeStart method, then assign the values you want to begin the range to the key index fields. Next call SetRangeEnd, and assign the values you want to end the range to the same key index fields. Finally, call the ApplyRange method to apply the range and filter the data visible to the application.

The corresponding method EditRangeEnd indicates to keep existing range values and update with the succeeding assignments. SetRangeEnd differs from EditRangEnd in that it clears all the elements of the range filter to the default values (or NULL). EditRangeEnd leaves the elements of the range filter with their current values.

Note   With Paradox or dBASE tables, these methods work only with indexed fields. With SQL databases, they can work with any columns specified in the IndexFieldNames property.

Example

```
{
    Table1.SetRangeStart(); // Set the beginning key */
    Table1.FieldByName("City")->AsString = "Felton";
    Table1.SetRangeEnd();    // Set the ending key */
    Table1.FieldByName("City")->AsString = "Scotts Valley";
    Table1.ApplyRange();     // Tell the dataset to establish the range
}
```

SetRangeStart method

Applies to   TTable component

void SetRangeStart(void);

The SetRangeStart method prepares the table to have the next assignments to key fields become the starting values of a range.

To establish a range on a table, call the SetRangeStart method, then assign the values you want to begin the range to the key index fields. Next call SetRangeEnd, and assign the values you want to end the range to the same key index fields. Finally, call the ApplyRange method to apply the range and filter the data visible to the application.

The corresponding method EditRangeStart indicates to keep existing range values and update with the succeeding assignments. SetRangeStart differs from EditRangeStart in that it clears all the elements of the range filter to the default values (or NULL). EditRangeEnd leaves the elements of the range filter with their current values.

Note   With Paradox or dBASE tables, these methods work only with indexed fields. With SQL databases, they can work with any columns specified in the IndexFieldNames property.

Example

```
{
    Table1.SetRangeStart(); // Set the beginning key
    Table1.FieldByName("City")->AsString = "Ben Lomond";
    Table1.SetRangeEnd();    // Set the ending key
    Table1.FieldByName("City")->AsString = "Scotts Valley";
    Table1.ApplyRange();     // Tell the dataset to establish the range
}
```

SetSelTextBuf method

Applies to   TDBEdit, TDBMemo components

void SetSelTextBuf (LPCSTR Buffer);
The SetSelTextBuf method sets the selected text in the database edit box or memo control to the text pointed to by Buffer.

SetText method

Applies to   TStrings components

void SetText(const string& text);
The SetText method writes an entire list of strings at one time. It is meant to be used with components that contain multiple strings where you would find it convenient to treat all the strings as one block. For example, SetText would be useful with a database memo component, which can hold multiple strings.

Specify the text you want to write as the value of the text parameter.

Example   The following code uses SetText to write the contents of a database edit box to a database memo:

```
string theText;
theText.assign( DBEdit1.Text );

DBMemo1.SetText(theText);
```

SetTextBuf method

Applies to   All data-aware controls

void SetTextBuf(const string& lpsz);
The SetTextBuf method sets the control's text to the text in the buffer pointed to by lpsz. Lpsz must point to a null-terminated string.

Show method

Applies to   All data-aware controls

void Show( );
The Show method makes a control visible by setting its Visible property to true.

ShowGridLines property

Applies to   TDBGrid component

bool ShowGridLines;
The ShowGridLines property determines whether lines appear between the rows and columns on a data grid. If true, the lines appear; if false, no lines appear.

Example

```
DBGrid1.ShowGridLines = true;
DBGrid1.Refresh( );
```

Size property

Applies to   All TField, TFieldDef, TMemoryStream components

Size property for field definitions

Applies to   TFieldDef component

uint16 Size;
Run-time and read-only. The Size property reports the size of the TFieldDef component. Size is meaningful only for a TFieldDef component with one of the following TFieldType values: ftString, ftBCD, ftBytes, ftVarBytes, ftBlob, ftMemo, or ftGraphic. For string and byte fields, Size is the number of bytes reserved in the table for the field. For a BCD field, it is the number of digits following the decimal point. For a BLOB, memo, or graphic field, it is the number of bytes in the field.

Size property for fields

Applies to   All TField components

uint16 Size;

For a TStringField, Size is the number of bytes reserved for the field in the dataset. For a TBCDField, it is the number of digits following the decimal point. For a TBlobField, TBytesField, TVarBytesField, TMemoField, or TGraphicField, it is the size of the field as stored in the table.

Size property for streams

Applies to   TMemoryStream component

int32 Size;

Run-time and read-only. The Size property returns the Size of the stream.

Sort method

Applies to   TStrings component

void Sort(void);

The Sort method sorts the strings in a string component in alphabetical order.

Example   The following code sorts MyStringList:

```
MyStringList.Sort();
```

Sorted property

Applies to   TDBComboBox, TDBLookupCombo, TDBListBox, TDBLookupList, TStrings components

Description   The Sorted property determines whether or not a list will be sorted in alphabetical order.

Sorted property for combo and list boxes

Applies to   TDBComboBox, TDBLookupCombo, TDBListBox, TDBLookupList components

bool Sorted;

The Sorted property indicates whether the items in a list box or combo box are arranged alphabetically. To sort the items, set the Sorted value to true. If Sorted is false, the items are unsorted.

If you add or insert items when Sorted is true, the items are placed in alphabetical order automatically.

Example   This code adds four strings to a database list box. Note that the strings are not in alphabetical order. Once the strings are added, setting the Sorted property to true sorts the strings so they appear in alphabetical order:

```
DBListBox1.Items->Add("Not");
DBListbox1.Items->Add("In");
DBListBox1.Items->Add("Alphabetical");
DBListBox1.Items->Add("Order");
DBListBox1.Sorted = true;
```

Sorted property for TStrings components

Applies to   TStrings component

bool Sorted;

The value of the Sorted property determines the order of the strings in the list of strings maintained by the string component. If Sorted is true, the strings are sorted in ascending order. If Sorted is false, the strings are not sorted.

Example   Three strings are added to a string list. The strings are sorted and then added to a database list box:

```
TStrings MyList;
MyList.Add("Plants");
MyList.Add("Animals");
MyList.Add("Minerals");
MyList.Sorted = true;
DBListBox1.Items->AddStrings(MyList);
```

Source property

Applies to   TBatchMove component

TDataSet Source;

The Source property specifies a source dataset corresponding to an existing source table for a batch move operation. When the batch move executes, the operation begins on the dataste specified as the value of Source.

SQL property

Applies to   TQuery component

TStrings* SQL;

The SQL property holds the text of the SQL statement that executes when the Open or ExecSQL is called. Once you have used the Open method to run the query, you must call the Close method before you can change the text of the SQL statement in the SQL property.

You can create the text for the SQL property:

- At run time, by closing any current query with Close, clearing the SQL property with Clear, and then specifying the SQL text with the Add or SetText methods.

- At run time, you can also use the LoadFromFile method to assign the text in an SQL script file to the SQL property.

A TQuery component can use the SQL property to access data from:

- Paradox or dBASE tables, using local SQL. The allowable syntax is a subset of ANSI-standard SQL and includes basic SELECT, INSERT, UPDATE, and DELETE statements.

- Databases on the Local InterBase Server, using InterBase SQL. For information on syntax and limitations, see the InterBase Language Reference.

- Databases on remote database servers. You must have installed the appropriate SQL Link available from Borland's SQL Links software. Any standard statement in the server's SQL is allowed. For information on SQL syntax and limitations, see your server documentation.

Visual Database Tools also supports heterogeneous queries against more than one server or table type (for example, data from an Oracle table and a Paradox table).

Note The SQL property can contain only one complete SQL statement at a time. In general, multiple statements are not allowed. Some servers support multiple statement "batch" syntax; if the server supports this, such statements are allowed.

StartTransaction method

Applies to   TDataBase component

void StartTransaction(void);

The StartTransaction method begins a transaction at the isolation level specified by the TransIsolation property. If a transaction is currently active, an EDatabaseError exception is raised.

Modifications made to the database will be held by the server until the Commit method is called to commit the changes or the Rollback method is called to cancel the changes.

Use this method only when connected to a server database.

Example

```
Database1.StartTransaction();
// Update one or more records in tables linked to Database1
...
Database1.Commit();
```

State property

Applies to   TDataSet, TDBCheckBox, TDBDataSet, TDataSource, TQuery, TStoredProc, TTable components

State property for check boxes

Applies to   TDBCheckBox component

TCheckBoxState State;
Run-time only. The State property determines the various states a check box control can have. These are the possible values:

Value	Meaning
cbUnchecked	The check box has no check mark, indicating the user hasn't selected the option.
cbChecked	The check box has a check mark in it, indicating the user has selected the option.
cbGrayed	The check box is gray, indicating a third state that is neither checked nor unchecked. Your application determines the meaning of a grayed check box.

State property for data sources

Applies to   TDataSource component

TDataSetState State;
Run-time and read-only. The State property reports the current status of the dataset referred to by the datasource component. The value of State is the same as that of the State property of DataSet, except that when Enabled is false or DataSet has not been assigned a value, State is Inactive. The possible values are those of the TDataSetState type:

Value	Meaning
dsInactive	The dataset is not active. To activate the dataset, set the Active property to true, or call the Open method.
dsBrowse	The user can view records in the dataset, but cannot change them or insert new records. This is the default state.
dsEdit	The user can modify records in the dataset.
dsInsert	The user can insert new records into the dataset.
dsSetKey	The dataset is in SetKey mode. The next assignments to the fields that make up the dataset's index key become the search key for the dataset. Call the SetKey method to put the dataset in SetKey mode.
dsCalcFields	Only calculated fields may be changed. This is the mode of the dataset when the OnCalcFields occurs.

State property for datasets

Applies to   TDataSet, TDBDataSet, TQuery, TStoredProc, TTable components

TDataSetState State;
Run-time and read-only. The State property specifies the current state of the dataset. The possible values are those of the TDataSetType type:

Value	Meaning
dsInactive	The dataset is not active. To activate the dataset, set the Active property to true, or call the Open method.
dsBrowse	The user can view records in the dataset, but cannot change them or insert new records. This is the default state.
dsEdit	The user can modify records in the dataset.
dsInsert	The user can insert new records into the dataset.
dsSetKey	The dataset is in SetKey mode. The next assignments to the fields that make up the dataset's index key become the search key for the dataset. Call the SetKey method to put the dataset in SetKey mode.
dsCalcFields	Only calculated fields may be changed. This is the mode of the dataset when the OnCalcFields occurs.

Example

```
// Open the dataset if it is not already
if( Table1.State == dsInactive )
  Table1.Active = true;
```

StmtHandle property

Applies to   TQuery, TStoredProc components

hDBIStmt StmtHandle;
Run-time and read-only. The StmtHandle property enables an application to make direct calls to the Borland Database Engine API using the result of the last query. You should not need to use this property, unless your application requires some functionality not available in the Visual Database Tools.

StoredProcName property

Applies to   TStoredProc component

string StoredProcName;
StoredProcName is the name of the stored procedure on the server.

Oracle servers allow more than one stored procedure with the same name. Set the Overload property to specify the procedure to execute on an Oracle server.

Stretch property

Applies to   TDBImage component

```
bool Stretch;
```
Setting the Stretch property to true permits bitmaps and metafiles to assume the size and shape of the image control. When the image control is resized, the image resizes also. The Stretch property has no effect on icons.

If you prefer to have the image control resize to fit the native size of the image, set the AutoSize property to true.

Example   This example uses a database image component on a form. When the form is created, the specified image is loaded and stretched to fit the boundaries of the image component.

```
TMyFormClass::SetupWindow()
{
  DBImage1.Stretch = true;
  DBImage1.Picture = TheHpic;
}
```

Strings property

Applies to   TStrings component

```
string Strings[ int index ];
```
Run-time only. With the Strings property, you can access a specific string of a string component. Specify the position of the string in the component as the value of the index parameter. The index of the Strings property is zero-based, so the first string has an Index value of 0, the second has an Index value of 1, and so on. To find out what the index of a particular string is, call the IndexOf method.

Example   This code adds strings to a database list box and then changes the value of the second string:

```
DBListBox1.Items->Add("One");
DBListBox1.Items->Add("Two");
DBListBox1.Items->Add("Three");
DBListBox1.Items->Strings[1] = "Second";
```

Because Strings is the default property of a string component, you can omit the reference to Strings in the preceding code. For example, you can write the code like this:

```
DBListBox1.Items->Add("One");
DBListBox1.Items->Add("Two");
ListBox1.Items->Add("Three");
DBListBox1.Items[1]  = "Second";
```

Style property

Applies to   TDBComboBox, TDBListBox, TDBLookupCombo, TDBLookupList components

Style property for list boxes

Applies to   TDBListBox, TDBLookupList components

TListBoxStyle Style;

The Style property determines how a list box displays its items. By default, Style is lbStandard, meaning that the list box displays each item as a string. By changing the value of Style, you can create owner-draw list boxes, meaning that items can be graphical and of either fixed or varying height. These are the possible values for Style:

Value	Meaning
lbStandard	All items are strings, with each item the same height.
lbOwnerDrawFixed	Each item in the list box is the height specified by the ItemHeight property.
lbOwnerDrawVariable	Items in the list box can be of varying heights.

Owner-draw list boxes can display items other than strings. For example, a list box could display graphical images along with or instead of its strings. Owner-draw list boxes require more programming, however, because the application needs information on how to render the image for each item in the list.

Each time an item is displayed in an lbOwnerDrawFixed list box, the OnDrawItem event occurs. The event handler for OnDrawItem draws the specified item. The ItemHeight property determines the height of all the items.

Each time an item is displayed in an lbOwnerDrawVariable list box, two events occur. The first is the OnMeasureItem event. The code you write for the OnMeasureItem handler can set the height of each item. Then the OnDrawItem event occurs. The code you write for the OnDrawItem handler draws each item in the list box using the size specified by the OnMeasureItem handler.

Style property for combo boxes

Applies to   TDBComboBox, TDBLookupCombo components

TComboBoxStyle Style;

The Style property determines how a database lookup combo box displays its items. These are the possible values:

Value	Meaning
csDropDown	Creates a drop-down list with an edit box in which the user can enter text. All items are strings, with each item having the same height. For database combo boxes, the combo box displays the contents of the field of the current record. The user can choose another item from the drop-down list and change the value of the field or type a new value in the edit box.
csSimple	Creates an edit box with a list that is always displayed (does not drop down). For database combo boxes, the current contents of the linked field displays in the combo box. The user can change the contents of the field by typing in a new value.

Value	Meaning
csDropDownList	Creates a drop-down list with no attached edit box, so the user can't edit an item or type in a new item. All items are strings, with each item having the same height. For database combo boxes, the edit box is blank unless the current contents of the field matches one of the specified Items in the drop-down list. The user can change the contents of the field only by selecting one of the strings from the drop-down list.
csOwnerDrawFixed	Each item in the combo box is the height specified by the ItemHeight property. For database combo boxes, the combo box is blank unless the current contents of the field matches one of the specified Items in the drop-down list. The user can change the contents of the field only by selecting one of the strings from the drop-down list.
csOwnerDrawVariable	Items in the combo box can be of varying heights. For database combo boxes, the combo box is blank unless the current contents of the field matches one of the specified Items in the drop-down list. The user can change the contents of the field only by selecting one of the strings from the drop-down list.

The default value is csDropDown.

Note If the value of the LookupDisplay property differs from the value of the LookupField property, the database lookup combo box functions as if its Style is csDropDownList, regardless of the value of the Style property.

Example The following code sets the style of DBLookupCombo1 to have a drop-down list with no edit box:

```
DBLookupCombo1.Style = csDropDownList;
```

TabIndex property (TabOrder at run time)

Applies to All data-aware controls

int TabIndex;
The TabIndex property indicates the position of the control in its parent's tab order, the order in which controls receive focus when the user presses the Tab key.

Initially, the tab order is always the order in which the components were added to the form, but you can change this by changing the TabIndex property. The value of the TabIndex property is unique for each component on the form. The first component added to the form has a TabIndex value of 0, the second is 1, the third is 2, and so on. These values determine where a control is in the tab order.

Each component has a unique tab-order value within its parent. If you change the TabIndex property value of one component to be the same as the value of a second component, the TabIndex value for all other components changes automatically. For example, suppose a component is sixth in the tab order. If you change the component's TabIndex property value to 3 (making the component fourth in the tab order), the component that was originally fourth in the tab order now becomes fifth, and the component that was fifth becomes sixth.

If you attempt to give a component a TabIndex value greater than the number of components on the form minus one (because numbering starts with 0), Resource

Workshop won't accept the new value, but will enter the value that assures the component will be the last in the tab order.

The control with the TabIndex value of 0 is the control that will have the focus when the form first appears.

TabIndex is meaningful only if the TabStop property is true.

When you access the TabIndex property programmatically, refer to it as TabOrder.

Example   This example ensures that the database check box on the form is the first in the tab order, and therefore, the active control whenever the form appears:

```
TMyFormClass::SetupWindow()
{
  DBCheckBox1.TabStop = true;
  DBCheckBox1.TabOrder = 0;
}
```

TableName property

Applies to   TTable component

string TableName;
The TableName property is the name of the underlying database table.

Note   Before you can change the value of this property, you must close by calling the Close method or setting the Active property to false.

TableType property

Applies to   TTable component

TTableType TableType;
The TableType property specifies the type of the underlying database table. This property is not used for SQL tables.

If TableType is set to ttDefault, the table's file-name extension determines the table type. If the value of TableType is not ttDefault, the table is always of the specified TableType, regardless of its file-name extension.

Value	Meaning
ttASCII	Text file
ttDBase	dBASE table
ttParadox	Paradox table

Note   The TTable must be closed to change this property.

TabOrder property (TabIndex at design time)

Applies To All data-aware controls

int TabOrder;
The TabOrder property indicates the position of the control in its parent's tab order, the order in which controls receive the focus when the user presses the Tab key.

Initially, the tab order is always the order in which the components were added to the form, but you can change this by changing the TabOrder property. The value of the TabOrder property is unique for each component on the form. The first component added to the form has a TabOrder value of 0, the second is 1, the third is 2, and so on. These values determine where a control is in the tab order.

Each component has a unique tab-order value within its parent. If you change the TabOrder property value of one component to be the same as the value of a second component, the TabOrder value for all other components changes automatically. For example, suppose a component is sixth in the tab order. If you change the component's TabOrder property value to 3 (making the component fourth in the tab order), the component that was originally fourth in the tab order now becomes fifth, and the component that was fifth becomes sixth.

If you attempt to give a component a TabOrder value greater than the number of components on the form minus one (because numbering starts with 0), Resource Workshop won't accept the new value, but will enter the value that assures the component will be the last in the tab order.

The control with the TabOrder value of 0 is the control that will have the focus when the form first appears.

TabOrder is meaningful only if the TabStop property is true.

When you access the TabOrder property at design time, Resource Workshop uses the VBX standard property name TabIndex.

Example This example ensures that the database check box on the form is the first in the tab order, and therefore, the active control whenever the form appears:

```
TMyFormClass::SetupWindow()
{
  DBCheckBox1.TabStop = true;
  DBCheckBox1.TabOrder = 0;
}
```

TabStop property

Applies To All data-aware controls

bool TabStop;
The TabStop property determines if the user can tab to a control. If TabStop is true, the control is in the tab order. If TabStop is false, the control is not in the tab order; therefore, the user can't press the Tab key to move to the control. The default value is true.

Example   This code removes DBListBox1 from the tab order so that the user can't use the Tab key to get to the list box:

```
DBListBox1.TabStop = false;
```

Tag property

Applies to   All components you can see at design time.

string Tag;

The Tag property is available to store a string as part of a component. While the Tag property has no particular meaning, your application can use the property to store a string for its special needs.

TAlign typedef   dbtype.h

typedef enum {alnNone, alnTop, alnBottom, alnLeft, alnRight, alnClient} TAlign;

TAlign defines the possible values of the Align property.

TAlignment typedef   dbtype.h

typedef enum {taLeftJustify, taRightJustify, taCenter} TAlignment;

TAlignment is the type of the Alignment property.

TBatchMode typedef   bdti.h

typedef enum {batAppend, batUpdate, batAppendUpdate, batDelete, batCopy}TBatchMode;

The TBatchMode type is the set of values which are passed to the BatchMove method of a TTable or the Mode property of a TBatchMove component.

TBatchMove component   bdto.h

A batch move component enables you to perform operations on groups of records or entire datasets. It is usually used to download data from a server to a local data source for analysis or other operations, or to upsize a database from a desktop data source to a server.

Specify the dataset from which data is to be moved as the value of the Source property. Specify the name of the table to which the data is to be transferred as the value of the Destination property. The destination table may or may not already exist. If it doesn't exist, the batch move operation creates it.

Use the Mode property to specify the operations to perform. If the source and destination datasets have different column names and you want to control how those fields are transferred, use the Mappings property.

To abort the batch move operation if a problem arises (for example, the data won't fit in a field in the destination table), set the AbortOnProblem property to true. To abort the operation when an integrity (key) violation occurs, set the AbortOnKeyViol to true.

To examine the records that caused the batch move operation to abort, specify tables to hold the problem records as the value of the KeyViolTableName and ProblemTableName properties. To examine which records were replaced or deleted during the batch move operation, name a table as the value of the ChangedTableName property. All of these tables are created during the batch move operation if you have specified a table name for these properties.

If the character set of the destination table is different from that of the source dataset, set the Transliterate property to true, so the conversion to the new character set occurs.

Public constructors and destructor

Constructors

Form 1   TBatchMove(PITBatchMove p)
Constructs a TBatchMove object which attaches to the given PITBatchMove COM interface pointer. The new TBatchMove saves the PITBatchMove COM object (incrementing its reference count) for later use.

Form 2   TBatchMove(const TBatchMove& p)
Constructs a TBatchMove object which attaches to the PITBatchMove COM object associated with the given TBatchMove object (which was passed by reference). The new TBatchMove saves the associated PITBatchMove COM object (incrementing its reference count) for later use.

Form 3   TBatchMove(PTBatchMove p)
Constructs a TBatchMove object which attaches to the PITBatchMove COM object associated with the given TBatchMove object (which was passed by pointer). The new TBatchMove saves the associated PITBatchMove COM object (incrementing its reference count) for later use.

Form 4   TBatchMove(void)
Constructs a new TBatchMove object. Internally, a new PITBatchMove COM object is created for later use.

Form 5   TBatchMove(HWND hdlg, int idc)
Constructs a TBatchMove object which attaches to the PITBatchMove COM object associated with the VBX specified by the given dialog box HWND and control id. The new TBatchMove saves the associated PITBatchMove COM object (incrementing its reference count) for later use.

Destructor

virtual ~TBatchMove()
Deletes the TBatchMove and reduces the reference count on the associated PITBatchMove COM object. If the reference count on the associated PITBatchMove COM object reaches zero, it is deleted.

Properties

AbortOnKeyViol
ChangedCount
Destination
KeyViolCount
KeyViolTableName
Mappings
Mode
MovedCount
Name
ProblemCount
ProblemTableName
RecordCount
Source
Transliterate

Methods

Assign
Execute

TBCDField component   **bdto.h**

A TBCDField represents a field of a record in a dataset. It is represented as a Binary
Coded Decimal (BCD) value. Use TBCDField for a floating-point number with a fixed
number of digits following the decimal point. The range depends on the number of
digits after the decimal point, since the accuracy is 18 digits.

Set the DisplayFormat property to control the formatting of the field for display
purposes, and the EditFormat property for editing purposes. Set the Size property to
define the number of BCD digits following the decimal point. Use the Value property to
access or change the current field value.

The TBCDField component has the properties, methods, and events of the TField
component.

Public constructors and destructor

Constructors

Form 1   TBCDField(PITField p)
Constructs a TBCDField object which attaches to the given PITField COM interface
pointer. The new TBCDField saves the PITField COM object (incrementing its reference
count) for later use.

Form 2   TBCDField(const TField& p)
Constructs a TBCDField object which attaches to the PITField COM object associated with the given TField object (which was passed by reference). The new TBCDField saves the associated PITField COM object (incrementing its reference count) for later use.

Form 3   TBCDField(PTField p)
Constructs a TBCDField object which attaches to the PITField COM object associated with the given TField object (which was passed by pointer). The new TBCDField saves the associated PITField COM object (incrementing its reference count) for later use.

Form 4   TBCDField(void)
Constructs a new TBCDField object. Internally, a new PITField COM object is created for later use.

Form 5   TBCDField(PTBDTComponent Owner)
Constructs a new TBCDField object. Internally, a new PITField COM object is created for later use. The Owner parameter specifies the DataSet which owns the new TBCDField. It can be NULL, to specify that there is no Owner.

Destructor

virtual ~TBCDField()
Deletes the TBCDField and reduces the reference count on the associated PITField COM object. If the reference count on the associated PITField COM object reaches 0, it is deleted.

Properties

AsBoolean
AsDateTime
AsFloat
AsInteger
AsString
Calculated
CanModify
Currency
DataSet
DataSize
DataType
DisplayFormat
DisplayText
EditFormat
EditMask
FieldName
FieldNo
Index (tfield components)
IsIndexField
IsNull
MaxValue

> MinValue
> Name
> Precision
> ReadOnly
> Required
> Size
> Text
> Value

Methods

> Assign
> AssignValue
> Clear
> GetData
> IsValidChar
> SetData

Events

> OnChange
> OnGetText
> OnSetText
> OnValidate

TBlobField component   bdto.h

A TBlobField component represents a field of a record in a dataset. It is represented by a value consisting of an arbitrary set of bytes of indefinite size.

To copy values from another field to a BLOB field, call the Assign method. To load a field's contents from a file or a stream, use the LoadFromFile and LoadFromStream methods, respectively. When you want to save the contents of a BLOB field to a file or a stream, call SaveToFile or SaveToStream.

The TBlobField component has the properties, methods, and events of the TField component from which it descends.

Public constructors and destructor

Constructors

Form 1   TBlobField(PITField p)
Constructs a TBlobField object which attaches to the given PITField COM interface pointer. The new TBlobField saves the PITField COM object (incrementing its reference count) for later use.

Form 2   TBlobField(const TField& p)
Constructs a TBlobField object which attaches to the PITField COM object associated with the given TField object (which was passed by reference). The new TBlobField saves the associated PITField COM object (incrementing its reference count) for later use.

Form 3   TBlobField(PTField p)
Constructs a TBlobField object which attaches to the PITField COM object associated with the given TField object (which was passed by pointer). The new TBlobField saves the associated PITField COM object (incrementing its reference count) for later use.

Form 4   TBlobField(void)
Constructs a new TBlobField object. Internally, a new PITField COM object is created for later use.

Form 5   TBlobField(PTBDTComponent Owner)
Constructs a new TBlobField object. Internally, a new PITField COM object is created for later use. The Owner parameter specifies the DataSet which owns the new TBlobField. It can be NULL, to specify that there is no Owner.

Form 6   TBlobField(PTBDTComponent Owner, TFieldType DataType)
Constructs a new TBlobField object. Internally, a new PITField COM object is created for later use. The Owner parameter specifies the DataSet which owns the new TBlobField. It can be NULL, to specify that there is no Owner. DataType is the type of field to be created.

Destructor

virtual ~TBlobField()
Deletes the TBlobField and reduces the reference count on the associated PITField COM object. If the reference count on the associated PITField COM object reaches 0, it is deleted.

Properties

▶ AsBoolean
▶ AsDateTime
▶ AsFloat
▶ AsInteger
▶ AsString
Calculated
▶ CanModify
▶ DataSet
▶ DataSize
▶ DataType
▶ DisplayText
EditMask
FieldName
▶ FieldNo
Index

▷ IsIndexField
▷ IsNull
Name
ReadOnly
Required
Size
▷ Text

Methods

Assign
AssignValue
Clear
GetData
IsValidChar
LoadFromFile
LoadFromStream
SaveToFile
SaveToStream
SetData

Events

OnChange
OnGetText
OnSetText
OnValidate

TBookmark typedef   bdti.h

typedef LPVOID TBookmark;

The TBookmark type is the type of the Bookmark parameter you use to call the
GetBookmark, GotoBookmark, and FreeBookmark methods of a dataset component.

TBooleanField component   bdto.h

A TBooleanField represents a field of a record in a dataset. A Boolean field is either true
or false, but the display string in a data-aware control can be varied.

Set the DisplayValues property to control the formatting of the field for display
purposes or input recognition. Use the Value property to access or change the current
field value.

The TBooleanField component has the properties, methods, and events of the TField
component.

Public constructors and destructor

Constructors

Form 1 TBooleanField(PITField p)
Constructs a TBooleanField object which attaches to the given PITField COM interface pointer. The new TBooleanField saves the PITField COM object (incrementing its reference count) for later use.

Form 2 TBooleanField(const TField& p)
Constructs a TBooleanField object which attaches to the PITField COM object associated with the given TField object (which was passed by reference). The new TBooleanField saves the associated PITField COM object (incrementing its reference count) for later use.

Form 3 TBooleanField(PTField p)
Constructs a TBooleanField object which attaches to the PITField COM object associated with the given TField object (which was passed by pointer). The new TBooleanField saves the associated PITField COM object (incrementing its reference count) for later use.

Form 4 TBooleanField(void)
Constructs a new TBooleanField object. Internally, a new PITField COM object is created for later use.

Form 5 TBooleanField(PTBDTComponent Owner)
Constructs a new TBooleanField object. Internally, a new PITField COM object is created for later use. The Owner parameter specifies the DataSet which owns the new TBooleanField. It can be NULL, to specify that there is no Owner.

Destructor

virtual ~TBooleanField()
Deletes the TBooleanField and reduces the reference count on the associated PITField COM object. If the reference count on the associated PITField COM object reaches 0, it is deleted.

Properties

▶ AsBoolean
▶ AsDateTime
▶ AsFloat
▶ AsInteger
▶ AsString
 Calculated
▶ CanModify
▶ DataSet
▶ DataSize
▶ DataType
▶ DisplayText
 DisplayValues

EditMask
FieldName
▶FieldNo
Index
▶IsIndexField
▶IsNull
Name
ReadOnly
Required
▶Size
▶Text
Value

Methods

Assign
AssignValue
Clear
GetData
IsValidChar
SetData

Events

OnChange
OnGetText
OnSetText
OnValidate

TBorderStyle typedef   dbtype.h

typedef enum {bsNone, bsSingle}TBorderStyle;
TBorderStyle is the type of the BorderStyle property for controls.

TBtnState typedef   dbtype.h

typedef enum {btnOff, btnOn, btnDisabled}TBtnState;
The TBtnState type is the data type of the button properties of a TDBNavigator
component. The button properties are: BtnCancel, BtnDelete, BtnEdit, BtnFirst,
BtnInsert, BtnLast, BtnNext, BtnPost, BtnPrevious, and BtnRefresh.

TBytesField component   bdto.h

A TBytesField represents a field of a record in a dataset. It is represented by a value
consisting of an arbitrary set of bytes with indefinite size.

Use the Assign method to copy values from another field to a TBytesField.

The TBytesField component has the properties, methods, and events of the TField component.

Public constructors and destructor

Constructors

Form 1   TBytesField(PITField p)
Constructs a TBytesField object which attaches to the given PITField COM interface pointer. The new TBytesField saves the PITField COM object (incrementing its reference count) for later use.

Form 2   TBytesField(const TField& p)
Constructs a TBytesField object which attaches to the PITField COM object associated with the given TField object (which was passed by reference). The new TBytesField saves the associated PITField COM object (incrementing its reference count) for later use.

Form 3   TBytesField(PTField p)
Constructs a TBytesField object which attaches to the PITField COM object associated with the given TField object (which was passed by pointer). The new TBytesField saves the associated PITField COM object (incrementing its reference count) for later use.

Form 4   TBytesField(void)
Constructs a new TBytesField object. Internally, a new PITField COM object will be created for later use.

Form 5   TBytesField(PTBDTComponent Owner)
Constructs a new TBytesField object. Internally, a new PITField COM object will be created for later use. The Owner parameter specifies the DataSet which owns the new TBytesField. It can be NULL, to specify that there is no Owner.

Destructor

virtual ~TBytesField()
Deletes the TBytesField and reduces the reference count on the associated PITField COM object. If the reference count on the associated PITField COM object reaches 0, it is deleted.

Properties

▶ AsBoolean
▶ AsDateTime
▶ AsFloat
▶ AsInteger
▶ AsString
  Calculated
▶ CanModify
▶ DataSet

▶ DataSize
▶ DataType
▶ DisplayText
EditMask
FieldName
▶ FieldNo
Index
▶ IsIndexField
▶ IsNull
Name
ReadOnly
Required
Size
▶ Text

Methods

Assign
AssignValue
Clear
GetData
IsValidChar
SetData

Events

OnChange
OnGetText
OnSetText
OnValidate

TComboBoxStyle typedef   dbtype.h

typedef enum{ csSimple, csDropDown, csDropDownList, csOwnerDrawFixed, csOwnerDrawVariable }
    TComboBoxStyle;
The TComboBoxStyle type is the type of the Style property for a combo box
(TDBComboBox and TDBLookupCombo components).

TCurrencyField component   bdto.h

A TCurrencyField represents a field of a record in a dataset. It is represented as a binary
value with a range from (positive or negative) 5.0 * 10-324 to 1.7 * 10308. It has an
accuracy of 15 digits. Use TCurrencyField for fields that hold currency values.

Set the DisplayFormat property to control the formatting of the field for display purposes, and the EditFormat property for editing purposes. Use the Value property to access or change the current field value.

The TCurrencyField component has the properties, methods, and events of the TField component.

Public constructors and destructor

Constructors

Form 1   TCurrencyField(PITField p)
Constructs a TCurrencyField object which attaches to the given PITField COM interface pointer. The new TCurrencyField saves the PITField COM object (incrementing its reference count) for later use.

Form 2   TCurrencyField(const TField& p)
Constructs a TCurrencyField object which attaches to the PITField COM object associated with the given TField object (which was passed by reference). The new TCurrencyField saves the associated PITField COM object (incrementing its reference count) for later use.

Form 3   TCurrencyField(PTField p)
Constructs a TCurrencyField object which attaches to the PITField COM object associated with the given TField object (which was passed by pointer). The new TCurrencyField saves the associated PITField COM object (incrementing its reference count) for later use.

Form 4   TCurrencyField(void)
Constructs a new TCurrencyField object. Internally, a new PITField COM object is created for later use.

Form 5   TCurrencyField(PTBDTComponent Owner)
Constructs a new TCurrencyField object. Internally, a new PITField COM object is created for later use. The Owner parameter specifies the DataSet which owns the new TCurrencyField. It can be NULL, to specify that there is no Owner.

Destructor

virtual ~TCurrencyField()
Deletes the TCurrencyField and reduces the reference count on the associated PITField COM object. If the reference count on the associated PITField COM object reaches 0, it is deleted.

Properties

- ▸ AsBoolean
- ▸ AsDateTime
- ▸ AsFloat
- ▸ AsInteger
- ▸ AsString

Calculated
▶CanModify
Currency
DataSet
▶DataSize
▶DataType
DisplayFormat
▶DisplayText
EditFormat
EditMask
FieldName
▶FieldNo
Index
▶IsIndexField
▶IsNull
MaxValue
MinValue
Name
Precision
ReadOnly
Required
▶Size
▶Text
▶Value

Methods

Assign
AssignValue
Clear
GetData
IsValidChar
SetData

Events

OnChange
OnGetText
OnSetText
OnValidate

TCursor typedef   dbtype.h

typedef enum{ crDefault, crArrow, crCross, crIBeam, crIcon, crSize, crSizeNESW, crSizeNS, crSizeNWSE, crSizeWE, crUpArrow }TCursor;

The TCursor type defines the different kinds of standard cursors a component can have. TCursor is the type of the Cursor property and the DragCursor property.

TDatabase component   bdto.h

The TDatabase component is not required for database access, but it provides additional control over factors that are important for client/server applications. If you do not create an explicit TDatabase component for a database, and an application opens a table in the database, then a temporary (virtual) TDatabase component is created.

DatabaseName is the name of the database connection that can be used by dataset components. In other words, this is the name of the local alias defined by the component that will show up in the DatabaseName drop-down list of dataset components.

AliasName is the name of an existing BDE alias defined with the BDE Configuration Utility. The specified alias determines the default parameter settings for connecting to a database for the TDatabase component, which appear as the value of the Params property.

DriverName is the name of a BDE driver, such as STANDARD (for dBASE and Paradox), ORACLE, SYBASE, INFORMIX, or INTERBASE. This property clears if AliasName is set, because an AliasName specifies a driver type.

The DataSets property of TDatabase is an array of references to the active datasets in the TDatabase. The DatasetCount property is an integer that specifies the number of active datasets.

To open or close the database, set the Connected property to true. You can avoid having to log in to the server each time the database is opened if you set the KeepConnection property to true. You can choose for your application to prompt the user for a user name and password each time the application logs in to the database server by setting the LoginPrompt prompt to true.

The TDatabase component controls server transactions. Call the StartTransaction method to begin a transaction, the RollBack method to cancel it, or the Commit method to commit the changes. The TransIsolation property specifies the transaction isolation level to request on the server.

Public constructors and destructor

Constructors

Form 1   TDatabase(PITDatabase p)
Constructs a TDatabase object which attaches to the given PITDatabase COM interface pointer. The new TDatabase saves the PITDatabase COM object (incrementing its reference count) for later use.

Form 2   TDatabase(const TDatabase& p)
Constructs a TDatabase object which attaches to the PITDatabase COM object associated with the given TDatabase object (which was passed by reference). The new TDatabase

saves the associated PITDatabase COM object (incrementing its reference count) for later use.

Form 3   TDatabase(PTDatabase p)

Constructs a TDatabase object which attaches to the PITDatabase COM object associated with the given TDatabase object (which was passed by pointer). The new TDatabase saves the associated PITDatabase COM object (incrementing its reference count) for later use.

Form 4   TDatabase(void)

Constructs a new TDatabase object. Internally, a PITDatabase COM object is created for later use.

Form 5   TDatabase(HWND hdlg, int idc)

Constructs a TDatabase object which attaches to the PITDatabase COM object associated with the VBX specified by the given dialog box HWND and control id. The new TDatabase saves the associated PITDatabase COM object (incrementing its reference count) for later use.

Destructor

virtual ~TDatabase()

Deletes the TDatabase and reduces the reference count on the associated PITDatabase COM object. If the reference count on the associated PITDatabase COM object reaches 0, it is deleted.

Properties

AliasName
Connected
DatabaseName
▶ DatasetCount
▶ Datasets
DriverName
▶ Handle
▶ IsSQLBased
KeepConnection
▶ Locale
LoginPrompt
Name
Params
▶ Temporary
TransIsolation

Methods

Assign
Close
CloseDatasets

Commit
Open
Rollback
StartTransaction
ValidateName

Events

OnLogin

TDataChange_MFUNCTOR macro

TDataChange_MFUNCTOR(object, memberFunc)
This macro constructs the event sink object, which is of type TDataChangeSink, binding
it to the handler method that responds when an event of a TDataSource component
occurs.

Parameter	Meaning
object	Identifies the event sink object; use the *this pointer
memberFunc	Identifies the event handler that responds to the OnDragOver event

TDataChangeSink typedef   bdto.h

typedef TBdtEventSinkV2<TDataSource& sender, TField* field> TDataChangeSink;
The TDataChangeSink is the type of the event sink for the OnDataChange event of a
TDataSource component.

TDataChangeSource typedef   bdto.h

typedef TBdtEventSourceV2<TDataSource& sender, TField* field> TDataChangeSource;
The TDataChangeSource is the type of the event source for the OnDataChange event of
a TDataSource component.

TDataSet component   bdto.h

The TDataSet component provides Visual Database Tools access to datasets, whether
they be tables, or the results of a query or a stored procedure. TDataSet is the immediate
ancestor of the TDBDataSet component, from which TTable, TQuery, and TStoredProc
inherit directly. Usually, applications use the TTable, TQuery, and TStoredProc
components instead of TDataSet.

The DataSource property identifies the origin of the data displayed in the dataset
component. You open a dataset either by setting its Active property to true, or by calling

the Open method. Setting Active to false is equivalent to calling the Close method. After a dataset is connected to one or more data source components, you can temporarily disconnect it from the data sources with the DisableControls method. EnableControls restores the connections.

The State property indicates the current state of the dataset; for example, whether it is being edited, browsed, or whether a record is being inserted.

The CanModify property determines whether the data in the dataset can be changed; if CanModify is true, your application can call the Edit method that prepares the dataset for changes. If you want to discard any changes made to the current record, call the Cancel method, and the dataset returns to browse state. If Modified is true, the contents of one or more fields in the dataset has changed. To return all fields of the current record to their default values, call ClearFields.

Your application can insert records in the dataset by calling the Insert method, and append records by calling Append. Once records have been changed in some way, either through inserting, appending, or editing, calling the Post method writes the current record to the database, although, in many cases, posting occurs automatically.

You can access a particular field using the Fields property, or by calling the FieldByName method. FieldCount returns the number of fields in the dataset, and FieldDefs returns the definitions of the fields in the dataset.

The RecordSize and RecordCount properties determine the size of the records and the number of records in the dataset, respectively.

The AtBOF property is true if the current record is at the beginning of the dataset. The AtEOF property is true if the current record is the last record in the dataset. The First method moves the cursor to the first record in the dataset and Last moves it to the last record. The Next method advances the cursor one record, and Prior moves the cursor backward one record. With the MoveBy method you can specify the number of records you want to advance the cursor on a dataset.

You can save current record information with the GetBookmark method, and then later return to that record using GotoBookmark. Release the bookmark by calling FreeBookmark.

Dataset components have several events. Many of them occur just before a TDataSet component method is executed. For example, BeforeOpen occurs before Open runs, and BeforePost occurs before Post runs. The names of all such events begin with Before: BeforeClose, BeforeCancel, and so on. Within their event handlers, specify special processing you want to occur before the corresponding method executes. For example, you would write code that you want to execute before the Open method runs in the BeforeOpen event.

Each Before event is paired with an After event, such as AfterClose, AfterCancel, and so on. Place code you want to execute after a method executes in its corresponding After event.

When a new record is added to a dataset, the OnNewRecord occurs.

You use the OnCalcFields event to calculate the value of calculated fields. How often the OnCalcFields event occurs depends on the value of the AutoCalcFields property.

Public constructors and destructor

Constructors

Form 1   TDataSet(PITDataSet p)

Constructs a TDataSet object which attaches to the given PITDataSet COM interface pointer. The new TDataSet saves the PITDataSet COM object (incrementing its reference count) for later use.

Form 2   TDataSet(const TDataSet& p)

Constructs a TDataSet object which attaches to the PITDataSet COM object associated with the given TDataSet object (which was passed by reference). The new TDataSet saves the associated PITDataSet COM object (incrementing its reference count) for later use.

Form 3   TDataSet(PTDataSet p)

Constructs a TDataSet object which attaches to the PITDataSet COM object associated with the given TDataSet object (which was passed by pointer). The new TDataSet saves the associated PITDataSet COM object (incrementing its reference count) for later use.

Form 4   TDataSet(void)

Constructs an unassigned TDataSet object. Internally, the PITDataSet COM object is set to NULL. This is for internal use only.

Destructor

virtual ~TDataSet()

Deletes the TDataSet and reduces the reference count on the associated PITDataSet COM object. If the reference count on the associated PITDataSet COM object reaches 0, it is deleted.

Properties

Active
▶ AtBOF
▶ AtEOF
AutoCalcFields
▶ CanModify
DataSource
DefaultFields
▶ FieldCount
▶ FieldDefs
▶ Fields
▶ Handle
▶ Locale
▶ Modified
Name
▶ RecordCount
RecordSize
▶ State

Methods

Append
AppendRecord
Assign
Cancel
CheckBrowseMode
ClearFields
Close
CursorPosChanged
Delete
DisableControls
Edit
EnableControls
FieldByName
FindField
First
FreeBookmark
GetBookmark
GetCurrentRecord
GetFieldNames
GotoBookmark
Insert
IsLinkedTo
Last
MoveBy
Next
Open
Post
Prior
Refresh
SetFields
UpdateCursorPos
UpdateRecord

Events

AfterCancel
AfterClose
AfterDelete
AfterEdit
AfterInsert
AfterOpen
AfterPost
BeforeCancel
BeforeClose

BeforeDelete
BeforeEdit
BeforeInsert
BeforeOpen
BeforePost
OnCalcFields

TDataSetNotify_MFUNCTOR macro

TDataSetNotify_MFUNCTOR(object, memberFunc)
This macro constructs the event sink object, which is of type TDataSetNotifySink,
binding it to the handler method that responds when an event of a TDataSet component
occurs.

Parameter	Meaning
object	Identifies the event sink object; use the *this pointer
memberFunc	Identifies the event handler that responds to the OnDragOver event

TDataSetNotifySink typedef   bdto.h

typedef TBdtEventSinkV1<TDataSet& sender> TDataSetNotifySink;
The TDataSetNotifySink is the type of the event sink for all the following events of a
TDataSet component:

AfterCancel	BeforeCancel	OnCalcFields
AfterClose	BeforeClose	OnNewRecord
AfterDelete	BeforeDelete	
AfterEdit	BeforeEdit	
AfterInsert	BeforeInsert	
AfterOpen	BeforeOpen	
AfterPost	BeforePost	

TDataSetNotifySource typedef   bdto.h

typedef TBdtEventSourceV1<TDataSet& sender> TDataSetNotifySource;
The TDataSetNotifySource is the type of the event source for all the following events of
a TDataSet component:

AfterCancel	BeforeCancel	OnCalcFields
AfterClose	BeforeClose	OnNewRecord
AfterDelete	BeforeDelete	

AfterEdit	BeforeEdit
AfterInsert	BeforeInsert
AfterOpen	BeforeOpen
AfterPost	BeforePost

TDataSetState typedef

typedef enum{ dsInactive, dsBrowse, dsEdit, dsInsert, dsSetKey, dsCalcFields }TDataSetState;

The TDataSetState type is the set of values of the State property of a dataset component.

TDataSource component

TDataSource is the interface between a dataset component and data-aware controls on forms. TDataSource attaches to a dataset through the Dataset property. Data-aware controls, such as database edit boxes and data grids, attach to a TDataSource through their DataSource properties. Usually each dataset component has only one data source, but you can have as many data source components connected to a dataset as needed.

The Dataset property identifies the dataset from which the data is obtained. Set the Enabled property to false to clear and disable the data-aware controls. Check the current status of the dataset with the State property. To monitor changes to both the dataset and attached data-aware controls, assign a method to the OnDataChange event. To monitor changes in the dataset's state, assign a method to the OnStateChange event. To update the dataset prior to a post, assign a method to the OnUpdateData event.

Public constructors and destructor

Constructors

Form 1   TDataSource(PITDataSource p)

Constructs a TDataSource object which attaches to the given PITDataSource COM interface pointer. The new TDataSource saves the PITDataSource COM object (incrementing its reference count) for later use.

Form 2   TDataSource(const TDataSource& p)

Constructs a TDataSource object which attaches to the PITDataSource COM object associated with the given TDataSource object (which was passed by reference). The new TDataSource saves the associated PITDataSource COM object (incrementing its reference count) for later use.

Form 3   TDataSource(PTDataSource p)

Constructs a TDataSource object which attaches to the PITDataSource COM object associated with the given TDataSource object (which was passed by pointer). The new TDataSource saves the associated PITDataSource COM object (incrementing its reference count) for later use.

Form 4   TDataSource(void)
Constructs a new TDataSource object. Internally, a PITDataSource COM object is created for later use.

Form 5   TDataSource(HWND hdlg, int idc)
Constructs a TDataSource object which attaches to the PITDataSource COM object associated with the VBX specified by the given dialog box HWND and control id. The new TDataSource saves the associated PITDataSource COM object (incrementing its reference count) for later use.

Destructor

virtual ~TDataSource()
Deletes the TDataSource and reduces the reference count on the associated PITDataSource COM object. If the reference count on the associated PITDataSource COM object reaches 0, it is deleted.

Properties

AutoEdit
Dataset
Enabled
Name
State

Methods

Assign
Edit
IsLinkedTo

Events

OnDataChange
OnStateChange
OnUpdateData

TDataSourceNotify_MFUNCTOR macro

TDataSourceNotify_MFUNCTOR(object, memberFunc)
This macro constructs the event sink object, which is of type TDataSourceNotifySink, binding it to the handler method that responds when an event of a TDataSource component occurs.

Parameter	Meaning
object	Identifies the event sink object; use the *this pointer
memberFunc	Identifies the event handler that responds to the OnDragOver event

TDataSourceNotifySink typedef

bdto.h

typedef TBdtEventSinkV1<TDataSource& sender> TDataSourceNotifySink;
The TDataSourceNotifySink is the type of the event sink for the OnStateChange and OnUpdateData events of a TDataSource component.

TDataSourceNotifySource typedef

bdto.h

typedef TBdtEventSourceV1<TDataSource& sender> TDataSourceNotifySource;
The TDataSourceNotifySource is the type of the event source for the OnStateChange and OnUpdateData events of a TDataSource component.

TDateField component

bdto.h

TDateField represents a field in a record in a dataset. It contains a value which is a date.

Set the DisplayFormat property to control the formatting of the field for display purposes, and the EditFormat property for editing purposes. Use the Value property to access or change the current field value.

The TDateField component has the properties, methods, and events of the TField component.

Public constructors and destructor

Constructors

Form 1   TDateField(PITField p)
Constructs a TDateField object which attaches to the given PITField COM interface pointer. The new TDateField saves the PITField COM object (incrementing its reference count) for later use.

Form 2   TDateField(const TField& p)
Constructs a TDateField object which attaches to the PITField COM object associated with the given TField object (which was passed by reference). The new TDateField saves the associated PITField COM object (incrementing its reference count) for later use.

Form 3   TDateField(PTField p)
Constructs a TDateField object which attaches to the PITField COM object associated with the given TField object (which was passed by pointer). The new TDateField saves the associated PITField COM object (incrementing its reference count) for later use.

Form 4   TDateField(void)
Constructs a new TDateField object. Internally, a new PITField COM object will be created for later use.

Form 5   TDateField(PTBDTComponent Owner)
Constructs a new TDateField object. Internally, a new PITField COM object will be created for later use. The Owner parameter specifies the DataSet which owns the new TDateField. It can be NULL, to specify that there is no Owner.

Destructor

virtual ~TDateField()
Deletes the TDateField and reduces the reference count on the associated PITField COM object. If the reference count on the associated PITField COM object reaches 0, it is deleted.

Properties

▶ AsBoolean
▶ AsDateTime
▶ AsFloat
▶ AsInteger
▶ AsString
Calculated
▶ CanModify
▶ DataSet
▶ DataSize
▶ DataType
DisplayFormat
▶ DisplayText
EditMask
FieldName
▶ FieldNo
Index
▶ IsIndexField
▶ IsNull
Name
ReadOnly
Required
▶ Size
▶ Text
Value

Methods

Assign
AssignValue
Clear

GetData
IsValidChar
SetData

Events

OnChange
OnGetText
OnSetText
OnValidate

TDateTimeField component

bdto.h

A TDateTimeField component represents a field of a record in a dataset. It contains a value consisting of a date and time.

Set the DisplayFormat property to control the formatting of the field for display purposes, and the EditFormat property for editing purposes. Use the Value property to access or change the current field value.

The TDateTimeField component has the properties, methods, and events of the TField component.

Public constructors and destructor

Constructors

Form 1 TDateTimeField(PITField p)
Constructs a TDateTimeField object which attaches to the given PITField COM interface pointer. The new TDateTimeField saves the PITField COM object (incrementing its reference count) for later use.

Form 2 TDateTimeField(const TField& p)
Constructs a TDateTimeField object which attaches to the PITField COM object associated with the given TField object (which was passed by reference). The new TDateTimeField saves the associated PITField COM object (incrementing its reference count) for later use.

Form 3 TDateTimeField(PTField p)
Constructs a TDateTimeField object which attaches to the PITField COM object associated with the given TField object (which was passed by pointer). The new TDateTimeField saves the associated PITField COM object (incrementing its reference count) for later use.

Form 4 TDateTimeField(void)
Constructs a new TDateTimeField object. Internally, a new PITField COM object is created for later use.

Form 5   TDateTimeField(PTBDTComponent Owner)
Constructs a new TDateTimeField object. Internally, a new PITField COM object is
created for later use. The Owner parameter specifies the DataSet which owns the new
TDateTimeField. It can be NULL, to specify that there is no Owner.

Form 6   TDateTimeField(PTBDTComponent Owner, TFieldType DataType)
Constructs a new TDateTimeField object. Internally, a new PITField COM object is
created for later use. The Owner parameter specifies the DataSet which owns the new
TDateTimeField. It can be NULL, to specify that there is no Owner. DataType is the type
of field to be created.

Destructor

virtual ~TDateTimeField()
Deletes the TDateTimeField and reduces the reference count on the associated PITField
COM object. If the reference count on the associated PITField COM object reaches 0, it is
deleted.

Properties

▶ AsBoolean
▶ AsDateTime
▶ AsFloat
▶ AsInteger
▶ AsString
Calculated
▶ CanModify
▶ DataSet
▶ DataSize
▶ DataType
DisplayFormat
▶ DisplayText
EditMask
FieldName
▶ FieldNo
Index
▶ IsIndexField
▶ IsNull
Name
ReadOnly
Required
▶ Size
▶ Text
▶ Value

Methods

Assign
AssignValue
Clear
GetData
IsValidChar
SetData

Events

OnChange
OnGetText
OnSetText
OnValidate

TDBCheckBox component   dbchkbx.h

A check box presents an option to the user; the user can check it to select the option, or uncheck it to deselect the option. A database check box (TDBCheckBox) is much like an ordinary check box, except that it is aware of the data in a particular field of a dataset.

You can link a database check box with a dataset by specifying the data source component (TDataSource) that identifies the dataset as the value of the check box's DataSource property. Specify the field in the dataset you want to access as the value of the check box's DataField property.

If the contents of a field in the current record of the dataset equals the string of the ValueChecked property, the database check box is checked. If the contents matches the string specified as the value of the ValueUnchecked property, the check box is unchecked.

When the user checks or unchecks a database check box, the string specified as the value of the ValueChecked or ValueUnchecked property becomes the value of the field in the dataset, as long as the value of the ReadOnly property is false and the dataset is in edit mode. If you want the user to be able to view the data in the field but not modify it, set ReadOnly to true. For more information, see "Updating Fields."

Public constructors and destructor

Constructors

Form 1   TDBCheckBox(TWindow* Parent, int ID, LPCSTR Title, int Left, Int Top, Int Width, int Height,
               TModule* Module=0);
Creates a new check box object with the following parameters:

- Parent identifies the parent window object.

- ID identifies the check box component.

- Title contains the title of the window.
- Left, Top, Width, and Height identify the window position. If this is a child component, the position is relative to the parent client area.
- Module identifies the owner of the check box component.

Form 2 TDBCheckBox(TWindow* Parent, int ID, TModule* Module=0);
Creates a check box by loading it from an existing dialog resource.

- Parent identifies the parent window object.
- ID identifies the check box.
- Module identifies the owner of the check box.

Destructor

~TDBCheckBox()
Deletes the check box component.

Properties

About
▶ Align
Alignment
AllowGrayed
BackColor
BoundsRect
Caption
Checked
▶ ComponentIndex
Cursor
DataChanged
DataField
DataSource
DragCursor
DragMode
Enabled
FontBold
FontItalic
FontName
FontSize
FontStrikethru
FontUnderline
ForeColor
Height
HelpContext
Index
Left
Name

▶Owner
▶Parent
ReadOnly
State
TabOrder
TabStop
Tag
Top
ValueChecked
ValueUnchecked
Visible
Width

Methods

BeginDrag
BringToFront
CanFocus
ClientToScreen
Dragging
EndDrag
Focused
GetTextBuf
GetTextLen
Hide
Invalidate
Refresh
Repaint
ScaleBy
ScreenToClient
ScrollBy
SendToBack
SetBounds
SetTextBuf
Show
Update

Events

OnClick
OnDragDrop
OnDragOver
OnEndDrag
OnEnter
OnExit
OnKeyDown

OnKeyPress
OnKeyUp
OnMouseDown
OnMouseMove
OnMouseUp

TDBCheckBoxDrag_MFUNCTOR macro

TDBCheckBoxDrag_MFUNCTOR(object, memberFunc)
This macro constructs the event sink object, which is of type TDBCheckBoxDragSink, binding it to the handler method that responds when the OnDragDrop and OnEndDrag events of a TDBCheckBox component occur.

Parameter	Meaning
object	Identifies the event sink object; use the *this pointer
memberFunc	Identifies the event handler that responds to the OnDragDrop event

TDBCheckBoxDragOver_MFUNCTOR macro

TDBCheckBoxDragOver_MFUNCTOR(object, memberFunc)
This macro constructs the event sink object, which is of type TDBCheckBoxDragOverSink, binding it to the handler method that responds when the OnDragOver event of a TDBCheckBox component occurs.

Parameter	Meaning
object	Identifies the event sink object; use the *this pointer
memberFunc	Identifies the event handler that responds to the OnDragOver event

TDBCheckBoxDragOverSink typedef   dbevent.h

typedef TBdtEventSinkV5<TDBCheckBox& sender, TVbxControl& source, SHORT X, SHORT Y,
    TDragState state> TDBCheckBoxDragOverSink;
The TDBCheckBoxDragSink is the type of the event sink for the OnDragOver event of a TDBCheckBox component.

Parameter	Meaning
sender	The TDBCheckBox component
source	The control being dragged and dropped
X	The X parameter of the coordinates of the mouse positioned over the control

Parameter	Meaning
Y	The Y parameter of the coordinates of the mouse positioned over the control
state	Possible values:
	0 The dragged object enters a control in which it can be dropped
	1 The dragged object is moved within a control in which it can be dropped
	2 The dragged object is moved within a control in which it can be dropped

TDBCheckBoxDragOverSource typedef dbevent.h

typedef TBdtEventSourceV5<TDBCheckBox& sender, TVbxControl& source, SHORT X, SHORT Y,
    TDragState state> TDBCheckBoxDragOverSource;

The TDBCheckBoxDragSource is the type of the event source the OnDragOver event of a TDBCheckBox component.

Parameter	Meaning
sender	The TDBCheckBox component
source	The control being dragged and dropped
X	The X parameter of the coordinates of the mouse positioned over the control
Y	The Y parameter of the coordinates of the mouse positioned over the control
state	Possible values:
	0 The dragged object enters a control in which it can be dropped
	1 The dragged object is moved within a control in which it can be dropped
	2 The dragged object leaves a control in which it can be dropped

TDBCheckBoxDragSink typdef dbevent.h

typedef TBdtEventSinkV4<TDBCheckBox& sender, TVbxControl& source, SHORT X,
    SHORT Y> TDBCheckBoxDragSink;

The TDBCheckBoxDragSink is the type of the event sink for the OnDragDrop and OnEndDrag events of a TDBCheckBox component.

Parameter	Meaning
sender	The TDBCheckBox component
source	The control being dragged and dropped
X	The X parameter of the coordinates of the mouse positioned over the control
Y	The Y parameter of the coordinates of the mouse positioned over the control

TDBCheckBoxDragSource typedef dbevent.h

typedef TBdtEventSourceV4<TDBCheckBox& sender, TVbxControl& source, SHORT X,
    SHORT Y> TDBCheckBoxDragSource;

The TDBCheckBoxDragSource is the type of the event source for the OnDragDrop and OnEndDrag events of a TDBCheckBox component.

Parameter	Meaning
sender	The TDBCheckBox component
source	The control being dragged and dropped
X	The X parameter of the coordinates of the mouse positioned over the control
Y	The Y parameter of the coordinates of the mouse positioned over the control

TDBCheckBoxKey_MFUNCTOR macro

TDBCheckBoxKey_MFUNCTOR(object, memberFunc)
This macro constructs the event sink object, which is of type TDBCheckBoxKeySink, binding it to the handler method that responds when the OnKeyUp and OnKeyDown events of a TDBCheckBox component occur.

Parameter	Meaning
object	Identifies the event sink object; use the *this pointer
memberFunc	Identifies the event handler that responds to the OnKeyUp and OnKeyDown events

TDBCheckBoxKeyPress_MFUNCTOR macro

TDBCheckBoxKeyPress_MFUNCTOR(object, memberFunc)
This macro constructs the event sink object, which is of type TDBCheckBoxKeyPressSink, binding it to the handler method that responds when the OnKeyPress event of a TDBCheckBox component occurs.

Parameter	Meaning
object	Identifies the event sink object; use the *this pointer
memberFunc	Identifies the event handler that responds to the OnKeyPress event

TDBCheckBoxKeyPressSink typedef   dbevent.h

typedef TBdtEventSinkV2<TDBCheckBox& sender, SHORT AsciiCode> TDBCheckBoxKeyPressSink;
The TDBCheckBoxKeyPressSink is the type of the event source for the OnKeyPress event of a TDBCheckBox component.

Parameter	Meaning
sender	The TDBCheckBox component
asciiCode	A single character key

TDBCheckBoxKeyPressSource typedef

dbevent.h

typedef TBdtEventSourceV2<TDBCheckBox& sender, SHORT AsciiCode> TDBCheckBoxKeyPressSource;
The TDBCheckBoxKeyPressSource is the type of the event source for the OnKeyPress event of a TDBCheckBox component.

Parameter	Meaning
sender	The TDBCheckBox component
asciiCode	A single character key

TDBCheckBoxKeySink typedef

dbevent.h

typedef TBdtEventSinkV3<TDBCheckBox& sender, TVbxControl& source, SHORT* scanCode, TShiftState state> TDBCheckBoxKeySink;
The TDBCheckBoxKeySink is the type of the event sink for the OnKeyUp and OnKeyDown events of a TDBCheckBox component.

Parameter	Meaning
sender	The TDBCheckBox component
scanCode	A virtual key code. You can find a list of virtual key codes in the Windows API Help.
state	Possible values:
	1 The *Shift* key is held down
	2 The *Ctrl* key is held down
	4 The *Alt* key is held down

TDBCheckBoxKeySource typedef

dbevent.h

typedef TBdtEventSourceV3<TDBCheckBox& sender, TVbxControl& source, SHORT* scanCode, TShiftState state> TDBCheckBoxKeySource;
The TDBCheckBoxKeySource is the type of the event source for the OnKeyUp and OnKeyDown events of a TDBCheckBox component.

Parameter	Meaning
sender	The TDBCheckBox component
scanCode	A virtual key code. You can find a list of virtual key codes in the Windows API Help.
state	Possible values:
	1 The *Shift* key is held down
	2 The *Ctrl* key is held down
	4 The *Alt* key is held down

TDBCheckBoxMouse_MFUNCTOR macro

TDBCheckBoxMouse_MFUNCTOR(object, memberFunc)

This macro constructs the event sink object, which is of type TDBCheckBoxMouseSink, binding it to the handler method that responds when an OnMouseDown, OnMouseUp, or OnMouseMove event of a TDBCheckBox component occurs.

Parameter	Meaning
object	Identifies the event sink object; use the *this pointer
memberFunc	Identifies the event handler that responds to the mouse events

TDBCheckBoxMouseSink typedef   dbevent.h

typedef TBdtEventSinkV5<TDBCheckBox& sender, TMouseButton mouseButton, TShiftState state, SHORT x, SHORT y> TDBCheckBoxMouseSink;

The TDBCheckBoxMouseSink is the type of the event sink for the OnMouseDown, OnMouseUp, and OnMouseMove events of a TDBCheckBox component.

Parameter	Meaning
sender	The TDBCheckBox component
mouseButton	Possible values are:
	1 Left mouse button
	2 Right mouse button
	4 Middle mouse button
state	Possible values are:
	1 *Shift* key
	2 *Ctrl* key
	4 *Alt* key
x	The position of the mouse pointer on the x-axis in screen pixels
y	The position of the mouse pointer on the y-axis in screen pixels

TDBCheckBoxMouseSource typedef   dbevent.h

typedef TBdtEventSourceV5<TDBCheckBox& sender, TMouseButton mouseButton, TShiftState state, SHORT x, SHORT y> TDBCheckBoxMouseSource;

The TDBCheckBoxMouseSource is the type of the event source for the OnMouseDown, OnMouseUp, and OnMouseMove events of a TDBCheckBox component.

Parameter	Meaning
sender	The TDBCheckBox component
mouseButton	Possible values are:
	1 Left mouse button
	2 Right mouse button
	4 Middle mouse button
state	Possible values are:
	1 *Shift* key
	2 *Ctrl* key
	4 *Alt* key
x	The position of the mouse pointer on the x-axis in screen pixels
y	The position of the mouse pointer on the y-axis in screen pixels

TDBCheckBoxNotify_MFUNCTOR macro   dbevent.h

TDBCheckBoxNotify_MFUNCTOR(object, memberFunc)

This macro constructs the event sink object, which is of type TDBCheckBoxNotifySink, binding it to the handler method that responds when the OnClick, OnEnter, or OnExit event of a TDBCheckBox component occurs.

Parameter	Meaning
object	Identifies the event sink object; use the *this pointer
memberFunc	Identifies the event handler that responds to the OnClick, OnEnter, or OnExit event

TDBCheckBoxNotifySink typedef   dbevent.h

typedef TBdtEventSinkV1<TDBCheckBox& sender> TDBCheckBoxNotifySink;

The TDBCheckBoxNotifySink is the type of the event sink for the OnClick , OnEnter, and OnExit events of a TDBCheckBox component.

TDBCheckBoxNotifySource typedef   dbevent.h

typedef TBdtEventSourceV1<TDBCheckBox& sender> TDBCheckBoxNotifySource;

The TDBCheckBoxNotifySource is the type of the event source for the OnClick , OnEnter, and OnExit events of a TDBCheckBox component.

TDBComboBox component

A TDBComboBox component is a data-aware combo box control. It allows the user to change the value of the field of the current record in a dataset either by selecting an item from a list or by typing in the edit box part of the control. The selected item or entered text becomes the new value of the field if the database combo box's ReadOnly property is false. For more information, see "Updating Fields."

How a database combo box appears and behaves depends on the value of its Style property.

You can link the database combo box with a dataset by specifying the data source component (TDataSource) that identifies the dataset as the value of the memo's DataSource property. Specify the field in the dataset you want to access as the value of the DataField property.

You specify the values the user can choose from in the combo box with the Items property. For example, to allow the user to choose from five different values in the combo box list, specify five strings as the value of Items. You can add, delete, and insert items to the combo box using the Add, Delete, and Insert methods of the Items component, which is of type TStrings. For example, to add a string to a database combo box, you could write this line of code:

```
DBListBox1.Items->Add("New item");
```

The ItemIndex property indicates which item in the database combo box is selected.

Sort the items in the list with the Sorted property.

At run time, you can select all the text in the edit box of the database combo box with the SelectAll method. To find out which text the user selected, or to replace selected text, use the SelText property. To select only part of the text or to find out what part of the text is selected, use the SelStart and SelLength properties.

Public constructors and destructor

Constructors

Form 1   TDBComboBox(TWindow* Parent, int ID, LPCSTR Title, int Left, Int Top, Int Width, int Height, TModule* Module=0);
Creates a new combo box object with the following parameters:

- Parent identifies the parent window object.

- ID identifies the combo box component.

- Title contains the title of the window.

- Left, Top, Width, and Height identify the window position. If this is a child component, the position is relative to the parent client area.

- Module identifies the owner of the combo box component.

Form 2   TDBComboBox(TWindow* Parent, int ID, TModule* Module=0);
Creates a combo box by loading it from an existing dialog resource.

- Parent identifies the parent window object.

- ID identifies the combo box.

- Module identifies the owner of the combo box.

Destructor

~TDBComboBox()
Deletes the combo box component.

Properties

About
▶ Action
▶ Align
BackColor
▶ BoundsRect
▶ Canvas
Caption
▶ ComponentIndex
Cursor
DataChanged
DataField
DataSource
DragCursor
DragMode
DropDownCount
DropDownWidth
Enabled
FontBold
FontItalic
FontName
FontSize
FontStrikethru
FontUnderline
ForeColor
▶ Handle
Height
HelpContext
Index
ItemHeight
▶ ItemIndex
Items
Left

MaxLength
Name
▶Owner
▶Parent
ReadOnly
▶SelLength
▶SelStart
▶SelText
Sorted
Style
TabOrder
TabStop
Tag
Top
Visible
Width

Methods

BeginDrag
BringToFront
CanFocus
Clear
ClientToScreen
CopyToClipboard
CutToClipboard
Dragging
EndDrag
Focused
GetTextBuf
GetTextLen
Hide
Invalidate
PasteFromClipboard
Refresh
Repaint
ScaleBy
ScreenToClient
ScrollBy
SelectAll
SendToBack
SetBounds
SetFocus
SetTextBuf
Show
Update

Events

OnChange
OnClick
OnDblClick
OnDragDrop
OnDragOver
OnDrawItem
OnDropDown
OnEndDrag
OnEnter
OnExit
OnKeyDown
OnKeyPress
OnKeyUp
OnMeasureItem

TDBComboBoxDrag_MFUNCTOR macro

TDBComboBoxDrag_MFUNCTOR(object, memberFunc)

This macro constructs the event sink object, which is of type TDBComboBoxDragSink, binding it to the handler method that responds when the OnDragDrop and OnEndDrag events of a TDBComboBox component occur.

Parameter	Meaning
object	Identifies the event sink object; use the *this pointer
memberFunc	Identifies the event handler that responds to the OnDragDrop event

TDBComboBoxDragOver_MFUNCTOR macro

TDBComboBoxDragOver_MFUNCTOR(object, memberFunc)

This macro constructs the event sink object, which is of type TDBComboBoxDragOverSink, binding it to the handler method that responds when the OnDragOver event of a TDBComboBox component occurs.

Parameter	Meaning
object	Identifies the event sink object; use the *this pointer
memberFunc	Identifies the event handler that responds to the OnDragOver event

TDBComboBoxDragOverSink typedef   dbevent.h

typedef TBdtEventSinkV5<TDBComboBox& sender, TVbxControl& source, SHORT X, SHORT Y, TDragState state> TDBComboBoxDragOverSink;

The TDBComboBoxDragSink is the type of the event sink for the OnDragOver event of a TDBComboBox component.

Parameter	Meaning
sender	The TDBComboBox component
source	The control being dragged and dropped
X	The X parameter of the coordinates of the mouse positioned over the control
Y	The Y parameter of the coordinates of the mouse positioned over the control
state	Possible values:
	0 The dragged object enters a control in which it can be dropped
	1 The dragged object is moved within a control in which it can be dropped
	2 The dragged object leaves a control in which it can be dropped

TDBComboBoxDragOverSource typedef   dbevent.h

```
typedef TBdtEventSourceV5<TDBComboBox& sender, TVbxControl& source, SHORT X, SHORT Y,
    TDragState state> TDBComboBoxDragOverSource;
```
The TDBComboBoxDragSource is the type of the event source for the OnDragOver event of a TDBComboBox component.

Parameter	Meaning
sender	The TDBComboBox component
source	The control being dragged and dropped
X	The X parameter of the coordinates of the mouse positioned over the control
Y	The Y parameter of the coordinates of the mouse positioned over the control
state	Possible values:
	0 The dragged object enters a control in which it can be dropped
	1 The dragged object is moved within a control in which it can be dropped
	2 The dragged object leaves a control in which it can be dropped

TDBComboBoxDragSink typedef   dbevent.h

```
typedef TBdtEventSinkV4<TDBComboBox& sender, TVbxControl& source, SHORT X,
    SHORT Y> TDBComboBoxDragSink;
```
The TDBComboBoxDragSink is the type of the event sink for the OnDragDrop and OnEndDrag events of a TDBComboBox component.

Parameter	Meaning
sender	The TDBComboBox component
source	The control being dragged and dropped
X	The X parameter of the coordinates of the mouse positioned over the control
Y	The Y parameter of the coordinates of the mouse positioned over the control

TDBComboBoxDragSource typedef   dbevent.h

typedef TBdtEventSourceV4<TDBComboBox& sender, TVbxControl& source, SHORT X,
        SHORT Y> TDBComboBoxDragSource;
The TDBComboBoxDragSource is the type of the event source for the OnDragDrop and
OnEndDrag events of a TDBComboBox component.

Parameter	Meaning
sender	The TDBComboBox component
source	The control being dragged and dropped
X	The X parameter of the coordinates of the mouse positioned over the control
Y	The Y parameter of the coordinates of the mouse positioned over the control

TDBComboBoxDrawItem_MFUNCTOR macro

TDBComboBoxDrawItem_MFUNCTOR(object, memberFunc)
This macro constructs the event sink object, which is of type
TDBComboBoxDrawItemSink, the handler method that responds when the
OnDrawItem event of a TDBComboBox component occurs.

Parameter	Meaning
object	Identifies the event sink object; use the *this pointer
memberFunc	Identifies the event handler that responds to the OnDrawItem event

TDBComboBoxDrawItemSink typedef   dbevent.h

typedef TBdtEventSinkV4<TDBComboBox& sender, SHORT index, TRect rc,
        TOwnerDrawState state> TDBComboBoxDrawItemSink;
The TDBComboBoxDrawItemSink is the type of the event sink for the OnDrawItem
event of a TDBComboBox component.

Parameter	Meaning
sender	The TDBComboBox component
index	The index of the item in the control that identifies the position of the item in the list
rc	A rectangle in which to draw
state	The state of the selected item. These are the possible values: 0 The item is selected 1 The control is disabled 2 The item currently has focus

TDBComboBoxDrawItemSource typedef

dbevent.h

typedef TBdtEventSourceV4<TDBComboBox& sender, SHORT index, TRect rc,
    TOwnerDrawState state> TDBComboBoxDrawItemSource;

The TDBComboBoxDrawItemSource is the type of the event source for the
OnDrawItem event of a TDBComboBox component.

Parameter	Meaning
sender	The TDBComboBox component
index	The index of the item in the control that identifies the position of the item in the list
rc	A rectangle in which to draw
state	The state of the selected item. These are the possible values:
	0 The item is selected
	1 The control is disabled
	2 The item currently has focus

TDBComboBoxKey_MFUNCTOR macro

TDBComboBoxKey_MFUNCTOR(object, memberFunc)

This macro constructs the event sink object, which is of type TDBComboBoxKeySink,
binding it to the handler method that responds when the OnKeyUp and OnKeyDown
events of a TDBComboBox component occur.

Parameter	Meaning
object	Identifies the event sink object; use the *this pointer
memberFunc	Identifies the event handler that responds to the OnKeyUp and OnKeyDown events

TDBComboBoxKeyPress_MFUNCTOR macro

TDBComboBoxKeyPress_MFUNCTOR(object, memberFunc)

This macro constructs the event sink object, which is of type
TDBComboBoxKeyPressSink, binding it to the handler method that responds when the
OnKeyPress event of a TDBComboBox component occurs.

Parameter	Meaning
object	Identifies the event sink object; use the *this pointer
memberFunc	Identifies the event handler that responds to the OnKeyPress event

TDBComboBoxKeyPressSink typedef

dbevent.h

typedef TBdtEventSinkV2<TDBComboBox& sender, SHORT AsciiCode> TDBComboBoxKeyPressSink;

The TDBComboBoxKeyPressSink is the type of the event source for the OnKeyPress event of a TDBComboBox component.

Parameter	Meaning
sender	The TDBComboBox component
asciiCode	A single character key

TDBComboBoxKeyPressSource typedef   dbevent.h

typedef TBdtEventSourceV2<TDBComboBox& sender, SHORT AsciiCode> TDBComboBoxKeyPressSource;
The TDBComboBoxKeyPressSource is the type of the event source for the OnKeyPress event of a TDBComboBox component.

Parameter	Meaning
sender	The TDBComboBox component
asciiCode	A single character key

TDBComboBoxKeySink typedef   dbevent.h

typedef TBdtEventSinkV3<TDBComboBox& sender, TVbxControl& source, SHORT* scanCode,
    TShiftState state> TDBComboBoxKeySink;
The TDBComboBoxKeySink is the type of the event sink for the OnKeyUp and OnKeyDown events of a TDBComboBox component.

Parameter	Meaning
sender	The TDBComboBox component
scanCode	A virtual key code. You can find a list of virtual key codes in the Windows API Help.
state	Possible values:
	1 The *Shift* key is held down
	2 The *Ctrl* key is held down
	4 The *Alt* key is held down

TDBComboBoxKeySource typedef   dbevent.h

typedef TBdtEventSourceV3<TDBComboBox& sender, TVbxControl& source, SHORT* scanCode,
    TShiftState state> TDBComboBoxKeySource;
The TDBComboBoxKeySource is the type of the event source for the OnKeyUp and OnKeyDown events of a TDBComboBox component.

Parameter	Meaning
sender	The TDBComboBox component
scanCode	A virtual key code. You can find a list of virtual key codes in the Windows API Help.

Parameter	Meaning
state	Possible values:
	1 The *Shift* key is held down
	2 The *Ctrl* key is held down
	4 The *Alt* key is held down

TDBComboBoxMeasureItem_MFUNCTOR macro

TDBComboBoxMeasureItem_MFUNCTOR(object, memberFunc)

This macro constructs the event sink object, which is of type TDBComboBoxMeasureItemSink, the handler method that responds when the OnMeasureItem event of TDBComboBox component occurs.

Parameter	Meaning
object	Identifies the event sink object; use the *this pointer
memberFunc	Identifies the event handler that responds to the OnMeasureItem event

TDBComboBoxMeasureItemSink typedef   dbevent.h

typedef TBdtEventSinkV3<TDBComboBox& sender, SHORT index,
     SHORT height*> TDBComboBoxMeasureItemSink;

The TDBComboBoxDrawItemSink is the type of the event sink for the OnMeasureItem event of a TDBComboBox component.

Parameter	Meaning
sender	The TDBComboBox component
index	The index of the item in the control that identifies the position of the item in the list
height	The height of the item to be drawn

TDBComboBoxMeasureItemSource typedef   dbevent.h

typedef TBdtEventSourceV3<TDBComboBox& sender, SHORT index,
     SHORT height*> TDBComboBoxMeasureItemSource;

The TDBComboBoxDrawItemSource is the type of the event source for the OnMeasureItem event of a TDBComboBox component.

Parameter	Meaning
sender	The TDBComboBox component
index	The index of the item in the control that identifies the position of the item in the list
height	The height of the item to be drawn

TDBComboBoxNotify_MFUNCTOR macro dbevent.h

TDBComboBoxNotify_MFUNCTOR(object, memberFunc)
This macro constructs the event sink object, which is of type TDBComboBoxNotifySink, binding it to the handler method that responds when an OnChange, OnClick, OnDblClick, OnEnter, or OnExit event of a TDBComboBox component occurs.

Parameter	Meaning
object	Identifies the event sink object; use the *this pointer
memberFunc	Identifies the event handler that responds to the click, OnChange, OnDropDown, OnEnter, or OnExit event

TDBComboBoxNotifySink typedef dbevent.h

typedef TBdtEventSinkV1<TDBComboBox& sender> TDBComboBoxNotifySink;
The TDBComboBoxNotifySink is the type of the event sink for the OnChange, OnClick, OnDblClick, OnDropDown, OnEnter, and OnExit events of a TDBComboBox component.

TDBComboBoxNotifySource typedef dbevent.h

typedef TBdtEventSourceV1<TDBComboBox& sender> TDBComboBoxNotifySource;
The TDBComboBoxNotifySource is the type of the event source for the OnChange, OnClick, OnDblClick, OnDropDown, OnEnter, and OnExit events of a TDBComboBox component.

TDBDataSet component bdto.h

The TDBDataSet component is an immediate descendant of the TDataSet component, and therefore, it inherits all the properties, methods, and events of that component. Usually, you won't be working with TDBDataSet, but instead using its direct descendants, TTable, TQuery, and TStoredProc.

The DatabaseName property identifies the name of the database to access. It can be a defined BDE alias, a directory path for Desktop Database files, or an application-specific alias defined by a database component (TDatabase).

The Database property is a read-only and run-time only property that identifies the database component associated with the dataset. Use the DBHandle and DBLocale properties to make direct calls to the Borland Database Engine application programming interface.

Public constructors and destructor

Constructors

Form 1 TDBDataSet(PITDBDataSet p)
Constructs a TDBDataSet object which attaches to the given PITDBDataSet COM interface pointer. The new TDBDataSet saves the PITDBDataSet COM object (incrementing its reference count) for later use.

Form 2 TDBDataSet(const TDBDataSet& p)
Constructs a TDBDataSet object which attaches to the PITDBDataSet COM object associated with the given TDBDataSet object (which was passed by reference). The new TDBDataSet saves the associated PITDBDataSet COM object (incrementing its reference count) for later use.

Form 3 TDBDataSet(PTDBDataSet p)
Constructs a TDBDataSet object which attaches to the PITDBDataSet COM object associated with the given TDBDataSet object (which was passed by pointer). The new TDBDataSet saves the associated PITDBDataSet COM object (incrementing its reference count) for later use.

Form 4 TDBDataSet(void)
Constructs an unassigned TDBDataSet object. Internally, the PITDBDataSet COM object is set to NULL. This is for internal use only.

Destructor

~TDBDataSet()
Deletes the TDBDataSet and reduces the reference count on the associated PITDBDataSet COM object. If the reference count on the associated PITDBDataSet COM object reaches 0, it is deleted.

Properties

Active
▶ AtBOF
▶ AtEOF
AutoCalcFields
▶ CanModify
DataBase
DatabaseName
DataSource
DBHandle
DBLocale
DefaultFields
▶ FieldCount
▶ FieldDefs
▶ Fields
▶ Handle

▶Locale
▶Modified
Name
▶RecordCount
RecordSize
▶State

Methods

Append
AppendRecord
Assign
Cancel
CheckBrowseMode
ClearFields
Close
CursorPosChanged
Delete
DisableControls
Edit
EnableControls
FieldByName
FindField
First
FreeBookmark
GetBookmark
GetCurrentRecord
GetFieldNames
GotoBookmark
Insert
InsertRecord
IsLinkedTo
Last
MoveBy
Next
Open
Post
Prior
Refresh
SetFields
UpdateCursorPos
UpdateRecord

Events

AfterCancel
AfterClose
AfterDelete
AfterEdit
AfterInsert
AfterOpen
AfterPost
BeforeCancel
BeforeClose
BeforeDelete
BeforeEdit
BeforeInsert
BeforeOpen
BeforePost
OnCalcFields
OnNewRecord

TDBEdit component   dbedit.h

A TDBEdit component is a data-aware edit box with all the capabilities of an ordinary edit box.

Unlike an ordinary edit box, you can use the database edit box to enter data into a field, or to simply display data from a field in a dataset. Link the database edit box with a dataset by specifying the data source component (TDataSource) that identifies the dataset as the value of the edit box's DataSource property. Specify the field in the dataset you want to access as the value of the DataField property.

Your application can tell if the text displayed in the edit box changed by checking the value of the Modified property. To limit the number of characters users can enter into the edit box, use the MaxLength property.

If you want to prevent the user from modifying the contents of the field linked to the edit box, set the ReadOnly property to true. For more information, see "Updating Fields."

You can choose to have the text in an edit box automatically selected whenever it becomes the active control with the AutoSelect property. At run time, you can select all the text in the edit box with the SelectAll method. To find out which text in the edit box the user has selected or to replace selected text, use the SelText property. To clear selected text, call the ClearSelection method. To select only part of the text or to find out what part of the text is selected, use the SelStart and SelLength properties.

You can cut, copy, and paste text in an edit box using the CutToClipboard, CopyToClipboard, and PasteFromClipboard methods.

Your application can use an edit box that displays a specified character rather than the actual character typed into it. If the edit box is used to enter a password, onlookers won't be able to read the typed text. Specify the special character with the PasswordChar property.

If you want the edit box to automatically resize to accommodate a change in font size, use the AutoSize property.

Public constructors and destructor

Constructors

Form 1   TDBEdit(TWindow* Parent, int ID, LPCSTR Title, int Left, Int Top, Int Width, int Height, TModule* Module=0);
Creates a new edit object with the following parameters:

- Parent identifies the parent window object.

- ID identifies the edit component.

- Title contains the title of the window.

- Left, Top, Width, and Height identify the window position. If this is a child component, the position is relative to the parent client area.

- Module identifies the owner of the edit component.

Form 2   TDBEdit(TWindow* Parent, int ID, TModule* Module=0);
Creates an edit by loading it from an existing dialog resource.

- Parent identifies the parent window object.

- ID identifies the edit component.

- Module identifies the owner of the edit component.

Destructor

~TDBEdit()
Deletes the edit component.

Properties

About
▷ Align
▷ AutoSelect
AutoSize
BackColor
BorderStyle
▷ BoundsRect
Caption
CharCase
▷ ComponentIndex

Cursor
DataChanged
DataField
DataSource
DragCursor
DragMode
Enabled
FontBold
FontItalic
FontName
FontSize
FontStrikethru
FontUnderline
ForeColor
Height
HelpContext
Index
Left
MaxLength
▶Modified*
Name
▶Owner
▶Parent
PasswordChar
ReadOnly
▶SelLength
▶SelStart
▶SelText
TabOrder
TabStop
Tag
Top
Visible
Width

Methods

BeginDrag
BringToFront
CanFocus
Clear
ClearSelection
ClientToScreen
CopyToClipboard
CutToClipboard
Dragging

EndDrag
Focused
GetSelTextBuf
GetTextBuf
GetTextLen
Hide
Invalidate
PasteFromClipboard
Refresh
Repaint
ScaleBy
ScreenToClient
ScrollBy
SelectAll
SendToBack
SetBounds
SetSelTextBuf
SetTextBuf
Show
Update

Events

OnChange
OnClick
OnDblClick
OnDragDrop
OnDragOver
OnEndDrag
OnEnter
OnExit
OnKeyDown
OnKeyPress
OnKeyUp
OnMouseDown
OnMouseMove
OnMouseUp

TDBEditDrag_MFUNCTOR macro

TDBEditDrag_MFUNCTOR(object, memberFunc)

This macro constructs the event sink object, which is of type TDBEditDragSink, binding it to the handler method that responds when the OnDragDrop and OnEndDrag events of a TDBEdit component occur.

Parameter	Meaning
object	Identifies the event sink object; use the *this pointer
memberFunc	Identifies the event handler that responds to the OnDragDrop event

TDBEditDragOver_MFUNCTOR macro

TDBEditDragOver_MFUNCTOR(object, memberFunc)

This macro constructs the event sink object, which is of type TDBEditDragOverSink, binding it to the handler method that responds when the OnDragOver event of a TDBEdit component occurs.

Parameter	Meaning
object	Identifies the event sink object; use the *this pointer
memberFunc	Identifies the event handler that responds to the OnDragOver event

TDBEditDragOverSink typedef   dbevent.h

typedef TBdtEventSinkV5<TDBEdit& sender, TVbxControl& source, SHORT X, SHORT Y,
    TDragState state> TDBEditDragOverSink;

The TDBEditDragSink is the type of the event sink for the OnDragOver event of a TDBEdit component.

Parameter	Meaning
sender	The TDBEdit component
source	The control being dragged and dropped
X	The X parameter of the coordinates of the mouse positioned over the control
Y	The Y parameter of the coordinates of the mouse positioned over the control
state	Possible values:
	0 The dragged object enters a control in which it can be dropped
	1 The dragged object is moved within a control in which it can be dropped
	2 The dragged object leaves a control in which it can be dropped

TDBEditDragOverSource typedef   dbevent.h

typedef TBdtEventSourceV5<TDBEdit& sender, TVbxControl& source, SHORT X, SHORT Y,
    TDragState state> TDBEditDragOverSource;

The TDBEditDragSource is the type of the event source for the OnDragOver event of a TDBEdit component.

Parameter	Meaning
sender	The TDBEdit component
source	The control being dragged and dropped
X	The X parameter of the coordinates of the mouse positioned over the control
Y	The Y parameter of the coordinates of the mouse positioned over the control
state	Possible values:
	0 The dragged object enters a control in which it can be dropped
	1 The dragged object is moved within a control in which it can be dropped
	2 The dragged object leaves a control in which it can be dropped

TDBEditDragSink typedef   dbevent.h

```
typedef TBdtEventSinkV4<TDBEditx& sender, TVbxControl& source, SHORT X,
        SHORT Y> TDBEditDragSink;
```
The TDBEditDragSink is the type of the event sink for the OnDragDrop and OnEndDrag events of a TDBEdit component.

Parameter	Meaning
sender	The TDBEdit component
source	The control being dragged and dropped
X	The X parameter of the coordinates of the mouse positioned over the control
Y	The Y parameter of the coordinates of the mouse positioned over the control

TDBEditDragSource typedef   dbevent.h

```
typedef TBdtEventSourceV4<TDBEdit& sender, TVbxControl& source, SHORT X,
        SHORT Y> TDBEditDragSource;
```
The TDBEditDragSource is the type of the event source for the OnDragDrop and OnEndDrag events of a TDBEdit component.

Parameter	Meaning
sender	The TDBEdit component
source	The control being dragged and dropped
X	The X parameter of the coordinates of the mouse positioned over the control
Y	The Y parameter of the coordinates of the mouse positioned over the control

TDBEditKey_MFUNCTOR macro

```
TDBEditKey_MFUNCTOR(object, memberFunc)
```

This macro constructs the event sink object, which is of type TDBEditKeySink, binding it to the handler method that responds when the OnKeyUp and OnKeyDown events of a TDBEdit component occur

Parameter	Meaning
object	Identifies the event sink object; use the *this pointer
memberFunc	Identifies the event handler that responds to the OnKeyUp and OnKeyDown events

TDBEditKeyPress_MFUNCTOR macro

TDBEditKeyPress_MFUNCTOR(object, memberFunc)
This macro constructs the event sink object, which is of type TDBEditKeyPressSink, binding it to the handler method that responds when the OnKeyPress event of a TDBEdit component occurs.

Parameter	Meaning
object	Identifies the event sink object; use the *this pointer
memberFunc	Identifies the event handler that responds to the OnKeyPress event

TDBEditKeyPressSink typedef · dbevent.h

typedef TBdtEventSinkV2<TDBEdit& sender, SHORT AsciiCode> TDBEditKeyPressSink;
The TDBEditKeyPressSink is the type of the event source for the OnKeyPress event of a TDBEdit component.

Parameter	Meaning
sender	The TDBEdit component
asciiCode	A single character key

TDBEditKeyPressSource typedef · dbevent.h

typedef TBdtEventSourceV2<TDBEdit& sender, SHORT AsciiCode> TDBEditKeyPressSource;
The TDBEditKeyPressSource is the type of the event source for the OnKeyPress event of a TDBEdit component.

Parameter	Meaning
sender	The TDBEdit component
asciiCode	A single character key

TDBEditKeySink typedef dbevent.h

typedef TBdtEventSinkV3<TDBEdit& sender, TVbxControl& source, SHORT* scanCode,
    TShiftState state> TDBEditKeySink;

The TDBEditKeySink is the type of the event sink for the OnKeyUp and OnKeyDown
events of a TDBEdit component.

Parameter	Meaning
sender	The TDBEdit component
scanCode	A virtual key code. You can find a list of virtual key codes in the Windows API Help.
state	Possible values:
	1 The *Shift* key is held down
	2 The *Ctrl* key is held down
	4 The *Alt* key is held down

TDBEditKeySource typedef dbevent.h

typedef TBdtEventSourceV3<TDBEdit& sender, TVbxControl& source, SHORT* scanCode,
    TShiftState state> TDBEditKeySource;

The TDBEditKeySource is the type of the event source for the OnKeyUp and
OnKeyDown events of a TDBEdit component.

Parameter	Meaning
sender	The TDBEdit component
scanCode	A virtual key code. You can find a list of virtual key codes in the Windows API Help.
state	Possible values:
	1 The *Shift* key is held down
	2 The *Ctrl* key is held down
	4 The *Alt* key is held down

TDBEditMouse_MFUNCTOR macro

TDBEditMouse_MFUNCTOR(object, memberFunc)

This macro constructs the event sink object, which is of type TDBEditMouseSink,
binding it to the handler method that responds when an OnMouseDown, OnMouseUp,
or OnMouseMove event of a TDBEdit component occurs.

Parameter	Meaning
object	Identifies the event sink object; use the *this pointer
memberFunc	Identifies the event handler that responds to the mouse events

TDBEditMouseSink typedef · dbevent.h

typedef TBdtEventSinkV5<TDBEdit& sender, TMouseButton mouseButton, TShiftState state,
SHORT x, SHORT y> TDBEditMouseSink;

The TDBEditMouseSink is the type of the event sink for the OnMouseDown,
OnMouseUp, and OnMouseMove events of a TDBEdit component.

Parameter	Meaning
sender	The TDBEdit component
mouseButton	Possible values are:
	1 Left mouse button
	2 Right mouse button
	4 Middle mouse button
state	Possible values are:
	1 *Shift* key
	2 *Ctrl* key
	4 *Alt* key
x	The position of the mouse pointer on the x-axis in screen pixels
y	The position of the mouse pointer on the y-axis in screen pixels

TDBEditMouseSource typedef · dbevent.h

typedef TBdtEventSourceV5<TDBEdit& sender, TMouseButton mouseButton, TShiftState state,
SHORT x, SHORT y> TDBEditMouseSource;

The TDBEditMouseSource is the type of the event source for the OnMouseDown,
OnMouseUp, and OnMouseMove events of a TDBEdit component.

Parameter	Meaning
sender	The TDBEdit component
mouseButton	Possible values are:
	1 Left mouse button
	2 Right mouse button
	4 Middle mouse button
state	Possible values are:
	1 *Shift* key
	2 *Ctrl* key
	4 *Alt* key
x	The position of the mouse pointer on the x-axis in screen pixels
y	The position of the mouse pointer on the y-axis in screen pixels

TDBEditNotify_MFUNCTOR macro · dbevent.h

TDBEditNotify_MFUNCTOR(object, memberFunc)

This macro constructs the event sink object, which is of type TDBEditNotifySink, binding it to the handler method that responds when an OnChange, OnClick, OnDblClick, OnEnter, or OnExit event of a TDBEdit component occurs.

Parameter	Meaning
object	Identifies the event sink object; use the *this pointer
memberFunc	Identifies the event handler that responds to the click, OnChange, OnEnter, and OnExit events

TDBEditNotifySink typedef dbevent.h

typedef TBdtEventSinkV1<TDBEdit& sender> TDBEditNotifySink;
The TDBEditNotifySink is the type of the event sink for the OnChange, OnClick, OnDblClick, OnEnter, and OnExit events of a TDBEdit component.

TDBEditNotifySource typedef dbevent.h

typedef TBdtEventSourceV1<TDBEdit& sender> TDBEditNotifySource;
The TDBEditNotifySource is the type of the event source for the OnChange, OnClick, OnDblClick, OnEnter, and OnExit events of a TDBEdit component.

TDBGrid component dbgrid.h

The TDBGrid component accesses the data in a database table or query and displays it in a grid. Your application can use the data grid to insert, delete, or edit data in the database, or simply to display it.

The most convenient way to move through data in a data grid and to insert, delete, and edit data is to use the database navigator (TDBNavigator) with the data grid.

You can change the appearance and behavior of a data grid with its properties. For example, you can choose to allow the user to use the Tab key to move to a new column by setting the AllowTabs property to true. Setting ShowGridLines to true draws visible borders between the rows and columns of the data grid. If you want headings at the top of each grid column, set the DataSetColumnName property to true.

If you want the user to be able only to view the data and not to edit it, set the ReadOnly property of the data source (TTable or TQuery component) to true. If you want the user to be able to edit the data, the dataset must be in Edit state, and the ReadOnly property of the data must be false. The user can cancel an edit by pressing *Esc*.

Users don't really insert or edit the data in a field using the data grid until they move to a different record or close the application. If you use the database navigator, clicking its Post button will post changes. You can also post changes in any event handlers you include for your data grid, such as for the OnExit event.

To customize the order the fields appear in the grid, use the Fields editor.

Public constructors and destructor

Constructors

Form 1   TDBGrid(TWindow* Parent, int ID, LPCSTR Title, int Left, Int Top, Int Width, int Height, TModule* Module=0);
Creates a new grid object with the following parameters:

- Parent identifies the parent window object.

- ID identifies the grid component.

- Title contains the title of the window.

- Left, Top, Width, and Height identify the window position. If this is a child component, the position is relative to the parent client area.

- Module identifies the owner of the grid component.

Form 2   TDBGrid(TWindow* Parent, int ID, TModule* Module=0);
Creates a grid by loading it from an existing dialog resource.

- Parent identifies the parent window object.

- ID identifies the grid component.

- Module identifies the owner of the grid component.

Destructor

~TDBGrid()
Deletes the grid component.

Properties

About
▷ Align
AllowResize
AllowTabs
BackColor
BorderStyle
▷ BoundsRect
Caption
ComponentIndex
DataField
DataSetColumnName
DataSource
DragCursor
DragMode
Enabled
Height
HelpContext

Index
Left
Name
Owner
Parent
ShowGridLines
TabOrder
TabStop
Tag
Top
Visible
Width

Methods

BeginDrag
BringToFront
CanFocus
ClientToScreen
Dragging
EndDrag
Focused
GetTextBuf
GetTextLen
Hide
Invalidate
Refresh
Repaint
ScaleBy
ScreenToClient
ScrollBy
SendToBack
SetBounds
SetTextBuf
Show
Update

Events

OnClick
OnDblClick
OnDragDrop
OnDragOver
OnEndDrag
OnEnter

OnExit
OnKeyDown
OnKeyPress
OnKeyUp

TDBGridDrag_MFUNCTOR macro

TDBGridDrag_MFUNCTOR(object, memberFunc)
This macro constructs the event sink object, which is of type TDBGridDragSink, binding it to the handler method that responds when the OnDragDrop and OnEndDrag events of a TDBGrid component occur.

Parameter	Meaning
object	Identifies the event sink object; use the *this pointer
memberFunc	Identifies the event handler that responds to the OnDragDrop event

TDBGridDragOver_MFUNCTOR macro

TDBGridDragOver_MFUNCTOR(object, memberFunc)
This macro constructs the event sink object, which is of type TDBGridDragOverSink, binding it to the handler method that responds when the OnDragOver event of a TDBGrid component occurs.

Parameter	Meaning
object	Identifies the event sink object; use the *this pointer
memberFunc	Identifies the event handler that responds to the OnDragOver event

TDBGridDragOverSink typedef   dbevent.h

typedef TBdtEventSinkV5<TDBGrid& sender, TVbxControl& source, SHORT X, SHORT Y,
    TDragState state> TDBGridDragOverSink;
The TDBGridDragSink is the type of the event sink for the OnDragOver event of a TDBGrid component.

Parameter	Meaning
sender	The TDBGrid component
source	The control being dragged and dropped
X	The X parameter of the coordinates of the mouse positioned over the control
Y	The Y parameter of the coordinates of the mouse positioned over the control
state	Possible values:
	0 The dragged object enters a control in which it can be dropped
	1 The dragged object is moved within a control in which it can be dropped
	2 The dragged object leaves a control in which it can be dropped

TDBGridDragOverSource typedef
dbevent.h

typedef TBdtEventSourceV5<TDBGrid& sender, TVbxControl& source, SHORT X, SHORT Y,
   TDragState state> TDBGridDragOverSource;

The TDBGridDragSource is the type of the event source for the OnDragOver event of a
TDBGrid component.

Parameter	Meaning
sender	The TDBGrid component
source	The control being dragged and dropped
X	The X parameter of the coordinates of the mouse positioned over the control
Y	The Y parameter of the coordinates of the mouse positioned over the control
state	Possible values:
	0 The dragged object enters a control in which it can be dropped
	1 The dragged object is moved within a control in which it can be dropped
	2 The dragged object leaves a control in which it can be dropped

TDBGridDragSink typedef
dbevent.h

typedef TBdtEventSinkV4<TDBGridx& sender, TVbxControl& source, SHORT X,
   SHORT Y> TDBGridDragSink;

The TDBGridDragSink is the type of the event sink for the OnDragDrop and
OnEndDrag events of a TDBGrid component.

Parameter	Meaning
sender	The TDBGrid component
source	The control being dragged and dropped
X	The X parameter of the coordinates of the mouse positioned over the control
Y	The Y parameter of the coordinates of the mouse positioned over the control

TDBGridDragSource typedef
dbevent.h

typedef TBdtEventSourceV4<TDBGrid& sender, TVbxControl& source, SHORT X,
   SHORT Y> TDBGridDragSource;

The TDBGridDragSource is the type of the event source for the OnDragDrop and
OnEndDrag events of a TDBGrid component.

Parameter	Meaning
sender	The TDBGrid component
source	The control being dragged and dropped
X	The X parameter of the coordinates of the mouse positioned over the control
Y	The Y parameter of the coordinates of the mouse positioned over the control

TDBGridKey_MFUNCTOR macro

TDBGridKey_MFUNCTOR(object, memberFunc)

This macro constructs the event sink object, which is of type TDBGridKeySink, binding it to the handler method that responds when the OnKeyUp and OnKeyDown events of a TDBGrid component occur.

Parameter	Meaning
object	Identifies the event sink object; use the *this pointer
memberFunc	Identifies the event handler that responds to the OnKeyUp and OnKeyDown events

TDBGridKeyPress_MFUNCTOR macro

TDBGridKeyPress_MFUNCTOR(object, memberFunc)

This macro constructs the event sink object, which is of type TDBGridKeyPressSink, binding it to the handler method that responds when the OnKeyPress event of a TDBGrid component occurs.

Parameter	Meaning
object	Identifies the event sink object; use the *this pointer
memberFunc	Identifies the event handler that responds to the OnKeyPress event

TDBGridKeyPressSink typedef   dbevent.h

typedef TBdtEventSinkV2<TDBGrid& sender, SHORT AsciiCode> TDBGridKeyPressSink;

The TDBGridKeyPressSink is the type of the event source for the OnKeyPress event of a TDBGrid component.

Parameter	Meaning
sender	The TDBGrid component
asciiCode	A single character key

TDBGridKeyPressSource typedef   dbevent.h

typedef TBdtEventSourceV2<TDBGrid& sender, SHORT AsciiCode> TDBGridKeyPressSource;

The TDBGridKeyPressSource is the type of the event source for the OnKeyPress event of a TDBGrid component.

Parameter	Meaning
sender	The TDBGrid component
asciiCode	A single character key

TDBGridKeySink typedef dbevent.h

typedef TBdtEventSinkV3<TDBGrid& sender, TVbxControl& source, SHORT* scanCode,
  TShiftState state> TDBGridKeySink;

The TDBGridKeySink is the type of the event sink for the OnKeyUp and OnKeyDown events of a TDBGrid component.

Parameter	Meaning
sender	The TDBGrid component
scanCode	A virtual key code. You can find a list of virtual key codes in the Windows API Help.
state	Possible values:
	1 The *Shift* key is held down
	2 The *Ctrl* key is held down
	4 The *Alt* key is held down

TDBGridKeySource typedef dbevent.h

typedef TBdtEventSourceV3<TDBGrid& sender, TVbxControl& source, SHORT* scanCode,
  TShiftState state> TDBGridKeySource;

The TDBGridKeySource is the type of the event source for the OnKeyUp and OnKeyDown events of a TDBGrid component.

Parameter	Meaning
sender	The TDBGrid component
scanCode	A virtual key code. You can find a list of virtual key codes in the Windows API Help.
state	Possible values:
	1 The *Shift* key is held down
	2 The *Ctrl* key is held down
	4 The *Alt* key is held down

TDBGridNotify_MFUNCTOR macro dbevent.h

TDBGridNotify_MFUNCTOR(object, memberFunc)

This macro constructs the event sink object, which is of type TDBGridNotifySink, binding it to the handler method that responds when an OnClick, OnDblClick, OnEnter, or OnExit event of a TDBGrid component occurs.

Parameter	Meaning
object	Identifies the event sink object; use the *this pointer
memberFunc	Identifies the event handler that responds to the click, OnEnter, and OnExit events

TDBGridNotifySink typdef

typedef TBdtEventSinkV1<TDBGrid& sender> TDBGridNotifySink;
The TDBGridNotifySink is the type of the event sink for the OnClick, OnDblClick, OnEnter, and OnExit events of a TDBGrid component.

TDBGridNotifySource typedef

typedef TBdtEventSourceV1<TDBGrid& sender> TDBGridNotifySource;
The TDBGridNotifySource is the type of the event source for the OnClick, OnDblClick, OnEnter, and OnExit events of a TDBGrid component.

TDBImage component

The TDBImage component displays a graphic image from a BLOB (binary large object) stored in a field of the current record of a dataset. You can also modify the image if the ReadOnly property is set to false. For more information about editing field values, see "Updating Fields."

You can link the database image with a dataset by specifying the data source component (TDataSource) that identifies the dataset as the value of the image's DataSource property. Specify the field in the dataset you want to access as the value of the image's DataField property.

You can control when the image appears in the database control with the AutoDisplay property.

You can change the size at which the BLOB is displayed by using the Stretch property.

You can cut, copy, and paste images in the database image control. While your application is running and the database image control has the focus, use the Windows cut, copy, and paste keys (*Ctrl+X, Ctrl+C,* and *Ctrl+V*).

Public constructors and destructor

Constructors

Form 1   TDBImage(TWindow* Parent, int ID, LPCSTR Title, int Left, Int Top, int Width, int Height, TModule* Module=0);
Creates a new image object with the following parameters:

- Parent identifies the parent window object.

- ID identifies the image component.

- Title contains the title of the window.

- Left, Top, Width, and Height identify the window position. If this is a child component, the position is relative to the parent client area.

- Module identifies the owner of the image component.

Form 2   TDBImage(TWindow* Parent, int ID, TModule* Module=0);
Creates a image by loading it from an existing dialog resource.

- Parent identifies the parent window object.

- ID identifies the image component.

- Module identifies the owner of the image component.

Destructor

~TDBImage()
Deletes the image component.

Properties

About
▸ Align
AutoDisplay
AutoSize
BackColor
BorderStyle
BoundsRect
Caption
Center
▸ ComponentIndex
Cursor
DataChanged
DataField
DataSource
DragCursor
DragMode
Enabled
ForeColor
Height
HelpContext
Index
Left
Name
Owner
▸ Parent
Picture
ReadOnly
Stretch

TabOrder
TabStop
Tag
Top
Visible
Width

Methods

BeginDrag
BringToFront
ClientToScreen
CopyToClipboard
CutToClipboard
Dragging
EndDrag
Focused
GetTextBuf
GetTextLen
Hide
Invalidate
LoadPicture
PasteFromClipboard
Refresh
Repaint
ScaleBy
ScreenToClient
ScrollBy
SendToBack
SetBounds
SetTextBuf
Show
Update

Events

OnClick
OnDblClick
OnDragDrop
OnDragOver
OnEndDrag
OnEnter
OnExit
OnKeyDown
OnKeyPress

OnKeyUp
OnMouseDown
OnMouseMove
OnMouseUp

TDBImageDrag_MFUNCTOR typdef

TDBImageDrag_MFUNCTOR(object, memberFunc)
This macro constructs the event sink object, which is of type TDBImageDragSink, binding it to the handler method that responds when the OnDragDrop and OnEndDrag events of a TDBImage component occur.

TDBImageDragOver_MFUNCTOR macro

TDBImageDragOver_MFUNCTOR(object, memberFunc)
This macro constructs the event sink object, which is of type TDBImageDragOverSink, binding it to the handler method that responds when the OnDragOver event of a TDBImage component occurs.

Parameter	Meaning
object	Identifies the event sink object; use the *this pointer
memberFunc	Identifies the event handler that responds to the OnDragOver event

TDBImageDragOverSink typedef   dbevent.h

typedef TBdtEventSinkV5<TDBImage& sender, TVbxControl& source, SHORT X, SHORT Y,
    TDragState state> TDBImageDragOverSink;
The TDBImageDragSink is the type of the event sink for the OnDragOver event of a TDBImage component.

Parameter	Meaning
sender	The TDBImage component
source	The control being dragged and dropped
X	The X parameter of the coordinates of the mouse positioned over the control
Y	The Y parameter of the coordinates of the mouse positioned over the control
state	Possible values:
	0 The dragged object enters a control in which it can be dropped
	1 The dragged object is moved within a control in which it can be dropped
	2 The dragged object leaves a control in which it can be dropped

TDBImageDragOverSource typedef   dbevent.h

typedef TBdtEventSourceV5<TDBImage& sender, TVbxControl& source, SHORT X, SHORT Y,
    TDragState state> TDBImageDragOverSource;

The TDBImageDragSource is the type of the event source for the OnDragOver event of a
TDBImage component.

Parameter	Meaning
sender	The TDBImage component
source	The control being dragged and dropped
X	The X parameter of the coordinates of the mouse positioned over the control
Y	The Y parameter of the coordinates of the mouse positioned over the control
state	Possible values:
	0 The dragged object enters a control in which it can be dropped
	1 The dragged object is moved within a control in which it can be dropped
	2 The dragged object leaves a control in which it can be dropped

TDBImageDragSink typedef   dbevent.h

typedef TBdtEventSinkV4<TDBImagex& sender, TVbxControl& source, SHORT X,
    SHORT Y> TDBImageDragSink;

The TDBImageDragSink is the type of the event sink for the OnDragDrop and
OnEndDrag events of a TDBImage component.

Parameter	Meaning
sender	The TDBImage component
source	The control being dragged and dropped
X	The X parameter of the coordinates of the mouse positioned over the control
Y	The Y parameter of the coordinates of the mouse positioned over the control

TDBImageDragSource typedef   dbevent.h

typedef TBdtEventSourceV4<TDBImage& sender, TVbxControl& source, SHORT X,
    SHORT Y> TDBImageDragSource;

The TDBImageDragSource is the type of the event source for the OnDragDrop and
OnEndDrag events of a TDBImage component.

Parameter	Meaning
sender	The TDBImage component
source	The control being dragged and dropped
X	The X parameter of the coordinates of the mouse positioned over the control
Y	The Y parameter of the coordinates of the mouse positioned over the control

TDBImageKey_MFUNCTOR macro

TDBImageKey_MFUNCTOR(object, memberFunc)

This macro constructs the event sink object, which is of type TDBImageKeySink, binding it to the handler method that responds when the OnKeyUp and OnKeyDown events of a TDBImage component occur.

Parameter	Meaning
object	Identifies the event sink object; use the *this pointer
memberFunc	Identifies the event handler that responds to the OnKeyUp and OnKeyDown events

TDBImageKeyPress_MFUNCTOR macro

TDBImageKeyPress_MFUNCTOR(object, memberFunc)

This macro constructs the event sink object, which is of type TDBImageKeyPressSink, binding it to the handler method that responds when the OnKeyPress event of a TDBImage component occurs.

Parameter	Meaning
object	Identifies the event sink object; use the *this pointer
memberFunc	Identifies the event handler that responds to the OnKeyPress event

TDBImageKeyPressSink typedef   dbevent.h

typedef TBdtEventSinkV2<TDBImage& sender, SHORT AsciiCode> TDBImageKeyPressSink;

The TDBImageKeyPressSink is the type of the event source for the OnKeyPress event of a TDBImage component.

Parameter	Meaning
sender	The TDBImage component
asciiCode	A single character key

TDBImageKeyPressSource typedef   dbevent.h

typedef TBdtEventSourceV2<TDBImage& sender, SHORT AsciiCode> TDBImageKeyPressSource;

The TDBImageKeyPressSource is the type of the event source for the OnKeyPress event of a TDBImage component.

Parameter	Meaning
sender	The TDBImage component
asciiCode	A single character key

TDBImageKeySink typedef
dbevent.h

typedef TBdtEventSinkV3<TDBImage& sender, TVbxControl& source, SHORT* scanCode,
   TShiftState state> TDBImageKeySink;

The TDBImageKeySink is the type of the event sink for the OnKeyUp and OnKeyDown events of a TDBImage component.

Parameter	Meaning
sender	The TDBImage component
scanCode	A virtual key code. You can find a list of virtual key codes in the Windows API Help.
state	Possible values:
	1 The *Shift* key is held down
	2 The *Ctrl* key is held down
	4 The *Alt* key is held down

TDBImageKeySource typedef
dbevent.h

typedef TBdtEventSourceV3<TDBImage& sender, TVbxControl& source, SHORT* scanCode,
   TShiftState state> TDBImageKeySource;

The TDBImageKeySource is the type of the event source for the OnKeyUp and OnKeyDown events of a TDBImage component.

Parameter	Meaning
sender	The TDBImage component
scanCode	A virtual key code. You can find a list of virtual key codes in the Windows API Help.
state	Possible values:
	1 The *Shift* key is held down
	2 The *Ctrl* key is held down
	4 The *Alt* key is held down

TDBImageMouse_MFUNCTOR macro

TDBImageMouse_MFUNCTOR(object, memberFunc)

This macro constructs the event sink object, which is of type TDBImageMouseSink, binding it to the handler method that responds when an OnMouseDown, OnMouseUp, or OnMouseMove event of a TDBImage component occurs.

Parameter	Meaning
object	Identifies the event sink object; use the *this pointer
memberFunc	Identifies the event handler that responds to the mouse events

TDBImageMouseSink typedef

typedef TBdtEventSinkV5<TDBImage& sender, TMouseButton mouseButton, TShiftState state, SHORT x, SHORT y> TDBImageMouseSink;

The TDBImageMouseSink is the type of the event sink for the OnMouseDown, OnMouseUp, and OnMouseMove events of a TDBImage component.

Parameter	Meaning
sender	The TDBImage component
mouseButton	Possible values are:
	1 Left mouse button
	2 Right mouse button
	4 Middle mouse button
state	Possible values are:
	1 *Shift* key
	2 *Ctrl* key
	4 *Alt* key
x	The position of the mouse pointer on the x-axis in screen pixels
y	The position of the mouse pointer on the y-axis in screen pixels

TDBImageMouseSource typedef

typedef TBdtEventSourceV5<TDBImage& sender, TMouseButton mouseButton, TShiftState state, SHORT x, SHORT y> TDBImageMouseSource;

The TDBImageMouseSource is the type of the event source for the OnMouseDown, OnMouseUp, and OnMouseMove events of a TDBImage component.

Parameter	Meaning
sender	The TDBImage component
mouseButton	Possible values are:
	1 Left mouse button
	2 Right mouse button
	4 Middle mouse button
state	Possible values are:
	1 *Shift* key
	2 *Ctrl* key
	4 *Alt* key
x	The position of the mouse pointer on the x-axis in screen pixels
y	The position of the mouse pointer on the y-axis in screen pixels

TDBImageNotify_MFUNCTOR macro   dbevent.h

TDBImageNotify_MFUNCTOR(object, memberFunc)

This macro constructs the event sink object, which is of type TDBImageNotifySink, binding it to the handler method that responds when an OnClick, OnDblClick, OnEnter, or OnExit event of a TDBImage component occurs.

Parameter	Meaning
object	Identifies the event sink object; use the *this pointer
memberFunc	Identifies the event handler that responds to the click, OnEnter, and OnExit events

TDBImageNotifySink typedef   dbevent.h

typedef TBdtEventSinkV1<TDBImage& sender> TDBImageNotifySink;

The TDBImageNotifySink is the type of the event sink for the OnClick, OnDblClick, OnEnter, and OnExit events of a TDBImage component.

TDBImageNotifySource typedef   dbevent.h

typedef TBdtEventSourceV1<TDBImage& sender> TDBImageNotifySource;

The TDBImageNotifySource is the type of the event source for the OnClick, OnDblClick, OnEnter, and OnExit events of a TDBImage component.

TDBListBox component   dblist.h

The TDBListBox component is a data-aware list box. It lets the user change the value of the field of the current record in a dataset by selecting an item from a list. The selected item becomes the new value of the field. For more information about editing field values, see "Updating Fields."

Link the database list box with a dataset by specifying the data source component (TDataSource) that identifies the dataset as the value of the memo's DataSource property. Specify the field in the dataset you want to access as the value of the DataField property.

You specify the values the user can choose from in the list box with the Items property. For example, if you want the user to choose from five different values in the list box, specify five strings as the value of Items. Just as with an ordinary list box, you can add, delete, and insert items in the list box using the Add, Delete, and Insert methods of the Items component, which is of type TStrings. For example, to add a string to a database list box, you could write this line of code:

```
DBListBox1.Items->Add("New item");
```

The ItemIndex property indicates which item in the list box is selected. If you want to prevent the user from being able to select an item in the list box, set the ReadOnly property to false.

Public constructors and destructor

Constructors

Form 1 TDBListBox(TWindow* Parent, int ID, LPCSTR Title, int Left, Int Top, Int Width, int Height, TModule* Module=0);
Creates a new list box object with the following parameters:

- Parent identifies the parent window object.

- ID identifies the list box component.

- Title contains the title of the window.

- Left, Top, Width, and Height identify the window position. If this is a child component, the position is relative to the parent client area.

- Module identifies the owner of the list box component.

Form 2 TDBListBox(TWindow* Parent, int ID, TModule* Module=0);
Creates a list box by loading it from an existing dialog resource.

- Parent identifies the parent window object.

- ID identifies the list box component.

- Module identifies the owner of the list box component.

Destructor

~TDBListBox()
Deletes the list box component.

Properties

About
▸ Action
▸ Align
BackColor
BorderStyle
▸ Canvas
Caption
ComponentIndex
Cursor
DataChanged
DataField
DataSource

DragCursor
DragMode
Enabled
FontBold
FontItalic
FontName
FontSize
FontStrikethru
FontUnderline
ForeColor
Height
HelpContext
Index
IntegralHeight
ItemHeight
▶ItemIndex
Items
Left
Name
▶Owner
▶Parent
ReadOnly
Sorted
Style
TabOrder
TabStop
Tag
Top
▶TopIndex
Value
Visible
Width

Methods

BeginDrag
BringToFront
CanFocus
Clear
ClientToScreen
Dragging
EndDrag
Focused
GetTextBuf
GetTextLen
Hide

Invalidate
ItemAtPos
ItemRect
Refresh
Repaint
ScaleBy
ScreenToClient
ScrollBy
SendToBack
SetBounds
SetTextBuf
Show
Update

Events

OnClick
OnDblClick
OnDragDrop
OnDragOver
OnDrawItem
OnEndDrag
OnEnter
OnExit
OnKeyDown
OnKeyPress
OnKeyUp
OnMeasureItem
OnMouseDown
OnMouseMove
OnMouseUp

TDBListBoxDrag_MFUNCTOR macro

TDBListBoxDrag_MFUNCTOR(object, memberFunc)
This macro constructs the event sink object, which is of type TDBListBoxDragSink, binding it to the handler method that responds when the OnDragDrop and OnEndDrag events of a TDBListBox component occur.

Parameter	Meaning
object	Identifies the event sink object; use the *this pointer
memberFunc	Identifies the event handler that responds to the OnDragDrop event

TDBListBoxDragOver_MFUNCTOR macro

TDBListBoxDragOver_MFUNCTOR(object, memberFunc)

This macro constructs the event sink object, which is of type TDBListBoxDragOverSink, binding it to the handler method that responds when the OnDragOver event of a TDBListBox component occurs.

Parameter	Meaning
object	Identifies the event sink object; use the *this pointer
memberFunc	Identifies the event handler that responds to the OnDragOver event

TDBListBoxDragOverSink typedef   dbevent.h

typedef TBdtEventSinkV5<TDBListBox& sender, TVbxControl& source, SHORT X, SHORT Y, TDragState state> TDBListBoxDragOverSink;

The TDBListBoxDragSink is the type of the event sink for the OnDragOver event of a TDBListBox component.

Parameter	Meaning
sender	The TDBListBox component
source	The control being dragged and dropped
X	The X parameter of the coordinates of the mouse positioned over the control
Y	The Y parameter of the coordinates of the mouse positioned over the control
state	Possible values:
	0 The dragged object enters a control in which it can be dropped
	1 The dragged object is moved within a control in which it can be dropped
	2 The dragged object leaves a control in which it can be dropped

TDBListBoxDragOverSource typedef   dbevent.h

typedef TBdtEventSourceV5<TDBListBox& sender, TVbxControl& source, SHORT X, SHORT Y, TDragState state> TDBListBoxDragOverSource;

The TDBListBoxDragSource is the type of the event source for the OnDragOver event of a TDBListBox component.

Parameter	Meaning
sender	The TDBListBox component
source	The control being dragged and dropped
X	The X parameter of the coordinates of the mouse positioned over the control
Y	The Y parameter of the coordinates of the mouse positioned over the control

Parameter	Meaning
state	Possible values:
	0 The dragged object enters a control in which it can be dropped
	1 The dragged object is moved within a control in which it can be dropped
	2 The dragged object leaves a control in which it can be dropped

TDBListBoxDragSink typedef — dbevent.h

```
typedef TBdtEventSinkV4<TDBListBoxx& sender, TVbxControl& source, SHORT X,
        SHORT Y> TDBListBoxDragSink;
```
The TDBListBoxDragSink is the type of the event sink for the OnDragDrop and OnEndDrag events of a TDBListBox component.

Parameter	Meaning
sender	The TDBListBox component
source	The control being dragged and dropped
X	The X parameter of the coordinates of the mouse positioned over the control
Y	The Y parameter of the coordinates of the mouse positioned over the control

TDBListBoxDragSource typedef — dbevent.h

```
typedef TBdtEventSourceV4<TDBListBox& sender, TVbxControl& source, SHORT X,
        SHORT Y> TDBListBoxDragSource;
```
The TDBListBoxDragSource is the type of the event source for the OnDragDrop and OnEndDrag events of a TDBListBox component.

Parameter	Meaning
sender	The TDBListBox component
source	The control being dragged and dropped
X	The X parameter of the coordinates of the mouse positioned over the control
Y	The Y parameter of the coordinates of the mouse positioned over the control

TDBListBoxDrawItem_MFUNCTOR macro

```
TDBListBoxDrawItem_MFUNCTOR(object, memberFunc)
```
This macro constructs the event sink object, which is of type TDBListBoxDrawItemSink, the handler method that responds when the OnDrawItem event of a TDBListBox component occurs.

Parameter	Meaning
object	Identifies the event sink object; use the *this pointer
memberFunc	Identifies the event handler that responds to the OnDrawItem event

TDBListBoxDrawItemSink typedef   dbevent.h

typedef TBdtEventSinkV4<TDBListBox& sender, SHORT index, TRect rc,
    TOwnerDrawState state> TDBListBoxDrawItemSink;

The TDBListBoxDrawItemSink is the type of the event sink for the OnDrawItem event of a TDBListBox component.

Parameter	Meaning
sender	The TDBListBox component
index	The index of the item in the control that identifies the position of the item in the list
rc	A rectangle in which to draw
state	The state of the selected item. These are the possible values:
	0 The item is selected
	1 The control is disabled
	2 The item currently has focus

TDBListBoxDrawItemSource typedef   dbevent.h

typedef TBdtEventSourceV4<TDBListBox& sender, SHORT index, TRect rc,
    TOwnerDrawState state> TDBListBoxDrawItemSource;

The TDBListBoxDrawItemSource is the type of the event source for the OnDrawItem event of a TDBListBox component.

Parameter	Meaning
sender	The TDBListBox component
index	The index of the item in the control that identifies the position of the item in the list
rc	A rectangle in which to draw
state	The state of the selected item. These are the possible values:
	0 The item is selected
	1 The control is disabled
	2 The item currently has focus

TDBListBoxKey_MFUNCTOR macro

TDBListBoxKey_MFUNCTOR(object, memberFunc)
This macro constructs the event sink object, which is of type TDBListBoxKeySink, binding it to the handler method that responds when the OnKeyUp and OnKeyDown events of a TDBListBox component occur.

Parameter	Meaning
object	Identifies the event sink object; use the *this pointer
memberFunc	Identifies the event handler that responds to the OnKeyUp and OnKeyDown events

TDBListBoxKeyPress_MFUNCTOR macro

TDBListBoxKeyPress_MFUNCTOR(object, memberFunc)
This macro constructs the event sink object, which is of type TDBListBoxKeyPressSink, binding it to the handler method that responds when the OnKeyPress event of a TDBListBox component occurs.

Parameter	Meaning
object	Identifies the event sink object; use the *this pointer
memberFunc	Identifies the event handler that responds to the OnKeyPress event

TDBListBoxKeyPressSink typedef   dbevent.h

typedef TBdtEventSinkV2<TDBListBox& sender, SHORT AsciiCode> TDBListBoxKeyPressSink;
The TDBListBoxKeyPressSink is the type of the event source for the OnKeyPress event of a TDBListBox component.

Parameter	Meaning
sender	The TDBListBox component
asciiCode	A single character key

TDBListBoxKeyPressSource typedef   dbevent.h

typedef TBdtEventSourceV2<TDBListBox& sender, SHORT AsciiCode> TDBListBoxKeyPressSource;
The TDBListBoxKeyPressSource is the type of the event source for the OnKeyPress event of a TDBListBox component.

Parameter	Meaning
sender	The TDBListBox component
asciiCode	A single character key

TDBListBoxKeySink typedef dbevent.h

typedef TBdtEventSinkV3<TDBListBox& sender, TVbxControl& source, SHORT* scanCode,
    TShiftState state> TDBListBoxKeySink;

The TDBListBoxKeySink is the type of the event sink for the OnKeyUp and
OnKeyDown events of a TDBListBox component.

Parameter	Meaning
sender	The TDBListBox component
scanCode	A virtual key code. You can find a list of virtual key codes in the Windows API Help.
state	Possible values:
	1 The *Shift* key is held down
	2 The *Ctrl* key is held down
	4 The *Alt* key is held down

TDBListBoxKeySource typedef dbevent.h

typedef TBdtEventSourceV3<TDBListBox& sender, TVbxControl& source, SHORT* scanCode,
    TShiftState state> TDBListBoxKeySource;

The TDBListBoxKeySource is the type of the event source for the OnKeyUp and
OnKeyDown events of a TDBListBox component.

Parameter	Meaning
sender	The TDBListBox component
scanCode	A virtual key code. You can find a list of virtual key codes in the Windows API Help.
state	Possible values:
	1 The *Shift* key is held down
	2 The *Ctrl* key is held down
	4 The *Alt* key is held down

TDBListBoxMeasureItem_MFUNCTOR macro

TDBListBoxMeasureItem_MFUNCTOR(object, memberFunc)

This macro constructs the event sink object, which is of type
TDBListBoxMeasureItemSink, the handler method that responds when the
OnMeasureItem event of TDBListBox component occurs.

Parameter	Meaning
object	Identifies the event sink object; use the *this pointer
memberFunc	Identifies the event handler that responds to the OnMeasureItem event

TDBListBoxMeasureItemSink typedef

typedef TBdtEventSinkV3<TDBListBox& sender, SHORT index, SHORT height*> TDBListBoxMeasureItemSink;
The TDBListBoxDrawItemSink is the type of the event sink for the OnMeasureItem event of a TDBListBox component.

Parameter	Meaning
sender	The TDBListBox component
index	The index of the item in the control that identifies the position of the item in the list
height	The height of the item to be drawn

TDBListBoxMeasureItemSource typedef

typedef TBdtEventSourceV3<TDBListBox& sender, SHORT index, SHORT height*>
The TDBListBoxDrawItemSource is the type of the event source for the OnMeasureItem event of a TDBListBox component.

Parameter	Meaning
sender	The TDBListBox component
index	The index of the item in the control that identifies the position of the item in the list
height	The height of the item to be drawn

TDBListBoxMouse_MFUNCTOR macro

TDBListBoxMouse_MFUNCTOR(object, memberFunc)
This macro constructs the event sink object, which is of type TDBListBoxMouseSink, binding it to the handler method that responds when an OnMouseDown, OnMouseUp, or OnMouseMove event of a TDBListBox component occurs.

Parameter	Meaning
object	Identifies the event sink object; use the *this pointer
memberFunc	Identifies the event handler that responds to the mouse events

TDBListBoxMouseSink typedef

typedef TBdtEventSinkV5<TDBListBox& sender, TMouseButton mouseButton, TShiftState state, SHORT x, SHORT y> TDBListBoxMouseSink;
The TDBListBoxMouseSink is the type of the event sink for the OnMouseDown, OnMouseUp, and OnMouseMove events of a TDBListBox component.

Parameter	Meaning
sender	The TDBListBox component
mouseButton	Possible values are:
	1 Left mouse button
	2 Right mouse button
	4 Middle mouse button
state	Possible values are:
	1 *Shift* key
	2 *Ctrl* key
	4 *Alt* key
x	The position of the mouse pointer on the x-axis in screen pixels
y	The position of the mouse pointer on the y-axis in screen pixels

TDBListBoxMouseSource typedef   dbevent.h

typedef TBdtEventSourceV5<TDBListBox& sender, TMouseButton mouseButton, TShiftState state, SHORT x, SHORT y> TDBListBoxMouseSource;

The TDBListBoxMouseSource is the type of the event source for the OnMouseDown, OnMouseUp, and OnMouseMove events of a TDBListBox component.

Parameter	Meaning
sender	The TDBListBox component
mouseButton	Possible values are:
	1 Left mouse button
	2 Right mouse button
	4 Middle mouse button
state	Possible values are:
	1 *Shift* key
	2 *Ctrl* key
	4 *Alt* key
x	The position of the mouse pointer on the x-axis in screen pixels
y	The position of the mouse pointer on the y-axis in screen pixels

TDBListBoxNotify_MFUNCTOR macro   dbevent.h

TDBListBoxNotify_MFUNCTOR(object, memberFunc)

This macro constructs the event sink object, which is of type TDBListBoxNotifySink, binding it to the handler method that responds when an OnClick, OnDblClick, OnEnter, or OnExit event of a TDBListBox component occurs.

Parameter	Meaning
object	Identifies the event sink object; use the *this pointer
memberFunc	Identifies the event handler that responds to the click, OnEnter, and OnExit events

TDBListBoxNotifySink typedef dbevent.h

typedef TBdtEventSinkV1<TDBListBox& sender> TDBListBoxNotifySink;
The TDBListBoxNotifySink is the type of the event sink for the OnClick, OnDblClick, OnEnter, and OnExit events of a TDBListBox component.

TDBListBoxNotifySource typedef dbevent.h

typedef TBdtEventSourceV1<TDBListBox& sender> TDBListBoxNotifySource;
The TDBListBoxNotifySource is the type of the event source for the OnClick, OnDblClick, OnEnter, and OnExit events of a TDBListBox component.

TDBLookupCombo component dblkuplb.h

A TDBLookupCombo component is a data-aware combo box that "looks up" a value in a lookup table.

For example, imagine that DataSource1 identifies a table called Customers, and DataSource2 identifies a table called Orders. The Orders table contains a CustNo field which has a number that identifies the customer who placed the order. When the user moves through the records in the Orders table, you want the database lookup combo box to display the name of the customer, and you want the drop-down list of the combo box to display all customer names. You can do this, because the Customers table also contains a CustNo field. It identifies the customer by number (CustNo) as well as by the customer's name.

To have the combo box look up the customer name, set the DataSource property value of the combo box to DataSource2, which refers to the Orders table. Set the DataField property value to CustNo. The LookupSource is the data source that refers to the table the combo box uses to look up the name of the customer—in this case, DataSource1— because the Customers table contains the name of the customer.

Set the LookupField property to CustNo. LookupField links the two tables on the value that identifies the customer by number. In this example, both the DataField value and the LookupField value have the same field name, but this isn't required. If the Active property of both tables is true, the database combo box displays the value of the CustNo field. You want to display the customer's name—not the customer number—so set the LookupDisplay property to Name, the field that contains the full name of the customer. Now the user moves through the records in the Orders table, the name of the customer who placed the order appears in the database lookup combo box.

You can choose to display multiple fields in the drop-down list of the combo box by entering a list of fields to display as the value of the LookupDisplay property. To display the resulting columns the way you want, use the Options property.

If the ReadOnly property is false, the user can select a displayed value in the database lookup combo box and the corresponding value in current record of the primary dataset updates with a new value. Using the Customers and Orders example, when the user selects a customer name in the lookup table using the database lookup combo box, the value of the CustNo field in the primary dataset updates accordingly.

The Style property determines whether the user can edit a selected item in the combo box or enter a new value and therefore change the value in the lookup table, or simply select items without being able to edit them.

The DropDownCount and DropDownWidth properties determine how long and how wide the drop-down list of the combo box is.

The Value property is the string the combo box uses to identify which record in the lookup table to display; it is the contents of the DataField for the current record. The DisplayValue is the actual displayed string in the combo box.

Public constructors and destructor

Constructors

Form 1
```
TDBLookupCombo( TWindow* Parent, int ID, LPCSTR Title, int Left, Int Top, Int Width, int Height,
      TModule* Module=0 );
```
Creates a new lookup combo object with the following parameters:

- Parent identifies the parent window object.

- ID identifies the lookup combo box component.

- Title contains the title of the window.

- Left, Top, Width, and Height identify the window position. If this is a child component, the position is relative to the parent client area.

- Module identifies the owner of the lookup combo box component.

Form 2
```
TDBLookupCombo( TWindow* Parent, int ID, TModule* Module=0 );
```
Creates a lookup combo by loading it from an existing dialog resource.

Creates a new lookup combo object with the following parameters:

- Parent identifies the parent window object.

- ID identifies the lookup combo box component.

- Module identifies the owner of the lookup combo box component.

Destructor

```
~TDBLookupCombo()
```
Deletes the lookup combo component.

Properties

About
▷ Align
AutoSelect
BackColor
▷ BoundsRect
Caption
▷ ComponentIndex
Cursor
DataChanged
DataField
DataSource
▷ DisplayValue
DragCursor
DragMode
DropDownCount
DropDownWidth
Enabled
FontBold
FontItalic
FontName
FontSize
FontStrikethru
FontUnderline
ForeColor
Height
HelpContext
Index
ItemHeight
▷ ItemIndex
Left
LookupDisplay
LookupField
LookupSource
MaxLength
Name
Options
▷ Owner
▷ Parent
ReadOnly
▷ SelLength
▷ SelStart
▷ SelText
Sorted
Style

TabOrder
TabStop
Tag
Top
▷Value
Visible
Width

Methods

BeginDrag
BringToFront
CanFocus
Clear
ClientToScreen
CloseUp
Dragging
DropDown
EndDrag
Focused
GetTextBuf
GetTextLen
Hide
Invalidate
Refresh
Repaint
ScaleBy
ScreenToClient
ScrollBy
SelectAll
SendToBack
SetBounds
SetTextBuf
Show
Update

Events

OnChange
OnClick
OnDblClick
OnDragDrop
OnDragOver
OnDropDown
OnEndDrag

OnEnter
OnExit
OnKeyDown
OnKeyPress
OnKeyUp
OnMouseDown
OnMouseMove
OnMouseUp

TDBLookupComboDrag_MFUNCTOR macro

TDBLookupComboDrag_MFUNCTOR(object, memberFunc)

This macro constructs the event sink object, which is of type TDBLookupComboDragSink, binding it to the handler method that responds when the OnDragDrop and OnEndDrag events of a TDBLookupCombo component occur.

Parameter	Meaning
object	Identifies the event sink object; use the *this pointer
memberFunc	Identifies the event handler that responds to the OnDragDrop event

TDBLookupComboDragOver_MFUNCTOR macro

TDBLookupComboDragOver_MFUNCTOR(object, memberFunc)

This macro constructs the event sink object, which is of type TDBLookupComboDragOverSink, binding it to the handler method that responds when the OnDragOver event of a TDBLookupCombo component occurs.

Parameter	Meaning
sender	The TDBLookupCombo component
source	The control being dragged and dropped
X	The X parameter of the coordinates of the mouse positioned over the control
Y	The Y parameter of the coordinates of the mouse positioned over the control
state	Possible values:
	0 The dragged object enters a control in which it can be dropped
	1 The dragged object is moved within a control in which it can be dropped
	2 The dragged object leaves a control in which it can be dropped

TDBLookupComboDragOverSink
dbevent.h

typedef TBdtEventSinkV5<TDBLookupCombo& sender, TVbxControl& source, SHORT X, SHORT Y,
TDragState state> TDBLookupComboDragOverSink;

The TDBLookupComboDragSink is the type of the event sink for the OnDragOver
event of a TDBLookupCombo component.

Parameter	Meaning
sender	The TDBLookupCombo component
source	The control being dragged and dropped
X	The X parameter of the coordinates of the mouse positioned over the control
Y	The Y parameter of the coordinates of the mouse positioned over the control
state	Possible values:
	0 The dragged object enters a control in which it can be dropped
	1 The dragged object is moved within a control in which it can be dropped
	2 The dragged object leaves a control in which it can be dropped

TDBLookupComboDragOverSource
dbevent.h

typedef TBdtEventSourceV5<TDBLookupCombo& sender, TVbxControl& source, SHORT X, SHORT Y,
TDragState state> TDBLookupComboDragOverSource;

The TDBLookupComboDragSource is the type of the event source the OnDragOver
event of a TDBLookupCombo component.

Parameter	Meaning
sender	The TDBLookupCombo component
source	The control being dragged and dropped
X	The X parameter of the coordinates of the mouse positioned over the control
Y	The Y parameter of the coordinates of the mouse positioned over the control
state	Possible values:
	0 The dragged object enters a control in which it can be dropped
	1 The dragged object is moved within a control in which it can be dropped
	2 The dragged object leaves a control in which it can be dropped

TDBLookupComboDragSink typedef
dbevent.h

typedef TBdtEventSinkV4<TDBLookupCombox& sender, TVbxControl& source, SHORT X, SHORT Y>
TDBLookupComboDragSink;

The TDBLookupComboDragSink is the type of the event sink for the OnDragDrop and
OnEndDrag events of a TDBLookupCombo component.

Parameter	Meaning
sender	The TDBLookupCombo component
source	The control being dragged and dropped

Parameter	Meaning
X	The X parameter of the coordinates of the mouse positioned over the control
Y	The Y parameter of the coordinates of the mouse positioned over the control

TDBLookupComboDragSource typedef dbevent.h

typedef TBdtEventSourceV4<TDBLookupCombo& sender, TVbxControl& source, SHORT X, SHORT Y>
    TDBLookupComboDragSource;

The TDBLookupComboDragSource is the type of the event source for the OnDragDrop and OnEndDrag events of a TDBLookupCombo component.

Parameter	Meaning
sender	The TDBLookupCombo component
source	The control being dragged and dropped
X	The X parameter of the coordinates of the mouse positioned over the control
Y	The Y parameter of the coordinates of the mouse positioned over the control

TDBLookupComboKey_MYFUNCTOR macro

TDBLookupComboKey_MFUNCTOR(object, memberFunc)

This macro constructs the event sink object, which is of type TDBLookupComboKeySink, binding it to the handler method that responds when the OnKeyUp and OnKeyDown events of a TDBLookupCombo component occur.

Parameter	Meaning
object	Identifies the event sink object; use the *this pointer
memberFunc	Identifies the event handler that responds to the OnKeyUp and OnKeyDown events

TDBLookupComboKeyPress_MFUNCTOR macro

TDBLookupComboKeyPress_MFUNCTOR(object, memberFunc)

This macro constructs the event sink object, which is of type TDBLookupComboKeyPressSink, binding it to the handler method that responds when the OnKeyPress event of a TDBLookupCombo component occurs.

Parameter	Meaning
object	Identifies the event sink object; use the *this pointer
memberFunc	Identifies the event handler that responds to the OnKeyPress event

TDBLookupComboKeyPressSink typedef dbevent.h

typedef TBdtEventSinkV2<TDBLookupCombo& sender,,
    SHORT AsciiCode> TDBLookupComboKeyPressSink;

The TDBLookupComboKeyPressSink is the type of the event source for the OnKeyPress event of a TDBLookupCombo component.

Parameter	Meaning
sender	The TDBLookupCombo component
asciiCode	A single character key

TDBLookupComboKeyPressSource typedef dbevent.h

```
typedef TBdtEventSourceV2<TDBLookupCombo& sender, SHORT AsciiCode>
    TDBLookupComboKeyPressSource;
```
The TDBLookupComboKeyPressSource is the type of the event source for the OnKeyPress event of a TDBLookupCombo component.

Parameter	Meaning
sender	The TDBLookupCombo component
asciiCode	A single character key

TDBLookupComboKeySink typedef dbevent.h

```
typedef TBdtEventSinkV3<TDBLookupCombo& sender, TVbxControl& source, SHORT* scanCode,
    TShiftState state> TDBLookupComboKeySink;
```
The TDBLookupComboKeySink is the type of the event sink for the OnKeyUp and OnKeyDown events of a TDBLookupCombo component.

Parameter	Meaning
sender	The TDBLookupCombo component
scanCode	A virtual key code. You can find a list of virtual key codes in the Windows API Help.
state	Possible values:
	1 The *Shift* key is held down
	2 The *Ctrl* key is held down
	4 The *Alt* key is held down

TDBLookupComboKeySource typedef dbevent.h

```
typedef TBdtEventSourceV3<TDBLookupCombo& sender, TVbxControl& source, SHORT* scanCode,
    TShiftState state> TDBLookupComboKeySource;
```
The TDBLookupComboKeySource is the type of the event source for the OnKeyUp and OnKeyDown events of a TDBLookupCombo component.

Parameter	Meaning
sender	The TDBLookupCombo component
scanCode	A virtual key code. You can find a list of virtual key codes in the Windows API Help.

Parameter	Meaning
state	Possible values:
	1 The *Shift* key is held down
	2 The *Ctrl* key is held down
	4 The *Alt* key is held down

TDBLookupComboMouse_MFUNCTOR macro

TDBLookupComboMouse_MFUNCTOR(object, memberFunc)

This macro constructs the event sink object, which is of type TDBLookupComboMouseSink, binding it to the handler method that responds when an OnMouseDown, OnMouseUp, or OnMouseMove event of a TDBLookupCombo component occurs:

Parameter	Meaning
object	Identifies the event sink object; use the *this pointer
memberFunc	Identifies the event handler that responds to the click, OnChange, OnEnter, and OnExit events

TDBLookupComboMouseSink typedef   dbevent.h

typedef TBdtEventSinkV5<TDBLookupCombo& sender, TMouseButton mouseButton, TShiftState state, SHORT x, SHORT y> TDBLookupComboMouseSink;

The TDBLookupComboMouseSink is the type of the event sink for the OnMouseDown, OnMouseUp, and OnMouseMove events of a TDBLookupCombo component.

PTDBLookupComboMouseSource typedef   dbevent.h

typedef TBdtEventSourceV5<TDBLookupCombo& sender, TMouseButton mouseButton, TShiftState state, SHORT x, SHORT y> TDBLookupComboMouseSource;

The TDBLookupComboMouseSource is the type of the event source for the OnMouseDown, OnMouseUp, and OnMouseMove events of a TDBLookupCombo component.

Parameter	Meaning
sender	The TDBLookupCombo component
mouseButton	Possible values are:
	1 Left mouse button
	2 Right mouse button
	4 Middle mouse button
state	Possible values are:
	1 *Shift* key

Parameter	Meaning
	2 *Ctrl* key
	4 *Alt* key
x	The position of the mouse pointer on the x-axis in screen pixels
y	The position of the mouse pointer on the y-axis in screen pixels

TDBLookupComboNotify_MFUNCTOR macro   dbevent.h

TDBLookupComboNotify_MFUNCTOR(object, memberFunc)

This macro constructs the event sink object, which is of typeTDBLookup-
ComboNotifySink, binding it to the handler method that responds when an OnClick,
OnDblClick, OnDropDown, OnEnter, or OnExit event of a TDBLookupCombo
component occurs.

Parameter	Meaning
object	Identifies the event sink object; use the *this pointer
memberFunc	Identifies the event handler that responds to the click, OnChange, OnEnter, and OnExit events

TDBLookupComboNotifySink typedef   dbevent.h

typedef TBdtEventSinkV1<TDBLookupCombo& sender> TDBLookupComboNotifySink;

The TDBLookupComboNotifySink is the type of the event sink for the OnChange,
OnClick, OnDblClick, OnDropDown, OnEnter, and OnExit events of a
TDBLookupCombo component.

TDBLookupComboNotifySource typedef   dbevent.h

typedef TBdtEventSourceV1< TDBLookupCombo& sender> TDBLookupComboNotifySource;

The TDBListBoxNotifySource is the type of the event source for the OnChange,
OnClick, OnDblClick, OnDropDown, OnEnter, and OnExit events of a TDBListBox
component.

TDBLookupList component   dblkuplb.h

A TDBLookupList component is a data-aware list box that "looks up" a value in a
lookup table.

For example, imagine that DataSource1 identifies a table called Books, and DataSource2
identifies a table called BookOrders. The BookOrders table contains a Volume field that
use a number to identify the book the customer ordered. When the user moves through
the records in the BookOrders table, you want the database lookup list box to display

the titles of the books. You can do this because the Books table also contains a field that identifies the book by number (Volume) as well as by the title of the book.

For the database lookup list box to look up the title of the book, set the DataSource property value of the list box to DataSource2, which refers to the BookOrders table. Set the DataField property value to Volume. The LookupSource is the data source that refers to the table the combo box uses to look up the title of the book in this case, DataSource1 because the Books table contains the book's title.

Set the LookupField property to Volume. LookupField links the two tables on the value that identifies the book by number. In this example, both the DataField value and the LookupField value have the same field name, but this isn't required. If the Active property of both tables is true, the database list box now displays the value of the Volume field. You want to display the title of the book not the volume number so set the LookupDisplay property to Title, the field that contains the title of the book. Now as the user moves through the records in the BookOrders table, the title of the ordered book appears in the database lookup list box.

You can display multiple fields in the list box by entering the list of fields to display as the value of the LookupDisplay property, separating each field with a semicolon. To display the resulting columns the way you want, use the Options property.

If the ReadOnly property is false, the user can select a displayed value in the database lookup list box and the corresponding value in current record of the primary dataset updates with a new value. Using the Books and BookOrders example, when the user selects a title in the lookup table using the database lookup list box, the value of the CustNo field in the primary dataset updates accordingly.

The Value property is the string the combo box uses to identify which record in the lookup table to display. The DisplayValue is the actual string displayed in the list box.

Public constructors and destructor

Constructors

Form 1   TDBLookupList(TWindow* Parent, int ID, LPCSTR Title, int Left, Int Top, Int Width, int Height,
       TModule*Module=0);
Creates a new lookup list object with the following parameters:

- Parent identifies the parent window object.

- ID identifies the lookup list box component.

- Title contains the title of the window.

- Left, Top, Width, Height identify the window position. If this is a child component, the position is relative to the parent client area.

- Module identifies the owner of the lookup list box component.

Form 2   TDBLookupList(TWindow* Parent, int ID, TModule* Module=0);
Creates a lookup list by loading it from an existing dialog resource.

- Parent identifies the parent window object.

- ID identifies the lookup list box component.

- Module identifies the owner of the lookup list box component.

Destructor

~TDBLookupList()
Deletes the lookup list component.

Properties

About
▶ Align
BackColor
BorderStyle
▶ BoundsRect
Caption
▶ ComponentIndex
Cursor
DataChanged
DataField
DataSource
▶ DisplayValue
DragCursor
DragMode
Enabled
▶ FieldCount
FontBold
FontItalic
FontName
FontSize
FontStrikethru
FontUnderline
ForeColor
Height
HelpContext
Index
IntegralHeight
ItemHeight

▶ItemIndex
Left
LookupDisplay
LookupField
LookupSource
Name
Options
▶Owner
▶Parent
ReadOnly
▶SelectedField
Sorted
Style
TabOrder
TabStop
Tag
Top
▶Value
Visible
Width

Methods

BeginDrag
BringToFront
CanFocus
ClientToScreen
Dragging
EndDrag
Focused
GetTextBuf
GetTextLen
Hide
Invalidate
Refresh
Repaint
ScaleBy
ScreenToClient
ScrollBy
SendToBack
SetBounds
SetFocus
SetTextBuf
Show
Update

Events

OnClick
OnDblClick
OnDragDrop
OnDragOver
OnEndDrag
OnEnter
OnExit
OnKeyDown
OnKeyPress
OnKeyUp

TDBLookupListDrag_MFUNCTOR macro

TDBLookupListDrag_MFUNCTOR(object, memberFunc)

This macro constructs the event sink object, which is of type TDBLookupListDragSink, binding it to the handler method that responds when the OnDragDrop and OnEndDrag events of a TDBLookupList component occur.

Parameter	Meaning
object	Identifies the event sink object; use the *this pointer
memberFunc	Identifies the event handler that responds to the OnDragDrop event

TDBLookupListDragOver_MFUNCTOR macro

TDBLookupListDragOver_MFUNCTOR(object, memberFunc)

This macro constructs the event sink object, which is of type TDBLookupListDragOverSink, binding it to the handler method that responds when the OnDragOver event of a TDBLookupList component occurs.

Parameter	Meaning
object	Identifies the event sink object; use the *this pointer
memberFunc	Identifies the event handler that responds to the OnDragOver event

TDBLookupListDragOverSink typedef   dbevent.h

typedef TBdtEventSinkV5<TDBLookupList& sender, TVbxControl& source, SHORT X, SHORT Y,
    TDragState state> TDBLookupListDragOverSink;

The TDBLookupListDragSink is the type of the event sink for the OnDragOver event of a TDBLookupList component.

Parameter	Meaning
sender	The TDBLookupList component
source	The control being dragged and dropped
X	The X parameter of the coordinates of the mouse positioned over the control
Y	The Y parameter of the coordinates of the mouse positioned over the control
state	Possible values:
	0 The dragged object enters a control in which it can be dropped
	1 The dragged object is moved within a control in which it can be dropped
	2 The dragged object leaves a control in which it can be dropped

TDBLookupListDragOverSource typedef dbevent.h

```
typedef TBdtEventSourceV5<TDBLookupList& sender, TVbxControl& source, SHORT X, SHORT Y,
    TDragState state> TDBLookupListDragOverSource;
```
The TDBLookupListDragSource is the type of the event source the OnDragOver event of a TDBLookupList component.

Parameter	Meaning
sender	The TDBLookupList component
source	The control being dragged and dropped
X	The X parameter of the coordinates of the mouse positioned over the control
Y	The Y parameter of the coordinates of the mouse positioned over the control
state	Possible values:
	0 The dragged object enters a control in which it can be dropped
	1 The dragged object is moved within a control in which it can be dropped
	2 The dragged object leaves a control in which it can be dropped

TDBLookupListDragSink typedef dbevent.h

```
typedef TBdtEventSinkV4<TDBLookupListx& sender, TVbxControl& source, SHORT X,
    SHORT Y>TDBLookupListDragSink;
```
The TDBLookupListDragSink is the type of the event sink for the OnDragDrop and OnEndDrag events of a TDBLookupList component.

Parameter	Meaning
sender	The TDBLookupList component
source	The control being dragged and dropped
X	The X parameter of the coordinates of the mouse positioned over the control
Y	The Y parameter of the coordinates of the mouse positioned over the control

TDBLookupListDragSource typedef

dbevent.h

typedef TBdtEventSourceV4<TDBLookupList& sender, TVbxControl& source, SHORT X,
    SHORT Y> TDBLookupListDragSource;

The TDBLookupListDragSource is the type of the event source for the OnDragDrop and
OnEndDrag events of a TDBLookupList component.

Parameter	Meaning
sender	The TDBLookupList component
source	The control being dragged and dropped
X	The X parameter of the coordinates of the mouse positioned over the control
Y	The Y parameter of the coordinates of the mouse positioned over the control

TDBLookupListKey_MFUNCTOR macro

TDBLookupListKey_MFUNCTOR(object, memberFunc)

This macro constructs the event sink object, which is of type TDBLookupListKeySink,
binding it to the handler method that responds when the OnKeyUp and OnKeyDown
events of a TDBLookupList component occur.

Parameter	Meaning
object	Identifies the event sink object; use the *this pointer
memberFunc	Identifies the event handler that responds to the OnKeyUp and OnKeyDown events

TDBLookupListKeyPress_MFUNCTOR macro

TDBLookupListKeyPress_MFUNCTOR(object, memberFunc)

This macro constructs the event sink object, which is of type
TDBLookupListKeyPressSink, binding it to the handler method that responds when the
OnKeyPress event of a TDBLookupList component occurs.

Parameter	Meaning
object	Identifies the event sink object; use the *this pointer
memberFunc	Identifies the event handler that responds to the OnKeyPress event

TDBLookupListKeyPressSink typedef

dbevent.h

typedef TBdtEventSinkV2<TDBLookupList& sender, SHORT AsciiCode> TDBLookupListKeyPressSink;

The TDBLookupListKeyPressSink is the type of the event source for the OnKeyPress
event of a TDBLookupList component.

Parameter	Meaning
sender	The TDBLookupList component
asciiCode	A single character key

TDBLookupListKeyPressSource typedef dbevent.h

typedef TBdtEventSourceV2<TDBLookupList& sender, SHORT AsciiCode> TDBLookupListKeyPressSource;
The TDBLookupListKeyPressSource is the type of the event source for the OnKeyPress event of a TDBLookupList component.

Parameter	Meaning
sender	The TDBLookupList component
asciiCode	A single character key

TDBLookupListKeySink typedef dbevent.h

typedef TBdtEventSinkV3<TDBLookupList& sender, TVbxControl& source, SHORT* scanCode, TShiftState state> TDBLookupListKeySink;
The TDBLookupListKeySink is the type of the event sink for the OnKeyUp and OnKeyDown events of a TDBLookupList component.

Parameter	Meaning
sender	The TDBLookupList component
scanCode	A virtual key code. You can find a list of virtual key codes in the Windows API Help.
state	Possible values:
	1 The *Shift* key is held down
	2 The *Ctrl* key is held down
	4 The *Alt* key is held down

TDBLookupListKeySource typedef dbevent.h

typedef TBdtEventSourceV3<TDBLookupList& sender, TVbxControl& source, SHORT* scanCode, TShiftState state> TDBLookupListKeySource;
The TDBLookupListKeySource is the type of the event source for the OnKeyUp and OnKeyDown events of a TDBLookupList component.

Parameter	Meaning
sender	The TDBLookupList component
scanCode	A virtual key code. You can find a list of virtual key codes in the Windows API Help.
state	Possible values:
	1 The *Shift* key is held down

Parameter	Meaning
	2 The *Ctrl* key is held down
	4 The *Alt* key is held down

TDBLookupListNotify_MFUNCTOR macro dbevent.h

TDBLookupListNotify_MFUNCTOR(object, memberFunc)

This macro constructs the event sink object, which is of type TDBLookupListNotifySink, to the handler method that when an OnClick, OnDblClick, OnEnter, or OnExit event of a TDBLookupList component occurs.

Parameter	Meaning
object	Identifies the event sink object; use the *this pointer
memberFunc	Identifies the event handler that responds to the OnClick and OnDblClick events

TDBLookupListNotifySink typedef dbevent.h

typedef TBdtEventSinkV1<TDBLookupList& sender> TDBLookupListNotifySink;

The TDBLookupListNotifySink is the type of the event sink for the OnClick, OnDblClick , OnEnter, and OnExit events of a TDBLookupList component.

TDBLookupListNotifySource typedef dbevent.h

typedef TBdtEventSourceV1<TDBLookupList& sender> TDBLookupListNotifySource;

The TDBLookupListNotifySource is the type of the event source for the OnClick, OnDblClick, OnEnter, and OnExit events of a TDBLookupListBox component.

TDBLookupListOptions typedef dbtype.h

```
typedef enum {
  loColLines = 0x01,
  loRowLines = 0x02,
  loTitles   = 0x04,
}TDBLookupListOption;
struct _TDBLookupListOptions {
  unsigned int loColLines : 1;
  unsigned int loRowLines : 1;
  unsigned int loTitles   : 1;
  _TDBLookupListOptions( unsigned short int u ) { *this = *(_TDBLookupListOptions*)&u; };
  operator unsigned short int() { return *(unsigned short int*)this; }
};
typedef struct _TDBLookupListOptions TDBLookupListOptions;
```

The TDBLookupListOptions type defines the possible values contained in the Options set of a database lookup combo box (TDBLookupCombo) or database lookup list box (TDBLookupList).

TDBMemo component   dbmemo.h

A TDBMemo component displays text for the user and lets the user display and enter data into a field much like a TDBEdit component. The TDBMemo component permits multiple lines to be entered or displayed, including text BLOBs (binary large objects).

Unlike an ordinary memo control, you can use the database memo to enter data into a field or to simply display data from a field of the current record in a dataset. Link the database memo with a dataset by specifying the data source component (TDataSource) that identifies the dataset as the value of the memo's DataSource property. Specify the field in the dataset you want to access as the value of the Data-Field property.

If you want the user to be able to view the data in the field but not able to change it, set the ReadOnly property to true. For more information about editing field values, see "Updating Fields."

Your application can tell if the value of Text changes by checking the value of the Modified property. To limit the number of characters users can enter into the database memo, use the MaxLength property.

You can add, delete, insert, and move lines in a database memo control using the Add, Delete, and Insert methods of the Lines component, which is of type TStrings. For example, to add a line to a memo, you could write this line of code:

```
DBMemo1.Lines->Add("Another line is added");
```

You can cut, copy, and paste text to and from a database memo control using the CutToClipboard, CopyToClipboard, and PasteFromClipboard methods.

If the memo displays a BLOB field, you can control when the text appears in the memo with the AutoDisplay property. You can also load the text using the LoadMemo method.

Several properties affect how the database memo appears and how text is entered. You can choose to supply scroll bars in the memo with the ScrollBars property. If you want the text to break into lines, set WordWrap to true. If you want the user to be able to use tabs in the text, set WantTabs to true.

At run time, you can select all the text in the memo with the SelectAll method. To find out which text in the memo the user has selected, or to replace selected text, use the SelText property. To select only part of the text or to find out what part of the text is selected, use the SelStart and SelLength properties.

Public constructors and destructor

Constructors

Form 1   TDBMemo(TWindow* Parent, int ID, LPCSTR Title, int Left, Int Top, Int Width, int Height, TModule* Module=0);
Creates a new memo object with the following parameters:

- Parent identifies the parent window object.

- ID identifies the memo component.

- Title contains the title of the window.

- Left, Top, Width, Height identify the window position. If this is a child component, the position is relative to the parent client area.

- Module identifies the owner of the memo component.

Form 2   TDBMemo(TWindow* Parent, int ID, TModule* Module=0);
Creates a memo by loading it from an existing dialog resource.

- Parent identifies the parent window object.

- ID identifies the memo component.

- Module identifies the owner of the memo component.

Destructor

~TDBMemo()
Deletes the memo component.

Properties

About
▷ Align
Alignment
AutoDisplay
BackColor
BorderStyle
▷ BoundsRect
▷ ComponentIndex
Cursor
DataChanged
DataField
DataSource
DragCursor
DragMode
Enabled
FontBold
FontItalic

FontName
FontSize
FontStrikethru
FontUnderline
ForeColor
Height
HelpContext
Index
Left
Lines
MaxLength
▶Modified
Name
▶Owner
▶Parent
ReadOnly
ScrollBars
SelLength
SelStart
SelText
TabOrder
TabStop
Tag
Top
Visible
WantReturns
WantTabs
Width
WordWrap

Methods

BeginDrag
BringToFront
CanFocus
Clear
ClearSelection
ClientToScreen
CopyToClipboard
CutToClipboard
Dragging
EndDrag
Focused
GetSelTextBuf

GetTextBuf
GetTextLen
Hide
Invalidate
LoadMemo
PasteFromClipboard
Refresh
Repaint
ScaleBy
ScreenToClient
ScrollBy
SelectAll
SendToBack
SetBounds
SetFocus
SetSelTextBuf
SetTextBuf
Show
Update

Events

OnChange
OnClick
OnDblClick
OnDragDrop
OnDragOver
OnEndDrag
OnEnter
OnExit
OnKeyDown
OnKeyPress
OnKeyUp
OnMouseDown
OnMouseMove
OnMouseUp

TDBMemoDrag_MFUNCTOR macro

TDBMemoDrag_MFUNCTOR(object, memberFunc)
This macro constructs the event sink object, which is of type TDBMemoDragSink,
binding it to the handler method that responds when the OnDragDrop and OnEndDrag
events of a TDBMemo component occur.

Parameter	Meaning
object	Identifies the event sink object; use the *this pointer
memberFunc	Identifies the event handler that responds to the OnDragDrop event

TDBMemoDragOver_MFUNCTOR macro

TDBMemoDragOver_MFUNCTOR(object, memberFunc)

This macro constructs the event sink object, which is of type TDBMemoDragOverSink, binding it to the handler method that responds when the OnDragOver event of a TDBMemo component occurs.

Parameter	Meaning
object	Identifies the event sink object; use the *this pointer
memberFunc	Identifies the event handler that responds to the OnDragOver event

TDBMemoDragOverSink typedef   dbevent.h

typedef TBdtEventSinkV5<TDBMemo& sender, TVbxControl& source, SHORT X, SHORT Y,
    TDragState state> TDBMemoDragOverSink;

The TDBMemoDragSink is the type of the event sink for the OnDragOver event of a TDBMemo component.

Parameter	Meaning
sender	The TDBMemo component
source	The control being dragged and dropped
X	The X parameter of the coordinates of the mouse positioned over the control
Y	The Y parameter of the coordinates of the mouse positioned over the control
state	Possible values:
	0 The dragged object enters a control in which it can be dropped
	1 The dragged object is moved within a control in which it can be dropped
	2 The dragged object leaves a control in which it can be dropped

TDBMemoDragOverSource typedef   dbevent.h

typedef TBdtEventSourceV5<TDBMemo& sender, TVbxControl& source, SHORT X, SHORT Y,
    TDragState state> TDBMemoDragOverSource;

The TDBMemoDragSource is the type of the event source the OnDragOver event of a TDBMemo component.

Parameter	Meaning
sender	The TDBMemo component
source	The control being dragged and dropped

Parameter	Meaning
X	The X parameter of the coordinates of the mouse positioned over the control
Y	The Y parameter of the coordinates of the mouse positioned over the control
state	Possible values:
	0 The dragged object enters a control in which it can be dropped
	1 The dragged object is moved within a control in which it can be dropped
	2 The dragged object leaves a control in which it can be dropped

TDBMemoDragSink typedef   dbevent.h

typedef TBdtEventSinkV4<TDBMemox& sender, TVbxControl& source, SHORT X,
     SHORT Y> TDBMemoDragSink;

The TDBMemoDragSink is the type of the event sink for the OnDragDrop and OnEndDrag events of a TDBMemo component.

Parameter	Meaning
sender	The TDBMemo component
source	The control being dragged and dropped
X	The X parameter of the coordinates of the mouse positioned over the control
Y	The Y parameter of the coordinates of the mouse positioned over the control

TDBMemoDragSource typedef   dbevent.h

typedef TBdtEventSourceV4<TDBMemo& sender, TVbxControl& source, SHORT X,
     SHORT Y> TDBMemoDragSource;

The TDBMemoDragSource is the type of the event source for the OnDragDrop and OnEndDrag events of a TDBMemo component.

Parameter	Meaning
sender	The TDBMemo component
source	The control being dragged and dropped
X	The X parameter of the coordinates of the mouse positioned over the control
Y	The Y parameter of the coordinates of the mouse positioned over the control

TDBMemoKey_MFUNCTOR macro

TDBMemoKey_MFUNCTOR(object, memberFunc)

This macro constructs the event sink object, which is of type TDBMemoKeySink, binding it to the handler method that responds when the OnKeyUp and OnKeyDown events of a TDBMemo component occur.

Parameter	Meaning
object	Identifies the event sink object; use the *this pointer
memberFunc	Identifies the event handler that responds to the OnKeyUp and OnKeyDown events

TDBMemoKeyPress_MFUNCTOR macro

TDBMemoKeyPress_MFUNCTOR(object, memberFunc)

This macro constructs the event sink object, which is of type TDBMemoKeyPressSink, binding it to the handler method that responds when the OnKeyPress event of a TDBMemo component occurs.

Parameter	Meaning
object	Identifies the event sink object; use the *this pointer
memberFunc	Identifies the event handler that responds to the OnKeyPress event

TDBMemoKeyPressSink typedef   dbevent.h

typedef TBdtEventSinkV2<TDBMemo& sender, SHORT AsciiCode> TDBMemoKeyPressSink;

The TDBMemoKeyPressSink is the type of the event source for the OnKeyPress event of a TDBMemo component.

Parameter	Meaning
sender	The TDBMemo component
asciiCode	A single character key

TDBMemoKeyPressSource typedef   dbevent.h

typedef TBdtEventSourceV2<TDBMemo& sender, SHORT AsciiCode> TDBMemoKeyPressSource;

The TDBMemoKeyPressSource is the type of the event source for the OnKeyPress event of a TDBMemo component.

Parameter	Meaning
sender	The TDBMemo component
asciiCode	A single character key

TDBMemoKeySink typedef

dbevent.h

typedef TBdtEventSinkV3<TDBMemo& sender, TVbxControl& source, SHORT* scanCode,
TShiftState state> TDBMemoKeySink;

The TDBMemoKeySink is the type of the event sink for the OnKeyUp and OnKeyDown
events of a TDBMemo component.

Parameter	Meaning
sender	The TDBMemo component
scanCode	A virtual key code. You can find a list of virtual key codes in the Windows API Help.
state	Possible values:
	1 The *Shift* key is held down
	2 The *Ctrl* key is held down
	4 The *Alt* key is held down

TDBMemoKeySource typedef

dbevent.h

typedef TBdtEventSourceV3<TDBMemo& sender, TVbxControl& source, SHORT* scanCode,
TShiftState state> TDBMemoKeySource;

The TDBMemoKeySource is the type of the event source for the OnKeyUp and
OnKeyDown events of a TDBMemo component.

Parameter	Meaning
sender	The TDBMemo component
scanCode	A virtual key code. You can find a list of virtual key codes in the Windows API Help.
state	Possible values:
	1 The *Shift* key is held down
	2 The *Ctrl* key is held down
	4 The *Alt* key is held down

TDBMemoMouse_MFUNCTOR macro

TDBMemoMouse_MFUNCTOR(object, memberFunc)

This macro constructs the event sink object, which is of type TDBMemoMouseSink,
binding it to the handler method that responds when an OnMouseDown, OnMouseUp,
or OnMouseMove event of a TDBMemo component occurs.

Parameter	Meaning
object	Identifies the event sink object; use the *this pointer
memberFunc	Identifies the event handler that responds to the mouse events

TDBMemoMouseSink typedef

dbevent.h

typedef TBdtEventSinkV5<TDBMemo& sender, TMouseButton mouseButton, TShiftState state, SHORT x, SHORT y> TDBMemoMouseSink;

The TDBMemoMouseSink is the type of the event sink for the OnMouseDown, OnMouseUp, and OnMouseMove events of a TDBMemo component.

Parameter	Meaning
sender	The TDBMemo component
mouseButton	Possible values are:
	1 Left mouse button
	2 Right mouse button
	4 Middle mouse button
state	Possible values are:
	1 *Shift* key
	2 *Ctrl* key
	4 *Alt* key
x	The position of the mouse pointer on the x-axis in screen pixels
y	The position of the mouse pointer on the y-axis in screen pixels

TDBMemoMouseSource typedef

dbevent.h

typedef TBdtEventSourceV5<TDBMemo& sender, TMouseButton mouseButton, TShiftState state, SHORT x, SHORT y> TDBMemoMouseSource;

The TDBMemoMouseSource is the type of the event source for the OnMouseDown, OnMouseUp, and OnMouseMove events of a TDBMemo component.

Parameter	Meaning
sender	The TDBMemo component
mouseButton	Possible values are:
	1 Left mouse button
	2 Right mouse button
	4 Middle mouse button
state	Possible values are:
	1 The *Shift* key
	2 The *Ctrl* key
	4 The *Alt* key
x	The position of the mouse pointer on the x-axis in screen pixels
y	The position of the mouse pointer on the y-axis in screen pixels

TDBMemoNotify_MFUNCTOR macro

dbevent.h

TDBMemoNotify_MFUNCTOR(object, memberFunc)

This macro constructs the event sink object, which is of type TDBMemoNotifySink, binding it to the handler method that responds when an OnChange, OnClick, OnDblClick, OnEnter, or OnExit event of a TDBMemo component occurs.

Parameter	Meaning
object	Identifies the event sink object; use the *this pointer
memberFunc	Identifies the event handler that responds to the click, OnChange, OnEnter, and OnExit events

TDBMemoNotifySink typedef   dbevent.h

typedef TBdtEventSinkV1<TDBMemo& sender> TDBMemoNotifySink;
The TDBMemoNotifySink is the type of the event sink for the OnChange, OnClick, OnDblClick, OnEnter, and OnExit events of a TDBMemo component.

TDBMemoNotifySource typedef   dbevent.h

typedef TBdtEventSourceV1<TDBMemo& sender> TDBMemoNotifySource;
The TDBMemoNotifySource is the type of the event source for the OnChange, OnClick, OnDblClick, OnEnter, and OnExit events of a TDBMemo component.

TDBNavigator component   dbnvgtr.h

The TDBNavigator component (a database navigator) is used to move through the data in a database table or query and perform operations on the data, such as inserting a blank record or posting a record. It is used with the data-aware controls, such as the data grid, which provide access to the data, either for editing or for simply displaying it.

You link the database navigator with a dataset when you specify a data source component that identifies the dataset as the value of navigator's DataSource property.

The database navigator consists of multiple buttons.

When the user chooses one of the navigator buttons, the appropriate action occurs on the dataset the navigator is linked to. For example, if the user clicks the Insert button, a blank record is inserted in the dataset.

This table describes the buttons on the navigator:

Button	Purpose
Cancel	Cancels edits to the current record, restores the record display to its condition prior to editing, and turns off Insert and Edit states if they are active.
Delete	Deletes the current record and makes the next record the current record.
Edit	Puts the dataset into Edit state so that the current record can be modified.
First	Sets the current record to the first record in the dataset, disables the First and Prior buttons, and enables the Next and last buttons if they are disabled.

Button	Purpose
Insert	Inserts a new record before the current record, and sets the dataset into Insert and Edit states.
Last	Sets the current record to the last record in the dataset, disables the Last and Next buttons, and enables the First and Prior buttons if they are disabled.
Next	Sets the current record to the next record and enables the First and Prior buttons if they are disabled.
Post	Writes changes in the current record to the database.
Previous	Sets the current record to the previous record and enables the Last and Next buttons if they are disabled.
Refresh	Redisplays the current record from the dataset, thereby updating the display of the record on the form.

Using the properties associated with each of these button types, you can decide which operations are allowed on the data and when.

Public constructors and destructor

Constructors

Form 1 TDBNavigator(TWindow* Parent, int ID, LPCSTR Title, int Left, Int Top, Int Width, int Height,
       TModule* Module=0);
Creates a new database navigator object with the following parameters:

- Parent identifies the parent window object.

- ID identifies the database navigator.

- Title contains the title of the window.

- Left, Top, Width, Height identify the window position. If this is a child component, the position is relative to the parent client area.

- Module identifies the owner of the database navigator.

Form 2 TDBNavigator(TWindow* Parent, int ID, TModule* Module=0);
Creates a database navigator by loading it from an existing dialog resource.

- Parent identifies the parent window object.

- ID identifies the database navigator.

- Module identifies the owner of the database navigator.

Destructor

~TDBNavigator()
Deletes the database navigator component.

Properties

About
▶ Align

▶BoundsRect
BtnCancel
BtnDelete
BtnEdit
BtnFirst
BtnInsert
BtnLast
BtnNext
BtnPost
BtnPrevious
BtnRefresh
Caption
▶ComponentIndex
ConfirmDelete
Cursor
DataSource
DragCursor
DragMode
Enabled
Height
HelpContext
Index
Left
Name
▶Owner
▶Parent
TabOrder
TabStop
Tag
Top
Visible
Width

Methods

BeginDrag
BringToFront
CanFocus
ClickButton
ClientToScreen
Dragging
EndDrag
Focused
GetTextBuf
GetTextLen
Hide

Invalidate
Refresh
Repaint
ScaleBy
ScreenToClient
ScrollBy
SendToBack
SetBounds
SetTextBuf
Show
Update

Events

OnClick
OnDblClick
OnDragDrop
OnDragOver
OnEndDrag
OnEnter
OnExit
OnResize

TDBNavigatorClick_MFUNCTOR macro

TDBNavigatorClick_MFUNCTOR(object, memberFunc)
This macro constructs the event sink object, which is of type TDBNavigatorClickSink,
the handler method that responds when OnClick event of the TDBNavigator occurs.

Parameter	Meaning
object	Identifies the event sink object; use the *this pointer
memberFunc	Identifies the event handler that responds to the OnClick event

TDBNavigatorClickSink typedef   dbevent.h

typedef TBdtEventSinkV2<TDBNavigator& sender, TNavigateBtn button,> TDBNavigatorClickSink;
The TDBNavigatorClickSink is the type of the event sink for the OnClick event of a
TDBNavigator component.

Parameter	Meaning	
sender	The TDBNavigator component	
button	BtnFirst	The button that moves to the first record in the dataset

Parameter	Meaning	
	BtnPrevious	The button that moves to the previous record in the dataset
	BtnNext	The button that moves to the next record in the dataset
	BtnLast	The button that moves to the last record in the dataset
	BtnInsert	The button that puts the dataset in Insert state
	BtnDelete	The button that deletes the current record from the dataset
	BtnEdit	The button that puts the dataset in Edit state
	BtnPost	The button that posts the current record to the dataset
	BtnCancel	The button that cancels changes made to the current record
	BtnRefresh	The button that refreshes the display of the dataset

TDBNavigatorClickSource typedef   dbevent.h

typedef TBdtEventSourceV2<TDBNavigator& sender, TNavigateBtn button,> TDBNavigatorClickSource;
The TDBNavigatorClickSource is the type of the event source for the OnClick event of a TDBNavigator component.

Parameter	Meaning	
sender	The TDBNavigator component	
button	BtnFirst	The button that moves to the first record in the dataset
	BtnPrevious	The button that moves to the previous record in the dataset
	BtnNext	The button that moves to the next record in the dataset
	BtnLast	The button that moves to the last record in the dataset
	BtnInsert	The button that puts the dataset in Insert state
	BtnDelete	The button that deletes the current record from the dataset
	BtnEdit	The button that puts the dataset in Edit state
	BtnPost	The button that posts the current record to the dataset
	BtnCancel	The button that cancels changes made to the current record
	BtnRefresh	The button that refreshes the display of the dataset

TDBNavigatorDrag_MFUNCTOR macro

TDBNavigatorDrag_MFUNCTOR(object, memberFunc)
This macro constructs the event sink object, which is of type TDBNavigatorDragSink, binding it to the handler method that responds when the OnDragDrop and OnEndDrag events of a TDBNavigator component occur.

Parameter	Meaning
object	Identifies the event sink object; use the *this pointer
memberFunc	Identifies the event handler that responds to the OnDragDrop event

TDBNavigatorDragOver_MFUNCTOR macro

TDBNavigatorDragOver_MFUNCTOR(object, memberFunc)

This macro constructs the event sink object, which is of type TDBNavigatorDrag OverSink, binding it to the handler method that responds when the OnDragOver event of a TDBNavigator component occurs.

Parameter	Meaning
object	Identifies the event sink object; use the *this pointer
memberFunc	Identifies the event handler that responds to the OnDragOver event

TDBNavigatorDragOverSink typedef   dbevent.h

typedef TBdtEventSinkV5<TDBNavigator& sender, TVbxControl& source, SHORT X, SHORT Y,
    TDragState state> TDBNavigatorDragOverSink;

The TDBNavigatorDragSink is the type of the event sink for the OnDragOver event of a TDBNavigator component.

Parameter	Meaning
sender	The TDBNavigator component
source	The control being dragged and dropped
X	The X parameter of the coordinates of the mouse positioned over the control
Y	The Y parameter of the coordinates of the mouse positioned over the control
state	Possible values:
	0 The dragged object enters a control in which it can be dropped
	1 The dragged object is moved within a control in which it can be dropped
	2 The dragged object leaves a control in which it can be dropped

TDBNavigatorDragOverSource typedef   dbevent.h

typedef TBdtEventSourceV5<TDBNavigator& sender, TVbxControl& source, SHORT X, SHORT Y,
    TDragState state> TDBNavigatorDragOverSource;

The TDBNavigatorDragSource is the type of the event source for the OnDragOver event of a TDBNavigator component.

Parameter	Meaning
sender	The TDBNavigator component
source	The control being dragged and dropped

Parameter	Meaning
X	The X parameter of the coordinates of the mouse positioned over the control
Y	The Y parameter of the coordinates of the mouse positioned over the control
state	Possible values:
	0 The dragged object enters a control in which it can be dropped
	1 The dragged object is moved within a control in which it can be dropped
	2 The dragged object leaves a control in which it can be dropped

TDBNavigatorDragSink typedef   dbevent.h

```
typedef TBdtEventSinkV4<TDBNavigator& sender, TVbxControl& source, SHORT X,
    SHORT Y>TDBNavigatorDragSink;
```
The TDBNavigatorDragSink is the type of the event sink for the OnDragDrop and OnEndDrag events of a TDBNavigator component.

Parameter	Meaning
sender	The TDBNavigator component
source	The control being dragged and dropped
X	The X parameter of the coordinates of the mouse positioned over the control.
Y	The Y parameter of the coordinates of the mouse positioned over the control

TDBNavigatorDragSource typedef   dbevent.h

```
typedef TBdtEventSourceV4<TDBNavigator& sender, TVbxControl& source, SHORT X,
    SHORT Y> TDBNavigatorDragSource;
```
The TDBNavigatorDragSource is the type of the event source for the OnDragDrop and OnEndDrag events of a TDBNavigator component.

Parameter	Meaning
sender	The TDBNavigator component
source	The control being dragged and dropped
X	The X parameter of the coordinates of the mouse positioned over the control.
Y	The Y parameter of the coordinates of the mouse positioned over the control

TDBNavigatorNotify_MFUNCTOR macro

TDBNavigatorNotify_MFUNCTOR(object, memberFunc)

This macro constructs the event sink object, which is of type TDBNavigatorNotifySink, the handler method that responds when the OnDblClick, OnEnter, OnExit, or OnResize event of the TDBNavigator occurs.

Parameter	Meaning
object	Identifies the event sink object; use the *this pointer
memberFunc	Identifies the event handler that responds to the OnDblClick, OnEnter, OnExit, or OnResize event

TDBNavigatorNotifySink typedef   dbevent.h

typedef TBdtEventSinkV1<TDBCheckBox&> TDBNavigatorNotifySink;

The TDBNavigatorNotifySink is the type of the event sink the OnDblClick, OnEnter, OnExit, or OnResize event a TDBNavigator component.

TDBNavigatorNotifySource typedef   dbevent.h

typedef TBdtEventSourceV1<TDBCheckBox&> TDBNavigatorNotifySource;

The TDBNavigatorNotifySource is the type of the event source for the OnDblClick, OnEnter, OnExit, or OnResize event a TDBNavigator component.

TDBRadioGroup component   dbradio.h

The TDBRadioGroup component displays a group of data-aware radio buttons. Only one of the radio buttons can be selected at a time, so the radio buttons present a set of mutually exclusive choices. Using a database radio button group box, you can force the user to select one of the presented options in a field. The database radio group box can display the valid values in a field when the field is limited to a few possibilities. For example, if only the values Red, Green, and Blue are valid in the field, the group box can have Red, Green, and Blue radio buttons.

Link the database radio group box with a dataset by specifying the data source component (TDataSource) that identifies the dataset as the value of the group box's DataSource property. Specify the field in the dataset you want to access as the value of the group box's DataField property.

The radio buttons are added to the group box when strings are entered as the value of the Items property. The strings entered in the Items property become the captions of the radio buttons if there are no strings in the Values property. If there are strings in the Values property, the first string is associated with the first radio button, the second with the second radio button, and so on. The Values string for a radio button is the value in the field of the current record that selects the radio button.

If the user selects a radio button and the ReadOnly property is false, the Values string for the radio button becomes the contents of the field for the current record in the dataset.

For more information about editing field values, see "Updating Fields." The Value property contains the contents of the field of the current record in the dataset.

You can display the radio buttons in a single column or in multiple columns by setting the value of the Columns property.

Public constructors and destructor

Constructors

Form 1
TDBRadioGroup(TWindow* Parent, int ID, LPCSTR Title, int Left, Int Top, Int Width, int Height,
    TModule* Module=0);
Creates a new radio group object with the following parameters:

- Parent identifies the parent window object.

- ID identifies the radio group.

- Title contains the title of the window.

- Left, Top, Width, Height identify the window position. If this is a child component, the position is relative to the parent client area.

- Module identifies the owner of the radio group.

Form 2
TDBRadioGroup(TWindow* Parent, int ID, TModule* Module=0);
Creates a radio group by loading it from an existing dialog resource.

- Parent identifies the parent window object.

- ID identifies the radio group.

- Module identifies the owner of the radio group.

Destructor

~TDBRadioGroup()
Deletes the radio group component.

Properties

About
▷ Align
BackColor
▷ BoundsRect
Caption
Columns
▷ ComponentIndex

Cursor
DataChanged
DataField
DataSource
DragCursor
DragMode
Enabled
▶ Fields
FontBold
FontItalic
FontName
FontSize
FontStrikethru
FontUnderline
ForeColor
Height
HelpContext
Index
▶ ItemIndex
Items
Left
Name
▶ Owner
▶ Parent
ReadOnly
TabOrder
TabStop
Tag
Top
▶ Value
Values
Visible
Width

Methods

BeginDrag
BringToFront
CanFocus
ClientToScreen
Dragging
EndDrag
Focused

GetTextBuf
GetTextLen
Hide
Invalidate
Refresh
Repaint
ScaleBy
ScreenToClient
ScrollBy
SendToBack
SetBounds
SetFocus
SetTextBuf
Show
Update

Events

OnChange
OnClick
OnDblClick
OnDragDrop
OnDragOver
OnEndDrag
OnEnter
OnExit

TDBRadioGroupDrag_MFUNCTOR macro

TDBRadioGroupDrag_MFUNCTOR(object, memberFunc)
This macro constructs the event sink object, which is of type TDBRadioGroupDragSink, binding it to the handler method that responds when the OnDragDrop and OnEndDrag events of a TDBRadioGroup component occur

Parameter	Meaning
object	Identifies the event sink object; use the *this pointer
memberFunc	Identifies the event handler that responds to the OnDragDrop event

TDBRadioGroupDragOver_MFUNCTOR macro

TDBRadioGroupDragOver_MFUNCTOR(object, memberFunc)

This macro constructs the event sink object, which is of type TDBRadioGroupDragOverSink, binding it to the handler method that responds when the OnDragOver event of a TDBRadioGroup component occurs.

Parameter	Meaning
object	Identifies the event sink object; use the *this pointer
memberFunc	Identifies the event handler that responds to the OnDragOver event

TDBRadioGroupDragOverSink typedef

dbevent.h

typedef TBdtEventSinkV5<TDBRadioGroup& sender, TVbxControl& source, SHORT X, SHORT Y, TDragState state> TDBRadioGroupDragOverSink;

The TDBRadioGroupDragSink is the type of the event sink for the OnDragOver event of a TDBRadioGroup component.

Parameter	Meaning
sender	The TDBRadioGroup component
source	The control being dragged and dropped
X	The X parameter of the coordinates of the mouse positioned over the control
Y	The Y parameter of the coordinates of the mouse positioned over the control
state	Possible values:
	0 The dragged object enters a control in which it can be dropped
	1 The dragged object is moved within a control in which it can be dropped
	2 The dragged object leaves a control in which it can be dropped

TDBRadioGroupDragOverSource typedef

dbevent.h

typedef TBdtEventSourceV5<TDBRadioGroup& sender, TVbxControl& source, SHORT X, SHORT Y, TDragState state> TDBRadioGroupDragOverSource;

The TDBRadioGroupDragSource is the type of the event source the OnDragOver event of a TDBRadioGroup component.

Parameter	Meaning
sender	The TDBRadioGroup component
source	The control being dragged and dropped
X	The X parameter of the coordinates of the mouse positioned over the control
Y	The Y parameter of the coordinates of the mouse positioned over the control
state	Possible values:
	0 The dragged object enters a control in which it can be dropped
	1 The dragged object is moved within a control in which it can be dropped
	2 The dragged object leaves a control in which it can be dropped

TDBRadioGroupDragSink typedef

dbevent.h

typedef TBdtEventSinkV4<TDBRadioGroupx& sender, TVbxControl& source, SHORT X,
    SHORT Y> TDBRadioGroupDragSink;

The TDBRadioGroupDragSink is the type of the event sink for the OnDragDrop and OnEndDrag events of a TDBRadioGroup component.

Parameter	Meaning
sender	The TDBRadioGroup component
source	The control being dragged and dropped
X	The X parameter of the coordinates of the mouse positioned over the control
Y	The Y parameter of the coordinates of the mouse positioned over the control

TDBRadioGroupDragSource typedef

dbevent.h

typedef TBdtEventSourceV4<TDBRadioGroup& sender, TVbxControl& source, SHORT X,
    SHORT Y> TDBRadioGroupDragSource;

The TDBRadioGroupDragSource is the type of the event source for the OnDragDrop and OnEndDrag events of a TDBRadioGroup component.

Parameter	Meaning
sender	The TDBRadioGroup component
source	The control being dragged and dropped
X	The X parameter of the coordinates of the mouse positioned over the control
Y	The Y parameter of the coordinates of the mouse positioned over the control

TDBRadioGroupNotify_MFUNCTOR macro

dbevent.h

TDBRadioGroupNotify_MFUNCTOR(object, memberFunc)

This macro constructs the event sink object, which is of type TDBRadioGroupNotifySink, binding it to the handler method that responds when an OnClick, OnDblClick, OnEnter, or OnExit event of a TDBRadioGroup component occurs

Parameter	Meaning
object	Identifies the event sink object; use the *this pointer
memberFunc	Identifies the event handler that responds to the OnClick, OnDblClick, and OnChange events

TDBRadioGroupNotifySink typedef
dbevent.h

typedef TBdtEventSinkV1<TDBRadioGroup& sender> TDBRadioGroupNotifySink;
The TDBRadioGroupNotifySink is the type of the event sink for the OnChange, OnClick, and OnDblClick events of a TDBRadioGroup component.

TDBRadioGroupNotifySource typedef
dbevent.h

typedef TBdtEventSourceV1<TDBRadioGroup& sender> TDBRadioGroupNotifySource;
The TDBRadioGroupNotifySource is the type of the event source for the OnChange, OnClick, and OnDblClick events of a TDBRadioGroup component.

TDBText component
dbtext.h

The TDBText component is a data-aware control that displays text on a form. Your application can display the contents of a field in the current record of a dataset in a database text control, but the user won't be able to modify the field's contents.

Link the database text control with a dataset by specifying the data source component (TDataSource) that identifies the dataset as the value of the label's DataSource property. Specify the field in the dataset you want to access as the value of the label's DataField property.

The text of a database text control is the value of its Caption property. How the text of the caption aligns within the label is determined by the value of the Alignment property. You can have the text control resize automatically to fit a changing caption if you set the AutoSize property to true. If you prefer to have the text wrap, set WordWrap to true.

Public constructors and destructor

Constructors

Form 1　TDBText(TWindow* Parent, int ID, LPCSTR Title, int Left, Int Top, Int Width, int Height, TModule* Module=0);
Creates a new text object with the following parameters:

- Parent identifies the parent window object.

- ID identifies the text component.

- Title contains the title of the window.

- Left, Top, Width, Height identify the window position. If this is a child component, the position is relative to the parent client area.

- Module identifies the owner of the text component.

Form 2   TDBText(TWindow* Parent, int ID, TModule* Module=0);
          Creates a text by loading it from an existing dialog resource.

- Parent identifies the parent window object.

- ID identifies the text component.

- Module identifies the owner of the text component.

Destructor

~TDBText()
Deletes the text component.

Properties

About
▶ Align
Alignment
AutoSize
BackColor
BorderStyle
BoundsRect
Caption
▶ ComponentIndex
Cursor
DataChanged
DataField
DataSource
DragCursor
DragMode
Enabled
▶ Fields
FontBold
FontItalic
FontName
FontSize
FontStrikethru
FontUnderline
ForeColor
Height
HelpContext
Index
Left
Name

▶Owner
▶Parent
TabOrder
TabStop
Tag
Top
Visible
Width
WordWrap

Methods

BeginDrag
BringToFront
CanFocus
Clear
ClientToScreen
Dragging
EndDrag
Focused
GetTextBuf
GetTextLen
Hide
Invalidate
Refresh
Repaint
ScaleBy
ScreenToClient
ScrollBy
SendToBack
SetBounds
SetTextBuf
Show
Update

Events

OnClick
OnDblClick
OnDragDrop
OnDragOver
OnEndDrag
OnMouseDown
OnMouseMove
OnMouseUp

TDBTextDrag_MFUNCTOR macro

TDBTextDrag_MFUNCTOR(object, memberFunc)
This macro constructs the event sink object, which is of type TDBTextDragSink, binding it to the handler method that responds when the OnDragDrop and OnEndDrag events of a TDBText component occur.

Parameter	Meaning
object	Identifies the event sink object; use the *this pointer
memberFunc	Identifies the event handler that responds to the OnDragDrop event

TDBTextDragOver_MFUNCTOR macro

TDBTextDragOver_MFUNCTOR(object, memberFunc)
This macro constructs the event sink object, which is of type TDBTextDragOverSink, binding it to the handler method that responds when the OnDragOver event of a TDBText component occurs.

Parameter	Meaning
object	Identifies the event sink object; use the *this pointer
memberFunc	Identifies the event handler that responds to the OnDragOver event

TDBTextDragOverSink typedef — dbevent.h

typedef TBdtEventSinkV5<TDBText& sender, TVbxControl& source, SHORT X, SHORT Y,
        TDragState state> TDBTextDragOverSink;
The TDBTextDragSink is the type of the event sink for the OnDragOver event of a TDBText component.

Parameter	Meaning
sender	The TDBText component
source	The control being dragged and dropped
X	The X parameter of the coordinates of the mouse positioned over the control
Y	The Y parameter of the coordinates of the mouse positioned over the control
state	Possible values:
	0 The dragged object enters a control in which it can be dropped
	1 The dragged object is moved within a control in which it can be dropped
	2 The dragged object leaves a control in which it can be dropped

TDBTextDragOverSource typedef

dbevent.h

typedef TBdtEventSourceV5<TDBText& sender, TVbxControl& source, SHORT X, SHORT Y,
    TDragState state> TDBTextDragOverSource;

The TDBTextDragSource is the type of the event source the OnDragOver event of a TDBText component.

Parameter	Meaning
sender	The TDBText component
source	The control being dragged and dropped
X	The X parameter of the coordinates of the mouse positioned over the control
Y	The Y parameter of the coordinates of the mouse positioned over the control
state	Possible values:
	0 The dragged object enters a control in which it can be dropped
	1 The dragged object is moved within a control in which it can be dropped
	2 The dragged object leaves a control in which it can be dropped

TDBTextDragSink typedef

dbevent.h

typedef TBdtEventSinkV4<TDBTextx& sender, TVbxControl& source, SHORT X,
    SHORT Y> TDBTextDragSink;

The TDBTextDragSink is the type of the event sink for the OnDragDrop and OnEndDrag events of a TDBText component.

Parameter	Meaning
sender	The TDBText component
source	The control being dragged and dropped
X	The X parameter of the coordinates of the mouse positioned over the control
Y	The Y parameter of the coordinates of the mouse positioned over the control

TDBTextDragSource typedef   dbevent.h

typedef TBdtEventSourceV4<TDBText& sender, TVbxControl& source, SHORT X,
    SHORT Y>TDBTextDragSource;

The TDBTextDragSource is the type of the event source for the OnDragDrop and
OnEndDrag events of a TDBText component.

Parameter	Meaning
sender	The TDBText component
source	The control being dragged and dropped
X	The X parameter of the coordinates of the mouse positioned over the control
Y	The Y parameter of the coordinates of the mouse positioned over the control

TDBTextMouse_MFUNCTOR macro

TDBTextMouse_MFUNCTOR(object, memberFunc)

This macro constructs the event sink object, which is of type TDBTextMouseSink,
binding it to the handler method that responds when an OnMouseDown, OnMouseUp,
or OnMouseMove event of a TDBText component occurs.

Parameter	Meaning
object	Identifies the event sink object; use the *this pointer
memberFunc	Identifies the event handler that responds to the mouse events

TDBTextMouseSink typedef   dbevent.h

typedef TBdtEventSinkV5<TDBText& sender, TMouseButton mouseButton, TShiftState state, SHORT x,
    SHORT y> TDBTextMouseSink;

The TDBTextMouseSink is the type of the event sink for the OnMouseDown,
OnMouseUp, and OnMouseMove events of a TDBText component.

Parameter	Meaning
sender	The TDBText component
mouseButton	Possible values are:
	1 Left mouse button
	2 Right mouse button
	4 Middle mouse button

Parameter	Meaning
state	Possible values are:
	1 *Shift* key
	2 *Ctrl* key
	4 *Alt* key
x	The position of the mouse pointer on the x-axis in screen pixels
y	The position of the mouse pointer on the y-axis in screen pixels

TDBTextMouseSource typedef dbevent.h

typedef TBdtEventSourceV5<TDBText& sender, TMouseButton mouseButton, TShiftState state, SHORT x, SHORT y> TDBTextMouseSource;

The TDBTextMouseSource is the type of the event source for the OnMouseDown, OnMouseUp, and OnMouseMove events of a TDBText component.

Parameter	Meaning
sender	The TDBText component
mouseButton	Possible values are:
	1 Left mouse button
	2 Right mouse button
	4 Middle mouse button
state	Possible values are:
	1 *Shift* key
	2 *Ctrl* key
	4 *Alt* key
x	The position of the mouse pointer on the x-axis in screen pixels
y	The position of the mouse pointer on the y-axis in screen pixels

TDBTextNotify_MFUNCTOR macro dbevent.h

TDBTextNotify_MFUNCTOR(object, memberFunc)

This macro constructs the event sink object, which is of type TDBTextNotifySink, binding it to the handler method that responds when an OnClick, OnDblClick, OnEnter, or OnExit event of a TDBText component occur.

Parameter	Meaning
object	Identifies the event sink object; use the *this pointer
memberFunc	Identifies the event handler that responds to the OnClick and OnDblClick events

TDBTextNotifySink typedef

dbevent.h

typedef TBdtEventSinkV1<TDBText& sender> TDBTextNotifySink;
The TDBTextNotifySink is the type of the event sink for the OnClick, OnDblClick ,
OnEnter, and OnExit events of a TDBText component.

TDBTextNotifySource typedef

dbevent.h

typedef TBdtEventSourceV1<TDBText& sender> TDBTextNotifySource;
The TDBTextNotifySource is the type of the event source for the OnClick, OnDblClick ,
OnEnter, and OnExit events of a TDBText component.

TDragMode typedef

dbtype.h

typedef enum{ dmManual, dmAutomatic }TDragMode;
The TDragMode type defines the values for the DragMode property of controls.

TDuplicates typedef

bdti.h

typedef enum{ dupIgnore, dupAccept, dupError }TDuplicates;
The TDuplicates type defines the possible values of the Duplicates property of a string
component (TStrings).

TEditCharCase typedef

dbtype.h

typedef enum{ ccNormal, ccUpper, ccLower }TEditCharCase;
The TEditCharCase type defines the possible values for the CharCase property of a
database edit box (TDBEdit).

Temporary property

Applies to   TDatabase component

bool Temporary;
Run-time only. The Temporary property is true if the TDatabase component was
created because none existed when a database table was opened. Such a database will
automatically be destroyed when the table or query is closed. You can set Temporary to
false so that it will be preserved until you explicitly free it. If you explicitly created the
TDatabase component, then Temporary will be false, but you can set it to be true and it
will automatically be freed when the last dataset linked to it is closed.

Text property

Applies to   TField, TParam, TQuery components

Description   The Text property specifies a text string to appear in a component.

Text property for TField components

Applies to   All TField components

string Text;

Run-time only. Text contains the string value of the field a data-aware control uses for display when the control is in edit mode.

You can control the strings returned by Text by assigning an OnGetText event handler, or you can accept defaults, which depend on the field's data type. The strings are formatted according to the field component's EditFormat or DisplayFormat properties if they are set.

Text property for TQuery components

Applies to   TQuery component

string Text;

Run-time and read only. The Text property holds the actual text of the SQL query sent to the Borland Database Engine. In general, you should not need to examine this property. However, if you encounter problems with an SQL statement, you may want to inspect the Text property to be sure that the statement is as expected.

Example

```
string ActualSQLText;
ActualSQLText = Query1.Text;
ActualSQLText = "The SQL statement is: " + ActualSQLText;
MessageBox( ActualSQLText.c_str() , "Information" , MB_OK );
```

Text property for TParam components

Applies to   TParam component

string Text;

The Text property is similar to the AsString property. Accessing the Text property attempts to convert the current data to a string value and returns that value. If the current data is NULL, the value is an empty string.

Example

```
// Assign "1221" to the CustNo parameter
Parameters.ParamByName("CustNo")->Text = "1221";
```

TField component

Use TField components to access fields in a record. By default, a set of TField components is created automatically each time a dataset component is activated; the resulting set of TField components is dynamic, mirroring the actual columns in an underlying physical table at that time.

At design time, you can use the Fields Editor to create a persistent, unchanging set of TField components for a dataset. Creating TField components with the Fields Editor provides efficient, readable, and type-safe programmatic access to underlying data. It guarantees that each time your application runs, it uses and displays the same columns, in the same order, every time, even if the physical structure of the underlying database has changed.

Creating TField components at design time guarantees that data-aware components and program code that rely on specific fields always work as expected. If a column on which a persistent TField component is based is deleted or changed, then an exception is generated rather than running the application against a nonexistent column or mismatched data.

A TField component is an abstract component. The Fields property of a dataset is always one of the following TField descendants:

Component	Used for
TBCDField	Real numbers with a fixed number of digits after the decimal point. Accurate to 18 digits. Range depends on the number of digits after the decimal point. [Paradox only]
TBlobField	Arbitrary data field without a size limit
TBooleanField	True or false values
TBytesField	Arbitrary data field without a size limit
TCurrencyField	Currency values. The range and accuracy is the same as TFloatField.
TDateField	Date value
TDateTimeField	Date and time value
TFloatField	Real numbers with absolute magnitudes from 5.0*10-324 to 1.7*10308 accurate to 15 digits
TGraphicField	Arbitrary length graphic, such as a bitmap
TIntegerField	Whole numbers in the range -2,147,483,648 to 2,147,483,647
TMemoField	Arbitrary length text
TSmallintField	Whole numbers in the range -32,768 to 32,767
TStringField	Fixed length text data up to 255 characters
TTimeField	Time value
TWordField	Whole numbers in the range 0 to 65,535
TVarBytesField	Arbitrary data field up to 65,535 characters, with the actual length stored in the first two bytes.

Each TField component and its properties, methods, and events can be accessed programmatically. At run time, dynamically created components can be accessed through the Fields property of the dataset; at design time, use the Fields Editor to select a field component and use the Property Inspector to modify the field's properties.

Most TField descendants have the same properties, but some properties, such as AsBoolean or EditMask only apply to some fields. Use the AsBoolean, AsDateTime, AsFloat, AsInteger, or AsString properties as appropriate to access or modify the current value of the field. Test the CanModify property to see if the field can be changed. Use the DataSet property to reference the dataset of the field. Use the DataType property to test the type of the field. The DisplayText property will format the field for display purposes; Text will format it for editing purposes. Set the EditMask property to limit the characters entered to a selected set. Use the FieldName property to get the name of the field in the dataset. Test the IsNull property to see if the field has been assigned a value. Set the ReadOnly property to prevent or allow the user to change the value. Set the Visible property to control whether the field appears in a data grid. Call the Clear method to erase any data assigned. Call the GetData method to access the data in native format, or SetData to assign new data. Use the OnChange event to be notified when the value of the field is changed.

Use the OnGetText event to do your own formatting of the data for display or edit purposes, and the OnSetText event to convert the edited data back to native format. Use the OnValidate event to validate the data before it is stored into the record.

Public constructors and destructor

Constructors

Form 1   TField(PITField p)
Constructs a TField object which attaches to the given PITField COM interface pointer. The new TField saves the PITField COM object (incrementing its reference count) for later use.

Form 2   TField(const TField& p)
Constructs a TField object which attaches to the PITField COM object associated with the given TField object (which was passed by reference). The new TField saves the associated PITField COM object (incrementing its reference count) for later use.

Form 3   TField(PTField p)
Constructs a TField object which attaches to the PITField COM object associated with the given TField object (which was passed by pointer). The new TField saves the associated PITField COM object (incrementing its reference count) for later use.

Form 4   TField(void)
Constructs a new TField object. Internally, a new PITField COM object is created for later use.

Form 5   TField(PTBDTComponent Owner, TFieldType DataType)
Constructs a new TField object. Internally, a new PITField COM object is created for later use. The Owner parameter specifies the DataSet which owns the new TField. It can be NULL, to specify that there is no Owner. DataType is the type of field to be created.

Destructor

virtual ~TField()
Deletes the TField and reduces the reference count on the associated PITField COM object. If the reference count on the associated PITField COM object reaches 0, it is deleted.

Properties

▸ AsBoolean
▸ AsDateTime
▸ AsFloat
▸ AsInteger
▸ AsString
Calculated
▸ CanModify
▸ DataSet
▸ DataSize
▸ DataType
▸ DisplayText
EditMask
FieldName
▸ FieldNo
Index
▸ IsIndexField
▸ IsNull
Name
ReadOnly
Required
▸ Size
▸ Text

Methods

Assign
AssignValue
Clear
GetData
IsValidChar
SetData

Events

OnChange
OnGetText
OnSetText
OnValidate

TFieldDef component   bdto.h

The TFieldDef component corresponds to a physical field of a record in a table underlying a dataset. TFieldDef components are created automatically for dataset components. A field definition has a corresponding TField component, but not all TField components have corresponding TFieldDef components. For example, calculated fields do not have TFieldDef components.

Public constructors and destructor

Constructors

Form 1   TFieldDef(PITFieldDef p)
Constructs a TFieldDef object which attaches to the given PITFieldDef COM interface pointer. The new TFieldDef saves the PITFieldDef COM object (incrementing its reference count) for later use.

Form 2   TFieldDef(const TFieldDef& p)
Constructs a TFieldDef object which attaches to the PITFieldDef COM object associated with the given TFieldDef object (which was passed by reference). The new TFieldDef saves the associated PITFieldDef COM object (incrementing its reference count) for later use.

Form 3   TFieldDef(PTFieldDef p) ·
Constructs a TFieldDef object which attaches to the PITFieldDef COM object associated with the given TFieldDef object (which was passed by pointer). The new TFieldDef saves the associated PITFieldDef COM object (incrementing its reference count) for later use.

Form 4   TFieldDef(void)
Constructs a new TFieldDef object. Internally, a new PITFieldDef COM object is created for later use.

Form 5   TFieldDef(PTFieldDefs Owner, const string& Name, TFieldType DataType, uint16 Size, bool Required, int FieldNo)
Constructs a new TFieldDef object. Internally, a new PITFieldDef COM object is created for later use. Specify the following parameters when using this constructor:

- Owner specifies the TFieldDefs which owns the new TFieldDef. The Owner parameter can be NULL, to specify that there is no Owner.
- Name specifies the Name property of the new TFieldDef.
- DataType specifies the DataType property of the new TFieldDef.
- Size specifies the Size property of the new TFieldDef.
- Required specifies the Required property of the new TFieldDef.
- FieldNo specifies the FieldNo property of the new TFieldDef.

Destructor

virtual ~TFieldDef()
Deletes the TFieldDef and reduces the reference count on the associated PITFieldDef COM object. If the reference count on the associated PITFieldDef COM object reaches 0, it is deleted.

Properties

▶ DataType
▶ FieldNo
▶ Name
▶ Required
▶ Size

Methods

CreateField

TFieldDefs component

A TFieldDefs component holds the TFieldDef components that represent the physical fields underlying a dataset.

The Count property is the total number of TFieldDef components in the TFieldDefs component. The Items property is an array of pointers to the TFieldDef components.

To locate a field definition entry in Items by name, call the Find or IndexOf methods. To remove all TFieldDef components from a TFieldDefs component, call the Clear method. Use the Update method to obtain information about the fields in a dataset without opening it.

Public constructors and destructor

Constructors

Form 1   TFieldDefs(PITFieldDefs p)
Constructs a TFieldDefs object which attaches to the given PITFieldDefs COM interface pointer. The new TFieldDefs saves the PITFieldDefs COM object (incrementing its reference count) for later use.

Form 2   TFieldDefs(const TFieldDefs& p)
Constructs a TFieldDefs object which attaches to the PITFieldDefs COM object associated with the given TFieldDefs object (which was passed by reference). The new TFieldDefs saves the associated PITFieldDefs COM object (incrementing its reference count) for later use.

Form 3   TFieldDefs(PTFieldDefs p)
Constructs a TFieldDefs object which attaches to the PITFieldDefs COM object associated with the given TFieldDefs object (which was passed by pointer). The new TFieldDefs saves the associated PITFieldDefs COM object (incrementing its reference count) for later use.

Form 4   TFieldDefs(void)
Constructs a new TFieldDefs object. Internally, a new PITFieldDefs COM object is created for later use.

Form 5   TFieldDefs(TDataSet& DataSet)
Constructs a new TFieldDefs object. Internally, a new PITFieldDefs COM object is created for later use. The new TFieldDefs is initialized with the FieldDefs from the given DataSet.

Destructor

virtual ~TFieldDefs()
Deletes the TFieldDefs and reduces the reference count on the associated PITFieldDefs COM object. If the reference count on the associated PITFieldDefs COM object reaches 0, it is deleted.

Properties

▶ Count
▶ Items

Methods

Add
AddFieldDesc
Assign
Clear
Find
IndexOf
Update

TFieldGetText_MFUNCTOR macro

TFieldGetText_MFUNCTOR(object, memberFunc)
This macro constructs the event sink object, which is of type TFieldGetTextSink, binding it to the handler method that responds when an event of a TField component.

Parameter	Meaning
object	Identifies the event sink object; use the *this pointer
memberFunc	Identifies the event handler that responds to the OnDragOver event

TFieldGetTextSink typedef   bdto.h

typedef TBdtEventSinkV3<TField& sender, string& text, bool displayText> TFieldGetTextSink;
The TFieldGetTextSink is the type of the event sink for the OnGetText event of a TField component.

Parameter	Meaning
sender	This TField component
text	The text contained in the field
displayText	If true, the text is in display format; if false, the text is not formatted for display

TFieldGetTextSource typedef

bdto.h

typedef TBdtEventSourceV3<TField& sender, string& text, bool displayText> TFieldGetTextSource;
The TFieldGetTextSource is the type of the event source for the OnGetText event of a
TField component.

Parameter	Meaning
sender	This TField component
text	The text contained in the field
displayText	If true, the text is in display format; if false, the text is not formatted for display

TFieldNotify_MFUNCTOR macro

TFieldNotify_MFUNCTOR(object, memberFunc)
This macro constructs the event sink object, which is of type TFieldNotifySink, binding
it to the handler method that responds when an event of a TDataSource component
occurs.

Parameter	Meaning
object	Identifies the event sink object; use the *this pointer
memberFunc	Identifies the event handler that responds to the OnDragOver event

TFieldNotifySink typedef

bdto.h

typedef TBdtEventSinkV1<TField& sender> TFieldNotifySink;
The TFieldNotifySink is the type of the event sink for the OnChange and OnValidate
events of a TField component.

TFieldNotifySource typedef

bdto.h

typedef TBdtEventSourceV1<TField& sender> TFieldNotifySource;
The TFieldNotifySource is the type of the event source for the OnChange and
OnValidate events of a TField component.

TFieldSetText_MFUNCTOR macro

TFieldSetText_MFUNCTOR(object, memberFunc)
This macro constructs the event sink object, which is of type TFieldSetTextSink, binding
it to the handler method that responds when an event of a TField component.

Parameter	Meaning
object	Identifies the event sink object; use the *this pointer
memberFunc	Identifies the event handler that responds to the OnDragOver event

TFieldSetTextSink typedef   bdto.h

typedef TBdtEventSinkV2<TField& sender, const string& text> TFieldSetTextSink;

The TFieldSetTextSink is the type of the event sink for the OnSetText event of a TField component.

Parameter	Meaning
sender	This TField component
text	The text contained in the field

TFieldSetTextSource typedef   bdto.h

typedef TBdtEventSourceV2<TField& sender, const string& text> TFieldSetTextSource;

The TFieldSetTextSource is the type of the event source for the OnSetText event of a TField component.

Parameter	Meaning
sender	This TField component
text	The text contained in the field

TFieldType typedef   bdti.h

typedef enum{ ftUnknown, ftString, ftSmallint, ftInteger, ftWord, ftBoolean, ftFloat, ftCurrency, ftBCD, ftDate, ftTime, ftDateTime, ftBytes, ftVarBytes, ftBlob, ftMemo, ftGraphic }TFieldType;

The TFieldType type is the set of values of the DataType property of a TField component or TFieldDef component.

TFloatField component   bdto.h

A TFloatField represents a field of a record in a dataset. It is represented as a binary value with a range from (positive or negative) $5.0 * 10-324$ to $1.7 * 10308$. It has an accuracy of 15 digits. Use TFloatField for fields that hold floating-point numbers.

Set the DisplayFormat property to control the formatting of the field for display purposes, and the EditFormat property for editing purposes. Use the Value property to access or change the current field value.

The TFloatField component has the properties, methods, and events of the TField component.

Public constructors and destructor

Constructors

Form 1 TFloatField(PITField p)

Constructs a TFloatField object which attaches to the given PITField COM interface pointer. The new TFloatField saves the PITField COM object (incrementing its reference count) for later use.

Form 2 TFloatField(const TField& p)

Constructs a TFloatField object which attaches to the PITField COM object associated with the given TField object (which was passed by reference). The new TFloatField saves the associated PITField COM object (incrementing its reference count) for later use.

Form 3 TFloatField(PTField p)

Constructs a TFloatField object which attaches to the PITField COM object associated with the given TField object (which was passed by pointer). The new TFloatField saves the associated PITField COM object (incrementing its reference count) for later use.

Form 4 TFloatField(void)

Constructs a new TFloatField object. Internally, a new PITField COM object is created for later use.

Form 5 TFloatField(PTBDTComponent Owner)

Constructs a new TFloatField object. Internally, a new PITField COM object is created for later use. Owner specifies the DataSet which owns the new TFloatField. It can be NULL, to specify that there is no Owner.

Form 6 TFloatField(PTBDTComponent Owner, TFieldType DataType)

Constructs a new TFloatField object. Internally, a new PITField COM object is created for later use. Owner specifies the DataSet which owns the new TFloatField. It can be NULL, to specify that there is no Owner. DataType is the type of field to be created.

Destructor

virtual ~TFloatField()

Deletes the TFloatField and reduces the reference count on the associated PITField COM object. If the reference count on the associated PITField COM object reaches 0, it is deleted.

Properties

▷ AsBoolean
AsDateTime
▷ AsFloat
▷ AsInteger
▷ AsString
Calculated
▷ CanModify
Currency
▷ DataSet
▷ DataSize
▷ DataType
DisplayFormat
▷ DisplayText
EditFormat
EditMask
FieldName
▷ FieldNo
Index
▷ IsIndexField
▷ IsNull
MaxValue
MinValue
Name
Precision
ReadOnly
Required
▷ Size
▷ Text
▷ Value

Methods

Assign
AssignValue
Clear
GetData
IsValidChar
SetData

Events

OnChange
OnGetText
OnSetText
OnValidate

TGraphicField component   **bdto.h**

A TGraphicField represents a field of a record which is represented by a value
consisting of an arbitrary set of bytes with indefinite size. The bytes should correspond
to graphics data.

Use the Assign method to transfer another component to a TGraphicField. Use the
LoadFromFile method to load a field's contents from a file. Use LoadFromStream
method to load a field from a Stream. Use SaveToFile method to write a field's contents
to a file. Use SaveToStream method to write a field's contents to a Stream.

Use SaveToBitmap to obtain an HBITMAP and an HPALETTE when you want to
display the grpahic using Windows GDI functions.

The TGraphicField component has the properties, methods, and events of the TField
component.

Public constructors and destructor

Constructors

Form 1   TGraphicField(PITField p)
Constructs a TGraphicField object which attaches to the given PITField COM interface
pointer. The new TGraphicField saves the PITField COM object (incrementing its
reference count) for later use.

Form 2   TGraphicField(const TField& p)
Constructs a TGraphicField object which attaches to the PITField COM object associated
with the given TField object (which was passed by reference). The new TGraphicField
saves the associated PITField COM object (incrementing its reference count) for later
use.

Form 3   TGraphicField(PTField p)
Constructs a TGraphicField object which attaches to the PITField COM object associated
with the given TField object (which was passed by pointer). The new TGraphicField
saves the associated PITField COM object (incrementing its reference count) for later
use.

Form 4   TGraphicField(void)
          Constructs a new TGraphicField object. Internally, a new PITField COM object is
          created for later use.

Form 5   TGraphicField(PTBDTComponent Owner)
          Constructs a new TGraphicField object. Internally, a new PITField COM object is
          created for later use. Owner specifies the DataSet which owns the new TGraphicField. It
          can be NULL, to specify that there is no Owner.

Destructor

virtual ~TGraphicField()
Deletes the TGraphicField and reduces the reference count on the associated PITField
COM object. If the reference count on the associated PITField COM object reaches 0, it is
deleted.

Properties

▷ AsBoolean
▷ AsDateTime
▷ AsFloat
▷ AsInteger
▷ AsString
  Calculated
▷ CanModify
▷ DataSet
▷ DataSize
▷ DataType
▷ DisplayText
  EditMask
  FieldName
▷ FieldNo
  Index
▷ IsIndexField
▷ IsNull
  Name
  ReadOnly
  Required
  Size
▷ Text

Methods

Assign
AssignValue
Clear
GetData
IsValidChar
LoadFromBitmap
LoadFromFile
LoadFromStream
SaveToBitmap
SaveToFile
SaveToStream
SetData

Events

OnChange
OnGetText
OnSetText
OnValidate

TIndexDef component   bdto.h

The TIndexDef component describes the index for a table.

Use the Fields property to obtain a list of the fields that make up the index. To find the name of the the index, check the value of the Name property. You can examine the Options to learn about specific characteristics of the index.

Use the Expression property to read expressions in dBASE indexes.

Public constructors and destructor

Constructors

Form 1   TIndexDef(PITIndexDef p)
Constructs a TIndexDef object which attaches to the given PITIndexDef COM interface pointer. The new TIndexDef saves the PITIndexDef COM object (incrementing its reference count) for later use.

Form 2   TIndexDef(const TIndexDef& p)
Constructs a TIndexDef object which attaches to the PITIndexDef COM object associated with the given TIndexDef object (which was passed by reference). The new TIndexDef saves the associated PITIndexDef COM object (incrementing its reference count) for later use.

Form 3   TIndexDef(PTIndexDef p)

Constructs a TIndexDef object which attaches to the PITIndexDef COM object associated with the given TIndexDef object (which was passed by pointer). The new TIndexDef saves the associated PITIndexDef COM object (incrementing its reference count) for later use.

Form 4   TIndexDef(void)

Constructs a new TIndexDef object. Internally, a new PITIndexDef COM object is created for later use.

Form 5   TIndexDef(PTIndexDefs Owner, const string& Name, const string& Fields, TIndexOptions Options)

Constructs a new TIndexDef object. Internally, a new PITIndexDef COM object is created for later use. Specify the following parameters when using this constructor:

- Owner specifies the TIndexDefs which will own the new TIndexDef, Name specifies the Name property of the new TIndexDef. It can be NULL, to specify that there is no Owner.

- Fields specifies the Fields property of the new TIndexDef.

- Options specifies the Options property of the new TIndexDef.

Destructor

virtual ~TIndexDef()

Deletes the TIndexDef and reduces the reference count on the associated PITIndexDef COM object. If the reference count on the associated PITIndexDef COM object reaches 0, it is deleted.

Properties

▸ Expression
▸ Fields
▸ Name
▸ Options

TIndexDefs component   bdto.h

The TIndexDefs component holds the set of available indexes for a table.

The Items property contains the all the TIndexDef components that make up the TIndexDefs component. The Count property reports the number of TIndexDef components.

You can add an index to the TIndexDefs component with the Add method or simply copy the values of one TIndexDefs component to another using the Assign method. To clear all indexes from TIndexDefs, call the Clear method. To obtain the TIndexDef component for a specific field, call the FindIndexForFields method. You can find the position of the entry in the list of indexes found in the Items property using the IndexOf method.

Public constructors and destructor

Constructors

Form 1 TIndexDefs(PITIndexDefs p)
Constructs a TIndexDefs object which attaches to the given PITIndexDefs COM interface pointer. The new TIndexDefs saves the PITIndexDefs COM object (incrementing its reference count) for later use.

Form 2 TIndexDefs(const TIndexDefs& p)
Constructs a TIndexDefs object which attaches to the PITIndexDefs COM object associated with the given TIndexDefs object (which was passed by reference). The new TIndexDefs saves the associated PITIndexDefs COM object (incrementing its reference count) for later use.

Form 3 TIndexDefs(PTIndexDefs p)
Constructs a TIndexDefs object which attaches to the PITIndexDefs COM object associated with the given TIndexDefs object (which was passed by pointer). The new TIndexDefs saves the associated PITIndexDefs COM object (incrementing its reference count) for later use.

Form 4 TIndexDefs(void)
Constructs a new TIndexDefs object. Internally, a new PITIndexDefs COM object is created for later use.

Form 5 TIndexDefs(TTable& Table)
Constructs a new TIndexDefs object. Internally, a new PITIndexDefs COM object is created for later use. The new TIndexDefs is initialized with the IndexDefs from the given Table.

Destructor

virtual ~TIndexDefs()
Deletes the TIndexDefs and reduces the reference count on the associated PITIndexDefs COM object. If the reference count on the associated PITIndexDefs COM object reaches 0, it is deleted.

Properties

▶ Count
▶ Items

Methods

Add
Assign
Clear

FindIndexForFields
IndexOf
Update

TIndexOptions typedef   bdti.h

typedef enum {ixPrimary = 1, ixUnique = 2, ixDescending = 4, ixCaseInsensitive = 8, ixExpresssion = 16}TIndexOptions;
The TIndexOptions type is the set of values that can be used in creating a new index. It is used by the AddIndex method of a dataset component. You can combine TIndexOptions values by using the binary "or" operator " | ".

TIntegerField component   bdto.h

A TIntegerField component represents a field of a record in a dataset. It is represented as a numeric value with a range from -2,147,483,648 to 2,147,483,647. Use TIntegerField for fields that hold large, signed whole numbers.

Set the DisplayFormat property to control the formatting of the field for display purposes, and the EditFormat property for editing purposes. Use the Value property to access or change the current field value. Set the MinValue or the MaxValue property to limit the smallest or largest value permitted in a field.

The TIntegerField component has the properties, methods, and events of the TField component.

Public constructors and destructor

Constructors

Form 1 TIntegerField(PITField p)
Constructs a TIntegerField object which attaches to the given PITField COM interface pointer. The new TIntegerField saves the PITField COM object (incrementing its reference count) for later use.

Form 2 TIntegerField(const TField& p)
Constructs a TIntegerField object which attaches to the PITField COM object associated with the given TField object (which was passed by reference). The new TIntegerField saves the associated PITField COM object (incrementing its reference count) for later use.

Form 3 TIntegerField(PTField p)
Constructs a TIntegerField object which attaches to the PITField COM object associated with the given TField object (which was passed by pointer). The new TIntegerField saves the associated PITField COM object (incrementing its reference count) for later use.

Form 4   TIntegerField(void)
Constructs a new TIntegerField object. Internally, a new PITField COM object is created for later use.

Form 5   TIntegerField(PTBDTComponent Owner)
Constructs a new TIntegerField object. Internally, a new PITField COM object is created for later use. Owner specifies the DataSet which will own the new TIntegerField. It can be NULL, to specify that there is no Owner.

Form 6   TIntegerField(PTBDTComponent Owner, TFieldType DataType)
Constructs a TIntegerField object. Internally, a new PITField COM object is created for later use. Owner specifies the DataSet which owns the new TIntegerField. It can be NULL, to specify that there is no Owner. DataType is the type of field to be created.

Destructor

virtual ~TIntegerField()
Deletes the TIntegerField and reduces the reference count on the associated PITField COM object. If the reference count on the associated PITField COM object reaches 0, it is deleted.

Properties

▶ AsBoolean
▶ AsDateTime
▶ AsFloat
▶ AsInteger
▶ AsString
Calculated
▶ CanModify
▶ DataSet
▶ DataSize
▶ DataType
DisplayFormat
▶ DisplayText
EditFormat
EditMask
FieldName
▶ FieldNo
Index
▶ IsIndexField
▶ IsNull
MaxValue
MinValue

Name
ReadOnly
Required
▶Size
▶Text
▶Value

Methods

Assign
AssignValue
Clear
GetData
IsValidChar
SetData

Events

OnChange
OnGetText
OnSetText
OnValidate

TLeftRight typedef   dbtype.h

typedef enum {lrLeftJustify, lrRightJustify}TLeftRight;
TLeftRight is the type of the Alignment property of check boxes.

TListBoxStyle typedef   dbtype.h

typedef enum{ lbStandard, lbOwnerDrawFixed, lbOwnerDrawVariable }TListBoxStyle;
The TListBoxStyle type is the type of the Style property for a list box (TDBListBox and
TDBLookupList components).

TLocale typedef   bdti.h

typedef LPVOID TLocale;
The TLocale typedef is the type of a Locale or DBLocale property. These properties are
only used or needed when making direct calls to the Borland Database Engine.

TLockType typedef   bdti.h

typedef enum {ltReadLock, ltWriteLock}TLockType;
The TLockType type is the type of the t parameter used by the LockTable and
UnlockTable methods.

TLogin_MFUNCTOR macro

TLogin_MFUNCTOR(object, memberFunc)
This macro constructs the event sink object, which is of type TLoginSink, binding it to
the handler method that responds when the OnLogin of a TDatabase component occurs.

Parameter	Meaning
object	Identifies the event sink object; use the *this pointer
memberFunc	Identifies the event handler that responds to the OnDragOver event

TLoginSink typedef   bdto.h

typedef TBdtEventSinkV2<TDatabase& sender, TStrings& loginparams> TLoginSink;
The TLoginSink is the type of the event sink for the OnLogin event of a TDatabase
component.

Parameter	Meaning
sender	The TSession component
loginparams	The parameters used to log in to the database

TLoginSource typedef   bdto.h

typedef TBdtEventSourceV2<TDatabase& sender, TStrings& loginparams> TLoginSource;
The TLoginSource is the type of the event source for the OnLogin event of a TDatabase
component.

Parameter	Meaning
sender	The TSession component
loginparams	The parameters used to log in to the database

TMemoField component   bdto.h

A TMemoField represents a field of a record in a dataset. It is represented by a value
consisting of an arbitrary set of bytes with indefinite size. The bytes should correspond
to text data.

Use the Assign method to transfer another component to a TMemoField. Use the LoadFromFile method to load a field's contents from a file. Use LoadFromStream method to load a field from a Stream. Use SaveToFile method to write a field's contents to a file. Use SaveToStream method to write a field's contents to a Stream.

The TMemoField component has the properties, methods, and events of the TField component.

Public constructors and destructor

Constructors

Form 1 TMemoField(PITField p)
Constructs a TMemoField object which attaches to the given PITField COM interface pointer. The new TMemoField saves the PITField COM object (incrementing its reference count) for later use.

Form 2 TMemoField(const TField& p)
Constructs a TMemoField object which attaches to the PITField COM object associated with the given TField object (which was passed by reference). The new TMemoField saves the associated PITField COM object (incrementing its reference count) for later use.

Form 3 TMemoField(PTField p)
Constructs a TMemoField object which attaches to the PITField COM object associated with the given TField object (which was passed by pointer). The new TMemoField saves the associated PITField COM object (incrementing its reference count) for later use.

Form 4 TMemoField(void)
Constructs a new TMemoField object. Internally, a new PITField COM object is created for later use.

Form 5 TMemoField(PTBDTComponent Owner)
Constructs a new TMemoField object. Internally, a new PITField COM object is created for later use. Owner specifies the DataSet which owns the new TMemoField. It can be NULL, to specify that there is no Owner.

Destructor

virtual ~TMemoField()
Deletes the TMemoField and reduces the reference count on the associated PITField COM object. If the reference count on the associated PITField COM object reaches 0, it is deleted.

Properties

▷ AsBoolean
▷ AsDateTime
▷ AsFloat
▷ AsInteger

▷ AsString
Calculated
▷ CanModify
▷ DataSet
▷ DataSize
▷ DataType
▷ DisplayText
EditMask
FieldName
▷ FieldNo
Index
▷ IsIndexField
▷ IsNull
Name
ReadOnly
Required
Size
▷ Text
▷ Transliterate

Methods

Assign
AssignValue
Clear
GetData
IsValidChar
LoadFromFile
LoadFromStream
SaveToFile
SaveToStream
SetData

Events

OnChange
OnGetText
OnSetText
OnValidate

TMemoryStream component   bdto.h

The TMemoryStream component manages the reading of data from and writing of data to a stream.

To read data from a stream into a buffer, use the ReadBuffer method. To write data from a buffer to a stream, call the WriteBuffer method. When you want to assign data from one stream to another, call the CopyFrom method.

The Position property returns and sets the current position within the stream. The Size property returns the size of the stream from the current position within the stream.

Public constructors and destructor

Constructors

Form 1 TMemoryStream(PITStream p)
Constructs a TMemoryStream object which attaches to the given PITStream COM interface pointer. The new TMemoryStream saves the PITStream COM object (incrementing its reference count) for later use.

Form 2 TMemoryStream(const TMemoryStream& p)
Constructs a TMemoryStream object which attaches to the PITStream COM object associated with the given TMemoryStream object (which was passed by reference). The new TMemoryStream saves the associated PITStream COM object (incrementing its reference count) for later use.

Form 3 TMemoryStream(PTMemoryStream p)
Constructs a TMemoryStream object which attaches to the PITStream COM object associated with the given TMemoryStream object (which was passed by pointer). The new TMemoryStream saves the associated PITStream COM object (incrementing its reference count) for later use.

Form 4 TMemoryStream(void)
Constructs a new TMemoryStream object. Internally, a new PITStream COM object is created for later use.

Destructor

virtual ~TMemoryStream()
Deletes the TMemoryStream and reduces the reference count on the associated PITStream COM object. If the reference count on the associated PITStream COM object reaches 0, it is deleted.

Properties

Position
Size

Methods

CopyFrom
Read
ReadBuffer

> Seek
> Write
> WriteBuffer

TMousePointer typedef   dbtype.h

typedef enum {crDefault, crArrow, crCross, crIBeam, crIcon, crSize, crSizeNESW, crSizeNS, crSizeNWSE,
    crSizeWE, crUpArrow}TMousePointer;

The TMousePointer type defines the different kinds of standard cursors a component
can have. TMousePointer is the type of the MousePointer property.

TNavigateBtn typedef   dbtype.h

typedef enum { nbFirst, nbPrior, nbNext, nbLast, nbInsert, nbDelete, nbEdit, nbPost, nbCancel,
    nbRefresh}TNavigateBtn;

The TNavigateBtn type defines the possible values returned by the BtnClick method.

TNumericField component   bdto.h

TNumericField is the base class for all numeric field types (TIntegerField, TFloatField,
TBCDField, TCurrencyField, TSmallintField, and TWordField). It represents a field of a
record in a dataset and has a numeric value.

Set the DisplayFormat property to control the formatting of the field for display
purposes, and the EditFormat property for editing purposes.

The TNumericField component has the properties, methods, and events of the TField
component.

Public constructors and destructor

Constructors

Form 1   TNumericField(PITField p)
Constructs a TNumericField object which attaches to the given PITField COM interface
pointer. The new TNumericField saves the PITField COM object (incrementing its
reference count) for later use.

Form 2   TNumericField(const TField& p)
Constructs a TNumericField object which attaches to the PITField COM object
associated with the given TField object (which was passed by reference). The new
TNumericField saves the associated PITField COM object (incrementing its reference
count) for later use.

Form 3   TNumericField(PTField p)
Constructs a TNumericField object which attaches to the PITField COM object
associated with the given TField object (which was passed by pointer). The new

TNumericField saves the associated PITField COM object (incrementing its reference count) for later use.

Form 4   TNumericField(void)
Constructs a new TNumericField object. Internally, a new PITField COM object is created for later use.

Form 5   TNumericField(PTBDTComponent Owner, TFieldType DataType)
Constructs a new TNumericField object. Internally, a new PITField COM object is created for later use. The Owner parameter specifies the DataSet which owns the new TNumericField. It can be NULL, to specify that there is no Owner. DataType is the type of field created.

Destructor

virtual ~TNumericField()
Deletes the TNumericField and reduces the reference count on the associated PITField COM object. If the reference count on the associated PITField COM object reaches 0, it is deleted.

Properties

▶ AsBoolean
▶ AsDateTime
▶ AsFloat
▶ AsInteger
▶ AsString
Calculated
▶ CanModify
Currency
DataSet
▶ DataSize
▶ DataType
DisplayFormat
▶ DisplayText
EditFormat
EditMask
FieldName
▶ FieldNo
Index
▶ IsIndexField
▶ IsNull
MaxValue
MinValue
Name
Precision
ReadOnly
Required

▶ Size
▶ Text
▶ Value

Methods

Assign
AssignValue
Clear
GetData
IsValidChar
SetData

Events

OnChange
OnGetText
OnSetText
OnValidate

Top property

Applies to   All data-aware controls

int Top;

The Top property determines the y coordinate of the top left corner of a control, relative to the form in pixels. For forms, the value of the Top property is relative to the screen in pixels.

For the Find and Replace dialog boxes, Top is a run-time only property. The default value is -1.

Example   The following line of code moves a database edit control 10 pixels up each time it executes:

```
DBEdit1.Top =DBEdit1.Top - 10;
```

TopIndex property

Applies to   TDBListBox component

int TopIndex;

The TopIndex property is the index number of the item that appears at the top of the database list box. You can use the TopIndex property to determine which item is the first item displayed at the top of the list box and to set it to the item of your choosing.

Example This code adds 20 items to a database list box, and then makes the third item in the list at the top of the list box:

```
int number = 0;
for( number = 0; number < 20; number++ )
{
    char buffer[25];
    sprintf( buffer, "Item %d" , number );
    DBListBox1.Items->Add( buffer );
}
DBListBox1.TopIndex = 2;
```

TOwnerDrawAction typedef   dbtype.h

```
typedef struct
{
  unsigned int oaDrawEntire:1;
  unsigned int oaSelect:1;
  unsigned int oaFocus:1;
}TOwnerDrawAction;
```

TOwnerDrawAction is the data type of the Action property used for owner-draw list boxes.

TOwnerDrawState typedef   dbtype.h

```
typedef struct
{
  unsigned int odSelected:1;
  unsigned int odGrayed:1;
  unsigned int odDisabled:1;
  unsigned int odChecked:1;
}TOwnerDrawState;
```

TOwnerDrawState is the data type of the State parameter of the OnDrawItem event used for owner-draw list boxes.

TParam component   bdto.h

The TParam component holds information about a parameter of a TQuery or TStoredProc. In addition to the parameter value, TParam stores the field type, name, and (for a stored procedure) the parameter type.

You generally do not need to create a TParam component explicitly, as the TQuery or TStoredProc component creates it as an element of its Params property as needed. All you must do is assign values to the parameters by assigning a value to one of these properties: AsBCD, AsBoolean, AsCurrency, AsDate, AsDateTime, AsFloat, AsInteger, AsSmallint, AsString, AsTime, or AsWord.

Public constructors and destructor

Constructors

Form 1   TParam(PITParam p)
Constructs a TParam object which attaches to the given PITParam COM interface pointer. The new TParam saves the PITParam COM object (incrementing its reference count) for later use.

Form 2   TParam(const TParam& p)
Constructs a TParam object which attaches to the PITParam COM object associated with the given TParam object (which was passed by reference). The new TParam saves the associated PITParam COM object (incrementing its reference count) for later use.

Form 3   TParam(PTParam p)
Constructs a TParam object which attaches to the PITParam COM object associated with the given TParam object (which was passed by pointer). The new TParam saves the associated PITParam COM object (incrementing its reference count) for later use.

Form 4   TParam(void)
Constructs a new TParam object. Internally, a new PITParam COM object is created for later use.

Form 5   TParam(PTParams AParamList, TParamType AParamType)
Constructs a new TParam object. Internally, a new PITParam COM object is created for later use. AParamList specifies the TParams object to which the new TParam is added, AParamType specifies the ParamType property of the new TParam. AParamList can be NULL, to specify that the new TParam is not added to an existing TParams object.

Destructor

virtual ~TParam()
Deletes the TParam and reduces the reference count on the associated PITParam COM object. If the reference count on the associated PITParam COM object reaches 0, it is deleted.

Properties

▶ AsBCD
▶ AsBoolean
▶ AsCurrency
▶ AsDate
▶ AsDateTime
▶ AsFloat
▶ AsInteger
▶ AsSmallInt
▶ AsString
▶ AsTime
▶ AsWord
Bound

▷ DataType
▷ IsNull
▷ Name
▷ ParamType
▷ Text

Methods

▷ Assign
▷ AssignField
Clear
GetData
GetDataSize
SetData

TParamBindMode typedef   bdti.h

typedef enum {pbByName, pbByNumber}TParamBindMode;
The TParamBindMode type defines the possible values of the ParamBindMode
property of a stored procedure (TStoredProc).

TParams component   bdto.h

The TParams component holds the parameters for a stored procedure or parameterized
query and provides the methods to create and access those parameters. The Count
property is the number of TParam components in the TParams component. The Items
property is an array of pointers to those TParam components.

To create a new parameter, call the CreateParam. You can call the AddParam method to
add a new parameter or the RemoveParam method to take one out of the set. To delete
all the parameters, call the Clear. If you want to find a particular TParam component by
its name, use the ParamByName method.

Public constructors and destructor

Constructors

Form 1   TParams(PITParams p)
Constructs a TParams object which attaches to the given PITParams COM interface
pointer. The new TParams saves the PITParams COM object (incrementing its reference
count) for later use.

Form 2   TParams(const TParams& p)
Constructs a TParams object which attaches to the PITParams COM object associated
with the given TParams object (which was passed by reference). The new TParams
saves the associated PITParams COM object (incrementing its reference count) for later
use.

Form 3   TParams(PTParams p)
Constructs a TParams object which attaches to the PITParams COM object associated with the given TParams object (which was passed by pointer). The new TParams saves the associated PITParams COM object (incrementing its reference count) for later use.

Form 4   TParams(void)
Constructs a new TParams object. Internally, a new PITParams COM object is created for later use.

Destructor

virtual ~TParams()
Deletes the TParams and reduces the reference count on the associated PITParams COM object. If the reference count on the associated PITParams COM object reaches 0, it is deleted.

Properties

Count
▷ Items

Methods

AddParam
Assign
AssignValues
Clear
CreateParam
ParamByName
RemoveParam

TParamType typedef   bdti.h

typedef enum {ptUnknown, ptInput, ptOutput, ptInputOutput,}TParamType;
The TParamType type is the set of values of the ParamType property of a TParam component.

TPassword_MFUNCTOR macro

TPassword_MFUNCTOR(object, memberFunc)

This macro constructs the event sink object, which is of type TPasswordSink, binding it to the handler method that responds when the OnPassword event of a TSession component occurs.

Parameter	Meaning
object	Identifies the event sink object; use the *this pointer
memberFunc	Identifies the event handler that responds to the OnDragOver event

TPasswordSink typedef bdto.h

typedef TBdtEventSinkV2<TSession& sender, bool& continue> TPasswordSink;
The TPasswordSink is the type of the event sink for the OnPassword event of a TSession component

Parameter	Meaning
sender	The TSession component
continue	If true, another attempt is made to access the database. If false, no further attempt is made to access the database

TPasswordSource typedef bdto.h

typedef TBdtEventSourceV2<TSession& sender, bool& continue> TPasswordSource;
The TPasswordSource is the type of the event source for the OnPassword event of a TSession component.

Parameter	Meaning
sender	The TSession component
continue	If true, another attempt is made to access the database. If false, no further attempt is made to access the database

TQuery component bdto.h

TQuery enables database applications to issue SQL statements to a database engine either the Borland Database Engine or an SQL server. TQuery provides the interface between an SQL server or the Borland Database Engine and TDataSource components. In turn, TDataSource components provide the interface to data-aware controls such as TDBGrid.

Specify the database you want to query as the value of the DatabaseName. Enter a single SQL statement to execute in the SQL property. To query dBASE or Paradox tables, use local SQL. To query SQL server tables, use passthrough SQL. The SQL statement can be a static SQL statement or a dynamic SQL statement.

At run time, an application can supply parameter values for dynamic queries with the Params property or the ParamByName method. Visual Database Tools also checks the value of the DataSource property when the application runs. If the field names of the specified data source match the names of the parameters in the SQL statement, those field values bind to the corresponding parameters.

To optimize a dynamic query, use the Prepare method.

A result set is the group of records returned by a query to an application. A TQuery can return two kinds of result sets:

- "Live" result sets: As with TTable components, users can edit data in the result set with data-aware controls. The changes are sent to the database when a Post occurs, or when the user tabs to a new control.

- "Read only" result sets: Users cannot edit data in the result set with data-aware controls.

If you want the query to provide a live result set, the SQL statement must conform to certain syntax requirements. If the SQL syntax does not conform to these requirements, the query result set is read-only.

To execute the SQL statement at design time, set the Active property to true . To execute the SQL statement at run time, call either the Open or ExecSQL method.

There are several methods available to navigate through the result set: First, Next, Prior, Last, and MoveBy. Test the AtBOF and AtEOF properties to determine if the cursor is at the beginning or end of the result set, respectively.

Call the Append or Insert method to add a record to the underlying database table. Call the Delete method to delete the current record. To let the user modify the fields or the result set, call the Edit method. To post those changes, call the Post method, or call the Cancel method to discard them.

TQuery derives from TDataSet through TDBDataSet and inherits all of their public properties, methods, and events.

Public constructors and destructor

Constructors

Form 1   TQuery(PITQuery p)
Constructs a TQuery object which attaches to the given PITQuery COM interface pointer. The new TQuery saves the PITQuery COM object (incrementing its reference count) for later use.

Form 2   TQuery(const TQuery& p)
Constructs a TQuery object which attaches to the PITQuery COM object associated with the given TQuery object (which was passed by reference). The new TQuery saves the associated PITQuery COM object (incrementing its reference count) for later use.

Form 3   TQuery(PTQuery p)
Constructs a TQuery object which attaches to the PITQuery COM object associated with the given TQuery object (which was passed by pointer). The new TQuery will save the associated PITQuery COM object (incrementing its reference count) for later use.

Form 4   TQuery(void)
Constructs a new TQuery object. Internally, a PITQuery COM object is created for later use.

Form 5   TQuery(HWND hdlg, int idc)
Constructs a TQuery object which attaches to the PITQuery COM object associated with the VBX specified by the given dialog box HWND and control id. The new TQuery saves the associated PITQuery COM object (incrementing its reference count) for later use.

Destructor

virtual ~TQuery()
Deletes the TQuery and reduces the reference count on the associated PITQuery COM object. If the reference count on the associated PITQuery COM object reaches 0, it is deleted.

Properties

Active
▶ AtBOF
▶ AtEOF
AutoCalcFields
▶ CanModify
▶ Count
▶ Database
DatabaseName
DataSource
▶ DBHandle
▶ DBLocale
▶ FieldCount
▶ FieldDefs
▶ Fields
▶ Handle
▶ Local
▶ Locale
▶ Modified
Name
▶ ParamCount
Params
▶ Prepared

RecordCount
RecordSize
RequestLive
SQL
▷State
▷StmtHandle
▷Text
UniDirectional
UpdateMode

Methods

Append
AppendRecord
Assign
Cancel
CheckBrowseMode
ClearFields
Close
CursorPosChanged
Delete
DisableControls
EnableControls
ExecSQL
FieldByName
FindField
First
FreeBookmark
GetBookmark
GetFieldNames
GotoBookmark
InsertRecord
Insert
MoveBy
Next
Open
ParamByName
Post
Prepare
Prior
Refresh
SetFields
UnPrepare
UpdateCursorPos
UpdateRecord

Events

AfterCancel
AfterClose
AfterDelete
AfterEdit
AfterInsert
AfterOpen
AfterPost
BeforeCancel
BeforeClose
BeforeDelete
BeforeEdit
BeforeInsert
BeforeOpen
BeforePost
OnCalcFields
OnNewRecord

TransIsolation property

Applies to   TDataBase component

TTransIsolation TransIsolation;
The TransIsolation property specifies the transaction isolation level used by an SQL server.

These are the possible values:

Value	Meaning
tiDirtyRead	Any change is returned, regardless of whether the record has been committed.
tiReadCommitted	Only committed versions of the record are returned; uncommitted changes are not reflected in the result.
tiRepeatableRead	Only the original record is returned for the duration of the transaction, even if another application has committed a change.

Database servers may support these isolation levels differently or not at all. If the requested isolation level is not supported by the server, then the next highest isolation level is used, as shown in the following table. For a detailed description of how each isolation level is implemented, see your server documentation.

Transliterate property

Applies to   TBatchMove, TMemoField, TStringField components bool TransLiterate;

For a batch move component, the Transliterate property controls whether character by character translations to another character are made as the data is transferred from the Source dataset to the Destination datasets. If different character sets are used by the source and destination datasets, Transliterate should be true, so that the transliteration to the Destination character set occurs.

For a string field component, the Transliterate property determines whether character by character translation to another character set when a field is displayed on another operating system platform.

For example, if you obtain data from a database that is represented by the OEM character set, but you want to display the data in a Windows application which uses the ANSI character set, Transliterate should be true. If it false, the data is displayed in its "raw" form, which may not be readable.

Transliterate is true by default.

Example

```
// Suppress translations
BatchMove1.Transliterate = false;
```

TScrollStyle typedef   dbtype.h

```
typedef enum {ScrollBars_0_None, ScrollBars_1_Horizontal, ScrollBars_2_Vertical,
    ScrollBars_3_Both}TScrollStyle;
```
The TScrollStyle type defines the different combinations of scroll bars a memo control or a grid can have. TScrollStyle is the type of the ScrollBars property of the TDBMemo component.

TSeekOrigin typedef   bdti.h

```
typedef enum{ soFromBeginning=0, soFromCurrent=1, soFromEnd=2 }TSeekOrigin;
```
TSeekOrigin is the type of the Origin parameter of the Seek method used by the TMemoryStream component.

TSession component   bdto.h

You should not explicitly create a TSession component, but you can use the global session variable to affect an application. Each time an application runs, a TSession component named Session is created automatically. You should not attempt to create any other TSession or destroy and recreate Session itself.

TSession provides global control over database connections for an application. The Databases property of TSession contains all the active databases in the session. The DatabaseCount property reports the number of active databases in the Session.

To maintain database connections even when no tables in the database are open, set the KeepConnections property to true. When you want to drop all inactive database connections, call the DropConnections method.

The NetFileDir property specifies the directory path of the BDE network control directory. The PrivateDir property specifies the path of the directory in which to store temporary files.

Properties

▶ DatabaseCount
▶ Databases
▶ Handle
▶ KeepConnections
▶ Locale
▶ Name
▶ NetFileDir
▶ PrivateDir

Methods

AddPassword
Assign
CloseDatabase
DropConnections
FindDatabase
GetAliasNames
GetAliasParams
GetDatabaseNames
GetDriverNames
GetDriverParams
GetPassword
GetStoredProcNames
GetTableNames
OpenDatabase
RemoveAllPasswords
RemovePassword

Event

OnPassword

TSmallintField component

bdto.h

A TSmallintField represents a field of a record in a dataset. It is represented as a numeric value with a range from -32,768 to 32,767. Use TSmallintField for fields that hold signed whole numbers.

Set the DisplayFormat property to control the formatting of the field for display purposes, and the EditFormat property for editing purposes. Use the Value property to access or change the current field value. Set the MinValue or the MaxValue property to limit the smallest or largest value permitted in a field.

The TSmallintField component has the properties, methods, and events of the TField component.

Public constructors and destructor

Constructors

Form 1   TSmallintField(PITField p)
Constructs a TSmallintField object which attaches to the given PITField COM interface pointer. The new TSmallintField saves the PITField COM object (incrementing its reference count) for later use.

Form 2   TSmallintField(const TField& p)
Constructs a TSmallintField object which attaches to the PITField COM object associated with the given TField object (which was passed by reference). The new TSmallintField saves the associated PITField COM object (incrementing its reference count) for later use.

Form 3   TSmallintField(PTField p)
Constructs a TSmallintField object which attaches to the PITField COM object associated with the given TField object (which was passed by pointer). The new TSmallintField saves the associated PITField COM object (incrementing its reference count) for later use.

Form 4   TSmallintField(void)
Constructs a new TSmallintField object. Internally, a new PITField COM object is created for later use.

Form 5   TSmallintField(PTBDTComponent Owner)
Constructs a new TSmallintField object. Internally, a new PITField COM object is created for later use. Owner specifies the DataSet which will own the new TSmallintField. It can be NULL, to specify that there is no Owner.

Destructor

virtual ~TSmallintField()
Deletes the TSmallintField and reduces the reference count on the associated PITField COM object. If the reference count on the associated PITField COM object reaches 0, it is deleted.

Properties

▶ AsBoolean
▶ AsDateTime
▶ AsFloat
▶ AsInteger
▶ AsString
Calculated
▶ CanModify
▶ DataSet
▶ DataSize
▶ DataType
DisplayFormat
▶ DisplayText
EditFormat
EditMask
FieldName
▶ FieldNo
Index
▶ IsIndexField
▶ IsNull
MaxValue
MinValue
Name
ReadOnly
Required
▶ Size
▶ Text
▶ Value

Methods

AssignValue
Assign
Clear
GetData
IsValidChar
SetData

Events

OnChange
OnGetText
OnSetText
OnValidate

TStoredProc component

bdto.h

The TStoredProc component enables applications to execute server stored procedures. To specify the database in which the stored procedure is defined, set the DatabaseName property to the name of the database. Specify the name of the stored procedure on the server as the value of the StoredProcName property.

A stored procedure has a Params property that holds its input and output parameters, similar to a TQuery component. The order of the parameters in the Params property is determined by the stored procedure definition. An application can set the values of input parameters and get the values of output parameters in the Params property as can be done with TQuery parameters. You can also use the ParamByName method to access the parameters by name. If you are not sure of the ordering of the input and output parameters for a stored procedure, use the Parameters Editor.

Before an application can execute a stored procedure, you must prepare it. You can prepare the stored procedure:

• At design time with the Parameters Editor.

• At run time with the Prepare method.

A stored procedure can return either a singleton (one row) result or a result set (multiple rows) with a cursor, if the server supports it. Execute a stored procedure with the ExecProc method, if the stored procedure returns a singleton result or call the Open method, if the stored procedure returns a result set.

Public constructors and destructor

Constructors

Form 1   TStoredProc(PITStoredProc p)
Constructs a TStoredProc object which attaches to the given PITStoredProc COM interface pointer. The new TStoredProc saves the PITStoredProc COM object (incrementing its reference count) for later use.

Form 2   TStoredProc(const TStoredProc& p)
Constructs a TStoredProc object which attaches to the PITStoredProc COM object associated with the given TStoredProc object (which was passed by reference). The new TStoredProc saves the associated PITStoredProc COM object (incrementing its reference count) for later use.

Form 3   TStoredProc(PTStoredProc p)
Constructs a TStoredProc object which attaches to the PITStoredProc COM object associated with the given TStoredProc object (which was passed by pointer). The new TStoredProc saves the associated PITStoredProc COM object (incrementing its reference count) for later use.

Form 4   TStoredProc(void)
Constructs a new TStoredProc object. Internally, a PITStoredProc COM object is created for later use.

Form 5   TStoredProc(HWND hdlg, int idc)

Constructs a TStoredProc object which attaches to the PITStoredProc COM object associated with the VBX specified by the given dialog box HWND and control id. The new TStoredProc saves the associated PITStoredProc COM object (incrementing its reference count) for later use.

Destructor

virtual ~TStoredProc()

Deletes the TStoredProc and reduces the reference count on the associated PITStoredProc COM object. If the reference count on the associated PITStoredProc COM object reaches 0, it is deleted.

Properties

Active
▶ AtBOF
▶ AtEOF
AutoCalcFields
▶ CanModify
▶ Database
DatabaseName
DBHandle
▶ DBLocale
DescriptionsAvailable
▶ FieldCount
▶ FieldDefs
▶ Fields
▶ Handle
▶ Locale
▶ Modified
Name
Overload
ParamBindMode
▶ ParamCount
Params
▶ Prepared
▶ RecordCount
▶ State
▶ StmtHandle
StoredProcName

Methods

Append
AppendRecord
Assign

Cancel
CheckBrowseMode
ClearFields
Close
CopyParams
CursorPosChanged
Delete
DisableControls
Edit
EnableControls
ExecProc
FieldByName
FindField
First
FreeBookmark
GetBookmark
GetFieldNames
GetResults
GotoBookmark
Insert
InsertRecord
Last
MoveBy
Next
Open
ParamByName
Post
Prepare
Prior
Refresh
SetFields
UnPrepare
UpdateCursorPos
UpdateRecord

Events

AfterCancel
AfterClose
AfterDelete
AfterEdit
AfterInsert
AfterOpen
AfterPost
BeforeCancel
BeforeClose

BeforeDelete
BeforeEdit
BeforeInsert
BeforeOpen
BeforePost
OnCalcFields
OnNewRecord

TStringField component   bdto.h

A TStringField component represents a field of a record in a dataset. A field of TStringField is physically stored as a sequence of up to 255 characters. Use TStringField for fields that contain text, such as names and addresses.

Use the Value property to access or change the current field value.

The TStringField component has the properties, methods, and events of the TField component.

Public constructors and destructor

Constructors

Form 1   TStringField(PITField p)
Constructs a TStringField object which attaches to the given PITField COM interface pointer. The new TStringField saves the PITField COM object (incrementing its reference count) for later use.

Form 2   TStringField(const TField& p)
Constructs a TStringField object which attaches to the PITField COM object associated with the given TField object (which was passed by reference). The new TStringField saves the associated PITField COM object (incrementing its reference count) for later use.

Form 3   TStringField(PTField p)
Constructs a TStringField object which attaches to the PITField COM object associated with the given TField object (which was passed by pointer). The new TStringField saves the associated PITField COM object (incrementing its reference count) for later use.

Form 4   TStringField(void)
Constructs a new TStringField object. Internally, a new PITField COM object is created for later use.

Form 5   TStringField(PTBDTComponent Owner)
Constructs a new TStringField object. Internally, a new PITField COM object is created for later use. Owner specifies the DataSet which will own the new TStringField. It can be NULL, to specify that there is no Owner.

Destructor

virtual ~TStringField()

Deletes the TStringField and reduces the reference count on the associated PITField COM object. If the reference count on the associated PITField COM object reaches 0, it is deleted.

Properties

▶ AsBoolean
▶ AsDateTime
▶ AsFloat
▶ AsInteger
▶ AsString
Calculated
▶ CanModify
▶ DataSet
▶ DataSize
▶ DataType
▶ DisplayText
EditMask
FieldName
▶ FieldNo
Index
▶ IsIndexField
▶ IsNull
Name
ReadOnly
Required
Size
▶ Text
Transliterate
▶ Value

Methods

Assign
AssignValue
Clear
GetData
IsValidChar
SetData

Events

OnChange
OnGetText
OnSetText
OnValidate

TStrings component

String components are used by various components to manipulate strings. For example, the Items property of a list box control is of type TStrings. When you add or delete items in a list box, you are adding and deleting them from a list box string component.

You can add, delete, insert, move, and exchange strings using the Add, Delete, Insert, Move, and Exchange methods of a string component. The Clear method clears all the strings in the list of strings. The Count property contains the number of strings in the list. Each string component has a Strings property that lets you access a particular string by its position in the list of strings. To find the position of a string in the list, use the IndexOf method.

To add several strings at once to a list of strings, use the AddStrings method. You can assign one string component to another using the Assign method.

Each string can be associated with a object. If you want to add a string and an object to string list at the same time, use the AddObject method. You can access a particular object by its position in the list of objects using the Objects property. To find the position of the object in the list, use the IndexOfObject method. To insert an object, call the InsertObject method. The Delete, Move, Clear, and Exchange methods operate on the object associated with a string as well as on the string itself. For example, calling Clear removes all strings and all their associated objects.

You can store strings in a file and then load them all at one using the LoadFromFile method. To save the strings to a file, use the SaveToFile method.

Public constructors and destructor

Constructors

Form 1   TStrings(PITStrings p)
Constructs a TStrings object which attaches to the given PITStrings COM interface pointer. The new TStrings saves the PITStrings COM object (incrementing its reference count) for later use.

Form 2   TStrings(const TStrings& p)
Constructs a TStrings object which attaches to the PITStrings COM object associated with the given TStrings object (which was passed by reference). The new TStrings saves the associated PITStrings COM object (incrementing its reference count) for later use.

Form 3   TStrings(PTStrings p)

Constructs a TStrings object which attaches to the PITStrings COM object associated with the given TStrings object (which was passed by pointer). The new TStrings saves the associated PITStrings COM object (incrementing its reference count) for later use.

Form 4   TStrings(void)

Constructs a new TStrings object. Internally, a new PITStrings COM object is created for later use.

Form 5   TStrings(const string& p)

Constructs a new TStrings object. Internally, a new PITStrings COM object is created for later use. The new TStrings is initialized with the given string.

Destructor

virtual ~TStrings()

Deletes the TStrings and reduces the reference count on the associated PITStrings COM object. If the reference count on the associated PITStrings COM object reaches 0, it is deleted.

Properties

▶ Count
Duplicates
▶ Objects
Sorted
▶ Strings
▶ Values

Methods

Add
AddObject
AddStrings
Assign
Clear
Delete
Equals
Exchange
Find
GetText
IndexOf
IndexOfObject
Insert
InsertObject
LoadFromFile
Move

SaveToFile
SetText
Sort

Events

OnChange event

TStringsNotify_MFUNCTOR macro

TStringsNotify_MFUNCTOR(object, memberFunc)
This macro constructs the event sink object, which is of type TStringsNotifySink, binding it to the handler method that responds when the OnChange event of a TStrings component occurs.

Parameter	Meaning
object	Identifies the event sink object; use the *this pointer
memberFunc	Identifies the event handler that responds to the OnDragOver event

TStringsNotifySink typedef   bdto.h

typedef TBdtEventSinkV1<TStrings&> TStringsNotifySink;
The TStringsNotifySink is the type of the event sink for the OnChange event of a TStrings component.

TStringsNotifySource typedef   bdto.h

typedef TBdtEventSourceV1<TStrings&> TStringsNotifySource;
The TStringsNotifySource is the type of the event source for the OnChange event of a TStrings component.

TTable component   bdto.h

The TTable component provides live access to database tables through the Borland Database Engine. TTable is the interface between the Borland Database Engine and TDataSource components. The TDataSource components then provide the interface to data-aware controls such as TDBGrid.

Set the DatabaseName property to specify the database to access. Set the TableName property to specify the table to access. Set the ReadOnly property to true unless you want to change the contents of the table. Set the Exclusive property to true if you do not want any other application to access the table while you are using it. Use the IndexName property to use the table with a secondary index. Use the MasterFields and MasterSource properties to create a link to a master table in a master-detail relationship.

Call the GotoCurrent method to move the cursor to the same position as another TTable linked to the same database table.

Set the Active property to true or call the Open method to open a TTable, putting it in Browse mode. Set Active to false or call Close to close the TTable. Call the First, Next, Prior, Last, and MoveBy, methods to navigate through the table. Call the SetKey, FindKey, FindNearest, GotoKey, and GotoNearest methods to search the database table for specific values.

Test the AtBOF and AtEOF properties to determine if the cursor has reached the beginning or end of the table, respectively. Call the Append, AppendRecord, Insert, or InsertRecord methods to add a record to the table. Call the Delete method to delete the current record. Call the Edit method to allow an application to modify records in the table, and Post to send the changes to the database or Cancel to discard them.

Use the EditRangeStart, EditRangeEnd, SetRangeStart, SetRangeEnd, ApplyRange, and SetRange methods to limit the range of records returned to the application and the CancelRange method to remove the limit.

Public constructors and destructor

Constructors

Form 1   TTable(PITTable p)
Constructs a TTable object which attaches to the given PITTable COM interface pointer. The new TTable saves the PITTable COM object (incrementing its reference count) for later use.

Form 2   TTable(const TTable& p)
Constructs a TTable object which attaches to the PITTable COM object associated with the given TTable object (which was passed by reference). The new TTable saves the associated PITTable COM object (incrementing its reference count) for later use.

Form 3   TTable(PTTable p)
Constructs a TTable object which attaches to the PITTable COM object associated with the given TTable object (which was passed by pointer). The new TTable saves the associated PITTable COM object (incrementing its reference count) for later use.

Form 4   TTable(void)
Constructs a new TTable object. Internally, a new PITTable COM object is created for later use.

Form 5   TTable(HWND hdlg, int idc)
Constructs a TTable object which attaches to the PITTable COM object associated with the VBX specified by the given dialog box HWND and control id. The new TTable saves the associated PITTable COM object (incrementing its reference count) for later use.

Destructor

virtual ~TTable()
Deletes the TTable and reduces the reference count on the associated PITTable COM object. If the reference count on the associated PITTable COM object reaches 0, it is deleted.

Properties

Active
▶ AtBOF
▶ AtEOF
AutoCalcFields
▶ CanModify
▶ Database
DatabaseName
▶ DBHandle
▶ DBLocale
Exclusive
▶ FieldCount
▶ FieldDefs
▶ Fields
▶ Handle
▶ IndexDefs
▶ IndexFieldCount
IndexFieldNames
▶ IndexFields
IndexName
▶ KeyExclusive
▶ KeyFieldCount
▶ Locale
MasterFields
MasterSource
▶ Modified
Name
ReadOnly
▶ RecordCount
▶ State
TableName
TableType
UpdateMode

Methods

AddIndex
Append
AppendRecord
ApplyRange
BatchMove
Cancel
CancelRange
CheckBrowseMode

ClearFields
Close
CreateTable
CursorPosChanged
Delete
DeleteIndex
DeleteTable
DisableControls
Edit
EditKey
EditRangeEnd
EditRangeStart
EmptyTable
EnableControls
FieldByName
FindField
FindKey
FindNearest
First
FreeBookmark
GetBookmark
GetFieldNames
GetIndexNames
GotoBookmark
GotoCurrent
GotoKey
GotoNearest
Insert
InsertRecord
Last
LockTable
MoveBy
Next
Open
Post
Prior
Refresh
RenameTable
SetFields
SetKey
SetRange

SetRangeEnd
SetRangeStart
UnlockTable
UpdateRecord

Events

AfterCancel
AfterClose
AfterDelete
AfterEdit
AfterInsert
AfterOpen
AfterPost
BeforeCancel
BeforeClose
BeforeDelete
BeforeEdit
BeforeInsert
BeforeOpen
BeforePost
OnCalcFields
OnNewRecord

TTableType typedef   bdti.h

typedef enum {ttDefault, ttParadox, ttDBase, ttASCII} TTableType;
The TTableType type is the set of values of the TableType property of a TTable
component.

TTimeField component   bdto.h

A TTimeField represents a field of a record in a dataset. It represents a value consisting
of a time.

Set the DisplayFormat property to control the formatting of the field for display
purposes. Use the Value property to access or change the current field value.

The TTimeField component has the properties, methods, and events of the TField
component.

Public constructors and destructor

Constructors

Form 1   TTimeField(PITField p)
Constructs a TTimeField object which attaches to the given PITField COM interface pointer. The new TTimeField saves the PITField COM object (incrementing its reference count) for later use.

Form 2   TTimeField(const TField& p)
Constructs a TTimeField object which attaches to the PITField COM object associated with the given TField object (which was passed by reference). The new TTimeField saves the associated PITField COM object (incrementing its reference count) for later use.

Form 3   TTimeField(PTField p
Constructs a TTimeField object which attaches to the PITField COM object associated with the given TField object (which was passed by pointer). The new TTimeField saves the associated PITField COM object (incrementing its reference count) for later use.

Form 4   TTimeField(void
Constructs a new TTimeField object. Internally, a new PITField COM object is created for later use.

Form 5   TTimeField(PTBDTComponent Owner)
Constructs a new TTimeField object. Internally, a new PITField COM object is created for later use. Owner specifies the DataSet which will own the new TTimeField. It can be NULL, to specify that there is no Owner.

Destructor

virtual ~TTimeField()
Deletes the TTimeField and reduces the reference count on the associated PITField COM object. If the reference count on the associated PITField COM object reaches 0, it is deleted.

Properties

▷ AsBoolean
▷ AsDateTime
▷ AsFloat
▷ AsInteger
▷ AsString
Calculated
▷ CanModify
▷ DataSet
▷ DataSize
▷ DataType
DisplayFormat

DisplayText
EditMask
FieldName
▶ FieldNo
Index
▶ IsIndexField
▶ IsNull
Name
ReadOnly
Required
▶ Size
▶ Text
Value

Methods

Assign
AssignValue
Clear
GetData
IsValidChar
SetData

Events

OnChange
OnSetText
OnValidate
OnGetText

TTransIsolation typedef   bdti.h

typedef enum {tiDirtyRead, tiReadCommitted, tiRepeatableRead}TTransIsolation;
The TTransIsolation type is used by the TransIsolation property and it is the set of
values that can be used to start a transaction. These values control how records which
have been modified by another application will be returned to your application by the
server.

TUpdateMode typedef   bdti.h

typedef enum {upWhereAll, upWhereChanged, upWhereKeyOnly}TUpdateMode;
The TUpdateMode is the type of the UpdateMode property for a table or query.

TVarBytesField component

bdto.h

A TVarBytesField represents a field of a record which is represented by a value consisting of an arbitrary set of up to 65535 bytes. The first two bytes are a binary value define the actual length.

Use the Assign method to copy values from another field to a TVarBytesField.

The TVarBytesField component has the properties, methods, and events of the TField component.

Public constructors and destructor

Constructors

Form 1   TVarBytesField(PITField p)
Constructs a TVarBytesField object which attaches to the given PITField COM interface pointer. The new TVarBytesField saves the PITField COM object (incrementing its reference count) for later use.

Form 2   TVarBytesField(const TField& p)
Constructs a TVarBytesField object which attaches to the PITField COM object associated with the given TField object (which was passed by reference). The new TVarBytesField saves the associated PITField COM object (incrementing its reference count) for later use.

Form 3   TVarBytesField(PTField p)
Constructs a TVarBytesField object which attaches to the PITField COM object associated with the given TField object (which was passed by pointer). The new TVarBytesField saves the associated PITField COM object (incrementing its reference count) for later use.

Form 4   TVarBytesField(void)
Constructs a new TVarBytesField object. Internally, a new PITField COM object is created for later use.

Form 5   TVarBytesField(PTBDTComponent Owner)
Constructs a new TVarBytesField object. Internally, a new PITField COM object is created for later use. Owner specifies the DataSet which will own the new TVarBytesField. It can be NULL, to specify that there is no Owner.

Destructor

virtual ~TVarBytesField()
Deletes the TVarBytesField and reduces the reference count on the associated PITField COM object. If the reference count on the associated PITField COM object reaches 0, it is deleted.

Properties

▷ AsBoolean
▷ AsDateTime
▷ AsFloat
▷ AsInteger
▷ AsString
Calculated
▷ CanModify
▷ DataSet
▷ DataSize
▷ DataType
▷ DisplayText
EditMask
FieldName
▷ FieldNo
Index
▷ IsIndexField
▷ IsNull
Name
ReadOnly
Required
Size
▷ Text

Methods

Assign
AssignValue
Clear
GetData
IsValidChar
SetData

Events

OnChange
OnGetText
OnSetText
OnValidate

TVarRecs component

bdto.h

TVarRecs components are used to manipulate data of various types. Each TVarRecs component can hold multiple data items. TVarRecs components are used by methods that require an array of values of any type, such as AppendRecord, FindKey, and SetFields.

To add a data item of any type to a TVarRecs component, call the Add method. The Clear method removes all data items from TVarRecs. The Count property reports how many data items are in TVarRecs. To access a particular data item, use the Items property.

Public constructors and destructor

Constructors

Form 1   TVarRecs(int c = 0, LPVARIANT p = 0)
Constructs a new TVarRecs object initialized with a copy of the data from the given LPVARIANT pointer. The c parameter specifies the number of elements of data to be copied.

Form 2   TVarRecs(const TVarRecs& p)
Constructs a new TVarRecs object initialized with a copy of the data from the given TVarRecs (which was passed by reference).

Form 3   TVarRecs(PTVarRecs p)
Constructs a new TVarRecs object initialized with a copy of the data from the given TVarRecs (which was passed by pointer).

Destructor

virtual ~TVarRecs()
Deletes the TVarRecs.

Properties

▶Count
▶Items

Methods

Add
Clear

TWordField component

A TWordField represents a field of a record in a dataset. It is represented as a numeric value with a range from 0 to 65,535. Use TWordField for fields that hold unsigned whole numbers.

Set the DisplayFormat property to control the formatting of the field for display purposes, and the EditFormat property for editing purposes. Use the Value property to access or change the current field value. Set the MinValue or the MaxValue property to limit the smallest or largest value permitted in a field.

The TWordField component has the properties, methods, and events of the TField component.

Public constructors and destructor

Constructors

Form 1 TWordField(PITField p)

Constructs a TWordField object which attaches to the given PITField COM interface pointer. The new TWordField saves the PITField COM object (incrementing its reference count) for later use.

Form 2 TWordField(const TField& p)

Constructs a TWordField object which attaches to the PITField COM object associated with the given TField object (which was passed by reference). The new TWordField saves the associated PITField COM object (incrementing its reference count) for later use.

Form 3 TWordField(PTField p)

Constructs a TWordField object which attaches to the PITField COM object associated with the given TField object (which was passed by pointer). The new TWordField saves the associated PITField COM object (incrementing its reference count) for later use.

Form 4 TWordField(void)

Constructs a new TWordField object. Internally, a new PITField COM object is created for later use.

Form 5 TWordField(void)

Constructs a new TWordField object. Internally, a new PITField COM object is created for later use.

Destructor

virtual ~TWordField()

Deletes the TWordField and reduces the reference count on the associated PITField COM object. If the reference count on the associated PITField COM object reaches 0, it is deleted.

Properties

▶ AsBoolean
▶ AsDateTime
▶ AsFloat
▶ AsInteger
▶ AsString
Calculated
▶ CanModify
▶ DataSet
▶ DataSize
▶ DataType
DisplayFormat
▶ DisplayText
EditFormat
EditMask
FieldName
▶ FieldNo
Index
▶ IsIndexField
IsNull
MaxValue
MinValue
Name
ReadOnly
Required
▶ Size
▶ Text
▶ Value

Methods

Assign
AssignValue
Clear
GetData
IsValidChar
SetData

Events

OnChange
OnGetText
OnSetText
OnValidate

UniDirectional property

Applies to   TQuery component

bool UniDirectional;

The UniDirectional property determines whether an application can move only forward or can move both forward and backward in the result set of a query.

To restrain the application to moving forward in the result set of a TQuery component, set the UniDirectional property to true. When UniDirectional is true, an application requires less memory (because the records do not have to be cached), but the application cannot move backward in the result set.

UniDirectional is false by default.

UnlockTable method

Applies to   TTable component

void UnlockTable(TLockType t);

The UnlockTable method removes a lock previously placed on a table with the LockTable method. The type of lock removed from the table is specified with the t parameter; these are the possible values:

Value	Meaning
ltReadLock	By placing a read lock on the table, the session prevents other sessions from writing to the physical table underlying a TTable component. Other sessions will still be able to read the table, but they won't be able to write to it, nor will they be able to place a write lock on it. Other TTable components in the same session will still be able to read and write to the physical table.
ltWriteLock	By placing a write lock on the table, the session prevents all other sessions from placing any locks on the physical table underlying a TTable component. Other sessions will be able to read the table, but they won't be able to write to it, nor will they be able to place any type of lock on it. Other TTable components in the same session will still be able to read and write to the physical table.

For each call to UnlockTable, the table must have been locked previously with LockTable using the same lock type. If the same lock type isn't specified, the table remains locked.

These methods are primarily intended for use with Paradox and dBASE tables.

UnPrepare method

Applies to   TQuery, TStoredProc component

Description   UnPrepare method for queries and stored procedures

UnPrepare method for stored procedures

Applies to   TStoredProc component

void UnPrepare(void);
The UnPrepare method notifies the server that the stored procedure is no longer
needed, allowing the server to release any resources allocated to the stored procedure.

UnPrepare method for queries

Applies to   TQuery component

void UnPrepare(void);
The UnPrepare method sets the Prepared property to false. This ensures that the SQL
property is translated again before the request is submitted to the server. In addition, the
server is notified that it can release any resources allocated for optimization purposes, as
a new request is sent before (or in conjunction with) a call to the Open or ExecSQL
method.

Preparing a query consumes some database resources, so it is good practice for an
application to unprepare a query once it is done using it. When you change the text of a
query at run time, the query is automatically unprepared and closed.

Update method

Applies to   All data-aware controls; TFieldDefs, TIndexDefs components

Description   The Update method repaints or refreshes a component.

Update method for data-aware controls

Applies to   All data-aware controls

void Update( );
The Update method calls the Windows API UpdateWindow function, which processes
any pending paint messages.

Example

```
RadioGrp1.Invalidate( );
RadioGrp1.Update( );
```

Update method for field definitions

Applies to   TFieldDefs component

void Update(void);
The Update method refreshes the TFieldDef entries in the Items property to reflect the current state of the fields in the underlying dataset. It does so without opening the dataset.

Update method for index definitions

Applies to   TIndexDefs component

void Update(void);
The Update method refreshes the entries in the Items property to reflect the current dataset. Use this method to obtain index information without opening the dataset.

UpdateCursorPos method

Applies to   TDataSet, TDBDataSet, TQuery, TStoredProc, TTable components

void UpdateCursorPos(void);
The UpdateCursorPos method sets the current position of the dataset's underlying Borland Database Engine's cursor to the current cursor position of the dataset. The UpdateCursorPos method is useful if you make direct calls to the Borland Database Engine.

UpdateMode property

Applies to   TQuery, TTable components (live result sets only)

TUpdateMode UpdateMode;
The UpdateMode property determines how an application finds records that are being updated in a SQL database. This property is important in a multiuser environment when users may retrieve the same records and make conflicting changes to them.

When a user posts an update, a Visual Database Tools application uses the original values in the record to find the record in the database. This approach is similar to an optimistic locking scheme. UpdateMode specifies which columns the application uses to find the record. In SQL terms, UpdateMode specifies which columns are included in the WHERE clause of an UPDATE statement. If the application cannot find a record with the original values in the columns specified (if another user has changed the values in the database), the update doesn't take place and an EDatabaseError exception occurs.

The UpdateMode property may have the following values:

Value	Meaning
WhereAll	Every column is used to find the record being updated. WhereAll is the default. This is the most restrictive mode.
WhereKeyOnly	Only the key columns are used to find the record being updated. This is the least restrictive mode and should be used only if other users will not be changing the records being updated.
WhereChanged	Key columns and columns that have changed are used to find the record being updated.

Example   Consider a COUNTRY table with columns for NAME (the key), CAPITAL, and CONTINENT. Suppose you and another user simultaneously retrieve a record with the following values:

• NAME = "Philippines"

• CAPITAL = "Nairobi"

• CONTINENT = "Africa"

Both you and the other user notice that the information in this record is incorrect and should be changed. Now, suppose the other user changes CONTINENT to "Asia", CAPITAL to "Manila", and posts the change to the database. A few seconds later, you change NAME to "Kenya" and post your change to the database.

If your application has UpdateMode set to WhereKey on the dataset, a Visual Database Tools application compares the original value of the key column (NAME = "Philippines") to the current value in the database. Since the other user did not change NAME, your update occurs. You think the record is now ["Kenya," "Nairobi," "Africa"] and the other users think it is ["Philippines," "Asia," "Manila"]. Unfortunately, it is actually ["Kenya," "Asia," "Manila"], which is still incorrect, even though both you and the other user think you have corrected the mistake. This problem occurred because you had UpdateMode set to its least restrictive level, which does not protect against such occurrences.

If your application had UpdateMode set to WhereAll, the Visual Database Tools application would check all the columns when you attempt to make your update. Because the other user changed CAPITAL and CONTINENT, you would not be allowed to make the update. When you retrieved the record again, you would see the new values entered by the other user and realize that the mistake had already been corrected.

UpdateRecord method

Applies to   TDataSet, TDBDataSet, TQuery, TStoredProc, TTable components

void UpdateRecord(void);
The UpdateRecord method notifies each TDataSource component that the current record is about to be posted to the dataset. Each data source in turn notifies all data-

aware controls so that they can update the fields of the record from the current values displayed in the controls. UpdateRecord is called automatically by Post, but an application can also use it separately to bring the current record up to date without posting it.

ValidateName method

Applies to   TDatabase component

void ValidateName(const string& name);
The ValidateName method checks to be sure that your application uses only one database with the same name. If your application attempts to use more than one database with the same name, an EDatabaseError exception is raised.

Value property

Applies to   TBCDField, TBooleanField, TBlobField, TBytesField, TCurrencyField, TDateField, TDateTimeField, TDBListBox, TDBLookupList, TDBRadioGroup, TFloatField, TGraphicField, TIntegerField, TMemoField, TSmallintField, TStringField, TTimeField, TVarBytes components

Description   The Value property specifies a value associated with a component that is linked to a field in a dataset record.

Value property for radio groups

Applies to   TDBRadioGroup component

string Value;
The value of the Value property is the current contents of the field for the current record in the dataset. When the user selects a radio button, the value of the Value property changes to the value of the Items string for the radio button. The new value of the Value property becomes the value of the field for the current record in the dataset.

If the ReadOnly property of the database radio group box is true, the user won't be able to select a button or change the contents of the field.

Example   This code displays the changed value of a field in a message box:

```
char buffer[100];
wsprintf( message, "Field %s has changed to %s", DBRadioGroup1.DataField.c_str(),
DBRadioGroup1.Value.c_str() );
MessageBox( message, "Information", MK_OK );
```

Value property for list boxes

Applies to   TDBListBox, TDBLookupList components

string Value;
Run-time only. The value of the Value property is the contents of the DataField for the current record in the primary dataset. As the user moves through the primary dataset, the value of the Value property changes.

By explicitly changing the Value property value at run time, you change the contents of the field.

Example   The following code changes the Value property, and thus, the value of the field in the connected dataset to "Green."

```
DBLookupCombo1.Value = "Green";
```

Value property for fields

Applies to   TBCDField, TBooleanField, TCurrencyField, TDateField, TDateTimeField, TFloatField, TIntegerField, TSmallintField, TStringField, TTimeField, TWordField components
string Value;   // TStringField
int32 Value;   // TIntegerField, TSmallintField, TWordField
double Value;   // TBCDField, TCurrencyField, TFloatField
bool Value;   // TBooleanField
DATE Value;   // TDateField, TDateTimeField, TTimeField
Run-time only. Value is the actual data in a field. Use Value to read data directly from and write data directly to a field component.

Example

```
StringField1.Value = "Visual Database Tools";
```

ValueChecked property

Applies to   TDBCheckBox component

string ValueChecked;
If the value of the ValueChecked property is equal to the data in the field of the current record of the dataset, the database check box is checked.

You can enter a semicolon-delimited list of items as the value of ValueChecked. If any of the items matches the contents of the field of the current record in the dataset, the check box is checked. For example, you can specify a ValueChecked string like this:

```
DBCheckBox1.ValueChecked = "True;Yes;On";
```

If the string True, Yes, or On is the contents of the field specified as the database check box's DataField, the check box is checked. The case of the specified strings is not checked.

If the contents of the field of the current record matches a string specified as the value of the ValueUnchecked property, the check box is unchecked. If the contents of the field matches no string in either ValueChecked or ValueUnchecked, the check box appears gray.

If the user checks a database check box, the string that is the value of the ValueChecked property is placed in the database field, as long as the ReadOnly property is false. If the value is a semicolon-delimited list of items, the first item in the list is inserted as the contents of the field of the current record.

The default value of ValueChecked is the string "True."

Example   The following code toggles the value of the ValueChecked property of DBCheckBox1 from "True" to "False" or from "False" to "True."

```
void DBCheckBox::foo()
if( ! DBCheckBox1.ValueChecked.compare( "True" ) )
  DBCheckBox1.ValueChecked = "False";
if( ! DBCheckBox1.ValueChecked.compare( "False" ) )
  DBCheckBox1.ValueChecked = "True";
```

Values property

Applies to   TDBRadioGroup, TStrings components

Description   The Values property is used by string and string list components, and by database radio group boxes.

Values property for strings

Applies to   TStrings component

string Values[const string& name];

The Values property gives you access to a specific string in a list of strings. The strings must have a unique structure before you can use the Values property array to access them:

```
Name=Value
```

The Name that identifies the string is to the left of the equal sign (=), and the current Value of the Name identifier is on the right side of the equal sign. There should be no spaces present before or after the equal sign.

Such strings are commonly found in .INI files. For example, here are a few strings taken from the writer's WIN.INI file:

```
Beep=yes
NullPort=None
BorderWidth=3
CursorBlinkRate=530
DoubleClickSpeed=572
Programs=com exe bat pif
```

The strings that make up the Params property of a database component (TDatabase) have the same format. The most common use of the Values property is to modify a string within the Params property array.

To modify a string in a list of strings that have the required format, identify the string to modify with the Name constant parameter, which serves as an index into the list of strings, and assign a new value.

Example   Assume that a string that identifies the password needed to access a database exists in the Params string list. You can change the acceptable password using this code:

```
Database1.Params->Values("Password") = "TopSecret";
```

If there is no password string, the same code creates one at the bottom of the list of strings and assigns the "TopSecret" string as its value.

You can also assign the value of the string to a variable. For example, this code assigns the current value of the password string to a variable called StringValue:

```
string StringValue;
StringValue = Database1.Params->Values("Password");
```

Values property for radio groups

Applies to   TDBRadioGroup component

TStrings Values;

Each string in the Items property for a database radio group box places a radio button in the group box with an accompanying caption. If the contents of a field for the current record is the same as one of the strings in Items, the corresponding radio button is selected. If the user selects one of the radio group buttons and the ReadOnly property of the database radio group is false, the contents of the field changes to the corresponding Items string.

Often, you might not want the same string that serves as the caption of a radio button to become the contents of the field. Or, you might want a different value in the data field (other than the caption of a radio button) to select a radio button. In this case, use the Values property. You can specify a string in the Value property for each string in the Items list. The first string in Values corresponds to the first string in the Items, and therefore, the first radio button in the group box.

For example, suppose you have two strings in the Items property for a database radio group: Yes and No. If there are no strings in the Values property, the data field must contain either the value Yes or No to select one of the radio buttons. If the user selects one of these buttons, the string Yes or No becomes the contents of the data field.

If the data field contains values such as Y or N, rather than Yes or No, you can specify Y or N as Values strings. This way, the Yes or No radio buttons are selected when a Y or N value appears in the data field. When the user selects one of the radio buttons, Y or N becomes the value of the field of the current record.

Example This example uses a database radio group box connected to field in a dataset. The field contains the values "Y," "N," or "M." You want the captions of the radio buttons to be "Yes," "No," or "Maybe," so the code adds these three strings to the Items property array. The actual values that are in the field and that can entered into the field are the "Y," "N," and "M" strings, so these are added to the Values property array.

```
VOID TMyFormClass::SetupWindow( VOID )
{
  DBRadioGroup1.Items->Add( "Yes" );
  DBRadioGroup1.Items->Add( "No " );
  DBRadioGroup1.Items->Add( "Maybe" );
  DBRadioGroup1.Values->Add( "Y" );
  DBRadioGroup1.Values->Add( "N" );
  DBRadioGroup1.Values->Add( "M" );
  ...
}
```

When the code runs, three radio buttons appear in the group box. If the current record in the dataset contains any of the values contained in the Values property, the appropriate radio button is checked. When the user selects a radio button, the corresponding string in the Values property is entered into the field.

ValueUnchecked property

Applies to TDBCheckBox component

string ValueUnchecked;

If the value of the ValueUnchecked property is equal to the data in the field of the current record of the dataset, the database check box is unchecked.

You also can enter a semicolon-delimited list of items as the value of ValueUnchecked. If any of the items matches the contents of the field of the current record in the dataset, the check box is unchecked. For example, you can specify a ValueUnchecked string like this:

```
DBCheckBox1.ValueUnchecked = "False;No;Off";
```

If the string False, No, or Off is the contents of the field specified as the database check box's DataField, the check box is unchecked.

If the contents of the field of the current record matches a string specified as the value of the ValueChecked property, the check box is checked. If the contents of the field matches no string in either ValueChecked or ValueUnchecked, the check box appears gray.

If the user checks a database check box, the string that is the value of the ValueUnchecked property is placed in the database field, as long as the ReadOnly property is false. If the value is a semicolon-delimited list of items, the first item in the list is inserted as the contents of the field of the current record.

The default value of ValueUnchecked is the string "False."

Example The following code changes ValueUnchecked to "NO." When the value of the linked field is "NO," DBCheckBox1 is unchecked.

```
DBCheckBox1.ValueUnchecked = "NO";
```

Visible property

Applies to All data-aware controls; all TField components

bool Visible;

The Visible property determines if a field can be displayed in a component. If Visible is false, the field is not displayed. If Visible is true, the field is displayed.

The default value is true.

WantReturns property

Applies to TDBMemo component

bool WantReturns;

The WantReturns property determines whether return characters the user enters in the database memo by pressing Enter affect the text in the memo, or go to the dialog box. If WantReturns is true and the user presses Enter, a return character is entered in the database memo. If WantReturns is false and the user presses Enter, a return is not entered in the memo, but instead goes to the dialog box. For example, if there is a default button on a dialog box, pressing Enter would choose the button instead of affecting the memo's text.

To enter return characters in a memo when WantReturns is false, press Ctrl+Enter.

WantTabs property

Applies to TDBMemo component

bool WantTabs;

The WantTabs property determines if tabs are enabled in a database memo control. To enable tabs in a memo, set WantTabs to true. To turn tabs off, set WantTabs to false.

Caution If WantTabs is true, the user can't use the Tab key to select the next control on the form. The user can tab into a memo control, but can't tab out.

Width property

Applies to   All data-aware controls

int Width;

The Width property determines the horizontal size of the control or form in pixels. When you increase the Width property value, the form or control becomes wider. If you decrease the value, the form or control becomes narrower.

Example   The following code doubles the width of a database edit control:

```
DBedit1.Width = DBEdit1.Width * 2;
```

WordWrap property

Applies to   TDBMemo, TDBText components

bool WordWrap;

The WordWrap property determines if text in a database text or database memo control wraps at the right margin so that it fits in the control. You can give the user access to the lines which aren't visible in a database memo control by setting its ScrollBars property to add horizontal, vertical, or both scrollbars to the memo control. There should be no reason to use a horizontal scroll bar if WordWrap is true.

The database memo control must be tall enough to display at least one line of text to allow the user to edit its contents, even if WordWrap is true.

The default value is false.

Example   This example allows text a user enters in the Memo1 control to wrap to the next line, if the control is not large enough to hold the text:

```
DBMemo1.WordWrap = true;
```

Write method

Applies to   TMemoryStream component

int32 Write(LPVOID Buffer, int32 Count);

The Write method writes data from a buffer to a stream. Specify the buffer with the Buffer parameter. Use the Count parameter to specify the number of bytes that are written from the buffer to the stream. The Write method returns the number of bytes written to the buffer.

WriteBuffer method

Applies to   TMemoryStreamComponent component

void WriteBuffer(LPVOID Buffer, int32 Count);

The WriteBuffer method writes data from a buffer to a stream. Specify the buffer with the Buffer parameter. Use the Count parameter to specify the number of bytes that are written from the buffer to the stream.

Borland Windows Custom Controls reference

Part VI describes technical aspects of the Borland Windows Custom Controls (BWCC) and contains information that might be useful or of interest to the advancd resource designer:

- BWCC functions

- Defining a derivative dialog class.

- Technical description of Borland Windows custom controls

- Using BWCC controls in non-dialog windows

19

Borland Windows Custom Controls API

The topics in this chapter describe technical aspects of the Borland Windows Custom Controls (BWCC) and contains information that might be useful or of interest to the advanced resource designer:

- BWCC functions
- Defining a derivative dialog class
- Technical description of Borland Windows custom controls
- Using BWCC controls in non-dialog windows

Borland Windows Custom Controls functions

BWCC.DLL exports these additional functions:

- *BWCCGetPattern*
- *BWCCGetVersion*
- *BWCCIntlInit*
- *BWCCIntlTerm*
- *BWCCMessageBox*
- *BWCCRegister*

BWCCGetPattern

BWCCGetPattern()
This function, which takes no parameters, returns a handle to the brush used to paint the background of *BorDlg class dialogs*. Since this brush could be a patterned brush, you must align it by calling *UnrealizeObject* and *SetBrushOrg* before selecting it into a device context. Do not delete this brush by calling *DeleteObject*!

BWCCGetVersion

BWCCGetVersion()
This function, which takes no parameters, returns the current version of BWCC.DLL. The value it returns is defined in BWCC.H as BWCCVERSION:

Value	Platform
0x0200	Windows 3.x
0x10200	Win32, Win32s, Windows NT

BWCCIntlInit

BWCCIntlInit (UINT language)
This function (call on startup) selects a language (see BWCC.H for language choices) for text and bitmaps (it returns TRUE for success or FALSE for failure). If you do not use this function. BWCC uses its default resource language, which depends on which translated version you have. Each BWCC client can use a different language.

BWCCIntlTerm

BWCCIntlTerm (VOID)
This function frees memory (use on exit) after you use *BWCCIntlInit*. This function returns TRUE (success) or FALSE (failure).

BWCCMessageBox

BWCCMessageBox()
This function, which is call-compatible with the Windows standard function *MessageBox*, displays a message box that is consistent with the Borland dialog box style.

BWCCRegister

BWCCRegister (HINSTANCE hInst)
This function is used to register an instance of the application with BWCC.DLL. It is required for 32-bit applications and should be called when the application is initialized.

Defining a derivative dialog class

To create your own dialog window class (for example, if you want the dialog box to have its own icon), you must "derive" your class from the BORDLG class.

To derive a class from BORDLG, do the following:

1 Your dialog window function should call *BWCCDefDlgProc*, note the Windows standard *DefDlgProc* for messages that it does not process.

2 The window proc must call *BWCCDefDlgProc* for the following messages:

- WM_CTLCOLOR
- WM_ERASEBKGND
- WM_NCCREATE
- WM_NCDESTROY
- WM_PAINT

Technical description of Borland Windows Custom Controls

This section describes each of these Borland Windows Custom Controls classes:

- BORBTN control
- BORCHECK control
- BORRADIO control
- BORSHADE control
- BORSTATIC control
- BORDLG dialog class

Most of the subsection headings are self-explanatory, with the possible exception of the following:

- **Class Name** gives the Resource Workshop name in quotation marks, followed by the identifier name—C define or Pascal constant.

- **Window Styles** include **Types** and **Options**. Within each class there may be several *types* of controls. Types dictate the overall appearance and functionality of the control. Options are those available to each control type.

- **Messages** include **Commands** and **Notifications**. Commands are messages to a control. Notifications are a special type of WM_COMMAND message used by controls. The control ID of the control is passed in the *wParam* of the message, while the *lParam* contains both the notification type and the window handle of the control. The notification type is contained in the high-order word of *lParam* and can be extracted using the HIWORD macro; the window handle is contained in the low-order word of *lParam* and can be extracted using the LOWORD macro.

BORBTN control

Function
Bitmapped push buttons and "splash panels"

Class name
"borbtn" (BUTTON_CLASS)

Types inherited from standard Windows controls

BS_DEFPUSHBUTTON
BS_PUSHBUTTON
Defines the two standard Windows push button types.

The BS_DEFPUSHBUTTON type identifies the "default" push button. When the user presses the Enter key in a dialog box, the ID of the default button is in the *wParam* of the WM_COMMAND message sent to the parent window of the button. The Windows dialog manager sends a BN_CLICKED notification from that button to the dialog window.

There are two exceptions:

- If another button gains keyboard focus through a Tab keystroke, that key temporarily becomes the default button and is referenced in the BN_CLICKED notification.

- If keyboard focus is in an edit control for which the ES_WANTRETURN flag is set, the *Enter* key inserts a carriage return into the text in the edit control.

Type unique to BWCC

BBS_BITMAP
This type is used to display "splash panels," which are bitmaps the user does not interact with.

Options unique to BWCC

BBS_OWNERDRAW
This option causes the control to send WM_DRAWITEM to its parent at run time, for specialized drawing.

BBS_PARENTNOTIFY
This option causes the control to generate the following notification messages at run time:

- BBN_SETFOCUS
- BBN_SETFOCUSMOUSE
- BBN_GOTATAB
- BBN_GOTABTAB

Commands inherited from standard Windows controls

BM_GETSTATE
This message determines whether a button is highlighted, has focus, and whether it is "checked" (checking does not, however, apply to buttons). The 0x0004 bit of the return value indicates that the button is highlighted (drawn with a heavy outline around the button); the 0x0008 bit indicates that the button has the focus (a dotted line surrounds the text caption).

BM_SETSTATE
This message changes the "highlight" state of a button. If the *wParam* of the message is nonzero, the button is highlighted (drawn as if it were pressed).

BM_SETSTYLE
The Windows dialog manager uses this message to toggle between the BS_DEFPUSHBUTTON and BS_PUSHBUTTON types.

Command unique to BWCC

BBM_SETBITS
The application uses this message to pass a set of bitmap handles to the button. Normally, the buttons use the button control ID to automatically load bitmaps from the resources of the user. If the bitmaps do not exist, the button caption is drawn into a default bitmap by using a lighter-weight version of the dialog font. To use this message, you must first create three bitmap images of a single button:

- The button without keyboard focus
- The button with keyboard focus, but not pressed
- The button when it is "pressed" (or highlighted)

After creating the bitmaps, you must put the handles to these bitmaps into an array and pass a far pointer to this array in the *lParam* of the BM_SETBITS message.

Notifications inherited from standard Windows controls

BN_CLICKED
The button sends this message when it has been "pressed" by the user, either by clicking while the mouse pointer is within the button window or by either of the following keyboard actions:

- The user presses the Spacebar or the Enter key when the button has keyboard focus.

- The user presses the accelerator key for the the button when keyboard focus is in another control.

To associate an accelerator key with a button, place an ampersand before the ASCII value of the key in the text of the button (for example, "&Yes"). Note that case is not significant for button accelerators.

BN_DOUBLECLICKED
The button sends this message when it has been double-clicked by the user. The notification is sent at the time of the second mouse button-down message.

Notifications unique to BWCC

The following notifications are available if you have specified the BBS_PARENTNOTIFY style:

BBN_GOTABTAB
The button sends this notification to its parent window when the user presses *Shift+Tab* (back-tab) while keyboard focus is in the button. The parent can then intervene in the processing of the keystroke by returning a nonzero value.

BBN_GOTATAB
The button sends this notification to its parent window when the user presses the *Tab* key while keyboard focus is in the button. The parent can then intervene in the processing of the keystroke by returning a nonzero value.

BBN_SETFOCUS

The button sends this notification to its parent window when it gains keyboard focus through an action other than a mouse click.

BBN_SETFOCUSMOUSE

The button sends this notification to its parent window when it gains keyboard focus through a mouse click.

WM_DRAWITEM

If you specify the BBS_OWNERDRAW style for the button, it sends a WM_DRAWITEM message to its parent window. The *lParam* of the message contains a far pointer to a DRAWITEMSTRUCT structure. The fields of that structure are described in the Windows SDK documentation for this message, but with the following enhancement.

For Windows owner-draw buttons, the *itemID* field of the DRAWITEMSTRUCT structure is unused. Borland buttons use this field to pass their type. If the button is a default push button, this field contains the value BS_DEFPUSHBUTTON. Otherwise, it contains the value BS_PUSHBUTTON.

The other fields and the values passed in them are:

- *CtlType*: ODT_BUTTON
- *CtlID*: The control ID of the button (GetWindowWord(hWnd, GWW_ID))
- *itemAction*: ODA_DRAWENTIRE, unless the repaint is being caused by a focus change, in which case this field contains ODA_FOCUS
- *itemState*: The combination of the following values, depending on the current state of the button:
  - ODS_FOCUS: if the button has keyboard focus
  - ODS_DISABLED: if the button is disabled
  - ODS_SELECTED: if the button is highlighted
- *hwndItem*: The window handle of the control
- *hDC*: A device context for the window, with all values in the default state returned by *GetDC*
- *rcItem*: The client rectangle of the control

Button resource ID numbering scheme

The Microsoft resource compiler does not provide user-specified control initialization data when it parses the Windows dialog template data structure. Because of this, Resource Workshop uses the control ID field as a base from which to derive the resource IDs of the bitmaps required by a button. For each bitmap button, there are six images: three for EGA and monochrome devices, and three for VGA and higher-resolution devices.

The bitmap resource IDs are derived from the button control using the following formulas:

Formula	Bitmap type
Control ID + 1000	Normal VGA-resolution image
Control ID + 3000	Pressed VGA-resolution image
Control ID + 5000	Focused VGA-resolution image
Control ID + 2000	Normal EGA-resolution image
Control ID + 4000	Pressed EGA-resolution image
Control ID + 6000	Focused EGA-resolution image

BORBTN example (C)

```
HBITMAP hBits[3];
HWND   hWndButton = GetDlgItem( hWnd, ID_FOO);

hBits[0] = MakeNormalBitmap(...);
hBits[1] = MakeHighlightBitmap(...);
hBits[2] = MakeFocusBitmap(...);

SendMessage( hWndButton, BBM_SETBITS, 0, (LONG) (LPSTR) hBits);
```

BORBTN example (Pascal)

```
procedure SetBitmaps(Wnd: HWnd);

var
  Bits: array[0..2] of HBitmap;
  WndButton: HWnd;

begin
  WndButton := GetDlgItem(Wnd, id_Foo);

  Bits[0] := MakeNormalBitmap(...);
  Bits[1] := MakeHighlightBitmap(...);
  Bits[2] := MakeFocusBitmap(...);

  SendMessage(WndButton, BBM_SETBITS, 0, @@Bits);
end;
```

Note If the bitmaps for a button are initialized in this manner, the application must destroy the bitmaps by calling DeleteObject before it terminates. The application typically makes this call in the WM_DESTROY message handler for the parent window of a button.

BORCHECK control

Function
Better-looking check boxes

Class name
"borcheck" (CHECK_CLASS)

Types inherited from standard Windows controls

BS_3STATE
A nonautomatic check box that switches between three states: checked, unchecked, and indeterminate.

BS_AUTO3STATE
An automatic version of BS_3STATE.

BS_AUTOCHECKBOX
A check box that automatically changes state when clicked.

BS_CHECKBOX
A nonautomatic check box. Application program intervention is required to change its visual state after it has been "clicked."

Option inherited from standard Windows controls

BS_LEFTTEXT
This option causes the text associated with the button to be displayed to the left of the button, rather than to the right of the button.

Options unique to BWCC

BBS_OWNERDRAW
This option causes the control to send WM_DRAWITEM to its parent at run time, for specialized drawing.

BBS_PARENTNOTIFY
This option causes the control to generate the following notification messages at run time:

- BBN_SETFOCUS
- BBN_SETFOCUSMOUSE
- BBN_GOTATAB
- BBN_GOTABTAB

Commands inherited from standard Windows controls

BM_GETCHECK

This message causes the control to return its current "check" state. The return value is 0 if the control is unchecked; 1 if checked; and 2 if indeterminate (applies only for 3-state check boxes).

BM_SETCHECK

This message changes the state of a check box. If the *wParam* of the message is 0, the check box is drawn empty; if 1, the check box is checked; and if 2, it is drawn with with a pattern indicating the indeterminate state.

BM_GETSTATE

This message determines whether a check box is highlighted, has focus, and whether it is checked. The low-order two bits (0x0003) of the return value contain the check state: 0 indicates unchecked; 1 indicates checked; and 2 indicates the indeterminate state for 3-state check boxes. The 0x0004 bit of the return value indicates that the check box is highlighted (drawn with a heavy outline); the 0x0008 bit indicates that the button has the focus (a dotted line surrounds the text caption).

BM_SETSTATE

This message changes the highlight state of a check box. If the *wParam* of the message is a nonzero value, the check box is highlighted.

Notifications inherited from standard Windows controls

BN_CLICKED

Described in the BORBTN section.

BN_DOUBLECLICKED

Described in the BORBTN section.

Notifications unique to BWCC

The following notifications are sent to the parent window only if the programmer has specified the BBS_PARENTNOTIFY style:

- BBN_SETFOCUS
- BBN_SETFOCUSMOUSE
- BBN_GOTATAB
- BBN_GOTABTAB

For a description of these notifications, see the BORBTN section in this chapter.

WM_DRAWITEM

The description of this notification is identical to the one in the BORBTN section with the following exception: For automatic check boxes, the *itemID* field of the DRAWITEMSTRUCT structure contains the value BS_AUTOCHECKBOX or BS_AUTO3STATE. Otherwise, it contains the value BS_CHECKBOX or BS_3STATE.

BORRADIO control

Function
Better-looking radio buttons

Class name
"borradio" (RADIO_CLASS)

Types inherited from standard Windows controls

BS_AUTORADIOBUTTON
An "automatic" radio button. When the user selects one of these buttons, it is automatically marked (with a circle or diamond), and the previously selected button within the group is deselected, without the intervention of the application program.

BS_RADIOBUTTON
A nonautomatic radio button. The button merely informs the application program that it has been "checked" (pressed) via the BN_CLICKED notification. The application is responsible for calling the *CheckRadioButton* function to change the state of a button and the state of the other buttons it is grouped with.

Option inherited from standard Windows controls

BS_LEFTTEXT
This option causes the text associated with the button to be displayed to the left of the button, rather than to the right of the button.

Options unique to BWCC

BBS_OWNERDRAW
This option causes the control to send WM_DRAWITEM to its parent at run time, for specialized drawing.

BBS_PARENTNOTIFY
This option causes the control to generate the following notification messages at run time:

- BBN_SETFOCUS
- BBN_SETFOCUSMOUSE
- BBN_GOTATAB
- BBN_GOTABTAB

Commands inherited from standard Windows controls

BM_GETCHECK
This message causes the button to return its current "check" state (the message names and descriptions all use check box imagery). If it is checked (pressed), it returns a nonzero value. Otherwise, it returns zero.

BM_GETSTATE

This message determines whether a button is highlighted, has focus, and whether it is checked. The low-order two bits (0x0003) of the return value contain the check state: 0 indicates unchecked and 1 indicates checked. The 0x0004 bit of the return value indicates that the button is highlighted (drawn with a heavy outline around the circle or diamond); the 0x0008 bit indicates that the button has the focus (a dotted line surrounds the text caption).

BM_SETCHECK

This message changes the check state of a button. If the *wParam* of the message is nonzero, the button is checked (filled with a circle or a diamond).

BM_SETSTATE

This message changes the highlight state of a button. If the *wParam* of the message is nonzero, the button is highlighted.

Notifications inherited from standard Windows controls

BN_CLICKED

Described earlier in this chapter.

BN_DOUBLECLICKED

Described ealier in this chapter.

Notifications unique to BWCC

The following notifications are sent to the parent window only if the programmer has specified the BBS_PARENTNOTIFY style.

- BBN_SETFOCUS
- BBN_SETFOCUSMOUSE
- BBN_GOTATAB
- BBN_GOTABTAB

WM_DRAWITEM

The description of this notification is identical to the one under BORBTN, with the following exception: For automatic radio buttons, the itemID field of the DRAWITEMSTRUCT structure contains the value BS_AUTORADIOBUTTON. Otherwise, it contains the value BS_RADIOBUTTON.

BORSHADE control

Function

Panels and dividers

Class name

"borshade" (SHADE_CLASS)

Types unique to BWCC

BSS_GROUP

This style draws a "chiseled" gray box with a recessed appearance.

BSS_HBUMP

This style draws a horizontal dividing line that can be used to separate sections of a gray group shade (BSS_GROUP or BSS_RGROUP).

BSS_HDIP

This style draws a horizontal dividing line that can be used to separate sections of a dialog box.

BSS_RGROUP

This style draws a "chiseled" gray box with a raised appearance.

BSS_VBUMP

This style draws a vertical dividing line that can be used to separate sections of a gray group shade (BSS_GROUP or BSS_RGROUP).

BSS_VDIP

This style draws a vertical dividing line that can be used to separate sections of a dialog box.

Options unique to BWCC

BSS_CAPTION

This option applies only to the BSS_GROUP and BSS_RGROUP types. It causes the caption of the group shade box (if any) to be appear above the recessed (or raised) portion of the box. The dimensions of the box include the caption as well as the box.

BSS_CTLCOLOR

This option applies only to the BSS_GROUP and BSS_RGROUP types. It causes the control to send registered messages to its parent prior to erasing. The parent can then provide a different brush for painting the group box background, and make other changes to the HDC as needed. To use this mechanism, you must first register a special message using the Windows *RegisterWindowMessage()* API. In the file BWCC.h, you will find the following definition:

```
#define BWCC_CtlColor_Shade "BWCC_CtlColor_Shade"
```

Include the following static declaration in your program (the following examples are in C):

```
WORD hCtlColor_Shade;
```

Then, in your application initialization function, register the message:

```
hCtlColor_Shade=RegisterWindowMessage(BWCC_CtlColor_Shade);
```

In your window procedure, dialog box window procedure, or most commonly your dialog procedure, test for the message:

```
if (msg == hCtlColor_Shade)
{
   ...
}
```

The parameters for the message are the same as for WM_CTLCOLOR, and the message is handled in the same manner. For example, the text foreground and background colors and the background mode in the HDC may be modified, in order to change the appearance of the caption. A background brush may be also returned. (As with normal WM_CTLCOLOR handling, be sure not to create a new brush every time the message is processed.)

In order to return a brush from a dialog procedure (as opposed to from a dialog box window procedure or a window procedure), you must place the value of the brush into offset DWL_MSGRESULT in the window structure with *SetWindowLong()* and then return TRUE. Here is an example:

```
if (msg == hCtlColor_Shade)
{
  SetTextColor( (HDC) wParam, RGB(255,0,0) ); // red text
  SetBkColor( (HDC) wParam, RGB(128,128,128) ); // gray
  SetBkMode ( (HDC) wParam, OPAQUE);
  SetWindowLong( hwndDlg, DWL_MSGRESULT,
  GetStockObject(WHITE_BRUSH) );
  return TRUE;
}
```

The Windows include files provide a macro that combines the last two steps: *SetDlgMsgResult(hwnd, msg, result)*, which you would use with *hCtlColor_Shade* as the second parameter.

BSS_LEFT, BSS_CENTER, BSS_RIGHT
These options apply only to the BSS_GROUP and BSS_RGROUP types, and control the horizontal placement of the caption.

BSS_NOPREFIX
This option applies only to the BSS_GROUP and BSS_RGROUP types, and is the equivalent of the SS_NOPREFIX option for static text: it causes any ampersands (&) within the caption to be treated as normal characters, rather than causing the next character to be underlined.

Command unique to BWCC

```
RegisterWindowMessage(BWCC_CtlColor_Shade)
```

BORSTATIC control

Function
static text with a gray background

Class name
"borstatic" (STATIC_CLASS)

Types inherited from standard Windows controls

SS_CENTER
The text is center-justified in the control.

SS_LEFT
The text is left-justified in the control.

SS_LEFTNOWORDWRAP
The text is left-justified within the control and does not word wrap.

SS_RIGHT
The text is right-justified in the control.

SS_SIMPLE
The text is left-justified in a single line within the control and does not word wrap.

Option inherited from standard Windows controls

SS_NOPREFIX
Ampersands (&) within the text do not cause the following character to be underlined.

BORDLG dialog class

Function
"Turbo" fast dialog box drawing

Class name
"bordlg" (BORDLGCLASS)
This custom dialog window class implements the "turbo painting" of Borland custom controls by keeping its own private list of controls within a dialog box and painting those controls itself. It also automatically provides a patterned background on VGA and higher-resolution displays. If you want your dialogs to have the "Borland look," specify this dialog class in your dialog box template. (As an alternative to specifying "bordlg" as the class, you may also call *BWCCDefDlgProc()*, as discussed in section 1 of this chapter.)

Types inherited from standard Windows controls
All valid styles for a standard Windows dialog box.

Commands inherited from standard Windows controls

WM_CTLCOLOR
If the user has provided a dialog procedure, it is called with the WM_CTLCOLOR message. If it returns a nonzero value, then no further processing takes place, and that value is returned. Otherwise, the processing depends on which CTCOLOR value is specified. For list boxes, the background is set to a gray brush. For static and button controls, the background mode is set to transparent; the text color to COLOR_WINDOWTEXT; for non-monochrome monitors, the background color is set to COLOR_GRAYTEXT; and a gray background brush is returned.

For CTLCOLOR_DLG, the steel-gray dialog background brush is returned, but it is first unrealized and the origin of the HDC is reset to match the dialog box.

For other CTLCOLOR values, *DefWindowProc()* is called and its value returned.

WM_DESTROY

This message simply frees the control list attached to the dialog window and then calls *DefDlgProc()*, returning its value.

WM_ERASEBKGND

This message first sends a WM_CTLCOLOR message with CTLCOLOR_DLG to the dialog procedure of the user (if any) to get a background brush for the dialog. If zero is returned, the chiseled-steel brush is used. But before painting the background, the control structure is iterated and any Borland group shades and Borland static text controls are painted with a gray background (for speed). (Note, however, that the brush used for group shades may be modified by an additional CTLCOLOR-like message, as described in the BORSHADE section.)

The background brush is realigned with the top left corner of the dialog window and the dialog background is painted with it, excluding any rectangles that were painted for group shades and static text controls. Finally, WM_ERASEBKGND returns TRUE, to indicate to Windows that no further erasing is necessary.

WM_NCCREATE

This message sets up a structure, which is attached as a property to the dialog window. As Borland controls are then created, they will register themselves with the dialog window, and information about each control will be added to this structure. This is the mechanism used to provide turbo-painting.

After attaching the structure, WM_NCCREATE calls *DefDlgProc()* and returns its value.

WM_PAINT

This message iterates through the control structure described above and paints each of the Borland controls. For each control that is painted, its window is validated, so that it will not itself get WM_PAINT or WM_ERASE messages.

After all Borland controls are painted, a thin frame is drawn around the dialog to provide a sense of depth, and zero is returned.

Using BWCC controls in non-dialog windows

If you want your non-dialog windows to look like the *BorDlg windows* (with the steel-gray background and light gray background for static controls), BWCC.DLL provides two functions that replace the Windows standard "Def" window functions and that should be called in place of them:

- For MDI child windows, call *BWCCDefMDIChildProc* instead of the Windows standard function *DefMDIChildProc*.

- For all other windows, call *BWCCDefWindowProc* instead of the Windows standard function *DefWindowProc*.

As described earlier for *BWCCDefDlgProc*, your window proc must call either *BWCCDefMDIChildProc* or *BWCCDefWindowProc* for the following messages:

- WM_CTLCOLOR
- WM_NCCREATE
- WM_NCDESTROY
- WM_PAINT
- WM_ERASEBKGND

Note   BWCC does not provide a replacement function for *DefFrameProc*.

Creating custom control classes

Windows provides standard control classes, such as list boxes and radio buttons, that you can add to your dialog box resources. In addition to these standard classes, Resource Workshop also lets you create and use custom control classes, which must be in a DLL (dynamic-link library). This file describes the functions you'll need to use to make your custom controls accessible to Resource Workshop.

The DLL file of custom controls must contain functions that let Resource Workshop work with the custom controls just as it works with the standard Windows controls. In particular, you must implement the *ListClasses* function and export it by name. This function provides information to Resource Workshop about the custom control classes in the DLL.

You must also provide the following functions for each custom control window class:

- *Info*
- *Style*
- *Flags*

These functions can have any name. They must, however, be exported by the DLL, and pointers to them must be supplied in the *ListClasses* function.

Using C to create custom controls

Four functions are provided for creating custom controls:

- *ListClasses* function
- *Info* function
- *Style* function
- *Flags* function

ListClasses function (C)

```
HGLOBAL CALLBACK ListClasses( LPSTR szAppClass, UINT wVersion, LPFNLOADRES fnLoad,
        LPFNEDITRES fnEdit);
```

ListClasses is a programmer-implemented function that passes information about the custom control classes back to Resource Workshop. Exporting *ListClasses* marks your DLL as supporting this custom control specification.

If *ListClasses* is present in the DLL, Resource Workshop calls the function, passing information about itself along with two utility function variables used in editing the custom control.

ListClasses should return a handle to global memory allocated by calling *GlobalAlloc*. The memory referenced by this handle holds a structure of type CTLCLASSLIST, which describes the controls in the library. CTLCLASSLIST is described later in this section. The handle is freed by Resource Workshop and should not be freed by the DLL.

Return value
Returns a global handle to the data structure.

Parameters

fnEdit
A pointer to a function that a custom control can use to start a resource editor for any resource in the project being edited by Resource Workshop. It takes two parameters: a resource type name and a resource name.

fnLoad
A pointer to a function that a custom control can use to get a binary version of any resource in the project being edited by the calling application—the equivalent of the Windows API function *LoadResource*. The function takes two parameters: a resource type name and a resource name. The custom control must free the global handle (if any) returned by the function.

szAppClass
The class name of the application's main window. The class name can be used by the custom control to determine if it is running under a resource editor. If *szAppClass* is "rwswnd", the calling application is Resource Workshop.

wVersion
The version number of the calling application. The major version is in the high-order byte and the minor version in the low-order byte. For example, version 1.02 is 0x0102.

Data structures

```
typedef struct
{
  LPFNINFO  fnRWInfo;        // Info function
  LPFNSTYLE fnRWStyle;       // Style function
  LPFNFLAGS fnFlags;         // Flags function
  char  szClass[ CTLCLASS]; // Class name

} RWCTLCLASS, FAR *LPRWCTLCLASS;

typedef struct {
  short  nClasses;            // Number of classes in list
```

```
           RWCTLCLASS Classes[];        // Class list
       } CTLCLASSLIST, FAR *LPCTLCLASSLIST;
```

The CTLCLASSLIST structure contains a variable number of RWCTLCLASS strucures, the number of which is determined by the *nClasses* field.

Each control class in the DLL must have a corresponding RWCTLCLASS structure in the CTLCLASSLIST. The *szClass* field contains the name with which the class was registered. For example, if you called *RegisterClass* giving the class name "MYBUTTON", *szClass* must be "MYBUTTON".

The function variables *Info*, *Style*, and *Flags*—which correspond to the pointers *fnRWInfo*, *fnRWStyle*, and *fnFlags*—are described in the following sections.

Info function (C)

HGLOBAL CALLBACK Info(void);
Resource Workshop calls the *Info* function to retrieve information about the control class, including the string to add to the control menu and the bitmap to add to the tool palette. The function returns a memory handle that can be allocated by *GlobalAlloc*. This handle must refer to memory that contains a RWCTLINFO structure. Like *ListClasses*, the handle returned by *Info* is freed by Resource Workshop and should not be freed by the DLL. Resource Workshop calls this function once when it loads the DLL.

Parameters
None.

Data structures
The RWCTLINFO structure, defined by a typedef in the file CUSTCNTL.H, has two basic parts:

- The first part has a fixed length and provides information about the whole control class.

- The second part is a variable-length array of fixed-length records. Each record provides information about a particular type or subclass of the control.

```
/* general size definitions */
#define  CTLTYPES12  /* number of control types*/
#define  CTLDESCR22  /* size of control menu name */
#define  CTLCLASS20  /* max size of class name */
#define  CTLTITLE94  /* max size of control text   */

typedef struct {
   UINTwVersion;              // control version
   UINTwCtlTypes;             // control types
   charszClass[CTLCLASS];     // control class name
   charszTitle[CTLTITLE];     // control title
   charszReserved[10];        // reserved for future
   RWCTLTYPE Type[CTLTYPES];  // control type list
} RWCTLINFO;
```

```
typedef RWCTLINFO *RWPCTLINFO;
typedef RWCTLINFO FAR *LPRWCTLINFO;
```

hDropCurs

A cursor to be used while dragging the control from the tool palette.

hToolBit

A handle to a bitmap which will be placed on the tool palette. Resource Workshop requires the bitmap be a 22x22 black and gray bitmap containing a 2-pixel border that is white on the top and left and black on the bottom and right. You can use the bitmaps contained in BITBTN.RES as templates.

szClass

The name of the class as registered with Windows. This is duplicated from the CTLCLASSLIST structure to retain upward compatiblity with the Windows custom control specificiation.

szDescr

The description of the control subtype. Resource Workshop uses the to text construct a menu item that the user can use to create an instance of your custom control.

szReserved

Space reserved for future expansion. Must be cleared to null characters (0).

Type

An array of subtype description structures of type RWCTLTYPE.

```
/*
 * RWCTLTYPE DATA STRUCTURE
 *
 * This data structure is returned by the control options
 * function while inquiring about the capabilities of a
 * particular control. Each control may contain various types
 * (with predefined style bits) under one general class.
 *
 * The width and height fields provide the application with
 * a suggested size. Use pixels or dialog units for the
 * values in these fields. If you use pixels, turn on the
 * most significant bit (MSB). If you use dialog units, turn
 * off the MSB.
 *
 */

typedef struct {
  UINT wType;              // type style
  UINT wWidth;            // suggested width
  UINT wHeight;           // suggested height
  DWORDdwStyle;           // default style
  char szDescr[CTLDESCR]; // menu name
  HBITMAP  hToolBit;      // Toolbox bitmap
  HCURSOR  hDropCurs;     // Drag and drop cursor
} RWCTLTYPE, FAR * LPRWCTLTYPE;
```

wCtlTypes

The number of control sub-types defined in the *Type* array.

wHeight

The default height for the control. Resource Workshop uses this value if, for example, the control is created by dragging the icon from the tool palette. *wHeight* is in dialog coordinates unless the most significant bit is set, in which case the value is in pixels. For example, a value of "32" is 32 in dialog coordinates, but the value "32 | 0x8000" is in pixels.

wStyle

The default style Resource Workshop uses to create the window. This is the key field that you use to distinguish one subtype from another.

wType

A user-defined value used to indicate the subtype of the control. This value is not used by Resource Workshop.

wVersion

The version number of the custom control library. The major version is in the high-order byte and the minor version is in the low-order byte. For example, version 1.02 is 0x0102. Resource Workshop doesn't use this.

wWidth

The default width for the control. Resource Workshop uses this value if, for example, the control is created by dragging the icon from the tool palette. *wWidth* is in dialog coordinates unless the most significant bit is set, in which case the value is in pixels. For example, a value of "32" is 32 in dialog coordinates, but the value "32 | 0x8000" is in pixels.

Style function (C)

```
BOOL CALLBACK Style( HWND hWnd, HGLOBAL hCtlStyle, LPFNSTRTOID lpfnStrToId,
                     LPFNIDTOSTR lpfnIdToStr);
```

The *Style* function makes it possible for you to edit your custom control. You must first create an appropriate dialog box in Resource Workshop and then implement a Boolean function that displays that dialog box. Resource Workshop calls this function whenever you initiate a request to edit the custom control. Resource Workshop passes the function a handle to the window that is the parent of the dialog, a handle to memory containing the RWCTLSTYLE structure, and two function variables for string conversion.

Return value

If the user changes any options for the control, this function's return value is TRUE. If the user does not make changes or if an error prevents changes, the return value is FALSE.

Parameters

hCtlStyle

A handle to global memory containing the RWCTLSTYLE structure to be edited.

hWnd

A handle to the parent window of the dialog box displayed by this function.

lpfnIdToStr

A function variable that converts the control ID in the wId field of RWCTLSTYLE to a string for editing. The ID can be converted back into a word by calling *lpfnStrToId*. This function variable lets the user see the symbolic constant that represents the control ID instead of the word value.

lpfnStrToId

A function variable that converts a string into a control ID for the *wId* field of RWCTLSTYLE. This lets the user enter the control ID using a constant identifier. This routine evaluates the string as an expression, returning the result. The ID can convert back into a string by calling *lpfnIdToStr*.

Data structures

```
/*
 * CONTROL-STYLE DATA STRUCTURE
 *
 * The class style function uses this data structure
 * to set or reset various control attributes.
 *
 */

typedef struct {
  UINT wX;                       // x origin of control
  UINT wY;                       // y origin of control
  UINT wCx;                      // width of control
  UINT wCy;                      // height of control
  UINT wId;                      // control child id
  DWORDdwStyle;                  // control style
  char szClass[CTLCLASS];        // control class name
  char szTitle[CTLTITLE];        // control text
  BYTE CtlDataSize;              // control data size
  BYTE CtlData[ CTLDATALENGTH];  // control data
} RWCTLSTYLE;

typedef RWCTLSTYLE *    PRWCTLSTYLE;
typedef RWCTLSTYLE FAR *    LPRWCTLSTYLE;
```

CtlData

This field holds up to 255 bytes of control-specific data. The amount used must be recorded in the *CtlDataSize* field. The use of this data area is user-defined. When you save your project, Resource Workshop saves the *CtlData* array into the .RC or .RES file.

To enable a custom control to access this array from within your program at run time, *lParam* of the WM_CREATE message points to a CREATESTRUCT data structure. The CREATESTRUCT structure contains a field, *lpCreateParams*, that is a pointer to the extra data you stored in the *CtlData* array. If the pointer is NULL, there is no *CtlData*.

The *CtlDataSize* variable is not available to your program. To make the size data accessible to your program, the *CtlData* array should either contain a fixed amount of data, or its first byte should contain the length of the data.

The *Style* function first converts the ID to a string by passing the numerical ID value to LPFNIDTOSTR. The *Style* function then displays the string in the dialog box.

If the user changes the string returned by LPFNIDTOSTR, the *Style* function verifies the string by passing it to LPFNSTRTOID, which determines if the string is a valid constant expression. If LPFNSTRTOID returns a zero in the LOWORD, the ID is illegal and is displayed in the dialog box, so the user can change it to a valid ID. If LPFNSTRTOID is successful, it returns a nonzero value in the LOWORD and the ID in the HIWORD.

CtlDataSize
Windows lets controls in a resource file have up to 255 bytes of control-defined data. This field indicates how much of that space is being used by the control. The data is stored in *CtlData*.

dwStyle
The style flags of the control.

szClass
The class name of the control.

szTitle
The title of the control.

wCx
The width of the control (dialog coordinates).

wCy
The height of the control (dialog coordinates).

wId
The control's ID value. This value must be converted to a string by calling *lpfnIdToStr* before being displayed for editing. It must be converted back into a word for storage by calling *lpfnStrToId* after editing.

wX
The horizontal (X) location of the control in dialog coordinates.

wY
The vertical (Y) location of the control in dialog coordinates.

Flags function (C)

UINT CALLBACK Flags(DWORD dwFlags, LPSTR lpStyle, UINT wMaxString);
Resource Workshop uses the *Flags* function to translate the style of a control into text. Resource Workshop inserts the text into the .RC file being edited. The function must only convert the values unique to the control. For example, if you were creating a *Flags* function for the Windows button class, you would only examine the lower sixteen bits of *Flags* and translate them into one of the bs_*XXXX* constants.

Return value

Returns the number of bytes copied into the destination string. Returns 0 if the *Flags* word is not valid or the string exceeds *MaxString* in length.

Parameters

dwFlags

The control style to be translated into text. This field is derived from the *dwStyle* field of the RWCTLSTYLE structure passed to the *Style* function variable.

lpStyle

The location to write the translated text.

wMaxString

The maximum number of bytes the *Flags* function can write into *Style*.

BIVBX library functions reference

Part VII presents information about using the BIVBX library functions defined in the header file bivbx.h, which is located in your include directory. This part empowers you to choose the correct VBX functions to initialize VBX support, return a VBX control handle, initialize a dialog window, handle events, and so forth.

BIVBX library functions

This chapter contains information about using the BIVBX library functions defined in the header file, bivbx.h, located in your include directory. If you are using VBX controls with your C, C++, or ObjectWindows applications, you will need to read this information so that you can use the correct VBX functions to initialize VBX support, return a VBX control handle, initialize a dialog window, handle events, and so forth.

For more information about using VBX controls in your C, C++, or ObjectWindows programs, see the online text file, VBX.TXT, which describes how to use VBXGEN, a utility program designed to generate a header file from a VBX control library.

Initialization functions

VBXInit
BOOL VBXInit(HINSTANCE instance, LPCSTR classPrefix)
This function initializes VBX support for the program instance *instance* and must be called before any other VBX function. The *classPrefix* argument specifies the string prefix used when registering VBX window classes (NULL defaults to "BiVbx"). This function returns TRUE if successful or FALSE if unable to initialize.

VBXTerm
void VBXTerm(void)
This function terminates VBX support for the current program instance. No other VBX functions should be called after this function.

VBXEnableDLL
BOOL VBXEnableDLL(HINSTANCE instApp, HINSTANCE instDLL)
This function enables VBX support for a DLL. It should be called prior to loading dialog resources from an instance other than the main program. It returns TRUE if successful or FALSE if an error occurs.

Controls

VBXGetHct1
HCTL VBXGetHctl(HWND window)
This function returns the VBX control handle associated with the window *window* or NULL if *window* is not a valid VBX control.

VBXGetHwnd
HWND VBXGetHwnd(HCTL control)
This function returns the window handle associated with the VBX control *control* or NULL if *control* is not a valid VBX control.

VBXCreate
HCTL VBXCreate(HWND windowParent, UINT id,
        LPCSTR library, LPCSTR cls,
        LPCSTR title, DWORD style,
        int x, int y, int w, int h, int file)
This function creates a new instance of the control *cls* located in the VBX library *library*. The *style* argument specifies the control window style and can be set to 0 to use the default style. The *file* argument specifies a form file and is should be set to 0 for dynamically created controls. This function returns NULL if it is unable to load the VBX library and create the control. *x*, *y*, *w*, and *h* are related system coordinates.

Dialogs

VBXInitDialog
BOOL VBXInitDialog(HWND window, HINSTANCE instance, LPSTR id)
This function is used to initialize a dialog window *window* loaded from a resource *id* (located in *instance*) by creating VBX controls for each child window of class VBControl located in the dialog template. It should be called by the dialog procedure when it receives the WM_INITDIALOG message. It returns TRUE if successful, or FALSE if an error occurs. Resource *id* must be of DLGINIT type.

Properties

VBXGetArrayProp
BOOL VBXGetArrayProp(HCTL control, int index, LPVOID value, int element)
This function retrieves the value of element *element* of property *index* of control *control* and places it into the buffer located at *value*. It returns TRUE if successful, or FALSE if an error occurs.

VBXGetArrayPropByName
BOOL VBXGetArrayPropByName(HCTL control, LPSTR name, LPVOID value, int element)
This function retrieves the value of element *element* of property *name* of control *control* and places it into the buffer located at *value*. It returns TRUE if successful, or FALSE if an error occurs.

VBXGetNumProps

int VBXGetNumProps(HCTL control)

This function returns the number of properties supported by the control *control* or -1 if an error occurs.

VBXGetProp

BOOL VBXGetProp(HCTL control, int index, LPVOID value)

This function retrieves the value of property *index* of control *control* and places it into the buffer located at *value*. It returns TRUE if successful, or FALSE if an error occurs.

VBXGetPropByName

ERR VBXGetPropByName(HCTL control, LPSTR name, LPVOID value)

This function retrieves the value of property *name* of control *control* and places it into the buffer located at *value*. It returns TRUE if successful, or FALSE if an error occurs.

For both VBXGetProp and VBXGetPropByName, *value* should be large enough to contain the property data type. Enumerated properties must have sizeof(value) >= sizeof(short).

VBXGetPropIndex

int VBXGetPropIndex(HCTL control, LPCSTR name)

This function returns the index of the property *name* of control *control* or -1 if an error occurs.

VBXGetPropName

LPCSTR VBXGetPropName(HCTL control, int index) [OBSOLETE: use VBXGetPropNameBuf]

This function returns the name of property *index* of control *control* or NULL if an error occurs.

VBXGetPropNameBuf

int VBXGetPropNameBuf(HCTL control, int index, LPSTR buffer, int len)

This function copies up to *len* bytes of the name of property *index* of control *control* into *buffer*. It returns the number of bytes copied or 0 if an error occurs.

VBXGetPropType

USHORT VBXGetPropType(HCTL control, int index)

This function returns the type (e.g., PTYPE_BOOL) of property *index* of control *control* or -1 if an error occurs. The property types are:

Type Name	C Type
PTYPE_CSTRING	HSZ
PTYPE_SHORT	short
PTYPE_LONG	long
PTYPE_BOOL	short
PTYPE_COLOR	COLORREF
PTYPE_ENUM	short
PTYPE_REAL	float
PTYPE_XPOS	long (twips)
PTYPE_XSIZE	long (twips)

Type Name	C Type
PTYPE_YPOS	long (twips)
PTYPE_YSIZE	long (twips)
PTYPE_PICTURE	HPIC
PTYPE_BSTRING	HLSTR

VBXIsArrayProp

BOOL VBXIsArrayProp(HCTL control, int index)

This function returns TRUE if the property *index* of control *control* is an array.

VBXSetArrayProp

BOOL VBXSetArrayProp(HCTL control, int index, LONG value, int element)

This function sets the value of element *element* of property *index* of control *control* to *value*. It returns TRUE if successful, or FALSE if an error occurs.

VBXSetArrayPropByName

BOOL VBXSetArrayPropByName(HCTL control, LPSTR name, LONG value, int element)

This function sets the value of element *element* of property *name* of control *control* to *value*. It returns TRUE if successful, or FALSE if an error occurs.

VBXSetProp

BOOL VBXSetProp(HCTL control, int index, LONG value)

This function sets the value of property *index* of control *control* to *value*. It returns TRUE if successful, or FALSE if an error occurs.

VBXSetPropByName

BOOL VBXSetPropByName(HCTL control, LPSTR name, LONG value);

This function sets the value of property *name* of control *control* to *value*. It returns TRUE if successful, or FALSE if an error occurs.

Events

When a VBX control generates an event, it sends a WM_VBXFIREEVENT message to its parent. The *lParam* argument of the message contains a far pointer to a VBXEVENT structure which describes the event:

```
typedef struct VBXEVENT
{
  HCTL    Control;
  HWND    Window;
  int        ID;
  int        EventIndex;
  LPCSTR  EventName;
  int        NumParams;
  LPVOID  ParamList;
} VBXEVENT, FAR * LPVBXEVENT, NEAR * NPVBXEVENT;
```

Control   The handle for the control that caused the event

Window   The window handle for the above control

ID	The control identifier for the above window
EventIndex	The index into the event list for that control
EventName	The name of the event (click, mouse move, etc.>)
NumParams	The number of arguments passed to the event
ParamList	A pointer to an array (of size *NumParams*) of event arguments in reverse order (i.e., *Arg0 == e->ParamList[e->NumParams-1]*)

VBX_EVENTARGNUM
<type> VBX_EVENTARGNUM(event,type,index)
This macro retrieves an argument *index* of type *type* from VBX event *event*. Note that 0 is the first argument index.

Example
```
int x = VBX_EVENTARGNUM(event,int,0);
int y = VBX_EVENTARGNUM(event,int,1);
```

VBX_EVENTARGSTR
HLSTR VBX_EVENTARGSTR(event,index)
This macro retrieves a string argument *index* of type HLSTR from VBX event *event*. Note that 0 is the first argument index. For example:
```
HLSTR s = VBX_EVENTARGSTR(event,2);
```

VBXGetEventIndex
int VBXGetEventIndex(HCTL control, LPCSTR name)
This function returns the index of event *name* of control *index* or -1 if an error occurs.

VBXGetEventName
LPCSTR VBXGetEventName(HCTL control, int index) [OBSOLETE: use VBXGetEventNameBuf]
This function returns the index of event *index* of control *control* or NULL if an error occurs.

VBXGetEventNameBuf
int VBXGetEventNameBuf(HCTL control, int index, LPSTR buffer, int len)
This function copies up to *len* bytes of the name of event *index* of control *control* into *buffer*. It returns the number of bytes copied or 0 if an error occurs.

VBXGetNumEvents
int VBXGetNumEvents(HCTL control)
This function returns the number of events supported by the control *control* or -1 if an error occurs.

Methods

VBXMethod
BOOL VBXMethod(HCTL control, int method, long far * args)
This function invokes method *method* on control *control* with arguments *args*. Note that this function is not normally called by application programs and is described here as a

means of invoking custom control methods. It returns TRUE if successful or FALSE if an error occurs.

VBXMethodAddItem
BOOL VBXMethodAddItem(HCTL control, int index, LPCSTR item)
This function invokes the standard "add item" method on control *control* where *index* is the index of the item to be added (*item*). The exact meaning of "add item" is dependent on the type of VBX control. It returns TRUE if successful or FALSE if an error occurs.

VBXMethodDrag
BOOL VBXMethodDrag(HCTL control, int action)
This function invokes the standard "drag" method on control *control* where *action* is one of the following:

0   Cancel a drag operation

1   Begin a drag operation

2   "Drop" the control at the current location

It returns TRUE if successful or FALSE if an error occurs.

VBXMethodMove
BOOL VBXMethodMove(HCTL control, long x, long y, long w, long h)
This function invokes the standard "move" method on control *control*. The default behavior for this method is to position the control at *x*, *y*, *w*, and *h*. It returns TRUE if successful or FALSE if an error occurs.

VBXMethodRefresh
BOOL VBXMethodRefresh(HCTL control)
This function invokes the standard "refresh" method on control *control*. The default behavior for this method is to update the contents of the control window before returning. It returns TRUE if successful or FALSE if an error occurs.

VBXMethodRemoveItem
BOOL VBXMethodRemoveItem(HCTL control, int item)
This function invokes the standard "remove item" method on control *control* where *index* is the index of the item to be removed. The exact meaning of "remove item" is dependent on the type of VBX control. It returns TRUE if successful or FALSE if an error occurs.

Conversions

VBX controls make use of a combination of twips and pixel measurements. The following functions are used to convert between these different measurement units:

VBXTwp2PixY
SHORT VBXTwp2PixY(LONG twips)
This function converts a Y coordinate *twips* from twips to pixels.

VBXTwp2PixX
SHORT VBXTwp2PixX(LONG twips)
This function converts an X coordinate *twips* from twips to pixels.

VBXPix2TwpY
LONG VBXPix2TwpY(SHORT pixels)
This function converts a Y coordinate *pixels* from pixels to twips.

VBXPix2TwpX
LONG VBXPix2TwpX(SHORT pixels)
This function converts an X coordinate *pixels* from pixels to twips.

Dynamic strings

VBX controls make extensive use of moveable zero-terminated strings, or "dynamic strings." The following functions are used to manipulate those strings:

VBXCreateCString
HSZ VBXCreateCString(HANDLE segment, LPSTR string)
This function creates a new string by allocating from the local heap in *segment* and initializing to *string*. It returns 0 if an error occurs.

VBXGetCStringLength
int VBXGetCStringLength(HSZ string)
This function returns the length of dynamic string *string* or 0 if an error occurs.

VBXGetCStringPtr
LPSTR VBXGetCStringPtr(HSZ string) [OBSOLETE: use VBXGetCStringBuf]
This function returns a pointer to the contents of the dynamic string *string* or 0 if an error occurs.

VBXGetCStringBuf
int VBXGetCStringBuf(HSZ string, LPSTR buffer, int len)
This function copies up to *len* bytes of the dynamic string *string* into *buffer*. It returns the number of bytes copied or 0 if an error occurs.

VBXDestroyCString
HSZ VBXDestroyCString(HSZ string)
This function destroys the dynamic string *string*. It returns *string*.

VBXLockCString
LPSTR VBXLockCString(HSZ string) [OBSOLETE: use VBXLockCStringBuf]
This function locks the string *string* and returns a pointer to the contents or 0 if an error occurs.

VBXLockCStringBuf
int VBXLockCStringBuf(HSZ string, LPSTR buffer, int len)
This function locks the dynamic string *string>* and copies up to *len* bytes of the string contents into *buffer*. It returns the number of bytes copied or 0 if an error occurs.

VBXUnlockCString
void VBXUnlockCString(HSZ string)
This function unlocks the string *string*.

Pictures

VBX controls can support a variety of "picture" property types, including bitmaps, metafiles, and icons. These types are represented by a single structure which contains a union of the different types:

```
typedef struct PICTURE
{
  BYTE Type;
  union
  {
    struct
    {
      HBITMAP  Bitmap;
      HPALETTE Palette;
    } Bitmap;
    struct
    {
      HANDLE Metafile;
      int xExtent;
      int yExtent;
    } Metafile;
    struct
    {
      HICON Icon;
    } Icon;
  } Data;
  BYTE Unused0;
  BYTE Unused1;
  BYTE Unused2;
  BYTE Unused3;
} PICTURE, FAR * LPPICTURE, NEAR * NPPICTURE;

#define PICTURE_EMPTY     0
#define PICTURE_BMP       1
#define PICTURE_META      2
#define PICTURE_ICON      3
```

VBXCreatePicture
HPIC VBXCreatePicture(LPPICTURE picture)
This function creates and returns a new picture handle from a picture buffer *picture* or 0 if an error occurs.

The following code creates an icon picture:

```
PICTURE pic;
HPIC hpic;
pic.Type = PICTURE_ICON;
pic.Icon.Icon.Icon = LoadIcon( NULL, IDI_ASTERISK );
hpic = VBXCreatePicture( &pic );
```

VBXDestroyPicture
void VBXDestroyPicture(HPIC pic)
This function decrements the reference count on the picture handle *pic* and destroys it if the count becomes 0.

VBXGetPicture
HPIC VBXGetPicture(HPIC pic, LPPICTURE picture)
This function copies the contents of the picture handle *pic* into the picture buffer *picture* and returns *pic* if successful or 0 if an error occurs.

VBXGetPictureFromClipboard
ERR VBXGetPictureFromClipboard(HPIC FAR *pic, HANDLE data, WORD format)
This function creates a new picture handle **pic* from a clipboard data handle *data* and format *format* and returns non-zero if an error occurs. Valid Clipboard formats include CF_BITMAP, CF_METAFILEPICT, CF_DIB and CF_PALETTE.

VBXReferencePicture
HPIC VBXReferencePicture(HPIC pic)
This function increments the reference count on the picture handle *pic* and returns *pic* if successful or 0 if an error occurs.

Basic strings

VBX controls make use of moveable string buffers (not zero terminated), or "Basic strings." The following functions are used to manipulate those strings:

VBXCreateBasicString
HLSTR VBXCreateBasicString(LPVOID buffer, USHORT len)
This function creates a Basic string of length *len* and initial contents of *buffer*. It returns 0 if an error occurs.

VBXGetBasicStringPtr
LPSTR VBXGetBasicStringPtr(HLSTR string) [OBSOLETE: use VBXGetBasicStringBuf]
This function returns a pointer to the contents of the Basic string *string* or 0 if an error occurs.

VBXGetBasicStringBuf
int VBXGetBasicStringBuf(HLSTR string, LPSTR buffer, int len)
This function copies up to *len* bytes of the Basic string *string* into *buffer*. It returns the number of bytes copied or 0 if an error occurs.

VBXDestroyBasicString
void VBXDestroyBasicString(HLSTR string)
This function destroys the Basic string *string*.

VBXGetBasicStringLength
USHORT VBXGetBasicStringLength(HLSTR string)
This function returns the length of the Basic string *string* or 0 if an error occurs.

VBXSetBasicString
ERR VBXSetBasicString(HLSTR far * string, LPVOID buffer, USHORT len)
This function replaces the contents of the Basic string *string* with *len* bytes from *buffer*. It returns nonzero if an error occurs.

Form files

These functions are for use with the header files generated by VBXGEN.

VBXCreateFormFile
HFORMFILE VBXCreateFormFile(LONG len, LPVOID data)
This function creates a temporary form file from a buffer *data* of *len* bytes of data. The form file returned can be used as an argument to the *VBXCreate()* function. It returns -1 if an error occurs.

VBXDeleteFormFile
BOOL VBXDeleteFormFile(HFORMFILE file)
This function deletes the form file *file* and frees any resources associate with it. It returns TRUE if successful, or FALSE if an error occurs.

32-bit issues

TVbxEventHandler as a base class
ObjectWindows windows and dialogs, including those generated by AppExpert, which use VBX controls must have *TVbxEventHandler* as a base class if built as a 32-bit application. This can done manually or with ClassExpert.

To manually make a TVbxEventHandler as a base class:

```
class TMyDialog : public TDialog
  :
DEFINE_RESPONSE_TABLE1(TMyDialog, TDialog)
```

should be

```
class TMyDialog : public TDialog, public TVbxEventHandler
  :
DEFINE_RESPONSE_TABLE2(TMyDialog, TDialog, TVbxEventHandler)
```

To make a TVbxEventHandler as a base class using ClassExpert

1 Select the target in the project window.

2 Select View | Class Expert.

3 Select the desired window or dialog class in the Classes window.

4 Select the Control Notifications item in the Events window.

5 Select a VBX control under the Control Notifications item.

6 Select a VBX event under the VBX control item.

7 Use a local menu to add a handler for the selected event.

8 ClassExpert will make sure that the window or dialog class is derived from *TVbxEventHandler*.

If *TVbxEventHandler* is not used as a base class, the VBX control will not appear.

Choosing data types

It's important to use the correct data type when getting property values from a VBX control. This is not always obvious. For example, the following code looks quite reasonable and works in 16-bit:

```
int count;
VBXGetPropByName( hCtl, "Count", &count );
```

This same code will not work in 32-bit since *count* is now 32-bits wide and the emulator (which is 16-bit) only writes 16-bits of information. The lower 2 bytes of *count* are left uninitialized. The best way to fix this is to make *count* a short:

```
short count;
VBXGetPropByName( hCtl, "Count", &count );
```

Please refer to the table in Section 4 for appropriate data types.

Windows NT

VBX events are not forwarded to ObjectWindows child objects under Windows NT. They are, however, correctly forwarded to the parent object.

Index

T